Encyclopedia of

Library and Information Sciences, Fourth Edition

Volume 3

Encyclopedia of

Library and Information Sciences, Fourth Edition

Volume 3

From: *Epistemology* To: *Information Retrieval Experimentation*

Encyclopedia Edited By

John D. McDonald

and

Michael Levine-Clark

CRC Press
Taylor & Francis Group
Boca Raton London New York

CRC Press is an imprint of the
Taylor & Francis Group, an **informa** business

First published 2018 by CRC Press

Published 2019 by CRC Press
Taylor & Francis Group
6000 Broken Sound Parkway NW, Suite 300
Boca Raton, FL 33487-2742

First issued in paperback 2020

© 2018 by Taylor & Francis Group, LLC
CRC Press is an imprint of the Taylor & Francis Group, an informa business

No claim to original U.S. Government works

ISBN-13: 978-1-4665-5259-3 (HB Set)
ISBN-13: 978-0-8153-8626-1 (Vol. 3) (hbk)

ISBN-13: 978-0-3675-7010-1 (PB Set)
ISBN-13: 978-0-3675-7018-7 (Vol. 3) (pbk)

**Visit the Taylor & Francis Web site at
http://www.taylorandfrancis.com
and the CRC Press Web site at
http://www.crcpress.com**

Encyclopedia of Library and Information Sciences, Fourth Edition

Brief Contents

Encyclopedia of Library and Information Sciences, Fourth Edition

Editors-in-Chief

John D. McDonald
Analytics and Assessment, EBSCO Information Services

Michael Levine-Clark
University of Denver Libraries, Denver, Colorado

Editorial Advisory Board

Encyclopedia of Library and Information Sciences, Fourth Edition

Editors-in-Chief

John D. McDonald

Michael Levine-Clark

Editorial Advisory Board

Contributors

June Abbas / *School of Library and Information Studies, University of Oklahoma, Norman, Oklahoma, U.S.A.*

Richard Abel / *Portland, Oregon, U.S.A.*

Eileen G. Abels / *College of Information Science and Technology, Drexel University, Philadelphia, Pennsylvania, U.S.A.*

Tia Abner / *American Medical Informatics Association (AMIA), Bethesda, Maryland, U.S.A.*

Donald C. Adcock / *Dominican University, River Forest, Illinois, U.S.A.*

Kendra S. Albright / *School of Library and Information Science, University of South Carolina, Columbia, South Carolina, U.S.A.*

Mikael Alexandersson / *University of Gothenburg, Gothenburg, Sweden*

Joan M. Aliprand / *Cupertino, California, U.S.A.*

Jacqueline Allen / *Dallas Museum of Art, Dallas, Texas, U.S.A.*

Romano Stephen Almagno / *International College of St. Bonaventure, Rome, Italy*

Connie J. Anderson-Cahoon / *Southern Oregon University Library, Ashland, Oregon, U.S.A.*

Karen Anderson / *Archives and Information Science, Mid Sweden University, ITM, Härnösand, Sweden*

Rick Anderson / *University of Utah, Salt Lake City, Utah, U.S.A.*

Silviu Andrieş-Tabac / *Institute of Cultural Heritage, Moldova Academy of Sciences, Chişinău, Republic of Moldova*

Peng Hwa Ang / *Wee Kim Wee School of Communication and Information, Nanyang Technological University, Singapore*

Hermina G.B. Anghelescu / *School of Library and Information Science, Wayne State University, Detroit, Michigan, U.S.A.*

Leah Arroyo / *American Association of Museums, Washington, District of Columbia, U.S.A.*

Terry Asla / *Senior Lifestyles Researcher, Seattle, U.S.A.*

Shiferaw Assefa / *University of Kansas, Lawrence, Kansas, U.S.A.*

Ilse Assmann / *Radio Broadcast Facilities, SABC, Johannesburg, South Africa*

Maija-Leena Aulikki Huotari / *University of Oulu, Oulu, Finland*

Henriette D. Avram / *Library of Congress, Washington, District of Columbia, U.S.A.*

Sven Axsäter / *Department of Industrial Management and Logistics, Lund University, Lund, Sweden*

Murtha Baca / *Getty Research Institute, Los Angeles, California, U.S.A.*

Roger S. Bagnall / *Institute for the Study of the Ancient World, New York University, New York, New York, U.S.A.*

Nestor Bamidis / *GSA-Archives of Macedonia, Thessaloniki, Greece*

Franz Barachini / *Business Innovation Consulting—Austria, Langenzersdorf, Austria*

Rebecca O. Barclay / *Rensselaer Polytechnic Institute, Troy, New York, U.S.A.*

Judit Bar-Ilan / *Department of Information Science, Bar-Ilan University, Ramat Gan, Israel*

Alex W. Barker / *Museum of Art and Archaeology, University of Missouri, Columbia, Missouri, U.S.A.*

John A. Bateman / *University of Bremen, Bremen, Germany*

Marcia J. Bates / *Department of Information Studies, Graduate School of Education and Information Studies, University of California, Los Angeles (UCLA), Los Angeles, California, U.S.A.*

Philippe Baumard / *School of Engineering, Stanford University, Stanford, California, U.S.A., and University Paul Cézanne, Aix-en-Provence, France*

David Bawden / *City, University of London, London, U.K.*

Jennifer Bawden / *Museum Studies Program, Faculty of Information Studies, University of Toronto, Toronto, Ontario, Canada*

David Bearman / *Archives & Museum Informatics, Toronto, Ontario, Canada*

William K. Beatty / *Northwestern University Medical School, Chicago, Illinois, U.S.A.*

A.R. Bednarek / *University of Florida, Gainesville, Florida, U.S.A.*

Clare Beghtol / *Faculty of Information Studies, University of Toronto, Toronto, Ontario, Canada*

Lori Bell / *Alliance Library System, East Peoria, Illinois, U.S.A.*

Danna Bell-Russel / *Library of Congress, Washington, District of Columbia, U.S.A.*

William Benedon / *Benedon & Associates, Encino, California, U.S.A.*

Anna Bergaliyeva / *Kazakhstan Institute of Management, Economics and Strategic Research (KIMEP), Almaty, Kazakhstan*

Sidney E. Berger / *Phillips Library, Peabody Essex Museum, Salem, Massachusetts, U.S.A.*

Andrew J. Berner / *University Club of New York, New York, New York, U.S.A.*

Sean F. Berrigan / *Policy, Library and Archives Canada, Ottawa, Ontario, Canada*

John W. Berry / *NILRC: Network of Illinois Learning Resources in Community Colleges, Dominican University, River Forest, Illinois, U.S.A.*

Michael W. Berry / *Department of Electrical Engineering and Computer Science, University of Tennessee, Knoxville, Tennessee, U.S.A.*

Suresh K. Bhavnani / *Center for Computational Medicine and Bioinformatics, University of Michigan, Ann Arbor, Michigan, U.S.A.*

Tamara Biggs / *Chicago History Museum, Chicago, Illinois, U.S.A.*

Frank Birkebæk / *Roskilde Museum, Roskilde, Denmark*

Ann P. Bishop / *Graduate School of Library and Information Science, University of Illinois at Urbana-Champaign, Urbana, Illinois, U.S.A.*

Julia Blixrud / *Association of Research Libraries, Washington, District of Columbia, U.S.A.*

Gloria Bordogna / *Italian National Research Council, Institute for the Dynamics of Environmental Processes, Dalmine, Italy*

Steve Bosch / *Administration Department, University of Arizona, Tucson, Arizona, U.S.A.*

Kimberly S. Bostwick / *Ecology and Evolutionary Biology, Cornell University Museum of Vertebrates, Ithaca, New York, U.S.A.*

Natalia T. Bowdoin / *University of South Carolina Aiken, Aiken, South Carolina, U.S.A.*

Patrick J. Boylan / *Department of Cultural Policy and Management, City University, London, U.K.*

Amy E. Brand / *CrossRef, Lynnfield, Massachusetts, U.S.A.*

Judy Brooker / *Australian Library and Information Association, Deakin, Australian Capital Territory, Australia*

Terrence Brooks / *iSchool, University of Washington, Seattle, Washington, U.S.A.*

Vanda Broughton / *School of Library, Archive and Information Studies, University College London, London, U.K.*

Cecelia Brown / *School of Library and Information Studies, University of Oklahoma, Norman, Oklahoma, U.S.A.*

Jos de Bruijn / *Digital Enterprise Research Institute, University of Innsbruck, Innsbruck, Austria*

Steve Bryant / *BFI National Archive, Herts, U.K.*

Alan Bryden / *International Organization for Standardization, Geneva, Switzerland*

Jeff E. Bullard / *Free Library of Philadelphia, Philadelphia, Pennsylvania, U.S.A.*

Kathleen Burns / *Beinecke Rare Book and Manuscript Library, Yale University, New Haven, Connecticut, U.S.A.*

Brenda A. Burton / *Library, Kirkland & Ellis LLP, Chicago, IL, U.S.A.*

E. Burton Swanson / *Anderson School of Management, University of California, Los Angeles, Los Angeles, California, U.S.A.*

Donald I. Butcher / *Canadian Library Association, Ottawa, Ontario, Canada*

Kevin Butterfield / *Wolf Law Library, College of William and Mary, Williamsburg, Virginia, U.S.A.*

Alex Byrne / *University of Technology, Sydney—Sydney, New South Wales, Australia*

Brian Byrne / *Discipline of Psychology, School of Behavioural, Cognitive and Social Sciences, University of New England, Armidale, New South Wales, Australia, Australian Research Council Centre of Excellence in Cognition and its Disorder, Australia, and National Health and Medical Research Council Centre of Research Excellence in Twin Research, Australia*

Bernadette G. Callery / *School of Information Sciences, University of Pittsburgh, Pittsburgh, Pennsylvania, U.S.A.*

Paul D. Callister / *Leon E. Bloch Law Library, University of Missouri-Kansas City School of Law, Kansas City, Missouri, U.S.A.*

Perrine Canavaggio / *International Council on Archives, Paris, France*

Sarah R. Canino / *Dickinson Music Library, Vassar College, Poughkeepsie, New York, U.S.A.*

Robert Capra / *School of Information and Library Science, University of North Carolina, Chapel Hill, North Carolina, U.S.A.*

Nicholas Carroll / *Hastings Research, Inc., Las Vegas, Nevada, U.S.A.*

Ben Carterette / *Department of Computer and Information Sciences, University of Delaware, Newark, Delaware, U.S.A.*

Vittorio Castelli / *T.J. Watson Research Center, IBM, Yorktown Heights, New York, U.S.A.*

Jane Rosetta Virginia Caulton / *Library of Congress, Washington, District of Columbia, U.S.A.*

Richard Cave / *Formerly at the Public Library of Science, San Francisco, California, U.S.A.*

Roderick Cave / *Loughborough University, Loughborough, U.K.*

Marcel Caya / *Department of History, University of Quebec at Montreal (UQAM), Montreal, Quebec, Canada*

Frank Cervone / *Purdue University Calumet, Hammond, Indiana, U.S.A.*

Leslie Champeny / *Alaska Resources Library and Information Services (ARLIS), Anchorage, Alaska, U.S.A.*

Lois Mai Chan / *School of Library and Information Science, University of Kentucky, Lexington, Kentucky, U.S.A.*

Sergio Chaparro-Univazo / *Graduate School of Library and Information Science, Simmons College, Boston, Massachusetts, U.S.A.*

Mary K. Chelton / *Graduate School of Library and Information Studies, Queens College Flushing, New York, U.S.A.*

Hsinchun Chen / *Department of Management Information Systems, University of Arizona, Tucson, Arizona, U.S.A.*

Jianhua Chen / *Computer Science Department, Louisiana State University, Baton Rouge, Louisiana, U.S.A.*

Eric R. Childress / *OCLC, Dublin, Ohio, U.S.A.*

Michael A. Chilton / *Department of Management, Kansas State University, Manhattan, Kansas, U.S.A.*

TzeHuey Chiou-Peng / *Spurlock Museum, University of Illinois at Urbana-Champaign, Urbana, Illinois, U.S.A.*

Hyun-Yang Cho / *Department of Library and Information Science, Kyonggi University, Suwon, South Korea*

Jae-Hwang Choi / *Department of Library and Information Science, Kyungpook National University, Daegu, South Korea*

Carol E.B. Choksy / *School of Library and Information Science, Indiana University, Bloomington, Indiana, U.S.A.*

Su Kim Chung / *University Libraries, University of Nevada–Las Vegas, Las Vegas, Nevada, U.S.A.*

James Church / *University Libraries, University of California, Berkeley, Berkeley, California, U.S.A.*

Barbara H. Clubb / *Ottawa Public Library, Ottawa, Ontario, Canada*

Arlene Cohen / *Pacific Islands Library Consultant, Seattle, Washington, U.S.A.*

Barbara Cohen-Stratyner / *New York Public Library for the Performing Arts, New York, U.S.A.*

Edward T. Cokely / *Center for Adaptive Behavior and Cognition, Max Planck Institute for Human Development, Berlin, Germany*

Arthur H. Cole / *Harvard University, Cambridge, Massachusetts, U.S.A.*

John Y. Cole / *Center for the Book, Library of Congress, Washington, District of Columbia, U.S.A.*

Patrick Tod Colegrove / *DeLaMare Science & Engineering Library, University Libraries, University of Nevada, Reno, Reno, Nevada, U.S.A.*

Edwin T. Coman, Jr. / *University of California, Riverside, California, U.S.A.*

Nora T. Corley / *Arctic Institute of North America, Montreal, Quebec, Canada*

Sheila Corrall / *Department of Information Studies, University of Sheffield, Sheffield, U.K.*

Erica Cosijn / *Department of Information Science, University of Pretoria, Pretoria, South Africa*

Richard J. Cox / *School of Computing and Information, University of Pittsburgh, Pittsburgh, Pennsylvania, U.S.A.*

Barbara M. Cross / *Records and Information Management, Sony Pictures Entertainment, Culver City, California, U.S.A.*

Kevin Crowston / *School of Information Studies, Syracuse University, Syracuse, New York, U.S.A.*

Adrian Cunningham / *National Archives of Australia (NAA), Canberra, Australian Capital Territory, Australia*

Judith N. Currano / *University of Pennsylvania, Philadelphia, Pennsylvania, U.S.A.*

Susan Curzon / *University Library, California State University–Northridge, Northridge, California, U.S.A.*

Ingetraut Dahlberg / *Bad Koenig, Germany*

Nan Christian Ploug Dahlkild / *Royal School of Library and Information Science, Copenhagen, Denmark*

Jay E. Daily / *University of Pittsburgh, Pittsburgh, Pennsylvania, U.S.A.*

Kimiz Dalkir / *Graduate School of Library and Information Studies, McGill University, Montreal, Quebec, Canada*

Prudence W. Dalrymple / *Drexel University College of Computing & Informatics, Philadelphia, Pennsylvania, U.S.A.*

Marcel Danesi / *Department of Anthropology, University of Toronto, Toronto, Ontario, Canada*

Xuan Hong Dang / *Computer Vision and Image Understanding, Institute for Infocomm, A* STAR, Singapore*

Yan Dang / *Department of Management Information Systems, University of Arizona, Tucson, Arizona, U.S.A.*

Evelyn Daniel / *School of Information and Library Science, University of North Carolina at Chapel Hill, Chapel Hill, North Carolina, U.S.A.*

Richard A. Danner / *School of Law, Duke University, Durham, North Carolina, U.S.A.*

Regina Dantas / *Museu Nacional, HCTE, Universidade Federal do Rio de Janeiro, Rio de Janeiro, Brazil*

Daniel C. Danzig / *Consultant, Pasadena, California, U.S.A.*

Robert Allen Daugherty / *University Library, University of Illinois at Chicago, Chicago, Illinois, U.S.A.*

Charles H. Davis / *Indiana University, Bloomington, IN, U.S.A., and School of Library and Information Science, Indiana University, Bloomington, Indiana, U.S.A.*

Gordon B. Davis / *Carlson School of Management, University of Minnesota, Minneapolis, Minnesota, U.S.A.*

Mary Ellen Davis / *American Library Association, Chicago, Illinois, U.S.A.*

Peter Davis / *International Centre for Cultural and Heritage Studies, Newcastle University, Newcastle upon Tyne, U.K.*

Sheryl Davis / *University Library, University of California, Riverside, Riverside, California, U.S.A.*

Ronald E. Day / *School of Library and Information Science, Indiana University, Bloomington, Indiana, U.S.A.*

Cheryl Dee / *School of Library and Information Science, University of South Florida, Tampa, Florida, U.S.A.*

Robert DeHart / *Department of History, Middle Tennessee State University, Murfreesboro, Tennessee, U.S.A.*

Brenda Dervin / *School of Communication, Ohio State University, Columbus, Ohio, U.S.A.*

Brian Detlor / *Information Systems, McMaster University, Hamilton, Ontario, Canada*

Don E. Detmer / *American Medical Informatics Association (AMIA), Bethesda, Maryland, U.S.A.*

Stella G. Dextre Clarke / *Information Consultant, Oxfordshire, U.K.*

Catherine Dhérent / *National Library of France, Paris, France*

Anne R. Diekema / *Gerald R. Sherratt Library, Southern Utah University, Cedar City, Utah, U.S.A.*

Susan S. DiMattia / *DiMattia Associates, Stamford, Connecticut, U.S.A.*

Gloria Dinerman / *The Library Co-Op, Inc., Edison, New Jersey, U.S.A.*

Jesse David Dinneen / *School of Information Studies, McGill University, Montreal, Quebec, Canada*

Bernard Dione / *School of Librarianship, Archivists Information Science (EBAD), Cheikh Anta Diop University, Dakar, Senegal*

Dieyi Diouf / *Central Library, Cheikh Anta Diop University of Dakar, Dakar, Senegal*

Keith Donohue / *National Historical Publications and Records Commission, Washington, District of Columbia, U.S.A.*

Ann Doyle / *X̱wi7xwa Library, First Nations House of Learning, University of British Columbia, Vancouver, British Columbia, Canada*

Carol D. Doyle / *Government Documents Department and Map Library, California State University, Fresno, California, U.S.A.*

Marek J. Druzdzel / *School of Information Sciences and Intelligent Systems Program, University of Pittsburgh, Pittsburgh, Pennsylvania, U.S.A., and Faculty of Computer Science, Bialystok Technical University, Bialystok, Poland*

Kathel Dunn / *National Library of Medicine, Bethesda, Maryland, U.S.A.*

Luciana Duranti / *School of Library, Archival and Information Studies, University of British Columbia, Vancouver, British Columbia, Canada*

Joan C. Durrance / *School of Information, University of Michigan, Ann Arbor, Michigan, U.S.A.*

Maria Economou / *Department of Communication and Cultural Technology, University of the Aegean, Mytilini, Greece*

Gary Edson / *Center for Advanced Study in Museum Science and Heritage Management, Museum of Texas Tech University, Lubbock, Texas, U.S.A.*

Mary B. Eggert / *Library, Kirkland & Ellis LLP, Chicago, IL, U.S.A.*

Daniel Eisenberg / *Florida State University, Tallahassee, Florida, U.S.A.*

Innocent I. Ekoja / *University Library, University of Abuja, Abuja, Nigeria*

Sarah Elliott / *International Centre for Cultural and Heritage Studies, Newcastle University, Newcastle upon Tyne, U.K.*

David Ellis / *Department of Information Studies, Aberystwyth University, Wales, U.K.*

Jill Emery / *Portland State University Library, Portland, Oregon, U.S.A.*

Zorana Ercegovac / *InfoEN Associates, Los Angeles, California, U.S.A.*

Timothy L. Ericson / *School of Information Science, University of Wisconsin-Milwaukee, Milwaukee, Wisconsin, U.S.A.*

Elena Escolano Rodríguez / *National Library of Spain, Madrid, Spain*

Leigh S. Estabrook / *Graduate School of Library and Information Science, University of Illinois at Urbana- / Champaign, Champaign, Illinois, U.S.A.*

Mark E. Estes / *Alameda County Law Library, Oakland, California, U.S.A.*

Beth Evans / *Library, Brooklyn College, City University of New York, Brooklyn, New York, U.S.A.*

Joanne Evans / *Centre for Organisational and Social Informatics, Monash University, Melbourne, Victoria, Australia*

Dominic J. Farace / *Grey Literature Network Service, TextRelease/GreyNet, Amsterdam, The Netherlands*

David Farneth / *Special Collections and Institutional Records, Getty Research Institute, Los Angeles, California, U.S.A.*

Sharon Fawcett / *Office of Presidential Libraries, National Archives and Records Administration, College Park, Maryland, U.S.A.*

Dieter Fensel / *Institute of Computer Science, University of Innsbruck, Innsbruck, Austria, and National University of Ireland, Galway, Galway, Ireland*

Thomas L. Findley / *Leo A. Daly/Architects & Engineers, Omaha, Nebraska, U.S.A.*

Karen E. Fisher / *Information School, University of Washington, Seattle, Washington, U.S.A.*

Nancy Fjällbrant / *Chalmers University of Technology Library, International Association of Technological University Libraries, Gothenburg, Sweden*

Julia Flanders / *Brown University, Providence, Rhode Island, U.S.A.*

Nancy Flury Carlson / *Westinghouse Electric Corporation, Pittsburgh, Pennsylvania, U.S.A.*

Roger R. Flynn / *School of Information Sciences and Intelligent Systems Program, University of Pittsburgh, Pittsburgh, Pennsylvania, U.S.A.*

Helen Forde / *Department of Information Studies, University College London, London, U.K.*

Douglas J. Foskett / *University of London, London, U.K.*

Susan Foutz / *Institute for Learning Innovation, Edgewater, Maryland, U.S.A.*

Christopher Fox / *Department of Computer Science, James Madison University, Harrisonburg, Virginia, U.S.A.*

Carl Franklin / *Consultant, Columbus, Ohio, U.S.A.*

Jonathan A. Franklin / *Gallagher Law Library, University of Washington, Seattle, Washington, U.S.A.*

Thomas J. Froehlich / *School of Library and Information Science, Kent State University, Kent, Ohio, U.S.A.*

Steve Fuller / *Department of Sociology, University of Warwick, Coventry, U.K.*

Crystal Fulton / *School of Information and Communication Studies, University College Dublin, Dublin, Ireland*

Carla J. Funk / *Medical Library Association, Chicago, Illinois, U.S.A.*

Jonathan Furner / *Department of Information Studies University of California, Los Angeles, Los Angeles, California, U.S.A.*

Dennis Galletta / *Katz Graduate School of Business, University of Pittsburgh, Pittsburgh, Pennsylvania, U.S.A.*

D. Linda Garcia / *Communication Culture and Technology, Georgetown University, Washington, District of Columbia, U.S.A.*

Holly Gardinier / *Honnold/Mudd Library, Libraries of The Claremont Colleges, Claremont, California, U.S.A.*

Sally Gardner Reed / *Association of Library Trustees, Advocates, Friends and Foundations (ALTAFF), Philadelphia, Pennsylvania, U.S.A.*

Janifer Gatenby / *Online Computer Library Center (OCLC), Leiden, The Netherlands*

Ramesh C. Gaur / *Kalanidhi Division, Indira Gandhi National Centre for the Arts (IGNCA), New Delhi, India*

Lee Anne George / *Association of Research Libraries, Washington, District of Columbia, U.S.A.*

David E. Gerard / *College of Librarianship Wales, Cardiganshire, Wales, U.K.*

Malcolm Getz / *Department of Economics, Vanderbilt University, Nashville, Tennessee, U.S.A.*

Mary W. Ghikas / *American Library Association, Chicago, Illinois, U.S.A.*

Nicholas Gibbins / *School of Electronics and Computer Science, University of Southampton, Southampton, U.K.*

Gerd Gigerenzer / *Center for Adaptive Behavior and Cognition, Max Planck Institute for Human Development, Berlin, Germany*

Tommaso Giordano / *Library, European University Institute, Florence, Italy*

Lilian Gisesa / *Kenya National Archives, Nairobi, Kenya*

Edward A. Goedeken / *Iowa State University, Ames, Iowa, U.S.A.*

Warren R. Goldmann / *National Technical Institute for the Deaf, Rochester Institute of Technology, Rochester, New York, U.S.A.*

David Gordon / *Milwaukee Art Museum, Milwaukee, Wisconsin, U.S.A.*

David B. Gracy II / *School of Information, University of Texas at Austin, Austin, Texas, U.S.A.*

Karen F. Gracy / *School of Library and Information Science, Kent State University, Kent, Ohio, U.S.A.*

Renny Granda / *Universidad Central de Venezuela, Caracas, Venezuela*

Paul Gray / *School of Information Systems and Technology, Claremont Graduate University, Claremont, California, U.S.A.*

Jane Greenberg / *Metadata Research Center, School of Information and Library Science, University of North Carolina at Chapel Hill, Chapel Hill, North Carolina, U.S.A.*

Karen Greenwood / *American Medical Informatics Association (AMIA), Bethesda, Maryland, U.S.A.*

Jill E. Grogg / *Libraries, University of Alabama, Tuscaloosa, Alabama, U.S.A.*

Melissa Gross / *School of Information, Florida State University, Tallahassee, Florida, U.S.A.*

Andrew Grove / *Guest Faculty, Information School, University of Washington, Seattle, Washington, U.S.A.*

Dinesh K. Gupta / *Department of Library and Information Science, Vardhaman Mahaveer Open University, 3 Kota, India*

Laurel L. Haak / *Open Researcher and Contributor ID, Inc. (ORCID), U.S.A.*

Kate Hagan / *American Association of Law Libraries, Chicago, Illinois, U.S.A.*

Kathleen Hall / *Leon E. Bloch Law Library, University of Missouri-Kansas City School of Law, Kansas City, Missouri, U.S.A.*

Virginia M.G. Hall / *Center for Educational Resources, The Sheridan Libraries, Johns Hopkins University, Baltimore, Maryland, U.S.A.*

Wendy Hall / *Intelligence, Agents, Multimedia Group, University of Southampton, Southampton, U.K.*

Stuart Hamilton / *International Federation of Library Associations and Institutions, The Hague, The Netherlands*

Maureen L. Hammer / *Knowledge Management, Batelle Memorial Institute, Charlottesville, Virginia, U.S.A.*

Jong-Yup Han / *Research Information Team, KORDI, Seoul, South Korea*

Debra Gold Hansen / *School of Library and Information Science, San Jose State University, Yorba Linda, California, U.S.A.*

Derek L. Hansen / *University of Maryland, College Park, Maryland, U.S.A.*

Eugene R. Hanson / *Shippensburg State College, Shippensburg, Pennsylvania, U.S.A.*

Jane Hardy / *Australian Library and Information Association, Deakin, Australian Capital Territory, Australia*

Julie Hart / *American Association of Museums, Washington, District of Columbia, U.S.A.*

Hiroyuki Hatano / *Surugadai University, Saitama, Japan*

Robert M. Hayes / *Department of Information Studies, University of California, Los Angeles, Los Angeles, California, U.S.A.*

Caroline Haythornthwaite / *Graduate School of Library and Information Science, University of Illinois at Urbana- / Champaign, Champaign, Illinois, U.S.A.*

Penny Hazelton / *Gallagher Law Library, University of Washington, Seattle, Washington, U.S.A.*

P. Bryan Heidorn / *Graduate School of Library and Information Science, University of Illinois at Urbana-Champaign, Champaign, Illinois, U.S.A.*

Helen Heinrich / *Collection Access and Management Services, California State University–Northridge, Northridge, California, U.S.A.*

Doris S. Helfer / *Collection Access and Management Services, California State University–Northridge, Northridge, California, U.S.A.*

Markus Helfert / *School of Computing, Dublin City University, Dublin, Ireland*

Jean Henefer / *School of Information and Communication Studies, University College Dublin, Dublin, Ireland*

Steven L. Hensen / *Rare Book, Manuscript and Special Collections Library, Duke University, Durham, North Carolina, U.S.A.*

Pamela M. Henson / *Archives, Smithsonian Institution, Washington, District of Columbia, U.S.A.*

Peter Hernon / *Graduate School of Library and Information Science, Simmons College, Boston, Massachusetts, U.S.A.*

Dorothy H. Hertzel / *Case Western Reserve University, Cleveland, Ohio, U.S.A.*

Francis Heylighen / *Free University of Brussels, Brussels, Belgium*

Randolph Hock / *Online Strategies, Annapolis, Maryland, U.S.A.*

Theodora L. Hodges / *Berkeley, California, U.S.A.*

Sara S. Hodson / *Huntington Library, San Marino, California, U.S.A.*

Judy C. Holoviak / *American Geophysical Union, Washington, District of Columbia, U.S.A.*

Aleksandra Horvat / *Faculty of Philosophy, University of Zagreb, Zagreb, Croatia*

Ali Houissa / *Olin Library, Cornell University, Ithaca, New York, U.S.A.*

Pamela Howard-Reguindin / *Library of Congress Office, Nairobi, Kenya*

Han-Yin Huang / *International Centre for Cultural and Heritage Studies, Newcastle University, Newcastle upon Tyne, U.K.*

Kathleen Hughes / *American Library Association, Chicago, Illinois, U.S.A.*

Betsy L. Humphreys / *National Library of Medicine, Bethesda, Maryland, U.S.A.*

Charlene S. Hurt / *University Library, Georgia State University, Atlanta, Georgia, U.S.A.*

Sue Hutley / *Australian Library and Information Association, Deakin, Australian Capital Territory, Australia*

John P. Immroth / *University of Pittsburgh, Pittsburgh, Pennsylvania, U.S.A.*

Peter Ingwersen / *Royal School of Library and Information Science, University of Copenhagen, Copenhagen, Denmark*

Vanessa Irvin / *Library and Information Science Program, Information and Computer Sciences Department, University of Hawaii at Mānoa, Honolulu, Hawaii, U.S.A.*

Karla Irwin / *University Libraries, University of Nevada–Las Vegas, Las Vegas, Nevada, U.S.A.*

October R. Ivins / *Ivins eContent Solutions, Sharon, Massachusetts, U.S.A.*

Kalervo Järvelin / *School of Information Science, University of Tampere, Tampere, Finland*

Jean Frédéric Jauslin / *Federal Department of Home Affairs (FDHA), Swiss Federal Office of Culture, Bern, Switzerland*

V. Jeyaraj / *Hepzibah Institute of Conversion, Chennai, India*

Scott Johnston / *McPherson Library, University of Victoria, Victoria, British Columbia, Canada*

Trevor Jones / *Mountain Heritage Center, Western Carolina University, Cullowhee, North Carolina, U.S.A.*

William Jones / *Information School, University of Washington, Seattle, Washington, U.S.A.*

Jay Jordan / *OCLC Online Computer Library Center, Inc., Dublin, Ohio, U.S.A.*

Corinne Jörgensen / *School of Information Studies, Florida State University, Tallahassee, Florida, U.S.A.*

Gene Joseph / *Aboriginal Library Consultant, Langley, British Columbia, Canada*

Daniel N. Joudrey / *School of Library and Information Science, Simmons College, Boston, Massachusetts, U.S.A.*

Heidi Julien / *Library and Information Studies, State University of New York–Buffalo, Buffalo, New York, U.S.A.*

Janet Kaaya / *Department of Information Studies, University of California, Los Angeles, California, U.S.A.*

Philomena Kagwiria Mwirigi / *Kenya National Library Service (KNLS), Nairobi, Kenya*

Athanase B. Kanamugire / *Library Consultant, Dhahran, Saudi Arabia*

Paul B. Kantor / *School of Communication and Information, Rutgers University, New Brunswick, New Jersey, U.S.A.*

Sofia Kapnisi / *International Federation of Library Associations and Institutions, The Hague, the Netherlands*

Nelson Otieno Karilus / *Kenya National Library Service (KNLS), Nairobi, Kenya*

Amy M. Kautzman / *University of California, Berkeley, Berkeley, California, U.S.A.*

Karalyn Kavanaugh / *Account Services Manager, EBSCO Information Services, Birmingham, Alabama, U.S.A.*

Caroline Kayoro / *Kenya National Library Service (KNLS), Nairobi, Kenya*

Andreas Kellerhals / *Federal Department of Home Affairs (FDHA), Swiss Federal Archives, Bern, Switzerland*

John M. Kennedy / *Indiana University, Bloomington, Indiana, U.S.A.*

Kristen Kern / *Portland State University, Portland, Oregon, U.S.A.*

Christopher S.G. Khoo / *School of Communication and Information, Nanyang Technological University, Singapore*

Tapan Khopkar / *University of Michigan, Ann Arbor, Michigan, U.S.A.*

Irene Muthoni Kibandi / *Kenya National Library Service (KNLS), Nairobi, Kenya*

Ruth E. Kifer / *Dr. Martin Luther King, Jr. Library, San Jose State University, San Jose, California, U.S.A.*

Seong Hee Kim / *Department of Library and Information Science, Chung-Ang University, Seoul, South Korea*

Pancras Kimaru / *Kenya National Library Service (KNLS), Nairobi, Kenya*

Karen E. King / *Washington, District of Columbia, U.S.A.*

William R. King / *University of Pittsburgh, Pittsburgh, Pennsylvania, U.S.A.*

Susan K. Kinnell / *Consultant, Santa Barbara, California, U.S.A.*

Laurence J. Kipp / *Harvard University, Cambridge, Massachusetts, U.S.A.*

Thomas G. Kirk, Jr. / *Earlham College Libraries, Earlham College, Richmond, Indiana, U.S.A.*

Breanne A. Kirsch / *Library, Emerging Technologies, University of South Carolina Upstate, Spartanburg, South Carolina, U.S.A.*

Vernon N. Kisling, Jr. / *Marston Science Library, University of Florida, Gainesville, Florida, U.S.A.*

Adam D. Knowles / *San Diego, California, U.S.A.*

Rebecca Knuth / *Library and Information Science Program, University of Hawaii, Honolulu, Hawaii, U.S.A.*

Michael Koenig / *College of Information and Computer Science, Long Island University, Brookville, New York, U.S.A.*

Jesse Koennecke / *Cornell University Library, Cornell University College of Arts and Sciences, Ithaca, New York, U.S.A.*

Jes Koepfler / *Museum Studies Program, Faculty of Information Studies, University of Toronto, Toronto, Ontario, Canada*

Amelia Koford / *Blumberg Memorial Library, Texas Lutheran University, Seguin, Texas, U.S.A.*

Toru Koizumi / *Library, Rikkyo University, Tokyo, Japan*

Josip Kolanović / *Croatian State Archives, Zagreb, Croatia*

Sjoerd Koopman / *International Federation of Library Associations and Institutions, The Hague, the Netherlands*

Donald Kraft / *Department of Computer Science, U.S. Air Force Academy, Colorado Springs, Colorado, U.S.A.*

Allison Krebs / *University of Arizona, Tucson, Arizona, U.S.A.*

Judith F. Krug / *Office for Intellectual Freedom, American Library Association, Chicago, Illinois, U.S.A.*

D.W. Krummel / *Emeritus, Graduate School of Library and Information Science, University of Illinois at Urbana-Champaign, Champaign, Illinois, U.S.A.*

Carol Collier Kuhlthau / *Department of Library and Information Science, Rutgers University, New Brunswick, New Jersey, U.S.A.*

Krishan Kumar / *Former Head, Department of Library and Information Science, University of Delhi, New Delhi, India*

Sanna Kumpulainen / *Library, Tampere University of Technology, Tampere, Finland*

Michael J. Kurtz / *National Archives at College Park, U.S. National Archives and Records Administration, College Park, Maryland, U.S.A.*

Zhenhua Lai / *Department of Management Information Systems, University of Arizona, Tucson, Arizona, U.S.A.*

Mounia Lalmas / *Department of Computing Science, University of Glasgow, Glasgow, U.K.*

Heather M. Lamond / *Massey University Library, Palmerston North, New Zealand*

F.W. Lancaster / *Graduate School of Library and Information Science, University of Illinois at Urbana-Champaign, Urbana, Illinois, U.S.A.*

Ronald L. Larsen / *School of Information Sciences, University of Pittsburgh, Pittsburgh, Pennsylvania, U.S.A.*

Ray R. Larson / *School of Information, University of California—Berkeley, Berkeley, California, U.S.A.*

Jesús Lau / *Library Services Unit USBI Veracruz (USBI VER), University of Veracruz, Veracruz, Mexico*

Judith V. Lechner / *Department of Educational Foundations, Leadership, and Technology, Auburn University, Auburn, Alabama, U.S.A.*

Christopher A. Lee / *School of Information and Library Science, University of North Carolina at Chapel Hill, Chapel Hill, North Carolina, U.S.A.*

Janet Lee / *University of Denver, Denver, Colorado, U.S.A, and Regis University, Denver, Colorado, U.S.A.*

Catherine Leekam / *Museum Studies Program, Faculty of Information Studies, University of Toronto, Toronto, Ontario, Canada*

Kjell Lemström / *Department of Computer Science, University of Helsinki, Helsinki, Finland*

Timothy F. Leslie / *Department of Geography and Geoinformation Science, George Mason University, Fairfax, Virginia, U.S.A.*

Noémie Lesquins / *Scientific Mission (DSR), National Library of France, Paris, France*

Rosalind K. Lett / *Information-2-Knowledge, Atlanta, Georgia, U.S.A.*

Allison V. Level / *Colorado State University, Fort Collins, Colorado, U.S.A.*

Michael Levine-Clark / *Penrose Library, University of Denver, Denver, Colorado, U.S.A.*

Anany Levitin / *Department of Computing Sciences, Villanova University, Villanova, Pennsylvania, U.S.A.*

Marjorie Lewis / *Canaan, New York, U.S.A.*

Elizabeth D. Liddy / *School of Information Studies, Syracuse University, Syracuse, New York, U.S.A.*

Silje C. Lier / *Software & Information Industry Association, Washington, District of Columbia, U.S.A.*

Jane E. Light / *Dr. Martin Luther King, Jr. Library, San Jose Public Library, San Jose, California, U.S.A.*

Paul M. Lima / *Canadian Heritage Information Network (CHIN), Gatineau, Quebec, Canada*

Louise Limberg / *Swedish School of Library and Information Science, University of Borås and University of Gothenburg, Borås, Sweden*

Shin-jeng Lin / *Department of Business Administration, Le Moyne College, Syracuse, New York, U.S.A.*

Sarah Lippincott / *Educopia Institute, Atlanta, Georgia, U.S.A.*

Peter Johan Lor / *School of Information Studies, University of Wisconsin-Milwaukee, Milwaukee, Wisconsin, U.S.A., and Department of Information Science, University of Pretoria, Pretoria, South Africa*

Beth Luey / *Fairhaven, Massachusetts, U.S.A.*

Joseph Luke / *Kazakhstan Institute of Management, Economics and Strategic Research (KIMEP), Almaty, Kazakhstan*

Claudia Lux / *Central and Regional Library of Berlin (ZLB), Berlin, Germany*

Marianne Lykke / *Information Interaction and Architecture, Royal School of Library and Information Science, Aalborg, Denmark*

Elena Macevičiūtė / *Faculty of Communication, Vilnius University, Vilnius, Lithuania, and Swedish School of Library and Information Science, University of Borås, Borås, Sweden*

Juan D. Machin-Mastromatteo / *Universidad Central de Venezuela, Caracas, Venezuela*

Barbara A. Macikas / *American Library Association, Chicago, Illinois, U.S.A.*

Leslie Madsen-Brooks / *Boise State University, Boise, Idaho, U.S.A.*

William J. Maher / *Archives, University of Illinois at Urbana-Champaign, Urbana, Illinois, U.S.A.*

Thomas Mann / *Library of Congress, Washington, District of Columbia, U.S.A.*

Sylva Natalie Manoogian / *Department of Information Studies, University of California, Los Angeles, Los Angeles, California, U.S.A.*

Daniel Marcu / *Information Sciences Institute, University of Southern California, Marina del Rey, California, U.S.A.*

James W. Marcum / *Fairleigh Dickinson University, Madison, New Jersey, U.S.A.*

Francesca Marini / *School of Library, Archival and Information Studies, University of British Columbia, Vancouver, British Columbia, Canada*

Johan Marklund / *Department of Industrial Management and Logistics, Lund University, Lund, Sweden*

Dian I. Martin / *Small Bear Technical Consulting, LLC, Thorn Hill, Tennessee, U.S.A.*

Susan K. Martin / *Lauinger Library, Georgetown University, Washington, District of Columbia, U.S.A.*

Paul F. Marty / *College of Communication and Information, Florida State University, Tallahassee, Florida, U.S.A.*

Dan Marwit / *Lee H. Skolnick Architecture + Design Partnership, New York, New York, U.S.A.*

Laura Matzer / *Arizona Museum for Youth, Mesa, Arizona, U.S.A.*

Robert L. Maxwell / *Special Collections and Metadata Catalog Department, Brigham Young University, Provo, Utah, U.S.A.*

Hope Mayo / *Houghton Library, Harvard University, Cambridge, Massachusetts, U.S.A.*

Sally H. McCallum / *Network Development and MARC Standards Office, Library of Congress, Washington, District of Columbia, U.S.A.*

Gavan McCarthy / *eScholarship Research Centre, University of Melbourne, Melbourne, Victoria, Australia*

Ian McGowan / *Former Librarian, National Library of Scotland, Edinburgh, U.K.*

Roger McHaney / *Department of Management, Kansas State University, Manhattan, Kansas, U.S.A.*

I.C. McIlwaine / *University College London, School of Library, Archive and Information Studies, London, U.K.*

Sue McKemmish / *Centre for Organisational and Social Informatics, Monash University, Melbourne, Victoria, Australia*

Marie E. McVeigh / *JCR and Bibliographic Policy, Thomson Reuters - Scientific, Philadelphia, Pennsylvania, U.S.A.*

Linda Mboya / *National Museums of Kenya, Nairobi, Kenya*

Judith Adams Meadows / *State Law Library of Montana, Helena, Montana, U.S.A.*

K. van der Meer / *Faculty of Electrical Engineering, Mathematics and Computer Science, Delft University, the Netherlands; Information and Library Science, IOIW, Antwerp University, Belgium; and D-CIS, Delft, The Netherlands*

Bharat Mehra / *School of Information Sciences, University of Tennessee, Knoxville, Tennessee, U.S.A.*

Margaret Ann Mellinger / *OSU Libraries & Press, Oregon State University, Corvallis, Oregon, U.S.A.*

Elizabeth E. Merritt / *American Association of Museums, Washington, District of Columbia, U.S.A.*

David Millman / *Academic Information Systems, Columbia University, New York, U.S.A.*

Jack Mills / *North-Western Polytechnic, London, U.K.*

Kevin L. Mills / *National Institute of Standards and Technology, Gaithersburg, Maryland, U.S.A.*

Staša Milojević / *Department of Information Studies, University of California, Los Angeles, Los Angeles, California, U.S.A.*

Marla Misunas / *Collections Information and Access, San Francisco Museum of Modern Art, San Francisco, California, U.S.A.*

Joan S. Mitchell / *OCLC Online Computer Library Center, Inc., Dublin, Ohio, U.S.A.*

Yoriko Miyabe / *Rikkyo University, Tokyo, Japan*

Diane Mizrachi / *University Libraries, University of California–Los Angeles, Los Angeles, California, U.S.A.*

William Moen / *Texas Center for Digital Knowledge, University of North Texas, Denton, Texas, U.S.A.*

Abdul Moid / *University of Karachi, Karachi, Pakistan*

Hermann Moisl / *Center for Research in Linguistics, University of Newcastle upon Tyne, Newcastle upon Tyne, U.K.*

Ole Magnus Mølbak Andersen / *Danish State Archives, Copenhagen, Denmark*

Mavis B. Molto / *Utah State University, Logan, Utah, U.S.A.*

Philip Mooney / *Heritage Communications, Coca-Cola Company, Atlanta, Georgia, U.S.A.*

Reagan W. Moore / *San Diego Supercomputer Center, University of North Carolina at Chapel Hill, Chapel Hill, North Carolina, U.S.A.*

Mersini Moreleli-Cacouris / *Department of Library Science and Information Systems, Technological Educational Institute (TEI) of Thessaloniki, Sindos, Greece*

Paul K. Moser / *Department of Philosophy, Loyola University Chicago, Chicago, Illinois, U.S.A.*

Clara C. Mosquera / *Library, Kirkland & Ellis LLP, Chicago, IL, U.S.A.*

David J. Muddiman / *Leeds Metropolitan University, Leeds, U.K.*

Nancy C. Mulvany / *Bayside Indexing Service, Fort Collins, Colorado, U.S.A.*

Sue Myburgh / *School of Communication, University of South Australia, Adelaide, South Australia, Australia*

Elli Mylonas / *Brown University, Providence, Rhode Island, U.S.A.*

Jeremy Myntti / *J. Willard Marriott Library, Salt Lake City, Utah, U.S.A.*

Jacob Nadal / *ReCAP: The Research Collections and Preservation Consortium, Princeton, New Jersey, U.S.A.*

Diane Nahl / *Information and Computer Sciences Department, University of Hawaii, Honolulu, Hawaii, U.S.A.*

Robert Nardini / *Vice President, Library Services, ProQuest Books, La Vergne, Tennessee, U.S.A.*

Arnold vander Nat / *Department of Philosophy, Loyola University Chicago, Chicago, Illinois, U.S.A.*

Charles M. Naumer / *Information School, University of Washington, Seattle, Washington, U.S.A.*

Sophie Ndegwa / *Kenya National Library Service (KNLS), Nairobi, Kenya*

Dixie Neilson / *University of Florida, Gainesville, Florida, U.S.A.*

Sarah Beth Nelson / *School of Information and Library Sciences, University of North Carolina at Chapel Hill, Chapel Hill, North Carolina, U.S.A.*

Stuart J. Nelson / *National Library of Medicine, Bethesda, Maryland, U.S.A.*

Stephanie Nemcsok / *Museum Studies Program, Faculty of Information Studies, University of Toronto, Toronto, Ontario, Canada*

Ken Neveroski / *College of Information and Computer Science, Long Island University, Brookville, New York, U.S.A.*

Jennifer Ng / *Museum Studies Program, Faculty of Information Studies, University of Toronto, Toronto, Ontario, Canada*

Melissa Niiya / *Portland Public Schools, Portland, Oregon, U.S.A.*

Angela Noseworthy / *Museum Studies Program, Faculty of Information Studies, University of Toronto, Toronto, Ontario, Canada*

Barbara E. Nye / *Ictus Consulting, LLC, Pasadena, California, U.S.A.*

Charles Nzivo / *Kenya National Library Service (KNLS), Nairobi, Kenya*

Dennis O'Brien / *Maps and Wayfinding, LLC, Mystic, Connecticut, U.S.A.*

Karen Lynn O'Brien / *American Library Association, Chicago, Illinois, U.S.A.*

Kieron O'Hara / *Intelligence, Agents, Multimedia Group, University of Southampton, Southampton, U.K.*

Elizabeth O'Keefe / *Morgan Library and Museum, New York, U.S.A.*

Denise I. O'Shea / *Fairleigh Dickinson University, Teaneck, New Jersey, U.S.A.*

Douglas W. Oard / *College of Information Studies, University of Maryland, College Park, Maryland, U.S.A.*

Maria Oldal / *Morgan Library and Museum, New York, U.S.A.*

Lorne Olfman / *School of Information Systems and Technology, Claremont Graduate University, Claremont, California, U.S.A.*

Bette W. Oliver / *Austin, Texas, U.S.A.*

Annette Olson / *Biological Resources Division, U.S. Geological Survey, Reston, Virginia, U.S.A.*

Hope A. Olson / *School of Information Studies, University of Wisconsin-Milwaukee, Milwaukee, Wisconsin, U.S.A.*

Lawrence J. Olszewski / *OCLC Library, Dublin, Ohio, U.S.A.*

Kok-Leong Ong / *School of Information Technology, Deakin University, Burwood, Victoria, Australia*

Tim Owen / *Chartered Institute of Library and Information Professionals (CILIP), London, U.K.*

John C. Paolillo / *School of Informatics and School of Library and Information Science, Indiana University, Bloomington, Indiana, U.S.A.*

Eun Bong Park / *Library Service Department, National Library of Korea, Seoul, South Korea*

Soyeon Park / *Department of Library and Information Science, Duksung Womens University, Seoul, South Korea*

Gabriella Pasi / *Department of Informatics, Systems and Communication, University of Studies of Milano Bicocca, Milan, Italy*

Norman Paskin / *Tertius Ltd., Oxford, U.K.*

Christiane Paul / *Whitney Museum of American Art, New York, U.S.A.*

Ellen Pearlstein / *Information Studies and UCLA / Getty Program in the Conservation of Ethnographic and Archaeological Materials, University of California, Los Angeles, Los Angeles, California, U.S.A.*

Kathleen de la Peña McCook / *School of Library and Information Science, University of South Florida, Tampa, Florida, U.S.A.*

Steve Pepper / *Department of Linguistics, University of Oslo, Oslo, Norway*

Manuel A. Pérez-Quiñones / *Department of Software and Information Systems, University of North Carolina, Charlotte, North Carolina, U.S.A.*

Paul Evan Peters / *University of Pittsburgh, Pittsburgh, Pennsylvania, U.S.A.*

Jakob Heide Petersen / *Danish Agency for Libraries and Media, Copenhagen, Denmark*

Mary Jane Petrowski / *American Library Association, Chicago, Illinois, U.S.A.*

Katharine J. Phenix / *Northglenn Branch, Rangeview Library District, Northglenn, Colorado, U.S.A.*

Robert B. Pickering / *Gilcrease Museum, and Museum Science and Management Program, University of Tulsa, Tulsa, Oklahoma, U.S.A.*

Janice T. Pilch / *Rutgers University Libraries, Rutgers University, New Brunswick, New Jersey, U.S.A.*

Thomas E. Pinelli / *Langley Research Center, National Aeronautics and Space Administration (NASA) Hampton, Virginia, U.S.A.*

Daniel Pitti / *Alderman Library, Institute for Advanced Technology in the Humanities, University of Virginia, Charlottesville, Virginia, U.S.A.*

Elena Ploşniţă / *Science Department, National Museum of Archaeology and History of Moldova, Chisinau, Republic of Moldova*

Gabriela Podušelová / *Slovak National Museum, Bratislava, Slovak Republic*

Danny C.C. Poo / *School of Computing, Department of Information Systems, National University of Singapore, Singapore*

Martine Poulain / *Department of Libraries and Documentation, National Institute for the History of Art (INHA), Paris, France*

Tammy Powell / *National Library of Medicine, Bethesda, Maryland, U.S.A.*

Stephen Prine / *Library of Congress, Washington, District of Columbia, U.S.A.*

Mary Jo Pugh / *Editor, American Archivist, Walnut Creek, California, U.S.A.*

Ajit K. Pyati / *University of Western Ontario, London, Ontario, Canada*

Aimée C. Quinn / *Government Publications Services, Brooks Library, Central Washington University, Ellensburg, Washington, U.S.A.*

Jennie Quiñónez-Skinner / *University Library, California State University–Northridge, Northridge, California, U.S.A.*

Debbie Rabina / *School of Library and Information Science, Pratt Institute, New York, New York, U.S.A.*

Katalin Radics / *Research Library, University of California—Los Angeles, Los Angeles, California, U.S.A.*

Carl Rahkonen / *Harold S. Orendorff Music Library, Indiana University of Pennsylvania, Indiana, Pennsylvania, U.S.A.*

Jocelyn Rankin / *Centers for Disease Control and Prevention Library, Atlanta, Georgia, U.S.A.*

Samuel J. Redman / *Department of History, University of California, Berkeley, Berkeley, California, U.S.A.*

Thomas C. Redman / *Navesink Consulting Group, Little Silver, New Jersey, U.S.A.*

Barbara Reed / *Recordkeeping Innovation, Sydney, New South Wales, Australia*

Marcia Reed / *Getty Research Institute, Los Angeles, CA, U.S.A.*

CarrieLynn D. Reinhard / *Department of Communication, Business, and Information Technologies, Roskilde University, Roskilde, Denmark*

Harold C. Relyea / *Congressional Research Service, Library of Congress, Washington, District of Columbia, U.S.A.*

Steve Ricci / *Department of Information Studies/Film and Television, University of California–Los Angeles, Los Angeles, California, U.S.A.*

Ronald E. Rice / *Department of Communication, University of California–Santa Barbara, Santa Barbara, California, U.S.A.*

John V. Richardson, Jr. / *Department of Information Studies, University of California, Los Angeles, Los Angeles, California, U.S.A.*

Soo Young Rieh / *School of Information, University of Michigan, Ann Arbor, Michigan, U.S.A.*

Kevin S. Rioux / *Division of Library and Information Science, St. John's University, Queens, New York, U.S.A.*

Julian Roberts / *Wolfson College, University of Oxford, Oxford, U.K.*

Lyn Robinson / *City, University of London, London, U.K.*

Diane Robson / *University Libraries, Media Library, University of North Texas, Denton, Texas, U.S.A.*

Michael Rodriguez / *Michigan State University Libraries, East Lansin, Michigan, U.S.A.*

Juraj Roháč / *Department of Archival Science and Auxiliary Historical Sciences, Comenius University in, Bratislava, Slovak Republic*

Mark Roosa / *Pepperdine University, Malibu, California, U.S.A.*

Jonathan Rose / *Department of History, Drew University, Madison, New Jersey, U.S.A.*

Howard Rosenbaum / *School of Library and Information Science, Indiana University, Bloomington, Indiana, U.S.A.*

Catherine Sheldrick Ross / *Faculty of Information and Media Studies, University of Western Ontario, London, Ontario, Canada*

Shannon Ross / *Canadian Heritage Information Network (CHIN), Gatineau, Quebec, Canada*

Richard Rubin / *School of Library and Information Science, Kent State University, Kent, Ohio, U.S.A.*

Lynne M. Rudasill / *University of Illinois at Urbana-Champaign, Champaign, Illinois, U.S.A.*

Michael Rush / *Beinecke Rare Book and Manuscript Library, Yale University, New Haven, Connecticut, U.S.A.*

Mariza Russo / *Faculty of Administration and Accounting Sciences (FACC), Federal University of Rio de Janeiro, Rio de Janeiro, Brazil*

Athena Salaba / *Kent State University, Kent, Ohio, U.S.A.*

Romelia Salinas / *California State University, Los Angeles, Los Angeles, California, U.S.A.*

Airi Salminen / *Department of Computer Science and Information Systems, University of Jyväskylä, Jyväskylä, Finland*

Michael J. Salvo / *Department of English, Purdue University, West Lafayette, Indiana, U.S.A.*

Robert J. Sandusky / *University Library, University of Illinois at Chicago, Chicago, Illinois, U.S.A.*

Tefko Saracevic / *School of Communication and Information, Rutgers University, New Brunswick, New Jersey, U.S.A.*

Chris Sauer / *Said Business School, University of Oxford, Oxford, U.K.*

Rejéan Savard / *School of Library and Information Science, University of Montreal, Montreal, Quebec, Canada*

Reijo Savolainen / *School of Information Sciences, University of Tampere, Tampere, Finland*

Barbara Schaefer / *Geneseo, New York, U.S.A.*

Silvia Schenkolewski-Kroll / *Department of Information Science, Bar-Ilan University, Ramat Gan, Israel*

Lael J. Schooler / *Center for Adaptive Behavior and Cognition, Max Planck Institute for Human Development, Berlin, Germany*

Joachim Schöpfel / *Department of Library and Information Sciences (IDIST), GERiico Laboratory Charles de Gaulle University Lille 3, Villeneuve d'Ascq, France*

Catherine F. Schryer / *Department of English Language and Literature, University of Waterloo, Waterloo, Ontario, Canada*

Marjorie Schwarzer / *Museum Studies Department, John F. Kennedy University, Berkeley, California, U.S.A.*

Jo Ann Secor / *Lee H. Skolnick Architecture + Design Partnership, New York, New York, U.S.A.*

Sara Selwood / *Department of Cultural Policy and Management, City University, London, U.K.*

Frank B. Sessa / *University of Pittsburgh, Pittsburgh, Pennsylvania, U.S.A.*

Mark Sgambettera / *Bronx County Historical Society, Bronx, New York, U.S.A.*

Ayman Shabana / International Institute, University of California, Los Angeles, Los Angeles, California, U.S.A.

Nigel Shadbolt / *School of Electronics and Computer Science, University of Southampton, Southampton, U.K.*

Kalpana Shankar / *School of Informatics, Indiana University, Bloomington, Indiana, U.S.A.*

Debora Shaw / *School of Library and Information Science, Indiana University, Bloomington, Indiana, U.S.A.*

Conrad Shayo / *Department of Information and Decision Sciences, California State University—San Bernardino, San Bernardino, California, U.S.A.*

Elizabeth Shepherd / *Department of Information Studies, University College London, London, U.K.*

Beverly K. Sheppard / *Institute for Learning Innovation, Edgewater, Maryland, U.S.A.*

Ross Shimmon / *Faversham, U.K.*

Snunith Shoham / *Department of Information Science, Bar-Ilan University, Ramat Gan, Israel*

Lyudmila Shpilevaya / *New York Public Library, New York, New York, U.S.A.*

David Shumaker / *School of Library and Information Science, Catholic University of America, Washington, District of Columbia, U.S.A.*

Judith A. Siess / *Information Bridges International, Inc., Champaign, Illinois, U.S.A.*

John Edward Simmons / *Museologica, Bellefonte, Pennsylvania, U.S.A.*

Anestis Sitas / *Aristotle University of Thessaloniki, Thessaloniki, Greece*

Roswitha Skare / *Institute of Culture and Literature, UiT The Arctic University of Norway, Tromsø, Norway*

Katherine Skinner / *Educopia Institute, Atlanta, Georgia, U.S.A.*

Lee H. Skolnick / *Lee H. Skolnick Architecture + Design Partnership, New York, New York, U.S.A.*

Mette Skov / *Department of Communication and Psychology, Aalborg University, Aalborg, Denmark*

Bobby Smiley / *Vanderbilt University, Heard Libraries, Nashville, Tennessee, U.S.A.*

Linda C. Smith / *School of Information Sciences, University of Illinois at Urbana-Champaign, Champaign, Illinois, U.S.A.*

Lois Smith / *Human Factors and Ergonomics Society, Santa Monica, California, U.S.A.*

Lori Smith / *Linus A. Sims Memorial Library, Southeastern Louisiana University, Hammond, Louisiana, U.S.A.*

Patricia A. Smith / *Colorado State University, Fort Collins, Colorado, U.S.A.*

Scott A. Smith / *Langlois Public Library, Langlois, Oregon, U.S.A.*

A. Patricia Smith-Hunt / *Science Library, Preservation Services, University of California, Riverside, Riverside, California, U.S.A.*

Karen Smith-Yoshimura / *Online Computer Library Center (OCLC), San Mateo, California, U.S.A.*

Diane H. Sonnenwald / *University College Dublin, Dublin, Ireland*

Nour Soufi / *Library Cataloging and Metadata Center, University of California, Los Angeles, Los Angeles, California, U.S.A.*

Barbara M. Spiegelman / *Churchill Associates, Pittsburgh, Pennsylvania, U.S.A.*

Robert P. Spindler / *Department of Archives and Manuscripts, Arizona State University, Tempe, Arizona, U.S.A.*

Joie Springer / *Information Society Division, UNESCO, Paris, France*

Suresh Srinivasan / *National Library of Medicine, Bethesda, Maryland, U.S.A.*

Guy St. Clair / *Knowledge Management and Learning, SMR International, New York, New York, U.S.A.*

Cheryl L. Stadel-Bevans / *National Archives and Records Administration, College Park, Maryland, U.S.A.*

Jill Stein / *Institute for Learning Innovation, Edgewater, Maryland, U.S.A.*

Marcia K. Stein / *Museum of Fine Arts, Houston, Houston, Texas, U.S.A.*

Jela Steinerová / *Department of Library and Information Science, Comenius University in, Bratislava, Slovak Republic*

Dick Stenmark / *Department of Applied IT, IT University of Gothenburg, Gothenburg, Sweden*

Andy Stephens / *OBE, Board Secretary, Head of International Engagement, The British Library, London, U.K.*

Margaret Stieg Dalton / *School of Library and Information Studies, University of Alabama, Tuscaloosa, Alabama, U.S.A.*

Katina Strauch / *Addlestone Library, College of Charleston, Charleston, South Carolina, U.S.A.*

Robert D. Stueart / *Graduate School of Library and Information Science, Simmons College, Boston, Massachusetts, U.S.A.*

Paul F. Stuehrenberg / *Yale Divinity Library, New Haven, Connecticut, U.S.A.*

Brian William Sturm / *School of Information and Library Sciences, University of North Carolina at Chapel Hill, Chapel Hill, North Carolina, U.S.A.*

Anna Suorsa / *University of Oulu, Oulu, Finland*

Brett Sutton / *Aurora University, Aurora, Illinois, U.S.A.*

Sarah Sutton / *Mary and Jeff Bell Library, Texas A&M University-Corpus Christi, Corpus Christi, Texas, U.S.A.*

Destinee Kae Swanson / *Adams Museum & House, Inc., Deadwood, South Dakota, U.S.A.*

H.L. Swanson / *GSOE, University of California, Riverside, California, U.S.A.*

Miriam E. Sweeney / *School of Library and Information Studies, University of Alabama, Tuscaloosa, Alabama, U.S.A.*

Shelley Sweeney / *University of Manitoba, Winnipeg, Manitoba, Canada*

Jean Tague-Sutcliffe / *Graduate School of Library and Information Science, University of Western Ontario, London, Ontario, Canada*

Masaya Takayama / *National Archives of Japan, Tokyo, Japan*

Sanna Talja / *Department of Information Studies and Interactive Media, University of Tampere, Tampere, Finland*

G. Thomas Tanselle / *Vice President, John Simon Guggenheim Memorial Foundation, New York, New York, U.S.A.*

Ivan Tanzer / *Museum Studies Program, Faculty of Information Studies, University of Toronto, Toronto, Ontario, Canada*

Melissa Terras / *UCL Department of Information Studies, UCL Centre for Digital Humanities, University College London, London, U.K.*

Mike Thelwall / *School of Computing and Information Technology, University of Wolverhampton, Wolverhampton, U.K.*

Lynne M. Thomas / *Rare Books and Special Collections, Northern Illinois University, DeKalb, Illinois, U.S.A.*

Lawrence S. Thompson / *University of Kentucky, Lexington, Kentucky, U.S.A.*

Jens Thorhauge / *Danish Agency for Libraries and Media, Copenhagen, Denmark*

Anne Thurston / *International Records Management Trust, London, U.K.*

Michael Tiemann / *Open Source Initiative, Chapel Hill, North Carolina, U.S.A.*

Christinger Tomer / *School of Information Sciences, University of Pittsburgh, Pittsburgh, Pennsylvania, U.S.A.*

Elaine G. Toms / *Faculty of Management, Dalhousie University, Halifax, Nova Scotia, Canada*

Jack Toolin / *Whitney Museum of American Art, New York, U.S.A.*

Jennifer Trant / *Archives & Museum Informatics, Toronto, Ontario, Canada*

Barry Trott / *Williamsburg Regional Library, Williamsburg, Virginia, U.S.A.*

Alice Trussell / *Hale Library, Kansas State University, Manhattan, Kansas, U.S.A.*

John Mark Tucker / *Abilene Christian University, Abilene, Texas, U.S.A.*

James M. Turner / *School of Library and Information Sciences, University of Montreal, Montreal, Quebec, Canada*

Louise Tythacott / *Centre for Museology, University of Manchester, Manchester, U.K.*

George Tzanetakis / *Department of Computer Science, University of Victoria, Victoria, British Columbia, Canada*

Franklyn Herbert Upward / *Centre for Organisational and Social Informatics, Monash University, Melbourne, Victoria, Australia*

Richard Urban / *Graduate School of Library and Information Science, University of Illinois, Champaign, Illinois, U.S.A.*

Rachel E. Vacek / *University of Michigan, Ann Arbor, Michigan, U.S.A.*

Ron Van den Branden / *Centre for Scholarly Editing and Document Studies, Royal Academy of Dutch Language and Literature, Gent, Belgium*

Sydney C. Van Nort / *The City College of New York, The City University of New York, New York, U.S.A.*

Edward Vanhoutte / *Centre for Scholarly Editing and Document Studies, Royal Academy of Dutch Language and Literature, Gent, Belgium*

Rebecca Vargha / *Information and Library Science Library, University of North Carolina at Chapel Hill, Chapel Hill, North Carolina, U.S.A.*

Jana Varlejs / *School of Communication, Information and Library Studies, Rutgers University, New Brunswick, New Jersey, U.S.A.*

Jason Vaughan / *Library Technologies, University of Nevada, Las Vegas University Libraries, Las Vegas, Nevada, U.S.A.*

Dale J. Vidmar / *Southern Oregon University Library, Ashland, Oregon, U.S.A.*

Diane Vizine-Goetz / *OCLC Online Computer Library Center, Inc., Dublin, Ohio, U.S.A.*

Ellen M. Voorhees / *Information Technology Laboratory, National Institute of Standards and Technology, Gaithersburg, Maryland, U.S.A.*

Sharon L. Walbridge / *Libraries Washington State University, Pullman, Washington, U.S.A.*

Stephanie Walker / *Brooklyn College, City University of New York, Brooklyn, New York, U.S.A.*

Virginia A. Walter / *Department of Information Studies, University of California, Los Angeles, Los Angeles, California, U.S.A.*

Mark Warschauer / *School of Education, University of California, Irvine, CA, U.S.A.*

Nigel M. Waters / *Department of Geography and Geoinformation Science, George Mason University, Fairfax, Virginia, U.S.A.*

Kathryn M. Wayne / *Art History/Classics Library, University of California, Berkeley, California, U.S.A.*

Frank Webster / *City University, London, U.K.*

Jeff Weddle / *School of Library and Information Studies, University of Alabama, Tuscaloosa, Alabama, U.S.A.*

Judith Weedman / *School of Library and Information Science, San Jose State University, Fullerton, California, U.S.A.*

Stuart L. Weibel / *Office of Research and Special Projects, OCLC Research, Dublin, Ohio, U.S.A.*

Jennifer Weil Arns / *School of Library and Information Science, University of South Carolina, Columbia, South Carolina, U.S.A.*

Bella Hass Weinberg / *Division of Library and Information Science, St. John's University, Queens, New York, New York, U.S.A.*

Volker M. Welter / *Department of the History of Art and Architecture, University of California, Santa Barbara, Santa Barbara, California, U.S.A.*

Caryn Wesner-Early / *ASRC Aerospace & Defense, US Patent & Trademark Office, Alexandria, Virginia, U.S.A.*

Lynn Westbrook / *School of Information, University of Texas at Austin, Austin, Texas, U.S.A.*

Howard D. White / *College of Computing and Informatics, Drexel University, Philadelphia, PA, U.S.A., and College of Information Science and Technology, Drexel University, Philadelphia, Pennsylvania, U.S.A.*

Layna White / *San Francisco Museum of Modern Art, San Francisco, California, U.S.A.*

Michael J. White / *Engineering and Science Library, Queen's University, Kingston, Ontario, Canada*

Sarah K. Wiant / *School of Law, Washington and Lee University, Lexington, Virginia, U.S.A.*

Stephen E. Wiberley, Jr. / *University of Illinois at Chicago, Chicago, Illinois, U.S.A.*

Gunilla Widén-Wulff / *Information Studies, Åbo Akademi University, Åbo, Finland*

Bradley J. Wiles / *Hill Memorial Library, Louisiana State University, Baton Rouge, Louisiana, U.S.A.*

Mary I. Wilke / *Center for Research Libraries, Chicago, Illinois, U.S.A.*

Barratt Wilkins / *Retired State Librarian of Florida, Tallahassee, Florida, U.S.A.*

Peter Willett / *Department of Information Studies, University of Sheffield, Sheffield, U.K.*

Kate Williams / *University of Illinois at Urbana-Champaign, Champaign, Illinois, U.S.A.*

Kirsty Williamson / *Caulfield School of IT, Monash University, Caulfield, Victoria, Australia and School of Information Studies, Charles Sturt University, Wagga Wagga, New South Wales, Australia*

Concepción S. Wilson / *School of Information Systems, Technology and Management, University of New South Wales, Sydney, New South Wales, Australia*

Ian E. Wilson / *Librarian and Archivist of Canada 2004–2009, Ottawa, Ontario, Canada*

Kristen Wilson / *North Carolina State University Libraries, Raleigh, North Carolina, U.S.A.*

Thomas D. Wilson / *Publisher/Editor in Chief, Information Research, U.K.*

Catherine C. Wilt / *PALINET, Philadelphia, Pennsylvania, U.S.A.*

Charles Wilt / *Association for Library Collections and Technical Services (ALCTS), Chicago, Illinois, U.S.A.*

Niels Windfeld Lund / *Institute of Culture and Literature, UiT The Arctic University of Norway, Troms , Norway*

Michael F. Winter / *Shields Library, University of California, Davis, California, U.S.A.*

Erica Wiseman / *Graduate School of Library and Information Studies, McGill University, Montreal, Quebec, Canada*

Steve W. Witt / *University of Illinois at Urbana-Champaign, Champaign, Illinois, U.S.A.*

Blanche Woolls / *iSchool, San Jose State University, San Jose, California, U.S.A.*

Louisa Worthington / *Public Library Association, Chicago, Illinois, U.S.A.*

Jadwiga Woźniak-Kasperek / *Institute of Information and Book Studies, University of Warsaw, Warsaw, Poland*

Judith Wusteman / *School of Information and Communication Studies, University College Dublin, Dublin, Ireland*

Iris Xie / *School of Information Studies, University of Wisconsin–Milwaukee, Milwaukee, Wisconsin, U.S.A.*

Yiyu Yao / *Department of Computer Science, University of Regina, Regina, Saskatchewan, Canada, and International WIC Institute, Beijing University of Technology, Beijing, China*

Janis L. Young / *Library of Congress, Washington, District of Columbia, U.S.A.*

Priscilla C. Yu / *University Library, University of Illinois at Urbana-Champaign, Urbana, Illinois, U.S.A.*

Jana Zabinski / *American National Standards Institute, New York, New York, U.S.A.*

Lisl Zach / *iSchool, Drexel University, Philadelphia, Pennsylvania, U.S.A.*

Olga Zaitseva / *Kazakhstan Institute of Management, Economics and Strategic Research (KIMEP), Almaty, Kazakhstan*

Marcia Lei Zeng / *School of Library and Information Science, Kent State University, Kent, Ohio, U.S.A.*

Yi Zeng / *International WIC Institute, Beijing University of Technology, Beijing, China*

Višnja Zgaga / *Museum Documentation Center, Zagreb, Croatia*

Jun Zhang / *Pitney Bowes, Shelton, Connecticut, U.S.A.*

Yulei Zhang / *Department of Management Information Systems, University of Arizona, Tucson, Arizona, U.S.A.*

Kai Zheng / *Department of Health Management and Policy, University of Michigan, Ann Arbor, Michigan, U.S.A.*

Ning Zhong / *Department of Life Science and Informatics, Maebashi Institute of Technology, Maebashi-City, Japan, and International WIC Institute, Beijing University of Technology, Beijing, China*

Maja Žumer / *University of Ljubljana, Slovenia*

Vladimir Zwass / *Computer Science and Management Information Systems, Fairleigh Dickinson University, Teaneck, New Jersey, U.S.A.*

Encyclopedia of Library and Information Sciences, Fourth Edition

Contents

Volume I

Volume I (*cont'd.*)

Volume I (*cont'd.*)

Volume II

Volume II (*cont'd.*)

Volume III

Volume III (*cont'd.*)

Volume III (*cont'd.*)

Volume IV

Volume IV (*cont'd.*)

Volume V

Volume V (*cont'd.*)

Volume VI

Volume VI (*cont'd.*)

Volume VII (*cont'd.*)

Introduction to the Encyclopedia of Library and Information Sciences, Fourth Edition

How to Use This Encyclopedia

Entries are arranged alphabetically in this encyclopedia (see end papers for alphabetical list). The editors of this edition (ELIS-4) have decided to forego the Topical Table of Contents that was provided in ELIS-3 by editors Marcia Bates and Mary Niles Maack. At the time of publication of ELIS-3, the Topical TOC was crucial for readers to get a sense of how subjects were grouped and an understanding of the field or subfield through the clustering of categorical entries in the print edition. ELIS-4 is envisioned as a primarily online reference work where a Topical TOC does not serve the same purpose. The print edition is served well by the main TOC as well as the detailed index, while entries in the online version are easily discoverable through title, author, keyword, and full text searches.

In sum, relevant entries can be found by
1. Entry title (alphabetical arrangement of entries in the encyclopedia or listing in the end papers)
2. Specific name or keyword, including the index at the end of each volume

If the first name or keyword searched is not found, try several more variations—either different words or a different order of words. Most topics are described in several ways in the literature of a discipline, and the first term or phrase that comes to mind may not be the one used here.

Scope of the Encyclopedia

The title of the third edition, *Encyclopedia of Library and Information Sciences*, ended with the letter "s" because the encyclopedia was broadened to cover a spectrum of related and newly emerging information disciplines, including archival science, document theory, informatics, and records management, among others. The fourth edition continues this trend but with an extensive focus on the aspects of library and information sciences that have been heavily impacted by the adoption and reliance on online information distribution. This focus is reflected in the inclusion of numerous new entries such as digital preservation, altmetrics, web-scale discovery services, demand-driven acquisitions, and global open knowledgebases. Alongside these entries based on entirely new topics, the expanded use of the Internet for information has led to new treatment of traditional LIS topics such as resource description and access (RDA) that reflects the adoption of new standards for cataloging.

ELIS-4 also seeks to build upon the description of professional practice to round out the theoretical perspective that previous editions covered very well. Both current editors are academic research librarians and thus, focused heavily on addressing gaps in the encyclopedia related to academic research information while still relying heavily on the structure established by editors of ELIS-3. For example, ELIS-3 introduced country profiles and ELIS-4 builds upon that with new entries for New Zealand and a third on Brazil, in addition to revisions for Slovakia, Netherlands, Canada, Belarus, Kazakhstan, and Brazil among others. This edition also expands the number of entries for named cultural and information entities that did not appear in previous editions, such as the National Library of Medicine, North American Serials Interest Group (NASIG), the International Association of Scientific, Technical and Medical Publishers (STM), and ASLIB, as well as entities like the HathiTrust that have been established since the last edition was published. A number of new entries describing important information conferences such as the Acquisitions Institute at Timberline, the Charleston Conference, and Electronic Resources in Libraries (ER&L) also help round out the encyclopedia and further the description of the current state of academic research librarianship.

ELIS-4 also continues the tradition of designating important entries of historical or theoretical importance as "ELIS Classics." These are entries by major figures in the library and information sciences or those that describe core concepts in LIS theory, practice, or education that appeared in earlier editions of the encyclopedia. The current editors preserved the approximately 40 previous "ELIS Classics" and designated 13 previous entries as new "ELIS Classics."

There are more than 550 entries, of which more than 20 are new, another 93 are revisions to prior entries that have been brought up to date by their authors or by new authors, about 30 are ELIS Classics, and about 400 are reprinted from an earlier edition since they have remained relevant to the present. It is important to note that the editors also had to make some choices related to retiring entries that were no longer relevant—due to the passage of time and the development of the field, the technologies and theories described in those entries were deemed to be out of scope for the new edition and thus not revised or reprinted.

Encyclopedia Authors

As in past editions, the authors writing for the encyclopedia are major researchers, librarians and practitioners, and leaders in the fields and subfields in the disciplines in which they are writing. Noted scholars are well represented, and a number of authors are former leaders in LIS associations, including the American Library Association (ALA), the Association for College and Research Libraries (ACRL), the International Federation of Library Associations and Institutions (IFLA), the American Society for Information Science and Technology (ASIS&T), and the American Association of Library and Information Science Education (ALISE). In addition, there are many contributors who are current or former directors of major institutions. As in past editions, the editors are very proud of the range and diversity of authors who have written these entries for the encyclopedia and we thank them for sharing their expertise with the current and future readers and researchers in the field.

Finally, the editors for ELIS-4 have grappled with the challenges of entry generation that was noted by previous editors in nearly every edition: that not all ideas, topics, and potential entries were able to be completed for publication in this edition. While we made a valiant attempt to include entries identified by ELIS-3 editors but not secured for publication in that edition, we sometimes could not find authors willing to take those topics on. Similarly, we were sometimes unable to secure revisions to entries from new authors when previous authors were unable to perform that task. To the greatest extent possible, we endeavored to replace authors when entries were deemed important enough to appear in ELIS-4 but initial or previous authors had to decline or defaulted. No doubt, the editors of ELIS-5 will also pick up the mantle and attempt to round out the encyclopedia with entries for anything that ELIS-4 missed. As noted by editors Bates and Niles Maack in ELIS-3, this problem of missing topics was also acknowledged by Allen Kent, editor of the first edition of ELIS. Kent stated in 1973, "I have prepared this presentation to make sure the lessons of Diderot-d'Alembert are recalled in terms of encyclopedia-making as an exercise in the art of the possible."

Background and Development of the Encyclopedia

The first edition of ELIS, under the editorship principally of Allen Kent and Harold Lancour, was published between 1968 and 1982. The 33 volumes of the first edition were published in alphabetical sequence during those years. After the "Z" volume appeared in 1982, a number of supplements were published at roughly the rate of two per year, up to and including volume 73, which appeared in 2003. Miriam Drake was appointed editor for the second edition, which appeared in 2003, both online and in paper. The second edition came out at one time in four large-format volumes, with a supplement in 2005 [3]. Kent and Lancour covered a wide range of librarianship, information science, and some computer science topics. Drake, an academic library director, emphasized academic libraries, and the ELIS-2 volumes contained many profiles of major academic libraries and professional library associations.

The third edition, under the editorship of Marcia Bates and Mary Niles Maack, reflected a growing convergence among the several disciplines that concern themselves with information and the cultural record. As information science educators and noted researchers in the field, their focus was on growing the encyclopedia in the theoretical fields of information sciences as well as drawing together the associated information and cultural disciplines such as archival sciences and museum studies within the overall field of LIS.

For this edition, we have focused on developing the encyclopedia to reflect the changing nature of information production and consumption through online and digital forms. We have also endeavored to fill in gaps in the description of important people, places, and theories in the information sciences, and further enhanced the description of important concepts related to the provision of research information and the field's major institutions.

We continue to see the audience for the encyclopedia just as previous editors have: as principally consisting of 1) the educated lay person interested in one or more of its topics, 2) students learning about a topic, and 3) professionals and researchers in the several fields who want to learn about something new, or to be refreshed on a familiar topic.

We honored the previous editors by reengaging their superb Editorial Advisory Board with significant new additions of experts known to the current editors. (See listing in the front matter.) These leaders and experts from as many disciplines as are in the encyclopedia provided excellent guidance and feedback for the editors as they began the process of new topic generation, evaluation of previous entries, and offering to author or review numerous entries throughout the process of publication.

All new and revised entries were reviewed by one or more outside expert reviewer as well as one or more of the editors. Referees provided invaluable feedback to authors, including noting errors or omissions as well as making suggestions on additional aspects of the topic to cover. While we made every reasonable attempt through this process to check the accuracy of every entry and every fact, undoubtedly readers will find some topics explained more thoroughly or accurately than others. Indeed, due to the time frame from the beginning of the generation of the fourth edition and the time of publication, readers will reasonably note that some topics have been quickly superseded due to this passage of time, so the date of acceptance of the entry will be noted on each entry since several years may have passed since the writing of the entry and the publication of this edition.

Acknowledgments

This edition of the encyclopedia was possible only through the countless hours that the editors, John McDonald and Michael Levine-Clark, spent reviewing the previous encyclopedia entries, outlining the topics that were missing or that were newly emerging in the field, and identifying appropriate expert authors to write those new entries. In addition, the editors devoted extensive time to corresponding with previous authors encouraging them to revise their entries, and finding replacement authors for important entries that needed revisions but whose original authors were unavailable.

Both editors wish to acknowledge the expertise of each other and their knowledge of our field, their extensive network of contacts, and their ability to work closely together to ensure the success of this encyclopedia. Neither of them could have completed this project alone.

They acknowledge and thank the Taylor & Francis Group editors, Claire Miller and Rich O'Hanley, as well as Susan Lee, who passed away at the early stages of the preparation of this edition, and more recently, Alexandra Torres, who supported and kept the editors and authors on track over the course of the years of work on this edition of the encyclopedia.

The editors thank the authors who wrote and revised entries, and the huge number of reviewers who refereed the entries. Without their dedication, expertise, and willingness to share their knowledge with others, there would be no encyclopedia. They also wish to thank the Editorial Advisory Board for their advice, suggestions of topics and authors, their hours spent writing or reviewing for the final edition. They also wish to thank the previous editors, Marcia Bates and Mary Niles Maack, whose organization and structure for ELIS-3 provided an excellent blueprint for ELIS-4.

Encyclopedia of Library and Information Sciences, Fourth Edition

Volume 3

Pages 1455–2180

Encyclopedia of Library
and Information Sciences,
Fourth Edition

Volume 3

Pages 1455–2180

Epistemology

Paul K. Moser
Department of Philosophy, Loyola University Chicago, Chicago, Illinois, U.S.A.

Abstract

Philosophers and others have long tried to formulate an explanation of the nature, origin, and scope of knowledge. Epistemology is the philosophical project of formulating such an explanation. It has occupied philosophers at least since the time of Plato, and it continues to provide a central field of study in contemporary philosophy. If we claim to have genuine knowledge in any area of inquiry, or information gathering, we should be prepared to offer the kind of explanation of knowledge that is constitutive of epistemology.

INTRODUCTION

Epistemology is the theory of knowledge, the philosophical study of the nature, origin, and scope of knowledge. Classical and contemporary epistemologists have debated (1) what knowledge consists in (e.g., justified true belief); (2) what knowledge is based on (e.g., sensory experience and/or pure reason); and (3) what the extent of our knowledge is (e.g., objective, conceiver-independent facts as well as subjective, conceiver-dependent facts). Debates over such topics have occupied epistemologists since the time of Plato. Contemporary epistemologists have not put an end to such debates by any means, but they have made some distinctive contributions. This entry surveys such topics.

ANALYZING KNOWLEDGE

In analyzing (the concept of) knowledge, epistemologists seek to identify the essential, defining constituents of knowledge. The standard analysis of knowledge stems from Plato's *Theaetetus*, and proposes that knowledge is justified true belief. Despite its distinctive heritage, this analysis faces a serious challenge called "the Gettier Problem." In 1963, Edmund Gettier published a crucial challenge to the view that if you have a justified true belief that *P*, then you know that *P*. One of Gettier's counterexamples to this view is the following. Smith is justified in believing the false proposition that (a) Jones owns a Ford. On the basis of (a), Smith infers, and thus is justified in believing, that (b) either Jones owns a Ford or Brown is in Barcelona. As it happens, Brown is in Barcelona, and so (b) is true. So, although Smith is justified in believing the true proposition (b), Smith does not know (b).

Gettier-style counterexamples illustrate the reality of cases where a person has justified true belief that *P* but lacks knowledge that *P*. The Gettier problem is the problem of finding a modification of, or an alternative to, the standard analysis of knowledge that sidesteps problems from Gettier-style counterexamples. Many epistemologists take the main lesson of Gettier-style counterexamples to be that propositional knowledge requires a fourth condition beyond the justification, truth, and belief conditions. No specific fourth condition has attracted a consensus, but some approaches to a fourth condition have become prominent. A proposed "defeasibility condition," for example, requires that the justification appropriate to knowledge be "undefeated" in that some appropriate subjunctive conditional concerning defeaters of justification be true of that justification. One simple defeasibility fourth condition requires of Smith's knowing that *P* that there be no true proposition, *Q*, such that if *Q* became justified for Smith, *P* would no longer be justified for Smith. So, if Smith knows, on the basis of visual perception, that Jeanne removed books from the library, then Smith's coming to believe the true proposition that Jeanne's identical twin removed books from the library would not undermine the justification for Smith's belief concerning Jeanne herself. A different approach avoids subjunctive conditionals of that sort, and implies that propositional knowledge requires justified true belief that is sustained by the collective totality of actual truths. This approach requires a detailed account of when justification is undermined and restored. After four decades of vigorous research, however, contemporary epistemologists have still not come up with a widely accepted solution to the Gettier problem. The Gettier problem is, nonetheless, epistemologically important, because our having a precise understanding of propositional knowledge requires our having a Gettier-proof analysis of such knowledge.

MODERN EMPIRICISM

Contemporary Anglo-American epistemology began with the departure of Bertrand Russell (1872–1970) and G. E.

Encyclopedia of Library and Information Sciences, Fourth Edition DOI: 10.1081/E-ELIS4-120043676

Moore (1873–1958) from Kantian and Hegelian idealism. They opposed idealism not only with the ontological claim that there are mind-independent facts, but also with the epistemological claim that they *know* that there are such facts. The ground for the latter epistemological claim, according to Russell, is "common sense, uninfluenced by philosophy or theology."[29]

What exactly is common sense? Surprisingly, Russell and Moore do not say in any detail. Russell speaks of common sense *uninfluenced by philosophy or theology*. Why, however, should we regard such common sense as a philosophically adequate ground for challenging idealism and supporting its opposite, realism? In particular, why should we regard such common sense as a reliable source of *correct* belief regarding idealism and realism? Russell excludes from his ground for realism common sense influenced by philosophy or theology.

On what ground may one recommend that commonsense beliefs uninfluenced by philosophy or theology are reliable or any more reliable than other commonsense beliefs? Commonsense beliefs influenced by certain kinds of physics, chemistry, biology, astronomy, sociology, psychology, or politics, for example, can be just as unreliable as commonsense beliefs influenced by certain kinds of philosophy or theology. A popular belief uninfluenced by philosophy or theology could still be highly unreliable owing to influence from other sources: for example, prejudicial political views.

The commonsense epistemology of Russell rests on *empiricism*: the view that the empirical input of the senses (e.g., visual, auditory, tactile, or gustatory experiences) is evidence appropriate to genuine knowledge. Russell sides with such empiricists as Locke, Berkeley, and Hume, against the rationalist view that a priori knowledge—knowledge independent of specific experience—can provide knowledge of what actually exists. Russell sides with such rationalists as Descartes and Leibniz, however, on the view that logical principles, whether deductive or inductive, are not known on the basis of evidence from experience. All evidence from experience, Russell claims, *pre*supposes logical principles. Russell does allow, though, that our knowledge of logical principles is elicited or caused by experience. He thus permits a distinction between the *evidence* and the *cause* of a belief. In sum, Russell holds that "all knowledge which asserts existence is empirical, and the only a priori knowledge concerning existence is hypothetical, giving connections among things that exist or may exist, but not giving actual existence."[26] Russell's empiricist epistemology is thus moderate, allowing for some a priori knowledge.

Russell[25,26] distinguishes between knowledge *by acquaintance* and knowledge *by description*, and between knowledge of *things* and knowledge of *true propositions*. Knowledge of things can be either knowledge of things by acquaintance or knowledge of things by description. Knowledge by description requires knowledge of a true proposition: knowledge *that* something is the case. Knowledge by acquaintance, in contrast, consists of direct non-propositional awareness of something, not of knowledge of truths. Russell holds that "to say that *S* has acquaintance with *O* is essentially the same thing as to say that *O* is presented to *S*."[25] Russell would say that readers are acquainted with the color of these printed words as they read them.

Russell's epistemology attributes decisive epistemological significance to the natural sciences, so much so that the sciences are given epistemological priority over common sense. Russell acknowledges that the sciences begin with commonsense notions, such as notions of causation, space, time, and things, but that the sciences often need to revise or to eliminate such common notions to achieve their explanatory purposes. Russell observes that we typically start our theorizing from "naive realism," the view that things are as they seem. We initially think that the objects we perceive really are as they appear to us: that pomegranates are red, that ice is cold, and so on. The natural sciences, however, offer a strikingly different view of the objects we perceive, a view entailing that the features ascribed to external objects by naive realism do not really inhere in the external objects themselves. Russell thus remarks that "naive realism leads to physics, and physics, if true, shows that naive realism is false."[28]

Philosophy, according to Russell, serves an important purpose, because it identifies how fundamental commonsense notions can be reconstructed to benefit the explanatory aims of the sciences. Russell denies, however, that philosophy offers a kind of knowledge ultimately different from scientific knowledge. He holds that "philosophy involves a criticism of scientific knowledge, not from a point of view ultimately different from that of science, but from a point of view less concerned with details and more concerned with the harmony of the whole body of special sciences."[27]

Why, however, should we take science as our final epistemological authority? This question will be especially urgent for people inclined to skepticism about the reliability of science. Russell offers little by way of reply: "For my part, I assume that science is broadly speaking true…. But against the thoroughgoing sceptic I can advance no argument except that I do not believe him to be sincere."[31] This reply will probably convince nobody with any cognitive caution. Russell understands the *truth* of statements as their describing *facts* that may be objective in that they transcend experience.[28,30] He gives no reason, however, for thinking that everyone doubtful of science's providing such truth is insincere. Epistemologists, among others, have long debated whether perception, memory, and the procedures of the natural sciences deliver objective truths. We cannot cogently settle this debate by assuming that beliefs based on perception, memory, or the sciences are broadly true, and that people doubting this assumption are insincere.

Russell's epistemology will not be helped here by the classical pragmatist view of William James (1842–1910), John Dewey (1859–1952), and C. I. Lewis (1883–1965) that knowledge has an unavoidable pragmatic component, viz., an element of "active interpretation." Often we do seek a pragmatic rationale for a manner of interpretation: we then wonder about the practical consequences of wielding certain concepts (or, ways of classifying), relative to our explanatory purposes. Such a pragmatic rationale concerns the instrumental effectiveness of certain concepts in achieving our theoretical purposes, whatever those purposes happen to be. Traditional epistemologists, however, have wondered whether we can assess concepts relative to something more objective and less variable, viz., relative to the reliability of their portrayal of the objective, conceiver-independent world. Some philosophers hold that the latter kind of assessment, in terms of objective reliability, is distinctively "epistemological," and that a merely pragmatic rationale can be, and often is, irrelevant to such epistemological assessment. They assume that epistemological assessment is centrally concerned with objective, purpose-independent truth, and reliable indications of such truth. Pragmatic success can sometimes proceed with beliefs that are unreliable and even false, such as when it is convenient for our (theoretical) purposes to maintain an unreliable, false view on something.

Given a coherent notion of objective, purpose-independent correctness, we can distinguish epistemological from pragmatic assessment. A notion of purpose-independent correctness allows that the concepts we use in theorizing often depend on our purposes in theorizing. A key issue, however, is whether it makes sense to talk of the purpose-independent correctness of concepts. A critic of pragmatism will suggest that the external world is featured in certain mind-independent ways (e.g., many of its objects have "natural" boundaries), and that our classificatory concepts can be more or less accurate, or reliable, in how they "fit" the mind-independent features of the external world. Given such coherent talk of accurate fitting, we can raise a distinctively epistemological issue about whether we know that our concepts accurately fit the external world. This issue drives much of traditional epistemology, and raises a skeptical problem noted in this entry's concluding section.

EXPLAINING EPISTEMIC JUSTIFICATION

According to the "standard analysis" of knowledge suggested in Plato's *Theaetetus*, we know that *P* if and only if we have a *justified* true belief that *P*. We might believe a true groundless guess (say, about the winning horse at the track), but would not thereby *know* that this guess is true. On the traditional analysis, knowledge requires not only that a belief condition and a truth

condition be satisfied, but also that the satisfaction of the belief condition be *suitably related* to the satisfaction of the truth condition. The latter requirement leads to a justification condition for knowledge, a condition that excludes such coincidental phenomena as lucky guesswork.

Contemporary epistemologists have given careful attention to the defining and explanatory conditions for *epistemic* justification, the kind of justification appropriate to knowledge. They typically have allowed for justified false beliefs, and this allowance is called *fallibilism* about justification. Fallibilism allows, for example, that the Ptolemaic astronomers before Copernicus were justified in holding their geocentric model of the universe, even though it turned out later to be a false model. In addition, justification for a proposition, according to most contemporary epistemologists, need not logically entail the proposition justified: It need not be such that necessarily if the justifying proposition is true, then the justified proposition is true too. When justification does logically entail what it justifies, we have *deductive* justification. *Inductive* justification, in contrast, does not logically entail what it justifies; it rather is such that if the justifying proposition is true, then the justified proposition is, to some extent, *probably* true. Contemporary epistemologists do not share a single account of the kind of probability appropriate to inductive justification. Most contemporary epistemologists agree, however, that epistemic justification is *defeasible*, that a justifying proposition can cease to be justifying for a person when that person acquires additional justification. For instance, one's justification for thinking that there is a pool of water on the road ahead can be defeated by new evidence one acquires upon approaching the relevant spot on the road.

A major topic of controversy in contemporary epistemology concerns the kind of justification we have for our beliefs about the external world, including the belief that conceiver-independent physical objects exist. Most contemporary epistemologists hold that such beliefs are justified only inductively, in terms of justification that does not logically entail the beliefs justified. Some skeptics, doubting that we have epistemic justification for the belief that external objects exist, have required deductive support for that belief; others have questioned whether we can even have inductive, probabilistic justification here. Epistemologists have no consensus here; nor is consensus anywhere in sight.

Some skeptics have used a *regress argument* to contend that we are not justified in believing anything about the external, conceiver-independent world (see Oakley[22]). This argument stems from the question whether, and if so how, we are justified in holding any belief about the external world *on the basis of other beliefs*, that is, on the basis of *inferential* justification. A skeptic's use of the regress argument aims to show that each of the available accounts of inferential justification fails, and thus that such justification is not to be had. The initial skeptical worry is: if our belief that external objects exist is supposedly justified on the basis of another belief, how is the latter, allegedly justifying belief itself justified? Is it justified by a further belief? If so, how is the latter belief itself justified? We seem to be threatened by an endless regress of required justifying beliefs, a regress that seems too complex to employ in our actual everyday reasoning or information gathering. Our options, according to many contemporary epistemologists, are straightforward. Either 1) explain how an endless regress of required justifying beliefs is not actually troublesome; 2) show how we can terminate the threatening regress; or 3) accept the skeptical conclusion that inferential justification is impossible.

A simple example illustrates the problem of inferential justification. While walking along the base of the highest mountain in Oregon, Mount Hood, we decide that a climb would be enjoyable, but that the current dangers of a snowstorm are too great. Our belief that mountain climbing today is dangerous is supported by other beliefs we have. We believe, for example, that (a) local meteorologists have predicted blizzard conditions today on Mt. Hood, (b) there is foreboding cloud cover overhead, and (c) the meteorologists' reports and the presence of the foreboding clouds are reliable indicators of an impending snowstorm. Our belief that mountain climbing today is dangerous receives support from our belief that (a), (b), and (c) are true. What, however, supports (a), (b), and (c) for us? Other beliefs we have will naturally contribute support here, and thus the chain of inferential justification will continue. Part of our support for (a) might be our belief that (d) we have seen internet reports today from some local meteorologists; and part of our support for (b) might be our belief that (e) we see foreboding cloud cover overhead. Our support for (d) and (e) might be similarly inferential, and thus extend the chain of inferential justification further.

Nonskeptical epistemologists have offered two noteworthy replies to the regress problem concerning inferential justification. One reply is *epistemic coherentism*: the view that all justification is inferential and systematic in virtue of "coherence relations" among beliefs. Justification for any belief, according to epistemic coherentism, ends in a system or network of beliefs with which the justified belief coheres. We should not confuse a coherence theory of *justification*, epistemic coherentism, with a coherence theory of *truth*. A coherence theory of truth, of the sort endorsed by Brand Blanshard,[1] aims to specify the meaning of "truth," or the essential nature of truth; a coherence theory of justification aims to explain the nature not of truth, but of the kind of justification appropriate to knowledge. Recent advocates of epistemic coherentism, of one version or another, include Wilfrid Sellars,[32–34] Nicholas Rescher,[23,24] Gilbert Harman,[11,12] Keith Lehrer,[13,14] and Laurence BonJour.[3]

Advocates of epistemic coherentism have tried to answer two pressing questions. First, what kind of coherence relation is crucial to justified belief? Second, what kind of belief-system must a justified belief cohere with? Regarding the first question, many proponents of epistemic coherentism acknowledge logical entailment and explanation as coherence relations among beliefs. Explanatory coherence relations are instantiated when some of one's beliefs effectively explain why some other of one's beliefs are true. For example, my belief that it is snowing outside might effectively explain the truth of my belief that my office windows are wet. Regarding the second question, not just any belief-system will serve the purpose of epistemic coherentism. Some belief-systems, such as those consisting of science-fiction propositions, seem obviously erroneous, and thus seem unable to provide a basis for epistemically justified belief. However one answers the previous two questions; epistemic coherentism implies that the justification of any belief depends on that belief's coherence relations to other beliefs. Such coherentism suggests that justified belief is systematic, given that it emphasizes the role of interconnectedness of beliefs in epistemic justification.

Skeptics will ask why we should regard coherence among one's beliefs as a reliable indication of empirical truth, of how things actually are in the empirical world. Consider, in addition, the following so-called *isolation objection* to epistemic coherentism: Epistemic coherentism entails that one can be epistemically justified in accepting a contingent empirical proposition that is incompatible with, or at least improbable, given one's total empirical evidence.[17–19] A proponent of this objection does not restrict empirical evidence to empirical propositions believed or accepted by a person.

The isolation objection becomes directly applicable to coherence theories of justification once we expand the scope of empirical evidence beyond the propositions (or, judgments) believed or accepted by a person. Suppose, for example, that one's empirical evidence includes the subjective nonpropositional contents (e.g., visual images) of one's *non*belief perceptual and sensory awareness-states, such as one's seeming to perceive something or one's feeling a pain. Such contents, being nonpropositional, are not among what one believes or accepts. One might, of course, accept *that one is having* a particular visual image, but this does not mean that the image itself is a proposition one accepts. If we include the nonpropositional contents of nonbelief perceptual and sensory states in one's empirical evidence, the isolation objection will bear directly on coherence theories of justification. Coherence theories, by definition, make epistemic justification depend just on coherence relations among propositions one believes or accepts. They thus neglect the evidential significance of the nonpropositional contents of nonbelief perceptual and sensory states. Proponents of epistemic coherentism have not yet achieved a uniform resolution of the problem raised by the isolation objection.

A second nonskeptical reply to the regress problem is *epistemic foundationalism*, the view that epistemic justification has a two-tier structure: some instances of justification are noninferential, or foundational, and all other instances of justification are inferential, or nonfoundational, in that they derive ultimately from foundational justification. This structural view was outlined in Aristotle's *Posterior Analytics* (as a view about knowledge), and it received an extreme formulation in Descartes' *Meditations*. It is also represented, in one form or another, in the twentieth-century epistemological works of Bertrand Russell,[28] C. I. Lewis,[15,16] and Roderick Chisholm,[4,5,7] among many others.

Versions of foundationalism about justification differ on two matters: the explanation of noninferential, foundational justification, and the explanation of how justification can be transmitted from foundational beliefs to nonfoundational beliefs. Some philosophers, following Descartes, have assumed that foundational beliefs must be *certain* (e.g., indubitable or infallible). Such an assumption underlies *radical* foundationalism, a view requiring not only that foundational beliefs be certain, but also that such beliefs guarantee the certainty of the nonfoundational beliefs they support. Two considerations explain why radical foundationalism attracts very few epistemologists. First, very few, if any, of our perceptual beliefs are certain; and, second, the beliefs that might be candidates for certainty (e.g., the belief that I am thinking) are insufficiently informative to guarantee the certainty of our highly specific inferential beliefs concerning the external world (e.g., beliefs suitable to physics, chemistry, biology, and astronomy).

Most contemporary foundationalists accept *modest* foundationalism, the view that foundational beliefs need not possess or provide certainty, and need not deductively support justified nonfoundational beliefs. Foundationalists typically characterize a *noninferentially justified, foundational* belief as a belief whose epistemic *justification* does not derive from other beliefs, but they leave open whether the *causal* basis of foundational beliefs includes other beliefs. Further, they typically hold that foundationalism is an account of a belief's (or a proposition's) *having* justification for a person, not of one's *showing* that a belief has justification or is true.

Modest foundationalists can choose from three influential approaches to noninferential, foundational justification: (1) self-justification; (2) justification by nonbelief, nonpropositional experiences; and (3) justification by a reliable nonbelief origin of a belief. Recent proponents of self-justification have included Roderick Chisholm[4] and C. J. Ducasse.[9] They contend that a foundational belief can justify itself, apart from any evidential support from something else. In contrast, proponents of foundational justification by nonbelief experiences avoid commitment to literal self-justification. They hold, following C. I. Lewis,[15,16] that foundational perceptual beliefs can be justified by nonbelief sensory or perceptual experiences (e.g., my nonbelief experience involving seeming to see a rectangular screen) that either make true, are best explained by, or otherwise support those foundational beliefs (e.g., the belief that there is, or at least appears to be, a rectangular screen here). Proponents of foundational justification by reliable origins hold that noninferential justification depends on nonbelief belief-forming processes (e.g., perception, memory, introspection) that are truth-conducive to some extent, in virtue of tending to produce true rather than false beliefs. The latter view invokes the reliability of a belief's nonbelief origin, whereas the previous view invokes the particular sensory or perceptual experiences that underlie a foundational belief. Despite the disagreement here, proponents of modest foundationalism typically agree that noninferential justification, at least in most cases, can be defeated upon expansion of one's justified beliefs. The justification for our belief that there is a blue screen before us, for example, might be defeated by the introduction of new evidence that there is a bright blue light shining on the screen.

Foundationalists must explain not only the conditions for noninferential justification, but also how justification is transmitted from foundational beliefs to inferentially justified, nonfoundational beliefs. Modest foundationalists, unlike radical foundationalists, allow for nondeductive, merely probabilistic connections that transmit justification. They have not, however, reached agreement on the exact nature of such connections. Some modest foundationalists hold that some kind of "inference to a best explanation" can account for transmission of justification in many cases. For example, the belief that there is a computer screen before us can, in certain circumstances, provide a best explanation of various foundational beliefs about our perceptual inputs. This, however, is a controversial matter among epistemologists.

A special problem threatens versions of foundationalism that restrict noninferential justification to subjective beliefs about what one *seems* to see, hear, feel, smell, and taste. Those versions must explain how such subjective beliefs can provide justification for beliefs about conceiver-independent physical objects. Clearly, such subjective beliefs do not logically entail beliefs about physical objects. Since extensive hallucination is always possible, it is always possible that one's subjective beliefs are true while the relevant beliefs about physical objects are false. Perhaps a foundationalist, following Chisholm[5] and Cornman,[8] can invoke a set of nondeductive relations to explain how subjective beliefs can justify beliefs about physical objects. This remains, however, as a challenge, since no set of such relations has attracted widespread acceptance from foundationalists. We should note, though, that some versions of foundationalism allow for the noninferential justification of beliefs about physical objects, and thus avoid the problem at hand.

In sum, then, the regress problem for inferential justification has a troublesome resilience about it. Coherentism and foundationalism, may provide a viable solution to the problem, but only after a resolution of the problems noted above. Let us turn briefly now to some complications facing the scope of knowledge.

SKEPTICISM

Epistemologists have long debated the scope of human knowledge. The more restricted we take the scope of knowledge to be, the more skeptical we are. Two influential types of skepticism are *knowledge*-skepticism and *justification*-skepticism. Unrestricted knowledge-skepticism implies that no one knows anything, and unrestricted justification-skepticism implies the more extreme view that no one is even justified in believing anything. Some forms of skepticism are stronger than others. Knowledge-skepticism in its strongest form implies that it is *impossible* for anyone to know anything. A weaker form would deny the *actuality* of our having knowledge, but leave open its possibility. Many skeptics have restricted their skepticism to a particular domain of supposed knowledge: for example, knowledge of the external world, knowledge of other minds, knowledge of the past or the future, or knowledge of non-empirical items. Limited skepticism is more common than unrestricted skepticism in the history of epistemology.

Arguments supporting skepticism take many different forms. One of the most difficult is *the problem of the criterion*, a version of which comes from the sixteenth-century skeptic Michel de Montaigne:

> To adjudicate [between the true and the false] among the appearances of things, we need to have a distinguishing method; to validate this method, we need to have a justifying argument; but to validate this justifying argument, we need the very method at issue. And there we are, going round on the wheel.

This line of skeptical argument originated in ancient Greece, with epistemology itself (see Sextus Empiricus, *Outlines of Pyrrhonism*, Book II). It forces us to face these questions: how can we specify *what* we know without having specified *how* we know, and how can we specify *how* we know without having specified *what* we know? Is there any reasonable way out of this threatening circle? This is one of the most difficult epistemological problems, and a defensible epistemology must offer a plausible solution to it. Contemporary epistemology still lacks a widely accepted reply to this urgent problem. One influential reply from Roderick Chisholm[6] rules out skepticism from the start, with the assumption that we do know some specific propositions about the external world. Chisholm endorses a *particularist* reply that begins with an answer

to the question of what we know. Such a reply seems, however, to beg a key question against the skeptic. A *methodist* (not to be confused with Christian Methodists) reply to the problem of the criterion begins with an answer to the question of how we know. Such a reply risks divorcing knowledge from our considered judgments about particular cases of knowledge. It also must avoid begging key questions raised by skeptics.

Cognitively relevant access to *anything* by us humans depends on such belief-forming, or information-gathering, processes as perception, introspection, judgment, memory, testimony, intuition, and common sense. Such processes, however, are subject to skeptical question regarding their reliability, and cannot themselves deliver non-questionbegging support for their own reliability. Put bluntly, we cannot assume a position independent of our own cognitively relevant processes to deliver a non-questionbegging indication of the reliability of those processes. This seems to be the human cognitive predicament; and nobody has yet shown how we can escape it. This, too, is a straightforward consideration favoring the conclusion that we must take skepticism quite seriously.

Questions under dispute in a philosophical context cannot attract non-questionbegging answers from mere *presumption* of the correctness of a disputed answer. If we allow such questionbegging in general, we can support *any* disputed position we prefer. We may then simply beg the key question in any dispute regarding the preferred position. Given that strategy, argument becomes superfluous in the way circular argument is typically pointless. Questionbegging strategies promote an undesirable arbitrariness in philosophical debate. They are thus rationally inconclusive relative to the questions under dispute.

Our question about the reliability of our belief-forming, or information-gathering, processes should be coherent. For instance, we should not demand non-questionbegging evidence indicating the reliability of vision, for example, while we call into question, and thus refuse, *any available evidence* indicating the reliability of belief-forming processes. That would be to demand that we stand somewhere to assess reliability while we are not allowed to stand anywhere at all. Such a demand would undermine itself in virtue of a kind of incoherence: *demand incoherence*. One *can* coherently question the reliability of all evidence available to us, and some skeptics do just this. In that case, however, one *cannot* coherently demand that we supply non-questionbegging evidence indicating the reliability of our belief-forming processes. If *all* available evidence, including that from any of our belief-forming processes, is under question, then *no* evidence will be non-questionbegging. As a result, a demand for non-questionbegging evidence cannot coherently include *unrestricted* questioning of all available evidence. Any demand, then, that we establish the reliability of our belief-forming processes must allow that some evidence not be under question regarding reliability. Otherwise, a kind of incoherence threatens.

Arguably, we have a firm place to stand in answering questions about evidence and reasonable belief: we may stand firmly on our semantic, concept-forming intentions that give meaning to our terms. Consider the term "epistemic reason." Philosophers of different outlooks share the general notion of an epistemic reason as a *(possibly fallible) truth-indicator*. An epistemic reason for a belief thus indicates, perhaps with only a degree of probability, that the belief is true. Our meaning-forming intentions to use terms in a certain way give semantic content to our talk of an "epistemic reason for a belief."

We may form a settled semantic intention to use "truth-indicator" and "epistemic reason" as follows: a visual experience, for example, of an *apparent* pomegranate in a situation with no accessible contrary evidence is a (fallible) truth-indicator and thus an epistemic reason for a visual belief that an actual pomegranate exists. This semantic intention, owing to its meaning-conferring role for us, could then serve as a directly accessible semantic truth-maker for our ascription of an epistemic reason for a visual belief that an actual pomegranate exists. It would then be *part of what we mean* by "epistemic reason" that *such* an ascription captures an epistemic reason for a visual belief that an actual pomegranate exists. Our semantic intentions concerning "epistemic reasons" may thus serve as ultimate, even if revisable, truth-makers for ascriptions of an epistemic reason.

Skeptics might object that our semantic intentions can be "mistaken," say in virtue of failing to capture language-independent justification. We can sidestep such an objection, however, because reality (the objective world) does not settle how *in particular* we must seek truth. For better or worse, it does not settle *which specific variant* (or specific concept) of justification, warrant, or knowledge is binding on a truth-seeker. Even so, a person seeking to acquire truth and to avoid error should accommodate any necessary conditions for truth-acquisition (e.g., logical consistency in a belief) and for reliable and warranted belief.

Skeptics cannot convincingly hold nonskeptics to a specific concept or strategy of truth-acquisition that recommends skepticism. In particular, skeptics cannot cogently require an epistemic concept or strategy for us that undermines the aforementioned kind of epistemic reason (for visual beliefs) grounded in semantic intentions regarding "epistemic reason." A problem here for skeptics is that the aforementioned kind of epistemic reason is, so far as we can tell, at least as effective for judicious truth-acquisition as anything skeptics offer. In addition, skeptics lack firm footing to propose that such a semantically grounded epistemic reason is defective as a fallible truth-indicator.

Skeptics cannot plausibly charge us with question begging or circular reasoning here. It is *part of what we mean* by "epistemic reason" that the kind of ascription in question captures an epistemic reason for a visual belief that an actual pomegranate exists. So, we may now shift the burden of argument to the skeptic, and call this *the skeptic's burden*. We have produced a skeptic-resistant truth-indicator grounded in cognitively significant semantic intentions. We have also challenged skeptics, among others, to avoid demand incoherence. The skeptic's burden is now *properly* the skeptic's. Until this burden is met, we may endorse the reasonableness of some of the beliefs delivered by our belief-forming processes. We may even endorse the reasonableness of belief in the reliability of some of our belief-forming processes.

Traditional epistemology began with skeptical questions in ancient Greece, and contemporary epistemology must face similar questions. In facing skeptical questions, we can learn much about epistemology and its quest to explain the nature, origin, and scope of human knowledge. We can also improve our understanding of well-founded information gathering.

CONCLUSION

Epistemology, as the philosophical study of knowledge, will be valuable as long as knowledge is valuable. When pursued aright, it illuminates the nature, sources, and limits of knowledge. In doing so, it contributes to a critically important area of human understanding. Clearly, this discipline will not run out of controversy and difficulty in its important explanatory pursuits.

REFERENCES

1. Blanshard, B. *The Nature of Thought*; Allen & Unwin: London, 1939; Vol. 2.
2. Blanshard, B. Reply to Nicholas Rescher. In *The Philosophy of Brand Blanshard*; Schilpp, A., Ed.; Open Court: LaSalle, IL, 1980; 589–600.
3. BonJour, L. *The Structure of Empirical Knowledge*; Harvard University Press: Cambridge, MA, 1985.
4. Chisholm, R. Theory of Knowledge in America. *The Foundations of Knowing*; University of Minnesota Press: Minneapolis, MN, 1982; 109–193.
5. Chisholm, R. *Theory of Knowledge*, 2nd Ed.; Prentice Hall: Englewood Cliffs, NJ, 1977.
6. Chisholm, R. The problem of the criterion. *The Foundations of Knowing*; University of Minnesota Press: Minneapolis, MN, 1982; 61–75.
7. Chisholm, R. *Theory of Knowledge*, 3rd Ed.; Prentice Hall: Englewood Cliffs, NJ, 1989.
8. Cornman, J. *Skepticism, Justification, and Explanation*; Reidel: Dordrecht, 1980.
9. Ducasse, C.J. Propositions, truth, and the ultimate criterion of truth. *Truth, Knowledge, and Causation*; Routledge & Kegan Paul: London, 1968.

10. Gettier, E. Is justified true belief knowledge?. Analysis **1963**, *23*, 121–23 Reprinted in *Empirical Knowledge*, 2nd Ed.; Moser, P., Ed.; Rowman & Littlefield: Lanham, ML, 1996; 237–240.

11. Harman, G. *Thought*, Princeton University Press: Princeton, 1973.

12. Harman, G. *Change in View*, The MIT Press: Cambridge, MA, 1986.

13. Lehrer, K. *Knowledge*, Clarendon Press: Oxford, 1974.

14. Lehrer, K. *Theory of Knowledge*, Westview: Boulder, CO, 1990.

15. Lewis, C.I. *Mind and the World-Order*, Scribner: New York, 1929.

16. Lewis, C.I. *An Analysis of Knowledge and Valuation*, Open Court: LaSalle, IL, 1946.

17. Moser, P. *Empirical Justification*, Reidel: Dordrecht, 1985.

18. Moser, P. Lehrer's coherentism and the isolation objection. In *The Current State of the Coherence Theory*; Bender, J.W., Ed.; Reidel: Dordrecht, 1989; 29–37.

19. Moser, P. *Knowledge and Evidence*; Cambridge University Press: Cambridge, MA, 1989.

20. Moser, P. *Philosophy After Objectivity*; Oxford University Press: New York, 1993.

21. Moser, P., Ed. *Empirical Knowledge: Readings in Contemporary Epistemology*, 2nd Ed.; Rowman & Littlefield: Lanham, MD, 1996.

22. Oakley, I.T. An argument for scepticism concerning justified belief. Am. Philos. Quart. **1976**, *13*, 221–228.

23. Rescher, N. *The Coherence Theory of Truth*; Clarendon Press: Oxford, 1973.

24. Rescher, N. *Cognitive Systematization*; Basil Blackwell: Oxford, 1979.

25. Russell, B. Knowledge by acquaintance and knowledge by description. *Mysticism and Logic*; Doubleday: Garden City, NY, 1957; 202–224.

26. Russell, B. *The Problems of Philosophy*; Oxford University Press: London, 1912.

27. Russell, B. *Philosophy*, Norton: London, 1927.

28. Russell, B. *An Inquiry Into Meaning and Truth*; Allen & Unwin: London, 1940.

29. Russell, B. My mental development. In *The Philosophy of Bertrand Russell*; Schilpp, P.A., Ed.; Northwestern University Press: Evanston, IL, 1944; 3–20.

30. Russell, B. *Human Knowledge: Its Scope and Limits*; Simon & Schuster: New York, 1948.

31. Russell, B. Logical positivism. In *Logic and Knowledge*; March, R.C., Ed.; Allen & Unwin: London, 1956; 367–382.

32. Sellars, W. Empiricism and the philosophy of mind. *Science, Perception, and Reality*; Routledge & Kegan Paul: London, 1963.

33. Sellars, W. Epistemic principles. In *Action, Knowledge, and Reality*; Castañeda, H.N., Ed.; Bobbs-Merrill: Indianapolis, 1975; 332–348.

34. Sellars, W. More on givenness and explanatory coherence. In *Justification and Knowledge*; Pappas, G.S., Ed.; Reidel: Dordrecht, 1979; 169–181.

BIBLIOGRAPHY

1. Alston, W. *Beyond "Justification" : Dimensions of Epistemic Evaluation*; Cornell University Press: Ithaca, NY, 2005.

2. Audi, Robert. *Epistemology: A Contemporary Introduction to the Theory of Knowledge*, 2nd Ed.; Routledge: London, U.K., 2003.

3. BonJour, L. *Epistemology*, Rowman & Littlefield: Lanham, MD, 2002.

4. Moser, P., Ed. *The Oxford Handbook of Epistemology*; Oxford University Press: New York, 2002.

5. Moser, P., vander Nat, A., Eds. *Human Knowledge: Classical and Contemporary Approaches*; Oxford University Press: New York, 2003.

6. Moser, P.; Mulder, D.H.; Trout, J.D. *The Theory of Knowledge: A Thematic Introduction*; Oxford University Press: New York, 1998.

Ethical and Legal Aspects of Archival Services

Sara S. Hodson
Huntington Library, San Marino, California, U.S.A.

Abstract

Archivists deal with legal and ethical issues every day in the course of administering collections of personal papers. This entry will discuss legal and ethical aspects of archival services in three areas: acquisitions, access, and terms of use, in the context of research libraries and manuscript repositories. It will not deal with government, corporate, or institutional archives.

INTRODUCTION

Archivists who work in government or institutional archives oversee the noncurrent records generated by their organization. Other archivists, sometimes called curators or manuscript librarians, who work in libraries or manuscript repositories, administer collections of personal papers or organizational records that have been acquired from the outside, either by gift or by purchase. Both types of archivists face a variety of legal and ethical challenges as they oversee the materials entrusted to their care, and, despite the helpful codes of ethics compiled by the library and archival professions, these challenges often require archivists to make difficult decisions for which there is insufficient guidance. In one article, there is not sufficient space to treat adequately all types of archival settings, so this entry will discuss the legal and ethical issues that archivists must deal with for collections of personal papers.

The legal and ethical issues they face often fall within three broad areas of archival enterprise: acquisitions, access, and terms of use. The area of acquisitions encompasses both gifts and purchases of archival material, and includes such legal issues as the establishment and transfer of clear title, legal documentation of the terms of a transfer, and establishing fair market value. Ethical aspects of acquisitions include the courtesies of working with dealers, donors, and sister institutions.

The second area—access—consists of making research material available according to fair and equitable policies and procedures, within the guidelines of one's institution. For government archives, security and freedom of information determine access, and for institutional and organizational archives, access might be governed by the presence of sensitive or proprietary information in the records. For collections of personal papers, with which this entry is concerned, questions of access often revolve around the question of privacy and confidentiality.

The third legal and ethical area relates to terms of use. This generally pertains to copyright restrictions, literary

rights, and fees for publication or reproduction from original material.

ACQUISITIONS

In libraries and manuscript repositories, archivists acquire material by both gift and purchase from individuals or organizations outside their own institution, rather than by transfer from within the institution. This material may consist of collections of personal papers relating to prominent people, or they may be the records of an organization that are transferred to the repository for long-term safe-keeping. Certain legal considerations apply to such acquisitions, for both gifts and purchases.

First, the archivist must try to determine whether the donor or seller has clear title to the material and therefore has the right to transfer it to the repository. A certain degree of trust must obviously apply to such transactions, but the archivist should explore with the donor or seller the ownership of the material, albeit with delicacy and finesse. The best approach is to ask questions of the donor/seller, to learn as much as possible about the ownership and other history of the material. Such information is enormously useful in any event, to provide intellectual and historical context for the material, but it can also provide valuable clues as to the legal status of its ownership. For example, the donor/seller might recount a story of the papers turning up in a trunk in the attic or garage, or being held in safe deposit boxes by successive family members, or she might tell of holding onto the records of her activist organization in her den until the bulk reached a proportion she couldn't handle any longer.

Stories like these, when they appear plausible and straightforward, generally tend to indicate that ownership is not in doubt. The key for archivists, though, is to ask questions and to listen carefully. Equally important, archivists should trust their instincts. If something sounds wrong, it may well be wrong. The biggest danger signals of all are donors or sellers (the latter, especially) who say

Encyclopedia of Library and Information Sciences, Fourth Edition DOI: 10.1081/E-ELIS4-120044292

they obtained their items at a swap meet or on eBay, for example. The rise of online auction sites has increased the opportunities and the motivations for the sale of stolen goods and, as a result, archivists must examine especially carefully all items that are offered for sale by an individual who either cites an online auction as his/her source or recounts a suspect story about the provenance, i.e., the ownership history.

Once the archivist is satisfied that the seller or donor has clear legal title, and that there is no other joint owner lurking in the wings, and if the material on offer fits the institution's collecting policy, the next step is to prepare a deed of gift or of sale setting forth the terms of transferring the material to the repository. Such documents are essential, but they have not always been employed by institutions acquiring manuscripts or other rare material.[1] For more than half the twentieth century, curators or archivists simply relied on a handshake to seal a transaction. This practice, however, fell out of use during the 1960s, once its obvious failings were recognized, and when archivists increasingly had to deal with the aftermath of undocumented gifts, in the form of donors suddenly appearing to reclaim collections for which institutions had no paperwork to prove ownership.

Deeds of gift and of sale may be quite simple or more elaborate, depending on the institution's preference and on the needs of each transaction. The basic elements include the date, the name, address and phone number of the donor/seller, the conditions of transfer (sale price, for example, and the transfer or retention of copyright or literary rights), a description of the papers being transferred, a note about the disposition of duplicate or undesired material, and a note about any restrictions on the use of the papers, e.g., identification of items to be sealed for privacy reasons. The document should be signed by the donor/seller and by the archivist or other representative of the repository, and each party should receive a copy.[2,3]

A similar document is a deed of deposit, which sets forth terms under which a repository accepts material not as a permanent acquisition but on temporary deposit. Deposits often become gifts, but archivists should accept deposits only with the greatest care. The deed of deposit must fully outline the terms of the deposit, leaving nothing to chance and nothing as merely an understanding. Archivists should take care not to accept open-ended deposits, i.e., having no terminal date. Open-ended deposits can hold an archivist hostage, subject to the demands of the depositor, with no end in sight. It is far preferable to state an end-date, by which time the collection is to be kept by the repository or returned to the depositor. Also, the deed of deposit should indicate whether the depositor will pay the cost of processing and housing the collection if he or she reclaims it. The amount of these costs should be clearly spelled out.

For either sale or gift transactions, it may be advisable or necessary to have the material's fair market value determined by an outside appraiser. With sale situations, it is better for an objective, outside appraiser to establish a fair price for material than for either the seller or purchaser to set a price. Both of the parties involved in the transaction have agendas, the seller to gain the maximum return for the material, and the purchasing repository to spend as little money as possible. Only an outside party, in the form of a qualified appraiser, can approach the situation with the necessary objectivity. There are rare book and manuscript dealers nationwide who know the market and can perform appraisals for a fee. Dealers and appraisers often specialize in particular formats (manuscripts, books, or photographs, for example) or subjects (literature or western history, for example), so archivists do well to locate an appraiser who specializes in the type of material at hand, in order to secure the best possible appraisal. Most but not all dealers are members of the Antiquarian Booksellers of America (ABAA), an organization that sets forth its own code of ethics to which its members are expected to adhere.[4] When engaging an appraiser, the archivist or seller should ascertain what the fee will be and should avoid anyone who sets a fee that is a percentage of the appraised value of the material, a clear conflict of interest.

Appraisals are required in gift situations, if the donor wishes to take a tax deduction for the appraised value of the papers. As with sale situations, the appraisal should never be performed by a party holding interest in the transaction but always by an objective outsider. An appraiser doing the work for a tax deductible gift will prepare a detailed appraisal report providing his or her credentials, a narrative about the material and about the market history of its value, and a list of the items and their fair market value. The question of who is to pay the fee should be discussed and agreed upon before the appraisal begins. Repositories' policies vary about the question of who pays an appraisal fee. Often, institutional policy requires that the donor pay for the appraisal, but some institutions stipulate that, if the institution pays the fee, then the donor must reduce his or her tax deduction by the amount of the appraisal fee. Archivists must learn the policy of their institution and should obtain legal advice if necessary.

There is one category of donation for which the donor can not obtain a tax deduction—self-generated papers. According to statute of the Internal Revenue Service (IRS), an individual who donates his or her own papers may take as a deduction only the value of the materials themselves, i.e., the paper or other surface, not of the text or art created on those materials. This came about when papers donated by former President Richard Nixon carried inflated market value, yielding a bountiful tax deduction. Since that time, donations by the creators of personal papers to repositories have declined, since the only incentive is altruistic, with no financial benefit.

In a cruel irony, family members, collectors, and others who have acquired an individual's creations may take a full tax deduction for the market value of those creations. Thus, an author, composer, or artist cannot derive any real tax benefit for donating his/her own works, but others can. Moreover, the IRS has taken a strict construction of the code, deeming incoming correspondence, for example, as "self-generated" since it comes in response to letters sent by the creator of the papers. This means that a creator cannot receive a tax benefit from any part of his papers, even those parts written by others. In addition, the creator cannot give papers to a spouse or other family member in order to derive benefit. The IRS watches for such efforts to circumvent the tax code.

When papers are donated to a repository by someone other than its creator, and when the material holds sufficient fair market value, then the donor can receive a tax deduction for the appraised value. As in sale situations involving private sellers, an outside appraiser is engaged to evaluate the papers, and the appraiser writes a full report after examining the material. In addition to the report, the appraiser generates and signs an IRS 8283 form, which is then signed by the donor and the repository before the document becomes part of the donor's tax filing.

Beyond the legal considerations surrounding gifts, purchases, and deposits, there are ethical aspects to the acquisition of archival material by libraries and manuscript repositories. With regard to purchases, archivists work with private sellers, manuscript dealers, and auction houses. With all three, archivists should proceed with honor and the highest of ethics. In working with private sellers, who may never have undertaken such a transaction before, archivists should never take advantage of the person's inexperience. As already discussed, an outside appraisal should be secured in order to determine a fair purchase price.

When working with manuscript dealers, archivists should develop good relationships and behave with courtesy and consideration. Dealers are archivists' allies and will often make referrals and contact archivists when appropriate material comes to them for resale or on consignment. In addition, dealers are often the first to learn of archival thefts, when a thief brings items to sell. Dealers know major library holdings and especially the collections of repositories in their geographic area, and they are likely to recognize stolen material when it comes in the door and to contact the repository that has suffered the theft. When archivists develop an ongoing relationship with a dealer, it is often possible to request that material be sent on approval, giving the archivist a chance to examine it before committing to purchase it. In such instances, it is crucial that the archivist treat this as a privilege and not abuse it, either by holding onto the material at length and then finally sending it back, or by treating material carelessly or damaging it before returning it.

In auctions, which are the most competitive of purchase situations, archivists must nonetheless proceed with integrity. Archivists often use agents to bid for them, especially when auctions take place a continent or half a world away.

An agent examines the items and reports to the archivist, who then issues clear, unambiguous bidding instructions. When engaging an agent, the archivist should ask questions about the agent's fee and policies, to ensure a compatible working relationship. Archivists must avoid collusion with other individuals and must refrain from bidding on an item unless seriously interested in it. Occasionally, it is possible for an archivist to defer to a colleague from another repository, but this can be risky, since it involves delicate discussion about each repository's intentions.

As with purchase situations, ethics come into play when archivists deal with donors, and, as with purchases, the fundamental principle is to behave honorably. Many donors have never been in this situation before, and they don't know how to approach a repository or what to expect. It is incumbent on archivists to explain, fully and honestly, every step and aspect of the donation process, so the donor understands the choices and possibilities involved. Occasionally, donors will behave as though they don't know much about the gift process, when in fact they have visited other libraries and are listening to see if an archivist's explanation matches that heard elsewhere. Whether a donor has prior knowledge of the gift process or not, archivists must offer a straightforward, even selfless description of the gift situation. In working with donors who are family members, especially spouses or life partners, of a deceased creator of papers, the archivist should be especially patient and sensitive to the emotional wrench caused by parting with a collection. It is important to give donors time and space to say good-bye to material that is, to a great extent, the tangible representation of a beloved individual.

For purchases and gifts alike, archivists must be willing to refer collections to other libraries, if appropriate. A healthy spirit of competition among repositories is fine, but it must never become ruthless. Archivists must be willing to defer to their colleagues in other repositories when appropriate, no matter how much they might covet the material in question. The bottom line with acquisitions, and the higher ethic, is for archivists to ensure that collections go to the most appropriate home, wherever that might be. Therefore, archivists should know the holdings of other repositories and should pursue cordial relationships with their colleagues, in order to foster interinstitutional cooperation for the good of the materials they preserve.

ACCESS

Just as archivists must proceed fairly and impartially when acquiring manuscripts and archival collections, so must they provide access to their collections in a fair and equitable manner. In the past, and up to the 1960s, research libraries holding rare materials including archival collections, often granted to researchers exclusive access to certain collections and would then turn away other researchers seeking to use the same material. This practice led to the tying up of collections for years, and sometimes decades, when researchers would hang on to their exclusive right of access like grim death, moving forward at a glacial rate while other researchers waited in frustration on the sidelines. A more recent instance of this kind of exclusive access occurred with the Dead Sea Scrolls, which, for several decades after their discovery in 1947, were available for research only among a small circle of "authorized" editors who closely guarded their own right of use and passed on that right to favored graduate students or other recipients. Other scholars seeking access to the Scrolls were turned away. Only in 1992 was this exclusive and exclusionary Scrolls cartel broken, when William A. Moffett, the library director at the Huntington Library, boldly opened the library's set of Scroll photographs to all researchers, in contravention of explicit threats from the cartel of official editors.[5]

In another dubious access practice that persisted in research institutions into the 1960s, many libraries allowed access to certain groups or categories of researchers, while denying it to others. In this kind of selective access, whose terms were often dictated by donors of collections, the use of manuscript material might be denied on the basis of religion, gender, or ethnic group. For example, one collection had long been closed to women and to people of British heritage. As soon as a new chief curator (a woman, and of British extraction) was appointed in the late 1960s, she quietly lifted this restriction. In another example, a collection had been off-limits to Jews, Catholics, and the donor's nephew. Again, this unfair, inequitable, and onerous restriction was quietly lifted with a change in administration. By the late 1960s, research libraries began to abandon both types of restriction—the exclusive use for a given researcher, and the exclusion of certain people—in favor of fair and equitable access for all researchers.

Since the late 1960s, the most common way in which archival material might be restricted is for reasons of privacy and confidentiality.[6] Repositories increasingly collect modern archival material, containing letters, diaries, and other material written by or referring to people still living. For this reason, archivists must be aware of privacy issues and of the possible presence of sensitive material in the collections they oversee. The Code of Ethics of the Society of American Archivists (SAA) includes this statement about privacy in archival collections: "Archivists protect the privacy rights of donors and individuals or groups who are the subject of records." (The code also protects patron confidentiality, continuing: "They [archivists] respect all users' right to privacy by maintaining the confidentiality of their research and protecting any personal information collected about them in accordance with the institution's security procedures.")[7]

Typically, the sealing of items or files in an archival collection comes at the request of the donor of the collection, or as a result of discussion between the donor and the archivist. When material is sealed for reasons of privacy, this restriction must apply to all people who use the collection. That is, it must not apply only to selected individuals or groups of people, and no exceptions should be made to the administration of the restriction.

Certain categories of data are protected by law and may not be seen by researchers under any circumstance. These categories include medical records, personnel records, student records, and attorney–client files. Archivists overseeing such materials must know the law regarding them and must ensure that they are never made available to researchers. Many repositories refrain from even acquiring these kinds of records, because they are so problematic.

For other archival material that falls outside these legal categories, the question of safeguarding privacy can be extremely difficult, especially when there is no directive from a donor or when there is no family member or other person in a position to advise the archivist about potentially sensitive material in a collection. In the absence of guidance from someone knowledgeable about a collection, an archivist who identifies sensitive items is faced with a tough challenge. It can be risky, and potentially improper, for an archivist to take upon himself or herself the responsibility of restricting private or sensitive material. Archivists tend to have a highly developed sense of ethics and therefore often worry about possibly violating the privacy of individuals represented in collections they oversee. However, they tread in dangerous territory when they begin to act on their own to seal manuscripts in order to protect the privacy of the individuals represented in the collections. To do so is a presumptuous act, and archivists who are tempted to take that action must examine their motives to ensure that they are not engaging in censorship. For example, an archivist might discover in a collection a series of recent letters that discuss someone's sexual preference or reveal an abortion obtained without a husband's knowledge. Should the archivist take on the responsibility of sealing such material, or should he or she avoid making such a difficult, even subjective judgment?

While the SAA Code of Ethics advises archivists to safeguard the privacy of those whose papers are entrusted to their care, it does not, and can not, provide specific advice about how to proceed in such challenging circumstances. Instead, archivists must navigate on their own the turbulent currents that roil the privacy/openness seas. Most institutions have policies for dealing with sensitive documents, and most of these policies land in the gray area somewhere between the extremes of sealing on a wide scale, on the one hand, and sealing nothing, on the other. One British library hewed to the restrictive end of the continuum, as a matter of policy sealing all letters written by individuals still living. This approach held the seemingly unassailable virtue of consistency, but for most Americans it was too draconian and it kept a vast amount of research material unavailable. At the other end of the continuum, some American repositories seal nothing, asserting that their archivists are unqualified to make the difficult judgments required in restricting material. This approach also possesses the virtue of consistency, and it can ensure that a repository is unlikely to be held liable for breaching privacy since it seals nothing. Most repositories, however, land somewhere between these two practices, occupying the difficult gray area of restricting under some circumstances.

The difficulty of attempting to safeguard privacy in archival collections has been made even more problematic by virtue of the rise of the Internet and electronic files. The current trend toward digitizing archival documents and posting them on the Internet profoundly increases the potential risk to the privacy of those represented in the documents. Posting a private or confidential document on the Internet where millions of people might read it constitutes a far greater threat to privacy than is the case when a few researchers read that document in a library's reading room. In addition to the documents themselves, the finding aids that describe and catalog the documents in collections can breach privacy to a greater degree when they are posted online. For example, a collection of documents relating to a girls' reformatory can carry a note cautioning researchers in the reading room not to use the girls' names in publications. But, if the online finding aid includes a list of the files, by name, the girls' privacy would be violated. Thus, both for the collections themselves and for the catalog records and finding aids that provide access to those collections, archivists must stop and think about the privacy implications of posting on the Internet. This is not to assert that documents and finding aids in general should not be made available over the Internet, but just a cautionary note to be aware of privacy and confidentiality when determining which materials should be posted online.

TERMS OF USE

Once a research library has acquired a manuscript collection, by either gift or purchase, and when it is opened for research access, the archivist must begin to deal with the third general area of legal and ethical issues—copyright, literary rights, and the publication or other use of the material. For more than 200 years, the United States has had copyright statutes in place, granting authors, artists, composers, and other creators of original works the exclusive right to control, and benefit from, the publication, reproduction, and further use of their creations. Throughout this time, attorneys and other interested parties have struggled to balance creators' rights against the rights of others to quote from or use in part the works created.

The copyright act has changed over the years, and the basic provision of the current law provides copyright protection for the life of the author plus 70 years, although there are further provisions based on the date of creation

and whether a work is anonymous. The statute's provisions are strict and do not allow copying unless the archives owns the copyright. However, there are two special exceptions to the law. First, the doctrine of fair use (Section 107) allows copies of a copyrighted work to be made "for purposes such as criticism, comment, news reporting, teaching (including multiple copies for classroom use), scholarship, or research." Second, in order to assist libraries, archives, and scholars, Congress enacted Section 108, which allows an institution to copy certain works if the purpose is preservation, security, or replacement of the work. The allowance is complicated and holds certain conditions that an institution must meet in order to proceed within the guidelines of Section 108, so archivists would be well advised to consult the copyright law itself, as well as interpretive sources.

The single best source for details about the copyright law provisions and for helpful charts, including a "copyright decision tree," is the Copyright Information Center at Cornell University, and there are many other very useful sources for explanation and interpretation of the copyright law.[8-10] It can be difficult to identify and locate the current owner of copyright, but a helpful Web site, called "WATCH: Writers, Artists and Their Copyright Holders" has been created and is maintained by the Harry Ransom Center at the University of Texas, Austin, in collaboration with the University of Reading Library. This site maintains a data base of copyright holders that can be searched by author, artist, or other creator name and that provides the name and contact information of the copyright holder.[11]

Similar to copyright is the right of first publication of an unpublished, original creation. This right is known as the literary rights, and modern collections in particular often arrive in a repository carrying material whose literary rights are held by the creator or by his/her heirs. Donors or sellers of collections seldom are willing to transfer their literary rights to the repository, choosing instead to retain those rights in order to reap whatever profit might accrue to the publication or reproduction of the works. When receiving a new acquisition in which literary rights are at issue, the archivist should always ask about the rights and should inquire whether the donor, creator, or family would be willing to pass the rights to the institution, either immediately or eventually. The gift or sale document should describe fully the disposition of literary rights so the institution is fully informed and will be able to refer researchers to the holder of the rights in order to obtain permission to publish or reproduce.

Even though a library or repository might only occasionally receive either the copyright or literary rights along with the collection material, the institution does hold the physical property rights. When the material is given or sold to the repository, and the gift or sale document has been signed, the physical items themselves become the property of the institution. Thus, there are two forms of ownership of documentary material—the copyright or literary rights, and the physical property rights—and these separate rights can be held simultaneously by different parties. Moreover, once a work has gone out of copyright, or once the literary rights are no longer an issue, the physical property rights still apply. This allows the owning repository to charge use fees to researchers, film makers, and others who wish to quote from, publish, or reproduce material from the repository's collections.

The question of whether libraries and archives should charge use fees holds some degree of controversy among library and archival professionals. Some feel that researchers and others wishing to use material, especially material in the public domain, should not have to pay any fee at all. Others feel that users should pay for the privilege of publishing or otherwise making use of unique material held in a repository. Among the institutions that charge use or publication fees, most use a graduating scale of fees, charging higher fees for commercial use and lower fees or no fees at all for scholarly or nonprofit use. This issue becomes more complicated with regard to material whose literary rights are held by an individual or estate that takes an active role in administering those rights. Archivists often go ahead with charging use fees when a literary rights holder is involved, but they may decide to defer to the literary rights holder, especially in cases when commercial use involves hefty payments to the literary rights holder.

CONCLUSION

As the foregoing discussion indicates, archivists must face many ethical and legal challenges every day, as they administer the collections entrusted to them. There can be many different types of legal and ethical dilemmas, but many fall within three areas: acquisitions, access to collections, and terms for the use of the collections. In these areas, and in all facets of their work, archivists must not only follow the laws that apply to archival enterprise, but they must also strive to hew to a high level of ethical behavior. Although doing so will always be challenging since many situations fall within gray areas, archivists have many resources at hand to assist them in making the decisions that face them as they follow the codes and tenets of their profession.

REFERENCES

1. Browar, L. An oral contract isn't worth the paper it's printed on. Rare Books Manuscr. Librarianship **1991**, 6 (2), 100–107.
2. Peterson, T.H. The gift and the deed. In *A Modern Archives Reader*, Daniels, M.F., Walch, T., Eds.; National Archives and Records Service: Washington, DC, 1984; 139–145.
3. Hunter, G.S. *Developing and Maintaining Practical Archives*; Neal-Schuman Publishers, Inc.: New York, 2003; 105–106.
4. http://www.abaa.org.
5. Hodson, S.S. Freeing the dead sea scrolls: A question of access. Am. Archivist **1993**, 56 (Fall), 690–703.
6. Behrnd-Klodt, M.; Wosh, P.J., Eds. *Privacy & Confidentiality Perspectives*; The Society of American Archivists: Chicago, IL, 2005.
7. http://www.archivists.org/governance/handbook/app.ethics. asp?prnt_y. For other professional standards and guidelines regarding ethics, including privacy, see also the ACRL/SAA Joint Statement on Access to Original Research Material (1994), http://www.ala.org/ala/mgrps/divs/acrl/standards/jointstatement.cfm, and the ACRL Guidelines: Competencies for Special Collections Librarians (2008), http://www.ala.org/ala/mgrps/divs/acrl/standards/comp4 specollect.cfm.
8. http://www.copyright.cornell.edu/public_domain/.
9. Behrnd-Klodt, M. *Navigating Legal Issues in Archives*; The Society of American Archivists: Chicago, IL, 2008; 203–271.
10. Shapiro, M.S.; Miller, B.I. *A Museum Guide to Copyright and Trademark*; American Association of Museums: Washington, DC, 1999.
11. http://tyler.hrc.utexas.edu/.

Ethical Aspects of Library and Information Science

Richard Rubin
Thomas J. Froehlich
School of Library and Information Science, Kent State University, Kent, Ohio, U.S.A.

Abstract

This entry discusses many of the ethical considerations in the library and information science professions: collection development, censorship, privacy, reference services, copyright, administrative concerns, information access, technology-related issues, and problems with conflicting loyalties. It surveys the factors that affect ethical deliberations in the information professions: social utility, survival, social responsibility, and respect for individuality. It also looks at professional factors in ethical deliberations, such as professional codes of ethics, and the values that support ethical principles of professional conduct: truth, tolerance, individual liberty, justice and beauty. In the final section, it indicates the kinds of actions to promote ethical conduct at the organizational, professional and individual levels. As a final caveat, it indicates that ethical decisions require deliberation and reflection. While one can articulate values, factors, codes, and actions, they inform ethical reflection that must often confront and negotiate dilemmas and tensions.

INTRODUCTION

Many of the individuals who occupy our most important professions, such as politicians, lawyers, business executives, and bankers are given low marks for their ethics and honesty.[1] A cursory glance at daily newspapers reveals religious leaders who have less than moral lifestyles, politicians who lie and benefit from the public purse, and businessmen who manipulate financial markets and unduly influence public policy.

Despite the general sense of ethical decline, the ethical dimensions of our personal and professional behavior are transparent in day-to-day activities. The actions we take everyday are reflexive in terms of ethical conduct; our days are not replete with ethical reflection. Rather, we operate with a subconscious ethical system, whether poorly or well developed, that emerges into consciousness only when a special event or situation makes us doubt or defend our judgments or actions. At these times individuals try to make explicit the values and beliefs that underlie their actions or judgments.

Consider what situations occur in the library and information workplace that create this type of ethical dissonance:

1. When we are about to lie to someone
   a. Indicating that there is no problem when there is.
   b. Giving someone a good performance review when he or she has performed poorly.
   c. Lying about why a person did not get a job.
   d. Reporting in sick when we are not sick.
   e. Reporting or recording inaccurate data in business reports.

2. When we believe that we are about to do someone harm
   a. Permitting a young person open access to Internet sites we feel could be psychologically harmful.
   b. Disciplining or terminating an employee.
   c. Violating an individual's privacy or disclosing a confidence.
   d. Unobtrusive monitoring of a patrons Internet use.
3. When we believe we are about to receive something we did not deserve
   a. Receiving too much money in our paycheck and not reporting it.
   b. Receiving credit that someone else should have.
   c. Misrepresenting the quality of our work.
4. When we deprive someone of information or ideas
   a. Censoring or restricting library materials.
   b. Withholding information from a fellow employee to encourage his or her failure.
   c. Withholding information concerning the inadequacies of an information source or database.
5. When we are asked by someone in authority to act in an unlawful or unethical fashion
   a. Falsifying or backdating a record to hide unlawful activity.
   b. Being encouraged to misrepresent oneself to get information from an unknowing source.
   c. Being asked to deceive others for the "best interests" of the organization.

Most individuals feel ethical qualms in these situations, and there is general agreement that there should be standards of conduct to limit unethical actions on the part of information workers. Buckley, for example, has proposed

Encyclopedia of Library and Information Sciences, Fourth Edition DOI: 10.1081/E-ELIS4-120044430

that the "Golden Rule" has application in understanding our ethical obligations in reference work.[2] In addition, ethical constraints apply not only to individuals but to organizations. Institutions, including libraries and other information organizations, are not value-neutral; they act, make choices, affect human beings, and receive, allocate, and disseminate resources in ways analogous to individuals. Many corporations and industries have recognized the importance of organizational and employee ethics, which often manifest themselves in ethical codes. Fleisher and Blenkhorn report that over 95% of all major corporations use ethical codes.[3]

Some of the issues and values that underlie ethical action in libraries and other information organizations will be discussed below. Of course, such a brief exposition cannot cover all of the ethical issues and concerns involved in library and information service. This discussion is meant to provide a framework to help structure further ethical analysis. In addition, there are several other limitations:

1. First, there are many different types of library and information services. Not only are there different types of libraries (academic, public, school, and special), but the information services could include database searchers, information consultants, and chief information officers. Trying to find a common ethical basis for these many different types of information providers and administrators may not be possible. Although general ethical principles will be advanced in this discussion, specific types of information workers especially those in for-profit enterprises may not find the discussion completely relevant to their type of information work.
2. Second, the discussion presented is based primarily on Western ethical traditions. The ideas suggested or values advanced may not apply in the same way to other cultural traditions. For work on intercultural information ethics, see Capurro.[4]
3. Third, this essay proposes one view of ethical conduct among information providers. Other views are possible; indeed, alternative perspectives should be encouraged so that diverse ethical dimensions can be exposed and analyzed.

MAJOR AREAS OF CONCERN: AN EXAMINATION OF THE LITERATURE

The library and information professions have recognized the ethical dimension of information work through irregular discussions in professional publications. The focus on ethics in librarianship and information science has become even sharper in the last few years, due to the growth of the Internet, the application of library and information skills to new domains related to the Internet, and the convergence of information-related disciplines. In 1989, the University of Illinois, Graduate School of Library and Information Science, sponsored a conference on ethics.[5] Since then, the body of ethical literature in the library profession has increased and the domain of concern has been enlarged to "information ethics" (see Smith[6] for an overview and Froehlich[7] for a brief history). The literature includes some writers who have attempted to identify specific factors that produce ethical friction, and who have advanced rules of conduct (e.g., Rubin[8] and Baker[9]).

The potential for ethical conflicts in library and information services is considerable. Among the major issues that have appeared in the literature are the following.

Selecting Materials and Censorship

Many selectors confront the unpleasant possibility that the selection of certain materials will cause controversy in the local community. Such controversy could generate considerable anger and negative publicity and jeopardize library budgets and the jobs of librarians. Similarly, the librarian may believe that certain materials actually have a harmful effect on patrons, most notably children. This belief might be supported by other members of the community. Ethical tensions are bound to arise in such circumstances. To what extent is refusal to select items justified because of the possibility of controversy in the community and the expectation that some materials may harm others? These problems are some of the many associated with ethical issues in acquisitions and censorship.[10–14]

Privacy Issues

Privacy issues have grown in importance and have been of increased concerns to librarians and other information professionals especially since September 11th. As the powers of government have expanded in order to catch terrorists, so has the capacity of government to entrap innocents in the Net. With the passage of the USA Patriot Act, the new crime of "domestic terrorism" was created. The law expanded the power of government to issue wiretaps, obtain search warrants, and gather records that at earlier times were unavailable or required a court to determine probable cause.[15] Today, such organizations as the American Library Association (ALA) express a need for constant vigilance to protect the rights of patrons to use new and traditional sources of information without unnecessary surveillance. The ALA has supported a variety of activities including supporting amendments to the USA Patriot Act, most notably the freedom to read protection act, to exempt libraries and bookstores from some of the more invasive aspects of the law.[16] The ALA has also supported a variety of resolutions exhorting the need to protect citizens from undue intrusions on their privacy. These include the "Resolution Reaffirming the Principles of Intellectual Freedom in the Aftermath of Terrorist

Attacks," and "Resolution on the USA Patriot Act and Related Measures That Infringe on the Rights of Library Users."[17,18]

Not only are libraries concerned with monitoring of Internet use or use of other electronic databases, but they are also concerned with more traditional records such as circulation records. Even if the Patriot Act did not exist, circulation records have been at the core of privacy issues in libraries for many years. Requests for such records have come from parents of children, police, prosecutors, courts, and the FBI.[19] From the perspective of librarians, revealing such information would create a "chilling effect" on borrowers, who, if they believe their reading habits were made public, would subject them to embarrassment. Consequently, patrons would not take out certain books or have online searches conducted on some controversial topics if they felt they could be subjected to public scrutiny or the scrutiny of unsympathetic individuals.[20] On the other hand, as a public institution, there are those who would argue that such records are public records, and the right of the citizenry to know what is happening in a public institution outweighs the privacy rights of individuals. Similarly, in circumstances in which a crime has been committed and the request for circulation records comes from law enforcement agencies and the courts, librarians also feel a public duty to cooperate with such agencies.

Another typical privacy issue relates to the age of the library user. For example, does a library user under the age of 18 have the right to privacy in terms of materials used, and does that right vary? For example, if a teenager takes a book out of a library, does the parent or guardian have a right to know the titles of those books, especially if there are fines on the material and the parent is responsible for the material? If a teenager has a right to privacy in the use of materials, what about a pre-teen—someone who is six or eight years old? What if the material is secured from a school library? Are there additional legal burdens in that case?[21]

Privacy issues may also involve the monitoring of library users in regard to copyright violations or unlawful use of digital resources. On many occasions one may observe a patron making multiple copies of copyrighted material, or copying an entire book. Similarly, an individual may be observed accessing material that may be a violation of law, i.e., accessing child pornography. To what extent is the librarian ethically obligated to surveil and report such individuals, or, at the least, to warn the individual that such conduct is unlawful and to desist?[22]

Reference Services

The fundamental tenet of reference service is to provide the information requested by the patron or client. Given the importance of this service, a variety of ethical questions arise, including the following:

1. To what extent does ability to pay for an information services raise ethical issues? Is it ethical to charge for certain types of reference services (e.g., online services) even if charging tends to discriminate against those who cannot afford the service?[23,24]
2. Is it ethical to provide different levels of reference service? For example, is it proper to provide library board members or influential politicians quicker, better, and more comprehensive service than regular patrons?
3. Is it ethical to use support staff to answer reference questions that should be answered by degreed librarians.[25]
4. Is it ethical to provide reduced time in the reference interview to a patron because the librarian is in a hurry to serve other patrons?
5. Is it ethical to limit information if you believe the information may harm the patron?
6. What is the degree to which an information provider should divulge the inadequacies of the information being provided or the information systems providing it?
7. What are the ethical limits for the information provider in obtaining information? For example, to what extent can the information provider deceive others to get information or invade other information systems without permission or without identifying their purpose?
8. To what extent can a librarian provide medical and legal reference services without giving the impression that legal or medical advice is being proffered?[26–28]
9. To what extent is a reference librarian obligated to report school or college plagiarism or other student's inappropriate use of the Internet to the appropriate educational authorities?
10. What is the obligation of a reference librarians to violate (interpret very liberally) a digital rights management contract that severely restricts use by librarians or patrons?

For additional issues related to reference services see Bunge,[29] Katz and Fraley,[30] and Ulvik and Salvesen.[31]

Copyright Issues

Information activities generally require the use of print, nonprint, and electronic sources. The copying or transferring of such information is often a necessity. While a primary motivation of publishers and electronic database producers is the profit earned through sale or lease of their product, the motivation of many information providers, most notably librarians, is access to information for the patron at the lowest cost. An ethical tension arises when the information needed is difficult or impossible to obtain efficiently without violating copyright restrictions. One's ethical feelings regarding obeying the law and respect for the rights of copyright owners conflicts with one's ethical obligation to provide the information. The issue is further complicated in the digital environment because of the concerns of electronic information providers concerned about excessive copyright abuse of their content. This has led to new treaties and laws including the WIPO treaty, the Digital Millennium Copyright Act, and the Teach Act—each attempting to balance the interests of the user or information intermediary (e.g., the librarian or information specialist) with the interest of the copyright owner. In addition, greater restrictions arise regarding electronic information because the providers of the digital information often require that a license be signed before access is provided. Such licenses may contain no "fair use" provision or right of first sale available under copyright law. This may prevent redistribution of useful content.[22]

Administrative Issues

There are many opportunities for library managers and administrators to encounter ethical situations in the workplace. Oftentimes certain actions seem necessary in the organizational context, which, in other circumstances, might be problematic. Among the areas of ethical tension are the following:

1. Purposely withholding information.
2. Making deceptive statements, providing distorted or false information, or acting deceptively.
3. Violating the privacy of individuals, e.g., monitoring employee e-mails or use of the Internet.
4. Being motivated by personal likes, dislikes, anger, or desire for retribution when making a decision.
5. Being motivated by personal gain when making a decision.
6. Acting in a discriminatory fashion.

For issues related to library administration and personnel see Heim,[32] Rubin,[8] Baker,[9] and Du Mont.[33]

Issues of Access

Of considerable concern to librarians and other information professionals is free access to information. Is information access a privilege or a basic right? If it is a right, is it a right to all sorts of information (e.g., expensive online services) or to information bearing upon the basic needs of life (e.g., health, housing, governmental issues, etc.)?[34] Arguments have been put forth for services for which a library could charge by Williams.[35] Access issues have been aggravated because the costs to acquire, store, catalog, and retrieve materials have escalated, partly because of the rapid growth of information and partly because of the increasing need for and costs of technologies to cope

with this growth. Put another way, the new technological means for information storage and transmission exacerbate the differences of information "haves" and "havenots" in the world. Is there an ethical obligation to equalize the differences? Also in the electronic environment, questions of monitoring access has arisen. This has become particularly sensitive with the passage of the Child Internet Protection Act which requires some type of Internet filtering in schools and public libraries that receive certain types of federal funds. The monitoring of patron use of materials and services generally raises concern over the "chilling effect" this may cause on the use of materials that may be considered useful but controversial. Hence librarians are placed in the position of enforcing a law which may inhibit individuals from finding the information they want and need.[36] Other access issues concern access to data collected by various local, state, and federal agencies, such as through the Freedom of Information Act (FOIA). In the post-9/11 era, there have been significant restrictions of governmental information that was traditionally available. For example, information on water resources, electrical grids, or locations of power plants, or other aspects of the U.S. infrastructure may now be unavailable to the citizens who financially support them.[15]

Cataloging issues may also be seen as issues of access; materials cataloged in various ways can either facilitate or pose a barrier to access. Ethical issues may arise for example when decisions are made regarding whether simplified or more complex cataloging rules are applied or whether to place materials in particular subject areas (where do creationist texts go—in religion or science?).[37] For ethical issues and suggestions for a code of ethics for catalogers, see Bair.[38]

Technology-Related Issues

Many of the problems that have been raised existed prior to the extensive use of information technologies, but these issues are magnified or aggravated through their applications in information environments. For example, circulation records collected in a centralized electronic storage computer provides additional vulnerability to invasions of privacy and confidentiality. Similarly, records of Internet searches may be saved electronically revealing the nature of information being sought and consulted by patrons. In addition, there are issues that have arisen because of the technologies themselves. The technologies are of two types: (1) intellectual technologies; and (2) computer technologies. Classification, cataloging, and indexing can be seen as intellectual technologies. As such, they provide a mechanism for providing access to the universe of available information; but at the same time, they may distort that universe, for example, classification schemes reflect the biases of the general population,[39] and the very act of providing access to information, by applying a limited, inaccurate, obsolete, or faulty set of descriptors to a particular citation, creates impediments to access.[40]

There are also ethical issues associated with computer technologies that in part extend the intellectual technologies and that create their own sets of problems. One set of problems is related to electronic access. For example, incompetent searchers, ones insufficiently trained to deal with commands, syntax, and qualifiers of access and/or who is unfamiliar with the differences in databases, not only prevents access to the information for the patron, but also conceals their incompetence from themselves.[41] Another set of problems concerns the library or information center–vendor relationships,[42,43] including the use of consultants, fair bidding, licensing, and award practices.[44]

Conflicting Loyalties

There are many varieties of ethical conflicts that emerge in the context of the information professions. There are conflicts between loyalties to oneself, one's organization, and the profession. For example, very often in information work information professionals demonstrate more loyalty to their organizations than to their professions,[45] primarily because of economic motivations. This is unfortunate to the degree that such acquiescence to local authority may result in an endorsement of unjust pay scales or the inappropriate use of nonprofessionals. Martha Montague Smith provides a structure for articulating conflicting loyalties in a professional environment, and suggests that there are five possible levels of orientation in the workplace: (1) ideal ethics, which represents the highest aspirations or goals of an individual or group; (2) practical working ethics, which represents high aspirations, yet conformable to institutional, professional, and personal goals, is enduring but is also flexible and adaptable; (3) pressure ethics, which represents a scenario in which internal and/or external pressures split institutional or professional goals from those of workers; (4) subversive ethics, which represents a situation in which a small or large group of people advance what they perceive to be worthy goals for the profession or organization by working outside the system of articulated or tacit organizational goals; and (5) survival ethics, which represents a situation in which institutional demands threaten employee integrity, safety, or security to such an extent that individuals isolate themselves within the organization.[46] These are various scenarios that information professionals may undertake, given a particular context of institutional life. What this framework underscores is that not only do ethical conflicts arise throughout the history of one's work in an organization, but that one's response to them may vary, depending on factors that affect organization life. While professionals should strive for the level of "practical working ethics," it is often the case that circumstances, such as declining budgets or forays at censorship of library

materials by patrons or groups, predispose professionals to operating at lower levels, such as "survival ethics." And of course, one may well be operating at different orientations with regard to different problems, one may undertake a stance of "practical working ethics" except for forays of censorship against the library, in which one's mode may be that of "subversive ethics."

Societal Issues

It is easy when discussing ethical issues of the information profession to forget that information agencies have a significant impact locally, nationally, and internationally. It is important to consider the ethical ramifications of this impact. Among the issues that foster ethical concern are the following:

1. To what extent does centralization over the control of information create a monopoly over the amount and quality of information being provided, and who receives the information?
2. To what extent do information technologies developed in Western societies, especially English-speaking societies, create a condition of cultural dominance over non-English speaking countries?
3. To what extent does information provided to lesser developed countries adversely affect the stability and health of those societies?

Such is a preliminary look at diverse ethical issues that arise in the information professions. The ALA has endorsed the importance of ethical conduct through the ALA *Code of Ethics*,[47] a history of which is given in Lindsey and Prentice[48] and through the ALA Committee on Professional Ethics. Similarly, the American Society for Information Science and Technology (ASIS&T) has issued the *ASIS&T Professional Guidelines*.[49] But they are not without their problems (see, e.g., Barnes[50]) so much so that they are frequently challenged for revision (see, e.g., Finks[51]).

It is impossible in this brief entry to list all the resources available on ethical issues. For a fairly comprehensive bibliography, one can consolidate those provided by Hauptman et al.[52] listed in the "General Introductions and Bibliographies" section of the Bibliography at the end of this entry. In addition to the articles cited here, resources are also provided in the sections: "Journals and Web Sites" and "Bibliography on Specific Topics."

FACTORS AFFECTING ETHICAL DELIBERATIONS IN THE INFORMATION PROFESSIONS

Libraries and other information organizations are subject to competing demands from a variety of sources, including the public, clients, board members, administrators, and staff. Attempts to satisfy these demands often produce ethical tensions. Some authors have attempted to identify the ethical influences on librarians. McMenemy, Poulter, and Burton, for example, identified five influences: the employers ethical code; the professional association's ethical code, pressure from the customer to provide service, personal ethical beliefs, and society's ethical norms (p. 11).[37] We would contend that when decisions are made, there are at least four factors that affect the deliberative process. These factors may not be consciously considered by the individuals making the decision, but are at least conceptually implicit and underlie the decision-making process. Such factors are not in and of themselves ethical principles; they are frequently considerations that come into play when ethical deliberations are attempted. Attempting to balance them often produces ethical frictions. It is therefore important to understand clearly the nature of these factors.

The Factor of Social Utility

All organizations have a purpose or a function. One might say, for example, that a public library's purpose is to meet the educational, cultural, informational, or recreational needs of its patrons or clients through the provision of materials and services. Insofar as the library performs such a socially valued service, it has a right to act in a way that would maintain and promote such activity.

Information organizations acting in this manner may make decisions that produce ethical qualms. For example, an organization may have to terminate an employee who is performing poorly because such performance interferes with the proper function of the organization. The employee may be a likeable individual whose performance may be the result of illness or personal problems, yet the decision to take action may be rationally based on the responsibility of the organization to execute its proper functions. Furthermore, the *Library Bill of Rights* of the ALA affirms the "Books and other library resources should be provided for the interest, information, and enlightenment of all people of the community the library serves" (p. 14).[53] Such an assertion articulates a concern for the factor of social utility.

The Factor of Survival

One obvious purpose of organizations is to survive. This principle has been recognized in management theory for many years and is a simple recognition that organizations view their perpetuation as a central function. It is also grounded in philosophical traditions in which self-interest is recognized as a fundamental component of moral reasoning [[54], Book III, Prop. 55; 55, Chap. XIV].

It is easy to envision an ethical issue in which survival is threatened. For example, if there is considerable public outcry concerning certain "objectionable" materials in a library, the librarian may have to choose between removing library materials or facing a taxpayer's revolt. One is therefore tempted to censor library materials to ensure the physical survival of the library. This also highlights how the wish to preserve the library as a financially viable institution can come into conflict with a significant goal of the library—freedom of access to a diverse collection of materials. Ethical dissonance is bound to arise when one hopes to preserve the existence of the library by sacrificing in part its social utility (e.g., by reducing the number of hours a library is open so the library can continue to exist despite a constrained budget).

Factor of Social Responsibility

Another consideration involves the broader purpose that institutions—especially public ones—have. That is a purpose to serve the society at large and to promote the altruistic goals of that society. To this end, organizations might purchase and use recyclable materials whenever possible, promote "green libraries" that promote sustainable development in their own actions, in their patrons, or in the community,[56,57] prohibit smoking on their premises, or employ only hiring and promotion policies that encourage equal employment opportunity and affirmative action. Of course, determining what "greater good" to satisfy is problematic, and would depend on the institutional values of the organization, the attitudes of those who direct an organization, and the political, economic, and environmental conditions in which the information organization is embedded. One may, for example, believe that the use of recyclable materials increases costs and hence negatively affects the survival and social utility of the organization. One may feel uneasy about affirmative action programs to the extent that they treat people as members of classes rather than as individuals. Nonetheless, when ethical deliberations are being made, organizations, especially those that provide a social service such as libraries, may take into account the need to accomplish and comport with broader social goals. This factor conforms to the second statement of the *Library Bill of Rights*: "Libraries should provide materials and information presenting all points of view on current and historical issues. Materials should not be proscribed or removed because of partisan or doctrinal disapproval." (p. 14).[53] There is a tension between this statement and factor and the corresponding statement acknowledging the factor of social utility—one patron's meat is another patron's poison—but the library must provide a complete selection of coldcuts; that is, in providing information representing all points of view, the library may be acquiring material useful to one patron but offensive to others (e.g., *The Joy of Gay Sex*). The problem is that if some patrons obsess about "the poison," the survival of the library may also be at stake.

The Factor of Respect for Individuality

This factor recognizes that all individuals deserve to be treated with dignity and respect because they arc people. It is a concept embedded in ethical traditions, most notably through the works of the eighteenth century German transcendental philosopher, Immanuel Kant, whose moral imperative required that we "Act in such a way that you treat humanity, whether in your own person or in the person of another, always at the same time as an end and never simply as a means."[58]

Respect for the individual has many implications for information functions. In terms of patrons or clients, it implies an obligation of the organization to collect materials and provide services that reflect diverse individual interests, wants, and needs, not just mass appeal. For public libraries in particular, this obligation has been noted by several writers as fundamental to the library's collection-building function.[59,60] This factor also implies that the organization provide service to people as individuals and not merely as members of a particular class, age group, race, sex, or ethnic background. In terms of employees, this factor implies that the library must treat its employees fairly, with respect and dignity. The organization must be responsive to individual employees' feelings, wants, and needs. In addition, it implies that employees should treat each other in the same fashion and that administrators are also entitled to their *individual* opinions on issues, despite the position they may have to take in their managerial roles.

Such a factor may, however, generate ethical concerns. For example, in serving individual needs, should a public library sacrifice "mass appeal"? After all, appealing to the average consumer has the salutary effect of promoting taxpayer support (i.e., of increasing circulation), and reducing the likelihood of complaining patrons who are unhappy when materials representing unorthodox points of view are included in the collection. Ethical qualms might also be generated in terms of staff treatment; for example, when we fail to uniformly apply personnel policies by making exceptions for "individual circumstances." We might be threatening the survival of the organization by subjecting it to potential legal liabilities and labor unrest. Finally, ethical qualms can be generated when we feel that we are not treating ourselves with respect. For example, we may be asked by others (employers, clients, competitors) to do something we believe is unethical. Acting in this manner diminishes us.

In attempting to make ethical judgments, these factors are constantly present. As ethical concerns arise, one might phrase concern for these factors in four questions:

1. To what extent is the survival of the organization threatened?
2. To what extent will the purpose of the organization be benefited or harmed?
3. To what extent is the organization or employee socially responsible or irresponsible when acting in a particular manner?
4. To what extent are the actions of the organization (or individuals acting in its behalf) harming or benefiting other individuals, organizations, or the profession?

The relative importance of these four factors depends on the specific situation and the seriousness of the effects. How should we make ethical judgments when so many competing factors are in operation? Before offering one possible answer it is necessary to examine a second ethical perspective, the professional dimension of ethical behavior.

PROFESSIONAL FACTORS IN ETHICAL DELIBERATIONS

The professional aspects of ethical behavior deal with the obligations and duties of information professionals while serving in the capacity of information providers. The Association for Library and Information Science Education (ALISE) has noted that ethical education "should be encouraged as an important aspect of education, research, scholarship, service, and practice in library and information studies and in other related profession." ALISE encourages "special attention to information ethics..."[61] As noted previously, most of our work decisions are made and actions taken with little or no ethical reflection. In this sense, we rely on our basic ethical training acquired in childhood and on our formal training regarding information work. This latter point is important, because it suggests that if our actions are often performed by habit rather than deliberation, then to the extent that information professionals are socialized into the ethics of the discipline, the greater the chance that these ethical standards become part of our basic ethical framework and will be consummated in day-to-day work life. It also places in relief the recognition that ethical training cannot be limited to "professionals." Indeed, calling codes of conduct professional ethics diminishes their scope and underestimates the ethical responsibilities of all library workers. Nor should the concept of professional ethics imply that these ethics are different than those we use in everyday life, or that they should take precedence over those of everyday life. Professional ethics should be viewed as ordinary ethical standards applied in a particular environment.

The ALA has attempted through its code of ethics to provide ethical guidance, and it serves as a touchstone for the ethical socialization of librarians. This code states the following:

(i) We provide the highest level of service to all library users through appropriate and usefully organized resources; equitable service policies; equitable access; and accurate, unbiased, and courteous responses to all requests.

(ii) We uphold the principles of intellectual freedom and resist all efforts to censor library resources.

(iii) We protect each library user's right to privacy and confidentiality with respect to information sought or received and resources consulted, borrowed, acquired, or transmitted.

(iv) We respect intellectual property rights and advocate balance between the interests of information users and rights holders.

(v)   We treat coworkers and other colleagues with respect, fairness, and good faith, and advocate conditions of employment that safeguard the rights and welfare of all employees of our institutions.

(vi) We do not advance private interests at the expense of library users, colleagues, or our employing institutions.

(vii) We distinguish between our personal convictions and professional duties and do not allow our personal beliefs to interfere with fair representation of the aims of our institutions or the provision of access to their information resources.

(viii) We strive for excellence in the profession by maintaining and enhancing our own knowledge and skills, by encouraging the professional development of coworkers, and by fostering the aspirations of potential members of the profession.[47]

Adopted June 28, 1997, by the ALA Council; Amended January 22, 2008.

Published professional codes serve useful purposes. They provide support and guidance when ethical concerns arise and serve as a tool for the inculcation of values in library employees that are ideally assimilated into daily behavior. But articulation of such a code is frequently misleading; one must understand the values inherent in it. This points up the central defect of such a code. The "thinking" behind the code is obscure, because only a very few were present at the deliberations that created it or because the formalized, collective product reflects a compromise among divergent viewpoints. Understanding the thinking behind code is critical in understanding its meaning. But the thinking behind ethical codes is often dialectical and didactic, representing an articulation of perspectives, competing views, and the tensions among them. When one fails to recognize this evolution or rationale for codes, the codes are seen as finished and foster dogmatic beliefs. One merely invokes a provision of a code instead of offering cogent reasons that would justify the conduct prescribed by the code.

Ordinary ethical principles provide the framework for, and are not inconsistent with, the professional values of the information profession. Within that ordinary ethical framework, the information professional includes the values inherent in the information profession. Such values should personally guide the information professional when acting in this capacity. It is therefore ironic that the ALA code specifically mandates that individuals separate their personal philosophy and attitude from those of their institutions or professional bodies (provision VII). What is actually desirable is that the individuals come to realize that there are important values of library and information service that should be a part of our own values when we serve in the capacity of information provider. This does not mean that individuals must give up other values to subscribe to those of the profession; rather, it is a recognition that the values of library and information service are worthy of admission to our individual value structure when we become information professionals. This sense of professional ethics becomes most important when individuals experience internal value conflicts while serving as information professionals, for example, when an individual who opposes abortion is asked to provide information on the topic. Although one may be personally opposed to abortion, one can also personally subscribe to the professional responsibility to be objective and to provide different points of view.

THE VALUES OF INFORMATION PROFESSIONS

It is fruitful to explore what values support the ethical principles of individual professional conduct. Understanding these values improves our ability to recognize ethical situations and to make ethical decisions and balance the competing organizational factors.

There are at least five values of the information professions that can serve as values of the individual as well as the organization (for a discussion of different values that are associated with the profession see Finks[62]). These values can be characterized in the following manner.

The Value of Truth

Information professionals have as one of their important ends the advancement of truth and the search for knowledge. Certainly promoting truth fulfills a fundamental mission of the library (social utility) and meets a broader social end of improving the society as a whole (social responsibility).

The commitment to truth does not imply that information professionals, most notably library workers, should attempt to suppress materials they believe are untrue (or to promote materials they believe to be true, for that matter). To the contrary, as John Swan has aptly noted, untruths are essential to stimulate our thinking and reveal pathways in the search for truth (p. 49).[60] The search for truth requires that the library provide an array of knowledge and information and access to expertise, so that individuals can apply their efforts in this search. Information professionals must act so that patrons and clients have the greatest opportunity to search for knowledge and truth.

This concept of truth as a value also pertains to the internal activities of the organization. Relations among employees and administrators and between workers must have truthfulness as a value. Such actions as deception, withholding of information that is essential to the performance of others, and falsification of records abrogate this value. This does not mean that administrators or managers are ethically obligated to answer any question put to them. There may be occasions in which the appropriate response is to refuse to answer. Examples include answers that would violate confidentiality. Rather, the value of truth implies that when answers are given they are truthful. Information professionals must act so that employees treat each other truthfully in their actions and communications.

The Value of Tolerance

The value of tolerance is closely aligned with that of truth and its search. Many people seem to hold the belief that there is one truth, but libraries function on the assumption that many people believe many truths. A belief in the value of the pursuit of truth does not imply that "the Truth" is in fact achievable in all areas of life (science, ethics, religion, politics). One must tolerate diverse truths, and even if there were one truth, different people may use different avenues to attain it or to attain different aspects of it at a time.

It has been said many times in the writings of the library profession that the free exchange of ideas forms the basis of democracy and library services. A similar case can be made for most forms of information dissemination within and outside libraries. It is an ethical obligation of information professionals to promote exposure to different ideas, even those that are unorthodox. Decisions concerning library and information service that affect the free flow of such ideas ipso facto generate ethical concern. This does not require that information professional accept or be tolerant in all aspects of their life. One may, for example, not subscribe to the value of tolerance within the home. It requires only that one's set of values reflects tolerance of ideas in the information workplace; that is, when one is performing library or information work, one must accept as a value that people have a right to information that one might find offensive. Parenthetically, the value of tolerance may not be as strongly held within the workplace. An employee, for example, whose remarks to other staff consistently cause demoralization and lower productivity might be disciplined or removed. But from the perspective of information service, it is essential that library professionals act so that library and information services increase the flow of ideas.

The Value of Individual Liberty

Library and information service is meant to assist individuals in their individual pursuit to have a better life. This does not mean that each time an information worker answers a question it profoundly alters a patron's life, but it does imply that every time questions are answered correctly the patron is able to accomplish a task, resolve a problem, or plan their future just a little better. In this way, the profession assumes that not only individuals, but organizations and society as a whole are changed, and, in the long run, improved by ideas. Improvement may mean many different things: providing information to a scientist to discover a new drug; stimulating the imagination of a child by providing reading or viewing material; providing training information to adults; or providing programming for mothers or the elderly. Actions that would impair this important function interfere with the basic liberties of people to make their lives better and generate ethical friction. Information professionals should therefore act so that library and information services respond to the information wants and needs of users.

The Value of Justice

This value pertains both to information users and to fellow information professionals within a given organization. From the public perspective, it implies that all citizens have equal access to library services. But even in nonpublic settings, it implies that all individuals should receive the best quality service. Similarly, for both private and public information organizations, it implies that the delivery of inferior information service on the basis of race, sex, religion, origin, disability, sexual orientation, or age is a violation of such a value.

But the concept of justice is complex, and a distinction noted by the philosopher John Rawls is especially appropriate in the information context. Rawls realized that justice cannot be understood merely as equality, but as "fairness" (p. 168–169).[63] One may, for example, accept as just the fact that the library director and maintenance worker are paid unequally. This is an important distinction because it implies that ethical action requires fair rather than equal service or treatment. Unequal service might, in fact, be an ethical obligation if the needs of individuals differ. This recognizes, for example, that children may receive unequal service because their needs are different from those of adults, or that less knowledgeable adults may require different levels of service. The value of justice implies that we do not necessarily provide equal service, but that we provide service that recognizes individual circumstances. This does not imply that equality is absent in the concept of justice or library ethics. Equality of *access* to information services is certainly inherent in the concept of public library and information service, and fairness in access is inherent in any information service. The information professional must act so that library services are provided fairly to all users.

The value of justice also applies to the internal workings of library and information services. Employees should be treated fairly and consistently by managers and administrators, and equal access to opportunities within information organizations must be provided. In addition, this value implies that employees should treat each other fairly. To this end, the library professional must act so that employees are treated and treat each other fairly.

The Value of Beauty

The value of beauty suggests that librarians have a deep and abiding respect for those works that please and educate. This includes works that occupy a notable position in literature and the arts. Such works arc valued because they broaden and deepen human understanding. It also includes works that provide pleasure and recreation to all individuals. Such a value implies that librarians make such collections available. Similarly, it is common that such collections come under attack by censors who feel that even classics (e.g., *Huckleberry Finn*), should be restricted or removed. Librarians must act so that works that provide aesthetic experiences be maintained, preserved, and available to users. Such a consideration may also imply an obligation that materials of high literary quality not be sacrificed with excessive attention to mass appeal (e.g., excessive quantities of gothic romances).

ACTIONS THAT PROMOTE ETHICAL CONDUCT

If one assumes that these values play an important role in ethical actions for information professionals, then it is important to determine what actions information organizations and librarians can take to promote ethical actions. These actions can be seen from three perspectives: organizational, individual, and professional.

Organizational Actions

When attempting to balance the factors that generate ethical tensions in organizations, the values of library and information service are pivotal concerns. For example, when library staff, supervisors, administrators, or board members make decisions or take actions that could affect the organization's utility or survival, one must also reflect on the central values that make the library what it is. To the extent that one sacrifices these values to other ends, one must accept the diminution of ethical standards. Few complex decisions in the workplace produce wholly satisfactory resolutions, even when the decision maker believes that no better decision could be reached. There is often a residue of uneasiness, sometimes because one suspects that an ethical dimension has been abandoned for the sake of utility or self-interest. It is every information professional's responsibility to maintain an ethical environment, but this is also a special responsibility of the management because of the increased ethical burden. Below are a variety of actions that the leadership of information organizations might take to meet this burden:

1. *Have a board and administration committed to leading by example.* Each individual is responsible for his or her own ethical actions. But these actions are also, in part, modeled by the behavior of those in authority. Rules and regulations are important and influence employee actions, but the ethical environment is a culture that is shaped as much or more by example than by rule. For this reason, the actions of board members, administrators, and supervisors must be ethically exemplary.
2. *Establish a written ethics policy.* The library's commitment to ethical behavior should be formally stated along with the rationale for that behavior. A professional code may be part of this commitment, but it is not in and of itself sufficient. The policy should include a clear statement on the part of the board and administration regarding their commitment to ethical conduct in relation to the patrons, the profession, and the organization. For example, it should be an ethical responsibility of staff
    a. To promote a sense of confidence about the organization and its purpose with the public or appropriate clientele.
    b. To make the organization as effective and efficient as possible both internally and with its relations with the public or clientele.
    c. To strive for personal and professional growth.
    Such a written policy should also include what will happen to employees who violate these ethical obligations, and how such violations can be reported. Although it is hoped that employees, once they understand the rationale for ethical behavior, will comport with that behavior, the organization should have some means to sanction those who violate ethical conduct. Otherwise, some employees may interpret the organization's position as "lip service." However, unusually severe punishments, especially for first infractions, are undesirable, because it would tend to inhibit reporting of such infractions if observed by others (p. 76).[57] Penalties for ethical violations should be progressive, with early violations being dealt with through discussion. Whenever violations occur, action should be taken swiftly, and continued violations should be dealt with harshly.
3. *Conduct orientations that include discussions of ethics.* When new employees are hired, it is important not only to provide them with general information concerning the mechanics of the organization, but also to begin the process of socialization, inculcating the values of public service. In such a discussion, the new employee should receive a clear understanding of what constitutes ethical and unethical conduct. Emphasis should be placed on the important role that the organization plays and the organization's commitment to the values noted above.

4. *Conduct staff development and training programs*. It is not enough to mention ethical concerns at the time of hire. Employees must experience ongoing reinforcement. This will increase the chance that ethical actions will become habitual. Emphasis should not be placed on the rules themselves, but on the values and deliberations that underlie such rules. It should be assumed that individuals want to behave ethically, especially when they understand how important such conduct is, and how destructive unethical conduct can be in terms of loss of trust and confidence of the public or of other staff. Programs and meetings on ethical issues should therefore be a regular part of staff development and training for all staff and might include case studies in which staff actually go through ethical deliberations that reveal the conflicting tensions within information organizations.

5. *Hire and promote individuals with ethical awareness*. There are many aspects that must be considered when hiring and promoting individuals. One area to explore is how they deal with job-related ethical issues. It should be kept in mind that organizational environments are very powerful. A newly hired employee may possess considerable scruples, but if the prevailing ethics of the organization tolerates unethical conduct, then new hires, in order to fit in, may well adapt rather than attempt to change the environment.

Professional Actions

Ethical conduct should also be promoted by the information profession itself to ensure that the standards of conduct are consistent with the highest levels of professional service.

1. *Create a code of conduct*. A professional association can be seen as the voice of a profession. The most obvious channel used by a profession is to establish a written code of ethics and create sanctions for those who violate it. These sanctions, found in such professions as law and medicine, include temporary or permanent suspension of a professional's ability to practice. Codes, however, may not have sanctions and it may be undesirable for all professions to have them. The ALA has no sanctions for its code of ethics, nor does ASIS&T for its professional guidelines, and hence, comportment with these codes is strictly voluntary. Although sanctions can promote certain types of behavior, they may do so for the wrong reason—fear of punishment. The purpose of an ethical code is first and foremost to promote ethical understanding. Focusing on penalties diverts attention from understanding the values that should determine our conduct.

2. *Offer training and advice in ethical conduct*. Professional associations are also obligated to reinforce their codes of conduct by providing programming and information on ethical issues. Associations such as the ALA and ASIS&T provide such programs, usually at their conference sites. In addition, the ALA has divisions that deal with ethical concerns, including the Committee on Ethics, which considers ethical issues and infrequently provides materials that promote discussion of ethical concerns (e.g., the *Ethics Sin List*[65] and the Intellectual Freedom Committee which deals with ethical issues when they coincide with intellectual freedom issues). It is notable, however, that the Committee on Ethics does not operate like the Intellectual Freedom Committee in that it does not promulgate official interpretations of the code of ethics or intervene in ethical matters outside the association. Similarly, the Professional Committee of ASIS&T issued the ASIS&T Professional Guidelines, but does not promulgate its interpretations or intervene in ethical matters outside the association.

Individual Actions

Ethical actions are associated most often with the conduct of individuals, and there is a clear obligation for information professionals to act ethically in regard to the provision of library and information services.

Information professionals are obligated to act ethically on at least three different levels: they have a responsibility to their profession, to their employer–clients–system users, and to the society as a whole. The ASIS&T Professional Guidelines has set forth the following provisions (abridged):

1. *Responsibilities to employers/clients/system users*
   To act faithfully for their employers or clients in professional matters;
   To uphold each user's, provider's, or employer's right to privacy and confidentiality and to respect whatever proprietary rights belong to them by limiting access to, providing proper security for and ensuring proper disposal of data about clients, patrons, or users;
   To treat all persons fairly.

2. *Responsibility to the profession*
   To truthfully represent themselves and the information systems which they utilize or which they represent...

3. *Responsibility to society*
   To improve the information systems which they work or which they represent to the best of their means and abilities...
   To promote open and equal access to information, within the scope permitted by their organization, and to resist procedures that promote unlawful

discriminatory practices in access to and provision of information...[[49]], adopted May 30, 1992].

These principles can easily be applied to librarians as well as information scientists and other kinds of information professionals.

ETHICAL DILEMMAS

Even with these responsibilities clearly delineated, there are times when the values of information provision appear to conflict with other personal or social or cultural values. This conflict is most conspicuous when the values of information professionals appear to conflict with commonly accepted notions of moral or right conduct. A common example, involving a public library, highlights this type of situation:

> An adolescent child comes to the librarian in a public library and asks for a book on how to commit suicide. The child looks very depressed and upset. The librarian is aware of a book that would provide substantial amount of accurate and up-to-date information on committing suicide. The librarian is also aware that the material would really be understandable to the patron. What should the librarian do?

Admittedly, this situation is contrived and its occurrence would be very rare. Nonetheless, it places into relief a situation in which the information provider's general concept of right conduct (the belief that one should not intentionally harm another person) seems to conflict with one's obligation to respect individuals and their right to information. Of course, implicit in this situation is the belief that the individual will in fact commit suicide. If this was actually known, then providing the information could hardly be defended by invoking provisions of the ALA code of ethics or any other professional code. Nor could one sensibly say that one is obligated to find this information for the patron because of a person's "right to information." Such a rationalization is contrary to our everyday ethical notions of right conduct.

But the situation described above is extraordinary and presupposes knowledge seldom, if ever, available to the information professional. In almost every case, the knowledge of the librarian regarding the patron is imperfect and very limited. This is due to the fact that most patron contacts are very brief. Librarians seldom have substantial information about the personal lives of their patrons or their psychological condition, nor are they qualified to evaluate this information. Consequently, the librarian has little or no ability to predict what a patron will do with the information and the consequences of the patron's actions. In the vast portion of circumstances, acting consistently with the values of the information profession does not require that one give up one's ordinary concept of moral

action; rather it is to accept the ethical obligation to recognize the individual's right to information. Such an obligation could only be violated with clear knowledge that significant harm to others will result. It is also to recognize that the information provider's predictive ability regarding the consequences of the information provided is minimal at best. The duty of the librarian is to accept the right of individuals to receive information and to use that information. Although librarians may be concerned as to how certain information may be used, without sure knowledge of such misuse and the substantial harmful consequences of the use, it becomes too easy for the information professional to project those consequences inaccurately, with harmful ethical consequences of their own.

The dilemma posed by the suicide example brings out another point about the purpose of information giving. One can view information provision simply as an obligation to answer a specific question, but this is an inappropriate and impoverished model for the information professional. The purpose of information giving should be seen in the broader context of resolving an information need of problem. This is consistent with the notion that the purpose of information giving is to assist the patrons in living their lives in the manner they see fit. It is the "problem context" or "problem environment" of the patron[[66]] that is the focus of the information provider. In this context, information providers need to know the context in which information is requested. If, in the unlikely ethical situation posed, a librarian actually had a strong suspicion that a patron was going to use the information to commit suicide, the information provider would in fact be obligated to locate additional information (perhaps the name and telephone numbers of suicide counseling agencies or community mental health agencies) that might resolve the problem in a manner that would promote the health of the individual. In other words, the information question involved how to commit suicide, the information problem was actually unstated: "How can I deal with a life so difficult that I wish to end it?"

There is no simple way to resolve the myriad of ethical problems that confront information professionals, but the fact that ethical issues are complex does not relieve us of the burden to act ethically.[[67]] On the contrary, the absence of ethical concerns would make the information profession very dangerous. As the information professions mature, expand, and grow in importance, information professionals need to redouble their efforts to define their ethical responsibilities and find the means to ensure that all professionals are aware of and accept their ethical obligations.

REFERENCES

1. Honesty/Ethics in Professions, Gallup Report. Available at http://www.gallup.com/poll/1654/Honesty-Ethics-Professions.aspx. (accessed February 12, 2008).

2. Buckley, C.E. Golden rule reference: Face to face and virtual. Ref. Libr. **2006**, *45*, 129–136.

3. Fleische, C.S.; Blenkhorn, D.L., Eds.; *Managing Frontiers in Competitive Intelligence*; Quorum Books: Westport, CT, 2001.

4. Capurro, R. Intercultural information ethics. In *Localizing the Internet. Ethical Aspects in Intercultural Perspective*; Capurro, R., Frühbauer, J., Hausmanninger, T., Eds.; Fink: Munich, Germany, 2007; 21–38. Available at http://www.capurro.de/iie.html.

5. Lancaster, F.W., Ed.; *Ethics and the Librarian;* Graduate School of Library and Information Science, University of Illinois: Urbana-Champaign, IL, 1989.

6. Smith, M.M. Information ethics. In *Annual Review of Information Science and Technology (ARIST)*; Williams, M., Ed.; Learned Information: Medford, NJ, 1997; Vol. 32, 339–366.

7. Froehlich, T.J. A brief history of information ethics. *Textos Universitaris de Biblioteconomia i Documentació (BiD) (Catalan Digital J.)*; December 2004. Available at http://www.ub.edu/bid/.

8. Rubin, R.R. Ethical issues in library personnel management. J. Libr. Admin. **1991**, *14*(4), 1–16.

9. Baker, S.L. Needed: An ethical code for library administrators. J. Libr. Admin. **1992**, *16*(4), 1–17.

10. Asheim, L. Not censorship but selection. Wilson Libr. Bull. **1953**, *28*, 63–67.

11. Summerford, S. The public library: Offensive by design. Pub. Libr. **1987**, *26*, 60–62.

12. Hole, C. Who me, censor?. Top News. **1984**, *40*(2), 147–153.

13. West, C. The secret garden of censorship: Ourselves. Libr. J. **1984**, *108*(15), 1651–1653.

14. Legal and ethical issues in acquisitions; (entire issue). Strauch, K.; Strauch, B., Eds.; 1990; (3).

15. Susman, T.M. Libraries and the USA Patriot Act. In *The Bowker Annual: Library and Book Trade Almanac*; Bogart, D., Ed.; Information Today: Medford, NJ, 2004; 229–252.

16. Munoz, R.E. The legal analysis of the ALA's support of the Freedom to Read Protection Act. J. Inform. Ethics. **2004**, *13*, 58–77.

17. American Library Association, Resolution reaffirming the principles of intellectual freedom in the aftermath of terrorist attacks. American Library Association: Chicago, IL, 2002. Available at http://www.ala/org.

18. American Library Association, Resolution on the USA Patriot Act and related measures that infringe on the rights of library users. American Library Association: Chicago, IL, 2003. Available at http://www.ala/org.

19. Foerstel, H. *Surveillance in the Stacks: The FBI's Library Awareness Program*; Greenwood Press: Westport, CT, 1991.

20. Isbell, M.K.; Cook, M.K. Confidentiality of online bibliographic searches: Attitudes and practices. Res. Q. **1986**, *25* (4), 483–487.

21. Penway, A.L. The Buckley Amendment: Student privacy versus parents' right to know. *Intellectual Freedom Manual*; 5th Ed. American Library Association: Chicago, IL, 1996; 323–327.

22. Harris, L.E. Monitoring legal and illegal use of digital content: How can your enterprise effectively keep tabs on use?. Inform. Outlook, August 2007.

23. Intne, S.S.; Schement, J.R. The ethic of free service. Libr. J. **1987**, *112*(16), 50–52.

24. Caren, L. Issues facing private academic libraries considering fee-based programs. Ref. Libr. **1998**, *22*, 37–49.

25. McKinzie, S. For ethical reference, pare the paraprofessionals. Am. Libr. **2002**, *33*, 42.

26. Kirkwood, C.C.; Watts, T.J. Legal reference service: Duties and liabilities. Legal Ref. Serv. Q. **1983**, *3*(2), 67–82.

27. Puckett, M.; Ashley, P.; Craig, J.P. Issues in information malpractice. Med. Red. Sere. Q. **1991**, *10*(2), 33–46.

28. Hurych, J.M.; Glenn, A.C. Ethics in health sciences librarianship. Bull. Med. Libr. Assoc. **1987**, *75*(4), 342–348.

29. Runge, C.A. Ethics and the reference librarian. In *Ethics and the Librarian*; Lancaster, F.W., Ed.; Graduate School of Library and Information Science, University of Illinois: Urbana-Champaign, IL, 1989; 45–61.

30. Ethics and reference services. (entire issue). Katz, B., Fraley, R., Eds.; 1982; (4).

31. Ulvik, S.; Salvesen, G. Ethical reference practice. New Libr. World. **2007**, *108*, 342–353.

32. Heim, K.M. Human resource management: Ethics in personnel. In *Ethics and the Librarian*; Lancaster, F.W., Ed.; Graduate School of Library and Information Science, University of Illinois: Urbana-Champaign, IL, 1991; 101–114.

33. Du Mont, R.R. Ethics in librarianship: A management model. Libr. Trends. **1991**, *40*(2), 201–215.

34. Dowlin, K.E. Access to information: A human right?. *The Bowker Annual Library and Book Trade Information*; 32nd Ed.; Simora, F., Ed.; R. R. Bowker: New York, 1987; 64–68.

35. Williams, S.F. To charge or not to charge: No longer a question?. Ref. Libr.s **1989**, *19*, 125–137.

36. Wyatt, A.M. Do librarians have an ethical duty to monitor patrons' internet usage in the public library?. J. Inform. Ethics. **2006**, *15*, 70–79.

37. McMenemy, D.; Poulter, A.; Burton, P.F. *A Handbook of Ethical Practice: A Practical Guide to Dealing with Ethical Issues in Information and Library Work*; Chandos: Oxford, 2007; 46–48.

38. Bair, S. Toward a code of ethics for cataloging. Tech. Serv. Quart. **2005**, *23*(1), 13–26.

39. Berman, S. DDC 19: An indictment. *The Joy of Cataloging: Essays, Reviews and Other Explosions*; 1981; 177–185.

40. Froehlich, T.J. Ethics, ideology, and the practices of information systems ASIS '90: Information in the Year 2000: From Research to Applications: Proceedings of the American Society for Information Science (ASIS) 53rd Annual Meeting Learned Information: Medford, NJ, 1990; 245–255.

41. Shaver, D.B.; Hewison, N.S.; Wykoff, L.W. Ethics for online intermediaries. Spec. Libr. **1985**, *76*(4), 238–245.

42. Crowe, L.; Anthes, S.H. The academic librarian and information technology: Ethical issues. Coll. Res. Libr. **1988**, *49* (2), 123–130.

43. Boissonnas, C.M. The cost is more than that elegant dinner: Your ethics are at steak. Libr. Ac. **1987**, *11*(2), 145–152.

44. Stahl, W.M. Automation and ethics: A view from the trenches. Libr. Hi Tech. **1986**, *4*(4), 53–57.

45. White, H.S. The conflict between professional and organizational loyalty. Libr. J. **1991**, *116*(9), 59–60.

46. Smith, M.M. Infoethics for leaders: Models of moral agency in the information environment. Libr. Trends. **1992**, *40*(30), 553–570.
47. American Library Association, Librarians' code of ethics. Adopted June 28, 1997, by the ALA Council; Amended January 22, 2008. Available at http://www.ala.org (accessed May 3, 2008).
48. Lindsey, J.A.; Prentice, A.E. *Professional Ethics and Librarians*; Oryx: Phoenix, AZ, 1985.
49. ASIS professional guidelines. Bull. Am. Soc. Inform. Sci. **1994**, *20*(2), 4. Available at http://www.asis.org/professionalguidelines.html (accessed May 5, 2008).
50. Barnes, R.E. Some thoughts on professional ethics codes. Bull. Am. Soc. Inform. Sci. **1986**, *21*(4), 1920.
51. Finks, L.W. Librarianship needs a new code of ethics. Am. Libr. **1991**, *22*(1), 84–88.
52. Kaplan, S.J. Information ethics: An annotated bibliography. In *Information Ethics: Concerns for the Information Industry*; Mintz, A., Ed.; McFarland: Jefferson, NC, 1990; 53–61.
53. American Library Association, Office for Intellectual Freedom, Library bill of rights. *Intellectual Freedom Manual*. Available at http://www.ala.org/ala/oif/statementspols/statementsif/librarybillrights.cfm (accessed May 7, 2008).
54. de Spinoza, B. Ethics. *The Great Books of the Western World*; Encyclopedia Britannica: Chicago, IL, 1952; Vol. 31, 355–463.
55. Hobbes, T. Leviathan. *The Great Books of the Western World*; Encyclopedia Britannica: Chicago, IL, 1952; Vol. 23, 45–283.
56. Ephraim, P.E. The greening of libraries. Libr. Manage. **2003**, *24*(3), 160–163.
57. Boyden, L.; Weiner, J. Sustainable libraries: Teaching environmental responsibility to communities. Bottom Line. **2000**, *13*(2), 74–82.
58. Kant, I. *Foundations of the Metaphysics of Morals, and What is Enlightenment?*; Bobbs-Merrill: Indianapolis, IN, 1959.
59. Bob, M.C. The case for quality book selection. Libr. J. **1982**, *107*(16), 1707–1710.
60. Swan, J.C. Untruth or consequences. Libr. J. **1986**, *111*(12), 44–52.
61. Association for Library and Information Science Education (ALISE), Position statement on information ethics in LIS education. Available at http://www.alise.org/mc/page.do?sitePageId = 58273 (accessed May 7, 2008).
62. Finks, L.W. Values without shame. Am. Libr. **1989**, *20*(4), 252–254.
63. Rawls, J. Justice as fairness. Philos. Rev. **1958**, *67*, 164–194.
64. Gellerman, S.W. Managing ethics from the top down. Sloan Mgt. Rev. **1989**, *30*(2), 73–79.
65. Ethic Sin List. American Library Association: Chicago, IL, 1989. Available at http://w2.eff.org/censorship/Academic_edu/CAF/library/order.form.ala.
66. Durrance, J.C. Information needs: Old song, new tune. *Rethinking the Library*; GPO: Washington, DC, 1989; 159–178.
67. Budd, J.M. Towards a practical and normative ethics for librarianship. Libr. Q. **2006**, *76*(3), 251–269.

BIBLIOGRAPHY

General Introductions and Bibliographies

1. Alfino, M.; Pierce, L. *Information Ethics for Librarians*; McFarland: Jefferson, NC, 1997.
2. Capurro, R. Moral issues in information science. J. Inform. Sci. **1985**, *11*(2), 113–123.
3. Cox, R.J. *Ethics, Accountability, and Recordkeeping in a Dangerous World*; Facet Publishing: London, U.K., 2006.
4. Foskett, D.J. *The Creed of the Librarian: No Politics, No Religion, No Morals*; Library Association: London, U.K., 1962.
5. Froehlich, T.J. Ethical considerations of information professionals. In *Annual Review of Information Science and Technology (ARIST)*; Williams, M., Ed.; Learned Information: Medford, NJ, 1992; 291–324.
6. Froehlich, T.J. Library and information professions. In *The Encyclopedia of Ethics*; Becker, L.C., Ed.; Garland: New York, 1992; 711–716.
7. Hauptman, R. *Ethical Challenges in Librarianship*; Oryx: Phoenix, AZ, 1988.
8. Hauptman, R. *Ethics and Librarianship*; McFarland: Jefferson, NC, 2002.
9. Lancaster, F.W., Ed.; *Ethics and the Librarian*; Graduate School of Library and Information Science, University of Illinois: Urbana, IL, 1989.
10. Mason, R.O. Mason, F.M. Culnan, M.J. *Ethics of Information Management*; Sage Publications: Thousand Oaks, CA, 1995.
11. McMenemy, D.; Poulter, A.; Burton, P.F. *A Handbook of Ethical Practice: A Practical Guide To Dealing With Ethical Issues In Information And Library Work*; Chandos: Oxford, 2007.
12. Mintz, A.P., Ed.; *Information Ethics: Concerns for Librarianship and the Information Industry*; McFarland: Jefferson, NC, 1990.
13. Severson, R.W. *Principles of Information Ethics*; M.E. Sharpe: Armonk, NY, 1997.
14. Smith, M.M. Information ethics. In *Annual Review of Information Science and Technology (ARIST)*; Williams, M., Ed.; Learned Information: Medford, NJ, 1997; Vol. 32, 339–366.

Journals and Web Sites

1. American Library Association. Available at http://www.ala.org.
2. Ethicomp Journal. Available at http://www.ccsr.cse.dmu.ac.uk/journal/previousissue.html.
3. Ethics and Information Technology **1999**, Springer.
4. J. Inform. Ethics, Jefforson, NC: McFarland, Fall **1992** Hauptman, R., Ed. (ISSN 1061–9321).
5. Information Ethics at the School of Information Sciences at the University of Pittsburgh. Available at http://www2.sis.pitt.edu/~ethics/.
6. International Review of Information Ethics **2004** Accessible at The International Center for Information Ethics (ICIE). Available at http://icie.zkm.de/.

7. The UNESCO Observatory of the Information Society. Available at http://www.unesco.org/webworld/observatory.

On Specific Topics

1. Agnew, G. Martin, M. Digital rights management: Why libraries should be major players. *The Bowker Annual Library and Book Trade Almanac*; Information Today: Medford, NJ, 2003; 267–278.
2. Bair, S. Toward a code of ethics for cataloging. Tech. Serv. Quart. **2005**, *23*(1), 13–26.
3. Doctor, R.D. Social equity and information technologies: Moving toward information democracy. In *Annual Review of Information Science and Technology (ARIST)*; Williams, M., Ed.; Learned Information: Medford, NJ, 1992; Vol. 27, 43–96.
4. Durrance, J.C. The generic librarian: Anonymity versus accountability. Res. Q. **1983**, *22*(3), 278–283.
5. Frankel, M. Professional codes: Why, how, and with what impact?. J. Bus. Ethics. **1989**, *9*, 109–115.
6. Froehlich, T.J. Ethical issues in the consultant–library relationship. In *Using Consultants in the Library and Information Centers: A Management Handbook*; Garten, E., Ed.; Greenwood Press: Westport, CT, 1992; 155–172.
7. Goehner, D.M. Vendor–library relations: The ethics of working with vendors. *Understanding the Business of Library Acquisitions*; American Library Association: Chicago, IL, 1990; 137–151.
8. Kostrewski, B.J.; Oppenheim, C. Ethics in information science. J. Inform. Sci. Prin. Prac. **1980**, *1*(5), 277–283.
9. Lievrouw, L.A. Farb, S. Information and equity. *Annual Review of Information Science and Technology (ARIST)*; Information Today: Medford, NJ, 2003; Vol. 37, 499–540.
10. *Legal Issues for Library and Information Managers*; Hayworth: New York, 1987.
11. Parker, D.B.; Swope, S.; Baker, B.N. *Ethical Conflicts in Information and Computer Science, Technology and Business*; Q.E.D. Information Sciences: Wellesley, MA, 1990.
12. Preer, J. Special ethics for special librarians?. Spec. Libr. **1991**, *8*(1), 12–18.
13. Rubin, R.R. Ethical issues in library personnel management. J. Libr. Admin. **1991**, *14*(4), 1–16.
14. Serebnick, J.; Harter, S.P. Ethical practices in journal publishing: A study of library and information science periodicals. Libr. Q. **1990**, *60*(2), 91–119.
15. Swan, J.C. Peattie, N. *The Freedom to Lie: A Debate About Democracy*, McFarland: Jefferson, NC, 1989.
16. Woodward, D. Teaching ethics for information professionals. J. Educ. Libr. Inform. Sci. **1989**, *30*(2), 132–135.

Ethical Issues in Information Systems

Vladimir Zwass
*Computer Science and Management Information Systems, Fairleigh Dickinson University,
Teaneck, New Jersey, USA*

Abstract

Information technology and information systems built around its artifacts can have powerful effects on individuals, both in their private life and in the workplace. As professionals and users, we should use ethical principles and codes of ethics to avoid and prevent deleterious effects of technology. Infoethics is the application of ethical theories to the development and use of information systems. The principal infoethical issues are privacy, accuracy, property (in particular, intellectual property), and access. These issues have come into a sharp focus as we spend ever more of our time online and as our actions are mediated by systems available over the Internet. Ethical decisions in the information-related domains are made by identifying the issues involved and applying ethical theories—classified as consequentialist and deontological—in the decision-making process.

INTRODUCTION

Information technology (IT) offers potent tools that can serve to fulfill an individual's life, to further organizational goals, pursue national and international interest, or support environmentally sustainable regional development. The same technology can also be used to infringe on property in a digital form, invade individuals' private sphere, and to hold them in fear of omnipresent surveillance. The way the technology is deployed depends on our decisions as professionals and as users of information systems. It also depends on the policies enacted by the government and business organizations, and on legislation. All of us, therefore, should make the relevant decisions guided not only by the economic, organizational, and technological aspects of information systems, but also in consideration of their effects on individuals. Our knowledge of ethics helps us in making such decisions. Furthermore, this knowledge can inform the evolution of the relevant public and organizational policies. What we may call infoethics is the application of ethical thinking to the development and use of information systems.

Ethics and Codes of Ethics

Ethics is a study of the principles of right and wrong that ought to guide human conduct. Ethics concerns itself with what values are worth pursuing in life and what acts are right. Therefore, ethics is a study of morality.

Human behavior and decision-making fall into three domains, as shown in Fig. 1. The legal domain governs a variety of relatively well-defined behaviors, specified by law enforceable in the courts of a given country or within a local jurisdiction. International bodies increasingly address legal issues that cross national borders. Computer crime and abuse, such as the destructive deployment of malware (e.g., computer viruses or worms) or misrepresentation of electronic identity toward financial gain, are the breaches of law and fall into this domain.

However, not every legal action is ethical. The domain of ethics is governed by the general norms of behavior and by specific codes of ethics. To see whether your decision-making in a given case involves an ethical issue, you may apply the "sunshine test": "What if I read about my decisions and subsequent actions in tomorrow's paper?" Ethical considerations go beyond legal liability, and the breach of norms not punishable by law meets with social opprobrium. Only if the action is both legal and ethical, does it fall in the discretionary domain, where we properly act entirely according to our preferences.

Knowledge of ethics as it applies to the issues arising from the development and use of information systems, which we may call infoethics, helps us to make decisions in our professional life. Professional knowledge is generally assumed to confer a special responsibility in its domain. This is why the professions have evolved codes of ethics, that is, sets of principles intended to guide the conduct of the members of the profession. The principal code of ethics for information systems professionals is the Association for Computing Machinery (ACM) Code of Ethics and Professional Conduct, binding on the members of the ACM.[2] The code should be familiar also to all whose professional life is affected by information systems. We have reproduced the fundamental statements of the ACM Code in Fig. 2. In addition, corporations and other employers should establish their own codes of infoethics. Such corporate codes have been shown to influence the behavior of people who would otherwise not think that an important ethical issue was involved in their decision-making.[3,4]

To select a course of action in an ethical dilemma, we turn to ethical theories.

Encyclopedia of Library and Information Sciences, Fourth Edition DOI: 10.1081/E-ELIS4-120053310

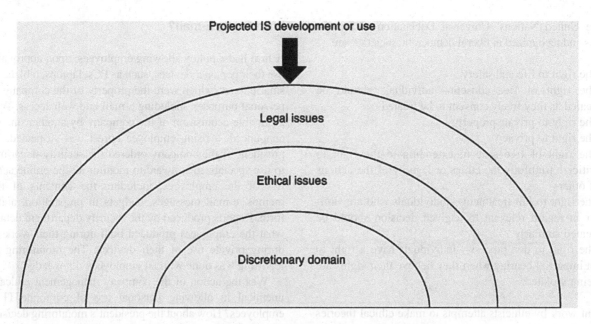

Fig. 1 Domains of pursuit in problem-solving or opportunity-seeking with information systems.
Source: From Zwass.[1]

Ethical Theories

Ethical theories give us the foundation for ethical decision-making. Some of them are grounded in an individual's pursuit of virtue, such as justice or generosity. While important in the development of the moral sense of individuals, these lend themselves, only to a limited degree, to a reasoned decision-making process. There are two fundamental effective approaches to ethical reasoning:

- Consequentialist theories tell us to choose the action with the best possible consequences. Thus, the utilitarian theory that prominently represents this approach holds that our chosen action should produce the greatest overall good for the greatest number of people affected by our decision. The difficulties lie in predicting the consequences of an action, and in deciding what the "good" is and how to measure and compare the resulting "goods." The approach may also lead to sacrificing the rights of a minority. A social contract

among the members of social groups implies the need to consider the lot of all these members. There are certain acts that are wrong in themselves and should be always avoided. These unethical acts interfere with the rights of others, the rights that may be derived from the other principal group of ethical theories.

- Deontological theories argue that it is our duty to do what is right. Your actions should be such that they could serve as a model of behavior for others—and, in particular, you should act as you would want others to act toward you. Our fundamental duty is to treat others with respect—and thus not to treat them *solely* as a means to our own purposes. These theories have been assailed by the claims that varieties of cultures exist, with differing norms and models of behavior.

Treating others with respect means not violating their rights. It is, therefore, vital that we recognize the rights of each human individual. The principal individual rights, enshrined

1. Contribute to society and human well-being.
2. Avoid harm to others.
3. Be honest and trustworthy.
4. Be fair and take action not to discriminate.
5. Honor property rights including copyrights and patents.
6. Give proper credit for intellectual property.
7. Respect privacy of others.
8. Honor confidentiality.

Fig. 2 General moral imperatives of the ACM Code of Ethics and Professional Conduct.
Source: From ACM Code of Ethics and Professional Conduct.[2]

in the United Nations' Universal Declaration of Human Rights and recognized in liberal democratic societies, are

1. The right to life and safety
2. The right of free consent—individuals should be treated as they freely consent to be treated
3. The right to private property
4. The right to privacy
5. The right of free speech, extending to the right to criticize truthfully the ethics or legality of the actions of others
6. The right to fair treatment—individuals who are similar in regard relevant to a given decision should be treated similarly
7. The right to due process—individuals have a right to an impartial hearing when they believe their rights are being violated.

Recent work by ethicists attempts to make ethical theories more effective in practice. An ethical theory that supports a process of deliberation between the future system users and its developers is discourse ethics, grounded in the theory of communicative action of Jürgen Habermas.[5] The emerging empirical moral psychology attempts to relate the actual human behavior in ethically challenging situations to the precepts of ethical theories.[6] Thus, we learn empirically about the implicit or explicit use of ethical theories by information-systems professionals in their decision-making processes.[7] This helps us inculcate values and ethical decision-making modes. The application of ethical theories is best illustrated by considering practical cases, which we will now proceed to do.

SCENARIOS IN THE ETHICAL DOMAIN

Consider the following three scenarios, adapted from Parker.[8] We will come back to these scenarios after we discuss the tenets of infoethics.

Transactional Information on Smart Cards

The manager of the smart-card division of a financial institution has developed a new debit card as a smart card, containing a microprocessor chip with memory. Unbeknownst to its holder, not only the amount spent was debited, but also detailed data about every purchase transaction were stored on the card. As a result, any merchant presented with the card could evaluate the credit history of the cardholder. The financial institution was also planning to allow the merchants to upload the data from the smart cards to their own servers. This would enable the retailers to use personal information about their customers for promotional purposes.

Consider these questions: Do you believe that there are any ethical issues involved? If so, what ethical principles were breached?

Who Owns E-mail?

A firm had a policy allowing employees, upon approval, to use their personal devices, such as PCs, laptops, tablets, and smartphones, which were the property of the company, for personal purposes, including e-mail and web access. When a possible acquisition of the company by another one was announced, a rising employee unrest was suspected. The president of the company ordered the security department to use specialized software to monitor all the online activities of the employees, including the contents of their memos, e-mail messages, budgets in preparation, and so forth. Reports produced by the security department detailed what the employees produced both during their work and during private use of their devices. The monitoring and reporting was done without employees' knowledge.

Was the action of the company management ethical or unethical in allowing personal use of corporate IT by employees? How about the president's monitoring decision?

Let's Just Release This System

A project leader in the corporate information systems division was assigned by her manager, the vice president of sales for the company, a task to develop a new Internet-based billing system. When the work was being assigned, the project leader thought that the time and human resources provided were adequate to complete the project. However, due to an unexpected turnover of computing specialists, it became clear that the system could not be completed as designed within the available budget and time frame. The project leader warned her superior about the impending problem. She was forced to deliver a "bare bones" system, without adequate error detection, exception handling, security safeguards, and audit trail. When the system was fielded, it became a source of problems in customer service. Many customers were billed incorrectly and, following heated exchanges, switched suppliers. Cases of fraud were discovered but proved impossible to trace. Business losses resulted and the project leader was blamed.

Was the action of the project leader ethical in knowingly implementing an inadequate system? How would you evaluate the actions of her superior in ordering an inadequate system into production?

The following general discussion of infoethics will allow us to discuss the issues involved in these cases.

ETHICAL ISSUES IN THE DEVELOPMENT AND USE OF INFORMATION SYSTEMS

The welfare of individuals and their specific rights, postulated by the ethical theories we discussed, need to be safeguarded in the environment of an information society. The principal ethical issues of concern with regard to information systems may be categorized as privacy, accuracy, property, and access.[9]

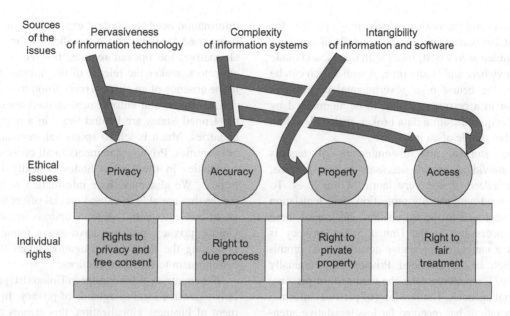

Fig. 3 Ethical issues, their sources, and the underlying individual rights.
Source: From Zwass.[1]

We have shown these principal ethical issues as the four circles in Fig. 3. As shown in the figure, we can trace these issues to their sources: 1) the pervasive role and immense capabilities of systems for collecting, aggregating, storing, communicating, and accessing information in our information society; 2) the complexity of IT; and 3) the intangible nature of information and digital goods, such as digitized music or software. We also show in the figure the specific individual rights whose potential violation brings the issues to a head.

Tracing an ethical issue to its source and understanding the individual rights that could be violated help us understand the issue itself. For example, the intellectual property (IP) rights embodied in digital goods, such as software, are relatively easily violated because software is intangible and can be easily copied at a marginal cost close to zero. At the same time, the development costs of software are very high. Since IT pervades so many aspects of our lives, particularly after the infusion of the Internet–web compound, our privacy can be more easily violated than in the absence of this technology. Indeed, without computerized databases accessible over the Internet, fed by information systems that process our purchases, loan applications, insurance policies, and other transactions, it would hardly be possible to assemble the detailed record of our lives within fractions of seconds. With the broad move to business analytics based on the many trillions of facts collected about individuals as "big data," our lives can be laid bare through the use of IT. Access to the information-based systems enhances our lives and the commercial activity in uncountable ways, as it exposes us to privacy risks. At the same time, those bereft of access to the technology are impaired in many of the life's pursuits and their right to fair treatment is violated. An individual in a modern society who cannot make use of the Internet is deprived of a principal source of information,

transactions, and relationships, and the means of self-expression. A handicapped person without effective access to IT in a society where such use is needed to work is not treated fairly. We will now proceed to consider the four ethical issues in the following sections.

PRIVACY

Privacy is often considered the most important ethical issue raised by information systems. Privacy is the right of individuals to retain certain information about themselves without disclosure and to have control over the information collected about them. When our privacy is invaded, we are embarrassed, diminished, and perceive a loss of autonomy—a loss of control over our lives. Invasion of privacy is a potent threat in an information society. Individuals can be deprived of opportunities to form desired professional and personal relationships or can be politically neutralized through surveillance and gathering of data from the myriad databases that provide information about them. Most authorities agree that it is necessary to uphold the right to privacy as a basic individual right; Justice Louis Brandeis, over a century ago, called this right "the most valued by the civilized man." Even though this right is not guaranteed by the Bill of Rights in the United States, that constitutional document stresses that other rights, beyond those enumerated there, are retained by the people. The right to privacy is considered to be such a right.

Concern about privacy had existed for many years before computer-based IT entered human affairs. Yet, computer-related technologies, and especially the massive use of the Internet–web compound, create opportunities for privacy invasion that had not existed previously. As much of our lives are now lived online, traces are left of our behaviors and activities which may persist for decades. Databases containing minute details of our lives can be assembled at low cost, fused with others, and made accessible anywhere and at any time. A web search can be conducted at the behest of a governmental or business institution, or in a personal pursuit, to be augmented by information acquired from a data broker, that will yield a comprehensive profile of an individual.

Collection, storage, and dissemination of records concerning individuals are all necessary to our business, government, indeed, to the very fabric of our lives. To balance this need with privacy protection, both legislation and ethical approach to the acquisition and use of these records are necessary. In the United States, privacy is protected by a variety of legislative acts, the most prominent of which is the amended Privacy Act originally enacted in 1974, which regulates the treatment of personal data by federal agencies. The handling of personal information by corporations has received far less legislative attention, and the essential legal mechanism in this case is the law of contract. A 1999 U.S. law requires financial institutions to send out their privacy policies to their customers. The Health Insurance Portability and Accountability Act (HIPAA) provides privacy protection for medical records. However, gaps in legislation and in its enforcement make it difficult to protect privacy through the legal system and leave much of the privacy issue in the domain of ethics.

The Privacy Act and the legislation that follows it specify the limitations on the data records that can be kept about individuals and are based on what is known as Fair Information Practice Principles. These principles also underlie the guidelines set by the Organization for Economic Cooperation and Development (OECD). These fundamental privacy safeguards are the following:

- Individuals should be given notice of the information practices of the entity that wishes to collect personal information from them.
- No use can be made of the records for other than the original purposes without the individuals' consent.
- Individuals have the right of inspection and correction of records about them.
- The collecting agency is responsible for the integrity and security of the record-keeping system.
- There is a mechanism in place to enforce the safeguards and offer redress.

These principles lie at the foundation of the Consumer Privacy Bill of Rights fostered by the United States executive branch as the framework aiming at limiting the scope and increasing the transparency of data collection practices by business organizations.[10] Ensuring privacy in the face of rapidly expanding technological possibilities for its invasion is not easy. Controversies arise and the trade-offs involved test the ethical frameworks. Many privacy advocates favor an opt-in practice in soliciting personal information. In this case, the individual releasing the information needs to consent expressly to the information being used for the purpose specified by the requester. An alternative, the opt-out regime, favored by information collectors, makes the release of the information a default in the absence of an express prohibition by the individual.

Legislation and enforcement in the area of privacy in the United States are behind those in a number of other countries. Much is left to spotty self-regulation by business entities. Privacy statements to all clients by financial companies in the United States typically include such tropes: "We also may share information with other companies that are able to extend special offers we feel might be of value to you." Opt-out options are cumbersome. Online privacy policies have been found to aim at protecting the firms from litigation rather than reflect a commitment to fair data practices.[11]

The countries of the European Union (EU) offer particularly extensive legal safeguards of privacy. In the environment of business globalization, this creates difficulties in transborder data flow, that is, transfer of data across national borders. Countries with more stringent measures for privacy protection object to a transfer of personal data into the states where this protection is more lax. Therefore, a number of U.S. corporations have signed the so-called safe harbor agreement, complying with the EU privacy standards. The United Nations has stated the minimum privacy guarantees to be incorporated into national legislation. The harmonization of privacy regimes across borders remains a challenge.

Privacy safeguards, such as privacy policies posted on websites, even when audited by independent agencies (e.g., TRUSTe, http://truste.org), are insufficient to protect this information from abuse. A common loophole is the dissolution of the original firm that had collected the information under certain safeguards, for example, during a merger or an acquisition. Conflicts arise between an individual's right to privacy and the right of a larger community to protect itself.[12] Such issues include the rights of governments to decipher encrypted messages in the cases of suspected terrorism or crime, or the rights of parents to have access to the records of sex offenders who may endanger their children's welfare. In discharging their responsibility to enhance national security, governments may move to take away the ability of individuals to remain anonymous in a variety of situations, for example, by demanding identification in the airports.

The marketing and personalization of products and services acquired and sometimes also delivered over the web requires personal information about the consumer. Recommender systems that facilitate our online transactions rely on the minute knowledge of our buying habits. Effective m-commerce, that is, relationships and transactions conducted over smartphones and other mobile devices, indeed calls for consumer intimacy: The more information the system stores about the user, the higher is the speed and quality of the interaction.[13] Pervasive information systems that introduce ubiquitous computing and sensing technology into everyday objects magnify the exposure to potential intrusions on privacy.[14] Fair Information Practice Principles should serve as the essential decision-making guideline. Matching of the online profile with personally identifiable data is of particular concern. Privacy concerns should inform technological solutions in system fielding; such concerns are, for example, debated before the radio-frequency identification tags are deployed on a wider scale.[15] There are various methods of de-identification in data sets, which should be considered before releasing the data from the originating organization.[16]

Information systems have made it possible to conduct systematic monitoring and surveillance of persons and groups. Among the technologies are the video-based systems that monitor city traffic for infractions, as well as the systems that monitor the use of rental cars to account for driving habits. The use of cookies and monitoring of the clickstream by websites, while facilitating commercial transactions and marketing, is troubling to many. Device fingerprinting allows monitoring users' online behavior even in the absence of cookies.[17] Tracking an individual's whereabouts with a geographic positioning system, embedded in a cell phone, although useful in m-commerce, presents a danger to privacy. Notably, human mobility traces are unique and can easily lead to identification.[18] Focused and context-specific data collection is a basis for privacy.

Aggregation and analysis of "big data" enables a broad product and process innovation, with evidence-based decision-making in various sectors of the economy. Of special concern is the personally identifiable information (PII), that is, the information that can be traced to an identifiable individual. The powerful and economically important use of the "big data" also creates new privacy risks with the commodification of data, including in many cases PII, and the loss of control over their flow and aggregation.[19,20] Since the value of the "big data" emerges mostly in its multiple and varied secondary uses, great care has to be exercised over the aggregation.[21] There are many options available to IT designers to build systems that foster limitations on the collection and transmission of PII with, among other measures, "privacy patterns" to be used in building the relevant software.[22]

Two database phenomena create specific threats of privacy invasion. The first, database fusion, makes it possible to merge separate facts collected about an individual in multiple databases in order to develop a comprehensive profile of a person. If minute facts about an individual are put together in this fashion in a context unrelated to the purpose of the data collection and without the individual's consent or ability to rectify inaccuracies, serious damage to the person's rights may result. The dispersion of personal data among several independent databases is one safeguard against invasion of privacy. The other concern relates to statistical databases that contain large numbers of personal records, but are intended to supply only statistical information (the U.S. census database is the best example). A snooper, however, may deduce personal information by constructing and asking a series of statistical queries that would gradually narrow the

field down to a specific individual. To prevent such disclosure, limitations on the allowed queries need to be placed (e.g., a query would not be answered if the answer would refer to fewer than 10 persons).

Active generation of online content by users leads to exposures we are just learning to control. Cocreation of value by users and consumers, along with the producers, through user-generated content and through conducting their relationships online has become a major economic factor.[23] Users are offered access at no charge to a great variety of social networks and expression media – and the content they produce and the traces they leave become the property of the sites. For example, these sites have become media for the management, or even manipulation, of one's public persona. Such reputation management often surrenders various aspects of the individual's privacy, to the individual's future regret. Social norms in that respect are in a state of flux.[24]

As privacy norms are being formed and as laws are emerging, it is important to consider the context of the system use and the expectations of privacy in that context, be it private life, school, or workplace.[25] The complexity of this consideration comes from the pervasiveness of IT throughout the various—and interlocking—contexts of our lives. Although we cannot "engineer privacy," there are numerous practices that can serve the goal of controlled approach to data.[26] As stated in Fig. 2, the ACM Code of Ethics obligates information systems professionals to "respect the privacy of others" and goes further to offer specific guidelines on how to do that.

ACCURACY

Pervasive use of information in our societal affairs means that we have become more vulnerable to misinformation. Accurate information is error-free, complete, and relevant to the decisions that are to be based on it. Accurate information is grounded in high-quality, secure information systems, constructed by responsible professionals. OECD data quality principle states that the data "should be accurate, complete, and kept up-to-date."[10] Although stories about inaccurate information surface most frequently with regard to the credit-reporting industry, they reflect a generally low level of data quality control throughout the public and private sectors of the economies.

Inaccurate information can prevent an applicant from obtaining a credit card—or a job. When people rely on inaccurate information, other people may be deprived of their right to due process. An incorrect medical record can threaten your life. A weather report that incorrectly forecast the trajectory of a storm because the data from a failed buoy were unavailable to the computerized model sent a sailor to his death.[9] French police officers, in hot pursuit of a car recorded as stolen in their database, opened fire and wounded a law-abiding driver. The records of the car recovery by the legitimate owner and of the subsequent sale of the car were missing from the database. Multiple accidents involving massive radiation overdose administered by the radiation-therapy system Therac-25 have been traced to imperfectly tested software.[27]

Is the development of information systems that provide accurate information just the question of professional competence? In the third scenario presented in "Scenarios in the Ethical Domain," a "bare-bones" system was knowingly forced through by a firm's executive and knowingly implemented by a project leader. Similar events could have been behind any of the systems that led to the loss of individual welfare—or life—in the cases we just described. Beyond that, there exist various sources of possible bias in information systems—and the information system developers should be aware of that. The bias of concern to infoethics represents a persistent discrimination against certain categories of individuals and groups reflected in the design of an information system, which negatively affects the accuracy of information provided.[28] Data analysis grounded in the "big data" may extrapolate individuals' behavior from that of "people like them" and, possibly, punish an individual for the expected, rather than the actual, deeds.[21] Professional integrity is an essential guarantor of information accuracy.

An ethical approach to information accuracy calls for the following:

- A professional should not misrepresent his or her qualifications to perform a task.
- A professional should indicate to his or her employer the consequences to be expected if his or her judgment is overruled. The ACM Code of Ethics and Professional Conduct speaks of the professional's obligation to "avoid harm to others" by carefully assessing potential impacts of an information system to be implemented.
- System safeguards, such as the controls and audits, are necessary to maintain information accuracy. Regular audits of data quality should be performed and acted upon.
- Individuals should be given an opportunity to correct inaccurate information held about them in databases. The sources of inaccuracies should be tracked down and eradicated.
- Contents of databases containing data about individuals should be reviewed at frequent intervals, with obsolete data discarded.

Regrettably, some information-systems professionals are likely to choose implementing a system with quality problems in the conditions known as moral hazard, that is when they have an incentive to act in their own interests and against the interests of their employer, while being able to hide this.[29] The same research has also shown that the ethical climate of an organization can influence these actions in the positive direction.

Accuracy problems have wider societal implications. A claim has been made that the absence of proper controls in some computerized election systems may threaten basic constitutional rights. An independent assessment of the e-voting systems certified for use in the State of California, as one example, showed serious security vulnerabilities.[30] Democratic process will require substantive information-accuracy safeguards before a wide move to electronic voting.

PROPERTY

The right to property is largely secured in the legal domain. However, intangibility of information is at the source of dilemmas that take clarity away from the laws, passing many problems into the domain of ethics. At issue are primarily the rights to IP: the intangible property that results from an individual's or a corporation's creative activity. The web, which has become a uniquely valuable medium for legitimate distribution of data, information, and knowledge in a digital form, has also become a common means for breaching the rights to this property.

IP, such as software or other digital content, is protected by three legal mechanisms: copyright, patent, and trade secret. These means serve to protect the investment of creators and to ensure public good by encouraging disclosure so that further innovations can be made by others. Indeed, the copyright and patent laws are designed to assist in the public disclosure and thus further technological progress. Copyright registration, which is easy to obtain, protects the form of expression (e.g., a given program) rather than the idea itself (e.g., an algorithm). Because the underlying problem solution is more valuable than its coded expression, this is a limited protection. Patents, which are more difficult to secure, protect novel and nonobvious discoveries that fall in the United States within the subject matter of the U.S. Patent Act. Many patent applications for software failed to prove that they qualify under this "subject-matter" criterion. However, a U.S. Federal Appeals court has affirmed in 1994 the patentability of sufficiently innovative software. Because of the limitations of copyrights and patents with respect to intangible products, software developers most often rely on trade-secret protection. Trade-secret law protects the confidentiality of IP through licenses or nondisclosure agreements.

An elaborate software system is expensive to create. The same software, or another digital product, can be copied at a negligible cost. Such is the nature of IP, which includes software, books, video, and music. Piracy in the form of selling illegally reproduced software has become a serious problem in international trade. In a number of countries, far more than the three quarters of the sales of U.S. software packages are illegal copies. Worldwide software piracy costs the U.S. software industry many billions of dollars annually. Because the legal system trails the pace of technology and because ethical guidance is sought in framing the legal issues, many controversies spill over into the ethical domain.

To "honor property rights" is one of the eight general moral imperatives of the ACM Code of Ethics.

The legal system and ethicists are grappling with many unresolved issues, such as

- To what extent can information and knowledge be considered property?[31]
- How to reconcile the public's right to access with the rights to IP and to privacy?
- What makes one digital product distinct from another?
- Would computer-generated works have a human author? If not, how would the property rights be protected?

In the case of property rights to electronic collections of data, such as directories, the U.S. courts have ruled that the copyright law protects only collections that display some creativity in the selection or arrangements of the data and does not protect such labor-intensive but nonoriginal collections as telephone white pages. Yet, the distinctions are often too fine to make a difference.

The industrial ecosystems producing digital goods, such as the music industry, have been transformed by the arrival of the web as a mass medium. Owing to the compression of the content and to the broadband telecommunications technologies, high-quality music and video can be streamed or downloaded. Music and video producers and sellers can be bypassed by consumers communicating in peer-to-peer mode and propagating copies of digital products. The technological domain offers, if only temporarily, a variety of methods of protecting this property, such as digital watermarks, as well as a broad encryption-based technology of digital rights management (DRM). The Digital Millennium Copyright Act, promulgated in 1998 to protect digital property, has made it illegal to circumvent a technological measure that controls access to a protected digital property. Taken together with the DRM technologies, the act goes beyond the preexisting copyright law and is likely to be challenged— justifiably, in much credible opinion.[32] As we may conclude, many legal issues regarding IP remain unresolved. This is why it is particularly important to approach this property from an ethical standpoint to ensure that our decisions do not violate property rights of others.

ACCESS

It is a hallmark of an information society that access to information and knowledge is mediated by IT, notably the Internet–web, most of the workforce is employed in the processing of information and transformation of knowledge, and most of the goods and services available for consumption are information-related. To gain full access to the benefits of such a society, an individual must possess at least four things: 1) the intellective skills to deal with information; 2) access to IT, including the Internet–

web; 3) access to information; and 4) access to a free expression over the digital media. If we consider these issues on national and global scales, we see that inequalities persist. Because each of us in a human society draws an economic benefit from the equality of opportunity and because each of us is ethically concerned about fairness, the issue of capable access to information and IT redefines our concern for literacy.

IT does not have to be a barrier to opportunities. Quite the contrary, when deployed purposefully, it can *provide* opportunities not previously accessible. Internet access can bring the contents of the world's libraries, participation in the world's markets, and the advice of the world's experts to a remote location. Intensive work is being done on developing assistive technologies that enhance access of the handicapped to the IT, and, thus, in many cases, to the social and economic mainstream. Assistive technologies for the blind include screen displays that work in an auditory mode through screen-reading software and speech synthesizers, and screens that work in a tactile mode with the use of a Braille display. Access to trustworthy electronic virtual communities, designed with ethical principles in mind, is a great source of support to people bearing afflictions.[33]

Indeed, with the phenomenal growth of shared computational resources, PCs, smart mobile devices, and of the Internet–web services, the accessibility of IT has grown vastly. But it has not grown equally. Access to the Internet is necessary to participate in the benefits of an information society and economy. Yet, several regions of the world, notably many of the countries of sub-Saharan Africa, remain with limited access. Significant digital divide persists between the developed and poor countries both in the information technologies and complementary assets, such as qualified professionals. Various digital divides also exist in developed countries. Action to eradicate these divides and expand the domain of inclusion in the Internet benefits is an important ethical concern.

Another ethical concern is the expansion of access to the content available online. The claims of IP have to be balanced by the needs of expanding the commonwealth of accessible knowledge and information.[34] The One Laptop per Child global initiative brings low-cost laptop computers, connected to the web, within the reach of children in poor countries. The Digital Commons initiative provides open access to the knowledge contributed by scholarly journals, as well as to the books not protected by copyright. The movement toward open source and free software makes both the digital products and the tools for their further development accessible to all. A broad understanding of access is gaining worldwide support.

Numerous countries limit their citizens' access to free expression over the web, erecting digital firewalls to filter and limit the content. Considering the power of the smartphone-armed citizens to organize disrupt dictatorial regimes, this is not surprising. The conscience of the IT professionals—and their ethics codes—will guide them on how to render their service.

MAKING ETHICAL DECISIONS

Let us consider how to make decisions applying ethical principles in the information-related domains—and then apply them to the scenarios presented earlier. The following decision-making sequence can be adopted:

- Examine the issues to see whether they fall in the ethical domain. Seek appropriate professional guidance if the issues seem to be in the legal domain. Apply the "sunshine test" to see whether the issue is ethical or discretionary: Would your decision withstand public disclosure?
- If you believe that ethical issues are involved, would a course of action you are considering violate individual rights? Would the action violate a professional code of ethics?
- Choose the course of action that would not result in an ethical breach.

Let us now view, in this light, our three scenarios presented earlier.

Transactional Information on Smart Cards

The ethical issue of privacy is involved. The legality of the action can be challenged. However, it is obvious that the developers and the users of the system invaded privacy of the debit-card holders with the system that gathered and released data about them without their knowledge. People may consent to their personal data being stored for a specific purpose; however, no such consent was sought. The individuals were also deprived of their right to inspect and, if appropriate, correct their personal data. Furthermore, the financial institution's prospective plans imply an even broader breach of privacy by indiscriminate, uncontrolled release of transactional information to third parties and should not be pursued. A breach of ethics may have financial consequences to all parties. A possible consumer outcry may render the system useless. Such an argument may indeed carry the day, if you need to defend your recommendation to not go ahead with developing a similar system.

Who Owns E-Mail?

Certainly, the management decision to allow employees the use of the company-owned computers and systems for private purposes violates no ethical principles. We could judge this to be a discretionary action and not an ethics issue. An employee stands in a different relationship to a workplace than a consumer does to a marketplace. But the monitoring action was taken without employees' knowledge and clearly it is a violation of their right to privacy and, thus, highly unethical if there was a justified

presumption of privacy. However, employers have a right to set policy—and an obligation to make the employees aware of their terms of employment. Should you, as an employer, wish to pursue this course of action, such acceptable use policy has to be drawn up. Perhaps the employees should be able to label certain communications as private, with the employer undertaking an obligation to respect their rights. The least invasive forms of computer-based work monitoring should be adopted. Thus, monitoring of performance, rather than of behaviors or personal characteristics, is preferred.

Let's Just Release This System

The vice president not only made a poor business decision (that would place the issue in the discretionary domain). By knowingly forcing the development of a defective system, he violated his duty to do what is right. What about the action of the project leader? The ACM Code obligates a professional to "give comprehensive and thorough evaluations of computer systems and their impacts, including analysis of possible risks."[2] The project leader failed to do so in this case by agreeing to implement a defective system and by failing to call her superior's action to the attention of higher authorities.

These three scenarios show that ethical decision-making protects not only professional integrity and upholds the social contract. The expediency of "cutting ethical corners" often produces adverse business results.

CONCLUSION

Information technologies have the power to affect significantly the quality of our personal and working lives. Therefore, all knowledge workers and system users, and particularly computing professionals, face IT-related problems whose solution involves ethical considerations. Purely technological or legal means of protecting individual rights affected by information systems are insufficient in separation from the tenets of infoethics.

The four principal infoethical issues, privacy, accuracy, property, and access, are subjects of professional and organizational codes of ethics, which should be familiar to computer professionals. Our lives have been vastly enriched by the ability to form relationships and express ourselves on social media and social network sites, to form and nurture e-commerce enterprises, and to educate and entertain ourselves online. In the workplace, the use of IT may have positive or negative impacts on the worker, depending on the way the technology is deployed. Potential positive impacts include the increased ability to develop and exercise individual skills, and integration of work into meaningful tasks that can be performed with a large degree of autonomy. Potential negative impacts include reducing skills, routinization of work, and excessive monitoring of workers. Computer-based performance monitoring should be made the least invasive and should be organized in accordance with ethical principles. Infoethical principles should be inculcated in the workplace as a component of the corporate culture. Ethical practices can and should be incorporated in the software engineering and other computer science curricula.[35] On the deeper level, our moral lives require reexamination in the face of the new technologies that confront our ethical principles.[36]

An information society both drives and is driven by incessant innovation. Emerging technologies present threats to the ethical uses of information systems, as well as the means to deal with these threats.[37] Beyond that, they offer the promise of a better life in an increasingly more inclusive global society. The proper deployment of emerging technologies has to be informed by the decision-making processes keeping in view the ethical issues raised by information systems.

REFERENCES

1. Zwass, V. Foundations of Information Systems; Irwin/McGraw-Hill: Boston, MA, 1998; 612–616.
2. ACM Code of Ethics and Professional Conduct, http://www.acm.org/about/code-of-ethics (accessed Feb 28, 2008).
3. Pierce, M.A.; Henry, J.W. Computer ethics: The role of personal, informal, and formal codes. J. Bus. Ethics 1996, 15, 425–437.
4. Kreie, J.; Cronan, T.P. Making ethical decisions. Commun. ACM 2000, 43 (12), 66–71.
5. Mingers, J.; Walsham, G. Toward ethical information systems: The contribution of discourse ethics. MIS Q 2010, 34 (4), 833–854.
6. Appiah, K.A. Experiments in Ethics; Harvard University Press: Cambridge, MA, 2008.
7. Thong, J.Y.L.; Yap, C.-S. Testing an ethical decision-making theory: The case of soft-lifting. J. Manage. Inform. Syst. 1998, 15 (1), 213–237.
8. Parker, D.B.; Swope, S.; Baker, B.N. Ethical Conflicts in Information and Computer Science, Technology and Business; QED Information Sciences: Wellesley, MA, 1990.
9. Mason, R.O. Four ethical issues of the information age. MIS Q 1986, 10 (1), 5–12.
10. Consumer Data Privacy in a Networked World: A Framework for Protecting Privacy and Promoting Innovation in the Global Digital Economy, White House Report, Journal of Privacy and Confidentiality, 2012, 4 (2), 95–142.
11. Pollach, I. What's wrong with online privacy policies? Commun. ACM 2007, 50 (9), 103–108.
12. Etzioni, A. The Limits of Privacy; Basic Books: New York, 1999.
13. Zwass, V. Electronic commerce and organizational innovation: Aspects and opportunities. Int. J. Electron. Comm. 2003, 7 (3), 7–37.
14. Kourouthanassis, P.E.; Giaglis, G.M. Systems Pervasive Information, Advances in Management Information Systems; M.E. Sharpe: Armonk, NY, 2008, 10.
15. Garfinkel, S.; Rosenberg, B. RFID: Applications, Security, and Privacy; Addison-Wesley: Upper Saddle River, NJ, 2006.
16. Daries, J.P.; Privacy, anonymity and big data in social sciences. Commun. ACM 2014, 57 (9), 56–63.
17. Nikiforakis, N.; Acar, G. Browse at your own risk. IEEE Spectrum 2014, August, 30–35.
18. de Montjoye, Y.-A.; Unique in the crowd: The privacy bounds of human mobility, Scientific Reports 3, No. 1376. 2013, http://www.nature.com/srep/2013/130325/srep01376/full/srep01376.html (accessed June 1, 2017).
19. Tanner, A. What Stays in Vegas: The World of Personal Data—Lifeblood of Big Business—And the End of Privacy as We Know It; Public Affairs: New York, 2014.
20. Gaff, B.M.; Sussman, H.E.; Geetter, J. Privacy and big data. Computer 2014, 47 (6), 7–9.
21. Mayer-Schönberger, V.; Cukier, K. Big Data: A Revolution that Will Transform how We Live, Work, and Think; Houghton Mifflin Harcourt: Boston, MA, 2013.
22. Goodman, E. Design and ethics in the era of big data. Interactions, 2014, 21 (3), 22–24.
23. Zwass, V. Co-creation: Toward a taxonomy and an integrated research perspective. Int. J. Electron. Commun. 2010, 15 (1), 11–48.
24. Solove, D.J. The Future of Reputation: Gossip, Rumor, and Privacy on the Internet; Yale University Press: New Haven, CT, 2007.
25. Nissenbaum, H. Privacy in Context: Technology, Policy, and the Integrity of Social Life; Stanford University Press: Stanford, CA, 2010.
26. Gurses, S. Can you engineer privacy? Commun. ACM 2014, 57 (8), 20–23.
27. Neumann, P.G. Computer-Related Risks; ACM Press/Addison-Wesley: New York/Reading, MA, 1995.
28. Friedman, B.; Nissenbaum, H. Bias in computer systems. ACM Trans. Inf. Syst. 1996, 14 (3), 330–347.
29. Tuttle, B.; Harrell, A.; Harrison, P. Moral hazard, ethical considerations, and the decision to implement an information system. J. Manage. Inform. Syst. 1997, 13 (4), 7–28.
30. Bishop, M.; Wagner, D. Risks of e-voting. Commun. ACM 2007, 50 (11), 120.
31. Branscomb, A.W. Who Owns Information? From Privacy to Public Access; Basic Books: New York, 1994.
32. Lessig, L. Code and Other Laws of Cyberspace; Basic Books: New York, 1999.
33. Leimeister, J.M.; Ebner, W.; Krcmar, H. Design, implementation, and evaluation of trust-supporting components in virtual communities for patients. J. Manage. Inform. Syst. 2005, 21 (4), 101–135.
34. McFarland, M.C. Intellectual property, information, and the common good. In Readings in Cyberethics, 2nd Ed.; Spinello, R.A.; Tavani, H.T., Eds.; Jones and Bartlett: Sudbury, MA, 2004; 294–304.
35. Huff, C.; Furchert, A. Toward a pedagogy of ethical practice. Commun. ACM 2014, 57 (7), 25–27.
36. Cavalier, R.J. The Impact of the Internet on Our Moral Lives; State University of New York Press: Albany, NY, 2005.
37. Rundle, M.; Conley, C. Ethical Implications of Emerging Technologies: A Survey; UNESCO: Paris, France, 2007, http://unesdoc.unesco.org/images/0014/001499/149992E.pdf (accessed Mar 22, 2008).

Ethiopia: Libraries, Archives, and Museums

Shiferaw Assefa
University of Kansas, Lawrence, Kansas, U.S.A.

Abstract

This entry explores the historical development of the national, public, academic school and special libraries, museums and galleries in Ethiopia. The country's effort to collect and preserve its documentary heritage started during the Aksumite period (fourth to eighth century A.D) and continued informally until the National Library was established in 1944. Since then, public and other types of libraries have been established and modestly expanded in the country. In addition, the collection and preservation of cultural objects and the development of museums and galleries goes back to the same Aksumite period when churches and monasteries served as custodians and preservers of these objects. The growth of museums and galleries can initially be attributed to the interest demonstrated for Ethiopian cultural and historical objects by foreigners who came to Ethiopia and to the archaeological discoveries carried out by different expeditions during the time of Menelik II (1889–1913) and thereafter. Since then, there has been a fairly slow growth of museums and galleries in the country as a result of an acute shortage of financial resources and trained manpower.

HISTORICAL INTRODUCTION

Ethiopia is located in the horn of East Africa. It lies between latitudes 3°15′ and 18° north of the equator and between 33° and 48° to the east of the Meridian. It is bordered by the Sudan on the west, Somalia and Djibouti on the east, Eritrea on the north, and Kenya on the south. The country has been called a cultural mosaic, due to its 80 different languages and dialects and as many, if not more, cultural varieties. The languages found in the country belong to the two major phyla found in Africa: Afro-Asiatic and Nilo-Saharan. The Afro-Asiatic phylum includes the majority of the languages of Ethiopia: the Ethio-Semitic languages of which Amharic and Tigrinya are the best known and the largest members, Cushitic, of which the major languages are Oromo and Somali, and Omotic languages that are entirely spoken in Ethiopia of which Wolaytta is the largest one.[1] The Nilo-Saharan languages found in the country include Berta, Suri, Me'en, Murle, Kwegu, Majang, and others.

Ethiopia is one of the oldest nations in the world, with great antiquities, cultures, and traditions stretching back 3000 years. It is one of the world's great crossroads, where the peoples and cultures of Africa, the Middle East, and the Mediterranean have interacted for thousands of years. The history of Ethiopia as an organized polity began around 100 B.C. in the northern region of the country. One of the most powerful early kingdoms of Ethiopia was the kingdom of Aksum, which had a complex society. During Aksum's prosperous centuries, it enjoyed contacts with the Mediterranean world, the Nile Valley, and the Indian Ocean as far as China.[2] Archaeological findings attest to the prosperity of Aksum by the third and fourth century C.E.

The Aksumite kingdom had its own urban centers, coinage in gold, silver, and bronze, buildings, exceptional monuments, and extensive trade contacts within Africa and beyond. Trade most likely was the main source of the kingdom's revenue and wealth. Its exports included ivory, rhinoceros horn, live animals, aromatic spices, and frankincense. Aksum started to decline during the seventh century C.E. as a result of: (1) the rise of Islam in the Arabian Peninsula, which limited its access to the sea; (2) geographical degradations in the capital and surrounding areas; and (3) internal political troubles.[3] This forced the power and the capital to move to the south and a new dynasty known as the Zagwe Dynasty (Cushitic speaking) came to power around 1137 C.E. It ruled the country until 1270. As devout Christians, the rulers of the Zagwe Dynasty constructed churches and monasteries including the rock-hewn churches of Lalibela. The southward expansion continued for several centuries. In 1270 C.E., power was transferred from the Cushitic speaking people to the Amhara, another Semitic speaking group. The Amhara stayed in power until the Imperial government of Haile Selassie was overthrown by the military in 1974. The current government came to power after it had defeated the military government of Mengistu Hailemariam in 1991. Throughout the history of the country, contacts between the Semitic, Cushitic, and other ethnic groups found in the country continued as the capital moved further south and the kingdom expanded and created a unique cultural diversity. This resulting ethnic and cultural diversity has given rise to many unique and dynamic visual traditions. Ethiopia has also had its own language and its own script for more than 2000 years. Inscriptions on stones that were crafted in the first century C.E. testify to the antiquity of writing.

Encyclopedia of Library and Information Sciences, Fourth Edition DOI: 10.1081/E-ELIS4-120043539

In addition, for more than 1500 years quite a number of manuscripts (the very earliest ones on vellum) were produced.

Ethiopia accepted Christianity in the fourth century C.E. As a result, many churches were built and a significant number of religious texts were translated into Geez, the liturgical language. Eminent church scholars attracted disciples, and centers of learning developed where calligraphy, manuscript illumination, music, and poetry were taught. Each church and monastery retained a collection of religious literature used for services, teaching, and scholarship.[4] Hence, the churches, monasteries, and a few respected elderly church dignitaries served as the custodians of the manuscripts and literary works of the country. This trend continued until 1863 when Emperor Thewodros II (1855–1868) put together the largest and the finest collection of Ethiopian manuscripts that well exceeded 981[4] from the donation of a church at his mountain fortress of Magdalla. The manuscripts were collected from churches, monasteries, and individuals. They were, however, seized by the British when Thewodros was defeated in 1868. The Napier expedition that defeated the king destroyed many manuscripts and looted several others. Some of these manuscripts were returned to Ethiopian Churches while others were kept by the British officers and soldiers. Some 350 came into the possession of the British Museum.

Although the printing of Ethiopic texts in Europe dates back to the late fifteenth century in Mainz, Germany (in the woodcut specimen by Erhard Reuwich),[5] print technology was not introduced in Ethiopia until the reign of Thewodros. The first printing machine was established at Macaw on the Red Sea coast in 1863.[4,6,7] When we look closely at the establishment of printing machines in Ethiopia, we find that all of them were primarily introduced to produce religious materials for the consumption of the local people. However, in the beginning of the twentieth century, increased contacts with the outside world made secular education necessary. The country started to build elementary schools. With the increasing number of schools, the need for textbooks also grew. This in turn encouraged the government to establish its own printing press in 1921 in Addis Ababa (the capital city of Ethiopia) which was called Berhanena Selam in 1923.[7] Although Ethiopia has a long history of language, script, and manuscripts, the history of printing and publishing is very short. The real development of printing started in the twentieth century, and proceeded very slowly. More and more printed materials began to emerge in the early 1930s to serve the erudite Ethiopians and foreigners that resided in the country. This advanced the idea of organizing a central reading room, collecting and making accessible all materials which existed in print.

In 1936, the then emperor Haile Selassie I, commenced a small library with books he collected in different European languages which either he bought or was presented with.[8] However, these were only accessible to people in his closest circle.

In another development, Italians who occupied the country during World War II from 1936 to 1941 organized a Central Government Library in Addis Ababa for Italian East Africa, which also included Ethiopia, Eritrea, and Italian Somaliland with a branch in Asmara, the current capital of Eritrea.

LIBRARIES

The National Library and the Development of Public Libraries

The national library

Research shows that efforts to collect and keep in one center the country's documentary heritage dates back to the Aksumite era (the kingdom that flourished between the fourth and eighth centuries A.D.), and churches and monasteries were used to produce manuscripts and to serve as the first "traditional" libraries or storage houses as indicated earlier. However, the intent to organize a National Library commenced only during the time of Emperor Menelik II (1844–1913).[8] His effort to establish a National Library did not come to fruition for reasons not known. After quite some time had elapsed, "Yehizb Meshaf Bet," and now the National Archives and Library of Ethiopia (NALE) [formerly known as National Library of Ethiopia (NLE)], was established on May 5, 1944. Its foundation signifies the beginning of the modern library in Ethiopia. In his speech to announce the establishment of the National Library, Haile Selassie emphasized that he laid the foundation of the National Library for the liberation of the minds of his people.[9]

Serke Berhan Gebreegzy was appointed as the first director of the organization. The initial collection of the library came largely from the East African Italian Government Library. At its inception, the National Library was under the auspices of the Antiquities Administration and had two divisions: the public library and the research library. The public library division was the most important resource for the city of Addis Ababa. One of the functions the National Library was to serve as a Central Lending Public Library. It also had a children's collection housed in a separate building. Finally, in the 7 years preceding the revolution (1967), the public library division embarked upon opening one library per year in a provincial town in order to organize a public library system.[9] The research library division contained materials and books that were transferred from the colonial collection, United Nations documents received on deposit, a number of manuscripts, an Ethiopian Studies collection, and books published in Ethiopia acquired from publishers on the basis of a letter from the Ministry of the Pen requesting the five printing houses to deposit to the library three copies of every title printed (in 1951). Since this was not promulgated by a separate act of parliament, it could not be enforced. Thus, the lukewarm and spontaneous response from the publishers resulted in the acquisition of few publications.

In the early days of the Ethiopian revolution, the libraries were threatened to be purged in order to get rid of "reactionary" literature. However, to the credit of heads of the different libraries and other intellectuals, books and other materials were not destroyed. More importantly, in 1975 the National Library came under the Department of National Library and Archives of the Ministry of Culture and Sports with four divisions: the public library, the technical services, national library, and archives. The overall objectives of the department were to serve as the center of studies and bibliographic information, to play a central role in leading and coordinating libraries in the country, and to serve the nation as a whole.[10]

The most important development in the history of libraries in the country was the Legal Deposit Proclamation no. 50 of 1976, which required all printed matter to be deposited in three copies in the National Library.[10] This has allowed the library to increase the gathering of book and other published material tremendously. The current collection includes 58,854 books, 33,627 periodicals, 859 manuscript, 9239 microfilms, 2650 bound newspapers, and 4408 CDs, audios, and videos.[10]

Since the establishment of the National Library, three problems have hindered it from achieving its goals: shortage of financial resources, dearth of qualified professional librarians, and space to catalog and store the materials acquired. These problems and others, except the problem of space, still prevail.

The acquisition of library materials for the National Library significantly benefited from the project sponsored by the United States for the microfilming, cataloging, repair, and return of manuscripts in churches and monasteries in Ethiopia. This project was launched in 1971 and steadily continued the filming of manuscripts from church and monastic libraries, private libraries, souvenir shops, and bazaars. For a long time, the copies of the microfilms were housed in the Ministry of Culture which created the Microfilm and Microfiche section of the Department of Libraries and Archives. They were also accessible for viewing for the public.[11] In 1987, the NALE was newly reorganized to incorporate and assume the responsibilities of the former Ethiopian Microfilm and Microfiche Library in addition to its function as a Department of Library and Archives under the Ministry of Information and Culture.

Since the 1980s, the Legal Deposit and Bibliography section of the Department of Libraries and Archives has published a series of bibliography indexes in Amharic and English entitled "Ethiopian Publications." The indexes are similar to those that are produced by the university library as mentioned below. They list all materials published in the country and abroad about Ethiopia, collected annually by the Legal Deposit and Bibliography section.

The National Library has taken on broader duties and responsibilities imposed upon it despite the sector not having been given enough attention to play a proper role in the country's social and economic activities. Now the organization, by proclamation 191/1999, has been authorized to receive three copies of every item published in the country, including visual and audiovisual materials, as legal deposit. These then form the basis of the bibliographical indexes called "Ethiopian Publications." NALE also serves as a registry of ISBN and ISSN numbers in order to create a union catalog in the country. In addition to acquiring materials by being the legal depository of the country, NALE gathers documents through purchase and donations. Other numerous duties were also assigned to the organization, such as serving as an information center and being the treasury of Ethiopian literary heritage, which requires the collecting of oral traditions including poems, hymns, and proverbs.

Much has been done to tackle the problems of libraries and archives. Special attention has been given to the development of libraries. NALE was established to serve as an information center and has become accountable to the profession at the national level. Other duties of the NALE staff include the editing, publishing, and distribution of the National Bibliography and periodicals index publications.[10] NALE is also required to serve as a training center. Moreover, NALE is accorded the responsibility of acquiring and returning to the country the originals or the copies of the priceless literary heritage of the country that have been taken out of the country.

The formation and growth of this information center can play a vital role in the country's development. NALE, in cooperation with the World Bank, inaugurated its Development Information Service Center in 2004 with duties that include: providing Internet access to the library users; providing information on the activities and mission of the World Bank; and making available up-to-date information on HIV/AIDS prevention programs.

Some of the major problems that continue at the NALE are limited financial resources; shortage of trained professional librarians and archivists; scarcity of modern computers and other types of machinery that could be used by technical services and library patrons; and much needed space for more storage, work space, public use areas, and offices.[8] The idea to construct a new building and to move the collection into this building came up in the 1950s, but it did not materialize until 2006. With the help of various sponsors and nongovernmental organizations, a corner stone was laid in 2002. The construction work began toward the end of the year and was completed in August 2006.[13] This temporarily solved the space problem that National Museum had for a long time.

The development of public libraries

The number of public libraries found in Ethiopia has now reached 249 (IFLA 2007).[8] Interestingly enough, 100 of these libraries are located in Addis Ababa.[13] Their sizes and collection of items varies greatly. As indicated earlier, the major functions of the National Library are providing service to the public and the development and expansion of public libraries in the country. In this regard, the public library division continued to render service to the public and promoted the expansion of public libraries in the southern part of the country, whereas the new technical services division was assigned to acquire and catalog for the National Library and for the public library in Addis Ababa. The plan was to extend its cataloging expertise to other public library branches located outside the capital city. Currently, there seems to be a concentrated effort to expand public libraries in the regional and rural areas of the country. The users of the majority of the public libraries are high school and college students from the surrounding areas. The major problems that the public libraries face today are limited financial resources, lack of trained librarians, and a shortage of space.

Academic Libraries

The Addis Ababa University (AAU), the oldest institution of higher education in the country, was established in 1950. Its library system is the largest in Ethiopia. It was established in 1961 (Fig. 1). The library system has seven branches, including law, medical, engineering, science, agriculture, and public health. The library has a collection of over half a million items.[12,13] The main library and some of the branches serve patrons 24 hr a day.

The main library has computers for users to access the library's catalog and also houses about 12 computers usually reserved for graduate students. In addition, the current government has opened a number of public universities in the different regions of the country with various subject specialties.[14] Moreover, quite a number of private universities have also been created.

As far as the development and growth of academic libraries in Ethiopia are concerned, we need to touch upon the collection of AAU [first known as University College of Addis Ababa (UCAA)], which was then named in the 1960s as Haile Selassie I University and other regional universities found in the country. A unique competitive relationship exists between the University College of Addis Ababa Library and the National Library. The UCAA Library was established in the 1950s and it employed well-qualified librarians. Its collection exceeded that of the National Library in a short period of time as a result of the donations it received. Over time, the UCAA collection became more important for research purposes than that of the National Library. Interestingly, it was the UCAA library that held the first exhibition of books published in Amharic (the national language) and later

Fig. 1 F. Kennedy Memorial Library of Addis Ababa University.

made available its first bibliography in 1964.[13] The collection of the UCAA library steadily grew whereas that of the National Library grew more slowly.

Other universities outside the capital city that have libraries with significant collections are University of Gondar, Bahir Dar University, Haramaya University, and Jimma University.

The first university library to be discussed is the University of Gondar Library. The University of Gondar is located 738 km from the capital city. The City of Gondar was the capital city of Ethiopia from 1636 to 1868. The University was inaugurated in 2004. It is an expansion of the former Gondar College of Medical Sciences that was established in 1954. The college library was also founded in the same year in order to serve the health professionals trainees, the faculty, and the staff. This is one of the few libraries in the country with "open access" whereby students are allowed to browse the bookshelves by themselves. It also has an online catalog for its users to access the collection. The library houses a good collection of scientific, health, business, and computer science materials. In addition, its collection has strength in information technology, computing, nursing, engineering, and medicine. The total collection of the university exceeds 100,000 items, which includes books, serials, and other materials. The library also offers access to more than 10,000 electronic journals, electronic books, video programs, slide images, and track music.[15]

The second institution to be considered is the Bahir Dar University located some 575 km from the capital city— Addis Ababa. Bahir Dar University was established in 1993 by combining the old Polytechnic Institute, which was established in 1963 under the cooperation between the government of the Soviet Union and the Imperial government of Ethiopia, with the Bahir Dar Academy of Pedagogy, which was established in 1972 by a cooperative agreement and contribution made by the Ethiopian government and UNESCO/UNDP. Thus, the current library houses the collections of both institutions. The University Library system has five libraries: the main library, the Law Library, Freshman Library, the Engineering Library that is located in the Engineering Faculty campus, and the Textile Industry Institution Library. The collection of the libraries has about 86,000 printed books.[16]

The third institution to examine is Haramaya University and its libraries which is located 510 km east of the capital in the town of Haramya. Haramaya University was established in 1952, and was formerly known as the Imperial Ethiopian College of Agriculture and Mechanical Arts which then became Alemaya University of Agriculture (1985). It was founded by an agreement made by the then government of Ethiopia and the United States of America, and at the beginning, the Oklahoma State University was given the responsibility for finding staff from abroad and for running the academic research and extension programs. The college was also responsible for coordinating

the agricultural research and extension programs in the country. The library system of the university has four branches: the main library, the School of Graduate Studies Library, and the Female Students' Library are located in the main campus in the town of Haramaya, whereas the Health Sciences Library, which was opened in 2003, is situated in the city of Harar. The collection in the main campus consists of 140,350 items that cover a wide range of academic subjects currently offered by the university.[17]

The last university library to be considered is the Jimma University Library. Jimma University is located about 335 km southwest of the capital. It was established in 1999 by merging the former Jimma College of Agriculture, which was founded in 1952, and Jimma Institute of Health Sciences, which was founded in 1983.

The university library system was created in 1985 to promote the instructional, research, and public service goals of the university community through the acquisition of necessary materials. The University Library has seven branches, each specializing in a particular subject area: Health Science Library, Education Library, Technology Libraries, Social Science Library, Law Library, Graduate Studies Library, and College of Agriculture Library. The total collection is about 131,715 items which includes books, monographs, texts, journals, magazines, and databases. It also offers full text electronic databases and audiovisual materials.

School Libraries

In IFLA's 2007 World Report,[18] the government of Ethiopia did not provide the number of school libraries found in the country. During the time of Emperor Menelik II, the first high school Teferi Makonnen was opened in 1908 in Addis Ababa. In the 1960s and 1970s, the Ministry of Education made a concerted effort to improve library services in schools with the help of a UNESCO expert who came to study and make recommendations on the development of various kinds of libraries for Ethiopia.

Efforts were made to improve the library services in high schools in the 1960s and 1970s. The Ministry of Education started to train school librarians and to purchase books following the recommendations of the UNESCO expert Paton (1964).[18] However, school libraries still have a shortage of books and trained manpower.

Special Libraries

In Ethiopia, there were about 100 special libraries which are affiliated with the various ministries and governmental departments, research centers or institutes, and international organizations in the 1990s.[19] The majority of the special government libraries are located in the ministries and parastatal organizations and serve the various professionals working for them. Examples of these include the governmental libraries of the Ministry of Agriculture and Commission for Water in Addis Ababa, and parastatal libraries, such as those of the Ethiopian Institute of Agricultural Research (EIAR) and the Medical Research Library of Ethiopia.[19] Here below, we will discuss the EIAR Library and Documentation Center, the Ethiopian Orthodox Library–Museum, and the Ministry of Foreign Affairs Library.

The EIAR Library and Documentation Center is located in Addis Ababa. It was established in 1966.[19] The EIAR Library and Document Center's collection includes a variety of materials on agriculture. It has print, electronic resources, and CD-ROMs, such as books and journals for the staff of the research center, postgraduate students, and other research and development workers from other institutions.[20]

The Ethiopian Orthodox Library–Museum was inaugurated on July 13, 2004 in Addis Ababa. The objectives of the library–museum are to preserve books and other historical relics for the coming generation and to assist local and international scholars in carrying out research on the Ethiopian Orthodox Church.

The Ministry of Foreign Affairs has its own library located in the premises of the ministry. The collection of the library is mainly used by the staff members of the ministry. The library houses international documents on political, social, and economic conditions of the country and other countries around the world. The library receives free publications locally from different publishers as well as from international organizations abroad.

Among the major international special libraries found in Ethiopia, the UN Economic Commission for Africa's (ECA) library and the library for the International Livestock Research Institute (ILRI) will be considered.

The ECA library was opened in 1959 to cater to the administrative and information needs of the commission and its member states. The collection of the library includes African government documents, periodicals, pamphlets, maps, microfiches, CD-ROMs, videotapes, books on Africa, bibliographic databases, and online databases.

ILRI, a nonprofit organization, was established in 1994 by merging the former International Livestock Center for Africa founded in 1974 and International Laboratory for Animal Diseases created in 1973. The headquarters of the institute is in Nairobi, Kenya with a principal campus in Addis Ababa. The organization focuses on issues around livestock management in poor countries. The library (information center) in Addis was launched in the 1980s.[19] It has a diverse collection of books, journals, and CD-ROMs in print and online forms, as well as microfiche, videotapes, journals, theses, conference proceedings, maps, photographs, newspapers, and other forms of literature. The library also houses a unique microfiche collection of 30,000 unpublished documents from research centers in over 25 countries of sub-Saharan Africa.

Other special libraries that provide invaluable service to the community are the British Council, Alliance Française, and the German and Italian Cultural Institutes.

Library Education

As indicated earlier, one of the responsibilities of the National Library of Ethiopia has been to organize formal professional training to allow the trainees to acquire proper knowledge of the profession and its practices.[19] To this effect, the formal organized professional training in the library profession started in 1959[7] with a few short courses organized by the Ministry of Education in the evenings. The instructors came from the United States of America, the National Library itself, the United Nations Economic Commission for Africa Library, and the University College of Addis Ababa. To further strengthen the profession, the first Ethiopian graduate student was sponsored to obtain a higher degree in librarianship in the United States in the 1960s.

In 1966, the Haile Selassie I University introduced librarianship courses as a UNESCO teacher-training project.[21] The main objective of this project was to produce librarians who would be working in small school libraries.[8] In addition, the university began to offer 1-year full-time and 2-year part-time library science courses in order to produce mid-level librarians. More people were sent abroad for training in the library profession, and those started to return in the 1970s. Moreover, a new Bachelors degree program in Library Science was introduced in 1988. Finally, with the assistance of the International Development Research Center (IDRC) and UNESCO, a new program leading to a masters degree in information science began with the establishment of the School of Information Science (SISA) at AAU (formerly known as Haile Selassie I University) in 1989. Unfortunately, the training of librarians in undergraduate degree and diploma programs has ceased in the university since 1994 and some activities have been undertaken in private colleges to fill this gap. Thus, the dearth of mid-level library professionals still prevails in the country.

Professional Association

Another important item that needs to be addressed for the development of the library profession is the existence of some kind of association that can promote professional development and leadership in the field. The Ethiopian Library Association (ELA) was first established as a library club in 1961. It was then registered and achieved its official status in 1969. ELA was unable to play its role because of bad image of the profession, migration of professionals to the West, and dissatisfied professionals. Presently, ELA does not exist as a professional organization; however, there is a movement toward reestablishing the association.[22] Just a year ago a new library, archives and information systems association was formed which was sponsored by the British Council and is called Ethiopian Library, Information Science and Archives Professional Association.

THE NATIONAL ARCHIVES

The National Archives of Ethiopia was established in 1979 as a main division of the NALE. The main objectives of this section were to gather and store documents of historical importance. In 1999, by virtue of proclamation 179/1999, the National Archives was clearly separated from the National Library in spite of the fact that it is housed in the same building with the National Library and still shares the same Board of Directors. The new responsibilities it has assumed are wider in scope. Some of its responsibilities are cataloging all the newly gathered materials: collecting chronicles, letters, historical documents and photographs, articles and research papers, correspondence, publications, maps, and materials concerning law and the judiciary; preserving priceless archival materials exposed to dangers (such as publications at an organization that is defunct or closed); and preventing any archival materials from being taken out of the country.

Currently, the National Archives houses 3218 folders of archives, 537 Plans and Maps, 665 bound audit and financial matters archives, and 2487 photographs. In addition, under special custody, it has 422 files and 38 bound archives. When considering the sources of these archival materials, the first collection came from the Ministry of the Grand Palace, Palace of the Crown Prince, and others. The collection of the National Archive includes letters by Ethiopian Kings, such as Emperor Thewodros' letter (1855–1868) to Queen Victoria explaining misunderstandings between the two; Emperor Yohannes IV's letter (1872–1889) to Queen Victoria explaining the threat his country faced with Muslims; and Emperor Menelik II's (1889–1893) letter to Nicolas II of Russia about his victory against the invading Italians and his interest in fostering the relationship between their countries. Most of the archival items collected are in Amharic, Geez, French, Italian, English, and Arabic.

As mentioned earlier, the origins for the collection of the National Archives are a wide range of organizations and private collections housed in individual residences. The Archive Repository and Research section was required to sort out and move all the items that were stored in the Prime Minister's office. These documents cover the administrations of Emperor Menelik (1889–1913), Lij Iyassu (1913–1916), Empress Zewditu (1916–1930), Haile Selassie I (1930–1974), Mengistu Hailemariam (1974–1991), and the current Prime Minister, Melesse Zenawi.

In addition, in the 1980s and 1990s, the National Archives collected materials from private sources. For instance, in 1981 the National Archives acquired the personal archives of Dejazmach Zewde Gabre Sellassie, who served as departmental attaché in the Ministry of Foreign Affairs, mayor of Addis Ababa and who also held other positions in other ministries. Some of the valuable items that were transferred are maps and archives in Amharic, English, Italian, French, Geez, and Tigrigna. The collection consists of handwritten, typed, and published materials.[21]

The second individual collection that was transferred to the National Archives was that of Aleka Taye Gabre Mariyam. The National Archives acquired it in 1993. The significance of the transfer of this collection is that Aleka Taye was a famous intellectual who served as instructor of Amharic and Geez languages, visited many countries, and befriended royalties. Most of the materials in his collections were handwritten, including the Book of Philosophers, the History of the Wanderer, the History of the Royalties in Geez, and the Book of Religion.[23]

The third valuable archival material that was transferred was the collection of Dejazmach Kebede Tessema who served as a palace attendant, the first mayor of Addis Ababa, vice-member of the legislative body, and vice-president of the same legislative body. His collection includes research conducted to alleviate prostitution, and letters he exchanged with various patriots since 1940.[23]

Finally, the fourth significant collection that was transferred to the National Archives was the collection of Bilata Mersie Hazen Wolde Kirkos, who served as a teacher, school director, Secretary of the Commission formed to resolve the British–French border dispute in French-Somaliland, and High Court judge. His collection comprises a historical account of ministerial appointments in Ethiopia and a list of ministers appointed, an account of confrontation between Egypt and Ethiopia, and the history of the national flag.[23]

The National Archives issues guidebooks and calendars for its users. Guidebooks are items that provide information on the available archival materials that are owned by the National Archives whereas calendars list the archival materials compiled on the basis of the guidebooks.[23]

MUSEUMS AND GALLERIES

Museums and galleries are the two types of institutions that collect and preserve cultural objects of a society. In most cases, museums are cultural centers where public properties are housed whereas galleries are privately owned for the purpose of collecting and exhibiting art objects. In addition, the main purpose of galleries seems to be promoting emerging artists and selling their works to art collectors and museums (in its current use of the term in Ethiopia).

The emergence of museums and galleries in Ethiopia goes back to the introduction of Christianity to the country in fourth century A.D. Since that time, religious centers, such as churches and monasteries, became custodians and preservers of ethnographic and religious objects. The emergence and growth of museums in Ethiopia can be divided into three periods: 1) from the formative period until the occupation of the country by Italians (1936–1941); 2) from the liberation to 1974 when the revolution started; and 3) the expansion of museums since 1974.

Museums

The shaping of museums before the Italian occupation

As mentioned earlier, the collection and preservation of cultural items in Ethiopia seems to begin after Christianity was introduced in the fourth century A.D. Some of the items that were gathered by the religious institutions include clothes, books, parchments, paintings, and crosses (either religious or secular in type). Kings and members of the ruling class also kept items of historical importance in their own private collections. The major problem with church or private collections was access to them by the general public. However, the endeavor to systematically collect objects of historical importance started during the reign of Menelik II immediately after the Battle of Adwa (1896). One of the reasons for the development of museums and galleries was the interest exhibited by foreigners, who came especially to Addis Ababa, for art works. According to Professor Richard Pankhurst,[4] the only person who opened a gallery and sold art objects was a certain Greek named Giyorgis, who fought against Italians alongside with Menelik II in the Battle of Adwa. In addition, this demand by travelers for art objects created cultural awareness among the local people at the same time.

The emergence of museums in Ethiopia was further advanced by the archaeological discoveries carried out by Europeans. The first one was a German Expedition that came to the north city of Aksum in 1906. Moreover, in the 1920s and 1930s, a group of artists who were educated in painting in France returned to the country. This created a demand for their products. The efforts of systematically collecting and preserving cultural and historical objects continued to grow under Haile Selassie I, who signed a cultural and scientific agreement with the French government. More importantly, the temporary occupation of Ethiopia during World War II had fundamentally changed the demand for and supply of touristic objects and this development was also seen as a new dimension of economic benefits among artists.

Development of museums from 1941 to 1971

The second major stage in the growth of museums and galleries was the time period between 1941 and 1974. The first significant step that was taken by Haile Selassie I was the organizing of a museum-like section that was attached to the National Library in 1944. In this section, precious objects of high value representing the ruling class members were stored, including cloaks, ceremonial clothes, and household objects. This led to the establishment of what is now called the National Museum of Ethiopia (Fig. 2; it seems nobody knows when this name was actually given to the museum-like building).

The second significant stage in the development of museums and galleries in Ethiopia during this period arose when the University College of Addis Ababa (UACC) was opened in 1950. Soon after its opening, the UACC began to sign cultural agreements with foreign governments. For instance, in 1952, UACC signed a cultural agreement with the French government that allowed the French archaeological mission into the country in 1954. The mission performed its archaeological excavations in the northern part of the country (Tigray and Eretria).

The 1906 German and 1950s French archaeological missions were rewarded with rich archaeological findings that included potteries, stone tools, and inscriptions.[4] Quite a number of their findings are now exhibited and preserved in the National Museum and Aksum Archaeological Museum, whereas some are stored in a facility near the Archaeological Museum in the city of Aksum.

Another important event in the development of museums and galleries in the 1950s was the celebration of the Silver Jubilee of the imperial period of Emperor Haile Selassie I. He invited foreign heads of states and other dignitaries to witness this celebration. For this event, he wanted an exhibition on the rich heritage of Ethiopia. UACC was given the responsibility to organize such an exhibition.[24] The Chief Librarian at UACC at that time, Professor Chojnacki, commenced to direct the collection of cultural objects from the different ethnic groups of the country through students (the students did some of the collecting). The efforts of gathering cultural objects from the various ethnic groups were also aided by the Ethnological Society (a professional association of scholars) that was established in 1951.[25] This in turn led to the creation of the Institute of Ethiopian Studies Museum in 1963 in Addis Ababa (Fig. 3).

Finally, there were two other national and international events that played important roles in the development of museums in Ethiopia. The national event was the small exhibition of 1958 that displayed the cultural items that were discovered by the German and French archaeological excavations conducted in the northern part of the country. The emperor himself visited the exhibition. This particular event at the same time increased the awareness of the public and led to having a permanent exhibition open to the general public. The international event that indirectly had an important role in the development of museums was that Ethiopia increasingly became a center for African and

Fig. 2 National museum of Ethiopia.

international affairs. The Organization of African Unity (OAU) was established on May 25, 1963. The Emperor wanted an exhibition to be organized at the university for this historic moment, and the responsibility was assigned to the then University Librarian Professor Chojancki. This resulted in the founding of the Institute of Ethiopian Studies and its museum as well. The items displayed in this museum include

Fig. 3 The institute of Ethiopian studies.

icons, triptychs, diptyches, religious and folk paintings, processional crosses, hand crosses, neck crosses, miscellaneous church objects as far as religion and art were concerned while its objects of material culture include agricultural implements, basketry, gourds, horn and ivory ware, leather objects, jewelry, metal objects, musical instruments, national costumes, outdoor life objects, pottery, weapons, other objects not classified.[25,26]

An important fact to mention is that the archaeological artifacts collected by the expeditions accumulated over time. Thus, citizens of Ethiopia wanted to know the past and there was a need to open a museum where the items could be displayed for the general public to view. This is the third stage in the development of museums in Ethiopia in the mid-1960s when the Ministry of Finance transferred the former office of the Ministry of Foreign Affairs to the National Museum on a temporary basis. Even at this time, there still is no law that formally establishes a national museum in the country. In 1966, the imperial government passed a proclamation that established the Office of Archaeology and Antiquities Administration as a result of the increasing archaeological findings that require proper preservation and handling for future researchers.

Finally, in 1968, there was a new milestone in the development of museums in the country. The Society of Friends of the Institute of Ethiopian Studies Museum (SOFIES) was founded as an organization that assumed the responsibility for collecting Ethiopian cultural objects within or outside the country, by organizing fund-raising activities in order to buy them back.

In summary, the development of museums in Ethiopia during the imperial time was modest. There were no plans or visions how to establish and run them. We can say they are mainly the products of the tremendous amount of artifacts uncovered by the archaeological missions conducted by foreigners and the interest showed by SOFIES.

Development of museums since 1974

In 1974, the military junta known as the Dergue overthrew the regime of Emperor Haile Sellassie I and assumed power until 1991. It was during this period that many ethnographic museums began to emerge in the different parts of the country. However, the development and the growth of the galleries took a different path as they were privately owned.

Some of the ethnographic museums that were established during this period include the Wollega Museum, the Harar Museum, the Dessie Museum, the Mekele Museum, and the Jimma Museum even though it was created earlier in 1973. The majority of these museums were founded with cultural objects collected by the different communities in their respective regions. In addition, in the capital city, Addis Ababa, another historical and ethnographic museum was founded in 1984.

We attempt to provide a brief description of these ethnographic museums here below.

The Addis Ababa Museum was first established in 1984 in dedication to the Founding Congress of the Workers Party of Ethiopia (WPE) on the tenth anniversary of the Ethiopian Revolution. Then, it became the city museum in 1986 during the centenary anniversary of its founding. The museum's exhibition consists of items that reflect the culture, social affairs, health, education, and housing and urban development of the city. In addition, the armed forces exhibition displays the Ethiopian national struggle against foreign invaders and aggressors and the growth of Ethiopia's modern armed forces.

The Jimma Museum is located about 340 km southwest of the capital city. It was in 1973 when the then Emperor Haile Sellassie I visited the city of Jimma that the collection of the cultural objects began. In 1989/90, the local office of the Ministry of Culture acquired these collections and started to run it as a museum. The museum currently displays royal objects from the local king Jimma Aba Jifar (1878–1932), cultural objects from the various areas in the region, Koran Holy Books on parchment, Christian Holy Books also on parchment, and paintings.[4]

The Wollega Museum was created in 1987 and is located 334 km west of Addis Ababa. The items collected for this museum predominantly represent the Oromo culture and the early rulers of the kingdom. The museum building is one of the two buildings in the country that show the architectural design of a museum. The objects in this museum include royal objects of the rulers of the kingdom, traditionally curved wooden chairs, photographs, and paleoanthropological and geological items.[27]

The Dessie Museum is located in the city of Dessie which is 400 km from the capital city. It was established in 1981. This museum displays fossils, bones, ancient manuscripts, weapons captured from the Italians during the battle of Adwa, pottery, handicrafts, ethnic costumes from the area around, a book written in Arabic about the introduction of Christianity, wooden products, musical instruments, leg bracelets, necklaces and neck crosses, baskets, and artifacts from King Mikael, Menelik II, and Haile Sellassie I.[27]

The Mekelle Museum (Yohannes VI) is another ethnographic museum located north of the capital. It was established in the compound of the palace of Emperor Yohannes IV (1872–1889). The items on display include clothing of dignitaries, family pictures of the Emperor, his bed, a jar, containers made of goat skin, ceramics, books, neck crosses, bracelets, a gold-plated knife, and a statue of Mussolini in front of the museum.

Finally, the Harar National Museum and Community Museum, created in 1981, are located in the eastern old city of Harar. The Harari (an Ethio-Semitic ethnic group) Community Museum houses cultural objects that completely represent its own ethnic group whereas the items displayed in the Harar National Museum come from the various ethnic groups that are found in the region. The items exhibited in the two museums include pottery, gourd, and wood-cut products.[27]

In summary, during the time of the Dergue and thereafter, museums saw a modest growth in the country. However, this growth cannot be enough when considering the many ethnic groups that exist in the country.

An Overview of the Development of Galleries

The beginning of galleries in Ethiopia is associated with the two brothers Assefa and Serek Yimaneberhan. They were graduates of the Menelik II Secondary School which had a painting and art training section. They had informal training by their father who was a traditional painter. After they had completed their school, the two brothers opened an art gallery, or some prefer to call it an art studio at Arat Kilo (just on the opposite side of their school) in the 1950s. Their works were not sold to the general public but they were commissioned to paint by the various offices of the military and prominent individuals. This gallery closed because of financial difficulties the two brothers faced in the 1950s.[27]

In another development, foreigners who resided in the country had keen interest in art works in the country. Some of them had the opportunity to open their own art galleries. One such gallery (souvenir shop) worthy of mentioning was the one opened by Madam Riva of Italian origin in 1957/1958 in Addis Ababa (Piazza area). Her shop sold paintings and antiquities of Italian, Greek, Ethiopian, and other origins.[27]

The second foreigner to open another gallery in the country was an Armenian. It was opened in the early 1960s. It was called Belvedere Gallery and was organized in a better way than the earlier one. It is in this gallery that Ethiopian artists began to display their works to the general public for the first time. The gallery continued to play that role until the 1974.

The development of galleries in the early 1970s started to decline. This decline could be attributed to the political situation that prevailed in the country at that time. In 1974, the Emperor was overthrown by the military and soon after a Marxist style of government that discouraged private ownership of property was formed. Thus, the role of the galleries was taken over by big hotels and foreign cultural centers, such as the Alliance Française, the German Cultural Center, and others. Artists commenced to use these new venues to exhibit their works.

Currently, there seems to be a significant increase in the growth and development of galleries in the country. The regime that is in power has created a suitable atmosphere for private investment and ownership of private property. As a result of this, galleries have started to reemerge in the country. One of the galleries that operates at this time is St. George Interior Decoration and Art Gallery that was founded in 1991. The gallery displays traditional tables, chairs, headrests of kings, decorated cotton clothes, jewelries, and modern and traditional paintings. The gallery acquires its cultural objects from different parts of the country.[28]

In 1996, another gallery named Goshu Art Gallery was established in Addis Ababa. The owners of the gallery, who are artists themselves, opened it in order to promote artists and art in the country. The items exhibited in the galley include traditional and modern paintings, sculptures from West Africa, masks and decorated vases from Yemen, and household items with Ethiopian touches. In addition, the owners use this galley to exhibit their own art works.[27,29]

Another art gallery that was also created in 1996 was Asni Gallery. It is housed in a traditional villa in Addis Ababa whose architecture is very interesting by itself. This art gallery features modern art. The last gallery is the Universal Arts and Crafts that was opened in 2000 in Addis Ababa too.[27] The gallery displays household ornaments, African art, Imperial Furniture, oriental art, lampshades, and paintings.[27] These are some of the significant galleries that are found mainly in the capital city Addis Ababa.

The development of museums and galleries in Ethiopia shows the same kind of problems shared by the National Library and Archives. The first and the most important problem is a lack of financial support coupled with a shortage of professionally trained manpower. In addition, the museums lack space for the objects to be properly displayed to the people who come to visit them.

In conclusion, the development of the National Library, National Archives, and museums and galleries requires proper planning, financing, trained-manpower, and legislation in order for the country to successfully utilize its rich cultural heritage. There are some indications pointing to this direction, but it needs a real commitment from the government, the people, and other organizations that have a stake in it.

References

1. Appleyard, D.; Martin, O. The horn of Africa: Ethiopia, Eritrea, Djibouti, and Somalia. In *Language and National Identity in Africa*; Simpson, A., Ed.; Oxford University Press: London, U.K., 2008; 267–290.
2. Finneran, N. *Archaeology of Ethiopia*, Routledge: London, U.K., 2007.
3. Munro-Hay, S.C. *Aksum*, Edinburg University Press: Edinburg, T.X., 1991.
4. Pankhurst, R. The foundation of education, printing, newspapers, book production, libraries and literacy in Ethiopia. Ethiopia Observer, **1962**, *6*(3), 241–290.
5. Wijnman, H.F. *An Outline of the Development of Ethiopian Typography in Europe*, Brill: Leiden, the Netherlands, 1960.

6. Ourgay, M. Libraries in Ethiopia before 1900. Int. Libr. Rev. **1991**, *23*(3), 391–399.

7. Gupta, S. The development of education, printing and publishing in Ethiopia. Int. Info. Libr. Rev. **1993**, *26*(3), 169–180.

8. Hryćko, K. An outline of the National Archives and Library of Ethiopia. Aethiopica **2007**, *10*, 92–105.

9. Derbie, A. The National Library of Ethiopia: Problems and Prospects. Senior Essay **2002**.

10. Pankhurst, R. Libraries in post-revolutionary Ethiopia. Info. Manage. **1988**, *4*(4), 239–245.

11. http://www.nale.gov.et 2008.

12. Paiva, M. *Final Report ALA/USIA Library Fellow Report*, 1997.

13. Paiva, M. *A Quick Glimpse at Public and Academic Libraries in Addis Ababa*, Ethiopia, 2008; (http://www.against-the grain.com).

14. Mingestab, A. Ethiopia. World Encyclopedia Libr. Info. Serv. **1993**, 285–287. 3rd Ed.

15. http://www.ugondar,edu.et 2008.

16. http://www.telecom.net.et/~bdu 2008.

17. http://www.haramaya.edu.et 2008.

18. IFLA. Ethiopia. *World Report*, 2007.

19. Alemie, L. Special libraries and document centers in Ethiopia. Libr. Rev. **1993**, *42*(5), 15–23.

20. http://www.eiar.gov.et 2008.

21. Tsigemelak, D. Libraries and librarianship in Ethiopia: Status, prospects and challenges *Where Transition and Transformation Converge*, Paper Presented on the 97th Annual Conference of the Special Libraries Association Baltimore, MD June, 11–14, 2006.

22. Giorgis, K.W. Library education in Ethiopia. Int. Libr. Rev. **1973**, *5*(4), 453–461.

23. http://www.nale.gov.et 2008.

24. Pankhurst, R. Leadership in Ethiopia Past-War Library Development: The National Library vs. the University Library. Proceeding of the 5th International Conference of Ethiopian Studies, Chicago, April 13–16, 1978; 601–610. IL, Session B, 1979.

25. Chojnacki, S. Some notes on the occasion of the 25th Anniversary of the Institute of Ethiopian Studies Silver Jubilee Anniversary of the IES, Proceeding of the Symposium 1990; Addis Ababa University: Addis Ababa 27–38.

26. Kebede, G. A brief background to the IES Museum and major sections *Silver Jubilee Anniversary of IES*, Proceedings of the Symposium 1990; Addis Ababa University: Addis Ababa 61–73.

27. Burka, T. *Museums and Galleries in Ethiopia*, 2004; Unpublished M.A. thesis.

28. http://www.stgeorgeart.com 2008.

29. http://www.goshugalleries.com 2008.

Everyday Life Information Seeking

Reijo Savolainen
School of Information Sciences, University of Tampere, Tampere, Finland

Abstract

Information seeking may be analyzed in two major contexts: job-related and nonwork. The present entry concentrates on nonwork information seeking, more properly called everyday life information seeking (ELIS). Typically, ELIS studies discuss the ways in which people access and use various information sources to meet information needs in areas such as health, consumption, and leisure. The entry specifies the concept of ELIS and characterizes the major ELIS models. They include the Sense-Making approach (Dervin), the small world theory (Chatman), the ecological model of ELIS (Williamson), ELIS in the context of way of life (Savolainen), the model of information practices (McKenzie), and the concept of information grounds (Fisher). ELIS practices tend to draw on the habitual use of a limited number of sources, which have been found useful in previous use contexts. Since the late 1990s, the Internet has increasingly affected the ELIS practices by providing easily accessible sources. Even though the popularity of the networked sources has grown rapidly, they will complement, rather than replace, more traditional sources and channels.

INTRODUCTION

Information seeking is a major constituent of information behavior or information practices, that is, the entirety of ways in which people seek, use, and share information in different contexts.[1–3] Information seeking may be analyzed in two major contexts: job-related and nonwork. The present entry concentrates on nonwork information seeking, more properly called everyday life information seeking (ELIS). Typically, ELIS studies discuss the ways in which people use various information sources to meet information needs in areas such as health, consumption, and leisure.

Due to space restrictions, the present entry focuses on ELIS research conducted in the field of information studies or library and information science since the 1990s. First, for this reason, certain types of studies relevant to ELIS will not be discussed. These studies include marketing and consumer research, communication studies (e.g., audience research), and public library use studies. Second, specific questions of ELIS such as search strategies during interactions with Internet search engines will not be considered in the present entry. The entry is structured as follows. In the next section, the concept of ELIS will be clarified. Then, the ways in which various sources and channels are used in ELIS will be discussed, and the major conceptual models of ELIS will be characterized. The last section concludes the entry.

THE CONCEPT OF ELIS

Thus far, a rich variety of themes has been explored in ELIS studies. They have focused on people belonging to diverse groups such as the following:

- Young adults[4–6]
- Adolescents making career decisions[7]
- Elderly people[8,9]
- Abused or battered women[10,11]
- Women struggling with overweight[12]
- People diagnosed with cancer[13,14]
- Homeless parents[15]
- Unemployed people[16]
- Immigrants[17–19]
- Hobbyists of various kinds, for example, amateur genealogists, coin collectors, and cooks[20–23]
- Environmental activists[24,25]

As these examples suggest, the phenomena of ELIS can be approached from a number of viewpoints, for example, by concentrating on the demographic features of information seekers, or investigating information needs and seeking of young people. The issues of ELIS can also be explored by focusing on the problems faced by people, for example, losing one's job, or having a chronic disease such as diabetes. Finally, ELIS can be investigated in the context of leisure activities such as hobbies.

Particularly in the early years of ELIS research, concepts such as citizen information needs and seeking were utilized to denote information seeking taking place outside work tasks.[26] Even though the concept of citizen information needs and seeking is illuminating in itself, it is rather narrow because it primarily refers to people's rights and obligations toward social institutions as voters or participants in activities of civil society. Alternative concepts such as nonwork information seeking are problematic due to its residual nature and negative connotations: nonwork information seeking is implied to be less significant because it deals with

Encyclopedia of Library and Information Sciences, Fourth Edition DOI: 10.1081/E-ELIS4-120053403

something that is not associated with daily work.[27] The definition problem is further aggravated by the fact that issues of job-related and nonwork information seeking tend to overlap and they may be interwoven in everyday settings.[28] For example, seeking information about computer courses may serve both professional ends and hobbies.

Terminological problems originating from the false dichotomy of work-related and "nonwork" information seeking may be avoided by taking the concept of ELIS as starting point.[27] The key word is everyday life, which refers to a set of attributes characterizing relatively stable and recurrent qualities of both work and free time activities. The most central attributes of everyday life are familiar, ordinary, and routine, and they qualify the structural conditions of action (e.g., the recurrent "rhythms" of work and leisure hours). These characteristics of familiar, ordinary, and routine become real only in the process in which they are reproduced, day after day.

From this perspective, information seeking may occur in both work-related and leisure-related contexts of everyday life. Because the field of work-related information seeking is relatively well defined and the term work-related information seeking is self-explanatory, usually there is no need to use the more specific expression of "work-related information seeking in the context of everyday life." Thus, the concept of ELIS may be reserved to denote information acquisition taking place in less clearly specified contexts and activities such as hobbies and household care. These activities and contexts are seen as important in their own right; they are not only residuals of work-related phenomena. Hence, the positive term ELIS indicates that ELIS is not inferior to work-related information seeking.

Generally defined, the concept of ELIS refers to the acquisition of various informational (both cognitive and expressive) elements, which people employ to orient themselves in daily life or to solve problems not directly connected with the performance of professional tasks or full-time study.[27] Similar to work-related information seeking, ELIS may have two modes. On the one hand, ELIS may refer to seeking of problem-specific information (e.g., finding a fact). On the other hand, ELIS may manifest itself in the seeking of orienting information (i.e., monitoring of everyday events by using various sources and channels).

EVERYDAY INFORMATION NEEDS

A considerable number of ELIS studies focus on the ways in which information sources are used to meet various information needs. The specificity of research settings varies from general-level surveys of source usage to studies on ELIS focusing, for example, on health issues.[29–31] However, due to space restrictions, the present entry concentrates on general-level studies.

Strictly defined, the tradition of ELIS research dates back to the early 1970s, when extensive surveys were launched in the United States to investigate ordinary people's information needs and seeking. At that time, the first attempts were made to elaborate conceptual and methodological tools for ELIS studies. Marcia Bates[32] pioneered by introducing the concept of life information in 1974: By "life information" is meant information needed for successful living. The area of need ranges all the way from sheer survival (stay away from dogs that walk funny and foam at the mouth) to the most advanced forms of self-realization (where can I study ceramics or transcendental meditation?). Thus defined, the aforementioned concept includes "vast amounts of information about how to do many different things in one's culture that will be acceptable and lead to one's survival and emotional satisfaction."[32]

Somewhat later, Brenda Dervin, a communication scholar, created innovative approaches to enrich traditional ELIS survey research settings. Douglas Zweizig also contributed significantly to methodological issues, primarily in the field of public library use studies.[33,34] One of the pioneering surveys of ELIS was based on interviews with about 1000 people in Baltimore in 1972. The informants represented various demographic groups. This massive study revealed almost 9000 everyday life questions or problems reported by the interviewees. These problems were categorized into problem areas indicating daily information needs as follows:[35]

- Neighborhood
- Consumer habits
- Housing and household maintenance
- Crime and safety
- Education
- Employment
- Transportation
- Health
- Recreation
- Discrimination
- Financial matters
- Legal problems
- Public assistance

Later surveys have demonstrated that these need areas are largely also valid today. For example, a nationwide project on citizenship information conducted in Great Britain in 1997 revealed similar areas of everyday information needs.[36] Apparently, the major information need areas are relatively stable, and the variation between (Western) countries is rather insignificant.

THE USE OF INFORMATION SOURCES

ELIS studies have also identified the most popular information sources and channels used to meet people's information needs. Traditionally, human sources are preferred in ELIS. An extensive telephone survey conducted in

New England, the United States, in 1979 showed that three out of four respondents had drawn on their own experience in problem solving; in addition, friends, neighbors, and relatives appeared to be popular sources.[37] Later studies have demonstrated that people tend to favor familiar sources such as newspapers, television news, and health professionals because they have functioned well in earlier use contexts.[38] Overall, ELIS seems to be characterized by a conservative attitude: people tend to draw on familiar information sources that are often used almost routinely.[38]

Since the late 1990s, particularly e-mail and Word Wide Web (WWW) have been widely accepted as new tools for communication and information seeking. The surveys indicate that people use the networked services for various purposes (e.g., keeping in contact with others by e-mail, seeking health information from web pages, buying products and services, and participating in online discussions).[38–40] For example, a study conducted in Sweden demonstrated that in the early 2000s, the Internet had already gained a fairly significant place in the informants' communication and information-seeking practices, providing a wide variety of sources for different purposes of use.[41] The Internet was also found to be useful as a source of market information (e.g., flight schedules, car rentals, objects for sale, and job opportunities). The preference for the networked sources was also strengthened by the availability of search engines such as Google.

Along with the development of Web 2.0 technologies, the forums of social media have become increasingly popular in ELIS. These forums provide user-generated content (UGC) such as blog postings, answers available on social reference sites, and Wikipedia entries that can be used to support everyday problem solving and decision making. Empirical studies have demonstrated that blogs and online discussion forums can provide useful sources of information for people struggling with health problems, for example.[42,43] In addition, social media forums such as Question & Answering (QA) services, for example, Yahoo! Answers, and virtual communities such as *Tripadvisor* have gained popularity as sources of ELIS.[44,45] Even though UGC can provide rich sources of information since UGC originates from "real experiences by real people,"[46] the credibility of UGC may be an issue because it is often a mixture of fact and opinion, impression and sentiment, founded and unfounded tidbits, and experience.[46] Although the networked sources have gained popularity, the Internet has not been able to replace other media such as the telephone, television, radio, and newspaper with ELIS. On the contrary, the network sources and services complement them both in job-related and nonwork contexts.[47,48]

THEORIES AND MODELS OF ELIS

Compared to job-related information seeking, the number of theoretical frameworks and models of ELIS is still quite low. This is partly due to the relatively short tradition of this subfield and the smaller number of researchers who are active in ELIS issues.

The Sense-Making Methodology (Dervin)

Brenda Dervin can be counted among the most influential researchers of ELIS since the early 1970s. Her early studies focused on the communication practices of urban poor people.[49] In the early 1970s, Dervin began to develop the sense-making approach as a methodology focusing on human communication and the design of communication-based systems and activities. Since then, the theoretical and methodological bases of the sense-making approach, currently referred to as sense-making methodology (SMM),[50] have been transformed and refined. The SMM has been applied in numerous contexts to explore information needs and seeking of specific groups of people.[50–52] Dervin employs the metaphors of situation, gaps, and uses to depict information seeking and use them as a sense-making process. Metaphorically, the situation stands for the time–space context, where the individual becomes aware of the insufficiency of one's earlier definition of a situation. Gaps refer to questions or information needs elicited in situations of this kind. Uses stand for the ways in which information being sought or received from various sources helps to bridge the gap and to create a new sense. Examples of uses include getting ideas and understanding, being able to plan ahead, deciding what to do, and getting out of a bad situation.[51] More generally, information seeking and use may be approached by drawing on the metaphor of gap-bridging. However, this metaphor does not suggest a substantive conception of information seeking and use. The metaphor gives methodological and heuristic guidance to posit contextual questions as to how people interpret information in order to make sense of it. These questions focus on the ways in which cognitive, affective, and other elements useful for sense-making process are constructed and shaped in order to bridge the gap.[50–55]

Although the SMM draws heavily on metaphorical formulations, it has gained empirical support. It strengthens the hypothesis that information seeking is a constructive process based on the utilization of categories of situation, gaps, and uses. For example, a study focused on blood donors who were asked to describe the process of donating: What happened first in the donating situation? What are the questions they themselves posed? How did they hope the answers to their questions would help them?[56] Other sense-making studies have focused, for example, on the information needs and seeking of cancer patients.[57] The SMM has inspired, for example, Julien's investigation focusing on barriers to adolescents' information seeking for career decision making;[7] and the study of Pettigrew et al.[58] reviewing the ways in which people use public library-community network systems.

In sum, the SMM has contributed significantly to the conceptual and methodological development of ELIS research. By emphasizing the role of individuals trying to bridge gaps in everyday situations and the nature of information as a situation-bound human construct, sense making has advocated the user-based approach, as opposed to the traditional information system-centered viewpoint. Thus, Dervin has not only introduced a new viewpoint to ELIS studies but has also more broadly contributed to the theoretical and methodological breakthrough of the user-centered approach to information-seeking studies.[59]

ELIS in the Context of Small World (Chatman)

Elfreda Chatman is one of the most distinguished researchers in the field of ELIS studies. In the 1980s and 1990s, she conducted a highly original ethnographic research project focusing on information-seeking behavior of people living in the margins of society. The project was characterized by an attempt to develop a genuine social scientific theory, which describes ELIS in the context of "small world." This concept refers to social environments where individuals live and work, bound together by shared interests and expectations, and often economic status and geographic proximity as well.[60] In small-scale communities of these kinds, activities are routine and fairly predictable. Everyday information seeking and sharing are oriented by generally recognized norms and role expectations based on beliefs shared by members of the community.

Chatman explored ways in which poor people seek, use, and communicate information within the context of their everyday settings. In a study characterizing the information world of low-skilled workers, Chatman[61] examined the information needs and seeking behavior of female janitors at a university. It appeared that they had a narrow, concrete, and local view of the world restricted to the most familiar social milieu. Thus, information originating outside of this "small world" was not of great interest to them. The repertoire of information sources appeared to be narrow. Much daily information came from television. To some extent, information was also sought in newspapers. Most informants felt that personal experience was the most reliable source of information. They favored "first-level information" received through personal experiences or hearsay from someone who is accepted as having knowledge of the matters to be discussed. In contrast, the value of "second-level" information received from outsiders was suspected and often ignored because this type of information is not compatible with the common sense reality of the small world.

The specific features, characteristic of information seeking in the small world, were also studied among elderly women residing in a retirement complex.[62] Ethnographic analysis was conducted to ascertain their information and recreational needs and to explore the most popular information sources. The informants appeared to be active users of mass media. In contrast to the janitor study, the informants of this study favored quality TV programs, and they read books and magazines quite frequently but were not active users of public library.

Based on the aforementioned studies, Chatman[63] concluded that everyday information seeking of small world people is affected by four major factors forming the basis of the theory of information poverty: risk taking, secrecy, deception, and situational relevance. For example, the women of the retirement community avoided risk taking by not telling anyone about declining health concerns, thus giving up to seeking information or gaining emotional support.[63] The notion of secrecy is closely related to risk taking in that the elderly women concealed physical and mental ailments. Third, deception represents a deliberative attempt to act out a false social reality.[63] In this way, one engages in activities in which personal reality is consciously and forcefully distorted, and the individual tries to appear better than one really is. Finally, situational relevance is instrumental in explaining information poverty. Potentially useful information will be not used because people living in a small world do not see a generalized value of sources provided by outsiders intended to respond to their situation. The source is ignored because it is not legitimized by "contextual others."[63]

To specify the ideas of small world, Chatman[64] developed "a theory in the round," based on the ethnographic study of female prisoners. The concept of "life in the round" refers to a dynamic world based largely on approximation; in this world, things are understood implicitly.[64,65] When people live in the round, imprecision is largely accepted and inexactitude is tolerated. In this context, "members move in and out of the round depending on their need for more systematic, precise, and defined information."[66] Understanding life in the round results when information is clear enough to give sensible meaning to things. The most important consequence of this construct for the practice of ELIS is that life in the round adversely affects information seeking in day-to-day situations; people will not search for information if there is no need to do so. Small world inhabitants ignore information if they perceive that their world is working without it (i.e., they have enough certainty, comfort, and situational predictability so that the need to seek information is negated).[66] Individuals will cross information boundaries only if 1) information is perceived as critical, 2) there is a collective expectation that the information is relevant, and 3) a perception exists that the life lived in the round is no longer functioning.[64]

Chatman[67] summarized the theoretical developments in a theory of "normative behavior." The theory may be seen as an elaboration and extension of the theory of life in the round. In brief, the normative theory of behavior suggests that ELIS is affected by the worldview and norms characteristic of specific communities. In addition, ELIS is affected by the ways in which actors are classified into insiders or outsiders. Ultimately, norms and roles determine what kind of information sources will be preferred, accepted, and used.

Chatman's research project on the information-seeking practices of marginalized people inspired other projects (e.g., the study of Hersberger[15] focusing on the ways in which homeless parents living in family shelters seek for everyday information). The research line opened by Chatman is promising both theoretically and methodologically. Importantly, Chatman's research project exemplifies the genuine need to utilize the repertoire of social scientific theories and ethnographic approaches to enhance our understanding of information seeking as an integral part of everyday action in social contexts.

The Ecological Model of ELIS (Williamson)

By drawing on the findings of an empirical study in which some 200 older adults were interviewed in Australia in 1992–1994, Kirsty Williamson[8,68] developed an ecological model of information seeking and use. It can be called ecological because it sets information seeking and use in the context of social and cultural factors, which may have an influence on the ways of selecting and using information sources and channels. The model suggests that, although people purposefully seek information in response to perceived needs, they also monitor their world and receive information incidentally. The ways in which they monitor the everyday world is mediated by social–cultural backgrounds and values, physical environments, and personal characteristics (e.g., their states of health), as well as their socioeconomic situations and lifestyles.

The model suggests that in purposeful and incidental information seeking, information sources of various types are given differing importance. The intimate personal networks (family and friends) are closest to the user and are probably also perceived by the user as most easily accessible. The other source types are located farther in the "ecology of sources" [i.e., wider personal networks (clubs, churches, and voluntary organizations) and the mass media (newspapers, television, radio, and magazines)]. Institutional sources such as professionals, government departments, and other organizations are perceived to be even more remote in this sense. The ecological model has been applied in empirical studies focusing on ELIS of diverse groups such as blind and visually impaired people.[69] The strength of the ecological model is that it allows information seekers to be conceptualized as both individuals and members of social groups. The model also takes into attention the influence of particular physical and social environments. The individual is seen as a creative and thinking entity, but within contexts that involve various kinds of biological and social constraints.

ELIS in the Context of Way of Life (Savolainen)

"Way of life" is a social scientific concept that provides a broad context to investigate individual and social factors affecting ELIS. Reijo Savolainen[27] defined the concept of way of life as "order of things," which is based on the choices that individuals make. "Things" stand for various activities taking place in the daily life world, including not only jobs but also necessary reproductive tasks such as household care and voluntary activities (hobbies); "order" refers to preferences given to these activities. Because, in most cases, the order of things is a relatively well-established constellation of work and nonwork activities taking place in a day or a week, this constellation is easily taken to be the most natural or normal way of organizing one's everyday life. Correspondingly, people have a "cognitive order" indicating their perceptions of how things are when they are "normal." Through their choices, individuals have practically engaged in a certain order of things, and it is in their own interest to adhere to that order as long as they find it meaningful. Thus at least implicitly, most people seek for an internal coherence in everyday matters because it gives them better chances to plan their choices and act meaningfully.

The most central issues of way of life manifest themselves in the structure of the time budget, described as a relation between working and leisure time, models of consumption of goods and services, and nature of hobbies.[27] The structure of the time budget reveals the proportions of time spent on work, necessary activities outside work such as household care, and, finally, the time devoted to recreational activities such as hobbies. By analyzing the models of consumption, one may draw a picture that indicates the share of money spent on the acquisition of various goods or services (e.g., books). The analysis of hobbies sheds light on the substance of way of life because the nature of hobbies informs us of the things that people find most pleasant. The analysis also reveals the role of informational interests (for instance, newspaper reading) in leisure time.

Because the meaningful order of things may not reproduce itself automatically, individuals are required to take active care of it. This caring activity can be defined as mastery of life, implying the importance of the coherence of the everyday life projects at large. The nature of these projects may vary. As aptly specified by Hektor,[41] some life projects may be generic in that that they are common to most people (e.g., household care). Other projects are specific because they originate from an individual's life situation (e.g., child rearing or one's specific interests, i.e., hobbies).

Mastery of life serving one's life projects may be either passive or active. It is passive when people are satisfied with seeing that everything is going on as expected, at least on the whole.[27] Active mastery of life is associated with pragmatic problem solving in cases where the order of things has been shaken or threatened. Mastery of life is a general preparedness to approach everyday problems in certain ways in accordance with one's values. Information seeking is an integral component of mastery of life, which aims at the elimination of continual dissonance between perceptions of "how things are at this moment" and "how they should be." If there is no dissonance, mastery of life goes on quite routinely and the information seeking attached to it can be characterized as a rather passive monitoring of everyday life events. In other cases, mastery of life may grow into active problem solving aimed at restoring the disturbed order, usually requiring active seeking of practically effective information.

Savolainen[27] utilized the aforementioned model in an empirical study conducted in Finland. The study focused on two groups: teachers and industrial workers. The empirical study strengthened the assumption that way of life directs information seeking in a significant way. Teachers were more eager to seek factual information from various media, and they took a more critical stand toward the supply of light entertainment from radio, television, newspapers, and magazines. The interviews revealed that personal interest and current life situation also affect media use. There appeared to be teachers not particularly interested in the culture or politics sections of newspapers; similarly, some workers preferred documentaries and other serious programs and took a critical view of entertainment.

Later on, Savolainen[38] elaborated the aforementioned framework into the model of everyday information practices. This model differentiates three modes of everyday information practices: information seeking, information use, and information sharing. The model makes use of the ideas of social phenomenology[70] by approaching information seeking, use, and sharing in the context of life world in which everyday projects of diverse kinds are embedded. For example, looking for a new job and concern for the environment exemplify such projects. Everyday information practices may serve as tools to achieve the goals of these projects. Furthermore, the model suggests that the concept of information source horizon is central for the constitution of everyday information practices since this horizon indicates the ways in which people prefer information sources and thus navigate the information world. The ideas of the model were used in an empirical study examining information practices among environmental activists and unemployed people.[38]

Information Practices (McKenzie)

One of the newest models of ELIS is proposed by Pamela McKenzie.[71] The model was developed in the context of health information seeking by pregnant women. McKenzie specifies a two-dimensional model of context-bound information practices. The model describes four modes: active seeking, active scanning, nondirected monitoring, and obtaining information by proxy. When seeking information, the modes may appear in varying order, depending on the information need at hand and the situational factors. The modes can take place in two phases: first, at times of connecting information sources; and, second, interacting with them. Thus, the second phase implies the use of the information source to which one has been connected. The indications of use are, for example, reading a text or actively asking specifying questions when consulting a doctor.

By drawing on the aforementioned model, the process of health information seeking may be described as follows.[71] Active seeking can be defined as the most directed mode of information practice. Consulting a previously identified source (e.g., a family physician), re-reading an entry in an encyclopedia, or conducting a systematic known-item search in a medical database exemplifies active seeking. Active scanning refers to semidirected browsing or scanning in likely locations (e.g., medical books in a bookstore, or web pages discussing diabetes). Nondirected scanning involves serendipitous encounter with, and recognizing, a source (e.g., incidentally getting a useful idea from a TV program on how to reduce smoking). Finally, obtaining information by proxy may take place when interacting with information sources through the initiative of another agent: either the information source or some other gatekeeper or intermediaries. For example, an individual interested in the stopping of smoking may receive e-mails from her friend informing about new web pages related to this topic. Alternatively, her friend may have bought a new book on this topic and lends it to the information seeker.

McKenzie's model exemplifies the major tenets of recent studies on information seeking. Information seeking is seen as a highly dynamic and context-dependent activity, drawing on a number of modes that may appear in various orders. The model also exemplifies the growing complexity of ELIS processes (e.g., the ways in which various information resources perceived to be accessible afford ELIS to meet the needs of orienting and problem-specific information).

Information Grounds (Fisher)

Drawing on a series of ethnographic studies, Karen Fisher (née Pettigrew) and her colleagues have developed the concept of information grounds that stands for a spatio-temporally sensitive context of ELIS.[72] Information grounds may be defined as an environment temporarily created by the behavior of people who have come together to perform a given task, but from which emerges a social atmosphere that fosters the spontaneous and serendipitous sharing of information.[73] In other words, information grounds stand for an individual's combined perceptions of place, people, and information.[74,75] Examples of everyday information grounds include medical clinics, hair salons, bars, clubs, daycare centers, metro buses, bookstores, and libraries.[17] Grounds of these kinds stand for information-rich places where people indicate an awareness that an appropriate source might be located.

A major characteristic of information grounds is that they can occur anywhere, in any type of temporal setting, and are predicated on the presence of individuals. Second, people gather at information grounds for a primary, instrumental purpose other than information sharing and seeking. Third, social interaction is a primary activity at information grounds, and information flow is a by-product. Fourth, people engage in formal and informal information sharing, and information flow occurs in many directions.[73] Even though information grounds primarily serve the needs of information sharing, they are also interesting from the viewpoint of ELIS. While people share information, they may also ask specifying questions related to the topic of discussion. Purposive information seeking occurs when someone voluntarily visits an information ground with the purpose of obtaining information.[71] Nonpurposive information seeking takes place when someone serendipitously encounters information without prior intent.[73]

In a study focusing on information sharing and seeking at the foot clinic, Pettigrew[73] found that everyday information flow did not occur solely from nurses to customers, but the latter appeared to be ripe sources of everyday information for the nurses themselves. Multiple persons participated in exchanges and customers shared information while waiting for treatment and afterward. It also appeared that information needs were rarely stated as direct requests but instead emerged subtly as people shared their situations with one another and chit-chatted. This suggests that information sharing may give rise to occasional seeking of information. On the other hand, information may also be shared in the context of information encountering because the information received this way may be passed on to others. Another study explored how new immigrants use coping skills and literacy programs run by Queens Public Library, New York.[17] Then, the study showed that the immigrants share information in multiple directions often as a part of social interaction and that topics of information seeking could arise quite serendipitously as well as through framing via the literacy program's subjects. Finally, a survey drawing on telephone interviews of residents in East King County, the United States, showed that people favor information grounds by diverse criteria.[74] However, a common denominator was the opportunity to share common interests or needs, and the feeling as if other people understood their needs, and that these people may be trusted. For example, a healthcare facility can provide opportunities to talk with people having similar life experiences.

In the most recent characterization of information grounds, the concept is specified by referring to the people–place–information trichotomy.[75] More specifically,

information grounds are perceived as a social construct rooted in an individual's combined perceptions of place, people, and information. As the numerous examples of recent studies[74–76] suggest, the construct of information grounds has not been explicated in a final form; on the contrary, the approach is continually elaborated, both conceptually and empirically.

CONCLUSION

Studies conducted since the 1970s indicate that everyday life information needs and seeking are affected by a number of cognitive, emotional, cultural, and situational factors. ELIS has two major modes. On the one hand, people may seek for orienting information by monitoring daily events through the media; newspapers, television, and the Internet are the most central sources of orienting information. On the other hand, they may seek for problem-specific information. Most frequently, information seeking of this kind is triggered by needs related to health issues, consumer problems, housing, and various kinds of hobbies. To meet these needs, people tend to favor a limited number of easily accessible sources, which have been found useful in previous use contexts.

To a large extent, the major features of ELIS may be condensed into the principles of information seeking proposed by Harris and Dewdney.[77] Most importantly, these principles suggest that the needs for problem-specific information arise from the situations in which information seekers find themselves; that is, any need for information is situationally based and dependent on a particular context. People also tend to look for the information that is most accessible, sometimes referred to as the principle of the least effort. It also seems that daily information-seeking habits change quite slowly. One of the recurrent findings of ELIS research is people's tendency to favor human sources due to easy access to them and the opportunity to get immediate feedback. However, source preferences may vary in differing information need situations. Depending on their requirements, for example, Wikipedia may be preferred over human sources in cases in which facts about an issue are urgently needed. Since the late 1990s, the Internet has increasingly affected ELIS practices by providing easily accessible sources. Even though the popularity of the networked sources has grown rapidly, it seems that they will complement, rather than replace, more traditional sources and channels.

As the daily information environment becomes more complex and information seeking is affected by an increasing number of contextual factors, there is a need to elaborate the research settings of ELIS. The major challenge is to study contextually the dynamic (situation-bound, sometimes nonlinear and cyclical) processes of ELIS as related to the recurrent patterns of information seeking. More reflective attention is being devoted to the ways in which the researchers gain access to the everyday life settings of the informants and conceptualize the phenomena of ELIS.[78] One indication of the progress made in this respect is the elaboration of the theoretical and methodological bases, as exemplified by Chatman's project to develop a social scientific theory of ELIS. Recent examples of promising lines of research include the approaches to information grounds[72] and information practices.[38,71] In addition, there is a growing interest in the role of the affective factors, such as emotions and feelings, in the study of health-related[13,14] and hobby-related information seeking[21,79] in particular. The study of affective factors is also important because they often make it understandable why people avoid information although it may be readily available.[14] These developments suggest that the best way to elaborate the picture of ELIS both conceptually and empirically is to thematize it as a contextual everyday practice that incorporates cognitive, affective, and sociocultural elements.[3,38,67,80] However, ELIS is not rendered meaningful as a separate practice because it is often connected to practices of using and sharing information.

REFERENCES

1. Wilson, T.D. Human information behaviour. Inf. Sci. **2000**, *3* (2), 49–56. http://www.inform.nu/Articles/Vol3/v3n2p49-56.pdf (accessed September 2014).
2. Savolainen, R. Information behavior and information practice. Reviewing the "umbrella concepts" of information seeking studies. Libr. Q. **2007**, *77* (2), 109–132.
3. Case, D.O. *Looking for Information. A Survey of Research on Information Seeking, Needs and Behavior*, 3rd Ed.; Emerald: Bingley, U.K., 2012.
4. Shenton, A.K.; Dixon, P. Models of young people's information seeking. J. Libr. Inf. Sci. **2003**, *35* (1), 5–22.
5. Agosto, D.E.; Hughes-Hassell, S. People, pages, and questions: an investigation of the everyday life information-seeking behaviors of urban young adults. Libr. Inf. Sci. Res. **2005**, *27* (2), 141–163.
6. Abbas, J.; Agosto, D.E. Everyday life information behavior of young people. In *The Information Behavior of a New Generation: Children and Teens in the 21st Century*; Beheshti, J., Large, A., Eds.; The Scarecrow Press: Lanham, MD, 2013; 65–91.
7. Julien, H.E. Barriers to adolescents' information seeking for career decision making. J. Am. Soc. Inf. Sci. **1999**, *50* (1), 38–48.
8. Williamson, K. Discovered by chance: the role of incidental information acquisition in an ecological model of information use. Libr. Inf. Sci. Res. **1998**, *20* (1), 23–40.
9. Niemelä, R.; Huotari, M.-L.; Kortelainen, T. Enactment and use of information and media among older adults. Libr. Inf. Sci. Res. **2012**, *34* (3), 212–219.
10. Harris, R.; Stickney, J.; Grasley, C. et al. Search for help and information: abused women speak. Libr. Inf. Sci. Res. **2001**, *23* (2), 123–141.
11. Westbrook, L. Information myths and intimate partner violence: sources, contexts and consequences. J. Am. Soc. Inf. Sci. Technol. **2009**, *60* (4), 828–836.
12. Bar-Ilan, J.; Shalom, N.; Shoham, S. et al. The role of information in a lifetime process: a model of weight maintenance by women over long time periods. Inf. Res. Int. Electron. J. **2006**, *11* (4), http://InformationR.net/ir/11–4/paper263.html (accessed September 2014).
13. Lambert, S.D.; Loiselle, C.G.; Macdonald, E. An in-depth exploration of information-seeking behavior among individuals with cancer. Part 1: understanding differential patterns of active information seeking. Cancer Nurs. **2009**, *32* (1), 11–23.
14. Lambert, S.D.; Loiselle, C.G.; Macdonald, E. An in-depth exploration of information-seeking behavior among individuals with cancer. Part 2: understanding differential patterns of information disinterest and avoidance. Cancer Nurs. **2009**, *32* (1), 26–36.
15. Hersberger, J. Everyday information needs and information sources of homeless parents. New Rev. Inf. Behav. Res. **2001**, *2*, 119–134.
16. Perttilä, R.; Ek, S. Information behaviour and coping functions of long-term unemployed people in Finland. Libri **2010**, *60* (2), 107–116.
17. Fisher, K.E.; Durrance, J.C.; Hinton, M.B. Information grounds and the use of need-based services by immigrants in Queens, New York: a context-based, outcome evaluation approach. J. Am. Soc. Inf. Sci. **2004**, *55* (8), 754–766.
18. Fisher, K.E.; Marcoux, E.; Miller, L.S. et al. Information behaviour of migrant Hispanic farm workers and their families in the Pacific Northwest. Inf. Res. Int. Electron. J. **2004**, *10* (1), http://InformationR.net/ir/10-1/paper199.html (accessed September 2014).
19. Caidi, N.; Allard, D.; Quirke, L. Information practices of immigrants. In *Annual Review of Information Science and Technology*; Cronin, B., Ed.; Information Today, Inc.: Medford, NJ, 2010; Vol. 44, 493–531.
20. Case, D.O. A model of the information seeking and decision making of online coin buyers. Inf. Res. Int. Electron. J. **2010**, *15* (4), 4. http://informationr.net/ir/15-4/paper448.html (accessed September 2014).
21. Fulton, C. The pleasure principle: the power of positive affect in information seeking. Aslib Proc. New Inf. Persp. **2009**, *61* (3), 245–261.
22. Hartel, J. Information activities and resources in an episode of gourmet cooking. Inf. Res. Electron. J. **2006**, *12* (1), http://InformationR.net/ir/12–1/paper282.html (accessed September 2014).
23. Skov, M. Hobby-related information-seeking behaviour of highly dedicated online museum visitors. Inf. Res. Electron. J. **2013**, *18*(4), http://InformationR.net/ir/18-4/paper597.html (accessed September 2014).
24. Savolainen, R. Information source horizons and source preferences of environmental activists: a social phenomenological approach. J. Am. Soc. Inf. Sci. Technol. **2007**, *58* (12), 1709–1719.
25. Savolainen, R. Source preferences in the context of seeking problem-specific information. Inf. Process. Manage **2008**, *44* (1), 274–293.
26. Durrance, J.C. *Armed for Action: Library Response to Citizen Information Needs*; Neal-Schuman: New York, 1984.

27. Savolainen, R. Everyday life information seeking: approaching information seeking in the context of "way of life" Libr. Inf. Sci. Res. **1995**, *17* (3), 259–294.

28. Given, L.M. The academic and the everyday: investigating the overlap in mature undergraduates' information-seeking behavior. Libr. Inf. Sci. Res. **2002**, *24* (1), 17–29.

29. Harris, R.M.; Wathen, C.N.; Fear, J.M. Searching for health information in rural Canada. Where do residents look for health information and what do they do when they find it? Inf. Res. Electron. J. **2006**, *12* (1), http://InformationR.net/ir/12-1/paper274.html (accessed September 2014).

30. Pálsdóttir, A. The connection between purposive information seeking and information encountering. A study of Icelanders' health and lifestyle information seeking. J. Doc. **2010**, *66* (2), 224–244.

31. Johnson, J.D.; Case, D.O. *Health Information Seeking*; Peter Lang: New York, 2012.

32. Bates, M.J. Speculations on the sociocultural context of public information provision in the seventies and beyond. In *Library and Information Service Needs of the Nation: Proceedings of a Conference on the Needs of Occupational, Ethnic, and other Groups in the United States*, Sponsored by the National Commission on Libraries and Information Science; Cuadra, C.A., Bates, M.J., Eds.; U.S. G.P.O: Washington, DC, 1974; 51–76.

33. Zweizig, D.; Dervin, B. Public library use, users, uses: advances in knowledge of the characteristics and needs of the adult clientele of American public libraries. In *Advances in Librarianship*; Voigt, M.J., Harris, M.H., Eds.; Academic Press: New York, 1977; Vol. 7, 231–255.

34. Dalrymple, P.W. A quarter century of user-centered study: the impact of Zweizig and Dervin on Library Information Science Research. Libr. Inf. Sci. Res. **2001**, *23* (2), 155–165.

35. Warner, E.; Murray, A.D.; Palmour, V.E. *Information Needs of Urban Citizens*, Final Report; U.S. Department of Health, Education and Welfare, Office of Education, Bureau of Libraries and Learning Resources: Washington, DC, 1973.

36. Marcella, R.; Baxter, G. The information needs and the information seeking behaviour of a national sample of the population in the United Kingdom, with special reference to needs related to citizenship. J. Doc. **1999**, *55* (2), 159–183.

37. Chen, C.; Hernon, P. *Information Seeking: Assessing and Anticipating User Needs*; Neal-Schuman: New York, 1982.

38. Savolainen, R. *Everyday Information Practices: A Social Phenomenological Perspective*; The Scarecrow Press: Lanham, MD, 2008.

39. Savolainen, R. "Living encyclopedia" or idle talk? Seeking and providing consumer information in an Internet newsgroup. Libr. Inf. Sci. Res. **2001**, *23* (1), 67–90.

40. Rieh, S.Y. On the web at home: information seeking and web searching in the home environment. J. Am. Soc. Inf. Sci. Technol. **2004**, *55* (8), 743–753.

41. Hektor, A. *What's the Use? Internet and Information Behavior in Everyday Life*; Linköping University: Linköping, Sweden, 2001.

42. Savolainen, R. Requesting and providing information in blogs and internet discussion forums. J. Doc. **2011**, *67* (5), 863–886.

43. Godbold, N. Usefully messy: how people use rich, complex descriptions to make sense in online renal discussion groups. In *Social Information Research*; Widén, G.; Holmberg, K., Eds.; Emerald: Bingley, U.K., 2012; 43–73.

44. Savolainen, R. The structure of argument patterns on a social Q&A site. J. Am. Soc. Inf. Sci. Technol. **2012**, *63* (12), 2536–2548.

45. Savolainen, R. Providing informational support in an online discussion group and a Q&A site: the case of travel planning. J. Assoc. Inf. Sci. Technol. **2015**, *66* (3), 450–461.

46. Kim, S.-B.; Choi, K.W.; Kim, D.-Y. The motivations of college students' use of social networking sites in travel information search behavior: the mediating effect of interacting with others. J. Travel Tour. Mark. **2013**, *30* (3), 238–252.

47. Nguyen, A.; Western, M. The complementary relationship between the Internet and traditional mass media: the case of online news and information. Inf. Res. Int. Electron. J. **2006**, *11* (3), http://InformationR.net/ir/11–3/paper259. html (accessed September 2014).

48. Williamson, K.; Qayyum, A.; Hider, P.; Liu, Y-H. Young adults and everyday-life information: the role of news media. Libr. Inf. Sci. Res. **2012**, *34* (4), 258–264.

49. Greenberg, B.S.; Dervin, B. *Use of the Mass Media by the Urban Poor: Findings of Three Research Projects, with an Annotated Bibliography*; Praeger: New York, 1970.

50. Dervin, B.; Loreman-Wernet, L.; Lauterbach, E. *Sense-Making Methodology Reader: Selected Writings of Brenda Dervin*; Hampton Press: Cresskill, NJ, 2003.

51. Dervin, B. An overview of sense-making research: concepts, methods and results to date, International Communication Association Annual Meeting, Dallas, TX, 1983 (mimeo).

52. Dervin, B. From the mind's eye of the 'user': the sense-making qualitative-quantitative methodology. In *Qualitative Research in Information Management*; Glazier, J.D., Powell, R.R., Eds.; Libraries Unlimited: Englewood, CO, 1992; 61–84.

53. Dervin, B. On studying information seeking methodologically: the implications of connecting metatheory to method. Inf. Process. Manag. **1999**, *35* (6), 727–750.

54. Savolainen, R. The sense-making theory: reviewing the interests of a user-centered approach to information seeking and use. Inf. Process. Manag. **1993**, *29* (1), 13–28.

55. Savolainen, R. Information use as gap-bridging: the viewpoint of sense-making methodology. J. Am. Soc. Inf. Sci. Technol. **2006**, *57* (8), 1116–1125.

56. Dervin, B.; Nilan, M.S.; Jacobson, T.L. Conducting helpful communications research. An approach with blood donors, Annual Meeting of the International Communication Association, Boston, MA, 1982 (mimeo).

57. Dervin, B.; Nilan, M.; Krenz, C. et al. *When Cancer Strikes: How Cancer Patients Make Sense of Their Health Situations*, Report Presented to the National Cancer Institute; National Cancer Institute: Washington, DC, 1982.

58. Pettigrew, K.E.; Durrance, J.; Unruh, K.T. Facilitating community information seeking using the internet: findings from three public library-community network systems. J. Am. Soc. Inf. Sci. Technol. **2002**, *53* (11), 894–903.

59. Dervin, B.; Nilan, M. Information needs and uses. In *Annual Review of Information Science and Technology*;

Williams, M.E., Ed.; Knowledge Industry, Inc.: White Plains, NY, 1986; Vol. 21, 3–33.

60. Burnett, G.; Besant, M.; Chatman, E.A. Small worlds: normative behavior in virtual communities and feminist bookselling. J. Am. Soc. Inf. Sci. Technol. 2001, 52 (7), 536–547.

61. Chatman, E.A. Life in a small world: applicability of gratification theory to information-seeking behavior. J. Am. Soc. Inf. Sci. 1991, 42 (6), 438–449.

62. Chatman, E.A. The Information World of Retired Women; Greenwood Press: Westport, CT, 1992.

63. Chatman, E.A. The impoverished life-world of outsiders. J. Am. Soc. Inf. Sci. 1996, 47 (3), 193–206.

64. Chatman, E.A. A theory of life in the round. J. Am. Soc. Inf. Sci. 1999, 50 (3), 207–217.

65. Fulton, C. Chatman's life in the round. In Theories of Information Behavior; Fisher, K.E., Erdelez, S., McKechnie, L., Eds.; Information Today, Inc.: Medford, NJ, 2005; 79–82.

66. Pettigrew, K.; Fidel, R.; Bruce, H. Conceptual frameworks in information behavior. In Annual Review of Information Science and Technology; Williams, M.E., Ed.; Information Today, Inc.: Medford, NJ, 2001; Vol. 35, 43–78.

67. Chatman, E.A. Framing social life in theory and research. New Rev. Inf. Behav. Res. 2000, 1, 23–17.

68. Williamson, K. The information needs and information seeking-behaviour of older adults: an Australian study. Information Seeking in Context, Proceedings of an International Conference on Research in Information Needs, Seeking and Use in Different Contexts, Tampere, Finland, August 14–16, 1996, Vakkari, P., Savolainen, R., Dervin, B., Eds.; Taylor Graham: London, U.K., 1998; 337–350.

69. Williamson, K.; Schauder, D.; Bow, A. Information seeking by blind and sight impaired citizens: an ecological study. Inf. Res. Int. Electron. J. 2000, 5 (4), http://informationr.net/ir/5-4/paper79.html (accessed September 2014).

70. Wilson, T.D.; Savolainen, R. Social phenomenology. In Theory in Information Behaviour Research; Wilson, T.D., Ed.; Eiconics Ltd.: Sheffield, U.K., 2013; 172–200. https://www.smashwords.com/books/view/336724 (accessed September 2014).

71. McKenzie, P.J. A model of information practices in accounts of everyday life information seeking. J. Doc. 2003, 59 (1), 19–40.

72. Fisher, K.E.; Naumer, C.M. Information grounds: theoretical basis and empirical findings on information flow in social settings. In New Directions in Human Information Behavior; Spink, A.; Cole, C., Eds.; Springer: Dordrecht, the Netherlands, 2006; 93–111.

73. Pettigrew, K.E. Waiting for chiropody: contextual results from an ethnographic study of the information behavior among attendees at community clinics. Inf. Process. Manag. 1999, 35 (6), 801–817.

74. Fisher, K.E.; Naumer, C.; Durrance, J. et al. Something old, something new: preliminary findings from an exploratory study about people's information habits and information grounds. Inf. Res. Int. Electron. J. 2005, 10 (2), http://InformationR.net/ir/10-2/paper223.html (accessed September 2014).

75. Fisher, K.E.; Landry, C.F.; Naumer, C. Social spaces, casual interactions, meaningful exchanges: 'information ground' characteristics based on the college student experience. Inf. Res. Int. Electron. J. 2007, 12 (2), http://informationr.net/ir/12-2/paper291.html (accessed September 2014).

76. Fisher, K.E.; Landry, C.F. Understanding the information behavior of stay-at-home mothers through affect. In Information and Emotion: The Emergent Affective Paradigm in Information Behavior Research and Theory; Nahl, D., Bilal, D., Eds.; Information Today, Inc.: Medford, NJ, 2007; 211–233.

77. Harris, R.M.; Dewdney, P. Barriers to Information: How Formal Help Systems Fail Battered Women; Greenwood Press: Westport, CT, 1994.

78. Carey, R.F.; Kechnie, L.E.F.; McKenzie, P. Gaining access to everyday life information seeking. Libr. Inf. Sci. Res. 2001, 23 (4), 319–334.

79. Laplante, A.; Downie, J.S. The utilitarian and hedonic outcomes of music information-seeking in everyday life. Libr. Inf. Sci. Res. 2011, 33 (3), 202–210.

80. Hasler, L.; Ruthven, I.; Buchanan, S. Using Internet groups in situations of information poverty: topics and information needs. J. Assoc. Inf. Sci. Technol. 2014, 65 (1), 25–36.

Evidence-Based Practice

Prudence W. Dalrymple
Drexel University College of Computing & Informatics, Philadelphia, Pennsylvania, U.S.A.

Abstract

Evidence-based practice (EBP) is the conscientious, explicit, and judicious use of current best evidence in making decisions. Its aim is to gather, assess, and apply research results that are pertinent to questions that arise in the course of everyday professional practice. Its focus is pragmatic rather than theoretic. Evidence-based library and information practice (EBLIP) comprises a set of principles and practices derived from EBP, primarily the health professions. These principles are described and referenced to examples from the library and information science (LIS) literature. While EBLIP's strongest proponents are found among health sciences librarians, efforts to incorporate evidence into practical decision-making may be found in other sectors in the library and information professions. It is also used as a rationale to encourage enlarging and improving the evidence base of library and information science as a discipline. EBLIP is an international movement of library and information professionals from a number of countries, especially the United Kingdom, Scandinavia, North America, and Australia. As a relatively new movement within the professions, EBP continues to evolve, with changing emphases depending on discipline, region, organization, and topic. Increasing use of qualitative methods and interest in data-driven decisions may affect the role of EBP in LIS.

INTRODUCTION

Evidence-based practice (EBP) is the conscientious, explicit, and judicious use of current best evidence in making decisions. Its aim is to gather, assess, and apply research results that are pertinent to questions that arise in the course of everyday professional practice in a variety of fields. Although EBP encourages the conduct and use of research, it focuses primarily on using research results to solve everyday problems, rather than on undertaking basic research that may or may not have a practical application. EBP is an approach increasingly used in the professions, most notably those in health, education, policy, and social service, in addition to library and information science (LIS). Evidence-based library and information practice (EBLIP) comprises a set of principles and practices derived from EBP in other sectors and espoused by library and information professionals from a number of countries, especially the United Kingdom, Scandinavia, North America, and Australia.

EBLIP evolved during the 1990s as a result of health science librarians' involvement in evidence-based medicine (EBM). As medical librarians participated in the EBM initiatives, they began to explore the feasibility of applying EBM principles to the problems facing a rapidly evolving library world. EBLIP encourages improving the research skills of practicing librarians in order to build a research base that can be applied to improving professional practice in libraries and other information-intensive organizations. As such, its focus is pragmatic rather than theoretical.

While EBLIP's strongest proponents are found among health sciences librarians, efforts to incorporate evidence into practical decision-making may be found in other sectors of the library and information professions. It is also used as a rationale to encourage enlarging and improving the evidence base of the discipline. As a relatively new movement within the professions, EBP continues to evolve, with changing emphases depending on the discipline, region, organization, and topic.

This evolution has benefitted from the biennial, international conferences on EBLIP that began in 1999 and have been held at various locations in Europe, Canada, Australia, and the United States. An open-access, peer-reviewed quarterly journal, *Evidence-Based Library and Information Practice*, was established in 2006 to "provide a forum for librarians and other information professionals to discover research that may contribute to decision-making in professional practice."[1] The journal's international editorial board includes many of the most prolific writers and strongest advocates for EBLIP. In addition to research reports and commentary, it publishes evidence summaries of previously published research. The journal complements the major text in the field *Evidence-Based Practice for Information Professionals: A Handbook*[2] and adds to the growing body of literature in the field, much of which has been published in the *Journal of the Medical Library Association*, in *Hypothesis*, the newsletter of the Research Section of the Medical Library Association (MLA), and in *Health Information and Libraries Journal*.

Encyclopedia of Library and Information Sciences, Fourth Edition DOI: 10.1081/E-ELIS4-120053417

Beginnings in Clinical Medicine

The EBM movement resulted from the observation that clinicians pursued answers to only a few of the information needs they identified during daily practice because they lacked time and access to current, high-quality resources, including critical reviews of the literature that were organized and presented systematically. Increased pressures on clinicians' time due in part to changes in professional practice, and the growth of the biomedical literature, led to concerns that clinicians were making clinical decisions based on tradition and personal inclination rather than on established, scientific evidence. Few of the clinicians' information needs were expressed as actual questions, and even fewer generated searches for answers.[3] EBM advocates challenge clinicians to become lifelong, self-directed learners, to seek out and apply the results of systematic reviews and meta-analyses, and to practice audit and feedback about their clinical decisions.

By most measures, EBM is a central tenet of clinical practice. EBM is now a part of most medical school curricula, it has been endorsed by the Institute of Medicine, thousands of systematic reviews have been published, and numerous electronic databases and digital devices deliver evidence-based summaries to the clinician at the bedside. Despite this success, EBM has also been criticized as an attempt to make practice formulaic ("cookbook medicine") and to remove professional judgment and values from decision-making. Such criticism prompted Sackett,[4] the author of a major EBM text, *Clinical Epidemiology*, to reassert the need for a balance between scientific evidence and clinical judgment. Although EBM continues to be critiqued, few dispute the need to collect, filter, synthesize, and apply the available information to clinical practice.[5,6]

EBP in the Information Professions

Advocates for evidence-based information practice have written extensively to encourage colleagues to adopt evidence-based methods, but at the same time they acknowledge that LIS provides few evidence tools and even fewer incentives for adoption. Not only is the comparatively small research base a barrier to EBP, cultural and communications gaps exist between researchers and practitioners. These gaps, which have been attributed to a myriad of factors—from lack of educational preparation to "semantic impenetrability" and lack of practical utility—have prompted calls to action to address them.[7] The MLA's research policy *Using Scientific Evidence to Improve Information Practice* (1995) and its successor *The Research Imperative* (2007) envision health information practice whose "core consists of verified scientific evidence, with LIS professionals as creators, managers, and active users of such evidence."[8,9] The revised policy also links EBP with quality improvement, stating that evidence

[will be] identified, applied, and assessed in a continuous loop of quality improvement with research as the critical underlying construct.[9] Evidence-based principles are beginning to diffuse through other sectors of library and information practice as indicated by the variety of evidence summaries published in the journal *Evidence-Based Library and Information Practice*.

COMPONENTS OF EVIDENCE-BASED PRACTICE

Though they may be described in a variety of ways and the details may differ according to domain, the components of EBP remain constant. They are

- Formulate the question
- Search for the evidence
- Evaluate the evidence
- Apply the results
- Evaluate the effect

Formulate the Question

In EBP, formulating a question is the ability to state the problem at hand in the form of an answerable question. This step is often preceded by recognizing an information need or "gap" that prompts the question. For example, researchers have analyzed the ways in which physicians decide to pursue answers to questions and studies of the information needs in other domains have found similar patterns.[10] Once an information need is identified, the need is transformed into an answerable question following a specific pattern. In clinical medicine, the pattern is known as PICO, a mnemonic translated as problem (or patient or population), intervention (prognostic finding or exposure), comparison (with the alternative, including placebo for trials), and outcome (or effect). Examples that apply PICO to clinical questions may be found at many websites such as https://www-ncbi-nlm-nih-gov. ezproxy2.library.drexel.edu/pmc/?term=3140151. A template for use when formulating either of two different types of PICO searches in PubMed is available at http://www.pubmedhh.nlm.nih.gov/nlm/picostudy/pico3.html. These examples are drawn from clinical medicine, but Booth has taken these models and developed SPICE—setting, perspective, intervention, comparison, and evaluation—an approach that is specific to LIS questions. SPICE stands for facets of a problem that are relevant library and information practice.[11]

Acknowledging the importance of stating questions in an answerable form has prompted efforts to develop a taxonomy or classification of questions. For example, some basic types of questions in clinical medicine are those having to do with diagnosis, treatment, etiology, prognosis, or prevention, each of which is one facet of a clinical situation.[10] Similar work has been undertaken with regard to

Table 1 Classification of library questions.

Question from *Hypothesis*[a]	Revised question	Domain	Potential resources
How can we predict the future usability of a print monograph collection in this electronic environment?	In academic libraries, how do electronic subscriptions affect usage of the print monograph collection?	Collections	LISA, Library Literature, CINAHL
Are students who have been taught information skills more or less likely to continue to further study?	Among students, does being taught information skills by a librarian affect future academic pursuit?	Education	ERIC, MEDLINE, Educational research abstracts, PsycInfo
Is there a way to measure the economic value of the medical library within a hospital?	In hospitals, does having a medical library vs. not having a library impact the hospital's economic viability?	Management	ABI Inform, CBCA, EconLit, MEDLINE
How do we apply outcomes-based evaluation to services in order to realistically demonstrate the impact of what we do?	In presentations to library boards, does the use of outcomes-based evaluation of library services impact upon board members' perception of the importance of library services?	Marketing/ Promotion	ABI Inform, CBCA, Library Literature
OPAC vs. library Web sites/databases for e-journal/e-book management—why…?	IN managing e-journal access and retrieval, is using an OPAC vs. a library Web site database for indexing those journals a more user-friendly medium?	Information access and retrieval	LISA, Library Literature, CINAHL. MEDLINE
Can we prove that librarians are more effective at answering reference questions and running literature searches than library technicians?	In reference transactions, do librarians, as compared to library technicians, provide a more complete answer? In literature searching, does a librarian search vs. a library technical search yield higher quality results?	Reference/ Enquiries	LISA, Library Literature, CINAHL, MEDLINE

[a] http://www.mlanet.org/p/cm/ld/fid=737&tid=511&sid=647.

questions in LIS. An illustrative list of questions generated by practicing health science librarians restated as EBL questions and mapped onto six domains of library practice appears in Table 1.[12] In addition, Eldredge[13] has proposed three question types—prediction, intervention, and exploration—which can be linked to research designs. Such efforts sharpen questions and help focus on an appropriate research design that will produce useful evidence that can be tapped to solve practical problems.[13]

Search for Evidence

The next step in EBP is the search for evidence. The purpose of the search for evidence is to enable both researchers and decision-makers to quickly access what is known about a particular topic. In addition to the usual criteria of relevance and recall, an evidence-based search uses special techniques to filter the retrieval, retaining only those items that meet criteria for quality. Indeed, the process of filtering evidence ("quality filtering") prompted medical librarians to engage in evidence-based activities on behalf of healthcare practitioners.[14,15] Evidence searching in biomedicine is greatly facilitated by using various "filters" that can restrict retrieval to specific study designs such as randomized controlled trials (RCTs).[16] These filters limit retrieval to research studies and sort them by research design. When these tools are fully deployed, they constitute an infrastructure of systematic reviews, meta-analyses, guidelines, and statements of best practice that can support evidence-based medical practice.

An infrastructure comparable to that found in medicine does not yet exist in LIS; its modest research base is dispersed across many cognate disciplines such as computer science and technology, education, management, and other social sciences where there are many different approaches to research. While standards for structured abstracts, such as those required by MLA, can simplify the process of retrieving a body of relevant work, they have yet to be universally adopted, and indexing terms do not typically identify study design.[17,18] Lacking this infrastructure, most LIS searchers employ citation searching, pearl-growing, or snowball strategies enhanced with text words to identify research studies from which evidence can be extracted.

Systematic Review and Evidence Appraisal

The literature search is part of the larger process referred to as a systematic review. A systematic review is a concise summary of the best available evidence that addresses a well-formulated question. It differs from the traditional literature review in that it includes a detailed description of the search strategy, the date(s) of searches, and databases searched (including hand searches) because it is expected that it will be replicated and updated. A systematic review aggregates and synthesizes research findings rated by the strength of their evidence—their validity or freedom from bias, their reliability or trustworthiness; and their applicability or impact. Differences in these dimensions are usually a function of the research design itself,

Table 2 EBL levels of evidence, revised.

Prediction	Intervention	Exploration
Systematic review	Systematic review	Systematic review
Meta-analysis	Meta-analysis	Summing up[a]
Prospective cohort study	RCTs	Comparative study[b]
Retrospective cohort study	Prospective cohort study	Qualitative studies[c]
Survey	Retrospective cohort study	Survey
Case study	Survey	Case study
Expert opinion[d]	Case study	Expert opinion[d]
	Expert opinion[d]	

[a–d] Eldredge, J. The most relevant and answerable research questions facing the practice of health sciences librarianship. *Hypothesis* 2001 15 (1), 9-14,17. http://www.mlanet.org/p/cm/ld/fid=737&tid=511&sid=647.

and because research varies in rigor, each study must be retrieved and reviewed, and the evidence extracted and rated according to a specified protocol. The process of rating the evidence is called evidence appraisal. The results of the appraisal are presented in a format referred to as an evidence table that orders the research according to the strength of its design.

A hierarchy of evidence was first developed in clinical medicine, where the RCT was placed at the top of the hierarchy, reflecting its importance in determining effectiveness of therapeutic interventions. RCTs are rare in LIS; nevertheless, research evidence can be appraised, and several approaches to appraising LIS evidence in LIS have been proposed. Eldredge's[13] hierarchy of evidence is one of the most well known and resembles the one used in clinical medicine; see Table 2.

In addition to classifying the levels of evidence, critical appraisal of evidence entails detailed analysis of each study selected for inclusion. There are numerous dimensions that can be used; in medicine, for example, there are estimated to be as many as 40 systems used to appraise or grade evidence. These systems incorporate both quantitative and qualitative measures, the former being represented by measures such as statistical power and effect size, while qualitative measures may use designations such as "gold star" or "fatal flaw."[19]

Because the systematic reviews are fundamental to EBP, bringing them together in a searchable database serves an important purpose. The Cochrane Collaboration, begun in 1993, is the oldest and largest collaborative effort in which hundreds of researchers cooperate to search the medical literature, appraise the evidence, and publish systematic reviews.[20] While the majority of these are only tangentially related to LIS EBP, they can sometimes be useful; see, for example, the Cochrane Collaboration review on opinion leaders, as well as the collection of Methodology Reviews. In addition to the Cochrane Collaboration, the Cochrane Library collects other databases containing high-quality, independent evidence.

In LIS, Glynn[21] has developed a critical appraisal tool for LIS that effectively combines questions aimed at internal validity such as research design and execution, with external validity such as whether the evidence is meaningful in a particular setting. Answering these questions can help determine the value of a research report to an organization and problem at hand.

Another evidence-based resource of potential use to LIS is the Campbell Collaboration whose mission is to provide high-quality, sound evidence for practitioners and the public when making decisions about public policy, particularly in education, criminology, social welfare, and other policy areas.[22]

Meta-Analysis in LIS

Meta-analysis is another important part of EBP in many fields. It is a procedure in which statistical techniques are used to summarize the data of several comparable studies. To conduct a meta-analysis, the study design must be sufficiently detailed and transparent to assure that the studies are comparable. Unfortunately, the research base in LIS lacks standards for reporting research, making it difficult to draw conclusions across multiple studies. Despite these limitations, there are some examples of meta-analysis in LIS research. See, for example, Trahan's[23] meta-analysis comparing computerized searching to paper-based searching, Chen and Rada's[24] meta-analysis of hypertext systems, Saxton's[25] meta-analysis of reference services, and Koufogiannakis and Wiebe's[26] meta-analysis of methods for teaching information literacy skills.

In order to accomplish the goal of providing a succinct summary of what is known in an area to facilitate and support decision-making, an alternative to meta-analysis known as meta-synthesis has emerged in LIS. Although meta-analysis is usually conducted using quantitative data, the approach described by Light and Pillemer[27] can produce useful, reliable summaries of research using many different research designs. Their checklist of 10 questions to ask in assessing a review can be particularly useful in LIS because of its applicability to education, policy, and other social science studies. Urquhart describes the technique of meta-synthesis and applies it to information behavior research.[28] Ke and Cheng examine issues surrounding the application of meta-analysis techniques in LIS, and they conclude that although the body of research in LIS is not currently large enough to support robust meta-analyses or meta-syntheses, the benefits are sufficient to warrant taking steps toward that goal.[29]

Apply the Results

Applying the results from a systematic review is a goal of EBP, but it is often this step that presents the great barrier. In medicine, the phrase "from bench to bedside" is frequently invoked to illustrate the transition that must take

Booth, A. Australian supermodel? A practical example of evidence-based library and information practce (EBLIP). *Health Inform. Libr. J.* **2006**, *23* (1), 69–72.

Bradley. D,R., et al. Real-time, evidence-based medicine inslruchon: a randomized controlled trial in a neonatal inlensive care unit. *J. Med. Libr. Assoc.* **2006**, *90* (2), 194–201.

Brettle, A. Information skills training: a systematic review of the literature. *Health Inform, Libr. J.* **2003**, *20* (Supp.1), 3–9.

LaPelle, N.R., Luckmann, R. Simpson, E.R. Martin, E,R. Identifying strategies to improve access to credible and relevant information for public health professionals: A qualitative study. *BMC Public Health* **2006**, *6*, 89.

Marshall, J.G. The impact of the hospital library on clinical decision making: the Rochester study. *Br. Med. Libr. Assoc.* **1992**. *80* (2), 169–178.

Marshal, J,G. Neufeld, V.R. A randomized trial of librarian educational participation in clinical settings. *J. Med. Educ.* **1981**, *56* (5), 409–416.

McKnight, M. Interlibrary loan availability of nursing journals through DOCLINE and OCLC: A five-state survey. *Br. Med. Libr. Assoc.* **2000**, *88* (3), 254-5.

Pearce-Smith, N. A journal club is an effective tool for assisting librarians in the practice of evidence-based librarianship: A case study. *Heallh Inform. Libr. J.* **2006**, *23* (1), 32–40.

Weightman, A.L; Williamson, J. The value and impact of information provided through library services for patient care: A systematic review. Health Inform. *Libr. J.* **2005**, *22* (1), 4–25.

Fig. 1 Examples of evidence-based research from LIS.
Source: From The Research Imperative: The Research Policy Statement of the Medical Library Association, by C. Perryman and J. Marshall. In *Appendix 2 Selected Bibliography: Evidence-Based Librarianship*, file:///C:/Users/pwd28/Downloads/2007_mla_research_imperative_full.pdf (accessed January 13, 2017); Reprinted from Dalrymple, P.W., The application of systematic research, in *Administration and Management in Health Sciences Libraries*; Forsman, R.B., Ed.; Medical Library Association and Scarecrow Press, Lanham, MD, Vol. 8, 173–194, 2000, Current Practice in Health Sciences Librarianship. With permission from the Medical Library Association.

place for the results of research to be used in patient care. While much has been written about the slow pace with which research is translated into practice, caution must be exercised to avoid exposing patients to therapies whose effectiveness has not been established or whose side effects not fully explored.

In LIS practice, applying evidence obtained from systematic reviews requires an organizational culture that values research and provides incentives and opportunities to practice the basics of EBP. The lack of easily accessible evidence tools and the relatively small research base in LIS contrasts with clinical medicine and creates additional challenges for creating a culture of EBP.

Two recent initiatives have attempted to address this problem. EBLIP advocates conducted Delphi studies in North America and Sweden and developed a research agenda whose objective is to create an evidence base for LIS practice by encouraging a collaborative community of EBP LIS professionals willing to address each of the research questions. This community of practice would undertake both basic research and systematic reviews of existing research to augment the current evidence base supporting LIS practice.[30]

Another approach advocates building an "evidence base" that can support data-driven decisions. Nicholson proposed aggregating data from multiple sources into a data warehouse that can be used to explore patterns in the data.[31] While such an approach might lead to "fishing expeditions," current advances and refinements in data mining techniques are promising. An advantage of using

data is that they reflect the "real world" in all its diversity, rather than an "artificial" or "ideal" world created as part of a research study. This approach—referred to as practice-based evidence—contrasts with EBP and has only very recently been considered. The Association for Research Libraries' LibQUAL+ suite of services to solicit, track, understand, and act upon users' opinions of service quality that can be adapted locally may be regarded as an example of practice-based evidence because it uses a systematic approach to data collection and analysis.[32] Comparing the evidence to the local situation on variables such as user population, budget and funding source, circulation, collection size and characteristics, as well as overall mission and values can help the practitioner assess whether the outcomes presented in the evidence are comparable to the local context and therefore applicable to the problem under consideration.[33]

Fig. 1 lists examples of LIS research that exemplify evidence-based approaches to solving problems of library and information practice.[34] To encourage additional work along these lines, EBP researchers and advocates have written extensively on the transfer of research to practice, and the EBLIP literature contains numerous articles that provide practical suggestions for implementing EBP.[33–39]

Evaluate the Effect

The final step in EBP is evaluation, which includes an assessment of the effort itself and using that assessment in future planning. In this regard, EBLIP benefits from and uses typical evaluation and assessment techniques. Among them are performance and output measures, quality improvement, audit and feedback, benchmarking, and other performance indicators, to name just a few. Some advocates for EBP have noted that Schön's notion of reflective practice is particularly compatible with the spirit of inquiry implied by the term "reflective practitioner."[40,41] Through reflective practice, EBLIP professionals engage in a cycle of inquiry, evaluation, reflection, and renewed inquiry that suggests the initial character of EBM—conscientious and judicious, as well as scientific, practice.

SUMMARY

EBLIP is an approach to professional work in which scientific evidence provides the basis for systematic problem-solving. EBLIP encourages both the conduct and the application of practical research in order to improve information practice.

REFERENCES

1. Evidence-Based Library and Information Practice is at https://ejournals.library.ualberta.ca/index.php/EBLIP/ (accessed January 11, 2017).
2. Booth, A.; Brice, A. *Evidence-Based Practice for Information Professionals: A Handbook*; Facet Publishing: London, U.K., 2004.
3. Covell, D.G.; Uman, G.C.; Manning, P.R. Information needs in office practice: Are they being met? Ann. Intern. Med. **1985**, *103* (4), 596–599. [CrossRef], [PubMed], [Web of Science®].
4. Sackett, D.L.; Rosenberg, W.M.; Gray, J.A.; Haynes, R.B.; Richardson, W.S. Evidence based medicine: What it is and what it isn't. Br. Med. J. **1996**, *312* (7023), 71–72. [CrossRef], [PubMed], [Web of Science®], [CSA].
5. Upshur, R.E. Looking for rules in a world of exceptions: Reflections on evidence-based practice. Perspect. Biol. Med. **2005**, *48* (4), 477–489.
6. Miles, A.; Loughlin, M. Continuing the evidence-based health care debate in 2006: The progress and price of EBM. J. Eval. Clin. Pract. **2006**, *12* (4), 385–398.
7. Genoni, P.; Haddow, G.; Ritchie, A. Why don't librarians use research?. In *Evidence-Based Practice for Information Professionals: A Handbook*; Booth, A., Brice, A., Eds.; Facet Publishing: London, U.K., 2004; 49–60.
8. Using Scientific Evidence to Improve Information Practice. The Research Policy Statement of the Medical Library Association; Medical Library Association: Chicago, IL, 1995; file:///C:/Users/pwd28/Downloads/1995_mla_research_policy_statement.pdf (accessed January 13, 2017).
9. The Research Imperative: The Research Policy Statement of the Medical Library Association. file:///C:/Users/pwd28/Downloads/2007_mla_research_imperative_full.pdf (accessed January 13, 2017).
10. Ely, J.W.; Osheroff, J.A.; Gorman, P.N.; Ebell, M.H.; Chambliss, M.L.; Pifer, E.A.; Stavri, P.Z. A taxonomy of generic clinical questions: Classification study. Br. Med. J. **2000**, *321* (7258), 429–432. [CrossRef], [PubMed], [Web of Science®], [CSA].
11. Booth, A. Formulating answerable questions. In *Evidence-Based Practice for Information Professionals: A Handbook*; Booth, A., Brice, A., Eds.; Facet Publishing: London, U.K., 2004; 65–66.
12. Crumley, E.; Koufogiannakis, D. Developing evidence-based librarianship: Practical steps for implementation. Health Inform. Lib. J. **2002**, *19*, 61–70. [CrossRef], [PubMed], [CSA].
13. Eldredge, J. Evidence-based librarianship: Levels of evidence. Hypothesis **2002**, *16* (3), 10–13.
14. Kuller, A.B.; Wessel, C.B.; Ginn, D.S.; Martin, T.P. Quality filtering of the clinical literature by librarians and physicians. Bull. Med. Libr. Assoc. **1993**, *81* (1), 38–43. [CSA].
15. Scherrer, C.S.; Dorsch, J.L. The evolving role of the librarian in evidence-based medicine. Bull. Med. Libr. Assoc. **1999**, *87* (3), 322–328. [PubMed], [CSA].
16. Wilczynski, N.L.; Morgan, D.; Haynes, R.B. Hedges team an overview of the design and methods for retrieving high-quality studies for clinical care. BMC Med. Infor. Decis. Making **2005**, *21*, 5–20.
17. Beverley, C. Searching the library and information science literature. In *Evidence-Based Practice for Information Professionals: A Handbook*; Booth, A., Brice, A., Eds.; Facet Publishing: London, U.K., 2004; 89–103.
18. Bayley, L.; Eldredge, J.D. The structured abstract: An essential tool for researchers. Hypothesis **2003**, *17* (1), 11–14.
19. West, S.; King, V.; Carey, T.S. Systems to rate the strength of scientific evidence: Summary. AHRQ Evidence Report Summaries **2002**. https://www.ncbi.nlm.nih.gov/books/NBK11930/ (accessed January 13, 2017).
20. The Cochrane Collaboration. http://www.cochrane.org (accessed January 11, 2017).
21. Glynn, L. A critical appraisal tool for library and information research. Libr. Hi Tech. **2006**, *24* (3), 387–399. [CrossRef].
22. Campbell Collaboration. https://www.campbellcollaboration.org/ (accessed January 11, 2017).
23. Trahan, E. Applying meta-analysis to library and information science research. Libr. Quart. **1993**, *63* (1), 73–91.
24. Chen, C.; Rada, R. Interacting with hypertext: A meta-analysis of experimental studies. Hum. Comput. Interact **1996**, *11* (2), 125–156. [Taylor & Francis Online], [Web of Science®], [CSA].
25. Saxton, M.L. Meta-analysis in library and information science: Method, history and recommendations for reporting research. Libr. Trends **2006**, *55* (1), 158–170.
26. Koufogiannakis, D.; Wiebe, N. Effective methods for teaching information literacy skills to undergraduate students: A systematic review and meta-analysis. Evid. Based Libr. Inform. Pract. **2006**, *1* (3), 3–43. http://ejournals.library.ualberta.ca/index.php/EBLIP/article/view/76/153 (accessed September 17, 2007).
27. Light, R.J.; Pillemer, D.B. *Summing Up: The Science of Reviewing Research*; Harvard University Press: Cambridge, MA, 1984.
28. Urquhart, C. Meta-synthesis with information behavior research. In *New Directions in Information Behaviour*

(Library and Information Science); Spink, A., Heinström, J., Eds.; Emerald Group Publishing Ltd. **2011**, *1*, 37–66.

29. Ke, Q.; Cheng, Y. Applications of meta-analysis to library and information science research: Content analysis. Libr. Info. Sci. Res. **2015**, *37* (4), 370–382. http://dx.doi.org/10.1016/j.lisr. 2015.05.004 (accessed December 8, 2015).

30. Eldredge, J.D.; Holmes, H.N.; Ascher, M.T. Moving the EBLIP community's research agenda forward. Evid. Based Libr. Inf. Pract. *10* (2), 170–173. June 2015. ISSN 1715-720X. Available at: https://ejournals.library.ualberta.ca/index.php/EBLIP/article/view/24336/18409. (accessed December 7, 2015.

31. Nicholson, S. Approaching librarianship from the data; using bibliomining for evidence-based librarianship. Libr. Hi Tech. **2006**, *24* (3), 369–375.

32. LIBQUAL+, a program of the Association of Research Libraries is at: https://www.libqual.org/home (accessed January 11, 2017).

33. Dalrymple, P.W. The application of systematic research. In *Administration and Management in Health Sciences Libraries*; Forsman, R.B., Ed.; Medical Library Association and Scarecrow Press: Lanham, MD, 2000; *8*, 173–194. Current Practice in Health Sciences Librarianship.

34. Perryman, C.; Marshall, J. The Research Imperative: The Research Policy Statement of the Medical Library Association. Appendix 2 Selected Bibliography: Evidence-based Librarianship. file:///C:/Users/pwd28/Downloads/2007_mla_research_imperative_full.pdf (accessed January 13, 2017).

35. Lakos, A.; Phipps, S.E. Creating a culture of assessment: A catalyst for organizational change. Portal Libr. Acad. **2004**, *4* (3), 345–361. http://muse.jhu.edu/login?uri=/journals/portal_libraries_and_the_academy/v004/4.3lakos (accessed September 19, 2007) [CrossRef], [Web of Science®].

36. Glynn, L. The current state of EBL. Evid. Based Libr. Inform. Pract. **2006**, *1* (2), 1–2. http://ejournals.library.ualberta.ca/index.php/EBLIP/article/view/64/126 (accessed September 19, 2007).

37. Plutchak, T.S. Building a body of evidence. J. Med. Libr. Assoc. **2005**, *93* (2), 193–195.

38. Haddow, G.; Klobas, J.E. Communication of research to practice in library and information science: Closing the gap. Libr. Inform. Sci. Res. **2004**, *26* (1), 29–43. [CrossRef]C.

39. Urquhart, C.; Brice, A.; Cooper, J.; Spink, S.; Thomas, T. The development of virtual communities of practice that support evidence based practice. Evid. Based Libr. Inform. Pract. **2010**, *5* (1), 48–63.

40. Schön, D.A. *The Reflective Practitioner: How Professionals Think in Action*; Basic Books: New York, 1983.

41. Grant, M.J. The role of reflection in the library and information sector: A systematic review. Health Inform. Libr. J. **2007**, *24* (3), 155–166.

Exhibition Design

Lee H. Skolnick
Dan Marwit
Jo Ann Secor
Lee H. Skolnick Architecture + Design Partnership, New York, New York, U.S.A.

Abstract

Exhibition design, sometimes called exhibit design, is the conceptualizing, planning, and creating of exhibitions—built, spatial environments that communicate with audiences moving through them. As a field of practice, exhibition design has only recently begun gaining definition and standards. Meanwhile, it is flourishing worldwide, as exposition attendance soars, retail environments reinvent themselves, and cultural institutions increasingly appeal to tourism and promote themselves as centers of entertainment, as well as education. Bringing together a constellation of disciplines, exhibitions are designed by teams working through a phased process that translates a script into an immersive experience. Audiences engaging with the experiences interpret them through interactions with their elements, including their architecture, colors, lighting, graphics, artifacts, and media. Design teams continually develop understandings of their audiences as they plan and arrange exhibitions' elements in context. As exhibition design expands in the beginning of the twenty-first century, it turns up new challenges, but as with all design fields, exhibition design views challenges as opportunities.

INTRODUCTION

Exhibition design, sometimes called exhibit design, is the conceptualizing, planning, and creating of exhibitions—built, spatial environments that communicate with audiences moving through them. Broadly, any exhibition can be categorized as either cultural or commercial, but more commonalities than differences are shared across this border. Really it is the permutation of many particularities, including content, intention, size, setting, duration, expected audience, and experience type that determine what an exhibition can be and how it gets designed.

In the world of museums, there are those that use artifacts, archival images, and text to document events for visitors with preexisting knowledge, and those that engage wide audiences in explorations of phenomena, ideas, and themes through interactivity and play. Among visitor centers, many attract year-round tourism to civic icons, while others showcase corporate accomplishments to employees and invited guests only. From trade shows to international expos, independent environments compete on the same floor for the attention of industry associates or the general public, whose interests in a new product, brand, or philosophy can translate into investment. Any of these exhibitions can be open for a matter of days or decades, and designing them requires attending to their distinct natures appropriately.

All exhibitions are designed by teams. To be sure, the exhibition designer's contribution is the core of the work, as the final product is inevitably a physical environment that functions and directs people in intended ways.

However, in order to create a total design, subteams, who together determine the story that guides the design, give the design its shape and tone, plan and create vital elements, and build and install the actual components.

Because the field of exhibition design is quite young, few exhibition designers, or design team members for that matter, have come to their titles through a course of exhibition design study. Rather, most approached the field through one of several avenues: designers through architecture, industrial design, commercial package design, and furniture design; and other team members through education, anthropology, and creative writing. Each of these has some bearing in exhibition design, but also requires designers and team members to think beyond their fields and work cooperatively, as none address all of an exhibition's needs.

Like all processes, the exhibition design process follows a sequence of phases, moving from concept design to schematic design, into design development, and finally fabrication documents and fabrication and installation. Each of these phases, often referred to differently by different designers, can be further delineated into smaller steps, and are typically completed in a reiterative fashion. Culminating in the production of documents that signify milestones and transitions, the phases keep team members working toward common goals in a shared time frame, and enable ongoing assessment of a project's progress that is captured and presented. A truer exploration of exhibition design would require quite a bit more space, and a few exceptional books have been written for that purpose, including David Dernie's *Exhibition Design*, Larry

Encyclopedia of Library and Information Sciences, Fourth Edition DOI: 10.1081/E-ELIS4-120044031

Klein's *Exhibits: Planning and Design*, Kathleen McLean's *Planning for People in Museum Exhibitions*, and Jan Lorenc, Lee Skolnick, and Craig Berger's *What Is Exhibition Design?* Also, because the field is one that is constantly reinventing itself, a richer understanding of exhibition design can be had with some continual study. Periodicals, like *Exhibitor* and *Exhibitionist* would encourage this, as would attendance at conferences, like the annual American Association of Museums conference. Finally, the best way to discover the burgeoning field of exhibition design is to visit exhibitions. Each one is so different from the next that comparisons made between them would awaken any curious person to the craft invested in them.

A last note: The background shared by the writers is mostly of cultural exhibition design in American settings. Much has been done to reach outside this limited scope, but the history of exhibition design in Europe, and the excitingly expanding field in both Europe and Asia are topics that easily warrant entire articles all their own. Exhibition design has unquestionably become a worldwide phenomenon, and its ubiquitous trends are reaching into other fields everywhere. While this entry is reliable in its overview of exhibition design, there is much more to explore, and readers are enthusiastically encouraged to do so.

HISTORY

The origins of exhibition design are at once self-evident and evasive. Humans naturally arrange objects for the communication of particular statements. We do it in our homes and other environments. Arguably, creating exhibitions is innate, and people have been doing it since the day they realized they could manipulate their surroundings.[1]

European Roots

Appearing in biblical passages and Roman history, trade fairs are as ancient as trade, itself, but trade fair exhibitions as they appear today have their roots in European history, as do exhibitions in museums.[2,3] The first of the known major fairs, which has continued since at least 1165, was the *Leipziger Messe* in Leipzig, Germany.[4] Meanwhile, the origins of museums has been traced to the European Age of Enlightenment, when proponents of the Age's interest in making sense of the world, cultivated the first natural history collections in *wunderkammern*, or *cabinets of curiosity*.[5] Essentially the province of royalty and the Church, several *wunderkammern* grew into renowned institutions, the *Modern Museums of Copenhagen* and the *Louvre* among them.[6,7] While most *wunderkammern*, overflowing with collectibles and exotic rarities, were meant to impress onlookers with their owner's prestige, a number showed early signs of design,

like thematically arranged floor plans and inclusion of interpretive text.[8,9]

Transition to Planned Experiences

In 1786, Charles Willson Peale brought museums to the public, opening *Peale's American Museum* in Philadelphia, PA.[10] While Peale's museum set a new precedent for curation, that of collecting and displaying culturally representative objects for the benefit of its visitors, its displays followed from the *wunderkammern*, voluminous, and somewhat indiscriminate. This style would hold sway until the *Museum of Modern Art* in New York shifted the paradigm in the 1940s with minimally displayed arrangements of "empathetic" pieces.[1]

Meanwhile, in the commercial sphere, exhibition design took a leap forward in 1851 with *The Great Exhibition of the Works of Industry of All Nations*.[11] Planned by Prince Albert and Henry Cole of England, the *Great Exhibition* was the first truly international exhibition. Bringing 13,000 exhibitors and 6,000,000 visitors together under the roof of Joseph Paxton's *Crystal Palace*, the *Great Exhibition* set the standard for future expositions, and led to the formation of formal oversight organizations, like the *Bureau International des Expositions*. In the coming years, expos grew increasingly impressive, with permanent structures designed by reputable engineers and architects, including the *Eiffel Tower* by Gustave Eiffel for the 1889 *Universal Exhibition*, the current *Museum of Science and Industry* for the 1893 *World's Columbian Exposition* in Chicago, and the *German Pavillion* by Ludwig Mies van der Rohe for the 1929 *Barcelona International Exposition*.[12–14] Also in the nineteenth century's latter half, department stores began appearing worldwide. Their competition for an emerging spending culture led them to install exhibitions of power and branding in their entrances and main floors.[15] *Wanamakers* in Philadelphia built a *Grand Court* with a commanding bald eagle as its dome.

Toward a Contemporary Vision

In 1939, expositions moved into a new era. With the *New York World's Fair's* theme *Tomorrow's World*, expos began addressing humanity and cultural issues, rather than technology and inventions.[16] Amusement rides and stage set architecture set the scene for designers to begin creating entire environments at fairs, one more exciting than the last. Following this course, the 1964 New York World's Fair marked a seminal moment with 140 full pavilions, four designed by the Walt Disney Corporation, and one by Charles and Ray Eames. Disney, equipped with a team of *Imagineers* and a list of *Mickey's Ten Commandments*, had by this time opened Disneyland in California, 1955.[17] The Eames team, with their chairs that both broke and set the mold, had already opened a number of exhibitions, including the *American Pavilion* in Moscow, 1959, and *Mathematica* in 1961, which remained open at the Los Angeles Museum of Science and Industry until 1998, and has since been duplicated at several institutions.[18]

Also at this time, many larger American institutions, like the National Museum of American History and the Field Museum of Natural History, created exhibition planning departments, shifting power away from curators. These departments created *blockbuster* exhibitions, like the Field's *Tut*, that drew enormous crowds and set a new pace for museum exhibition design. In this atmosphere, museums began rethinking the purpose of exhibitions and the structures of the departments responsible for them. Michael Spock of the field museum advocated for including into design teams educators and content developers who could translate scholarship into stories for general audiences. Frank Oppenheimer of the Exploratorium in San Francisco challenged the nature of museum exhibitions altogether, populating them with interactive experiences from which visitors derived their own interpretations. A series of workshops at the Field in 1982, sponsored by the W. K. Kellogg Foundation demonstrated the effectiveness of a team approach to designing museum exhibitions, an approach that has been adopted and adapted by museums far and wide.[19]

Today, at the onset of a new century, fairs, trade shows, and expos around the world draw attendance rates rivaling those of the Olympic Games.[20] Museums and visitor centers find themselves competing for expanding tourism and audiences looking for entertainment as much as education.[21] Design firms are increasingly contracted to plan both cultural and commercial exhibitions, and the resulting cross-pollination is benefiting both arenas.[22] Undoubtedly, exhibition design is flourishing, and work by firms in Japan, Korea, and other Asian nations is inspiring exciting movement worldwide.[22]

ELEMENTS

All exhibitions are compositions of space, architectural elements, materials, graphics, color, lighting, and acoustics. Most also include objects, artifacts and images, and increasingly media components. The available variety of materials and methods is remarkably vast, and expanding rapidly with technological advances. The possible uses of them in shaping immersive, transcendent experiences for visitors are as many as the needs of each individual exhibition, and those needs are governed by the exhibition's narrative and context.[23]

Narrative

The narrative, also variably known as the script, messaging, or storyline, is in plain terms what the exhibition is about. It is developed from a body of knowledge, a corporate philosophy, a set of ideas, concepts or messages or a promotion of a brand, and subsequently completed with additional research as necessary. Structuring the information to be presented in the exhibition, the narrative also suggests how the information should be accessed and interpreted. Thus, it sets the foundation for decisions about how the environment will communicate with its visitors.[24]

Context: Physical and Cultural

An exhibition set inside a building not yet constructed, allows opportunities to work with an architect in tailoring important features to the exhibition's needs. These can include circulation, ceiling heights, natural lighting, and access to mechanical, electrical, and plumbing systems. However, more often designers plan exhibitions for existing buildings, working either with or around the context's features.[23] Meanwhile, the situation of an exhibition in a surrounding culture determines who might attend it, and how it might be interpreted by attendees, as well as by press outlets, schools, various communities, and other groups. Depending on its reach, an exhibition's cultural context can require wrestling with every detail of its narrative and design, especially in the handling of controversial topics.

Space

Space is the volumetric area that the exhibition organizes and thematically conditions. It is usually contained by structural walls, a floor and a ceiling within an interior, or imaginarily assigned within a larger interior, as with the space designated to a trade show booth. An exhibition can also be outside, but its space is still limited and its organization is still in the designer's hands. To organize space, designers consider aesthetic and experiential properties, including scale, proportion and balance, site line, and visitor flow, among others. All together, these properties choreograph the positioning of exhibition elements in relationship to one another.[25]

Architectural Elements

Architectural elements are those that are constructed to define the exhibition's space and display its feature elements. Walls built to partition spaces, ramps pitched to steer visitor flow, platforms created to elevate experiences, and built forms inserted for interpretive effect are just a few examples. In interactive exhibitions, these elements also serve a second purpose of housing and protecting mechanics and audio/visual and computer equipment. Furniture built for comfort or as part of an experience, and cases that contain collection items or display products are also architectural elements that have design qualities all their own, and whose appearance in the space further defines it.

Materials: Construction and Finishes

Materials are used to build the exhibition's architecture, enable the mounting and presentation of other elements, and evoke particular associations and sensations. Construction materials, often hidden from view, are usually generic, like wood, steel, drywall, and fiberboard. Finishes are materials that exhibition visitors see, or that support the other elements that visitors see, like affixed graphics and painted colors. Traditionally, these materials have been finished woods and different grades of glass, as in the display cases of object-based exhibitions.[26] Recently, technological advances have opened an expansive repertoire of materials to designers, including ranges of new metals, plastics, and laminates, making it easier to evoke emotions and interpret information and themes through shape and texture. New materials also aid in placing graphics and colors in desired locations, as their properties make them lightweight and receptive to paint and adhesives.[27]

Graphics

Graphics are two-dimensional designs applied to surfaces. In some instances, they are painted directly onto finishes. More often, they are created with computer software, printed on substrates with adhesive backings, and applied to surfaces prior to their installation. Featuring text, diagrams, and images, graphics are used to deliver information and suggest context. Composed of typefaces, color palettes, patterns, and illustrations, graphics are also used to set an exhibition's tone, and unify its interpretive and navigational systems. As computer and printing technology advances, graphics are increasingly designed to cover large exhibition surfaces, like entire walls, floors, and ceilings.[28,29]

Color, Lighting, and Acoustics

Color, lighting, and acoustics can be grouped together as environmentally interpretive tools. They are often the most effective tools in transporting visitors to believable places, or immersing them in convincing ideas. Colors conjure emotions and psychological associations, especially in juxtaposition or cooperation with one another. Lighting both makes things visible and sets a range of moods. Acoustics control sound, dampening it in some places, and allowing it to escalate in others. Together, these elements make a richly interpretive exhibition experience possible, and also strongly influence its feeling.[30]

Objects, Artifacts, and Images

Objects, artifacts, and images are often a client or institution's reason for creating an exhibition, in the first place. In many cases, the display of one or more of these elements is intended to create a brand by which an institution or business becomes known to the public. They can be small enough to require a microscope, or large enough to fit groups of people inside; sensitive enough to warrant controlled conditions, or best experienced through touch and manipulation. Exhibition designers create environments that both highlight these elements as attractions and storytelling elements, and protect them as necessary.

Media

Media in exhibitions commonly refers to on-screen media, which includes film, video, and interactive virtual experiences. Increasingly, media is becoming a standard expectation. A handful of exhibitions have even been designed with media as their central themes, or with media pieces serving as pinnacle experiences. Media has become highly sophisticated, able to respond to users in surprising ways, and to perform ever more complex functions. Fully immersive media experiences are now not only possible, but are even becoming commonplace. Balancing these powerful experiences with the rest of an exhibition has become an important challenge for designers.

PROCESS

From start to finish, the creation of an exhibition can take several weeks to several years, depending on its size and the complications of its content, context, and physical requirements. Certainly, every designer has his or her own approach to bringing an exhibition from nonexistent to open to the public, but all create through a process that advances through a series of work phases.[31] Referring to the phases, designers often use different terminology, but commonly they are known in sequence as concept, schematic, design development, fabrication documents, and fabrication and installation.

From here, the process appears step-by-step and direct. However, the progression of an exhibition's design is rarely so simple and linear. Rather, designers work in what is called a reiterative fashion, meaning that within each phase iterations of designs are completed, reviewed, and revised until satisfactory. On a macro level, whole phases can be reiterated until complete; on a micro level, single drawings or written descriptions can cycle in their own reiterative processes. Further emphasizing the process' reiterative direction, exhibition designers typically allow for returns to previous process phases either to complete unfinished steps, or to revise designs as new information and insights emerge. In mapping a process at a project's outset, designers try to plan ahead for these motions, doing their best to keep to schedule and within budget.

Throughout the exhibition design process, a succession of document sets, or packages is produced. Each set signifies a benchmark, simultaneously presenting the culmination of the designer's work up to that point, and establishing the new foundation from which the work will continue. Titled after the process phases they complete, the document sets are typically known as concept, schematic, design development, and fabrication documents. In the fabrication and installation phase, there are no benchmark documents, as the culmination of this phase is the opening of the exhibition itself.

Concept

The concept phase marks the initiation of an exhibition design project. Its primary goal is the establishment of the exhibition's foundations, and its principal work is characterized by research, brainstorming, and exploration. To determine what the exhibition will be about, initial research into its topic is conducted, structured into a hierarchy or framework, and developed into a preliminary script. The script determines the exhibition's perspective or approach to the topic, and with it in place, the exhibition's general look, feel, and function begin to bloom through a series of brainstorming sessions. From the sessions, designers make explorations, sketching architecture, and exhibit ideas that could appropriately translate the script into an experience.

The concept document set can include:

- Concept outline, exhibition criteria, preliminary script.
- Sketches or diagrams of the whole space and its components.
- Analyses of projected attendance and circulation.
- Initial rough budget projections.
- Preliminary schedule.
- Suggestions of graphic style, copy style, and object and artifact placements.
- Suggestions for marketing and outreach.

Schematic

During the schematic phase, the approved concept is used to create a preliminary design for the entire exhibition. The goal of the schematic phase is to identify the exhibition's components and make them imaginable, while leaving room for their details to be developed and debated. Extending from the preceding phase, script writing, brainstorming, and exploration continue until the concept is fully fleshed out, and a design for the entire exhibition can be proposed and discussed. Making this possible, designers begin seriously assessing the physical context in which the exhibition will be installed, as well as the host's resources for marketing, outreach, and staffing.

The schematic document set can include:

- Finished preliminary script.
- Revised project budget and schedule.

- Floor plans.
- Sketches of vignettes and component elevations.
- Foam core spatial models and mock-ups, or photographs of them.

Design Development

While the body of the exhibition has been made imaginable by the schematic designs, its details still need to be elaborated. The goal of the design development phase is to specify the exhibition's details. The thrust of the phase is in making definite choices about the tangible things that will compose the three-dimensional environment, including materials, colors, graphics, text, equipment, lighting schemes, A/V scripts, and computer software. The decision-based character of design development shifts the focus of the exhibition design process from imagining possibilities to making the chosen possibilities work.

The design development document set can include:

- Plan, elevation, and sectional drawings of all exhibition components.
- Written descriptions of all exhibition components.
- Preliminary *schedules*, lists of materials, graphics, A/V equipment, and hardware and descriptions of their uses.
- Updated project budget and schedule.

Fabrication Documents

In the fabrication documents phase, the decisions made in the design development phase are incorporated into a set of technical drawings and specifications. The goal of the fabrication documents phase is twofold: first, to produce documents so highly detailed that they can serve as instructions for fabricating the exhibition; second, to identify a fabricator. Every detail of the exhibition, down to its literal nuts and bolts, is specified, recorded in *schedules* and indicated in hard-line drawings. Once this is done, designers open a competitive bidding process, unless a trusted fabricator is already known. Designers also open bidding for other contractors, including media producers, graphics producers, and copywriters, if they have not yet been chosen.

The fabrication document set can include:

- Hard-line, dimensioned plan, elevation, section, and "exploded" drawings of every exhibition component with close-ups of important details and specifications of materials and hardware.
- Finalized *schedules*.
- Plans for lighting, electricity, A/V connections, mechanics, and plumbing.
- Final project budget and schedule.

Fabrication and Installation

The final phase, fabrication and installation, takes the exhibition from drawing and study to actuality. The goal of this phase is a successful opening, and to get there takes meticulous decisions on behalf of clients. First, the fabrication drawings are delivered to the chosen fabricator. The fabricator reviews them and returns them as *shop drawings* with suggestions of necessary, and sometimes creative revisions. The designer then reviews the revisions, and either approves them or makes further suggestions. This back and forth shuttling continues until the fabricator is confident he or she can build precisely what the designer wants. Ensuring the fabrication meets the design's intents, the designer makes frequent visits to the fabricator's shop during this phase, as well as to the studios of other contractors. Present at the exhibition's installation, designers watch over details to the very end.

No documents are delivered during the fabrication and installation phase. The culmination of the phase is the exhibition's opening.

UNDERSTANDING AUDIENCE

Throughout the process, designers strive to understand their audience as best they can, and get ideas from them about how to better the exhibition's design.[32] To reiterate the point: Any exhibition is a medium for communication. Its very purpose for being built rests on the fact that people will visit it.[33] Who those people are— children, adults, scholars, the general public, etc.—determines the verbal, visual, and experiential language most appropriate for the dialog.[34–36] Cultivating an understanding of the audience not only encourages an exhibition's success, it recognizes its responsibility. To this end, many designers conduct formal studies of their audiences at different phases of the process. Often, contracted evaluators are hired to perform these studies more systematically and objectively.[37]

Initial Understanding: Front-End

During the concept phase, or even prior to it, many designers conduct *front-end evaluations*. Learning what an audience already knows and feels about an exhibition's topic can help set the parameters of its script and influence its possible presentation and tone. Considering an audience's abilities and learning styles helps produce exhibits that are suitable for them. Certainly, fair generalizations about an exhibition's intended audience can be made with demographics, learning theories, and past precedents, but many designers prefer to "meet" their audiences, or representatives thereof, through formal studies, such as questionnaires, focus groups, and interviews.

Informed Understanding: Formative

Arguably, the most useful evaluation, *formative evaluation*, can be conducted in the schematic design phase, when it becomes possible to gauge audience reactions accurately before moving into the latter decision-making phases.[38] By providing them with drawings, designers can ask evaluation participants direct questions about a fairly imaginable exhibition. By presenting them with foam-core mock-ups, designers can observe participants' interactions with their designs, often adjusting the mock-ups to test various possibilities. Follow-up interviews and questionnaires provide insights into what audiences are deriving from their experiences. Results and recommendations from these tests are used to finalize schematic plans and prepare for making determined design decisions in the next phase.

Specific Understanding: Prototyping

During the design development phase, concerns about the operations of particular exhibit components arise. Because the level of detail is so specific in this phase, it becomes possible to build full-scale *prototypes* of these components. If the budget allows, designers can try variations of actual materials and mechanics until the component works exactly as intended. Including audiences in prototype testing can be extremely informative, as very reliable observations can be made from their engagements with and reactions to the exhibition.

Final Understanding: Summative

No better reaction to an exhibition can be gauged than that of an actual audience in the actual space. Often, designers add a postopening phase to the exhibition design process during which modifications can be made to exhibit components that for all their planning do not result as intended. Formal studies of audiences during this phase, known as *summative evaluations*, time and observe interactions and behaviors, and gather audience responses through interviews. The findings of these studies can often point to simple solutions to apparent issues, or lessons for the next project.

DESIGNERS AND DESIGN TEAMS

Because by their nature, exhibitions are cross-disciplinary experiences, they are designed by teams. Depending on the size of the exhibition, teams can be comprised of individuals, or entire departments. In many cases, coordination of the players' contributions, and assurance of their mutual understanding of a shared process are as crucial for a project's success as any individual's talent.

The assembling of a team can be the task of a lead team member, or a manager who serves a more supervisory role. In most design firms and museum exhibition departments, team members are chosen from full-time staff. Meanwhile, it is not uncommon for firms and departments to complete teams by hiring freelance workers. In some cases, teams are formed solely for the project at hand. In still other cases, teams can include a core team surrounded by peripheral ones, made up of hired experts, volunteer advisors, interested community members, and so on. In any instance, when assembling a team, the goal is to select compatible team members, whose talents and interests match the needs of the exhibition, some of which will unfold as the project develops.[39,40]

Making decisions together, and communicating in general, are critical tasks for exhibition design teams, especially those working on large projects that take years to complete. Many models exist for structuring teams and enabling their collective efforts.[41] They range on a spectrum from linear hierarchies, with one chief decision maker, to egalitarian committees that strive for consensus.

Similar to teams working in other fields of design and communications media, exhibition design teams generally divide their responsibilities into at least two sides (not a technical term, but one commonly used), one to handle the development of the story, *content*, and the other to handle its telling, *design*. Often, teams also include a third side, *project management*, to coordinate the actions of the whole team and supervise the production of the entire project.

Within their sides, individual team members work toward common goals, but it is through the collaboration between sides that an exhibition is fully designed. Both content and design bring their work to the table, and management ensures that the story and its telling remain within the project's feasibility. Thus, some permeability between sides is usually important for best practice. A team whose members respect each other's roles, but can think in each other's terms is the most likely to succeed with greatest ease.

Content Team

Responsible for the story itself, team members on the content side can include curators, educators, exhibit developers, interpretive planners, content developers, content coordinators, researchers, and writers. Collectively, their role is to cultivate the ideas, topics, and information to be conveyed in the exhibition, and articulate them in a manner that visitors will be able to grasp. The process of doing so typically follows a reiterative course of accumulating, editing and arranging knowledge that relies on research, organization, analysis, association, and story-writing skills.

In the design of exhibitions that are rich in objects and artifacts, content team members also maintain knowledge of available collections and external sources. Sometimes, entire stories are constructed around the showing of a single item. Other times, it is through categorizing items and selecting the most totemic ones that a story emerges. Knowing what is obtainable, and understanding how the inclusion and omission of particular objects and artifacts will affect a story is the job of content team members.

Once a compelling story has been developed, the collective role of content team members becomes that of ensuring that the design expresses it, and that the expression is appropriate to the intended visitors. Often, this calls for responses to evaluation findings, and additional research and development to inform the details of the story as its translation manifests.

Design Team

Determining how to tell the story, the design side of the team can comprise a variety of designers from various disciplines, including graphics, media, lighting, and acoustics, all of whose work is coordinated by a lead exhibit designer, typically also supervising the efforts of junior exhibit designers. Oftentimes, draftspeople, model makers, illustrators, and other talents are added to the design side to aid its diverse disciplines. All together, design team members give the exhibition dimensionality that people can enter, navigate, use, and share.

Beginning with rough sketches, designers' transition to drawings, and finally hard-line drawings as they reiteratively conceptualize, plan, and detail the visual and experiential communication of the content. Inevitably, the act of drawing reveals problems in the exhibition's functionality and challenges to its proper expressions. Solving these problems is part of designing exhibits, and doing so often requires invention. Most designers welcome such detours, viewing their pursuit as opportunities to make their designs unique and successful.

As the exhibition develops, the various designers' work affects each other. Graphics influence the exhibition's look, light reflects on graphic surfaces in unexpected ways, audio from media transforms acoustic spaces. Meanwhile, each of the design contributions carries material concerns. Lighting grids need to be suspended and electrically wired, graphics need substrates that adhere to surfaces, and acoustics call for very specific finishes. Each of these is researched, sized, and specified by the design side, and the responsibility for all of it fitting together, both conceptually and tangibly, resides with design team members.

Project Management Side

Responsible for the exhibition's opening on time and within budget, the management side of the team usually includes one project manager. Typically the liaison between the team and the project's client, the project manager drafts a scope and a schedule and budget for its completion, and communicates progress, delays, and changes between parties. Because the project manager remains aware of time, money, and the client's concerns, design teams frequently look to him or her to remind them of parameters on their creativity. While this can be a politically sensitive position, it is a critical one. Not only does it help the team accomplish the job properly, but it also protects team members from investing beyond the project's bounds, keeping them from overworking and making sure they'll be available when needed for the next project.

Because bringing an exhibition to its fruition involves the weaving together of so many efforts over time, coordination is the project manager's principal and constant task.[42] With the many team members working independently on their ends of the project, the project manager resides at the center, keeping everyone apprised of each other's progress, and helping maintain the team's camaraderie and morale. At times, this can require great tact, as any one team member's progress can easily influence changes, or even pose difficulties in that of another.

CONCLUSION: CONTEMPORARY TRENDS AND CHALLENGES

The current state of exhibition design is an effervescent one. Still relatively young, and certainly younger than the museums and expos it services, its movement toward becoming a formalized field has accelerated in recent years, but its standards of practice have yet to be codified. Only a handful of design schools teach it as a subject, and only in rare instances is it offered as a full course or major.[43–45] Professionals of various types are filling its positions, and their writings about their own experiences are some of the first. Meanwhile, exhibition design is growing by leaps and bounds, and gaining momentum around the world, as cultural institutions, corporations, businesses, public awareness campaigns, city governments, and more call upon the unique mode of communication that only exhibitions can offer.

The Next Big Way to Present the Next Big Thing

Over the last few decades, attendance rates at international expos have skyrocketed into the tens of millions. Meanwhile, casinos like New York, New York, and retail chains like Apple, Niketown, and IKEA have realized the power of reshaping their stores into total, experiential environments.[46] In both arenas, the goal of communication is to present the next big thing, be it a product, brand, lifestyle, or philosophy. Competition in the commercial sphere has become intense and fast-paced, and designers are constantly looking for the next big way to present the next big thing. As a result, in many ways, commercial exhibition design has become a proving ground for many new technologies, materials, and strategies.[47]

More and more frequently, these new technologies, materials, and strategies are also being incorporated into cultural exhibition design. One possible reason is that most exhibition design firms work in both arenas, often supplementing their abilities in the cultural sphere with earnings from the commercial sphere. Another is the recently emergent phenomenon of in-house teams collaborating with contracted designers, who give shape to expertly researched content in institutions whose staff knows the audience quite well.

New Perspectives of Interpretation

In years past, knowing an audience was less valued by cultural institutions who viewed themselves as having a more authoritative role. The shift toward gauging visitor expectations and interests, often through focus groups, surveys, and other tools familiar to the commercial sector, is a recent one that is swiftly setting a new paradigm. Responding to visitors, cultural institutions have learned how to maintain and expand their public reach. Enabling this response, designers increasingly plan exhibitions that are more able to communicate with particular audiences. To do so, many design teams have added educators to their talent and educational theory to their tool kits.[48] Not limited to cultural exhibitions, commercial designers have also begun to consider experiential learning, constructivism, multiple intelligence theory, theories of intrinsic motivation, and others as helpful guides in creating communicative environments.[49–52]

Universal Access

Along the same lines, a recent phenomenon is the requirement of planning for people with disabilities. While designers have always taken this into consideration, as one goal has always been to reach as many people as possible, allowing for universal access has in many places become enforceable by law. In the United States, title III, section 36.101 of the Americans with Disabilities Act (ADA) of 1990 "prohibits discrimination on the basis of disability... and requires places of public accommodation and commercial facilities to be designed...in compliance with the accessibility standards established" by the ADA.[53,54] As stated in explicit terms, exhibition designers, like the designers of any nonresidential facility, are now legally obligated to plan environments that do not exclude physically impaired people. The ramifications of this are enormous, as are the opportunities. On one hand a suite of new constraints are imposed; on the other hand, implementing standards like the ADA's positions designers to revolutionize communities by creating wholly inclusive environments.

New Narratives

The trend in museums to respond to visitors' interests has engendered the rise in popularity of issue-based exhibitions, made possible by a popular push away from object-based exhibitions and towards concept-based ones. As race, death, health, fear, and other conceptual explorations become crowd-draws for museums, exhibitions are changing shape to suit a very different genre of narrative. Designers increasingly plan environments that embody questions and journeys, rather than simply representations of topical times and places.[55]

New Technology

One undeniable force that has transformed exhibition design in just the last few years is digital technology and the hurrying pace of its advances. Computers are now small enough and powerful enough to easily be hidden from view, while providing incredibly rich experiences. Video and screen-based interactivity can deliver massive amounts of self-discovered information without consuming much space. The temptation to fill an exhibition with digital experiences is a pressing one for many designers, and often something close to that is requested by a client.

Meanwhile, computers' shrinking dimensions and escalating abilities are placing more of them in more people's homes and pockets, equipping people with rich experiences that require no environmental contexts. The need to create digital experiences that are unique, or more sophisticated than what is available to consumers, has become demanding for exhibition designers. Likewise, the challenge of designing real environments equally or more exciting than virtual ones has become an actual pressure.[56]

One emerging solution is the design of digital experiences that are integrated into exhibition environments.[57] As technologies like motion tracking and multitouch flat screens become more accessible, this solution has grown more viable. Another emerging solution is the invention of new technologies and varieties of interfaces. Speaking to both solutions, a new industry is burgeoning.[58–60] Digital designers contracting with exhibition designers are gaining popularity, often winning bids for jobs as collaborative teams.

New Technology Backstage

The influence of technology's innovations is also revolutionizing exhibition design behind the scenes. Software applications, like *Photoshop*, *Illustrator*, *AutoCAD*, *3D Studio Max*, *Sketch Up*, *Revit*, and *Vectorworks*, have nearly rendered obsolete traditional design tools, like compasses, shape palettes, drafting tables, and pencils. At the same time, the Internet has become an indispensable resource for content developers and researchers, as well as a location for idea-exchange forums hosted by design communities, like the Association of Science-Technology Center's *Exhibit Files* Web site and blog.[61] E-mail and FTP's have expedited communications between teams and clients, and also made it possible to easily collaborate across oceans. The effect of this sweeping change of tools is not only immeasurable, but also hardly complete.

Accounting for Sustainability

All exhibitions are made of materials whose processing and transportation extracts natural resources and emits greenhouse gasses.[23,62] Lighting, video projections, and other electrically powered elements drain large amounts of energy and produce pollution when sources of power are fossil-fuel-burning power plants. Publicly supported regulations and institutions like the World Green Building Council are setting standards for designers to follow, and making those standards achievable by helping grow an economy for them. As these concerns swell in the public conscience, designers have an opportunity to serve as vanguards by creating sustainable exhibitions visited by millions of people.

Looking Forward

In any field of design, the root of the practice is in presenting information and emotion in new and more effective fashions. Responsively, designers view the challenges of the day as abundances of promising opportunities. As today's exhibition designers plan environments that engage people in experiences in compelling new ways, they raise the field from its youth to its fruition. As they stay aware of trends and plan one step ahead of them, they raise the bar.

REFERENCES

1. Dernie, D. Introduction. *Exhibition Design*; Laurence King Publishing Ltd: London, U.K., 2006; 6–19.
2. Ezekiel 27:10. In *The Oxford Study Bible*; Suggs, J.M., Sakenfeld, K.D., Mueller, J.R., Eds.; Oxford University Press: New York, 1992; 885–886.
3. Europe and India. In *Teaching World History*; Roupp, H., Ed.; M.E. Sharpe: Amonk, NY, 1997; 171–172.
4. http://www.leipziger-messe.de/LeMMon/LMGWeb_E. NSF/pages/messeeng?OpenDocument.
5. Impey, O. MacGregor, A. Introduction. *The Origins of Museums*; House of Stratus: North Yorkshire, U.K., 2001; xvii–xx.
6. Lorenc, J. Skolnick, L. Berger, C. A brief history of exhibition design. *What Is Exhibition Design?*, Rotovision: Hove, U.K., 2007; 12–17.
7. Gundestrup, B. From the royal Kunstkammer to the modern museums of Copenhagen. In *The Origins of Museums*;

Impey, O., MacGregor, A., Eds.; House of Stratus: North Yorkshire, U.K., 2001; 177–188.

8. Olmi, G. Science—honour—metaphor: Italian cabinets of the sixteenth and seventeenth centuries. In *The Origins of Museums*; Impey, O., MacGregor, A., Eds.; House of Stratus: North Yorkshire, U.K., 2001; 1–18.

9. Laurencich-Minelli, L. Museography and ethnographical collections in Bologna during the sixteenth and seventeenth centuries. In *The Origins of Museums*; Impey, O., MacGregor, A., Eds.; House of Stratus: North Yorkshire, U.K., 2001; 19–28.

10. Alexander, E.P. The natural history museum. *Museums in Motion: An Introduction to the History and Functions of Museums*; The American Association for State and Local History: Nashville, TN, 1979; 39–60.

11. http://www.lib.umd.edu/ARCH/honr219f/1851lond.html.

12. http://www.tour-eiffel.fr/teiffel/uk/.

13. http://expomuseum.com/1893/.

14. http://www.youtube.com/watch?v=e5xb551wtnI.

15. Leach, W. Interiors. *Land of Desire*; Random House, Inc.: New York, 1993; 71–90.

16. http://park.org/Pavilions/WorldExpositions/new_york.html.

17. http://thisdayindisneyhistory.homestead.com/WorldsFair.html.

18. http://www.eamesoffice.com/index2.php?mod=exhibitions.

19. Klein, L. Museum exhibition. *Exhibits*; Madison Square Press: New York, 1986; 62–89.

20. http://www.answers.com/topic/trade-fair?cat=biz-fin.

21. Stefanovich, A. Driving innovation in museums American Association of Museums Annual Meeting Chicago, IL May, 16, 2007.

22. Lorenc, J. Skolnick, L. Berger, C. Portfolios. *What Is Exhibition Design?*, Rotovision: Hove, U.K., 2007; 140–249.

23. Lorenc, J. Skolnick, L. Berger, C. Process. *What Is Exhibition Design?*, Rotovision: Hove, U.K., 2007; 104–139.

24. Caulton, T. Exhibit devlopment. *Hands-On Exhibitions: Managing Interactive Museums and Science Centers*; Routledge: London, U.K.,1998; 39–56.

25. McLean, K. Transforming space. *Planning for People in Museums*; Association of Science-Technology Centers: Washington, DC, 1993; 115–130.

26. Witteborg, L.P. Raw materials. In *Good Show!*; Stevens, A.P., Ed.; Smithsonian Institution: Washington, DC, 1982; 145–156.

27. Cuffaro, D.F. Paige, D. Blackman, C.J. Laituri, D. Covert, D.E. Sears, L.M. Nehez-Cuffaro, A. Material selection. *Process, Materials and Measurements: All the Details Industrial Designers Need to Know But Can Never Find*; Rockport Publishers: Gloucester, MA, 2006; 78–87.

28. http://www.segd.org/about/what_egd.html.

29. Calori, C. What is environmental graphic design?. *Signage and Wayfinding Design: A Complete Guide to Environmental Graphic Design Systems*; John Wiley & Sons, Inc.: Hoboken, NJ, 2007; 2–13.

30. Dernie, D. Lighting. *Exhibition Design*; Laurence King Publishing Ltd.: London, U.K., 2006; 136–159.

31. Dean, D. The exhibition development process. *Museum Exhibition: Theory and Practice*; Routledge: London, U.K., 1994; 8–18.

32. http://www.visitorstudies.org/.

33. Dean, D. Audiences and learning. *Museum Exhibition: Theory and Practice*; Routledge: London, U.K., 1994; 19–32.

34. Hooper-Greenhill, E. Communication in theory and practice. *Museums and Their Visitors*, Routledge: London, U.K., 1994; 35–53.

35. Panero, J. Zelnik, M. Introduction. *Human Dimension & Interior Space: A Source Book of Design Reference Standards*; Whitney Library of Design: New York, 1979; 15–20.

36. Ruth, L.C. Introduction. *Design Standards for Children's Environments*; McGraw Hill: New York, 2000; vii–x.

37. Diamond, J. Planning an evaluation project. *Practical Evaluation Guide: Tools for Museums & Other Informal Educational Settings*; AltaMira Press: Walnut Creek, CA, 1999; 15–24.

38. McLean, K. Doing it right. *Planning for People in Museums*; Association of Science-Technology Centers: Washington, DC, 1993; 68–80.

39. Klein, L. What is an exhibit?. *Exhibits*; Madison Square Press: New York, 1986; 62–89.

40. McLean, K. Teams and schemes: The cast of players. *Planning for People in Museums*; Association of Science-Technology Centers: Washington, DC, 1993; 35–47.

41. Smithsonian Institution, Office of Policy and Analysis, Exhibition making models. *The Making of Exhibitions: Purpose, Structure, Roles and Process*; Smithsonian Institution: Washington DC, 2002; 5–10.

42. Bine, J. A project manager is. *Exhibitionist Spring 2006, Spring,* 70–71.

43. http://www.pratt.edu/newsite/index.php?group_id=62&div_id=5375.

44. http://www3.fitnyc.edu/graduatestudies/exhibition.

45. http://www.uarts.edu/academics/cad/ms/mepd.html.

46. Klingmann, A. The lessons of Las Vegas. *Brandscapes*; MIT Press: Cambridge, MA, 2007; 189–205.

47. Vranckx, B. Leisure. *Exhibit Design: High Impact Solutions*; Collins Design: New York, 2006; 202–253.

48. Hooper-Greenhill, E. Forces for change. *Museums and Their Visitors*; Routledge: London, U.K., 1994; 6–34.

49. Dewey, J. Criteria of experience. *Experience and Education*; Simon and Schuster, Inc.: New York, 1938; 33–50.

50. Hein, G. Significance of constructivism for museum education. *Museums and the Needs of the People*; International Committee on Museums Meeting: Israel, 1991.

51. Gardener, H. The idea of multiple intelligences. *Frames of Mind*; Basic Books: New York, 1983; 3–11.

52. Csikszentmihalyi, M.; Hermanson, K. Intrinsic motivation in museums: what makes visitors want to learn?. Mus. News, May/June **1995**, *74* (3), 3438.

53. http://www.justice.gov/crt/ada/reg3a.html#Anchor-Appendix 52467.

54. Majewski, J. On striving for accessible exhibition design. *Smithsonian Guidelines for Accessible Exhibition Design*; Smithsonian Accessibility Program: Washington, DC, 1996; iii–iv.

55. Skolnick, L. Towards a new museum architecture. In *Reshaping Museum Space: Architecture, Design, Exhibitions*; MacLeod, S., Ed.; Routledge: New York, 2005; 118–130.

56. Thomas, S. Introduction. In *The Digital Museum: A Think Guide*; Din, H., Hecht, P., Eds.; American Association of Museums: Washington, DC, 2007; 1–8.

57. Mouw, M. Spock, D. Immersive media: creating theatrical storytelling experiences. In *The Digital Museum: A Think Guide*; Din, H., Hecht, P., Eds.; American Association of Museums: Washington, DC, 2007; 45–56.

58. http://snibbe.com/.

59. http://www.localprojects.net/lpV2/.

60. http://www.mine-control.com/.

61. http://www.exhibitfiles.org/.

62. Cuffaro, D.F. Paige, D. Blackman, C.J. Laituri, D. Covert, D.E. Sears, L.M. Nehez-Cuffaro, A. Sustainable design. *Process, Materials and Measurements: All the Details Industrial Designers Need to Know But Can Never Find*; Rockport Publishers: Gloucester, MA, 2006; 172–177.

Facet Analysis [ELIS Classic]

Douglas J. Foskett
University of London, London, U.K.

Abstract
The brothers Foskett, Anthony and Douglas, have both made major contributions to the theory and practice of subject analysis and description. Here, Douglas Foskett explains facet analysis, a vital technique in the development of both classification schemes and thesauri. Foskett himself created faceted classification schemes for specific disciplines, drawing from the philosophy of the great Indian classificationist, S.R. Ranganathan.

—ELIS Classic, from 1972

INTRODUCTION

The term "facet analysis" was first introduced into discussions of bibliographical classification by S.R. Ranganathan to denote the technique of separating the various elements of complex subjects in relation to a set of abstract fundamental concepts. The *Colon Classification*[1,2] is the only example of a general classification scheme covering the whole of knowledge that is entirely based on facet principles, but many other special schemes have been made using this technique, and a simple account of the methodology was presented to the Washington Conference on Scientific Information in 1958.[3] Ranganathan has expounded the theory and practice in many writings; the basic theoretical work is the *Prolegomena to Library Classification*, of which the third edition has appeared,[4] and advances in his research are regularly reported in the Indian journal *Library Science with a Slant to Documentation*. Perhaps the best introductions to his work, however, remain a paper to the British Society for Visiting Scientists given in 1948[5] and a monograph prepared for the Library Research Monograph series of the University Library in Copenhagen.[6] In the latter, Ranganathan defines facet analysis as

> the mental process by which the possible trains of characteristics which can form the basis of classification of a subject are enumerated and the exact measure in which the attributes concerned are incident in the subject are determined. Facets are inherent in the subject.

B.C. Vickery, in a contribution for the Classification Research Group (q.v.), writes that "a faceted classification is a schedule of standard terms to be used in the subject description of documents,"[7] and he has shown the relation of facet analysis to the general analysis of information in his article "Analysis of Information" (q.v.).

BACKGROUND

Classification, both the word and the process, begins with the Greeks, who used it for the purpose of forming definitions of *things*. For Plato, to know things meant to place them in their correct class according to their permanent, ideal form, or essence, and Aristotle in his *Logic* analyzed in detail the processes by which one could identify things by starting with a group or class of objects, and then eliminating all members of the class except the one aimed at, by enumerating specific properties not possessed by the others. Thus, by starting with the class, or *genus*, one could arrive at the individual, or *species* by enumerating properties that stated differences between one species and another. This form of division is still best seen in the so-called "classificatory sciences," especially Zoology and Botany, in which the genera may be divided into the individual animals and plants; we may start with a class such as vertebrates, and by the division on the basis of successive characteristics we arrive at a chain of subclasses such as mammals—(primates)—anthropoid—apes (chimpanzees). This sort of classificatory process proved of great value for the development of these sciences, and the description of individual species is still of value today. We can, for example, profit by the description of individual libraries and information services, studying their similarities and differences to arrive at a more general theory of what these organizations should be like under ideal conditions.

One of the most important aspects of the achievement of Melvil Dewey in the decimal classification was to show how the use of the decimal fraction notation could provide a systematic sequence of subjects, which mirrored this form of classification and which would therefore arrange books or other documents, such as index cards, in a pattern that would be readily recognized by the specialist in any subject as corresponding to the way in which he thought

Encyclopedia of Library and Information Sciences, Fourth Edition DOI: 10.1081/E-ELIS4-120008985

about his subject. But the literature of specialist subjects in all fields, including the "classificatory sciences," is no longer mainly a literature of description of individual species, as it was to a great extent in the nineteenth century. The field of knowledge has advanced in complexity, and specialist writing now consists much more of the discussion of the relations and interconnections subsisting between entities than of mere descriptions of the entities themselves. We need, therefore, a scheme of categories of terms which will do more than imitate the genus–species relation.

Dewey had already realized that this problem existed and provided for a certain element of synthesis as well as analysis in his schedules. He knew that any subject might in principle at least be subdivided geographically, but rather than enumerating a complete geographical table under each subject, he introduced the technique of adding on the schedule from the class 900, inserting a zero in front of the 9 to indicate that this was the point at which a new aspect (or facet) of the subject was about to be introduced. This process was carried much further by the International Federation for Documentation (q.v.) in its revisions of the universal decimal classification, and in his bibliographic classification, H.E. Bliss used the systematic auxiliary schedules to carry out the classificatory process which he called "composite specification."

All of these schemes, however, failed to provide a systematic basis for the use of synthesis in classifying a complex subject, and the inevitable result is a mixture of subjects in the same array, arrived at by applying different characteristics of division in one series instead of one at a time. In the Dewey decimal classification, for example, we find arrays like this:

370	Education
370.1	Theory
370.7	Study
370.71	Meetings
370.72	Conferences
370.73	Teachers' Colleges
370.732	Courses and programs

It is obvious that "Courses and programs" are not *species* (i.e., special types) of "Teachers' Colleges," and that "Teachers' Colleges" themselves are not *species* of "Study"; on the other hand, "Conferences" might reasonably be called *species* of "Meetings." The true nature of the various hierarchies are not demonstrated; all terms are enumerated as if the genus–species relation were the only one, and all subdivisions were examples of it.

The aim of the writer of a document is to study phenomena in the round; he observes all the aspects of a given entity—its appearance, its structure, and the interrelationships and interactions that exist between one entity or group of entities and another. He tries to describe a

universe that is dynamic and not static, and this means that it is not sufficient to rely any longer on schemes of classification that attempt to force all types of relation into a pattern that actually exhibits only the generic relation.

Perhaps the simplest way of illustrating this is to consider a technology. The aim of a technology is to take some material or object, such as a piece of steel or aluminum, or a measure of some substance, and then to work on it to change it into something else. We apply an activity or operation to the entity or raw material and turn it into another entity—the end product. Thus, we have two types of entity terms (raw material and end product) and the operation terms (which might be stamping, extruding, heating, and so on).

The purpose of facet analysis is to provide a framework within which all these various types of terms can be accommodated, together with rules for their combination as required by the literature. It uses the term "analysis" to replace the older term "division" because division implies the breaking up of a single entity, but analysis has a wider connotation and may be applied to the study of complexes as well as of entities. A facet can be said to be all the classes produced when a subject is divided by one and only one characteristic. Classes in a scheme of classification are represented by words or terms, and a facet is therefore a list of terms in which each term stands in the same relation to the subject of which it is a part. A facet may consist of entity terms, such as elements in chemistry, or crops in agriculture; forms of entities, such as solid, liquid, gas; operations made on entities, such as combustion, forging, harvesting; tools for operations, such as presses, x-rays for therapy, microscopes; states of being, such as health and disease.

In applying facet analysis to a subject, the first step is to examine a representative sample of the literature and enumerate the subject of each article, book, or abstract. It soon becomes clear that the terms encountered may be grouped together in sets according to their relation to the subject and to each other, that they represent, in fact, the various aspects of the subject, each of which can be studied apart from the others, at least conceptually, even though in practice it may be impossible to separate them into groups of static entities apart from the phenomena in which they are observed. Consider the following subjects from journal articles in the field of occupational safety and health:

The lighting of underground roadways in coal mines.
The protection of workers against ionizing radiations.
The examination and testing of dust masks.
Dermatologic aspects of the chromate problem.
Guarding of machines used by blind workers.
Registration of accidents in nuclear reactors.

From these, and other subjects like them, one can easily deduce the following facets:

Classes of workers (blind, etc.)
Industries (where hazards exist: coal mines, reactors)
Sources of hazards (things causing danger: dust, chromates, radiation, machines)
Accidents and diseases (results of hazards: dermatitis)
Prevention (masks, guarding)
Administration (registration, etc.)

It can readily be seen now that the basic difference between a faceted classification and a merely enumerative one is that here the terms are itemized as elementary terms and are not combined into complexes for insertion in the schedules of the scheme. For classifying documents, terms are used mainly in a postcoordinate manner because they are not precoordinated in the schedules, except insofar as a generic hierarchy may still legitimately be inserted into a facet. In a faceted scheme for education, we can find, in the "Educand" facet, the following sequence:

Exceptional children
　Handicapped children
　　Physically handicapped children
　　　Blind
　　　Deaf
　　　Brain-injured

Terms signifying other aspects, such as curriculum subjects or teaching methods, will likewise be enumerated only as elementary terms in separate facets, and any combination of elementary terms that may appear in the literature can therefore be catered for as it arises.

One particular kind of facet is called a differential facet. This is a facet of a class in which the terms are secondary to another facet and may differ according to the term to which they are attached in the primary facet. If we look at the subject "Food Technology," for example, we can enumerate the various groups of foodstuffs in the primary facet: meat products, dairy products, vegetable products, and so on; in the "Process or Operations" facet, the types of process vary according to the food group. The operations for processing dairy or cereal products are different from those used in processing meat or fish products. Thus, although the name of the facet may be a general term such as "Process" or "Operation," the individual terms in the facet will fall into several separate groups depending on the term in the product facet to which they apply.

To find a sound theoretical basis for the choice and sequence of facets in a scheme, Ranganathan advanced the solution of relating facets to a set of fundamental abstract notions, which he called time, space, energy, matter, and personality. Every facet of a basic class is regarded as a concrete manifestation of one of these. The time facet is for chronological division, and the space facet for geographical division; these are clear and are to be found in virtually every classification scheme. Energy and matter, illustrated in a technology by raw material and process, are

not so easily identified in some other subjects in the social sciences and humanities, for example. Personality, if interpreted as the end product in a technology, or the educand in education, can be seen to be a recognizable entity with an identity that is unique and clearly separable from other entities, but it has certainly caused more difficulty and controversy than any of Ranganathan's other fundamental categories. Nevertheless, for him it is the most important of the categories, because it is the personality facet that contains the terms that give the class itself its own identity in the field of knowledge.

It is clear that many compound subjects found in the literature will display more than three basic facets, excluding space and time, which normally will only appear once. To meet this situation, Ranganathan introduced the idea of levels and rounds of facets. In Class I, Botany, of the Colon Classification, the individual plants are classified into natural groups as the First Level Personality; for example:

1	Cryptogamia
2	Thallophyta
22	Algae, seaweeds
23	Fungi
237	Basidiomycete
2375	Mushroom
5	Phanerogamia
7	Monocotyledon
8	Dicotyledon

But parts of plants are also personality terms and are placed as Second Level Personality in the same facet as the plants themselves (i.e., before the appearance of any other facet). For example:

1	Basic and regional
13	Root
14	Stem
16	Flower

The two levels of the personality facet are joined by a comma. Thus, the notation symbol for the plant gentian is I 8516, and the symbol for the flower of the gentian is I 8516,16; the preceding comma enables us to distinguish between the 16, which indicates the division gentian of the group Dicotyledons, and the 16, which indicates the part flower and which could be added in the same way to the symbol for any other plant.

Rounds of facets are necessary because each type of term may appear more than once in a compound subject. In a technology, we may very well find the tool specified which carries out a certain operation on a certain raw material to produce a certain end product. A tool is an entity and in the context of the manufacture of the tool it would appear as the primary personality. But it is not primary in the context of using it for the production of another entity; that entity is the primary personality because that is the entity on which primary attention is focused. Similarly, in the class agriculture, fertilizers are regarded as personality terms, but agriculture is not concerned with the production but with the use of fertilizers. The crop is the primary focus of attention in agriculture and is, therefore, the First Round Personality facet. This facet is followed by an operation or energy facet that contains, among others, these terms:

1	Soil
2	Manure
4	Disease
7	Harvesting

The symbol that introduces an energy term is the colon. Thus, the notation for the crop turnip is J 332, and the symbol for the subject, the manuring of turnips is J 332 : 2. After this, the different kinds of fertilizer that may be used for the manuring of turnips are listed as the Second Round Personality facet. Ranganathan has postulated that there are no subdivisions (second levels) of any energy term, so that Second Round Personality terms do not require any indicating symbol but may run straight on after the symbol for the appropriate energy term:

1	Green manure
2	Farm
4	Fertilizer
41	Nitrogenous
42	Phosphatic

The combined symbol for "the use of phosphates in the cultivation of turnips" is therefore J 332 : 242. A full explanation of these devices has been given by Ranganathan in his Rutgers seminar.[2]

There is no doubt at all that these fundamental categories are easy to identify in some subjects and particularly in science and technology. They have been used with success as a checking device for subject analysis in relation to the decimal classification in the *British National Bibliography* and in relation to an alphabetical index in the *British Technology Index* (q.v.). It is very useful to have in mind some generalized idea of the structure of subjects when either constructing a classification scheme or when classifying documents. Unfortunately, it is not so easy to see the application in the Social Sciences or the Humanities, and the Classification Research Group and other research workers, particularly on the Continent, have tended to follow a more pragmatic approach and, while using facet analysis, to give the facets a more precise name limited to the subject field being classified. Examples are given by Vickery in another Rutgers seminar;[8] whether the technique is allied to the notion of fundamental categories or not, however, it certainly provides the most powerful tool yet devised for the analysis of subjects, both for classifying documents and for search strategy in information retrieval.

There are some who seem to think that the arrival of computers has relieved librarians and information officers of the necessity to perform this operation and that all that will be required in the future is for clerical workers to file text into the machine in the natural language of authors and file requests in the natural language of users, and take for granted these two varieties of natural language will match. Operating experience (with perhaps the exception of stores that are so small as to be insignificant for real-life purposes) shows the contrary; and most machine-based systems now are provided with some form of vocabulary control, usually in the form of a "thesaurus." Although many of the early thesauri were no more than what had hitherto been called by librarians "subject headings lists," it has lately been realized that the efficiency of these lists, both for input and search strategy, is greatly increased if there is, in addition to the alphabetical list, a second list of the same terms arranged into categories. In one case these have been called "facets,"[9] and the superiority of this Barhydt-Schmidt thesaurus of educational terms over the alphabetic thesaurus issued by the U.S. Office of Education is so marked that the latter has included in its second edition a rough and not very ready approximation to a set of categories called "descriptor groups."

The most effective combinations to date have been those produced by D. Soergel for a chemical company in Germany and by Jean Aitchison as a new version of the faceted classification scheme compiled for the English Electric Co. and described in Vickery's Rutgers seminar.[8] The new version has been called a Thesaurofacet,[10] and Jean Aitchison has also published a simplified account of the technique.[11] She has used the faceted structure to present a pattern of the most basic relationships subsisting between the phenomena denoted by the terms in the system and has complemented this by introducing all the other manifold relationships that may appear in the actual literature into the thesaurus, which now acts as both an entry vocabulary to the system for precisely named terms and a detailed and highly structured alphabetical index to the faceted classification. The characteristic features of each technique have been exploited to achieve a very complete pair of structured vocabularies with the maximum of economy: relations that are more satisfactorily displayed in one list are not repeated in the other. The two lists are linked by the notation of the classification scheme.

Thesaurus Entry		
Jets		CWJ
RT	Jet condensers	
	Jet dispersal valves	
	Jet dispersers	
	Jet pumps	
	Jet rectifiers	
	Nozzles	
NT (A)	Jets (Hovercraft)	REJ
	Plasma jets	EXQ

Classification Schedule	
CWJ	Jets
CWK	Jet streams
CWL	Plumes
CWM	Wall jets
CWO	Couette flow
CWP	Jet mixing
CWQ	Propulsive jets
EXP	Plasma experimental apparatus
EXQ	Plasma jets
EXR	Plasma guns
EXT	Plasma arcs
REI	Hovercraft components
REJ	Jets (hovercraft)

CONCLUSION

Information science, unlike information theory, is concerned with meaning and communication as well as with the transfer of messages. Communication means conveying the meaning of a message so that the recipient is able to fit it into the pattern of ideas that already exists in his mind. Library systems should be so formed that they can do this; they should attempt to correspond with the structure of reality, which writers attempt to describe so that the system of terms in the writer's mind may be inserted into a matrix that can be used in turn as a pattern for matching with the system of terms in a user's mind.

It should be a lattice system able to form the same relations as those existing in the infinitely varied phenomena of Nature, and not a single hierarchy, however "logical," such as those on which the traditional library classification schemes are based. Facet analysis provides such a lattice system. It corresponds to the way in which specialists think about their subjects and has, therefore, a vital role to play in modern library and information services, including those that make use of the most sophisticated of machines.

REFERENCES

1. Ranganathan, S.R. *Colon Classification*, 7th Ed.; Asia: Bombay, 1971.
2. Ranganathan, S.R. *The Colon Classification*, Graduate School of Library Service, Rutgers, The State University: New Brunswick, NJ, 1965.
3. Foskett, D.J. The construction of a faceted classification for a special subject. *Science, Humanism and Libraries* Crosby Lockwood: London, U.K., 1964.
4. Ranganathan, S.R. *Prolegomena to Library Classification*, 3rd Ed.; Asia: Bombay, India, 1967.
5. Ranganathan, S.R. Self-perpetuating scheme of classification. J. Doc. **1949**, *4*, 223–244.
6. Ranganathan, S.R. *Philosophy of Library Classification*, Munksgaard: Copenhagen, Denmark, 1951.
7. Vickery, B.C. *Faceted Classification*, Aslib: London, U.K., 1960.
8. Vickery, B.C. *Faceted Classification Schemes*, Graduate School of Library Service, Rutgers, The State University: New Brunswick, NJ, 1966.
9. Barhydt, G.; Schmidt, C.T. *Information Retrieval Thesaurus of Educational Terms*, Case Western Reserve Univ. Press: Cleveland, OH, 1968.
10. Aitchison, J.; et al. *The Thesaurofacet*; English Electric Co.: Rugby, U.K., 1969.
11. Aitchison, J. The thesaurofacet: A multi-purpose retrieval language tool. J. Doc. **1970**, *26*, 187–203.

Faceted Application of Subject Terminology (FAST)

Eric R. Childress
Diane Vizine-Goetz
OCLC, Dublin, Ohio, U.S.A.

Abstract

FAST (faceted application of subject terminology) is a faceted subject heading vocabulary derived chiefly from the Library of Congress Subject Headings (LCSH), a widely-used subject heading system published and maintained by the Library of Congress (LC). A controlled vocabulary with simple application rules and a design well suited to Linked Data applications, FAST has been developed through a multi-year collaboration of OCLC Research and the Library of Congress with advice from the library community. OCLC is responsible for the ongoing development of FAST.

INTRODUCTION

Faceted application of subject terminology (FAST) is an enumerative, faceted subject heading vocabulary that consists of eight categories of terms, or facets, that cover key attributes of information resources (topics, persons, organizations, events, places, titles of works, time, and form/genre). Derived chiefly from the Library of Congress Subject Headings (LCSH), FAST retains the rich vocabulary of LCSH and benefits greatly from the ongoing development of LC-controlled vocabularies. In contrast to LCSH, which provides authority records for main headings and subdivisions but not all valid combinations allowed by LCSH application rules, all authorized FAST headings, except FAST chronological headings, are established in an authority file. The FAST authority file is available in multiple representations including MAchine-Readable Cataloging (MARC) and Resource Description Framework (RDF). Individual FAST authority records can also be accessed through a web interface and as Linked Data.

FAST was developed to meet the need for a general-use subject vocabulary that is easy to learn, apply, and control. As a controlled vocabulary that consists of eight independent but complementary facets, FAST is designed to work well in a Linked Data environment and in information systems that support post-coordinate retrieval and faceted navigation. Ongoing development of FAST includes synchronizing with LCSH, providing tools for users, and enhancing FAST records with supplemental information.

BACKGROUND

History of the FAST Project

The origins of the FAST project can be traced to work with Dublin Core (DC) features in the Cooperative Online Resource Catalog (CORC) service (1998–2002). CORC included a novel metadata editor that allowed input and modification of metadata in both DC and MARC views[1] and the ability to easily shift between DC and MARC views by virtue of a sophisticated crosswalk.[2] OCLC staff members and CORC participants valued this feature, but it revealed difficulties in mapping LCSH between DC and MARC. The chief issue was that valid LCSH topical strings can include multiple aspects (e.g., topic, place, time, form) in the same MARC tag, but in DC each aspect typically belongs to different DC elements. The machine logic required to properly map parts of LCSH constructed headings between MARC and DC was judged impractical, and in a best-case scenario would only have allowed a one-way mapping.

With this issue in mind, OCLC Research staff members began exploring the possibility of faceting LCSH into a new vocabulary. If the project was successful, LCSH's rich vocabulary would be recast to be more amenable to use in contexts where metadata was expressed in DC or other non-MARC formats or in workflows that relied on staff unfamiliar with LCSH application rules.[3,4]

Influences

The release of the report, *Subject Data in the Metadata Record*, in 1999 further inspired the FAST team to persist in its efforts to simplify and adapt LCSH. The report included the following recommendations:

> *Schemes for supplying subject data should, to the fullest possible extent:*
>
> - *be simple and easy to apply and comprehend;*
>   - *be intuitive so that sophisticated training in subject indexing and classification, while highly desirable, is not required in order to implement them;*

Encyclopedia of Library and Information Sciences, Fourth Edition DOI: 10.1081/E-EISA-120053275

- *be scalable for implementation from the simplest to the most sophisticated;*
- *be logical so that it requires the least effort to understand and to implement; and,*
- *be appropriate to the specific discipline and subject, and to the domain of implementation such as libraries, museums, archives, information services, the scientific community, and personal knowledge management.*[5]

These objectives resonated with the general goals of the FAST project. While never expressly adopted by the team, the subcommittee's recommendations have influenced the team in its decision-making over the course of the project.

FAST AND LCSH

FAST is derived from LCSH and benefits significantly from LCSH's strengths as a large, general vocabulary maintained by LC. As a widely adopted vocabulary, LCSH covers all subject areas, imposes synonym and homograph control, includes many cross-references, and is updated regularly by LC. LCSH has been added to tens of millions of metadata descriptions including nearly 100 million in WorldCat. The FAST authority file is built chiefly from three sources: 1) the LCSH authority file, 2) millions of constructed LCSH present in WorldCat, and 3) the NACO Authority file. Constructed headings, representing authorized combinations of LCSH, serve as literary warrant and effectively focus FAST on the universe of things represented in library collections. As LCSH evolves and improves, FAST is adapted to reflect the changes and enhancements.

The individual terms in the FAST vocabulary are divided into seven subject facets and a form/genre facet.[6] The headings in the subject facets are used to describe what a work is *about*; the terms in form/genre facet are used to represent what a resource or document *is*, for example, an encyclopedia. The facets are named

- Topical
- Geographic name (place)
- Corporate name (organization)
- Personal name
- Title of work
- Event name
- Chronological (date or time period)
- Form/genre

FAST is intended for use in post-coordinate retrieval; however, FAST does contain multiple concept headings. They appear as compound phrases (e.g., *agriculture and state*), prepositional phrases (e.g., *conservation of natural resources*), and as main heading/subdivision combinations (e.g., *natural gas—conservation*).[7] Headings

such as these reflect the vocabulary of LCSH and will be familiar to users of LC Subject Headings. Where FAST differs from LCSH is in the rules for combining subdivisions. In FAST, all terms in the heading must come from the same facet. Topical headings can only be combined with topical subdivisions, geographic names with other geographic names. A main heading may not be combined with a subdivision from another facet.

FACETS

Topical Headings

FAST topical headings look very similar to established topical headings in LCSH. Topical headings in FAST are made up of topical main headings and main heading/subdivision combinations that have been used in WorldCat bibliographic records, including topical heading/free-floating subdivision combinations and expansions of multiple headings.[8] Topical headings are the majority of subject headings used in cataloging.[9] The following are examples of FAST topical headings:

> AIDS (disease)
> Church work with youth
> Cities and towns
> Murder—investigation
> Political science
> Roads—design and construction
> Roads—design and construction—safety measures
> Travel
> Water—pollution
> Women—employment
> Women—employment reentry—public opinion

Geographic Names

The FAST geographic name facet contains place names that are the subject of a work, including names of countries and political or administrative divisions within countries, states, cities, and towns. These names are referred to as jurisdictional names. FAST also includes names for natural features and man-made structures, referred to as nonjurisdictional names. Jurisdictional names are derived primarily from the NACO Authority File, and nonjurisdictional names are derived from LCSH.

Jurisdictional names
China
France
Texas
Wales

Nonjurisdictional names
Arizona—Grand Canyon
Maritime Provinces
North America
Pacific Ocean

In FAST, the structure of geographic names is hierarchal and is based on the *MARC Code List for Geographic Areas*.[10] The heading begins with the first-level name and may contain two additional levels. First-level names are normally names of countries or larger areas except for Australia, Canada, Great Britain, and the United States. For these areas, second-level entities such as provinces and states are treated as first level names (Texas rather than United States—Texas). Additional geographic entities are given special treatment in FAST including extinct cities, bodies of water, and extraterrestrial bodies.[11] The following are examples of geographic name headings:

First-level names
Atlantic Ocean
North America
Texas

Second-level names
Arizona—Grand Canyon
Atlantic Ocean—Baltic Sea
England—London
France—Provence

Third-level name
California—Los Angeles—Sunset Boulevard
England—London—Chelsea
New York (State)—New York—Central Park

Personal Names, Corporate Names, and Title of Work

Personal and corporate names and titles of works are established as FAST headings. They are based on headings in the NACO Authority File. Only the names that have been used at least once as a subject in a WorldCat bibliographic record are established in FAST.

Personal Names

Personal name headings in FAST look much like established headings in the NACO Authority File. They may not be combined with subdivisions from other facets, but contain one or more following elements:

- Personal name (surname and/or forename)
- Numeration
- Words associated with a name
- More complete form of the name
- Date(s)

The following are examples of personal name headings:

Austen, Jane, 1775–1817
Beyoncé, 1981-
Downey, Robert, Jr., 1965-
Francis, Pope, 1936-
Marie Antoinette, Queen, consort of Louis XVI, King of France, 1755–1793
Milne, A. A. (Alan Alexander), 1882–1956
Sting (Musician)

Corporate Names

Corporate name headings are established for corporate bodies, which include public and private organizations, associations, institutions, governments, government agencies, commercial firms, nonprofit enterprises, and religious bodies. Corporate name headings may not be combined with subdivisions from other facets, but they may contain one or more elements for subordinate units combined with the main heading. The following are examples of FAST corporate name headings:

Canada. Parliament. House of Commons
eBay (Firm)
European Union
Metropolitan Museum of Art (New York, N.Y.)
Peace Corps (U.S.)
United States National Aeronautics and Space Administration
World Bank

Title of Work

A FAST heading for title of work is the title of a work used as subject heading. For example, a critical work about *Pride and Prejudice* by Jane Austen would have the FAST heading Pride and Prejudice (Austen, Jane) as a subject heading. Headings for titles fall into three main categories: anonymous works, works of known personal authorship, and works from corporate bodies.[12] FAST headings for titles begin with the title followed by the name of the creator except for anonymous works. Dates of authors/creators are not included unless the dates are necessary to avoid conflicts. The following are examples of titles of works:

Beowulf
Dame aux camélias (Play) (Dumas, Alexandre, 1824–1895)
Declaration of Independence (United States)
Divina commedia (Dante Alighieri)
Pride and Prejudice (Austen, Jane)
Romeo and Juliet (Shakespeare, William)
Trois mousquetaires (Dumas, Alexandre, 1802–1870)
Winnie-the-Pooh (Milne, A. A.)

Qualifiers are added to titles to identify the type of work or distinguish between works with the same title, for example:

> Romeo and Juliet (Choreographic work : Balanchine and Nijinska)
> Romeo and Juliet (Motion picture : 1936)
> Romeo and Juliet (Motion picture : 1968)

Event Names

In FAST, an event is defined as something that occurs during a particular time period. An event may be recurring or a single occurrence. FAST event headings are derived from LCSH topical and geographic headings and chronological subdivisions, conference names and meeting names in the NACO Authority File, and subject fields in WorldCat bibliographic records. There are four main types of event headings:

1. Military conflicts—headings for wars, battles, and sieges, etc., include the place and date as the qualifier unless it is redundant.

   > Cuban Missile Crisis (1962)
   > Revolution (France : 1789–1799)
   > Soviet Occupation of Afghanistan (1979–1989)
   > World War (1914–1918)

2. Conferences and meetings

   > G8 Summit
   > Paris Peace Conference (1919–1920)
   > South by Southwest Music and Media Conference

3. Sporting events

   > Stanley Cup (Hockey)
   > British Open (Golf tournament)
   > World Cup (Rugby football)

4. Other types of events, for example, strikes, festivals, natural disasters

   > Burning Man (Festival)
   > Fukushima Nuclear Disaster (Japan : 2011)
   > Indian Ocean Tsunami (2004)

Only event names that have been used at least once as a subject in a WorldCat bibliographic record are established in FAST.

Chronological

FAST chronological headings contain either a single date or date range consisting of a beginning date and an ending date. Either the beginning date or the ending date can be open. An individual date usually consists of only a year. The chronological facet is not controlled but relies on syntax rules for formulating headings.[13] The following

are examples of four types of commonly occurring chronological headings:

1. Single date
   1975
   1941 (December 7)

2. Beginning date
   Since 2000

3. Ending date
   To 1900

4. Date range
   2003–2011

Form and Genre Headings

FAST form and genre headings are derived from LCSH. Form and genre terms are used to describe what a work *is* in contrast to what a work is *about*. Form headings are used to indicate form of presentation or arrangement, intended audience, or physical medium. Genre headings indicate categories of works characterized by plot, theme, setting, etc. The following are examples of form and genre headings:

> Atlases
> Catalogs
> Fiction
> Guidebooks
> Periodicals
> Photographs
> Scores

APPLICATION RULES

When applying any subject vocabulary, catalogers and indexers must also choose between summarization and depth indexing. A cataloger employing summarization will apply subject terms based the overall theme or content of the resource. A metadata specialist using the depth indexing approach will attempt to represent all significant aspects of a work. Either method is appropriate for use with FAST.

As the first step in assigning FAST, a cataloger or other user applies personal judgment to determine which attributes (e.g., topic, geographic name, event, etc.) are primary for the resource being described, and whether the resource should also be categorized as a particular form or genre. The next step is to categorize the concepts by FAST facets and then select the appropriate heading from the FAST authority file. The FAST database contains all valid main headings and main heading/subdivision combinations and selected tracings for variant and related headings. If no FAST heading for a particular topic has been established, then either a broader heading or multiple headings may be assigned to represent the topic. It is common practice in subject cataloging to use the most specific term available in the vocabulary to describe the resource. For example, for a resource about mice, the FAST heading, Mice, should be used instead of the headings, Rodents or Mammals.

DEVELOPMENT AND MAINTENANCE OF FAST

Generating FAST Headings

FAST headings are generated from 1) established headings in the LCSH Authority File, 2) headings extracted from WorldCat bibliographic records, and 3) name headings in the NACO Name Authority File. The initial steps in the development of FAST were to algorithmically facet and validate all unique LCSH topical and geographic headings in WorldCat records. The validity of a heading from WorldCat was calculated based on frequency of use, source of cataloging, and various validation tables built from LC subject cataloging guidelines. A MARC 21 authority record was then created for each validated heading. As part of the generation and updating of FAST authority records, metrics for frequency of use of a given heading are generated and included in the FAST authority record. Table 1 provides a mapping of the facets to the appropriate fields in MARC21 bibliographic and authority records.

The FAST authority file is available for download[14] as a single file or by individual facet. In a particular application, some facets may not be required, or one or more of the facets may be used with another controlled vocabulary. The following are examples of a FAST topical authority record and a FAST geographic authority record, respectively:

```
LDR00000cz a2200037n 45 0
001 fst01099527
003 OCoLC
```

Table 1   Mapping of FAST facets to MARC 21 fields

FAST facet	MARC 21 format for authority data	MARC 21 format for bibliographic data
Chronological	148	648
Corporate name	110	610
Event name	111	611
Form/genre	155	655
Geographic name	151	651
Personal name	100	600
Title of work	130	630
Topical	150	650

```
005 20090915093506.0
008 041024nn anznnbabn || ana d
016 7#$a fst01099527$2 OCoLC
040 ##$a OCoLC$b eng$c OCoLC$f fast
053 #0$a QL737.R6$b QL737.R688$c Zoology
053 #0$a SB994.R6$c Agricultural zoology
150 ##$a Rodents
450 ##$a Rodentia
550 ##$a Mammals$0 (OCoLC)fst01006948
688 ##$a LC (2014) Subject Usage: 111 (239)
688 ##$a WC (2014) Subject Usage: 1,944 (3,626)
750 #0$a Rodents$0 (DLC)sh 85114803
LDR 00000cz a2200037n 45 0
001 fst01222022
003 OCoLC
005 20120706140721.0
008 060620nn anznnbabn || ana d
016 7#$a fst01222022$2 OCoLC
034 ##$d W0785815$e W0785815$f N0405637$g
    N0405637$2 geonames
040 ##$a OCoLC$b eng$c OCoLC$f fast
043 ##$a n-us-pa
151 ##$a Pennsylvania$z Punxsutawney
451 ##$a Pennsylvania$z Punxsy
670 ##$a GeoNames [algorithmically matched]$b
    ppl;40°56′37″N 078°58′15″W
688 ##$a LC (2014) Subject Usage: 16
688 ##$a WC (2014) Subject Usage: 99
751 #0$a Punxsutawney (Pa.)$0 (DLC)n 82132956
751 #7$a Punxsutawney$0 (GeoNames)5207307$2
    geonames$w nnna
751 #0$a Punxsutawney (Pa.)$0 (viaf)146606875$0
    (uri)http://viaf.org/viaf/146606875
```

FAST geographic name records include latitude, longitude, and geographic feature type when available. The sources of this information are LCSH and NACO authority records, and the GeoNames database. Software was created to match FAST geographic names to entries in the GeoNames database as part of the development of FAST.

Maintaining the FAST Authority File

Each month new and changed LCSH and new main heading/subdivision combinations from WorldCat are incorporated into the FAST Authority file. Headings from WorldCat must meet thresholds for literary warrant. Most of the updates are algorithmically determined; however, the more complicated mappings may require manual editing or review. When a valid FAST heading changes, its previously authorized form is maintained in a tracing field (MARC 4xx $wnne). Authority records for all previously valid headings are marked as obsolete (record status changed to "x" and retained in the FAST authority file.

TOOLS AND IMPLEMENTATIONS

Tools

Several tools are available from OCLC Research to help users understand and apply FAST.

FASTConverter

FASTConverter is a web application that converts LCSH headings to FAST headings.[15] This tool helps users become familiar with FAST and see the differences between LCSH and FAST. When a bibliographic record contains valid LCSH, it is possible to programmatically generate the corresponding set of FAST headings. Each subject heading is processed separately to create one or more FAST headings. The resulting FAST headings are then sorted and duplicate headings are removed. Conversion of sample sets of records allows for the evaluation of FAST as a subject cataloging system.

A central component of the FAST project is computer code that efficiently converts LCSH to FAST headings in bibliographic files. FASTConverter provides access to the conversion process for manually entered headings or for small sets of bibliographic records. LCSH headings can be entered as text, with conversion results displayed as plain text; or, MARC21 format bibliographic files can be uploaded for conversion. A link to the converted file is returned. Conversion files are limited to 50,000 bytes, or approximately 500 records. The following is an example of a set of LCSH headings before and after conversion to FAST:

LCSH before conversion

Personal name headings

Lacks, Henrietta, 1920-1951—Health
Lacks, Henrietta, 1920–1951

Topical headings

Cancer—Patients—Virginia—Biography
African American women—History
Human experimentation in medicine—United States—
    History
HeLa cells
Cancer—Research
Cell culture
Medical ethics

FAST headings after conversion

Personal name headings

Lacks, Henrietta, 1920–1951

Topical headings

African American women
Cancer—Patients
Cancer—Research
Cell culture
Health

HeLa cells
Human experimentation in medicine
Medical ethics

Geographic names

United States
Virginia

Form/genre headings

Biography
History

The same headings, as they would appear in a MARC 21 bibliographic record, are shown later. Each FAST heading includes a link to its corresponding FAST authority record in subfield $0. The inclusion of FAST authority record numbers in subfield $0 facilitates the automated validation and maintenance of FAST headings in bibliographic records.

Headings before conversion

> 600 10$a Lacks, Henrietta, $d 1920–1951 $x Health.
> 650 #0$a Cancer $x Patients $z Virginia $v Biography.
> 650 #0$a African American women $x History.
> 650 #0$a Human experimentation in medicine $z United States $x History.
> 650 #0$a HeLa cells.
> 650 #0$a Cancer $x Research.
> 650 #0$a Cell culture.
> 650 #0$a Medical ethics.

FAST headings after conversion

> 600 17 $a Lacks, Henrietta, $d 1920–1951 $2 fast $0 (OCoLC)fst01914767
> 650 #7 $a African American women $2 fast $0 (OCoLC)fst00799438
> 650 #7 $a Cancer $x Patients $2 fast $0 (OCoLC) fst00845411
> 650 #7 $a Cancer $x Research $2 fast $0 (OCoLC) fst00845497
> 650 #7 $a Cell culture $2 fast $0 (OCoLC)fst00850172
> 650 #7 $a Health $2 fast $0 (OCoLC)fst00952743
> 650 #7 $a HeLa cells $2 fast $0 (OCoLC)fst00952578
> 650 #7 $a Human experimentation in medicine $2 fast $0 (OCoLC)fst00963042
> 650 #7 $a Medical ethics $2 fast $0 (OCoLC) fst01014081
> 651 #7 $a United States $2 fast $0 (OCoLC) fst01204155
> 651 #7 $a Virginia $2 fast $0 (OCoLC)fst01204597
> 655 #7 $a Biography $2 fast $0 (OCoLC)fst01423686
> 655 #7 $a History $2 fast $0 (OCoLC)fst01411628

assignFAST

The assignFAST service provides autosuggest-style searching of the FAST subject heading database. The feature is accessible through a web-based user interface and through an application programming interface (API).[16] The user interface is ideal for day-to-day cataloging tasks. When a user of the web application starts typing, suggested authorized headings and variant headings are displayed. When a user selects either type of heading, the application presents a correctly formatted heading that can be copied into a cataloging interface. The API allows software developers to integrate the feature into another service or application.[17] The API enables easy selection of controlled FAST headings and can eliminate cut and paste operations.

searchFAST

SearchFAST is a full-featured search interface to the FAST authority file[18] that simplifies the process of heading selection. The user interface provides a search box, brief results list, and full view of a selected record on a single page. To increase searching accuracy, the application provides several indexes and the ability to restrict the results to a desired facet. Search results are ranked by usage, which positions the most likely candidate headings near the top of the results list. Search results can also be sorted alphabetically and in facet order. The user interface includes an autosuggest feature that makes the selection process even easier.

Implementations

WorldCat and FAST

Beginning in September 2013—in response to interest and requests from member libraries and to make OCLC's use of FAST easier to implement—OCLC began systematically adding FAST headings to WorldCat bibliographic records.[19] The records affected are those with LCSH assigned, and the routines are applied only to records that are attributed as being English-language-of-cataloging. The FAST enrichments are presented to users of WorldCat.org (a discovery interface) and Connexion (a cataloging interface) when users view an individual record, and also appear in Linked Data serializations of WorldCat that OCLC supports.

Metadata editing tools and FAST

OCLC WorldShare Record Manager provides a convenient means of adding FAST headings for users that are using the "text" view in the editor. This feature was made available as part of Record Manager in 2014.[20]

MarcEdit, a popular open source metadata editing tool maintained by Terry Reese, has a "Generate FAST Headings" tool feature. This feature as was added to MarcEdit in October 2013 and makes use of the assignFAST API.[21]

The BIBFRAME Scribe prototype by Zepheira demonstrates how to catalog materials in a native BIBFRAME

serialization. Scribe includes a search-and-FAST component in its editing toolkit.[22]

Backstage LibraryWorks provides a FAST validation service to its customers. The service can determine whether a given heading in a bibliographic record is a valid FAST heading.[23]

Agencies using FAST

Based on a study[24] by OCLC and other sources, at the writing of this entry a small number of institutions are known to be using FAST routinely. These include

- Bodleian Libraries, University of Oxford (UK)
- Chronicling Illinois & The Papers of Abraham Lincoln projects (US)
- Cornell University Libraries (US)[25]
- Databib.org (US)
- National Library of New Zealand (New Zealand)
- OCLC (US)
- RMIT Publishing (Australia)
- University of North Dakota (US)

Common applications include the use of FAST in metadata for digital materials (Oxford, Chronicling Illinois, Papers of Abraham Lincoln, University of North Dakota), journal articles (National Library of New Zealand, RMIT), datasets (Databib), and inside discovery tools (Cornell, OCLC).

RESEARCH

FAST Linked Data

During the initial phases of the FAST project, OCLC made a copy of the FAST authority file available up request, in MARC 21 authority format, to a small number of parties. As OCLC began releasing publicly accessible data sets, the FAST team pursued publishing FAST for open access.

In late 2011 with the support of LC, OCLC made the FAST authority file available as a data set under the ODC-By open license.[26] Formats offered include RDF, MARC 21, and MARC XML. FAST incorporates links to corresponding LCSH authorities. In addition, many of the geographic headings have links to the GeoNames geographic database[27] and personal names, corporate names, and titles of works records link to the VIAF (Virtual International Authority File) database[28] hosted by OCLC. FAST as linked data (expressed as schema.org) also appears in many worldcat.org linked data representations of WorldCat bibliographic data. An example of a FAST authority record as RDF is shown next:

```
<rdf:Description rdf:about="1222022">
<dct:identifier>1222022</dct:identifier>
```

```
<skos:inScheme  rdf:resource="ontology/
   1.0/#fast"/>
<rdf:type  rdf:resource="http://schema.
   org/Place"/>
<skos:inScheme  rdf:resource="ontology/
   1.0/#facet-Geographic"/>
<skos:prefLabel>Pennsylvania--
   Punxsutawney</skos:prefLabel>
<schema:name>Pennsylvania--
   Punxsutawney</schema:name>
<skos:altLabel>Pennsylvania--Punxsy</
   skos:altLabel>
<schema:name>Pennsylvania--Punxsy</
   schema:name>
<schema:sameAs>
<rdf:Description  rdf:about="http://id.
   loc.gov/authorities/names/n82132956">
<rdfs:label>Punxsutawney  (Pa.)</rdfs:
   label>
</rdf:Description>
</schema:sameAs>
<skos:relatedMatch>
<skos:Concept rdf:about="http://id.loc.
   gov/authorities/names/5207307">
<rdfs:label>Punxsutawney</rdfs:label>
</skos:Concept>
</skos:relatedMatch>
<schema:sameAs>
<rdf:Description      rdf:about="http://
   viaf.org/viaf/146606875">
<rdfs:label>Punxsutawney  (Pa.)</rdfs:
   label>
</rdf:Description>
</schema:sameAs>
<schema:geo>
<schema:GeoCoordinates>
<schema:latitude>40.94361</schema:
   latitude>
<schema:longitude>-78.97083</schema:
   longitude>
</schema:GeoCoordinates>
</schema:geo>
</rdf:Description>
```

OCLC Research Prototypes

OCLC Research develops prototypes and demonstrations systems to test ideas and processes. FAST appears in several OCLC Research prototypes. The following are some examples:

mapFAST

mapFAST is a mashup of FAST geographic and event authority data and Google Maps. The prototype is designed to provide map-based access to bibliographic records.[29] Mobile versions are also available.

WorldCat Identities

WorldCat Identities provides a characterization for every name in WorldCat. It includes a list of works by and about the identity, a FAST tag cloud of places, topics, etc., closely related to works by and about the person, links to coauthors, and more.[30]

Classify

Classify is an Functional Requirements for Bibliographic Records (FRBR)-based prototype designed to support the assignment of classification numbers and subject headings for books, DVDs, CDs, and other types of materials. FAST headings are used for the subject index and on the summary display.[31]

CONCLUSION

FAST, with its simple application rules, modular design, and tools for automated application and maintenance, is well positioned to meet the needs of catalogers and indexers challenged to provide efficient subject access to growing numbers of diverse resources. However, the future of FAST as a subject access tool will depend on the continued updating and development of the vocabulary, application of FAST to content, and a growing partnership with the community of FAST users.

ACKNOWLEDGMENTS

We acknowledge the careful reading and feedback from their fellow FAST Team members, Rick Bennett and Kerre Kammerer (both of OCLC Research). We also thank Edward T. O'Neill (OCLC Research, retired), Lynn El-Hoshy (Library of Congress, retired) and the late Lois Mai Chan (University of Kentucky, retired) for their indirect contributions as we have drawn upon their work, thinking, and writing as inspiration while preparing this entry.

REFERENCES

1. Hickey, T.B. CORC: cooperative online resource catalog. J. Libr. Admin. 2001, 34(3/4), 317–323. doi:10.1300/J111v34n03_11.
2. Childress, E. Crosswalking metadata in the OCLC CORC service. J. Internet Catalog. 2001, 4(1/2), 81–881. doi:10.1300/J141v04n01_08.

3. Chan, L.M.; O'Neill, E.T. *FAST: Faceted Application of Subject Terminology: Principles and Applications*; Libraries Unlimited: Santa Barbara, CA, 2010; 53–56.
4. http://www.oclc.org/research/themes/data-science/fast/history.html (accessed June 2017).
5. American Library Association. Subcommittee on Metadata and Subject Analysis. In *Subject Data in the Metadata Record: Recommendations and Rationale: A Report from the ALCTS/CCS/SAC/Subcommittee on Metadata and Subject Analysis*. Report. July 1999. http://www.ala.org/alcts/resources/org/cat/subjectdata_record (accessed June 2017).
6. The FAST Form/Genre headings are being aligned with Library of Congress Genre/Form Terms (LCGFT). http://id.loc.gov/authorities/genreForms.html (accessed June 2017).
7. Chan, L.M.; O'Neill, E.T. *FAST: Faceted Application of Subject Terminology: Principles and Applications*; Libraries Unlimited: Santa Barbara, CA, 2010; 71–72.
8. Introduction to Library of Congress subject headings, Library of Congress. http://www.loc.gov/aba/publications/FreeLCSH/lcshintro.pdf (accessed June 2017).
9. http://experimental.worldcat.org/marcusage/viz/starburst-tags.html (accessed June 2017).
10. MARC code lists for geographic areas. http://www.loc.gov/marc/geoareas/ (accessed June 2017).
11. Chan, L.M.; O'Neill, E.T. *FAST: Faceted Application of Subject Terminology: Principles and Applications*; Libraries Unlimited: Santa Barbara, CA, 2010; 87–96.
12. Chan, L.M.; O'Neill, E.T. *FAST: Faceted Application of Subject Terminology: Principles and Applications*; Libraries Unlimited: Santa Barbara, CA, 2010; 121–122.
13. Chan, L.M.; O'Neill, E.T. *FAST: Faceted Application of Subject Terminology: Principles and Applications*; Libraries Unlimited: Santa Barbara, CA, 2010; 99–102.
14. http://www.oclc.org/research/themes/data-science/fast/download.html (accessed June 2017).
15. http://experimental.worldcat.org/fast/fastconverter/ (accessed June 2017).
16. http://experimental.worldcat.org/fast/assignfast/ (accessed June 2017).
17. http://www.oclc.org/developer/develop/web-services/fast-api/assign-fast.en.html (accessed June 2017).
18. http://fast.oclc.org/searchfast/ (accessed June 2017).
19. OCLC. Enriching WorldCat with FAST. News release, September 25, 2013. OCLC. http://www.oclc.org/news/announcements/2013/enriching-worldcat-with-fast.en.html (accessed March 2015). Available on Wayback: https://web.archive.org/web/20150919121937/http://www.oclc.org/news/announcements/2013/enriching-worldcat-with-fast.en.html.
20. OCLC. WorldShare Record Manager. Program documentation. OCLC.org. http://www.oclc.org/support/services/record-manager.en.html (accessed June 2017).
21. Reese, T. MarcEdit 5.9 Update. *Terry's Worklog* (blog), October 10, 2013. http://blog.reeset.net/archives/1212 (accessed June 2017).
22. Zephira. About the BIBFRAME Scribe Prototype. Program documentation. Zephira.com. http://editor.bibframe.zepheira.com/static/about.html# (accessed June 2017).
23. Miller, J.D.; Naun, C.C. *FAST for cataloging and discovery: E-Forum summary*. ALA.org. 2013. http://www.ala.org/alctsnews/features/fast-cataloging (accessed June 2017).
24. Mixter, J.; Childress, E. *FAST (Faceted Application of Subject Terminology) Users: Summary and Case Studies*. OCLC: Dublin, OH, August 2013. http://www.oclc.org/content/dam/research/publications/library/2013/2013-04.pdf (accessed June 2017).
25. Cornell University Libraries. FAST headings for cataloging (LTS Procedure #127). Cornell.edu. http://lts.library.cornell.edu/lts/pp/cat/127FAST (accessed March 2015). Available on Wayback machine https://web.archive.org/web/20160129155707/https://lts.library.cornell.edu/lts/pp/cat/127FAST#F.
26. OCLC. OCLC Releases FAST (Faceted application of subject terminology) as linked data. News release. December 14, 2011. OCLC.org. http://www.oclc.org/news/releases/2011/201171.en.html (accessed June 2017).
27. http://www.geonames.org/ (accessed March 2015).
28. http://viaf.org/ (accessed March 2015).
29. http://experimental.worldcat.org/mapfast/ (accessed June 2017).
30. http://www.oclc.org/research/themes/data-science/identities.html (accessed June 2017).
31. http://www.oclc.org/research/themes/data-science/classify.html (accessed June 2017).

BIBLIOGRAPHY

1. Arash, J.; Mahdi, A.E. Classification of scientific publications according to library controlled vocabularies: a new concept matching-based approach. Libr. Hi Tech **2013**, *31*(4), 725–747. doi:10.1108/LHT-03-2013-0030.
2. Bennett, R.; O'Neill, E.T.; Kammerer, K.; Shipengrover, J.D. MapFAST: a FAST geographic authorities mashup with Google maps. Code4Lib J. **2011**, *14*. http://journal.code4lib.org/articles/5645.
3. Chan, L.M. Subject vocabulary for web resources. In *CASLIN*, Proceedings of CASLIN 2001, Popis a Zpřístupnění Dokumentů: Nová Výzva, Beroun, Czech Republic, 2001. http://klement.nkp.cz/caslin/caslin01/sbornik/subjectvoc.html.
4. Chan, L.M.; Childress, E.; Dean, R.; O'Neill, E.T.; Vizine-Goetz, D. A faceted approach to subject data in the Dublin core metadata record. J. Internet Catalog. **2001**, *4*(1/2), 35–47. doi:10.1300/J141v04n01_05..
5. Dean, R. FAST: development of simplified headings for metadata. Catalog. Classif. Q. **2004**, *39*(1/2), 331–352. doi:10.1300/J104v39n01_03.
6. O'Neill, E.T.; Bennett, R.; Kammerer, K. Using authorities to improve subject searches. Catalog. Classif. Q. **2014**, *52*(1), 6–19.
7. O'Neill, E.; Chan, L.M.; Childress, E.; Dean, R.; El-Hoshy, L.; Vizine-Goetz, D. Form subdivisions: their identification and use in LCSH. Libr. Resour. Tech. Serv. **2001**, *45*(4), 187–197.
8. O'Neill, E.T.; Chan, L.M. *FAST (Faceted Application of Subject Terminology): A Simplified LCSH-based Vocabulary*. Publication no. 010-E. August 2003. https://archive.ifla.org/IV/ifla69/papers/010e-ONeill_Mai-Chan.pdf.

9. O'Neill, E.T.; Childress, E.; Dean, R.; Kammerer, K.;
   Vizine-Goetz, D.; Chan, L.M.; El-Hoshy, L. FAST: Fac-
   eted application of subject terminology. In *Subject
   Retrieval in a Networked Environment: Proceedings of the
   IFLA Satellite Meeting Held in Dublin, OH, August 14–16,
   2001 and Sponsored by the IFLA Classification and
   Indexing Section, the IFLA Information Technology*
   Section, and OCLC, UBCIM Publications, New Series;
   K.G. Saur. München, Germany, 2003; Vol. 25, 140–146.

10. Vizine-Goetz, D. FAST headings as tags for WorldCat. In
    Subject Access: Preparing for the Future, IFLA Series on
    Bibliographic Control. International Federation of Library
    Associations and Institutions (IFLA): Berlin, Germany,
    2011; Vol. 42, 181–188.

Federal Electronic Information in the United States

Carol D. Doyle
Government Documents Department and Map Library, California State University, Fresno, California, U.S.A.

Abstract

The dissemination of federal information in electronic form, and in particular the use of the Internet, offer the opportunity to provide more timely, convenient, and widespread access to government information resources. However, identifying and locating needed government information can be difficult and frustrating for users attempting to navigate the fragmented and complex federal information landscape. This fragmentation is seen in the overwhelming number of federal Web sites that lack central coordination, even within a specific organizational hierarchy (e.g., departmental or legislative). It also appears in the varying media and formats in which the information may be offered and in the use of partnerships and privatization to distribute government information. Navigation is made more difficult by the fact that government information offered via the Web frequently changes location or apparently entirely disappears. The existence of multiple comprehensive locators, GPO Access, FedWorld, and the GILS, all established at the direction of Congress, and the Executive Branch's FirstGov, illustrates the lack of an overall strategy for the provision of access to federal information. The development of a comprehensive government-wide policy framework is needed to realize the promise offered by technology to improve public access to government information.

INTRODUCTION

Information producers and users alike have embraced electronic information technologies for the production and dissemination of electronic information resources. Information producers seek savings in the costs of producing and disseminating information, and both producers and users benefit from more timely dissemination of information and the greater ability to manipulate data disseminated in electronic formats. Because personal computers have become more affordable to a larger segment of the population and access to the Internet has become more widespread, electronic information resources have become increasingly accessible to individuals, businesses, and government agencies.

The federal government is one of the largest producers of information in the world. It has collected and disseminated information in a variety of electronic media and formats. Tangible information products have included magnetic tapes, to 5¼- and 3½-inch floppy disks, CD-ROMs, and DVDs. In addition to tangible products, throughout the 1990s there has been increasing on-line access to information housed in a wide variety of government databases and files accessible via dial-up bulletin boards and via the Internet. The electronic transformation of the Federal Depository Library Program (FDLP) began in 1989 with the distribution of the first CD-ROM to depository libraries, Census Test Disk Number 2, one of a number of pilot projects on disseminating electronic information to depository libraries, which were the result of much lobbying by the depository community. Through

the 1990s, the CD-ROM was the primary means of electronic information dissemination by FDLP. The number of titles distributed on CD-ROM peaked in 1998 and thereafter began a steady decline as online access replaced a growing number of titles formerly distributed on CD-ROM, print, and microfiche. By fiscal year 2001, about 60% of the titles in the FDLP were available online.[1]

Also in 2001, the 107th Congress was considering two electronic government (e-gov) bills, and the president had embraced the concept of a "citizen-centered electronic government."[2] Information technologies today play a major and ever-increasing role in the conduct of government business, and the access of citizens to information by and about their government will continue to be influenced by this transformation to an electronic federal information environment. Many of the policy issues being discussed today were first raised in the 1980s and early 1990s. These issues include questions of centralized versus decentralized dissemination and access points for federal electronic information and the role of the Government Printing Office (GPO) and the FDLP; concerns about the electronic information technologies creating the "information rich" and the "information poor"; concerns about the lack of a comprehensive policy framework addressing the life cycle of federal electronic information and the necessity of not only archiving or preserving it but also of ensuring persistent public access; and concerns about privacy, security, and ensuring the authenticity of federal electronic information resources. Other issues, such as debates over defining information as a public good or as a

Encyclopedia of Library and Information Sciences, Fourth Edition DOI: 10.1081/E-ELIS4-120008881

commodity, and the privatization of government information, are also long-standing concerns that have resurfaced in part because of other pressures such as reducing the cost of government and the information industry's concerns over the proper roles of government and private business in the dissemination of government information.

MAJOR FEDERAL INFORMATION LAWS AND REGULATIONS

An informed citizenry has long been considered to be one of the cornerstones of our system of government, and our nation has a long tradition of providing public access to government information. In 1813, to inform the people of the actions of their government, an act was passed to authorize the distribution of the House and Senate Journals to selected libraries and historical institutions.[3] By the late 1880s, the Government Printing Office was responsible for the depository library program. The depository system was expanded in the 1850s by the addition of congressionally designated libraries and was considered to be a "safety net" for making federal government information available to the public without cost to the individual user. The regional depositories, which were mandated to receive and retain a copy of all government publications, ensured long-term public access to the nation's historical record.

Throughout the past several decades, there has been a pronounced lack of a coherent overall policy framework for handling the dissemination of federal electronic information resources. Developments in information technology have made necessary a reexamination of the federal information laws and regulations that were created with printed information resources in mind, to incorporate access to electronic government information. New laws that addressed various aspects of the new information environment have been proposed during this time, and some have been enacted. An overview of the major laws and regulations related to government information dissemination can aid in understanding the current policy environment as well as public expectations for access to federal electronic information resources.

Title 44 United States Code: Public Printing and Documents

Title 44 of the U.S. Code is the statutory authority that gives the GPO's Superintendent of Documents responsibility for acquiring, classifying, cataloging, distributing to libraries, and ensuring the preservation of government publications. This centralized distribution system has been described as a funnel:

> Before the advent of the Internet, a primary method of access to federal information was one in which the U.S.

Government Printing Office (GPO) acted as a funnel through which agency produced information resources were distributed to federal depository libraries. Depository libraries, physically dispersed throughout the United States, offered local access to federal information. This model has typified most existing federal information dissemination programs, including the Patent and Trademark Office's depository library program, the GPO sales program, and the Education Resources Information Clearinghouse and National Technical Information Service.[4]

When agencies began to disseminate information in tangible electronic formats and online, the language of Title 44 was no longer adequate to accomplish its intent, providing for a centralized system to ensure the dissemination of and free public access to government information. The lack of statutory authority specifically requiring the dissemination of electronic information resources through the GPO to depository libraries has meant uneven compliance with the spirit of the law. Although some agencies have continued to use the GPO to distribute both their print and electronic information products, others have followed the guidance of the Office of Management and Budget (OMB), which, up until 1996, did not consider electronic products to be subject to Title 44. The various legislative efforts to revise the definition of government publications to include electronic information have all failed, including an attempt in the 105th Congress with Senate Bill 2288, the Wendell H. Ford Government Publications Reform Act of 1998, which sought a comprehensive reform of public printing and dissemination of government information in Title 44. The bill enjoyed the support of the library community and of the GPO, which saw it as "an important step forward in updating and modernizing the ability of the public to gain access to government information."[5] It failed primarily because of opposition from private publishing and information technology groups.[6]

The Paperwork Reduction Act (44 USC § 3501 et seq.)

The Paperwork Reduction Act (PRA), as first enacted in 1980 and amended in 1986, was an attempt to reduce the burden on the public of federal information collection and reporting requirements. This early PRA focused on cost-savings and efficiency, and one of its main effects was to discourage agencies from disseminating their information. In the PRA of 1995 (P.L. 104-13), public access to government information was specifically established as a responsibility of federal agencies. The PRA of 1995 instructs agencies to contribute to the Government Information Locator Service (GILS), an online inventory of federal government information that describes the content and location of their publications and records. It also established an Office of Information and Regulatory

Affairs (OIRA) within the Office of Management and Budget (OMB) to oversee agency information resources management activities and to develop information resources management policies, principles, standards, and guidelines. OMB's role in information resources management was revised and clarified by the PRA of 1995, in which the OMB was assigned oversight responsibility for information technology and for the life cycle of information resources in all formats. Under the PRA, each executive branch agency is responsible for its information resources management activities. The Information Technology Management Reform Act of 1996 (P.L. 104-106, Division E) amended the PRA by establishing a Central Information Officer (CIO) in each agency with the responsibility for its information technology programs and information resources management functions.

The primary directive issued by OMB in relation to its oversight of government information resources management policy is Circular A-130, *Management of Federal Information Resources*.[7] As first issued in 1985, Circular A-130 treated government information as a commodity and encouraged executive branch agencies to look to the private sector for the dissemination of their information resources and to price their products based on cost-recovery. It also discouraged the distribution of agency information through the GPO and the FDLP. Revisions to the Circular in the 1990s reversed the OMB's earlier policy of limiting the government's role in disseminating its information. Circular A-130 now affirms that the free flow of information between the government and public is essential to a democratic society and that agencies are responsible for providing information to the public. It limits user fees to a level sufficient only to recover the cost of dissemination and also specifies that agency publications, including those disseminated electronically, must be provided to the GPO for distribution to depository libraries, a provision sought by the depository community for many years.

Government Printing Office Electronic Information Access Enhancement Act of 1993 (P.L. 103-40)

Although the definition of government publications in Title 44 has not yet been amended to include electronic information resources, the GPO was given a formal role in providing access to federal electronic information with the passage of the Government Printing Office Electronic Information Access Enhancement Act of 1993. Popularly known as the GPO Access Act, it directs the Superintendent of Documents to:

1. Maintain an electronic directory of federal electronic information.
2. Provide a system of online access to the *Congressional Record*, the *Federal Register*, and other appropriate

publications distributed by the Superintendent of Documents.
3. Operate an electronic storage facility for the federal electronic information made available on that system.
4. Accommodate as feasible, agency and departmental requests to have their information included in the system.

GPO Access debuted in June 1994. Although free access was given to depository libraries, an access fee to recover the cost of dissemination was charged to other users as provided for by the act. Free access was extended to the general public in December 1995.[8]

Electronic Freedom of Information Act Amendments of 1996 (PL 104-231)

The Freedom of Information Act (FOIA) of 1966 (5 USC § 552) delineated the public's right of access to unpublished and unclassified federal agency records while protecting personal privacy and government security. As was the case with the definition of government publication in Title 44, agencies were not consistently interpreting the FOIA to include access to records in electronic form. The 1996 Electronic Freedom of Information Act (EFOIA) amended the FOIA and expanded the definition of a record to include electronic formats. It also mandated the establishment of "electronic reading rooms" to facilitate public access to major government records.

High Performance Computing Act of 1991 (P.L. 102-194)

The development of a national supernetwork of networks or "information superhighways" forming the backbone of a National Information Infrastructure (NII) was supported by the High Performance Computing Act of 1991. The act provided for a number of interrelated programs including high-performance computing research and development, the establishment of the National Research and Education Network (NREN) linking research institutions, government, and industry, and research and development of software and hardware. Federal agencies were to work with private network service providers, libraries, educational institutions, and others, to ensure that researchers, educators, and students had access to the network. The network would in turn provide access to a variety of electronic information resources including information from federal agencies and departments.

In 1993, the Clinton administration launched its National Information Infrastructure (NII) initiative to create partnerships between business, government, academia, and the public with the purpose of developing and extending access to the NII. Among the goals of the initiative were universal access, and improving the accessibility of government information.[9] The High Performance Computing Act was amended in 1998 by the Next Generation Initiative Research Act (P.L. 105-305), which continues the development of the NII by providing for the improving Internet capabilities, reliability, security, stability, and performance, and the development of advanced Internet applications. The act specifically recognized that an increasingly important role of the Internet is keeping citizens informed of the actions of their government.

IDENTIFYING AND LOCATING FEDERAL ELECTRONIC INFORMATION

Agencies are producing an increasing volume of their information products and services on a decentralized, local basis through the Internet. Nevertheless, public access to these web-based information resources may be limited, since they are not consistently included in the various existing government programs that foster information dissemination or information access, such as the FDLP, GPO Access, or NTIS.[10]

GPO Access

In today's Internet environment, there is a strong trend to decentralized dissemination of federal electronic information, yet the GPO still plays a valuable role in providing access to federal electronic information. Through its GPO Access system it provides free access to a wide variety of federal government electronic information resources such as databases housed on the GPO Access servers containing regulatory, congressional, and agency information. GPO Access also hosts federal agency files available for download via GPO's Federal Bulletin Board, hosts some federal agency Web sites, and provides a variety of tools to locate government information. GPO's *Catalog of U.S. Government Publications*, one of the major indexes to federal government publications, contains not only records for tangible products distributed through the FDLP but also records for and links to resources in the FDLP Electronic Collection, a virtual library comprised of core regulatory and legislative information on GPO servers and selected remotely accessible products.[11,12] A few of the other GPO Access finding aids include topical pathfinders to U.S. government information developed by volunteer government information librarians, an index to federal agency Internet sites, developed by government information librarians at Louisiana State University, and links to indexes created by federal agencies to identify their publications.

The National Technical Information Service

The National Technical Information Service (NTIS) has been another major clearinghouse of government information, specializing in government-funded scientific, technical, engineering, and business related information. Under direction by the American Technology Pre-Eminence Act (ATPA) of 1991 (P.L. 102-245) to develop a comprehensive inventory of federal government information products and services, by 1992 it introduced FedWorld, a gateway to information available through federal agency bulletin boards.[13] Today, FedWorld bills itself as "the online locator service for a comprehensive inventory of information disseminated by the Federal Government." Still offering its electronic gateway of more than 100 government bulletin boards, it also offers searching of agency Web sites and databases hosted by FedWorld and links to other government Web sites; a FedWorld FTP site contains more than 10,000 federal government data files. Although access to FedWorld is free, a number of the databases it offers are not.

The Government Information Locator Service (GILS)

Under the PRA of 1995, each agency is to establish and maintain an electronic agency information locator service to identify its major public information systems, holdings, and dissemination products, including electronic information resources. GILS records describe the information available in a resource and tell how to obtain or access the resource. Records describing resources accessible via the Internet should include a link to the resource.[14] Taken as a whole, this distributed system of agency information locators forms the federal GILS.[15] Uneven agency compliance with this decentralized approach to creating a governmentwide system has been one of its weaknesses. Other limitations are the lack of a single point of access that would truly define a federal GILS and that all agency GILS databases cannot be searched simultaneously. GPO Access offers the only cross-agency searching of GILS records, although it is limited to the 32 agency GILS databases it houses. It has also created pointer records describing and linking to the GILS of other agencies.[16] FedWorld's GILS page offers a search form and list of agency GILS databases, but only one can be selected and searched at a time.[17] Users have also been disappointed with the results of GILS searches because they expect to retrieve the full text of the resource instead of a description of it and information on how to get it.[18]

Subject Portals

Most federal government entities are using the Web to provide public access to varying amounts of information by and about them. In 1995, at the direction of the House of Representatives, the Library of Congress developed a Web site called THOMAS to make federal legislative information freely available to the public over the Internet.[19] THOMAS provides a search bill summary, status and text, voting, the Congressional Record, and committee information, It also provides links to congressional reports and Web sites, directories, guides to the legislative process, and historical documents. Much of THOMAS' content, the text of congressional bills, reports, the *Congressional Record*, is obtained from the GPO, and THOMAS offers users the option of linking to the pdf. or text versions of these legislative resources on GPO Access.

The Department of Energy's Office of Scientific and Technical Information (OSTI) is a shining example of agency use of the Internet to make its information resources available to the public. In partnership with GPO, OSTI introduced its *DOE Information Bridge* in 1995, giving access to the full text of research and development reports from DOE national laboratories and grantees.[20] OSTI has followed this well-received database with a number of others including the GreyLIT Network, a collaboration with the Department of Defense, NASA, and the Environmental Protection Agency.[21] GreyLIT provides access to the full text of technical reports generated through federally funded research and development projects, resources that were previously difficult to identify and locate. OSTI is now involved in a partnership with a coalition of science agencies to create Science.gov, a unified gateway to their scientific and technical information resources in the physical and life sciences. Science.gov is projected to become public in early 2002.[22,23]

FedStats, the "gateway to statistics from over 100 U.S. Federal agencies" is another cross-agency information-access partnership, providing a single location from which to discover federal government statistical information maintained on agency Web servers.[24] Access points include alphabetical lists of topics and agencies and an option to search across all or selected agency Web sites. Other departments and agencies, such as the U.S. Department of Agriculture (USDA), partner with educational institutions for assistance with disseminating their electronic information resources. The Mann Library at Cornell University hosts the Department of Agriculture Economics and Statistics System containing reports and data sets from USDA economics agencies.[25]

Web Search Engines

FirstGov is the latest "comprehensive" locator to emerge from the federal government.[26] An executive branch initiative administered by the General Services Administration, FirstGov was launched in September 2000 amidst a storm of publicity. Introduced by President Clinton, FirstGov was embraced by the Bush administration as an essential building block of a citizen-centered e-government.[27] It is touted as the "only official U.S. Government portal to 47 million pages of government information, services, and online transactions" and offers both a search engine and topical and agency directories.[28] On its release, it was found lacking in its general and apparently haphazard topical directory structure and in the poor performance and simple search

features offered by its search engine.[29] Its search engine has since improved, and the directory structure is currently under revision. Publicity for FirstGov overlooks the existence of GPO Access and other governmentally sponsored locators such as THOMAS, and how these other information providers and locators are to be integrated with FirstGov is not clear. Currently, FirstGov includes links to the GPO Access and DOE databases and to THOMAS under its "Reference Shelf." Although initially FirstGov did poorly in comparison to other major search engines at retrieving GPO Access pages, GPO Access has had some success in working with FirstGov to improve its search engine's retrieval from databases on the GPO Access servers. One study found FirstGov gave the best performance of 23 major search engines in retrieving information from GPO Access.[30]

Several other search engines focus on government Web sites, including usgovsearch and Google Uncle Sam.[31,32] Usgovsearch is a joint venture between NTIS and Northern Light and searches the citations and abstracts of material in the NTIS database, selected government Web sites, and Northern Light's Special Collection, a library of full-text journals, books, magazines, newswires, and reference sources. Searching usgovsearch is free, but there is a charge to retrieve the text of material from the NTIS Archive and the Special Collection. Google Uncle Sam is an option offered by the popular Google search engine that restricts searches to .gov and .mil domains. Although using Google Uncle Sam does limit retrieval to government Web sites, it also includes other levels of government using the .gov domain such as state government Web sites, and it omits Web sites in .org, .edu., .net, and .com domains with government information such as those created with partners in educational institutions. However, a great advantage either version of Google has over other search engines, including FirstGov, derives from the fact that a large amount of government information is posted to the Web as pdf files and other non-HTML formats, and Google is the only search engine to search non-HTML file types such as pdf and Microsoft Office documents.

Despite FirstGov's claims that its search engine searches every word of every U.S. government document, no single search engine retrieves all of the government information available on or through the Internet. Because of different searching and ranking methods, different search engines find and offer overlapping but different retrieval sets. Nonetheless, some or all material lurking in the "invisible Web" and the "opaque Web" eludes every search engine. This includes material that is accessible to the search engine but is not indexed for reasons including restrictions on the depth of crawl (amount of material indexed on a single site), frequency with which sites are revisited and reindexed, or that the crawler is not aware of the web page. It also includes pages not accessible to search engines such as databases that require registration to search and resources that require interaction such as the selection of variables that generates a custom page.[33] The Census Bureau's American FactFinder, THOMAS, and the GPO Access databases are examples of deep Web resource.[34] The best strategy to use in searching for federal government information accessible via the Web is to use multiple search engines in combination with subject directories, the various cross-agency tools such as offered by GPO Access, and NTIS, and to mine government agency sites by browsing and using their own site search engines and databases.

OTHER INFORMATION POLICY ISSUES

Variation and Obsolescence of Media and Formats

The variety of formats and media used to distribute government information was shown in the *Assessment of Electronic Government Information Products*.[35] This wide variety, together with the frequent lack of accompanying documentation, creates difficulties in providing access. Access to information distributed in older formats and media, such as the 5¼-inch floppy disks, is also threatened and sometimes lost because the required equipment or software is no longer available. Historical research and time series comparisons can be hindered because over time agencies have distributed data in a variety of formats and media. Several projects initiated by depository librarians are attempting to ameliorate some of these barriers to access. The GODORT CD-ROM Documentation Service provides bibliographic, content, use, technical, and management information for government-produced and government-related CD-ROMs, DVDs, and floppy disks.[36] The Floppy Disk Project at the Indiana University Bloomington campus provides a central location through which floppy disks that were distributed through the FDLP, and of which many are no longer accessible locally, can be located and downloaded.[37] Two projects illustrative of attempts to deal with the variation in user interfaces are the Oregon State University's Government Information Sharing Project, which provides Web access to a variety of federal statistical information issued through the FDLP on CD-ROM, and the University of California's announced Counting California, which has developed a single interface to data compiled by a growing number of federal, state, and local agencies.[38,39]

Economics of Access to Information

The initial use of electronic publishing technologies by agencies was to produce a less expensive printed product. It is now common for information to remain in electronic form from creation through dissemination. Although this may yield cost savings for the publisher, it can be viewed as a cost increase for the end user who now bears the cost of the equipment and software required to gain access to the electronic product, as well as the cost of printing the material as needed. Because it is becoming increasingly necessary for citizens to have access to computers and the Internet to connect with government information and services, there have been a variety of studies and reports on measures of "digital inclusion." Census Bureau surveys have shown a dramatic increase in the percentage of households with computers, from 8.2% to 51% between 1984 and 2000, and households with access to the Internet have increased from 18.0% in 1997 to 41.5% in 2000.[40] Although there were increases in computer ownership and Internet access across socioeconomic and geographic groups, "noticeable divides still exist between those with different levels of income and education, different racial and ethnic groups, old and young, single and dual-parent families, and those with and without disabilities."[41] However, an even greater divide is apparent when looking at high-speed, high-capacity, or broadband connections, because only half of those with access to the Internet have the option of a broadband connection. The 12% of Internet users who do subscribe to a broadband service tend to be of a higher income level and live in large metropolitan areas.[42]

The burden of the cost shift to the information user is exacerbated by the trend to commercialize or privatize government information. Commercialization refers to agencies that, by choice or by mandate, treat government information resources as a commodity and recover costs or generate revenues from their sale. An example of this is the National Technical Information Service, which is mandated by the American Technology Pre-Eminence Act of 1991 to be self-supporting. It sells access to its own database as well as to many of the agency databases it distributes, for example, the Department of Labor's Davis-Bacon Wage Determination Database. The Davis-Bacon database has been made available without charge through GPO, unlike some other commercialized resources such as the federal courts' PACER (Public Access to Court Electronic Records) system. PACER is funded through the collection of user fees by direction of congress and provides access to electronic versions of the opinions of the lower federal courts. Although some of the courts provide users free access to the actual opinions, others only link to the fee-based PACER. No free alternatives are available to the user because PACER is not made available without charge to depository libraries. The dissemination practices even within a commercialized program are not necessarily consistent, as seen with STAT-USA, an agency in the Economics and Statistics Administration of the U.S. Department of Commerce It is also required by law to be self-sustaining but manages to acknowledge Title 44 by providing depository libraries with one-password access to its main databases, State of the Nation, and GLOBUS and NTDB. It does not, however, extend this to its USA Trade® Online database, a

STAT-USA and U.S. Census Bureau, Foreign Trade Division collaboration.[43–46]

Privatization refers to federal agencies making exclusive contracts with the private sector, which "adds value" to and disseminates government information resources. A well-publicized example of privatization and the problems it can create for public access is the U.S. Department of Justice's contract with the West Publishing Company to maintain its database of case law and digests:

> JURIS includes a mix of non-copyrightable, public domain government information with proprietary information created by West Publishing Company. The JURIS database exemplifies the loss of government information to the public when an agency enters into an exclusive contract with a private entity without including in the licensing agreement provisions for public access mandated under Title 44. To this day, parts of the JURIS database, including its public domain content, is still controlled by West Publishing Company and public access, even under the Freedom of Information Act (FOIA), is prohibited.[47]

In contrast, although its dissemination subsystem is privatized, the U.S. Security and Exchange Commission's EDGAR (Electronic Data Gathering, Analysis, and Retrieval) database provides free public access through the SEC Web site.[48] The private sector has been vocal in its campaign to claim a larger and more exclusive role in the dissemination of government information resources and sees any value-adding activity as an encroachment onto the private sector's turf.[49] In the electronic information environment, an agency that creates software to provide public access to its own databases is seen by the information industry to be adding value and, therefore, engaging in inappropriate competition. The information industry also objects to projects such as PubScience, the Department of Energy's (DOE) database of citations with abstracts to peer-reviewed journal literature in the physical sciences and other disciplines of concern to the DOE.[50] DOE created the database and makes it available to the public for free as part of its mission to provide for the accessibility and dissemination of scientific information. The challenge to PubScience raises concerns that similar agency indexing projects, such as the National Library of Medicine's PubMed and the Education Department's ERIC database, may be forthcoming.[51–53]

The Safety Net

Disparities in access to information technology and the varying abilities to of citizens to pay the access fee for commercialized or privatized information has raised concerns that the government is participating in the creation of an information-rich and an information-poor situation. The government has recognized the necessity of connecting

libraries to the Internet to help provide access to those without access at home.[54] However, access to the information technology is only part of the equation. Librarians have long maintained that to ensure equitable access in the spirit of Title 44, depository libraries should have free access to databases and other electronic information products created by the government whether they are distributed by the government.

Privacy, Security, and Authenticity

The push to widespread implementation of e-government initiatives has heightened concerns for data privacy, security, and authenticity, and aspects of these issues are directly relevant to a discussion of federal electronic information resources. The Privacy Act of 1976 (P.L. 93-579) addressed aspects of personal privacy protection and restricted the ability of the federal government to collect and disclose personal information. It was amended in 1988 by the Computer Matching and Privacy Protection Act (P. L. 100-503), which regulates federal agency use of personally identifiable records in computer matching programs. The 1998 amendment applies only to records in systems subject to the Privacy Act and excludes matches performed for certain purposes such as statistics, law enforcement, and research. Maintaining the confidentiality of data is an ongoing concern for, as technologies continue to make it easier to access and share data, agencies and researchers see efficiencies and advantages in sharing and "repurposing" or linking data collected from multiple sources:

> Record linkage projects like these raise privacy issues, such as whether consent to linkage was obtained; whether linkages required sharing identifiable data with other organizations; and whether "deidentified" linked data are subject to reidentification risks when released for research or other uses.[55]

If people are not convinced about the confidentiality of their responses to government surveys and other data collection efforts, the reliability of those surveys and databases will decrease. Access to government data might be severely curtailed as an answer to privacy concerns, a reaction researchers and the data community hope to avoid.[56]

Another privacy concern is the collection of personal information about individuals who use government Web sites. OMB's Memorandum M-99-18 directed agencies to post on privacy policies on their principal Web sites to disclose what information is collected, why, and how it will be used. It was followed by M-00-13, which specified that the presumption should be that "cookies," which can be used to track an individual's use of Web sites, will not be used by federal Web sites.[57,58]

The Computer Security Act of 1987 (P.L. 100-235) established minimum security standards for federal computer systems. The Government Information Security Reform, Act (P.L.106-398 Title X, subtitle G) was an amendment to the PRA of 1995 requiring each agency to develop, implement, and maintain a security program and plan. Each agency must ensure the integrity, confidentiality, authenticity, availability, and nonrepudiation of information and information systems. Authenticity and nonrepudiation were addressed by the Government Paperwork Elimination Act (GPRA) of 1998 (P.L.105-277 Title XVII), which also amended the PRA to facilitate e-government by requiring agencies to make electronic versions of their forms available and allow the use of electronic signatures to file the forms electronically. One of the applications of electronic signature technologies is to ensure the recipient of downloaded federal electronic information that they have received a complete and unaltered copy of that information. The GPO is pursuing the use of public key infrastructure (PKI) technology to validate that the user has received the official text of congressional bills that reside on GPO Access.[59]

Permanent Public Access

Elimination of tangible government resources without a clear and systematic policy for electronic preservation and retention could greatly increase the number of fugitive federal documents and result in the deletion of important unique materials from computer systems.[60]

Historically, libraries in the Federal Depository Library Program were responsible for providing permanent access at no cost to the public for the government information products in tangible formats that were distributed through the program. Their role in providing permanent access focuses on public access to reference copies of publications and is distinct from that of the National Archives and Records Administration, which preserves an official copy of federal government records, including electronic records in its Center for Electronic Records. Permanent access in the electronic environment involves technological aspects of preservation, such as refreshing or transferring data from one medium to another and reformatting information due to software or platform obsolescence.[61] It also involves making the information accessible to the public on a continuing and indefinite basis in some online mode and/or through the collections of depository libraries. With the decentralized dissemination of online publications and databases combined with the lack of a centralized information policy, it is alarming but not surprising that much federal electronic information is neither making it into the depository system as tangible products for dissemination and permanent public access, nor are agencies themselves ensuring permanent access to their own information resources. Electronic-only publications

are easily revised or removed altogether, including annual reports and statistical publications from previous years.[62] Dynamic databases, allowing the creation of a "publication" tailored to an individual user that ceases to exist at the end of the session, are an advantage of the on-line environment, yet they are also endangered information if provisions are not made for the permanent accessibility of either the database or at the least, of prepackaged publications derived from the database.

The GPO has taken a number of steps to address the issues regarding preservation of and access to federal electronic information. The FDLP Electronic Collection Archive, established by authority of the GPO Access Act, contains "publications which are identified, described, and pointed to as part of the FDLP Electronic Collection and which are not part of the FDLP in any other form nor guaranteed to be permanently available by their issuing agency or entity."[63] GPO also coordinates a Permanent Public Access Working Group with participants from federal agencies, national libraries, congressional committees, the GPO and the FDLP, and public interest organizations.[64] Partnership agreements between GPO and federal agencies, such as DOE and the National Library of Medicine, ensure that content from their Web sites will be permanently available. The GPO also enters into content partnerships with depository libraries, who agree to host part of the electronic Permanent Online Collection for free use by the public. Two examples of content partnerships are Department of State Foreign Affairs Network (DOSFAN), a partnership with the U.S. Department of State and the University of Illinois at Chicago, and the "cybercemetary" at University of North Texas Libraries, which provides permanent online access to electronic publications of selected federal government agencies that have ceased operation.[65] Although these initiatives by the GPO to ensure permanent public access are still evolving, there is still much federal electronic information that is being missed by these efforts. Concerns have also been voiced about the loss of the safe redundancy offered by the depository system with multiple copies housed in collections across the nation and the shift of responsibility for permanent public access from libraries to the government. In response, it has been suggested that GPO acquire agency databases and digital versions of government publications posted on agency Web sites and make them available for selection by digital depository libraries.[66]

CONCLUSION

The dissemination of federal information in electronic form, and in particular the use of the Internet, offer the opportunity to provide more timely, convenient, and widespread access to government information resources. However, identifying and locating needed government information can be difficult and frustrating for users attempting to navigate the fragmented and complex federal information landscape. This fragmentation is seen in the overwhelming number of federal Web sites that lack central coordination, even within a specific organizational hierarchy (e.g., departmental or legislative). It also appears in the varying media and formats in which the information may be offered and in the use of partnerships and privatization to distribute government information. Navigation is made more difficult by the fact that government information offered via the Web frequently changes location or apparently entirely disappears. The existence of multiple comprehensive locators, GPO Access, FedWorld, and the GILS, all established at the direction of Congress, and the Executive Branch's FirstGov, illustrates the lack of an overall strategy for the provision of access to federal information. Although overlap and multiple points of access are not inherently bad, the lack of a unified vision and coordination of effort, as well as competition for funding, weaken the overall effort to provide access to federal information.

The development of a comprehensive governmentwide policy framework is needed to realize the promise offered by technology to improve public access to government information. Such a framework should incorporate the strong foundation of the past as embodied in the Federal Depository Library Program. Five principles for the dissemination of and access to federal government information were offered in the *Study to Identify Measures Necessary for a Successful Transition to a More Electronic Depository Library Program*:

1. The Public has the right of access to government information.
2. The government has an obligation to disseminate and provide broad public access to its information.
3. The government has an obligation to guarantee the authenticity and integrity of its information.
4. The government has an obligation to preserve its information.
5. Government information created or compiled by government employees or at government expense should remain in the public domain.[67]

Long overdue and made more urgent because much government information is increasingly available only electronically, perhaps the current move to e-government with its discussions of electronic access to government information and services will help bring about a review and reform of national information policy. A new comprehensive federal information policy framework that incorporates these historical principles and encompasses federal electronic information resources would recognize the vital role government information plays in the nation's economy, scientific, technical, and educational endeavors, and in our system of governance.

REFERENCES

1. Library programs service. FY 2001 annual report. Adm. Notes **2001**, *22*(15), 15–21. Available at http://www.access.gpo.gov/su_docs/fdlp/pubs/annrprt/01lpsar.html (accessed November 2001).
2. E-Government Act of 2001. Senate Bill 803 and House Bill 2458, 107th Congress. The President's Management Agenda: Fiscal Year 2002. Executive Office of the President, Office of Management and Budget, Washington, DC, 2001. Available at http://www.whitehouse.gov/omb/budget/fy2002/mgmt.pdf (accessed November 2001).
3. 3 Stat. 140 (1813).
4. Aldrich, D.M. Depository libraries, the internet, and the 21st century?. J. Gov. Inf. **1996**, *23*(4), 381–391.
5. DiMario, M.F. Public Printer, U.S. Government Printing Office, Washington, DC. *The Wendall H. Ford Government Publications Act of 1998: Hearings…, Congress. Senate. Committee on Rules and Administration*; S. Hrg. 105-1070, GPO: Washington, DC, 1998; 41–43. Prepared Statement.
6. Relyea, H.C. Public printing reform and the 105th congress. Gov. Inf. Q. **1999**, *16*(2), 129–147.
7. *Management of Federal Information Resources*, Office of Management and Budget, 2000; Nov. OMB Circular No. A-130; Available at http://www.whitehouse.gov/omb/circulars/a130/a130.html (accessed November 2001).
8. GPO Access. Available at http://www.access.gpo.gov/su_docs/index.html (accessed November 2001).
9. U.S. Information Infrastructure Task Force. *The National Information Infrastructure: Agenda for Action*, Information Infrastructure Task Force: Washington, DC, 1993. http://www.ibiblio.org/nii/toc.html (accessed November 2001).
10. U.S. National Commission on Library and Information Science. *A Comprehensive Assessment of Public Information Dissemination: Final Report*, NCLIS: Washington, DC 2001; Vol. 1. Available at http://www.nclis.gov/govt/assess/assess.vol1.pdf (accessed November 2001).
11. Catalog of U.S. Government Publications. http://www.access.gpo.gov/su_docs/locators/cgp/index.html (accessed November 2001).
12. Federal Depository Library Program. *Managing the FDLP Electronic Collection: A Policy and Planning* Document. GPO: Washington, DC 1998. Available at http://www.access.gpo.gov/su_docs/fdlp/pubs/ecplan.html.
13. FedWorld. Available at http://www.fedworld.gov/ (accessed November 2001).
14. *Guidance on the Government Information Locator Service*, Office of Management and Budget. 1998 Feb OMB Memorandum M 98-05; Available at http://www.whitehouse.gov/omb/memoranda/m9805.html (accessed November 2001).
15. The Federal GILS website. Available at http://www.gils.net/ (accessed November 2001).
16. GILS on GPO Access. Available at http://www.access.gpo.gov/su_docs/gils/ (accessed November 2001).
17. FedWorld's GILS page. Available at http://www.fedworld.gov/gils/index.htm (accessed November 2001).
18. Moen, W.E.; McClure, C.R. *An Evaluation of the Federal Government's Implementation of the Government Information Locator Service (GILS): Final Report*, U.S. General

Services Administration, Office of Information Technology Integration: Washington, DC 1997. Available at http://www.access.gpo.gov/su_docs/gils/gils-eval/index.html (accessed November 2001).

19. THOMAS. Available at http://thomas.loc.gov/ (accessed November 2001).

20. DOE Information Bridge. Available at http://www.osti.gov/bridge/ (accessed November 2001).

21. GreyLIT Network. Available at http://www.osti.gov/graylit/ (accessed November 2001).

22. Daukantas, P. Agencies lay groundwork for Science.gov portal. Gov. Comput. News **2001**, 7 Nov. Available at http://www.gcn.com/vol1_no1/daily-updates/17459-1.html (accessed November 2001).

23. Science.gov Alliance. *Strengthening the Public Infrastructure for Science*, National Technical Information Service, 2001. Available at http://www.science.gov/workshop/finalworkshopreport.pdf (accessed November 2001).

24. FedStats. Available at http://www.fedstats.gov/ (accessed November 2001).

25. U.S. Department of Agriculture Economics and Statistics System. Available at http://usda.mannlib.cornell.edu/usda/usda.html (accessed November 2001).

26. FirstGov. Available at http://www.firstgov.gov/ (accessed November 2001).

27. U.S. Office of Management and Budget. *A Blueprint for New Beginnings: A Responsible Budget for America's Priorities*, OMB: Washington, DC 2001. Available at http://www.whitehouse.gov/news/usbudget/blueprint/budtoc.html (accessed November 2001).

28. About FirstGov. http://www.firstgov.gov/top_nav/about.html (accessed November 2001).

29. *Comments on Firstgov Web Site*, American Library Association, October 18, 2000. Government Information Technology Committee; Government Document Round Table and Government Information Subcommittee; American Library. Available at http://www.nclis.gov/govt/assess/comment.

30. U.S. Government Printing Office, Electronic Product and Services Specialists, EIDS. *An Analysis of the Visibility of GPO Access in Major Internet Search Engines and Directories*, U.S. Government Printing Office, 2001. Available at http://Fedbbs.access.gpo.gov/library/download/SRCENG/Eval06.pdf (accessed November 2001).

31. usgovsearch. Available at http://usgovsearch.northernlight.com/ (accessed November 2001).

32. Google Uncle Sam. Available at http://www.google.com/unclesam (accessed November 2001).

33. Sherman, C.; Price, G. The invisible web. Searcher **2001**, 9 (6), 62–74.

34. American FactFinder. Available at http://factfinder.census.gov (accessed November 2001).

35. U.S. National Commission on Library and Information Science. *Report on the Assessment of Electronic Government Information Products*, GPO: Washington, DC 1999. Available at http://www.access.gpo.gov/su_docs/nclisassessment/report.html (accessed November 2001).

36. GODORT CD-ROM Documentation Service. Available at http://www.lib.uiowa.edu/govpubs/gitco_docs/gitco.html (accessed November 2001).

37. CIC Government Publications Task Force Floppy Disk Project. Available at http://www.indiana.edu/~libgpd/mforms/floppy/floppy.html (accessed November 2001).

38. Government Information Sharing Project. Available at http://govinfo.kerr.orst.edu/aboutus.html (accessed November 2001).

39. Counting California. http://countingcalifornia.cdlib.org/ (accessed November 2001).

40. U.S. Census Bureau. *Home Computers and Internet Use in the United States, August 2000*, Census Bureau: Washington, DC 2001. Current Population Reports. Special Studies P23-207. Available at http://www.census.gov (accessed November 2001).

41. U.S. National Telecommunications and Information. *Falling Through the Net: Toward Digital Inclusion, A Report on Americans' Access to Technology Tools*, NTIA: Washington, DC 2000. Available at http://www.ntia.doc.gov/ntiahome/digitaldivide/index.html (accessed November 2001).

42. U.S. General Accounting Office. *Telecommunications: Characteristics and Choices of Internet Users*, GAO: Washington, DC 2001. GAO-01-345. Available at http://www.gao.gov/new.items/d01345.pdf (accessed November 2001).

43. Davis Bacon Wage Determination Database via GPO Access. Available at http://www.gpo.gov/davisbacon/ (accessed November 2001).

44. PACER. Available at http://pacer.psc.uscourts.gov/ (accessed November 2001).

45. STAT-USA. Available at http://stat-usa.gov (accessed November 2001).

46. USATrade Online. Available at http://www.usatradeonline.gov (accessed November 2001).

47. Oakley, R.L. *The Wendall H. Ford Government Publications Act of 1998: Hearings...*, U.S. Government Printing Office, 1998; 97–100 Responses from.

48. SEC EDGAR. Available at http://www.sec.gov/edgar.shtml (accessed November 2001).

49. Stiglitz, J.E.; Orszag, P.R.; Prszag, J.M. *The Role of Government in a Digital Age*, Computer and Communications Industry Association: Washington, DC 2000. Available at http://www.ccianet.org/digital_age/report.pdf (accessed November 2001).

50. PubScience. Available at http://pubsci.osti.gov/ (accessed November 2001).

51. Butler, D. Budget proposal casts doubt over physics portal's future. Nature Webdebates. june 28, 2001. Available at http://www.nature.com/nature/debates/e-access/Articles/butler.html (accessed November 2001).

52. PubMed. Available at http://www.ncbi.nlm.nih.gov/PubMed/ (accessed November 2001).

53. ERIC. Available at http://www.eric.ed.gov/searchdb/searchdb.html (accessed November 2001).

54. U.S. National Telecommunications and Information Administration. *Connecting the Nation: Classrooms, Libraries, and Health Care Organizations in the Information Age. Update 1995*, NTIA: Washington, DC 1995. Available at http://www.ntia.doc.gov/connect.html (accessed November 2001).

55. U.S. General Accounting Office. *Record Linkage and Privacy: Issues in Creating New Federal Research and*

Statistical Information, GAO: Washington, DC 2001, GAO-01-126SP. Available at http://www.gao.gov/new.items/d01126sp.pdf (accessed November 2001).

56. Jacobs, J.; Peterson, K. The technical IS political. Of Signif. **2000**, *3*(1), 25–35.

57. *Privacy Policies on Federal Web Sites*, OMB Memorandum M-99-18 Office of Management and Budget, June 1999. Available at http://www.whitehouse.gov/omb/memoranda/m99-18.html (accessed November 2001).

58. *Privacy Policies and Data Collection on Federal Web Sites*, OMB Memorandum M-00-13 Office of Management and Budget, June 2000. Available at http://www.whitehouse.gov/omb/memoranda/m00-13.html (accessed November 2001).

59. Recommendations and responses. Adm. Notes **2001**, *22*(6), 11–17. Available at http://www.access.gpo.gov/su_docs/fdlp/council/rfa00.html (accessed November 2001).

60. McMullen, S.U.S. government information: Selected current issues in public access vs private competition. J. Gov. Inf. **2000**, *27*(5), 581–593.

61. *Study to Identify Measures Necessary for a Successful Transition to a More Electronic Federal Depository Library Program*, GPO Publication 500.11 U.S. GPO: Washington, DC 1996. Available at http://www.access.gpo.gov/su_docs/dpos/rep_cong/efdlp.html (accessed November 2001).

62. American Library Association, Government Documents Round Table. *Electronic Information No Longer Available on the Internet*, American Library Association, 1998. Available at http://sunsite.berkeley.edu/GODORT/9808missing.html (accessed November 2001).

63. U.S. Government Printing Office, Superintendent of Documents. *The Federal Depository Library Program Electronic Collection (FDLP/EC) Archive*, Last updated November. 20, 2000. Available at http://www.access.gpo.gov/su_docs/fdlp/ec/ecarc.html (accessed November 2001).

64. Permanent Public Access to U.S > Government Information Working Group. Available at http://www.access.gpo.gov/ppa/ (accessed November 2001).

65. FDLP Partnerships. Available at http://www.access.gpo.gov/su_docs/fdlp/partners/index.html (accessed November 2001).

66. Peterson, K.; Cowell, E.; Jacobs, J. Government documents at the crossroads. Am. Libr. **2001**, *32*(8), 52–55.

67. *Study to Identify Measures Necessary for a Successful Transition to a More Electronic Federal Depository Library Program*, U.S. Government Printing Office, 1996.

Film and Broadcast Archives

Karen F. Gracy
School of Library and Information Science, Kent State University, Kent, Ohio, U.S.A.

Karen E. King
Washington, District of Columbia, U.S.A.

Abstract

Film and broadcast archives serve as repositories for moving image and sound resources. Whether found in commercial or noncommercial settings, these archives aim to collect, describe, preserve, and make accessible audiovisual materials for users. Archives face many challenges in maintaining film, video, and audio materials, including physical deterioration, format obsolescence, and storage requirements. Audiovisual collections also require significant investment in appraisal, metadata generation for description, and access technologies. The abandonment of the motion picture film as a format for distribution and exhibition and the narrowing window of opportunity to transfer analog magnetic media will continue to drive the archival agenda. Copyright legislation, such as the Copyright Term Extension Act and the Digital Millennium Copyright Act, also complicate the mission of audiovisual archives to preserve and provide access to their materials.

INTRODUCTION

This entry aims to familiarize readers with the mission, goals, and activities of film and broadcast archives, which serve as the repositories for moving image and sound resources. These organizations, which may be found in commercial and noncommercial settings, aim to collect, describe, preserve, and make accessible audiovisual materials for users. While commercial archives tend to focus on the maintenance of collections for the purposes of republication in ancillary markets such as CDs and DVDs, web streaming, or for reuse in new productions, noncommercial archives more often aim to serve users interested in using moving images and audio for educational, artistic, or research purposes. Film and broadcast collections can be found in a variety of settings, including libraries, museums, archives, universities, radio and television news stations, corporations, and many other organizations where these materials are produced and used for education, information, or entertainment purposes.

Film and broadcast archives face unique challenges in providing the same sort of services that are often taken for granted by libraries and traditional archives. Audiovisual material requires different approaches and tools for its appraisal, description, access, and preservation. Yet, the current demand for visual and aural resources to enrich education, scholarship, news services, and entertainment means that institutions and organizations must invest in these rich sources of information.

This entry discusses the major institutions and organizations involved in audiovisual archiving, the scope of activities in which they are involved (including preservation, appraisal, cataloging and description, and access), and key issues archives are currently facing, including the transition from analog to digital formats, intellectual property concerns, funding for preservation of film and broadcast material, and educational opportunities for audiovisual archivists.

DEFINITION AND CHARACTERIZATION OF MOVING IMAGE ARCHIVES

Film Archives

Although collections of motion pictures were accumulated early on after the introduction and commercial exploitation of film in the 1890s, primarily by the distributors and exhibitors of early films, the prevailing attitude at the time of those involved in the motion picture industry was that films were disposable commodities rather than being seen as the subjects of study or artistic appreciation. This attitude changed quickly as intellectuals and film fans began to articulate the importance of motion pictures as cultural artifacts and information sources and clamored for the long-term retention of films for posterity.

The desire to provide a more permanent haven for film accelerated as the silent era drew to a close, when many motion picture studios attempted to jettison their libraries in the wake of sound film. The fear that the first decades of film would be lost encouraged several individuals to found organizations dedicated to the protection and exhibition of what were considered to be treasures of film heritage.[1]

Encyclopedia of Library and Information Sciences, Fourth Edition DOI: 10.1081/E-ELIS4-120053311

By the early 1930s, the first film archives recognized as such emerged in the United States and Europe. Operating primarily as either national repositories or collections within larger cultural institutions, these archives soon formed an international association known as the International Federation of Film Archives (FIAF) in 1938.[2] Founding members of FIAF included the Cinémathèque Française, the Museum of Modern Art Film Library in New York, the British Film Institute (BFI) National Film Library, and Germany's Reichsfilmarchiv. The establishment of cultural institutions devoted to the care of film heritage was evidence that films were beginning to be taken seriously as cultural artifacts and information sources. Readers interested in further information about the history of the film archive movement should consult Steven Ricci's article on this subject, found in this volume.

Collections of motion picture film were first amassed in the early decades of the twentieth century, as producers of films—production companies—began to build up their film libraries. Early film archives had mixed success in getting studios to donate material from their libraries to archive collections, due to fears that archives would somehow exploit films in violation of copyright law.[1] Some of this initial antagonism was overcome by the 1970s, however, as studios began to look for ways to unburden themselves from the expenses of storing large quantities of nitrate film and later, 16 mm television prints.[3] In this manner, a number of archives in the United States acquired access copies of the first half-century of motion picture production. Due to copyright deposit requirements, the Library of Congress has amassed the largest collection of film in the United States, and one of the largest in the world. Table 1 summarizes the most prominent film collections in the United States, including size of collections and strengths. For an extensive list of film archives and research centers throughout the world, please consult the website of the Library of Congress, which maintains a directory.[4] Many commercial copyright owners maintain their own library of titles and footage, and thus must also be considered as important sources for film resources. These libraries are maintained primarily for the purposes of commercial exploitation, rather than as public resources, however.

Outside of the United States, many archives have acquired copies of films through deposit laws that require production companies to give copies of films, particularly those financed in whole or in part by the government, to the national archive. For a complete list of European Union countries that have deposit laws, please consult the list compiled by the International Federation of Film Producers Associations (FIAPF).[5]

Broadcast Archives and Collections

Until quite recently, producers of broadcast radio and television in the United States had an inconsistent record of preserving their productions for long-term retention. While some earliest productions were captured on transcription discs (in the case of radio), or on film (for early television), the switch to videotape, which began in the 1950s with the introduction of the earliest formats and became near universal by the late 1960s/early 1970s, meant that content often was seen as more disposable. Due to the expense of the new magnetic medium, it was quite common for commercial stations to erase and reuse the newly adopted tape. While certain news and entertainment segments were seen as having potential for reuse in other programs, others were quickly deleted to make way for new programming. Yet, many commercial stations still own unique historic material that has great use in education, research, and other uses.[6] The television and video archives movement in North America was a response to the new use of videotape for education and documentation. Furthermore, the 1976 revision of the American copyright law encouraged off-air taping of hard news broadcasts and established the new American Television and Radio Archives.[7]

Broadcast archives and collections exist in many different sizes and formats throughout the world. Table 2 summarizes the most well-known broadcast archives collections in the United States, Europe, and Asia, including size of collections and strengths.

The following section will describe various archives and collections throughout the world, which may be categorized as academic, museum, government, or station collections.

Academic Collections

The United States has many different academic broadcast collections covering both television and radio, commercial and noncommercial. First, Special Collections in Mass Media & Culture (SCMMC), as a unit of Special Collections and University Archives at the University of Maryland Libraries, holds a wide-ranging assortment of resources documenting the history of commercial, public, and educational radio and television broadcasting, through its two component collections, the National Public Broadcasting Archives (NPBA) and the Library of American Broadcasting. SCMMC also has substantial secondary resources in the areas of cinema, print journalism, and humor studies.[8]

The first organized library of radio history was the Broadcast Pioneers Library, which began in 1972. From 1964 to 1971, former National Broadcasting Company (NBC) executive William S. Hedges collected items for the Broadcast Pioneers History Project. These materials, comprising approximately 13,000 items, including correspondence, articles, and speeches, formed the core collection of the Broadcast Pioneers Library and were housed in the National Association of Broadcasters' (NAB) headquarters in Washington, DC, until 1994. That year, it

Table 1 Major motion picture archives in the United States (collections consisting of at least 10,000 titles, items, or equivalent).

Archive	Collection size	Collection strengths
Academy Film Archive[a]	Over 190,000 items	Academy Award–nominated films; film and television programs relating to the Academy Awards shows; documentary film holdings including the collection of the International Documentary Association; home movies and amateur films, particularly those related to the history of Hollywood, the motion picture industry, and the history of the Los Angeles region
Archive Films (parent company is Getty Images)[b]	31,000 titles	Documentaries; news footage; actualities; industrial films
George Eastman House[c]	More than 28,000 titles; collection of stills, posters, and papers with over 3 million artifacts	Silent film; personal film collections of directors Kathryn Bigelow, Ken Burns, Cecil B. DeMille, Norman Jewison, Spike Lee, and Martin Scorsese; largest collection of nitrate Technicolor negatives in the United States
Human Studies Film Archives, Smithsonian Institution[d]	Approximately eight million feet of film and video	Ethnographic film
Indiana University Libraries Moving Image Archive[e]	More than 86,000 items	Educational film and video collections, many produced by Indiana University
Library of Congress[f]	More than 400,000 titles (approximately 750,000 items)	Studio features; independent features, documentaries;newsreels; animation; trailers
Museum of Modern Art (NY)[g]	More than 22,000 films; four million film stills	International cinema; silent film (particularly Biograph and Edison companies, and the films of D.W. Griffith); circulating collection of more than 1200 16 mm prints that include many classics of world cinema
National Archives and Records Administration[h]	Nearly 300,000 motion picture films; more than 200,000 sound and video recordings	Universal Newsreel collection; motion pictures created by the U.S. Armed Forces; Ford Motor Company Collection; U.S. Atomic Energy Commission
Northeast Historic Film[i]	900 collections; 29,000 individual items	Film and videotape related to the northern New England region (Maine, New Hampshire, Vermont, and Massachusetts); major collections include film and videotape originating from television stations or created primarily for broadcast, industrial works created by and for corporate and industrial entities, professionally created fictional works, titles made by independent creators intended for public viewing, and amateur films
Pacific Film Archive[j]	More than 16,000 films and videos	International features (particularly Japan, Soviet Union, Eastern Europe, and Central Asia); studio features; independent features; documentaries; experimental/avant-garde films; educational films; animation; trailers
UCLA Film and Television Archive[k]	More than 350,000 films and 160,000 television programs; 27 million feet of newsreel footage	35 mm collections from Paramount Pictures, Twentieth Century Fox, Warner Bros., Columbia Pictures, New World Pictures, Orion Pictures, RKO Pictures, and Republic Pictures; Hearst Metrotone newsreels; 16 mm film collection of over 5000 titles; animation; live-action shorts; personal donations from William Wyler, Jean Renoir, King Vidor, George Pal, Stanley Kramer, Tony Curtis, and Robert Aldrich

(Continued)

Table 1 Major motion picture archives in the United States (collections consisting of at least 10,000 titles, items, or equivalent). *(Continued)*

Archive	Collection size	Collection strengths
Walter J. Brown Media Archive and Peabody Awards Collection, University of Georgia Libraries[l]	250,000 titles in film, video, and audio formats; 5 million feet of newsfilm clips	Entries for the Peabody Awards for broadcast journalism; newsfilm and amateur film (focusing on the Southeast and Atlanta regions, particularly Civil Rights era documentation); documentaries

[a] **Source:** Academy of Motion Picture Arts and Sciences, http://www.oscars.org/filmarchive/about/index.html (accessed December 7, 2016).

[b] **Source:** *AMIA Compendium of Moving Image Cataloging Practice*, ed. Abigail Leab Martin; Association of Moving Image Archivists: Beverly Hills, CA, 2001.

[c] **Source:** George Eastman House International Museum of Photography and Film, https://www.eastman.org/moving-image (accessed December 7, 2016).

[d] **Source:** Human Studies Film Archives, Smithsonian Institution, http://www.anthropology.si.edu/naa/home/hsfahistory.html (accessed December 7, 2016).

[e] **Source:** http://libraries.iub.edu/iulmia (accessed December 7, 2016).

[f] **Source:** *AMIA Compendium of Moving Image Cataloging Practice*, ed. Abigail Leab Martin; Association of Moving Image Archivists: Beverly Hills, CA, 2001.

[g] **Source:** Museum of Modern Art, http://www.moma.org/explore/collection/film (accessed December 7, 2016).

[h] **Sources:** National Archives and Records Administration, https://www.archives.gov/research/start/by-format.html#film (accessed December 7, 2016). *AMIA Compendium of Moving Image Cataloging Practice*, ed. Abigail Leab Martin; Association of Moving Image Archivists: Beverly Hills, CA, 2001.

[i] **Sources:** Northeast Historic Film, http://www.oldfilm.org (accessed December 7, 2016). *AMIA Compendium of Moving Image Cataloging Practice*, ed. Abigail Leab Martin; Association of Moving Image Archivists: Beverly Hills, CA, 2001.

[j] **Sources:** Pacific Film Archive, http://www.bampfa.berkeley.edu/about/bampfa-collection (accessed December 7, 2016). *AMIA Compendium of Moving Image Cataloging Practice*, ed. Abigail Leab Martin; Association of Moving Image Archivists: Beverly Hills, CA, 2001.

[k] **Sources:** UCLA Film and Television Archive, https://www.cinema.ucla.edu/collections/explore-collections (accessed December 7, 2016). *AMIA Compendium of Moving Image Cataloging Practice*, ed. Abigail Leab Martin; Association of Moving Image Archivists: Beverly Hills, CA, 2001.

[l] **Sources:** Walter J. Brown Media Archive and Peabody Awards Collection, University of Georgia Libraries, http://www.libs.uga.edu/media/about/history.html (accessed December 7, 2016). *AMIA Compendium of Moving Image Cataloging Practice*, ed. Abigail Leab Martin; Association of Moving Image Archivists: Beverly Hills, CA, 2001.

moved to the University of Maryland and changed its name to the Library of American Broadcasting (LAB). The LAB collection, which is one of the most extensive collections in the history of broadcasting, includes audiovisual materials, books, photographs, pamphlets, periodicals, manuscripts, oral histories, and scripts pertaining to the history of the field.[9]

The NPBA is another academic broadcast collection. Since it began in June 1990 at the University of Maryland, NPBA's mission has been to preserve and make accessible the archival record of the major organizations of public broadcasting, to archive personal papers of individuals who made significant contributions to educational and public broadcasting, and to provide archival services to several Washington, DC, metropolitan area public stations. While NPBA's first concern is textual material, it also has a growing audiovisual component.[10]

Other academic collections of note include the Wisconsin Historical Society's Mass Communications History Collections, the UCLA Film & Television Archive, and the Vanderbilt Television News Archive. The Wisconsin Historical Society's Mass Communications Collection began in 1955 with the purpose of documenting the importance of mass media in twentieth century American life. Its collections include the records of NBC, the Association of Education in Journalism and Mass Communications, and National Educational Television (NET), as well as

the papers of David Brinkley, H.V. Kaltenborn, and Howard K. Smith.[11]

The UCLA Film & Television Archive, the second largest moving image archive in the United States, began in 1965, when the Academy of Television Arts and Sciences and the UCLA Theater Arts Department created the ATAS/UCLA Television Library. In 1976, the Television Library merged with the Film Archive to become the UCLA Film & Television Archive.[12]

Finally, the Vanderbilt Television News Archive began in August 1968 with the mission of preserving and providing access to television newscasts from U.S. national news networks. It operates in conjunction with the Motion Picture, Broadcasting and Recorded Sound Division of the Library of Congress, providing copies for the Library's permanent collection.[13]

Museums and Libraries

Prominent museums and libraries with broadcasting collections include the Museum of Broadcast Communications (MBC), the Paley Center for Media, and the Thousand Oaks Library collection. The MBC, located in Chicago, Illinois, is a combination of archive, media arts center, educational institution, and museum. Since 1987, the MBC collects and preserves historic and contemporary broadcasting content in order to educate and entertain

Table 2 Major broadcast archives and collections worldwide (consisting of at least 10,000 titles, items, or equivalent).

Archive	Collection size	Collection strength
Special Collections in Mass Media and Culture–Library of American Broadcasting (LAB), National Public Broadcasting Archives (NPBA)[a]	10,000 books and monographs, 8,000 broadcasting industry pamphlets, 93,000 audiotapes of various formats, 20,000 audio CDs, 11,000 videotapes of various formats, 1,000 films and kinescopes, 8,000 recorded discs, 2,500 radio and television scripts, 300,000 photographs	Extensive collections making the past and present of commercial and noncommercial broadcasting widely accessible. Key NPBA collections include Archives of the Corporation for Public Broadcasting, National Public Radio, Children's Television Workshop, WAMU-FM Programming Archives, C. Scott Fletcher Papers, and James Day Papers. Key LAB collections include WNET-Thirteen Arthur Godfrey Collection, *Vox Pop* Program Collection, Radio Advertising Bureau (RAB) Collection
Wisconsin Historical Society. Mass Communications History Collections[b]	1000 ft^3 of paper collections, more than 5000 audio recordings, and more than 500 films	Papers of significant individuals, organizations, corporations in mass communications including NET, David Brinkley, and Joseph Hanna
UCLA Film and Television Archives[c]	More than 350,000 films and 160,000 television programs, more than 100,000 News and Public Affairs programs, more than 2,000 radio programs	Materials cover broadcast history such as DuMont TV, the Hearst Metrotone News, news and public affairs taped off-air from 1979 to 2003
Vanderbilt Television News Archive[d]	More than 60,000 news broadcasts from NBC, ABC, CBS, Fox, and CNN	Materials span the presidential administrations from Johnson to Obama. Notable topics covered include political conventions, presidential speeches, events of September 11, 2001, the Persian Gulf War, and the wars in Afghanistan and Iraq
Museum of Broadcast Communications (MBC)[e]	Scores of radio memorabilia, working radio and television studios, etc. 62,000 ft^2 facility that includes the National Radio Hall of Fame	Films, videos, photographs, audio recordings, and scripts representing genres including television entertainment, television news, and instructional/educational programming
Paley Center for Media[f]	Nearly 140,000 programs and advertisements	Documents the intersection between media and society through collections and public events
Library of Congress[g]	Approximately 80,000 television programs	Examples include the NBC Collection comprising a wide variety of genre programming and the NET Collection with more than 10,000 titles from early noncommercial U.S. television
WGBH Media Archives and Preservation Center[h]	More than 1 million audiovisual materials accessed through Open Vault	Examples include television series like "Vietnam: A Television History," "American Playhouse," and "The French Chef"
Pacifica Radio Archives[i]	More than 50,000 recordings	Programs document political, cultural, and artistic movements since the 1950s
United Kingdom		
British Broadcasting Company (BBC) Sound Archive[j]	Over 1 million discs, 185,000 tapes, and many other sound and video recordings from all over the world	Includes off-air radio programs since 1960, and off-air television programs since 1980. Subjects include music, drama, literature, oral history, and wildlife sound
BBC Written Archives Centre[k]	Thousands of files, scripts, and working papers	Documents BBC history from formation in 1922 to the 1980s; other topics include history and development of mass communication and changes in popular culture
National Archive, British Film Institute[l]	Nearly one million film and television titles.	Rich resource of British television programming

(Continued)

Table 2 Major broadcast archives and collections worldwide (consisting of at least 10,000 titles, items, or equivalent). *(Continued)*

Archive	Collection size	Collection strength
National Media Museum[m]	More than 3.5 million items of television history including television receivers, studio equipment, and video recorders	Documents the technological evolution of television and film
Japan		
Nippon Hoso Kyokai (NHK)[n]	More than 8 million news and program items	Documents Japanese programs, both current and historical
Canada		
Canadian Broadcasting Company (CBC) Program Archives[o]	Millions of discs, tapes, films, photographs, written records, and computer files	Documents 70 years of Canadian radio and television history
Australia		
Australian Broadcasting Corporation (ABC) Archives and Library Services[p]	More than 100,000 radio and television programs, photographs, and documents	Documents Australian media created since 1932
National Film and Sound Archive[q]	More than 2.3 million films, radio programs, television programs, videos, audiotapes, etc.	Documents Australia's audiovisual heritage

[a] **Sources**: Special Collections in Mass Media and Culture (SCMMC), http://www.lib.umd.edu/special/collections/massmedia/home (accessed December 7, 2016). C. Howell, Collection Leader, SCMMC (personal communication, November 4, 2014).

[b] **Sources**: A.E. Bridger, Archivist – Bibliographic Information Systems, Library –Archives Division, Wisconsin Historical Society (personal communication, September 18, 2014).
WHS – Mass Communications History Collections Factsheet, http://www.wisconsinhistory.org/pdfs/la/WHS-MassCommFactSheet.pdf (accessed December 7, 2016).

[c] **Source**: UCLA Film and Television Archive –Explore Collections URL, https://www.cinema.ucla.edu/collections/explore-collections (accessed December 7, 2016).

[d] **Source**: Vanderbilt TV News Archive URL, http://tvnews.vanderbilt.edu/web/tvnews/about/ (accessed December 7, 2016).

[e] **Source**: Museum of Broadcast Communications - About Us – URL, http://www.museum.tv/about_us.htm (accessed December 7, 2016).

[f] **Sources**: Paley Center URL, http://www.paleycenter.org/ (accessed December 7, 2016).
Mission and History. About Us – Paley Center, http://www.paleycenter.org/about-mission-history/ (accessed December 7, 2016).

[g] **Source**: Murphy, W.; Library of Congress. *Television and Video Preservation 1997: A Report on the Current State of American Television and Video Preservation: Report of the Librarian of Congress*, Library of Congress: Washington, DC, 1997.

[h] **Sources**: WGBH Open Vault – About; Open Vault - Series: http://openvault.wgbh.org/about/ (accessed December 7, 2016). http://openvault.wgbh.org/series (accessed December 7, 2015).

[i] **Source**: Pacifica Radio Archives – About the Archives, http://www.pacificaradioarchives.org/about-archives (accessed December 7, 2016).

[j] **Source**: BBC Sound Archive – About, http://www.bl.uk/subjects/sound (accessed December 7, 2016).

[k] **Source**: BBC Written Archives Centre, http://www.bbc.co.uk/informationandarchives/access_archives/bbc_written_archives_centre (accessed December 7, 2016).

[l] **Source**: British Film Institute National Archive, http://www.bfi.org.uk/archive-collections (accessed December 7, 2016).

[m] **Source:** National Media Museum – Television Collection, http://www.nationalmediamuseum.org.uk/Collection/Television.aspx (accessed December 7, 2016).

[n] **Sources:** NHK International, http://www.nhkint.or.jp/en/foundation/ (accessed December 7, 2016).
NHK Video Bank, http://www.nhkint.or.jp/en/footage (accessed December 7, 2016).

[o] **Source:** CBC Digital Archives, http://www.cbc.ca/archives/ (accessed December 7, 2016).

[p] **Source:** ABC Archives, http://www.abc.net.au/archives/ (accessed December 7, 2016).

[q] **Sources:** About Us – National Film and Sound Archive, http://www.nfsa.gov.au/about/ (accessed December 7, 2016). National Film and Sound Archives of Australia, Annual Report, 2013–14.

visitors and researchers through various outreach activities including public programs, exhibits, on-site visits to the archives, and online access.[14] Formerly known as The Museum of Television and Radio, the Paley Center has a large collection of television and radio programming documenting 100 years of media history.[15]

The American Radio Archives, found in the Special Collections Department of the Thousand Oaks Library System, California, has an extensive broadcast document collection including thousands of radio and television scripts, pamphlets, sound recordings, manuscripts, and personal papers. The library also holds personal papers of people such as Norman Corwin and Rudy Vallee.[16]

Government

The Library of Congress began collecting and preserving radio and television programs in the 1940s. In 1976, the Copyright Act established the American Television and Radio Archives at the Library of Congress, which is now administered by the Motion Picture, Broadcasting and Recorded Sound Division.[17] This collection contains approximately 80,000 television programs, focusing on prime-time entertainment series. For example, the NBC Collection consists of a wide variety of genre programming including sports and children's programs from 1948 to 1977. Its NET Collection has over 10,000 titles from early noncommercial U.S. television.[18] In 1993, after years of negotiations, the Library of Congress agreed to accession all programs aired and retained by Public Broadcast Service (PBS), which could exceed over 100,000 items.[17]

The National Archives and Records Administration (NARA) is the other governmental body with a significant amount of broadcast-related material. Examples include the Records of the Federal Communications Commission (FCC).[19] and the Records of the National Telecommunications and Information Administration (NTIA).[20]

Broadcasting Stations

Many stations either have their own archives or work with local universities and historical societies when appropriate. For example, while the NPBA cannot serve as a central repository for all public broadcasting stations, NPBA's mission includes advising stations to create archival agreements with local universities and historical societies.[10] One prominent public broadcasting station archive is the WGBH Media Archives and Preservation Center. Established in 1978 as part of the Film Operations Department, its collection mostly consists of nearly 1 million audio, video, and digital assets. With funding support from the Andrew W. Mellon Foundation, the WGBH MLA created Open Vault, an online media archive content delivery system for academic and research use.[21]

The Pacifica Radio Archives, described as "... one of the oldest and most important audio collections in the world," has audio material from five member stations ranging from documentaries to poetry readings. Its mission is to "... appraise, collect, organize, describe, and preserve the creative work generated by or produced in association with Pacifica Radio...and to make it available for reference and research use".[22]

INTERNATIONAL

On the international scene, broadcast collections tend to be less widely dispersed, as stations are usually government owned. This section will look at broadcast archives and their respective repositories in the United Kingdom, Japan, Canada, and Australia.

United Kingdom

In the United Kingdom, the broadcasting collections range from materials aired by the public service television entity, the British Broadcasting Company (BBC), and the commercial broadcasters, Independent Television News (ITN) and Thames Television, as well as material located at the BFI.

The BBC began under a Royal Charter of Incorporation in 1927, granted when the company was a radio organization. The BBC is mostly funded through a license fee

system with supplemental income through foreign sales and cable and satellite contracts. It is a national broadcaster based in London with eight regional studios in England and other studios in Wales, Scotland, and Northern Ireland.[23] Selected BBC radio and television programs are archived in the BBC Sound Archive at the British Library with its holdings reflecting trends and interests of different generations. The holdings include off-air radio programs since 1960 and off-air television programs since the late 1980s with subjects such as music, drama, literature, oral history, and wildlife sound.[24] The BBC written documentation is archived in the BBC Written Archives Centre, located in Reading. The Centre has material that documents the history of past programming (more than 3 years old), the history and development of mass communication, and changes in tastes and popular culture.[25]

Commercial television in the United Kingdom began in the mid-1950s when Parliament established the Independent Television Authority (ITA) on July 30, 1954. Other commercial television companies such as Thames Television, Associated-Rediffusion, London Weekend Television, Granada Television Network, and Channel 4 decided to work together to compete with the BBC for audience share. Jointly they own ITN, a profit-making news business.[23] Part of ITN Source, one of the largest moving image libraries in the world, the Archive began in 1955 with the first ITN news program broadcast. In 1998, after housing ITN's news programs since 1955, the ITN Archive signed a deal to sell Reuters' news library. In 2002, ITN Archive began managing the Channel 4 Archive clip-sales business, and in 2003, it started marketing and managing the historic British Pathé film archive with footage dating back to 1896. Other deals benefiting the ITN Archive include the representation of Granada Television clips in 2003, the representation of U.S. Fox News and Fox Movietone archives in 2004 and becoming a key launch partner with Google Video in 2006.[26] Researchers can search for and order footage to be used under a license agreement.[27]

The National Television and Film Archive at the BFI, located in London, is another rich resource of British television programming, holding around 625,000 programs.[28] Their television holdings are through donations and through various agreements with the broadcasters including Independent Television (ITV) and Channels 4 and 5. The Archive also selects examples of regional programs and has an access arrangement with the BBC in which researchers can view material produced by BBC1 and BBC2 since August 1990 and from BBC3 and BBC4 since their inception.[29] The Archive offers a variety of services to researchers, both nationally and internationally, including a researchers' guide of film libraries and archives listings and a searchable film and television database.[30]

The National Media Museum, located in Bradford, UK, is part of the National Museum of Science and Industry

(NMSI) Museums Group.[31] The Television Collection represents the evolution of television production since the late nineteenth century to the present. Types of materials include television recorders, television cameras, and television receivers.[32]

Japan

While Japanese experimental television began in 1939, World War II ended research until the early 1950s, which saw the beginnings of Nippon Hoso Kyokai (NHK) and Nippon Television (NTV). NHK, Japan's public broadcasting system, began in 1926 as a radio network. After World War II, the Occupation Authorities issued the Radio Law, the Broadcast Law, and the Radio Regulatory Commission Law, all to reduce government control over broadcasting. Due to these regulations, NHK is independent from the government and is mostly funded through consumer fees. Its programming, divided into two networks, includes news, cultural and entertainment programs on NHK Sogo, and educational programs on NHK Kyoiku.[33] The Japanese network, NHK, established its archives in February 2003 in commemoration of the 50th anniversary of television in Japan. In its Tokyo headquarters, the NHK Archives has over 500,000 programs that visitors can view on-site.[34]

Canada

The Canadian Broadcasting Company (CBC), a public network operating under a parliamentary mandate, has its archives in Toronto. These archives hold more that 70 years of radio and television history on millions of discs, tapes, films, photographs, written records, and computer files. Originally a low priority, the CBC gradually realized that archiving past material was worthwhile, especially after technology made production cheaper and storage easier.

The work of the archives staff includes the ongoing capture of new material, doing research and technical preparation for programming, and selling and sourcing of archival content to broadcasters and other third parties. The archives' first priority is the capture, cataloging, and storage of new material. The archive also tries to gain intellectual and physical control over its backlog of material.[35]

Australia

The Australian Broadcasting Company archive materials are located in various repositories. The ABC Archives and Library Services serve the needs of ABC Radio, Television, and Multimedia as well as external customers worldwide. To this end, the Archive selects, catalogs, and preserves material representing an audiovisual record of Australian history.[36–38]

Researchers can find additional Australian broadcasting material at the National Film and Sound Archive (NFSA) in Acton. The NFSA's mission is to collect, store, preserve, and make available Australia's audiovisual history.[39] Through this mission, the NFSA supplies footage and recordings for use in television and radio productions. With expert technicians skilled in preservation practices, the NFSA transfers, duplicates, restores, and reformats materials in all formats.[40]

SCOPE OF ACTIVITIES OF FILM AND BROADCAST ARCHIVES

Preservation of Audiovisual Material

Film

While digital formats are now the dominant mode of motion picture production, postproduction, distribution, and exhibition, analog formats continue to predominate in most film archives and may continue to do so for many years. Over the last 100 years many motion picture formats have been marketed, as new developments in film gauge, composition, and aspect ratios emerged. Flammable nitrate-based film, used for the first 50 years of commercial film production, was replaced in the mid-1950s by acetate "safety" film. (Note that nitrate was only used for 35 mm motion picture film, never for the amateur or semiprofessional gauges of 8 or 16 mm film [Fig. 1].) There have been numerous color and sound systems over the decades as these technologies were engineered and perfected. Fortunately, for film archivists, the drive toward standardization spearheaded by the Society of Motion Picture Engineers (now the Society of Motion Picture and Television Engineers (SMPTE)) has resulted in relatively few modern analog motion picture formats currently in use (in comparison to the bewildering array of digital formats now available).[41] Table 3 summarizes the most common analog film formats. Those readers interested in a concise introduction to film technology should consult Enticknap.[42]

For most noncommercial film archives, as well as for many commercial ones interested in protecting their assets, preservation is seen as a core function. While archives focused on copying of decaying nitrate film to acetate in the early days as their primary preservation treatment, the emphasis for most archives now is on providing appropriate, secure storage facilities that control temperature and relative humidity, protect against damage from natural disaster and fire, and reduce airborne pollutants such as the acetic acid produced by the deteriorating acetate film. By placing collections in good storage facilities that slow down the rate of physical deterioration for motion picture film, archives can extend the life of their

Fig. 1 Reel of 16 mm motion picture film. The 16 mm format was commonly used for television production as well as government, business, medical, and industrial filmmaking from the 1930s through the 1980s until it was largely supplanted by videotape technology.
Source: Photograph courtesy of Tom Connors.

Table 3 Common analog film formats.

Gauge	Users	Bases
35 mm	Professional market	Cellulose nitrate (1894–1953)
		Cellulose diacetate (1909–1940s)
		Cellulose triacetate (1948–present)
		Polyester (1950s–present)
16 mm/Super 16	Professional, industrial, educational; also used by artists and amateur filmmakers	Cellulose acetate, various esters (16 mm: 1923–present; Super 16: 1971–present)
		Polyester (1950s–present)
8 mm/Super 8	Consumer market (amateur/home movies; small gauge enthusiasts)	Cellulose acetate, various esters (8 mm: 1932–present; Super 8: 1965–present)

Sources: *Film Preservation Guide: The Basics for Archives, Libraries, and Museums*; National Film Preservation Foundation: San Francisco, CA, 2004. Horak, J.C., Introduction to film gauges, http://archive.today/xt5rw (accessed December 7, 2016). *Restoration of Motion Picture Film*; Read, P. and Meyer, M.P., Eds.; Butterworth-Heinemann: Oxford, U.K., 2000.

collections and obtain a longer window for making preservation decisions.

Analog Audio and Videotape Materials

According to the organization Independent Media Arts Preservation (IMAP), electronic media is especially vulnerable because the short life expectancy of magnetic tape rules out its use as a permanent, archival storage medium.[43] Additionally, most analog audio and video formats are already or close to becoming obsolete—tape formats, machine, computer hardware, and software are constantly being upgraded—making it difficult to maintain machines for playback of older media.[43] The earliest videotape, the 2" Quadruplex, introduced in 1954, required large, compressed-air-driven machines that can only be run and maintained by engineers trained to operate them (Fig. 2).

Later analog formats, such as ¾" U-matic, VHS, Betamax, and Betacam, each require their own machines, all of which are becoming increasingly rare and which do not read other formats (see Figs. 3 and 4). Though newer

digital formats such as Digital Betacam, DVCAM, and Digital 8 are recommended for preservation masters, these formats also have problems with tape stability and incompatibility with other formats. For an overview of videotape formats, see Tables 4 and 5.[44]

Problems with magnetic tape as a storage medium include natural deterioration such as binder hydrolysis, also known as "sticky shed syndrome," in which the tape's binder coating absorbs moisture in high heat and humidity and leaves a gummy residue on the tape and machine surfaces.[43] Signal loss is a common risk for analog formats. Signal loss can occur as a result of either physical damage to the tape or degradation of the tape components (most often the binder). Archivists are encouraged to reformat these tapes through expert vendors after cleaning and to rehouse originals in nonacidic, nonreactive containers.

Audio formats, both analog and digital, also have their preservation issues. Radio archives can have many formats including transcription discs dating from 1929, wire recordings from the 1930s, acetate-based magnetic recording tape dating from 1948, digital audiotape recordings

Fig. 2 Ampex 2 in. Quadruplex machine, located at the Library of Congress Packard Campus for Audio-Visual Conservation.
Source: Photograph courtesy of Karen F. Gracy.

Fig. 3 One inch Type C videotape, developed by Ampex and Sony and used as a broadcasting standard from the late 1970s through the early 1990s, replaced the cumbersome 2 in. Quadraplex format.
Source: Photograph courtesy of Tom Connors.

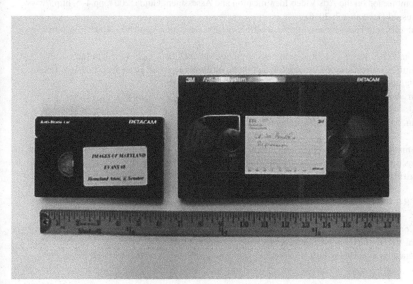

Fig. 4 The family of Betacam products, including Betacam (1982), Betacam SP (1986), and Digital Betacam (1993), are all one-half inch in width. Tapes come in S and L sizes (Betacam videotape recorders accept both sizes, but Betacam cameras use the S size exclusively). The Superior Performance (SP) variety was the format of choice for preservation purposes for many years, although it is now considered to be an endangered format in the wake of Sony's decision in 2002 to cease production of recorders and players.
Source: Photograph courtesy of Tom Connors.

Table 4 Video—analog formats.

Name	Year introduced	Years used	Users
2" Quadruplex[a]	1956	1956–early 1980s	First video format, for in-studio use
1" [Philips, Grundig, etc.][b]	1964	1964–early 1970s	Industrial, consumer markets
½" open reel[c]	1965	1965–late 1970s	Industrial, educational, consumer markets. Examples include artists, independent producers, community organizers, schools, television stations
1" Ampex (A-Format)[d]	1965	1965–early 1980s	Industrial, educational, consumer markets
EIAJ ¼" VT-100/110/120 B&W open reel[e]	1969	1969–end 1970s	Consumer, education markets
¾" U-matic/¾" U-matic SP[f]	¾" U-matic, 1971/¾" U-matic SP, 1986	¾" U-matic, 1971–present/¾" U-matic SP, 1986–present	Industrial, educational markets. Used in 1970s and 1980s for electronic news. 1990s—artists, community activists, academic institutions, production houses
EIAJ-2 Cartridge color video NV-5120[g]	1971	1971–early 1980s	Industrial, educational, consumers markets
VCR-1500/VCR-1700[h]	1971	1971–early 1980s	Consumer, educational markets
V-Cord[i]	1974	1974–end 1970s	Consumer, educational markets
Akai VK[j]	1975	1975–early 1980s	Home Video, Educational markets
Betamax[k]	1975	1975–late 1980s in the United States	Developed for consumer, industrial, and educational markets. Users included schools, community centers, artists
1" B-format, Philips–Bosch[l]	1976	1976–present	Professional, broadcast markets
VHS/VHS-C/S-VHS[m]	VHS, VHS-C, 1976/S-VHS, 1987	VHS, VHS-C, 1976–present/S-VHS, 1987–present	VHS: consumer marketVHS-C: consumer, educational marketsS-VHS: consumer, educational, and industrial markets
1" Type C[n]	1978	1978–1980s	In-studio use. Also used as a preservation master format in the late 1980s and early 1990s
Quasar VX[o]	1978	1978	Home video market
Video 2000/VR-2000 mono/VR-2000 stereo[p]	1979	1979–1980s	Home video market
CVC[q]	1981	1981–1984	Consumer, educational markets
Betacam/Betacam SP[r]	Betacam, 1982/Betacam SP, 1986	Betacam, 1982–present/Betacam SP, 1986–present	Broadcast industrial, educational, professional markets. Betacam SP—preservation master in the last 10–15 years
U-matic-HB, BVU[s]	1982	1982–early 1990s	Broadcast professional market
Panasonic M/MII[t]	1982	1982–early 1990s	Professional market
Video8/Hi8[u]	Video8, 1984/Hi8, 1989	Video8, 1984 to present/Hi8, 1989 to present	Video8, consumer market. Hi8—consumer, industrial, and educational markets

[a] **Sources**: The Little Reference Guide for Small Video Tape Collections, Video formats: Quadruplex 2 in., http://www.little-archives.net/guide/content/1quadruplex.html (accessed December 7, 2016). Texas Commission on the Arts Video Identification and Assessment Guide, 2004, pp 4–5, http://www.arts.texas.gov/wp-content/uploads/2012/04/video.pdf (accessed December 7, 2016).

[b] **Source**: The Little Reference Guide, Video formats: 1 in. different brand names, http://www.little-archives.net/guide/content/2_1inch_diff.htm (accessed December 7, 2016).

[c] **Sources**: The Little Reference Guide, Video formats: ½ in. EIAJ, http://www.little-archives.net/guide/content/2_half_inch_sony.htm (accessed December 7, 2016), ½ inch different brands; http://www.little-archives.net/guide/content/2_half_inch_diff.htm (accessed December 7, 2016). Texas Commission, pp 8–9, http://www.arts.texas.gov/wp-content/uploads/2012/04/video.pdf (accessed December 7, 2016).

[d] **Source**: The Little Reference Guide, Video formats: 1 in. Ampex, http://www.little-archives.net/guide/content/2_1inch_ampex.htm (accessed December 7, 2016).

[e] **Source**: The Little Reference Guide, Video formats: ¼ in. EIAJ, http://www.little-archives.net/guide/content/3_kwart_inch_akai.htm (accessed December 7, 2016).

[f] **Sources**: The Little Reference Guide, Video formats: U-matic LB, http://www.little-archives.net/guide/content/5_umaticlb.htm (accessed December 7, 2016). Texas Commission, pp 10–12, http://www.arts.texas.gov/wp-content/uploads/2012/04/video.pdf (accessed December 7, 2016).

[g] **Source**: The Little Reference Guide, Video formats: Cartridge National, http://www.little-archives.net/guide/content/7_cardridge.htm (accessed December 7, 2016).

[h] **Source**: The Little Reference Guide, Video formats: VCR-1500 / 1700, http://www.little-archives.net/guide/content/6_vtr.htm (accessed December 7, 2016).

[i] **Source**: The Little Reference Guide, Video formats: V-Cord, http://www.little-archives.net/guide/content/20_v_cord.htm (accessed December 7, 2016).

[j] **Source**: The Little Reference Guide, Video formats: Akai VK, http://www.little-archives.net/guide/content/6b_akai.htm (accessed December 7, 2016).

[k] **Sources**: The Little Reference Guide, Video formats: Betamax, http://www.little-archives.net/guide/content/9_betamx.htm (accessed December 7, 2016).

(Continued)

Table 4 Video—analog formats. *(Continued)*

Texas Commission, pp 13–14, http://www.arts.texas.gov/wp-content/uploads/2012/04/video.pdf (accessed December 7, 2016).

^l **Source**: The Little Reference Guide, Video formats: B-format, http://www.little-archives.net/guide/content/2_1inch_b_format.htm (accessed December 7, 2016).

^m **Sources**: The Little Reference Guide, Video formats: VHS / S-VHS / VHS-C, http://www.little-archives.net/guide/content/8_vhs.htm (accessed December 7, 2016). Texas Commission, pp 15–16, http://www.arts.texas.gov/wp-content/uploads/2012/04/video.pdf (accessed December 7, 2016).

ⁿ **Sources**: The Little Reference Guide, Video formats: C-format, http://www.little-archives.net/guide/content/2_1inch_sony_ampex.htm (accessed December 7, 2016). Texas Commission, pp 6–7, http://www.arts.texas.gov/wp-content/uploads/2012/04/video.pdf (accessed December 7, 2016).

^o **Source**: The Little Reference Guide, Video formats: Quasar VX, http://www.little-archives.net/guide/content/10_quasar_vx.htm (accessed December 7, 2016).

^p **Source**: The Little Reference Guide, Video formats: Video 2000, http://www.little-archives.net/guide/content/11_video_2000.htm (accessed December 7, 2016).

^q **Source**: The Little Reference Guide, Video formats: CVC, http://www.little-archives.net/guide/content/21_cvc_format.htm (accessed December 7, 2016).

^r **Sources**: The Little Reference Guide, Video formats: Betacam SP, http://www.little-archives.net/guide/content/15_betacam_sp.htm (accessed December 7, 2016). Texas Commission, pp. 17–19, http://www.arts.texas.gov/wp-content/uploads/2012/04/video.pdf (accessed December 7, 2016).

^s **Source**: The Little Reference, Video formats: U-matic-HB (High Band) BVU, http://www.little-archives.net/guide/content/12_umatichb.htm (accessed December 7, 2016).

^t **Source**: The Little Reference Guide, Video formats: Panasonic M / MII, http://www.little-archives.net/guide/content/13_m_format.htm (accessed December 7, 2016).

^u **Sources**: The Little Reference Guide, Video formats, Video 8 – Hi 8 (HB), http://www.little-archives.net/guide/content/14_video8_hi8.htm (accessed December 7, 2016). Texas Commission, pp 20–22, http://www.arts.texas.gov/wp-content/uploads/2012/04/video.pdf (accessed December 7, 2016).

dating from 1962, audiocassettes dating from 1963, compact discs dating from 1983, and Super Audio CD (SACD) and streaming audio from 1999.[45] These formats require compatible machines, some of which have become increasingly obsolete (see Figs. 4 and 5).[46] The fragility of transcription discs, usually coated with lacquer or, during World War II, made of breakable glass, makes these materials particularly at risk and in need of reformatting.[47]

Digital Formats

Preservation of digital audio has progressed significantly in the last 20 years. Echoing the transition to digital in audio production and distribution, archivists have embraced digital technology as the primary method to preserve audio for the future. As most analog audio formats have now become obsolete, with the exception of LP records, most archives have chosen to migrate their analog recordings on cylinders, discs, and magnetic tape to an uncompressed digital format such as Broadcast WAV for long-term preservation purposes.[48] The significant storage requirements of uncompressed digital video have thus far hindered wide-scale adoption of digital formats as target preservation formats in the conversion of analog moving images to digital storage systems. The rapid decline of motion picture film manufacturing in the wake of transition to digital distribution and exhibition for most commercial film releases, combined with carrier degradation and obsolescence of most analog video formats, will hasten many archives' decision to migrate their significant analog film and video collections to digital formats.[49,50] While the moving image archiving community still works

primarily with analog material, the influx of digital material has begun and most archives are grappling with a potential solution for long-term preservation of digitized and born-digital material.[51]

Appraisal

Film

For many years, the appraisal of films was seen as an unusual, even dangerous, activity. Given the number of films lost due to deterioration or discarded by their owners when no longer profitable, early film archivists aimed to save as much as they could.[52] While some archivists, such as Iris Barry, film curator at the Museum of Modern Art, were quite selective in what was chosen as part of the collection, other archivists preferred to "take the films now and ask questions later," reserving judgment on films until further assessment of their value could be undertaken.[53] The latter attitude toward appraisal often meant that collections grew beyond the capabilities of the facility and staff who worked at the archive. Even today, it is rare to find appraisal as part of the institutional mission and activities. An atypical example is films collected for the NARA, which are subject to the record retention and disposal schedules created for government agencies. Outside of such government archives, however, appraisal has rarely been formalized as an archival activity, and what little has been done has often been scattershot. Interestingly, some archives are more likely to be interested in monetary appraisal, for purposes of accepting a film collection from a private donor, than in an assessment of the material's archival values.[53]

Table 5 Video—digital formats.

Name	Year introduced	Years used	Users
D1[a]	1986	1996	Professional market, broadcast sector
D2[b]	1988	1988–present	High-end professional market. Used as mastering format
HDV-1000[c]	1988	1988–present	Professional market, broadcast sector
D3[d]	1990	1990–present	High-end professional market. Used as mastering format
DCT[e]	1992	1992–present	Professional market, broadcast sector
Digital Betacam (DigiBeta)[f]	1993	1993–present	Developed for professional market. Used for electronic news gathering, broadcast television—industry standard. Advertising, high-end TV programming, corporate—mastering format. Format for video preservation masters
D5[g]/D5-HD[h]	1994	1994–present	D5: Professional market, broadcast sector/D5-HD: Professional market
D9 Digital-S[i]	1995	1995–present	Professional market, broadcast sector
DVCAM[j]	1995	1995–present	Industrial, educational, professional markets. Used for electronic news gathering, cable television, field production. Used as mastering format by artists, independent producers
MiniDV (DV or DVC)[k]	1995	1995–present	Consumer, industrial, educational markets. Users: artists, community activists
D6[l]	1995	1995–present	Digital Cinema
D7 (DVCPRO-25)[m]/D7 (DVCPRO-50)[n]	1995/1998	1995–present/ 1998–present	Industrial, educational, professional markets. Used for electronic news gathering, cable television, field production
Digital Beta SX[o]	1996	1996–present	Professional market, broadcast sector
D11-HDCAM[p]	1997	1997–present	Professional market, broadcast sector
Digital8[q]	1999	1999–present	Consumer market, educational sector
D10-MPEG IMX[r]	2001	2001–present	Professional market, broadcast sector

[a] **Source:** The Little Reference Guide for Small Video Tape Collections, Video formats: D1, http://www.little-archives.net/guide/content/di_d1.htm (accessed December 7, 2016).

[b] **Sources:** The Little Reference Guide, Video formats: D2, http://www.little-archives.net/guide/content/di_d2.htm (accessed December 7, 2016); Texas Commission on the Arts Video Identification and Assessment Guide, pp 23–24. http://www.arts.texas.gov/wp-content/uploads/2012/04/video.pdf (accessed December 7, 2016).

[c] **Source:** Little Reference Guide, Video formats: HDV-1000, http://www.little-archives.net/guide/content/di_hdv1000.htm (accessed December 7, 2016).

[d] **Sources:** The Little Reference Guide, Video formats: D3, http://www.little-archives.net/guide/content/di_d3.htm (accessed December 7, 2016); Texas Commission, pp 25–26, http://www.arts.texas.gov/wp-content/uploads/2012/04/video.pdf (accessed December 7, 2016).

[e] **Source:** The Little Reference Guide, Video formats: DCT, http://www.little-archives.net/guide/content/di_dct.htm (accessed December 7, 2016).

[f] **Sources:** The Little Reference Guide, Video formats: Digital Betacam, http://www.little-archives.net/guide/content/di_beta.htm (accessed December 7, 2016); Texas Commission, pp 27–28, http://www.arts.texas.gov/wp-content/uploads/2012/04/video.pdf (accessed December 7, 2016).

[g] **Source:** The Little Reference Guide, Video format: D5, http://www.little-archives.net/guide/content/di_d5.htm (accessed December 7, 2016).

[h] **Source:** The Little Reference Guide, Video Format: D5-HD, http://www.little-archives.net/guide/content/di_d5hd.htm (accessed December 7, 2016).

[i] **Source:** The Little Reference Guide, Video Format: D9 Digital-S http://www.little-archives.net/guide/content/di_d9.htm (accessed December 7, 2016).

[j] **Sources:** The Little Reference Guide, Video Format: DVCAM, http://www.little-archives.net/guide/content/di_dvcam.htm (accessed December 7, 2016); Texas Commission, pp 29–30, http://www.arts.texas.gov/wp-content/uploads/2012/04/video.pdf (accessed December 7, 2016).

[k] **Sources:** The Little Reference Guide, Video format: DV, http://www.little-archives.net/guide/content/di_dv.htm (accessed December 7, 2016); Texas Commission, pp 31–32. http://www.arts.texas.gov/wp-content/uploads/2012/04/video.pdf (accessed December 7, 2016).

[l] **Source:** The Little Reference Guide, Video Format: D6, http://www.little-archives.net/guide/content/di_d6.htm (accessed December 7, 2016).

[m] **Sources:** The Little Reference Guide, Video Format: D7 (DVCPRO-25), http://www.little-archives.net/guide/content/di_d725.htm (accessed December 7, 2016); Texas Commission, pp. 33–34, http://www.arts.texas.gov/wp-content/uploads/2012/04/video.pdf (accessed December 7, 2016).

[n] **Source:** The Little Reference Guide, Video format: D7 (DVCPRO-50), http://www.little-archives.net/guide/content/di_d750.htm (accessed December 7, 2016).

[o] **Source:** The Little Reference Guide, Video format: Digital Beta SX, http://www.little-archives.net/guide/content/di_betasx.htm (accessed December 7, 2016).

[p] **Source:** The Little Reference Guide, Video format: D11-HDCAM, http://www.little-archives.net/guide/content/di_d11.htm (accessed December 7, 2016).

[q] **Sources:** The Little Reference Guide, Video format: Digital 8, http://www.little-archives.net/guide/content/di_digital8.htm (accessed December 7, 2016), Texas Commission, pp 35–36, http://www.arts.texas.gov/wp-content/uploads/2012/04/video.pdf (accessed December 7, 2016).

[r] **Source:** The Little Reference Guide, Video format: D10 MPEG IMX, http://www.little-archives.net/guide/content/di_imx.htm (accessed December 7, 2016).

Radio

Sound archivists often acquire materials from collectors in an ad hoc fashion instead of based on a set records management schedule. As a result, they often have to weed out unwanted materials to make a more cohesive collection. Due to limits on space, staffing, and finances, archives cannot be unlimited storehouses, keeping every sound recording in perpetuity. Those who advocate retention of all materials often forget that archivists do not have

Fig. 5 One-quarter inch magnetic audiotape, once considered the gold standard for preserving sound recordings, has been largely abandoned in favor of transfer to digital formats stored on high-density magnetic tape formats (such as LTO), hard drives, or secure servers.
Source: Photograph courtesy of Tom Connors.

unlimited time to go through hundreds of hours of material to appraise, process, and make it available for research. Unlike textual materials, audio recordings must be listened to in real time. The audiovisual archivist must use disciplined appraisal methods to keep materials selected in accordance with archival principles. If possible, the archivist should be involved in prearchival control by working with collectors to ensure that material is recorded on good quality audiotape to maintain minimum technical standards.

The basic principle of selection, which is a craft rather than an exact science or an art, is to preserve material with evidential or research value in order to ensure a balanced, representative collection relevant to the nature of the subject matter and the archive's purpose. Two types of selection processes, as defined by Rolf Schuursma, are coarse and fine mesh.[54] With coarse selection, the archivist evaluates complete collections without investigating individual recordings. The result is a larger but less manageable collection, especially if there is little documentation.

With fine mesh selection, the archivist examines each recording, providing documentation and adequate cataloging. This selection type is good for material that enters the archives in small groups or singly. Another type of selection process, sampling, is especially useful for radio broadcasting material. One example, based on the policy of the Public Television Archive of PBS, has the archive keep the first, last, and representative episodes of a series. Radio archives also use this process to keep one news broadcast daily as the main broadcast. Material that is then weeded out is not always destroyed but may be stored elsewhere or offered to another archive.

Television

In 1995, NPBA curator Thomas Connors and then WGBH Archivist Mary Ide received a Bentley Fellowship to research appraisal standards for public television materials. In his article, "Appraising Public Television Programs: Toward an Interpretive and Comparative

Evaluation Model," Connors offered a three-tiered ranking scheme to evaluate programs for preservation.[10] For this scheme, the archivist would examine the following elements for each program: provenance, cost of retention, implications of selection decisions, reference potential, and critical values. The archivist would then rank the programs into three tiers. The first-tier programs would be reformatted for permanent retention. If resources become available, then the second-tier programs would be reformatted. Finally, the third-tier programs would be kept in their original format.

Approaching the appraisal question from the station's point of view, Mary Ide and Leah Weisse described the retention criteria of the WGBH Media Archives and Preservation Center in their 2003 article "Developing Preservation Appraisal Criteria for a Public Broadcasting Station".[55] Every WGBH-produced program sent selected production elements, records, and multiple masters to the Archives. Soon, to save retention costs, the WGBH Archives began to implement a preservation selection standard in order to create a quality collection of program content. This production standard was based on four values: institutional, informational, reuse, and the cost of retention. For institutional values, the WGBH Archives kept track of the program category and genre to maintain a balanced selection as mandated in the WGBH mission statement. Thus, the Archives would describe programs by category such as humanities, music, or science and by genre such as documentary, public affairs, or instruction. Next, for informational values, the Archives looked at the level of cataloging, whether from the shot level by the production staff to descriptive video and closed-captioning after the production has finished. This information is useful for future research and reuse. Reusing a program also plays a factor as to whether it is worth preserving, as maintaining an archive of editorial content saves the station research time and money. Thus, the Archives work with both WGBH Enterprises and the Media Library to determine marketing possibility through possible footage sales. When the Archive has determined what to keep, the next value considered is the cost of retention. There, the Archives looks at such costs as tape transfers, storage, processing and cataloging masters for preservation, adding new catalog information to the Archives database, and the reshelving of newly dubbed material.

Cataloging and Description

Just as archivists need to preserve materials, they also need to know what they have. To reach this goal, the archivist describes the material and creates a record of who authored a work, its format, how many copies the archive has, the work's value, and who owns the copyright. However, there are many challenges in cataloging and describing audiovisual media. Often, the media object does not have accompanying labels and must be played in order to determine its contents. Due to the potential danger of damaging older audiovisual material by playing it, archivists often create an incomplete catalog record until they can make a preservation copy and can then update the record.

The organization and description of film and broadcast material has not followed the same path of standardization that helped librarians assume intellectual and physical control over library resources. Sound and moving image cataloging schemas often grew organically within institutions and corporations, with the primary goal of facilitating the retrieval of particular titles, broadcasts, or footage. The approach of a museum registrar describing a collection of avant-garde films was likely to be quite different from the method of a librarian cataloging outtakes for a stock footage house or an archivist organizing a set of corporate in-house productions. While some catalogers have adapted their descriptions to currently existing standards like Resource Description and Access (RDA), Machine-Readable Cataloging (MARC), and the Library of Congress Subject Headings (LCSH), others have created in-house rules for description and subject access.

Digitized and born-digital materials require new ways of cataloging and providing access to material through the use of metadata standards. Metadata, or data about data, helps describe, explain, and locate information about various types of textual and nontextual objects. The three types of metadata include descriptive, such as title, author, and keywords; structural, such as the information about how the parts of complex digital objects relate to one another, for example, the information needed to order individual shots and synchronize picture and soundtrack to create audio or video news stories; and administrative, such as access information and creation information.[56]

Audiovisual archivists have developed or adapted several metadata standards to meet the functional requirements of describing, preserving, and providing access to moving images. Some archives, particularly those within library organizations, have tailored the Metadata Object Description Schema (MODS) standard, an XML-based derivative of MARC, to describe audiovisual media in collections. For those working outside the library community, other standards have been developed to address the particular needs of moving images. The PBCore data standard was originally developed for the public broadcasting community but has been adopted by other organizations with audiovisual collections that are looking for a way to describe their media items' intellectual content, property rights, and formats. The PBCore standard is based on the Dublin Core Metadata Element Set, with added fields that are specific to the requirements of describing audiovisual media.[57] Audiovisual archivists have also developed application profiles for media description that employ elements from metadata standards such as the Metadata Encoding and Transmission Standard (METS), which is used for bundling and encoding descriptive, administrative, and structural metadata regarding objects within a digital library, and the Preservation Metadata: Implementation Strategies standard (PREMIS), which supports the long-term preservation of digital objects. Other archivists may adopt metadata standards used by the commercial motion picture and television community that are more appropriate for materials in production environments, including MPEG-7 (the Multimedia Content Description Interface), MPEG-21 (a standard for expressing rights, permissions, and restrictions on the use of moving images and sound), and SMPTE standards (including the SMPTE Data Dictionary and the MXF container format for digital audio and video media, which can record various types of metadata in its file header).[58]

Audiovisual Cataloging Resources

A number of cataloging resources have emerged that take existing sets of rules or headings and tailor them to the needs of moving image and sound description. One such rule set is the *Archival Moving Image Materials (AMIM)* standard, which is based on the *Anglo-American Cataloguing Rules (AACR)*.[59] Another rule set is the *FIAF Moving Image Cataloguing Manual*, developed by representatives of institutional members of the FIAF. The FIAF rules have recently been revised to reflect the Functional Requirements for Bibliographic Records (FBRR) model and aim to be compatible with multiple metadata schemas such as Dublin Core and MARC.[60]

While catalogers have often taken terms from LCSH to assign indexing terms, particularly for nonfiction films, the Moving Image Genre-Form Guide (MIGFG) term list was specifically created to give film seekers access to films by type or category and often is used to supplement LCSH.[61] Similarly, the Radio Form/Genre Terms Guide (RADFG) provides a list of subject headings for sound archivists cataloging such material.[62]

For materials such as stock footage and news stories, which often lack the hallmarks of authorship such as formal titles, catalogers have often developed separate databases using software like FileMaker Pro or Microsoft Access and created their own thesauri specific to the collection at hand, rather than attempt to integrate records of moving image resources with preexisting catalogs. While the variety of resources created by moving image catalogers often served the internal needs of the organization well, such homegrown systems were rarely interoperable with other systems.

Access

Whether the material is textual or audiovisual, researchers want access to it. Preservation and cataloging are key methods for providing this access. However, the Library of Congress television and video preservation report notes that obstacles to access include "... underfunding in public archives, lack of descriptive cataloging and reference copies, copyright interests, and very restrictive usage policies" (p. 9).[17] Other problems, as noted in the Council on Library and Information Resources (CLIR) 2004 report, *Survey of the State of Audio Collections in Academic Libraries*, include physical deterioration, lack of staff, intellectual property rights, and space problems.[63]

On-site

While audiovisual archives, particularly those found in public institutions, have always had the capability to provide on-site access to materials in their collections, preservation imperatives and copyright restrictions have often made it difficult or impossible for institutions to lend films to users for off-site use. Larger archives had the resources to create study centers, which users could visit for the purposes of requesting titles to view that have been transferred to CD, video, or DVD, while smaller archives must often make do with a few listening or viewing stations. One problem for many archives is the inability to provide even on-site access to users, either because they lack the proper equipment to view material or because they do not want to risk damage to fragile, often deteriorating, material by screening it for users before it has been transferred to a more stable format.

Online

With recent advances in audio and moving image digitization and streaming technologies, many archives are exploring the Internet's promise for increasing access to collections and reaching new users who are unable to travel to the archive to listen to recordings or view films and videos. While copyright restrictions still limit archives' ability to provide access to many materials in the online environment, for those films and broadcasts that are in the public domain or for which archives have the rights to distribute, archives can now provide digitized versions of sound recordings, films, and videos for downloading or streaming. Users can integrate digital audio and moving images into new works or research much more easily than before. The explosion in video sharing services such as YouTube and Vimeo also offers a new template for archives to consider when designing sites for accessing material—users can now provide valuable information through tagging and commenting activities that may enrich the catalog.[64]

Projection of Motion Picture Film

The lure of online access has the unfortunate side effect of overshadowing an important mode of access to analog film materials: presentation through projection. In the wake of the digital transition, the number of working projectors for the 35 mm format has dwindled rapidly. The National Association of Theatre Owners reported that conversion of motion picture theaters to digital projection had occurred for approximately 94% of all commercial venues in the United States by May 2014.[65] In the current environment, where most theaters have abandoned the 35 mm format, specialized venues such as museums, archives, and universities with large collections of features on 16 and 35 mm may be the only locations where users will be able to see film as a projected medium.[42]

The 16 mm format, once the mainstay for schools, churches, nonprofit organizations, and others to show educational, industrial, amateur, and other types of nontheatrical films, has largely been abandoned in the wake of video, DVD, and other digital forms of exhibition. Used equipment for 16 mm projection has been widely available in the past, although the challenges of maintaining such equipment and the preference for newer formats of such material by most users are the reasons why most institutions have jettisoned much of their 16 mm collections (buying DVD replacements where available, or transferring them to a newer format if no DVD replacement can be found).[66]

The 8 mm and the Super 8 formats are no longer used by most amateur and home moviemakers, who long ago adopted video formats (initially flocking to the analog video formats first introduced in the 1980s and, more recently, to digital video formats). These small gauge film formats continue to have a fan base, however, with enthusiasts such as experimental filmmakers and archivists. While these collections are found much more often in personal collections than in institutional settings, the rediscovery and celebration of small gauge films by organizations such as Home Movie Day means that more and more of this valuable material may find its way into archives and museums.[67]

ISSUES AND TRENDS AFFECTING FILM AND BROADCAST ARCHIVE WORK

Developing Digital Archiving Systems to Support Production, Access, and Storage

As the film and broadcast industries continue to adopt new modes of production, distribution, and exhibition, archives must prepare themselves to care for the new formats generated by production companies, artists, researchers, and amateur filmmakers. The digital formats of today will challenge archivists to develop solutions to problems such as rapid media and format obsolescence, restrictive copyright laws hindering preservation and access imperatives, and creating preservation-ready repositories for reliable and affordable long-term storage of digital moving images (Fig. 6).

While many archives have focused attention on obtaining appropriate storage facilities for their analog collections and maintaining machines to access film and video elements, they also have been contemplating requirements for accessioning, maintaining, and making accessible digital moving image collections. While media asset management systems predominate in commercial organizations where systems must support production environments, many noncommercial organizations are

Fig. 6   DAT uses 4 mm tape and its dimensions are roughly half that of the Philips compact audiocassette. Its recording quality represented a great improvement over analog magnetic tape; however, it has been used largely by professionals rather than being a consumer format. Sony ceased production of DAT recorders in 2005, which adds it to the long list of obsolete magnetic tape formats.
Source: Photograph courtesy of Tom Connors.

choosing to construct digital storage repositories according to the Open Archival Information System (OAIS) model in order to meet needs to preserve the content, integrity, and authenticity of moving image material and manage the migration of files in obsolete formats to current formats. Specific features that are desired of these new preservation-oriented systems include support of on- and off-site ingest; centralized metadata creation and maintenance (where metadata can be acquired throughout production workflows, as well as in later assessment and cataloging workflows); automated migration of analog and digital files to uncompressed, nonproprietary formats; hierarchical storage management; selection criteria for long-term preservation; quality control; and environmental control for data storage systems. Larger organizations with significant resources may prefer to build customized in-house systems, but other smaller organizations are exploring the adoption of open-source solutions in whole or in part to accomplish preservation and access goals. The Hydra repository and associated software components is one such open-source solution being employed by organizations such as WGBH, Indiana University Libraries, Stanford University Libraries, and Northwestern University Library.[68]

Copyright Legislation

Copyright legislation such as the Copyright Term Extension Act (CTEA) of 1998 (Public Law 105–298) and the Digital Millennium Copyright Act (DCMA) of 1998 (Public Law 105–304) often restrict the ability of archives to fulfill their missions of preservation and access, particularly those noncommercial archives holding large quantities of copyrighted material still considered to have commercial value. The CTEA has ensured that most material from the sound era of motion pictures remains under copyright (except for those titles whose copyright lapsed back when the United States required copyrights to be renewed for continued protection). For films still under copyright, archives cannot distribute them freely (access is limited to on-site viewing), must pay copyright owners for any public exhibitions, and have limited powers to make copies of them for preservation purposes.

The DCMA further limits archives in achieving preservation goals by forbidding them from circumventing mechanisms meant to protect copyrighted material such as digital rights management (DRM) systems and encoding and encryption schemas, in order to make copies for preservation purposes. While archivists have lobbied the Copyright Office to provide exemptions for preservation work, no rulings from the Office have yet given archivists the power to do so. Some hope may be drawn from a 2006 exemption that allows university educators to rip clips from DVDs and other digital files in order to make compilations for use in the classroom as part of film or media studies courses.[69]

In certain motion picture genres, such as silent, educational, and industrial films, many titles have fallen into the public domain or are no longer cared for by their owners, who may no longer be in business. These films have been dubbed "orphans" by the moving image archiving community, and interest in protecting and preserving them has grown exponentially in the last decade, particularly as federal grant programs have targeted them as strong candidates for preservation funding. The Orphans Film Symposium, first established in 1999 by Dan Streible and fellow enthusiasts (known as orphanistas), has become the premier event for archivists, scholars, educators, and others eager to celebrate these films.[70]

Attempts to remedy the problem of copyright limbo for orphan works through the introduction of legislation to the U.S. Congress in 2006 failed due to opposition by photographers, illustrators, and textile designers. Since then, the U.S. Copyright Office has been investigating this issue through studies and public comment periods; these activities may eventually lead to some sort of exemption to the current copyright law.[71]

The issue of copyright is also important in the field of broadcast archives. The Copyright Law of 1976 encouraged scholarly use of audiovisual material by permitting off-air taping for educational purposes.[46] Under the law, retention of off-air videotapes for classroom use is limited to 45 calendar days and further use requires a license from the copyright owner. However, unlike the American Society of Composers, Authors, and Publishers (ASCAP), there is no copyright clearinghouse, and researchers thus have problems finding accurate copyright information on older programs. The 1997 Library of Congress report on television and video preservation recommends that interested parties discuss issues such as revising fair use guidelines and policies for off-air recording, especially concerning programs without clearly identifiable copyright ownership.[17]

Copyright limitations affect access to materials both on-site and remotely. For example, Vanderbilt Television News Archive provides limited access to its collection via streaming video due to copyright consideration. While it makes dubs of news programs on request, the archive considers the tapes to be loans.[13] Another example is the Paley Center for Media, which encourages researchers to view programs on-site. The Paley Center does not have any rights to the tapes that were donated to the Center, which are "only to be viewed or listened to in the Paley Center by the general public".[72]

For government collections, deposit laws vary from country to country and are not always equally applied. For example, the collections in the Library of Congress Television Archive offer a broad but incomplete view of television history. Reasons for incomplete runs of television series include the Library's earlier practices of selectively keeping deposit copies for copyright protection, earlier producers deciding not to register their programs, problems with legal definitions of publication, and the underestimation of broadcast recordings as a scholarly resource. In 1966, the Motion Picture Section's reference staff started answering television questions, and the acquisition of programs began to expand.[73]

Building New Storage Facilities for Audiovisual Media

In the last 20 years, many archives have focused on the construction of the new storage facilities for their collections, in an effort to prolong the life span of fragile film and video material in danger of decay. The Museum of Modern Art in New York completed the Celeste Bartos Film Preservation Center in Hamlin, Pennsylvania, in 1996; Northeast Historic Film, a small archive in Bucksport, Maine, built a cold storage facility in 2003 that rents space to other institutions in the New England area seeking a place to store their moving images; the Library of Congress built the National Audio-Visual Conservation Center in Culpeper, Virginia (which opened in 2006 and includes facilities for storage of digital moving images as well as analog film and video elements); and the UCLA Film & Television Archive relocated all conservation activities to a new facility in Santa Clarita, California in 2015 (Fig. 7).[74–77]

Other smaller collections found within larger institutions may also be benefiting from trends of academic libraries such as the University of Toronto, the University of Pittsburgh, the University of California, Berkeley, the Harry Ransom Center at the University of Texas at Austin, and, the University of Texas at Arlington, to create cold storage facilities to house those types of photographic and magnetic media that require colder temperatures and lower relative humidity than print collections.[78]

Funding for Audiovisual Preservation

Funding for Film Preservation

In the last two decades, the sources of funding to support film preservation activities have changed significantly.

Whereas the primary funding source in the 1970s and 1980s was the federally funded American Film Institute-National Endowment for the Arts (AFI-NEA) grant program, cuts in federal funding to the NEA in 1994 led to the discontinuation of this program. In 1997 the National Film Preservation Foundation (NFPF) was established by the National Film Preservation Act of 1996. As a public charity, its goals are to support preservation of orphan films by facilitating fundraising from individuals, organizations, and corporations and encouraging in-kind contributions of goods and services from laboratories and suppliers of preservation materials.[79] To date, the NFPF has contributed to the preservation of over 2,000 films.[80] Other federal grant sources funding film preservation have included the National Endowment for the Humanities (NEH) and the National Historic Publications and Records Commission (NHPRC).

Archives have come to rely increasingly on the donations from private individuals and foundations in recent years to fund capital expenditures, such as new storage facilities and study centers, or to defray costs of digitization and access projects. The Film Foundation, the David and Lucile Packard Foundation, and the IBM Corporation have supported major projects at film archives in recent years.[81,82] Archives have worked together with studio copyright owners such as Sony, Paramount, and Walt Disney, which often contribute funds for laboratory services and lend production elements to assist with preservation projects.

Funding for Television and Video Preservation

The Library of Congress television preservation report notes that often funding of television and video preservation has been inadequate, with some exceptions. Many foundations reject video preservation grant applications because videotape is perceived as inadequate for long-term preservation. While federal agencies such as the NHPRC and the NEH have awarded funds to public archives primarily to improve access, there has been little

Fig. 7 Exterior of the Packard Campus for Audio-Visual Conservation. **Source:** Photograph courtesy of the Library of Congress.

coordination and communication among the different agencies.[17]

Based on the recommendations of the Library of Congress report, the National Television and Video Preservation Foundation (NTVPF) was created to raise private funds and provide grants for preservation projects in institutions with television and videotape collections.[83] Since its inception, NTVPF has awarded grants for projects such as ten hours of videotapes from the Experimental Television Center in 2004.[84] NTVPF is currently dormant, with no new grants being announced in the last decade. The future of this foundation is not clear at the time of this writing, unfortunately.

The American Archive of Public Broadcasting is another funded television preservation project. In 2007, the Corporation for Public Broadcasting (CPB) started an inventory of public media content from participating stations resulting in over two million records representing a wide range of media content including complete programs, unedited interviews, and live music sessions. The first 40,000 hours of content digitized for permanent preservation and public access was funded by CPB.[85] The American Archive of Public Broadcasting, instituted in 2013, continues to preserve public television programming through funding from CPB.[86]

Funding for Radio Preservation

In the area of radio, funding for preservation comes primarily from the following sources. The GRAMMY Foundation awards grants to archives for planning, assessment, consultation, or implementation of preservation projects.[87] One prominent recipient of preservation grants from the GRAMMY Foundation is the Pacifica Radio Archive's weekly radio show *From the Vault*.[88] Other funding sources for preservation and access have come from the NEH's Preservation and Access program and the Save America's Treasures program (cosponsored over the years by various government and civilian agencies including the National Park Service (NPS), the National Trust for Historic Preservation, NEA, and the Institute of Museum and Library Services (IMLS)), which have also made grants relating to preservation and access projects.[89–92]

Education and Professionalization Opportunities for Film and Broadcast Archivists

Graduate Programs in Moving Image Preservation and Archiving

The Library of Congress report Redefining Film Preservation strongly urged the moving image archiving community to develop educational programs at the graduate level to produce archivists trained to care for the burgeoning collections of analog and digital material in U.S. repositories.[93] Within a decade, several programs had been established, including the L. Jeffrey Selznick School of Film Preservation at the George Eastman House (established in 1996; the School began to offer a joint M.A. degree combined with a Certificate in Film Preservation with the University of Rochester in 2005); the M.A. in Moving Image Archive Studies at the University of California, Los Angeles (2002); and the Moving Image Archiving Program at New York University (2003). Internationally, several programs are available in Canada, Europe, and Australia. Additionally, moving image archiving courses have been added to the curricula at several library and information science (LIS) programs in the United States, making educational opportunities much more widely available. The Library of Congress maintains a current list of moving image archiving educational opportunities available both in the United States and abroad.[94]

Similar recommendations have been made to train a new generation of sound archivists.[95] These suggestions have yet to result in many formal educational training opportunities at the graduate level, unfortunately. Several LIS schools have begun to offer electives in sound archiving and reformatting, including the University of Texas at Austin and UCLA, which have regularly offered courses in this area.

Moving Image and Recorded Sound Archives Associations

In North America, the primary professional association serving the moving image archiving community is the Association of Moving Image Archivists (AMIA).[96] As noted earlier, FIAF also plays an important role; however, it must be acknowledged that only institutions can be members of FIAF, while AMIA has both individual and institutional membership, which allows it to facilitate communication among archivists more directly than FIAF. For sound archivists, the national organization that supports the profession is the Association of Recorded Sound Collections (ARSC).[97] Other international associations that provide leadership in the field include the Southeast Asia-Pacific Audiovisual Archive Association (SEAPAVAA), the International Association of Sound and Audiovisual Archives (IASA), the International Federation of Television Archives (IFTA/FIAT), the International Council on Archives (ICA), and the International Federation of Library Associations and Institutions (IFLA). Many of these organizations offer opportunities for continuing education through their annual conferences, particularly AMIA and ARSC. FIAF holds a Summer School for training film archivists every other year as well.

CONCLUSION

To summarize, the authors defined the scope, mission, and activities of film and broadcast archives, focusing particularly on archival functions including preservation, appraisal, description, and access to moving image and sound material.

Several important factors emerged as critical issues for film and broadcast archives. First, film and broadcast material requires extensive description, which is not fully supported by traditional library descriptive tools such as Resource Description and Access or MARC. Metadata standards developed or revised specifically to address preservation and access activities, particularly for newer digital formats, have been developed or adapted by the film and broadcast archiving communities, including PREMIS, PBCore, the FIAF Moving Image Cataloging Manual, MXF, MPEG-7, and MPEG-21 to provide archivists with opportunities to make full descriptions of legacy and digital formats. Adoption of these standards will facilitate interoperability among film and broadcast archive repositories, and may lead to increased information sharing among archives and facilitate searching across collections.

Second, appraisal methods for audiovisual archives must continue to be developed and refined to establish best practices for selecting film and broadcast materials for long-term retention. Models developed in the area of appraisal for television broadcast material should be tested for other audiovisual media and digital materials.

Third, preservation concerns such as format obsolescence, as well as copyright considerations, can often complicate efforts to provide access to audiovisual archives. Archives will need to be proactive in advancing archival interests in the areas of copyright reform and development of new formats suitable for long-term storage of audiovisual media.

Finally, audiovisual archives, while continuing to emphasize the importance of caring for legacy formats, must now deal directly with the effects of the digital transition and its accompanying new paradigms for preservation and access. These new directions and responsibilities require financial support both from within their institutions and from external sources. Archivists will need to lobby their own organizations and government agencies for the continued support of funding for preservation and access activities, as digital repositories are designed and launched to care for moving image and sound archives into the future.

REFERENCES

1. Houston, P. *Keepers of the Frame: The Film Archives*; British Film Institute: London, U.K., 1994.
2. FIAF. http://www.fiafnet.org (accessed December 7, 2016).
3. Melville, A. National Film Preservation Board. In *Film Preservation 1993: A Study of the Current State of American Film Preservation: Report of the Librarian of Congress*; National Film Preservation Board of the Library of Congress: Washington, DC, 1993.
4. Library of Congress. National Film Preservation Board. Public moving image archives and research centers https://www.loc.gov/programs/national-film-preservation-board/resources/public-research-centers-and-archives/ (accessed December 7, 2016).
5. http://www.fiapf.org/pdf/cannes05/EUfilmdepositchart.pdf (accessed December 7, 2016).
6. Local Television. *A Guide to Saving Our Heritage*; Association of Moving Image Archivists: Los Angeles, CA, 2003.
7. Murphy, W.T. Genesis of a profession: Origins of the Film and Television Archives Advisory Committees. Mov. Image **2011**, *11* (1), 105.
8. Mass Media & Culture, Special Collections & University Archives, University of Maryland Libraries-About us. http://www.lib.umd.edu/special/collections/massmedia/about-us (accessed December 7, 2016).
9. Gerri, J. Museums and archives of radio. In *The Museum of Broadcast Communications Encyclopedia of Radio*; Stirling, C., Keith, M., Eds.; Fitzroy Dearborn Publishers: New York, 2004; *2*, 970–975.
10. Connors, T. Appraising public television programs: Toward an interpretive and comparative evaluation model. Am. Archiv. **2000**, *63* (1), 105.
11. Wisconsin Historical Society, Library-Archives Division. Mass communications history collections. http://www.wisconsinhistory.org/pdfs/la/WHS-MassCommFactSheet.pdf (accessed December 7, 2016).
12. Archive history-UCLA Film & Television Archive. https://www.cinema.ucla.edu/about-archive (accessed December 7, 2016).
13. Vanderbilt Television News Archive-About. https://tvnews.vanderbilt.edu/about (accessed December 7, 2016).
14. The Museum of Broadcast Communications. http://www.museum.tv/about_us.htm (accessed December 7, 2016).
15. The Paley Center for Media. http://www.paleycenter.org (accessed December 7, 2016).
16. List of the Special Collections, Thousand Oaks Library. http://www.tol.lib.ca.us/pages/new/screens/listcollections.html (accessed December 7, 2016).
17. Murphy, W. Library of Congress. In *Television and Video Preservation, 1997: A Report on the Current State of American Television and Video Preservation: Report of the Librarian of Congress*; Library of Congress: Washington, DC, 1997.
18. Negra, D. Archives for television materials. In *Museum of Broadcast Communications Encyclopedia of Television*; Newcomb, H., O'Dell, C., Watson, N., Eds.; Fitzroy Dearborn Publishers: Chicago, IL, 1997; *1*, 76–78.
19. Records of the Federal Communications Commission [FCC]. http://www.archives.gov/research/guide-fed-records/groups/173.html (accessed December 7, 2016).
20. Records of the National Telecommunications and Information Administration [NTIA]. http://www.archives.gov/research/guide-fed-records/groups/417.html (accessed December 7, 2016).
21. WGBH Open Vault-About us. http://openvault.wgbh.org/about/ (accessed December 7, 2016).
22. Pacifica Radio Archives-About. http://www.pacificaradioarchives.org/about-archives (accessed December 7, 2016).

23. Alvarado, M. British programme production companies. http://www.museum.tv/eotv/britishprogr.htm (accessed December 7, 2016).

24. British Library-Sound recordings. http://www.bl.uk/collection-guides/radio-broadcast-recordings (accessed December 7, 2016).

25. BBC-Written Archives Centre. http://www.bbc.co.uk/informationandarchives/access_archives/bbc_written_archives_centre (accessed December 7, 2016).

26. ITN Source-About us. http://www.itnsource.com/en/aboutus (accessed December 7, 2016).

27. ITN Source-Licensing information. http://www.itnsource.com/en/helpandsupport/licensing-and-information (accessed December 7, 2016).

28. British Film Institute National Archive. http://www.bfi.org.uk/archive-collections (access December 7, 2016).

29. British Film Institute National Archive, About the BFI National Archive. http://www.bfi.org.uk/archive-collections/about-bfi-national-archive (accessed December 7, 2016).

30. British Film Archive-Searching and access. http://www.bfi.org.uk/archive-collections/searching-access-collections (accessed December 7, 2016).

31. National Media Museum-About us. http://www.nationalmediamuseum.org.uk/aboutus (accessed December 7, 2016).

32. National Media Museum-TV collection. http://www.nationalmediamuseum.org.uk/Collection/Television (accessed December 7, 2016).

33. Fox, J. Japan, http://www.museum.tv/eotv/japan.htm (accessed December 7, 2016).

34. NHK International. http://www.nhkint.or.jp/en/#/home (accessed December 7, 2016).

35. CBC digital archives. http://www.cbc.ca/archives/about/our-work.html (accessed December 7, 2016).

36. Australia-ABC Archives. http://www.abc.net.au/archives/ (accessed December 7, 2016).

37. ABC Archives-FAQ (holdings). http://www.abc.net.au/archives/contact.htm (accessed December 7, 2016).

38. ABC Archives-Open archives. http://www.abc.net.au/archives/openarchives.htm (accessed December 7, 2016).

39. National Film and Sound Archive. http://www.nfsa.gov.au (accessed December 7, 2016).

40. NFSA-Preservation Services. https://www.nfsa.gov.au/preservation/preservation-services. (accessed December 7, 2016).

41. Society of Motion Picture and Television Engineers. Standards facilitate interoperability. http://www.smpte.org/standards (accessed December 7, 2016).

42. Enticknap, L. *Moving Image Technology from Zoetrope to Digital*; Wallflower Press: London, U.K., 2005.

43. IMAP: Preservation 101. http://www.imappreserve.org/pres_101/index.html (accessed December 7, 2016).

44. Texas Commission on the Arts. *Videotape Identification and Assessment Guide*, 2004. http://www.arts.texas.gov/wp-content/uploads/2012/04/video.pdf (accessed December 7, 2016).

45. Yale University, Audio Timeline, excerpted from Preparing for the brave new world of sound recordings cataloging by Mary Huismann, University of Minnesota 2006, http://www.library.yale.edu/cataloging/music/audiotimeline.htm (accessed December 7, 2016).

46. Bensman, M.R.; Godfrey, D. Forward. In *Reruns on File: A Guide to Electronic Media*; Lawrence Erlbaum Associates: Hillsdale, NJ, 1992; xvii–xxvii.

47. The State of Recorded Sound Preservation in the United States: A National Legacy at Risk in the Digital Age. *Council on Library and Information Resources and the Library of Congress*. August 2010; 22. http://www.clir.org/pubs/reports/pub148/pub148.pdf (accessed December 7, 2016).

48. International Association of Sound and Audiovisual Archives Technical Committee. IASA-TC 03: The Safeguarding of the Audio Heritage: Ethics, Principles and Preservation Strategy. Version 3, December 2005. http://www.iasa-web.org/sites/default/files/downloads/publications/TC03_English.pdf (accessed December 7, 2016).

49. Alexander, H.; Blakely, R. The triumph of digital will be the death of many movies. New Republic, September 12, 2014. http://www.newrepublic.com/article/119431/how-digital-cinema-took-over-35mm-film (accessed December 7, 2016).

50. Lacinak, C. *The Cost of Inaction: A New Model and Application for Quantifying the Financial and Intellectual Implications of Decisions Regarding Digitization of Physical Audiovisual Media Holdings*. http://www.avpreserve.com/wp-content/uploads/2014/07/COICalculator.pdf (accessed December 7, 2016).

51. Science & Technology Council, The Academy of Motion Picture Arts and Sciences. *Digital Dilemma 2: Perspectives from Independent Filmmakers, Documentarians and Non-profit Audiovisual Archives*; AMPAS: Hollywood, CA, 2012.

52. Slide, A. *Nitrate Won't Wait: A History of Film Preservation in the United States*; McFarland & Co: Jefferson, NC, 1992.

53. Kula, S. *Appraising Moving Images: Assessing the Archival and Monetary Value of Film and Video Records*; Scarecrow Press: Lanham, MD, 2003.

54. Harrison, H. Archival appraisal. In *Audiovisual Archives: A Practical Reader*; Harrison, H., Ed.; UNESCO: Paris, France, 1997; 126–143.

55. Ide, M.; Weisse, L. Developing preservation appraisal criteria for a public broadcasting station. Mov. Image **2003**, *3* (1), 146–157.

56. Understanding metadata. http://www.niso.org/publications/press/UnderstandingMetadata.pdf (accessed December 7, 2016).

57. About | PBCore. http://pbcore.org (accessed December 7, 2016).

58. de Jong, A. *Metadata in the Audiovisual Production Environment: An Introduction;* Nederlands Instituut voor Beeld en Geluid; Hilversum: The Netherlands, 2003. https://www.prestocentre.org/system/files/library/resource/0000020986_Publicatie%20Annemieke%20de%20Jong%20-2%20%28Metadataboek_compleet_Eng-version_2003 %29.pdf (accessed December 7, 2016).

59. *Archival Moving Image Materials: A Cataloging Manual*, 2nd Ed.; Cataloging Distribution Service, Library of Congress: Washington, DC, 2000.

60. http://www.filmstandards.org/fiaf/wiki/doku.php?id=history_of_the_project (accessed December 7, 2016).

61. The Moving Image Genre-Form Guide. http://www.loc.gov/rr/mopic/migintro.html (accessed December 7, 2016).

62. The Radio Genre/Forms Term Guide. http://www.loc.gov/rr/record/frmgen.html (accessed December 7, 2016).

63. Smith, A. Council on Library and Information Resources, *Survey of the State of Audio Collections in Academic Libraries*; Council on Library and Information Resources: Washington, DC, 2004. http://www.clir.org/pubs/reports/pub128/pub128.pdf (accessed December 7, 2016).

64. Andreano, K. The missing link: Content indexing, user created metadata, and improving scholarly access to moving image archives. Mov. Image **2007**, *7* (2), 82–99.

65. Cinema Technologies, http://natoonline.org/initiatives/cinema-technologies/ (accessed December 7, 2016).

66. Rossi-Snook, E. Persistence of vision: Public library 16 mm film collections in America. Mov. Image **2005**, *5* (1), 1–27.

67. Center for Home Movies; Home Movie Day. http://www.centerforhomemovies.org/hmd/ (accessed December 7, 2016).

68. Elnabli, S. One body, many heads: *Preservation and access from Project Hydra*; Association of Moving Image Archivists, Savannah, GA, October 9, 2014, http://www.slideshare.net/AvalonMediaSys/avalon-media-system (accessed December 7, 2016).

69. U.S. Copyright Office—Anticircumvention rulemaking. http://copyright.gov/1201/2006/ (accessed December 7, 2016).

70. The Orphan Film Symposium. http://www.nyu.edu/orphanfilm/ (accessed December 7, 2016).

71. U.S. Copyright Office—Orphan works. http://copyright.gov/orphan/ (accessed December 7, 2016).

72. FAQ-The Paley Center for Media. http://www.paleycenter.org/about-mission-history-FAQ#clip-availability (accessed December 7, 2016).

73. Television (Motion Picture and Reading Room), Library of Congress. http://www.loc.gov/rr/mopic/tvcoll.html (accessed December 7, 2016).

74. https://www.moma.org/research-and-learning/research-resources/film preservation (accessed December 7, 2016).

75. Storage-Northeast Historic Film. http://www.oldfilm.org/content/storage (accessed December 7, 2016).

76. The Packard Campus (A/V Conservation)-Library of Congress. http://www.loc.gov/avconservation/packard/ (accessed December 7, 2016).

77. BAR Architects-Our work (film archive and preservation center). http://www.bararch.com/work/arts-entertainment/project/film-archive-and-preservation-center (accessed December 7, 2016).

78. UT Arlington Central Library begins construction on cold storage vault for millions of historic photographic negatives. http://www.uta.edu/news/releases/2014/08/library-cold-storage.php (accessed December 7, 2016).

79. National Film Preservation Foundation-About the NFPF. http://www.filmpreservation.org/about (accessed December 7, 2016).

80. National Film Preservation Foundation. Report to the U.S. Congress for the Year Ending December 31, 2013. http://www.filmpreservation.org/userfiles/image/PDFs/nfpf_ar2013.pdf (accessed http://www.filmpreservation.org/userfiles/image/PDFs/nfpf_ar2013.pdf).

81. The Film Foundation. http://www.film-foundation.org (accessed December 7, 2016).

82. Friedman, J. IBM lends support to Hearst project; *UCLA Film and Television Archive Newsletter*: April/May, 2003; 6.

83. Independent Media Arts Preservation (IMAP)-Funding for preservation. http://www.imappreserve.org/info_res/funders.html (accessed December 7, 2016).

84. Experimental Television Center-Funding from NTVPF. http://www.experimentaltvcenter.org/etc-history (accessed December 7, 2016).

85. Library of Congress Archive of American Public Broadcasting press release. http://loc.gov/today/pr/2013/13-203.html (accessed December 7, 2016).

86. Archive of American Public Broadcasting-About. http://americanarchive.org/about-the-american-archive/ (accessed December 7, 2016).

87. Grammy Foundation grants. http://www.grammy.org/grammy-foundation/grants (accessed December 7, 2016).

88. Pacifica Radio Archive radio documentaries. http://www.pacificaradioarchives.org/radio-documentaries (accessed December 7, 2016).

89. NEH grants. http://www.neh.gov/grants (accessed December 7, 2016).

90. Save America's Treasures Grants. http://www.nps.gov/preservation-grants/sat/ (accessed December 7, 2016).

91. National Endowment for the Arts, News release, February 1, 2011. Save America's Treasures grant program announces $14.3 million in grants: Federal-private partnership funds historic preservation and conservation. https://www.nps.gov/aboutus/news/release.htm?id=1116 (accessed December 7, 2016).

92. American Architectural Foundation. Save America's Treasures. http://www.archfoundation.org/category/center-for-design-cultural-heritage/save-americas-treasures/ (accessed December 7, 2016).

93. *Redefining Film Preservation*: A National Plan. *National Film Preservation Board*; Library of Congress: Washington, DC, 1994. https://www.loc.gov/programs/national-film-preservation-board/preservation-research/film-preservation-plan/redefining-film-preservation/ (accessed December 7, 2016).

94. National Film Preservation Board, Library of Congress. Film schools & careers in preservation. http://www.loc.gov/film/schools.html (accessed December 7, 2016).

95. *Capturing Analog Sound for Digital Preservation: Report of a Roundtable Discussion of Best Practices for Transferring Analog Discs and Tapes*; Council on Library and Information Resources, Library of Congress: Washington, DC, 2006. http://www.clir.org/pubs/reports/pub137/pub137.pdf (accessed December 7, 2016).

96. Association of Moving Image Archivists. Home page. http://www.amianet.org (accessed December 7, 2016).

97. ARSC (Association of Recorded Sound Collections). http://www.arsc-audio.org/index.php (accessed December 7, 2016).

BIBLIOGRAPHY

1. Cox, M.; Tadic, L.; Mulder, E. *Descriptive Metadata for Television: An End-to-End Introduction*; Focal Press: Burlington, MA, 2006.

2. The Film Preservation Guide. *The Basics for Archives, Libraries, and Museums*; National Film Preservation Foundation: San Francisco, CA, 2004.

3. Fossati, G. *From Grain to Pixel: The Archival Life of Film in Transition*; Amsterdam University Press: Amsterdam, the Netherlands, 2009.

4. IASA Technical Committee. Standards *Recommended Practices and Strategies: IASA-TC 04, Guidelines on the Production and Preservation of Digital Audio Objects*; Bradley, Kevin, Ed.; Second edition 2009. (= Standards, Recommended Practices and Strategies, IASA-TC 04). http://www.iasa-web.org/tc04/audio-preservation (accessed December 7, 2016).

5. Dietrich, S. *Audio and Video Carriers: Recording Principles, Storage and Handling, Maintenance of Equipment, Format and Equipment Obsolescence*, 2008. http://www.tape-online.net/docs/audio_and_video_carriers.pdf (accessed December 7, 2016).

Film Archiving: History

Steve Ricci
Department of Information Studies/Film and Television, University of California–Los Angeles, Los Angeles, California, U.S.A.

Abstract

This entry provides an overview of the evolution of motion picture archiving from its beginnings as an uncoordinated set of craft-oriented skills to its modern status as a profession. It discusses the role of the profession's major historical associations including the International Federation of Film Archives, the American Film Institute, the Library of Congress, and the Association of Moving Image Archivists.

This entry retraces the evolution of the field of motion picture archiving in order to provide the cultural and philosophical background to the extraordinary practical challenges that public-sector archives currently face. The two most useful books on the history of film preservation are Anthony Slide's *Nitrate Won't Wait* (Jefferson, North Carolina: McFarland, 2000) and Penelope Huston's *Keepers of the Frame* (London: British Film Institute, 1984).While Slide focuses on the major film archives in the United States, Huston concentrates on the large international institutions. Around the world, only 15%, at best, of all silent films survive. This means that almost 90% of what was screened during the first 30 years of cinema history cannot be seen by today's audiences. It is estimated that roughly half of the 21,000 feature films made in America prior to 1950 have been lost. If we then consider that much of what actually remains suffers from general wear and tear, color fading, deep scratches, shrinkage, and sprocket damage, and that only a small percentage of the extant films have been professionally restored and preserved, the picture is perhaps as bleak as it is barren. Although precise statistics vary somewhat, most estimates already tell us that significant moving image inventories are lost. Author Frank Thompson estimates the percentage of lost silent films at 80%.[1] In the documentary *Keepers of the Frame* (Produced by Randy Gitsch, 1999), the estimated loss is 90%.

According to Penelope Houston, "it is generally assumed that some 75–80% of all silent cinema has been lost, most of it gone beyond recall unless caches still exist in the unexplored recesses of the archives or in the holdings of private collectors"—*Keepers of the Frame: The Film Archives* (London: British Film Institute, 1994). Moving Image Collections asserts that "only 10% of pre-1929 films survive."

The "Silent Era" Web site states that "educated guesses estimate that only 10–15% of the films made during the silent era survive today."[2]

Exactly how much of America's film production has already been lost remains difficult to say. The most familiar statistic, which has attained its authority primarily through repetition, is that we have lost 50% of all titles produced before 1950.[6] This estimate may not be inaccurate so long as one qualifies it in three ways. First, it would apply only to full-length fiction films. Anecdotal evidence suggests that survival rates for other film types, even major studio newsreels and shorts, are lower. Second, among those studio features, there is a sharp break in survival rates at 1929, the year that sound film became the industry standard. Features of the 1930s have been recently documented to survive at a rate of no less than 80%, probably closer to 90%.[7] However, fewer than 20% of the features of the 1920s survive in complete form; for features of the 1910s, the survival rate falls to slightly above 10% (and those in copies generally made from projection prints, not negatives, which are almost entirely lost)...Third and last, the familiarity of that 50%-before-1950 statistic also implies, by omission, that there are few preservation problems with films produced after that year—something which is not the case, as will be discussed (p. 56).[3]

Historical memory of the world's moving image heritage is incomplete in three profound ways. Many films are permanently lost. Much of what remains is in immediate need of archival attention, and some of these films may never be able to be restored to an integral state. Even after the remaining titles have been repaired or reconstructed, it is extremely rare that these works can be exhibited to the public in a manner that even remotely resembles their original presentations.

Contemporary moving image archives, particularly in the public sector, face unprecedented practical challenges and a new set of opportunities. On the one hand, the soon-to-be expected disappearance of duplicating stocks constitutes a new threat to the long-term preservation of moving images on film. The major manufacturers of photographic raw stock have, over time, introduced, replaced, or simply discontinued numerous types of negative, reversal, and print stocks. For example, many of the 16 mm color reversal stocks, which were once the medium of choice for

Encyclopedia of Iron, Steel, and Their Alloys DOI: 10.1081/E-ELIS4-120044979

television news films, are no longer available. Starting in the early 1990s, just as announcements began to appear about the anticipated deployment of digital cinema projection and distribution, Kodak significantly reduced its budget for research and development of new film stocks. These reductions certainly reflected the wide-spread transition from consumer still photography to digital cameras. One of the more troubling developments, however, is that newer moving image stocks do not accurately reproduce the visual qualities of Kodak's earlier products. This most recent technical problem represents potential loss that could far exceed the combined effects of nitrate and acetate deterioration. These two forms of chemical deterioration, which progressively destroy the film emulsion and/or its base, are responsible for the greatest loss of legacy films from the history of cinema. Cellulose nitrate was the dominant 35 mm film stock until the early 1950s until it was replaced first by cellulose acetate and then by polyester stocks. The latter types are generically referred to as "safety" film. What becomes of the millions of hours of unprotected archival footage when the ability to accurately copy film to film disappears? In 1993, it was estimated that 97 million feet of unique nitrate film footage, held in tax-exempt archives, was yet to be preserved. This estimate is even more staggering if we consider that a good portion of the original film-to-film duplications were done very quickly, and that current laboratory techniques have significantly improved. In other words, much of what was accomplished in the modern archival era needs to be redone.

On the other hand, new technologies may constitute new opportunities for the acquisition, preservation, and documentation of moving images. The technical capabilities of a digital future are regularly described as virtually limitless, unchained by the scarcity of time or material resources. Although it may be too early to assess precisely the long-term effect that these technologies (DVD, High Definition Television, Internet) will have upon moving image culture, they will certainly provoke intriguing ethical and theoretical questions. Given the vertiginous pace at which post-production technologies and new delivery platforms are evolving, the vital role of public-sector archives as agencies for historical memory will undergo a paradigmatic shift. Kay Hoffman has suggested that these changes are as significant as the most significant historical upheaval in all of cinema history:

> The fundamental consequences of digitalization for movie production, post-production, and distribution can only be compared with the sea change brought about by the transition from silent to sound film at the end of the 1920s.[4]

In comparison to traditional records and document-based archives, moving image archiving is a recent phenomenon. Its first formal association came only in 1938 with the establishment of the International Federation of Film Archives (FIAF). On the one hand, this relatively new field does share many of the core functions of traditional archives, including collection development, preservation, documentation, and access. On the other hand, it diverges from these traditional archival institutions given the priority it has historically assigned to both the restoration and exhibition of archival materials. For example, the first lines of FIAF's Web site emphasize the importance of exhibition as part of its core mission: ". . . . the world's leading archives whose purpose has always been to ensure the proper preservation and showing of motion pictures."[5]

In contrast, the welcoming message to the International Council on Archives' Web site instead emphasizes key terms such as evidence, memory, and records. "Archives, by providing evidence of human actions and transactions, underlie the rights of individuals and of states, and are fundamental to democracy and good governance. Archives safeguard the memory of mankind by preserving records of its past."[6]

Moving image archives also confront special challenges, perhaps shared only by photographic archives, generated by the complex question of what constitutes "any" original item. Throughout their entire history, moving images have generally been manifested in works existing in multiple copies, in multiple versions, and often in multiple physical formats. Moreover, the very separations between a work's carrier and its message, between its material status and its presentation, between structure and event, require additional attention to each and every level of archival practice. As we will discuss later on, these unique characteristics are both practical and philosophical in nature.

Although the field of moving image archiving has a comparatively short history, it has already moved through several distinct phases: 1) 1938–WWII: the early years of FIAF; 2) 1946–1970: preservation reigns; "Nitrate Won't Wait"; 3) 1970–present: the craft becomes a profession (AMIA) the era of Access. The mass circulation of moving images was a distinctive phenomenon of the twentieth century. Moving image media have been subject to a particularly accelerated rate of technological and cultural change. Precisely because of this accelerated evolution we can already point to at least three significant historical benchmarks or phases. Each of these phases was characterized by a substantial reconceptualization of some of the field's core goals and methods.

Archiving motion pictures has been practiced and discussed since almost the birth of the cinema itself. As early as 1898, photographer and documentarian Boleslaw Matuszewski, in his often cited essay *A New Source of History*, called for the creation of a proto-archive, a "Depository of Historical Cinematography." Matuszewski argued that the value of such an enterprise was found in cinema's "unique" ability to record history. "The cinematographe does not perhaps show history in its complete form, but what it does show is indubitable and constitutes absolute truth.... It is an eyewitness par excellence, reliable and infallible."[7] From the time of this clarion call until the establishment of FIAF in 1938, it would be difficult to describe either a systematic response to Matuszewski or a system of shared practices codified by archival groups or associations. It is true, however, that during this pre-history, several major archival institutions began to operate, including the Imperial War Museum (1917), the Academy of Motion Picture Arts and Sciences (1927), the British Film Institute/National Film Library (1933) (For a detailed discussion on the evolution of the British Film Institute's archival operations, see Dupin),[8] the Film Library of the Museum of Modern Art (1935), and the Cinémathèque Française (1935). But it was only with FIAF that the loosely affiliated, individual archives made efforts toward establishing "universal" codes of conduct, and thus advanced toward the transformation of independent national archives into an international network with shared goals.

These initial efforts were characterized by two dominant philosophical orientations. On the one hand, some archives (most notably the Cinémathèque Francaise under Henri Langlois) concentrated on the exhibition of films as works of art. On the other hand, the British Film Institute (under Ernst Lindgren) focused almost exclusively on the long-term preservation and cataloging of its collections. Although it led to numerous internal battles, this foundational contradiction went unresolved, philosophically and practically, until the late 1970s. Despite the various maneuvers carried out by the field's charismatic figures, FIAF's inability to arrive at standards needed to define archiving as a profession of consistent practices was inextricably linked to Cold War tensions between its member nations. For decades, the Association's Western-nation members were concerned about the potentially disproportionate influence that Soviet-block institutions might exert on international cultural policy. Thus, FIAF's extraordinarily detailed statutes and rules effectively sought to achieve a political stalemate on many archival issues in light of the external Cold War political tensions.

Remarkably, the philosophical tension between "preservation" and "exhibition" would not be undone until FIAF's Lisbon Congress in 1989. The event, entitled "Rediscovering the Role of Film Archives: To Preserve and to Show, "crystallized growing consensus over the rights (actually, the "duty" and obligations) of professional archives with respect to the exhibition of films. Under the umbrella of various publications and manifestos, this particular historical turn was expressed by the capstone mantra "To Preserve, To Show." Public exhibition was thus recast as an organic result of the preservation mandate and accorded equal legitimacy and validation in the ideology of the Federation. Significantly, the new episteme led to a general liberalization of FIAF's statutes and rules. As the Cold War's cultural stalemate dissolved,

reformations within FIAF resulted in the admission of regional institutions, archives which prominently featured nonfiction materials, and, particularly, archives from the developing world.

During this first historical phase, a number of public-sector archives began to operate in the United States. Long before the advent of the American Film Institute (AFI) these had evolved into serious film preservation institutions. However, a common genealogy of the archival profession can be charted in relationship to the AFI, which had engaged in archival activities from almost its inception in 1967. Although the AFI had formally administered National Endowment for the Arts (NEA) preservation funds starting in 1971, it would not be until 1979 that the program would achieve a measure of budgetary and policy autonomy from the AFI's traditional commitment to its film school. In these "early" years, funding was devoted to the acquisition and preservation of silent films and was dispensed to only a few of the country's larger archives. From 1979 to 1982, 53% of the AFI/NEA funds went to silent film preservation and approximately 87% of the total was distributed to three nonprofit archives: the Museum of Modern Art, George Eastman House, and UCLA Film and Television Archive. During these years, the Motion Picture and Sound Recording Branch of the Library of Congress duplicated hundreds of American film titles. But, it too is an agency of the federal government, the Library was ineligible to receive NEA funding.[9]

The decade of the 1970s witnessed the rapid expansion in public-sector archives and the birth of the modern archival movement in the United States. During this brief period of time, the tax-exempt archives vastly enlarged their holdings by acquiring studio collections (nitrate original negatives, fine grain masters, and prints) of classical "Hollywood" feature films that the major film studios were about to destroy. For a number of reasons, the establishment of the National Center for Film and Video Preservation in 1984 (the NCFVP *at* the AFI) was the apex of this evolution. Under the ubiquitous slogan of "nitrate won't wait," the cause of film preservation gained culture-wide visibility and film archiving made significant progress in its professional standing. Interestingly, Robert Rosen, the director of UCLA's Film and Television Archive (who also served as the first director of the NCFVP) has referred retrospectively to the period leading up to the Center as the "buccaneer" years of film archiving.[10] Not only would the NCFVP come to serve as the secretariat for the nascent Association of Moving Image Archivists (AMIA), it revitalized an AFI project to build a complete catalog of American Motion Pictures and established the National Moving Image Database (NAMID). Although the NAMID project would eventually be commercialized by the AFI, it was a significant step toward conceptualizing the totality of the archival field insofar as it was designed to acquire and share holdings information for the totality of archival materials held in both the private and public repositories.

It is important to point out that the evolution of the field took place neither in a cultural vacuum nor only on a national level. One of the chief public voices in support of both archival practice and discourses on their importance came from the scholarly world and specifically from cultural and media historians. The cultural corollary for the birth of the modern archival movement was most clearly in evidence at FIAF's Brighton Congress in 1978. The Congress symposium focused specifically on newly restored films from the period 1900 to 1906. In addition to representatives of archives from around the world, Brighton also welcomed a new generation of scholars who would soon play a central role in the development of film education both in the United States and abroad, including Richard Abel, Robert Allen, Andre Gaudreault, Tom Gunning, Miriam Hansen, Charlie Musser, and Janet Staiger. In a special section of *Cinema Journal* dedicated to the "historical turn" in film studies, Musser described this evolution as a "...new integration of academic and archive-based history and fostered tendencies that contributed to the formulation of a new historiography." One of the most fundamental changes involved a new approach or attitude toward the subject.[11]

Since this approchement, if not partnership between archivists (as custodians of history) and scholars (as writers of history), other significant forces have come into play.

CONCLUSIONS

Two benchmarks which characterize the contemporary moving image archive field in the public sector are the arrival of new digital technologies and the establishment of graduate-level degree programs in moving image archiving (at UCLA, NYU, and the University of Amsterdam). Paradoxically, the added archival capabilities offered by the new technologies only increase the need for additional advanced training of new generations of archivist. Although the new delivery platforms (such as DVDs, Blu-Ray, and the Internet) increase the professions capability to provide access to its collections, the exponential growth in content far exceeds the public sector's ability to serve as professional repositories.

The establishment of the AMIA in 1991 expressed both the need to codify professional behavior and a fundamental shift toward democracy within the field. A particularly good example is AMIA's MIC project, an attempt to provide a common portal for the cataloging of moving image collections.[12] As a membership-based organization, AMIA accepts archivists from across the entire spectrum of archive types and passions. Whereas participation within FIAF is limited to institutional members, literally anyone can join AMIA. Furthermore, this "structural" democracy ignores the distinction between

private and public sectors, thereby theoretically narrowing the hierarchical and economical divisions between professionals. Even FIAF, which for decades had maintained hierarchical distinctions between types of members (full, associate, provisional) has in recent years sought to stimulate participation by moving away from its historically restrictive membership rules to a more open code of ethics in 1999. FIAF's code was constructed in part because the Association found it difficult to actually enforce certain aspects of its membership rules. Adherence to the Code, however, is now a precondition of membership.

Benefiting, in some cases, from the lessons learned by other archival traditions, film archiving, in its relatively recent move toward professionalism, has also recently placed increased importance on the issue of access to archival resources. Key benchmarks include, by the late 1980s, both the Motion Picture and Sound Recording Branch of the Library of Congress and the UCLA Film and Television Archive placing extensive information about their holdings online. For decades, public-sector archives had been reticent to share such information. Recognizing the importance of the access issue, FIAF itself created a specialist commission on the topic and went so far as to devote a special issue to this topic, a professional manual for access in its *Journal of Film Preservation*.[13] Another significant benchmark has been the shift of emphasis in the types of films and media objects to be collected, preserved, and accessed.

The vast majority of public spending on archives in the "buccaneer" years and the early modern era was applied to laboratory costs associated with film-to-film duplication of classical Hollywood feature narratives. And although the movement toward film preservation had picked up considerable steam during these years, the level of federal funding continually decreased. In 1980, the highest annual disbursement (federal support for preservation through the NEA/AFI grants) was $514,215 (for a fuller account of the AFI's early contributions to film preservation, see Mann).[14] By 1992, the total Federal funding had declined to $355,600 which allowed for the preservation of only 26 feature titles. In part, precisely because the AFI/NCFVP had failed in its mission to stop the erosion of Federal support and secure meaningful new sources of funding, to raise sufficient funds for film and television preservation, the field turned to a new organizational model, and embarked on a series of initiatives; including a much expanded commitment to film preservation on the part of the Library of Congress, the creation of the National Film Registry, and most significantly, the creation of a new, Congressionally funded entity, the National Film Preservation Foundation (NFPF) devoted solely to funding preservation and access projects among archives. Since 1997, the field has looked to the NFPF for financial support and cultural leadership.

This shift was accompanied by a broad reconceptualization of the idea of film preservation, influenced by the reformulation of technical standards for the long-term survival of legacy collections. Thus the realization that optimal storage conditions were as important to preservation as film-to-film transfers leads to the epochal conclusion that nitrate, for example, could indeed wait.

More importantly, the public-sector archives began to focus on the importance of nonclassical titles by validating orphan films, a category of media types that includes amateur productions, nonfiction films (particularly news reels), titles in the public domain, and works whose copyright status was unclear or unprotected by large corporate interests. Proponents of orphan film studies cite their value as complex historical and cultural artifacts. It is also true that their unclear or ambiguous legal status affords archives additional flexibility in their handling and use. Indications of this new focus are plentiful: the establishment of the European Association Inedits (which now includes 41 archives as members), the ongoing research presented at the annual *Orphans of the Storm* conference, the amateur cinema topic for FIAF's 1997 Congress in Cartagena, and the many *Home Movie Days* that have been organized throughout the United States. Whereas the AFI used to channel federal funding to large U.S. archives for the preservation of nitrate-era feature films, the NFPF's funding priorities now clearly express this change in emphasis. As outlined on its Web site and in its annual reports:

> The NFPF offers several types of grants to help public and non-profit institutions preserve and provide access to American orphan films. The grants are made possible through the National Preservation Act of 2005, the support of the Library of Congress, and the contributions of public spirited donors.[15]

The generally anti-classicist orientation leads the NFPF to also include avant-garde works in the category of the orphan film. Indeed, one of its funding programs directly supports the preservation and archival treatment of avant-garde productions (the Avant-Garde Masters Grants). While the particularly social orientation of the orphan film movement validates local identities and cultural diversity, it also shares some of the theoretical tenets of New Historicism. The keynote address for FIAF's 1997 Congress, for example, was delivered by Patricia Zimmerman, whose seminal *Reel Families* argues for the value of such voices in the construction of historical accounts that are alternative to traditional, grand narratives.[16] Orphan works make for *new sources* of history. Arguably, one century later, Matuszewski might feel an appropriate measure of vindication.

REFERENCES

1. Thompson, F.T. *Lost Films: Important Movies that Disappeared*, Carol Publishing Corporation: New York, March 1996.
2. "Presumed Lost," Silent Era, Silent Era: The Silent Film Website. Available at http://www.silentera.com/lost/index.html.
3. *Film Preservation 1993: A Study of the Current State of American Film Preservation Volume 1:* Report, June 1993. Report of the Librarian of Congress Available at http://www.loc.gov/film/study.html.
4. Hoffman, K. Celluloid goes digital. Mov. Image. **2004**, *4*(1), 161–163.
5. http://www.fiafnet.org.
6. http://www.ica.org.
7. Matuszewski, B. A new source of history, Film History *7*(3), 322–324. [Different translation than the author's].
8. Dupin, C. The origins and early development of the National Film Library: 1929–1936. J. Media Pract. **2006**, *7*(3), 199–217.
9. Report of the Librarian of Congress, 35–36.
10. Rosen, R. The UCLA film and television archive: A retrospective look. Mov. Image Fall **2002**, *2*(2).
11. Musser, C. Historiographic method and the study of early cinema. Cinema J. **2004**, *44*(1), 101.
12. http://mic.imtc.gatech.edu/.
13. Special Issue: Manual for access to the collections. J. Film Preserv. December **1997**, *55*, 1–55.
14. Mann, S.Z. The evolution of the American moving image preservation (1967–1977). Mov. Image Fall **2001**, *1*(2).
15. http://www.filmpreservation.org.
16. Zimmerman, P. *Reel Families: A Social History of Amateur Film*, Indiana University Press: Bloomington, IN, 1995.

France: Archives, Museums, and Libraries

Martine Poulain
*Department of Libraries and Documentation, National Institute for the History of Art (INHA),
Paris, France*

Abstract

There are many similarities in the history and the evolution of contemporary French archives, museums, and libraries. All three have their roots in the Ancien Régime, but it was the Revolution that imposed their administrative structure. Over the centuries, all three have evoked similar questions and have been the subject of identical political and intellectual debates. At the end of the twentieth and the beginning of the twenty-first century, all three have finally become the object of ambitious public policies. Last, all three are today confronted with profound transformations—often experienced at a dizzying pace of change.

INTRODUCTION

In geographical area, France is the largest country in the European Union (EU) and the second largest in Europe. It is has an extensive coastline, bordered on the north and west by the Atlantic Ocean and on the south by the Mediterranean Sea. The Alps, the Pyrenees, and the Rhine also provide natural boundaries. With an estimated population of 62,150,775 (July 2008) France is the second largest country in the EU. Governed under the constitution of the Fifth Republic, adopted in 1958, France has long time been a highly centralized state that has gradually ceded greater autonomy to local and regional authorities.

France not only has a long history of developing rich library and museum collections, it has been a leader in the field of archival training. The idea of the citizens' right to access archives dates from the French Revolution, and the principal of creating a national museum open to the public also dates from this period.

Since the nineteenth century, the central government has a tradition of offering financial support to national and local cultural institutions such as libraries, museums, and historic sites. This has lead to the continuous enrichment of cultural heritage institutions, and these institutions have in turn provided a stimulus for the growth of cultural tourism among French residents and visitors from abroad. Attracting 81.9 million foreign tourists in 2007, France was ranked as the most popular tourist destination in the world.

FRANCE—ARCHIVES, LIBRARIES, AND MUSEUMS

There are numerous similarities in the history and the evolution of archives, libraries, and museums. All three have their roots in the Ancien Régime, but it was the Revolution that imposed their administrative structure. Over the centuries, all three have evoked similar questions and have been the subject of identical political and intellectual debates. At the end of the twentieth and the beginning of the twenty-first century, all three have finally become the object of ambitious public policies. Today these three "places of memory" are all confronted with profound changes: the growth of collections, the technological revolution, the increase in costs, and the effects of globalization. Another important transformation has been the increase in the number and type of users, and archives as well as museums and libraries now welcome a much broader segment of the public. At the same time profound changes in professional philosophy have had a significant impact on the way in which resources and services of archives, libraries, and museums are conceptualized and how these three institutions are situated within the public space (Fig. 1).

ARCHIVES

According to the law on French archives (January 3, 1979), archives are defined as "the totality (ensemble) of documents, whatever their date, their form, or their format, produced or received by any person or corporate body, and by any agency or organism, public or private, in the course of their activity" (Article 1). This new definition is considerably broader than the one which prevailed in the past, and the current law is meant to give archives responsibility for conserving and making available the "memory of the nation."

From the Ancien Regime to the Present

The well-known *Encyclopédie* of Diderot et d'Alembert described archives as "deeds or charters that contain the rights, claims, privileges, and prerogatives of a household,

Encyclopedia of Library and Information Sciences, Fourth Edition DOI: 10.1081/E-ELIS4-120043451

Fig. 1 Map of France.
Source: *CIA The World Factbook*, https://www.cia.gov/library/publications/the-world-factbook/geos/fr.html

a city, or a kingdom." Until the twelfth century, sovereigns traveled with the collection of documents which proved their legitimacy. However, the theft of this "treasure" during a battle lead Philippe Auguste (1165–1223) to organize his archival documents and to make plans for their conservation in a fixed location. The succeeding kings continued and augmented this organization of royal and governmental records. Over time, the archives increased to the point that in 1774 France had 5700 archival depositories. During this time specific disciplines were constituted such as paleography, which is the science of deciphering ancient writing through expert knowledge of the inks used as well as the writing material (such as parchment, vellum, or paper). Paleographical skills that were initially developed in monasteries became essential competencies of the first archivists.

One of the foundational acts of the French Revolution was the creation of the National Archives (September 7, 1790) as "the depository of all the acts which form the constitution of the kingdom, its public law and its administrative division into *départements*." Throughout France the confiscation of the archives of the nobility lead to the establishment of bureaus for triage that were set up to process this historic influx of nearly a billion documents. The necessity of organizing the archives of the young republic lead to passage in June 1794 of a new law that established the right of citizens to have free access to the archives—a dramatic departure from the practices during the *Ancien Régime* when secrecy had been the rule. The départemental archives were created in 1796.

Nonetheless, during this period there were new concerns regarding the preservation of the national memory. Because the policies of the First Republic were diametrically opposed to those of the *Ancien Régime*, vandalism and destruction went with the establishment of new memory institutions: nearly two-thirds of the documents were eliminated, in most cases because they bore witness to the property and privileges of the hated nobility and clergy who produced them.

The archival institutions and practices established during the First Republic continued to be pursued during the nineteenth century even though France again became a monarchy. Archival knowledge continued to develop and new institutions were set up. The Ecole des Chartes, which still trains archivists, was created in 1821. In addition, the Daunou classification, an alphanumeric archival classification scheme, was developed; it is still in use today, although with modification. Despite advances in the field, by 1870 there were only 31 archivists at the National Archives. These archivists came under the authority of the Ministry of Public Instruction, and in 1897 the creation of a Directorate for Archives within the ministry underlined the importance of archives in regard to public policy. At the same time regulations were established regarding access to the archives and the appraisal and deselection of documents.

After 1945 public investment in archives was strengthened, but, as often is the case in France, this lagged behind the enormous growth in the number of documents that needed to be collected and preserved, and did not keep pace with the increased demands placed by the public. In 1959, the Directorate for the Archives became a part of the brand new Ministry of Culture headed by André Malraux.

Situated in the heart of Paris in a historic mansion, the National Archives has for a long time lacked adequate space to process, preserve, and make its collections available. For those documents created after 1945 a new facility was inaugurated in 1969 at Fontainebleau (in the Parisian region), but this building soon became inadequate. In 1988 at the Paris site a new building was made available to users. Finally in 2004, the complaints of historians and researchers and the continuous petitions of archivists resulted in a project of much greater scope: the construction of an archival campus (Cité des Archives) in the Paris suburbs. Designed by the architect Massimiliano Fuksas and scheduled to open in 2011, this building will have a 60,000 m^2 surface, and a stocking capacity of 320 linear kilometers.

Contemporary Structure of the French Archives

The Directorate for Archives within the Ministry of Culture has an advisory role in regard to the public archives of France as well as regulatory functions and the responsibility for encouraging good practice. In addition, the directorate is charged with the evaluation, control and appraisal of classification, description, and conservation of the archives as well as the provision of access to researchers and to citizens. The Directorate not only oversees the national archives, but also supervises the local, municipal, and départemental archives. In addition it supports the general development of archival science.

Created in 1988, the Superior Archives Council (Conseil supérieur des archives) is a consultative body for public and private archives and is concerned with both content and policy. The mandate of the Conseil supérieur is to analyze the situation and make recommendations but it has no administrative power.

The National Archives are responsible for the collection, conservation, and access to the administrative archives of the central government and its institutions. The ministries, public institutions, and all government agencies are required to deposit their archives in the National Archives which then processes them and makes them available. Only the Ministry of Defense and the Ministry of Foreign Affairs, for longstanding reasons of security, administer their own archives. Today the National Archives includes:

- The Historic Center of the National Archives (le Centre historique des archives nationales—CHAN) preserves and makes available archives covering the period from the Middle Ages to 1958; this collection occupies 100 linear kilometers of stacks.
- The Center for Contemporary Archives (le Centre des archives contemporaines—CAC) holds documents for the period from 1958 to the present day; it occupies 193 linear kilometers of archives.
- The Center for Overseas Archives (le Centre des archives d'outre-mer—CAOM) maintains the archives of the former "French Empire" with its colonies and overseas territories.
- The Center for Labor Archives (le Centre des archives du monde du travail—CAMT), is located in Roubaix, in the North of France. Opened in 1993, it is dedicated to preserving the papers of commercial enterprises and their workers. This new center provides evidence of the recognition by the government of a broadened contemporary conception of archives.

The collection, conservation, and access to archives is also carried out on at the level of the commune, the department, and the region. Local authorities in France include: 36,600 communes, 100 départements, and 26 regions. The regional archives have grown in importance along with the increasing power of the 26 regional administrative districts which were created in 1972 as political and administrative entities. The regional archives have also been enriched by the decentralization of the services of the central government.

The départemental archives collect the records of the 100 French administrative units known as departments. The importance of these collections has also increased as a result of the laws passed between 1983 and 1986; this legislation lead to the decentralization of public

responsibilities and strengthened the powers of the General Councils (Conseils généraux) that administer the départements. The départemental archives also administer the archives of small communes (fewer than 2000 inhabitants) that lack the resources necessary to maintain their own archives. The archives of the larger communes collect and maintain the records of the cities and towns. All of these local archives constitute a rich source of information on a wide range of subjects.

The law of June 20, 1992 enlarged the National Audiovisual Institute (Institut national de l'audiovisuel) legal deposit rights to all radio and television programming. As of 2008 these depository rights extended to most of the national television channels and to 17 public and private radio stations. This archives contains approximately 90% of all radio programs and 60% of all television programs created in France since the origins of radio and TV programming. By 2008, over 4,000,000 hr of programs could be consulted, and each year nearly 540,000 hr of radio and television programs are recorded. Nonetheless the French audiovisual archives prior to 1990 are vulnerable, because the recordings themselves (reel-to-reel tapes and cassettes) are threatened by physical deterioration due to chemical mutations over time. The disappearance of equipment needed to play these recordings also creates a threat to future access to these collections. If nothing were to be done, 835,000 hr of audiovisual archives would be lost between now and 2015 (almost one-third of the total). The preservation and the restoration of the original recordings and systematic digitization of these materials are both necessary. By the end of the twentieth century, when audio recordings and videos had expanded into the world of the Internet, the National Audiovisual Institute became interested in methods for the conservation of such materials originating from the Web.

Contestated Issues Concerning Access to Archives

The concerns for the conservation of archival collections and the protection of the confidentiality of individuals had for a long time been considered more important than access, and this was particularly true for contemporary archives. Without special authorization, no access was allowed to documents issued after 1940 (a particularly sensitive period). As a result of the law of 1979, the regulations became more flexible. The period of restricted access was reduced, and is as follows:

- 30 years after being issued all administrative archives of a general nature can be consulted, with a possibility of exemption.
- 60 years restriction is placed on any document containing information on the private life of individuals, the security of the state, or national defense.
- 100 years for any archive concerning documents relating to judicial affairs or pardons.

• 120 years after the birth of the individual concerned for documents regarding personnel records of administrative employees and professionals.

Exceptions to these rules are allowed for by the law, and they are often accorded. This liberalization represented a real breath of fresh air and has permitted considerable progress in regard to the consultation of contemporary archives and the scholarly study thus made possible.

It was the progressive opening up of the archives that made possible significant advances in the study of topics relating to the Second World War and this in turn encouraged a modification of the collective memory and a change in our understanding of this dark period of French history. Greater access to primary sources has allowed progress in the study of the French state of Philippe Pétain, as well as the collaboration and the resistance, and it has enabled scholars to revisit issues raised by earlier historians (such as Robert Paxton, an eminent example of a historian who was not allowed access to the many of these archives when he worked on his seminal book, *Vichy France*, 1940–1944. *Old Guard and New Order*, 1971).

Nonetheless other primary sources remain inaccessible, such as archives related to the war in Algeria. It took the concerted activism of historians before the Prime Minister finally issued two circulars, the first in 1997 and the second 2001 that increased access to the archives of the Nazi occupation and those of the last colonial war. Then in 2001 the law on the information society established the right of each citizen to have access to all archives that personally concerned him or her. The potential for historical study of the World War II period was also increased by the belated return, beginning in 1994, of many kilometers of French archives (mainly governmental administrative records), seized by the Nazis in the early years of the Occupation. At the end of the war when the Nazis were defeated by the Soviets, these French documents were confiscated by the Russians who considered the archives to be legitimate spoils of war. The repatriated French archives consist of 1.2 million archival folders. However, not all these "special archives" have yet been returned, and their processing is an immense task.

Despite the increasing availability of archival materials, many researchers continue to protest against restrictions to access, and consider "the secrets of the archives" as not being in conformity with the exigencies of scholarly research and democratic process.

Private archives

An important aspect of the nation's history and collective memory is not found in the various administrative archives described above. However, numerous initiatives have addressed a growing preoccupation with other sources of archives that can contribute to the national memory and identity. Out of a desire to encourage the deposit of private collections in public archives, the Directorate of Archives of France has been systematically inventorying the private papers held by the National Archives and the départemental archives. This information has been entered into the Database for Orientation and Research in the Archives (Base d'Orientation et de Recherche dans les Archives—BORA). When completed, it will be possible for scholars to locate several 1000 collections of private papers relevant to their research.

In 1993, when the Centre des archives du monde du travail was opened in the north of France, the region was experiencing significant social and economic problems due to the changes in industrial production. Nonetheless, the new center for labor archives was also one of the signs of the commitment of public institutions to create a space for alternate memories. Located in a building that had been constructed as a factory in the second half of the nineteenth century, this facility collects the archives of industrial enterprises, commercial firms, professional bodies, unions, employers, associations, and even the personal archives of individuals who had played an important role in the professional world. These archives are largely made up of collections of private organisms that have no legal obligation to deposit their papers.

There are also a very large number of private archives in French libraries which often welcome the archives of local leaders, historians, artists, writers, etc. It is at the Bibliothèque Nationale on the rue Richilieu, within the Department of Manuscripts, that the largest number of private papers are conserved; these include not only the papers of writers but also scholars and statesmen.

The concern for preserving the diverse facets of national heritage has increased. Created in 1988 at the initiative of scholars and professionals from the publishing world, the Institute for the History of Contemporary Publishing (l'Institut Mémoires de l'édition contemporaine—IMEC) brings together, organizes, and preserves archival materials and research related to major publishing houses and important periodicals. L'Institut Mémoires de l'édition contemporaine also holds the papers of editors, writers, artists, researchers, critics, graphic designers, booksellers, printers, periodical editors, literary agents, journalists, and acquisition editors.

In a completely different domain, Génériques, an association created in 1987, has for 10 years taken on the task of inventorying the resources of public archives concerning foreigners in France. In addition, Génériques is working to safeguard and preserve private archives (associations, unions, and activists) related to immigration. Its goal is to make these papers available to the public in the hope of encouraging historical studies of immigration as well as increasing public awareness of the contributions made by immigrant populations throughout the history of France.

Transformations

Contemporary changes affect not only professional practice but also the formats that must be preserved and the nature of the public who use services of the archives. The advent of documents "born digital" (*tout électronique*) also represents a major change. Basing their work on the international standards for the description of documents (General International Standard Archival Description—ISAD-G), archivists find that more and more they are describing documents that utilize the XML format. French archivists also use Encoded Archival Description Document Type Definition (EAD DTD), which can be applied to the description of both paper and electronic documents. These standards and formats have been adopted because they permit the precise description of documents and allow for the exchange of records as well as database searching. Archives are also confronted with the long-term conservation of electronic documents. In numerous countries there are rules stating that under certain conditions the same legal validity is accorded to the electronic text as to documents on paper. However, as the French specialist, Catherine Dhérent asserts:

> To describe digital texts, evaluate, and select them takes much more time than to organize archives in traditional formats or to prepare a finding aid like those used in the past—even one that is very detailed... The archivist must intervene much earlier in the life cycle of information.

In fact the initial structure of information is of primary importance, and from the time when electronic data is created, the intent to preserve these records must be factored into the software and the databases. Efforts to ensure effective records management and archival deposit must be integrated in all practices of those institutions concerned with preserving electronic records.

Archival services, like libraries, are also faced with the need to preserve Web sites, especially those of administrative authorities. Competencies expected of archivists now include application of new techniques for the capture of electronic data and the establishment of metadata, as well as knowing how to preserve digital documents. More than ever the archivists must plan in advance for tasks not made explicit and they must therefore become immersed in the professional or administrative milieu whose records they preserve and maintain. Archivists are no longer actors whose role begins after a document is written, but instead they must intervene early, anticipating the production of electronic texts in order to preserve them.

The public using archives has grown and diversified considerably during the last 30 years. In 1999, more than 300,000 individuals used the *départemental* and communal archives. Even though scholars and researchers are still numerous, the archives are now used by more and more people interested in genealogy who are researching their family history. One-third of the users of *départemental* and communal archives are academics or administrators and one-third are retirees; the remainder include university students and individuals from other professions. Half of the users are undertaking genealogical research. General history or local history is the central interest of the majority of these readers. Half of them consult documents from the nineteenth century, and half use earlier materials, from the Revolution or the *Ancien régime*—notably parish records or registers of civil records.

Issues relating to the maintenance and preservation of archives is now of concern to a significant number of persons interested in social history or engaged in researching their family roots. The increasing presence of amateur genealogists has lead the archives of France to collaborate with the French Genealogical Federation in order to establish the portal Nomina. Set up in 2005, Nomina offers simple direct access to a significant collection of references and resources that can aid genealogists. Through this portal one can search four databases of names; within 3 years these databases included 13 million names, and the number is rapidly growing.

New segments of society also seek to be represented in the archives. At the same time research topics have diversified and multiplied and as a result more varied kinds of archival documents are being consulted. For example, because of an increasing research interest in daily life, ordinary social practices are now an integral part of the field of investigation. As the interest in historical sources are accompanied by the explosion of digital texts, paper, and pixels combine to increase in a dramatic way the reach of memory institutions that are now part of global information society.

MUSEUMS

Since the 1980s, French museums have experienced enormous transformations such as: a significant increase in the number of museums; construction of new buildings and ambitious renovations; a large growth in the number of visitors; an increase of large ambitious temporary exhibitions; and greater administrative challenges for managers. Trends include the temptation to commercialize museum practices; the redoubled efforts to attract philanthropy; and projects to "delocalize" certain important museum with branches elsewhere in France or abroad.

From Princely Collections to Public Collections

French princes and nobles have always collected works of art as signs of their power and their refinement. By the seventeenth century, the taste for collecting spread to other collectors (labeled "curieux") whom Jean de La Bruyère, a satirical writer, mocked for their desire to simply amass an exhaustive collection. However, the "cabinets of curiosities" bore witness to the growing knowledge in the area of natural history. An interest in antiquities developed as well as greater attention to historical monuments. Scholars such as Pereisc, Caylus, Gaignères, or Montfaucon established the concept of cultural heritage (*patrimoine*), and certain collectors opened their galleries to other amateurs. It is thought that the first museum was opened in 1694 in Besançon thanks to the donation of a priest who willed his books and works of art to the city on the condition that his collection would be open for consultation two times per week.

Starting in 1748, the Royal Academy of Painting organized a Salon with the aim of exhibiting and promoting the painters recognized by the king; at this time historical paintings were especially favored. From 1750 onward 100 paintings from the royal collections were presented at the Luxembourg Palace, which could therefore be considered the first example of a public museum. Soon a growing number of agents became involved in shaping aesthetic taste in France and bringing new perspectives to the art world; these individuals included the artists themselves, art dealers, new kinds of collectors, and the first art critics.

At the same time the field of museology was invented and attention was given to questions relating to the selection of works, the kind of space best adapted for the exhibition of the collection, and reflections on how to classify and organize works of art. During the 1770s several provincial cities opened museums, but these were generally scientific and technical. At the same time "lycées" dedicated to works of art were established; these institutions were often as a result of the efforts of scholars, artists, and writers. In addition, there were schools for design set up to train apprentice artists.

Although buildings and works of art that symbolized the hated Ancien Régime were sometimes destroyed during the French Revolution, it was also the Revolution that established and organized cultural heritage institutions dedicated to the arts. In addition, the Revolution encouraged the creation of three types of museums: the fine arts museum, the natural history museum, and the local museum. The newly established republic scrupulously inventoried "paintings, drawings, and statues," "models and machines" and collections of natural history that were designated to become part of the Central Museum of the arts established at the Louvre in 1793. According to historian Dominique Poulot, this project was envisioned as a "world museum" (*"musée-monde"*). The intent was to return to the nation its treasures, reinterpreting them in the light of the new ideology of emancipation. These collections were enriched with art works brought back during the conquests of the Republic and later augmented by Napoleon I. The task of organizing these extensive collections fell to Dominique Vivant-Denon, one of the first directors of the Louvre. Similar pedagogical goals were envisioned for the Museum of Monuments, founded by Alexandre Lenoir who sought to illustrate the history of French architecture.

During the nineteenth century, the paintings exhibited at the Salon des artistes français which were selected by designated members of the Academy of Beaux-Arts became more and more numerous, going from 1900 in 1848 to 7000 in 1880. Over time, the criteria of the Academy were contested and a group of artists created an alternative venue called the "Salon des refusés" (also known as the Salon of the independents) where the works of the impressionists were welcomed. The setting of aesthetic standards and of artistic achievement escaped from the control of the state and the growth of salons was the prelude to an increase in other types of exhibitions.

At the same time, museums spread throughout France and their interests began to diversify. The idea of national heritage (*la mémoire nationale*) began to be defined through museums. The same trend was seen in local history (*la mémoire locale*): regionalism encouraged the flaunting of specific local identities, sometimes contesting the dominance of an identity restricted to characteristics considered national. At the end of the century the Third Republic (1870–1940) established a policy of public funding that enriched provincial museums through purchases by the central government. The construction of museums in large cities was integrated into urban public works projects, and thus the discourse of local identity was translated into stone. Situated in the center of the city the museum often shared the same building with the municipal library, and it was never far from city hall.

During the last decades of the nineteenth century museography progressed as a discipline. However, despite the construction of some new buildings, museums and their treasures became mausoleums without adequate financial support (much like the situation of libraries during the same period). The image of the French museum was dusty and conventional, without impact on the contemporary world of art. The irruption of modernity thus took the path of subverting or bypassing existing institutions. Thus, in France until very recently museums lacked an openness to contemporary art and they failed to respond to important cultural and aesthetic trends such as the regional or local aspects of nineteenth century culture or the focus on popular culture, heightened in the twentieth century by the emerging disciplines of anthropology and ethnography.

The first part of the twentieth century was difficult for museums. Museum curators found their selection of works contested by the avant-garde, while at the same time they were confronted with the growing financial power of private collectors, art dealers, and galleries and soon became marginalized in the art market. Allotted insufficient funds by administrative authorities, French museums became somewhat fossilized around collections that were not being renewed.

Nonetheless, during the 1930s a new kind of museology and new preoccupations came to the fore. These included the contribution of the ethnographic perspective to the understanding of non-Western civilizations as well as a growing interest in popular culture in France. Such trends lead to the creation of different types of museums, such as the renowned Anthropology museum (Musée de l'homme) and the Museum of Popular Arts and Traditions, whose respective founders, Jean Rivet and Georges-Henri Rivière, were guided by the modern museographical ideas.

Museology was also evolving, and the accumulation of collections gave way to greater selectivity, accompanied by more effective exhibition techniques and a pedagogical discourse which was intended to aid visitors who were no longer left on their own to confront works of art unaware of the context of their creation. Henri Focillon, a scholar and director of the museum of Lyon, laid the foundation for the International Council of Museums, created in 1946 at a time when the museum world was becoming interested in international exchanges with the goal of creating standards for museum practices.

As was the case in the domain of archives and libraries, public policy initiatives in the museum domain were redoubled after the Liberation. A 1945 law whose aim was to increase the administrative support of the central government distinguished three types of museums throughout the country; this typology was based on the size and value of the collections. The largest were given the status of national museums, followed by those designated as classified museums (musées classés) and finally by smaller museums that were inspected from time to time by representatives of the central government. The idea of monitoring museums should not be thought of as retrograde Jacobinism. On the contrary, at this time, it represented greater governmental support for museum development and stimulated the professionalization of museum practice.

André Malraux, writer and author of the *Imaginary Museum* (*Museum Without Walls* in the English translation) was well qualified to become the first Minister of Cultural Affairs in 1959. Basing his policies on a desire to promote an aesthetic shock (*choc esthétique*) in the confrontation between the public and the works of art, his goal was to "make accessible the great works of humanity, and especially of France, to the largest possible number of French people" (Law of 1959 founding the Ministry of Culture). Malraux not only initiated the renovation of museums, he also saw to the construction of cultural centers (*Maisons de la Culture*) in the heart of the larger cities. These centers were a kind of "space for the totality of culture" offering concerts, theatrical performances, debates, and sometimes they even included an "*artothèque*" lending art that could be displayed at home. The *artothèque* usually contained reproductions of paintings or works by young artists. Despite his best efforts, Malraux's objective of consecrating 1% of the national budget to the activities of the Ministry of Culture was not attained until 1981 when the Left gained power.

Museums Today

The law of January 4, 2002 renewed the statute for those museums that are administered by public authorities. This law designated 34 national museums, thus emphasizing their scope and importance; national institutions includes: the Chateau of Versailles, the Louvre, the Orsay Museum, the Rodin Museum, the Picasso Museum, and the Museum of Franco-American Cooperation at Blérancourt, etc. At the next level are 1173 "museums of France" which are administered by local authorities or by associations. These museums hold collections that are in part owned by the central government, but the museums themselves are now under the responsibility of local or regional authorities. The designation "museum of France" is defined by specific cultural and scientific criteria: these establishments must

conserve, restore, study, and enrich their collections; make their collections accessible to the general public; plan and implement educational activities with the goal of assuring to all equal access to culture; and contribute to research and to the advancement of knowledge and to its diffusion.

(article 2). A High Council for Museums (Haut Conseil des musées) brings together representatives from different kinds of museums.

The total number of museums in France today is between 5000 and 6000 institutions. Numerous museums are under the authority of ministries other than the Ministry of Culture; others are administered by territorial collectivities, by association or even by private individuals, such as collectors. The city of Paris also is responsible for numerous museums such as Carnavalet Museum of the History of Paris, the Museum of the Petit Palais, the Museum of the Art and History of Judaism, etc.

Within the Ministry of Culture the Directorate for the Museums of France provides funding for the 34 national museums over which it exercises a supervisory role. In addition, the Directorate has an overarching mission of orientation, programming, and coordinating museums throughout France. The Directorate also has the responsibility to:

- Monitor and provide technical and scientific advice to museums that are administered by municipalities, by départements or by associations.
- Implement the government's policy of contribution to the enrichment of national public collections.
- Establish and promulgate rules for the protection and conservation of works of art.

- Set rules for loans, and authorize or deny permission for works of art to leave French soil.
- Support the training of museum professionals.

Public collections of art are governed by the rule of inalienability; no works can be sold unless they are first "declassified." The evaluation of works to be declassified is carried out by museum advisors who belong to one of the 26 Regional Directorates of Cultural Affairs.

Other services that support and coordinate museums are also under the authority of the Directorate of the Museums of France. One of these is La Réunion des musées nationaux, an agency whose main mission is to acquire works of art to enrich the national collections; the Réunion also organizes major exhibits and edits their catalogs as well as selling any tie-in products. Another body known as Center for Museum Research and Conservation in France (le Centre de recherche et de restauration des musées de France) carries out research in the domain of restoration and conservation and participates in the implementation of new practices and techniques.

As in other cultural domains, the last 20 years were marked by growing power of territorial collectivities. By 2008, half of the museum professionals were employed by regional or local museums. In order to structure and coordinate their activities, the départements often employ a museum advisor (conseiller patrimoine) who attempts to promote networking. The fine arts museums of Northern France and of Pas-de-Calais coordinate their exhibition programs and their public relations work. In Auvergne, an association to promote local museums has been established. In large cities, the Directorate of Cultural Affairs employs a museum advisor who supports the development of museums and seeks to establish partnerships with other institutions within the city, especially in activities that relate to public relations and education.

Local museums in France are not limited to fine arts, even though here the tradition of local history museums is less developed than that in Great Britain or the United States. Numerous French museums are dedicated to history, prehistory, ancient archaeology, natural sciences, while other focus on specific social or economic activities. Since, the 1970s there has been a flowering of eco-museums as well as museums that collect objects related to popular culture, to professional, industrial or technological activities; in addition there are museums that collect artifacts representing the ethnographic heritage of France. There are over 200 of these kinds of museums throughout France—a fact which demonstrated the viability of a new socioeconomic orientation for museums.

Audacious Architecture

During the past 30 years there has been a spectacular development of museum buildings in France. Renowned architects have been commissioned for numerous new building projects and for the audacious renovation of existing museums. The landscape has been radically transformed. This wave of construction began in 1977 with the Centre Georges Pompidou designed in an unabashedly modernist style by Renzo Piano and Richard Rogers. The building consists of eight levels that are entirely modular. All the weight bearing supports as well as the water pipes and ducts for electrical cables, elevators, and air conditioning were pushed out to the exterior of the building, thus giving the center a unique appearance that has been compared to an oil refinery by certain critics.

During the 1980s, numerous museums in Paris and the provinces have been renovated or rebuilt. In 1985, a private mansion in the Marais historic district on the right bank of the Seine was transformed into the Picasso Museum by the architect Roland Simounet. A year later three architects and interior designers working under the direction of Gae Aulenti carried out an even more radical transformation of the Orsay railway station in Paris, creating exhibition space for a museum consecrated to the nineteenth century.

In the late 1980s Ieoh Ming Peï, a renowned architect who is known for numerous projects, especially the new wing of the National Gallery in Washington, D.C., was chosen to renovate, modernize, and enlarge the Louvre. Pei's audacious design was centered around a stunning glass pyramid in the heart of the Louvre's courtyard. Another group of notable architects, J. M. Wilmotte, Rudy Ricciotti, and Mario Bellini, have been commissioned to carry out the interior design of the galleries of Louvre. This expansion was carried out from 1981 to 1999.

Jean Nouvel, architect of the Institute the Arab World and the Cartier Foundation for Contemporary Art, constructed the Quai Branly Museum, dedicated to non-Western art; this innovative new museum opened in 2006. Numerous projects are now in the process of being constructed, such as a building in Paris by Frank Gehry which will house the private collection of François Pinault.

In the provinces, the construction of a new fine arts museum in Grenoble was followed by the Carré d'art (museum and library) in Nîmes designed by Norman Forster in 1993 and the Museum of modern art of Villeneuve d'Ascq. Important renovations were carried out in Lyon, Nantes, and Lille and many other cities. All these innovative constructions and renovations of French museums offer visitors the pleasure of viewing newly enhanced and enriched collections shown to their best advantage.

A Few Major Museums

The Louvre Museum occupies 160,106 m² of which 58,470 m² are used for exhibits. It is the third largest museum in the world after the Metropolitan Museum of Art in New York and the Hermitage Museum in Saint

Petersburg, Russia. In 1993, the Louvre became a public institution under the Ministry of Culture, and this change in its statute permitted the museum to enjoy greater autonomy. The collections of the Louvre cover the period from antiquity to 1848 and exhibits represent a wide geographical area from Europe to Iran, via Greece, Egypt, and the Near East. Among the most famous masterpieces are the Code of Hammurabi, the Venus de Milo, the Mona Lisa by Leonardo da Vinci, and Liberty Guiding the People by Eugène Delacroix. The renovation of the Louvre allowed for an increase of 30,000 m^2. The Pyramid of the Louvre is the center of gravity for the collections, and functions as the principal entry, allowing visitors access to the three wings of the Louvre palace: Richelieu, Sully, and Denon.

The *Orsay Museum* presents diverse works of the second half of the nineteenth century, from 1848 to the birth of Cubisme. By featuring artists born between 1820 and 1870, it provides the transition from the collections of the Louvre and the collection of the Museum of Modern Art at the Pompidou Center.

The *Pompidou Center* is the result of the vision of President Georges Pompidou (1911–1974) who wished to create an innovative cultural center in the heart of Paris— a center not only dedicated to fostering creativity in the plastic arts but also offering access to books, drawings and graphic design, music and cinema within the same building. The Pompidou Center houses an Institute for Contemporary Music, theaters for performing arts and movies, and the largest public library in Europe at the time—the Bibliothèque publique d'information (BPI). Occupying two levels of the Pompidou Center, the National Museum of Modern Art/Center for Industrial Creation holds 59,000 works, making it one of the most important collections of modern and contemporary art in the world (rivaled only by the New York Museum of Modern Art). Out of its vast collection, the Pompidou center offers 1330 works on permanent display, but it also has galleries for temporary exhibits as well as the Kandinsky library which offers a specialized collection of works related to twentieth century art. In the course of its three decades of existence, the Center has offered some remarkable exhibitions, such as *Paris–New York, Paris–Berlin, Paris–Moscow*, or later *Vienna, Turn of the Century* (1986).

The *City for Science and Industry (Cité des sciences et de l'industrie)*, designed by architect Adrien Fainsilber, opened in 1986 and has since become very popular with the public. The mission of the Cité is to promote an understanding of science and technology to the general public, especially targeting children and adolescents. In addition, it attempts to stimulate the interest of citizens in the challenges to society that are linked to scientific and industrial research. Located in the immense La Villette Park, this complex offers many theaters and auditoriums, a music conservatory, and a concert hall.

In the course of the twentieth century non-Western art began to occupy a major place within museum collections.

This development was due in part to the efforts of artists known as Fauves and Cubists, as well as to the work of ethnographers such as Claude Levi-Strauss and to writers and critics from Apollinaire to Malraux. The *Quai Branly museum*, opened in 2006, is entirely devoted to the arts of Africa, Asia, Oceania, and the Americas. Its goal is to stimulate the study of these objects using diverse perspectives, from ethnography to art history, and to recognize the importance of the civilizations and heritage of people sometimes marginalized by contemporary globalization of Western culture.

In 2007, a new national museum on the history of immigration (*la Cité nationale de l'histoire de l'immigration*) was opened. It is the goal of this new institution to collect, protect, interpret, and display artifacts relating to the history of immigration in France since the nineteenth century and to contribute to the development of new scholarly perspectives and to influence public attitudes (mentalités) by increasing the understanding of the role and contributions of immigrants in France. Narrative accounts, archival documents, photographs, drawings, and works of art are used to illustrate the history of immigrant experience. Among the important French historical museums one should also note those museums dedicated to the First or Second World War which have also benefited from recent building projects as well as new approaches to museology. Since 1988, more than 7 million people of all nationalities have visited the Peace Memorial dedicated to the Second World War in Caen, a city 73% destroyed during the summer of 1944.

The Museum Professions in Evolution

The curators of national or regional museums are trained at the National Heritage Institute (l'Institut national du patrimoine). Founded in 1990, the institute has as its mission the training of curators and conservators who work in cultural heritage institutions. These curators practice their profession in archives or museums; some conduct inventories and others work for organisms dealing with archaeology, historical monuments, or with other types of heritage collections in natural history, science or technology. Curators are appointed head of the national museums and major museums under local authorities; working under the curators are technical assistants (attachés de conservation) who belong to a national technical corps established in 1991. Trained in schools for territorial administrators, these technical assistants have become more and more numerous in museums operated by local authorities, and they direct some of the smaller local museums. Other staff in territorial museums include assistants and credentialed assistants with an expertise in conservation; both must pass a national examination. The guards are the most numerous museum employees, and they are given a double role of providing security and of welcoming the public.

The growth in the number of museums and the increase in temporary exhibitions has initiated or contributed to the professionalization of related occupations, such as registrars of works of art. It has also given rise to the function of exhibit planning, which is usually carried out by curators who are chosen either for their specialized subject knowledge or for their special competence in mounting temporary exhibits and organizing programs. Such exhibitions are often the moving force behind museums, attracting a different public than those who come to see the permanent collections. For major exhibits great care is taken as to the presentation, which is conceptualized by designers (scénographes). Finally, most museums now have a cultural service or an educational department which oversees a variety of interpretive activities offered to a diverse public of adults as well as children. These offerings include debates, meetings, concerts, lectures, or guided visits as well as pedagogical activities and special programs for schools.

For curators, scholarly expertise remains the primary requirement and they must be specialists in the art genre and period in which they work. Curators are increasingly engaged in research which primarily (but not solely), relates to catalogs focused on a single artist or accompanying a thematic exhibition. In addition to research and publication, the concern for documentation has lead museums to mount reproductions of their holdings online (http://www.culture.gouv.fr/culture/bdd/bdd3g.htm).

Opened in 2004, the National Institute for the History of Art (Institut national d'histoire de l'art—INHA) supports research in art history carried out by teacher–researchers in higher education institutions or by museum curators. To aid these researchers INHA has created databases, directories, dictionaries, and compilations of sources materials that are useful for research in art history. In addition, INHA has an important library with a rich collection of 1.7 million items that are used for specialized research in the history of art, archeology, and architecture. The institute also welcomes foreign researchers and contributes to the training of young researchers.

The School of the Louvre (Ecole du Louvre) is aimed at a broader public. Founded in 1882 and still located in the Louvre Palace, it offers courses in the history of art, archeology, epigraphy, history of civilization, and museology. It also welcomes individuals wishing to audit its courses, and offers evening courses and series of lectures for the general public.

The Growth of the Public

The great public success of museums and exhibits is not a recent phenomenon. The French Revolution inaugurated the doctrine that all citizens should share in the enjoyment of national treasures. From that time on a broad public has visited the Louvre and the Museum of French Monuments. It is estimated that number of museum visitors had tripled

by the end of the eighteenth century. The "grand tour" of Europe which became obligatory for wealthy families on the other side of the Atlantic also brought an increasing number of visitors to European museums, including some who came in search of their roots and their identity. At the same time growing crowds of French bourgeoisie were seen at the Salons: 360,000 persons at the Salon of 1870 and 500,000 at the Salon of 1874. Despite the bourgeoning interest in art, the public who visited museums remained dominated by scholars or members of the elite and the nineteenth century did not greatly add to this audience.

Since the 1980s, the museum-going public has increased and diversified due to a combination of factors: the investments by public authorities in museums; the renovation of key museums; and the attraction of temporary exhibits not restricted by a narrow scholarly discourse and therefore open to a much wider audience. If the public was eager to respond to these new incentives, it was because the structure of the French population had changed during the intervening years. There were many factors that stimulated a much greater demand for cultural activities. These included: the general lengthening of schooling; the increase of the number of graduates from secondary schools and higher educational institutions among the middle class; an increased life expectancy; and the growth of cities. Nonetheless, only 30% of French citizens visit at least one museum per year.

The Louvre is the most visited museum in the world with 8.5 million visitors in 2008; that year the Pompidou center welcomed 5.5 million visitors, and Versailles 3 million—mostly foreigners as is the case at the Orsay Museum. Major exhibitions bring crowds of people ready to stand in long lines waiting to enter exhibit halls so packed that it is difficult to calmly reflect on or enjoy the works of art displayed. Examples include an exhibit of the works of Manet in 1983 that drew 700,000 visitors; another on Renoir in 1985 welcomed 825,000 visitors; 660,000 came to view the Gauguin exhibit in 1989; for Toulouse-Lautrec in 1992 attendance was 700,000, and for, Cézanne in 1995 630,000. Nonetheless, the large audience for exhibitions remains marked by social distinctions: museum visitors are still drawn from among the highly educated and from those in higher social and economic levels. Broad democratization of the museum-going public is still far from being realized.

In order to respond to large scale changes that require heavy expenditures in museums, France encourages philanthropy. This is done by offering a substantial reduction in income tax for corporations. If the work of art purchased is considered a "national treasure" and has been refused a certificate for exportation, the individual donor or the corporation can benefit from a tax reduction equivalent to 90% of the price paid for the work of art.

In 2007, the Louvre and the emirate of Abu Dhabi provoked considerable controversy. The Louvre assisted the emirate in planning a museum that would bear the name of the Louvre for 30 years. French museums will organize traveling exhibitions and will loan works (300 initially, more subsequently). In return the emirate will deposit important sums of money [1 billion euros] into the account of a new International Agency for the Museums of France (Agence Internationale des Musées de France).

France, like a number of European countries, has not only developed a passion for heritage institutions and sites of memory ("lieux de mémoire") but has also succumbed to the vogue of the "patrimonialisation du monde." Everything represents heritage and every place is a site of memory in this movement that has led to both a greater openness and to a turning inward. If modernity and globalization extend one's perspectives and stimulate curiosity, these trends also stimulate a desire to return to one's roots, to be inscribed into a more circumscribed world, into a history and geography that are more familiar. Revealing an opening to the larger world, the celebration of heritage also bears witness to a certain fear of the future and a redoubled need to share common social beliefs and practices, a desire to belong to a community. Finally, as globalization has brought about mass cultural tourism, the great museums of France are welcoming an impressive number of foreign visitors.

LIBRARIES

Like museums, libraries have experienced unprecedented development at the end of the twentieth century. The provision of library resources and services has undergone a continuous reconceptualization and readjustment due to the transformation in educational and cultural policies, the evolution of professional practice, and the revolution in information technologies.

A Rich History

French libraries have had a very long, rich, and varied history. In the Middle Ages, monasteries were the major centers for the production of manuscripts, and their *scriptoria* were the source for many theological works. The monks were not only responsible for exegesis but also for the conservation and reproduction of manuscripts at a time when copying was the only means of reproducing and diffusing a work. Each manuscript was unique, because every copy could contain variants, glosses, and errors; it is this characteristic unicity that makes these manuscripts so valuable today. By the thirteenth century, the first universities and colleges established libraries where valuable large format, manuscript books were chained to lecterns. In contrast, the kings traveled with their books, and from 1483 onward the kings passed their collection intact from father to son. The royal library was first installed in a fixed location in the Chateau of Blois then moved to the Louvre

palace in the 1560s. Soon the first classification schemes and library catalogs were developed.

Meanwhile, the invention of printing and the era of religious disputes altered the world of books. Access to religious works in the vernacular was one of the challenges of the Protestant reformation, and around the same time scholars such as Erasmus of Rotterdam (1467–1534) and Michel de Montaigne (1533–1592) affirmed the right to personal reflection and free thought as an essential component of humanism. The library ("librairie") of these humanists was a personally selected collection of works that became a space outside of the control of the authorities.

In 1521, François I made legal deposit of printed books obligatory—an act that has continuously enriched the royal library with books published in France. Nonetheless, the establishment of legal deposit was an act characterized by mixed motives; on the one hand, it reflected the king's desire to collect and preserve all works published throughout the nation and, on the other hand, it represented his intent to control the printed word through the exercise of censorship. In addition to royal oversight there was also ecclesiastical control of French printing; the requirement that writings receive a license to be printed (*l'imprimatur*) from the Catholic church was one of the triumphs of the Counter-Reformation in face of the challenges by Protestant "heretics."

Meanwhile educated princes, nobles, and other cultivated people began to collect personal libraries, and some of these were quite important. In the seventeenth century, Cardinal Mazarin (1602–1661) owned one of the largest collections of his time, enriched by the efforts of Gabriel Naudé (1600–1653), a librarian active in the Republic of Letters. By the time of the Enlightenment in the eighteenth century, books and libraries had become instruments for the conquest of public space, then opened to the exercise of reason, dialog, and freedom of thought. At this time libraries were more numerous, offered more abundant collections, and were sometimes opened to the public. Even the Royal Library was open to the curious ("curieux") and to the amateurs two afternoons a week.

In France, the first establishment of libraries placed under public responsibility was an outcome of the emancipatory ideology and policy of the Revolution. These newly created libraries were supplied with books confiscated from the libraries of the aristocrats and the clergy, whose collections were sometimes expurgated. Between 4 and 7 million items were seized and placed in literary depositories (*dépôts littéraires*), then given to colleges; finally in 1803 they were entrusted to the communes. At this time the Royal library was renamed the Bibliothèque nationale (BN), and both the BN and a number of other large libraries were enriched by the works that were seized.

For a time this rich heritage was the glory of French libraries, and during the 1860s British librarians and members of parliament who wished to develop libraries in their country, held up French libraries as the example to imitate. Although the municipal collections throughout France were slowly cataloged, preserved, and made available to the public, these libraries acquired few new works and their services to the public were limited. Paradoxically, the richness of the collections became a dead weight on municipal libraries; neglected by the authorities, these institutions only attracted scholars and students who appreciated their rare and precious works. However, by the end of the nineteenth century the demand for reading materials increased in France.

Literacy became much more widespread, and the working class as well as women and children were becoming readers. These changes lead to the creation of popular libraries (*bibliothèques populaires*) which were financed by philanthropic organizations, by cities, by schools, and by religious bodies. Although the collections of these lending libraries were often limited, they included carefully selected books, often chosen with the intent of using "good books" to combat the taste for "bad books"; the founders of these libraries also hoped that the working classes would engage in reading instead of pursuing leisure activities considered bad. Nonetheless, in addition to nonfiction works these libraries did loan out novels (a genre that was considered illegitimate for a long time). These popular libraries initially met with great success and it is estimated that there were tens of thousands of them by the late nineteenth century when they began to rapidly disappear.

In the early years of the twentieth century, modernist librarians struggled to gain acceptance of a new model of free public libraries inspired by examples they found in Great Britain and the United States. After the First World War, these reformers were able to point to model public libraries constructed by the American Committee for Devastated France (Comité américain pour les régions dévastées—CARD), a philanthropic organization active in the reconstruction of villages destroyed by the German invasion.

Jessie Carson, a librarian from the New York Public Library was responsible for the CARD library projects, and she oversaw the creation of five small libraries installed in wooden barracks. Although the CARD libraries were modest, they were nonetheless significant in the history of public librarianship in France. Later Carson worked with CARD and with French library leaders to establish a Paris public library branch that featured open shelves and used American cataloging and classification systems. Another American philanthropic organization later gave the Paris municipal library system the first children's library with open shelves. Known as l'Heure joyeuse, this collection was directed for many years by Marguerite Gruny, who is considered a great pioneer of children's services in France.

After the Second World War important new policies for library development were put in place. Within the Ministry of Education a new Directorate for Libraries and for Public Library Services (*Direction des bibliothèques et de la lecture publique*) was established. At the départemental level the Directorate set up Central Lending Libraries (*Bibliothèques centrales de prêt-BCP*) in order to encourage the development of rural public library services in a country that still had a significant population living in rural areas. Charged with bringing the "food for the spirit" to homes in small communes and rural areas, these Central Lending Libraries deposited book boxes in schools and town halls, sent out bookmobiles that traversed the countryside, and later offered users direct access to the central facility whose shelves were filled with books.

The Directorate also promoted significant development of university libraries by assuring that they were allotted greatly increased financing, better facilities, and more staff. Significant investment in libraries and in the advancement of librarianship continued into the 1960s. This enabled the restructuring and strengthening of training for librarianship, and provided incentives for professional meetings and publications. In addition career opportunities in the field were improved, and the National Graduate Library School (Ecole nationale supérieure des bibliothèques) was established to train professionals at a level equivalent to a master's degree.

Despite considerable progress in the field, it was not enough to keep up with new demands placed on libraries by the rising educational and cultural level of the population and the rapid growth of specialized knowledge which stimulated an exponential growth in publishing. During the 1970s, French libraries again experienced a crisis. Renewed efforts first came at the local level as cities finally decided to develop new cultural policies to meet the needs of urban populations who were more highly educated than in the past. The opening of the new municipal library in Lyon in 1972 and that of the *Bibliothèque publique d'information* at the Centre Pompidou in Paris in 1977 clearly demonstrated the huge popular success of rich open-access collections that were regularly updated. At the same time there were numerous new construction projects as well as renovations of buildings and renewal of collections. At the same time libraries began offering books and other materials in a variety of formats. A new term, "médiathèque" (media center), was chosen to signify the wide range of materials and formats offered by these facilities whose development found a favor among city policy makers.

At the national level after 1981 the left wing coalition government vigorously supported the development of public library services. The renaissance of university and research libraries came somewhat later, and it was not until the late 1980s that universities received an important increase in funds to develop their libraries.

Today, there are several types of library systems or networks in France.

- Municipal libraries under the authority of cities; they may benefit from support from the central government, especially in regard to construction.
- Départemental libraries, governed by départemental authorities; their mission is to promote the development of library services in cities with fewer than 10,000 inhabitants;
- School libraries which include centers for documentation and information (CDI) offered by most secondary schools and middle schools, and library documentation centers (bibliothèques centres documentaries—BCD) found in a certain number of primary schools;
- Academic libraries that belong to universities and are placed under the authority of the ministry in charge of higher education;
- Libraries under the authority of the Ministry of Culture and directly financed by the ministry. These include for instance the Bibliothèque nationale de France (placed under the ministry in 1981) and the BPI at the Centre Pompidou.

The Transformation of Public Libraries

The development of public libraries in France has occurred along several important lines, and could be thought of as the implementation of professional philosophies and practices which originated in the nineteenth century, first being used in the young American democracy and then spreading to northern Europe. These practices, adapted to twenty-first century France, include:

- Providing extensive multimedia collections regularly updated and enriched.
- Facilitating easy use of the collections by offering readers direct access to all the types of materials from books to electronic resources and DVDs.
- Fostering a welcoming ambiance and an openness to all levels of readers from experienced scholars to novice users.
- Offering nonjudgmental services to all users, whether their reading needs are cultural, educational, informational, or recreational.

The above principles of service have been widely adopted and to them have been added two more principles that may be specifically French. First is the importance given to architecture and also to the use of space in a way that not only promotes the shared national heritage but also links cultural needs with the common good. Second is the desire to respect the tastes of the readers and, at the same time, to promote cultural policies which are characterized by a refusal of librarians to follow the simple supply and demand logic of the market place.

In 2006, France had a total of 2913 municipal libraries which employed 24,200 staff members and occupied 1.8 million m² of shelf space. Their collections provide users with access to 100 million items: 90.5 million printed materials (2.6 books per inhabitant only); 8.4 million pieces of music or discs; nearly 1.4 million films, videos, and still photographs, as well as language learning materials and an ever increasing number of electronic resources and digital documents of all types. Annually, municipal libraries acquire 4.9 million printed works (or 18 printed works per 100 inhabitants), purchased at a cost of 2.72 Euros per capita, and about 800,000 CDs or DVDs. However, it is audiovisual materials and electronic resources that have increased most rapidly, both in terms of their importance as a proportion of the collections and in terms of items loaned. These collections are largely available through direct access, which has radically transformed the relationship between the users and the knowledge or information they need. Now people can make use of the library without preconceived ideas and without knowing exactly what they are looking for.

The 97 départemental libraries (Bibliothèques départementales de prêt, BDP, which were known as Bibliothèques Centales de prêt prior to 1992) offer services to the 30 million inhabitants of France who live in 17,000 communes with a population of less than 10,000. They offer a total of 27 million print and nonprint materials (90 works for 100 inhabitants) in 17,000 libraries or book deposit stations, buying a total of 1.5 million documents a year (1 Euro per inhabitant per year). The départemental libraries also assist small municipal libraries and intercommunal libraries with their programming and operations. In addition, they provide support for the smallest library units known as *bibliothèquess-relais*," and they send rotating deposits of books to schools, daycare centers, town halls, or to prisons and retirement homes. In addition, they provide for bookmobiles (bibliobus or médiabus) that offer direct access to their collections and also provide training to volunteers who staff the small book depositories or libraries.

Now very well integrated into local educational and cultural policies, public libraries have increased their efforts to partner with other civic organizations; they participate in many kinds of cultural programs and activities, and they promote reading in disadvantaged neighborhoods through outreach programs. Public libraries also network with other educational and cultural institutions and organizations, such as schools and associations. In a number of cities, libraries work with diverse institutions and agencies to plan and coordinate city-read programs (ville-lecture).

One of the weaknesses of French administration is the extreme partition and dilution of political responsibilities among 36,700 communes, each of which has considerable autonomy within its jurisdiction. In contrast, other European countries started regrouping their smallest territorial divisions into larger units during the mid-1960s; for example in Great Britain there are only 209 local authorities. It seems that the time has finally come in France for cooperation and sharing responsibilities through inter-communal groupings. For the past decade and a half at the départemental level elected officials have often worked together in developing joint cultural policies and programs, and they have frequently taken on responsibility for promoting reading through various federated efforts.

School, Academic, and Research Libraries

For a long time French academic and school libraries have suffered from the indifference of public policy makers, a fact which remains paradoxical in a country with a strong intellectual tradition. In the long sweep of history there are a number of reasons for this situation. Those countries that were predominantly Catholic had a longstanding tradition of clerical control over the written word, because the church wished to monitor reading and "protect" readers. In contrast, Protestant countries claimed the right of individuals to have direct access to the Bible which was read in the vernacular. Meanwhile, in France aristocratic traditions favored an individual relationship with reading, which depended more on the wealth of personal collections, often inherited, than on the public provision of libraries. These aristocratic traditions in regard to education and cultural questions (so well analyzed by Alexis de Tocqueville), still have traces remaining today in contemporary attitudes, especially among the elite. Finally, educational system in France for a long time favored orality and privileged the spoken words of the teacher (maître) to the written word. Educational authorities also devalued the practice of gaining knowledge based on everyday experience and not simply by reading literary texts.

These factors explain why, despite significant funding in the nineteenth century, school libraries have had to wait until the mid-1970s to be given professionally trained personnel. It was not until the 1980s that school libraries were present in a large majority of schools. Centers for documentation in schools nowadays are expected to play a double role: supporting the instructional curriculum and providing increased opportunities for students to gain access to the broader culture. The CDI in secondary schools and middle schools teach young people to make use of all kinds of printed and electronic resources, and they now think of themselves as having a dynamic role of key agents for the modernization of the relationship that students have with knowledge.

Within universities and research institutes, the modernization of library collections and services has passed through several stages. In the traditional French system, universities are largely financed by the central government and are almost free to students. This has been changing since 1985 when universities entered into a contractual relationship with the government. University finances still depend on the number of students served, the level of study offered, and the disciplines covered, but now their

funding is also based on a four-year plan and on the evaluation of performance. Regional authorities also contribute to the support of universities, especially in the area of construction. In July 2007, a law was passed giving greater autonomy to the university in its relationship to the government, and university administrators were given much broader responsibilities.

Under these new regulations, university libraries have become "shared services" that are expected to coordinate acquisitions and prepare union catalogs to provide federated access to all resources offered on the campus. As in the past, university libraries have to provide learning materials for a more and more massive student body (1.4 million students, or 55% of all those students who have completed secondary school and have successfully passed their baccalauréat examination). At the same time these academic libraries must furnish researchers with specialized resources that are becoming more and more numerous and more onerous to acquire. There has been considerable tension between these two missions—to provide for both the needs of beginning students and advanced researchers. In the 1980s, specialized centers were established for the acquisition and diffusion of scientific and technical information (*Centres d'acquisition et de diffusion de l'information scientifique et technique—CADIST*); through this coordinated program certain university libraries that already had rich collections in a particular domain of knowledge were given national responsibilities.

Another example of cooperation is the Couperin consortium of French research libraries. Set up in 1999 to negotiate favorable pricing for electronic periodicals, Couperin also coordinates strategic initiatives in regard to publication and dissemination of international scientific and technical publications in the context of globalization. Another very important collaborative effort involves the creation of a union catalog containing information on the holdings of more than 2000 participating libraries in France. Known as the university documentation system (Système universitaire de documentation—SUDOC), this database, which joined Worldcat in 2008, contains over 8 million records and offers location information for 25 million items; it also provides information on periodical collections in 4200 institutions. In 2008, over 25 million data bases searches were conducted using the SUDOC catalog. In addition SUDOC collects, archives, and offers access to French theses in electronic format and offers a portal providing access to a number of other digital resources.

Academic libraries in France have experienced an impressive increase in the number of users. In 2006, 62% of all university students were active users and visited the library more than 50 times per year; statistics show that the total number of visits had doubled since 1990. University libraries throughout the country were open 58 hr per week on average. A total of 69 million volumes of printed works are available in all French university libraries (30 million books and 39 million of bounded volumes of periodical) and each year 1.4 million books are acquired (less than one volume per student). In addition, university libraries subscribe to 141,000 printed periodicals and 480,000 electronic periodicals. As elsewhere the impact of new technologies has been overwhelming and the increase in electronic resources has expanded exponentially; for example the number of subscriptions to electronic journals grew by 30% between 2004 and 2005. Although the expense per user for acquisitions varies, the average per capita acquisitions expense in French university libraries has increased fourfold since 1990 and in 2006 it had risen to 70 Euros. Training students to use library resources is strongly encouraged. In contrast to what has happened in other countries following the development of mass use of the Internet, in France the use of libraries is stable, although consultation of printed materials in the library has fallen slightly—by less than 4% (i.e., 13 items per person per year). Interlibrary loan has experienced a slight decline, and the provision of electronic documents is not yet sufficiently developed in France.

Modern Buildings and a Growing Public

A library tour in France offers fine examples of architecture including new construction and the renovation of historic buildings. If architectural achievement is shown through large projects (such as the wave of construction of municipal libraries with a regional vocation), smaller libraries also demonstrate the significance of the library in urban development policies as well as highlighting the talent of the architect. During the 1970s, the concept of the library as a temple or cathedral was rejected in favor of libraries integrated into fabric of the neighborhood, housed in newly constructed facilities that were intentionally modest. In contrast, the end of the twentieth century saw a triumphal return of the landmark library, with striking architecture that had a certain seductive power. Nonetheless this return to libraries that are monumental, or at least built on a grand scale, did not minimize questions concerning urban development or social issues. Sometimes it was decided that a new library building should be not situated in the city center, but should instead be located in an outlying suburb where it could give renewed life to a neighborhood that had a negative image. In such a location, the library could also serve to promote books among disadvantaged populations who were less likely to be readers. The construction of a library thus has become a major element of the cultural policy of cities and at the same time has become a factor in urban planning and social development.

Library space planning and interior design has not only been the object of considerable attention in France, but has also become the physical expression of the intellectual and utopian ideology of the contemporary *médiathèque*—a concept which calls for unimpeded passage from children's spaces to adult reading areas and reflects a holistic approach to cultural activities, bringing together reading, listening to music, watching documentary or feature films, and consulting electronic materials in all forms and formats. The new ideal of the *médiathèque* also represents a dramatic shift in focus—from collection-centered structures and practices to a user-centered orientation. The emphasis is now on the intellectually curious reader, open to all kinds of resources and services, disposing of free time to browse the shelves, and sample their diverse materials—a kind of all encompassing reader (*lecteur total*). The intellectual itineraries and journeys of this new type of reader are now the focal point of the library, which offers its collections and services with the unique goal of facilitating, enhancing, and maximizing their use. Several principles have become central in every library design project; these include attention to the flow of movement through the library; openness in the arrangement of spaces for reading and consultation; and requirements for transversality and fluidity.

At the beginning of the twenty-first century, 43% of the population in France visited libraries and 21% were registered library users. The percentage of the population visiting a library has doubled between 1989 and 2005. Municipal libraries have experienced the greatest increase: 35% of the population visits the library and 20% are registered, with children accounting for 35% of registered users. The modernization of libraries has stimulated an increase in the number of new users and once open access to the shelves became common librarians observed a considerable increase in visits by individuals who are not registered borrowers, and whose presence had previously been quite marginal in terms of library statistics. The library, which had once been above all a place where one came and quickly selected books to borrow, has now become a place where more people remain for a longer time, profiting from the collections, enjoying the ambiance and the comfortable space, and appreciating an opportunity for sociability with few constraining rules. Nonetheless, despite the spectacular increase in the use of municipal libraries, the percentage of the public who visit libraries in France has remained considerably lower than that in the United States, Great Britain, or in Scandinavia where libraries serve 60% to 80% of the population.

Sociological studies have often emphasized socio-cultural differences at play in regard to the use of libraries and in the reading of books. For example, young people visit libraries more than their elders, but less than they did 20 years ago and those groups who are over represented among library users include the most educated segments of the population, upper level professionals, and the middle classes in general. Gender is also a factor and women library users are more numerous than men. Finally registered borrowers are not necessarily loyal library users;

only one-third of them renew their membership each year. Furthermore, the number of books borrowed by registered users has declined among adults, only 18 books were taken out per borrower per year in 2006,

La Bibliothèque nationale de France

Despite major nineteenth- and twentieth-century efforts to enlarge the facilities of the Bibliothèque nationale on the rue Richelieu, it lacked adequate space. As a result, the tension between conservation and access to the collections became more and more acute. Confronting considerably increased demands, the Bibliothèque nationale was forced to consider drastic measures. In 1988, President Mitterrand announced his decision to provide France with "one of the largest and most modern libraries in the world." The design of the architect Dominique Perrault was selected. As in any profound change, the plans for a radically new library were plagued by early difficulties, including polemics as to how the project should be conceptualized, its location, and the conditions necessary for the conservation of the collections as well as how to provide access to the public.

Situated in the east of Paris with a surface of 207,000 m^2, the François-Mitterrand site of the BNF opened in 1998, offering two levels of complementary services and collections. The upper garden level, which is open to the general public, offers a seating capacity of 1700. Here one can consult a research collection in all areas of scholarship-science, the arts, history, literature, and law; the collection offers access to 300,000 works available on open shelves, 3,500 periodical subscriptions, 3,000 films, 10,000 musical recordings, a digital library, and numerous databases. Located on the lower garden level, the research library offers access to 10 million volumes of printed materials, 95,000 films, 900,000 sound recordings, and 60,000 multimedia materials. These vast collections have been acquired over many centuries through copyright deposit or as a result of gifts, collections bequeathed to the library, exchanges, and acquisitions by purchase. The reading rooms on the lower level offer seating for 1,900 users who have open access to 290,000 volumes and 4,000 periodicals as well as audiovisual and multimedia materials and electronic resources.

In addition to these new offerings are collections conserved in specialized départements located elsewhere in Paris. In the historic building on the rue Richelieu one can find:

- The Département for Prints and Photographs (15 million items acquired through copyright deposit).
- The Département of Occidental and Oriental Manuscripts (225,000 works including the collection of oriental manuscripts written in 100 languages on diverse writing materials, e.g., clay, papyrus, palm leaves, etc.).
- The Département of Maps and Plans (600,000 printed and manuscript maps 104 globes and 10,000 atlases).

- The Department of Coins and Medals and Antiquities, which originated in the collection of the kings of France, and now contains more than 530,000 items.
- The Department of Music which receives copyright deposit for printed music and also administers the Library and Museum of the Opera; the combined collections consist of 2 million items.
- The Department of Performing Arts has approximately 3 million items related to cinema as well as theater and opera. These collections will soon be renovated and opened for a wider consultation.

The BNF also administers Library of the Arsenal which has a rich collection of literary materials and works on the history of ideas from the sixteenth century to the nineteenth century (contains 1 million printed materials, 14,000 manuscripts). In addition the BN administers other units devoted to preservation and restoration.

Each year through copyright deposit the library adds 170,000 monographs, 34,000 pamphlets, 1.3 million issues of periodicals, numerous audiovisual materials and electronic resources, and nearly 40,000 specialized items. Items acquired through purchase include 60,000 volumes in foreign languages. The BNF has also been charged with responsibility for archiving the Web; this is carried out by Web crawlers programmed to automatically collect this data. However, to capture sites on the deep Web and to take into account frequent changes within each site, manually assisted procedures are needed.

The general catalog of the BNF maintains cataloging records for all kinds of media; in 2008 it contained 5 million authority records and over 10 million bibliographic records. In the course of its reorganization, the BNF has pursued important collaborative projects with other libraries in France that have rich cultural heritage collections and specialized research materials that complement those of the national library. These partnerships in specific focus areas include various kinds of cooperative efforts such as the retrospective conversion of catalogs, collective bibliographic databases and abstracts, joint conservation efforts, and collaborative digitization projects. One result of this kind of cooperation is the French union catalog (*le Catalogue collectif de France*) which includes descriptions of the collections of 4000 institutions and allows users to find the location of 15 million items.

Gallica, the French digital library project launched in 1997, offers access to 3,50,000 items, of which 90,000 digital works, more than 2,30,000 images, and many hours of audio recordings. This collection of images and printed works covers many disciplines such as history, literature, science, philosophy, law, economics, and political science. Although Gallica now contains mainly image files, in cooperation with the European Digital Library, it plans to make available searchable text files at a rate of 100,000 documents a year between 2008 and 2010.

Other digital projects involved cooperation between libraries and research institutes, governmental bodies, or scientific publishers. As the result of cooperative efforts of four publishing houses and the BNF the Cairn portal has been created to offer access in digital form to articles appearing since 2001 in 126 journals in humanities and social sciences. Another portal named Persée has been sponsored by the Ministry of Higher Education in order to provide access to other scholarly journals essential to the work of French researchers. Other important, large scale digitization projects are now underway in municipal libraries that contain important historical collections. Such initiatives are flourishing, and now many libraries find that their daily operations must include digitization of historic collections or preparation of electronic databases needed by the communities they serve.

CONCLUSION

The tidal wave brought by the Internet and the promise of digital collections has radically transformed the work of the libraries and archives, but also of museums, and it has also changed the practices and expectations of users. The entire documentary cycle (from the acquisition of materials to their use) has been radically transformed by this technological revolution that has modified how collections and constituted and processed, organized, and made available. In addition, it has profoundly transformed the nature of learning, the representation of knowledge and attitudes toward the written word.

ACKNOWLEDGMENT

This entry was translated by Mary Niles Maack.

BIBLIOGRAPHY

1. Baratin, M.; Jacob, C. *Le Pouvoir des bibliothèques: la mémoire des livres en Occident*, Albin Michel: Paris, France, 1996.
2. Bertrand, A.-M. *Les villes et leur bibliothèque. Légitimer et décider*, éditions du Cercle de la Librairie: Paris, France, 1999.
3. Chartier, A.-M.; Hébrard, J. avec la collaboration de Emmanuel Fraisse, Martine Poulain et Jean-Claude Pompougnac. *Discours sur la lecture, 1881–2000*; BPI-Centre Pompidou, Fayard: Paris, France, 2000.
4. Coeuré, S. *La mémoire spoliée. Les archives des Français, butin de guerre nazi puis soviétique*, Payot: Paris, France, 2007.
5. Combe, S. *Archives interdites*, L'Harmattan: Paris, France, 1991.
6. *Dictionnaire encyclopédique du livre*, sous la direction de Pascal Fouché, Daniel Péchoin, Philippe Schuwer, et la responsabilité scientifique de Pascal Fouché, Jean-Dominique Mellot, Alain Nave, Martine Poulain, Philippe Schuwer, 3 Vols. Éditions du Cercle de la Librairie, Paris, France, 2002–2010.
7. Dhérent, C. *Les archives électroniques. Manuel pratique*. Available at http://www.archivesdefrance.culture.gouv.fr/fr/archivistique/DAFmanuel%20version%207.htm.
8. Farge, A. *Le goût de l'archive*, Le Seuil: Paris, France, 1989.
9. Georgel, C. *La jeunesse des musées. Les musées de France au XIXe siècle*, éditions de la Réunion des musées nationaux: Paris, France, 1994 (dir.).
10. Hildesheimer, F. *Les Archives de France, mémoire de l'histoire*, Société des amis des archives de France: Paris, France, 1997.
11. http://www.archivesdefrance.culture.gouv.fr (accessed November 2008).
12. Laurent, S. *Archives "secrètes", secrets d'archives? Historiens et archivistes face aux archives sensibles*, CNRS éditions: Paris, France, 2003.
13. Malraux, A. *Le musée imaginaire*, Albert Skira: Paris, France, 1967.
14. Nora, P. *Les lieux de mémoire*, Gallimard: Paris, France, 1997.
15. Poulain, M. *Histoire des bibliothèques françaises. Les bibliothèques au XXe siècle, 1914–1990*, Promodis-éditions du Cercle de la librairie: Paris, France, 1992; (dir).
16. Poulot, D. *Patrimoine et musées. L'institution de la culture*, Hachette Education: Paris, France, 2001.
17. Poulot, D. *Histoire des musées de France, XVIIIe-XXe siècles*, La Découverte: Paris, France, 2005.
18. Recht, R. *Penser le patrimoine. Mise en scène et mise en ordre de l'art*, Hazan: Paris, France, 1998.

Functional Requirements for Subject Authority Data (FRSAD): Conceptual Model

Marcia Lei Zeng
Athena Salaba
Kent State University, Kent, Ohio, U.S.A.

Maja Žumer
University of Ljubljana, Slovenia

Abstract

Functional Requirements for Subject Authority Data (FRSAD) is the third model of the FRBR family developed by IFLA. This paper traces the history of the development of the model through the activities of the Working Group that developed the model (Part I), and describes the constructs of the FRSAD model, including the entities, attributes, and relationships defined in the FRSAD model (Part II). The paper also summarizes a number of issues around the model (Part III) and discusses application-related studies (Part IV).

I. IFLA FRSAR WORKING GROUP AND ITS ACTIVITIES

Background

In 1998, the International Federation of Library Associations and Institutions (IFLA) published the Functional Requirements for Bibliographic Records (FRBR) conceptual model, which identified entities, attributes, and relationships based on a logical analysis of typical data included in bibliographic records. The FRBR model divides the identified entities into three groups:[1]

1. Group 1 contains four entities that represent the different aspects of user interests in the products of intellectual or artistic endeavor. These are
   a. *Work*—A distinct intellectual or artistic creation
   b. *Expression*—An intellectual or artistic realization of a *work*
   c. *Manifestation*—A physical embodiment of an *expression*
   d. *Item*—A single exemplar of a *manifestation*
2. Group 2 contains entities defined as actors or those who are responsible for the intellectual or artistic content, the physical production and dissemination, or the custodianship of Group 1 entities. These are
   a. *Person*
   b. *Corporate body*
3. Group 3, as defined by FRBR in relation to Group 1 and 2, represents an additional set of entities that serve as subjects of intellectual or artistic endeavor *works*. They are
   a. *Concept*
   b. *Object*
   c. *Event*
   d. *Place*

Continuing the tradition set by the IFLA FRBR model, two new IFLA working groups (WG) were formed: the Working Group on the Functional Requirements for Numbering and Authority Records (FRANAR) and the Working Group on the Functional Requirements for Subject Authority Records (FRSAR).

FRANAR WG was established in 1999 to develop a conceptual model for authority records. The WG released a draft of the Functional Requirements for Authority Data (FRAD) model in 2007 and published the FRAD Final Report in 2009, parallel with the work of the FRSAR WG. The FRANAR WG defines authority records as aggregates of information regarding entities that are assigned as controlled access points in bibliographic records.[2] Although all three FRBR entity groups (with the "Family" entity added to Group 2 by FRAD) are covered in the FRAD conceptual model, its major focus has been given to Group 1 and 2 entities.

The FRSAR WG was formed in April 2005 to report to the IFLA Classification and Indexing Section. The original terms of reference were

- Build a conceptual model of Group 3 entities within the FRBR framework as they relate to the aboutness of *works*
- Provide a clearly defined, structured frame of reference for relating the data that are recorded in subject authority records to the needs of the users of those records
- Assist in an assessment of the potential for international sharing and use of subject authority data both within the library sector and beyond

Encyclopedia of Library and Information Sciences, Fourth Edition DOI: 10.1081/E-ELIS4-120049494

By definition, IFLA FRBR Group 3 entities "represent an additional set of entities that serve as the subjects of *works*. The group includes *concept* (an abstract notion or idea), *object* (a material thing), *event* (an action or occurrence), and *place* (a location)"[3] (emphasis added). This part of the FRBR model has been questioned as to whether it is sufficient to cover everything that can be viewed as a "subject" of a *work*, for example, "time."[4,5] One of the FRSAR terms of reference, as listed above, was to build a conceptual model of Group 3 entities within the FRBR framework as they relate to the "aboutness" of *works*. In this framework, all controlled access points related to all three entity groups, as defined by the FRBR conceptual model, have the potential to be the topics of a *work*. In other words, Group 1, 2, and 3 entities can have an "is-the-subject-of" relationship with the *work* (to be discussed in detail in the following sections.)

The FRSAR Working Group

The FRSAR WG was chaired by Marcia Lei Zeng (who was at the time the Chair of IFLA's Standing Committee of the Classification and Indexing Section) and cochaired by Maja Žumer (who was a member of the same Committee and also of the FRBR Review Group) and Athena Salaba (who also served as the secretary of the WG). In May 2005, an invitational workshop titled "FRBR in 21st Century Catalogues" was held in Dublin Ohio, hosted by OCLC. It was during this workshop that the FRSAR WG chairs started to invite WG members and Advisory Group (AG) members. Table 1 lists WG and AG members who served on this task and contributed to the development of the FRSAD conceptual model (Table 1). The WG divided tasks among members of two groups: the User Tasks Subgroup, led by Salaba and including members of Bultrini, Chan, Riesthuis, Miller, McGarry, and Zeng; and the Subject Entities Subgroup, led by Žumer and including members of Bultrini, Chan, Furner, O'Neill, Vizine-Goetz, and Zeng.

In addition to the whole group meetings held at IFLA Annual conferences, numerous meetings, combined with teleconference facility, were conducted from 2005 to 2009, not to mention many emails among the members. Kent State University, OCLC Headquarters (both located in Ohio, United States), and IFLA provided support or facilities for these meetings. The WG also conducted meetings in other related professional conferences, with the support of the hosting institutions, especially the University of Vienna, during the International Society for Knowledge Organization (ISKO) 2006 Conference, and the University of Montréal, during the ISKO 2008 Conference.

FRSAD Development Timeline

The WG started by defining user tasks as soon as the subgroups were formed. A survey on the use of subject authority data was conducted worldwide, and over 800

Table 1 IFLA FRSAR Working and Advisory Groups Membership

2005–2008 (74th IFLA)	2008 (74th IFLA)–2010 (76th IFLA)
WG members	**WG members**
Leda Bultrini, Italy	Leda Bultrini, Italy
Lois Mai Chan, USA	Lois Mai Chan, USA
Gerhard Riesthuis, The Netherlands	Jonathan Furner, USA
Athena Salaba, USA	Edward O'Neill, USA
Diane Vizine-Goetz, USA	Gerhard Riesthuis, The Netherlands
Ekaterina Zaytseva, Russia	Athena Salaba, USA
Marcia Lei Zeng, USA	Diane Vizine-Goetz, USA
Maja Žumer, Slovenia	Ekaterina Zaytseva, Russia
	Marcia Lei Zeng, USA
	Maja Žumer, Slovenia
AG members	**AG members**
Victoria Francu, Romania	Dorothy McGarry, USA
Jonathan Furner, USA	David Miller, USA
Hemalata Iyer, USA	(Liaison to ALA SAC)
Dorothy McGarry, USA	Päivi Pekkarinen, Finland
David Miller, USA (Liaison to ALA Subject Analysis Committee (SAC))	Barbara Tillett, USA
Edward O'Neill, USA (Liaison to OCLC FRBR and to ALA SAC)	
Päivi Pekkarinen, Finland	

responses were received between June and August of 2006. At the June 2006 ISKO Conference in Vienna, the WG had a full-day meeting to discuss the conceptual model according to the first term of reference given to the WG by IFLA (i.e., to build a conceptual model of Group 3 entities within the FRBR framework as they relate to the aboutness of *works*). At that point questions around "Group 3" started to emerge. The WG meetings at the 2006 IFLA Conference in Durban, South Africa, resulted in a number of alternative models. Based on two tests conducted by the WG members, extensive discussions of existing conceptual models of aboutness and the alternative FRSAD models examined during 2007 and 2008, the WG had a major breakthrough. Eventually a conceptual model was developed and finalized at the ISKO conference in Montréal and the IFLA conference in Québec City, Canada, in August 2008. A draft report was completed at the end of 2008, and reviewed by the Advisory Group members. The revised Draft Report was officially released for its worldwide review in June 2009. It received many comments by individuals and institutions, which provided a solid foundation for the WG to revise and prepare the Final Report. The FRSAD conceptual model was presented at the 75th IFLA General Conference and Assembly held in Milan, Italy, in August 2009. The Final Report, titled "Functional Requirements for Subject Authority Data (FRSAD): A Conceptual Model," was submitted for approval in April 2010 and was approved by the IFLA Standing Committee of the Classification and Indexing Section in June of the same year. In July 2010, the Chair of Division III Library Services, on behalf of the IFLA Professional Committee, informed the WG that the FRSAD Final Report was validated and released for publication by IFLA. The FRSAD Final Report was published as the 43rd volume of the IFLA Series on Bibliographic Control by De Gruyter Saur in May 2011 (Fig. 1).

The FRSAD Final Report contains seven chapters and four appendices. Some sections in the Final Draft, such as the research-based background, the development processes, and implementation examples, were moved to the appendices in the Final Report. The final chapters and appendices are

1. Background
2. Purpose and Scope
3. Entities
4. Attributes
5. Relationships
6. User Tasks
7. Conclusion
Appendix A. Modeling Aboutness
Appendix B. Relationship of FRSAD with FRBR and FRAD
Appendix C. FRSAD Model and Other Models
Appendix D. Examples from Subject Authority Systems

FRSAR Working Group Studies

The FRSAR WG identified four user groups of subject authority data. They are: 1) information professionals who create and maintain subject authority data, including cataloguers and controlled vocabulary creators; 2) information professionals who create and maintain metadata; 3) reference services librarians and other information professionals who search for information as intermediaries; and 4) end-users who search for information to fulfill their information needs.[6]

In an effort to define user tasks based on empirical data, the FRSAR WG deemed it necessary to conduct user studies. Two surveys were distributed in 2006. The first was a pilot study at the 2006 Semantic Technologies Conference (San Jose, California, USA). Most participants of this first study were either creators of semantic tools, including controlled vocabularies, taxonomies, and ontologies, or developers and managers of semantic technology systems. The second, an international survey among information professionals throughout the world, received about 800 responses. The majority of the participants were authority record creators, vocabulary creators and managers, catalogers, metadata librarians, and reference librarians.

Based on findings from these two surveys, which covered use scenarios for all user groups, four subject authority data user tasks were defined. Users may *find*, *identify*, and *select* a subject entity or entities and they may also

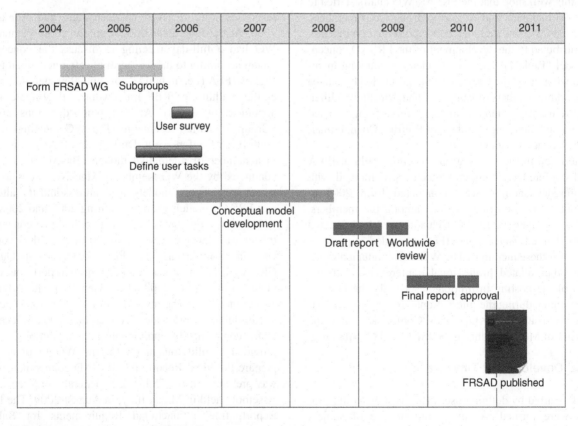

Fig. 1   FRSAD Working Group activities timeline.

Table 2 Comparison of the User Tasks Defined by FRBR, FRAD, and FRSAD

User Tasks		
FRBR (1998)	**FRAD (2009)**	**FRSAD (2011)**
Find entities of Group 1 that have entities from Groups 1, 2, and 3 as their subject	**Find** one entity or entities	**Find** one subject entity or entities
Identify	**Identify** an entity	**Identify**
Select		**Select**
Obtain		
	Contextualize, place in context, explore relationships	
	Justify the form of an access point	
		Explore a subject domain or relationships

choose to *explore* a subject domain and its terminology as well as the relationships that exist among subjects. Table 2 provides a comparison of the user tasks defined in FRBR, FRAD, and FRSAD.

The four user tasks for subject authority data defined by FRSAD[7] are

- **Find** one or more subjects and/or their appellations that correspond(s) to the user's stated criteria, using attributes and relationships
- **Identify** a subject and/or its appellation based on their attributes or relationships (i.e., to distinguish between two or more subjects or appellations with similar characteristics and to confirm that the appropriate subject or appellation has been found)
- **Select** a subject and/or its appellation appropriate to the user's needs (i.e., to choose or reject based on the user's requirements and needs)
- **Explore** relationships between subjects and/or their appellations (e.g., to explore relationships in order to understand the structure of a subject domain and its terminology)

As illustrated in Table 2, the *explore* user task is a new task introduced in FRSAD; whereas the *find*, *identify*, and *select* user tasks have been previously introduced in the FRBR and/or FRAD conceptual models.

In an attempt to verify the Group 3 entities originally defined by the FRBR model, the FRSAR WG collected comments found in published documents (refer to the next section, II.A) and conducted a small study to classify existing subject terms used by U.S. National Science Digital Library (NSDL) contributors into the categories based on FRBR entities (*Concept, Object, Event, Place*) plus *Time* and *Other*. These included about 3,000 terms assigned to NSDL metadata records. The terms were classified into six categories: concrete stuff, abstract stuff, event, time, place, and other. The study results indicated difficulties in the distinction between concrete and abstract concepts, as well as in categorizing named instances, which resulted in many subject terms being put into the "other" category. Findings of this study resulted in the development of FRSAD as a more abstract conceptual model.

II. THE FRSAD MODEL

A. The Development of the FRSAD Model

FRBR defines the many-to-many subject relationship between *work* and entities of Groups 1, 2, and 3 (Fig. 2). IFLA FRBR Group 3 entities are recognized as the subjects of *works* (i.e., the results of intellectual or artistic endeavor). They "represent an additional set of entities that serve as the subjects of *works*"[3] (emphasis added), in addition to any of the Group 1 and 2 entities, which can also be subjects of *works*. Group 3 includes *concept* (an abstract notion or idea), *object* (a material thing), *event* (an action or occurrence), and *place* (a location).[8]

From the time the FRSAR WG was formed, there seems to have been a general agreement in the FRBR research community that Group 3 entities should be revisited.[9] The WG was considering several scenarios. In addition to enhancing the FRBR model based on Group 3 entities by adding "time," the approaches of other existing models were discussed. These models include the <indecs> model,[10] Ranganathan's facets,[11] and the pragmatic list of entities developed by Buizza and Guerrini.[12] These models present solid references for revising the FRBR conceptual model. The WG analyzed and discussed possible solutions based on each of these models, from conservative (making minor amendments of FRBR Group 3) to radical (proposing a completely new model). However, the WG found that none of the existing models and the ones based on them could be universal enough to reflect the needs of today's subject authority data, considering particularly different domains and subject access tools. In 2007, the WG shifted focus from the revision of the FRBR model to the development of a more general and abstract model, justified by the WG studies, which confirmed that there is no universally applicable and useful categorization of subjects. At the 2008 IFLA Québec meeting, the group concluded the development of the model as represented in the following figure (Fig. 3).

In this framework, instances of all entity types of all three entity groups, as defined by the FRBR conceptual model, have the potential to be the topics of a *work*. In

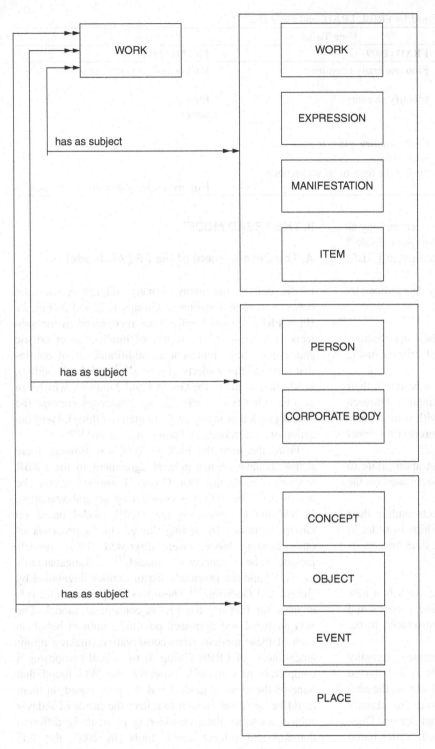

Fig. 2 Subject relationship as presented in FRBR 1988 final report Fig. 3.3 (Ref. 1, p. 15.).

other words, any instance of the Group 1, 2, and 3 entities can have an "is-subject-of" relationship with the *work*. The FRSAR Entity subgroup proposed a more abstract conceptual model. As presented in the following Figure 4, the model should be understood with two key points of view (Fig. 4):

1. This model confirms one of the basic relationships defined in FRBR: *WORK* has as subject *THEMA* / *THEMA* is subject of *WORK*.

a. *THEMA* is defined as any entity used as a subject of a work.[13]
b. *THEMA* includes any FRBR entities—existing Group 1 and Group 2 entities and, in addition, all other subjects of *works*. This is a very abstract view, enabling us to model relationships and attributes on a more general and abstract level.

A Greek term (also used in Latin), THEMA, is used to avoid misunderstanding in translating the English term.

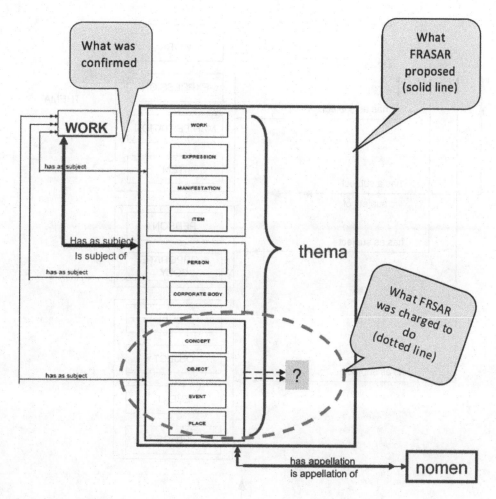

Fig. 3 FRSAD representation in 2008.

2. This model also proposes a new relationship: *THEMA* has appellation *NOMEN* / *NOMEN* is appellation of *THEMA*.

   a. *NOMEN* is defined as any sign or sequence of signs (alphanumeric characters, symbols, sound, etc.) that a thema is known by, referred to, or addressed as.[13]

   b. Examples include "love," "∞", or "595.733."

A Latin term, NOMEN, was chosen for the same reason as above.

This was a major breakthrough because, for many years, terms or labels representing concepts have been mixed with concepts in subject authority tools.

To simplify Figure 3, FRSAD model can be presented by the following illustration (Fig. 5):

Some important accents regarding the model:

- The "has as subject/is subject of" relationship is a many-to-many relationship. Any *work* can have more than one *thema*, and any *thema* can be the subject of more than one *work*.

- In general (i.e., in natural language or when mapping different vocabularies) the "has appellation/is appellation of" relationship is also a many-to-many relationship. A *thema* has one or more *nomen* and there may be a *nomen* referring to more than one *thema*.

- It is important, however, to note that, in a given controlled vocabulary and within a domain, a *nomen* should be an appellation of only one *thema*.

Attributes of *thema* and *nomen*, relationships between *themas* and between *nomens*, as well as *thema*-to-*nomen* relationships are all discussed in detail in the FRSAD report.

An Overview of the FRSAD Model

Presented below is an overview of the constructs in the FRSAD model: 1) the entities (*thema* and *nomen*), 2) the attributes of *thema* and *nomen* (Table 3), and 3) relationships between the entities (*work–thema* and *thema–nomen*)

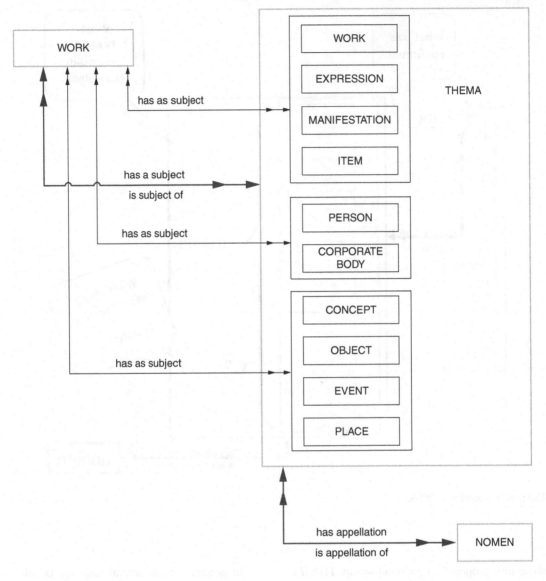

Fig. 4 FRSAD's relation to FRBR.

Fig. 5 FRSAD conceptual model.

and within the entities (*thema–thema* and *nomen–nomen*) (Table 4).

The importance of the *THEMA–NOMEN* model for the subject authority data is to separate *themas* from what they are known by, referred to, or addressed as. This enables us to define attributes and relationships for the appellation separately.

It is therefore up to application profiles, developed to support particular implementations, to deal with the complex *themas* by specifying the rules for creation of complex *nomens*. Rules guide creation of subject heading strings or faceted classification. This is therefore another area that is language/domain/system specific and should be addressed within application profiles.

Differences between FRBR, FRAD, and FRSAD

Two models, FRAD and FRSAD, are complementing and further developing some aspects of FRBR. All three have been labeled the "FRBR family," suggesting that they all

Table 3 Entities and Attributes in FRSAD

Thema

Type:	Entity
Definition:	Any entity used as a subject of a *work*.
Attributes:	Type of *thema*
	The category to which a *thema* belongs in the context of a particular KOS.
	Scope note
	A text describing and/or defining the *thema* or specifying its scope within the particular subject authority system.

Nomen

Type:	Entity
Definition:	Any sign or sequence of signs (alphanumeric characters, symbols, sound, etc.) that a thema is known by, referred to, or addressed as.
Attributes:	Type of *nomen*
	Category to which the *nomen* belongs.
	Scheme
	The scheme in which the *nomen* is established, including value-encoding schemes (particular subject heading lists, thesauri, classification systems, name authority lists, etc.) and syntax encoding schemes (standards for encoding dates, etc.).
	Reference source of *nomen*
	The source in which the *nomen* is found. It may also be modeled as a relationship with the appropriate Group 1 entity (*work, expression, manifestation*).
	Representation of *nomen*
	The data type in which the *nomen* is expressed.
	Language of *nomen*
	The language in which the *nomen* is expressed.
	Script of *nomen*
	The script in which a *nomen* is expressed.
	Script conversion
	The rule, system, or standard used to render the *nomen* in a different representation.
	Form of *nomen*
	Any additional information that helps to interpret the *nomen*.
	Time of validity of *nomen*
	The time period in which a particular instance of a *nomen* is/was used or is/was valid within a subject vocabulary system.
	Audience
	The community or user group for which this *nomen* is the preferred form.
	Status of *nomen*
	The status of a particular *nomen* in a subject authority system.

Table 4 Relationships Defined by FRSAD

Work-to-*thema* relationship
"has as subject"

Reverse:	"is subject of"
Domain:	*Work*
Range:	*Thema*
Cardinality:	Many-to-many

***Thema*-to-*nomen* relationship**
"has appellation"

Reverse:	"is appellation of"
Domain:	*Thema*
Range:	*Nomen*
Cardinality:	Many-to-many

***Thema*-to-*thema* relationship**
- Hierarchical relationship
"has broader *thema*"

Reverse:	"has narrower *thema*"
Domain:	*Thema*
Range:	*Thema*
Cardinality:	Many-to-many

"has narrower *thema*"

Reverse:	"has broader *thema*"
Domain:	*Thema*
Range:	*Thema*
Cardinality:	Many-to-many

- Associative relationship
"has related *thema*"

Reverse:	"has related *thema*"
Domain:	*Thema*
Range:	*Thema*
Cardinality:	Many-to-many

***Nomen*-to-*nomen* relationship**
"is equivalent to"

Reverse:	"is equivalent to"
Domain:	*Nomen*
Range:	*Nomen*
Cardinality:	Many-to-many

"has part"

Reverse:	"is part of"
Domain:	*Nomen*
Range:	*Nomen*
Cardinality:	Many-to-many

"is part of"

Reverse:	"has part"
Domain:	*Nomen*
Range:	*Nomen*
Cardinality:	Many-to-many

are considered parts of a larger general model. There exist some differences among them due to different modeling decisions made during their independent development over time. At the time of writing, the FRBR Review Group is working on the harmonization of FRBR, FRAD, and FRSAD. The project was completed in 2017 with a the new IFLA Library Reference Model (LRM), replacing all three FR family models.

Relationship of FRSAD with FRBR

The FRSAR WG follows FRBR in the methodology, specification, and presentation of entities and relationships. The "has as subject" (many-to-many) relationship, established between the *work* and the entity(ies) representing the aboutness of the *work*, is kept in its entirety in FRSAD. The four areas where some differences were introduced in FRSAD are as follows:

- The "Explore" task is added.
- *Thema* is introduced as a superclass of all entities that can be subjects of a *work*.
- No entity types are explicitly predefined in Group 3.
- *Nomen* is introduced (including attributes and relationships) and is defined as a separate entity instead of an attribute of an entity.

In Fig. 3.3 of the FRBR report, the depicted "subject" relationship has three boxes representing all three groups of entities, respectively, on the right side of the "has as subject" relationship. FRSAD has developed this further by creating a superclass (*thema*), thus enabling the modeling of the "has as subject" relationship on a more general level. *Thema* includes Group 1, Group 2, and all other entities that can be the subjects of a *work*. Therefore, the subject relationship can easily be modeled as "*work* has as subject *thema*."

FRSAD introduces a differentiation between a thing itself and its appellation. The appellation (name, label, etc.) is often modeled as an attribute of the entity it refers to (e.g., in FRBR). While seemingly simpler, such an approach makes it impossible to introduce the attributes (e.g., language, script) of appellations and relationships between appellations (e.g., between a former and a latter name). In FRSAD, *Nomen* is introduced as an entity to enable appropriate modeling.

Relationship of FRSAD with FRAD

The FRANAR WG was established in 1999 with the mandate to develop further FRBR in the area of authority files. Later, the decision was made by FRANAR to focus on Group 2 entities and *work* only. As a consequence, the FRSAR WG was established to cover the "has as subject" relationship and the appropriate entities. The FRAD and FRSAD models were therefore developed independently. The most significant differences are as follows:

- User tasks: "Contextualize" and "Justify" in FRAD vs. "Explore" in FRSAD
- *Subject* as an attribute of *work* in FRAD
- *Name* in FRAD vs. *Nomen* in FRSAD
- *Name*, *Identifier*, and *Controlled access point* as separate entities in FRAD vs. values of the attribute "Type of *Nomen*" in FRSAD

- *Rules* and *agency* as new entities in FRAD and not explicitly modeled in FRSAD

FRSAD's user task "explore" is a generalization of FRAD's "contextualize" and expresses better the user task of browsing, getting acquainted, becoming familiar with, and discovering. FRAD "justify," on the other hand, is a task of information professionals and not end users. It is an important task on its own, but in the context of metadata creation and not metadata use.

Although similar at first glance, FRAD's entity *name* (defined as "a character or group of words and/or characters by which an entity is known in the real world") and FRSAD's entity *nomen* are different. The FRSAD *nomen* is a more general entity, comprising any (textual or other) appellation both in the real world and in artificial systems. In relation to FRAD, *nomen* is a superclass of FRAD *name*, *identifier*, and *controlled access point*.

Rules and *agency* are not specifically modeled in FRSAD, because again they apply to the cataloging process. If needed, *rules* (which are applied in all phases of cataloging, not merely in creation of controlled access points) should be considered instances of *work*. *Agencies*, which apply the rules, should be considered instances of *corporate body*. If modeled, they are in a relationship with the attribute assignment event.

III. DISCUSSION ON FRSAD MODEL

Following the release of the FRSAD Draft Report for worldwide review in June 2009, the WG received a number of comments. Four major comment categories are presented and discussed below.

FRSAD Terminology

While many explicitly praised the choice of Latin terms for the main entities of FRSAD, some expressed concern about this choice: Latin terminology was labeled as old fashioned, confusing, and presumptuous. Meanwhile, no real alternative was suggested. The choice of Latin terms is explained in the FRSAD Final Report[14]:

The Working Group chose Latin terms, *thema* (plural *themata* or *themas*) and *nomen* (plural *nomina* or *nomens*), because they have no pre-existing meaning in our context, are culturally neutral, and do not require translation. For *thema*, other possible (English) terms include "subject," "topic," and "concept"; however, even discussions within the WG proved that there are very different views on granularity (some see "subject" and "topic" as synonyms, while others see "topic" as a component of "subject"). The WG needed to distinguish *thema* from the previously defined FRBR entity *concept* because *thema* is a superclass of all FRBR entities (to be explained in the next section). For *nomen*, it is the case that the term "name" is often considered synonymous to proper name. In addition, the WG needed to distinguish *nomen* from the FRAD entity *name* because *nomen* includes FRAD entities *name*, *identifier*, and *controlled access point*.

The terminology problems would be similar in languages other than English. The choice of Latin, which does not have to be translated, has already been tested in translating FRSAD presentations into all official IFLA languages. Translators reported no problems.

FRSAD Is General and Abstract

Soon after FRBR was published, Strunck[15] noted, "Some students find it unnecessarily complicated to operate with the abstract entities of the model as you cannot study these entities per se. They find the definitions of the entities to be academic and airy." The problem seems to persist with FRSAD.

The library community has no tradition of conceptual models; FRBR is the first of its kind. It is therefore understandable that practicing librarians are often focusing on detailed rules and not on the big picture. Modeling is difficult and cannot be mastered without some education. It would therefore be necessary to include those topics in the curricula of library schools and continuing education opportunities for professionals. Not only will this enable professionals to understand and contribute to the development of FRBR and related models, it will also help them to more efficiently communicate with developers of computer tools.

FRSAD's Applicability in Libraries

Some have commented that FRSAD does not closely model the current cataloging practice and is not directly applicable to Library of Congress Subject Headings (LCSH). While this is true, it is also intentional. A lot of developments in the area of subject access, including the development of different knowledge organization systems, are currently conducted outside the library domain. In addition, the mission and purpose of a conceptual model is not to blindly model the current practice but rather to question it and propose improved solutions in order to pave the way for better, more popular, and widely used bibliographic information systems.

The FRSAD Final Report addressed the applicability issue by including an appendix that provides examples using a variety of existing subject authority systems, including *The USP Dictionary of U.S. Adopted Names and International Drug Names*, *Getty Thesaurus of Geographic Names*, and *Medical Subject Headings (MeSH)*[16]:

This appendix provides examples found in implementations of existing subject authority systems through the perspective of the FRSAD model, presented

in four parts: 1) existing models of *thema* types; 2) *thema-thema* relationships presented in subject authority data (both in individual vocabularies and cross-schemes); 3) same *thema* represented by *nomens* from different schemes; and 4) examples of display records from controlled vocabularies or subject authority systems.

COMPLEXITY OF *THEMA*

According to these comments, *thema* is too general and does not appropriately cover the difference between simple and complex *themas*.

Although everybody intuitively understands that some topics are simpler than others (e.g., "cats" vs. "winter fishing in the Cuyahoga River"), a proper definition of complexity is difficult. It seems that we mostly associate the complexity of a *thema* with the complexity of its *nomen*. The problem is addressed in the FRSAD Final Report[17]:

Themas can vary substantially in complexity or simplicity. Depending on the circumstances (the subject authority system, user needs, the nature of the *work*, etc.) the aboutness of a *work* can be expressed as a one-to-one relationship between the *work* and the *thema*; this means that the totality of the aboutness is encompassed in a single *thema*. In other circumstances the relationship is one-to-many, meaning that the aboutness of the *work* is captured in two or more *themas*. It is virtually impossible to define what the universal "atomic" level of a *thema* might be, because any *thema* can be fragmented further. The argument can be reversed: simple *themas* may be combined or aggregated, resulting in more complex *thema(s)*. In each particular implementation the atomic level is specified and rules guide the creation of *nomens* for complex *themas*.

IV. APPLICATIONS OF FRSAD MODEL

Developed as a general conceptual model that focuses on the subject relationship, FRSAD provides a theoretical framework for all knowledge organization structures, systems, and services (KOS) and their data models. FRSAR WG aimed to develop this model in order to assist in an assessment of the potential for international sharing and use of subject authority data both within the library sector and beyond.

Because the *thema* entity class includes anything that is or has the potential of being or becoming a subject, not restricted to actual subjects of *works* within a particular collection, the FRSAD model is applicable in a wide range of activities related to the development and management of KOS. FRSAD's modeling of *nomen* as an entity also allows tremendous flexibility for modeling attributes and attribute values for *nomens* representing *themas*. The WG members have conducted a series of studies on the implementation of FRSAD for various KOS since the model was finalized, especially in controlled lists, subject headings systems, and thesauri, as well as taxonomies and classification systems. The studies have focused on the following issues[18,19]:

- The granularity of *themas* in different KOS vocabularies.
- Representation of *themas* by various appellation forms in these KOS vocabularies. These can be seen from different perspectives: single, compound, or multiple-word terms; pre-coordinated or stand-alone; notations with captions or category labels, etc.
- FRSAD model for authority data in general (i.e., not restricted to subject authority data).
- The potential of FRSAD for multilingual and multicultural community needs.
- Approaches for handling vocabulary mapping in situations where vocabularies have or have not already applied the FRSAD model.

The studies conducted by the WG have also confirmed that the FRSAD model coincided with the works of a number of other efforts of standardization for KOS construction, publishing, and interoperating, particularly:

- ISO 25964-1:2011 Thesauri and interoperability with other vocabularies—Part 1: Thesauri for information retrieval (published in 2011)[20]
- SKOS Simple Knowledge Organization System Reference. W3C Recommendation March 17, 2009[21]
- SKOS Core Vocabulary Specification. W3C Working Draft May 10, 2005[22]
- SKOS eXtension for Labels (SKOS-XL). In: SKOS Simple Knowledge Organization System Reference. W3C Recommendation March 17, 2009[23]

Conceptual models and data models have been developed or enhanced by the working groups of these standards, each with particular implementation targets in mind. FRSAD WG conducted careful studies and mappings to these models; the results have been presented in several conferences. In general, the conceptualization of the relationship between a concept (*thema*) and the representations of the concept (*nomen(s)*) is consistent with all these models. As indicated previously, FRSAD added a new entity, *nomen*, to the FRBR family. This enables the modeling of *nomen* by defining its attributes as well as relationships between instances of a *nomen*. This important conceptualization can be found to have echoes in the data models of ISO 25964. It is also paralleled by the newer version of the SKOS, which supplements an eXtension for Labels (SKOS-XL) (SKOS Simple Knowledge Organization System Reference, 2009, Appendix B) specification in 2009. SKOS has been widely used by the

Linked Data datasets of subject authorities such as the *Library of Congress Subject Headings (LCSH)*, *Dewey Decimal Classification (DDC)*, *AGROVOC*, and *Eurovoc*, as well as name authorities such as the *Library of Congress Name Authority File (LCNAF)* and *Virtual International Authority File (VIAF)*.[24]

Another important model FRSAD WG has studied is the Dublin Core Metadata Initiative (DCMI) Abstract Model, a DCMI Recommendation.[25] The FRSAD model is consistent with the DCMI abstract model in the sense that FRSAD allows any *thema* to be independent of any *nomen*, including any syntax that a *nomen* may use. Furthermore, it will enable the sharing, linking, and reuse of subject authority data among not only the subject vocabularies themselves but also metadata resources.

These studies conducted by the WG and the fact that FRSAD complies with the models presented in ISO 25964, SKOS, and the DCMI Abstract Model provide proof that the FRSAD model can meet the needs of subject authority data in both the conventional information management environment and the emerging Linked Data environment.

REFERENCES

1. *Functional Requirements for Bibliographic Records: Final Report*. IFLA Study Group on the Functional Requirements for Bibliographic Records. KG Saur: München, Germany, 1998. Available at: http://www.ifla.org/files/cataloguing/frbr/frbr.pdf (accessed August 2017).
2. Patton, G.E. *Functional Requirements for Authority Data—A Conceptual Model*. IFLA Working Group on Functional Requirements and Numbering of Authority Records (FRANAR). K.G. Saur: München, Germany, 2009.
3. Ref. 1, p. 16.
4. Heaney, M. Time is of the essence: Some thoughts occasioned by the papers contributed to the *International Conference on the Principles and Future Development of AACR*; Bodleian Library: Oxford, U.K., 1997.
5. Delsey, T. Modeling subject access: Extending the FRBR and FRANAR conceptual models. Cat. Classif. Q. **2005**, *39* (3/4), 49–61.
6. Zeng, M.L.; Žumer, M.; Salaba, M.Eds. *Functional Requirements for Subject Authority Data (FRSAD): A Conceptual Model*. IFLA Working Group on Functional Requirements for Subject Authority Records (FRSAR). De Gruyter Saur: Berlin/München, Germany, 2011.
7. Ref. 6, Section 6.2.
8. Ref. 1.
9. Ref. 5.
10. Rust, G.; Bide, M. The <indecs> metadata framework: Principles, model and data dictionary. Version2. Indecs Framework Ltd. 2000. Available at: http://www.doi.org/topics/indecs/indecs_framework_2000.pdf (accessed August 2017).
11. Ranganathan, S.R. In *Colon Classification*; Madras Library Association: Madras, India, 1933.

12. Buizza, P.; Guerrini, M. A conceptual model for the New Soggetario: Subject indexing in the light of FRBR. Cat. Classif. Q. **2002**, *34* (4), 31–45.

13. Ref.6, p. 12.

14. Ref.6, Section 3.3.

15. Strunck, K. About the use of "Functional Requirements for Bibliographic Records" in teaching cataloguing. 65th IFLA Council and General Conference, August 20–August 28, 1999. Bangkok, Thailand, Available at, http://ifla.org/IV/ifla65/papers/108-131e.htm. (accessed December 2012) Also available in International Cataloguing and Bibliographic Control **2000**, *29* (4), 68–70.

16. Ref. 6, Appendix D.

17. Ref. 6, Section 3.4.

18. Ref. 6.

19. Žumer, M.; Zeng, M.L.; Salaba, A. *FRSAD: Conceptual Modeling of Aboutness.* Third Millennium Cataloging Series, Libraries Unlimited: Santa Barbara, CA, 2012.

20. ISO 25964–1:2011. *Information and documentation—Thesauri and interoperability with other vocabularies—Part 1: Thesauri for information retrieval.* ISO/TC 46/SC 9 ISO 25964 Working Group. International Organization for Standardization, 2011.

21. *SKOS Simple Knowledge Organization System Reference (2009)*; Miles, A.; Bechhofer, S., Eds.; W3C Candidate Recommendation March 17, 2009. 2009. Available at: http://www.w3.org/TR/skos-reference/ (accessed August 2017).

22. *SKOS Core Vocabulary Specification*; Miles, A.; Bechhofer, S., Eds.; W3C Working Draft May 10, 2005, 2005. Available at:http://www.w3.org/TR/2005/WD-swbp-skos-core-spec-20050510/ (accessed August 2017).

23. SKOS eXtension for Labels (SKOS-XL). In *SKOS Simple Knowledge Organization System Reference*; Miles, A.; Bechhofer, S., Eds.; 2009. Appendix B. Available at: http://www.w3.org/TR/skos-reference/#xl (accessed August 2017).

24. Library Linked Data Incubator Group: Datasets, Value Vocabularies, and Metadata Element Sets. W3C Incubator Group Report, October 25, 2011. Isaac, A.; Waltes, W.; Young, J.; Zeng, M., Eds.; 2011. Available at: http://www.w3.org/2005/Incubator/lld/XGR-lld-vocabdataset-20111025/ (accessed August 2017).

25. Powell, A.; Nilsson, M.; Naeve, A.; Johnston, P.; Baker, T., Eds.; DCMI Abstract Model. Dublin Core Metadata Initiative, 2007. Available at: http://dublincore.org/documents/abstract-model/ (accessed August 2017).

Fuzzy Set Theory

Donald Kraft
Department of Computer Science, U.S. Air Force Academy, Colorado Springs, Colorado, U.S.A.

Gloria Bordogna
Italian National Research Council, Institute for the Dynamics of Environmental Processes, Dalmine, Italy

Gabriella Pasi
Department of Informatics, Systems and Communication, University of Studies of Milano Bicocca, Milan, Italy

Abstract

This entry presents a definition of fuzzy set theory and an overview of some applications to model flexible information retrieval systems. The entry focuses on a description of fuzzy indexing procedures defined to represent the varying significance of terms in synthesizing the documents' contents, the representation of structured documents so as to model a subjective view of document content, the definition of flexible query languages which allow the expression of soft selection conditions, and fuzzy associative retrieval mechanisms to model fuzzy pseudothesauri, fuzzy ontologies, and fuzzy categorizations of documents.

INTRODUCTION

The objective of this entry is to provide an overview of some applications of fuzzy set theory to design flexible information retrieval systems (IRSs). The term "flexible" implies that we consider IRSs that can represent and manage the uncertainty, vagueness, and subjectivity, which are characteristic of the process of information searching and retrieval.

Consider the notions that index terms offer only an approximate and incomplete view of a document's content, that query languages (such as those incorporating Boolean logic) do not usually allow users to express vague requirements for specifying selection conditions that are tolerant to imprecision, and that a document's relevance to the user's query is a subjective and an imprecise notion. We show how imprecision, vagueness, and subjectivity can be managed within the formal framework of fuzzy set theory. This means that retrieval mechanisms capable of both modeling human subjectivity and of estimating the partial relevance of documents to a user's needs can be designed.

The retrieval process is introduced as a fuzzy multi-criteria decision-making (MCDM) activity in the presence of vagueness. Documents constitute the set of the alternatives described using weighted index terms. The query specifies a set of soft constraints on the document representations that are created via indexing. The retrieval mechanism performs a decision analysis in the presence of imprecision to rank the documents on the basis of their partial satisfaction of the soft constraints.

This entry is organized as follows: in the section on "Current Trends in IR," the current trends and key issues in IR are discussed. In the section on "Fuzzy Retrieval Models," an overview of the basic notions of fuzzy set theory to model flexible IRSs are presented. In the section on "Fuzzy Document Indexing," a description of the tradiional fuzzy document representation is first illustrated. In addition, both a fuzzy representation of documents structured into logical sections that can be adapted to the subjective needs of a user and a fuzzy representation of HTML documents are presented. In the section on "Flexible Querying," a description of how the Boolean query language of IR can be extended so as to make it flexible and suitable to express soft constraints by capturing the vagueness of the user needs is presented. Both numeric and linguistic selection conditions are introduced to qualify term's importance, and it is shown how linguistic quantifiers are defined to specify soft aggregation operators of query terms. In the section on "Fuzzy Associative Mechanisms," a description of how fuzzy sets can serve to define associative mechanisms to expand the functionalities of IRSs are presented. The focus of current research trends in IR is on the semantic web, i.e., the capability to represent concepts and to model their semantic relationships: fuzzy sets provide notions that can be applied to this purpose allowing to model either fuzzy pseudothesauri and fuzzy ontologies and to build fuzzy categorizations of documents by fuzzy clustering techniques. In the section on "Fuzzy Performance Measures," fuzzy performance measures for IRSs are introduced and the conclusion summarizes the main contents of this entry.

Encyclopedia of Library and Information Sciences, Fourth Edition DOI: 10.1081/E-ELIS4-120043233

CURRENT TRENDS IN IR

In this section the current trends and the key issues in IR are introduced.

Current Trends in IR

Some of the current trends in IR research run the gamut in terms of expanding the discipline both to incorporate the latest technologies and to cope with novel necessities. In terms of novel necessities, with the diffusion of the Internet and the heterogeneous characteristics of users of search engines, which can be regarded as the new frontier of IR, a new central issue has arisen, generally known as the semantic web. It mainly consists in expanding IRSs with the capability to represent and manage the semantics of both user requests and documents so as to be able to account for user and document contexts. This need becomes urgent with cross-language retrieval, which consists in expressing queries in one language, and retrieving documents written in another language, that is what commonly happens when submitting queries to search engines. Cross language retrieval not only implies new works on text processing, e.g., stemming conducted on a variety of languages, new models of IR such as the development of language models, but also the ability to match terms in distinct languages at a conceptual level, by modeling their meaning.

Another research trend of IR is motivated by the need to manage multimedia collections with nonprint audio elements such as sound, music, and voice, and video elements such as images, pictures, movies, and animation. Retrieval of such elements can include consideration of both metadata and content-based retrieval techniques. The definition of new IRSs capable to efficiently extract content indexes from multimedia documents, and to effectively retrieve documents by similarity or proximity to a query by example so as to fill the semantic gap existing between low-level syntactic index matching and the semantics of multimedia document and query are still to come.

In addition, modern computing technology, including storage media, distributed and parallel processing architectures, and improved algorithms for text processing and for retrieval, has an effect on IRSs. For example, improved string searching algorithms have improved the efficiency of search engines. Improved computer networks have made the Internet and the World Wide Web a possibility. Intelligent agents can improve retrieval in terms of attempting to customize and personalize it for individual users. Moreover, great improvements have been made in retrieval systems interfaces based on human–computer interface research.

These novel research trends in IR are faced by turning to technologies such as natural language processing, image processing, language models, artificial intelligence, and automatic learning.

Also fuzzy set theory can play a crucial role to define novel solutions to these research issues since it provides suitable means to cope with the needs of the semantic web,[1,2] e.g., to model the semantic of linguistic terms so as to reflect their vagueness and subjectivity and to compute degrees of similarity, generalization, and specialization between their meanings.

Key Issues in IR

Modeling the concept of relevance in IR is certainly a key issue, perhaps the most difficult one, and no doubt the most important one. What makes a document relevant to a given user is still not fully understood, specifically when one goes beyond topicality (i.e., the matching of the topics of the query with the topics of the document). Of course, this leads to the realization that relevance is gradual and subjective.

A second key issue is the representation of the documents in a collection, as well as the representation of users' information needs, especially for the purpose of matching documents to the queries at a "semantic" level. This implies introducing incompleteness, approximation, and managing vagueness and imprecision.

Finally, a key issue is how to evaluate properly an IRS's performance. Here, too, one sees imprecision.

IMPRECISION, VAGUENESS, UNCERTAINTY, AND INCONSISTENCY IN IR

Very often the terms imprecision, vagueness, uncertainty, and inconsistency are used as synonymous concepts. Nevertheless when they are referred to qualify a characteristic of the information they have a distinct meaning.[3] Since IR has to do with information, understanding the different meanings of imprecision, vagueness, uncertainty, and inconsistency allows to better understanding the perspectives of the distinct IR models defined in the literature.

Vagueness and imprecision are related to the representation of the information content of a proposition. For example, in the information request, "find *recent* scientific chapters dealing with the *early* stage of infectious diseases by HIV," the terms *recent* and *early* specify vague values of the publication date and of the temporal evolution of the disease, respectively. The publication date and the phase of an infectious disease are usually expressed as numeric values; their linguistic characterization has a coarser granularity with respect to their numeric characterization. Linguistic values are defined by terms with semantics compatible with several numeric values on the scale upon which the numeric information is defined. Imprecision is just a case-limit of vagueness, since imprecise values have a full compatibility with a subset of values of the numeric reference scale.

There are several ways to represent imprecise and vague concepts. Indirectly, by defining similarity or proximity relationships between each pair of imprecise and vague concepts.

If we regard a document as an imprecise or vague concept, i.e., as bearing a vague content, a numeric value computed by a similarity measure can be used to express the closeness of any two pairs of documents. This is the way of dealing with the imprecise and vague document and query contents in the vector space model of IR. In this context the documents and the query are represented as points in a vector space of terms and the distances between the query and the documents points are used to quantify their similarity.

Another way to represent vague and imprecise concepts is by means of the notion of fuzzy set. The notion of a fuzzy set is an extension to normal set theory.[4] A set is simply a collection of objects. A fuzzy set (more properly called a fuzzy subset) is a subset of a given universe of objects, where the membership in the fuzzy set is not definite. For example, consider the idea of a person being middle-aged. If a person's age is 39, one can consider the imprecision of that person being in the set of middle-aged people. The membership function, μ, is a number in the interval [0, 1] that represents the degree to which that person belongs to that set. Thus, the terms *recent* and *early* can be defined as fuzzy subsets, with the membership functions interpreted as compatibility functions of the meaning of the terms with respect to the numeric values of the reference (base) variable. In Fig. 1, the compatibility function of the term *recent* is presented with the numeric values of the time-scale measured in years. Note that here a chapter that has a publication date of the current year or 1 year previous is perfectly *recent*; however, the extent to which a chapter remains *recent* declines steadily over the next 2 years until chapters older than 3 years have no sense of being *recent*.

In the next sections we will see how the notion of fuzzy set has been used in the IR context to represent the vague concepts expressed in a flexible query for specifying soft selection conditions of the documents.

Uncertainty is related to the truth of a proposition, intended as the conformity of the information carried by the proposition with the considered reality. Linguistic expressions such as "probably" and "it is possible that" can be used to declare a partial lack of knowledge about the truth of the stated information.

Further, there are cases in which information is affected by both uncertainty and imprecision or vagueness. For example, consider the proposition "probably document d is relevant to query q." Possibility theory[5,6] together with the concept of a linguistic variable defined within fuzzy set theory[7] provide a unifying formal framework to formalize the management of imprecise, vague, and uncertain information.[8]

However, the same information content can be expressed by choosing a trade-off between the vagueness and the uncertainty embedded in a proposition. For example, one can express the content of the previous proposition by a new one "document d is more or less relevant to query q." In this latter proposition, the uncertain term *probably* has been eliminated, but the specificity of the vague term *relevant* has been reduced. In point of fact, the term *more or less relevant* is less specific than the term *relevant*. A dual representation can eliminate imprecision and augment the uncertainty, like in the expression "it is *not completely probable* that document d fully satisfies the query q."

One way to model IR is to regard it as an uncertain problem.[9]

On the basis of what has been said about the trade-off between uncertainty and vagueness to express the same information content, there are two alternative ways to model the IR activity. One possibility is to model the query evaluation mechanism as an uncertain decision process. Here the concept of relevance is considered binary (crisp) and the query evaluation mechanism computes the probability of relevance of a document d to a query q. Such an approach, which does model the uncertainty of the retrieval process, has been introduced and developed by probabilistic IR models.[10–12] Another possibility is to interpret the query as the specification of soft "elastic" constraints that the representation of a document can satisfy to an extent, and to consider the term *relevant* as a gradual (vague) concept. This is the approach adopted in fuzzy IR models.[9,13] In this latter case, the decision process performed by the query evaluation mechanism computes the degree of satisfaction of the query by the representation of each document. This satisfaction degree, called the retrieval status value (RSV), is considered as an estimate of the degree of relevance (or is at least proportional to the relevance) of a given document with respect to a given user query. An RSV of 1 implies maximum relevance; an RSV value of 0 implies absolutely no relevance. And, an RSV value in the interval [0, 1] implies an intermediate level or degree of relevance. For example, an RSV value of 0.5 could imply an average degree of relevance.

Inconsistency comes from the simultaneous presence of contradictory information about the same reality. An example of inconsistency can be observed when submitting

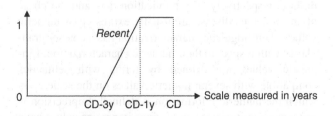

Fig. 1 Semantics of the term "recent" referring to the publication date of a scientific chapter. CD, current date; y, years.

the same query to several IRSs that adopt different representations of documents and produce different results. This is actually very common and often occurs when searching for information over the Internet using different search engines. To solve this kind of inconsistency, some fusion strategies can be applied to the ranked lists each search engine produces. In fact, this is what metasearch engines do.[14,15]

In this entry, we analyze the representation and management of vagueness as a means of improving the flexibility of IRSs. In particular, we will focus on the modeling of vagueness and in fuzzy IR models.

The document representation based on a selection of index terms is invariably incomplete. When synthesizing the content of a text manually by asking an expert to select a set of index terms, one introduces subjectivity in the representation. On the other hand, automatic full-text indexing introduces imprecision since the terms are not all fully significant in characterizing a document's content. However, these terms can have a partial significance that might also depend upon the context in which they appear, i.e., which document component.

In the query formulation, users often only have a vague idea of the information for which they are looking. Users therefore find it difficult to translate their needs into a precise request using a formal query language such as one employing Boolean logic.

A flexible IRS should be capable of providing more detailed and rich representations of documents and of interpreting vague queries in order to perform retrieval processes that tolerate, and account for, this vagueness.

FUZZY RETRIEVAL MODELS

Fuzzy retrieval models have been defined in order to reduce the imprecision that characterizes the Boolean indexing process, to represent the user's vagueness in queries, and to deal with discriminated answers estimating the partial relevance of the documents with respect to queries. Extended Boolean models based on fuzzy set theory have been defined to deal with one or more of these aspects.[16–24] Surveys of fuzzy extensions for IRSs and of fuzzy generalizations of the Boolean retrieval model can be found in Kraft[9] and Bordogna.[13]

Fuzzy "knowledge-based" models[25,26] and fuzzy associative mechanisms[27–30] have been defined to cope with the incompleteness that characterizes either the representation of documents or the users' queries. Miyamoto[31] illustrates a wide range of methods to generate fuzzy associative mechanisms.

It has been speculated that Boolean logic is passé, out of vogue. Yet, researchers have employed p-norms in the vector space model or Bayesian inference nets in the probabilistic model to incorporate Boolean logic into those models. In addition, the use of Boolean logic to separate a

collection of records into two disjoint classes has been considered, e.g., using the one-clause-at-a time (OCAT) methodology.[32] Moreover, even now retrieval systems such as Dialog and Web search engines such as Google allow for Boolean connectives. It should come as no surprise, therefore, to see extensions of Boolean logic based upon fuzzy set theory for IR.

It is noteworthy that most of the research on fuzzy retrieval has been conducted by a relatively few scholars. Moreover, that research has focused upon theoretical models, focusing primarily upon text retrieval, so that precious little testing has to date been conducted.

Extensions of Fuzzy Boolean Retrieval Models

The fuzzy retrieval models have been defined as generalizations of the classical Boolean model. These allow one to extend existing Boolean IRSs without having to redesign them. This was first motivated by the need to be able to produce proper answers in response to the queries. In essence, the classical Boolean IRSs apply an exact match between a Boolean query and the representation of each document. This document representation is defined as a set of index terms. These systems partition the collection of documents into two sets, the retrieved documents and the rejected (non-retrieved) ones. As a consequence of this crisp behavior, these systems are liable to reject useful items as a result of too restrictive queries, as well as to retrieve useless material in reply to queries.[33]

The softening of the retrieval activity in order to rank the retrieved items in decreasing order of their relevance to a user query can greatly improve the effectiveness of such systems. This objective has been approached by extending the Boolean models at different levels. We shall consider those levels in order to model retrieval using a MCDM model that allows the expression of the users' queries as soft constraints and produce discriminated answers.

Fuzzy techniques for documents' indexing

The aim here is to provide more specific and exhaustive representations of each document's information content. This means improving these representations beyond those generated by existing indexing mechanisms. We shall introduce the fuzzy interpretation of a weighted document representation and then later introduce a fuzzy representation of documents structured in logical sections that can be adapted to a user that has subjective criteria for interpreting the content of documents.[17] In this same vein, we shall describe an indexing procedure for HTML documents.[34]

Definition of flexible query languages

The objective here is to define query languages that are more expressive and natural than classical Boolean logic. This is done in order to capture the vagueness of user needs as well as to simplify user–system interaction. This has been pursued with two different approaches. First, there has been work on the definition of soft selection criteria (soft constraints), which allow the specification of the different importance of the search terms. Query languages based on numeric query term weights with different semantics have been first proposed as an aid to define more expressive selection criteria.[18,21,22,24,35] An evolution of these approaches has been defined that introduces linguistic query weights, specified by fuzzy sets such as *important* or *very important*, in order to express the different vague importance of the query terms.[36] Second, there is the approach of introducing soft aggregation operators for the selection criteria, characterized by a parametric behavior which can be set between the two extremes of intersection (AND) and union (OR) as adopted in Boolean logic. Boolean query languages have been extended and generalized by defining aggregation operators as linguistic quantifiers such as *at least k* or *about k*.[16]

As we shall see, the incorporation of weighted document representations in a Boolean IRS is a sufficient condition to improve the system via a ranking capability. As a consequence of this extension, the exact matching that is employed by a classical Boolean IRS is softened using a partial matching mechanism that evaluates the degree of satisfaction of a user's query for each document. This degree of satisfaction is the RSV that is used for ranking.

Fuzzy Associative Mechanisms

These associative mechanisms allow to automatically generating fuzzy pseudothesauri, fuzzy ontologies, and fuzzy clustering techniques to serve three distinct but compatible purposes. First, fuzzy pseudothesauri and fuzzy ontologies can be used to contextualize the search by expanding the set of index terms of documents to include additional terms by taking into account their varying significance in representing the topics dealt with in the documents. The degree of significance of these associated terms depends on the strength of the associations with a document's original descriptors. Second, an alternative use of fuzzy pseudothesauri and fuzzy ontologies is to expand the query with related terms by taking into account their varying importance in representing the concepts of interest. The importance of an additional term is dependent upon its strength of association with the search terms in the original query. Third, fuzzy clustering techniques, where each document can be placed within several clusters with a given strength of belonging to each cluster, can be used to expand the set of the documents retrieved in response to a query. Documents associated with retrieved documents, i.e., in the same cluster, can be retrieved. The degree of association of a document with the retrieved documents does influence its RSV. Another application of fuzzy clustering in IR is that of providing an alternative way, with respect to the usual ranked list, of presenting the results of a search.

FUZZY DOCUMENT INDEXING

In order to increase the effectiveness of IRSs, the indexing process plays a crucial role. In fact, it is not sufficient to provide IRSs with powerful query languages or sophisticated retrieval mechanisms to achieve effective results if the representation of documents oversimplifies their information content.

Vector Space, Probabilistic, and Generalized Boolean Indexing

The vector space model and the probabilistic models generally adopt a weighted document representation, which has improved the Boolean document representation by allowing the association of a numeric weight with each index term.[10,33] The automatic computation of the index term weights is based on the occurrences count of a term in the document and in the whole archive.[37–39] In this case, the indexing mechanism computes for each document d and each term t a numeric value by means of a function F. An example of F which has the index term weight increasing with the frequency of term t in document d but decreasing with the frequency of the term in all the documents of the archive is given by

$$F(d,t) = tf_{dt} \times g(\text{IDF}_t) \tag{1}$$

where

- tf_{dt} is a normalized term frequency, which can be defined as:

$$= tf_{dt} = \frac{\text{OCC}_{dt}}{\text{MAXOCC}_d};$$

- OCC_{dt} is the number of occurrences of t in d;
- MAXOCC_d is the number of occurrences of the most frequent term in d;
- IDF_t is an inverse document frequency which can be defined as: IDF_t

$$\text{IDF}_t = \log \frac{\text{N}}{\text{NDOC}_t};$$

- N is the total number of documents in the archive;
- NDOC_t is the number of documents indexed by t; and
- g is a normalizing function.

The computation of IDF_t is particularly costly in the case of large collections which are updated online.

The definition of such a function F is based on a quantitative analysis of the text, which makes it possible to model the qualitative concept of significance of a term in describing the information carried by the text. The adoption of weighted indexes allows for an estimate of the relevance, or of the probability of relevance, of documents to a query.[10,33]

Based on such an indexing function, and by incorporating Boolean logic into the query, the first fuzzy interpretation of an extended Boolean model has been to adopt a weighted document representation and to interpret it as a fuzzy set of terms.[40] From a mathematical point of view, this is a quite natural extension: the concept of the significance of index terms in describing the information content of a document can then be naturally described by adopting the function F, such as the one defined by Zadeh[5] as the membership function of the fuzzy set representing a document's being in the subset of concepts represented by the term in question. Formally, a document is represented as a fuzzy set of terms: $R_d = \sum_{t \in T} \mu_{Rd}/t$ in which the membership function is defined as $\mu_{Rd}:D \times T \rightarrow [0, 1]$. In this case, $\mu_{Rd}(t) = F(d, t)$, i.e., the membership value, can be obtained by the indexing function F. We describe later that through this extension of the document representation, the evaluation of a Boolean query produces a numeric estimate of the relevance of each document to the query, expressed by a numeric score or RSV, which is interpreted as the degree of satisfaction of the constraints expressed in a query.

Fuzzy set theory has been applied to define new and more powerful indexing models than the one based on the function specified in Eq. 1. The definition of new indexing functions has been motivated by several considerations. First, these F functions do not take into account the idea that a term can play different roles within a text according to the distribution of its occurrences. Moreover, the text can be considered as a black box, closed to users' interpretation. Such users might naturally filter information by emphasizing certain subparts on the basis of their subjective interests. This outlines the fact that relevance judgments are driven by a subjective interpretation of the document's structure, and supports the idea of *dynamic* and *adaptive* indexing.[17,41] By adaptive indexing, we mean indexing procedures which take into account the users' desire to *interpret* the document contents and to "build" their synthesis on the basis of this interpretation.

Fuzzy Representation of Structured Documents

We also consider the synthesis of a fuzzy representation of structured documents that takes into account the user needs.[17] A document can be represented as an entity composed of sections (e.g., *title*, *authors*, *introduction*, and *references*). For example, a single occurrence of the term in the *title* indicates that the chapter is concerned with the concept expressed by the term, while a single occurrence in the *reference* suggests that the chapter refers to other publications dealing with that concept. The information role of each term occurrence depends then on the semantics of the subpart where it is located. This means that to the aim of defining an indexing function for

structured documents the single occurrences of a term may contribute differently to the significance of the term in the whole document. Moreover, the document's subparts may have a different importance determined by the users' needs. For example, when looking for chapters written by a certain author, the most important subpart would be the *author name*; while when looking for chapters on a certain topic, the *title*, *abstract*, and *introduction* subparts would be preferred.

Of course, when generating an archive of a set of documents, it is necessary to define the sections which one wants to employ to structure each document. The decision of how to structure the documents, i.e., the type and number of sections, depends on the semantics of the documents and on the accuracy of the indexing module that one wants to achieve. A formal representation of a document will be constituted using a fuzzy binary relation: with each pair <section, term>, a significance degree in the interval [0, 1] is computed to express the significance of that term in that document section. To obtain the overall significance degree of a term in a document, i.e., the index term weight, these values are *dynamically* aggregated by taking into account the indications that a user explicits in the query formulation. Other non-fuzzy approaches have also introduced the concept of boosting factor to emphasize differently the contribution of the index terms occurrences depending on the document sections to the overall index term weights. However these approaches compute *static* index term weights during the indexing process, without taking into account the user interpretation.

On the contrary, in the fuzzy approach the aggregation function is defined on two levels. First, the user expresses preferences for the document sections (the equivalent of the boosting factors), specifying those sections that the system should more heavily weight in order to take proper account of the evaluation of the relevance of a given document to that user's query. Second, the user should decide which aggregation function has to be applied for producing the overall significance degree. This is done by the specification of a linguistic quantifier such as *at least one*, *at least k*, or *all*.[42] By adopting this document representation, the same query can select documents in different relevance order depending on the user's indicated preferences.

An indexing model has been proposed by which the occurrences of a term in the different documents' sections are taken into account according to specific criteria, and the user's interpretation of the text is modeled.[17] During the retrieval phase, the user can specify the distinct importance (preference) of the sections and decide that a term must be present in *all* the sections of the document or in *at least a certain number* of them in order to consider the term fully significant. A section is a logical subpart identified by s_i, where $i \in 1, .., n$ and n is the total number of the sections in the documents. We assume here that an archive contains documents sharing a common structure.

Formally, a document is represented as a fuzzy binary relation:

$$R_d = \sum_{(t, s) \in T \times S} \mu_d(t, s) / (t, s) \qquad (2)$$

The value $\mu_d(t, s) = F_s(d, t)$ expresses the significance of term t in section s of document d. A function $F_s: D \times T \rightarrow [0, 1]$ is then defined for each section s. The overall significance degree $F(d, t)$ is computed by combining the single significance degrees of the sections, the $F_s(d, t)$s, through an aggregation function specified by the user. This function is identified by a fuzzy linguistic quantifier such as *all*, *at least k*, or *at least 1*, which aggregates the significance degrees of the sections according to their importance values as specified by the user.

The criteria for the definition of F_s are based on the semantics of section s and are specified by an expert during the indexing of the documents. For example, for sections containing short texts or formatted texts, such as the *author* or *keywords*, a single occurrence of a term makes it fully significant in that section: in this case, it could be assumed that $F_s(d, t) = 1$ if t is present in s but 0 otherwise. On the other hand, for sections containing textual descriptions of variable length such as the *abstract* and *title* sections, $F_s(d, t)$ can be computed as a function of the normalized term frequency in the section as for example:

$$\mu_s(d,t) = tf_{dst} * IDF_t \qquad (3)$$

in which IDF_t is the inverse document frequency of term t [see definition (5)], tf_{dst} is the normalized term frequency defined as:

$$tf_{dst} = \frac{OCC_{dst}}{MAXOCC_{sd}}$$

in which OCC_{dst} is the number of occurrences of term t in section s of document d and $MAXOCC_{sd}$ is a normalization parameter depending on the section's length so as not to underestimate the significance of short sections with respect to long ones. For example, this normalization parameter could be computed as the frequency of the term with the highest number of occurrences in the section.

To simplify the computation of this value, it is possible to heuristically approximate it: during the archive generation phase, with an expert indicating the estimated percentage of the average length of each section with respect to the average length of documents (PERL$_s$). Given the number of occurrences of the most frequent term in each document d, MAXOCC$_d$, an approximation of the number of occurrences of the most frequent term in section s of document d is

$$MAXOCC_{sd} = PERL_s * MAXOCC_d$$

Term Significance

To obtain the overall degree of significance of a term in a document, an aggregation scheme of the $F_s(d, t)$s values has been suggested, based on a twofold specification of the user.[17] When starting a retrieval session, users can specify their preferences on the sections s by a numeric score $\alpha_s \in [0, 1]$ where the most important sections have an importance weight close to 1. Moreover, users can select a linguistic quantifier to specify the aggregation criterion; the quantifier can be chosen among *all* (the most restrictive one), *at least one* (the weakest one), or *at least k* which is associated with an intermediate aggregation criterion.

Within fuzzy set theory linguistic quantifiers used to specify aggregations are defined as ordered weighted averaging (OWA) operators.[43] When processing a query, the first step accomplished by the system for evaluating $F(d, t)$ is the selection of the OWA operator associated with the linguistic quantifier lq, OWA$_{lq}$. When the user does not specify any preferences on the documents' sections, the overall significance degree $F(d, t)$ is obtained by applying directly the OWA$_{lq}$ operator to the values $\mu_1(d, t), \ldots, \mu_n(d, t)$:

$$F(d,t) = OWA_{lq}(\mu_1(d,t), \ldots, \mu_n(d,t))$$

When distinct preference scores $\alpha_1, \ldots, \alpha_n$ are associated with the sections, it is first necessary to modify the values $\mu_1(d, t), \ldots, \mu_n(d, t)$ in order to increase the "contrast" between the contributions due to important sections with respect to those of less important ones. The evaluation of the overall significance degree $F(d, t)$ is obtained by applying the operator OWA$_{lq}$ to the modified degrees $a_1, \ldots, a_n$: $F(d, t) = OWA_{lq}(a_1, \ldots, a_n)$.

We can now briefly sketch a comparison of the effectiveness of a system adopting a simple weighted representation versus a system with this structured weighted representation. In particular, the different rankings of two documents obtained by adopting the two different representations are outlined by an example. The two documents considered in the archive of CNR research projects contain the term "genoma." Fig. 2 shows the normalized frequency of "genoma" in the sections of the two documents; as it can be noticed, the term "genoma" has the same total number of occurrences in both documents. Since the normalization factors are the same, by applying F as defined in Eq. 1, the significance of "genoma" in both documents gets the same value $F(d_1, genoma) = F(d_2, genoma) = 0.8$. Fig. 3 shows the significance degrees for each section in which the term "genoma" occurs. These degrees are obtained using the fuzzy representation of structured documents; since the title and keywords sections are short texts, μ_{title} and $\mu_{keywords}$ are defined so as to take values in $\{0, 1\}$. After estimating that the objective section takes up averagely 30% of the documents' length, and the

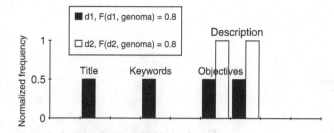

Fig. 2 Normalized frequency of "genoma" in the sections of the two documents.

description section is around 40%, $\mu_{\text{objective}}$ and $\mu_{\text{description}}$ are defined.

When the user does not specify any criterion to aggregate the single degrees of the sections, a default aggregation operator is used.[16,17] Since no importance is specified to differentiate the contributions of the sections, all of them are assumed to have the same importance weight of 1. Notice that the document d_1, which contains "genoma" in the *keywords* and title sections is now considered more significant with respect to document d_2 that contains the term just in the *objectives* and *description* sections.

These results could be reversed if the user specifies that the presence of the term "genoma" in the *objectives* section is fundamental. Fig. 4 illustrates this situation, showing the modified degrees of significances of the sections when the user sets the aggregation criterion equal to at *least 1* and $\alpha_{\text{objective}} = 1$, $\alpha_{\text{title}} = \alpha_{\text{keywords}} = \alpha_{\text{description}} = 0.5$, and $\alpha_i = 0$ otherwise.

The fact that the user can explicate the preferences on the section and the aggregation criterion by a linguistic quantifier allows a subjective interpretation of document content and gives the user the possibility of full control on the system behavior. This is not the case for other IR models, the probabilistic model (e.g., Bayesian updating of the probabilities as part of relevance feedback), and Rocchio's relevance feedback mechanism for the vector space model, or even the calculation of the rank for Web pages retrieved by Google using PageRank. In these models the retrieval criteria remain implicit and are not observable directly by the user.

Experimental Results

A comparison of the results produced by using the traditional fuzzy representation of documents and the fuzzy representation of structured documents can be found.[17] In this experiment, a collection of 2500 textual documents about descriptions of CNR research projects has been considered. The indexing module of the prototypal IRS named DOMINO, used for the experiment, has been extended in order to be able to recognize in the documents any structure simply by specifying it into a definition file. In this way it is not necessary to modify the system when dealing with a new collection of documents with a different structure. The definition of the documents sections has been made before starting the archive generation phase. During this phase it was also necessary to specify the criteria by which to compute the significance degrees of the terms in each section. Two kinds of sections have been identified: the "structured" sections, i.e., the research code, title, research leader, and the "narrative" sections, containing unstructured textual descriptions, i.e., the project description and the project objective. It has been observed that while the values of precision remain unchanged in the two versions of the system, the values of recall are higher by using the structured representation than those obtained by using the traditional fuzzy representation.

We illustrate another approach which produces a weighted representation of documents written in HTML.[34] An HTML document has a specific syntactic structure in which its subparts have a given format specified by the delimiting tags. In this context, tags are seen as syntactic elements carrying an indication of the importance of the associated text. When writing a document in HTML, an author associates varying importance to each of the different subparts of a given document by delimiting them by means of appropriate tags. Since a certain tag can be employed more than once, and in different positions inside the document, the concept of document subpart is not meant as a unique, adjacent piece of text. Such a structure is subjective and carries the interpretation of the document author. It can be applied in archives, which collect heterogeneous documents, i.e., documents with possibly different "logical" structures.

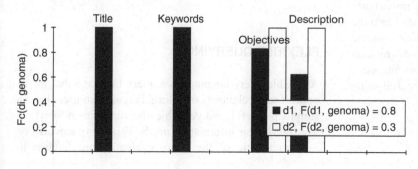

Fig. 3 Significance degrees of "genoma" in each section of the two documents.

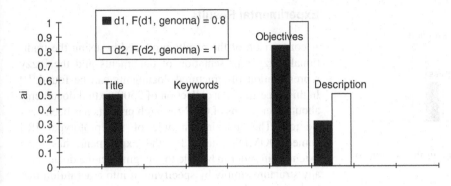

Fig. 4 Modified significance degrees of the term "genoma" in the documents sections.

When generating a HTML document, an author exploits the importance weights associated with different subparts of the text. If characters of different fonts are used, it is assumed that the larger the font, the more important the information carried by the text. Moreover, to use boldface or italics for characters generally means the highlighting of a portion of the text. Tags constitute then indicators of the importance of documents' subparts.

An indexing function has been proposed which provides different weights for the occurrences of a given term in the document, depending on the tags by which they are delimited.[34] The overall significance degree $F(d, t)$ of a term t in a document d is computed by first evaluating the term significance in the different document tags, and then by aggregating these contributions. With each tag, a function $F_{tag}: D \times T \to [0, 1]$ is associated together an importance weight $\mu_{tag} \in [0, 1]$. Note that the greater is the emphasis of the text associated with a tag, the greater is its importance weight. A possible ranking of the considered tags has been suggested[34] in decreasing order of tag importance. The definition of such a list is quite subjective, although based on objective assumptions suggested by commonsense. These rankings include notion such as a larger font for the characters in a portion of text yields greater importance of that portion of text, or text in boldface or italics or appearing in a list can be assumed as having a higher importance. Of course, other orderings could be defined.

To simplify the hierarchy of the tags, we see that certain tags can be employed to accomplish similar aims, so one can group them into different classes. It is assumed that the members of a class have the same importance weight. Text not delimited by any tag is included into the lowest class. A simple procedure to compute numeric importance weights starting from the proposed ranking can be achieved. The definition of F_{tag} follows the same mechanism as the previous approach.[17] The following normalized frequency is now proposed:

$$F_{tag}(d,t) = \frac{NOCC_{tag\ dt}}{MAXOCC_{tag\ d}}$$

in which $NOCC_{tag\ dt}$ is the number of occurrences of term t inside tag in document d, and $MAXOCC_{tag\ d}$ is the number of occurrences of the most frequent term inside the tag.

Once the single significance degrees of a term into the tags have been computed, these have to be aggregated in order to produce an overall significance degree of the term into the document. In the aggregation all the significance degrees should be taken into account, so as to consider the contribution of each tag, modulated by their importance weights. To this aim a weighted mean can be adopted:

$$A(F_{tag1}(d,t), \ldots, F_{tagn}(d,t)) = \sum_{i=1,\ldots,n} F_{tag\ i}(d,t) * w_i$$

in which $\sum_{i=1,\ldots,n} w_i = 1$. Starting from the list of tags in decreasing relative order of their importance, the numeric weights w_i are computed through a simple procedure. Assuming that tag_i is more important than tag_j iff $I < j$ (i and j being the positions of tag_i and tag_j respectively in the ordered list), the numeric importance weight w_i associated with tag_i can be computed as $w_i = (n - i + 1)/\sum_{i=1,\ldots,n} i$.

In the computation of the overall significance degree $F(d, t)$, the inverse document frequency of term t could be taken into account:

$$F(d,t) = \left(\sum_{i=1,\ldots,n} F_{tag\ i}(d,t) * w_i * g(IDF_t) \right)$$

in which the definition of $g(IDF_t)$ is given in formula (5).

FLEXIBLE QUERYING

A flexible query language is a query language that incorporates some elements of natural language so users have a simple, powerful, and yet subjective mechanism by which to express their information needs. Flexibility can also be a characteristic of the query evaluation mechanism to allow a tuning of the query's concepts' semantics with respect to the document collection, the user's subjective statement of information need, and even the user's application domain. Linguistic variables provide a suitable framework to generalize, to represent, and to manage the linguistics of the query's concepts. Thus, this approach can be used to formalize the semantics of linguistic terms introduced in a Boolean query language.

Flexible query languages have been defined as generalizations of Boolean query languages that employ Boolean logic. Within the framework of fuzzy set theory, we have the idea of a softening of the rigid, crisp constraints of a Boolean condition being strictly true (a document has a keyword) or false (the document does not contain the keyword).

A flexible query consists of either or both of two soft components. First, there can be selection conditions interpreted as soft constraints on the significance of the index terms in each document representation. Second, there can be soft aggregation operators, which can be applied to the soft constraints in order to define compound selection conditions. The atomic selection conditions for individual terms are expressed by pairs <term, weight>, in which the weight can be a numeric value in the interval [0, 1] that is used to identify a soft constraint or the weight can be a linguistic value for the variable *importance*. The compound conditions for combining terms via Boolean logic are expressed by means of linguistic quantifiers used as aggregation operators.

Query Evaluation Mechanism

Query processing within retrieval can be interpreted as a decision-making activity. Its aim is to evaluate a set of alternatives or possible solutions, in this case a set of documents, based upon some criteria or selection conditions in order to select the optimal list (perhaps ranked) of documents in response to a user's query.

In the case of a Boolean query, the alternatives are the document representations as described based on the presence or absence of index terms or keywords. The selection conditions, as expressed by terms specified in a query, define a set of constraints requiring the presence or absence of these terms within a document's representation. These conditions are expressed connected by aggregation operators, i.e., the Boolean logic operators of AND, OR, and NOT. The decision process is performed through an exact matching function, which is strictly dependent on the system query language. This decision process evaluates the global satisfaction of the query constraints for each document representation. Relevance is modeled as a binary property of the documents with respect to the user's query.

Given a fuzzy approach to retrieval, query processing can be regarded as a decision activity affected by vagueness. In fact, the query can be seen as the specification of a set of soft constraints, i.e., vague selection conditions, that the documents can satisfy to a partial extent. The documents described through the significance degrees of the index terms constitute the alternatives. The query evaluation mechanism is regarded as fuzzy decision process that evaluates the degree of satisfaction of the query constraints by each document representation by applying a partial matching function. This degree is the RSV and can be interpreted as the degree of relevance of the document to the query and is used to rank the documents. Then, as a result of a query evaluation, a fuzzy set of documents is retrieved in which the RSV is the membership value. In this case the definition of the partial matching function is strictly dependent on the query language, specifically on the semantics of the soft constraints.

A wish list of requirements that a matching function of an IRS must satisfy has been proposed.[18,24] Included in this list is the separability property that the evaluation of an atomic selection condition for an individual term in a query should be independent of the evaluation of the other atomic components or their Boolean connectors. The matching function should be based solely upon a function evaluating atomic conditions. Following the calculation of these evaluations, one can then aggregate them based upon the Boolean operators in the query. It has been shown that this property guarantees a homomorphic mapping from the space of all single terms to the space of all possible Boolean queries using these terms.[44] This property has been considered widely within fuzzy retrieval models, especially in the definition of flexible query languages.

By designing the partial matching mechanism from the bottom-up the separability property is ensured. First, each atomic selection condition or soft constraint in the query is evaluated by a function E for a given document. Then the aggregation operators are applied to the results starting from the inmost operator in the query to the outermost operator by a function E^*. This E function evaluates the soft constraints associated with the query atoms on the fuzzy set R_d representing each document, where these soft constraints are defined as fuzzy subsets. The membership value $\mu_{atom}(i)$ is the degree of satisfaction of the soft constraint associated with the atomic query *atom*, i.e., $E(<atom>, d) = \mu_{atom}(F(d, t))$. In other words, E evaluates how well the term t, which has an indexing weight $F(d, t)$ for document d, satisfies the soft constraint specified by *atom*. The result of the evaluation is a fuzzy set, $\sum_{d \in D} \mu_{atom}(F(d, t))/d$ in which $\mu_{atom}(F(d, t))$ is interpreted as the RSV of document d with respect to the query atom.

The function $E^*: D \times Q \to [0, 1]$, where Q is the set of all the proper queries in the query language, evaluates the final RSV of a document, reflecting the satisfaction of the whole query. The definition of E^* depends strictly upon the structure of the query language, specifically upon the aggregation operators used to combine the atomic components. The AND connective is classically defined as the minimum (min) operator, the OR connective as the maximum (max) operator, and the NOT connective as the one-minus (1−) or complement operator. These definitions preserve the idempotence property. A fuzzy generalization of the Boolean query structure has been defined in which the Boolean operators are replaced by linguistic quantifiers.[16] In this context, linguistic quantifiers are used as aggregation operators to determine the degree of satisfaction for the soft constraints. They allow to improve as well as to simplify the expressiveness of the Boolean query language.

Query Weights

To render a Boolean query language to be more user-friendly and more expressive, one can extend the atomic selection conditions by introducing query term weights.[22,23,45,46] An example of weighted query is the following: $<t_1, w_1>$ AND $(<t_2, w_2>$ OR $<t_3, w_3>)$ in which t_1, t_2, and t_3, are search terms with numeric weights w_1, w_2, and w_3 in the interval [0, 1]. These weights are implicitly given as being equal to 1 in the classical Boolean query language.

The concept of query weights raises the problem of their interpretation. Several authors have realized that the semantics of query weights should be related to the concept of the "importance" of the terms. Being well aware that the semantics of the query term weights influences the definition of the partial matching function, specifically of the E function, different semantics for the soft constraint imposed by a pair $<t, w>$ have been proposed in the literature trying to satisfy as much as possible properties of the wish list, in particular the separability property.

Early on, query weights were interpreted as a relative importance weight where the separability property does not hold. Two distinct definitions of E have been proposed for conjunctive and disjunctive queries, respectively.[22,47] Later, other models[23,24,46] used an interpretation of the query weights w as a threshold on the index term weight or as an ideal index term weight.[35,45]

Implicit query weights

The simplest extension of the Boolean model consists of the adoption of a weighted document representation but with a classical Boolean query language.[40] This retrieval mechanism ranks the retrieved documents in decreasing order of their significance with respect to the user query. In this case, an atomic query consisting of a single term t is interpreted as the specification of a pair $<t, 1>$ in which $w = 1$ is implicitly specified. The soft constraint associated with $<t, 1>$ is then interpreted as the requirement that the index term weight be "close to 1" and its evaluation is defined as $\mu_w(F(d, t)) = F(d, t)$. This means that the desired

documents are those with maximum index term weight for the specified term t, i.e., index term weights closest to 1. This interpretation implies that the evaluation mechanism tolerates the under satisfaction of the soft constraint associated with $<t, 1>$ with a degree equal to $F(d, t)$.

Relative importance query weights

Here, query weights are interpreted as measures of the "relative importance" of each term with respect to the other terms in the query.[22,47] This interpretation allows the IRS to rank documents so that documents are ranked higher if they have larger index term weights for those terms that have larger query weights. However, since it is not possible to have a single definition for the soft constraint μ_w that preserves the "relative importance" semantics independently of the Boolean connectors in the query, two distinct definitions of μ_w have been proposed, depending on the aggregation operators in the query. This approach, sadly, gives up the separability property. Two alternative definitions have been proposed for conjunctive and disjunctive queries.[22,47] The first proposal[22] yields

$\mu_w(F(d, t)) = wF(d, t)$ for disjunctive queries and
$\mu_w(F(d, t)) = \max(1, F(d, t)/w)$ for conjunctive queries;

while the second proposal[47] yields

$\mu_w(F(d, t)) = \min[w, F(d, t)$ for disjunctive queries
$\mu_w(F(d, t)) = \max[(1 - w), F(d, t)]$ for conjunctive queries

Notice that any weighted Boolean query can be expressed in disjunctive normal form (DNF) so that any query can be evaluated by using one of these two definitions.

Threshold query weights

To preserve the separability property, an approach treating the query weights as thresholds has been suggested.[23,46] By specifying query weights as thresholds the user is asking to see all documents "sufficiently about" a topic. In this case, the soft constraint identified by the numeric query weight can be linguistically expressed as "more or less over w." Of course, the lower the threshold, the greater the number of documents retrieved. Thus, a threshold allows a user to define a point of discrimination between under- and over satisfaction.

The simplest formalization of threshold weights has been suggested as a crisp threshold[23]

$$\mu_w(F(d,t)) = \begin{cases} 0 & \text{for } F(d, t) < w \\ F(d, t) & \text{for } F(d, t) \geq w \end{cases}$$

In this case, the threshold defines the minimally acceptable document. Due to its inherent discontinuity, this formalization might lead to an abrupt variation in the number of documents retrieved for small changes in the query weights. To remedy this, continuous threshold formalization has been suggested:[46]

$$\mu_w(F(d,t)) = \begin{cases} P(w) * \dfrac{F(d,t)}{w} & \text{for } F(d,t) < w \\[2mm] P(w) + Q(w) * \dfrac{(F(d,t) - w)}{(1 - w)} & \text{for } F(d,t) \geq w \end{cases}.$$

where $P(w)$ and $Q(w)$ might be defined as $P(w) = 1 + w/2$ and $Q(w) = 1 - w^2/4$.

For $F(d,t) < w$, the μ_w function measures the closeness of $F(d,t)$ to w; for $F(d,t) \geq w$, $\mu_w(F(d,t))$ expresses the degree of over satisfaction with respect to w, and under satisfaction with respect to 1.

Ideal query weights

Another interpretation for the query weights has been defined.[35,45] Here, the pair $<t, w>$ identifies a set of ideal or perfect documents so that the soft constraint μ_w measures how well $F(d, t)$ comes close to w, yielding

$$\mu_w(F(d,t)) = e^{\ln(k) * (F(d,t) - w)^2}$$

The parameter k in the interval [0, 1] determines the steepness of the Gaussian function's slopes. As a consequence, k will affect the strength of the soft constraint *close to w*. So, the larger the value of k is, the weaker the constraint becomes. This parametric definition makes it possible to adapt the constraint interpretation to the user concept of *close to w*.[36] The retrieval operation associated with a pair $<t, w>$ corresponds in this model to the evaluation of a similarity measure between the importance value w and the significance value of t in R_d: $w \approx F(d, t)$.

Comparisons of these query weight semantics

In order to analyze the results obtained by these different semantics associated with the query weight w, let us consider the archive represented by the fuzzy sets in Table 1. The rows are the documents, the columns are the terms, and the elements are the values of the index term weights, i.e., an element of row d_i and column t_j is the value $F(d_i, t_j)$. Let us consider the query: $q = <t_1, 1>$ AND $<t_2, 0.6>$ AND $<t_4, 0.2>$, as represented in Table 2.

Table 3 yields the results of the evaluation of q for each of the query weight semantics, assuming that the AND connective is evaluated using the MIN operator.

Table 1 Each row is a fuzzy set representing a document.

	t_1	t_2	t_3	t_4
d_1	1	0.9	1	0.2
d_2	0.7	0.6	0.3	0.8

Table 2 Query q (ANDed weighted pairs).

	t_1	t_2	t_4
q	1	0.6	0.2

Linguistic Query Weights

The main limitation of numeric query weights is their inadequacy in dealing with the imprecision which characterizes the concept of importance that they represent. In fact, the use of numeric query weights forces the user to quantify a qualitative and rather vague notion and to be aware of the weight semantics. Thus, a fuzzy retrieval model with linguistic query weights has been proposed[36] with a linguistic extension of the Boolean query language based upon the concept of a linguistic variable.[7] With this approach, the user can select the primary linguistic term "important" together with linguistic hedges (e.g., "very" or "almost") to qualify the desired importance of the search terms in the query. When defining such a query language the term set, i.e., the set of all the possible linguistic values of the linguistic variable *importance* must be defined. Such a definition depends on the desired granularity that one wants to achieve. The greater the number of the linguistic terms, the finer the granularity of the concepts that are dealt with. Next, the semantics for the primary terms must be defined. A pair $<t, important>$, expresses a soft constraint $\mu_{important}$ on the term significance values (the $F(d, t)$ values). The evaluation of the relevance of a given document d to a query consisting solely of the pair $<t, important>$ is based upon the evaluation of the degree of satisfaction of the associated soft constraint $\mu_{important}$.

The problem of giving a meaning to numeric weights reappears here in associating a semantic with the linguistic term *important*. The $\mu_{important}$ function is defined based on the ideal semantics of the numeric weight to yield[36]

$$\mu_{important}(F(d,t)) = \begin{cases} e^{\ln(k) * (F(d,t) - i)^2} & \text{for } F(d,t) < i \\ 1 & \text{for } i \leq F(d,t) \leq j \\ e^{\ln(k) * (F(d,t) - j)^2} & \text{for } F(d,t) > j \end{cases}$$

We see that if $F(d, t)$ is less than the lower bound i or greater than the upper bound j, the constraint is under satisfied. The strength of the soft constraint $\mu_{important}$ depends upon both the width of the range $[i, j]$ and the value of the k parameter. The values i and j delimit the

Table 3 Results of query q in Table 2 referred to documents in Table 1.

Query weight semantics	d_1	d_2
Ideal index term weight	0.3	0.6
Relative importance	0.8	0.6
Threshold on index term weight	0.2	0

level of *importance* for the user. We note that as the value $|i - j|$ increases, the soft constraint becomes less precise. So, for the case of the ideal semantics of numeric query term weights, k determines the sharpness of the constraint in that as k increases, the constraint increases in fuzziness.

We can define the $\mu_{\text{important}}$ function based upon the threshold semantics to yield[48]

$$\mu_{\text{important}}(F(d,t)) = \begin{cases} \frac{1+i}{2} * e^{\ln(k)*(F(d,t)-i)^2} & \text{for } F(d,t) < i \\ \frac{1+F(d,t)}{2} & \text{for } i \leq F(d,t) \leq j \\ \frac{1+j}{2} * \left(1 + \frac{F(d,t)-j}{2}\right) & \text{for } F(d,t) > j \end{cases}$$

We note that this compatibility function is continuous and nondecreasing in $F(d, t)$ over the interval $[0, 1]$. For $F(d, t) < i$, $\mu_{\text{important}}$ increases as a Gaussian function. For $F(d, t)$ in the interval $[i, j]$, $\mu_{\text{important}}$ increases at a linear rate. For $F(d, t) > j$, $\mu_{\text{important}}$ still increases, but at a lesser rate. The compatibility functions of non-primary terms, such as *very important* or *fairly important*, are derived by modifying the compatibility functions of primary terms. This is achieved by defining each linguistic hedge as a modifier operator. For example, the linguistic hedges are defined as translation operators in[48] to yield

$\mu_{\text{very important}}(x) = \mu_{\text{important}}(x)$

with $i_{\text{very}} = i + 0.2$ and $j_{\text{very}} = j + 0.2$ and $\forall x \in [0, 1]$.

$\mu_{\text{averagely important}}(x) = \mu_{\text{important}}(x)$

with $i_{\text{averagely}} = i - 0.3$ and $j_{\text{averagely}} = j - 0.3$ and $\forall x \in [0, 1]$.

$\mu_{\text{minimally important}}(x) = \mu_{\text{important}}(x)$

with $i_{\text{minimally}} = i - 0.5$ and $j_{\text{minimally}} = j - 0.5$ and $\forall x \in [0,1]$.

in which i and j are values in $[0, 1]$ delimiting the range of complete satisfaction of the constraint $\mu_{\text{important}}$. With these definitions, any value $F(d, t)$ of the basic domain of the *importance* variable fully satisfies at least one of the constraints defined by the linguistic query terms.

In Herrara–Viedma[49] a query language with linguistic query weights having heterogeneous semantics have been proposed so as to benefit of the full potential offered of fuzzy set to model subjective needs.

Linguistic Quantifiers to Aggregate the Selection Conditions

In a classical Boolean query language, the AND and OR connectives allow only for crisp (non-fuzzy) aggregations which do not capture any of the inherent vagueness of user information needs. For example, the AND used for aggregating M selection conditions does not tolerate the no satisfaction of but a single condition which could cause the no retrieval of relevant documents. To deal with this

problem, additional extensions of Boolean queries have been provided which involves the replacement of the AND and OR connectives with soft operators for aggregating the selection criteria.[33,50,51]

Within the framework of fuzzy set theory, a generalization of the Boolean query language has been defined based upon the concept of linguistic quantifiers that are employed to specify both crisp and vague aggregation criteria of the selection conditions.[16] New aggregation operators can be specified by linguistic expressions with self-expressive meaning, such as *at least k* and *most of*. They are defined to exist between the two extremes corresponding to the AND and OR connectives, which allow requests for *all* and *at least one of* the selection conditions, respectively. The linguistic quantifiers used as aggregation operators are defined by OWA operators.

Adopting linguistic quantifiers more easily and intuitively formulate the requirements of a complex Boolean query. For example, when desiring that *at least 2* out of the three terms "politics," "economy," and "inflation" be satisfied, one might formulate the Boolean query as:

(politics AND economy) OR (politics AND inflation) OR (economy AND inflation)

However, a simpler one can replace this,

*atleast*2(politics, economy, inflation)

This new query language via the nesting of linguistic quantifiers supports the expression of any Boolean query. For example the query

AND (<processing> OR <analysis>) AND <digital>

can be translated into the new, more synthetic and clear formulation:

all (<image>, *at least 1 of* (<processing>, <analysis>), <digital>).

A quantified aggregation function can be applied not only to single selection conditions, but also to other quantified expressions. Then, the E^* function evaluating the entire query yields a value in $[0, 1]$ for each document d in the archive D.

If S is the set of atomic selection conditions and Q is the set of legitimate Boolean queries over our vocabulary of terms, then the E^* function can be formalized by recursively applying the following rules

1. if $q \in S$ then $E^*(d, s) = \mu_w(F(d, t))$ in which $\mu_w(F(d, t))$ is the satisfaction degree of a pair $<t, w>$ by document d with w being either a numeric weight or a linguistic weight.

2. if $q = quantifier (q_1,\ldots,q_n)$ and $q_1,\ldots,q_n \in Q$ then

$$E * (d, q) = OWA_{quantifier}(E * (d, q_1), \ldots, E * (d, q_n))$$

3. $E*(d, NOT\ q) = 1 - E*(d, q)$

in which $OWA_{quantifier}$ is the OWA operator associated with *quantifier*.

The formal definition of the query language with linguistic quantifiers with the following quantifies has been generated[16]

- *all* replaces AND.
- *at least k* acts as the specification of a crisp threshold of value k on the number of selection conditions and is defined by a weighting vector $w_{at\ least\ k}$ in which $w_k = 1$, and $w_j = 0$, for $i \le k$—noting that *at least 1* selects the maximum of the satisfaction degrees so that it has the same semantics of OR.
- *about k* is a soft interpretation of the quantifier *at least k* in which the k value is not interpreted as a crisp threshold, but as a fuzzy one so that the user is fully satisfied if k or more conditions are satisfied but gets a certain degree of satisfaction even if $k-1, k-2,\ldots,1$ conditions are satisfied—this quantifier is defined by a weighting vector $w_{about\ k}$ in which $W_i = \dfrac{i}{\sum_{j=1}^{k} j}$ for $i \le k$, and $w_i = 0$ for $i > k$.
- *most of* is defined as a synonym of *at least $\frac{2}{3}n$* in which n is the total number of selection conditions.

With respect to non-fuzzy approaches that tried to simplify the Boolean formulations, the fuzzy approach subsumes the Boolean language, allows reformulating Boolean queries in a more synthetic and comprehensible way, and improves the Boolean expressiveness by allowing flexible aggregations.

Other authors have followed these ideas by proposing alternative formalization of linguistic query weights and flexible operators based on ordinal labels and ordinal aggregations,[52] thus reducing the complexity of the evaluation mechanism.

FUZZY ASSOCIATIVE MECHANISMS

Associative retrieval mechanisms are defined to enhance the retrieval of IRSs. They work by retrieving additional documents that are not directly indexed by the terms in a given query but are indexed by other, related terms, sometimes called associated descriptors. The most common type of associative retrieval mechanism is based upon the use of a thesaurus to associate index or query terms with related terms. In traditional associative retrieval, these associations are crisp.

Fuzzy associative retrieval mechanisms obviously assume fuzzy associations. A fuzzy association between two sets $X = \{x_1, \ldots, x_m\}$ and $Y = \{y_1, \ldots, y_n\}$ is formally defined as a fuzzy relation

$$f : X \times Y \to [0, 1]$$

where the value $f(x, y)$ represents the degree or strength of the association existing between the values $x \in X$ and $y \in Y$. In IR, different kinds of fuzzy associations can be derived depending on the semantics of the sets X and Y.

Fuzzy associative mechanisms employ fuzzy thesauri, fuzzy pseudothesauri, fuzzy ontologies, and fuzzy categorizations to serve three alternative, but compatible purposes: 1) to expand the set of index terms of documents with new terms; 2) to expand the search terms in the query with associated terms; and 3) to expand the set of the documents retrieved by a query with associated documents.

Fuzzy Thesauri

A thesaurus is an associative mechanism that can be used to improve both indexing and querying. It is well known that the development of thesauri is very costly, as it requires a large amount of human effort to construct and to maintain. In highly dynamic situations, i.e., volatile situations, terms are added and new meanings derived for old terms quite rapidly, so that the thesaurus needs frequent updates. For this reason, methods for automatic construction of thesauri have been proposed, named pseudothesauri, based on statistical criteria such as the terms' co-occurrences, i.e., the simultaneous appearance of pairs (or triplets, or larger subsets) of terms in the same documents.

In a thesaurus, the relations defined between terms are of different types. If the associated descriptor has a more general meaning than the entry term, the relation is classified as broader term (BT), while a narrower term (NT) is the inverse relation. Moreover, synonyms and near-synonyms are parts of another type of relationship associated by a related term (RT) connection.

The concept of a fuzzy thesaurus has been suggested,[27,31,53,54] where the links between terms are weighted to indicate the relative strengths of these associations. Moreover, fuzzy pseudothesauri are generated when the weights of the links are automatically computed by considering document relationships rather than concept relationships.[30,55]

The first work on fuzzy thesauri introduced the notion of fuzzy relations to represent associations between terms.[54,56] Let us look at a formal definition of a fuzzy thesaurus.[27,28] Consider T to be the set of index terms and C to be a set of concepts. Each term $t \in T$ corresponds to a fuzzy set of concepts $h(t)$:

$$h(t) = \{\langle c, t(c)\rangle | c \in C\}$$

in which $t(c)$ is the degree to which term t is related to concept c. A measure M is defined on all of the possible fuzzy sets of concepts, which satisfies:

$$M(\theta) = 0$$
$$M(C) < \infty$$
$$M(A) \leq M(B) \quad \text{if } A \subseteq B$$

A typical example of M is the cardinality of a fuzzy set. The fuzzy RT relation is represented in a fuzzy thesaurus by the similarity relation between two index terms, t_1 and $t_2 \in T$ and is defined as

$$s(t_1, t_2) = M[h(t_1) \cap h(t_2)] / M[h(t_1) \cup h(t_2)]$$

This definition satisfies the following:

- if terms t_1 and t_2 are synonymous, i.e., $h(t_1) = h(t_2)$, then $s(t_1, t_2) = 1$;
- if t_1 and t_2 are not semantically related, i.e., $h(t_1) \cap h(t_2) = \emptyset$, then $s(t_1, t_2) = 0$;
- $s(t_2, t_1) = s(t_1, t_2)$ for all $t_1, t_2 \in T$; and
- if t_1 is more similar to term t_3 than to t_2, then $s(t_1, t_3) > s(t_1, t_2)$.

The fuzzy NT relation, indicated as nt, which represents grades of inclusion of a narrower term t_1 in another (broader) term t_2, is defined as:

$$nt(t_1, t_2) = M[h(t_1) \cap h(t_2)] / M[h(t_1)]$$

This definition satisfies the following:

- if term t_1's concept(s) is completely included within term t_2's concept(s), i.e., $h(t_1) \subseteq h(t_2)$, then

$$nt(t_1, t_2) = 1;$$

- if t_1 and t_2 are not semantically related, i.e., $h(t_1) \cap h(t_2) = \emptyset$, then $nt(t_1, t_2) = 0$; and
- if the inclusion of t_1's concept(s) in t_2's concept(s) is greater than the inclusion of t_1's concept(s) in

$$t_3\text{'s concept(s), then } nt(t_1, t_2) > nt(t_1, t_3)$$

By assuming M as the cardinality of a set, s and nt are given as:

$$s(t_1, t_2) = \sum_{k=1}^{M} \min[t_1(c_k), t_2(c_k)] \bigg/ \sum_{k=1}^{M} \max[t_1(c_k), t_2(c_k)]$$
$$nt(t_1, t_2) = \sum_{k=1}^{M} \min[t_1(c_k), t_2(c_k)] \bigg/ \sum_{k=1}^{M} t_1(c_k)$$

A fuzzy pseudothesaurus can be defined by replacing the set C in the definition of $h(t)$ above with the set of documents D, with the assumption that $h(t)$ is the fuzzy set of documents indexed by term t. This yields

$$h(t) = \{(d, t(d)) | d \in D\}$$

in which $t(d) = F(d, t)$ is the index term weight defined above. F can be either a binary value defining a crisp representation, or it can be a value in [0, 1] to define a fuzzy representation of documents. The fuzzy RT and the fuzzy NT relations now are defined as:

$$s(t_1, t_2) =$$
$$\sum_{k=1}^{M} \min[F(t_1, d_k), F(t_2, d_k)] \bigg/ \sum_{k=1}^{M} \max[F(t_1, d_k), F(t_2, d_k)]$$
$$nt(t_1, t_2) = \sum_{k=1}^{M} \min[F(t_1, d_k), F(t_2, d_k)] \bigg/ \sum_{k=1}^{M} F(t_1, d_k)$$

Note that $s(t_1, t_2)$ and $nt(t_1, t_2)$ are dependent on the co-occurrences of terms t_1 and t_2 in the set of documents, D. The set of index terms of document d, i.e., $\{t \mid F(d, t) \neq 0$ and $t \in T\}$, can be augmented by those terms t_A which have $s(t, t_A) > \alpha$ and/or $nt(t, t_A) > \beta$ for parameters α and $\beta \in [0, 1]$.

Suppose that in the definition of F we have the set T as a set of citations which are used to index documents, rather than a set of terms. In this case, a fuzzy association on citations can be defined through the fuzzy relations of s and/or nt. By using citations, a user may retrieve documents that cite a particular author or a particular reference. In addition, a keyword connection matrix has been proposed to represent similarities between key-words in order to reduce the difference between relationship values initially assigned using statistical information and a user's evaluation.[57] A new method is also proposed in which keywords that are attached to a document and broader concepts are hierarchically organized, calculating the keyword relationships through the broader concepts.

Moreover, a thesaurus can be generated based on the max-star transitive closure for linguistic completion of a thesaurus generated initially by an expert linking terms.[58] In addition, a probabilistic notion of term relationships can be employed by assuming that if one given term is a good discriminator between relevant and nonrelevant documents, then any term that is closely associated with that given term (i.e., statistically co-occurring) is likely to be a good discriminator, too.[10] Note that this implies that thesauri are collection-dependent.

One can also expand on Salton's[59] use of the $F(d, t)$ values. Salton[60] infers term relationships from document section similarities. On the other hand, one can manipulate the $F(d, t)$ values in order to generate co-occurrence statistics to represent term linkage weights.[61] Here, a synonym link is considered, defined as:

$$\mu_{\text{synonym}}(t_1, t_2) = \sum_{d \in D} [F(d, t_1) \leftrightarrow F(d, t_2)]$$

where $F(d, t_1) \leftrightarrow F(d, t_2) = \min[F(d, t_1) \rightarrow F(d, t_2), F(d, t_1) \leftarrow F(d, t_2)]$ and $F(d, t_1) \rightarrow F(d, t_2)$ can be defined in variety of ways. For instance, $F(d, t_1) \rightarrow F(d, t_2)$, the implication operator, can be defined as $[F(d, t_1)^c \vee F(d, t_2)]$, where $F(d, t_1)^c = 1 - F(d, t_1)$ is the complement of $F(d, t_1)$ and $\vee$ is the disjunctive (OR) operator defined as the max; or it can be defined as $\min(1, [1 - F(d, t_1) + F(d, t_2)])$. Here, a narrower term link (where term t_1 is narrower than term t_2, so term t_2 is broader than term t_1), is defined as:

$$\mu_{\text{narrower}}(t_1, t_2) = \sum_{d \in D} [F(d, t_1) \leftrightarrow F(d, t_2)]$$

Note that fuzzy narrower relationships defined between fuzzy sets can help the purpose of identifying generalization and specialization of topics, while the fuzzy similarity relationship between fuzzy sets can be of aid to identify similar topics. Thus they serve to build a labeled graph of relationships between concepts, regarded as fuzzy sets of terms, in the specific domain of the collection.

Fuzzy Clustering for Documents

Clustering in IR is a method for partitioning D, a given set of documents, into groups using a measure of similarity (or distance) which is defined on every pairs of documents. Grouping like documents together is not a new phenomenon, especially for librarians. The similarity between documents in the same group should be large, while the similarity between documents in different groups should be small.

A common clustering method is based on the simultaneous occurrences of citations in pairs of documents. Documents are clustered using a measure defined on the space of the citations. Generated clusters can then be used as an index for IR, i.e., documents which belong to the same clusters as the documents directly indexed by the terms in the query are retrieved.

Similarity measures have been suggested empirically or heuristically, sometimes analogously to the similarity measures for documents matched against queries.[33,38,62] When adopting a fuzzy set model, clustering can be formalized as a kind of fuzzy association. In this case, the fuzzy association is defined on the domain $D \times D$. By assuming $R(d)$ to be the fuzzy set of terms representing a document d with membership function values $d(t) = F(d, t)$ being the index term weights of term t in document d, the symmetric fuzzy relation s, as originally defined above, is taken to be the similarity measure for clustering documents:

$$s(d_1, d_2) = \sum_{k=1}^{M} \min[d_1(t_k), d_2(t_k)] \bigg/ \sum_{k=1}^{M} \max[d_1(t_k), d_2(t_k)]$$

$$= \sum_{k=1}^{M} \min[F(t_k, d_1), F(t_k, d_2)] \bigg/ \sum_{k=1}^{M} \max[F(t_k, d_1), F(t_k, d_2)]$$

in which T is the set of index terms in the vocabulary and M is the number of index terms in T.

In fuzzy clustering, documents can belong to more than one cluster with varying degree of membership.[63] Each document is assigned a membership value to each cluster. In a pure fuzzy clustering, a complete overlap of clusters is allowed. Modified fuzzy clustering, also called soft clustering, uses thresholding mechanisms to limit the number of documents belonging to each cluster. The main advantage of using modified fuzzy clustering is the fact that the degree of fuzziness is controlled. The use of fuzzy clustering in IR have several applications, that span from unsupervised categorization of documents into homogenous overlapping topic categories, so as to offer users an overview of the contents of a collection or to organize the results of a search into labeled groups, thus allowing users to have an immediate view of what has been retrieved. With respect to crisp clustering, fuzzy clustering allows finding a document in several labeled groups, thus reflecting distinct interpretation of document's content.

FUZZY PERFORMANCE MEASURES

One problem with current criteria to measure the effectiveness of IRSs is the fact that Recall and Precision measures have been defined by assuming that relevance is a Boolean concept. In order to take into account the fact that IRSs rank the retrieved documents based on their RSVs that are interpreted either as a probabilities of relevance, similarity degrees of the documents to the query, or as degrees of relevance, Recall–Precision graphs are produced in which the values of precision are computed at standard levels of recall. Then the average of the precision values at different recall levels is computed to produce a single estimate.

Nevertheless, these measures do not evaluate the actual values of the RSVs associated with documents and do not take into account the fact that also users can consider relevance as a gradual concept. For this reason some authors have proposed some fuzzy measure of effectiveness. Buell and Kraft[46] proposed the evaluation of fuzzy recall and fuzzy precision, defined as follows:

$$\text{Fuzzy precision} = \frac{\sum_d \min(e_d, u_d)}{\sum_d e_d},$$

$$\text{Fuzzy recall} = \frac{\sum_d \min(e_d, u_d)}{\sum_d u_d}$$

where u_d is the user's evaluation of the relevance of document d (u_d can be binary or defined in the interval $[0, 1]$) and e_d is the RSV of document d computer by the IRSs. These measures take into account the actual values of e_d and u_d, rather than the rank ordering based in descending order on e_d.

These measures can be particularly useful to evaluate the results of fuzzy clustering algorithms.

CONCLUSIONS

This entry reviews the main objectives and characteristics of the fuzzy modeling of the IR activity with respect to alternative approaches such as probabilistic IR and vector space IR. The focus of the fuzzy approaches is on modeling imprecision and vagueness of the information with respect to uncertainty. The fuzzy generalizations of the Boolean Retrieval model have been discussed by describing the fuzzy indexing of structured documents, the definition of flexible query languages subsuming the Boolean language, and the definition of fuzzy associations to expand either the indexes or the queries, or to generate fuzzy clusters of documents. Fuzzy similarity and fuzzy inclusion relationships between fuzzy sets ave been introduced that can help to define more evolved fuzzy IR models performing "semantic" matching of documents and queries, which is the current trend of research in IR.

REFERENCES

1. Tho, Q.T.; Hui, S.C.; Fong, A.C.M.; Cao, T.H. Automatic fuzzy ontology generation for semantic web. IEEE Trans. Knowl. Data Eng. **2006**, *18*(6), 842–856.
2. Sanchez, E. *Fuzzy Logic and the Semantic Web*, Elsevier: Amsterdam, the Netherlands, 2006.
3. Motro, A. Imprecision and uncertainty in database systems. In *Fuzziness in Database Management Systems*; Bosc, P., Kacprzyk, J., Eds.; Physica-Verlag: Heidelberg, Germany, 1995; 3–22.
4. Zadeh, L.A. Fuzzy sets. Inform. Control. **1965**, *8*, 338–353.
5. Zadeh, L.A. Fuzzy sets as a basis for a theory of possibility. Fuzzy Set Syst. **1978**, *1*, 3–28.
6. Dubois, D. Prade, H. *Possibility Theory: An Approach to Computerized Processing of Uncertainty*, Plenum Press: New York, 1988.
7. Zadeh, L.A. The concept of a linguistic variable and its application to approximate reasoning. Inform. Sci. **1975**, *8*, 199–249 parts I, II. 301–357.
8. Bosc, P. Fuzzy databases. In *Fuzzy Sets in Approximate Reasoning and Information Systems*; Bezdek, J., Dubois, D., Prade, H., Eds.; The Handbooks of Fuzzy Sets Series Kluwer Academic Publishers: Boston, MA, 1999.
9. Kraft, D.; Bordogna, G.; Pasi, G. Fuzzy set techniques in information retrieval. In *Fuzzy Sets in Approximate Reasoning and Information Systems*; Bezdek, J.C., Dubois, D., Prade, H., Eds.; The Handbooks of Fuzzy Sets Series Kluwer Academic Publishers: Boston, MA, 1999; 469–510.
10. van Rijsbergen, C.J. *Information Retrieval*, Butterworths & Co. Ltd.: London, U.K., 1979.
11. Fuhr, N. Models for retrieval with probabilistic indexing. Inform. Process. Manage. **1989**, *25*(1), 55–72.
12. Crestani, F.; Lalmas, M.; van Rijsbergen, C.J.; Campbell, I. Is this document relevant? Probably. ACM Comput. Surv. **1998**, *30*(4), 528–552.
13. Bordogna, G.; Pasi, G. The application of fuzzy set theory to model information retrieval. In *Soft Computing in Information Retrieval: Techniques and Applications*; Crestani, F., Pasi, G., Eds.; Physica-Verlag: Heidelberg, Germany, 2000.
14. Yager, R.R.; Rybalov, A. On the fusion of documents from multiple collections information retrieval systems. J. Am. Soc. Inform. Sci. **1999**, *49*(13), 1177–1184.
15. Bordogna, G.; Pasi, G.; Yager, R. Soft approaches to information retrieval on the WEB. Int. J. Approx. Reason. **2003**, *34*, 105–120.
16. Bordogna, G.; Pasi, G. Linguistic aggregation operators in fuzzy information retrieval. Int. J. Intell. Syst. **1995**, *10*(2), 233–248.
17. Bordogna, G.; Pasi, G. Controlling information retrieval through a user adaptive representation of documents. Int. J. Approx. Reason. **1995**, *12*, 317–339.
18. Cater, S.C.; Kraft, D.H. A generalizaton and clarification of the Waller-Kraft wish-list. Inform. Process. Manage. **1989**, *25*, 15–25.
19. Buell, D.A. A problem in information retrieval with fuzzy sets. J. Am. Soc. Inform. Sci. **1985**, *36*(6), 398–401.
20. Kraft, D.H. Advances in information retrieval: Where is that /#*%@^ record?. In *Advances in Computers*; Yovits, M., Ed.; Academic Press: New York, 1985; 277–318.
21. Buell, D.A.; Kraft, D.H. A model for a weighted retrieval system. J. Am. Soc. Inform. Sci. **1981**, *32*(3), 211–216.
22. Bookstein, A. Fuzzy requests: An approach to weighted Boolean searches. J. Am. Soc. Inform. Sci. **1980**, *31*(4), 240–247.
23. Radecki, T. Fuzzy set theoretical approach to document retrieval. Inform. Process. Manage. **1979**, *15*(5), 247–260.
24. Waller, W.G.; Kraft, D.H. A mathematical model of a weighted Boolean retrieval system. Inform. Process. Manage. **1979**, *15*, 235–245.
25. Lucarella, D.; Zanzi, A. Information retrieval from hypertext: An approach using plausible inference. Inform. Process. Manage. **1993**, *29*(1), 299–312.
26. Lucarella, D.; Morara, R. FIRST: Fuzzy information retrieval system. J. Inform. Sci. **1991**, *17*(2), 81–91.
27. Miyamoto, S. Information retrieval based on fuzzy associations. Fuzzy Set Syst. **1990**, *38*(2), 191–205.
28. Miyamoto, S. Two approaches for information retrieval through fuzzy associations. IEEE Trans. Syst., Man Cybernet. **1989**, *19*(1), 123–130.

29. Murai, T.; Miyakoshi, M.; Shimbo, M. A fuzzy document retrieval method based on two-valued indexing. Fuzzy Set Syst. **1989**, *30*(2), 103–120.

30. Miyamoto, S.; Nakayama, K. Fuzzy information retrieval based on a fuzzy pseudothesaurus. IEEE Trans. Syst., Man and Cybernet. **1986**, *SMC-16*(2), 278–282.

31. Miyamoto, S. *Fuzzy Sets in Information Retrieval and Cluster Analysis*, Kluwer Academic Publishers: Dordrecht, the Netherlands, 1990.

32. Sanchez, S.N.; Triantaphyllou, E.; Kraft, D.H. A feature mining based approach for the classification of text documents into disjoint classes. Inform. Process. Manage. **2002**, *38*(4), 583–604.

33. Salton, G. McGill, M.J. *Introduction to Modern Information Retrieval*, McGraw-Hill: New York, 1983.

34. Molinari, A. Pasi, G. A fuzzy representation of HTML documents for information retrieval systems In Proceedings of the IEEE International Conference on Fuzzy Systems New Orleans September, 8–12, 1996; Vol. 1, 107–112.

35. Cater, S.C. Kraft, D.H. TIRS: A topological information retrieval system satisfying the requirements of the Waller–Kraft wish list In Proceedings of the Tenth Annual ACM/ SIGIR International Conference on Research and Development in Information Retrieval New Orleans, LA June, 1987; 171–180.

36. Bordogna, G.; Pasi, G. A fuzzy linguistic approach generalizing Boolean information retrieval: A model and its evaluation. J. Am. Soc. Inform. Sci. **1993**, *44*(2), 70–82.

37. Salton, G.; Buckley, C. Term weighting approaches in automatic text retrieval. Inform. Process. Manage. **1988**, *24*(5), 513–523.

38. Sparck Jones, K.A. *Automatic Keyword Classification for Information Retrieval*, Butterworths: London, U.K., 1971.

39. Sparck Jones, K.A. A statistical interpretation of term specificity and its application in retrieval. J. Doc. **1972**, *28*(1), 11–20.

40. Buell, D.A. An analysis of some fuzzy subset applications to information retrieval systems. Fuzzy Sets Syst. **1982**, *7*(1), 35–42.

41. Berrut, C.; Chiaramella, Y. Indexing medical reports in a multimedia environment: The RIME experimental approach. *ACM-SIGIR 89*, Boston, MA, 1986; 187–197.

42. Zadeh, L.A. A computational approach to fuzzy quantifiers in natural languages. Comput. Math. Appl. **1983**, *9*, 149–184.

43. Yager, R.R. On ordered weighted averaging aggregation operators in multi criteria decision making. IEEE Trans. Syst. Man Cybernet. **1988**, *18*(1), 183–190.

44. Bartschi, M. Requirements for query evaluation in weighted information retrieval. Inform. Process. Manage. **1985**, *21*(4), 291–303.

45. Bordogna, G.; Carrara, P.; Pasi, G. Query term weights as constraints in fuzzy information retrieval. Inform. Process. Manage. **1991**, *27*(1), 15–26.

46. Buell, D.A. Kraft, D.H. Performance measurement in a fuzzy retrieval environment In Proceedings of the Fourth International Conference on Information Storage and Retrieval Oakland, CA May 31–June 2, 1981; 16, 56–62 ACM/SIGIR Forum (1).

47. Yager, R.R. A note on weighted queries in information retrieval systems. J. Am. Soc. Inform. Sci. **1987**, *38*(1), 23–24.

48. Kraft, D.H.; Bordogna, G.; Pasi, G. An extended fuzzy linguistic approach to generalize Boolean information retrieval. J. Inform. Sci. Appl. **1995**, *2*(3), 119–134.

49. Herrera-Viedma, E.; Lopez-Herrera, A.G. A model of an information retrieval system with unbalanced fuzzy linguistic information. Int. J. Intell. Syst. **2007**, *22*(11), 1197–1214.

50. Paice, C.D. Soft evaluation of Boolean search queries in information retrieval systems. Inform. Technol.: Res. Develop. Appl. **1984**, *3*(1), 33–41.

51. Sanchez, E. Importance in knowledge systems. Inform. Syst. **1989**, *14*(6), 455–464.

52. Herrera, F.; Herrera-Viedma, E. Aggregation operators for linguistic weighted information. IEEE Trans. Syst. Man Cybernet. Part A: Syst. Hum. **1997**, *27*(5), 646–656.

53. Neuwirth, E.; Reisinger, L. Dissimilarity and distance coefficients in automation-supported thesauri. Inform. Syst. **1982**, *7*(1), 47–52.

54. Radecki, T. Mathematical model of information retrieval system based on the concept of fuzzy thesaurus. Inform. Process. Manage. **1976**, *12*(5), 313–318.

55. Nomoto, K.; Wakayama, S.; Kirimoto, T.; Kondo, M. A fuzzy retrieval system based on citation. Syst. Control. **1987**, *31*(10), 748–755.

56. Reisinger, L. On fuzzy thesauri. In *COMPSTAT 1974*; Bruckman, G., Ed.; Physica Verlag: Vienna, Austria, 1974; 119–127.

57. Ogawa, Y.; Morita, T.; Kobayashi, K. A fuzzy document retrieval system using the keyword connection matrix and a learning method. Fuzzy Set Syst. **1991**, *39*(2), 163–179.

58. Bezdek, J.C.; Biswas, G.; Huang, L.Y. Transitive closures of fuzzy thesauri for information-retrieval systems. Int. J. Man Mach. Stud. **1986**, *25*(3), 343–356.

59. Salton, G. *Automatic Text Processing: The Transformation, Analysis and Retrieval of Information by Computer*, Addison Wesley: Boston, MA, 1989.

60. Salton, G.; Allan, J.; Buckley, C.; Singhal, A. Automatic analysis, theme generation, and summarization of machine-readable texts. Science. **1994**, *264*(June 3), 1421–1426.

61. Kohout, L.J.; Keravanou, E. Bandler, W. Information retrieval system using fuzzy relational products for thesaurus construction In Proceedings IFAC Fuzzy Information Marseille, France; 1983 7–13.

62. Salton, G.; Bergmark, D. A citation study of computer science literature. IEEE Trans. Prof. Commun. **1979**, *22*(3), 146–158.

63. Bezdek, J.C. *Pattern Recognition with Fuzzy Objective Function Algorithms*, Plenum Press: New York, 1981.

Games and Gaming

Diane Robson
University Libraries, Media Library, University of North Texas, Denton, Texas, U.S.A.

Breanne A. Kirsch
Library, Emerging Technologies, University of South Carolina Upstate, Spartanburg, South Carolina, U.S.A.

Abstract

Games and gaming are more visible and viable in libraries as computer, console, and tabletop games gain popularity as a form of leisure and recreation. Even though libraries have supported games in one form or another for many years, this type of collection is still controversial. Librarians with the guidance of professional groups, scholars, and educators are working together to show the value of games in all types of libraries. Games and gaming in public libraries are growing beyond simply providing space for their recreational use to include targeted programs to increase diversity. They are also being used to encourage collaboration and learning across all ages. Many public libraries host game programs, facilitate game play, and even encourage game creation. All types of games are now more readily recognized for their educational value in school classrooms and libraries. School librarians encourage the use of games to meet educational goals, life skills, and digital citizenship in the classroom. Academic libraries and archives are not only building game collections to aid in programming, retention, and research, but also creating archival and digital repositories to aid future scholars. Despite the technology and digital rights management difficulties inherent to video games, libraries recognize the historical and cultural value of games and the need for this type of collection. Librarians are not only developing ways to support leisure, research, and game preservation, but also the creation of games in and for libraries.

INTRODUCTION

Games and gaming in libraries is a hot topic at the present time for many librarians who wish to attract users to the library. Game collections and gaming as an activity mean different things to different people in the library and community at large. Librarians are working together to provide access to this type of collection as well as promote the positive influences of games in the library.

This entry will give a basic definition of what games are and why they belong in the library. It will also give brief descriptions of how games are being used in public, school, and academic libraries to enhance recreation, learning, and scholarly research. Lastly, an overview of how librarians are not only collecting games but also creating games to help entertain and educate their patrons. Librarians are creating organizations and harnessing the positive influence of this dynamic and evolving format.

DEFINITION OF A GAME

What is a game? The definition of a game changes context according to the situation in which it is used. Kevin Maroney defines games as a form of play that has structure and set goals. The structure can include sequence and timing of the action. These actions can be strictly described in the rules or more flexible, such as those in a role-playing game where a player is limited by their specific attributes. Actions the players take in any game are to reach a set goal or objective and possibly win the game.[1] Jesper Juul adds to this by including player effort and attachment as necessary elements of a game. A player invests effort to influence the outcome and, therefore, becomes attached to that outcome.[2] This goes to show that games are not just physical objects with goals and structure but also an activity.[3] Each iteration of gameplay can be different than the one before as the players and their knowledge, ability, and expertise change. Games must be played, and gameplay is different every time a game is played. This means games are ever changing and players must react and refine their play to be successful. Play is a valuable part of learning and video and tabletop games let us play regardless of age or infirmity. It allows users to practice behaviors and experiment without any real-life consequences.[4] Gamers interact, collaborate, and engage with the game and each other as they seek to accomplish the game's goals.

Most library games fit this definition of a game. Library collections are most likely in the format of computer, console, and tabletop games. PC games or computer games are video games played on a personal computer. Video games can also be played on game consoles. These games are usually specific to a certain console type and model.

Encyclopedia of Library and Information Sciences, Fourth Edition DOI: 10.1081/E-EISA-120059523

Consoles, unlike PCs, were designed just for the purpose of playing games, although that has been changing to include Internet access and other uses with the latest console models.[5] Computer and console games are digital games that require hardware platforms to be playable. Tabletop games is an inclusive term that refers to games that can be played on a table's surface such as board games, card games, role-playing games, and dice to name a few. These games vary in their materials to include boards, pieces, dice, cards, paper, pencil, and role-playing guides, in book and digital form. These are just the predominant formats that a library might have in their collection. The world of games is very broad and varied.

GAMES IN THE LIBRARY

Gaming might appear to be a new type of activity in the library to many people; however, games have been in libraries, in one form or another, for the past 150 years.[6] As both tabletop and video games have become mainstream and connected to other types of mass media, gaming in libraries has gained visibility. Over the last 40 years, gamers have grown up and had children that may also game. This has led to gaming being a more readily accepted leisure activity for all ages.

The Entertainment Software Association Industry Facts show that 59% of Americans play video games. This means that 183 million people play video games in America. It's not just kids playing these games. The average age of a gamer is 31.[7] Why do people play video games? The author of *Reality is Broken*, Jane McGonigal, believes that games are fulfilling some of the needs that people are not getting from the real world. Engaging games teach and inspire gamers. Unable to find this type of fulfillment in their daily real-world life, people are turning to virtual worlds.[8] One benefit of games is the ability to fight, die, and rise up to try another strategy that can accomplish the games' given goals. People are able to vanquish villains, be a hero that saves the world, or simply have a successful farm in their virtual life. Games give this type of success to the average person.

Beyond the use of games for leisure, librarians have a duty to consider collections that have cultural significance. Music, movies, books, and games are more intertwined now than at any time in the past. Barwick, Dearnley, and Muir note that games deserve a rightful place in libraries because they are an important part of the history of play. Games are a part of our cultural legacy.[3] Although digital games are what usually come to mind when people think of a game collection, tabletop games have also had a resurgence in the last 10 years. Now tabletop games offer better design and deeper engagement while also being more accessible because of the Internet.[9] Librarians are ignoring a significant part of modern cultural heritage if they do not consider tabletop and digital games worth collecting for their user's benefit.

This resurgence in tabletop games and the continued popularity of video games as a type of mass media led to the creation of an American Library Association (ALA) Member Interest Group focused on games and gaming in libraries in 2008. In 2012, this group became the ALA Games and Gaming Round Table (GameRT). The GameRT website (http://www.ala.org/gamert/home) lists their mission as offering librarians a professional forum for ideas, resources, and support. As a professional group, GameRT is able to provide a positive voice and create awareness of the value of games and gaming in libraries.

Do Games Belong in a Library?

There has always been conflict around the inclusion of games and other new media in libraries. The idea of supporting leisure materials, regardless of format, has been debated by librarians for at least 150 years. Hayes and Morris note that collections including leisure materials struggle to be accepted by librarians but are generally the reason that the public uses libraries. Librarians in the past were asked by social reformers to provide only materials that improve both the user and society through their leisure activities. Problems arise in the fact that no one can agree to just what type of material this is.[10] Librarians today are still fighting this battle. Librarians in the process of establishing a new collection should keep in mind that almost every new type of library material was seen as a threat to literacy, even fiction novels.[11]

Not only do librarians need to deal with ingrained ideas about librarianship and library collections, they must also deal with how today's popular media portrays gaming. News stories tend to focus on controversial games or the negative aspects of games, while ignoring the vast number of players who play without any issues arising.[12] James Paul Gee articulates that the number of people who have killed others or aided them because of a book is vastly larger than those who have done so because of a game, movie, or television show.[13] Focusing only on the negative aspects of any material or format will only lead to an empty library that no one wants to visit or support.

Despite naysayers, some librarians have responded to the public's demand and started game collections. These librarians realize that games are a part of our culture and, as such, should be collected for their users' benefit. Libraries have a duty to provide materials for their users to be informed citizens. Many might say games don't count, whereas Sandy Farmer explains that entire conversations take place in society today that revolve around the cultural references that occur in games.[14] Providing access to these games allows users without home access to understand these references and participate in this part of culture. Library game collections still cause some controversy; however, the benefits of games and gaming are developing day by day. Game collections are merely another resource for the edification and leisure of library patrons.

Public Libraries and Gaming

Games and gaming fit the mission of many public libraries, which is to support the public's information and learning needs. Public libraries support these needs in many different ways. For example, The Mechanics' Institute Library of San Francisco has been supporting the public by hosting a chess club since 1854.[6] Public libraries are not only playing chess but are expanding to include other types of games and gaming programs in their libraries. Public library game programs exist for all ages. John Pappas at The Primos Library in Secane, Philadelphia, began a Golden Gamers Group for gamers aged 65+. Board games provide these gamers with a social experience that is also interactive and engaging.[15] Patrons at the Bainbridge Library in Bainbridge Island, Washington, get to solve a Murder Mystery, searching for clues throughout the library. Audrey Barbakoff initiated this type of game to help bring in a more diverse crowd and this program met its goal.[16] Gaming programs can be developed to cater to an individual library's needs.

Who is gaming in public libraries? In a survey from 2007, when the question was asked very broadly to include hosting a chess club or allowing web-based games to be played on public computers, the results were that 77% of public libraries support gaming. Nearly half of these libraries hosted gaming programs. 90% of the formal programming used board games, with 45% of this group noting the games were traditional games such as chess. Almost a quarter of libraries with game collections included console games, and a much smaller group, 7%, included computer games. Card games, other than those considered traditional such as Bridge, were used 19% of the time, with role-playing games being used 4% of the time.[17]

Some of these libraries support the in-house use of games as well as circulating them. Twenty percent of public libraries surveyed in 2007 circulated games, with board and card games being the most circulated types of games. These libraries also circulated computer games, puzzles, and console games.[17] In 2008, the Houston Public Library started circulating video games, controllers, and consoles. They estimate the average cost to be about $1 per library customer.[14] These circulating collections give patrons a chance to try out new games when they would not be otherwise able to do so because of costs or availability.

Games and gaming are a natural fit for public libraries. Public libraries have shown that games are a valuable part of their collection as well as a great resource for event programming. Thoughtful use of a library game collection can encourage collaboration and communities through play.

Games in School Libraries

Like in public libraries, games have been a fixture in public schools for years. Nicholson notes in his article,

"Playing in the past: a history of games, Toys, and Puzzles in North American Libraries," that various other libraries and library associations have encouraged the use of games to facilitate learning. The use of games in libraries was included in a guide published by the ALA in 1920 because games stimulate an interest in reading. Another *School Library Journal* article in 1979 promoted developing learning games.[17] The interest in using games and gaming for educational goals, like games themselves, is having a resurgence. This renewed interest is due to technology, new designer games, and recent changes in educational goals.

How are public schools using games? Scott Nicholson surveyed librarians to gather a census of gaming programs and practices in 2007. Of the 314 responses, 78 were school media libraries. Thirty percent of these school media libraries circulated games, with the majority, 19%, being board games. Nine percent circulated PC games and 3% circulated Nintendo, PlayStation, or Xbox console games. Web-based games were allowed in half of these school media libraries. Thirty-two percent of these libraries only allowed educational games, but 17% allowed recreational games during free periods. This survey also gathered data on the programs being offered in the school media libraries. Half of the programs were educational and half recreational. Problems with noise, space, and supervision were noted as being limitations for recreational school gaming programs.[18]

As the survey shows, school libraries are using games, but not to their full potential. School librarians, with the right resources, can help educators meet educational goals with games and gaming. Brian Mayer and Christopher Harris are two educators who are actively involved in integrating tabletop games into the classroom curriculum in their school district. They believe that using games, especially the new Eurogames, require students to explore, learn, and act on what they have learned. They often must gather information from several sources to be successful.[19] Many games can be aligned with the learning standards and outcomes while also allowing collaboration and cooperation among players. In classrooms, gameplay is often used as a reward; it can also function as a valuable part of the lesson. Games can be used, much like fiction is used in English classes, as a part of daily instruction to enhance learning and provide historical context.[19]

In the article "Three different paths for tabletop gaming in school libraries," three school librarians detail how they are using games educationally as well as recreationally to benefit their students. The first school, a high school in the United Kingdom, took the path of starting an after school board game club called "Unplugged." This club offers a haven for students. It allows them the benefit of team building and socializing with their peers.[20] Tabletop gaming clubs, for many librarians, is one of the easier ways to start a games and gaming collection because of the minimal costs and labor involved at the outset. A successful afterschool club confirms the benefits of gaming to educators and school administrators. This small step can lead to the start of a library game collection and eventually to the successful integration of games into classroom learning.

The second path is to have students act out a game of the "Trials of Socrates," based on the role-playing game series developed by Barnard College called "Reacting to the Past." To be successful in this game, students must study the time period, read The Iliad and The Odyssey, and hone their debate skills. These students learn by role-playing a character. They immerse themselves in a role with a background, alliances, and goals. The teacher acts as the game master. This type of learning through role-playing has led to the students and teachers becoming more creative. After this success, some of the teachers wrote a role-playing scenario to teach about the "Salem Witch Trials." This school also offers the students an opportunity to create their own games.[20]

The third path is to build a comprehensive library collection that aligns with state and national learning standards to help teach students through play. Brian Mayer, the specialist who curates this collection, actively facilitates gameplay in the classroom. This allows him to grow the collection to align with learning standards and incorporate life skills, such as fine motor skills, social skills, and problem-solving.[20] All three of these paths are beneficial to students; however, it requires buy-in from students and staff. The first step is always hardest and the same holds true for introducing games and gaming to an institution.

Information literacy can be developed using games. Digital citizenship, a form of information literacy for responsible participation in a networked society, is taught to students in schools using Minecraft. The virtual world, MinecraftEdu, was created in 2011 to help support learning. Students collaborate, communicate, and engage with each other in this world. Their virtual interactions inherently lead to virtual offenses and conflicts. This facilitated and monitored play allows these students to learn suitable online behaviors under the guidance of a teacher in an environment with minimal consequences.[21]

There are still obstacles for game collections in schools. The value of a game for use in a curriculum is measured by its educational components. Many games produced for the education market are lacking in their ability to engage users. This is because the educational value of a game cannot be determined by the label but by what the player brings and takes away from the game. Mass market games and even independent games can be educational because many of these games incorporate good learning principles, such as strategic thinking and problem-solving.[22] These games usually succeed where games designed with educational goals fail because they grab the buyer's attention and keep it to stay profitable. Many popular games motivate the user by offering challenges that require learning and research to be an effective player. These games have communities and wikis that discuss strategy, include statistical analysis of attributes for each class, expand on the lore or history of the game, and much more. Players are building up skills and literacies as they accomplish the game's goals.[23] Many games developed purely for the educational market are still falling short of their educational goal because they are skill and drill games. They are more palatable but often do not offer the user a chance to be a creative and innovative problem solver.[24] This is not to say that games designed to be educational should be ignored; however, librarians should look at all genres of games to find suitable items for their school library collection.

The use of facilitated and guided play using games and gaming in schools is valuable for students as they move through a world of technological and social change. The benefit of play is that it gives students a chance to learn from their mistakes and improve on their strategies as they encounter their world, both real and virtual, without worldly consequences. School librarians are seeing success in their integration of games into learning. This will continue to grow as students, teachers, and administrators become more comfortable with this media.

Games in Academic Libraries

Games and gaming collections in academic libraries have a slower growth than in public and school libraries. It's gaining momentum and acceptance as the need for research into games and their social impact grows. Academic libraries are starting to build collections to support research, programs that use games in their curriculum, as well as for student recreation and retention.

Do games belong in an academic library? The growth of games and gaming in society and as an industry has spurred several academic libraries to begin a collection to support its study and research. Laskowski and Ward note what issues need to be explored while building a video game collection in their paper, "Building next generation video game collections in academic libraries." They include the following as the main issues to explore, determining what students, instructors, and researchers need for their work: purchasing the appropriate hardware to support the required formats, navigating the software and licensing issues related to video games, and providing appropriate library support.[25] This type of collection development is dependent on the technology changes and evolution of video games and their platforms, whether PC or console. The amount of technology support in the library is important to the collection's goals. Without the appropriate technology, a collection will not be usable. Sustainability of game's accessibility and collection goals should be taken into account with all purchases and donations.[26]

Technology, digital rights management, and computer security on college campuses are big concerns for a video game collection. The technology related to games, like other digital technology, is in constant flux, so new hardware, formats, and digital updates are always on the horizon. Access to games is limited by digital rights management that the manufacturer includes and security networks on the campus or in the library. The viability of a digital game collection in a library is vulnerable to many factors out of their control. Despite these odds, academic libraries are building leisure and educational collections on their campuses.

Not only is the technology and accessibility of games changing, but the types of courses that might use games in the curriculum is changing fairly rapidly as well. Computer science programs with classes in game design will probably benefit from use of a collection; however, programs that use games exist in other academic departments as well, such as art and design, music composition programs, communications, and mass media. As the research in games and the culture that surrounds it changes, the library collection needs to change as well.

Tabletop games should not be overlooked when building an academic game collection. These games are generally much easier to collect than video games. However, they do bring their own set of issues as do other nonbook formats. A tabletop collection is a great way to introduce games and gaming into the library without the technology and digital rights management issues of video games. If the library does not have sufficient technology or administrative support for a video game collection, a successful tabletop collection can garner positive attention and eventually draw support for a video game collection. Small, successful steps are better than big fails for a gaming collection.

For most academic libraries, a gaming collection is much more than just a research resource; it can also be used for library programming and outreach. Library outreach seeks to introduce students to library services and help with retention—especially among first-year students—by building a sense of community. Library space is not limited to particular departments, so students from diverse programs can use it to meet and work together. Libraries with gaming collections and programming are particularly well suited for community building. Most gameplay includes social elements either through cooperative and collaborative play or discussion around single-player games. Gaming is like electricity for some college students today. It has always been a part of their lives even if they didn't actively take part in gaming while growing up.[27] With a little help from residence life coordinators, campus student groups, and social media, librarians can create a physical, social space for gaming in the library. The space alone may not help with retention, but it provides a level environment for interactions between faculty and students. These informal interactions can nurture a sense of belonging and self-worth.[28] All of these feelings are integral to building community and ultimately increasing retention. An enthusiastic librarian or staff member that encourages play can easily accomplish this kind of fun, safe space.

Gaming, teaching, technology, and research are rapidly evolving, and there is much to do to support research related to games. Academic libraries have an opportunity to move beyond collection building and into actively participating and collaborating in this interdisciplinary field.[25]

Digital Preservation

Another aspect of games in libraries is the preservation and collection of digital data related to video games. Many academic libraries have digital repositories that include collections of digital objects. The digital objects include audio, visual, and text items. These repositories are capturing items from the past as well as current projects to aid researchers. The Game Preservation Special Interest Group of the International Game Developers Association has a white paper, "Before it's too late: a digital game preservation white paper," addressing the need to preserve electronic games.[29]

Gaming enthusiasts with the technical expertise to convert games have emulated older games as a form of preservation, but with no regard for the rights of the creator. One of the largest old game collections is hosted on the Internet Archive. Part of the Internet Archives goal is to be "a searchable memory of society, and not just for scholars this time, but everyone".[30] This has led them to provide access to classic arcade, console, and computer games on their software website at https://archive.org/details/software. These games are emulated to work in an Internet browser. Although the Internet Archive does not own the rights to these games, the Electronic Frontier Foundation is working to make it legal for older abandoned games to be modified by fans to remain playable.[31]

Academic Libraries have their part to play in the preservation of games. Professional preservationists in libraries and museums are beginning to see the need to gather games and gaming data in their local repositories to aid in the preservation of gaming culture and history.[3] Librarians can aid in the preservation of games by encouraging scholars and students to add copies of their digital game data to a university repository for preservation and research purposes.

Creating Games in Libraries

A number of librarians have created games for use by library patrons. There are two main reasons librarians will create a game: for outreach purposes and for instruction. Outreach games, such as murder mysteries or scavenger hunts, can help students and library patrons become comfortable with the library and hopefully cause them to visit the library more often in the future.

Public libraries hold outreach events, such as murder mysteries for adults or literature-themed events, like Hunger Games for teens. These events are fun in nature and used to help promote the library as a community place where community events can be held.[32] The Daring Librarian shares an example of having students complete a QR Codes Quest (or scavenger hunt) to help them become familiar with library services at the school library.[33]

Academic libraries can hold scavenger hunts as a fun way to help first-year students learn about the library during an orientation period. For example, the University of South Carolina Upstate invited first-year students to complete a photo scavenger hunt using the social media site of their choice and tagging the library in their photos.[34] This is one of the promoted events during their orientation week. Students seem to enjoy taking selfies or photos of their new friends throughout the library. Some academic libraries make use of the murder mystery theme. The University of North Carolina Chapel Hill held a Clue event night at their special library to help students become comfortable being in the library.[35] With Clue, a number of librarians helped out as different characters and provided participants with hints if they asked the right questions. Additionally, students looked in different parts of the library for additional hints.

These outreach events can take time to prepare, but are usually successful with patrons. There are websites where murder mysteries can be purchased for use in libraries, but librarians can design their own murder mysteries from scratch. Lycoming College held a Harry Potter–themed night for students with activities and games designed around the books for a number of years and this was quite successful with the students.[36] This event was planned with the assistance of a number of librarians and faculty across campus. Assistants played different Harry Potter characters, as well as helping come up with games and activities.

One final type of outreach game that can be held in the library are large-scale, live-action games, such as *Capture the Flag* or *Humans versus Zombies*. These are events held inside libraries, often after the library is regularly closed, when large numbers of students can participate and have physical activities, such as using nerf guns to "kill" the zombies.[37] At large universities, these types of large-scale events can bring hundreds of students to the library.

Instruction is an important part of academic librarianship in addition to school librarianship. Quite a few librarians started creating their own games with instructional goals. While the outreach games and events have an instructional component, the major purpose of these events is having fun in the library. There are a number of ways to create games for instructional purposes: the easiest being a board game and the most advanced being a digital game or web application.

The University of South Carolina uses a board game as an exit activity. After an instruction session, the game is played for a quick review of the material covered during class.[38] The librarians used a map of the library that existed and added some numbers at key locations of the library. Students then answered questions about each location on the board. The students who correctly answer questions at the seven locations can leave first.

This is a quick and easy way to use games for instructional purposes. Board games are useable in any type of library and do not have to be complicated to create. Similar to board games, gamification can be used during library sessions. Gamification is essentially using game elements to make things more fun and engaging. For example, Kahoot! is a recent quiz tool that creates multiple-choice questions to give students a gamified review of material. The game elements of Kahoot! include a timer, sound effects, images, and score-keeping (https://getkahoot.com/). More gamification tools will likely become available in the not-too-distant future.

One of the best and most used digital games created by a librarian is *Goblin Threat* by Mary J. Snyder Broussard at Lycoming College (http://www.lycoming.edu/library/instruction/tutorials/plagiarismGame.aspx). Mary allowed a number of librarians to use her game in their classes to help students avoid plagiarism. When playing *Goblin Threat*, students must answer questions about plagiarism correctly to make the goblins disappear and save the university. The librarians at the University of South Carolina Upstate used this game as a fun final activity for students during their plagiarism prevention workshops and students often listed this as their favorite activity.

The University of South Carolina Upstate has created an Agoge Game based on the journey of becoming a Spartan to fit the university's mascot of Sparty, the Spartan (http://agoge.uscupstate.edu/agoge/agogegame.html). This game is based on Goblin Threat in its layout with multiple levels, answering questions correctly to advance, and a score. Music and images are included to create a more game-like atmosphere. Throughout the game, the warrior gains more armor and weapons after completing each level until they are a Spartan. This game was geared toward transfer students to test their information literacy skills. As an instructional tool, the game has embedded videos and screenshots of various library tools to help students who wish to learn more about the library.

The Game Making Interest Group within the Library and Information Technology Association of the ALA has a wiki that contains a wealth of game-making information (http://gamemakinginterestgroup.wikispaces.com). There are suggestions for incorporating games into instruction, as well as game creation best practices. A number of library game examples are included with links to more information and suggested readings (including books and articles about games in libraries and creating games). *Games in Libraries: Essays on Using Play to Connect and Instruct,* edited by Breanne A. Kirsch, provides more information about a number of the games discussed in this entry and suggestions on creating a library game.

CONCLUSION

Games and gaming in all types of libraries are evolving along with the gaming market and its consumers. Technology development will undoubtedly challenge libraries while educational changes will provide guidance. Librarians show that games, like any other media, have a recognizable cultural influence and deserve a space in libraries as a beneficial collection to students, scholars, and the community.

ACKNOWLEDGMENT

The authors would like to acknowledge Dr. Scott Nicholson and Mary J. Snyder Broussard for all of their scholarship and guidance related to games and gaming in libraries.

REFERENCES

1. Maroney, K. My entire waking life. Games J. **2001**, http://www.thegamesjournal.com/articles/MyEntireWakingLife.shtml (accessed February 2015).
2. Juul, J. In *The game, the player, the world: Looking for a heart of gameness*, Level Up: Digital Games Research Conference Proceedings, Utrecht, the Netherlands, 2003; Copier, M., Raessens, C., Eds.; Utrecht University: Utrecht, Netherlands, 2003. http://www.jesperjuul.net/text/gameplayerworld/ (accessed February 2015).
3. Barwick, J.; Dearnley, J.; Muir, A. Playing games with cultural heritage: a comparative case study analysis of the current status of digital game preservation. Games Cult. **2011**, *6* (4), 373–390. doi: 10.1177/1555412010391092 (accessed January 2015).
4. Csikszentmihalyi, M. In *Some paradoxes in the definition of play*. Play as Context: 1979 Proceedings of the Association for the Anthropological Study of Play; Cheska, A.T., Ed.; Leisure Press: West Point, NY, 1981.
5. Levy, L.; Novak, J. *Part 1: The Basics; Play the Game: The Parent's Guide to Video Games*; Course Technology/Cengage Learning: Boston, MA, 2007.
6. Nicholson, S. Playing in the past: a history of games, toys, and puzzles in North American libraries. Libr. Q. **2013**, *83* (4), 341–361. http://www.jstor.org/stable/10.1086/671913 (accessed February 2015).
7. The Entertainment Software. Association *Industry facts— The Entertainment Software Association*. http://www.theesa.com/about-esa/industry-facts/ (accessed February 2015).
8. McGonigal, J. Introduction. In *Reality Is Broken: Why Games Make Us Better and How They Can Change the World*, updated edition; Penguin Group: New York, 2011.
9. Duffy, O. Board games' golden age: Sociable, brilliant and driven by the Internet. The Guardian 2014. http://www.theguardian.com/technology/2014/nov/25/board-games-internet-playstation-xbox (accessed February 2015).
10. Hayes, E. Leisure role of public libraries: a historical perspective. J. Librariansh. Inf. Sci. **2005**, *37* (2), 75–81. doi:10.1177/0961000605055358 (accessed February 2015).
11. Sturges, P.; Barr, A. The fiction nuisance' in nineteenth-century British public libraries. J. Librariansh. Inf. Sci. **1992**, *24* (1), 23–32. doi:10.1177/096100069202400104 (accessed February 2015).
12. Kirriemuir, J. The librarian as video game player. N. Rev. Inf. Network. **2006**, *12* (1/2), 61–75. doi:10.1080/13614570701198262 (accessed January 2015).
13. Gee, J.P. *Good Video Games + Good Learning: Collected Essays on Video Games, Learning and Literacy*, 2nd Ed.; Peter Lang: New York, 2013.
14. Farmer, S. Gaming 2.0. Amer. Libr. Mag. **2010**, *41* (11), 32–34, http://americanlibrariesmagazine.org/2010/10/19/gaming-2-0/(accessed February 2015).
15. Pappas, J. The golden gamers: A 65 Library Gaming Group. Slideshare.net. 2014, http://www.slideshare.net/mesodma/the-golden-gamers-a-65-library-gaming-group (accessed February 2015).
16. Sooter, T. Bainbridge Librarian Earns National Attention for Efforts to Draw in Younger Adults. BSUN 2013, http://www.kitsapsun.com/news/local-news/bainbridge-librarian-earns-national-attention-to (accessed January 2015).
17. Nicholson, S. Go back to start: gathering baseline data about gaming in libraries. Libr. Rev. **2009**, *58* (3), 203–214.
18. Nicholson, S. Finish your games so you can start your schoolwork: a look of gaming in school libraries. Libr. Media Connect. **2008**, *26* (5), 52–55.
19. Mayer, B.; Harris, C. *Libraries Got Game Aligned Learning through Modern Board Games*; American Library Association: Chicago, IL, 2010.
20. Copeland, T.; Henderson, B.; Mayer, B.; Nicholson, S. Three different paths for tabletop gaming in school libraries. Libr. Trends **2013**, *61* (4), 825–835.
21. Waniewski, B. In this Minecraft classroom digital citizenship 101 is the topic of play. Fast Company **2012**, http://www.fastcompany.com/3003185/minecraft-classroom-digital-citizenship-101-topic-play (accessed February 2015).
22. Gee, J.P. Good video games and good learning. Phi Kappa Phi Forum, **2005**, *85* (2), 33–37. http://search.proquest.com/docview/235184729 (accessed January 2015).
23. Nicholson, S. *Everyone Plays at the Library: Creating Great Gaming Experiences for All Ages*; Information Today: Medford, CT, 2010.
24. Gee, J.P. *Good Video Games + Good Learning Collected Essays on Video Games, Learning and Literacy*, 2nd Ed.; Peter Lang: New York, 2013.
25. Laskowski, M.; Ward, D. Building next generation video game collections in academic libraries. J. Acad. Libr. **2009**, *35* (3), 267–273. doi:10.1016/j.acalib.2009.03.005 (accessed January 2015).
26. Robson, D.; Durkee, P. New directions for academic video game collections: strategies for acquiring, supporting, and managing online materials. J. Acad. Libr. **2012**, *38* (2), 79–84. doi:10.1016/j.acalib.2012.01.003 (accessed February 2015).
27. Levine, J. Case studies: academic libraries. Libr. Technol. Rep. **2006**, *42* (5), 38–44. http://search.proquest.com/docview/202708706 (accessed January 2015).
28. Kuh, G.D. The other curriculum: out-of-class experiences associated with student learning and personal development. J. High. Educ. **1995**, *66* (2), 123–155. http://www.jstor.org/stable/2943909 (accessed February 2015).
29. Monnens, D.; Vowell, Z.; Ruggill, J.E.; McAllister, K.S.; Armstrong, A. Before it's too late: a digital game preservation white paper. J. Play **2009**, http://www.journalofplay.org/sites/www.journalofplay.org/files/pdf-articles/2-2-special-feature-

digital-game-preservation-white-paper.pdf (accessed January 2015).

30. Brand, S. Future libraries—how people envision using Internet libraries. Internet Arch. **2014**, https://archive.org/about/ (accessed January 2015).

31. Newman, L.H. In *Rehabbing abandoned video games should be legal*, Slate 2014, http://www.slate.com/blogs/future_tense/2014/11/05/electronic_frontier_foundation_is_petitioning_to_put_abandoned_video_games.html (accessed February 2015).

32. Ward, H. Creating a literary gaming experience. In *Games in Libraries: Essays on Using Play to Connect and Instruct*; Kirsch, B.A., Ed.; McFarland & Company, Inc.: Jefferson, NC, 2014.

33. Jones, G. QR code quest scavenger hunt—Part deux!. The Daring Librarian. 2012, http://www.thedaringlibrarian.com/2012/05/qr-code-quest-scavenger-hunt-part-deux.html (accessed February 2015).

34. University of South Carolina Upstate Library. The great Spartan search: Monday, August 16, 2014, University of South Carolina Upstate Library Facebook Page 2014.

https://www.facebook.com/media/set/?set=a.10152302748360924.1073741829.49369060923&type=1 (accessed February 2015).

35. Jack, E.; McMichael, J. In the library with the candlestick: adapting Clue for the special collections library. In *Games in Libraries: Essays on Using Play to Connect and Instruct*; Kirsch, B.A., Ed.; McFarland & Company, Inc.: Jefferson, NC, 2014.

36. Snyder Broussard, M.J. No muggles in the library tonight! Harry Potter night at an academic library. Libr. Trends **2013**, *61* (4), 814. doi:10.1353/lib.2013.0017 (accessed February 2015).

37. Womack, H.; Smith, S.S.; Lock, M.B. Large-scale, live-action gaming events in academic libraries: how and why. Coll. Res. Libr. News, **2015**, http://crln.acrl.org/content/76/4/210.full (accessed September 2015).

38. Edwards, A.; Simmons, T. Your attention please!: Keeping the attention of your generation Y students. Presentation at the *Annual Conference of the South Carolina Library Association*, Columbia, SC, October 22, 2014.

Genealogical Literature and Its Users

Mavis B. Molto
Utah State University, Logan, Utah, U.S.A.

Abstract

Genealogical literature is the body of writings on genealogy, which is the study of ancestry and descent. This entry describes the history of genealogy, the users of genealogical literature, and the procedures and resources used in genealogical research. The steps in genealogical research consist broadly of a preliminary survey to identify what is already known about one's ancestors, using compiled sources, and then verifying and extending what is known, using original sources. A discussion of both compiled and original sources, along with reference tools and periodical, news, and networking sources, is included. Tables are presented outlining the major resources available in each of these areas, including resources for specific countries. Both print and online resources are identified.

INTRODUCTION

Definitions

Genealogical literature is the body of writings on genealogy, which in turn is the study of ancestry and descent. The term "genealogy" is sometimes used interchangeably with "family history." Powell explains the difference as follows:

"Genealogy, the study of ancestry and descent, refers more to the actual search for ancestors, while family history, the narrative of the events in your ancestors' lives, denotes the telling of your family's story. Family history is genealogy come alive."[1]

This entry will focus on the literature and resources that are used to identify one's ancestors (i.e., names, and dates and places of birth, death, and marriage), though some of the resources discussed may also include the additional information one may want to know in writing a detailed family history.

Interest in Genealogy and Expansion of the Literature

Genealogy is the second most popular hobby in the United States, after gardening, according to an ABC News report.[2] Polls show a steadily increasing interest among Americans in tracing their family history, with 60% "somewhat interested" in 2000 and 73% "interested" in 2005.[3] A study commissioned by Ancestry.com in 2014 found "Over the past decade, online family history research has grown in the United States by 14 times, with two-thirds (63%) of respondents in a recent study reporting that family history has become more important than ever."[4]

The increasing interest in genealogy is also evident in the growing number of theses and dissertations being written on various aspects of the genealogical literature and its users, with several examples discussed later.

Crandall, in the foreword to *Printed Sources*, describes the growing literature that is now available for genealogical research due to the increasing interest in genealogy:

"Genealogists are now much more numerous and genealogy much more popular than at any time in our national history. As this interest has proceeded, many authors and compilers have added immensely to the fast-growing multitude of printed sources for every kind of genealogy—compiled family or local histories, multi-ancestor works, new periodicals, guidebooks, printed source records, bibliographies, indexes, and reference works."[5]

Meyerink adds the following concerning the genealogical literature:

"... [There] has been an explosion of printed genealogical sources. Every day several new books are published by and for genealogists; some major genealogical publishers release three or more new books and reprints *every week*."[6]

He notes further:

"Although research methodology does not change rapidly, and original records are much the same as they were twenty or more years ago, there have been many changes in printed sources. In 1975 there were very few census indexes. The limited number of transcribed records meant limited access for the research. There were no computer programs or databases for family historians. Bibliographies and other research tools were fewer and much older than they are today."[6]

Overview

This entry consists of a description of the history of genealogy, the users of genealogical literature, and the procedures and resources used in genealogical research. A discussion of both compiled and original sources, along with reference tools and periodical, news, and networking sources, follows.

Encyclopedia of Library and Information Sciences, Fourth Edition DOI: 10.1081/E-ELIS4-120053703

HISTORY

Antiquity (to 1500)

A short history of genealogy is found in an article by Potter-Phillips, describing the keeping of genealogies in various ages, starting with Biblical times. References to genealogies are found in both the Old and New Testaments. The ancient Greeks, Assyrians, Egyptians, and Chinese also kept genealogies. Genealogies have been kept by many native peoples, including African clans, Maori and Inca peoples, and the North American Indians. During the Middle Ages in Europe, proving one's descent was required to claim the privileges of the nobility and gentry.[7]

Beginning of Record Keeping and Modern Interest (1500s to Mid-1800s)

The ancient genealogies were frequently fragmentary and unreliable. In modern times, laws have been established in various countries requiring that records be kept of birth, marriage, and death, which in turn provides the documentation needed to construct accurate genealogies.[7] However, even through the nineteenth century there were errors and lack of proof in genealogies because records were difficult to locate and examine.[8]

The following are some important events in the development of record keeping in the United States and Europe:

- 1538—In Britain, an edict from King Henry VIII required that ministers keep records of christenings, baptisms, marriages, and burials.
- Mid-1500s—The lands that later became Germany began keeping records similar to the British records, and the Scandinavian countries followed.
- 1630s—In the American colonies, civil records were required in the General Assembly of Virginia in 1632 and in the Massachusetts Bay Colony in 1639.
- 1837—Civil registration began in Britain.[7]

The first known genealogy in the United States was prepared in 1698: Pedigree of the Byrd family (at the Virginia Historical Society in Richmond).[9] Genealogy, however, has not always been popular in the United States, due to the societies from which the early colonizers came. Traditions of inheritance and caste had denied them opportunities in achieving success, thus they often wanted to forget their heritage. Also, the early pioneers did not have the time required to do the research to identify their ancestors.[8]

Rise of Organized Genealogical Endeavors (Mid-1800s to Early 1900s)

Bockstruck proposes that the beginning of genealogical research and publication in the United States occurred in the 1840s,[9] with Bidlack noting that the publication of

genealogical source materials did not begin until after the Civil War.[8] Wood describes the period 1848–1921 as a boom for genealogy.[10]

Important developments occurred in the mid- to late 1800s with regard to county histories and historical associations. The first county history in America was published in 1848, for the County of Westchester (New York). In 1876, a Joint Resolution of Congress recommended that each county prepare a historical sketch to present on the centennial anniversary of the nation's independence, with copies to be filed in the county clerk's office and the office of the Librarian of Congress.[9] In the latter half of the nineteenth century, historical associations were established in towns, counties, and states, and provided help in recording and preserving the local history.[8] Key events regarding the historical associations include

- 1845—New England Historic Genealogical Society was founded,[9] first genealogical society in the world.[7]
- 1876—American Centennial stimulated the formation of patriotic societies and interest in looking back.[8]
- 1876—Sons of the Revolution was organized in New York, first patriotic organization in America.[9]
- 1903—National Genealogical Society was founded, in Washington, District of Columbia.[9]

Scientific Genealogy and Growing Interest (Early 1900s–1969)

Mills reviews the history of genealogy, with a focus on the development of standards and scholarship. She describes various movements in genealogical scholarship and the emergence of "scientific" genealogy in the 1930s. The school of "scientific" genealogists was led by Donald Lines Jacobus (1887–1970), the father of American genealogy.[11] Jacobus was the first American to make his living as a genealogist, for which he gained entry to Who's Who in America for his accomplishments.[8] He established standards of genealogical scholarship[11] and published important genealogical guides and reference materials, including

- 1930—Genealogy as Pastime and Profession, the first real guide for the beginner in family history[8]
- 1933—Is genealogy an exact science?[12]
- 1932–1953—Index to Genealogical Periodicals[9]

Wood notes that prior to the 1970s organized genealogical research in North America tended to be a pastime for the white Euro-North American upper classes.[10] Both of the world wars, however, promoted an interest in genealogy among Americans, as soldiers found themselves in the lands of their ancestors.[8] After 1945, with the growing interest in genealogy, there was an increase in the number of hereditary societies[9] and an increase in genealogical source materials. Bidlack attributes the latter to the large number of people involved, along with the impact of technology, including offset printing, microfilm, copying machines, and, later, computers.[8]

Wood describes the 1950s as the beginning of modern genealogy.[10] Mills notes the establishment of several important organizations, beginning in 1940, which fostered the growth of standards and scholarship in the United States:[11]

> 1940—American Society of Genealogists, recognized as the field's scholastic honor society
> 1950—National Institute for Genealogical Research, based at the National Archives
> 1964—Samford University's Institute of Genealogy and Historical Research
> 1964—Board for Certification of Genealogists, created in Washington, District of Columbia, to establish standards and a register of qualified genealogists[8]

Genealogical Research Comes of Age (1969–1980s)

In 1969, the World Conference on Records, sponsored by the Church of Jesus Christ of Latter-day Saints (LDS Church), was held. This event promoted scholarship in genealogical research, as did the succeeding conference in 1980.[8] Filby, Kaminkow, and others published important reference works during this period, including

> 1970—*American and British Genealogy and Heraldry*, by P. William Filby (ALA)[9]
> 1972—*Genealogies in the Library of Congress: A Bibliography*, edited by Marion J. Kaminkow (Magna Carta Book Co.)[9]

In 1976, Alex Haley's book, *Roots: The Saga of an American Family*, was published and the popular television drama based on it began in 1977. Both stimulated interest in family history among a wider range of people, including minority groups.[10] Patrons at genealogical and historical libraries doubled and tripled during the 1970s,[8] including a 70% increase in use, in 1979, by genealogists at the National Archives and Records Administration.[10]

Prior to 1980, the image of genealogy was poor, since genealogy was often performed for exclusion and the promotion of social ambition. Changes in the 1980s prompted American historian Samuel P. Hays to maintain that a "new genealogy" had emerged. Wood, in a thesis, examines the "new genealogy" over the period 1969–2004, noting "a significant shift in the characteristics of genealogical research in North America at least" during this period. Characteristics of the new genealogy included:[10]

> More focus on archival research by those outside the social elites.

Interest in family history among a wider range of people.

Interest in more than illustrious or elite ancestral ties.

Interest in the historical context in which the family lived.

Flourishing of genealogical societies, publications, and codes of ethics.

Adoption of the Internet as a major research tool.

Improvement in the relationship between archivists and genealogists.

Genealogical research becoming the basis of media reports, plays, and books.

Genealogical research becoming an important aspect of medical care.

The Internet and Digitization (1990s–2000s)

The Internet and digitization have played major roles in developments pertaining to genealogy in the 1990s and on. Crandall notes that: "…CD-ROMs and the Internet … will not so much replace the older literature as place it in a new format."[5] Following are some of the genealogical websites established during the 1990s to early 2000s (see Table 1 for further details):

> 1993—RootsWeb
> 1996—Cyndi's List
> 1996—WorldGenWeb Project
> 1997—Ancestry.com
> 1999—FamilySearch
> 1999—Heritage Quest
> 2003—Linkpendium (beta version)
> 2005—MyHeritage

Over 40 million hits were received at the FamilySearch website on its first day of operation in 1999.[10] As the popularity of the genealogical websites has grown, so has the interest in building family trees online and in sharing the trees within families and communities. Sites that provide these capabilities include Ancestry.com, MyHeritage, and FamilySearch (see Table 1).

As the genealogical websites have evolved, so have efforts to digitize resources. Digitization, the process of converting data or an image to digital form,[13] is making possible the display of genealogical records on the Internet. Partnerships have been developed with genealogical providers to digitize extensive collections of genealogical materials. Several recent digitization projects are described below.

FamilySearch, a major player in the digitization efforts, announced partnerships in early 2014 with several commercial providers. Agreements were reached with Ancestry.com, Findmypast, and MyHeritage. The partnerships are seen as a way to accelerate digitization and to deal with the staggering amount of material needing digitization, as noted in the following:[14]

Table 1 General resources

Category	Title	Content and URL ($ = fee-based)
Directories—Intl.	Cyndi's List	http://www.cyndislist.com —Search by (1) category (place or topic), (2) keyword —Original directory of genealogical links —Over 300,000 links
Directories—U.S. emphasis	Linkpendium	http://www.linkpendium.com —Search by (1) surnames worldwide, (2) localities in the U.S., U.K., and Ireland —Largest directory of genealogical links —Over 10 million links
Intl.	Ancestry.com fee-based some free access also in library ed.	$ http://www.ancestry.com —16 billion historical records (many digitized) —U.S. records (census, court, immigration, military, and vital records) —International records (U.K., Europe, Canada, more) —70 million family trees —Family tree-building tools, Ancestry Community, family/local histories, reference tools
Intl.	FamilySearch	https://familysearch.org —Hundreds of millions of individual birth, christening, or marriage dates for deceased individuals —Original records (census, immigration, military, naturalization, probate, and vital records) —User-submitted family group records and pedigrees —Wiki research guides, by place and topic
Intl.	Google	https://www.google.com —Search for names, places, records, maps, and translations, using the search guidelines below: —Tips for using Google in genealogy searches, at: http://www.searchforancestors.com/google/searchtips.html —Google for genealogy, at: http://www.cyndislist.com/google/google-for-genealogy

(Continued)

Table 1 General resources *(Continued)*

Category	Title	Content and URL ($ = fee-based)
Intl.	MyHeritage fee-based some free access also in library ed. (Ebsco)	$ http://www.myheritage.com —Search engine built specifically for genealogy, searches hundreds of major genealogy databases in a single query —7.7 billion historical records —39 million family trees —Family tree builder, message boards
Intl.	WorldGenWeb Project	http://www.worldgenweb.org —Resource and reference information for each country, along with a surname query feature
Intl.	WorldVitalRecords fee-based (moderate)	$ http://www.worldvitalrecords.com —Scanned and indexed state and country vital records, family histories, books, gazetteers, and maps. —U.S. small town newspapers (especially strong) —MyHeritage family trees
U.K., U.S.	Archives.com fee-based (moderate)	$ http://www.archives.com —4.8 billion photos, newspapers, vital records —How-to articles, tutorials, Ancestry Community
U.K., U.S., Pacific	FindMyPast fee-based	$ http://www.findmypast.com —Over 2 billion census, church, migration, military, and vital records —User-created family trees —How-to articles
U.S. emphasis	Heritage Quest Online fee-based library ed. only (ProQuest)	$ http://www.heritagequestonline.com —Genealogical information for America since the late 1700s —U.S. census images (1790–1940) —Family history books —Periodical Source Index (PERSI) —Revolutionary War records —U.S. Congressional Serial Set (from 1789) —American State Papers

"Notwithstanding the astounding success of the FamilySearch indexing program and the tireless dedication of hundreds of thousands of volunteers, it will still take many generations to index and publish just the records contained in FamilySearch's Granite Mountain Records Vault. This estimate does not account for the more than 35 million new images of records that are digitized each month—and that rate is increasing."[14]

Another significant partnership, between FamilySearch International and GenealogyBank, was announced on October 1, 2014. The two groups plan to make over a billion records from historical obituaries searchable online. This initiative has been described as the largest online U.S. historical record access initiative yet.[15]

Many important U.S. records are being digitized through partnerships developed by the National Archives and Records Administration (NARA) with Ancestry, Fold3, and FamilySearch. The partners are digitizing selected NARA microfilm and original records and making the records available on their websites, with free searching allowed on some or all of the index terms. Free access to the records is available in the NARA Research Rooms and regional archives and Presidential libraries.[16]

USERS OF GENEALOGICAL LITERATURE

Interest in Genealogy

Genealogical researchers have various reasons for their interest in genealogy. In earlier periods of time, the motivation for creating genealogies had to do with proving one's descent so as to claim special privileges or social recognition. In more recent times, some have done genealogical research because of an interest in history. Others have sought meaning in their lives by developing ties with those in the past and present. Genealogical research is also performed to identify missing heirs of estates and to learn about hereditary diseases.

Still others have religious reasons for identifying their ancestors. The following explanation of LDS beliefs is found on the FamilySearch Wiki: "Members of the Church [of Jesus Christ of Latter-day Saints] believe that the family can continue beyond the grave.... Members of the church also believe that their deceased ancestors can receive this blessing of being eternally united with their families. This can be accomplished when Church members make covenants in temples in behalf of their ancestors, who may accept these covenants in the spirit world if they so choose."[17]

Studies of User Behavior and Needs

Most previous studies of genealogical users, in the library and information science and archival literature, have focused on managerial issues rather than the information needs and behavior of the users. A growing number of studies and dissertations are now focusing on the information-seeking behavior of genealogists. Several studies are discussed here, with the findings summarized in the following five areas: 1) goals in genealogical research; 2) how genealogists search; 3) how genealogists learn; 4) how genealogists manage information; and 5) unmet needs of genealogists.

Goals in genealogical research: Yakel found no clear end goal in the genealogist's search for information.[18] "The ultimate need is not for a fact or date, but to create a longer narrative, connect with others in the past and present, and find coherence in one's own life." Self-identification and self-discovery are thus important dimensions of genealogical research.[18] Yakel and Torres found, further, that genealogists as seekers of meaning are "less invested in proving the truth of stories and records, but more in uncovering coherent narratives."[19]

Antcliff Tucker, in a related dissertation, investigated whether people use family history to explore and articulate a sense of cultural identity. It was verified that family history research develops a sense of cultural identity, through discovery of one's particular genealogy and through connecting with ancestral places and with a cultural group. Certain of the findings coincided with two of Yakel's findings, namely, 1) "participants need to know their ancestors beyond a list of names and dates" and 2) "participants need to find and understand their ancestors' stories."[20]

How genealogists search: Duff and Johnson identified three stages that are followed in genealogical research. In the first stage, genealogists gather names of their family members. In the second stage, they collect further details about the individuals. In these two stages, genealogists search by name and place, consult specific record forms for particular time periods, and search maps and gazetteers for names of localities in their area of research. The third and final stage involves finding out about the society and time period in which their ancestors lived.[21]

Darby and Clough also looked at the research process used by genealogists and family historians, but with a different focus. A model was developed to describe the stages of activity carried out during a person's lifelong family history research. The authors provide a multiphase view of the research process, showing "(1) the different research phases themselves; (b) the inter-relationship between phases; (c) distinct phase-specific behaviours; and (d) phase-specific resource preferences."[22]

Lucas, finally, in a dissertation focused more narrowly on how genealogists resolve problems, identified two distinct processes that are used. The two steps consist of 1) the location and selection of sources and 2) an information selection process for finding information in the sources. Once a problem is solved, new problems are identified and researched in an iterative process.[23]

How genealogists learn: Duff and Johnson found that genealogists learn from one another. They tend to rely on their own expertise but when help is needed they consult most frequently with colleagues. A strong network exists among genealogists, through associations developed in taking courses and attending genealogical society meetings and through newsletters.[21] Fulton, in a related study of amateur genealogists researching their Irish ancestry, confirmed the importance of networking. Fulton found that networking and information sharing among fellow genealogists is an important means for advancing one's research.[24] Yakel adds that genealogists and family historians turn to genealogical organizations for "education, celebration, and support." They also use Internet resources, such as online databases, chat rooms, LISTSERVs, and sites providing contact information for libraries and archives.[18]

How genealogists manage information: The way genealogists and family historians manage information, according to a study by Yakel, is tied to how they conceptualize their role. Three roles were identified: narrators (telling a story), archivists (creating an archive of the research findings), and navigators (creating pedigree charts). The organizational devices used include genealogical software, notebooks, loose-leaf binders, and narratives.[18]

Unmet needs of genealogists: Archives are organized by provenance or creator, but genealogists usually seek information concerning specific people. Duff and Johnson found that while expert genealogists have learned to use the provenance-based finding aids, the finding aids are a challenge for novice genealogists. Time constraints are also an issue for genealogists using archives. Professionals work on an hourly basis and need to find efficient ways to retrieve information in the archives. Nonprofessionals have concerns about the limited hours of service, especially in the evenings and on weekends.[21]

USE OF LIBRARY CATALOGS AND CLASSIFICATION

Library catalogs and classification systems are important tools in providing access to the genealogical literature. Several studies and projects describe the problems and needs of genealogists in the use of the library catalog, and subject and classification systems. Though some of the studies were done prior to the implementation of the online library catalog, the findings remain relevant since many of the cataloging rules are still the same. The findings are described here.

Problems genealogists have with the library catalog: Users of genealogical libraries have been studied to identify the problems they have with the library catalog. The problems that occurred with the highest frequency at the Genealogical Library (Utah), in a study by Dilts, concerned 1) call numbers, 2) indirect locality entries in the catalog, 3) subject headings; and 4) filing rules. It was found, further, that these problems were often related to 1) patron inexperience with the Library (or catalog system), 2) the patron's use of incorrect or incomplete data, and 3) poor or inadequate cataloging.[25]

Bibliographic elements of most use to genealogists: In another study, by Johnson, patrons at the Genealogical Library (Utah) identified the following bibliographic elements as needed or helpful, each having a combined percentage of 90% or more: title, author, illustrations, content notes, bibliographic references, index notes, and locality tracings. It was concluded that the existing catalog should be replaced with an abbreviated short entry catalog, since most patrons did not understand the more detailed catalog entries.[26]

Analytic entry needs of genealogists: Sowers describes a project that identified how users approached research at the Kansas State Library. It was found they were often looking for specific information on individuals, events, institutions, etc. Subject access in the library catalog, however, was very broad. Following an experiment to create analytic entries in the catalog, for articles from the journal *Kansas History*, there was an immediate increase in the use of the articles and in interlibrary loan requests for the articles. The analytic entries provided access to the specific information the users were seeking.[27]

Subject access needs of genealogists: Genealogists often seek information on the county level. To meet this need, the Rowan Public Library (North Carolina) added county-level headings, along with relevant subdivisions, to the library catalog, for example: "Wilkes County (N.C.)—Marriage records." These headings complemented the authorized LCSH headings, for example: "Marriage records—North Carolina—Wilkes County."[28] With both kinds of headings in the catalog, access for the users was greatly improved.

Classification needs of genealogists: Genealogists have a need to browse library shelves by geographic area. The Rowan Public Library (North Carolina) designed a new classification for the History Room collection to accommodate this need, with materials arranged by geographic area and then by subject content, for example: KS KIN .34 [Kansas, Kingman County, marriage records]. In interviews, following the change, users said they liked the ease of use of the new system and being able to find materials for a county grouped together.[28]

PROCEDURES IN GENEALOGICAL RESEARCH

Genealogical research is performed to identify and learn about one's ancestors. Some researchers are satisfied with creating only a pedigree chart, showing their line of descent, with names, dates, and places of their ancestors' births, deaths, and marriages. Other researchers want to learn more, including information about their ancestors' occupations, education, moves, and religious beliefs. In this entry, the focus will be on the steps needed to identify the basic details about one's ancestors, relating to birth, death, and marriage.

Steps in Research

An introduction to genealogical and family history research is found on the FamilySearch Wiki, in a document entitled: *A Guide to Research*. The document describes five steps in the research process:

Step 1: Identify what you know about your family
Step 2: Decide what you want to learn about your family
Step 3: Select records to search
Step 4: Obtain and search the record
Step 5: Use the information[29]

Step 1 in the research process consists of identifying what one already knows about one's ancestors, including information obtained from other family members. In gathering information, it is useful to contact both close and more distant family members and relatives. The objective is to learn about any research they have done and any family histories or genealogies they may have.

As one identifies names, dates, and places for one's ancestors, the information can be recorded on pedigree charts and family group records. A pedigree chart is "A chart that shows an individual's direct ancestors, [including] parents, grandparents, great-grandparents, and so forth. A pedigree chart may contain birth, marriage, and death information."[30] A family group record is "A printed form that lists a family, parents and children, and gives information about dates and places of birth, marriage, and death."[30] For each pair of ancestors one identifies (e.g., a grandfather and a grandmother), one would complete a family group record, with information about the husband and wife and their children. Both the pedigree charts and the family group records can be printed from the FamilySearch website.

Step 2 consists of choosing one ancestor about whom one wants to know more. One normally starts with the generation closest to oneself and then works back. In step 3, one selects the resources one will search, including both compiled and original records (discussed later). In step 4, one obtains the records and searches them. Step 5, finally, consists of evaluating and using the information found, copying any new information to one's pedigree and family groups records, organizing newly found records, and sharing the information with others.

This entry will focus on step 3, selecting records to search, since this is the step that is concerned most directly with the genealogical literature and in particular with the resources one must use to identify one's ancestors. In determining which records to search, one usually proceeds as follows:

First, use compiled records to identify research already done on a given individual or family.

Second, use original records to locate new information about the individual or family.
As needed, use reference tools (background and finding aids) to assist in the two foregoing steps.

Classification and Evaluation of Genealogical Literature

The genealogical literature can be classified according to the types of resources used in the research process. Meyerink describes a classification that places genealogical resources into two broad classes:

1. "*Research sources* are those books and records which actually provide data that a researcher needs to solve a problem at hand. For family historians, these are the genealogical records which provide family data for charts and family group records."[6]
2. "*Reference tools* provide auxiliary information to help researchers find the right research sources. Reference tools include bibliographies, indexes, instructional material, and other reference aids."[6]

Research sources can, further, be subdivided into the following two classes:

1. "Original records are those sources that contain the first recording of an event...; they are generally recorded near the time of the event by someone who was present and associated with the event."[6]
2. . "Compiled records are those records that provide actual genealogical information whose content is derived from the research and evaluation of original records and/or other persons' research."[6]

Reference tools, in turn, can also be subdivided into two classes:

1. "Background information helps researchers understand the settings in which records were created..."[6]
2. "Finding aids indicate where specific information can be found..."[6]

The foregoing subclassification of research sources contrasts with the more traditional view of primary versus secondary sources. Meyerink proposes that the information in the sources should be classified as primary or secondary, while the sources themselves should be classified as original or compiled, as explained here:

"The traditional definition of a 'primary source' has been that it is a record created at the time of the event by someone associated with the event. For example, a death record is usually considered to be a primary source because it is created at the time of the event by someone associated with the event, such as the attending physician or a close relative. However, only *some* of the information in a death record is primary in nature.... Thus, on a death certificate, the death date and cause of death are primary information, but the dead person's birth date or parents' names are *not* primary information. Such information, which significantly predates the event being recorded, is secondary information...."[6]

In conducting genealogical research, it is important to evaluate the information one finds, including a determination of whether the information is primary or secondary, as noted above. Other areas needing evaluation include relevance, origin of the information, nature of the record, format of the record, directness of the evidence, consistency and clarity of the facts, and likelihood of the event(s).[6] Further guidance on evaluating information may be found in the how-to resources and guides listed in Table 4.

GENEALOGICAL RESOURCES

The genealogical literature will be discussed in further detail here, within the structure described earlier. Research sources will be described first, including compiled sources and original sources, followed by a discussion of reference tools. Some reference tools (e.g., indexes) will be discussed in conjunction with the original or compiled sources with which they are used. Resources that consist of a combination of original, compiled, and reference resources will be considered in the section that seems most pertinent. Periodical, news, and networking sources will be discussed separately, since these sources often contain a combination of resource types.

Tables have been prepared corresponding with the areas noted before, including

Table 1—General resources
Table 2—Compiled sources
Table 3—Original sources
Table 4—Reference tools
Table 5—Periodical, news, and networking sources

Table 1 identifies some of the major websites available for family history research. A few of the sites are megasites, providing links to many other sites. One can use the sites in Table 1 to access both compiled and original sources, as well as reference tools, for a variety of geographic areas.

Compiled Sources

Compiled sources, as described earlier, are used to identify research previously done. Table 2 contains a list of compiled sources commonly used to identify previous research, along with the finding aids used to access the sources (e.g., library catalogs may be used to locate family

Table 2 Compiled sources

Category	Title	Content and URL ($ = fee-based)
Biographies–Intl.	World Biographical Information System–DeGruyter	$ http://db.saur.de/WBIS —Over 6 million biographical entries
Family/local histories–Intl.	FamilySearch Catalog	https://familysearch.org —Click on: Search, Catalog [or Search, Books], then search by surname or place (as subject) —Large collection of published family and local histories, including 325,000+ digitized family and local histories and related publications —Overview of Family History Library resources, classes, and research assistance at: https://familysearch.org/locations/saltlakecity-library
Family/local histories–Intl.	Library of Congress Online Catalog	http://catalog.loc.gov —Search by family or locality (as subject) —Premier collection of U.S./foreign publications, including 50,000+ genealogies and 100,000+ local histories —Overview of LC Local History and Genealogy Reference Services, including genealogical materials, digitized materials, searching tips, and online orientations at: http://www.loc.gov/rr/genealogy/
Family/local histories–Intl.	WorldCat or other library/archive catalog in area of interest (national/state/local)	http://www.worldcat.org —Search by family (as subject), e.g., Walsh family —Search by locality (as subject), e.g., —Logan (Utah)–History, or Stuttgart (Germany)–Genealogy —Worldwide library records of published family and local histories

(Continued)

Table 2 Compiled sources *(Continued)*

Category	Title	Content and URL ($ = fee-based)
Family/local histories– Intl./U.S.	Periodical Source Index (PERSI)– Allen County Public Library Foundation	$ http://www.findmypast.com/persi —Search by family or locality to identify periodical articles about the family or locality
Pedigrees– Intl.	Genealogies– FamilySearch	https://familysearch.org —Click on: Search, Genealogies, then search by name —User-submitted lineage linked trees, including: Ancestral File (1979–2000, names merged) —Pedigree Resource File (1999- names not merged)
Pedigrees– Intl.	Family Tree– FamilySearch	https://familysearch.org —Click on: Family Tree, Find, then search by name (must create account) —Community-submitted pedigrees
Query services– by country	Query services– WorldGenWeb Project	http://www.worldgenweb.org —Surname queries by country (some) —Country- and county-specific e-mail lists (some)
Query services– by country	Message boards– Ancestry.com	http://boards.ancestry.com —Search bulletin boards by category —More than 198,000 bulletin boards
Society resources– Intl.	Family association and surname Websites	http://www.cyndislist.com/surnames —Search by surname to find association or surname websites —Search association or surname websites to locate genealogies, family histories, query lists, and information on the organization's library/archive, publications, and events http://www.cyndislist.com/societies

(Continued)

Table 2 Compiled sources *(Continued)*

Category	Title	Content and URL ($ = fee-based)
Society resources– Intl.	Genealogical and historical societies (national, state, local)	—Search by locality or ethnic group along with the word "societies" to find society websites —Search society websites to locate genealogical indexes and records, and information on the society's library/ archive, publications, and events
Society resources– U.S.	National Genealogical Society	$ http://www.ngsgenealogy.org —Quarterly publication, online courses, conferences, family group sheets, databases

histories). Six types of compiled sources are described, including

Biographies
Family histories and genealogies
Local histories
Pedigrees
Query services
Society and association resources

The latter two categories, "Query services" and "Society and association resources," may be thought of more as finding aids, but are included here since they can direct one to compiled sources that are important in the research process. Each of the six types of compiled sources is described below.

Biographies

A biography is "A history of an individual's life."[30] An early index of biographies, by Freemont Rider, consolidated all American biographical–genealogical records. This index has been published in two series:

1st series, *American Genealogical Index*, 1942–1952.[9]
2nd series, *The American Genealogical-Biographical Index to American Genealogical, Biographical, and Local History Materials*, 1952–2000 (with supplements).[9]

Table 3 Original sources

Category	Title	Content and URL ($ = fee-based)
Cemetery records	Find a Grave	http://www.findagrave.com —160,000 worldwide grave records
Emigration and immigration records	Emigration and Immigration Records and Resources– WeeMonster	http://www.germanroots.com/ei.html —Links to emigration, immigration, naturalization, and passenger list resources —Indexes and guides for ports in: U.S. (all ports), Canada, Europe
Vital records	International Vital Records Handbook (Kemp)	$ http://www.genealogical.com [*Search for title] —Genealogical Publishing Co., 7th ed., 2017 —Vital records information, by country
Vital records	Vitalrec.com	http://www.vitalrec.com/links2.html —Search by country (U.S., Canada, Europe, Pacific) —Links to vital record indexes, record ordering services, guides

Ethnic Groups

Category	Title	Content and URL ($ = fee-based)
By ethnic group	Cyndi's List	http://www.cyndislist.com —Search by ethnic group, then by type of record

Europe

Category	Title	Content and URL ($ = fee-based)
Denmark	Arkivalieronline–Statens Arkivers	https://www.sa.dk/content/dk (also in English) —Census, church, emigration, and probate records (some digitized)
E. Europe	Foundation for East European Family History Studies (FEEFHS)	http://www.feefhs.org —Umbrella organization for east/central Europe —Links to resources (by country/ethnic group) —Conferences, calendar, news

(Continued)

Table 3 Original sources *(Continued)*

Category	Title	Content and URL ($ = fee-based)
France	FranceGenWeb	http://www.francegenweb.org (English via help) —Links to databases, directories, by region
Germany	GenWiki– Verein für Computergenealogie	http://wiki-de.genealogy.net (also in English) —Portal for all German speaking areas —Links to databases, societies, mailing lists
Italy	Italy GenWeb	http://www.rootsweb.ancestry.com/~itawgw/ (in English) —Links to guides, records, by region
Norway	Arkivverket Digitalarkivet	http://arkivverket.no/Digitalarkivet (also in English) —Digitized census, church, probate, property, and tax records (some searchable online)
Spain	Spain GenWeb	http://www.genealogia-es.com —Links to databases, directories, by region
Sweden	SVAR (Svensk Arkivinformation)	$ https://sok.riksarkivet.se/svar-digitala-forskarsalen (also in English) —Digitized census, church, court, land, property, and vital records (some searchable online)
U.K.	U.K. BMD	http://www.ukbmd.org.uk —Links to websites offering online transcriptions of U.K. births, marriages, deaths, and censuses
U.K., Ireland	GENUKI– U.K. and Ireland Genealogy	http://www.genuki.org.uk —Portal for the U.K. and Ireland, by county/parish —Links to census, church, probate, and vital records

North, South, and Central America

Category	Title	Content and URL ($ = fee-based)
Canada	Genealogy and Family History– Library and Archives Canada	http://www.bac-lac.gc.ca/eng/discover/genealogy

(Continued)

Table 3 Original sources *(Continued)*

Category	Title	Content and URL ($ = fee-based)
Central/ South America	Central and South America– Cyndi's List	—Links to census, immigration, naturalization, and vital records http://www. cyndislist.com/ central-and-south-america/ —Links to sources for countries in Central/South America —Links to vital records, family histories
Mexico	Genealogy of Mexico	http://members. tripod.com/~Gary Felix/index1.htm —Names of early settlers of Mexico (from mission registers, civil records) —Spanish-American family histories
U.S.	Resources for Genealogists– National Archives and Records Administration	http://www.archives. gov/research/ genealogy —Indexes, how to find/access records —Links to both NARA and non-NARA sites for census, court, immigration, land, military, naturalization, passport, and vital records
U.S.	GenealogyBank– NewsBank, Inc.	$ http://www. genealogybank.com —Modern obituaries, news from 7000+ historical newspapers, military/ pension records, land grants —Social Security Death Index, 1962-(free)
Africa, Asia, and the Pacific		
Africa	Africa– Cyndi's List	http://www. cyndislist.com/africa —Links to sources for countries in Africa —Links to vital records (S. Africa), queries

(Continued)

Table 3 Original sources *(Continued)*

Category	Title	Content and URL ($ = fee-based)
Asia and Pacific	Asia and the Pacific– Cyndi's List	http://www. cyndislist.com/asia —Links to sources for countries in Asia and the Pacific —Links to vital records, queries

A large international biographical resource, the World Biographical Information System, currently provides access to over 6 million biographical entries (see Table 2).

Family histories and genealogies

A family history is defined as "A recorded account of the events occurring in one or more generations of a family."[30] A genealogy is "A published account of an individual's ancestors, descendants, or both."[30] These terms are sometimes used interchangeably. Family histories and genealogies are published both as books and as articles in periodicals, in print and online, and may include only basic genealogical information or a longer narrative history of the family and individuals.[6] The growth in family histories may be seen in the following figures:

  1698—First genealogy in the United States (Byrd family)[9]
  1862—108 family histories available (from a bibliography by William H. Whitmore)[9]
  1982—50,000 family histories available (estimated by Willard Heiss)[8]

One can search for genealogies and family histories in online catalogs, using subject terms such as "Jones family." Three large online catalogs providing access to numerous family histories are identified in Table 2: the Library of Congress Online Catalog, the FamilySearch Catalog, and WorldCat. A useful resource for identifying family histories in the periodical literature is the *Periodical Source Index* (see Table 2).

Family histories are being digitized in growing numbers. Family History Books is a collection of over 325,000 digitized genealogy and family history publications on the FamilySearch website. The resources come from several partner institutions, including the Allen County Public Library, Brigham Young University, the Houston Public Library, and the Family History Library in Salt Lake City.[31]

As family histories become digitized and searchable, massive amounts of text will be available online and the need to search effectively will increase. A dissertation designed to identify properties of family history literature

Table 4 Reference tools

Category	Title	Content and URL
Directories–Societies– U.S.	Federation of Genealogical Societies	http://www.fgs.org —Click on: Find a society —Information on 473 societies (mostly U.S.)
Directories–Societies, Libraries–Canada, U.S.	Directory of Genealogical and Historical Societies, Libraries and Museums in the US and Canada (Carson)	http://www.irongate.com [*Click on title] —Iron Gate Publishing, 2016 —Information on 47,000 societies, libraries, archives, and museums
Directories–Software	Software and Computers–Cyndi's List	http://www.cyndislist.com/software —Information on genealogical software and tools
Guides– by country / ethnic group	Guides to Tracing Family Trees–RootsWeb	http://rwguide.rootsweb.ancestry.com —Search by country, ethnic group, or record type
Guides– by country / state	Record Selection Tables–FamilySearch	https://familysearch.org/wiki/ —Search wiki by country or state, then click on Record Finder link to see Record Selection Table —Advice on records to search for specific information (e.g., to find names of parents)
Guides–Canada, U.S.	The Researcher's Guide to American Genealogy (Greenwood)	$ http://www.genealogical.com [*Search for title] —Genealogical Publishing Co., 3rd ed., c2000, reprinted 2005 —Text used in college and university courses on American genealogy
Guides– U.S.	Red Book: American State, County, and Town Sources (Eichholz)	http://www.ancestry.com/wiki [*Click on title] —Ancestry, Inc., 3rd ed., 2004 (digitized) —Information on records and holdings for every county in the U.S.

(Continued)

Table 4 Reference tools *(Continued)*

Category	Title	Content and URL
Guides– U.S.	The Source: A Guidebook to American Genealogy (Szucs and Luebking)	http://www.ancestry.com/wiki [*Click on title] —Ancestry, Inc., 3rd ed., 2006 (digitized) Information on original U.S. records —"The genealogist's Bible"
How to– Beginning research	Genealogy Online for Dummies (Helm & Helm)	$ http://www.dummies.com/ [*Search for title] —John Wiley & Sons, 7th ed., 2014 —Description of online and offline research techniques, social networks, and mobile aps
How to– Citations	QuickSheet: Your Stripped-Bare Guide to Citing Sources (Mills)	$ http://www.genealogical.com [*Search for title] —Genealogical Publishing Co., 2017 (2-pages) —Template for citing any type of source material
How to– Classes	Learning Center–FamilySearch	https://familysearch.org/learningcenter/ —Search for lessons by place or other topic
How to– Handwriting– U.S.	Reading Early American Handwriting (Sperry)	$ http://www.genealogical.com [*Search for title] —Genealogical Publishing Co., 1998, reprinted 2008 —Guide to reading early American handwriting
How to– Standards	The Genealogical Proof Standard– Board for Certification of Genealogists	http://bcgcertification.org/resources/standard.html —Click on Genealogy's Standards link to see list of elements to establish credibility and proof in genealogy
How to– Standards	QuickSheet: Your Stripped-Bare Guide to Historical Proof (Mills)	$ http://www.genealogical.com [*Search for title] —Genealogical Publishing Co., 2014 (2 pages)

(Continued)

Table 4 Reference tools *(Continued)*

Category	Title	Content and URL
		—Description of three ways to arrive at proof: evaluating the source, the information, and the evidence
Maps and gazetteers– Intl.	GEOnet Names Server–National Geospatial-Intelligence Agency	http://geonames.nga.mil/gns/html/ —Information on foreign place names sanctioned by the U.S. Board on Geographic Names
Maps and gazetteers– Intl.	Perry-Castañeda Library Map Collection– Univ. of Texas, Austin	http://www.lib.utexas.edu/maps —Online maps (current and historical) —Links to maps and gazetteers on other sites
Maps and gazetteers–U.S.	Geographic Names Information System– U.S. Geological Survey	http://geonames.usgs.gov/pls/gnispublic —Information on every place name in the U.S.

applicable to full text searching was completed by Molto relevant to this issue. Several properties of the literature were identified, including differences between male and female search term patterns. These differences would suggest gender-specific strategies when searching a full text family history database.[32,33]

Local histories

A local history is "An account of the historical events surrounding a particular area."[30] Local histories include county histories, as well as histories of particular communities. These resources are helpful in family history research, since they usually contain information about early residents of an area, especially those prominent in the community. The growth in local histories may be seen in the following figures:

1848—First county history in America published (County of Westchester, New York)[9]
1862—62 local histories available (from a bibliography by William H. Whitmore)[9]
1975—90,000 local histories available (from a bibliography by Marion J. Kaminkow)[8,9]

As with family histories, one can locate local histories through online catalogs, such as WorldCat (see Table 2).

One would search the catalog under a subject term, such as "Los Angeles (Calif.)—History," or "Stuttgart (Germany)—Genealogy."

Pedigrees

A pedigree chart, sometimes also referred to as a family tree, is "A chart that shows an individual's direct ancestors, [including] parents, grandparents, great-grandparents, and so forth. A pedigree chart may contain birth, marriage, and death information."[30] Pedigrees are available on many websites, including the FamilySearch website. Three FamilySearch resources that include extensive pedigrees are the Ancestral File, the Pedigree Resource File, and Family Tree (see Table 2). The websites listed in Table 1 provide additional possibilities for locating pedigrees.

Query services

A query, relevant to family history, is "A request for information, such as information about a particular ancestor."[30] A query service provides a medium (e.g., via a message board) for communicating with individuals researching or wanting information on the same person. Forums are a variation of a query service, allowing one to read or post comments about a particular family or individual. Query services are available through various websites, including Ancestry.com and WorldGenWeb Project (see Table 2). Query services are frequently hosted by genealogical societies and family associations, and query lists can be found in genealogical periodicals relevant to one's area of research.

Society and association resources

Genealogical and historical societies, such as the National Genealogical Society (United States), publish and archive numerous compiled resources (see Table 2). The societies often publish periodicals, which include family and local histories. They also gather pedigrees and genealogies from members of the organization, and house these materials in libraries or post the information on websites. Family and surname associations, likewise, provide access to compiled resources (e.g., pedigrees and histories), collected from members of the association (see Table 2). Directories can be used to identify societies and associations relevant to the ethnic group, locality, or surname being researched (see Table 4).

Original Sources

Once previously completed research has been identified, one can use original sources to verify the information or to extend what is known. Original sources, as previously described, contain information recorded near the time of

Table 5 Periodical, news, and networking sources

Category	Title	Content and URL ($ = fee-based)
Blogs– Intl.	Eastman's Online Genealogy Newsletter free and paid editions	http://blog.eogn.com —News about events, societies, companies, hardware/software, book reviews —Postings searchable under: Categories
Blogs– Intl.	GenealogyBlog (Meitzler)	http://www.genealogyblog.com —News about events, societies, companies, software, database content, book reviews —Postings searchable under: Categories
Periodicals–Computers	Internet Genealogy (print/PDF/app)	$ http://internet-genealogy.com —Moorshead Magazines, 2006- —Articles on online genealogical resources and strategies
Periodicals (scholarly)– U.S.	The American Genealogist (print)	$ http://americangenealogist.com —D. L. Jacobus, 1937- —Articles on difficult research problems, showing how to analyze and apply scholarly standards to the problem
Periodicals– U.S./Intl.	Family Tree Magazine (print/digital)	$ http://www.familytreemagazine.com —F &W Publications, 1999- (also UK edition) —Articles on record types, country-specific research, websites, and research tools
Periodicals–Indexes– U.S./Intl.	Periodical Source Index (PERSI)– Allen County Public Library Foundation	$ http://www.findmypast.com/persi —Index to names, places, and research methods, in English and French genealogical and local history periodicals, since 1800s —Growing number of links to digitized articles through the Findmypast partnership (July 19, 2013)
Social networks– Intl.	Popular social networks for genealogy– FamilySearch	https://familysearch.org/learn/wiki/en/ Popular_Social_Networks_for_Genealogy —Information on blogs, forums, message boards, podcasts, wikis

the event. Examples of original sources include birth records, marriage records, death records, probate records, land purchase records, census enumeration records, and pension records.[6] Some original records have been copied, in whole or in part, forming new resources known as abstracts, extracts, transcripts, or translations.[6] Indexes and other finding aids must be used to locate names in the original sources. More and more original records are becoming viewable and searchable online through digitization and massive indexing projects.

Tables 1 and 3 list resources that will assist one in locating original sources. Table 1 identifies general resources and Table 3 identifies resources pertaining to specific countries, geographic areas, and ethnic groups. Umbrella websites will direct one to other sites for the relevant information. Not all countries are included in Table 3, due to space limitations, but websites for major regions (e.g., Africa) will direct one to resources within that region.

Original sources are generally housed in archives. An archive is "A place where institutions such as governments, businesses, and churches keep their records and official documents."[30] Government sources (e.g., census records) are housed on either the national, state (or equivalent), or local level. For example, in the United States, the National Archives and Records Administration houses federal records, whereas the Massachusetts State Archive would house records pertaining to Massachusetts. Nongovernment sources are housed in repositories relevant to the organization. Church records, for example, would be housed by the local church or in a regional repository for the particular denomination.

The Family History Library in Salt Lake City maintains a vast repository of microfilmed and digitized records. The records are copies of original church, government, and other archival resources from throughout the world.[29] Access to the Library's microfilmed records is available at over 4700 branch FamilySearch centers located worldwide. The digital records can be viewed on the FamilySearch website. The Family History Library is managed by FamilySearch, previously known as the Genealogical Society of Utah which dates back to 1894.[34,35]

Following is a description of the major types of original records.

Vital records and civil registration

Vital records are "...birth, marriage, divorce, and death records created by governments."[30] Civil registration is an alternate term used in many countries to refer to the process of keeping vital records. These records are especially important in genealogical research, since they document dates and places of birth, death, and marriage.[29] Vital records, however, have not been kept until fairly recently in some countries. In Great Britain, for example, civil registration began in 1837.[7] Most government offices now keep vital records, and indexes to these records are available online for many countries (see Tables 1 and 3).

The following sources, described in Table 3 (International section), will direct one to vital records in specific countries:

International Vital Records Handbook
Vitalrec.com

National archives in various countries can also provide information on how and where to obtain vital records, as can the country-specific articles available on the FamilySearch Wiki.[36]

Church records

Church records are "Records kept by religious institutions."[30] Churches usually keep records of their christenings, baptisms, confirmations, marriages, and burials.[29] In some countries, especially those with state churches, church records are the most significant source for documenting births, deaths, and marriages in earlier time periods, since civil vital records were often not begun until the mid- to late 1800s. Information on church records in specific countries is available on the FamilySearch Wiki, in the country-specific articles.[36]

Cemetery records

Cemetery records include records kept by cemeteries, as well as information from headstones. Cemetery records and headstones contain names, birth dates, and death dates. One can often identify members of families in these records, since family members are usually buried near each other. Epitaphs may help establish the relationships between individuals.[29] The Find a Grave website is an excellent resource for viewing and searching headstone information (see Table 3). Information on cemetery records in specific countries is available on the FamilySearch Wiki, in the country-specific articles.[36]

Census records

A census is "An official count and description of the people living in a country, colony, state, county, township, or city."[30] Most national governments conduct periodic censuses. In the United States, the 1850 census was the first to list every member of a household, by name, sex, age, country or state of birth, and occupation. Census records are helpful in determining where one's ancestors lived.[29] Census information is available online for some countries (see Tables 1 and 3). Information on census records in specific countries is also available on the FamilySearch Wiki, in the country-specific articles.[36]

Probate records

Probate records are "Legal documents dealing with the distribution of an individual's property after his or her death."[30] Probate records may contain a copy of a person's will, if one exists, as well as names of family members and their relationships.[29] In some countries and time periods, people did not generally own property, so probate records are not available. Information on probate records in specific countries is available on the FamilySearch Wiki, in the country-specific articles.[36]

Military records

Military records are "Records detailing an individual's service in a country's armed forces."[30] The kinds of military records available vary by country, but may include service records, draft or conscription records, records of regular military forces, and veterans' benefit records. Indexes to a growing number of military records are available online (see Tables 1 and 3). Information on military records in specific countries is available on the FamilySearch Wiki, in the country-specific articles.[36]

Immigration and emigration records

Immigration records are "Records that document a person's arrival into a country."[30] Emigration records are "Record[s] documenting an individual's move to a different country."[30] Examples of these records include passenger lists, permissions to emigrate, and records of passports issued. Especially important are the passenger lists,[37] for which indexes are available online, through services such as Ancestry.com (see Table 1).

A helpful resource for tracing an ancestor's town of origin is Tracing immigrant origins, available on the FamilySearch Wiki. The following advice is given:

"The best approach is to start searching records created in the immigrant's new country, especially if you know little about the person. Only rarely is it better to use country-of-origin records first.... Obituaries are an excellent source of biographical information about immigrants.... Even if a place of origin is not given, an obituary may provide additional research clues...."[37]

Useful links for immigration and emigration information are found in the following resource: Emigration and Immigration Records and Resources (see Table 3). Information relevant to specific countries is available on the FamilySearch Wiki, in the country-specific articles.[36]

Other original records

Other types of original records include court, land, naturalization, taxation, business, medical, and school records. One should check all jurisdictions (e.g., town, county, state, and country) that may have kept records about one's ancestor.[29] Detailed descriptions of the many kinds of records available for specific countries can be found on the FamilySearch Wiki, in the country-specific articles.[36]

Reference Tools

Reference tools are often divided into two types: background information and finding aids. Each type is discussed here.

Background information

Reference tools that are useful in providing background information in the research process include[6]

Guides
How-to resources
Maps and gazetteers

A growing number of guides and how-to resources for genealogy have become available. Table 4 includes descriptions of some of these, including guides to research in particular countries. An example is Greenwood's *The Researcher's Guide to American Genealogy*. The Research Selection Tables, available on the FamilySearch Wiki, also provide research guidance, by country, state, and equivalent areas, including detailed information about which resources to use to find specific information about one's ancestors (see Table 4).

A basic how-to resource, listed in Table 4, is *Genealogy Online for Dummies*, by Helm and Helm. This resource provides an introduction to genealogical research. Other how-to resources from Table 4 include a citation guide, standards guides for establishing proof in genealogical research, a handwriting guide, and a reference to online classes. A prime source of information for maps and gazetteers (geographical dictionaries) is the Perry-Castañeda Library Map Collection, with links to maps from throughout the world (see Table 4).

Finding aids

Reference tools that serve as finding aids for locating information in record collections include[6]

Bibliographies
Catalogs
Directories
Indexes

Several finding aids are identified in Table 4, along with some additional references in Tables 2 and 5. Bibliographies, though not listed in the tables, are a useful finding aid for identifying published family histories.

The following bibliographies, edited by Kaminkow and by Filby, are classics in the genealogical literature:

1970—*American and British Genealogy and Heraldry*, by Filby[9]
1972–[1987]—*Genealogies in the Library of Congress* (including supplements) by Kaminkow[9]
1981—*A Complement to Genealogies in the Library of Congress*, by Kaminkow[9]

Library catalogs (listed in Table 2) are another type of finding aid for locating family histories and local histories. Directories (listed in Table 4) are helpful in identifying societies, libraries, museums, software, and other items of genealogical interest. Indexes, finally, are a finding aid that is useful for searching the periodical literature. Examples of periodical indexes are provided in the next section and in Table 5.

PERIODICAL, NEWS, AND NETWORKING SOURCES

A periodical is defined as "A periodical publication... with a fixed interval between the issues or numbers."[13] Periodicals often contain all three types of resources discussed earlier: compiled and original sources, as well as reference tools. Periodicals are available for specific countries, regions, and ethnic groups, as well as for other topics relevant to genealogy. Examples of several genealogical periodicals are provided in Table 5.

Society periodicals

Bidlack notes "At least half the genealogical journals and books being published today come from societies.... Below the state level there are scores of genealogical societies that publish periodicals devoted, usually, to a county."[8] Two of the earliest society periodicals, relevant to the United States, are

1. 1847—*The New England Historical and Genealogical Register*—oldest continuing genealogical periodical in the United States.[8]
2. 1912—*National Genealogical Society Quarterly*—including primary source material from throughout the United States.[8]

Non-society periodicals

Many non-society genealogical periodicals are also available. A periodical focusing on computers and technology in genealogy is *Internet Genealogy* (see Table 5). An example of a scholarly genealogical periodical is *The American Genealogist*, whereas a periodical useful for practical advice is *Family Tree Magazine* (see Table 5).

Periodical indexes

Indexes are important in providing access to the information found in genealogical periodicals. Jacobus produced the first index to periodicals, with others continuing his work in subsequent years:

1932–1953—*Index to Genealogical Periodicals*, by Donald Lines Jacobus[9]

1957–1963—*Annual Index to Genealogical Periodicals & Family Histories*, by Inez Waldenmaier[9]

1963–[2002]—*Genealogical Periodical Annual Index*, by various editors[9]

1987–present—*Periodical Source Index* (PERSI) (see Table 5)

The *Periodical Source Index* is the most comprehensive and up to date of the genealogical periodical indexes and may be accessed online from two vendors, with a growing number of links to articles that have been digitized (see Table 5).

News and networking

Periodicals and blogs are important sources for genealogical news. A blog is "a website that contains online personal reflections, comments, and often hyperlinks, videos, and photographs provided by the writer."[13] Blogs are especially useful for news, since they are often updated daily. Two genealogical blogs are described in Table 5: Eastman's *Online Genealogy Newsletter*, and the *GenealogyBlog*. Various social networking tools are also available for genealogists, for communicating with other researchers and for obtaining research advice (e.g., via podcasts and wikis). A FamilySearch Wiki article, entitled "Popular social networks for genealogists," describes these tools (see Table 5).

CONCLUSION

Interest in genealogy began in antiquity, with references to genealogical records found in both the Old and New Testaments. During the earlier periods, those tracing their genealogies were often interested in proving their nobility. In the United States, it was not until the 1970s that interest expanded to people of all classes and ethnic groups. The availability of printed records, from which to derive accurate genealogies, did not exist in some countries until the mid-1500s, with civil records not available until the 1700s and 1800s. Genealogy as a scholarly pursuit came into being in the 1930s in the United States. Since then, a growing number of resources have become available, including microfilmed and digitized records. The Internet has revolutionized the way research is done, by providing access to genealogical resources from one's home

computer. Genealogy is the second most popular hobby in the United States.

A growing number of user studies have been conducted to determine how genealogists perform their work. There is a need, however, for further research relevant to the growing use of the Internet in genealogical research. One concern relates to how genealogists can effectively navigate the Internet to access the many resources now available. More studies are also needed relating to the novice genealogist, since previous studies have focused on the professional.

REFERENCES

1. Powell, K. Genealogy or family history? About.com: Genealogy. http://genealogy.about.com/library/tips/blfamily history.htm (accessed December 2014); http://rpareinfo-gathering.blogspot.com/2013_06_01_archive.html (accessed May 2017).
2. Rodriguez, G. How genealogy became almost as popular as porn. Time 2014 (May 30). http://time.com/133811/how-genealogy-became-almost-as-popular-as-porn/ (accessed May 2017).
3. Americans' fascination with family history is rapidly growing PRNewswire 2005 (June 9). http://www.prnews wire.com/news-releases/americans-fascination-with-family-history-is-rapidly-growing-54590942.html (accessed May 2017).
4. Online family history research in United States grows by 14 times in past decade. Ancestry Press Releases 2014 (November 19). http://corporate.ancestry.com/press/press-releases/2014/11/Online-Family-History-Research-in-United-States-Grows-by-14-Times-in-Past-Decade-/ (accessed May 2017).
5. Crandall, R.J. Foreword. In *Printed Sources: A Guide to Published Genealogical Records*; Meyerink, K.L., Ed.; Ancestry, Inc.: Salt Lake City, UT, 1998, xi.
6. Meyerink, K.L., Ed. Introduction and foundations for research. In *Printed Sources: A Guide to Published Genealogical Records*; Ancestry, Inc.: Salt Lake City, UT, 1998, 1–29.
7. Potter-Phillips, D. History of genealogy. Family Chronicle 1999 (July/August). http://www.familychronicle.com/HistoryOfGenealogy.html (accessed May 2017).
8. Bidlack, R.E. Genealogy today. Libr. Trends **1983**, *32* (1), 7–23.
9. Bockstruck, L.D. Four centuries of genealogy: A historical overview. RQ **1983**, *23* (2), 162–170.
10. Wood, C.A. *Toward the new genealogy: Genealogical research in archives and the Saskatchewan Genealogical Society, 1969–2004 (Thesis)*; University of Manitoba: Winnipeg, MB, 2004.
11. Mills, E.S. Genealogy in the "information age": History's new frontier? National Geneal. Soc. Quart. **2003**, *91* (December), 260–277.
12. Jacobus, D.L. Is genealogy an exact science? Am. Geneal. **1933**, *10* (October), 65.
13. Merriam-Webster. http://www.merriam-webster.com/dictionary (accessed May 2017).
14. Brimhall, D. FamilySearch partnerships: Some questions and answers. FamilySearch Blog 2014 (February 26). https://familysearch.org/blog/en (accessed May 2017).

15. Nauta, P.G. Massive online US obituaries project will help find your ancestors. FamilySearch Blog 2014 (October 1). https://familysearch.org/blog/en/ (accessed May 2017).

16. Microfilm publications and original records digitized by our digitization partners; NARA: Washington, D.C., http://www.archives.gov/digitization/digitized-by-partners.html (accessed May 2017).

17. Mormons in the United States (National Institute); National Institute for Genealogical Studies, 2012. https://familysearch.org/wiki/en/Mormons_in_the_United_States_(National_Institute) (accessed May 2017).

18. Yakel, E. Seeking information, seeking connections, seeking meaning: Genealogists and family historians. Inform. Res. 2004, 10 (1), 1–11.

19. Yakel, E.; Torres, D.A. Genealogists as a "community of records." Am. Arch. 2007, 70 (spring/summer), 93–113.

20. Antcliff Tucker, E.M. Myth, memory and multiculturalism: Informing cultural identity through genealogical pursuit (PhD dissertation); New Mexico State University: Las Cruces, NM, 2012.

21. Duff, W.M.; Johnson, C.A. Where is the list with all the names? Information-seeking behavior of genealogists. Am. Arch. 2003, 66 (spring/summer), 79–95.

22. Darby, P.; Clough, P. Investigating the information-seeking behaviour of genealogists and family historians. J. Inform. Sci 2013, 39 (1), 73–84.

23. Lucas, S.A. The information seeking processes of genealogists (PhD dissertation); Emporia State University: Emporia, KS, 2008.

24. Fulton, C. Quid pro quo: Information sharing in leisure activities. Lib. Trends 2009, 57 (4), 753–768.

25. Dilts, G.D. Catalog use difficulties in a genealogical library (research paper); Brigham Young University: Provo, UT, 1979.

26. Johnson, L.A. A library user's needs in regards to bibliographic information in catalog entries of the Genealogical Society of Utah (research paper); Brigham Young University: Provo, UT, 1984.

27. Sowers, B. Enhancing a catalog with local and family history analytics. Technicalities 2003, 23 (6), 1, 11–14.

28. Blake, L.; Stallings, E.T. Arranging roots: Classification and subject headings for genealogical collections. Libr. Resour. Tech. Ser. 1997, 41 (4), 335–346.

29. A Guide to Research; FamilySearch: Salt Lake City, UT. https://familysearch.org/learn/wiki/en/A_Guide_to_Research (accessed May 2017).

30. A Glossary of Genealogical Terms; FamilySearch: Salt Lake City, UT. https://familysearch.org/wiki/en/A_Glossary_of_Genealogical_Terms (accessed May 2017).

31. Family History Books; FamilySearch: Salt Lake City, UT. https://books.familysearch.org/primo_library/libweb/action/search.do?vid=FHD_PUBLIC&backFromPreferences=true (accessed May 2017).

32. Molto, M.B. Textual regularities applicable to full text searching: The case of family history literature (PhD dissertation); University of California: Los Angeles, CA, 1989.

33. Molto, M.B. Improving full text search performance through textual analysis. Inform. Process. Manage. 1993, 29 (5), 615–632.

34. [Family History Library]; FamilySearch: Salt Lake City, UT. https://familysearch.org/locations/saltlakecity-library (accessed May 2017).

35. About FamilySearch; FamilySearch: Salt Lake City, UT. https://familysearch.org/about (accessed May 2017).

36. Family History Research Wiki; FamilySearch: Salt Lake City, UT. https://familysearch.org/learn/wiki/en/Main_Page (*search by country/state/province, then by type of record) (accessed May 2017).

37. Tracing Immigrant Origins; FamilySearch: Salt Lake City, UT. https://familysearch.org/wiki/en/Tracing_Immigrant_Origins (accessed December 2014).

BIBLIOGRAPHY

1. Carson, D.C. Directory of Genealogical and Historical Societies, Libraries and Museums in the US and Canada; Iron Gate Publishing: Niwot, CO, 2016.

2. Family History Research Wiki; FamilySearch: Salt Lake City, UT. https://familysearch.org/learn/wiki/en/Main_Page (accessed May 2017).

3. Guides to Tracing Family Trees; RootsWeb: Provo, UT. http://rwguide.rootsweb.ancestry.com (accessed May 2017).

4. Helm, M.; Helm, A.L. Genealogy Online for Dummies, 7th Ed.; John Wiley & Sons: Hoboken, NJ, 2014.

5. Kemp, T.J. International Vital Records Handbook, 6th Ed.; Genealogical Publishing Co.: Baltimore, MD, 2013.

6. Resources for Genealogists; National Archives and Records Administration: Washington, DC. http://www.archives.gov/research/genealogy (accessed May 2017).

Genre Theory and Research

Catherine F. Schryer
Department of English Language and Literature, University of Waterloo, Waterloo, Ontario, Canada

Abstract

This entry provides overviews on current genre theory and research that investigates texts in their social contexts. Specifically, the entry focuses on relevant theory in Rhetorical genre studies and Linguistics and provides illustrations from applied studies in Professional Communication and Composition research. Since much current research in genre theory utilizes social theories that deal with questions of structure and agency, relevant theories in that area are reviewed as well. Finally, the entry notes some of the pedagogical implications of genre research.

Information Studies scholars such as Andersen[1] have recognized the importance of the concept of genre especially for scholars in information disciplines. Andersen points out that the term genre does not just encompass classification of text types. Rather he suggests that using a nuanced understanding of genre to refer to "situated and typified document production and use" can assist researchers to have a "more informed understanding of the ways in which information systems help, or fail to help people in their work" (p. 341). In fact, from a variety of perspectives genre researchers have developed theoretical and methodological tools to investigate texts in their social contexts. This research could assist information discipline scholars in enriching their own understanding of the important social action of categorization.

This entry provides overviews into the two main areas investigating the concept of genre: Rhetorical genre studies (RGS) and Linguistics. Because genre scholars are concerned with the interaction between texts and their social contexts, some relevant social theories are also described. Finally, since many investigations into genre have occurred in educational or workplace settings devoted to training, several theories of particular importance to teaching and learning are also reviewed.

RHETORICAL GENRE STUDIES

Rhetorical genre studies surfaced in the North American academy in the early 1980s and was adopted and refined by researchers particularly in professional communication who recognized its importance for investigating workplace communication practices. From the RGS perspective, either genres are not just classifications of texts (such as poetry versus the novel) or classification itself as an enterprise means much more than simply slotting texts into various categories. As its name suggests, RGS

began among rhetorical scholars namely Bitzer,[2] Campbell and Jamieson[3] and most importantly, Miller[4] in reaction to traditional rigid systems of classifying texts according to regularly occurring features. Classical rhetoricians, Aristotle[5] for example, designated persuasive texts into one of three categories. A text or speech could be forensic, epideictic, or deliberative. Thus, forensic discourse tended to occur in law courts and focus on past actions in order to determine guilt or innocence; epideictic speeches, associated with the present, emerged in ceremonial occasions such as weddings or funerals and elaborated on praising or blaming an individual; and deliberative performances occurred in political venues and were intended to move their audiences to future action. This system, as useful as it might have been for classical rhetoricians, breaks down in the face of complex modern texts such as a report that might combine a forensic analysis of a problem together with a deliberative plan to address the problem. Nor does it account for the various ways that a report might appear in different organizations. In fact, what a report entails can differ significantly in government agencies, engineering companies, or hospitals. And yet people in these organizations do classify oral events and written documents such as reports and know among themselves what they mean and expect in a meeting, interview, case presentation, record, consultation letter, or any of the other multitudinous tasks that people accomplish in their daily lives.

Miller asserted that genres were, in fact, forms of social action—that they functioned to coordinate the work of organizations or to accomplish some kind of significant task for individuals. Miller based this argument on Campbell and Jamieson's insight that "a genre does not consist merely of a series of acts in which certain rhetorical forms recur...Instead a genre is composed of a constellation of recognizable forms driven by an internal dynamic" (p. 21). As Miller explains, this sense of an "internal dynamic" is

Encyclopedia of Library and Information Sciences, Fourth Edition DOI: 10.1081/E-ELIS4-120043259

crucial because it conveys the sense that these language events emerge as fusions of substantive and stylistic features in response to specific situations. Using Bitzer's notion of "exigence," Miller suggests that people in their social networks or contexts over time both recognize the need to respond (exigence) to specific situations and to typify those situations. For example, healthcare workers have long recognized the need to record their observations, consult with experts, and transfer information about patients in order to accomplish their work. Over time these practitioners developed ways to handle these needs and these strategies evolved into recognizable text types or oral speech events such as patient records, consultation letters, and case presentations. These already existing structures, fusions of content, style and organization, now facilitate practice in these settings, and newcomers have to learn how to wield them in order to get their work done.

Miller's insights were important for several reasons. She recognized the pragmatic function of genres (they get work done) and that this work occurred in social settings such as workplaces and not just in literary texts. She argued that genres constitute epistemological categories (types evolved and created by their users) and were composed of sets of content, stylistic features, and organizational structures that tended to re-occur within these typified events. In short, Miller's reconceptualization of genre as a theoretical concept opened the way for professional communication researchers to investigate texts in their social contexts. Researchers who operationalized and refined Miller's insights include Winsor[6] and Artemeva[7] in engineering, Smart,[8] Orlikowski and Yates,[9] and Schryer[10] in business communication, Spinuzzi[11] in software development, and Devitt[12] and Bawarshi[13] in composition studies.

Another important source for the renovation of genre theory was the work of Bakhtin[14] and his circle including Volosinov.[15] Although Bakhtin developed his ideas during the 1920s and into the 1930s (and mostly in reaction to de Saussurean linguistics and literary formalism) his dynamic ways of thinking about language did not enter into the North American academy until the 1970s and even the 1980s. Rhetoricians such as Bialostosky,[16] Kent,[17] Klancher,[18] anthropological linguists such as Hanks,[19] and professional communication researchers such as Schryer,[20] Cross,[21] Berkenkotter and Huckin[22] recognized the relevance of Bakhtin's insights for investigating texts in their contexts. As Dentith[23] notes, central to Bakhtin's thought is the basic principle "that communicative acts only have meaning, only take on their specific force and weight, in particular situations or contexts" (p. 3).

Two key terms—utterance and speech genre—evoke Bakhtin's dynamic way of conceptualizing language and constitute his major contribution to genre theory. As he explains in "The Problem of Speech Genres," the primary unit of communication is not the sentence or the word but the utterance. The utterance is "individual" and "concrete" and generated by participants in the "various areas of human activity" (p. 60). The utterance is inherently, he suggests, addressing and responding to another person or collective of people. This understanding of language stands in direct opposition to traditional linguists (such as de Saussure) who see language as an objective system with classifiable elements (langue) that the writer or speaker operationalizes (pp. 67–69). Instead Bakhtin sees that as we speak or write we are always shaping our language for real or imagined others. For example, a dictionary definition of the word *right* would indicate that it is an adjective meaning *correct*. However, note what happens in the following conversations.

1. A mother and teen-aged daughter are watching TV.
   Mother: Doesn't he (referring to news anchor) look good today?
   Daughter: Yeah, right (said quickly, emphatically, and sarcastically).
2. A mother is driving her adult son back to his apartment. He is a doctoral student trying to finish his dissertation.
   Son: You know, my advisor tells me that I have to produce three publishable articles before I complete my dissertation. So I think I am going to have to take an extra year to get everything done.
   Mother: Right (said very slowly while she nods her head).

In the first instance *right* does not mean correct but might mean something like *you must be out of your mind*. In the second instance *right* might mean something like *I respect your decision but can see some financial implications that we will have to discuss later*. The utterance captures this process wherein speakers and listeners, writers and readers, inflect on the fly their language to mean something appropriate for that person and that situation. Furthermore, as these examples suggest, an utterance "is a link in a very complexly organized chain of other utterances" (p. 69). The utterance *right* is a response to an utterance and could generate a host of other utterances.

This profoundly situated understanding of language might suggest that for Bakhtin communication is indeterminate and chaotic. However the concept of "speech genre" provides a balance. He suggests that although utterances are individual "each sphere in which language is used develops its own *relatively stable types* of these utterances" which he calls "*speech genres*" (original emphasis, p. 60). He indicates that genres are heterogeneous and range from "short rejoinders of daily dialogue. . .to the fairly variegated repertoire of business documents" and include the "diverse forms of scientific statements and all literary genres" (pp. 60–61). Bakhtin's theory can accommodate this diversity because he posits that speech genres are both centrifugal and centripetal.

The centrifugal quality of utterances or speech genres refers to the forces of change (de-normalizing, clowning, or mimicry) that occur within text types; whereas the centripetal quality refers to the social forces that attempt to keep an utterance stable. An important feature of Bakhtin's thought is that both actions (stabilizing and destabilizing) co-occur within utterances.

Because of their very heterogeneity, speech genres can be difficult to identify. However, Bakhtin provides some features that allow researchers to argue that a specific language event could be defined as participating in a genre. He notes that a change of speaking subjects or a sense of *finalization* marks the boundary of a speech genre (p. 76). Like Miller, Bakhtin sees that agents in their social milieus simply know when a speech event has been accomplished and when or if they can interrupt and start a new utterance or chain of utterances. Bakhtin points to three aspects whereby social agents can recognize that the speech event is complete and that they can respond: "1) semantic exhaustiveness of the theme; 2) the speaker's plan or speech will; and 3) typical compositional and generic forms of finalization" (pp. 76–77). In some contexts such as the military, the semantic resources can be limited (for example requests and orders) whereas in other contexts semantic resources can be rich as in creative or scientific endeavors. His understanding of genres as affected by the speaker's plan is particularly interesting as he suggests that speakers and listeners together enact a genre. He explains "We learn to cast our speech in generic forms and, when hearing others' speech, we guess its genre from the very first words; we predict a certain length...and a certain compositional structure; we foresee the end" (p. 79). In a way genres function very much like a piece of jazz. When the first performer lays down the track or musical line, the other performers improvise around it, and all the performers know by listening and looking at each other when the piece is completed. Many of our daily language events such as interviews, condolence letters, and classroom interactions have this felt sense of improvisation within structure. As Kent[17] explains, genres are like "guessing games we employ in order to produce utterances and to understand the utterances of others" (p. 46).

Finally, Bakhtin indicates that "typical compositional and generic forms" (p. 77) mark specific genres. In some contexts, especially those associated with power, these typical features can seem regulated, "compulsory and extremely stable" (p. 79). But in most situations genres are "flexible, plastic, and free" (p. 79). In other words, speakers and writers, when they launch into a genre, do not actually know which strategies they will use to accomplish their purpose but they also tend to stay within a generic range so as to accommodate their readers' or listeners' expectations.

Bakhtin's insights into genre shifted the ground for communication researchers in several important ways. First, his work obviously extends concepts of genre far beyond literary texts into examining the powerful genres such as records, reports, and letters that constitute our social worlds. Secondly, his insights, like those of Miller's, offer a way to theorize the process of classifying utterances. It really matters how social agents classify their text types or speech events. These classifications tell researchers a great deal about what a group values and recognizes as assisting in accomplishing its social purposes. At the same time, however, these same utterances are not simply instances of a category. Because each instance of a genre is addressed to a different context, audience, and time, it evokes a different set of strategies within an acceptable (to participants) range. In effect, genres are abstractions or ever changing sets of socially accepted strategies that participants can use to improvise their responses to a particular situation. As I[20] suggested in an early study of veterinary medical records, genres are "stabilized-for-now or stabilized enough sites of social and ideological action" (p. 200). This definition expresses the sense that genres are just stabilized enough so that agents can accomplish their social purposes but that genres are constantly evolving. Finally, Bakhtin's work suggests that utterances or genres are the socially situated ways that we learn to communicate. Rather like a singer who learns to sing by singing songs, we all learn to communicate through these constellations of resources.

RGS researchers, using a range of qualitative methods, have profited from a synthesis of Miller's and Bakhtin insights into order to investigate the social contexts that both structure and are structured by specific texts. To name just a few, Smart's[8] work has investigated reading and revision practices associated with banking; Hanks[19] has investigated historical government documents; and Bazerman[24] and Spinuzzi[11] have explored genres as existing in networks or systems.

GENRE RESEARCH IN LINGUISTICS

Although both RGS and genre researchers in linguistics recognize the relationship between texts and their social contexts, it is fair to say that RGS has often concentrated on investigating the social practices associated with text types; whereas genre research in linguistics has often focused on analyzing the textual features found in various text types. The development of genre studies has also experienced more controversy in linguistics than it has in RGS.

In fact, the recognition of the dynamic interaction between texts and their social contexts captures an intense debate that has been occurring within linguistics. For some time, applied and critical linguists have disparaged each other's projects. Applied linguists, mostly from the systemic functional linguistic (SFL) tradition, have critiqued critical discourse analysis (CDA) for its failure to develop rigorous methodologies, especially in terms of precise terminology for analyzing text.

According to Chapelle,[25] SFL views "language as a social semiotic a resource people use to accomplish their purposes by expressing meanings in context." Although SFL provides ways to analyze syntactic structures, as a theory it insists that the functions of language are central. Consequently, the dynamic interaction between social contexts and language are central for SFL. Much of SFL stems from the work of Halliday and his many collaborators.[26,27]

As Wodak[28] explains, CDA involves "an interdisciplinary approach to language study with a critical point of view" for the purpose of studying "language behavior in natural speech situations of social relevance." Kress[29] notes that CDA differs from other forms of linguistic analysis as it has an overt political agenda—exposing relations of power.

Luke[30] for example, points out that CDA does not have a consistent taxonomy. The CDA researchers such as Young and Harrison,[31] on the other hand, have challenged SFL to move beyond descriptions of linguistic structures to accounts that provide a "social critique by documenting structures of inequality" (p. 2).

The terms of this debate are echoed in applied linguistic genre research. Applied linguists, especially those interested in issues related to second language learning, literacy, and pedagogy have found the concept of genre particularly useful. One group, especially associated with English for Specific Purposes (ESP) (much of the ESP understanding of genre derives from Swales'[32] focus on text types as characterized by specific organizational structures or moves), has provided detailed descriptions of the moves or "schematic structures"[33] within genres as diverse as the research article,[34] grant proposals,[34,35] and business letters.[36] Another group, more influenced by SFL, has emphasized the social purposes of genres and has sought to explain not only the moves of specific genres but also lexical, grammatical, and cohesive patterns. The work of Cope and Kalantzis[37] and Martin[38] has contributed significantly to this group, often called the Sydney School. This school, in particular, points to the pedagogical implications of genre research and claims that the often tacit rhetorical and linguistic choices within powerful genres need demystification for those with less access to privileged forms of education. Consequently, these scholars call for more overt teaching of genres in order to resolve this inequity.

The Sydney School also critiques RGS researchers on two counts. They note that North American genre researchers through their dependence on qualitative studies have focused on exploring social context rather than texts and that RGS has failed to link genre research to pedagogical issues. RGS advocates, on the other hand, have critiqued linguistic genre research, especially the Sydney School, for abstracting genres from their social contexts and attempting to codify them.[39] The pedagogy

associated with this type of research, they suggest, fails to address issues related to situated learning. Gee et al.[40] effectively dramatize the issue by pointing to the discourses associated with law school. They point out that law students are not directly taught the strategies associated with legal discourse. Rather they are subjected to an immersion program wherein they learn "inside the procedures, rather than overtly about them" (p. 13). This immersion program works for two reasons. First, as Gee et al. point out, trying to spell out the rules of the game involved in doing law would only offer a "panacea" (p. 12). They assert that, "All that goes into thinking, acting, believing, valuing, dressing, interacting, reading, and writing *like a lawyer* cannot be put overtly into words" (p. 12) and the attempt to codify all these strategies would produce stilted performances. Secondly, learning inside procedures ensures that a learner "takes on perspectives, adopts a worldview, accepts a set of core values and masters an identity without a great deal of critical and reflective awareness" (p. 13). No field or organization wants its newcomers to question its basic values as such questioning would undermine the kinds of "fluent and fluid performances" (p. 13) that mark a speaker as a member of a field. Of course, Gee et al. suggest that field-specific discourses should be critiqued but not during the process of acquiring them.

Critical Discourse Analysts critique both RGS and other linguistic projects for being too descriptive and for failing to deal with issues of power and hegemony. As Luke[30] explains CDA advocates for "principled reading positions and practices for the critical analysis of the place and force of language, discourse, text, and image in changing contemporary social, economic, and cultural conditions" (p. 97). In fact, what sets CDA analyses apart is their, as Luke explains, "attempt to inform text analyses with broader social theory" (p. 101). This emphasis has resulted in diverse studies of public discourse,[41,42] racism,[43] and organizational discourse[44] that focus on issues of power and hegemony.

Until recently, RGS scholars, genre researchers in applied linguistics, and CDA scholars have not been addressing each other's research. In fact, these groups all offer useful resources for genre-focused projects. Genre research can only profit from a combination of RGS with its strong commitment to rigorous qualitative studies and the rich development of linguistic concepts in the work of Swales,[33] Hodge and Kress,[45] Stillar,[46] Hyland,[32] and Giltrow.[47]

SOCIAL CONTEXT THEORIES

Much of the integration within genre studies has been made possible by the incorporation of the social theories exploring the relationship between structure and agency. Genre research has always struggled with issues of agency. Critics of genre theory have complained that the concept of genre implies rigid discourse structures that impose actions on agents. In order to develop models of research that negotiate the difficult terrain between power, social structures, and agency, some genre researchers have turned to the theoretical and methodological resources present in social theories such as those of Giddens,[48,49] Bourdieu[50,51] and Engeström[52,53] that investigate the dynamic between agents (readers and writers), their products (genres), and social contexts. Central to Giddens'[50] work, for instance, is his insistence on the "mutual dependence of structure and agency" (p. 122). Giddens rejects structuralist and functionalist notions that conceptualize social structures as abstract systems outside of time. Such accounts describe agents as either fully in control of their own operations or as fully subject to their social contexts. For example, in de Saussurean linguistics, language users are conceptualized as fully in control of their language systems; whereas in Levi-Straussian structuralism, agents are at the mercy of systems (such as systems of myths) which compel them to articulate essentially the same structure (despite discrepant details). Neither account explains, in Giddens' view, the complex and nuanced way that human agents are affected by and reproduce their social environments. Rather Giddens suggests that agents bring with them their memories of past experiences and/or they use already existing structures—such as reports, meetings, memos, patient records, etc.—to guide them in their interactions with other social agents. These already constructed social structures are filled with "rules" or the resources and constraints that enable and constrain the constant reproduction of social life. However, as Giddens explains, these "rules" are not like the rigid rules present in a game of chess. Rather they are more fluid, emergent and dependent on the collective agreement of those involved in the interaction (pp. 118–120). He also asserts that agents can change these social structures in the midst of social interaction. As he puts it, "*All reproduction is necessarily production*, however; and the seed of change is there in *every act* which contributes towards the production of any 'ordered' form of social life" (p. 101, emphasis in original). For Giddens, in fact, all social contexts are ordered but changing social accomplishments—constantly being co-constructed by social agents.

Giddens' insights help explain how relationships exist between texts and their social contexts. For instance, my interdisciplinary research group[54] investigated the effect of medical case presentations on new physicians. We noted that the case presentation preexists the students who use it. It is filled with rules and resources that both constrain and enable the performance of their cases. These rules and resources resonated with professional attitudes and values. At the same time the case presentation can only exist if users reproduce it, and no case

presentation ever uses the exact same rules and resources as another case presentation even in the same setting even though the users recognize the case presentation as a recurrent event.

Giddens also offers useful methodological insights. He parallels his focus on agency with an insistence that agents "are able to explain most of what they do, if asked" (p. 93). Researchers need to include participant information in their data collection because social agents have access to both discursive and practical knowledge about their routine activities. Social agents, according to Giddens, are reflexively monitoring their own activities and have valuable explanations (discursive knowledge) of their practices. At the same time agents have tacit, "practical knowledge" or "knowledge embodied in what actors 'know how to do'" (p. 126) in their daily activities. Consequently, researchers need to develop methodologies that capture both kinds of knowledge.

My own work[55] and others such as Yates and Orlikowski[56,57] have profited from Giddens's insights. For instance, my interdisciplinary research group[55] also investigated the resources and constraints associated with forensic letters written by physicians charged with providing an opinion as to whether a child had experienced abuse or neglect. We identified many regular features associated with these letters and yet no two of these letters are the same. Yates and Orlikowski[56] also draw on a combination of rhetorical and structuration theories when they observe that workplaces genres such as the memo, the proposal, and the meeting are organizational genres "embedded in social processes" (p. 299) and that genres such as email both shape and are shaped by discursive practices in workplaces.[57]

Another social theorist, Bourdieu, offers significant theoretical and methodological insights in terms of addressing issues of power. For Bourdieu, the most important aspect of social agents is that they are *social* or inhabited by "habitus." Bourdieu[52] defines habitus as "socialized subjectivity" (p. 126). As Wacquant,[52] one of Bourdieu's main collaborators, explains, the habitus "consists of a set of historical relations 'deposited' within individual bodies in the form of mental and corporeal schemata of perception, appreciation and action" (p. 16). Habitus, thus, is not a passive kind of socialization; it produces an active engagement wherein social agents, because of their prior experiences, recognize how to respond appropriately and even strategically to "fields" (p. 14) or specific social contexts. To respond agents must have a range of resources that predispose them to react appropriately. Thus, for example, healthcare fields accept students from academic programs that predispose them to work within healthcare paradigms. These professions or fields then further shape students to perceive, communicate, and behave in professional or acceptable ways.

The concept of "field" or "market" or "game" is central to Bourdieu's way of conceptualizing disciplines, organizations, or social systems and their relationship to power. For Bourdieu,[52] society is not a seamless totality, but rather an "ensemble of relatively autonomous spheres of play" (p. 17). He[51] explains that a game, market, or field is a "structured space of positions in which the positions and their interrelations are determined by the distributions of different kinds of resources or capital" (p. 14).

In other words, agents are structured by their experiences within a field. At the same time they also structure or reproduce those fields but not in purely reductive ways. Rather, because agents occupy different positions within their fields (and thus have different access to power) and because fields themselves occupy different positions in relation to each other, agents enact different strategies (although only within a specific range). Bourdieu[58] calls these regulated, improvisational strategies, triggered by the interaction between habitus and field, "the logic of practice" (p. 112).

Integral to habitus is linguistic habitus,[52] or the improvisational communication strategies that agents use to enhance and distinguish their own position. Language, particularly that aspect of language called style, is deeply implicated in this struggle to succeed. Bourdieu observes that "style exists only in relation to agents endowed with schemes of perception and appreciation that enable them to constitute it as a set of systematic differences" (p. 39). Furthermore, this process of differentiation, or style production is deeply implicated in the reproduction of symbolic power. Bourdieu notes that:

> This production of instruments of production, such as rhetorical devices, genres, legitimate styles, and manners and, more generally, all the formulations destined to be "authoritative" and to be cited as examples of "good usage," confers on those who engage it a power over language (p. 58).

As instruments of production, some genres, especially those enacted by well-positioned agents in well-positioned fields such as medicine, can reproduce forms of symbolic power that can literally shape their receivers' views of the world. From Bourdieu's perspective, then, genres can be seen as constellations of regulated, improvisational strategies triggered by the interaction between individual socialization, or "habitus," and an organization or "field."

Bourdieu, like Giddens, also provides methodological insights. He suggests that two types of analyses are needed in order to undercover the structures that maintain and reproduce power.

> First, we push aside mundane representations to construct the objective structures (spaces of *positions*), the distribution of socially efficient resources that define the external constraints bearing on interactions and representations. Second, we reintroduce the immediate, lived experience of agents in order to explicate the categories of perception and appreciation. (p. 11, emphasis in original)

From a genre perspective, the first step entails the close reading of a set of text types, suspected to be participating in a genre, in order to describe and critique the kinds of strategies evoked within this discursive event. Already existing terminology from linguistics can prove useful at this stage. The second step involves interviewing readers and writers and asking them for explanations for their strategies and problem-solving techniques.

Bourdieu's insights resonate across much genre studies in work such as that done by Devitt[12] and Bawarshi.[13] My own work[10] has certainly profited from Bourdieu's work not only in terms of developing a critical perspective that can demonstrate that certain genres can enact forms of symbolic violence but also in terms of developing a methodology that can accommodate both linguistic and qualitative forms of analysis. Another researcher, Hanks,[19] from linguistic anthropology, has done groundbreaking work integrating Bakhtin and Bourdieu in order to create a model to investigate historical genres of subjugation in fifteenth century Mexico.

Finally, activity theory has provided additional insights to explain the complex, dialectical interaction of agents, and their social structures. According to Vygotsky,[59] activity theory emerged as a counterbalance to simplistic notions of socialization which either envisioned individual agents as self-contained preformed entities (psychological model) or as entities totally at the mercy of their environments (behaviorist model). Instead, Vygotsky envisioned agents as learning through using tools in purposeful, goal directed activities. He saw that these tools, both physical (hammers, pencils) and cultural (language, genres), preexist their users and mediate the interaction between agents and their social environments. By using tools, human agents internalized the values, practices, and beliefs associated with their social worlds. At the same time as they become experienced users, agents can, in the midst of purposeful activity, affect their social contexts or even modify their tools. Certainly in my group's research,[55] we saw that, by using the mediating tool of case presentations, healthcare students were internalizing the values and practices while involved in purposeful activities that would lead to their own ability to affect future social contexts (i.e., their ability to deal with their own future patients or clients).

Engeström[52,53] and other researchers such as Cole,[60] Scribner,[61] and Wertsch[62] have extended Vygotsky work into a model for the analysis of complex interactions between agents and social structures in professional and workplaces settings. While retaining the concepts of tools mediating the socialization of agents, they have expanded the analytical concepts within the notion of system to account for more of the dialectical, or rather dialogical, interactions that occur between social agents and between social agents and their settings. Engeström[63] defines an activity system as a system "that incorporates both the object-oriented productive aspect and the person-oriented communicative aspect of human conduct," and he suggests that a human activity system, "always contains the subsystems of production, distribution, exchange, and consumption (p. 67)."

Research integrating theories of genre together with activity system theory include Bazerman,[64] Russell,[65] Artemeva,[66] Spinuzzi,[11,67] Yates and Orlikowski,[68] and Varpio[69] among many others. Activity system theory has proved particularly valuable in terms of exploring "genre sets,"[64] systems of genre,[65,66] or genre repertoires,[68] in order to explain the ways that text types affect each other and create hybrid forms. Activity theory has also proved useful in terms of investigating the ways that systems of genres interact with various technologies.[69]

LEARNING THEORIES

As noted earlier, genre theorists have been debating the impact of their contextualized findings on education. Much of the debate has focused on whether genres should be taught directly at all. On one side of the debate are members of the Sydney School[38] who insist that genres need to be directly taught. On the other side of the debate are RGS scholars such as Freedman[70] and Dias et al. Dias et al.,[71] for instance, in their thought provoking comparison of writing practices in the workplace and the academy claimed that the school genres of the academy were "worlds apart" (p. 3) from workplace genres. Reflecting the purposes of schooling, educational genres typically create the circumstances wherein "epistemic" or knowledge-making tasks are evaluated on an individual basis (p. 44). As Dias et al. explain, "Within the classroom context each paper is graded in comparison to all others, and the institution has a vested interest in a quality spread" (p. 62). Workplace genres, on the other hand, mediate the interactions of agents in different ways. In workplace settings, for example, managers will intervene in writing processes as "the institutional goal is to elicit the best possible product from each employee each time writing is undertaken" (p. 62). In fact, Dias et al. conclude that the activity systems of education and workplaces differ so radically, that educational institutions cannot claim to be teaching the genres of workplace communication. This perspective, of course, is deeply troubling to educators in professional communication[72] who claim that the strategies that students learn in professional communication classrooms translate into useful practices in workplace settings.

Much of Dias et al.'s arguments stem from their understanding of activity theory and their realization that the activity systems of the workplace and education have inherently different purposes. However, their insights were also shaped by current research into learning theory particularly the concept of "communities of practice" (COP) as developed by Lave and Wenger[73] and later refined by Wenger.[74] This body of work focuses on apprenticeship experiences. Lave and Wenger describe a COP as "a set of relations among persons, activity and world, over time and in relation with other tangential and overlapping COP" (p. 98). Lave and Wenger and their many supporters also insist that learning is a natural and ubiquitous phenomenon and that it occurs most naturally and effectively within COPs through the process of "legitimate peripheral participation" (p. 34). As Lave and Wenger explain, "learning is an integral part of generative social practice in the lived-in world" (p. 35) and occurs naturally and constantly in groups consisting of expert and inexpert members. Less expert members learn through their involvement in legitimate (recognized by the group) practices. At first this involvement is peripheral (by observing, by being assigned part of the task, by being supervised) but eventually less expert members assume full participation in the group's activities.

More recently, research has challenged the either/or nature of this debate. Researchers such as Artemeva et al.[75] have pointed out that activity systems and COP overlap and that often strategies learned in one context can be transferred to another. Certainly Bourdieu's work on linguistic habitus predicts this kind of movement. At the same time students can also be taught to see text types not as rigid formalizations but as constellations of strategies that they can adjust to different circumstances. In other words, students can be taught to be 'savvy' users of genres. This kind of pedagogy as advocated by Giltrow[48] means[1] getting students to see the regularities often associated with specific text types such as academic research papers,[2] pointing to the range of different strategies that exist among different instances of the text types,[3] explaining the often ideological reasons for certain strategies,[4] and advocating that students chose their strategies according to the needs of their audience and situation rather than following a rote format.

CONCLUSION

This overview of research on genre theory and research can only provide snapshots of the rich discussions about genres or texts in their social contexts that are occurring in a variety of interdisciplinary settings. These discussions could be of value to researchers in the information sciences. Most importantly, they point to the important role of categorizing. As readers and writers, speakers and listeners, we anticipate (categorize) text types and improvise with each other on the fly. We are also constantly bringing resources from one text type to another and thus experiencing constant genre hybridity. In many ways information scientists are at the heart of much genre work as they often have to reflect in their categorization schemes the ever evolving social process that is genre.

REFERENCES

1. Andersen, J. The concept of genre in information studies. In *Annual Review of Information Science and Technology*; Cronin, B., Ed.; American Society for Information Science: Washington, DC, 2008; Vol. 43, 339–367.

2. Bitzer, L.F. The rhetorical situation. Philos. Rhetoric **1968**, *1*, 1–14.

3. Campbell, K.K.; Jamieson, K.H. Form and genre in rhetorical criticism: An introduction. In *Form and Genre: Shaping Rhetorical Action*; Campbell, K.K., Jamieson, K.H., Eds.; Speech Communication Association: Falls Church, VA, 1979; 9–32.

4. Miller, C. Genre as social action. Q. J. Speech **1984**, *70*, 151–167.

5. Aristotle, Rhetorica. In *The Basic Works of Aristotle*; Roberts, W.R., Trans. McKeon, R., Ed.; Modern Library: New York, 2001; 1325–1451.

6. Winsor, D. Ordering work: Blue-collar literacy and the political nature of genre. Writ. Commun. **2000**, *17* (2), 155–184.

7. Artemeva, N. The writing consultant as cultural interpreter: Bridging cultural perspectives in the genre of the periodic engineering report. Tech. Commun. Quart. **1998**, *7*, 285–299.

8. Smart, G. Genre as community invention: A central bank's response to its executives' expectations as readers. In *Writing in the Workplace: New Research Perspectives*; Spilka, R., Ed.; Southern Illinois University Press: Carbondale, IL, 1993; 121–140.

9. Orlikowski, W.J.; Yates, J. Genre repertoire: The structuring of communicative practices in organizations. Admin. Sci. Quart. **1994**, *39* (4), 541–574.

10. Schryer, C.F. Walking a fine line: Writing 'negative news' letters in an insurance company. J. Bus. Tech. Commun. **2000**, *14* (4), 445–497.

11. Spinuzzi, C. Compound mediation in software development: Using genre ecologies to study textual artifacts. In *Writing Selves/Writing Societies: Research from Activity Perspectives*; Bazerman, C., Russell, D., Eds.; The WAC Clearinghouse and Mind, Culture, and Activity: Fort Collins, CO, 2003; 97–124. http://wac.colostate.edu/books/selvessocieties/.

12. Devitt, A.J. *Writing Genres*; Southern Illinois University Press: Carbondale, IL, 2004.

13. Bawarshi, A.S. *Genre and the Invention of the Writer: Reconsidering the Place of Invention in Composition*; Utah State University Press: Logan, UT, 2003.

14. Bakhtin, M. The problem of speech genres. In *Speech Genres and Other Late Essays*; McGee, V.W., Trans., Emerson, C., Holquist, M., Eds.; University of Texas Press: Austin, TX, 1986; 60–102.

15. Volosinov, V.N. *Marxism and the Philosophy of Language*; Matejka, L.; Titunik, Trans., Harvard University Press: Cambridge, MA, 1986.

16. Bialostosky, D. Bakhtin and rhetorical criticism: A symposium. Rhetoric Soc. Q. **1992**, *22* (4), 1–28.

17. Kent, T. Hermeneutics and genre: Bakhtin and the problem of communicative intentions. In *Landmark Essays on Bakhtin, Rhetoric and Writing*; Farmer, F., Ed.; Laurence Erlbaum: Mahwah, NJ, 1998; Vol. 13, 33–50.

18. Klancher, J. Bakhtin's rhetoric. In *Reclaiming Pedagogy: The Rhetoric of the Classroom*; Donahue, P., Quandahl, E., Eds.; Southern Illinois University Press: Carbondale, IL, 1989; 83–96.

19. Hanks, W.F. Discourse genres in a theory of practice. Am. Ethnol. **1987**, *14* (4), 668–692.

20. Schryer, C.F. Records as genre. Writ. Commun. **1993**, *10* (2), 200–234.

21. Cross, G.A. Bakhtinian exploration of factors affecting the collaborative writing of an executive letter of an annual report. Res. Teach. Engl. **1990**, *24* (2), 173–203.

22. Berkenkotter, C.; Huckin, T. *Genre Knowledge in Disciplinary Communication: Cognition/Culture/Power*; Erlbaum: Hillsdale, NJ, 1993.

23. Dentith, S. *Bakhtinian Thought: An Introductory Reader*; Routledge: London, U.K., 1995.

24. Bazerman, C. Systems of genres and the enactment of social intentions. In *Genre and the New Rhetoric*; Freedman, A.; Medway, P., Eds.; Taylor & Francis: London, U.K., 1994; 79–101.

25. Chapelle, C.A. *Some notes on systemic functional linguistics*; http://www.isfla.org/Systemics/Definition/chapelle.html (accessed November 14, 2008).

26. Halliday, M.A.K.; Hasan, R. *Language, Context and Text: A Social Semiotic Perspective*; Deakin University Press: Geelong, Australia, 1985.

27. Halliday, M.A.K. *An Introduction to Functional Grammar*; Edward Arnold: London, U.K., 1985.

28. Wodak, R., Eds. *Language Power and Ideology: Studies in Political Discourse*; Benjamins Publishing Company: Amsterdam, the Netherlands/Philadelphia, PA, 1989.

29. Kress, G. Critical discourse analysis. Annu. Rev. Appl. Linguist. **1990**, *11*, 84–99.

30. Luke, A. Beyond science and ideology critique: Developments in critical discourse analysis. Annu. Rev. Appl. Linguist. **2002**, *22*, 96–110.

31. Young, L.; Harrison, C., Eds. *Systemic Functional Linguistics and Critical Discourse Analysis*; Continuum: London; New York, 2004.

32. Swales, J.M. *Genre Analysis: English in Academic and Research Settings*; Cambridge University Press: Cambridge, U.K., 1990.

33. Hyland, K. *Disciplinary Discourse: Social Interactions in Academic Writing*; Longman: Harlow, U.K., 2000.

34. Connor, U.; Mauranen, A. Linguistic analysis of grant proposals: European Union research grants. Engl. Specif. Purposes **1999**, *18* (1), 47–62.

35. Connor, U. Variation in rhetorical moves in grant proposals of United States humanists and scientists. Text **2000**, *20*, 1–28.

36. Bhatia, V.J. *Analyzing Genre: Language in Professional Settings*; Longman: London, U.K., 1993.

37. Cope, B.; Kalantzis, M. How a genre approach to literacy can transform the way writing is taught. In *The Powers of Literacy: A Genre Approach to Teaching Writing*; Cope, B., Kalantzis, M., Eds.; Falmer: London, U.K., 1993; 1–21.

38. Martin, J.R. *English Text: System and Structure*; Benjamins: Amsterdam, the Netherlands, 1992.

39. Freedman, A.; Medway, P., Eds. *Genre and the New Rhetoric*; Taylor & Francis: London, U.K., 1994.

40. Gee, J.P.; Hull, G.; Lankshear, C. *The New Work Order: Behind the Language of the New Capitalism*; Westview Press: Boulder, CO, 1996.

41. Chilton, P.; Schäffner, C. Discourse and politics. In *Discourse as Social Interaction*; Van Dijk, T.A., Ed.; Sage: Thousand Oaks, CA, 1997; 206–230.

42. Fowler, R. *Language in the News: Discourse and Ideology in the Press*; Routledge: London, U.K., 1991.

43. Van Dijk, T.A. *Racism and the Press*; Routledge: London, U.K., 1991.

44. Mumby, D.K. *Communication and Power in Organizations: Discourse, Ideology and Domination*; Ablex: Norwood, NJ, 1988.

45. Hodge, R.; Kress, G. *Social Semiotics*; Cornell University Press: Ithaca, NY, 1993.

46. Stillar, G.G. *Analyzing Everyday Texts: Discourse, Rhetoric and Social Perspectives*; Sage: Thousand Oaks, CA, 1998.

47. Giltrow, J. *Academic Writing: Writing and Reading in the Disciplines, 3rd Ed.*; Broadview Press: Mississauga, ON, Canada, 2002.

48. Giddens, A. *The Constitution of Society: Outline of the Theory of Structuration*; University of California Press: Berkeley, CA, 1984.

49. Giddens, A. Problems of action and structure. In *The Giddens Reader*; Cassell, P., Ed.; Stanford University Press: Stanford, CA, 1993; 88–175.

50. Bourdieu, P. *Language and Symbolic Power*, Raymond, G., Adamson, M., Trans., Thompson, J.B., Ed.; Harvard University Press: Cambridge, MA, 1991.

51. Bourdieu, P.; Wacquant, L. *An Invitation to Reflexive Sociology*; University of Chicago Press: Chicago, IL, 1992.

52. Engeström, Y. *Learning by Expanding: An Activity-Theoretical Approach to Developmental Research*; Orienta-Konsultit: Helsinki, Finland, 1987.

53. Engeström, Y. Activity theory and individual social transformation. In *Perspectives on Activity Theory*; Engeström, Y., Miettinen, R., Punamaki, R., Eds.; Cambridge University Press: Cambridge, MA, 1999; 19–38.

54. Schryer, C.F.; Lingard, L.; Spafford, M. Structure and agency in medical case presentations. In *Writing Selves/Writing Societies: Research from Activity Perspectives*; Bazerman, C., Russell, D., Eds.; The WAC Clearinghouse and Mind, Culture, and Activity: Fort Collins, CO, 2003; 62–96, http://wac.colostate.edu/books/selvessocieties/.

55. Schryer, C.F.; Afros, E.; Mian, M.; Spafford, M.M.; Lingard, L.A. (in press), The trial of the expert witness: Negotiating credibility in court documents in child abuse cases. Writ. Commun. **2009**, *26*, 215–246.

56. Yates, J.; Orlikowski, W. Genres of organizational communication: a structurational approach to studying communication and media. Acad. Manage. Rev. **1992**, *17*, 299–326.

57. Orlikowski, W.; Yates, J. Genre repertoire: The structuring of communicative practices in organizations. Acad. Manage. Rev. **1994**, *39*, 13–35.

58. Robbins, D. *The Work of Pierre Bourdieu: Recognizing Society*; Open University Press: Milton Keynes, U.K., 1991.

59. Vygotsky, L.S. *Mind in Society: The Development of Higher Psychological Processes*; Harvard University Press: Cambridge, MA, 1978.

60. Cole, M. Cultural psychology: Some general principles and a concrete example. In *Perspectives on Activity Theory*; Engeström, Y., Miettinen, R., Punamaki, R.L., Eds.; Cambridge University Press: Cambridge, MA, 1999; 87–106.

61. Scribner, S. Vygotsky's uses of history. In *Culture, Communication and Cognition: Vygotskian Perspectives*; Wertsch, J.V., Ed.; Cambridge University Press: New York, 1985; 119–145.

62. Wertsch, J.V., Ed. *The Concept of Activity in Soviet Psychology*; M.E. Sharpe: Armonk, NY, 1981.

63. Engeström, Y. Developmental studies of work as a testbench of activity theory: The case of primary care medical practice. In *Understanding Practice: Perspectives on Activity and Context*; Chaiklin, S., Lave, L., Eds.; Cambridge University Press: Cambridge, U.K., 1993; 63–103.

64. Bazerman, C. Systems of genre and the enactment of social intentions. In *Genre and the New Rhetoric*; Freedman, A., Medway, P., Eds.; Taylor & Francis: London, U.K., 1994; 79–99.

65. Russell, D.R. Rethinking genre in school and society: An activity theory analysis. Writ. Commun. **1997**, *14* (4), 504–554.

66. Artemeva, N. Approaches to learning genres. In *Rhetorical Genre Studies and Beyond*; Artemeva, N., Freedman, A., Eds.; Inkshed: Winnipeg, MB, 2006; 9–100.

67. Spinuzzi, C. *Tracing Genres through Organizations: A Sociocultural Approach to Information Design*; MIT Press: Cambridge, MA, 2003.

68. Yates, J.; Orlikowski, W. Genre systems: Structuring interaction through communicative norms. J. Bus. Commun. **2002**, *39* (1), 13–35.

69. Varpio, L.; Hall, P.; Lingard, L.; Schryer, C.F. Interprofessional communication & medical error: A reframing of research questions and approaches. Acad. Med. **2008**, *83* (10), S76–S81.

70. Freedman, A. Show and tell? The role of explicit teaching in the learning of new genres. Res. Teach. Engl. **1993**, *27* (3), 222–251.

71. Dias, P.; Freedman, A.; Medway, P.; Paré, A. *Worlds Apart: Acting and Writing in Academic and Workplace Contexts*; Erlbaum. Mahwah: NJ, 1999.

72. Fahnestock, J. Genre and rhetorical craft. Res. Teach. Engl. **1993**, *27* (3), 265–271.

73. Lave, J.; Wenger, E. *Situated Learning: Legitimate Peripheral Participation*; Cambridge University Press: Cambridge, U.K., 1991.

74. Wenger, E. *Communities of Practice: Learning, Meaning and Identity*; Cambridge University Press: Cambridge, U.K., 1998.

75. Artemeva, N.; Logie, S.; St. Martin, J. From page to stage: How theories of genre and situated learning help introduce engineering students to discipline-specific communication. Tech. Commun. Q. **1999**, *8* (3), 301–316.

Geographic Information Systems (GIS)

Timothy F. Leslie
Nigel M. Waters
Department of Geography and Geoinformation Science, George Mason University, Fairfax, Virginia, U.S.A.

Abstract

This entry, describing the world of geographic information systems (GIS), begins with a synopsis of the considerable academic debate over the classification of GIS as a tool or a science. The state of the art for GIS technology is described along with the current concern over the teaching of spatial thinking, a necessary prerequisite for the successful use of GIS. The importance of spatial autocorrelation in the statistical analysis of geographic data is explained. Recent developments including public participation GIS (PPGIS) and volunteer geographic information are recounted. The second part of the entry describes GIS applications and software packages along with the anticipated future for GIS. This entry concludes with a resource section that includes information on GIS Day and GIS conferences, journals, books, and organizations.

INTRODUCTION AND OVERVIEW

In 1998, *The Encyclopedia of Library and Information Science* published an entry on geographic information systems (GIS)[1] that reviewed both the history and the body of knowledge associated with GIS. A sequel in 2001[2] documented the progress made by the community during the following 3 years, with particular detail given to the "systems versus science" debate. For the sake of completeness and self-containment, this overview of the subject again begins with formal definitions of GIS. Next, the state of the art as it existed in 2008 is described. This is followed by a discussion of spatial thinking as conceptualized within the (generally American) educational system.

In recent years, GIS has come to represent a synthesis of science and application. The "systems versus science" debate has become passé. Internet applications have flourished, with many users unaware they were using GIS technology to create maps or obtain driving directions. This entry concludes with an overview of the near-term future of GIS and with a list of GIS resources, both online and traditional print materials. The present account does not provide a complete and comprehensive introduction to GIS, and readers wishing to learn the basics before consulting the rest of the entry are advised to go to the following online tutorials: the U.S. Geological Survey (USGS) GIS education Web site at http://education.usgs.gov/common/lessons/gis.html and the Environmental Systems Research Institute (ESRI) discussion of GIS presented at http://www.gis.com/whatisgis/. A comprehensive description of those topics belonging to the body of knowledge associated with GIS may be found in DiBiase et al.[3]

In addition, this entry does not review the history of GIS. The reader may consult the extensive discussion in Waters[1] or in Clarke.[4] A complete review may be found in Foresman[5] and comprehensive online resources are maintained with The GIS History Project (http://www.ncgia.buffalo.edu/gishist/). Chrisman[6] has described the transformation of computer mapping software into GIS at the Harvard Laboratory for Computer Graphics and Spatial Analysis during the 1960s and 1970s.

MODERN DEFINITIONS OF GIS

A terse, useful definition of GIS continues to elude the community. Two views of GIS pervade the literature, differing largely because of the difference in the "S" in the acronym. Those scholars that represent the "S" as systems include Clarke,[4] who provides a number of definitions of GIS. Clarke begins by stating that a GIS is a computer-based system for linking attribute data from a database with spatial information. He notes that a GIS can be described in various ways. Thus some authors have referred to GIS as a toolbox. Similarly, Burrough and McDonnell[7] state that GIS is a "a powerful set of tools for storing and retrieving at will, transforming and displaying spatial data from the real world for a particular set of purposes." Longley et al.[8] review definitions that describe GIS as both data analysis–data display tools and as map-making tools. These definitions emphasize the applied nature of GIS and are generally used by practitioners in the field, such as the government and related industry contractors. These definitions have become more entrenched with the increasing use of software programming packages and languages (e.g., Visual Basic, Python,

Encyclopedia of Library and Information Sciences, Fourth Edition DOI: 10.1081/E-ELIS4-120043922

and Java, among others) to create sets of procedures that specialized user groups can employ (e.g., transportation planners, see Kang and Scott[9]).

Alternatively, the "S" in GIS can be taken to represent Science (Mark[10]). This approach has been advocated by scholars who are actively developing new methods and who view themselves as more than simple toolmakers. Goodchild provides an overview of the differences between GISystems, GIScience and GIStudies at http://www.ncgia. ucsb.edu/giscc/units/u002/u002.html. According to Goodchild GIScience is the science behind the technology of GIS. It is also the science that keeps GIS at the research frontier. GIScience is thus a multidisciplinary field in which cartography, cognitive psychology, computer science, geodesy, geography, photogrammetry, and spatial statistics are all important contributors.

The tool versus science debate has been reviewed by Wright et al.[11] It has been resolved largely by the acceptance of both terms and an increased vagueness in the use of the GIS acronym. Within universities this dichotomy is evident in the number of "professional master's" programs available largely to fill the market for increased application courses and community-based GIS funding in the vein of GISystems. GIScience remains as a realm for continued research and software development, and is popular as a specialization, minor, or additional certificate in degree programs. Academic units with a mix of GIScience and GISystems activity remain healthy.

Finally, Chrisman[12] has defined GIS as an "organized activity by which people measure and represent geographic phenomena then transform these representations into other forms while interacting with social structures." This definition reflects the increased interest in the use of GIS for community planning and advocacy. It is such an important new trend that it has been variously referred to as community-based GIS and Public Participation GIS (PPGIS) and more recently as VGIS where the "V" in the acronym indicates volunteer involvement. These developments are described in further detail below.

GIS: THE STATE OF THE ART IN 2008

In 2008, GIS software packages for making maps and for displaying and analyzing spatial data in a variety of ways was commonplace. Large price differences existed, with GIS software packages ranging in cost from free (for GRASS and other open source initiatives) to a few hundred dollars (for Idrisi, MapInfo, and Maptitude) to tens of thousands of dollars (for enterprise versions of TransCAD and ArcServer). These packages generally come with a graphical interface and run on the Windows operating system, although Unix-friendly server editions are becoming common. Mac OS X and Linux are poorly represented, and can only run a subset of existing GIS software without

a Windows emulator or interpreter. Open source software has been particularly successful with these operating systems, to the point that dedicated teams focus on GIS-specific Linux distributions (see information on Debian-GIS at http://wiki.debian.org/DebianGis).

Conducting analysis with GIS software still requires extensive training and this is especially so if it is to be used for decision-making and policy implementation. Most GIS education and training is completed in university undergraduate programs. Post-degree diploma programs are also popular as are graduate level master's degree programs, and employers frequently pay for such education for their employees.

Web-based GIS applications and the use of software and data online are becoming increasingly common. Many of these Web-based devices are lowering the technical know-how necessary to interact with spatial data. GPS units are capable of calculating driving directions as well as tracking traffic information from a server and rerouting the user on the fly. Cell phones, such as the iPhone, can track their location, navigate users, and check the weather with a few touches of the screen.

Spatial data is still extremely costly in most countries where cost-recovery models are often used by government agencies (see Taylor[13] for an exhaustive discussion of this topic for various countries around the world). The United States is almost the lone exception to this approach to the provision of spatial data, and it is arguable that this has done much to spawn the world's most active and innovative GIS industry.

Although GIS, even today, cannot be considered more than a niche application it is now a common place subject in university curricula and is frequently used as a research tool by a large number of university disciplines.[1] In addition, it is being taught more and more in the K-12 curriculum in schools and is being used in an increasingly extensive number of applications in both the public and private sectors.

Public Participation GIS and Volunteered Geographic Information

During the last decade, GIS has been used more and more for community planning and social advocacy. Such developments have been variously described as Public Participation GIS and Participatory GIS with the acronyms PPGIS and PGIS, respectively, in common use. The most extensive set of resources for participatory GIS may be found at the portal Web site maintained by the integrated approaches to participatory development (IAPAD) organization at http://www.iapad.org/. IAPAD maintains a list for those interested in PGIS research and also stores numerous case studies which may be downloaded. In recent years it has promoted as participatory three-dimensional modeling (P3DM) of physical environments and the ethically responsible use of GIS to protect lands belonging to indigenous communities.

PGIS has now been well accepted by mainstream GIS researchers with highly regarded texts such as that by Craig et al.[14] devoted to this topic. For a number of years PGIS had its own series of conferences sponsored by the Urban and Regional Information Systems Association (URISA) although during 2006 and 2007 PGIS was again merged into URISA's main, annual conference. The PPGIS Web site (http://www.ppgis.net/) maintains an open forum on Participatory GIS and associated technologies.

Volunteered geographic information is an increasingly important and associated development. Software developments that include Google Earth, Google SketchUp, Wikimapia, and OpenStreetMap have allowed citizens with limited or indeed no specialized knowledge of GIS to upload their geographic knowledge to publicly accessible Web sites. This process of "geotagging" and its impact on the future of GIS is discussed by Goodchild.[15] The Geography Network (http://www.geographynetwork.com/) supports project Globe (http://www.globe.gov/GaN/analyze.html) which allows students in elementary schools to observe data, for example, the brilliance of the night sky. It is easy for these students to record their observations and upload them to a map where they can become part of a network of thousands of observations from schoolchildren around the world. As Goodchild notes, the children have become geographic sensors.

TEACHING SPATIAL THINKING

GIS Education continues to progress as spatial thinking has received attention at all educational levels. Many vendors of GIS software offer reduced or free versions of their packages for education institutions, and resource materials including data sets and lesson plans are widely available.

Schools

Recently the National Research Council has produced a major study[16] advocating the teaching of spatial thinking and GIS across the K-12 curriculum. The authors of the report argue that spatial thinking is a constructive mix of three elements: spatial concepts, methods of representation, and spatial reasoning. Indeed the Association of American Geographers has argued recently (http://aag.org/nclb/nclb.pdf) for changes to the U.S. No Child Left Behind Legislation that would see an appropriation of funding in this legislation for the teaching of geography and GIS.

It can be argued that GIS should be incorporated into the K-12 curriculum for several reasons. First, it helps with the teaching of geography, a core academic discipline. Major software manufacturers such as ERSI (http://

www.esri.com) have made available at no cost software such as ArcGIS Explorer which, at the time of writing is available with seven worldwide coverages that include various themes such as physical relief and political boundaries. Second, spatial thinking is advocated because it helps with other disciplines such as the physical, mathematical and environmental sciences. Third, it prepares students to be better citizens in that the data embedded within a GIS provides them with an understanding of other regions of their country and of other countries within the world. A GIS also prepares them to interact with the world in a more effective manner as an entrepreneur or merely as someone who can use an in-car navigation system more resourcefully.

Evidence to support improved spatial thinking and education in the National Research Council Report is contained in Chapter 4 and Appendix C of the study. Unfortunately, most of this research is dated and will have to be revisited if the council is to succeed in its goal of developing new GIS software that is age appropriate in its design, scope, and sequence.

Information on geographic information technology for teachers and the lay person may be found at http://geography.about.com/od/geographictechnology/Geographic_Technology.htm. A complete set of links summarizing articles, lesson plans, and software for teaching GIS in the K-12 curriculum is available at http://www.esi.utexas.edu/gk12/lessons.php.

GIS and geography teaching in elementary and secondary schools has moved forward quickly since 1990. Bednarz and Bednarz[17] take an optimistic view of the progress that has been made and how future challenges may be addressed. Doering (http://gis2.esri.com/library/userconf/educ02/pap5039/p5039.htm) has analyzed the effectiveness of various strategies for teaching about GIS in the K-12 curriculum (see also Doering and Veletsianos[18]).

Simply put, GIS is a highly effective way of teaching schoolchildren about their world. There is, however, a steep learning curve for teachers and professional development resources constantly need to be upgraded (McClurg and Buss[19]). Others have argued for a minimal GIS software package that increases in complexity with grade level and focuses on the introduction of geographical concepts appropriate to a child's intellectual development (Marsh et al.[20]).

Resources for teachers may be found at a link on the ESRI Web site at http://www.esri.com/industries/k-12/education/teaching.html. These resources include lesson plans for a variety of ages and skill levels A list of resources for teachers including annotated bibliographies of the use of GIS in the K-12 system may be found at the Web site http://gislounge.com/k-12-education-in-gis/. Links to resources on best practices and "white papers" discussing the future of GIS in school education may be found at this link on the ESRI Web site: http://www.esri.com/library/whitepapers/pdfs/higher_ed.pdf.

The work of the National Center for Geographic Information and Analysis (NCGIA) at the University of California at Santa Barbara in supporting the integration of GIS into the secondary school curriculum may be seen at the following Web site: http://www.ncgia.ucsb.edu/education/projects/SEP/sep.html. This Web site also contains links to other sites providing resources and support for K-12 GIS initiatives. Resources for schools in the United Kingdom and a sourcebook that may be ordered online can both be found at http://www.abdn.ac.uk/gis_school/.

A new trend is the linking of qualitative geography to GIS (Mei-Po Kwan[21]). This development may also unite interest in another new area of research, Children's Geographies (see the new journal of that name and introductory editorial by Matthews[22]). Children and youths may be used to supply volunteer information that can be incorporated into GIS (see discussion above and Dennis[23]).

Despite all these developments the reality is that in the year 2008 many schools still do not have the computers or the teacher expertise to take advantage of the resources that are available to them on the Internet. It can only be hoped that this will change in the coming years.

Universities

University education in GIS grew substantially after the introduction of the core curriculum in GIS by the NCGIA in 1990. The original core curriculum was designed to provide university faculty with notes for 75 lectures that represented a year-long introduction to the fundamental issues and concepts in GIS. This curriculum was remarkably successful and about 2000 copies were distributed to over 70 countries after being translated into at least eight languages (including Portuguese, Chinese, Hungarian, Japanese, Korean, Polish, Russian, and French). It may still be found at http://www.geog.ubc.ca/courses/klink/gis.notes/ncgia/toc.html.

The new Core Curriculum in GIScience may be found at http://www.ncgia.ucsb.edu/education/curricula/giscc/ and is still under development. It includes two sets of lecture notes specifically on teaching GIS within a university setting http://www.ncgia.ucsb.edu/education/curricula/giscc/units/u158/u158_f.html. A core curriculum for the closely related field of remote sensing may be found at http://userpages.umbc.edu/~tbenja1/umbc7/.

A related occurrence has been the NCGIA's development of CSISS (The Center for Spatially Integrated Social Science http://www.csiss.org/index.html).

GIS research and teaching in Universities in the United States has been substantially stimulated through the creation of the University Consortium for Geographic Information Science [UCGIS; (http://www.ucgis.org/)]. The UCGIS defines its mission to be "an effective, unified voice for the geographic information science research community." A listing of university-based, GIS courses in the United Kingdom may be found at http://www.agi.

org.uk/ under the Education Link. University based GIS research in the U.K. was also supported by the Regional Research Laboratory initiative.[1] Canadian GIS degree programs may be accessed at http://www.canadian-universities.net/Universities/Programs/Geography_and_GIS.html.

Masters courses

In recent years, master's degrees have proliferated at universities in the United States and in many other countries around the world. A listing of these programs, including distance-based offerings, may be found at http://www.ucgis.org/priorities/education/GIS_Cert+Masters_Prog/certificates.htm. Many of these master's degree programs now include modules on programming in GIS. Popular choices for programming languages include Visual Basic, Java, C, C#, and C++. Students find these courses most attractive and often feel that their education in the GISciences is not complete without some basic training in programming. The more important software vendors such as ESRI (see below) are moving away from their own, proprietary scripting languages toward industry standard languages such as Visual Basic.

In some cases these masters programs have been seen as terminal, professional degree programs which supply a need generated by the GIS industry. Others have seen them as the ideal "springboard" into Ph.D. research in Geography and other disciplines such as Archaeology that use spatially distributed data (see the Web site at http://www.le.ac.uk/geography/postgraduate/msc_gis_hg.html which discusses the Master of Science degree in GIS at the University of Leicester).

Colleges

The NCGIA has developed a core curriculum for technical programs taught in colleges and this may be accessed at http://www.ncgia.ucsb.edu/education/curricula/cctp/Welcome.html. GIS has found a particularly successful niche in technical colleges that offer postgraduate diploma programs. One of the oldest and most successful of these programs has been taught at the College of Geographic Sciences in Nova Scotia, Canada, since the early 1980s. A description of this program may be found at http://www.cogs.ns.ca/Programs/Geomatics/. A partial listing of some of the better known college programs in GIS may be found at http://www.ncgia.ucsb.edu/education/curricula/cctp/resources/example_courses/examples_f.html.

Virtual Campuses

Distance education is a well-established method of instruction in GIS and is sponsored by the UCGIS organization among others. A "white paper" on this topic may be found at (http://dusk.geo.orst.edu/disted/). Links to many

U.S. sites that offer distance education may be found at this location together with a link to the UNIGIS International site (http://www.unigis.org/) which has offices in 10 separate countries around the world. Perhaps one of the most outstandingly successful attempts at distance education is ESRI's virtual campus which may be found at http://training.esri.com/gateway/index.cfm?fa = trainingOptions. gateway. These courses may be either self study or instructor led.

While distance-based education represents an affordable and convenient way of learning about GIS or indeed any other subject it is not without its critics such as Noble.[24]

SOFTWARE PACKAGES

Software vendors have done much to popularize the use of GIS in academia, government, and industry. This they have achieved by sponsoring software distribution, conferences, Web sites, Web services, and trade newsletters. Here the activities of a number of the more important vendors and software developers are described. Most software vendors now support their own online listserves, Web knowledge banks, and other interactive communities in order to resolve problems for their user base. Information on Open Source GIS software may be found at the Open Source Geospatial Foundation Web site (http://www.osgeo.org/) and is discussed in more detail below. A survey of this software undertaken in late 2007 is available at http://www.foss4g2007.org/presentations/view.php?abstract_id=136. The rest of this section lists the leading commercial GIS software.

ESRI

Founded in 1969, ESRI (http://www.esri.com/) continues to dominate the industry as the GIS market leader. ESRI offers various configurations of its ArcGIS software. The current version of the ArcGIS software is 9.3 but new releases occur about every 6 months. The Desktop configuration has three components: ArcGIS Desktop, ArcGIS Engine, and ArcGIS Explorer (http://www.esri.com/products.html#arcgis). The Desktop product allows for the creation, editing, and analysis of geographic data and the development of professional, publication-quality maps. ESRI provides a server configuration for delivering maps and geographic data across an organization and over the Web. This configuration requires their ArcGIS Server and Image Server products. ESRI's Mobile GIS products include ArcGIS Mobile and ArcPad, products that allow the development of GIS products in the field and full use by clients with mobile devices including phones. ESRI offers data in various formats to populate these GIS products and also as Web services that are available online (http://www.esri.com/software/arcwebservices/index.

html). Other organizations that offer Web services include GIS factory (http://gisfactory.com/webservices.html) where the services include address finders, district finders, and route finders (http://gisfactory.com/whitepapers/wp_giswebservices.pdf).

ESRI sponsors the ArcWatch e-mail newsletter, the ArcUser magazine, and the ArcNews publication. In 2008 it will hold its 28th annual user conference (http://www.esri.com/events/uc/index.html), one of the most popular and enduring of all the yearly GIS conferences. Recently attendance at this premier, vendor-sponsored conference has been around 14,000 attendees. The functionality of the ESRI ArcGIS software has been augmented by a series of extensions that can be deployed to perform specific functions. For ArcGIS these include extensions for analysis, such as Spatial Analyst and Network Analyst, for productivity including, Publisher and Street Map, and solution based software such as Business Analyst and Military Analyst and, finally, Web services. A complete list of ESRI supported extensions may be found at http://www.esri.com/software/arcgis/about/desktop_extensions.html. Extensions developed by their partners may be found at http://gis.esri.com/partners/partners-user/index.cfm. A review of these extensions, organized by application type, is provided by Limp,[25] an article which may be accessed by registering at the GeoPlace Web site (http://www.geoplace.com), a GIS industry Web portal. Some extensions are packaged in the form of toolboxes that perform specific GIS operations that are often missing from the standard GIS packages. A prototypical example is Hawth's Tools that provides functionality for a variety of spatial, sampling, and animal movement operations and may be found at the spatial ecology Web site (http://www.spatialecology.com/htools/tooldesc.php).

IDRISI

One of the most popular, affordably priced, GIS products is Idrisi which was developed in 1987 by Ron Eastman and is now supported by Clark Labs at Clark University in Worcester, Massachusetts (http://www.clarklabs.org/). Idrisi's roots are as a raster GIS and as such it has been most widely used in resource management, land use change, and image processing applications. At the time of writing, the Andes Edition, the 15th major release, was the current version of this enormously popular GIS software package. The unusual name of the software owes its origins to the famed, twelfth century, Moroccan cartographer, Muhammad al-Idrisi. The Idrisi software is a fully functional GIS and image processing package that is now used in more than 175 countries. It has an especially rich and diverse set of processing modules for analytical research that include the first ever machine learning algorithms for use in a GIS and image processing system, soft classifiers, multi-criteria and multi-objective decision making that provided the first GIS implementation of

Saaty's Analytical Hierarchy Process (Saaty[26]), sophisticated geospatial statistics, and a dynamic modeling routine that is implemented through a graphical interface.

Intergraph

Intergraph is ESRI's chief competitor for the title of GIS market leader and has been providing GIS and related software for 35 years. Intergraph has a suite of GIS-related products including its GeoMedia products (http://www.intergraph.com/geomediasuite/). Intergraph also sponsors its own annual user's conference and publications including the trade publication, Insight, which is available online together with Intergraph's e-Connection Newsletter. Intergraph works with business partners such as Hansen Information Technologies (http://www.hansen.com/) to provide additional geospatial functionality, in this case for asset management and transportation and related solutions.

MAPINFO

Since 1986 MapInfo Corporation, Troy, New York (http://www.mapinfo.com/) has been producing affordable GIS software that is eminently suited to desktop mapping and such applications as geodemographics and target marketing. MapInfo emphasizes location-based intelligence especially in the field of business planning and analysis. It too supports an annual conference, the MapWorld Global User Conference, and provides customer support through online user groups.

Caliper Corporation

Caliper Corporation, Newton, Massachusetts (http://www.caliper.com/), produces one of the most sophisticated low-cost GIS desktop mapping products available, Maptitude. This software comes complete with extensive data sets from the U.S. Bureau of the Census and is ideal software for many GIS applications and has been favorably reviewed. A special version of Maptitude is available for building and analyzing political and other redistricting plans. Caliper Corporation's flagship product is Trans-CAD, a transportation GIS package that has the most complete set of transportation planning and related routines available in any GIS package. The latest release of this software, Version 5, is also produced as a Web mapping package that may be used for developing online transportation planning applications. One suggestion is that this software could be used to do online travel surveys greatly reducing the cost of traditional in-house, paper-based surveys (http://www.caliper.com/web/gist2002.pdf). Caliper Corporation is now marketing a GIS-based traffic simulation package, TransModeler.

Autodesk

Autodesk, San Rafael, California (http://www.autodesk.com), is the major software developer in the Computer Assisted Drafting market with its AutoCAD product. In recent years it has also added desktop mapping and GIS to its product line with its Map 3D product.

Bentley

In a 2006 study the Daratech organization (http://www.daratech.com/) rated Bentley Systems, Inc., as the number two provider of GIS systems worldwide. Their flagship GIS/CAD product, Microstation, was originally developed for Intergraph. It is now available as Bentley Map.

Manifold

Manifold (http://www.manifold.net/index.shtml), manufactured by CDA International Ltd., is a low cost GIS that is highly popular with organizations that have limited budgets and lack the technical expertise to work with open source software. It has an online users' support group (http://forum.manifold.net/forum/). It is a full featured GIS that in its current release of 8.0 offers 64 bit processing, an Internet map server, and is available in personal and enterprise editions.

Free and Open Source Software

There are numerous GIS packages now available in various amounts of free and open-source packages. GRASS (the geographic resources analysis support system) has made large strides in development since its release under the open source GPL license in 1999 (http://grass.itc.it/). It is designed primarily to work on Linux and other operating systems that use X windows (not to be confused with Microsoft Windows).

GeoDA is a specialized analysis tool used to examine spatial autocorrelation and related spatial regression analyses implemented on Windows. PySal (python spatial analysis library) is a shared set of libraries for both GeoDA and the STARS software that is available at the Regional Analysis Laboratory at San Diego State University (http://regionalanalysislab.org/).

Software, such as the crime analysis package, Crimestat (http://www.icpsr.umich.edu/CRIMESTAT/), are free and used frequently in the professional world, although they are not truly open source. GIS also shares a great deal of overlap with the postgreSQL and mySQL server backends, and postgis serves as "spatially-enabled" upgrade for postgreSQL and has been implemented in both the U.S. and U.K. Programs such as terraview (http://www.terralib.org/), and mapserver (http://mapserver.gis.umn.edu/) have more niche audiences but are also growing in popularity.

Geoexploration Systems

There now exist a number of competing technologies that have been described as geographic exploration systems (Ball[27]) or geoexploration systems. These technologies include Google Earth, Microsoft's Virtual Earth, NASA WorldWind, and ESRI's ArcGIS Explorer among others. They have become extremely popular since the introduction of "mashup" technology that allows even the neophyte user to combine their spatial data with real world environments across a nation or indeed across the globe. Visualization software such as GeoFusion (http://www.geofusion.com/) has been developed to improve download times, allow the integration of multiple data sets, and enhance the interface of these systems. Geoexploration systems have proved extremely useful in aiding the development of participatory GIS where nonspecialists use GIS technology for advocacy planning or to protect the rights of indigenous populations (see discussion above). Volunteer geographic information has been made far more effective by the ease of use of this new type of GIS.

Geographic social networking is a new development that represents the integration of social network technology such as MySpace, video technology such as YouTube, and geoexploration systems like Virtual Earth. This approach is being pioneered by The Carbon Project (http://www.thecarbonproject.com/).

SPATIAL AUTOCORRELATION

Spatial analysis continues to be the crux of GIScience's growth. The forms of analysis special to geographic information have continued to be developed and remain unique to the discipline (Gould[28]). Spatial autocorrelation, the problem of observations near each other having correlated regression residuals, and related analysis has become ubiquitous in the geography literature. Increases in computational resources have allowed for most desktop computers to be able to create weight matrices, calculate spatial autocorrelation, and map significance scores (Anselin;[29,30] and Anselin and Florax[31]). These tools were originally implemented in stand-alone software, but are increasingly part of commercial software such as Idrisi and ArcMap.

For more sophisticated forms of analysis, researchers are still forced to use packages such as SpaceStat (http://www.spacestat.com/) or the spatial statistics routines in S-Plus (http://insightful.com). Modern spatial analysis continues to focus on local models of spatial association (Fotheringham et al.[32]). These Local Indicators of Spatial Association (LISA) statistics, such as Local Moran's I, are frequent in the literature. Anselin's GeoDA software is the most frequently used software employed to examine these local autocorrelation statistics. GeoDA allows for the creation and analysis of weight matrices, as well as the use of

them to account for spatial autocorrelation in modified regression analysis. Another approach has been to allow the coefficients within regressions to vary over space. This method, termed geographically weighted regression, is promoted by Fotheringham and has received a mixed reception in the literature.

Markup Languages

Markup languages are the *lingua franca* of the Internet. Since its inception hypertext markup language (HTML) has been the dominant method for encoding information for text that is transmitted over the Internet. Essentially HTML does little more than provide a "picture" of a document for the Web user. All markup languages seek to provide information about the data that is transmitted over the Internet. When that data has unique characteristics, as is the case with spatial or geographical data, it requires its own markup language.

Geography markup language has been in development since 1998 and this has been largely due to the efforts of Ron Lake and his company Galdos Systems (http://www.galdosinc.com/). GML v3.0 was released as ISO Standard 19136 for the storage and transport of geographic data. GML is now the standard for the GeoWeb (http://www.geoweb.org/). It thus allows devices that are connected to the Internet to store and transmit geographical data across the Internet permitting the efficient use of Web services. Like XML, it has also spawned other related markup languages including CityGML which enables the storage and exchange of three dimensional objects that describe urban infrastructure (http://www.citygml.org/). In late 2007, CityGML was officially adopted by the Open Geospatial Consortium as the preferred markup language for urban infrastructure.

More commonly, GIS data on a server is accessed through flash and JavaScript applets that do not require the screen to refresh every time the user makes a change but instead the onscreen image will change "on the fly." This has vastly increased the usability of many online GIS applications. However, it also has made it far more difficult to create these GIS systems, with more advanced training required for these software and database packages.

GIS AND ITS APPLICATIONS

A major strength of GIS has been its ability to prove itself useful in a great many application areas. The reader may find detailed discussions of the use of GIS in the management of utilities, telecommunications, emergency management, land administration, urban planning, military applications, library management, health care, political redistricting, geodemographics and target marketing, agriculture and environmental monitoring in Longley et al.[8].

Each of these application areas has an extensive literature of its own and these are described in the various chapters included in Longley et al.'s comprehensive review of the discipline.

CERTIFICATION OF GIS PROFESSIONALS

An ongoing concern for GIS professionals has been the need for certification. Many individuals and organizations have argued that GIS professionals should be certified in a manner similar to the certification of engineers, geologists, psychologists, and others in professional disciplines. In 1998 the Urban and Regional Information Systems Association (URISA: http://www.urisa.org/) created a Certification Committee. After extensive industry-wide debate, the finalized portfolio-based certification program was established in 2003. This certification process was adopted and administered by the newly established GIS Certification Institute (http://www.gisci.org/). Certification involves establishing evidence of professional competence and ethical conduct. Until January 1, 2009, a "grandfathering" process was also permitted. At the end of 2007 almost 2000 individuals have availed themselves of the certification process.

GIS AND THE FUTURE

Judging the future of the discipline is difficult, as rapid advancements make such statements outdated by the time of publishing. Such is the case in a recent work by Reuter and Zipf (http://www.i3mainz.fh-mainz.de/publicat/zipf05/gis.where.next-reuter-zipf.pdf), that predicts the trajectory of a device to support trip planning that is partially implemented in a new release of the iPhone. As GIS presses onward, it will continue to be embedded within more and more electronics. While appliances such as refrigerators and stoves do not generally need location information, most devices that move today already have some sort of location-finding mechanism inside them. The future of these devices may rely on the ability to more precisely locate themselves, particularly inside buildings. Reuter and Zipf suggest this may come in a ground-based GPS system they term a "Global Universal Computer."

The amount of spatial data is blossoming and will likely continue to do so. As users mark important personal events and places linked to particular places, storage and retrieval of this data will become increasingly important. Reuter and Zipf suggest it is the storage and search of these items that will be most important. This technology may be crucial to historians and psychologists working to understand the reasons for individual behavior.

At some point, the lack of widespread spatial education will segment the population further, based on those who can use new integrated devices and those who cannot.

Technological advances will make up for some of this digital divide by simplifying interfaces. However, these new interfaces generally cannot wholly account for such differences and maintain full functionality without a significant paradigm shift.

Finally, it may be noted that GIS in the future will become more involved with the third and fourth dimensions. The third dimension is already being implemented in geographic exploration systems and the integration of products such as Google SketchUp (http://sketchup.google.com/) into Google Earth. The fourth dimension is time, a difficult concept to incorporate into traditional GIS software structures. Peuquet[33] has provided part of the theoretical paradigm for this new implementation and new versions of commercial software such as ESRI's ArcGIS 9.3 make it easier to create animated visualizations of geodatabases. 3-D/4-D GIS will be the new frontier.

BIBLIOGRAPHY AND ADDITIONAL RELATED RESOURCES

GIS Day

On November 14, 2007, GIS Day was held in over 80 countries around the World and in all 50 states in the United States. GIS Day is a grassroots movement in which GIS users and vendors (academics, government employees and entrepreneurs) open their doors to schoolchildren and all members of the general public in order to showcase the capabilities of GIS projects which they have developed (http://www.gisday.com/). The event is sponsored principally by the National Geographic Society, the Association of American Geographers, the University Consortium for Geographic Information Science, the United States Geological Survey, The Library of Congress, Sun Microsystems and Hewlett-Packard and ESRI, and by local GIS organizations. The next GIS Day will be held on November 18 and 17 in 2009 and 2010, respectively. The event is usually held as part of Geography Awareness Week, which has been sponsored by the National Geographic Society since 1987. The U.S. e-Government Web site using data from Daratech estimates that there are 1,000,000 users of GIS worldwide, half of whom are in the United States (http://www.whitehouse.gov/omb/egov/c-7-10-b-geospatial.html).

Books

The most important reference works for GIS are the so-called "Big-Books" of GIS. The first edition of this huge, two-volume review of the state of the art in GIS was edited by Maguire, Goodchild, and Rhind[34] and published in 1991, while the second edition was edited by Longley, Goodchild, Maguire, and Rhind[35] in 1999.

More recently, the second volume has been published in a paperback edition with editorial updates based on input from the individual chapter authors, various additional chapters, and a CD featuring all the chapters from the second edition (Longley et al.[36]). Popular textbooks discussing the concepts behind GIS include Longley et al.[37] and Clarke.[4] The latter author provides an extensive list of GIS books magazines and journals, conference proceedings, and professional organizations. Price's[38] text is a guide to operating the industry leading ArcGIS 9.2 software and includes a series of hands-on tutorials to aid the novice user.

A searchable GIS bibliography may be found at ESRI's Web site: http://training.esri.com/campus/library/index.cfm. Important publishers of GIS texts include ESRI (http://store. esri.com/esri/category.cfm?SID=2&Category_ID=35) and Taylor & Francis (http://gis.tandf.co.uk/). Longley et al.[37] provide a list of major GIS textbooks while Chrisman[6] describes the earliest days of the discipline. Vendor publications have been discussed above. Suffice it to note that most major vendors have a company publication designed to inform their user base of the latest developments in their software products and many of these are now available online.

Journals and Magazines

Some of the main academic journals in which GIS research is published include

Annals of the Association of American Geographers (http://www.aag.org/);
Canadian Geographer (http://www.blackwellpublishing. com/CG);
Cartographica (http://www.utpjournals.com/carto/ carto.html);
Cartographic Perspectives (http://www.nacis.org/index. cfm?x=5);
Cartography and GIS (http://www.cartogis.org/);
Computers, Environment, and Urban Systems (http:// www.elsevier.com/locate/compenvurbsys);
Computers and Geosciences (http://www.elsevier.com/ locate/cageo);
Conference Papers in GIS (http://srmwww.gov.bc.ca/ gis/papers/index.html);
ESRI User Conference Proceedings (http://gis.esri. com/library/userconf/index.html);
Geocarto International (http://www.geocarto.com/ geocarto.html);
Geographical Systems (http://link.springer.de/link/ser- vice/journals//10109/);
GeoInformatica (http://www.wkap.nl/journalhome. htm/1384-6175);
Geoscience E-Journals (http://paleopolis.rediris.es/ geosciences/);

Geographical Journal (http://www.ingentaconnect.com/ content/bpl/geoj/latest);
GeoJournal (http://www.ingentaconnect.com/content/klu/ gejo/latest);
GIS Law;
IEEE Transactions on Computer Graphics and Appli- cations (http://ieeexplore.ieee.org/xpl/RecentIssue. jsp?punumber=38);
IEEE Transactions on Geoscience and Remote Sensing (http://ieeexplore.ieee.org/xpl/RecentIssue.jsp? punumber=36);
International Journal of Geographical Information Science (http://www.tandf.co.uk/journals/titles/ 13658816.asp);
International Journal of Remote Sensing (http://www. tandf.co.uk/journals/frameloader.html?http://www. tandf.co.uk/journals/tf/01431161.html);
International Journal of Mapping Sciences and Remote Sensing (http://www.ingentaconnect.com/content/ bell/msrs/latest);
Journal of Geographical Systems (http://link.springer. de/link/service/journals/10109/index.htm);
Photogrammetric Engineering and Remote Sensing (http://www.asprs.org/publications/pers/www.asprs. org/publications/pers/);
Public Health GIS News and Information (http://www. cdc.gov/nchs/about/otheract/gis/gis_publichealthinfo. htm);
Remote Sensing Reviews (http://www.tandf.co.uk/ journals/online/0275–7257.asp);
Transactions in GIS (http://www.blackwellpublishing. com/journals/tgis/);
The Spatial Odyssey Website also has a list of GIS Journal Abstracts and Citations (http://libraries. maine.edu/Spatial/gisweb/journals/journals.html).

Many **magazines** are available in both an online and a paper version. Some of the more notable examples are

ArcNews Online (http://www.esri.com/news/arcnews/ arcnews.html);
ArcUser Online (http://www.esri.com/news/arcuser/ index.html);
Challenges: A news letter from UCGIS (http://dusk2. geo.orst.edu/ucgis/news/);
Asian surveying and mapping (http://www.asmmag. com/);
GEOWorld (http://www.geoplace.com/).

Other online GIS-oriented magazines include

Directions Magazine (http://www.directionsmag.com/);
Earth Observing Magazine (http://www.eomonline. com/);
GeoCommunity (http://www.geocomm.com/);

Geomatics Information and Trading Centre (http://www.gitc.nl/);

GeoSpatial Solutions (http://www.geospatial-online.com/);

GeoVision (http://www.gisvisionmag.com/);

Geomatics Info Magazine International (http://www.reedbusiness-geo.nl/Home.asp);

GPS World (http://www.gpsworld.com/);

Spatial News (http://spatialnews.geocomm.com/);

Mentor Software (http://www.mentorsoftwareinc.com/cc/ccdir.htm);

Position Magazine (http://www.positionmag.com.au/);

Professional Surveyor Magazine Online (http://www.profsurv.com/);

The CADD/GIS Technology Center CADD/GIS Bulletins Page (https://tsc.wes.army.mil/news/bulletins/).

Organizations

The following are some of the better known organizations with a strong interest in GIS:

The American Congress on Surveying and Mapping (ACSM) (http://www.acsm.net/);

The American Society for Photogrammetry and Remote Sensing (ASPRS) (http://www.asprs.org/);

The Association for Geographic Information (AGI) (http://www.agi.org.uk/);

The Association of American Geographers (AAG) (http://www.aag.org/ this organization has a specialty group devoted to GIS) (http://geography.sdsu.edu/aaggis/);

The International Geographical Union which has a Commission on Geographical Information Science (http://www.hku.hk/cupem/igugisc/);

The North American Cartographic Information Society (NACIS) (http://www.nacis.org/);

Geospatial Information and technology Association (http://www.gita.org/);

The Urban and Regional Information Systems Association (URISA) (http://www.urisa.org/).

Conferences

This section lists a number of the more important conferences other that the vendor-specific conferences mentioned above. Many of the general, omnibus GIS Conferences have in recent years folded as more specialized offerings take their place. These conferences have usually produced either a print proceedings or a proceedings on CD-ROM.

Most of the major GIS organizations such as URISA will also have annual and even regional GIS conferences. Some conferences are strictly devoted to a single theme and are strongly oriented toward training. This is true of the Web mapping conferences (http://www.gisconferences.com/). In 2007, the following was a selection of the conferences held across the globe:

ACM GIS conference in Bellevue, Washington

Africa GIS conference in Ouagadougou, Burkina Fasa

AGIC (Arizona Geographic Information Council); GIS conference in Prescott, Arizona

AGILE (Association Geographic Information Laboratories Europe); conference on GIS in Aalborg, Denmark

Annual CA Geographic Information Association conference in Cypress, California

Annual GIS conference, ASPRS and URISA in Vancouver, Washington

Annual GIS for Oil & Gas Conference in Aurora, Colorado

Annual International airport GIS conference in Budapest, Hungary

Annual Minnesota GIS conference in Rochester, Minnesota

Annual Missouri GIS conference in Osage Beach, Missouri

Annual NC GIS conference in Winston-Salem, North Carolina

Annual Ohio GIS conference in Columbus, Ohio

Annual Virginia GIS conference in Virginia Beach, Virginia

Arc GIS conference in Biloxi, Mississippi

Biennial GIS conference, Iowa Geographic Council in Sioux City, Iowa

California GIS conference in Oakland, California

Croatian GIS Association conference in Sinj, Croatia

Delaware GIS conference in Dover, Delaware

East Tennessee GIS conference in Pigeon Forge, Tennessee

Eastern Montana GIS conference in Miles City, Missouri

ESRI Asia-Pacific User Conference in New Delhi, India

ESRI Australia: GIS user conference in Sydney, Australia

ESRI Eastern Africa: GIS user conference in Kampala, Uganda

ESRI Federal Users GIS conference in Washington, District of Columbia

ESRI GIS solution expo in Danvers, Massachusetts

ESRI Health GIS conference in Scottsdale, Arizona

ESRI International User conference in San Diego, California

ESRI New Zealand: GIS user conference in New Zealand

ESRI South Asia user conference in Novotel Clarke Quay, Singapore

EUC (European User Conference) in Stockholm, Sweden

The GeoTec Event in Ottawa, Ontario, Canada

GI and GIS conference in Porto, Portugal

GIS conference, Office of Lt Governor, U.S. Virgin Islands

GIS Engineers Society conference in Trivandrum, India

GIS for public sector conference in London, U.K.

GIS for Urban Environmental summit in Johannesburg, South Africa

GIS in Rockies conference in Denver, Colorado

GIS in Transit in Tampa, Florida

GIS South Africa conference in Umhlanga Rocks, Durban

Historical GIS conference in Nagoya, Japan

Homeland Security GIS summit in Denver, Colorado

Illinois GIS conference (ILGISA) in Oak Brook, Illinois

Indiana GIS conference in Indianapolis, Indiana

Indonesian Geospatial Technology Exhibition in Jakarta, Indonesia

Intermountain GIS conference in Donnelly, Idaho

International conference of GIS/RS in Hydrology in Guangzhou, China

International conference on Health GIS in Bangkok, Thailand

International GIS crime mapping conference in Brussels, Belgium

Ireland GIS conference in Dublin, Ireland

Kentucky GIS conference in Louville, Kentucky

Kuwait GIS conference in Kuwait

Map Asia in Kulamanpur, Malaysia

Memphis Area Geographic Information Council GIS conference in Memphis, Tennessee

National GIS symposium in Saudi Arabia in Khobar, Saudi Arabia

Nebraska GIS Symposium in Omaha, Nebraska

Nordic GIS conference in Herning, Denmark

North Dakota GIS user conference in Bismarck, North Dakota

North Western PA GIS conference in Clarion, Pennsylvania

Northeast Arc Users Group: GIS conference in Burlington, Vermont

NSGIC (National States Geographic Information Council); in Madison, Wisconsin

NYS GIS conference in Liverpool, New York

PA GIS conference in Harrisburg, Pennsylvania

Pacific Islands GIS/RS conference in Suva, Fiji

Real estate GIS user conference in Scottsdale, Arizona

Rhode Island GIS conference in Narragansett, Rhode Island

ScanGIS—Scandinavian GIS Conference in As, Norway

Southern Forestry and Natural Resources Management GIS conferences in Kissimmee, Florida

Super map GIS conference in Beijing, China

Towson GIS conference in Towson, Maryland

UGIC (Utah Geographic Information Council)—GIS conference in Salt Lake City, Utah

URISA & IAAO 11th Annual GIS conference in Las Vegas, Nevada

URISA (urban regional information systems association)

VIGIC (Virgin Islands Geospatial Information Council)

Washington GIS conference in Lynnwood, Washington

GIS Dictionaries

The Association for Geographic Information has an online dictionary at http://www.geo.ed.ac.uk/agidict/welcome.html. For a published GIS dictionary McDonnell and Kemp's[39] International GIS Dictionary can be referred to.

ACKNOWLEDGMENT

The authors would like to thank Matt Ball for comments on an earlier draft.

REFERENCES

1. Waters, N.M. Geographic information systems. *Encyclopedia of Library and Information Science*; Marcel Dekker Inc.: New York, 1998; Vol. 63, 98–125 Supplement 26.
2. Waters, N.M. Geographic information systems. *Encyclopedia of Library and Information Science*, 2nd Ed.; Drake, M., Ed.; Marcel Dekker, Inc.: New York, 2003; 1106–1115.
3. Dibiase, D. Demers, M. Johnson, A. Kamp, K. Taylor Luck, A. Plewe, B. Wentz, E. *Geographic Information Science and Technology Body of Knowledge*, Association of American Geographers: Washington, DC, 2006.
4. Clarke, K.C. *Getting Started with Geographic Information Systems*, 4th Ed. Prentice Hall: Upper Saddle River, NJ, 2003.
5. In *The History of Geographic Information Systems: Perspectives from the Pioneers*; Foresman, T.W., Ed.; Prentice Hall: Upper Saddle River, NJ, 1997.
6. Chrisman, N. *Charting the Unknown: How Computer Mapping at Harvard Became GIS*, ESRI Press: Redlands, CA, 2006.
7. Burrough, P. McDonnell, R. *Principles of Geographical Information Systems*, 2nd Ed.; Oxford University Press: New York, 1998.
8. Longley, P. Goodchild, M.F. Maguire, D.J. Rhind, D.W. Introduction. In *Geographical Information Systems, Vol. 1, Principles and Technical Issues*; Longley, P., Goodchild, M.F., Maguire, D.J., Rhind, D.W., Eds.; Wiley: New York, 1999; 1–16.
9. Kang, H.; Scott, D.M. An integrated spatio-temporal GIS toolkit for exploring intra-household interactions. *Transportation* **2008**, *35*, 253–268.

10. Mark, D.M. Geographic information science: Defining the field. In *Foundations of Geographic Information Science*; Duckham, M., Goodchild, M.F., Worboys, M.F., Eds.; Taylor & Francis: New York, 2003; 3–18.

11. Wright, D.J.; Goodchild, M.F.; Proctor, J.D. Demystifying the persistent ambiguity of GIS as 'tool' versus 'science.'. Ann. Assoc. Am. Geogr. **1997**, *87*, 346–362.

12. Chrisman, N.R. What does GIS mean?. Trans. GIS **1999**, *3*, 175–186.

13. In *Policy Issues in Modern Cartography*; Taylor, D.R.F., Ed.; Elsevier Science: Oxford, U.K., 1998.

14. Craig, W.J. Harris, T.M. Weiner, D. *Community Participation and Geographical Information Systems*, CRC Press: Boca Raton, FL, 2002.

15. Goodchild, M.F. Citizens as sensors: The world of volunteered geography. GeoJournal **2007**, *69*, 211–221.

16. National Research Council. *Learning to Think Spatially*, The National Academies Press: Washington, DC, 2006.

17. Bednarz, S.W.; Bednarz, R.S. Geography education: The glass is half full and its getting fuller. Prof. Geogr. **2004**, *56*, 22–27.

18. Doering, A.; Veletsianos, G. An investigation of the use of real-time, authentic geospatial data in the K-12 classroom. J. Geogr. **2007**, *106*, 217–225.

19. McClurg, P.A.; Buss, A. Professional development: Teachers use of GIS to enhance student learning. J. Geogr. **2007**, *106*, 79–87.

20. Marsh, M.; Golledge, R.; Battersby, S.E. Geospatial concept understanding and recognition in G6-college students: A preliminary argument for minimal GIS. Ann. Assoc. Am. Geogr. **2007**, *97*, 696–712.

21. Kwan, M.P.; Knigge, L. Guest editorial: Doing qualitative research using GIS: An oxymoronic endeavor?. Environ. Plann. A **2006**, *38*, 1999–2002.

22. Matthews, H. Inaugural editorial: Coming of age for children's geographies. Child. Geogr. **2003**, *1*, 3–5.

23. Dennis, S. Prospects for qualitative GIS at the intersection of youth development and participatory urban planning. Environ. Plann. A **2006**, *38*, 2039–2002.

24. Noble, D. *Digital Diploma Mills*, Monthly Review Press: New York, 2003.

25. Limp, W.F. ArcGIS extensions: Quick take review. GeoWorld **2005**, *18*(7), 54–58.

26. Saaty, T.L. *Theory and Applications of the Analytic Network Process: Decision Making with Benefits, Opportunities, Costs, and Risks*, RWS Publishers: Artarmon, New South Wales, Australia, 2005.

27. Ball, M. *Digital reality: Comparing geographic exploration systems*. 2006. http://www.geoplace.com.

28. Gould, P.R. Is Statistix Inferens the geographical name for a wild goose?. Econ. Geogr. **1970**, *46*, 439–448.

29. Anselin, L. *Spatial Econometrics*, Kluwer: Dordrecht, the Netherlands, 1988.

30. Anselin, L. Local indicators of spatial autocorrelation. Geogr. Anal. **1995**, *27*, 93–115.

31. Anselin, L. Florax, R. *New Directions in Spatial Econometrics*, Springer-Verlag: Berlin, Germany, 1995.

32. Fotheringham, A.S. Brunsdon, C. Charlton, M. *Quantitative Geography: Perspectives on Spatial Analysis*, Sage: London, U.K., 2000.

33. Peuquet, D. *Representations of Space and Time*, Guilford: New York, 2002.

34. In *Geographical Information Systems*; Maguire, D.J., Goodchild, M.F., Rhind, D.W., Eds.; Longman: London, U.K., 1991.

35. In *Geographical Information Systems*; Longley, P., Goodchild, M.F., Maguire, D.J., Rhind, D.W., Eds.; Wiley: New York, 1999.

36. *Geographical Information Systems*, 2nd Ed.; Longley, P.A., Goodchild, M.F., Maguire, D.J., Rhind, D.W., Eds.; Wiley: New York, 2005.

37. Longley, P.A. Goodchild, M.F. Maguire, D.J. Rhind, D.W. *Geographic Information Systems and Science*, 2nd Ed; Wiley: New York, 2005.

38. Price, M. *Mastering ArcGIS 9.2*, McGraw-Hill: New York, 2008.

39. McDonnell, R. Kemp, K. *International GIS Dictionary*, Longman: London, U.K., 1995.

Geographical Literature: History [ELIS Classic]

Nora T. Corley
Arctic Institute of North America, Montreal, Quebec, Canada

Abstract

One of the objectives of the information disciplines is to study the universe of recorded information—that is, to study the documentary products of domains of human activity—and to come to understand such bodies of literature as social and historical phenomena in and of themselves. Corley traces the development of the discipline of geography in parallel to the development of the literature of geography.

—*ELIS Classic, from 1973*

INTRODUCTION

Geography is, by definition, the science that describes the surface of the earth: the land, the sea, the air, the distribution of animals and plants, man and his works, and the relationships of all of these elements. The word "geography" itself is derived from Greek words meaning "earth description."

Like other academic disciplines, geography has its own body of literature and its own peculiar ways of looking at the problems under investigation. As a science, geography dates back to antiquity, in fact, it is perhaps the oldest science of all. But scientific geography as we know it today dates back only to the end of the eighteenth century, when Kant, Humboldt, Peschel, Ratzel, and others defined the scope and content of geography, and dictated the methods of collecting, organizing, and presenting the material.

HISTORY

Primitive man has always been a keen observer of his own country and any he traveled through (even today Eskimos can give an extremely detailed description of an area that to the untrained and unfamiliar eye might otherwise be called featureless).

Geography was held in great esteem by the ancient Greeks, who traveled and accumulated facts, charted and mapped their world, and speculated about the knowledge they had gathered. The information they collected was of prime importance to their merchants, administrators, statesmen, and military.

Thales of Miletus (624–546 B.C.), thought to be one of the most talented men of all time, was one of the earliest geographers. In fact he founded Greek mathematics, astronomy, and physics, as well as geography. Thales realized that the surface of the earth was curved because of the different slant of the sun as one traveled north. He also noted that the slant of the sun's rays changed with the

seasons, and he invented the equator and the plane of the ecliptic. He also suggested that the earth could be divided by circles parallel to the equator and lines perpendicular to it, now known as lines of latitude and longitude.

Hecataeus (fl. 500 B.C.), sometimes called the father of geography, wrote about his travels to Egypt, Persia, Libya, Spain, and Italy; unfortunately only fragments of his narrative are extant. He considered the earth a flat disk surrounded by a river of ocean. His works were the first regional geography. His map was an extension of one made by Anaxemander who, along with Thales, Aristotle, and Eratosthenes, developed mathematical geography. They proved the earth to be a sphere; computed its size fairly accurately; established the latitude and longitude of many places; and began the practice of plotting maps on grids.

Homer, too, is sometimes referred to as the father of geography, as much of his poetry dealt with the geographical lore of the day, gleaned from the tales of ancient travelers.

A third claimant to this same title was Herodotus (ca. 485–428 B.C.), who was the first to designate Europe, Asia, and Africa as three distinct continents. Herodotus had traveled widely throughout the Near and Middle East, seeking out and questioning the intellectuals in each locality. He did not ascribe to the theory of a disk-shaped earth rimmed by a river of ocean. Instead he gave a detailed description of the world as he knew it as far east as India, west to the Pillars of Hercules, north to the forest boundary of the steppes, and south to the present Sudan. His work is distinguished by the excellent descriptions of town sites.

Theophrastes (ca. 370 B.C.) was the first to note the relationship between plants and climate, and so began the study of plant geography.

Eratosthenes (ca. 276–194 B.C.) was the curator of Ptolemy II's library in Alexandria, which contained some 40,000 books. He was reputed to be the most learned man of antiquity. His *Geographica* described the world as he knew it, summarizing the history and concepts of

Encyclopedia of Library and Information Sciences, Fourth Edition DOI: 10.1081/E-ELIS4-120008986

geography. He is credited with naming the subject, though he certainly did not invent it. Eratosthenes also calculated the circumference of the earth at 250,000 stadia (approximately 25,000 miles), coming very close to the actual figure.

Pomponius Mela (ca. A.D. 50) employed the concept of a world symmetrically divided into four by two narrow strips of ocean, despite the fact that realistic geographies had been written based on explorers' and travelers' reports. In his textbook, written in Latin (which made it influential in medieval times), he maintained that the unknown parts of the continents were not necessarily inhabited by people, and that those who lived at the "bottom" of the world were foot to foot with those at the "top," and so he called the former Antipodes (a term no longer used for a people, but rather for a place).

The Romans were not scientifically minded and so added little to geographic thought. Rather, they were concerned with more practical things such as the problems of commerce, administration, and military conquest. They did, however, contribute the *itinerarii* which were descriptions of their road systems—a kind of map, without scale or projection. They were designed only as a convenience to travelers.

Strabo (63 B.C.–A.D. 36) was a Greek regional geographer living in Rome. He summarized (in 17 volumes) the geographical knowledge of his time in his *Geographica*, which has survived.[1] Strabo relied heavily on other Greek authorities, but maintained that it was the geographer's task to describe the known world, to write about the different countries, and to discuss the differences between them. He used the reports of travelers and merchants, seamen's handbooks, and histories of Alexander's conquests as well as material relative to the Roman empire and its trade routes. Strabo's treatment of regional geography at the turn of the millenum is the most elaborate to survive. Since it was written in Greek and was not translated until a long time after, it did not have the influence that it deserved.

Ptolemy (Claudius Ptolemius) taught and studied in Alexandria from A.D. 127–151. His great general work *Geographike Syntaxis* dealt with map projections, included tables for latitude and longitude, and gave calculations for the length of day and night for various places depending on their distance from the equator. This work was far beyond the standard of its predecessors. It was translated into Arabic in A.D. 815 and much later (A.D. 1475) into Latin, thus becoming both a Christian and a Moslem authority.

Ptolemy considered *geography* as the description on mathematical principles of the whole world, *chorography* as a detailed account of a region, and *topography* as a minute account of a smaller area. The world, according to Ptolemy, stretched from Spain to China, and from Thule to south of the equator.

During the Middle Ages geography as a science almost disappeared. It was forbidden by the Christian Church as a pagan science; the theory of the spherical shape of the earth was denounced and the accepted concept was that of a flat disk with Jerusalem at the center. However, at this time geography was being encouraged by the Arabs. Their empire extended, at its height, over most of Europe, Asia, and Africa. In the eastern Mediterranean they came into contact with Greek learning and libraries. Because of Ptolemy's work, descriptive geography flourished. The continued existence of the Roman roads and the compulsory pilgrimages to Mecca encouraged people to travel throughout the empire, and so trade arose as a natural result; all of which influenced geography. The Arabs made accurate calculations of latitude and longitude and the size of the earth, but they made no improvement in the science of cartography. Arab maps were often distorted because of their love of flourish and ornamentation. However, their sea charts, which were based on a cylindrical projection, were highly thought of by the explorer Vasco da Gama. Regional geographical handbooks were written for travelers, merchants, and administrators by ibn Haukal, Masudi, and Idrisi. These were not translated and so had no influence in the West.

Because of the relatively easy travel throughout the Arab empire, it was possible for Marco Polo (1254–1324) to travel overland to China. His account of his journey, and his return by sea has been a widely read story since it was first published. *The Book of Marco Polo* (1296–1299) is an attempt at systematic geography. He was not writing from his own observation in every chapter, but assembled the best information that was available to him. This is particularly true of his chapter on the Indian Ocean. His adventures stimulated exploration in the Christian world, and though written in the thirteenth century, at the end of the next century it supplied Columbus with considerable support to his theories.

About 1357 the spurious *Travels* of Sir John Mandeville (ca. 1300–1372) were published and, thought to be authentic, they were very popular. The book was based on real travelers' tales and tall stories, as well as on Pliny and Solinus. The author also noted the spherical shape of the earth.

Beginnings of Modern Geography

Explorers

Modern geography began when man became aware of the fact that there were lands still to be discovered. Numerous people went exploring—found new worlds, circumnavigated the earth, and returned home with detailed observations and maps of what they had seen. They were exercising a modern geographer's technique—that of gathering data in the field. Their notes were used by contemporary writers of books and compilers of atlases.

About 1418 Henry the Navigator (1394–1460) established a school of geographers. Though he did not travel himself, Henry sent out many exploring expeditions, notably Vasco da Gama's in 1498 which opened the way to the Indies via the Cape of Good Hope. About the same time Columbus discovered America, and so did Cabot. Vespucci discovered South America and in 1520–1521 Magellan sailed completely around the world, proving for once and for all the sphericity of the earth and the continuity of the oceans. The narratives of these great explorations took an important place in the literature of geography during the great age of discovery.

Editions of Ptolemy's works continued to appear, enlarged with new tables. Sebastian Münster's (1489–1552) *Cosmographia universalis*,[2] a political and regional work based on Strabo, was the most complete attempt to rewrite the classics, and was most popular.

In 1570 Abraham Ortelius (1527–1598) published his *Theatrum Orbis Terrarum*[3] of regional and world maps. This was the first modern atlas. A few years before (1598) his friend Gerhard Kremer, better known as Mercator (1512–1594), had published his famous map projection, now known as the Mercator projection, for use in navigation.

Philipp Clüver (1580–1622), a German, published an *Introduction to Universal Geography*.[4] This was a brief account of mathematical geography, with regional descriptions of the world. It was an excellent work, and set a standard for regional geography that was long unsurpassed.

By 1642, when the Dutch mariner Abel Tasman (1602 or 1603–1659) completed the delineation of Australia, the land masses of the world, except for the Antarctic, were fairly well known. The next 150 years saw further exploration.

Writers

Another Dutchman, Varenius (Bernhard Varen, 1622–ca. 1650) published in 1650 the most notable geographical textbook of the time: *Geographia Generalis*.[5] This was the first book to include the new theory of the universe as set forth by Copernicus, Kepler, and Galileo. Varenius defined geography as a branch of mathematics, not wanting to limit it merely to the regional descriptions of countries. He included human geography only as a concession to custom. In 1672 his book was reprinted in London at the insistence of Sir Isaac Newton, who wished to have it as a text for his students at Cambridge. It was translated into English in 1732, but Varenius was considered a very difficult writer, and though his book, unfinished because of his early demise, was not expected to be read outside the universities, it was for centuries considered a standard text.

The English geographer Nathaniel Carpenter (fl. early seventeenth century) had some years before delineated geography in two books.[6] His methods and sources were similar to Varenius's, and he came to the same conclusions. Many of Carpenter's themes were drawn from the French

political theorist Jean Boden—especially in dividing the world into three climatic zones: torrid, temperate, and frigid; and attributing to the inhabitants of each region certain general characteristics. Carpenter was dogmatic on this aspect—men in colder climates were strong, tall and active; those of the warmer regions were languid; also people living in mountains or highlands were superior to those of the plains. He deemed Europe the most favored region in the world.

For a century after Varenius there was little geographical research; most interest was in the natural sciences. However, the unprecedented expansion of knowledge in these fields made it possible to give a more scientific description of the earth. By the early eighteenth century geography was taking its place as an independent science.

Geography as a Science

Though Jean Jacques Rousseau (1712–1779) was not a geographer, he made many interesting geographical observations. He noted that environment exercised influence on primitive man; the varieties of soils, climates, and the seasons introduced differences in their manner of living. He accepted these differences between northerners and southerners without going into the matter to any degree. He was apt to select unique instances to support his geographical arguments. He realized that the relationship between geography and history was not as simple as generally supposed.

Anton Friedrich Büsching (1724–1793) in his *Neue Erdbeschreibung*[7] described the surface of the earth, being as accurate as possible, without trying to explain facts or relationships. A regional description was made by political units, and he insisted on a very high standard of accuracy and on the critical handling of his sources. Büsching opened a new era in the science of geography—for the next 150 years, up until the beginning of the twentieth century, geography became almost solely a German science, and the significant developments were made by German scholars.

Next came Johann Rheinhold Forster (1729–1798), and his son, Johann Georg. The elder Forster had a keen scientific mind and great powers of observation. He collected facts, classified them and compared them, made generalizations, and sought explanations. His works were noted also for their contribution to human geography. He was one of the first to try to explain the relationship between man and his environment.

Johann Georg Forster (1754–1779) was not as gifted as his father but, as is often the case, he was more honored in his lifetime. He translated his father's famous *Observations* (1778);[8] he was a friend of Humboldt, who had been stimulated by the younger Forster's *Voyage around the world* (1777)[9] (based on the elder Forster's travels), and by whom he was often quoted.

The philosopher Emmanuel Kant (1729–1804) stressed physical geography in his lectures and writings, and he recognized its position in relation to the other natural sciences.

The nineteenth century saw the exploration of the interiors of the continents. The journals and diaries subsequently published by the explorers were an important contribution to regional geography, and later to historical geography. They described the country as they saw it, and in most cases, as it is no longer. In Canada there were Samuel Hearne, Sir Alexander Mackenzie, David Thompson, and Sir John Franklin; and later Sir John M'Clure, Sir Edward Parry, and others opened up the Canadian Arctic searching for Franklin's lost expedition. In the United States there were explorers such as Merriweather Lewis and William Clark, Zebulon Pike, Stephen Harriman Long, Benjamin Bonneville, and John C. Fremont.

In Africa there were such men as Mungo Park, David Livingstone, Stanley, Sir Richard Francis Burton, and John Hanning. In India Sir Francis Younghusband, Evariste Régis Huc, and Nikolai Przhevalsky. Sven Hedig and Sir Aurel Stein visited the interior of the Asian continent, and Ferdinand Baron von Richthofen made seven journeys into China. In Australia there was Captain Charles Stunt, Thomas Mitchell, Dr. Ludevig Leichhardt, Robert O'Hara Burke, and William John Wills.

The Antarctic continent did not come in for intensive exploration until the twentieth century, when Robert Falcon Scott and Sir Douglas Mawson and others made their mark. At the beginning of the twentieth century the Arctic also contributed some famous explorers: Robert E. Peary, Frederick Cook, Knud Rasmussen, Roald Amundsen, Fridtjof Nansen, Vilhjalmur Stefansson, and Otto Nordenskiöld.

MODERN GEOGRAPHY

It is generally agreed that modern geography was founded by two German masters of the subject: Alexander von Humboldt (1769–1859) and Karl Ritter (1779–1859). Humboldt was a great scientist and traveler. He traveled extensively throughout Latin America and Asia gathering data, mapping and sketching in the field, and returned home to write up his results. Ritter, on the other hand, was a historian who carefully considered and cataloged other researchers' data. Though these two scholars approached geography from different backgrounds, they both made such a significant contribution to the subject that the course they charted for the science of geography is still largely followed today.

Humboldt made his first foreign tour with J.R. Forster, whose methods of careful observation and treatment of facts, as well as his scientific description of landscapes, greatly impressed him. Humboldt spent five years in Latin American and the next 20 writing up his notes. His *Ansichten der Natur*,[10] written when he returned from Mexico in 1808, gave a suggestion of a pattern of regularity on the earth's surface and received widespread attention. In 1829 he went to the Urals to study the ore-bearing regions, and eventually ended his career as chamberlain to the King of Germany.

Humboldt's *Kosmos*,[11] published in five volumes, was a comprehensive survey of the universe. His was an empirical approach to research. He combined geography and astronomy in a classical fashion, but kept to the principle of the unity of nature.

Karl Ritter spent 20 years as tutor in a rich family and the rest of his life teaching (he was professor of geography at the University of Berlin), writing, and directing the Gesellschaft für Erdekunde. His great work was his *Die Erdkunde, im Vertältnis zur Natur und zur Geschichte des Menschen, oder Allgemeine, Vergleichende Geographie*,[12] a comparative regional geography of the world. It was never finished although 21 volumes were published on Asia and Africa. Ritter's approach, like Humboldt's, was empirical. He stressed comparison of phenomena in various regions rather than drawing conclusions from only one. His rule was to proceed from observation to observation and not from hypothesis or opinion to observation. Ritter's literary style was very difficult, often lacking clarity or precision of expression, and so he is frequently misunderstood. Though his books are today considered to be unreadable, his position as a father of geography has been established on the basis of the whole of his writings, and not on any one particular work.

The writings of the two great men were complementary. Humboldt gave method and form to systematic geography; Ritter founded regional geography. Unfortunately, they left no followers. Humboldt never taught, and Ritter's vacated chair was never filled. In their wake they left confusion and shifting points of view. Physical geography was stressed; there was a desire that it be considered a natural science. Human geography, thought to be unscientific, was treated only when necessary to the description of various regions.

One of the most notable geographical works of the nineteenth century was the *Physical Geography* (1848)[13] by Mary Somerville (1780–1872). This book showed an interest in historical geography and a concern for its basic physical foundations, thus anticipating two popular trends of the twentieth century.

Arnold Henry Guyot (1807–1884), a Swiss and a follower of Ritter's, wrote *The Earth and Man*,[14] which was translated into English in 1849. This book helped introduce German ideas to English-speaking geographers. Guyot set forth some of geography's significant problems and so helped define the limits of the new science. As professor of geography at Princeton he contributed to the advance of physical geography, stressing the study of structure, surface formations, and erosional processes.

Ritter's most successful pupil was Jean Jacques Elisée Reclus (1830–1905) whose *La Terre* (1867–1868)[15] was a systematic study in physical geography. His 19 volume *Nouvelle Géographie Universelle* (1875–1894)[16] was another complete regional geography of the world. This work shows a wide knowledge and understanding of contemporary advances in the natural sciences, and it also demonstrates a deep appreciation of natural beauty.

Pièrre Guillaume Frédéric LePlay (1806–1822) studied environmental influences on man in urban and rural areas, and so laid the foundations for regional surveys such as town and country planning. His *Ouvriers Européans* (1855)[17] in six volumes was based on carefully collected data, such as family budgets, a method that has since been used in many economic surveys.

Oscar Peschel (1826–1875) revolutionized morphological research. His work, systematic and empirical, tended to produce geomorphologists and climatologists first, and geographers second [*Neue Probleme der Vergleichende Erdkunde als Versuch einer Morphologie der Erdoberflache* (1870)[18]].

Friedrich Ratzel (1844–1904) developed systematic and scientific human geography, though he also made contributions to physical geography, geology, zoology, and ethnology. His *Anthropogeographie* (1882),[19] a word he coined, attempted to show in the first volume that man's distribution on earth was more or less controlled by nature. In the second volume he described man's existing distribution, going over Ritter's ground and developing his ideas. However, Ratzel's work differed from Ritter's in that he treated human geography regionally rather than systematically. His *Politische Geographie* (1897),[20] another term he coined, reshaped an old subject. Ritter's last great work *Die Erde und das Leben* (1901–1902)[21] sought to discuss the earth as an integral whole.

Baron Ferdinand von Richthofen (1833–1905) taught geography at Leipzig, where he stressed a unified geography based on the concepts of Humboldt and Ritter. Trained as a geologist, he developed scientific morphology in his studies of the loess regions of China. His *China. Ergebnisse eigener Reisen und darauf gegründeter Studien*[22] appeared in five volumes, partly posthumously, from 1877–1912, and set the seal on his reputation. A master of observation in the field, his first two volumes were immediately recognized as a great scientific work, and for them he received the Royal Geographical Society's Founders Medal. For many years von Richthofen was president of the Berlin Geographical Society and he founded the Oceanographical Institute of Berlin. He is still regarded as a dominant influence in modern German geography.

Paul Vidal de la Blache (1854–1922) was a distinguished scholar and the master of French geographers. Acknowledging his debt to Ritter who had strongly influenced him, he refashioned geography by his teaching and writing. Trained in history, geography, and the classics, and widely traveled, Vidal de la Blache united the study of sociology with geography, infusing the French school with a humane spirit which it has since retained.

In 1902 he prepared for Lavisses's *Histoire de la France* a masterly paper, *Tableau Geographique*,[23] which has become a classic in geographical literature and played a major role in developing the concept of regions. In it he analyzed and interpreted the "geographical personality" of France. Vidal de la Blache never completed a systematic work on human geography, but he expressed his views in many articles published in *Annales de Géographie*, which he founded. In his work he stressed three topics—physical geography, biogeography, and human geography. These were welded together to make up the territorial units within which a distinctive way of life flourished. He also believed that in seeking to understand a human region, history cannot be neglected; and so history and geography were joined together on a sounder basis than they were in the days of Carl Ritter. His most original and important work was *France de l'Est* (1917),[24] devoted to the study of the foundation of landscapes and rural societies in Alsace and Lorraine.

Jean Brunhes (1869–1930) was a pupil of Vidal de la Blache. His *La Géographie Humaine* (1910)[25] limited human geography to human phenomena that modify nature, and at the same time are modified or controlled by it, e.g., unproductive occupation (houses, settlements, roads); cultivation and stock raising; and destructive economy (mineral exploration, deforestation).

Another pupil, Albert Demangeon (1872–1940), studied the use of archives in establishing the past human geography of a region.[26] His study of Picardy is a model of regional geography.

Alfred Hettner (1859–1941) contributed to the methodology of geography.[27] To him geography was the study of the different characteristics of various regions, resulting from their soil types, plant cover, and the results of man's activity. Studying such phenomena on a worldwide scale enabled the geographer to establish a general comparative geography. In 1895 he founded the *Geographische Zeitschrift* as a forum for the general problems of geography.

Before Halford John Mackinder (1861–1947), British geography was largely centered on exploration. Geography did not become a "proper" subject until 1887 when Mackinder, at the age of 26, was appointed to Oxford University, half his salary being paid by the Royal Geographical Society. His great energy, and his gift for stimulating and brilliant generalizations were indelibly impressed on British geography.

In that same year he lectured to the Royal Geographical Society on the scope and methods of geography, defining it as "the science whose main function is to trace the interaction of man in society and as much of his environment as varies locally," and "the science of distribution, the science, that is, which traces the arrangement of things in general on the earth's surface." Mackinder's lectures, particularly those in historical geography, always drew large audiences.[28] In 1902 he published *Britain and the British*

Seas,[29] which is now considered as a classic of British geography; it summarizes the fundamental concepts based on his wide reading and thought, followed by a summary of British history in relation to this background.

His paper "The Geographical Pivot of History" brought him unexpected fame. In it he stated that the maritime age had passed and that land powers would be decisive; that the greatest land area was in the Old World, the heart of which lies within continental or arctic drainage; ringing this "heartland" is an inner crescent of marginal states, with an outer crescent of overseas powers (Great Britain, the United States of America, and Japan). If the balance of power should favor the pivot state, it would then expand over the marginal lands of Eurasia, permitting the vast continental resources to be used for building fleets of ships, thus permitting a world empire. Because of this threat the overseas powers would be obliged to maintain bridgeheads, thus forcing the "pivot allies" to develop their land forces and preventing them from maintaining large fleets.

Mackinder developed his "heartland" theme in *Democratic Ideals and Reality* (1919)[30] in which he maintained that whoever rules eastern Europe commands the Heartland; whoever rules the Heartland commands the World Island; and whoever rules the World Island commands the World. This theory attracted little attention when it first appeared, but was later taken over by German geopoliticians. Mackinder's influence is still strong, and his ideas are still being developed.

William Morris Davis (1850–1934), a pioneer geomorphologist, laid solid foundations for the study of modern physical geography and established geography as a subject in American universities.[31] His work exerted considerable influence on the subject, and he was the founder of the Association of American Geographers. In his studies of erosion cycles Davis did not forget the relationship of man's activities to various landforms. In this his influence was felt by other geographers. His emphasis on the time factor has since been established in the concept of "dynamic geography."

Davis's pupil Ellsworth Huntington (1876–1947) stressed the influence of climate on the life and activities of man and the relationships of the distribution of culture with the world's main climatic regions concluding, as did Carpenter, that western Europe was climatically the most favored region for human activities. Huntington trained originally as a geologist, but as a result of a trip to Tibet and central Asia changed to climatology. His hypotheses that central Asia would progressively break up as an influence in the historical and human geography of the continent caused much controversy. He wrote *The Pulse of Asia* (1907),[32] *Civilization and Climate* (1915),[33] and *The Mainsprings of Civilization* (1945)[34] which summarized much of his life's work.

Isaiah Bowman (1878–1950) is considered foremost among modern geographers. He began his career as a physiographer, and later was inspired and influenced by Davis. His first important publication, *Forest Physiography: Physiography of the United States and Principles of Soils in Relation to Forests* (1911),[35] constituted a sound basis for the study of North America's physical regions. *The New World: Problems in Political Geography* (1921)[36] is a valuable source of political and human geography as they were affected by the peace settlements made after World War I. Bowman was director of the American Geographical Society from 1915–1935, and was adviser to the American delegation to the Peace Conference at Versailles. He was always quick to seize opportunities to advance the status of geography in academic circles and the world of public affairs.

The foregoing gives only the barest outline of the history of the literature of geography up to the early years of the twentieth century. Those geographers so briefly discussed were the giants, but there were numerous others who also contributed to the science with their field work, their theories, or both. To have given proper credit to all concerned would have necessitated a several volume work.

As an academic discipline geography has continued to grow and mature, to the extent that no one geographer can any longer be competent in all branches of the field, specialization being necessitated by the new scope of the old subject. Always a dynamic field, geography is continuously changing its methods and tools, striving to provide accurate and useful descriptions of our planet.

Since World War II when the position of geography was consolidated, the number of geographers has greatly increased, as have university departments of geography and so, as a natural consequence, has the literature. Modern geographers, like their spiritual forebearers, are great travelers, theorists, and writers. Some do write books, but generally important works appear as articles in geographical journals (which in turn are usually published by geographical societies). The following is a list of thirty geographical serials[37] considered to be of "particularly broad international value and interest."

Annales de Géographie: Bulletin de la Société de Géographie, Paris, **1**, 1891, 6/yr.
Association of American Geographers. Annals, Washington, DC, **1**, 1911, 4/yr.
Australian Geographer, Geographical Society of New South Wales, Sydney, **1**, 1928, 2/yr.
Australian Geographical Studies, Institute of Australian geographers, Hobart, 1963, 2/yr.
Cahiers d'Outre-mer; Revue de Géographie de Bordeaux, Université, Faculté des Lettres et Sciences Humaines. Institut de Géographie; Institut d'Outre-Mer de Bordeaux; Société de Géographie de Bordeaux, Bordeaux, **1**, 1948, 4/yr.
Canadian Geographer. Géographe Canadien, Canadian Association of Geographers, Toronto, **1**, 1951, 4/yr.

Economic Geography, Clark University, Worcester, MA, **1**, 1925, 4/yr.

Die Erde. Zeitschrift der Gesellschaft für Erdkunde zu Berlin, Berlin, **1**, 1853, 4/yr.

Erdkunde: Archiv für wissenschaftliche Geographie, Bonn, **1**, 1947, 4/yr.

Geoforum. Journal of Physical, Human, and Regional Geosciences, Braunschweig, Germany, **1**, 1970, 4/yr.

Geografiska Annaler. Series A, Physical Geography, Svenska Sällskapet för Antropologi och Geografi, Stockholm, **47**, 1965, 4/yr.

Geografiska Annaler. Series B, Human Geography, Svenska Sällskapet för Antropologi och Geografi, Stockholm, **47**, 1965, 2/yr.

[The preceding two serials succeed *Geografiska annaler*, **1–46**, 1919–1964.]

Geographia Polonica, Polish Academy of Sciences, Institute of Geography, Warsaw, **1**, 1964, irregular.

Geographical Journal, Royal Geographical Society, London, **1**, 1893, 4/yr.

Geographical Magazine, London, **1**, 1935, 12/yr.

Geographical Review, American Geographical Society, New York, **1**, 1916, 4/yr.

Geographische Zeitschrift, **1–50**, 1895–1944; **51**, 1963, Wiesbaden, 4/yr.

Geography, Geographical Association, Sheffield, **1**, 1901, 4/yr.

Institute of British Geographers. Transactions, **1**, 1935, London, 3/yr.

Journal of Tropical Geography, Departments of Geography, University of Singapore and University of Malaya, Singapore, **1**, 1953, 2/yr.

Mediterranée; Revue Géographique des Pays Mediterranéens, Instituts de Géographie des Facultés des Lettres et Sciences Humanes d'Aix-en-Provence-Nice. Gap, **1–10**, 1960–1969; n.s., 1970, 4/yr.

New Zealand Geographer, New Zealand Geographical Society, Christchurch, **1**, 1945, 2/yr.

Norois; Revue Géographique de l'Ouest et des Pays de l'Atlantique Nord, Universités de Caen, Nantes, Orléans-Tours, Poitiers, Rennes, Rouen, Brest, et Limoges, Poitiers, **1**, 1954, 4/yr.

Österreichische Geographische Gesellschaft. Mitteilunge, Vienna, **1**, 1857, 3/yr.

Petermanns geographische Mitteilungen, Geographische Gesellschaft der Deutschen Demokratischen Republik, Gotha, **1**, 1855, 4/yr.

Revista Geográfica, Instituto Panamericano de Geografia e História. Comissão de Geografia, Rio de Janeiro, **1**, 1941, 2/yr.

Revue Géographique de l'Est, Instituts de géographie des Universités de Besançon, Dijon, Metz, Nancy, Reims, et Strasbourg, Nancy, **1**, 1961, 4/yr.

Soviet Geography: Review and Translation, American Geographical Society, New York, **1**, 1960, 10/yr.

Tijdschrift voor Economische en Sociale Geografie (Netherlands Journal of Economic and Social Geography), Koninklijk Nederlands Aardrijks-Kundig Genootschap, Rotterdam, **1**, 1910, 6/yr.

Zeitschrift für Geomorphologie. Annals of Geomorphology. Annales de Géomorphologie, Stuttgart, 1–11, 1925–1940; n.f. **1**, 1957, 4/yr.

CONCLUSION

It is in publications such as these that the modern classics of geographical literature can be expected to be found.

REFERENCES

1. Strabo. *The Geography of Strabo*, Harvard Univ. Press: Cambridge, MA, 1960–1961; 8 Vols (trans from Greek by H.L. Jones and J.R.S. Sterrett).
2. Münster, S. *Cosmographia universalis lib. VI...*, apud *Henrichum Petri, Basileae*, 1554.
3. Ortelius, A. *Theatrum Orbis Terrarum; ..., apud Christophorum Plantinum, Antverpiae*, 1584.
4. Clüver, P. *Philippi Cluverii Introductionis in universam geographiam, tam veterem quam novam, libri VI, apud I. Hondium, Amstelod*, 1629.
5. Varen, B. *Geographia Generalis, ex officina Eldeviriana, Amsterdam*, 1664.
6. Carpenter, N. *Geography Delineated Forth in Two Books. Containing the Sphaericall and Tropicall Parts Thereof*, Printed by I. Lichfield and W. Turner for H. Cripps, Oxford, 1625; 2 Vols. in 1.
7. Büsching, A.F. *A New System of Geography.... Carefully Translated from the Last Edition of the German Original*, A. Millar: London, 1762; 6 Vols.
8. Forster, J.R. *Observations Made during a Voyage Round the World, on Physical Geography, Natural History and Ethic Philosophy*, G. Robinson: London, U.K., 1778.
9. Forster, J.G. *A Voyage Around the World, in His Britannic Majesty's Sloop Resolution, Commanded by Capt. James Cook, During the Years 1772, 3, 4, and 5*, B. White [etc.]: London, U.K., 1777; 2 Vols.
10. von Humboldt, A. *Ansichten der Natur, mit wissenschaftlichen Erläuterungen*, Cotta: Stuttgart, Germany, 1849; 2 Vols. in 1.
11. von Humboldt, A. *Kosmos. Entwurf einer physischen Weltbeschreibung*, Cotta: Stuttgart, Germany, 1845–1862; 5 Vols. (English trans. by E.C. Otté, *Cosmos: A Sketch of a Physical Description of the Universe*; Harper: New York, 1860; 4 Vols.).
12. Ritter, K. *Die Erdkunde, im Verhältniss zur Natur und zur Geschichte des Menchen, oder Allgemeine, Vergleichend Geographie als sichere Grunlage des Studiums und Unterrichts in Physikalischen und historichen Wissenschaften*, Reimer: Berlin, Germany, 1822–1859; 19 parts in 21 Vols.

13. M. (Fairfax), Somerville. *Physical Geography*, Lea and Blanchard: Philadelphia, PA, 1848.

14. Guyot, A.H. *The Earth and Man: Lectures on Comparative Physical Geography, in Its Relation to the History of Mankind*, Gould, Kendall and Lincoln: Boston, MA, 1849 (trans. from the French by C.C. Kelton).

15. Reclus, E. *The Earth: Descriptive History of the Phenomena of Life of the Globe*, Harper: New York, 1872 (trans. by B.B. Woodward).

16. Reclus, E. *Nouvelle Géographie Universelle; la Terre et les Hommes*, Hachette: Paris, France, 1876–1894; 19 Vols. (*The Earth and Its Inhabitants*; Appleton: New York, 1882–1895; 19 Vols.).

17. LePlay, F. *Ouvriers Européans. Études sur les Travaux, la Vie Domestique, et la Condition Morale des Populations Ouvrières de l'Europe*, Imprimerie impèriale: Paris, France, 1855.

18. Peschel, O.F. *Neue Probleme der Vergleichenden Erdkunde als Versuch einer Morphologie der Erdoberfläche*, Duncker und Humblot: Leipzig, Germany, 1870.

19. Ratzel, F. *Anthropogeographie*, J. Engelhorn: Stuttgart, Germany, 1882–1912; 4 parts in 2 Vols.

20. Ratzel, F. *Politische Geographie. 3 aufl., durchgeseten und ergänzt von Eugen Oberhummer*, R. Oldenbourg: Munich, Germany, 1923.

21. Ratzel, F. *Die erde und das Leben*, Bibliographisches Institut: Leipzig, Germany, 1901–1902; 2 Vols.

22. von Richtofen, F.P.W. *China. Ergebnisse eigener Reisen und darauf gegründeter Studien*, Reimer: Berlin, Germany, 1877–1912; 5 Vols.

23. de la Blache, P.V. *La France, Tableau Géographique*, New Ed. Hachette: Paris, France, 1908 (text reprinted from Histoire de la France, published under the direction of E. Lavisse).

24. de la Blache, P.V. *France de l'Est (Lorraine–Alsace)*, A. Colin: Paris, France, 1917.

25. Brunhes, J. *La Géographie Humaine; Essai de Classification Positive, Principes et Exemples*, 3rd Ed. Alcan: Paris, France, 1925; 3 vols.

26. de Demangeon, A. *Problèmes de Géographie Humaine*, Armand Colin: Paris, France, 1942.

27. Hettner, A. *Die geographie, ihr Geschichte, ihr Wesen und ihre Methoden*, Hirt: Breslau, 1927.

28. Mackinder, H.J. *The Scope and Methods of Geography, and the Geographical Pivot of History; Being Papers Read to the Royal Geographical Society on 31 January 1887 (Proc. R.G.S. 1887, 9, 141–160) and on 25 January 1904 (Geogr. J. 1904, 23, 421–437) reprinted with an introduction by E.W. Gilbert*, Royal Geographical Society: London, U.K., 1951.

29. Mackinder, H.J. *Britain and the British Seas*, Appleton: New York, 1902.

30. Mackinder, H.J. *Democratic Ideals and Reality. With Additional Papers*, Norton: New York, 1962.

31. Davis, W.M.In *Geographical Essays*; Johnson, D.W., Ed.; Dover: New York, 1954; (Unabridged reproduction of the 1909 edition).

32. Huntington, E. *The Pulse of Asia, Illustrating the Geographic Basis of History*, Houghton Mifflin: Boston, MA, 1907.

33. Huntington, E. *Civilization and Climate*, Yale Univ. Press: New Haven, CT, 1915.

34. Huntington, E. *The Mainsprings of Civilization*, Wiley: New York, 1945.

35. Bowman, I. *Forest Physiography: Physiography of the United States and Principles of Soils in Relation to Forests*, Wiley: New York, 1911.

36. Bowman, I. *The New World: Problems in Political Geography*, World: Yonkers-on-Hudson, NY, 1921.

37. Chicago University Department of Geography. *Annotated World List of Selected Current Geographical Serials in English, French and German: Including Serials in Other Languages with Supplementary Use of English or Other International Languages,* 3rd Ed.; Research Paper, 1971; 137, by C.D. Harris, Chicago.

BIBLIOGRAPHY

Other Important Titles by Authors Cited in the Text

1. Bowman, I. *The Andes of Southern Peru, Geographical Reconnaissance along the Seventy-Third Meridian*; 1916, published for the American Geographical Society of New York by H. Holt, New York.

2. Bowman, I. *The Pioneer Fringe*, American Geographical Society: New York, 1931.

3. Brunhes, J. *Human Geography (abridged edited by M.J.-B. Delamarre and P. Deffontaines; trans. by E.F. Row)*, Harrap: London, 1952.

4. Peschel, O.F. *Geschichte der Erdkunde bis auf A. v. Humboldt und Carl Ritter (Geschichte der Wissenschaften in Deutschalnd. Neuere Zeit. 4. bd.)*, Cotta: Munich, Germany, 1865.

5. Ritter, K. *Allegemaine Erdkunde*, Reimer: Berlin, Germany, 1862.

6. Semple, E.C. *Influences of Geographic Environment, on the System of Ratzel's System of Anthropo-Geography*, Holt: New York, 1911, 1947.

7. Vidal de la Blache, P. *États et Nations de l'Europe Autour de France*, C. Delagrave: Paris, France, 1889.

8. Vidal de la Blache, P. *The Personality of France* (trans. from the French by H.C. Brehtuall), Christophers: London, U.K., 1928.

9. Vidal de la Blache, P.In *Principles of Human Geography* (trans. from the French by M.T. Bingham); de Martonne, E., Ed.; Constable: London, U.K., 1950.

10. Vidal de la Blache, P., Gallois, L.L.J., Eds. *Geographie Universelle;* Colin: Bris, 1927–1948; 15 Vols. in 23.

11. von Humboldt, A. *Voyage de Humboldt et Bonpland*, F. Schoell [etc.]: Paris, France, 1805–1834; 23 Vols. (often cited by title of Part I: "Voyage aux Regions Equinoxiales du Nouveau Continent").

12. von Humboldt, A. *Essai Politique sur le Royaume de la Nouvelle-Espagne*, F. Schoell: Paris, France, 1811; 2 Vols. (English trans. by J. Black, 1811, 4 Vols.).

13. von Humboldt, A. *Asie Centrale: Récherches sur les Chaines de Montagnes et la Climatologie Comparée*, Gide: Paris, France, 1843; 2 Vols.

14. von Richthofen, F.P.W. *Aufgaben und Methoden der heutigen Geographie*, Veit: Leipzig, Germany, 1883.
15. von Richthofen, F.P.W. *Atlas von China. Orographische und geologische Kartan ... zu des verfassers Werk: China, Ergebnisse eigner Reisen und darauf gegründeter Studien*, Reimer: Berlin, Germany, 1885–1912; 2 Vols.

History of Geography and Geographical Thought

1. Ackerman, E.A. *Geography as a Fundamental Research Discipline*, Department of Geography, Univ. Chicago, Research Paper Univ. Chicago Press: Chicago, IL, 1958.
2. Baker, J.N.L. *A History of Geographical Discovery and Exploration*, Harrap: London, U.K., 1931 (2nd Ed. 1937).
3. Baker, J.N.L. *The History of Geography Papers*, Barnes and Noble: New York, 1963.
4. Beazley, C.R. *The Dawn of Modern Geography*, John Murray: London, U.K., 1897–1906; 3 Vols.
5. Berg, L.S. *Ocherk istorii Russkoi geograficheskoi nauki (vplot' do 1923 goda)*, Akademiia nauk SSSR, Trudy komissi po istorii znanii, Leningrad, 1929; Vol. 4.
6. Bunbury, E.H. *A History of Ancient Geography, Among the Greeks and Romans from the Earliest Ages till the Fall of the Roman Empire (with a new introduction by W.H. Stahl)*, 2nd Ed. Dover: New York, 1959; 2 Vols. (Original Ed. 1883).
7. Bunge, W.W. *Theoretical Geography*. Lund Studies in Geography, Series C, General and Mathematical Geography Gleerup: Lund, Sweden, 1962.
8. Burton, H.E. *The Discovery of the Ancient World*, Harvard Univ. Press: Cambridge, MA, 1932.
9. Carpenter, R. *Beyond the Pillars of Heracles: the Classical World Seen through the Eyes of Its Discovers*, Delacorte: New York, 1966.
10. Cary, M. *The Geographical Background of Greek and Roman History*, Clarendon: Oxford, U.K., 1949.
11. Cary, M. Warmington, E.H. *The Ancient Explorers*, Dodd, Meade: New York, 1929.
12. Crone, G.R. *Modern Geographers: An Outline of Progress in Geography Since 1800 A.D.*, Royal Geographical Society: London, U.K., 1951.
13. Crone, G.R. *Background to Geography*, Museum Press: London, U.K., 1964.
14. Dickinson, R.E. *Makers of Modern Geography*, Praeger: New York, 1969.
15. Dickinson, R.E. Howarth, O.J.R. *The Making of Geography*, Clarendon: Oxford, U.K., 1933.
16. East, W.G. *The Geography behind History*, Rev and Enl. Ed. Nelson: London, U.K., 1966.
17. Fuson, R.H. *A Geography of Geography, Origins and Development of the Discipline*, William C. Brown: Dubuque, IA, 1969.
18. Febvre, L.P.V. *A Geographical Introduction to History* (trans. from the French by E.G. Mountford and J.H. Paxton), Kegan Paul: London, U.K., 1925.
19. Freeman, T.W. *A Hundred Years of Geography*, Aldine: Chicago, 1963.
20. Gerasimov, I.P. *Soviet Geography: Accomplishments and Tasks* (trans. from the Russian by L. Ecker, English Ed. edited by C.D. Harris), American Geographical Society, Occasional Publication American Geographical Society: New York, 1962.
21. Haggett, P. *Locational Analysis in Human Geography*, Arnold: London, U.K., 1966.
22. Hartshorne, R. *The Nature of Geography: A Critical Survey of Current Thought in the Light of the Past*, The Association of American Geographers: Lancaster, PA, 1939, 1942; [reissue of Ann. Assoc. Amer. Geographers, 29 (3 and 4)].
23. Hartshorne, R. *Perspective on the Nature of Geography*, 1959; published for the Association of American Geographers by R. McNally, Chicago.
24. Heawood, E. *A History of Geographical Discovery in the 17th and 18th Centuries*, Octagon: New York, 1965; (first issued in 1912).
25. Hyde, W.W. *Ancient Greek Mariners*, Oxford Univ. Press: New York, 1947.
26. James, P.E.; Jones, C.F., Eds. *American Geography: Inventory and Prospect*; 1954, published for the Association of American Geographers by Syracuse Univ. Press: Syracuse, NY.
27. Joerg, W.L.G. Recent geographical work in Europe. Geogr. Rev. **1922**, *12*, 431–483.
28. Kimble, G.H.T. *Geography in the Middle Ages*, Methuen: London, U.K., 1938.
29. Mood, F. *The English Geographers and the Anglo-American Frontier in the Seventeenth Century*, Univ. California Publication in Geography Univ. California Press: Berkeley, CA, 1944; Vol. 6 (9), 363–395.
30. Nansen, F. *Northern Mists: Arctic Exploration in Early Times* (trans. by A.G. Chater), Stokes: New York, 1911; 2 Vols.
31. Penrose, B. *Travel and Discovery in the Renaissance, 1420–1620*, Harvard Univ. Press: Cambridge, MA, 1952.
32. Taylor, E.G.R. *Tudor Geography: 1485–1583*, Methuen: London, U.K., 1930.
33. Taylor, E.G.R. *Later Tudor and Early Stuart Geography: 1583–1650; A Sequel to Tudor Geography, 1485–1583*, Methuen: London, U.K., 1934.
34. Taylor, T.G., Ed. *Geography in the Twentieth Century: A Study of Growth, Fields, Techniques, Aims and Trends, with chapters by K. Hare and others*; Philosophical Library: New York, 1951 (3rd Ed. Enl., 1957).
35. Thomson, J.O. *History Ancient of Geography*, Univ. Press: Cambridge, MA, 1965.
36. Tozer, H.F. *A History of Ancient Geography*, 2nd Ed. Univ. Press: Cambridge, 1964.
37. van Paassen, C. *The Classical Tradition of Geography*, Wolters: Groninger, the Netherlands, 1957.
38. Warmington, E.H. *Greek Geography*, Dent: London, England, 1934.
39. Warntz, W. *Geography Now and Then, Some Notes on the History of Academic Geography in the United States*, American Geographical Society, Research Series American Geographical Society: New York, 1964.
40. Wooldridge, S.W. *The Geographer as a Scientist. Essays on the Scope and Nature of Geography*, Thomas Nelson: London, U.K., 1956.
41. Wooldridge, S.W. East, W.G. *The Spirit and Purpose of Geography*, Hutchinson's Univ. Library: London, U.K., 1951; 176.
42. Wright, J.K. A plea for the history of geography. Isis **1925**, *8*, 477–491.

43. Wright, J.K. *The Geographical Basis of European History*, Holt: New York, 1928; 110 (The Berkshire Studies in European History).

44. Wright, J.K. *Geography in the Making: The American Geographical Society, 1851–1951*, American Geographical Society: New York, 1952; 437.

45. Wright, J.K. *The Geographical Lore at the Time of the Crusades: A Study in the History of Medieval Science and Tradition in Western Europe (with a new introduction by C.J.G. Glacken)*, Dover: New York, 1965; 563 (original published 1925).

46. Wright, J.K. *Human Nature in Geography: Fourteen Papers, 1925–1965*, Harvard Univ. Press: Cambridge, MA, 1966; 361.

Bibliographies of Geographical Literature

1. American Geographical Society. *Research Catalogue*, Hall: Boston, MA, 1962; 15 Vols.

2. *Bibliographie géographique internationale*, Association de géographes français: Paris, France, 1891; 1 , annual.

3. Burkett, J., Ed. *Concise Guide to the Literature of Geography, 1967*; Ealing Technical College: London, U.K., 1967; 47.

4. Chicago University Department of Geography. *International List of Geographical Serials*, 2nd Ed.; Research Paper, 1971; 138, compiled by C.D. Harris, J.D. Fellman, and J.A. Licate, Chicago, 267.

5. Church, M. *A Basic Geographical Library: A Selected and Annotated Book List for American Colleges*; Association of American Geographers, Commission on College Geography, Association of American Geographers: Washington, DC, 1966; 2 compiled by M. Church, R.E. Huke, and W. Zelinsky, 153.

6. Cox, E.G. *A Reference Guide to the Literature of Travel; Including Voyages, Geographical Description, Adventures, Shipwrecks and Expeditions*, Univ. Washington: Seattle, WA, 1935–1939; 3 Vols.

7. *Current Geographical Publications*; American Geographical Society: New York, 1938; 1 , 10/yr.

8. *Documentatio Geographica; Geographische Zeitschriften- und Serien-Literatur; Papers of Geographical Periodicals and Serials; Articles dans les Periodiques Geographiques*; Institut für Landeskunde: Bad Godesberg, 1966; 1, 6/yr., with annual cumulation and index.

9. *Geographical Abstracts*; Norwiche, 1966; 6/yr. (4 series: A, Geomorphology; B, Biogeography and Climatology; C, Economic Geography; D, Social Geography and Cartography) (supersedes Geomorphological Abstracts, 1–27, 1960–1965).

10. Harris, C.D. *Bibliographies and Reference Works for Research in Geography*, Univ. Chicago Press: Chicago, IL, 1967; 89 (supplement to Aids to Geographical Research, 2nd Ed., J.K. Wright and E.T. Platt, American Geographical Society: New York, 1947).

11. *New Geographical Literature and Maps*; Royal Geographical Society: London, U.K., 1951; 1 , 2/yr.

12. Norell, I.P. *Geographical Literature: A Brief Annotated Guide*, Preliminary Ed. San Jose State College: San Jose, CA, 1969; 78.

13. *Referativnyi Zhurnal: Geografiia*; Institut nauchnoi informatsii, Akademiia nauk SSSR: Moscow, Russia, 1956; 12/yr.

14. Wright, J.K. Platt, E.T. *Aids to Geographical Research: Bibliographies, Periodicals, Atlases, Gazetteers and Other Reference Books*, 2nd Ed.; American Geographical Society, Research Series American Geographical Society: New York, 1947; 22, 331.

Germany: Libraries, Archives, and Museums

Claudia Lux
Central and Regional Library of Berlin (ZLB), Berlin, Germany

Abstract

This entry discusses the role and status of German libraries, archives, and museums, with a focus on the two decades following the Reunification of Germany. Although the emphasis is on contemporary trends and issues, a short historical overview is provided. Major topics include: library legislation, public, school, and research libraries and programs for professional education as well as archival science and archival institutions (national, state, and local). There is also a discussion of museology and profiles of major museum in range of areas including archaeology, fine arts, national and local history, natural history, and science and technology. Digital projects are also discussed as are numerous cooperative efforts among libraries.

INTRODUCTION

The Federal Republic of Germany is situated in the center of Europe and is bounded on the north by the Baltic Sea and the North Sea. Germany has 16 Federal States (Länder) with the capital Berlin (Fig. 1). In February 2008, the population was over 82 million with a high percentage of inhabitants over 50 years old; migrants make up approximately 9% of the population. The strong economy manifested by a trade surplus is not always mirrored at the community or state level, as the money earned goes to global players. The percentage of unemployed persons in June 2008 remained at 7.5%. Since the Reunification of East and West Germany in 1990, there slight decline in population and the gap between rich and poor has increased.[1]

Germany is known as a nation of poets and thinkers—from Goethe and Schiller to Heine and Rilke, from Hegel and Kant to Adorno and Heidegger. It is a nation as proud of its cultural heritage as of its technical inventions like Gutenberg's printing press. Before the German Empire in 1871 was founded and even after, many formerly independent regions and small kingdoms had their own cultural activities. They supported musicians from Bach to Beethoven and commissioned works from celebrated artists such as Albrecht Duerer and Caspar David Friedrich. Local rulers and noble families built up collections of precious books, hand-painted maps, and beautiful art works and crafts. This pluralistic cultural heritage strongly influenced the decision for political federalism in culture and education when the Federal Republic of Germany (Bundesrepublik Deutschlan—BRD) was founded in 1949. A second reason was the still remaining resistance to the centralized censorship in culture and education during the terror regime of the Nazis.

In contrast to the BRD, a centralized structure in culture and education was kept in tact in East Germany during the years 1945–1990 when the German Democratic Republic (GDR) existed. After World War II, there were two very different political systems in Germany—one being embedded in the Western bloc with the political influence of the Allied Forces, and the other integrated into the Eastern bloc with an even stronger influence by the Soviet Union. Both systems had different impact on the respective cultural institutions. Different standards and methods were introduced. In the Western part, libraries developed step by step and open stacks were introduced, first in public libraries and from the end of the 1960s also in some university libraries. In contrast, all research libraries in the GDR had reading rooms with reference works and a catalog from which one could find the call number and then request the desired work from the collection that was kept in closed stacks. There were not many official contacts between the two parts of Germany during that time and certain libraries, archives, and museums whose collections had been divided during the bombing in the Second World War remained separated after the War because of the political split. Only after the Reunification did it become clear what the real losses were—not only from the First and the Second World War but also through Nazi Tyranny, the book burnings and destruction of many authors' books in the libraries. A cultural generation of poets, musicians, and artists were killed or emigrated and their art and books were destroyed. Shortly after World War II, the Russians took away many cultural works as compensation for their losses during the War. All the cultural activities in both parts of Germany were monitored, either by Allied troops from United States of America, France and Britain or by Russia. During the process of Reunification of West Germany and East Germany in 1990, federalism was revitalized and this became the foundation of new developments in culture and education.

Modern information services began to be established at the end of the 1970s and the beginning of the 1980s in

Encyclopedia of Library and Information Sciences, Fourth Edition DOI: 10.1081/E-ELIS4-120043729

Fig. 1 Map of Germany.
Source: *CIA World Factbook*: https://www.cia.gov/library/publications/the-world-factbook/geos/gm.html.

German libraries. There was increased progress toward the end of the 1990s and into the twenty-first century with the integration of many Internet services and digital libraries' available through the Internet. Archives and museums started to use technology some years later, but made great progress as soon as digitization became more common.

In December 2007, after 4 years of work, a Parliamentarian Enquête Commission on Culture in Germany finished its report.[2] The report gives an excellent overview of the legal framework for culture in Germany. Many specific recommendations for libraries and museums are presented and an important outcome of the work of this Commission is the strong commitment in support of a library law at the Länder level.

LIBRARY AND INFORMATION PROFESSIONALS IN GERMANY—SYSTEMS AND SERVICES

Brief Overview

The German library system with its approximately 11,500 libraries is organized on four levels of service provision to meet the public's information and literature need:[3]

Level 1: First level information needs should be met by small and middle-sized public libraries, i.e., by public libraries in villages or small towns, branch libraries, or bookmobiles.

Level 2: This level represents an increased need for books and information, to be met by city libraries especially by their central library.
Level 3: The needs for specialized information and literature are to be met cooperatively by some metropolitan libraries, special libraries, and university libraries in the region.
Level 4: This level refers to highly specialized needs that can only be met in cooperation on the part of designated special libraries, university libraries with their special collections, the three central specialized libraries, and last but not least, the libraries with national collections and services.

There is no general public library law at the national level, and at the state level public library legislation has just started to be enacted. In Thuringia, the first law concerning public libraries was passed at the state level in July 2008 and this puts libraries in an important position as educational and cultural institutions.[4] There are various laws on different governmental levels in regard to their responsibility for libraries. For example legislation regarding responsibilities of the National Library of Germany was renewed in 2007.[5] At the state level in Germany there is legislation from 2005 with regard to regional libraries (called Landesbibliothek).[6] Interlibrary loan between libraries in different states in Germany also requires an agreement of all states. To facilitate this, the Conference of the Ministers of Culture from all 16 Federal States—which is the highest cultural organ—has to formulate a common agreement, which is then passed by each state legislature individually before it can begin to function.

National Library and Information Services

The National Library of Germany was founded as the Deutsche Bücherei in 1912 by German publishers in cooperation with the Kingdom of Saxony and the city of Leipzig. In 1970, the Deutsche Bücherei Leipzig was assigned the function of being the central coordination institution for bibliography in the German Democratic Republic. In 1947, when Germany was divided, publishers of the Federal Republic of Germany founded the Deutsche Bibliothek in Frankfurt am Main as their bibliographical center. In 1969, it changed its status under public law and became a federal cooperative agency for all the states, with legal deposit and support by the Federal Republic of Germany. One year later in 1970, the Music Archives were created in West Berlin to receive deposits of all musical works and production. The Deutsche Bücherei Leipzig and the Deutsche Bibliothek with the Music Archives as a department were united in 1990 under a new name: "Die Deutsche Bibliothek." In June 2006, a new law changed the name of the institution into Deutsche

Nationalbibliothek (=German National Library). The same law reconfirmed support for the national legal deposit at this Library which receives two mandatory deposit copies of each of the more than 100,000 items published in Germany every year. According to the collections policy with regard to German language literature, the German National Library not only receives materials from Austria and the German-speaking part of Switzerland but also collects German-language publications worldwide. Now the law includes online publications to be collected by the library, cataloged, and stored as part of Germany's cultural heritage.[7] The German National Library compiles various series of the Deutsche National-bibliographie (=German National Bibliography), which can also be searched online.[8] The German National Library collects German imprints only from 1913 onward. Due to the history of numerous German kingdoms, it had never been possible to create a unified collection of all printed materials produced in Germany that would be comparable to other large national libraries in Europe. Therefore, the National Library is collaborating with a group of five libraries with significant collections in order to develop a complete collection of printed literature published in German-speaking countries from the beginning of Gutenberg's press, over 550 years ago. This venture is called *Arbeitsgemeinschaft Sammlung Deutscher Drucke (=Working Group for the Collection of German Imprints)* and has led to the creation of a combined virtual national library in which the participating libraries are responsible for the following periods shown in Table 1.[9]

A national library, besides collecting the nation's production of published works, often collects the most important scholarly literature from all over the world. Again in Germany this task is shared by several libraries on the national level. The Bayerische Staatsbibliothek (=Bavarian State Library) in Munich holds a multitude of Incunabula, but also has important international collections, as does the Staatsbibliothek zu Berlin—Preussischer Kulturbesitz (=State Library Berlin-Prussian Cultural Heritage). These two libraries are very important sources for humanities studies due to their collections of works in all European languages and special collections in Oriental, Asian, and East European languages. The State Library of Berlin is not a regular state library with legal deposit (the legal depository library for Berlin is the Central and

Table 1 Sammlung Deutscher Drucke.

1450–1600 Bayerische Staatsbibliothek in Munich
1601–1700 Herzog August Bibliothek in Wolfenbüttel
1701–1800 Staats- und Universitätsbibliothek of Göttingen
1801–1870 Universitätsbibliothek Johann Christian Senckenberg in Frankfurt/Main
1871–1912 Staatsbibliothek zu Berlin—Preussischer Kulturbesitz in Berlin
1913–Deutsche Nationalbibliothek in both Frankfurt/Main and Leipzig

Regional Library Berlin). However, it is a library with rich collections like those of a national library.

On the national level, Germany has three central subject libraries.[10] They collect national and international materials in their subject area quite comprehensively and function as national resource

- For science and technology at the Technische Informationsbibliothek (=Technical Information Library) in Hanover.
- For medicine and biology at the Deutsche Zentralbibliothek für Medizin (=German National Library of Medicine) in Cologne and Bonn.
- For economy at the Deutsche Zentralbibliothek für Wirtschaftswissenschaften (=German National Library of Economics) in Kiel and Hamburg.

Together with the two state libraries in Berlin and Munich and a few other institutions these are the key institutions for national licenses, fully financed up to now by the German Research Foundation [=Deutsche Forschungsgemeinschaft (DFG)]. The national licenses can be used by all faculty members and interested private persons in Germany.[11]

Germany—a country with so many different states in its history—has developed a refined system of financial support for special collections in university and state libraries to fulfill the need for highly specialized literature in research. This service can be provided thanks to the "special subject collections system" or nationwide library service of the Deutsche Forschungsgemeinschaft (=German Research Foundation). The German Research Foundation covers 50% of the cost of foreign literature in libraries participating in this program which are then designated as the special subject libraries for that subject area. Libraries participating in this system have to commit themselves to building up and maintaining this collection from their own budget and also to sending this material to another library via the interlending library system, when required. The special material may be searched by subject or region using WEBIS[12] software that enables the user to find the library with holdings on special subject area— for example Psychology in Trier, English language, and literature in Göttingen, etc. All these activities at the national level is seen as the level 4 in serving the information and literature need of the country. Six regional union catalogs facilitate access to these collections.[13] A search covering all these catalogs can be executed by the Karlsruher Virtueller Katalog (KVK) (=Karlsruhe Virtual Catalog),[14] The KVK also provides the possibility to search many different national library catalogs from Australia to the United States at the same time.

Academic and Research Libraries

Academic and research libraries have a long tradition in Germany. In the Holy Roman Empire (962–1806), the first university and university library was founded in Prague in 1348. In what is now Germany, the oldest university library is the library of the oldest university—the Ruprechts Karl University in Heidelberg, founded in 1386. In the following two centuries, many German dukes and kings founded universities for the education of the nobility. In 1388, the University of Cologne was founded and quite a few other university libraries like the ones in Erfurt, Würzburg, Leipzig, Rostock, Greifswald, Freiburg, Trier, and Tübingen were established.

Many university libraries did not develop substantial collections until 1800, some not even until the end of the nineteenth century when the Prussian empire started to build up special collections in the university libraries of Prussia. At that time Prussia covered a great part of east and northern Germany with boundaries stretching to the Rhineland. University libraries developed in the beginning of the twentieth century as did individual departmental libraries. During the Nazi regime, university libraries hid or destroyed works by Communist, Socialist, and Jewish authors, and the role of librarians in this dark period of the German history still has not yet been fully investigated.[15] In the GDR 1945–1990, university libraries became centralized institutions and were part of a regulated system with each library playing a special role in the access structure to Western literature. In the Federal Republic of Germany in the 1970s, many new university libraries were opened with the new concept of open stacks and often these institutions had only one single centrally organized library. This structure is in contrast to the two-level system still in existence in many universities where there is a main university library and many independent faculty and departmental libraries. After Reunification, libraries of the former East Germany received new buildings and upgraded their collections. Some university libraries have developed remarkable service ideas: the 24-hour library in Konstanz (Konstanz University library was the first university library in Germany with 24-hour-opening starting in 2001[16]); a cooperative subject list of accessible databases from 195 libraries organized by the university library of Regensburg;[17] and research on digital resources and repositories in projects of the university library of Goettingen.[18] Following a discussion of open access journals the Regenburg university library developed the Electronic Journals Library (=Elektronische Zeitschriftenbibliothek EZB)[19] with a very simple method: green for free access to full text, yellow for free access for users from certain institutions, and red no full text access available. Libraries of universities of applied science are oriented toward providing study materials and they have a high rate of duplication in their collections to serve the needs of their students.

At the same time, the European Union has started a reform of European Higher Education which was articulated in the Bologna Declaration of June 1999. The aim of this reform is to make academic degree standards and quality assurance standards more comparable and compatible throughout Europe.[20] Since the Bologna Process started, academic institutions in Germany are changing from a self-determined study system to a streamlined Bachelor's and Master's degree program with specified requirements for the students. Bachelor students often need the same books as before, but they frequently use library space for learning and they need information literacy training. To meet those needs, academic libraries have changed to provide far more space with wireless Lan connections, and librarians have been successful in integrating information literacy into the curriculum at some universities.

Public Libraries

German public libraries have gone through various dramatic changes during the 160 years of their existence. In the beginning, city libraries had to collect important publications needed by the administration and they were usually viewed as being open to the public even though only the upper class could have access to them. The first "true" public library was opened on October 24, 1828, in Grossenhain, Saxony, on the initiative of Karl Benjamin Preusker (1786–1871) and since 1995, October 24 is now designated as "Library Day" in Germany. The creation of this library came at the beginning of a political awakening of the German nation which cumulated in the March Revolution of 1848. Many public libraries were founded in the middle and the end of the nineteenth century, supported by private "Bildung" educational initiatives (the word Bildung means more than education, it includes the whole person). These initiatives included the "private reading room movement." At the same time there were official community activities like the opening of public reading rooms and public libraries, which were sometimes combined with the former city library.

At the end of the nineteenth century, more information about American public libraries reached Germany through the librarian Constantin Nörrenberg who reported on what he observed in his travels. In 1893 Constantin Nörrenberg took part in a library conference in Chicago. His report in 'Centralblatt für das Bibliothekswesen' suggested reforms in German libraries. These new ideas influenced the profession and stimulated the movement for creating Bücherhallen (public reading rooms) and public libraries. Many German public libraries were founded during the first years of the twentieth century and another wave of public libraries were founded after the First World War. From 1912 onward an intense dispute arose between Paul Ladewig (1858–1940) from Essen,[21] who supported a free and tolerant approach of library service and Walter Hofmann (1879–1952) from Leipzig who preferred a strong socio-pedagogical approach.[22] This dispute still has influence on public libraries in Germany today. Instead of combining the service for the general public with older and traditional works in the collection, German librarians in their tendency to be very exact, divided library collections and services clearly into research or scientific materials on one side and easy reading material for the entertainment of the public on the other side. After 1945, many new public libraries were founded in the GDR—not only in cities and villages but also in factories. A system of large public libraries called Wissenschaftliche Allgemeinbibliothek (General Research Library), was established to serve the scientific needs of the public. East Germany became known as "Leseland," a country of reading.

In Germany today small and medium-sized libraries have a good mixture of different books and media to offer at the basic level. In serving people at this level, the library provides a central access point for information and markets its services to everybody. Public libraries at this level are financed by local communities. The libraries' tasks at levels 1 and 2 include:

- Meeting the citizen's information needs, by facilitating access to the complex world of books and nonbook resources, including the Internet.
- Supporting the use of new technologies.
- Promoting reading and cultural work within their community.
- Inspiring people to spend their leisure time creatively,
- Motivating learning.
- Helping to integrate different user groups, such as people from different cultural and linguistic backgrounds.

According to the Bibliotheken 1993 libraries at level 2 have to meet the following standards:

- Two books or nonbook items per resident.
- A stock of current periodicals.
- 20% of the collection should be nonbook materials (CD, video, DVD etc.).
- Minimum opening hours of at least 35 hr a week.
- Participation in union cataloging and interlibrary lending systems.
- 5% of the collection should be current reference books that provide extensive information and information about products and prices, as well as about tested technical products.

Libraries at levels 1 and 2 should offer access to selected databases.[23] The traditional organizational system of the public library is still in existence: there is a central library either with district and branch libraries or just branch libraries. Some public libraries have special music libraries providing musical scores, books on music, and CDs. A special home delivery system for handicapped people delivers books and nonbooks materials; often this service is supported by volunteers. The mobile library stops at schools and at places outside the city center where there are no branch libraries. One mobile library can serve approximately 25,000 inhabitants.

During recent years, many new public libraries have been built in Germany. Some of these have very interesting architecture; examples include Münster and Ulm which have fascinated architects and librarians alike, and have sparked the development of new concepts for library architecture in Germany. One of the most famous public libraries is the Würzburg library which has won different prizes like the "Library of the Year" prize in 2003 and which was often at the top of the German library benchmarking public libraries of this size. German public libraries have developed interesting concepts for youth libraries all over the country, with good examples in Düsseldorf and Hamburg. The largest public library system in Germany is found in Munich with the traditional central library and many different branches. Munich was the first metropolitan library to use Radio Frequency Identification in bar codes.

The establishment of five or six Combi(Combination)-libraries, where research library and public library are integrated into one organization, illustrates a trend which is not only found in Germany but also in Europe and elsewhere. The most developed integration can be seen in the Central-and Regional-Library in Berlin, where the general books for the public and scientific information and scholarly works are all shelved together. The Zentral-und Landesbibliothek Berlin functions as a public library and as a state library with legal deposit for the city and state of Berlin. The combined Berlin library offers 3.2 million books and nonprint media in an integrated research and public library collection which provides users with a wide range of materials.

Other Libraries for the General Reader

"Factory" libraries are public libraries for the employees of the factory and their families. West Germany was a country with numerous factory libraries up to the 1970s and East Germany had many factory libraries until the change in the industry after Reunification. During the last decade, factory libraries decreased from several 100 to fewer than 50 during the 1990s and the German Association of Factory Libraries dissolved in 2004. In hospitals, libraries for the patients that provide a kind of public library service are still prevalent, but often they are administratively combined with the highly specialized library for the medical staff. Libraries in prisons received more attention when the prison library in Münster won the National Library Price in 2007.

Quite a number of public libraries are financed by the Christian churches with philosophy of practice based on their own cultural traditions. They have fewer opening hours and are run by volunteers.

School Libraries

In Germany only 5% of all public schools have any kind of school library. Some school libraries have a good collection of books and media, enough space, and high speed internet connections. Others have only a small collection of donated books, collected by parents and supported by volunteers. The reason for a lack of school libraries in Germany has its roots in the civil servant hierarchy in which librarians and teachers often have a different status and hence, schools do not usually have the means for employing a librarian for the school.

Special Libraries

Special libraries are often part of their institutions and are focused on internal services. Their collection policy often covers digital research data and grey literature in all kinds of formats. Librarians in these special libraries are often expected to synthesize detailed content information to suit their users' needs and in most cases, these special libraries are not open to the public, although some may allow use of the reading room. Nevertheless, special libraries play an important role in Germany's library services; innovative information services often develop from these libraries' activities in response to their highly specialized users' needs. There are special libraries of research institutes, such as Max-Planck Institutes or Fraunhofer Institutes, which serve the basic research programs in these institutes. These libraries are of high quality and very well financed. Many special libraries in Germany are one-person-libraries and these solo librarians have created a small, informal network for mutual support, and exchange of ideas. Germany has nearly 1000 special libraries, including those located in ministries and in administration, law libraries and medical libraries, and libraries of museums and art galleries.

Digital Library Collections and Services

Digitization is a very important activity of German libraries. From the small special library all the way up to the National Library, digitization is a topic of great interest. There are three important digitization centers, one at the German National Library and a second center at the University Library Göttingen and the third being the Google Library Digitization Project at the State Library Munich. Most of the projects focus on digitization of special collections, incunabula, and older manuscripts. The Google project in Munich is different as it is the first mass digitization project in Germany and is concentrated on the eighteenth- and nineteenth-century collection in Bavaria. There are quite a few other digitization projects which are heavily used, such as the address-books of Berlin from 1799 to 1943 at the Central and Regional Library in Berlin[24] or the digital Gutenberg Bible[25] at the University library of Göttingen. Many of the ongoing digitization projects are cofinanced by the German Science Foundation, which supports library technological development and cooperative research library activities for better science.

LIBRARY AND INFORMATION SCIENCE AS A DISCIPLINE AND A PROFESSION AND LIS EDUCATION

Library and Information Sciences is offered as a discipline in different types of institutions. There is only one academic university—the Humboldt University in Berlin—which offers a doctorate as well as a Bachelor's and Master's degree. Although the Master's degree will soon become the qualification needed by professional librarians an older system of credentialing is still in place. In the past, to become a professional academic librarian, the candidate must have already completed a university diploma or master's degree in some field like German literature, history, or physics, before he or she is admitted to a 2-year course of library and information science to get a second master's degree in this field. This qualifies him or her to work as a subject librarian at the university level and for different higher management positions including the head librarian position at larger public libraries.

Since the Bologna process has altered the European higher education practices, the former course for certified librarian or Diplom-Bibliothekar(in) at different universities for applied sciences has now changed to a Bachelor's degree in library and information science. This training program qualifies the candidate for cataloging and many other positions in university and research libraries as well as for management positions in small- to medium-sized public libraries and special libraries.

At the lower level, students who have completed the 10th grade (or German middle school) may enroll in a 3 year vocational training program to become a specialized employee in media and information services. This is an integrated qualification for work in libraries, archives, and audiovisual archives. This program is administered like other German vocational training programs, i.e., the training takes place alternating between 3 weeks in a library followed by 3 weeks of courses in a corresponding vocational school for the period of 3 years and requires a series of final examinations. This training program provides German libraries with well-qualified young staff able to carry out various tasks from simple cataloging to lending services and periodicals' maintenance to Web page management and so on. In Germany, it is very common that everybody in a library and information service does front desk work (check-out, reference desk, etc.), or public relations work combined with back office work like cataloging or acquisition.

Continuing education is a very important activity in German libraries. Each year the Bibliothekartag (German librarians' conference) is the most important continuing education meeting for German library and information professionals. There are many other possibilities for continuing education for librarians at the level of the Länder and a virtual marketplace makes it easy to find them all.[26]

Professional Associations

Cooperation is at the heart of *Bibliothek & Information Deutschland* (BID = Federal Union of German Library & Information Associations), the national federation of library associations, founded in 1989 as an umbrella organization of German library and information associations. This umbrella organization unites four major association:

1. *The Deutscher Bibliotheksverband* (DBV—German Library Association), represents 1700 institutions and includes both academic and public libraries. DBV was created in 1949 and in 1991, after being separated for 27 years, the German Library Association (East) and the German Library Association (West) reunited.
2. *The Berufsverband Information Bibliothek* (BIB—Association of Information and Library Professionals) has 6300 members and is the largest association of library and information professionals. It was founded in 2000 through a merger of four separate associations. Its members include many public librarians and library assistants.
3. *The Verein Deutscher Bibliothekare* (VDB—the Association of German Librarians) the oldest librarian association in Germany, was founded in 1900. Most of the library directors and many professional librarians in Germany are among its members. Its membership includes academic and research librarians with university degrees.
4. *The Deutsche Gesellschaft für Information* (DGI—German Society of Information) founded in 1948, represents documentalists and information specialists.

The German Library Association (DVB) has developed and has taken the leadership of a Competence Network of Services like the library statistics and the library portal for Germany.[27] This library portal is the best information source about libraries in Germany.

ARCHIVES AND ARCHIVAL SCIENCE IN GERMANY

Overview

Germany's archival law was issued in 1988 in the Federal Republic of Germany with amendments added in 2005[28] that apply to the freedom of information legislation concerning the accessibility of archives and official records by everybody. Following World War I the first national archival law of 1919 created a central archive for all historical records. Today, materials in all formats (printed materials, maps, data and images, and films and sound recordings) produced by government agencies at different levels must be collected by the Bundesarchiv (=Federal Archive). In a federal state like Germany there is a national archival law and there are archival laws in the different federal states (Länder) to regulate archiving of government records at all levels.[29] The national law of January 1988 establishes the basic rules for the legal deposit of official records for all administration and government agencies at the national level, and regulates the organization and the accessibility of these records. An important part of the archival law is the question of delayed access. In general, archival records are accessible to the public after 30 years; however, records containing personal information or having special security concerns (medical records, tax data, etc.), are not accessible for 60 years. Other personal data can be accessed 10 years after the death of the person, although there are exceptions to this concerning the official records of the German Democratic Republic. They are freely accessible by law.

The history of Germany with its many small kingdoms is reflected in the development of archives at the state and regional levels. In managing historical records of a territory, archivists must cope with many situations where boundaries recognized in the past often differ from the current political borders of the territory. An excellent overview on archives in Germany has been produced by the Archivschule Marburg which lists State archives at the level of the Länder, community archives, and all other kinds of archives in a full list.[30]

National Archives and Services

The Bundesarchiv (=Federal Archive) in Koblenz is the central Federal archives in Germany and is under the State Minister of Culture and Media of the Federal Republic of Germany. Some of its records go back to 1411, but the regular collection of records started in 1867, just 4 years before the Foundation of the German Empire in 1871. The Federal Archive is the successor of the Archives of the German Empire that was founded in 1919. The Federal Archive is responsible for collecting the records of all federal constitutional bodies, government, and courts, except the parliament. After Reunification in 1990, the development of eight branches of the Bundesarchiv shows the integration of the two parts of Germany very well. In Koblenz, the records of the Federal Republic of Germany are maintained, in Berlin the records of the German Reich and its successors since 1871, and all other records from 1495 to 1871 except the time from 1807 to 1814 when Napoleon occupied Germany (this archive is in Paris). The Berlin Branch of the national archive keeps the record of

East Germany and of a foundation which was created to protect the records and documents of parties and mass organizations of the GDR (Stiftung Archiv der Parteien und Massenorganisationen der DDR im Bundesarchiv).

As part of the Federal Archives the Berlin Film-Archive is the biggest film archive of the world. The Bayreuth Branch keeps records concerning lost property of Germans in former German territories and former GDR as the records on the search services of the Red Cross, which played an important role after the Second World War 1945.

The German Military Archive is kept in the Freiburg Branch of the Federal Archive and in Ludwigsburg the records of Nazi Crimes can be found. Many records were destroyed during the Second World War 1939–1945, as was a part of the former Military Archive of the Army.

There are four other important Archives at the national level: First:

- The Parlamentsarchiv des Deutschen Bundestags (=Archive of the German Bundestag) with all parliamentary records since the Federal Republic of Germany was founded in 1949, and some records from 1945 to 1949 of the military government of the Allies.
- Die Beauftragte für die Unterlagen des Staatssicherheitsdienstes der ehemaligen Deutschen Demokratischen Republik (=The Office of the Federal Commissioner for State Security Services of the former German Democratic Republic) preserves the records of the former Ministry for State Security in its archives and makes these available to private individuals, institutions, and the public in accordance with strict legal regulations. These legal regulations differ from the archive law, as there is a special law for this archive which makes it possible to have access to files on persons.[31] In the archive of the central office in Berlin and in the 14 archives of the outposts of the Federal Commissioner, one can find the records of the former intelligence service of the GDR which developed during the four decades of the existence of the Ministry for State Security. This archive is very active in public relations and often presents results of the research to the press when politicians or other public persons are confronted with their past—as victims or as employees of the Ministry of State Security in the German Democratic Republic.
- Another very important Archive at the national government level is the Politische Archiv des Auswärtigen Amtes (=The Political Archives of the Foreign Ministry) with all bilateral and international contracts from 1876 up to the present.
- Last but not least the Geheime Staatsarchiv Preußischer Kulturbesitz (=Secret Central Archives of Prussian Cultural Heritage)—a name applied in 1803—can be traced back to 1282 with a location in Brandenburg and it became an autonomous body

in 1598. This archive is no longer secret and provides access to records from 1188 to 1933 relating to Prussia including the history of the king's family and the archive of the Foundation Prussian Cultural heritage since 1957.

German State Archives (Landesarchives)

In the 16 federal states of Germany today, the central state archives or Landesarchive together with some archives of special territories contain important collections of official archives. Due to the historical existence of many duchies and kingdoms, "state" archives have been developed by small territorial units, not identical with the political boundaries of the German states (Länder) as they presently exist. There is still two-tiered structure of archival responsibilities in some of the German federal states, especially those with double names. Since 2003, there have been some organizational changes. First in the state of Saxony-Anhalt, later in North Rhine-Westphalia, Lower Saxony, and Saxony and Baden-Wuerttemberg, the archives of smaller territories have been integrated in one Hauptstaasarchiv (=central state archive) or Landesarchiv of the respective federal state. This practice has created a single streamlined organization in each these states, as well as a standardized appraisal policy, and it will prepare for the next step toward a digital future.[32] At the level of the Länder, the archives have the task to collect material of the state governments including the ministries, administrative units, and courts at this level. Just as the National Parliament has its own Bundestagsarchiv, the state parliaments also have their own parliamentary archives. Many archives on the level of the Länder also collect materials from parties and civil organizations. The archives in the new Länder of former East-Germany also have files from the former state-owned companies and factories. Parliaments of the Länder have their independent archives or deposit their archival materials at the state archive. The archives in North Rhine-Westphalia have collected a Linklist as a guide to using materials in all kind of archives in this region.[33]

Local Archives in Germany

Germany has a very strong community life with more than 12,000 cities, districts, and villages. At the local level, Germany has city archives and county archives. In addition to collecting the records of the local government and the local courts, these archives are active in obtaining materials about civil organizations and famous persons. Besides the official records at this level, many kinds of local organizations have created historical records. There is a saying that wherever there are three Germans, they will found an organization. In many cases, records of local groups may be collected in a community archive. Some of the local archives have special materials like calendar collections, leaflets and posters, and theater programs and postcards. To support communities with archival services and to give advice on archival problems, in some parts of Germany, such Brandenburg and Westfalen, service institutions for archives have been established to support the local level. As we have seen, the history of Germany as a country is more complicated than in centralized states, and this is mirrored at the local level, where the situation is even more complicated. Preparations for research in a local archive must be accompanied by a good knowledge of the region's history, what state it belonged to in which time period. Only with this detailed information is it easy to determine the correct archive that was responsible at that time for collecting the files. The principle that the archive must be organized according to the principles used by the government then in power is a very important principle for Germany's changing landscape of small territories over centuries.[34]

School Archives and University Archives

Archives of famous schools, especially of some of the early secondary schools (Gymnasien) in Germany, have been maintained very well. One example is the school archive of the Berlinische Gymnasium zum Grauen Klosters held in the Central and Regional Library in Berlin. This is a school which many famous people attended and where you still can find the grades of Bismarck, the first chancellor of the German Empire. All records of students and teachers have been kept since 1574.

All universities in Germany have their own university archives, which is often part of the university library and collect student data and documents of the university administration and manuscripts of famous professors. Some of the old university archives like Heidelberg have a long tradition but may have lost documents during times of war in the seventeenth, nineteenth, or twentieth century.

Film Archives and Other Audiovisual Archives

The most important film archive has already been mentioned as a part of the national archive. The most important audiovisual archives are those from the radio and television stations. The ARD Radio stations and other public radio and television stations have maintained public archives from the beginning of radio and television in Germany. The Deutsches Rundfunkarchiv in Potsdam is supported by all public radio and television stations in Germany and has to be especially mentioned because its collection includes the first public radio announcement from October 1923. Current activities includes the SWR 2 archive radio with presentation of interesting features from the archive.[35] The German Music Archives collect all audiovisual media on music and is part of the German National Library. Besides the Bundesarchive one of the

biggest image archive with 12 million images is the Bildarchiv Prussian Cultural Heritage. In Dresden, the Deutsche Fotothek, a famous archives with more than 800,000 photos, is a part of the university library.

Literary Archives

In the tradition of the classical literature, Germany has quite a few archives of literary figures—the extensive Goethe and Schiller archives in Weimar are only one model. The Literature Archive in Marbach is the main institution that holds manuscripts and typescripts of many German authors and poets. There are some other literature archives with a special focus on regional authors, more or less famous, like the Theodor Fontane Archive in Frankfurt/Oder.

Corporate Archives

Corporate archives are known for being less well organized and are often integrated into the archives of the Länder, state libraries, or university libraries. For example, the 200-year-old library and the corporate archives of the family of Thurn und Taxis, which started the first private postal system in Germany, was given to the university library in Regensburg as a deposit. Other large companies still have their own corporate archive like Krupp in Essen and are able to answer requests from interested persons. The family archives for family-owned concerns are often integrated with the documents of the firm. When companies are dissolved, regional economic archives collect some of those records. A good example is the Bergbauarchiv in Bochum for the coal mining industry of the Ruhr District.

Religious Archives

In Germany, the main type of religious archives are from the Catholic and the Protestant churches with their diocesan or state-level church archives. Protestant archives at the local church level are the most important local sources for genealogy research. Social activities for the poor and for orphans are also well documented in these archives.

Private Archives

Quite a few historical societies have their own archives as do important families. Many family archives of nobility or important men and women are found in Germany, and, if they are not collected by the state archive, they remain in the hands of the families. The nobility has played an important role in Germany in agriculture, economy, military, civil services, and as public persons. Therefore, the archives of nobility like the Deutsches Adelsarchiv (=German Nobility Archive) may have important historical records. In Germany, some active special interest groups have created important private archives as a grass-roots initiative: these include the women's archive, the migration archives, and others called Archive von unten (=Archive from the grassroots). One of these very special private initiatives that needs to be mentioned here is the Archiv der Jugendkulturen (=Archive of Youth Culture) in Berlin, a private institution which resembles both a library and an archive. This archive collects Fanzine, the magazines and flyers produced by fans, and they also collect all kinds of record about the fan culture. It relies on voluntary contributions. Nowadays, the fan culture is moving to the Net and the Fanzines are produced electronically. So, as in all other archives, this archive faces new challenges. The Archiv der Jugendkulturen produces an electronic list of these records, the Fanzine-Index.[36]

Digital Archival Collections and Digital Finding Aids

Digitization as a form to give access to archival materials is being discussed. The Bundesarchiv in Koblenz and the Berlin branch were very active in digitizing finding aids of their archives. Finding aids are presented at the homepage of the institution. All other archives are increasingly placing their finding lists on the Internet, like the Berlin Landesarchiv. In contrast to the libraries, the discussion on digitizing the material itself is not so intensive. The amount of time spent on doing digitization is judged in relation to the importance of the records. There are many projects on digitization supported by the German Science Foundation, focusing on the conversion of the finding aids. One of the first activities to digitize archival documents was the digitization of the pre-eighteenth century records of the Archive of Duderstadt. This was a project in connection with the Max Planck Institute of History in Göttingen. It was also a pilot program for long-term conservation.

In contrast to Germany's libraries, the archives do not enjoy the same kind of cooperation. During recent years this has changed and more cooperation and discussion has started. The digitization activities are growing, but prior to this there were many successful efforts to save archival records on microfilm. New cooperation has begun with the cooperative cataloging of manuscripts in Kalliope, a central catalog of manuscripts in Germany, run by the State Library Berlin Prussian Heritage.[37] There is information about 1.3 million manuscripts and for over 400,000 individuals. Approximately 300 libraries and archives are cataloging their manuscripts in this database, which is a partner of the BAM-Portal, a Web server for libraries, archives, and museums.

ARCHIVAL SCIENCE AND EDUCATION

Archival science becoming more important in Germany. Educational programs for archivists and records managers are offered at various levels and there are ongoing discussions concerning examinations, certification, university level programs, and continuing education.

Besides, the Fachangestellte für Medien und Informationsdienste with their integrated training program for work in libraries, information and media centers or archives, one category of the archivists employed in Germany are still trained according to the rules for civil servants. This means, to become an archivist, with a credential comparable to a bachelor's level degree, the Landesarchiv, or state archive select candidates with high school degree (Abitur). They go through a 3 year program including a 4 month training module at a school of administration and on-the-job training periods in the archive which has selected the student. At the end, the student passes a professional certification examination for civil servants in archival institutions. Then he or she is able to look for the middle management level position in German state archives.

The higher level of civil servants are selected by the State Archives. As a prerequisite, they must have finished a full course of university study, a master's degree, preferably in history, and they are encouraged to have a doctorate. Following an 8-month training period in the archive, the candidate for this level has 12-month program of study at the School for Archivists in Marburg, and a 1-month internship at the Bundesarchiv. Certain universities of applied science in Germany have changed the former Diplome-programs for archivists to bachelor and master's degree programs of study. The 3- to 4-year courses include one semester of work experience at an archive. At the University of Applied Science in Potsdam, preparations for the start of a nonconsecutive master course for working archivists have begun, following the distance learning model for librarians at the Humboldt University in Berlin. The consecutive master's course will start in 2010. The most famous school for archivists is the Archivschule Marburg, a university of applied science solely for archival studies. Its library is the special library for archival science in Germany.

Professional Associations

The main professional association of archivists is the *Verband Deutscher Archivare und Archivarinnen(VdA)* (=Association of Archivists) founded in 1946. With 2200 members it is the largest association of archivists in Europe. Archival appraisal is discussed in the position paper of a working group "Archival Appraisal" within the Association of German Archivists.[38] The association publishes papers on basic principles, standard procedures and as special problems like handling large quantities of similar case files, statistical records, electronic, and audiovisual records with checklists. These publications help to build a common level of appraisal in state and local archives in Germany. Since November 2008, the association has a new working group on archival documents of the twentieth and twenty-first century.[39]

Electronic Records

There is an ongoing discussion about using electronic records, about the complexity of permanent data retention and other issues. In many German archives, the focus is now changing to long-term preservation of electronic records—a very difficult task as government agencies and administrations use different technologies for their archival systems.

Preservation of Documents

Preservation and conservation is one of the main challenges in German Archives. Since 1961, a selection of archival documents of national and state archives are preserved additionally by preservation microfilming, supported by the Bundesamt für Bevölkerungsschutz und Katastrophenhilfe (=Federal Office of Civil Protection and Disaster Assistance).[40] Methods of restoration and conservation of the materials including removal of mould and deacidification are regularly discussed as paper made between 1840 and 1990 contains acid and German companies have devised different methods to extract the acid and stabilize the paper.

Other Issues

Archival pedagogic or user education is new to the archival field, as is public relations work for the archives in Germany. More and more activities are initiated by key archives for the public, including not only exhibitions but also discussions for students of middle school who are doing learning projects on history.

MUSEUMS AND MUSEOLOGY

National Museums

There are more than 6000 museums in Germany. Most of them are organized at the community level. At the level of the federal states (Länder), there are Landesmusseen (State museums), as well as other special and more important collections. Due to the federal structure, there is not one National Museum in Germany. Instead, there are several museums at the national level supported by the Federal Minister of Culture together with the Länder. Today, some of these museums are organized as a public foundation or a limited company, with representatives of the national government on the board of trustees, often together with those from the Länder.

The most important museum complex of this kind is the *Stiftung Preussischer Kulturbesitz* (=*The Prussian*

Cultural Heritage Foundation) and its museums, libraries, and archives. The Foundation was created in 1957, and two-thirds of its budget is financed by the Federal Government of Germany and by the 16 Länder.[41] It is one of the largest museum complexes worldwide and the most extensive in Germany with 25 individual institutions altogether. The Museum collection, called the *Staatliche Museen zu Berlin—Preussicher Kulturbesitz*, (=*Berlin State Museums—Prussian Cultural Heritage*) originated with collections of the treasures of the Prussian kings and emperors, and on the travels of important German archeologists. Since Re-unification of Germany in 1990, the collections and museums from the East and the West are united again. Most famous of these is the *Museumsinsel* (=*Museum Island*) in Berlin, a UNESCO World Heritage Site, with the Pergamon-Museum as its public magnet. This is surrounded by museums with extensive archeological artifacts and nineteenth-century collections. At the *Kulturforum Site* (=*Cultural Forum*) in the former West part of Berlin is another major complex of art museums with collections of paintings from more than five centuries and galleries with twentieth-century art. The *Dahlem Museums*, another part of the Prussian Cultural Heritage, combines museum collections of ethnology and Asian art. Collections of contemporary art, design, and photography; these collections are located at the Museum Hamburger Bahnhof, at Museum Berggruen and the New National Gallery and at other facilities of this Foundation which includes the *Institut für Museumsforschung* (=Institute of Museum Research) which produces documentation and statistics, as well as research on German museums.

The *Deutsche Historische Museum* (=*The Germany Historical Museum*), supported by the Federal Minister of Culture, was officially founded in 1987 after a long discussion about the need and relevance of a national museum of history. Opponents saw this as a growing tendency toward nationalism which was at the base of the Nazi ideology—still a sensitive topic in German society. The museum now offers German history from its beginnings, but places this history within the European context. After Re-unification of Germany, the museum moved back to the center of Berlin, and took over the collection of the former Historical Museum of German Democratic Republic.

The *Stiftung Haus der Geschichte der Bundesrepublik Deutschland* (=Foundation House of the History of the Federal Republic of Germany) in Bonn and Leipzig, documents the history and the democratic development of the Federal Republic of Germany since 1945. As the eastern branch of the Foundation, the Leipzig Forum of Contemporary History was opened on October 9, 1999, in recognition of Leipzig as the center of the peaceful revolution in East Germany 1989 which led to Re-unification of Germany. This History Museum collects items of from all media to art, graphic art and political caricatures, designs, textiles and objects of daily life, and currencies.

There is one contemporary art collection at the national level called *Bundeskunstsammlung*. Since 1970, the German Federal Republic collects German art from 1949 onwards. The whole collection is not located in one museum but is placed in embassies, ministries, and public spaces. Today, this collection includes 1200 pieces of art.[42]

Although culture is the responsibility of the Länder, there is a special law for a "blue list" of those cultural institutions from Western Germany which are cofinanced by the Federal Government. Accordingly, 20 important cultural institutions of Eastern Germany are listed in a so-called "bluebook" of the Federal Government. Some of the following museums of the Länder belong to one of the lists and receive national support as cultural beacons of national importance.

The Castles and Gardens of the Prussian Kings are combined in *the Stiftung Preußische Schlösser und Gärten Berlin-Brandenburg (=the Foundation of Prussian Castles and Gardens in Berlin and Brandenburg)*. It was founded in 1994 as a combination of two former institutions in West and East. The foundation maintains and documents the heritage of the castles and gardens including their collections of royal art and interior furnishings.

The *Klassik Stiftung Weimar (=Foundation of the Weimar Classics)* is a large museum complex comprising 11 sites: a library, the archives, and museums of Goethe and Schiller, palaces and historical houses as well as the parks in and around Weimar. The Weimar Classic forms the ensemble Classical Weimar, honoring this famous period in German culture.

Other institutions from the blue list include

- Kunsthalle Bremen (=Art Gallery Bremen).
- Bauhaus-Archiv Museum für Gestaltung (=Bauhaus-Archiv Museum of design) Berlin.
- Schiller Nationalmuseum (=Schiller National Museum) Marbach.
- Franckesche Stiftungen Halle (=Francke Foundations).
- Leibniz Science Society museums.
- The Römisch-Germanisches Zentralmuseum (=Roman-Germanic Central Museum) Mainz.
- Germanisches Nationalmuseum (=Germanic National Museum) Nürnberg.
- Deutsches Museum München (=German Museum Munich).
- Deutsches Bergbaumuseum (=German Mining Museum).
- Bochum, Deutsches Schifffahrtsmuseum (=German Maritime Museum) Bremerhaven.

Major Art Museums and Galleries

Altogether there are about 500 art museums in Germany. Germany's major art museums and galleries are in Berlin, but Munich, Dresden, Kassel, Hamburg, Cologne, Düsseldorf, and Stuttgart all have significant art museums and galleries. Especially famous are *Munich's Alte Pinakothek* with European masterpieces of the fourteenth to the eighteenth century (one room just for Rubens) and the *Neue Pinakothek* which covers nineteenth-century art. Munich also has the Pinakothek der Moderne which collects graphic art from the fifteenth century to the twenty-first century; it also includes one the first design collections that originated in 1907.[43] The *Staatliche Kunstsammlungen Dresden - The Old Masters Picture Gallery in Dresden*—displays Italian renaissance, Dutch and Flemish masterpieces, Spanish and French paintings of the seventeenth century and older German art as that by Dürer, Cranach, and Holbein. As one of the few museums from Germany represented in the virtual reality of the "Second Life," there are rooms from this Museum reproduced true to scale with all 750 masterpieces.[44] The New Masters Picture Gallery is well-known for modern art. The Staatsgalerie (=State Gallery) Stuttgart has art from the Middle Ages up to the modern period, although the Stuttgart Kunstmuseum (=Stuttgart art museum) concentrates on modern art. In Kassel princely state supported museums have very rich collections. The Hamburger Kunsthalle (Hamburg Art Gallery) supported by the Hamburger Kunstverein (Hamburg Art Society) is known for its art from the Northern Germany, from Holland, France, and Italy, with many masterpieces from the fourteenth century. Since 1995, it also has a contemporary section. The development of German artists belonging to the "Brücke" (Ludwig Kirchner, Emil Nolde, and others) is very well represented with 400 art works in the Brücke Museum in Berlin Grunewald. The Bauhaus, a design and architecture school from 1919 to 1933, is represented in the Bauhaus-Archiv Museum Berlin, and in museums in Dessau and Weimar, where the Bauhaus was founded. The art museum of the Land Berlin, the Berlinische Gallery, has a fine collection from 1870 until the present with special themes Fluxus and Dada. The Kunstsammlung von Nordrhein-Westfalen K20 K21 (=the Art Collection K 20 K21 of the Land North Rhine-Westphalia)[45] is a fabulous collection of the art of the twentieth century focused on Western European and American art (Picasso, Beuys, and Klee). Nearby, the Museum Ludwig of the city of Cologne collects twentieth century and contemporary art, too. This is one of the few museums with Russian avant-garde art of the 1920s and 1930s and is known as the third largest collection of Picasso's works in the world. Frankfurt City's Museumsufer—11 museums at the bank of the river Main—can be seen as a museum complex, representing all kinds of special art collections.

Science and Natural History Museums

Natural history museums in Germany often developed from university collections of minerals, fossils, plants, and insects. At a global level, Germany's various collections of millions of specimens are of great importance for biodiversity research. There is no one central national museum for natural history but instead, the specimens are divided among 12 major museums and more than 100 smaller ones. Germany's natural history museums comprise seven direct nodes of the *Global Biodiversity Information Facility. They* are responsible for collecting data representing seven major taxonomic groups:

- Insects at the Staatlichen Museum für Naturkunde Stuttgart (=State Museum of Natural Science in Stuttgart).
- terrestrial invertebrates at the Zoologische Staatssammlung München (=Zoological State Collections Munich).
- marine invertebrates at the Forschungsinstitut und Naturmuseum Senckenberg (=Research Institute and Museum of Nature Senckenberg) in Frankfurt.
- animals with vertebrae at the Zoologischen Forschungsinstitut und Museum Alexander Koenig (=Zoological research institute and museum Alexander König) in Bonn.
- botanical specimens at the Botanischer Garten und Botanisches Museum Berlin (=Botanic Garden and Botanic Museum Berlin).
- mycology at the Botanische Staatssammlung München (=Botanic State collection Munich).
- prokaryotes at the Deutsche Sammlung von Mikroorganismen und Zellkulturen Braunschweig (=German collection of prokaryotes and viruses).

In Germany, technical history museums have seen rapid development during recent decades. Due to a total economical change in certain regions in Western Germany and after the Re-unification in the East of Germany, large coal mines, and old steel production sites, as well as abandoned industry sites of different kinds, have been preserved, making Germany very rich in technical history sites. There are large museums of the former mining and steel industry and groups of volunteers run the museums in their leisure time, sometimes supported by the local governments. Other technical museums have a longer tradition, such as those displaying handicrafts and other items that represent the rich diversity of local traditions in Germany's small communities.

The Deutsches Museum (=German Museum) in Munich founded in 1903, has one of the richest technical collections of the world. Besides the traditional display of mechanical and technical inventions, the museum has created a transportation museum to explain the development of bicycles, cars, and trains, and in 1992 opened a special airplane museum with an old airport and maintenance hangar outside of Munich.

Established only during the 1970s, the *Stiftung Deutsches Technik Museum in Berlin (= Foundation of*

German Museum of Technology in Berlin) presents impressive exhibitions of technical masterworks ranging from locomotives to small scale technology. Many exhibits with a strong experiential character have been developed in order to involve visitors in all kinds of activities using new interactive concepts. The Museum has opened a new section in 2006—recognizable from afar by an example of the "Raisin bombers" aircraft during the Berlin Air Lift on its roof. The attached Sugar museum 6 km north shows 500 objects on the history of sugar and is typical of traditional museum culture in Germany.[46] It was founded in 1904 as a part of the sugar industry, before it came under the support of the city and state of Berlin. It is typical for the development of small industry museums in Germany to go from private institutions to ones that are supported by state or local authorities.

On the level of the Länder, important museums of crafts and technology are located in Mannheim, Hagen, Hamburg, and many other cities. From the German Radio Museum in Potsdam to the clock museum in Furtwangen or the famous toy museum in Nuremberg, many special museums possess rich collections of crafts and technological inventions. Since Germany is so famous for its organs, clavichords, and pianofortes as well as other instruments like violins, the museums of music must be mentioned. The collection of the *Musikinstrumentenmuseum (Museum of Musical Instruments)* in Berlin with more than 3000 instruments is one of the biggest in Germany.

All technical museums are a wonderful world for children and many of them have special tours for children or offer their location for birthday parties in the museum. However, there are only a few institutions specifically designated as children's museums in Germany, and most of these are based on private initiatives like the Exploratorium in Potsdam or the Machmit Museum (Hands-on Museum) in Berlin, where even a few objects like a special "path to feel" can be borrowed.

Many of the older universities in Germany have museum-like collections with plant and animal specimens, and technological artifacts from the history of their university. The most famous and oldest university museum is in Heidelberg. Marburg and Halle have important university museums and with them, the Berlin Humboldt-University collection are all famous in medicine and science. Altogether there are 700 collections existing at universities with significant objects of science, technology, medicine, history, and art.[47]

Historical, Anthropological, and Archeological Museums

Besides the large national institutions, there are more than 2000 historical museums and historical sites in Germany and many of these local museums were founded during the Nazi regime. During recent years important new themes have developed for these museums such as memory-culture (Erinnerungskultur), oral history, and multicultural collections. Local history museums are key to the historical understanding of the people, and now the museums exploring the oppression of the Nazi period are becoming important. Some of these museums consist of historical parks to explore the history of early settlements, old housing, and economy. Often positioned in the countryside, these outdoor museums have special functions in supporting regional tourism.

There are many historical sites associated with Germany's world-famous authors, philosophers, artists, and other historical personages. There are museum houses of Goethe and Schiller not only in Weimar but also in the towns of their birth, Frankfurt and Marbach, and the same is true for Bertold Brecht in Augsburg (his birthplace) and in Berlin where he lived and worked for so long.

Archeological finds in Germany cover a wide range of periods, starting with the Homo Neanderthalensis in the Neanderthal near Düsseldorf (130,000 years ago). The Hedeby Viking Museum, (eighth to eleventh century), and artifacts from the Roman era found along the Rhine and Mosel and exhibited in archeological sites and museums from Cologne to Trier, from Xanten to Mainz. Site museum also represent the complex history of German duchies and small kingdoms. From the Middle Ages to the Renaissance, from the Baroque to a new Gothic style all types of castles can be visited. Many castles and palaces are regional museums and there are special tours along the Rhine to visit the numerous, beautiful castles on the mountains there. More than 80 scenic holiday routes throughout Germany are integrating local museums into their proposed itineraries; these include museums related to fairy tales, toys, windmills, or asparagus, just to name a few.

Special museum sites have developed in Germany to honor the victims of the crimes of Nazi Terror—the Gedenkstätten (=the memorial sites of the Holocaust). They are more than a normal holocaust museum as they commemorate the site, where the Jews, the Communists, and the Roma were murdered. Many of the buildings of these sites still exist and show the brutality of that time. All these memorial sites have many activities for students and host regular lectures for the public.

ZOOS AND BOTANICAL GARDENS

In Germany, zoos and botanical gardens are not counted in the statistics of German museums.[48] Nevertheless, Germany has many zoos and the Berlin Zoo has the most animals and species of any zoo in the world. *Berlin Zoologischer Garten*, founded in 1841, has 13,722 animals of 1388 species and has now been combined with the Tierpark Berlin-Friedrichsfelde in former East Berlin, founded in 1954 with 7955 animals of 976 species.[49] Important zoos are Hagenbeck in Hamburg, Hellabrunn

in Munich, Wilhelm in Stuttgart and the Cologne Zoo. Altogether, there are more than 750 zoos listed in the German Zoo Database.[50]

Botanical gardens in Germany have existed since the sixteenth century. Often such gardens developed from former monastery gardens and were later affiliated with the neighboring university (as in Leipzig, 1539). Today, more than 90 botanical gardens offer great attractions. The *Berlin Botanischer Garten and Botanisches Museum* (=*Berlin Botanical Gardens and Botanical Museum*) with more than 22,000 plants is the third biggest botanical garden of the world. Every 2 years a new botanical garden is founded in Germany as the result of the Bundesgartenschau, a biannual Federal horticulture show.

DIGITAL MUSEUM EXHIBITS AND SERVICES

Creation of digital museums in Germany is just starting. As more and more museums have the documentation of their collections accessible in digital form, the museums are starting to put these materials online. Digital museums often just mean that the list of objects can be found on the museum Web site. Nevertheless, a few museums have scanned their objects and put these up in the Web. The German Historical Museum in Berlin has already digitized 250,000 items which are searchable via Internet.[51] Big museums like the German Historical Museums are in the forefront in developing virtual exhibitions. Together with Bonn, they are part of the LEMO, the Living Museum Online, a collection of Germany's history with interesting historical multimedia files from 1871 up to the present.[52] The Gemäldegalerie Dresden is one of the few German museums represented in virtual reality with attractive explanations accompanying its objects online. German museums have started a Web presentation to concentrate their virtual activities. This Virtual Library Museum has been created by the German Museum Association in cooperation with International Council of Museums (ICOM) Germany and the Museum Institute, and cosponsored by the Historisches Centrum Hagen. Thus, all museums in Germany with virtual activities, documentation, and Web sites are listed here.[53]

Museology as a Discipline and Profession

In November 2007, a very important conference on museum research took place in Berlin, sponsored by the Volkswagenstiftung—Volkswagen Foundation. More than 4000 museums were asked to respond to a questionnaire on research in museums. Research is an important part of museum activities and in 2008, as a follow up, the Volkswagen Foundation launched an initiative of research in museums with support of doctorate and post doctorate research in middle-sized museums, international research networking of curator; they also provided funds for making more information about research in museums available to the public. Major museums have research agendas, as has the Museum of Natural Science in Berlin. Currently, this research concentrate on six different research lines including biodiversity, evolution, impact research, and research history.

Education for Curatorship and Museum Administration

More than 50 universities and universities of applied science offer a wide range of courses from museology in Leipzig to museum studies in Berlin, and they teach practical knowledge of how to run a museum. Cultural management and museum paedagogics (museum education) are also research fields at some universities. Nevertheless, many museum curators have studied art history or have other traditional university degrees before the Bologna process in 1999 introduced the bachelor and master degrees in Germany. New developments in this field can be expected.

The "Voluntariat," (a museum assistant in German museums) is a 2 year, low-paid training period at an institution, which is prerequisite to gain a permanent position in one of the museums. After finishing a university master's degree or doctorate, one can apply for a "volontariat" at a museum. In contrast to training for librarianship, there is no clear museology curriculum, but only on-the-job training for these museum specialists. Therefore in 2007, a group was founded by the museum associations to establish regulations and standards for training museum assistants.

Professional Associations

The Deutscher Museumsbund (=German Museums Association), founded in 1917, is the premier organization for museums and its membership includes both institutions and individuals. The Association works closely with the Institute of Museum Research in Berlin which produces the German museum statistics each year and supports museum research. The statistics on museums only include museums that are open to the public and not commercial. The Institute is also the home of the central special library on museology in Germany. It was founded in 1979 in response to similar developments in the German Democratic Republic. The Museumsbund also cooperates with the National Committee of the International Council of Museums—ICOM Deutschland which supports international exchange programs. There is no strong cooperation between the regional associations of the German Museum Association. The most important meeting is an annual conference.

Small- and middle-sized museums are supported by some institutions in the Länder, which give advise and help. In some Länder like Bavaria and Baden-

Württemberg these are public institutions, in other Länder like Lower Saxony or Brandenburg, the Museum Association has this task. Therefore the regional museum organizations are important in the Länder.

Key Contemporary Issues

The museum associations have established various projects and research groups. The educational task of museums has been one of the main topics in German museum discussions for more than 30 years. Museum education programs are aimed at children as well as at adults, and their goal is to inform and support understanding of the museum objects. These discussions have focused on methods of integrating museum education: either as supplementary to the exhibition or as an integral part of the exhibition concept. There is a special association for museums' educational tasks. In cooperation between different partners some projects like http://www.schule-museum.de[54] have developed very successfully.

Other contemporary issues under discussion are visitor research, marketing museums, and managing volunteers. A lot of research is being done on conservation and restoration in museums and there is an active exchange of knowledge on disaster prevention. Research on museum visitors is a one of the most important aspects of modern museology in order to optimize exhibition content and location, and to analyze the impact of the museums. A working group on volunteers in museums has published a position paper and the discussion shows different views and activities with volunteers. For several years, the multicultural aspect of museum work has produced discussion and new activities now focus on the history of the Germany's immigrants in the local Heimatmuseums. The "Long Museum Nights" with museums being open without fees for the entire night first started in Berlin in 1997 and has become a very attractive event twice a year and a role model for other museum nights all over Germany.

In February 2006, the German Museum Association published standards for museums. These are not rigid regulations, but important guidelines to assist in developing individual activities along these standards. The German view on museums is determined by these regulations set out by the Museumsbund: professional supervision with adequate support for researchers and scientific specialists. Another basic principle: The original has to be placed in the center of all exhibitions.

CONCLUSION

Convergence and cooperation among the various information institutions in Germany have not been developed extensively and there are few strong ties between them. Libraries, archives, and museums have their specialized standards, different software tools, and different training programs. It is difficult to merge databases and information.

Provenance Research, a common topic for museums, archives, and libraries, is currently gaining important, as during World War II many collections were lost, confiscated or displaced. The Nazis seized art collections and libraries from Jewish civilians before they were deported to concentration camps. Many of these objects were placed in museums and libraries. After more than 50 years it is extremely important to clear up the "smudges" in ownership, to learn more about the lost and looted art, and to support the Washington Declaration from 1998 about restitution, which has also been reinforced by a declaration by the government of the Federal Republic of Germany. Libraries, archives, and museums are working together to identify Nazi-confiscated cultural property and place it into http://www.lostart.de, the Internet Portal of the Koordinierungsstelle für Kulturgutverluste (=the coordination office for lost cultural property) in Magdeburg.[55]

One model of cooperation is the BAM-Portal, a Web portal for libraries, archives, and museums, which helps libraries, archives, and museum to coordinate digital projects. This includes European digital projects like EUROPEANA which include Germany's cultural heritage at the European level. In future digitization will play a greater role in convergence between libraries archives and museums. Nestor,[56] the German network of expertise in digital long-term preservation, will become an important cooperation for libraries, archives, and museums and their future in the digital age.

REFERENCES

1. http://statistik.arbeitsamt.de/statistik/index.php?id = D.
2. Schlussbericht der Enquêtekommission Kultur in Deutschland. *Bundestagsdrucksache*, 16/7000 vom November 12, 2007.
3. Bundesvereinigung Deutscher, Bibliotheksverbände, Ed.; *Bibliotheken '93: Strukturen — Aufgaben — Positionen*; Deutsches Bibliotheksinstitut: Berlin, Germany, 1994. A good overview on German libraries is also found in: Seefeldt, J.; Syré, L: *Portale zu Vergangenheit und Zukunft — Bibliotheken in Deutschland*. Ed.: BID. - 3. überarb. Auflage. - Georg Olms-Verl.: Hildesheim, Germany, 2007.
4. *Thüringer Gesetz zum Erlass und zur Änderung bibliotheksrechtlicher Vorschriften — Thüringer Bibliotheksrechtsgesetz (ThürBibRG) — Vom 16*, 2008; Juli 243–244 Gesetz und Verordnungsblatt für den Freistaat Thüringe.
5. *Gesetz über die Deutsche Nationalbibliothek (DNBG) vom 22*, 2006; Juni 1338 In Bundesgesetzblatt I (BGBl. I) S.
6. *Gesetz über die Errichtung der Stiftung Zentral- und Landesbibliothek Berlin (Zentralbibliotheksstiftungsgesetz – ZLBG) in der Fassung vom 27*, 2005; February S. 134–139 In: Gesetz- und Verordnungsblatt für Berlin (GVBl).
7. http://www.d-nb.de/eng/netzpub/sammlung/ueber_np.htm.
8. http://dnb.d-nb.de.
9. http://www.ag-sdd.de/eng/index.htm.
10. http://www.goportis.de.
11. http://www.nationallizenzen.de/.
12. webis.sub.uni-hamburg.de (accessed November 10, 2008) All projects funded by the German Research Foundation DFG are listed here: Available at http://www.dfg.de/en/research_funding/scientific_instrumentation_ and_ infrastructure/scientific_library_services_and_information_ systems/project_funding/projects_funded/index.html (accessed February 7, 2009I).
13. http://www.gbv.de/vgm/links/links_0218.
14. http://www.ubka.uni-karlsruhe.de/kvk.html.
15. Happel, H.-G. *Das wissenschaftliche Bibliothekswesen im Nationalsozialismus: unter besonderer Berücksichtigung der Universitätsbibliotheken*, Saur: München, Germany, 1989.
16. http://www.ub.uni-konstanz.de/.
17. http://rzblx10.uni-regensburg.de/dbinfo/fachliste.php?lett = l.
18. http://rdd.sub.uni-goettingen.de/.
19. http://rzblx1.uni-regensburg.de/ezeit/index.phtml?bibid = AAAAA&colors = 7&lang = en.
20. http://ec.europa.eu/education/policies/educ/bologna/bologna_ en.html.
21. Ladewig, P. *Politik der Bücherei*, Wiegandt: Leipzig, Germany, 1912.
22. Hofmann, W. *Von alten und neuen Richtungen: eine Erwiderung und Ergänzung*, Zentralstelle: Leipzig, Germany, 1917.
23. In *Bibliotheken '93: Strukturen — Aufgaben – Positionen*; Bundesvereinigung Deutscher, Bibliotheksverbände, Ed.; Deutsches Bibliotheksinstitut: Berlin, Germany, 1994.
24. http://adressbuch.zlb.de/.
25. http://www.gutenbergdigital.de/.
26. http://www.wissenbringtweiter.de/home.php.
27. http://www.bibliotheksportal.de/hauptmenue/home/.
28. Bundesarchivgesetz vom 6. Januar 1988 In: Bundesgesetzblatt I (BGBl. I) p. 62), letzte Änderung von § 13 Abs. 2 durch das Gesetz vom 5. September 2005. In Bundesgesetzblatt I (BGBl. I) p. 2722.
29. The best overview about all archival laws in Germany can be found at. Available at http://www.archivschule.de/content/49.html The best overview about all archival laws in Germany can be found at.
30. http://www.archivschule.de/content/59.html.
31. *Stasi-Unterlagen-Gesetz in der Fassung der Bekanntmachung vom 18*, 2007; February p. 162 In: Bundesgesetzblatt I (BGBl. I).
32. Kretzschmar, R. Auf einer Stufe zukunftsfähig? Die staatliche Archivverwaltung Baden-Wuerttemberg in der Verwaltungsreform. Available at http://www.landesarchiv-bw.de/sixcms/media.php/25/VORTRAG_Kretzschmar.pdf (accessed October 11, 2008).
33. http://www.archive.nrw.de.
34. Burkhardt, M. 4. Von der Frage zur Quelle. Der Weg der Recherche Gebrauchsanleitung für Archive, historicum. net.Available at http://www.historicum.net/no_cache/persistent/artikel/3104/ (accessed November 10, 2008).
35. http://www.swr.de/swr2/wissen/archivradio/-/id = 2847740/ 10g9qhv/index.html.

36. http://www.jugendkulturen.de/.
37. http://www.kalliope-portal.de.
38. Positionen des Arbeitskreises Archivische Bewertung im VdA – Verband deutscher Archivarinnen und Archivare zur archivischen Überlieferungsbildung vom 15, 2004; October http://www.archiv.net/pdf/ak_bew_positionen 2004.pdf. (accessed November 11, 2008).
39. http:// www.vda.archiv.net/.
40. http://www.bbk.bund.de/cln_007/nn_398894/DE/02_Themen/ 12_Kulturgutschutz/04_Sicherungsverfilmung/Sicherungsver-filmung_node.html_nnn = true.
41. http://www.hv.spk-berlin.de/english/wir_ueber_uns/profil. php.
42. http://www.bundesregierung.de/Webs/Breg/DE/Bundesreg-ierung/BeauftragterfuerKulturundMedien/Kulturpolitik/Kun-stundKulturfoerderung/Bereiche/BildendeKunst/Bundeskuns-tsammlung/bundeskunstsammlung.html.
43. http://www.pinakothek.de/.
44. http://www.dresdengallery.com.
45. https://www.kunstsammlung.de/en/home.htm.

46. http://www.dtmb.de/Zucker-Museum/index.html.
47. http://publicus.culture.hu-berlin.de/sammlungen/ index.php.
48. Statistische Gesamterhebung an den Museen der Bundesrepublik Deutschland für das Jahr 2006. *Staatliche Museen zu Berlin — Preussischer Kulturbesitz, Institut für Museumskunde Heft 61*, Berlin, Germany, 2007. Available at http://museum.zib.de/ifm/mat61.pdf (accessed September 10, 2008).
49. Zoo Statistics from December 31, 2007. Available at http:// www.zoo-berlin.de/verstehen/zahlen-fakten.html Zoo Statistics from December 31, 2007.
50. http://www.zoo-infos.de/.
51. http://www.dhm.de/sammlungen/index_new.html.
52. http://www.dhm.de/lemo/home.html.
53. http://www.historisches-centrum de/index.php?id = 272.
54. http://www.schule-museum.de.
55. http://www.lostart.de.
56. http://www.langzeitarchivierung.de/index.php?newlang = eng.

Global Open Knowledgebase

Kristen Wilson
North Carolina State University Libraries, Raleigh, North Carolina, U.S.A.

Abstract
The Global Open Knowledgebase (GOKb) is a project to build an open-data, community-managed knowledge base that describes academic publications as they appear in the supply chain. GOKb was designed and implemented by the Kuali Open Library Environment founding partners and Jisc Collections, and is maintained by the Open Library Environment. This entry describes the history of the project and the core functionality of the GOKb service.

INTRODUCTION

This entry will introduce readers to the Global Open Knowledgebase (GOKb) project, including project history and core functionality.

GOKb is an open, community-managed repository of metadata describing electronic resources as they are represented with the academic publishing supply chain. Like existing commercial knowledge bases, GOKb includes standard metadata elements describing the components that support the marketing, sale, purchase, and hosting of electronic resources. Through GOKb, users can acquire information about the titles sold by a particular publisher, the package grouping used by the publisher for sales purposes, and the access platforms used to make resources available to library customers and their end users.

Founded in 2012, GOKb began a project of the Kuali Open Library Environment (OLE) founding partners, including North Carolina State University (NCSU), Indiana University, the University of Florida, Lehigh University, Duke University, the University of Chicago, the University of Maryland, the University of Michigan, and the University of Pennsylvania; and Jisc of the United Kingdom. NCSU served as the lead school for the project. As of 2016, GOKb continues to be supported by OLE.

FOUNDING AND BACKGROUND

The GOKb project was initially conceived as a way to provide an integrated knowledge base for Kuali OLE, a community-source library services platform (LSP) that began development in 2011. During the initial planning for GOKb, the organizers recognized that an open, global knowledge base could serve the needs of similar projects in addition to OLE. Knowledge Base Plus (KB+), an electronic resources management service provided by Jisc Collections of the United Kingdom, was already in development at the time and shared a need for a central repository of data describing the packages and titles managed by its users. KB+ was recruited as a partner in the development of GOKb and began collaborating closely in the initial planning phases of the project.

In 2012, the Andrew W. Mellon Foundation awarded the NCSU Libraries a $499,000 grant to serve as the lead institution in the development of GOKb. Kuali OLE and Jisc were named as partners in the project.[1] This grant funded the first phase of GOKb development, which ran through September 2014. Phase 1 included data model design, the development of a web-based interface for browsing and editing data, and the development of a rules-based tool for validation and data ingest.

At the conclusion of the Phase 1 grant funding period, the GOKb project launched a public preview designed to demonstrate the latest version of the GOKb software, including the web application, API, and co-reference service. The preview also contained a small amount of seed data to illustrate the different record types found within the system. Additional data was added throughout Phase 2 of the project. The preview period was intended as a demonstration of GOKb's potential, with the intent of attracting additional partners to the project.[2]

The Mellon Foundation awarded a $333,000 grant to the NCSU Libraries in 2014 for additional development of GOKb. This funding period ran through March 2016 and supported new development directions for GOKb including expansion of the data model to support e-books, implementation of linked data, and exploration of intersections with other projects addressing open access and open data in scholarly communication.[3]

The primary governing body of GOKb is a steering committee that contains representatives from OLE, NCSU, and other stakeholder groups. The steering committee is responsible for the operations of the GOKb project and has joint reporting responsibility to the OLE Board.[4] The GOKb project has one full-time staff position, the GOKb editor, which reports to the principal investigator of the project based at NCSU Libraries.

Encyclopedia of Library and Information Sciences, Fourth Edition DOI: 10.1081/E-ELIS4-120053601

RELATIONSHIP WITH OLE AND JISC

The GOKb development team worked closely with OLE participants to design a data model and tools that would support the management of electronic resources within the OLE LSP. These efforts included the development of an API that would allow OLE to consume data from GOKb and receive updates when changes were made at the global level. The benefits of the planned integration between these two systems included the ability to create local records linked to their global counterparts via a canonical identifier and to manage changes to these entities through a management dashboard. As changes were made within OLE, they could be communicated back to GOKb and shared across all users of the system.

In mid-2016, the OLE partners decided to cease development of the existing OLE LSP and proposed e-resource features, including integration with GOKb. Also in 2016, OLE became a participant in FOLIO, a new community collaboration to develop an open source LSP. Other FOLIO partners include EBSCO and Index Data. While GOKb is not explicitly part of the FOLIO roadmap at this time, the project partners have put forth a stated goal of integration with multiple knowledge bases, and GOKb remains a candidate for inclusion in the project.

GOKb also maintained a relationship with Jisc throughout most of its early development. At the time of GOKb's initial request for funding, Jisc had already begun development of the KB+ project, which aimed to create a knowledge base describing journal collections negotiated by university libraries within the United Kingdom. Leadership from both projects recognized the similarity of the data being collected and concluded that each could enhance the progress and quality of the overall effort through collaboration [5]. GOKb and KB+ functional experts and developers worked together to create a shared data model for both projects. KB+ originally intended to shift the management of its knowledge base data from a local environment to GOKb. However, changes to the mission and distribution model of KB+ prevented the change from being implemented.

The GOKb project remains closely aligned with OLE in its governance. While GOKb operated semi-independently throughout the grant-funded phases of the project, once the funding expired, its governance was folded more closely into the OLE project to ensure long-term sustainability. The OLE project partners provide ongoing financial support for GOKb through partner dues. Financial contributions primarily support the continuation of the GOKb editor position, which is part of the OLE core team of staff.

CORE FEATURES OF GOKB

GOKb expands on the traditional knowledge base feature set in a number of ways. While existing knowledge bases have offered a snapshot of electronic resources that exist at the current moment in time, GOKb's data model will include an expanded set of attributes to facilitate tracking of changes. GOKb can store information about changes to works, such as a bibliographic title change or a transfer between publishers. Additionally, the system uses a series of status to track information about resources that have ceased or are not yet available, thus allowing users to see how the contents of a package have or will change over the years it is offered for sale.[6]

Another key component of GOKb is its open-data model. GOKb's data are freely available under a Creative Commons 0 license, which allows use by anyone for any purpose without attribution. This openness means that GOKb's data can be consumed by its official partners, as well as any interested party, including commercial entities. The GOKb project has cited several benefits to the open-data approach, including the potential to partner with a wide variety of institutions and corporations, as well as the benefits of separating data from software.[6] By making well-structured, accurate metadata freely available across the industry, GOKb hopes to see adoption not just by library partners but also by academic publishers and library vendors, who can use GOKb's service to improve their own products.

The use of a community contribution model for data sourcing and maintenance is another differentiator for GOKb. Discussions with partners, as well a number of potential collaborators internationally, have highlighted the similar problems that institutions face when it comes to managing knowledge base data.[5] Users from across these institutions spend time on tasks such as reconciling publisher- and vendor-provided title lists against knowledge base data and investigating title changes. These activities commonly result in customers informing their commercial knowledge base vendors of a series of changes, which are then incorporated into that vendor's product.[2] By harnessing these efforts and capturing the outcome in a freely available, centralized environment, the GOKb project aims to increase the impact of this work by making it available across the entire community of libraries and vendors.

It is also important to note that GOKb differs from the traditional knowledge base in two major ways. First, GOKb is not a discovery knowledge base; rather, it is intended to support that management of electronic resource purchasing and licensing operations. GOKb does not support discovery tools such as a link resolver, MARC record service, or unified search index. This means that GOKb is not intended as a replacement for those products that rely on vended knowledge bases. Second, GOKb is not an environment for users to store information about their local entitlements. It exists purely as a data repository. It will be the role of partner systems to provide an interface that can consume GOKb's data and allow users to create local variations on the data.

DATA MODEL AND DATA ELEMENTS

GOKb uses a bill of materials data model to represent the elements that make up the e-resources landscape. This model represents the raw materials needed to create an end product. In the bill of materials model, raw materials are called "components" and the end product is a "combination" of those components.[7] In GOKb, for example, one of the core components is the title. Titles can be combined to form packages. A combination like a package can then be linked to another component, such as an organization, to create a new combination. The advantage of this model is that its flexibility makes it extensible. Components and combinations can always be linked in new ways to meet the changing landscape. If, for instance, GOKb was expanded to include article-level information, articles could be added as a new type of component, which could then be linked together to form a journal combination.[6]

The core components that make up the GOKb data model are titles, packages, platforms, and organizations. The title component describes a journal or other resource at the work level. Title history information, such as publication dates, current and past publishers, and relationships to other titles, are also stored on the title component (see Fig. 1). Packages represent groups of titles that are commonly sold together for a set price, while platforms represent the websites where those titles and packages are hosted. A unique feature of GOKb is a combination of components called the title instance package platform, or TIPP. The TIPP goes beyond simple bibliographic description to represent a resource as it is purchased and managed by a library. By creating an entity to represent this combination, GOKb provides a place to store metadata describing salable units. The TIPP record also allows GOKb to assign an identifier to this important concept as well as to link it to other components and make machine-readable statements about it.

Organization records can be linked to any component type to provide additional detail. Organizations can play different roles depending on their context. For example, the organization Springer can be related to a title in the role of publisher, while it may also be related to a platform in the role of platform provider.[2]

METHODS OF ACCESS

Web Application

The GOKb web application provides a public interface for browsing and searching of GOKb data, as well as an editing tool for project partners. Users can navigate the various components found in the knowledge base and explore combinations using links between records. The data in GOKb may provide general value as a reference tool, supplying such information as bibliographic metadata, details of changes over time, lists of available packages and their contents, and basic access information.

For project partners, the web application provides additional functionality, including the ability to edit the data found in most fields. This allows for easy correction of isolated errors or basic updates. The web application also allows users to perform a series of more complex actions, including title changes and transfers. Finally,

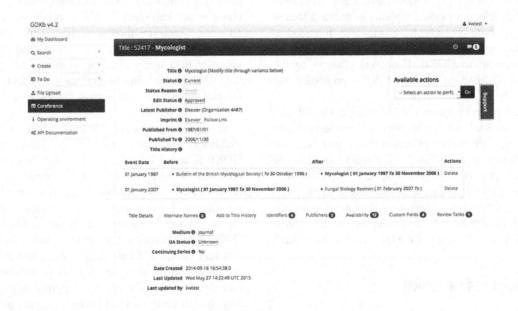

Fig. 1   A title record in GOKb.

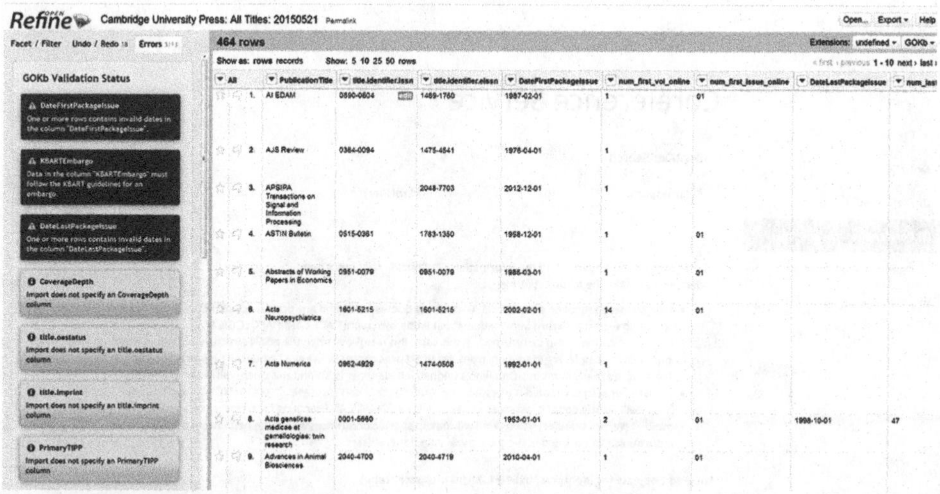

Fig. 2 The OpenRefine custom extension for GOKb.

the application contains a lightweight problem tracking system that allows users to create review tasks and assign them to themselves or other users. Review tasks are also generated automatically when new data ingested into GOKb conflicts with existing data in the knowledge base.

OpenRefine

GOKb uses an open-source data manipulation tool called OpenRefine to allow population of the knowledge base with large, externally sourced data sets. Through OpenRefine and a custom GOKb extension, users can validate data and upload it to the knowledge base. The GOKb extension applies a set of rules designed to help users modify data so that it complies with GOKb's data specification. Common transformations include renaming columns, adding missing information, reformatting dates and abbreviations, and resolving data conflicts like duplicate ISSNs (see Fig. 2). The GOKb extension for OpenRefine also provides a collaborative workspace and version control features, allowing users to share project files.

API

GOKb offers an API that allows external services to extract data from GOKb and credentialed users to contribute changes back to the knowledge base. The API uses the OAI-PMH protocol.[5]

Co-Reference Service

Many of the components in GOKb can support multiple identifiers. GOKb can collect and store identifiers across namespaces that describe roughly equivalent concepts. On the title record for example, GOKb may store title identifiers that include the ISSN and e-ISSN, DOI, and publisher's proprietary identifier. These identifiers are linked together through the title component, which is assigned a GOKb identifier. The co-reference service provides a crosswalk between identifiers by allowing users to search for any identifier and return a list of all identifiers associated with the same component. The co-reference service is not a registry and makes no assertions about the correctness of any of the identifiers stored within GOKb. The co-reference service can be accessed through the GOKb web application (see Fig. 3) or through the API using a JSON or XML query.[5]

CONCLUSION

The development of GOKb has established the principles and structure needed to create and provide a comprehensive, open repository of key metadata about scholarly publications. These core components include a data model to support the description of electronic resources, both in the present moment and as they change over time, multiple modes of access to support human and consumption; and a community of invested partners who can contribute expertise and resources to the collection and maintenance of knowledge base data. The work on GOKb to date serves as a strong proof of concept for the technical feasibility of and community interest in an open knowledge base. Future efforts for GOKb will include evaluating the potential for the project to increase its scale and continue building community interest.

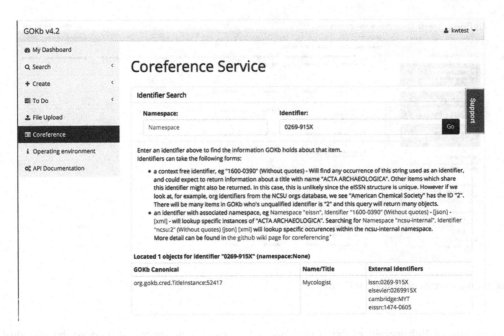

Fig. 3   The GOKb co-reference service.

REFERENCES

1. Duke, J. Kuali OLE, Jisc Announce GOKb Project. Adv. Libr. Technol. **2012**, *41* (7), 1–11.
2. Wilson, K. In *Bringing the Global Open Knowledgebase to Life: Data, Integrations, and Development.* Proceedings of the 34th Charleston Library Conference, http://dx.doi.org/10.5703/1288284315649 (accessed December 13, 2016).
3. http://news.lib.ncsu.edu/blog/2015/01/22/global-open-know ledgebase-receives-additional-mellon-funding-to-pioneer-community-sourced-management-of-digital-content-for-edu cation-and-research/ (accessed March 13, 2015).
4. About GOKb. http://gokb.org/about (accessed March 13, 2015).
5. Antelman, K.; Wilson, K. The Global Open Knowledgebase (GOKb): Open linked data supporting electronic resources management and scholarly communication. Insights **2015**, *28* (1), 42–50. doi:http://dx.doi.org/10.1629/uksg.217.
6. Wilson, K. Building the Global Open Knowledgebase (GOKb). Ser. Rev. **2013**, *39* (4), 261–265.
7. http://en.wikipedia.org/wiki/Bill_of_materials (accessed March 13, 2015).

Government Documents: Collection and Management

Aimée C. Quinn
Government Publications Services, Brooks Library, Central Washington University, Ellensburg, Washington, U.S.A.

Lori Smith
Linus A. Sims Memorial Library, Southeastern Louisiana University, Hammond, Louisiana, U.S.A.

James Church
University Libraries, University of California, Berkeley, Berkeley, California, U.S.A.

Abstract

Collecting and managing government information in the twenty-first century is a challenge to most libraries and librarians. Historically, government documents were difficult to collect and manage in a print environment; yet while the digital transformation of information makes some government publications more available, at the same time, the Internet allows for valuable content to be more readily removed. This entry examines government information in all its forms and formats to offer a comprehensive assessment of issues involved in the development and management of government information (publications, documents, etc.) collections in print, electronic, and digital formats. The goal of this entry is to explore how nineteenth-century bibliographic description shaped the twenty-first-century government information society and this particular field of librarianship is paving the way for future developers of collections. The first three sections of this essay focus on U.S. documents at the federal, state, and local levels; The fourth section concerns international publications. Each section will detail the relevant history and strategies for developing and managing a viable, fluid government publications collection.

INTRODUCTION

What is a government document? It is informational matter created by a government. The U.S. government defines it as any informational matter printed at government expense or as required by law, 44 USC 1901 (2012). Government documents librarianship is a field that is guided by this U.S. law. Government documents collections include materials found in libraries including digital objects, monographs, serials, periodicals, maps, technical reports, ephemera, kits, etc. The main difference is they emanate from government bodies. All government bodies produce documents. Libraries of all kinds (academic, public, school, and special) collect government documents. When most people think of government documents, images of unending pages of census figures and appropriation hearings come to mind, but few consider that one of the most popular government documents is the re-release of the Warren Commission Report. Think you are smarter than an 8th grade civics student? Then, you should check out the Civics Quiz on the Government Book Talk blog at http://govbooktalk.gpo.gov/?s=civics+quiz.

In this entry, the phrase "government documents" is used interchangeably with "government publications" and "government information." The form or format of a government document does not negate the laws that require printing or dissemination. This entry examines collecting

and managing government documents at the federal, state, local, and international levels of government. A bibliography along with relevant websites is included at the end. Please note, as the field changes, so too does this bibliography.

FEDERAL PUBLICATIONS

Historical Foundations

From the time Congress first started publishing the *Journal* as required by the *Constitution of the United States*, American libraries were interested in collecting government documents. Publications issued by the government cover all manner of subjects and disciplines ranging from weather reports and train schedules to budget analysis, judicial decisions, and administrative laws. Although the interest still exists, government documents are still as mysterious today as they were in 1860 when the Government Printing Office (GPO) was created to counter the growing corruption in printing contracts, the advent of newspaper patronage, and concerns about the cost of official publication. The foundation for what is today known as Federal Depository Library Program (FDLP) originated in the first 12 Congresses and later became centralized in the Printing Act of 1895 (28 Stat. 601) along with the

Encyclopedia of Library and Information Sciences, Fourth Edition DOI: 10.1081/E-ELIS4-120053405

Office of the Superintendent of Documents.[1] First, this act developed a federal depository library program as a means to consolidate printing, publishing, distribution, and dissemination of official government publications. Second, the act led to the development of a central collection of government documents by Adelaide Hasse, the inventor of the Superintendent of Documents (SuDocs) classification scheme. Ms Hasse began developing this classification scheme when she worked at the Los Angeles Public Library and later took her skills to Washington to begin developing a documents library at the GPO between 1895 and 1903.[2] Based on the principle of provenance, or issuing agency, rather than a subject-based scheme, it is an alphanumeric organization based on the status of the government agency. Her creation of a comprehensive list of publications from the Department of Agriculture was the first of many tools created to build, develop, and maintain library collections of government documents including the development of the *Monthly Catalog of United States Government Publications*, the basic finding tool for federal publication until the advent of the Internet. This act firmly established government printing, publishing, dissemination, and distribution of materials as *functions of both* the Legislative and Executive branches of government. Prior to the act, all materials were published at the express request of Congress and many libraries tried to develop their government collections based upon lists of publications rather than an overall strategy catering to local need. As the country grew, so did the government, and soon the Executive branch took over as the main producer of government information. One of the provisions of the Printing Act of 1895 was to create a depository library system to ensure all citizens had access to their government's activities via publication. *The fundamental purpose of the Federal Depository Library Program is to ensure that all Americans have permanent public access to their government's information regardless of form or format.*

The next major change to the FDLP was the Depository Library Act of 1962 (76 Stat. 352), which enhanced access to depository libraries by expanding the number of depository libraries per state and creating two types of depositories: regionals, which are required to keep permanently all government publications disseminated through the FDLP, and selectives, which may pick and choose which kinds of publications to house plus may dispose after 5 years. For a short history of the program, please see http://www.access.gpo.gov/su_docs/fdlp/history/macgilvray.html.

Today, the FDLP is a partnership between the GPO and 1,175 libraries representing most Congressional districts across the nation (see Table 1). GPO prints, digitizes, and disseminates government information products utilizing all information technologies available. Additionally, this agency is recognized as the authority for the bibliographic control, cataloging, and classification for all federal government publication. The GPO serves as a model for state

Table 1

Library Type	Number	Percent
Academic General	627	54%
Public Library	180	16%
Academic, Law Library	150	13%
Academic, Community College	56	5%
State Library	39	3%
Federal Agency Library	37	3%
Highest State Court Library	37	3%
Federal Court Library	11	1%
Special Library	14	1%
Service Academy	4	0%
TOTAL	1155	100%

Note: Special thanks to the U.S. Government Printing Office. Data accurate as of March 30, 2016.

and international government depository programs. Building upon both a history and tradition of public service, these depository programs are still germane in an electronic environment. While the publications themselves may not be tangible, knowledge of the interconnectedness of governments, how agencies work or in some cases do not work together and why government publications are developed differently than other information resources are all examples of why this field in librarianship is thriving. For additional information about the FDLP, please see http://www.fdlp.gov/.

Throughout its history, the U.S. government embraced technology. GPO frequently was in the forefront in implementing new technologies from handset to machine set typesetting to digitization and everything in between. In January 2014, Public Printer Davita Vance-Cook led the move to change the name of the 154-year printing establishment, Government Printing Office to the Government Publishing Office, in an effort to better describe the digital transformation beginning with Public Law 104–30. She testified: "It's time for our name to catch up with who we are and what we do. It's time for a new name for the digital age."

Transforming Government Information

In the introduction to the textbook *Fundamentals of Government Information*, the authors discuss the transition of the FDLP and the need for permanent public access to government information eloquently stating:

> The formats of government information have transitioned quickly in recent years. The print era evolved to the web era; then HTML and PDF documents became blogs and wikis, which became videos, which became ever-evolving websites … As revolutionary as this electronic migration has been for government information, many aspects of depository libraries and services are less changed.[3]

The information revolution taking place is changing the very nature of American society. Fondly called the

"Information Age," the twenty-first century is a time where every American is overwhelmed with too much content but little organization of information. The growth and permeation of the social media everywhere means that more information is available without the filters provided by proofreaders, editors, reviewers, etc., which was prevalent in the era of print publication. The digital divide of the previous decade is not the same concern it once was; instead, libraries are faced with a three-pronged dilemma of providing access to born digital information, preserving tangible collections, and creating safe digital spaces for users.

Aside from depository library programs, collecting government information is difficult regardless of where it is housed in a library, on a server, or in the cloud. Many librarians still comb the "media" for stories about government-funded studies, reports, proposed legislation, guidelines, and/or regulations to find what is most germane for their collection, regardless of whether they are available in electronic or tangible formats. The advent of digital information not only made finding information easier but also made removal of information just as simple. In fact, most library research conducted today is focused on the policies of electronic creation, dissemination, and preservation of government information. Current writing focuses on the sheer volume and integrity of electronic information. And yet, digital information is not immune to the guidelines limiting how it should be distributed via social media.[4] It is up to those librarians to work collaboratively in building permanent collections.

Congress enacted additional legislation such as the Government Printing Office Electronic Information Access Enhancement Act of 1993 (107 Stat 112) and the E-Government Act (116 Stat 2899) to further provide access to government information in electronic form, but neither piece of legislation provided GPO the same authority over electronic information produced by the U.S. government as print distribution of depository materials. There remain many questions of access and equity. This division is examined in detail.[5] The question remains with collecting and managing electronic information. "Who is responsible for permanent public access to electronic and digital content?" This question permeates depository librarianship in the early twenty-first century.

Depository Libraries and Management

As mentioned earlier, government information permeates society unlike other publications. Whether it is interest in the Iraq War or reading the "Starr Report" or filing a tax form, more and more Americans use government information more readily than ever. During the age of print, government publications followed a fairly narrow hierarchy for publication. It was mainly due to this form that the bibliographic control and organization of government documents is based on issuing agency rather than on subject. Thus, the SuDocs classification scheme became the primary means to organize print collections. This classification scheme further allowed for the FDLP to develop its mission and goals: to be the primary means of government information dissemination and preservation. Several print indexes and abstracts were developed in order to provide access to government publication. Building upon Adelaide Haase's list of USDA publications, bibliographic tools such as *The Monthly Catalog of U.S. Government Publications*, *GRA&I* (*Government Reports Announcements & Index*), *ERA* (*Energy Resources Abstracts*), and *RIE* (*Resources in Education*), plus the many products from the Congressional Research Service were developed in order to provide bibliographic access to government publications. While online equivalents of these print reference resources exist, they do not provide the same level of bibliographic control simply because the online equivalent works quite differently from the print. However, the GPO continues to work with their partners in the FDLP to use newer technologies to enhance access to government information and provide permanency of this information. This program is still one enduring example of how government works well in keeping the citizenry informed.

The success of the FDLP led to the creation of other depository programs including state, local, international, and foreign programs based upon a government providing copies of its public documents to libraries in exchange for those libraries housing the material, providing access to these materials, and in many cases, providing experts to assist the citizens in locating the information. This principle is the basic strategy librarians use when developing government publication collections. Not so long ago, this strategy of having agencies send materials directly through the GPO was a reasonable method for developing a depository collection. The U.S. Census Bureau and Patents & Trademark Office (PTO) both created successful depository programs after the initial success of the FDLP. Each agency looked at libraries as places where citizens could obtain specialized agency information.[6] In fact, the PTO Depository Program was more successful in some ways since the PTO instituted a plan to ensure that patent librarians were trained by the experts employed in the Office. Detailed descriptions of the various depository programs are widely discussed in the literature, but no better sources exist than the works of Laurence F. Schmeckebier, including his agency histories and his overview of government publications. While his books are nearing their century mark, their importance is still as great as when first published, especially given the challenges of managing government publications in an electronic environment.

The complexity of the modern world, coupled with ever-changing and increasing information policies and technologies, makes the dissemination of government information more challenging. Even before the beginning of printing, governments made policies to control the flow of information.

Information Policy

Jaeger defines information policy as "the combination of laws, regulations, rules, and guidelines that steer the creation, management, and use of information." The Internet transformed the entire way society views and uses information thus public policy on information is more on the mind of legislators and administrations. It is common knowledge that whoever controls the flow of information, controls the government, hence the fight within governments regarding the release of information.[7] Each session of Congress deals with more issues related to information, from freedom of information to protections of intellectual property; security and civil rights; and personal privacy versus the government's need for personally identifiable information.

One overwhelming challenge early in the depository process was when government agencies did not furnish copies of their publications to the GPO, leading to what is known as "fugitive documents" or those publications that belong in the program by law, but are not included, for various reasons internal to particular agencies. This same problem is echoed today by those agencies that continue to produce digital documents but provide no mechanism for digital preservation, thus denying permanent public access. Public access to government information is considered by many to be a right of citizenship, although there is no law or official policy enforcing that right. An example of this was seen in President Obama's revocation of EO 13233 by his own executive order.[8] This Executive Order offered the president to extend executive privilege to other members of the Executive Branch including appointed officials within the Cabinet or senior staff members. Another proviso of EO 13233 allowed a president to exert this privilege at any time over any document of any president. By rescinding this Executive Order, President Obama restored Congress' original intent of the law limiting the time allowed for the privilege and who can use this privilege. This example ensures the people the right to know what the president is doing. The principles of our society are built on a democratic framework that requires citizens to be informed of their government's actions. The *Constitution of the United States* outlines how that framework will work, including a provision that requires a journal be kept of proceedings and actions.

The importance of information policy and e-government is discussed in other chapters in this encyclopedia. As more scholars analyze these policies as part of their study, government publications become more preeminent in their work and analysis. The need for collecting and managing this material is still a vital role for librarians and administrators. While the federal government provides an overarching view of information policy, states and local governments each have their own opportunities and challenges in developing their information policies.[9]

STATE PUBLICATIONS

The formation of territories and state governments was authorized by acts that are included with other laws in the *United State Statutes at Large* and may also be found online at some individual state Web portals.[10] State government impacts daily life through taxes, education, public safety, economic growth, laws, and regulations. State government agencies communicate with the public in a number of ways. For some agencies, educating the public is an important part of their mission. Service-oriented agencies such as departments of health and human services have historically produced a large number of public documents. A public document, loosely defined, is any informational matter, regardless of format, which is produced for public distribution by state agencies or state institutions of higher learning. Vital statistics such as number of births, and number of and causes of deaths, are examples of public information found in state documents. Other examples include schedules of state elections, statistics about public schools, and instructions for acquiring a driver's license.

While the FDLP provides leadership, best practices, and regulations for federal publications, there is no central governing unit to manage access to state publications. Individual states are left to their own devices to develop, implement, and manage the lifecycle of state-produced public information. Using the FDLP as a model, many states have established state depository library programs.

In most cases, it is the state library or an equivalent agency that administers the state depository library program. Typically, depository programs are charged by their respective legislatures with collecting, indexing, distributing, and preserving state public documents.

Depository programs collect state documents by obtaining physical copies from state agencies or by acquiring and archiving electronic copies. Electronic copies are most commonly harvested from the web, received by e-mail, or uploaded by state agencies directly to a database or repository. Even though most depository laws require agency compliance, many agencies ignore them or selectively comply, resulting in an incomplete collection. Because state library resources are limited, efforts are typically made to collect at least core materials, items that are deemed the most important to preserve and make accessible. Items collected are commonly classified using a classification scheme developed specifically for that state's publications—though some programs do use Library of Congress (LC) or Dewey Decimal numbers—and recorded in a catalog, index, and/or list. Cataloging records are usually made available in the state library's online catalog and may or may not be added to a national bibliographic database such as *WorldCat*. Shipping lists and monthly checklists, organized lists of items received since the last listing, are often used to notify participants about the arrival of new items into the depository program.

Physical publications are typically distributed to a network of depository libraries throughout the state and often to the LC as well. Like state agencies, depository libraries are required to comply with the laws, rules, and regulations governing the depository program. They provide space for the collection, staffing to assist the public with finding state publications, and most often have to retain depository publications for a certain number of years and obtain permission before disposing of them. In some programs, depository libraries are required to make digital publications available by including bibliographic records with live links in their online catalogs. Archived copies of electronic publications are generally made available online via links in the state library's catalog, or in a dedicated, searchable state documents database or repository (i.e., *Iowa Publications Online* at http://publications.iowa.gov/). Collectively, the libraries in the network attempt to preserve access to state publications in perpetuity.

For a more detailed overview of key state publications and state depository library programs, consult Lori Smith and others' *Tapping State Government Information Sources* published in 2003.[11] In part one, Smith discusses general sources covering all 50 states, including publications that are both state government produced and commercially produced. Part two contains a chapter for each individual state with information regarding its depository system, as well as useful addresses and telephone numbers, indexes to state publications, essential titles, pertinent commercial publications, and its Web portal. For an overview of efforts to archive and preserve federal, state, and local digital documents, see *Managing Electronic Government Information in Libraries: Issues and Practices*.[12]

Beyond print publications and their electronic siblings, state governments provide a wealth of additional information and services online. Technology and electronic resources have led to the rise of e-government. According to a 2007 report from the National Association of State Chief Information Officers (NASCIO), the number of citizens using the Internet to access state agency information and transact business was increasing, and the sophistication of state government Web portals was improving.[13] In 2010, a Pew Research Internet Project publication reported that 82% of Internet users had accessed government information or utilized a government service online.[14] A 2011 report from the Pew Research Internet Project noted that the Knight Commission on the Information Needs of Communities in a Democracy had found that two key indicators of a successful "community information system" were "A vibrant public library, or other public center for information that provides digital resources and professional assistance," and "A majority

of government information and services online, accessible through a central and easy to use portal."[15]

Entities other than states have undertaken efforts at the national level to increase awareness of and access to state- and local-level documents. In 2007, the State and Local Documents Task Force (SLDTF) within the Government Documents Round Table (GODORT) of the American Library Association (ALA) created a "50 State Agency Database Registry" wiki.[16] Volunteers adopt one or more states and maintain lists of databases that agencies in that particular state have built. The SLDTF wiki also offers, among other things, a list of links to state depository system Web pages and a list of librarians within each state who are willing to facilitate the exchange of state publications between libraries in different states.[17]

The LC maintains Web pages featuring links to state and local government information from all 50 states.[18] The Law Library of Congress also has a Web page with links to legal information for states and territories.[19]

The LC collects state and local publications with a goal of building a research-level collection, which does not mean everything issued.[20] Administrative reports, publications issued by state legislative and judicial branches, and planning and policy statements are examples of the types of items collected. With the exception of a few counties, the LC does not collect publications of U.S. counties. It does manage a comprehensive collection of cartographic materials for all counties, cities, and towns. Publications from a select number of major population centers are also actively collected.

From 1910 to 1994, the LC published the *Monthly Checklist of State Publications*.[21] This publication was recognized as the national bibliography for U.S. state publications, but the demand for it decreased as online alternatives to it increased. Not everything in the *Checklist* was retained by the LC and not everything issued by a state was sent to the LC, resulting in an incomplete record of official state publications. Since the *Checklist* ceased, there has been no comprehensive bibliography to publications of the 50 states, but today a large part of what would have been included in the *Checklist* is available in Online Computer Library Center (OCLC) and Research Libraries Information Network (RLIN).

Many state checklists are now available online. In 1977, the SLDTF of ALA first approved guidelines for compiling and distributing state publications checklists.[22] At that time, checklists were seen as necessary for bibliographic control. They are now useful as a current awareness tool. For more information about a particular state, check *StateList: the Electronic Source for State Publications Lists*, a project of the University of Illinois at Urbana-Champaign.[23]

The *StateList* project uses the Web to make citizens aware of the publishing activities of state governments. In late 2014, a total of 37 states had provided links to state publication checklists and shipping lists currently available on the Internet.

The Center for Research Libraries (CRL) has acquired a collection of state documents that consists of the official publications of the legislative bodies, departments, and agencies of all 50 of the United States from the earliest period of state government through 1950. It also has holdings of legislative journals through 1990. Most of these materials are not in the CRL's catalog, but they are organized by state, by agency on the shelf. Additionally, the CRL has the pre-1951 *Records of the States of the United States of America: A Microfilm Compilation.*[24]

This is currently a static collection with no concerted effort to develop it further.

When looking for historical information on state documents prior to 1908, refer to the four volume set covering 1899 to 1908 entitled *State Publications: A Provisional List of the Official Publications of the Several States of the United States from Their Organization.*[25] For more state information prior to 1904, consult the multiple part set of the *Index of Economic Material in the Documents of the States of the United States* created between 1907 and 1922.[26] The next major reference tool would be the *Manual on the Use of State Publications.*[27] Published in 1940, it contained a detailed record of available bibliographic sources by state. In 1942, this was followed by *Government Document Bibliography in the United States and Elsewhere*, which included 20 pages of state bibliographic sources.[28] This source remained the authoritative source on state document bibliography until 1975 when *Government Publications: A Guide to Bibliographic Tools* was published.[29] Sixteen years later, in 1981, Margaret Lane's classic *State Publications and Depository Libraries: A Reference Handbook* was published.[30] In part one, Lane provides the characteristics of depository library legislation. In part two, there is a state publications literature review followed by lists of bibliographic items that represents the largest portion of the book. In part three, 2–10 pages of information are provided for individual states.

The trend for the future is clearly toward more emphasis on digital information. Some depository programs are already predominantly electronic and nearly all have a strong digital component. Debate will continue about the long-term efficacy of electronic archives, and more focus will be placed on issues such as state government transparency, cybersecurity, open access, and big data. As with the FDLP, attention will inevitably turn toward digitizing the older publications housed in depository libraries and making those materials freely available online as well.

LOCAL DOCUMENTS

Local documents "are those materials issued by local governmental agencies and their subunits including municipalities, counties, townships, villages, special districts, school boards, park districts, and the like. Typical types of local documents include municipal codes, building codes, zoning ordinances, annual reports of agencies, financial reports, minutes and proceedings of boards and committees, reports of committees and commissions, and any similar materials produced by governmental units."[31] One of the unique challenges for collecting local government documents is the plethora of local government entities, which leads to the lack of a central dissemination point. To provide some perspective on this challenge, according to the 2012 Census of Governments there are 90,107 governments in the United States, of which 90,056 were local governments. The breakdowns of these governments are

County: 3,031
Municipal: 19,519
Town or township: 16,360 special districts (school): 38,266
The state of Illinois alone has 6963 local governments.[32]

While difficult to collect, local government publications provide unique information about the community—everything from urban life, to local health, to tourism. Local agencies may or may not keep publications for historical purposes, so preservation is a major concern for information originally available on government websites and in print. Like state and federal publications, another key challenge is learning about the existence of the document. Few local government agencies set up depository library programs, although some individual agencies will add a library to a mailing list. As more local documents move to the Internet, it becomes harder to track them, much less provide any kind of bibliographic control. According to Alexander Stille: "One of the great ironies of the information age is that, while the late twentieth century will undoubtedly record more data than have been recorded at any other time in history, it will also almost certainly lose more information than has been lost in any previous era."[33] The nature of the information published online also differs from that which was traditionally published in print.

It is estimated that more than 75 percent of local governments now maintain web sites... Local government web sites tend to place an emphasis on showcasing the community's attractions to draw business and tourism to an area rather than featuring annual reports, in-depth statistical data, and full-text land use and planning documents. Annual budgets and summaries are sometimes posted, but it is rare to find more than the current year.[34]

As mentioned previously, effective depository systems are virtually nonexistent at the local level of government. Nearby libraries may receive a small number of locally produced government publications, but may need to actively pursue their acquisition. Public libraries often collect local documents and typically view providing access to them as a means of promoting and assisting citizens' involvement in government. The strength of local collections varies. There is a common practice to have open access to local documents that are organized by series such as "minutes" and "reports" and that have not been cataloged or added to a searchable database. To access information, it must first be findable, and publications that have not been cataloged or indexed are only minimally findable. A local government collection often includes names and contact information for agencies, departments, and elected officials. Other items collected may include the local municipal code, the annual budget for the city and/or county, and zoning ordinances. State and academic libraries, typically, are selective in regard to acquiring local-level publications.

For a more detailed overview of this topic, see *Local and Regional Government Information: How to Find It, How to Use It*.[35]

INTERNATIONAL PUBLICATIONS AND ORGANIZATIONS

Patrons also seek out international government information, and the first place they typically look will be a search engine. This is a rational decision but may lead to frustrations. Most recent international government information is online (free or priced—and sometimes both at once) and legacy collections are rapidly being digitized. In this environment, one could argue the role of the library is marginal, but things are not that simple. The volume of international government information is immense, and much of it is embedded in the "deep Web" of databases that must be queried. Some international government information is distributed exclusively on priced electronic libraries or sold in print and/or online formats by commercial publishers. Other international organizations (IOs) distribute Machine Readable Cataloging (MARC) records for their publications, which enhances discovery for patrons unaware of the nature of their work. In an environment of "too much information," libraries still have a valuable role to play in providing access, curation, and preservation of this material.

IGOs and NGOs

If the concept of international governmental organizations (IGOs) is unfamiliar to some, the *Yearbook of International Organizations* is a good source to start. Edited by the Union of International Associations and published by Brill, the *Yearbook* is not just a directory of names and addresses. The online version contains searchable entries of over 66,000 IOs including both intergovernmental organizations (IGOs) and international nongovernmental organizations (INGOs) in over 300 countries and territories. Approximately 1200 new organizations are added

each year.[36] The print *Yearbook* set of six volumes includes organizational descriptions with information broken down by subject, country, and region. A separate volume identifies organization publications and resources, and there are additional volumes for statistics and visualizations, memberships, and secretariats. Additional information is available at http://www.uia.org/yearbook.

IGOs are generally defined as 1) treaty-based, 2) made of three or more member states, and 3) having a secretariat for ongoing tasks. Statistics from the current *Yearbook of International Organizations Online* show that as of 2013/2014 there were 7710 IGOs.[37] Definitions of nongovernmental organizations (NGOs) vary, but generally NGOs are 1) individual/nongovernmental actors and 2) voluntary associations. NGOs are often specialized in their goals, and work to make improvements in the fields of the Environment, Human Rights, Education, Women's Issues, Humanitarian Aid, or Economic Development. Think-tanks and independent research institutes are sometimes also included.

Examples of well-known NGOs include Médecins Sans Frontières, The International Red Cross, Partners in Health, Transparency International, and Oxfam. More widely recognized NGOs are often based in developed countries, but this is changing as NGOs in China and the Global South become better known: examples include the Grameen Bank, BRAC, and Friends of Nature (自然之友). Statistics from the current *Yearbook of International Organizations Online* show that as of 2013/2014 there were 58,588 NGOs.[37]

Both IGOs and NGOs offer a wealth of statistical, historical, and administrative information that can help librarians serve their patrons' information needs. Libraries can develop and provide access to international information collections through a variety of avenues. Six IO collection development strategies and access models are discussed in this article. These include the following:

1. IGO depositories
2. IGO/NGO information on the Web
3. Digital MARC records
4. IGO publications offices
5. IGO priced databases
6. Third-party vendors that distribute IGO and NGO information IGO depository programs

IGO depositories

Historically, IGOs distributed documents and publications to a global network of depositories, chiefly based at national libraries and universities. With the widespread availability of free digital content, one could argue that IGO depository libraries have become irrelevant except as warehouses of historical print collections, destined for eventual digitization. We are indeed in the midst of a significant transformation. In 2010, the Asian Development Bank (ADB) announced it would cease print distribution of depository materials except a handful of flagship publications. Tangible depository publications from the Organization for Cooperation and Security in Europe (OSCE) are now issued exclusively on an annual DVD. Document distribution from the European Union (EU) depository program has declined significantly, with some EU agencies no longer publishing anything in print. In 2012, the United Nations (UN) Depository Library System office in New York ceased distribution of print publications, although some material is still dispatched via its global network of offices. The UN Dag Hammarskjöld Library is developing a digital depository for UN documents, but at present no UN Sales Publications will be available for download on this platform. UN Depository Libraries will need to subscribe to a fee-based digital library constructed in partnership by the Organization for Economic Cooperation and Development to search for and download publications within a consolidated database environment.

Details about the current UN Depository program is available at http://www.un.org/depts/dhl/deplib/index.html

And information about EU depositories is at http://www.euintheus.org/resources-learning/depository-libraries-in-the-us/.

However, IGO depository libraries or the information professionals working in them are not relics of a bygone era. Effective government information retrieval is an advanced skill and librarians at these depositories possess a wealth of knowledge and historical collections one can tap into for assistance. Any librarian needing assistance with international information can contact these specialists, or use the Web guides created by them as reference sources.

Freely available IGO and NGO information on the Web

All IGOs and NGOs now provide substantial amounts of information on their Web sites, and some have the taken the dramatic step of publishing virtually all of their unclassified documents online, free of charge. While there are certainly exceptions to this (see later text), the trend is unmistakable and linked to the open government, open access, and open data movements championed by libraries and civil society organizations.

IGOs, like the UN and the EU, and International Financial Organizations like the World Trade Organization (WTO) have published "documentation" (working documents and official records created by an organization in the course of conducting its business) online for years: examples include the United Nations Official Documents System (http://documents.un.org/), the World Bank's Projects and Operations (http://www.worldbank.org/projects), and the WTO's Documents Online (https://docs.wto.org/).

Other organizations such as the World Health Organization, which historically did not release any public documentation, now do so also (http://apps.who.int/gb/bd/). More IGOs are following suit. This movement allows access to IGO documentation scarcely imaginable only a few years ago as citizens now have digital access not just to publications produced and sold by IGOs, but also to information about their deliberative processes, budgets, decisions, and official records.

In addition, many IGOs now post previously priced "publications" (monographs and serials intended for use by the general public) freely online also. The World Bank, in a dramatic move in 2012, launched its "Open Access Policy," which requires that "Bank research outputs and knowledge products be deposited into the World Bank institutional repository (the OKR), allowing any user in the world to read, download, save, copy, print, reuse and link to the full text of the work, free of charge."[38] This is among the most liberal publications policies of any IGO, but others are not so transparent: conditions of reuse, copyright, and access vary tremendously. The EU posts publications online at no charge, but has a copyright statement that only permits reuse of content published by the European Commission and the Publications Office.[39] The UNESCO Open Access Policy is three pages long and quite complex.[40] Other IGOs publish all, or virtually all, of their publications free online, but when in doubt check the policy and investigate the availability of digital content—you may be surprised.

Other IGOs publish only a limited amount of free content: examples include the Council of Europe, the UN Tourism Organization, the International Monetary Fund (IMF), and the OECD. Some IGOs sell their titles to commercial publishers who may publish the item in print or distribute them via e-book aggregators. The OECD licenses most publications via its subscription database, the OECD iLibrary, but there are free titles also. Publications from the Council of Europe (again, with exceptions) are priced, both in print and as PDFs. The IMF is making its priced online statistics databases free in 2015, but will still license an "eLibrary complete," which will provide access to more than 14,000 IMF publications.

Furthermore, other IGOs offer both free and priced options for the essentially the same content. Some IGOs will sell a print publication on its bookstore, a priced digital copy on an electronic library, and a free digital version elsewhere its Web site. The World Bank eLibrary (http://elibrary.worldbank.org/) offers much of the same content found in the Open Knowledge Repository, but the eLibrary search is more robust and the historical content more extensive: it also includes MARC records. The subscription-based United Nations iLibrary (http://www.un-ilibrary.org/) also offers search and download features within a consolidated database environment—but in fact much of the same content can be found and downloaded elsewhere within the global network of UN agency web sites. But much of the same content should also be free online via the wide network of UN agencies and offices around the world.

The resulting situation is thus very complex. Librarians, when considering which option is best suited for their clientele, should carefully consider whether print, free online, or priced online content best meets their needs: the various options all have advantages and disadvantages. Careful research should be conducted for each organization of interest as there is no consistency across the board, and policies can change rapidly.

And then, there is Open Data. Not long ago the UN, World Bank, IMF, and other IGOs sold most of their numeric data on subscription databases, prompting world renowned open data advocate Hans Rosling to diagnose them (during the H1N1 flu outbreak) with "DbHd" "Database Hugging Disorder."[41] Slowly but steadily IGOs have been curing themselves of this malaise. The UN was among the first, when it changed the name of its priced *UNSTATS Common Database* to *UNData* (data.un.org) and made it freely available online. Other previously priced data sets, including *FAOStat* from the Food and Agriculture Organization (FAO) and *World Development Indicators* from the World Bank, are now entirely free. The IMF is scheduled to make its subscription-based numeric databases, including *International Financial Statistics*, freely available in 2015. But other data sets, notably from the OECD and the International Telecommunication Union remain priced, as does the "premium access version" of *UN Comtrade*, the UN's International Trade Database. What follows are some examples of freely available and commonly used IGO numeric databases:

United Nations—UNData: http://data.un.org/
European Union—Eurostat: http://epp.eurostat.ec. europa.eu/
World Bank Data: http://data.worldbank.org/
International Labour Organization—ILOStat: http:// www.ilo.org/ilostat

Digital MARC records

Even when international government information is online (free or priced), it may be buried so deep within a database that the information is virtually unfindable unless the patron knows in advance it exists. Some organizations have addressed this discoverability issue by assigning Digital Object Identifiers (DOIs) or Uniform Resource Identifiers (URIs) to publications, but not all. Here are two examples of IGO documents dealing with the Ebola Outbreak.

Economic Impact of the 2014 Ebola Epidemic: Short and Medium Term Estimates for West Africa. http:// hdl.handle.net/10986/20396
Liberia Ebola Emergency Response—Update N.1 http://www.fao.org/emergencies/resources/documents/resources-detail/en/c/243283/

The first document has a URI that is easily cited: the second is more problematic. But whether a patron would have found either of these documents on search engine is debatable: many patrons would not have thought of the World Bank or the FAO when researching Ebola. To address this problem, libraries may wish to upload digital MARC records into their catalogs that some IGOs make available. With MARC records, a patron does not need to know in advance about the work of an international organization: they can find these documents in a keyword search in the catalog. Examples of IGOs that offer this service include the following. Some are free; others are priced via Electronic library subscriptions.

OECD iLibrary (subscription-based): http://www.oecd-ilibrary.org/about/about
Asian Development Bank: http://www.adb.org/publications/marcrecords
World Bank eLibrary (subscription-based): http:// elibrary.worldbank.org/page/services_benefits
EU Bookshop Publications Services for Librarians: http://bookshop.europa.eu/en/publications-office-services-for-librarians-pbOA0114666/

Another way patrons can search for IGO and NGO publications of interest is to use one of the Google Custom Search Engines that conduct searches across hundreds of IGO and NGO Web sites. For more information and links to these please, see next.

IGO publications offices

A number of large IOs have online bookstores for print publications. Furthermore, even smaller IOs will have their publications either online for free or available for order and purchase. A few of the more popular IGO bookstores include

EU Bookshop: https://bookshop.europa.eu/en/home/
OECD Online Bookshop: http://www.oecdbookshop. org/
United Nations Publications: https://shop.un.org/
World Bank Publications: https://publications. worldbank.org/

The fact that many of these publications are free online has not stopped this business, and libraries may wish to consider print publications for clientele who prefer them, or for preservation and archival purposes.

IGO subscription databases

Another avenue of providing IO information to patrons is through IGO subscription databases. Even when much IGO content is free online, the benefit of acquiring these is that the information is consolidated into one place, allowing patrons to perform detailed searches by country, topic, or time period. Most databases include MARC records and some include longer runs of historic material. Examples include

> World Bank Elibrary: http://elibrary.worldbank.org/
> OECD iLibrary: http://www.oecd-ilibrary.org/
> IMF eLibrary/eLibrary Complete: http://www.elibrary. imf.org/
> UNWTO Elibrary: http://www.e-unwto.org/home/ main.mpx

Third-party vendors for IO information

Many libraries work through third-party vendors to obtain international publications. This can be useful for placing standing orders for specific categories of publications or obtaining difficult to find or out-of-print material. Some leading vendors include

> *Renouf Press*: http://www.renoufbooks.com/—"North America's leading distributor of governmental and international reports and documents."
> *Bernan Press*: http://www.bernan.com/—"A leading distributor of essential publications from the United States government and intergovernmental organizations."
> *Readex United Nations Documents Collections*: http:// www.readex.com/content/united-nations-documents— Only comprehensive digital index to United Nations documents from the founding of the UN to present, as well as a collection of UN documents on microfiche. The avenues a library takes to build collections will depend on the library's goals, patron needs, finances, and staffing resources. Many libraries use several means to add International Organization information to their collections.

Professional Organizations and Online Research Guides

Any librarian or informational professional interested in international information should consider joining the Government Documents Roundtable (GODORT) of the American Library Association. GODORT's International Documents Task Force (IDTF) is a group of professionals who work with or specialize in this field. Their Web site is located at http://wikis.ala.org/godort/index.php/ International_Documents and contains lists of current projects, research guides, and other valuable information. It also contains links to library research guides, some of which are listed next.

As a general note, many comprehensive government information guides have been "retired" as online search

has improved and governments have improved the usability of their own sites. What is increasingly done is librarians create research guides that explain the process of finding, understanding, and interpreting information for international organizations.

Finding IGOs

> Northwestern University's International Government Organizations: http://www.library.northwestern. edu/libraries-collections/evanston-campus/government-information/international-documents.
> Union of International Associations' Open Yearbook (free version of the priced yearbook): http://www. uia.org/ybio/.
> IGO Custom Search—Google custom search engine for IGOs, sponsored by GODORT and maintained by James Jacobs at Stanford University: http://wikis. ala.org/godort/index.php/IGO_search.
> Finding NGOs NGO Research Guide at Duke University: http://guides.library.duke.edu/ngo_guide.
> Idealist—Online directory of NGOs searchable by region and area of activity: http://www.idealist. org/.
> NGO Custom Search—Google custom search engine for NGOs sponsored by GODORT and maintained by James Jacobs at Stanford University: http://wikis. ala.org/godort/index.php/IGO_search/.

Finding foreign national governments

> Northwestern University's alphabetical list of foreign national government Web sites: http://www.library. northwestern.edu/govinfo/resource/internat/foreign. html
> Foreign Information by Country at the University of Colorado Boulder: http://ucblibraries.colorado.edu/ govpubs/for/foreigngovt.htm

Detailed information about specific organizations

> United Nations Dag Hammarskjöld Library Research Guides: http://research.un.org/en
> European Union Research Guide: http://www.law. georgetown.edu/library/research/guides/ EuropeanUnion.cfm
> WTO & GATT Research: http://nyulaw.libguides.com/ wto_gatt

CONCLUSION AND OUTLOOK

Given the rise of e-government, it is likely that future users will demand more online access to government information while tangible collections of materials will be few and far between. Requests for government information are growing across all nations and at all levels of governments. In many ways, all government information is becoming local in that demand is based on how the release of the information impacts the local community. In order to meet future demands, librarians must build their documents collections (both physical and virtual) based upon the overall mission, goals, and audience of an individual library.

In 2012, the U.S. Government Printing Office (later the U.S. Government Publishing Office) began a strategic planning process to outline the future of the Federal Depository Library Program. A series of forecast questionnaires and action plans will eventually result in a new national plan for the program that will attempt to ensure permanent access to published federal information, no matter the medium in which it is issued. On a grander scale, national and local governments around the globe will continue to grapple with controlling the flow of information. In the digital era, ensuring the security of information that is not intended for public release has become as great a challenge as ensuring ongoing access to public information.

REFERENCES

1. Morehead, J. *Introduction to United States Government Information Sources*, 6th Ed.; Libraries Unlimited: Englewood, CO, 1999.
2. Beck, C. *The New Woman as Librarian: The Career of Adelaide Hasse*; Scarecrow Press: Lanham, MD, 2006.
3. Forte, E.J.; Hartnett, C.J.; Sevetson, A.L. *Fundamentals of Government Information: Mining, Finding, Evaluating, and Using Government Resources*; Neal-Schuman Publishers, Inc.: New York, 2011.
4. Reilly, B.F. Jr. *Governments and the Digital Record: The Historian's Perspective*. Report on a Panel Discussion on Government Information and Societal Memory Convened by the American Historical Association, January, 2014. Prepared for the Center for Research Libraries, Global Resources Collection Forum. http://www.crl.edu/focus/summer-2014 (accessed October 10, 2014).
5. Bertot, J.C.; McClure, C.R.; Wright, C.B.; Jensen, E.; Thomas, S. *Public Libraries and the Internet 2008: Study Results and Findings*, 2008. http://www.ii.fsu.edu/Solutions/Public-Libraries-The-Internet/Reports (accessed October 10, 2014).
6. Hernon, P. Government information policy principles. Gov. Inf. Q. **1991**, *8* (4), 393–399.
7. Jaeger, P. Information policy, information access, and democratic participation: the national and international implications of the bush administration's information politics. Gov. Inf. Q. **2007**, *24* (4), 840–859.
8. Blanton, T.S. Information ethics and government power, from the White House e-mail to the Stasi files. In *Libraries and Democracy: The Cornerstones of Liberty*; Kranich, N., Ed.; American Library Association: Chicago, IL, 2001; 129–39.
9. Weaver, B.F. Library involvement in state government information policy development in the United States. Inspel **2002**, *36* (3), 171–182. http://www.ifla.org/VII/d2/inspel/02-3weba.pdf (accessed October 2014).
10. Government Printing Office. *United States Statutes at Large*; Government Printing Office: Washington, DC, 1937–present.
11. Smith, L.L.; Barkley, D.C.; Cornwall, D.D.; Johnson, E. W.; Malcomb, J.L. *Tapping State Government Information Sources*; Greenwood Press: Westport, CT, 2003.
12. Morrison, A.M. *Managing Electronic Government Information in Libraries: Issues and Practices*; American Library Association: Chicago, IL, 2008.
13. NASCIO. *Harmony Helps: A Progress Report on State Government Internet Presence*; NASCIO: Lexington, KY, 2007; 4. http://www.nascio.org/Publications/ArtMID/485/ArticleID/216/Harmony-Helps-A-Progress-Report-on-State-Government-Internet-Presence (accessed October 2014).
14. Smith, A. *Government Online*; Pew Research Internet Project: Washington, DC, 2010. http://www.pewinternet.org/2010/04/27/government-online/ (accessed October 2014).
15. Rainie, L.; Purcell, K. *How the Public Perceives Community Information Systems*; Pew Research Internet Project: Washington, DC, 2011. http://www.pewinternet.org/2011/03/01/how-the-public-perceives-community-information-systems/ (accessed October 2014).
16. State agency databases, http://wikis.ala.org/godort/index.php/State_Agency_Databases (accessed October 2014).
17. State and local documents, http://wikis.ala.org/godort/index.php/State_%26_Local_Documents (accessed October 2014).
18. Newspaper and current periodical reading room: state government information, http://www.loc.gov/rr/news/stategov/stategov.html (accessed October 2014).
19. The guide to law online, http://www.loc.gov/law/help/guide/states.php (accessed October 2014).
20. Government publications: United States, http://www.loc.gov/acq/devpol/govus.pdf (accessed October 2014).
21. Library of Congress Exchange and Gift Division. *Monthly Checklist of State Publications*; Government Printing Office: Washington, DC, 1910–1994.
22. Guidelines for state documents checklists. http://wikis.ala.org/godort/index.php/Accepted_Guidelines_for_State_Documents_Checklists (accessed October 2014).
23. University of Illinois at Urbana-Champaign. *StateList: The Electronic Source for State Publications Lists*; University of Illinois at Urbana-Champaign: Urbana-Champaign, IL, http://www.library.illinois.edu/doc/researchtools/guides/state/statelist.html (accessed October 2014).
24. Jenkins, W.S. *Records of the States of the United States of America: A Microfilm Compilation*; Library of Congress: Washington, DC, 1949–1951. https://dds.crl.edu/crldelivery/16951 (accessed October 2014).
25. Bowker, R.R. *State Publications: A Provisional List of the Official Publications of the Several States of the United States from Their Organization*; The Publishers' Weekly: New York, 1899–1908, 4 Vols.
26. Hasse, A. *Index of Economic Material in the Documents of the States of the United States...*; Department of Economics and Sociology of the Carnegie Institution of Washington: Washington, DC, 1907–1922, 13 Vols.

27. Wilcox, J.K. *Manual on the Use of State Publications*; American Library Association: Chicago, IL, 1940.

28. Childs, J.B. *Government Document Bibliography in the United States and Elsewhere*, 3rd Ed.; Library of Congress: Washington, DC, 1942.

29. Palic, V.M.; Childs, J.B. *Government Publications: A Guide to Bibliographic Tools*; Library of Congress/Government Printing Office: Washington, DC, 1975.

30. Lane, M. *State Publications and Depository Libraries: A Reference Handbook*; Greenwood Press: Westport, CT, 1981.

31. Nakata, Y.; Smith, S.L.; Ernst, W.B. *Organizing a Local Government Documents Collection*; American Library Association: Chicago, IL, 1979.

32. Government Organization summary report, 2012. http://www2.census.gov/govs/cog/g12_org.pdf (accessed October 2014).

33. Stille, A. Overload. New Yorker **1999**, *75* (2), 38.

34. Wilson, Y.; Richey, D. State and local documents roundup: a basic primer on collecting local government publications. Doc. People **2005**, *33* (4), 9–12.

35. Martin, M. *Local and Regional Government Information: How to Find It, How to Use It*; Greenwood Press: Westport, CT, 2005.

36. Union of International Associations. *The Yearbook of International Organizations*. Free online version, http://www.uia.org/yearbook/ (accessed October 12, 2014).

37. *Yearbook of International Organizations Online: Statistics, Visualizations and Patterns*; Union of International Associations: Brussels, Belgium; Leiden, the Netherlands: Brill, Subscription database, http://ybio.brillonline.com/ (accessed March 30, 2016).

38. World Bank Open Knowledge Repository FAQ, https://openknowledge.worldbank.org/faq (accessed October 10, 2014).

39. *The EU Internet Handbook*. Legal notices and copyright, http://ec.europa.eu/ipg/basics/legal/notice_copyright/index_en.htm (accessed October 12, 2014).

40. Open access policy concerning UNESCO publications, http://www.unesco.org/new/fileadmin/MULTIMEDIA/HQ/ERI/pdf/oa_policy_rev2.pdf (accessed October 12, 2014).

41. Hans Rosling at World Bank: open data (YouTube), https://www.youtube.com/watch?v=5OWhcrjxP-E (accessed October 12, 2014).

BIBLIOGRAPHY

1. American Library Association. *Guide to Country Information in International Governmental Organization Publications*; ALA GODORT/CIS: Bethesda, MD, 1996.

2. Archer, C. *International Organizations*, 2nd Ed.; Routledge: London, U.K./New York, 1992.

3. Barnum, G. Availability, access, authenticity, and persistence: creating the environment for permanent public access to electronic government information. Gov. Inf. Q. **2002**, *19* (1), 3845.

4. Brimmer, B. *Guide to the Use of United Nations Documents*. (Including Reference to the Specialized Agencies and Special U.N. Bodies); Oceana: Dobbs Ferry, NY, 1962.

5. Browne, M. The field of information policy: 1. Fundamental concepts. J. Inf. Sci. **1997**, *23* (4), 261–275.

6. Burger, R.H. *Information Policy: A Framework for Evaluation and Policy Research*; Ablex Press: Norwood, NJ, 1993.

7. Bush, G.W. Executive order 13233: access to presidential records. Fed. Regist. **2001**, *66* (214), 56025–56029.

8. Childs, J.B. Bibliographic control of federal, state, and local documents. Libr. Trends **1966**, *15* (1), 6–26.

9. Doty, P. Why study information policy? J. Educ. Libr. Inf. Sci. **1993**, *39* (1), 58–64.

10. *Electronic Freedom of Information Act Amendments of 1996*. 116 STAT. 2899 (Public Law 104–231).

11. Ghebali, V.-Y. *A Repertoire of League of Nations Serial Documents, 1919–1947*; Oceana Publications: Dobbs Ferry, NY, 1973.

12. Hajnal, P.I. *International Information: Documents, Publications, and Electronic Information of International Governmental Organizations*; Libraries Unlimited: Englewood, CO, 1997; Vols. 1–2.

13. Hajnal, P. *Directory of United Nations Documentary and Archival Sources*; Academic Council on the United Nations System: Hanover, NH; Kraus International: Millwood, NY.

14. Hamilton, A.; Madison, J.; Jay, J. *The Federalist Papers*; New American Library: New York, 1961.

15. Hernon, P. Information life cycle: it's place in the management of U.S. Government Information Resources. Gov. Inf. Q. **1994**, *11* (2), 143–170.

16. Hernon, P.; McClure, C.R.; Relyea, H.C. *Federal Information Policies in the 1990s*; Ablex Press: Norwood, NJ, 1996.

17. Hernon, P.; Purcell, G.R. *Developing Collections of U.S. Government Publications*. Foundations in Library Science, JAI Press: Greenwich, CT, 1982; Vol. 12.

18. Hernon, P.; Relyea, H.C. Government publishing: past to a present. Gov. Inf. Q. **1995**, *12* (3), 309–330.

19. Hernon, P.; Relyea, H.C.; Dugan, R.E.; Cheverie, J.F. *United States Government Information: Policies and Sources*; Libraries Unlimited: Westport, CT, 2002.

20. Horrigan, J.; Garrett, K.; Resnick, P. *The Internet and Democratic Debate*; Pew Internet & The American Life Project: Washington, DC, 2004.

21. *International Organizations Series*. Scarecrow Press: Metuchen, NJ, 14 Vols.

22. *International Organizations Series*; Transaction Publishers: New Brunswick, NJ; ABC-Clio: Oxford, U.K., 11 Vols.

23. Kram, L. Why continue to be a depository library if it is all on the Internet anyway? Gov. Inf. Q. **1998**, *15* (1), 57–71.

24. Kumar, M.J. Executive order 13233: further implementation of the Presidential Records. Act. Polit. Sci. Q. **2002**, *32* (1), 194–209.

25. Lenhart, A.; Horrigan, J.; Rainie, L.; Allen, K.; Boyce, A.; Madden, M.; O'Grady, E. *The Ever-Shifting Internet Population: A New Look at Internet Access and the Digital Divide*; Pew Internet & The American Life Project: Washington, DC, 2002.

26. Louis-Jacque, L.; Korman, J.S. *Introduction to International Organizations*; New York: Oceana/American Association of Law Libraries, 1996.

27. Morehead, J. *Essays on Public Documents and Government Policies*; Haworth Press: Binghamton, NY, 1986.

28. Morehead, J. *Introduction to United States Government Information Sources*, 6th Ed.; Libraries Unlimited: Westport, CT, 1999.

29. Morrison, A.; Mann, B. *International Government Information and Country Information: A Subject Guide*; Greenwood Press: Westport, CT, 2004.

30. Morrison, A.M. *Managing Electronic Government Information in Libraries: Issues and Practices*; American Library Association: Chicago, IL, 2008.

31. National Research Council; Committee on Intellectual Property Rights in the Emerging Information Infrastructure. *The Digital Dilemma: Intellectual Property in the Information Age*; National Academy Press: Washington, DC, 2000.

32. NCLIS. *Permanent Public Access To Electronic Federal Government Information*. NAS/CSTB Concept Paper; U.S. National Commission on Libraries and Information Science: Rockland, MD. March 30, 1990, revised 12 May 1999. https://www.gpo.gov/fdsys/pkg/GPO-NCLIS-ELECTRONIC/html/GPO-NCLIS-ELECTRONIC-1-1.htm (accessed March 30, 2016).

33. O'Mahony, D.P. The federal depository library program in transition: a perspective at the turn of the century. Gov. Inf. Q. **1998**, *15* (1), 13–26.

34. Perritt, H.H. *Public Information in the National Information Infrastructure*, Report to the Regulatory Information Service Center, the General Services Administration, and to the Administrator of the Office of Information and Regulatory Affairs; Office of Management and Budget: Washington, DC, 1994.

35. Quinn, A.C. Collection development in the electronic library. Doc. People **2001**, *29*(3).

36. Reilly, B.F. Jr. *Papers. Leviathan: Libraries and Government Information in the Age of Big Data*. Global Resources Research Forum. Center for Research Libraries: Chicago, IL, April 24–25, 2014. http://www.crl.edu/leviathan (accessed October 10, 2014).

37. Reinalda, B. *Routledge Handbook of International Organization*; Routledge: Abingdon, U.K., 2013.

38. Relyea, H.C. *Title 44, United States Code-Public Printing and Documents: A Brief Historical Overview*, Congressional Research Service Report No. 79–36 GOV; Congressional Research Service: Washington, DC, February 23, 1979.

39. Robinson, J.S. *Tapping the Government Grapevine: The User-friendly Guide to U.S. Government Information Sources*, 3rd Ed.; Oryx Press: Phoenix, AZ, 1998.

40. Rubin, R.E. *Foundations of Library and Information Science*; Neal-Schuman: New York, 2000.

41. Schaaf, R.W. Information policies of international organizations. Gov. Publ. Rev. **1990**, *17*, 49–61.

42. Schmeckebier, L.F. *The Government Printing Office: Its History, Activities, and Organization*; Johns Hopkins Press: Baltimore, MD, 1925.

43. Schmeckebier, L.F.; Eastin, R.B. *Government Publications and Their Use*, 2nd Ed. revised; Brookings Institute: Washington, DC, 1969.

44. Sears, J.L.; Moody, M.K. *Using Government Information Sources: Electronic and Print*, 3rd Ed.; Oryx: Phoenix, AZ, 2001.

45. Smith, D. *Management of Government Information Resources in Libraries*; Libraries Unlimited: Englewood, CO, 2003.

46. The World Bank. *Guide to the World Bank*; The World Bank: Washington, DC, 2003.

47. U.S. Congress, Joint Committee on Printing. *Government Depository Libraries: The Present Law Governing Designated Depository Libraries*; Government Printing Office: Washington, DC, 1981. Joint Committee Print, 97th Congress, 1st Session.

48. U.S. Congress, Office of Technology Assessment. *Federal Government Information Technology: Management, Security, and Congressional Oversight*; Government Printing Office: Washington, DC, 1986.

49. U.S. Congress, Office of Technology Assessment. *Office of Technology Assessment. Defending Secrets, Sharing Data*; Government Printing Office: Washington, DC, 1987.

50. U.S. Congress, Office of Technology Assessment. *Intellectual Property Rights in an Age of Electronics and Information*; Government Printing Office: Washington, DC, 1986.

51. U.S. Congress, Office of Technology Assessment. *Making Government Work: Electronic Delivery of Federal Services*; Government Printing Office: Washington, DC, 1993.

52. U.S. Congress, Office of Technology Assessment. *Informing the Nation: Federal Information Dissemination in an Electronic Age*; Government Printing Office: Washington, DC, 1988.

53. U.S. Government Printing Office, Permanent Public Access Working Group. *A Report on Meetings Hosted by the U.S. Government Printing Office, 1999–2000*; U.S. Government Printing Office: Washington, DC, 2000.

54. U.S. Government Printing Office, Superintendent of Documents Office. *Managing the FDLP Electronic Collection: A Policy and Planning Document*; U.S. Government Printing Office: Washington, DC, 1998.

55. U.S. Government Printing Office, Superintendent of Documents Office. *A Strategic Vision for the 21st Century*; Government Printing Office: Washington, DC, http://www.gpo.gov/congressional/pdfs/04strategicplan.pdf (accessed September 2008).

56. Walters, J.S. *U.S. Government Publication: Ideological Development and Institutional Politics from the Founding to 1970*; Scarecrow Press: Lanham, MD, 2005.

57. Warren, S.D.; Brandeis, L.D. The right to privacy. In *Ethical Issues in the Use of Computers*; Johnson, D.G., Snapper, J.W., Eds.; Wadsworth Publishing: Belmont, CA, 1985 (Original work published 1890), 172–183.

58. Weiss, S. Problems and solutions in a collecting local and municipal documents for a State University Library. J. Educ. Media Libr. Sci. **1996**, *34* (1), 1–9.

59. Wells, R.N. Jr. *Piece by Pieces: United Nations Agencies and Their Roles: A Reader and Selective Bibliography*; Scarecrow Press: Metuchen, NJ, 1991.

Greece: Archives

Nestor Bamidis
GSA-Archives of Macedonia, Thessaloniki, Greece

Abstract

This entry discusses the development of national and regional archives in Greece, focusing on the period from the early twentieth century to the present. College and university archives, private archives, and audiovisual archives are also discussed. Archival science is a new field in Greece. The Society of Greek Archivists was founded in 1990, and the first university level archival studies program was established in 1993 at Ionian University.

NATIONAL ARCHIVES AND SERVICES

The Greek national archive service is the "General State Archives" (Genika Archeia tou Kratous, GSA). It was established in 1914 by the Eleftherios Venizelos government and aimed at "the collection and supervision of all historical and public archives, including documents dated up to 50 years ago."[1] The foundation of the archive service was the result of the efforts of two exceptional men, the historian Spyridon Lamprou and the author and history researcher Giannis Vlachogiannis. The already existing Archives of the Ionian Islands, Crete, and Samos were incorporated into this service as well. Giannis Vlachogiannis, who donated his valuable collection to the Hellenic State, was the first director of the GSA. The next act was voted in 1939.[2] The legislation in force today concerning archives consists of the following Acts: 1946/1991 "GSA and other provisions"[3] and 2846/2000 "Archives of the Prime Minister, the Ministers, deputy ministers, and the General Secretariat of the Council of Ministers."[4] Access to public information is regulated by Act 1690/1999 (Article 5, "Access to documents"), in effect of article 5A of the Constitution, 2001[5] and Acts 1599/1986, article 16, "Right of access to administrative documents," and 1943/1991, article 6, "Publicity of administrative actions."

The Constitution of Greece:

All persons have the right to information, as specified by law. Restrictions to this right may be imposed by law only insofar as they are absolutely necessary and justified for reasons of national security, of combating crime or of protecting rights and interests of third parties.

All persons have the right to participate in the Information Society. Facilitation of access to electronically transmitted information, as well as of the production, exchange and diffusion thereof, constitutes an obligation of the State, always in observance of the guarantees of articles 9, 9A and 19.

The protection of personal data is regulated by Act 1472/1997 on the Protection of Individuals with regard to the Processing of Personal Data, enforcing article 9A of the Constitution, 2001:

All persons have the right to be protected from the collection, processing and use, especially by electronic means, of their personal data, as specified by law. The protection of personal data is ensured by an independent authority, which is constituted and operates as specified by law.

The GSA has been since then, with the exemption of a short period (1971–1985), fallen under the jurisdiction of the Ministry of National Education and Religious Affairs. The state archives service was reorganized in 1939 by an act in force until 1991, when it was substituted by Act 1946/1991.

The GSA operate according to the provisions of act 1946/1991 and constitute an autonomous, unified public service, under the auspices of the Ministry of Education and Religious Affairs. Issues concerning Archives are managed by the Direction of Libraries and General, with the administrative support of the Department of Historical Archives of the Ministry of Education and Religious Affairs.

The primary mission of the GSA, as described in article 9 of the above act, reads as follows:

- The supervision, preservation, collection, conservation, cataloging, micro photographing, arrangement, and indexing of the archival material of the country. Making all public and private records, documents, and manuscripts concerning the cultural heritage of the Greek nation and the administrative, economic, and social activities of the Hellenic State available to researchers for consultation;
- Location of public records of historical interest, their selection, acquisition, and transfer in the GSA, their preparation for consultation by the researchers and the creation of finding aids;
- Supervision of the special archives, which are founded and operate in public agencies;

Encyclopedia of Library and Information Sciences, Fourth Edition DOI: 10.1081/E-ELIS4-120045541

- Publication of archival studies and catalogs;
- Cooperation with the church authorities, monastic institutions, and other religious authorities for the preservation of archival material;
- Cooperation with owners of private archives, which have historical interest;
- Enrichment of its collections by purchase or acceptance of donations of archival material by private owners and copies of archival material in the possession of foreign countries or organizations; and
- Participation in scientific research, in cooperation with other scientific authorities as well as in all kinds of exhibits, in Greece and abroad.

The Archival Service is divided into the Central and the Regional Services. The head of the Service is the "Director of the General State Archives." The GSA of Greece are governed by a Board of nine members, whose duty is to decide, give expert opinion or advice on various matters concerning archives, based on proposals of the Director of the GSA.

The Central Service consists of the following departments: The General Index Department, the Contemporary Archives Department, the Organizing and Planning Department, the Department of Secretariat and Accounting, the Conservation and Reproduction Department, and the Reading Room and Library Department.

The regional services are divided into a) the Archives of the prefectures (nomoi) seated at the capitals of the prefectures, entitled and having the name "GSA—Archives of the Prefecture of . . ." and b) Archives operating in towns of the Prefectures and having the title "GSA— Local Archives of. . . ." The responsibilities of the regional services are relevant to those of the Central service. Today, the network includes 62 services, covering the mainland and all the islands of Greece.

Archives in any kind or form, of all public agencies, of judicial authorities, local authorities, educational institutions, and notaries are collected and deposited in the GSA. The holdings of the GSA also include private archives, and their acquisition is considered to be of great importance. For that reason, an effort is made for the enrichment of the private archives collections by purchasing archival material and by seeking active collaboration with donors, holders, or owners of private archives of historical interest.

The GSA at the Prefecture level collect and keep the archives of the public and local authorities, judicial records, notaries, and educational records as well as private collections.

INDIVIDUAL STATE ARCHIVES

A special mention should be made of certain Archives having significant archival material. They include the following:

- *The Central Service*, where archives date back to the period of the Struggle for Independence (early nineteenth century) and the establishment of the Greek State are kept.
- *The Historical Archives of Macedonia*, where archives created by the Ottoman government and concerning certain areas of Macedonia (Thessalonicki, Veroia, Kilkis, Katerini, and Chalkidiki) are deposited. This includes the archives of the Religious Court (1694–1912), archives of administrative and judicial acts (1875–1912), and estate and tax registers.
- *The Historical Archives of Epirus* (Ioannina) which keep archives of the General Administration of Epirus (1912–1940).
- *The Archives of the Ionian Islands* (Corfu, Kefalonia, Ithaca, Zakynthos, Lefkada, Kythira, and Paksoi), which keep archives of their governments before their union with Greece. These include archives of the Venetian domination the "Serenissima Signoria" of St. Mark (1500–1789), of the Democratic French (1789–1799), of the Ionian Government (1799–1807), of the Imperial French (1807–1814), of the Cambell's provisional government (1814–1817), and of the English Protectorate (1817–1864).
- *The Archives of the Prefecture of the Dodecanese*, where archives of the Italian administration, Ottoman manuscripts, archives of the Greek military administration, and of the General Administration of Dodecanese are deposited;
- *The Historical Archives of Crete* keeps archives of the Ottoman administration, as well as the official correspondence of the Cretan revolutions (1821–1835, 1866–1869, 1877–1878, 1895–1898 and 1905), archives of the Cretan State, of the German Occupation, during the Second World War, as well as private collections about important periods of Cretan history;
- *The Archives of Samos*, where collections (various documents—Ottoman, ecclesiastical, etc. of the eighteenth and nineteenth centuries) and archives of the Samian Hegemony (1834–1912) are saved.

STATE/PROVINCIAL AND LOCAL ARCHIVES

In Greece, all public Archives are incorporated in the GSA. As a result, archival agencies at the local authorities level (Provincial and Local Archives) are part of the State Archives. However, legislation concerning archives allows for the founding and operation of Archives by public sector agencies. Some of the most important are mentioned below:

- *Center for the History of Thessaloniki* The Center houses the municipal historical archive. Part of this archive is kept in the Center's building and is gradually becoming accessible to scholars. The Center also possesses a number of important private archival collections. It contains an important photographic collection, a map collection, and a collection of postcards printed in the beginning of the twentieth century.

- *Municipal Center for History and Documentation of Volos.*[6] he Center possesses today a rich archive, consisting of the Volos Municipality archive (1883–1982), numerous private archives concerned directly or indirectly with the city and its greater area, archives of old industrial enterprises, as well as important material of building plans, maps, aerial photos, slides/transparencies, and photographs. In the context of electronic processing of the archive collections and the compilation of an index, the Municipal Center for Historical Research and Documentation, in cooperation with the *National Documentation Center*, proceeded with the electronic publication of the search tools for the archival collection.

COLLEGE AND UNIVERSITY ARCHIVES

Some of the oldest and most important universities in Greece have gathered archival material related to their domain or to their own activity. To name a few:

- *The Historical Archive of the National and Capodistrian University of Athens*[7] was established in 1991 and since then has constituted an important research and administration unit of the University. From the beginning, the main goal was the gathering of archival material, scattered since the foundation of the University in 1837. Today, archives from that date up to 1970 are well organized, arranged, and described. Electronic finding aids are also available, as well as a growing number of digitized documents. The Historical Archive has created a solid infrastructure for the study of the history of university education and science. It also participates in research programs on Modern Greek and European history, in collaboration with universities and research centers all over Europe and contributes to the organization of archives and records management in other Universities, institutions, and business establishments.
- *The Aristotle University of Thessaloniki Historical Archives* Its educational, literary, social, and historic archival collections, concerning Macedonia (mainly from the beginning of the nineteenth century until 1950), are kept in different Departments of the University. The holdings of the historical archives include documentary records from the Teachers College of Thessaloniki (1933–1990), elementary and secondary private and public schools, educational authorities, hospitals, parishes, and monasteries.

OTHER ARCHIVES

There are also organizations maintaining important collections of specific interest, due to their nature or acquisition policy. Some representative examples include the following:

- *The National Bank of Greece Historical Archives (NBG)*[8] were set up for the preservation and display of archival material of the National Bank of Greece, deemed to be of historical importance. The NBG has demonstrated particular concern for its archival material since its early days. As a consequence, NBG possesses a comprehensive historical archive whose time span coincides practically with the history of the Modern Greek state. The material held in the NBG Historical Archives covers the Bank's history from 1841 to 1966, while it also contains originals or copies of various archives of other institutions or individuals entrusted to its safekeeping.
- The **Hellenic Literary and Historical Archive**[9] keeps an important collection of archival material (nineteenth and twentieth centuries), of historical, literary, social, economic, and artistic interest.
- The document collection of the *Foreign Ministry's Diplomatic and Historical Archive*[10] encompasses the period from the beginning of the Greek national liberation struggle in 1821 to the present day. The Service of Diplomatic & Historical Archives of the Hellenic Ministry of Foreign Affairs (M.F.A.) is responsible for safe-keeping, preserving, classifying, and utilizing the written, audiovisual and electronic archives of the Ministry, and managing the Library and the Film Archive of the M.F.A.

AUDIOVISUAL ARCHIVES

In recent years, special care has been taken in Greece for audiovisual archives, which have been preserved in public agencies.

- The *Secretariat General of Communication and Information*[11] maintains an important film archive (about 2100 titles), documenting important aspects of the political, economic, social and cultural life of Greece from 1908 to 1996. The material is divided into three categories: "Contemporary," "Chronicles," and "Documentary." A project of digitalization is currently aiming at facilitating the effective management and utilization of the film archive. According to Law 3444/2006, the film archive will be turned over to the National Audiovisual Archive.
- The task of the *Hellenic Audiovisual Institute Archive*[12] is the conservation and preservation of audiovisual and

born-digital material, for wide access by any interested party. The Archive manages audiovisual and born-digital material with informational-news, historical-political and, in general, social-cultural content, related to the heritage of the Hellenic State and Hellenism as a whole.

- The *Archive Museum of ERT* (Hellenic Broadcasting Corporation)[13] was established in 1990. It comprises the departments of the Museum, the Picture Archive, and the Audiovisual Archive. ERT's holdings of more than 15,000 reels of film, 300,000 negatives of pictures and photographic archives, are the most important ones of their sort in Greece. Since 1996, it has been operating as a maintenance and restoration workshop for films, while in 1999 it started operating as a restoration workshop for videotapes—the only one of its kind in Greece—as well as a workshop for the maintenance of photographic material.

The archival landscape in Greece could not be complete without mentioning the following institutions:

- Archive of Cinematograph and Archive of Documentaries of the Ministry of Foreign Affairs, http://www.mfa.gr/greek/the_ministry/history_archive/index.htm
- National Bank of Greece Cultural Foundation—Historical and Paleographical Archive, http://www.miet.gr/web/en/archive/
- Archives of Contemporary Social History, http://www.askiweb.gr
- Historical Archives of the Benaki Museum, http://www.benaki.gr
- Historical Archives of the Agricultural University of Athens, http://www.aua.gr/gr/arxeio/
- The American School of Classical Studies at Athens, http://www.ascsa.edu.gr/archives/Gennadius/Catalog1.htm
- The Konstantinos G. Karamanlis Foundation Historical Archive, http://www.Karamanlis-foundation.gr/gr/drastiriotites/arxeio.html
- Association for the salvage of Historical Archives 1940–1974 http://www.edia.gr/
- The Konstantinos K. Mitsotakis Foundation, http://www.ikm.gr/archive_purpose.cfm
- Army History Directorate, http://www.army.gr/html/GR_Army/dieuthinseis/DIS/index.html

DIGITAL ARCHIVAL COLLECTIONS AND ELECTRONIC FINDING AIDS

Most of the repositories mentioned above have digitized part of their collections and provide electronic finding aids, accessible over the Internet. During the last 5 years, a large number of digitization projects, funded by the EU

Information Society Operational Programme, have been launched and continue to be carried out.

ARCHIVAL STUDIES

Archival science is a relatively new field in Greece. Employment positions are available in the state archives (provided by law), while new prospects are being developed in the private (banks and corporations) and public (Local Administration, Police, Universities, and Research Centres) sectors.

A Department of Archival and Library Sciences was established at the Ionian University in 1993.[14] It is a 4-year course of study leading to a Bachelor's Degree. Graduates may work as archivists in the GSA or in the archival institutions of the public or private sector, mentioned above. The Departments of Library Studies and Information Systems of the Technological Educational Institutions of Athens and Thessaloniki provide basic courses in Archival science (in two of the eight semesters). Graduates may take positions as assistant archivists in GSA and other archival institutions, or record managers in public and private organisations. Continuing education programs are available through seminars and workshops organized by the GSA, as well as the Society of Greek Archivists.

PROFESSIONAL ASSOCIATIONS

The Society of Greek Archivists was established in 1990.[15] Society of Greek Archivists, the sole professional association of archivists in Greece, currently has more than 200 members, and includes archivists, historians, and researchers. Some of its main constitutional functions are attracting the attention of citizens and decision makers about the salvage and preservation of archives, promoting the national archival heritage, providing consultancy and expertise concerning the management of archives to various organizations, and promoting the archival training and education of the archives and record management professionals.

One of the main concerns of archival professionals is the management of electronic records as archival documents. Existing legislation is not adequate on this issue, while the implementation of the e-government project raises an important number of problems that should be resolved as soon as possible. This issue holds back the efforts of archivists concerning long-term preservation of the documents in their original form. Microfilming and digitization are starting to be widely used for improved access of archival information. On the other hand, there are institutions focused on managing special archival mediums, e.g., audiovisual *registrations*, maps, and plans. The GSA are promoting the standardization of best practices for the preservation of traditional and electronic documents.

REFERENCES

1. Greece. Parliament. Law 380 Concerning the Founding of the State Archives Agency. Greek Official Gazette. Volume One 334 (1914). National Press: Athens, 1914.
2. Greece. Parliament. Emergency Law 2027 Concerning the Reorganization of the General State Archives. Greek Official Gazette. Volume One 448 (1939). National Press: Athens, 1939.
3. Greece. Parliament. Law 1946 General State Archives and Other Provisions. Greek Official Gazette. Volume One 69 (1991). National Press: Athens, 1991.
4. Greece. Parliament. Law 2846 Archives of Prime Minister, Ministers, Vice-Ministers and the General Secretariat of the Council of Ministers. Greek Official Gazette. Volume One 229 (2000). National Press: Athens, 2000.
5. Greece. Parliament. The Constitution of Greece. Available at http://www.parliament.gr/politeuma.
6. Municipal Center for History and Documentation of Volos. Available at http://www.diki.gr.
7. Historical Archive University of Athens. Available at http://www.archive.uoa.gr.
8. National Bank of Greece Historical Archives. Available at http://www.nbg.gr/dp/hanbg/en/soc_archive.html.
9. Hellenic Literary and Historical Archive. Available at http://www.elia.org.gr/.
10. Ministry of Foreign Affairs, Diplomatic and Historical Archives. Available at http://www.ypex.gov.gr/www.mfa.gr/en-US/The+Ministry/Structure/Archives/ .
11. Secretariat General of Communication and Information, National Audiovisual Archive. Available at http://www.minpress.gr/minpress/en/index/other_pages-1/ministry-domi/ministry-audiovisual-archive.htm.
12. Hellenic Audiovisual Institute. Available at http://www.iom.gr.
13. Hellenic Broadcasting Corporation. Available at http://www.ert.gr/archive.
14. Ionian University. Department of Archival and Library Science. Available at http://www.ionio.gr/tab.
15. Society of Greek Archivists. Available at http://www.eae.org.gr.

Greece: Libraries

Anestis Sitas
Aristotle University of Thessaloniki, Thessaloniki, Greece

Mersini Moreleli-Cacouris
Department of Library Science and Information Systems, Technological Educational Institute (TEI) of Thessaloniki, Sindos, Greece

Abstract

This entry provides an overview of the development of different types of libraries in Greece. Although the authors make reference to what is known of similar cultural institutions in ancient Greece, the focus is on modern period from the Greek Enlightenment and the establishment of the modern state in the early nineteenth century to the present. Special attention is given to recent trends, challenges, and accomplishments.

INTRODUCTION

Greece, a peninsular country, plus an archipelago of many islands, is situated on the south-eastern edge of Europe. It contains an area of 131,957 km^2 and has a population of 10,964,020 (2001 census).[1] Greece was declared independent in 1830 and has been a parliamentary republic since 1974. It has been a member of the European Union since 1981. The 2007 GDP amounts to 209,268 billion €, and the per capita annual income is 22,700 € (estimated figure in 2006) (Fig. 1).

LIBRARIES

History

The first indications of libraries in the ancient Greek world can be found in the Minoan and Mycenaean periods. The Library of Peisistratos (about 560 B.C.) is considered to be the first public library in Athens. The most famous library, however, was the Library of Alexandria, founded by Ptolemy II Philadelphus (309–246 B.C.). During the Byzantine Empire, the first "imperial" library was set up in Constantinople in the fourth century. Nevertheless, the kind of libraries that flourished at the time were monastery libraries (Mount Athos, Meteora, Patmos).

After the Fall of Constantinople to the Turks (A.D. 1453), some libraries continued to operate, while others ceased to exist. During the Modern Greek Enlightenment (late eighteenth to early nineteenth centuries), many schools were established, most of which had a library available to serve the needs of the curriculum. That period is considered the starting point for the modern era of libraries. The Library of Zagora, on Mt. Pelion, one of the most significant libraries in those days, opened its doors in 1762. Since 1955, it has

been known as the Public Library of Zagora. Another library opened at that time was the Library of the Dimitsana School, in the Pelopennese, which began to operate in 1764. Its present name is Public Library of Dimitsana. Finally, in 1828, the Zosimaia School, in Ioannina (Epirus), set up its library, which has borne the name Zosimaia Central Public Library of Ioannina' since 1987.

Contemporary Libraries

Recently, as many as 1145 libraries were identified in a 1998 survey that aimed to record all libraries. Of all those libraries recorded, 61.4% were public libraries, 13.9% academic libraries, 2.9% school libraries, and 21.8% special libraries.[2]

As far as book production is concerned, 730 publishers released 9209 new titles in 2006.[3] A survey on reading behavior indicates that 43.8% of Greek citizens do not read at all, 19% read only "practical" books, 0.9% only professional books, and 2.4% read both practical and professional books. On an annual basis, 25.4% read a few books (one to nine) as opposed to 8.6% that read several books (over nine). When stating the way of obtaining their books, 70.8% indicate that they buy them themselves, 17.9% borrow them from their acquaintances, 4.7% borrow them from libraries, and 3.9% receive them as gifts.[4] 28.9% of the Greek population aged 16–74 have Internet access.[5]

For years, Greek libraries had been underdeveloped and provided poor services. There had never been a national plan for library and information development, and the involvement of various ministries, state, and local agencies in government created many problems in planning and coordinating services. The fact that the majority of Greek libraries belonged to the public sector, with limited funding available, made any efforts for improvement even harder. This has changed radically. Funding of libraries has

Encyclopedia of Library and Information Sciences, Fourth Edition DOI: 10.1081/E-ELIS4-120044028

Fig. 1 Map of Greece.
Source: Modified from *CIA The World Factbook.*[10]

undergone a positive change: more state funds are now made available and European Union funds have flowed into the country. Information technology has become a part of library operations and plays an important and dominant role in the dissemination of information. Users, introduced to the wealth of electronic sources, have become more demanding. The range, kind, and modes of services which are provided now reflect active organizations, and do not resemble the warehouse-type institutions of the past.[6]

National Library of Greece (NLG)

After the liberation of Greece, the National Library of Greece (NLG) began to operate in 1829 in Aigina, which was then the capital of Greece. It was established under the initial name of Public Library, by decree in 1832. In 1834, it was transferred to Athens, which had become the new capital of the Greek State. In 1842, it was incorporated into the library of the University of Athens, established in 1837 and in 1866, the above collections merged into a single library under the formal Greek title "Ethniki Vivliothiki tis Ellados" (The NLG).

Since 1903, it has been housed in a building that was erected with funding by the Vallianos brothers, merchants, ship owners, and bankers, who, in the nineteenth century had businesses in Russia, Marseille, Constantinople, and London. It was designed by the Danish architect Theophil Hansen and built under the supervision of Ernst Ziller, a prominent German architect, whose work constitutes a milestone in contemporary Greek architecture. On June

11, 2007, a memorandum of understanding was signed between the Greek State and the Stavros Niarchos Foundation, for the construction of a new building. The project is expected to be completed in 2013 (Fig. 2).

The NLG is under the authority of the Greek Ministry of National Education and its institutional framework is prescribed by Law 3149 (FEK A, 141/10–06–2003). Its collections include approximately five million documents, and it is the main legal depository library in Greece. It publishes the *National Bibliography* and it operates as the national center for the assignment of ISBN, ISSN, and ISMN numbering. The Library was granted the authority to transfer *Library of Congress Subject Headings* into a Greek database, translate them into Greek, and adopt them to the Greek context. Various bibliographic tools, such as the *Catalog of Greek Subject Headings* and a translation of IFLA's *UNIMARC Manual* into Greek, have been published. Access to the library's OPAC (Online Public Access Catalog) is now possible, enabling librarians to check their collections, locate and verify items and copy bibliographic data.

Parliament Library

The Greek Parliament Library (Vivliothiki tis Voulis) was founded in 1844. It is housed in three different buildings in Athens. The "Main Library" of the Parliament Building houses collections of social sciences, rare books dating from 1471 to 1850, and maps and engravings, as well as documents pertaining to modern Greek history. The "Benakeios Library" houses collections of humanities and sciences. It also contains the personal libraries of prominent Greek politicians and scholars. The "Old Tobacco Factory" was converted into a library and houses the Microphotography and Preservation Departments as well as the largest part of the collection of Greek newspapers and periodicals. Mainly for preservation reasons, the Library began in 1984 to microfilm its serial collections; the outcome was 14,500 microforms. Following this

Fig. 2 National Library of Greece.

project, the Library is digitizing its rare books and works of its art collections. Along with the National Library, the Parliament Library is one of the mandatory legal deposit agencies.

Public Libraries

When discussing Greek public libraries some clarifications need to be made. In the Greek context there are two kinds of public libraries, depending on the supervising and regulating authorities; the "dimosies" (public) and the "dimotikes" (municipal).

Public libraries operate within a common institutional framework and are under the authority of and funded directly by the Greek Ministry of National Education. Their operation is prescribed by Law 3149. Their by-laws have been established by Ministerial Decision 83064/IZ (FEK B, 1173/20–8–2003). There are 45 such libraries spread throughout the country.

On the other hand, municipal libraries belong to the respective municipalities that provide their funds. This results in the lack of uniform regulations concerning the operation of these libraries and, as a consequence, there is considerable diversity in the way municipal libraries are organized and funded. A network of mobile libraries has been in operation since the early 1960s, to serve small communities and schools in remote areas. Of those, 38 operate as part of public libraries, two operate under the Ministry of Macedonia-Thrace, and another 11 libraries operate, since 1992, under the Union of Local Authorities, offering services to an equal number of prefectures.

In 2003, within the framework of the European Union's Information Society Operational Program, Public Information Centers were set up in 45 public and 30 municipal libraries; funding for networking and computing was included. Also electronic equipment to facilitate people with special needs to access the centers' electronic sources, was acquired. A network of mobile libraries has been in operation since the early 1960s, to serve small communities and schools in remote areas. Of those, 38 operate as part of public libraries, 2 operate under the Ministry of Macedonia-Thrace and another 11 libraries operate, since 1992, under the Union of Local Authorities, offering services to an equal number of prefectures.

Central Public Library of Veroia, Macedonia: Founded in 1952. Since 1976, it has operated as a public library. Under the direction of Ioannis Trochopoulos, it has become a leader in the field, implementing new technologies, cooperating with libraries in other countries, and participating in European projects. In addition to its innovative services, it offers free Web page hosting to local cultural associations and educational bodies and maintains the portal of Greek public libraries (infolibraries. gr) (Fig. 3).

Central Public Library of Sparta, the Peloponnese: Founded in 1972. Since 1989, it has operated in a new

Fig. 3 Public Library of Veroia.

building. It is one of the first public libraries to provide equipment for people with special needs. Under the leadership of E. Tzinieri-Tzanetakou, and in cooperation with other institutions, it developed and published library standards and building specifications for Greek public and school libraries.

Municipal Library of Thessaloniki (Founded in 1932) Originally under the leadership of G.M. Cacouris, it is one of the few municipal library systems, that since 1984 has been organized in a modern way, based on international standards and staffed by professional librarians. It comprises the Central Library, which has been housed in a new building since 2000, and a network of 15 branch libraries, including very active children's libraries. The total of its collections amounts to 220,000 books. It has the most comprehensive collection of newspapers and periodicals in Northern Greece (Fig. 4).

The Vafopouleio Cultural Center, also under the authority of the Municipality of Thessaloniki, was founded in 1983 with funds provided by the eminent poet George Vafopoulos and his wife Soula Gerakopoulou. The Center, which includes Libraries, an Art Gallery, and a Theater has had a positive impact on the cultural life of Thessaloniki.

School Libraries

While the establishment of the first school libraries dates back to 1835, school libraries have yet to be valued by the Greek educational system. Libraries in a number of private secondary schools (Athens College, Anatolia College of Thessaloniki, and Pierce College) were until recently the only examples of well organized and functioning school libraries. The centralized Greek educational system, the outdated learning styles, the heavy schedules of students, the absence of professional librarians in schools, and the lack of appropriate space are some of the reasons for this pattern. Also, the prevalence of the one textbook

Fig. 4   Municipal Library of Thessaloniki.

for every subject, the same in all primary and secondary schools throughout the country, is another reason for the low priority libraries have in the educational system.

The situation of school libraries is changing. The 499 libraries, founded in secondary education schools in 1999, were the first properly organized state school libraries. They were provided for the first time with an institutional framework by a special decision of the Greek Ministry of National Education (19/11/2003, acc. no. 128800/G7/Es. F.11/1240). The development of EDUNet, a national network for primary and secondary education, connects school libraries with the international information world. ABEKT has been used for the automation of all library functions, ensuring standardization. The establishment of another 266 libraries in secondary education schools as well as the pilot establishment of 25 libraries in primary education schools are well under way.

Academic Libraries

In Greece, public higher education is comprised of 22 universities and 15 Technological Educational Institutions (TEIs). Until, the late 1970s the educational system did not require the use of libraries, especially for undergraduate studies. Students relied mainly on professors' lecture notes or on a single textbook. This, along with the fact that the Greek educational system in the nineteenth century was influenced by the German educational model, resulted in the creation of small departmental collections in every institution. Laws 1268 (art. 7, par. 7, FEK A, 87/16–07–1982) and 1404 (art. 49, par. 5, FEK A, 173/24–11–1983), and Law 3404 (art. 16, FEK A, 260/17–10–2005), which provides for the existence of only main libraries and libraries at the faculty level, have been adopted to rectify this fragmentation.

The necessity to converge on and participate in the integrated European educational environment of higher education, and generous funding from the European Union within the Community Framework of Support (from 1996 onwards) were critical for academic library development. Libraries were staffed with professional librarians, the necessary technological infrastructure was established, their collections were developed, and electronic services were organized and offered. National policies in certain areas were developed and common decisions were taken.

National and Capodistrian University of Athens: Founded in 1837, it was the first university in the Balkans and the Eastern Mediterranean. Due to the fact that the university buildings were scattered over a large area, 47 independent brunch libraries were created, which, following a decision of the Rectorial Council in 1998, were united to form 12 Central Libraries. Although they administratively belong to and are supervised by the respective academic departments, they are "managed by" the Library Management Center of the University of Athens.

Aristotle University of Thessaloniki: Founded in 1925, it is the largest academic institution in Greece. Although a large number of branch libraries were originally created, currently the libraries constitute a single system with one catalog and common by-laws. However, they are funded and economically managed independently. Apart from the main library (in operation since 1974), the system comprises of four subject and 40 branch libraries. It has been a pioneer in automating its collections, acquiring electronic sources, digitizing its material, and providing electronic services to its users (Fig. 5).

University of Macedonia of Economics and Social Sciences: This is a Thessaloniki-based university that was founded in 1948 and began its operation in 1957. Its library was established in 1962, and since 1993, under the leadership of its director Anna Fragkou, it has been reorganized, provides innovative services, and participates in many European projects. It is also the leader among academic libraries in providing services to students with special needs and organizing seminars and workshops to train librarians in this area.

University of Crete: It was founded in 1973 but began to operate in 1977. Its library includes the main library in Rethymno and three branches in Irakleio. Under the guidance of Michalis Tzekakis, it was the first large academic library in Greece to be organized as a single administrative

Fig. 5 Aristotle University of Thessaloniki Library.

Fig. 6 University of Crete Library.

unit, and served as a model for the organization and management of other academic libraries. Michalis Tzekakis is also to be noted for his pioneering efforts for the automation of academic libraries and their cooperation on the national level. It was one of the very first libraries to have connections and cooperate with foreign libraries and has carried out many advanced and innovative projects; on the national level. The most serious attempt to create software for the automation of library procedures was PTOLEMEOS, which was in operation in various libraries from 1985 to 2004 (Fig. 6).

University of Patras: Established in 1964, the library started to operate in 1966 to serve the needs of a new University. Committed to quality, change, and improvement, it was the first Greek library in 1988, under the leadership of Catherine Synellis, to subscribe to electronic databases. It is currently involved in digitization projects and quality assessment efforts.

Special Libraries

In the 1998 library survey, 341 special libraries were recorded. They include libraries operating in organizations of the public or private sector (35.2%), research institutions (17.9%), hospitals (19.4%), cultural institutions (12.9%), banks (4.4%), churches (5.3%), and prisons (5%).[2]

The Gennadius Library: It was created in 1922 when the personal collection of Ioannes Gennadios, a diplomat, was donated to the American School of Classical Studies at Athens. The Carnegie Foundation undertook to erect the building on land provided by the Greek State. It has the personal collections of Lord Byron and the scholar A. Korais as well as 42 archival collections (including the archives of Ali Pasha, the amateur archaeologist Heinrich Schliemann, the composer Dimitris Mitropoulos, and two Nobel prize winners—G. Seferis and O. Elytis, etc.).

Benaki Museum: Its library was established in 1931. It is the largest museum library in Greece. Since 1991, it has included as a branch the library of the N. Chatzikyriakos-Gkikas Gallery, holding the personal collection of the famous painter.

Music Library of Greece "Lilian Voudouri": Although there are two more music libraries operating in Greece (University of Thessaloniki and Ionian University in Corfu), this was the first Greek library to fully deserve its name. It was founded in 1997 by the Friends of Music Society. It houses books, sheets of music, and sound recordings, as well as the archives of composers, such as Mikis Theodorakis, etc.

Other special libraries worthy of mention are those of the Benaki Phytopathological Institute, the Center for Planning and Economic Research (KEPE) and the Technical Chamber of Greece (TEE).

DIGITAL LIBRARIES AND INSTITUTIONAL REPOSITORIES

Following the trend for the digitization of Europe's cultural heritage and the provision of a common access point, Greek cultural institutions have been active in this area. There are 75 digital collections to date. Of these, 30 are full-text collections, 15 are book databases, five combine the types above, 19 are defined as institutional repositories, and the remaining six are collections of online periodical articles. As regards the software used, 32 are open-source applications and 30 collections use commercial applications.[7] Besides the above projects, one of the largest Greek digitization projects is currently under way; public libraries and the NLG, will digitize their rare book collections, estimated to amount to 15 million pages.

Anemi: Created in 2006 by the Library of the University of Crete. It contains digitized material on Modern Greek culture. Digital Library, the first institutional repository of a Greek institution, has been in operation at the same university since 1997.

e-fimeris: The National Library Newspapers Digitization Project has the full text of five newspapers of the period 1893–1983.

Psifiothiki: It is being implemented by Aristotle University of Thessaloniki, starting in 2003. It includes newspaper and magazine articles on Greek philology and theater. The university's institutional repository is being implemented using the same database.

Digital Collections and Institutional Repository at NTUA (National Technical University of Athens): The digital collection began in 2005 and includes 300 books and periodical titles. The repository began to operate in 2007.

National Documentation Center, Digital Library: Creator and owner of 22 mainly bibliographic databases, such as Argos and the full-text database of Hellenic Doctoral Theses.

NETWORKS, CONSORTIA, AND UNION CATALOGS

Hellenic Academic Libraries (HEAL)-Link: The Association of Greek Academic Libraries was established during this trend toward modernization. Heal Link (Syndesmos Ellinikon Akadimaikon Vivliothikon), began to operate in 1997 and took its final legal form under Article 17 of Law 3404 (FEK A, 260/17–1–2005). Its members are 37 academic institutions, 17 research institutions, the Academy of Athens, the National Library, the Parliament Library, and the University of Cyprus. The Association is a significant innovation on the library scene, since this is the first time there is planning and action at a central level. Today all academic and research institutions have access to digital material and services, a central union catalog was created, and an interlibrary loan network started to operate. The number of e-journals and e-books that the libraries have access to through the consortium is quite impressive, when compared to the number of journals academic libraries had access to in the print world. Access to the full text of about 14,000 journals is provided, and while it started off with 202,500 downloads, in 2006 it reached about 4.5 million. Claudine Xenidou-Dervou, Librarian at Aristotle University of Thessaloniki, is recognized for her significant effort in the creation and maintenance of Heal-Link.

Zephyr: Virtual Union Catalogue of Greek Academic Libraries. Created in 2003 by the Technologies and Information Service of the University of Crete Library, it supports MARC21 and UNIMARC formats and its design is based on the Z39.50 protocol. It includes all bibliographic records of Greek academic libraries in real time.

Union Catalog of Greek Academic Libraries: It includes the catalogs of Greek academic libraries. Its participants are the Academy of Athens, the National Library,

the Pedagogical Institute, the University of Cyprus, and the Open University of Cyprus. Works on its creation began in 1997, while it first operated in 2005. It is a main (natural) slave type catalog. It uses the UNIMARC format.

Greek Public Libraries Union Catalog: It includes the collections of public libraries and began to operate in 1999. The Central Public Library o Levadeia undertook its creation, with support from the Greek Ministry of National Education and the EKT. It is an integrated catalog that has a master record for each document and supports the UNIMARC format. The records of 10 libraries have been included to date.

Union List of Serials: Since 1984, the EAT has developed and managed the national union catalog of scholarly journals held in Greek libraries, through which online ordering for interlibrary loan can be done. Some 250 Greek libraries of all types participate in the project and make their print journal collections nationally available.

Openarchives.gr: A search engine, based on open-source software, has been in operation since 2006. It conducts simultaneous searches of Greek digital libraries and institutional repositories.

OTHER RELEVANT BODIES

National Documentation Center (EKT): Pressure exercised by the Greek scientific community resulted in 1980 in the establishment of the National Documentation Center. The Center, supervised by the Ministry of Development General Secretariat for Research and Technology, is the national organization for the development of an information system for science and technology.

The Greek doctoral dissertations database, and 20 more bibliographic databases, along with union catalogs of various types of libraries, have been developed by the Center. It has also produced an integrated library automation system, ABEKT, which has solved automation problems in many small libraries, which otherwise could not have afforded to purchase a commercially available system.

Organization of Juvenile and Adolescent Libraries (O.P.E.B.): Founded by the late Anne Gruner Schlumberger, a librarian originally from France, who wished to offer opportunities for culture and education to children coming from rural or underprivileged areas. Originally supervised and coordinated by the Ministry of Agriculture, in conjunction with local agricultural Cooperatives, it has been, since 1993, under the supervision of the Greek Ministry of National Education (Law 2174/1993). Today there is a network of 29 O.P.E.B. supported libraries throughout Greece, including three libraries in prisons.

National Book Center of Greece (E.KE.BI): This independent legal entity was established in 1994 by the Ministry of Culture. Its goal is to formulate a national policy on books. Its main objective is to support and organize the book trade, with parallel activities focusing on readers and books. "The modernization, support, and animation of libraries" are also included among its interests.

The Book Monitoring Unit (PAB): It was established in 1997 under the aegis of the National Book Center and is responsible for statistics and measurements about book production. In 1998, it developed the electronic book database BIBLIONET which contains Greek books in print.

Total Quality Management Unit of Greek Academic Libraries (MOPAB): It has been in operation since 1999, under the responsibility of George Zachos, director of the University of Ioannina Library. Its main objectives are to collect, process, analyze, and present data on Greek academic libraries, and to develop assessment indicators concerning academic libraries.

Union of Hellenic Librarians and Information Scientists (E.E.B.E.P.): The professional association of Greek librarians was founded in 1968, originally under the name Union of Greek Librarians. It was renamed in 2004 to encompass the new developments in the field. G.M. Cacouris was the first elected president. Its membership is around 2000. Regional divisions exist in the Peloponnese, Crete, Thessaly, and Northern Greece.

Association of Archivists and Librarians in Greece (E.A.B.E.): Founded in 2000, it is the professional body of graduates of University departments of archives and library sciences.

LIBRARY AND INFORMATION SCIENCE STUDIES

The first efforts to provide formal library education programs were made in 1957 through training seminars. On the invitation of the Greek State, UNESCO commissioned Leon Carnovsky (in 1960), professor at the University of Chicago, and Preben Kierkegaard (in 1962), director of the Danish Library School, to study the situation and make appropriate suggestions. They both proposed the establishment of a library science school at the university level. A 1-year vocational school was set up by the YWCA in Athens in 1961 and operated until 1976.[8] G.M. Cacouris, as its director, and Maria Alexandraki, as member of its faculty, inspired, trained, and created employment opportunities for a large number of graduates. G.M. Cacouris also contributed to the establishment of library science departments at TEI, the new institutions founded in the early 1970s, in order to foster new emerging professions and applied disciplines.

In 1977, the Department of Library Science was set up at the TEI of Athens. Its name was changed to Department of Library Science and Information Systems in 2003, to reflect the new developments in the field. Alkmini Skandali and V. Moniarou, were among the first members of its faculty and worked for the development of a modern curriculum. Over 4000 students have graduated from the department to date. A second department was founded in 1981 at the TEI of Thessaloniki. Under the guidance of professors G.M. Cacouris and M. Moreleli-Cacouris, the

first library and information science collection in Greece was organized, exchange programs with schools in Europe and the United States were developed, and courses on information technology started to be taught. Over 2500 students have graduated from the department to date.[9]

In 1993 the Department of Archives and Library Sciences at the Ionian University, Corfu was founded. George Bokos, contributed to the development of its curriculum, and soon the department started offering doctoral degrees; also since 2003, course-based master's programs have been organized, in conjunction with the TEI of Athens department.

PUBLISHING ACTIVITIES AND CONFERENCES

The publication of *Cataloguing Rules* (1969, 1974) and *Librarian's Dictionary* (1974) by G.M. Cacouris, as well as the *Bibliography of Greek Library Science* by K. Delopoulos (1974) were the first efforts to publish professional material in Greek.

The E.E.B.E.P. published (and continues to publish) the first library periodical, *Libraries and Information (Vivliothikes kai Pliroforisi)*, Issue 1 (June 1984). In addition, the E.E.B.E.P. has published handbooks and organized seven Panhellenic conferences (the last one in 1993). The Department of Archives and Library Sciences of the Ionian University has been publishing a yearbook *Document* (Tekmirion), since 1998. Also, two short-lived titles *Modern Library and Information Services (Sygchroni Vivliothiki kai Ypiresies Pliroforisis)*, Issues 1 (March 2000) to 21 (August 2003) and *School Library (Vivliothiki sto Scholeio)*, Issues 1–3 (2001) were published by private publishers.

Libraries have started to implement Web 2.0 applications in order to communicate with their users. The EKT publishes the electronic newsletter *Public Libraries...on the Move (Oi Dimosies Vivliothikes ... kinountai)* (Issue 1/June 2004), and the Goethe Institute brings out the online magazine *Synergasia*, Issue 1 (April 2006).

The EKT also published the Greek translation of the 13th abridged edition of the DDC in 2001. Since 2002, it has developed and made available the first bilingual (Greek and English) *Thesaurus of Greek Terms of General Content*. AACR2 was published by TEI of Thessaloniki in 1996.

The annual conference of Greek academic libraries is an important event for the library community. It was first organized in 1992, and the library of a different institution organizes it every year.

CONCLUSION

With the establishment of library science departments and the provision of European Union funds from 1996 onwards, a new era has begun for Greek libraries. Libraries have managed to overcome the adversity of many decades, creating a modern environment that meets the needs of the information society. New buildings have been erected, older buildings have been renovated and up-to-date equipment has been acquired. The appointment of professional librarians has been a significant factor contributing to success. Greek libraries, funded by European Union Programs, have started the digitization of conventional material and the management of born-digital material, and the provision of innovative services. They have learned how to cooperate, conduct research projects, and actively claim their right to participate in the new globalized information environment.

REFERENCES

1. ESYE (National Statistical Service of Greece), *I Ellada me arithmous*, 2007 [Hellas in numbers]. Available at http://www.statistics.gr/gr_tables/hellas_in_numbers.pdf (accessed October 2007).
2. EKEBI, Ionian University, Department of Archival and Library Sciences. *Programma katagrafis kai kodikopoiisis ellinikon vivliothikon*, Athena, Greece, 1998 (Project for the recording and coding of Greek libraries).
3. EKEBI. *The Book Market in Greece* May 2007. Available at http://www.ekebi.gr/erevnes/2006en.pdf (accessed October 2007).
4. EKEBI. *B' Panellinia erevna anagnostikis symperiforas kai politistikon praktikon*, 2004 [2nd Pan-Hellenic research of reading behaviour and cultural practices]. Available at http://www.ekebi.gr/erevnes/anagn04/index.htm (accessed October 2007).
5. ESYE, *Diathesi syskevon texnologin pliroforisis & epikoinnias*, 2006 [Appliances disposal of technologies of information and communication], http://www.statistics.gr/gr_tables/S803_SFA_3_ICTSurvey_03.pdf (accessed October 2007).
6. Moreleli-Cacouris, M. Tsafou, S. Working in the new information environment: the changing role of libraries and library education in Greece in the new millennium. In *The Meeting of Librarians of the Balkan Countries: Cooperation, Education, Quality*, Proceedings of the International Meeting Belgrade, Serbia December, 5–8, 2001 Faculty of Belgrade University, National Library of Serbia: Belgrade, Serbia, 2002; 179–189.
7. Georgiou, P. Papadadou, P. Psifiako elliniko periechomeno kai anoikti prosvasi [Digital Greek content and open access] 16th Pan-Hellenic Conference of Academic Libraries Proceedings Piraeus, Greece; University of Piraeus Library: Piraeus, Greece, 2007; 224–241.
8. Moreleli-Cacouris, Mersini. In *Library Education in Greece*; Keller, D.H., Ed.; Greek Academic Libraries: present situation and future prospects; The Howard Press: New York, 1993; 39–53.
9. ESYE. *Information Given by National Statistical Service of Greece* 2007.
10. *CIA The World Factbook*. Available at https://www.cia.gov/library/publications/the-world-factbook/geos/gr.html.

Greece: Museums

Maria Economou
Department of Communication and Cultural Technology, University of the Aegean, Mytilini, Greece

Abstract
The entry provides some general statistics about the number of museums and their visitors in Greece. It then examines the development of the idea of the museum from antiquity to modern times, focusing mainly in the nineteenth century, when the modern Greek state was founded. The first museums in Greece were associated from their beginnings with the strengthening of national identity and its links with ancient Greece, while they had a public mission and a strong educational character. In modern times the Greek museum scene shows an increasing interest in current museological concerns and practices. The entry covers in greater detail the National Archaeological Museum, the Byzantine and Christian Museum, the National Gallery-Museum of Alexandros Soutsos, and the Benaki Museum.

INTRODUCTION

There are over 280 museums in Greece that operate under the supervision and the administrative control of the Ministry of Culture (founded in 1971). The majority of these are archeological (165). They are legal entities governed by public law, but the Ministry also supervises 105 museums which are legal entities governed by private law. Apart from these, there are also a number of private, local authority, university, church, and independent museums, but there is not a reliable, comprehensive list of these, as they do not belong to the list of museums supervised by the Ministry of Culture.

According to the 2006 National Greek Statistical Service survey, about 2,800,000 people (Greeks and non-Greeks) visited the state museums (more than a third of whom were admitted free of charge).[1] A 2007 Eurostat survey on European Cultural Values reported that only 25% of Greeks declared that they had visited a museum or gallery within the last 12 months (2006–2007) (average in the European Community: 41%), while a higher percentage, 33% had visited a historical monument (EC average: 54%).[2] The Acropolis Museum was by far the most visited (annual average of over 1 million visitors between 1998 and 2005, while the rest had less than 400,000 visitors annually, on average). The same survey reported that 28% of Greeks use the Internet for visiting museum or library Web sites.[3] According to another Eurostat survey, in Greece 2.1% (4382) of people in employment worked in the cultural sector in 2005, compared with 2.4% (4.9 million) in the remaining 27 countries of the European Union.[4]

FROM ANCIENT TO MODERN TIMES

For ancient Greeks, "mouseio" was the sacred precinct of the Muses, the space dedicated to the protectresses of the arts. During the Hellenistic period, the term referred by association to a research center and congregating point for the scholars of the time and was usually associated with a large library, like the one in Alexandria.

During the Roman period, noblemen and officers of the Roman army demonstrated their affinity with Greek education by forming collections of Greek art (mainly fifth to fourth century Athenian), often looted and brought back home. These were also used as symbols of political messages and of military victories. It is, however, during the Renaissance that the contemporary meaning of the museum evolved. It is then that the idea of the public role of the museum also evolved, followed by the notion of the specialist who studies and curates a collection.

In the nineteenth century, the idea of the museum in Greece was closely linked with its role as guardian and tangible evidence of the ancient Greek roots, thus strengthening the modern Greek national identity. Following the emergence of the independent state in 1830, the primary role of the museums aimed at the protection and safekeeping of antiquities, and not so much for their display. Furthermore, unlike most European museums, whose early beginnings were rooted in private collections, Greek museums had a public mission and a strong educational character. They addressed all members of society from the time they were founded, even though they were in practice accessible only to a small educated elite. The new Greek state recognized early in the 1830s the importance of protecting the ancient heritage. It founded the first national museum in 1829 in Aigina (first capital of the state) and established measures for the protection of antiquities. In those early days, several ancient monuments functioned temporarily as museums, like the Parthenon, the Pinakothiki in the Acropolis, and the Stoa of Hadrian in Athens, where the capital moved later. In the rest of Greece, the movable antiquities were collected and guarded in schools, churches,

Encyclopedia of Library and Information Sciences, Fourth Edition DOI: 10.1081/E-ELIS4-120045540

and public buildings, since there were no funds yet for building museums. The first purpose-built museums in Greece were the Acropolis Museum (1874) and the National Archaeological Museum in Athens (1866–1889).

The first museums in Greece were associated directly with the strengthening of national identity and its links with ancient Greece. The influence of neoclassicism which dominated in Europe, as it was filtered through the modern Greek Enlightenment, emphasized primarily the classical period, even though the collections of the museums covered a period from the prehistoric to the late-Roman times. The belief in the historical continuity of Hellenism and the imitation of the ideals of classical antiquity served the rising middle class, which, influenced by the principles of the Enlightenment, aimed at the reduction of the power of the church and at democratic government. With the arrival of the first modern king of Greece, Otto (or Othon) from Bavaria in 1832, whereby Greece became a new independent kingdom under the protection of the Great Powers (the United Kingdom, France, and the Russian Empire), and the import of western-European political and cultural standards, foreign to the Greek society, the middle class resorted to a sterile historicism and a strong worship of the ancestors.

After World War II there was an expansion and growth of many new museums in Greece; in addition to archaeological museums (which still kept their original role), there were also ethnographic and local history museums and many other types (such as children's museums, theater museums, etc). This expansion of public museums was followed by the creation of many private museums and the involvement of the cultural departments of several banks and private companies and individuals. There has also been a recent expansion of museums of modern and contemporary art.

As the role of science and technology and industrial archaeology became more widely recognized, related museums have also become more widespread in Greece, although their development is much later than in many other European countries. Activities of the Cultural and Technological Foundation of the Greek Bank of Industrial Development (ETVA) and later, of the Piraeus Bank Cultural Foundation, have been instrumental in preserving and promoting Greece's industrial and technological past and in creating related museums.

CURRENT DEVELOPMENTS AND CONCERNS

Currently, a dialog about modern museums' role and ways of operating is becoming more widespread (often influenced by related discussions in the United States and Western Europe). This is evidenced also by an increase in the number of conferences related to museums as well as the number of university undergraduate and postgraduate courses like the undergraduate courses and the MSc in Cultural Informatics with a Museology option offered by the Department of Cultural Technology and Communication of the University of the Aegean, the interdepartmental MA in Museum Studies of the University of Athens, the interdepartmental MA in Museology of the Aristotle University of Thessaloniki, and the MA in Cultural Management of the Hellenic Open University, specialized journals, (Such as the Museology Notebooks [Tetradia Mouseiologias] by the publisher Kaleidoskopio, and the online Journal of Museology, published by the Department of Cultural Technology and Communication of the University of the Aegean[5]) and publications. Apart from the theoretical discussions, since the late 1990s there have also been increasing signs of a greater professionalism in the functioning of museums and galleries in Greece; collaboration with trained museologists in the creation of museums, exhibitions, and services; and improved communication with visitors. There have also been encouraging steps to promote professional development and training, where the Greek Committee of the International Council on Museums (ICOM) plays an important role.

In the twenty first century, the opening of the Greek museums to the public is primarily evidenced by educational programs offered by museums, which are becoming more widespread. The early pioneers for these were in many cases private museums (like the Benaki Museum which started its educational programs in 1978, and the Museum of Cycladic Art of the N.P. Goulandris Foundation, from its first year of operation in 1986), but also the Department of Educational Programs of the Directorate of Prehistoric and Classical Antiquities of the Ministry of Culture which was founded in 1985. An important initiative in this direction was the Melina Project, which ran from 1995 till 2003 organized by the Ministries of Culture and Education and the General Secretariat of Adult Education, which supported programs of museums and cultural organizations for primary school pupils (incorporating theater, music, dance and movement, arts, and audiovisual expression).

Another sign of the influence of contemporary museological thinking has been evidenced in the exhibitions created in many Greek cultural organizations since the 1990s. Several of these aim to incorporate audiovisual and interactive media, special lighting, and advanced graphic design in order to support more effective communication of their messages. The use of new technologies is generally spreading behind the scenes to support the management and documentation of the collections as well as for enabling worldwide communication over the Internet and presentation of the collections in different contexts. These developments are followed by an increased interest in the use of standards in all areas of documentation, such as terminology, data organization, and structure. Most Greek museums have some form of computerized collections catalog (even though, with the exception of the Benaki Museum, none of these are available online yet). There have also been initiatives by the Ministry of Culture for designing and using a common system among state-run archaeological museums. Some Greek museums have also experimented with new technologies for presenting the collections, usually in the form of information kiosks positioned in or near exhibitions, and with electronic publications, such as CD-ROMs and DVDs on the highlights of their collections. The privately funded nonprofit Foundation of the Hellenic World in Athens, established in 1993, was one of the early pioneers in the use of Information and Communication Technology and particularly virtual reality, such as the CAVE-like system, and more recently, the virtual reality Tholos (Dome), an interactive theater with stereoscopic projection inaugurated in 2006, with a seating capacity of 132 visitors. These efforts create an interactive experience for visitors mainly about the ancient Greek past.

NATIONAL ARCHAEOLOGICAL MUSEUM

The National Archaeological Museum is the largest museum in Greece. It was initially founded in 1829 at the Orphanage of Aegina (the first public building built at the first capital of Greece, which housed also the National Library), and its first director was the scholar Andreas Moustoxydis. According to modern museological standards, the first National Museum resembled more a museum storage area and warehouse, as its primary role

was the protection of antiquities. A few years later, in 1833, the Archaeological Service was founded in Athens in order to compliment the Museum's role of protection with those of research, study, and excavation. The Museum was transferred to the new capital of Athens in 1834 and was then named "Central Archaeological Museum," housed initially at the Hephaisteion, the ancient temple of Hephaestus, until 1874 and then changing location several times. It is currently housed in a neoclassical building from the end of the nineteenth century (completed in 1889), which was designed by Ludwig Lange and later remodeled by the German architect Ernst Ziller. During World War II, parts of the collections were boxed, removed for safety and buried. After the war, the redisplay of the collections was organized by the then director Christos Karouzos and his wife Semni Karouzou. The building has undergone several expansions to accommodate the rapidly increasing collections. After its more recent refurbishment, it was reopened in 2004 (Fig. 1).

Although the original purpose of the Museum was to preserve and protect all the finds from the nineteenth century excavations in and around Athens, it was gradually enriched with finds from all over Greece. Its over 20,000 archaeological exhibits cover the beginnings of Prehistory to Late Antiquity in Greece and are organized in five large permanent collections: The Prehistoric Collection includes works of the civilizations that developed in the Aegean from the sixth millennium B.C. to 1050 B.C.

Fig. 1 National Archaeological Museum.
Source: From http://en.wikipedia.org/wiki/File:National_Archaeological_Museum_Athens_building.jpg.

(Neolithic, Cycladic, Mycenaean), and finds from the pre-historic settlement at Thera. The Sculptures Collection shows the development of ancient Greek sculpture from the seventh to the fifth centuries B.C. The Vases and Minor Objects Collection, which contains representative works of ancient Greek pottery from the eleventh century B.C. to the Roman period, includes the Stathatos Collection, a corpus of minor objects of all periods. The Metallurgy Collection includes statues, figurines, and minor objects. And, finally, there is the only Egyptian and Near Eastern Antiquities Collection in Greece with works dating from the predynastic period (5000 B.C.) to the Roman conquest. The Museum functions today as a Special Regional Service of the Ministry of Culture and its five permanent collections are administered autonomously.

BYZANTINE AND CHRISTIAN MUSEUM

The end of the nineteenth century saw the recognition of the role of the Byzantine, late Byzantine, and later period as the bridge connecting historically and culturally antiquity with contemporary Greece. The objects surviving from these periods were treated as testaments to the continuous character of Greek civilization which survived from ancient Greece. In this climate, the Christian Archaeological Society aimed for the creation of a Museum of Christian Archaeology since 1884, when the Museum was initially founded and its director Georgios Lampakis started collecting related objects (mainly religious relics), even though the Museum did not have yet a permanent home. In 1914, the Byzantine and Christian Museum was officially founded as a national organization with Professor Adamantios Adamantiou as its first director, who enriched the collections with objects of national history and art. In 1923, Professor Georgios Sotiriou was appointed the next director and started organizing the collections under scientific principles. In 1930, the government offered to the Museum the mansion of Villa Ilissia, originally the home of the Duchess of Plakentia.

In recent years, a large extension was designed with a basement and buildings partly aboveground, which was then complemented by a varied program of exhibitions and activities. The recently redisplayed collections of the Byzantine Museum show the course of Greek art from the fourth to the nineteenth century. The collections include icons, sculptural works, ceramics, mosaics, manuscripts, and small works representing the artistic production of the Greek mainland and of other regions of the Byzantine Empire.

NATIONAL GALLERY—MUSEUM OF ALEXANDROS SOUTSOS

The National Gallery was founded in 1900 after the bequest of the jurist and art lover Alexandros Soutsos to the Greek State aspiring to the creation of a "Museum of Fine Arts" a few years earlier. Its first curator was the painter Georgios Iakovidis and it was housed until 1939 at the Technical University buildings (Polytechneion), where the first nucleus of the collection was formed from 1878. After the war, it was housed in several different buildings until it was moved in 1976 to its current purpose-built location. The expansion of the collection and the new needs of the Gallery have led to plans for extending the current space.

The main foci of the collections are twofold: renaissance art (a small but important collection) and the representation of Greek painting through time (from the late Byzantine period until today). Temporary exhibitions are usually supported by sponsorships, which cover about 50% of the Gallery's budget. The mission of the National Gallery focuses on the enrichment of the collections, the care and study of artworks as well as in "the aesthetic cultivation of the public, the ongoing education through art and the pleasure that it offers, but also in national self-consciousness through the history of Greek art that expresses national life on a symbolic level." Responding to this role, the National Gallery-Alexandros Soutzos Museum aims to present its permanent collections in a manner that highlights both the evolution of art and the parallel development of the society which it expresses. In order to serve this mission more effectively and expand its activities in the periphery of Greece as well, it has also founded a series of annexes: the Koumantareios Art Gallery in Sparta, the annex of the National Gallery in Corfu, and one in Nafplion which opened in March 2004, as well as the National Sculpture Gallery, inaugurated in 2006 and housed at the former royal stables in the Alsos Stratou in the area of Goudi in Athens.

BENAKI MUSEUM

The Benaki Museum is the largest and oldest museum in Greece operating as a foundation under private law. Its nucleus was the extensive collections housed at the private neoclassical mansion of Antonis Benakis, scion of one of the leading families of the Greek diaspora of Alexandria, which were donated to the Greek state together with the building in 1931.

The Museum collections are organized under the following departments: Greece at the Benaki (which covers Greek cultural objects from antiquity until 1922, aiming to show the continuity of Hellenism through time), Greek artists of the twentieth century (including the Gallery of the Greek painter Nikos Chatzikyriakos-Gkikas and the Studio of artist Giannis Pappas), the Department of Childhood, Toys and Games, Coptic Art, Chinese Art, Pre-Columbian Art, and Islamic Art. The collections also include rich and wide-ranging archives (photographic, historical, performing arts, and modern Greek architecture ones).

Fig. 2 Benaki Museum Pireos Street Annex.
Source: From Photograph by Erieta Attali.

Despite various extensions of the original building, the continuously expanding collections, needs of the Museum, and modern museological demands led to a large project of decentralization of services and buildings. This follows the satellite concept with a number of autonomous branches (located at several impressive and in many cases historic buildings around Athens) organized around an initial central core (housed at the original main building, whose displays are currently devoted to narrating the history of Hellenism over time). The projects included the establishment of the New Benaki at 138 Peiraios Street (Fig. 2), one of the central development axes of Athens, at a recently refurbished building, which currently shows only changing exhibitions and performances (art, music, architecture, drama, cinema, dance) and functions as a cultural center, but is anticipated to also house the rare (in Greece) Chinese, African, Indian, and Pre-Columbian collections. Another part of this restructuring and expansion project included the creation of the Benaki Museum of Islamic Art, which is housed in a neoclassical building complex at the historical center of Athens (near the ancient Kerameikos cemetery) that was inaugurated in 2004. The collection of children's Toys and Games will be housed in the Kouloura Building, in Palaio Faliro, a seaside suburb of Athens.

Apart from the high quality and size of the collections, since its foundation, the Benaki Museum has played an important role in the Greek museological scene. It was the first to organize an educational program, a museum cafe, a museum shop, an association of Friends of the Museum, and an Information Technology Department.

REFERENCES

1. General Secretariat of National Statistical Service of Greece, Statistical data, Social Statistics, Culture-Sports-Entertainment, Visitors to Museums per month (December 2006). Available at http://www.statistics.gr/.
2. Special Eurobarometer 278. *European Cultural Values*, (Fieldwork: February–March 2007, Report publication: September 2007), 119–120. Available at http://ec.europa.eu/public_opinion/archives/ebs/ebs_278_en.pdf.
3. Special Eurobarometer 278. *European Cultural Values*, 125 (Fieldwork: February–March 2007, Report publication: September 2007).
4. Eurostat—European Commission. *Cultural Statistics*, Office for Official Publications of the European Communities: Luxembourg, 2007; 54. Available at http://www.aulaintercultural.org/article.php3?id_article=2711 (accessed November 2007).
5. http://www.aegean.gr/culturaltec/museology/.

Grey Literature *[ELIS Classic]*

Joachim Schöpfel
Department of Library and Information Sciences (IDIST), GERiico Laboratory Charles de Gaulle University Lille 3, Villeneuve d'Ascq, France

Dominic J. Farace
Grey Literature Network Service, TextRelease/GreyNet, Amsterdam, The Netherlands

Abstract
This entry provides an overview on the definition and evolution of grey literature in the emerging environment of digital resources and open access to scientific and technical information as well as the social sciences and humanities. First, it gives some empirical evidence on the importance of grey literature in scientific publications from different domains, especially library and information sciences (LIS), based on citation analysis. Other topics include the impact of Internet on the production of grey literature, the place of grey resources in open archives and institutional repositories, the development of bibliographic control and standardization, and the difficulties of identification and accessing grey documents. The entry ends with some predictions on the future of grey literature and open questions for research in LIS.

INTRODUCTION

A great part of scientific results are published first and/or exclusively in reports, conference proceedings, preprints, working papers, theses, dissertations, personal communications, technical notes, etc. In spite of their widespread differences, all these documents are known by library and information science (LIS) experts as "grey literature" because they share two common characteristics: they are outside of the realm of commercial publishers, and they are rather ephemeral—often poorly controlled by catalogs, databases, and bibliographies.

How important is grey literature for scientific publishing, are there distinctions between the different research domains? What is the usual definition of grey literature, does it change in the environment of digital libraries and New Technologies of Information and Communication (NTIC)? What types of science and technology information (STI) does the term "grey literature" cover, how is it disseminated, how can it be assessed? In which way is grey literature related to and impacted by open archive initiatives? Who does research on grey literature, and what are the frontline topics for LIS research?

The following entry addresses these and other questions but acknowledges that there still remain unanswered questions because of the rapid evolution of information technologies and practices. Nevertheless, we conclude with nine predictions on the future of grey literature.

WHAT EXACTLY IS GREY LITERATURE?

There are several definitions of grey literature, the most common being the so-called "Luxembourg definition," which was discussed and approved during the Third International Conference on Grey Literature in 1997: "[Grey literature is] that which is produced on all levels of government, academics, business and industry in print and electronic formats, but which is not controlled by commercial publishers." In 2004, at the Sixth International Conference on Grey literature in New York City, a postscript was added to the Luxembourg definition for purposes of clarification "...not controlled by commercial publishers i.e., where publishing is not the primary activity of the producing body."

This definition in itself contains two of the main characteristics of "grey" resources: On the one hand they are universal and ubiquitous, but on the other hand, they are difficult to identify and to obtain through conventional publishing circuits.[1] The Luxembourg definition is also vague enough to reflect the problem of determining exactly what a type of literature variously described as "ephemeral," "nonconventional," or "underground" really means. To quote two experts from the British Library, "grey literature is difficult to define."[2]

Another definition is from the U.S. Interagency Gray Literature Working Group, "Gray Information Functional Plan," January 18, 1995, that defines gray (or grey) literature as "foreign or domestic open source material that usually is available through specialized channels and may not enter normal channels or systems of publication,

Encyclopedia of Library and Information Sciences, Fourth Edition DOI: 10.1081/E-ELIS4-120043732

distribution, bibliographic control, or acquisition by book-sellers or subscription agents."[3]

In fact, the term traditionally covers three categories of documents—conference proceedings, reports, and doc-toral theses—that are often printed in short runs. Never-theless, the borderline with "white" or "conventional" literature is permeable, since some conference proceed-ings are published by commercial publishers, as mono-graphs in serial publications or journals, and the same is true for some reports. As for doctoral theses, especially in the humanities and social sciences, some are also found on the commercial publishing market.

However, regarding all the other documents that circu-late outside conventional publishing circuits, the lack of "commercial control" raises real problems for academics and scientists as well as for information professionals when it comes to locating and acquiring them. The lack of "commercial control" and promotion also often implies a lack of "bibliographic control." In other words, these documents are often inadequately referenced in catalogs and databases, so that searches through this category of scientific information require specialized knowledge on sources and circuits.

THE WHO'S WHO IN GREY

Information professionals—including archivists, librar-ians, researchers, and teachers—have been contributing to studies on grey literature for nearly 30 years now, compiling a rich corpus of articles and, since 1993, international conference papers on grey literature.[4] In 1985, several European national libraries and informa-tion centers founded European Association for Grey Lit-erature Exploitation (EAGLE) to identify and disseminate grey literature. In the 1990s, governmental initiatives in France resulted in particular in the estab-lishment of two national "one-stop shops" for accessing reports of general or scientific interest (La Documenta-tion Française, INIST-CNRS). Other countries have des-ignated "deposit and distribution centers" [such as the British Library[5] for the United Kingdom or the TIB (German National Library of Science and Technology) Hanover[6] for Germany] or established portals for scien-tific reports (such as GrayLit for U.S. Federal Agencies), which was discontinued in 2007.

From 1992 on, Farace, a former member of the EAGLE technical committee founded GreyNet, the Grey Literature Network Service,[7] which organizes the inter-national conference series on grey literature. Confer-ences in the GL-Series have since taken place in Amsterdam (1993 and 2003); Washington, D.C. (1995 and 1999); Luxembourg (1997); New York City (2004); Nancy, France (2005); New Orleans, Louisiana (2006); Antwerp, Belgium (2007); and the next in this series—the Tenth International Conference on Grey Literature—

returns to Amsterdam in December 2008. The more than 250 authors and researchers in the field of grey litera-ture, who have contributed over the past years to the above conference programs form as it were the WHOIS in grey literature along with the host and sponsoring organizations, whose financial contributions guarantee the continuity and longevity of research programs and projects in the various sectors of government, academics, business, and industry.

The Textrelease Web site[4] provides biographical notes for over 75 academics, scientists, and professionals who work and publish on grey literature.

Special tribute should be paid to five outstanding per-sonalities who made lasting contributions to specific areas in the field of grey literature in the four decades from 1960 to 2000:[8] A.M. Weinberg (the United States), author of the famous "Weinberg Report 2000"; V. Alberani (Italy), organizer of a national program for grey literature; C.P. Auger (the United Kingdom), who provided the first Roadmap of Grey Literature Systems and Services; P. Wattenberg from the German Max-Planck-Gesellschaft, who specialized in the infrastructure of grey literature for the Japanese JICST (now JST, Japan Science and Tech-nology Agency); and A. Zemskov (Russia) from VNTIC, the National Public Library for Science and Technology, where he explored the free access of information and grey literature.

To date, only one monograph has been published on grey literature.[9] In 1989, in his second edition for Bowker-Saur, Charles P. Auger re-titled his work "Use of Reports Literature" (Butterworths, 1975) to "Information Sources in Grey Literature." This title change was indica-tive of the fact that reports were only one type of grey literature among increasing sundry of other types; and that the term "grey literature" was most suited to capture this phenomenon. Auger's work saw a 4th edition in 1998. Unfortunately, however, in this his final edition, the rise of electronic grey literature was almost completely neglected. TGJ, *The Grey Journal* (ISSN for the print edition 1574–1796) from TextRelease/GreyNet in Amsterdam is the only current journal dedicated to this topic. Since its creation in 2005, some 70 articles were published in the first four volumes. TextRelease/GreyNet also maintained a cooperative publishing agree-ment with PRQ, Publishing Research Quarterly (2004–2007) whereby the annual spring issue of that journal was solely dedicated to articles on grey literature that origi-nated as conference papers within the GL-Conference Series; and this accounts for another 35 journal articles. Both TGJ and PRQ maintain licensing agreements with EBSCO Publishing, whereby the full-text of both TGJ and PRQ are online, available in the Library, Information Sci-ence & Technology Abstracts (LISTA)-FT database. Ear-lier IJGL, *International Journal on Grey Literature* (ISSN 1466–6189) was edited in 2000 by Emerald (former MCB University Press). However, it ceased publication after the first volume of four issues totaling 23 journal articles; these articles are nevertheless still available on the Emerald server. Most other articles on grey literature are published in other serials in LIS or journals from other scientific domains such as *The Lancet*, *Marine Policy*, and *European Psychiatry*.

While it is rather easy to identify specific landmarks in the history of grey literature studies, it is perhaps first more constructive to indicate timeframes in which grey literature has developed. Five such periods can be distinguished.

1. They begin with the years leading up to 1979 in which numerous uncontrolled terms such as ephemera, fringe literature, fugitive literature, nonconventional literature, non-published literature, report literature, research outputs, small-circulation literature, unconventional literature, unpublished literature, etc., were coined to capture the growing phenomenon.
2. The period 1980–1990 covered the development and launch of national and international programs on grey literature (1985 is the year in which the European network EAGLE was created).
3. The period 1990–2000 included the creation of GreyNet, the Grey Literature Network Service (1993 is the year in which the first international conference on grey literature was convened).
4. The years 2003–2005 covered the re-launch of the Grey Literature Network Service showcasing new projects in the context of the explosion of digital resources, the movement for open access to scientific and technical information, and the Web2.0 (these research results were presented at GL conferences in Amsterdam (NL, 2003), New York (US, 2004), and Nancy (FR, 2005). This growth occurred notwithstanding the fact that EAGLE and its System for Information on Grey Literature in Europe (SIGLE) database was also terminated in 2005.
5. The current timeframe from 2006 onward is one in which new cooperative research initiatives in the aftermath of EAGLE-SIGLE are on the rise.

One of the recent projects is the OpenSIGLE project,[10] an initiative powered by INIST to provide access to former SIGLE records in an open source context. In the spring of 2008, GreyNet signed on to the OpenSIGLE Repository in order to preserve and make openly available research results originating in the International Conference Series on Grey Literature.[11] And, in so doing, the OpenSIGLE Repository has become the intersection of more than 25 years of bibliographic information on grey literature with 15 years of research in the field. Another initiative is the collaboration of researchers in the field of grey literature on institutional levels involving cross-country and international partnerships. And yet another recent initiative was the pilot for a distance learning course on grey literature for (post)graduate students, one that was accredited by the University of New Orleans (UNO) and which is now available to other academic institutions. These and other such cooperative initiatives were introduced and discussed at the GL conference in New Orleans (US, 2006) as well as the GL conference in Antwerp (BE) in December 2007.

ON THE (RELATIVE) IMPORTANCE OF GREY LITERATURE

Grey literature has a role of its own as a means of distributing scientific and technical information,[12] and professionals insist on its importance for two main reasons: research results are often more detailed in reports, doctoral theses, and conference proceedings than in journals, and they are distributed in these forms up to 12 or even 18 months before being published elsewhere.[1] We might add that some results simply are not published elsewhere.

But how do researchers actually use grey literature? One way of evaluating this is to analyze the citations given in their publications. In order to obtain empirical evidence, we present two different approaches: first, results from a Franco-Dutch study launched in 2004 and revisited in 2005 with evidence for different scientific disciplines, and second, results from a small study of bibliographic references published in four different journals in LIS.

Citation Analyses

Let us look first at some results from the Franco-Dutch study[13,14] which analyzed 64 citation analyses published between 1987 and 2005, citing altogether several thousands references. Table 1 shows the proportion of grey literature cited in publications from different scientific disciplines.

The relative importance of grey literature is largely dependent on research disciplines and subjects, on methodological approaches, and on sources used. In some

Table 1 Proportions of grey literature citations in selected scientific domains

Field	Grey literature citations (in %)
Soil science	14
Biology	5–13
Veterinary medicine	6
Psychiatry (addiction)	1
Psychology	3
Engineering sciences	39–42
Economic sciences	9–17
Sociology	7–9
Education sciences	14–19

fields, especially the life sciences and medical sciences, there has been a traditional preference for conventional distribution media (journals), while in others, such as agriculture, aeronautics, and the engineering sciences in general, grey literature resources tend to predominate.

In particular, public administrations and public and industrial research laboratories produce a great deal of "grey" material, often for internal and in some cases "restricted" dissemination.[15]

Publications in LIS

For a more accurate idea of the way grey literature is used in LIS, we analyze recently published articles from four representative, refereed LIS journals with impact factor.

Emerald's *Journal of Documentation* (ISSN 0022-0418) published 13 articles in the first two issues of 2007 (vol. 63), with 472 bibliographic references. About 16% of these references are to grey literature.

The first issue of 2007 (vol. 43) of Elsevier's journal on *Information Processing & Management* (ISSN 0306-4573) contains 17 articles with a total of 469 references. Of them, 80% cite commercial material (e.g., serials, monographs, and conference series), while the other 20% are grey.

The journal *Information Technology & Libraries* (ISSN 0730-9295) is published by the American Library Association (ALA). The four issues in 2006 (that comprise vol. 25) contain 24 articles with 512 references, 36% of which are to grey literature.

Finally, when we examine the 18 papers comprising the second issue of 2007 (vol. 12) *Information Research* (ISSN 1368-1613), we find 374 bibliographic references, 18% of which are to grey documents. Note that "Information Research" is an international electronic open access journal from the University of Sheffield (U.K.).

Four journals, eight issues, 72 articles with 1827 bibliographic references is not a large sample. Nevertheless, let's sum up the evidence in the following three points:

Grey literature apparently plays a considerable part in the LIS, accounting on average around 20% of all sources used. This figure may be compared with the citation habits in economics and educational sciences (see above).

Even so, citations to grey material vary widely between different papers from 0% to 50% and more, depending at least in part on subject areas and methodologies.

Most of the noncommercial documents might be identified as unpublished material e.g., doctoral or master theses, reports, legal texts, working papers, lecture notes, Web sites, and even posted messages. This also holds for some conference proceedings and other serial resources, for the identification of the exact nature of the cited material poses difficulties. However, all of these above mentioned types of documents have in fact been published by

what can be referred to as corporate authors i.e., organizations responsible for producing the grey literature, but whose primary activity is not publishing.

ON THE TYPOLOGY OF GREY LITERATURE

To return now to the definition of grey literature, we indicated earlier that the term traditionally refers to reports, conference proceedings, and doctoral theses. We will now take a closer look at what these cover in reality. The SIGLE database has been supplied since the 1980s with information from organizations in several European countries. Its more than 800,000 references are distributed as follows (Table 2).

Reports are the most numerous by far among the different types of grey literature in the SIGLE database. But the "reports" category covers a wide variety of very different documents: institutional reports, annual or activity reports, project or study reports, technical reports, reports published by ministries, laboratories or research teams, etc. Some are disseminated by national and international public bodies; others are confidential, protected, or disseminated to a restricted readership, such as technical reports from industrial R&D laboratories. Some are voluminous, with statistical appendices, while others are only a few pages in length.

In the other categories, citation analyses[14] offer a tremendous range of grey resources. Besides theses and conference proceedings, they also include unpublished manuscripts, newsletters, recommendations and standards, patents, technical notes, product catalogs, data and statistics, presentations, personal communications, working papers, house journals, laboratory research books, preprints, academic courseware, lecture notes, and so on. GreyNet in fact maintains an extensive online listing of document types, which are categorized as grey literature (Table 3).

However diverse, these documents all share one thing in common, they contain unique and significant scientific and technical information that is often never published elsewhere. The lack of descriptive referencing and adequate circulation is therefore, as we have said earlier, a real problem for scientific communication.

Table 2 Distribution by the types of documents referenced in the SIGLE database

Document types	Proportion (in %)
Reports	62.7
Theses	31.7
Conferences	2.3
Data files	2.1
Translations	0.9
Other	0.3

Table 3 Document types in grey literature

A
Announcements
Annuals

B
Bibliographies
Blogs
Booklets
Brochures
Bulletin boards
Bulletins

C
Call for papers
Case studies
Catalogs
Chronicles
Codebooks
Conference papers
Conference proceedings
Country profiles
Course materials

D
Databases
Datasets
Datasheets
Deposited papers
Directories
Dissertations
Doctoral theses

E
E-prints
E-texts
Essays
Exchange agreements

F
Fact sheets
Feasibility studies
Flyers
Folders

G
Glossaries
Government documents
Green papers
Guidebooks

H
Handbooks
House journals

I
Image directories
Inaugural lectures
Indexes
Internet reviews
Interviews

(Continued)

Table 3 Document types in grey literature *(Continued)*

J
Journals
• Articles
• Grey journals
• In-house journals
• Noncommercial journals
• Synopsis journals

L
Leaflets
Lectures
Legal documents
Legislation

M
Manuals
Memoranda

N
Newsgroups
Newsletters
Notebooks

O
Off-prints
Orations

P
Pamphlets
Papers
Patents
Policy documents
Policy statements
Posters
Précis articles
Preprints
Press releases
Proceedings
Product data
Programs
Project information documents
Proposals

Q
Questionnaires

R
Readers
Registers
Reports
• Annual reports
• Bank reports
• Business reports
• Committee reports
• Compliance reports
• Draft reports
• Feasibility reports
• Government reports
• Intelligence reports
• Internal reports

(Continued)

Table 3 Document types in grey literature (Continued)

- Official reports
- Policy reports
- Progress reports
- Regulatory reports
- Site reports
- Stockbroker reports
- Technical reports

R (continued)

Reprints
Research memoranda
Research notes
Research proposals
Research registers
Research reports
Reviews
Risk analyses

S

Satellite data
Scientific protocols
Scientific visualizations
Serials
Show cards
Software
Specifications
Speeches
Standards
State of the art reviews
Statistical surveys
Statistics
Supplements
Survey results
Syllabi

T

Technical documentation
Technical notes
Tenders
Theses
Timelines
Trade directories
Translations
Treatises

W

Web site reviews
Web Pages
Web sites
White books
White papers
Working documents
Working papers

Y

Yearbooks

Source: From http://www.greynet.org/greysourceindex.html.

The Internet, however, is now altering the entire landscape. Not only because of changing user behavior, but also, and especially, because more and more grey literature is being published on the Web. As one study from the German Centre for Information in the Social Sciences has pointed out,[16] the switch from paper to digital does not necessarily mean that more grey literature is appearing. Instead, the Internet has radically changed access and distribution methods, accentuating the ephemeral and volatile nature of grey literature. This same study also drew attention to the fact that many journals and the journal articles contained therein can be categorized as grey literature i.e., where publishing is not the primary activity of the producing body. The fact that in Europe, for more than two decades the SIGLE database did not identify journals and journal articles as grey literature may account in part for the apparent neglect of these two types of grey documents.

And yet, another special type of grey material is also likely to gain more importance. Until now, raw data—the basis for many scientific publications—are widely unpublished and inaccessible. Today, public research organizations are starting to develop national and international strategies for the control and archiving of these files, the data, and statistics (scientific data infrastructure or eScience, see Hey and Trefethen[17]). The principle of open access to datasets is generally accepted (astronomy, life science, physics, etc.) but major Scientific, Technical, and Medical (STM) publishers, because of their historical role and responsibility in the dissemination of scientific results, claim that such data should become part of their portfolio of added value products much like scientific journals and articles. Up until the mid-1990s, the Dutch Social Science Information and Documentation Center (SWIDOC), an institute within the Netherlands Academy of Arts and Sciences (KNAW), maintained a paradigm, whereby current research information and statistical datasets were linked to reports and other grey literature. Unfortunately, this model was abandoned. However, with the rise of repositories such as OpenSIGLE, where attachments and links to a metadata record allow access to the enriched publication, this paradigm can now be fully realized. The coming years will determine who will gain control over the deposit and dissemination of these materials. Will it be the public bodies or corporate information companies, who win out? The question is not only political but economic as well.

GREY LITERATURE IN OPEN ARCHIVES

Since 1994, the movement toward open access to scientific information has been crystallizing around various initiatives to promote open archives.[18,19] The first preprint server, ArXiv, set up by P. Ginsparg at Los Alamos in 1991 was a means for distributing research results organized by and for physicists, without intermediaries. This initiative was entirely independent of any commercial circuit for scientific publications.[20] In this sense, the server (which today contains over 410,000 documents) corresponded exactly to the definition of grey literature.

However, the case is more complex. "Preprints"[21] would not have existed without the prospect of "print"—in other words, ArXiv would not have existed without scientific journals. Ginsparg's aim was simply to circulate results quickly and immediately. The point then was not to bring commercial publishing into question, since Ginsparg did not offer any alternative to the peer review system still run by the conventional publishing circuit. ArXiv was in fact creating a kind of symbiosis between grey literature and traditional publishing, which was linked to the highly specific organization of the nuclear physics community.

But the crisis that has hit scientific journals along with the appropriation of new technologies of information and communication has together helped to turn the means of distribution into an alternative model of scientific publishing. This model has two objectives, one being economic: in that it offers a cheaper alternative to scientific publications by increasing pressure on STM publishers introducing competitive and parallel publishing channels. The other being an administrative one: by facilitating control over scientific production issuing from various research organizations and universities by way of identifying and evaluating publications through a central database.

Given the methodological and interpretative diversity among different scientific communities, one may well wonder whether a system that has operated for more than 15 years in physics will be equally effective in other fields, especially in view of the constraints induced by research evaluation. However, we are seeing derivatives of that system in the social and human sciences spearheaded by organizations such as the New York Academy of Medicine (NYAM) with their Grey Literature Report,[22] the Centre for Information on Low External Input and Sustainable Agriculture (ILEIA) with their LEISA e-magazine and database,[23] and the New York University (NYU), School of Social Work with their Web-based resource Information for Practice.[24]

What is the part played by grey literature in this new environment? The international "Directory of Open Access Repositories" (OpenDOAR), established by the Universities of Nottingham and Lund,[25] identifies 1,115 different sites, including 250 from the United States and 94 from the United Kingdom (June 2008). OpenDOAR indexes some categories of grey literature, including theses[26] and conference proceedings, but also learning objects (especially university lectures) and research results (data sets). Table 4 shows the number of open archives that contain certain categories of grey literature.

At first sight, these figures seem to suggest that grey literature is relatively well represented in open archives: 50% contain doctoral theses, and about 40% contain conference proceedings, reports or working papers. However,

Table 4 Presence of different document types in the OpenDOAR archives (*N* = 1115)

Document types	Number of archives	% of OpenDOAR sites
Theses	585	51
Unpublished	533	46
Conferences	427	37
Multimedia	262	23
Special	193	17
Learning objects	166	14
Datasets	62	5
Reports	56	5
Software	26	2
Working papers	16	1

the picture becomes less clear with an analysis of archive descriptions, which show that the number of sites explicitly dedicated to grey literature is considerably smaller: less than 20% are identified for doctoral theses, only 5% for reports, and just 1% for conference proceedings. Probably, a lot of grey material is hidden in categories like "special" (letters, images, sound, sites, etc.), "unpublished" (preprints, etc.) or "multimedia." Observations made at the Seventh International Conference on Grey Literature in 2005 indicate that these documents are often swamped within the sheer mass of documents that are deposited in archives and/or difficult to identify. The development of open archives does not therefore seem to have altered the situation of grey literature to any great extent.

To sum up, we observe a steadily growing number of open archives that (also) contain grey literature. It is nearly impossible to give an overall number of grey documents in these repositories. And even if it were possible, those documents are not currently representative of the national output of scientific and technical information. Moreover, there are even fewer repositories in smaller countries, especially outside of Europe and North America; and, non-English material remains until now largely invisible and un-retrievable.

IMPROVING "BIBLIOGRAPHIC CONTROL"

We said earlier that the lack of "commercial control" of grey literature implies a lack of "bibliographic control." In other words, "grey" documents are often inadequately referenced in catalogs and databases.[27] This does not mean that there are no standards or recommendations for cataloging reports, conference proceedings, theses, and so on. However, contrary to the situation with journals and books, the absence of commercial stakes has contributed to a (relative) "success" of the rules that have been set out.

The way in which the different types of grey literature are referenced still depends more on choices made by the bodies that produce, collect, or distribute these documents, rather than on any national or international standard (ISO, ISBD). The failure of the International Standard Technical Report Number (ISRN) is symptomatic in this respect. France, having been the only country with an active ISRN agency (INIST) for several years, eventually had to agree to the ISO, thus abandoning the ISRN. The only remaining exception in France concerns doctoral theses submitted to French universities for which the academic union catalog Système universitaire de documentation (SUDOC) imposes a uniform bibliographic format.

On a European level, input requirements for the SIGLE database forced the network's member countries to attempt to harmonize their "grey" resources around a single SGML format. But input to SIGLE ceased in April 2005, and its EAGLE association has gone into liquidation.[28] The predictable outcome is that each organization will be returning to its own referencing methods and rules abandoning any kind of uniform bibliographic control.

The rapid development of the Internet, and its ever-multiplying online resources, is affecting bibliographic control in two ways.[16] In one way, this "wild growth" is speeding up the decline in the application of formal and controlled standards, with the risk that grey literature is becoming "even more greyish." However, in another way, the same risk has also boosted global awareness of the need to define a few minimal data—called metadata[29]—in order to provide a framework for referencing digital documents.

Examples include: a project aiming to adapt the Dublin Core to reports[30] or doctoral theses; the French "Thèses Electroniques Françaises" (TEF) initiative, which is working on a set of metadata and a single XML schema,[31] the "Text Encoding Initiative" (TEI) designed to develop and recommend, at international level, common tagging standards that are independent from IT upgrades,[32] and the creation in 2005 of a TEI support centre for Europe located in Nancy, which will also address the matter of grey literature.

The problem of poor standards and lack of uniformity in referencing documents deposited in institutional archives was the reason why JISC (Joint Information Systems Committee)[33] was established in the United Kingdom in 1993. Its task was to look into the interoperability of these archives and to describe their resources in order to facilitate identification by end-users.

One final example: after the Seventh International Conference on Grey Literature in 2005, P. de Castro and S. Salinetti from the Istituto Superiore di Sanità in Rome initiated the International Steering Committee on Grey Literature (GLISC), which would develop recommendations (the "Nancy Style") for the production and distribution of scientific and technical reports as well as other grey literature. The second version of the document is now published on the Web,[34] with translations into French, Italian, German, and Spanish.

This last example is symptomatic in some ways of the problem of bibliographic control of grey literature. It is an international issue to which national responses have only brought partial solutions, thereby actually increasing the diversity of data and the difficulties involved in identifying and locating documents. Since there are no set commercial issues at stake, improved referencing will always be dependent on the initiatives and willingness of producing and distributing organizations steered by a few committed information professionals.

ACCESS AND DISSEMINATION

Identifying, locating, and obtaining grey literature is generally not easy—and this is inherent to its nature. To get some idea of the problem, readers might attempt a search for some of the reports, working papers, Web pages, conference proceedings, and doctoral theses cited by the authors of the four LIS journals mentioned earlier in this entry.

For 20 years, the SIGLE database offered a solution at EU level, insofar as its partner organizations were under obligation to keep referenced documents at their end-users' disposal via lending or document delivery services.

Users today are faced with a huge variety of sites, archives, catalogs, and databases, which makes searches for "grey" information not only painstaking but sometimes prohibitive—taking into consideration the linguistic difficulties involved.

In view of the rapidly changing face of STI within the digital environment, all the major traditional centers collecting and distributing grey literature, such as the British Library, the Canadian Institute for Scientific and Technical Information,[35] the TIB in Hanover, and INIST have undertaken to develop free access services to these documents, especially theses and preprints, but also reports and other types of grey literature.[36]

What is now needed are portals and search tools that are specifically dedicated to "grey" documents. Elsevier started to index in their SCIRUS search engine NASA reports and dissertations, MIT courseware, working papers and communications from a number of institutions, as well as theses in electronic format from the United States, China, India, and other countries. The Office of Scientific and Technical Information (OSTI) at the U.S. Department of Energy (DOE), hosted the GrayLit Network's unique science portal of technical reports from U. S. Federal Agencies. Now that this portal has been discontinued, we look to OSTI/DOE's Keynote Address at the Tenth International Conference on Grey Literature (Amsterdam, December 2008) in order to see if and how the global science gateway, WorldWideScience.org and its multilateral governance structure, the WorldWideScience Alliance will incorporate scientific and technical grey literature (including the social sciences and humanities).[3] A European comparative initiative from members of the former EAGLE association to launch a metasearch engine dedicated to grey literature collections is still in draft stage.[37] In the meantime, users have no other choice but to conduct searches on their own using whatever means at hand (Google), or to remain with the search services provided by established organizations.

The short history of EAGLE indicates some challenges of grey resources. Initially funded by the Commission of the European Communities in order to provide access to European grey literature and improve bibliographic coverage,[1] EAGLE was faced 20 years after its creation with major problems that lead to its liquidation:[28] The SIGLE database offered no solutions for online cataloging, metadata harvesting, links to full-text, and other resources. National input became increasingly unrepresentative of the national production, and was continuously decreasing while digital documents were not referenced. And last but not least, the economic model of its nonprofit, low-budget association did not allow for necessary strategic decisions, because further investment for the development of the database was not provided by the European Union or by the member institutions.

THE FUTURE OF GREY LITERATURE

Grey literature will remain a challenge for information and documentation professionals as well as an interesting field for research activities in at least six areas:

The need for a new definition: The traditional definition of grey literature needs to be further refined and/or redefined by way of an accurate analysis of new means of access and distribution, in line with Mackenzie Owen's observation that "Grey does not imply any qualification (but) is merely a characterization of the distribution mode."[38] What we see is that the current "Luxembourg" definition moved from emphasis on the acquisition of grey literature to the production of grey literature. And now, the definition should reflect both.

The need for an economic model: Despite the absence of "commercial control," collecting, distributing, and searching grey literature all come at a price, which may in fact be much higher than for journal article and book searches. To date, there is no clear economic model in this area and further analysis is needed in terms of investments, direct and indirect costs, acquisition prices, and so on. The case of EAGLE underlines the need for public funding and a sustainable economic model to guarantee the bibliographic coverage and full-text, enriched dissemination of grey literature.

The need to oversee archiving practice: New technologies of information and communication facilitate resource archiving in general, and there is strong incentives from the "open access" movement. Nevertheless, the question of "who should archive what, where, when, and for how long" has remained largely unanswered.

Aware of information policy and the concomitant financial aspects involved, answers are rather urgently needed, even if they were to now address only part of grey literature resources.

The need for a new "value chain": In the Netherlands, Roosendaal has in the past few years, been examining the process whereby universities re-appropriate publications. In his work, he highlights the radical changes taking place in the "value chain" of scientific publication.[39] This type of research and evaluation of scientific publications brings to the forefront major issues in the context of emerging STI trends. What is the future of peer review? Which "quality label" applies to working papers or scientific communications on blogs or in open repositories? Does the community approach of Web 2.0 offer a viable solution for the need for quality standards of noncommercial STI materials? The impact of new technologies in information and communication on the dissemination of nonconventional literature is a complex matter, and the potential field for research is vast. To date, research and analyses have only broken ground giving way to a vast and virtually untapped field of investigation.

The need to clarify the legal aspects: In our study, the issue of intellectual property rights in grey literature has been deliberately left aside. Nevertheless, the legal status of grey resources and rights in their use (deposit, archiving, distribution, etc.) is (another) major challenge for the future of this form of STI publishing. The national and international legal environment is evolving rapidly, and all restrictions, exceptions, and technical constraints [Digital Rights Management (DRM), interoperability, etc.] of the new laws on intellectual property, author's rights, and copyright also apply to grey resources. Nevertheless, very few documentary analyses have addressed legal aspects in the field of grey literature and their subsequent economic consequences. This issue, however, will be taken up in a plenary session during the Tenth International Conference on Grey Literature (Amsterdam, December 2008). While the outcome of this forum may not be conclusive, much needed groundwork will have been covered.

The need for education and training: At the Sixth International Conference on Grey Literature (New York, 2004), the results of an online survey in which 102 respondents participated not only indicate that an increasing number information professionals involved in grey literature are also involved in teaching and instruction but also they were in agreement (69.2%) with the statement that grey literature constitutes a field in information studies. Over the past years, training courses, guest lectures, seminars, and workshops have been organized by information professionals on the topic of grey literature. Most of these endeavors have undoubtedly had some impact on this field of information. As mentioned earlier in this entry, an accredited college course on grey literature was carried out via UNO's distance education program in the fall semester 2007. And, it has been rescheduled for the spring

2009 semester. Education and training is fundamental to the future of grey literature—not only for LIS students and their instructors but also for information practitioners in government, business, and industry as well.

While the above six areas of consideration remain as yet to be fully addressed, there has been considerable effort on the part of INIST and GreyNet over the past 15 years to use the results of research compiled within the International Conference Series on Grey Literature,[13,14] and, at the same time, to involve the existing pool of GL authors and researchers, who have contributed to its information and knowledge base. Without them, the future of grey literature would have little or no direction based on empirical data and would be simply *speculative*. It would have remained among the myriad of uncontrolled terms listed earlier in this entry.

CONCLUDING REMARKS

In concluding our current review on the state of grey literature, we might offer the reader some prospects in further need of reflection.

It seems likely that:

1. Grey literature will not disappear, but will continue to play a significant role alongside commercial publishing. Our research has led us to believe that information discovery into the various types of grey literature available in print and electronic formats is ever increasing.
2. The borderline between "grey" and "white" (commercial) literature will become increasingly indistinct, particularly in an environment that is moving toward open access to STI. However, in our limited research we find that the approaches and appropriations to these two kinds of publications are still quite distinct.
3. The proportion of "grey" documents published on the Web will continue to increase. We see this development closely linked to the production of grey literature in e-environments, as well as to retrospective activities leading to republication.
4. The Internet will encourage a greater diversity in the types of "grey" resources available (raw research results, notes and personal comments, lectures, newsletters, product catalogs, etc.). Also as our own research indicates, grey journals and the articles contained therein even now challenge reports as being the mainstay of grey literature.

It also seems likely that:

5. Bibliographic control of grey literature will remain problematic despite the trend toward standardization of digital documents. We find that this has everything to do with the application and use of standards, which are in transition.
6. Open archives will offer more appropriate services and functions for at least some segments of grey literature i.e., preprints, doctoral theses, and reports. We mention these three types of grey literature, because they have come to form special collections making them more visible in and for repositories.
7. Some organizations—especially in the public sector (e.g., national libraries and STI centers) but also in the private sector (e.g., Elsevier, Google, etc.)—will develop tools and services to aid in the efficient exploitation of grey resources on the Web. This in all likelihood is based on the response by such organizations to our research efforts.

However, it seems unlikely that:

8. Searching and collecting grey literature will become as straightforward as it is for journals and books in the traditional publishing sector. We adjudge that the increase in grey over commercial publications is the main explanation for this.
9. New tools for collecting, depositing, and archiving will make grey literature less ephemeral and volatile than in the past. Our research indicates that until an organization formulates a policy on grey literature backed by budget appropriations, the implementation of technology cannot be guaranteed and thus the environment in which grey literature has coexisted in the past will remain unstable in the likely future.

REFERENCES

1. Abel, R. Book and journal publishing. In *Encyclopedia of Library and Information Science. 2nd Ed., First Update Supplement*; Drake, M., Ed.; Taylor & Francis: New York, 2005.
2. Wood, D.N.; Smith, A.W. SIGLE: A model for international co-operation. Interlend. Doc. Supply **1993**, *21* (1), 18–22.
3. GrayLit Network, A science portal of technical reports (discontinued October 2007) .
4. TextRelease, Program and Conference Bureau. http://www.textrelease.com (accessed June 2008).
5. Purday, J.; Crump, M. The British Library. In *Encyclopedia of Library and Information Science. 2nd Ed., First Update Supplement*; Drake, M., Ed.; Taylor & Francis: New York, 2005.
6. Umlauf, K. German academic libraries. In *Encyclopedia of Library and Information Science. 2nd Ed., First Update Supplement*; Drake, M., Ed.; Taylor & Francis: New York, 2005.
7. GreyNet, Grey Literature Network Service, http://www.greynet.org (accessed June 2008).

8. Farace, D.J.; Frantzen, J. Four winds on the grey landscape: A review of four information professionals, their work and impact on the field of grey literature. In *Fifth International Conference on Grey Literature: Grey Matters in the World of Networked Information*, GL5 Conference Proceedings, Amsterdam, the Netherlands, December 4–5, 2003; Farace, D., Frantzen, J., Eds.; TextRelease: Amsterdam, the Netherlands, 2004.

9. Auger, C.P. *Use of Reports Literature*; Butterworths: London, 1975.

10. http://opensigle.inist.fr/ (accessed June 2008).

11. http://opensigle.inist.fr/handle/10068/697753 (accessed June 2008).

12. Sondergaard, T.F.; Andersen, J.; Hjorland, B. Documents and the communication of scientific and scholarly information. Revising and updating the UNISIST model. J. Doc. **2003**, *59* (3), 278–320.

13. Schöpfel, J.; Stock, C.; Farace, D.J.; Frantzen, J. Citation analysis and grey literature: Stakeholders in the grey circuit. Grey J. **2005**, *1* (1), 31–40.

14. Farace, D.J.; Frantzen, J.; Schöpfel, J.; Stock, C.; Boekhorst, A.K. Access to grey content: An analysis of grey literature based on citation and survey data. In *Seventh International Conference on Grey Literature: Open Access to Grey Resources*, GL7 Conference Proceedings, Nancy, France, December, 5–6, 2005; Farace, D., Frantzen, J., Eds.; TextRelease: Amsterdam, the Netherlands, 2006.

15. Ullah, M.F.; Kanwar, S.S.; Kumar, P. A quantitative analysis of citations of research reports published by National Institute of Hydrology, Rorkee. Ann. Libr. Inform. Stud. **2004**, *51* (3), 108–115.

16. Artus, H.M. Old WWWine in New Bottles? Developments in electronic information and communication: Structural change and functional inertia. Grey J. **2005**, *1* (1), 9–16.

17. Hey, T.; Trefethen, A.E. Cyberinfrastructure for e-Science. Science **2005**, *308* (5723), 817–821.

18. Branin, J. Institutional repositories. In *Encyclopedia of Library and Information Science. 2nd Ed., First Update Supplement*; Drake, M., Ed.; Taylor & Francis: New York, 2005.

19. Simpson, P.; Hey, J.M.N. Institutional e-print repositories for research visibility. In *Encyclopedia of Library and Information Science. 2nd Ed. (online only)*; Drake, M., Ed.; Taylor & Francis: New York, 2005.

20. ArXiv, An e-print service in the fields of physics, mathematics, non-linear science, computer science, and quantitative biology. http://arxiv.org (accessed March 2007).

21. Harnad, S. E-prints: Electronic preprints and postprints. In *Encyclopedia of Library and Information Science. 2nd Ed.*, Drake, M., Ed.; Marcel Dekker: New York, 2003.

22. http://www.nyam.org/library/pages/grey_literature_report (accessed June 2008).

23. http://www.leisa.info/index.php?url=library-search.tpl (accessed June 2008).

24. http://www.nyu.edu/socialwork/ip/ (accessed June 2008).

25. OpenDOAR, Directory of Open Access Repositories. http://www.opendoar.org (accessed March 2007).

26. McMillan, G. Electronic these and dissertations. In *Encyclopedia of Library and Information Science. 2nd Ed.*, Drake, M., Ed.; Marcel Dekker: New York, 2003.

27. Hanson, E.R.; Daily, J.E. Catalogs and cataloging. In *Encyclopedia of Library and Information Science. 2nd Ed.*, Drake, M., Ed.; Marcel Dekker: New York, 2003.

28. Schöpfel, J.; Stock, C.; Henrot, N. From SIGLE to OpenSIGLE and beyond: An in-depth look at resource migration in the European context. In *Eighth International Conference on Grey Literature: Harnessing the Power of Grey*, GL8 Conference Proceedings, New Orleans, LA, December, 4–5, 2006; Farace, D., Frantzen, J., Eds.; TextRelease: Amsterdam, the Netherlands, 2007.

29. Greenberg, J. Metadata and the world wide web. In *Encyclopedia of Library and Information Science. 2nd Ed.*, Drake, M.A., Ed.; Marcel Dekker: New York, 2003.

30. Jeffery, K.G.; Lopatenko, A.; Asserson, A. Comparative study of metadata for scientific information: The place of CERIF in CRISs and scientific repositories. In *Current Research Information Systems*, Proceedings of 6th International Conference CRIS, 2002; Adamczak, W., Nase, A., Eds.; University Press: Kassel, Germany, 2002.

31. TEF (Thèses Electroniques Françaises). http://www.abes.fr/abes/documents/tef/index.html (accessed March 2007).

32. TEI (The Text Encoding Initiative), http://www.tei-c.org (accessed March 2007).

33. Austen, G. Joint information systems committee. In *Encyclopedia of Library and Information Science. 2nd Ed.*, Drake, M., Ed.; Marcel Dekker: New York, 2003.

34. GLISC Grey Literature International Steering Committee, *Guidelines for the Production of Scientific and Technical Reports: How to Write and Distribute Grey Literature*; Istituto Superiore di Sanità: Rome, Italy, 2007; http://www.glisc.info (accessed March 2007).

35. VanBuskirk, M.E.; Wallace, K.M. History of Canada Institute for Scientific and Technical Information (CISTI). In *Encyclopedia of Library and Information Science. 2nd Ed. (online only)*; Drake, M., Ed.; Taylor & Francis: New York, 2005.

36. Boukacem-Zeghmouri, C.; Schöpfel, J. Document supply and open access: An international survey on grey literature. Interlend. Doc. Supply **2006**, *34* (3), 96–104.

37. Schöpfel, J. MetaGrey Europe, A proposal in the aftermath of EAGLE-SIGLE. In *Seventh International Conference on Grey Literature: Open Access to Grey Resources*, GL7 Conference Proceedings, Nancy, France, December, 5–6, 2005; Farace, D., Frantzen, J., Eds.; TextRelease: Amsterdam, the Netherlands, 2006.

38. Mackenzie Owen, J.S. The expanding horizon of grey literature. In *Third International Conference on Grey Literature: Perspectives on the Design and Transfer of Scientific and Technical Information*, GL3 Conference Proceedings, Luxemburg, November, 13–14, 1997; Commission of the European Communities DGTIMER: Luxemburg, 1997; http://eprints.rclis.org/archiv/00002596 (accessed March 2007).

39. Roosendaal, H.E. Driving change in the research and HE information market. Learn. Publ. **2004**, *17* (1), 1–6.

HathiTrust

Rick Anderson
University of Utah, Salt Lake City, Utah, U.S.A.

Abstract

HathiTrust is a partnership of major research libraries working together to create and maintain a digital archive of the human cultural record. Its programming includes not only a digital library but also a growing array of programs and services to facilitate scholarship.

HathiTrust is an international partnership of research libraries formed for the purpose of preserving, curating, and making access available to the record of human knowledge.

HathiTrust was formally created in 2008, but its roots can be found in conversations that were taking place among research libraries in the early 2000s, a period during which it was becoming clear that cooperative, large-scale digitization of printed documents might soon become technically and fiscally feasible. A watershed moment came at the inception of Google's massive Google Print initiative, which within months had been expanded to encompass what came to be called the Google Library Project.

The Google Library Project is a partnership between Google and a number of major research libraries including those of the University of Michigan, Harvard University, Stanford University, and Oxford University, as well as the New York Public Library.[1] Under the agreements struck with these libraries, Google agreed to digitize portions of the libraries' collections; partner libraries received a copy of all digitized works. The libraries negotiated the right to share those digitized copies with other libraries, thus laying the foundation for the broad collaboration that underlies HathiTrust.

The Google Library Project eventually became an international initiative, attracting participants from Germany (the Bavarian State Library), Spain (Complutense University of Madrid), France (Bibliothèque Nationale de Lyon), and Japan (Keio University) among other countries.[2]

Among the earliest and most extensive libraries participating in this project were those affiliated with the Committee on Institutional Cooperation (CIC), a consortium of research libraries affiliated with universities in the Big Ten athletic conference, plus the University of Chicago.[3] In 2005, the members of this consortium began making plans for a shared repository to hold the digitized copies of books from their collections—not only for the purpose of permanent preservation but also to make the content of those books more readily available to readers and researchers. In 2008, the libraries of the University of California System joined the shared initiative, and the resulting program was redubbed HathiTrust.[4]

THE "HATHITRUST" NAME AND INITIAL GOALS

"Hathi" is the Hindi word for "elephant," and it was chosen at the outset of the collaborative project to "(underscore) the immensity of this undertaking" as well as to "evoke memory, wisdom, and strength," according to John Wilkin, who was at the time associate university librarian at the University of Michigan and the first executive director of HathiTrust.[5] Early in the process of forming the coalition and defining its mission, the partner institutions settled on a set of six initial goals:

1. To build a reliable and increasingly comprehensive digital archive of library materials converted from print that is co-owned and managed by a number of academic institutions
2. To dramatically improve access to these materials in ways that, first and foremost, meet the needs of the co-owning institutions
3. To help preserve these important human records by creating reliable and accessible electronic representations
4. To stimulate redoubled efforts to coordinate shared storage strategies among libraries, thus reducing long-term capital and operating costs of libraries associated with the storage and care of print collections
5. To create and sustain this "public good" in a way that ensures the greatest availability of materials to the public but offers additional value to members, mitigating the problem of "free riders"
6. To create a technical framework for the repository that provides significant centralized functionality, such as full-text search, but also supports distributed development of tools and services to allow partners and nonpartners to meet specific access needs of their user communities[4]

Encyclopedia of Library and Information Sciences, Fourth Edition DOI: 10.1081/E-ELIS4-120049495

SHORT- AND LONG-TERM FUNCTIONAL OBJECTIVES

In accordance with the goals outlined above, the HathiTrust partners also agreed on a set of short-term and long-term functional objectives. These were not meant to define the scope of HathiTrust's mission, but rather, in Wilkin's words, to help "articulate goals for a quickly emerging organization, a way to give some initial direction until other mechanisms could create a more nuanced roadmap." These objectives were

Short Term

1. Creation of a page-turner mechanism
2. Branding
3. Format validation, migration, and error-checking
4. Development of application programming interfaces that would allow partner libraries to access information and integrate it into local systems
5. Access mechanisms for persons with disabilities
6. A public discovery interface
7. The ability to publish virtual collections
8. A mechanism for the direct ingest of non-Google content

Long Term

1. Compliance with required elements in the Center for Research Libraries' (CRL) Trustworthy Repositories Audit and Certification (TRAC) criteria and checklist
2. Robust discovery mechanisms, such as full-text cross-repository searching
3. Development of an open service definition, to make it possible for partner libraries to develop other secure access mechanisms and discovery tools
4. Support for formats beyond books and journals
5. Development of data-mining tools for HathiTrust, and use by HathiTrust of analysis tools from other sources[6]

PRESERVATION AND ACCESS

From the beginning, a central tenet of the HathiTrust program was the twinned imperatives of preservation and access. The purpose of the initiative was never to create a "dark" archive but rather to focus simultaneously on two overarching goals: first, both curating and safeguarding the digitized documents; second, making them as freely and easily available as technology and the law would allow. To this end, the HathiTrust partners determined early on that—while it would recognize and respect all legal constraints around copyright and other intellectual

property law—the program would not accept for deposit documents whose original owners wished to keep them inaccessible, where access rights could be lawfully granted. Books and other documents that are in the public domain are, thus, freely available for the general public to view and download (though HathiTrust members have enhanced access capabilities, as will be discussed below), whereas documents currently protected by copyright are available for full-text searching; search results do not include views of full-page texts but instead indicate the number and locations of occurrences of the search terms across titles in the HathiTrust database, enabling the user to see which books contain significant occurrences of those terms. The researcher can then pursue access to the relevant books through his or her local library or bookstore.

CONTENT

As of January 2014, the HathiTrust digital collection contained just under 11 million volumes, comprising approximately 5.7 million book titles, 286,000 serial titles, and 3.8 million pages of text. Of its 11 million volumes, 3.5 million are in the public domain. Just over half of the books are in languages other than English; more than 400 languages are represented in the collection. While the great majority (roughly 82%) of the volumes in HathiTrust were originally published in the twentieth or twenty-first century, the collection includes books several centuries old, including more than 25,000 books published during the seventeenth century and just over 1,000 from before 1500. (Though it is worth noting that roughly 350,000 volumes in the collection are of either not-yet-determined or indeterminate date.) A very large majority of the volumes in the collection deal with disciplines in the humanities and social sciences, especially history and literature, in a wide variety of languages.

Because HathiTrust's collection is built on digitized materials taken primarily from large North American research libraries (which comprise the roughly 115-member Association of Research Libraries, or ARL), there is significant and growing overlap between HathiTrust content and the physical collections housed in most ARL libraries. In 2011, a white paper prepared by Constance Malpas of OCLC on the feasibility of "cloud-sourcing" research library collections noted that, for example,

> in June 2009, approximately 20% of titles in NYU's Bobst Library (as measured by holdings in WorldCat) were duplicated in the Hathi repository; by June 2010, the rate of duplication has increased to about 30%.[7]

Wilkin subsequently found that this pattern was "remarkably constant" across ARL libraries. Writing in 2011, he observed that as of June 2010 nearly every ARL library could depend on finding approximately 31% of its collection online in HathiTrust. The rate of overlap (continues) to grow; by June 2011, I estimate the overlap rate to have hit a median of about 45%, and (to) reach something like 50% overlap early next year.[6]

MEMBERSHIP

To join HathiTrust, an institution must submit summary information about its print holdings. This information is used to determine the amount of overlap between the institution's holdings and the contents of the HathiTrust collection; that overlap partially determines the institution's membership fee, which is calculated according to two formulas. The first combines an equally distributed share of the cost of hosting public-domain content with a sliding share (based on local holdings overlap) of the cost of hosting in-copyright materials. The second is a cost multiplier designed to generate a surplus sufficient to support new services and programmatic infrastructure for the organization. As of January 2014, the multiplier is 1.5, though the Board of Governors will review that value periodically.

Members of HathiTrust have the option (though are not required) to contribute digital documents of their own to the collection. As of January 2014, there are no additional costs associated with deposit, as long as the materials submitted are formatted and submitted according to HathiTrust specifications.[8]

A significant benefit of membership consists in enhanced access to the public-domain materials housed in the collection (that are not subject to third-party restrictions). While these materials are freely available to the general public for online discovery and reading as well as printing and download, nonmembers can only print and download such materials page by page. Users affiliated with member institutions are able to download and/or print entire books from the public domain collection as single .pdf files.

Another member benefit is the ability to make in-copyright materials available to users who have disabilities that make use of printed materials difficult or impossible; if the library in question currently holds (or once held) a physical copy of an in-copyright book held digitally by HathiTrust, that library can obtain a full .pdf copy of the book from HathiTrust on behalf of such a user, subject to a set of guidelines and restrictions designed to keep the program in compliance with copyright law. (HathiTrust provides one set of guidelines for institutions in the United States and another for those in Canada.)

HathiTrust also provides member institutions with limited access to materials falling under the provisions of Section 108 of the copyright law—"where the print copies of the works are damaged, deteriorating, lost or stolen, and a copy is not available on the market at a fair price."[9]

REPOSITORY CERTIFICATION

In March 2011, Hathitrust was certified by the CRL as being compliant with TRAC criteria.[10] This certification came as the result of a one-year audit that examined HathiTrust's organizational infrastructure, digital object management practices and technologies, technical infrastructure, and security practices. CRL found HathiTrust to be most solidly in compliance with regard to the latter category and most in need of improvement (though still certifiably robust) in the first; ongoing certification requires HathiTrust to report progress every two years in several areas, including significant changes in system architecture, new policies, additions to content, financial activities, and significant organizational events.[11]

GOVERNANCE

HathiTrust was originally chartered for a five-year period, from 2008 to 2012, with an expectation of formal review of its governance and structure in the third year.

Prior to 2012, HathiTrust was governed by an Executive Committee, which was composed of library administrators from its founding institutions: two members each from Indiana University, the University of Michigan, and the University of California system. In addition, the Committee included HathiTrust's executive director and one member drawn from another CIC institution. The Executive Committee was guided by a Strategic Advisory Board, the chair of which acted as a member of the Executive Committee ex officio. This arrangement was intended to be provisional until a new governance structure could be put in place with broader input from the HathiTrust membership. The organization contracted with Ithaka S&R to conduct a three-year review of the organization's progress.

In late 2011, HathiTrust held a Constitutional Convention for the purpose of creating a new and more permanent governance structure and set of bylaws. Over the course of two days, delegates from all HathiTrust partner institutions and consortia considered and voted on ballot proposals dealing with such issues as an approval process for development initiatives, the disposition of U.S. government documents, and the new governance structure.[12]

The governance structure settled upon in the Constitutional Convention provides for a Board of Governors consisting of 13 members: six appointed by the founding HathiTrust institutions, six elected by the membership, and the Executive Director (in a nonvoting role). Of these 13 board members, five (including the Executive Director, ex officio) serve as an Executive Committee. All board members are elected to a three-year term; however, in order to establish a staggered rotation of members (and thus ensure some degree of continuity), members of the inaugural board were assigned a variety of term lengths from three to five years.

INITIATIVES, TOOLS, AND SERVICES

In addition to serving as a permanent repository and offering search and download capabilities, HathiTrust has developed a variety of services designed to add value to the hosted content. Such development is ongoing; as of this writing, notable tools and services include:

HathiTrust Research Center

The HathiTrust Research Center (HTRC) is the research arm of HathiTrust and makes possible computational use of the HathiTrust digital library for nonprofit and educational researchers. A joint venture of Indiana University, the University of Illinois Urbana-Champaign, and HathiTrust, the HTRC provides a secure environment in which researchers can use text mining and other data-intensive research techniques to interrogate and analyze digitized texts on a massive scale. Currently, the HTRC environment allows researchers to conduct such analysis of public-domain titles, but HathiTrust is working toward agreements that would allow such use of in-copyright works as well.

HathiTrust has created e-mail listservs, a User Community wiki, and a portal for workset construction, and has hosted two annual 1-1/2-day "UnCamps" for those in the research community interested in learning how to make use of the HTRC's offerings.[13]

mPach

mPach is a project of the University of Michigan's Michigan Publishing program, in collaboration with the University of Michigan Library's Digital Library Production Service. It is designed to provide support for born-digital publications, and to that end, in collaboration with HathiTrust, mPach will provide a modular platform for the creation and publication of open-access journals and will offer integration with other open journal applications such as Open Journal Systems. As of January 2014, completion of the project is projected for sometime between October and December of that year.[14]

Zephir

Zephir is a bibliographic metadata management system developed for HathiTrust by the California Digital Library.[15] It is the first component of HathiTrust that has been developed and will be managed by an entity outside of the University of Michigan.

Copyright Review

HathiTrust member institutions have been working since 2008 to identify materials in the collection that are in the public domain. In some cases, this is easy to determine based on standard bibliographic data points, but in many cases such a determination requires significant work. This effort has resulted in the public availability of hundreds of thousands of titles.

Government Documents

In 2013, HathiTrust began a project to preserve and provide access to a comprehensive collection of U.S. federal government documents (which are in the public domain by definition). As of January 2014, this project is still underway, beginning with the creation of a formal registry of those documents including information about which of them are available in digital formats.[16]

Shared Print Monograph Archive

In an effort to help libraries reduce their long-term storage and preservation costs, HathiTrust is developing a framework for a distributed network of print monograph archives; the network's holdings will correspond to HathiTrust's digital collection.

DPN Participation

The Digital Preservation Network is a network of digital repositories working to "ensure that the complete scholarly record is preserved for future generations."[17] HathiTrust is working with that initiative to help define its technical, business, and administrative models. In November 2013, it announced its intention to become a "replicating node" in the DPN.[18]

ISSUES AND CONTROVERSIES

Because the HathiTrust is built on a multimillion-volume repository of digitized books, most of which are still under copyright, there have been questions and issues surrounding both the legality of the original digitization project (carried out primarily by Google, Microsoft, and the Internet Archive) and of HathiTrust's subsequent use of the collection.

Authors Guild v. Google

In 2005, Google was sued by the Authors Guild of America and the Association of American Publishers (AAP), both of whom asserted that Google's digitization project constituted massive copyright infringement.[19] A finding for the plaintiffs in either or both of these cases would have had significant implications for HathiTrust's ability to continue providing access to its collection. The lawsuits were eventually consolidated and the parties reached a settlement; however, the proposed settlement was rejected and a separate settlement was subsequently reached between Google and the AAP. The Authors Guild persisted with its suit, which was dismissed in 2013. As of January 2014, the Authors Guild intends to appeal that decision.

Authors Guild vs. HathiTrust et al.

In 2011, the Authors Guild filed suit against HathiTrust and the governing bodies of its founding universities, asking for "injunctive and declaratory relief" from what it characterized as "the systematic, concerted, widespread and unauthorized reproduction and distribution" of the digitized books in HathiTrust's collection. The lawsuit did not ask for damages, but rather asked the court to affirm and declare the illegality of HathiTrust's actions and to impound the digital books.[20]

One aspect of the case came to dominate public discussion; this was HathiTrust's plan to make "orphan works" available online to those who have "the right to check out these works from the Library's print collection for scholarly and educational purposes."[21] Orphan works are generally defined as titles that are under copyright, but whose copyright holder is unknown. Since orphan works are almost invariably out of print, they are unavailable for purchase in the primary book market (though used copies may be available in the secondary market). Michigan's justification for providing free—though limited—access to the full text of the digitized orphan works to its faculty and students was that since the copyright holders were unknown or could not be located, since the books were not commercially available anyway, and since access would be limited to a controlled population of Michigan-affiliated readers, the provision of them was very unlikely to harm any stakeholder in the work. In addition, HathiTrust publicly offered to curtail providing access to any orphan work whose copyright holder identified himself or herself and submitted a form provided for the purpose.

The program began in 2011 with the posting of a list of orphan works identified as candidates for this treatment; the list was to remain live for 90 days, during which copyright holders were invited to contact HathiTrust either to formally grant permission or to withhold it. Following the 90-day period, the books would be made available, but copyright holders could subsequently contact HathiTrust and request a takedown at any point thereafter, and HathiTrust promised to honor that request.[22]

The Authors Guild, however, objected quickly—noting, among other things, that it had succeeded without too much effort in identifying and locating rightsholders to several titles on HathiTrust's list of orphan works. Michigan subsequently removed some titles from the list and then announced a suspension of the program. In a public statement, the institution said that "the close and welcome scrutiny of the list of potential orphan works has revealed a number of errors, some of them serious. This tells us that our pilot process is flawed." The statement expressed the Michigan Library's intention to "create a more robust, transparent, and fully documented process," at which point it would "proceed with the work, because we remain as certain as ever that our proposed uses of orphan works are lawful and important to the future of scholarship and the libraries that support it."[23]

In October 2012, the court dismissed the Authors Guild's suit, finding in particular that its claims regarding the orphan works project were "not ripe for adjudication," given that the project had been stopped too soon for its ultimate nature and impact to be assessed.[24] The Authors Guild is appealing the decision.

REFERENCES

1. Google Books Library Partners, http://books.google.com/intl/en/googlebooks/library/partners.html (accessed January 2014).
2. Wikipedia, Google Books. http://en.wikipedia.org/wiki/Google_books (accessed January 2014).
3. History of CIC, http://www.cic.net/about-cic/history-of-cic (accessed January 2014).
4. York, J HathiTrust: The elephant in the library. Libr. Issues: Brief. Facul. Administr. 2012, 32 (3), 1–4.
5. HathiTrust, Launch of HathiTrust. October 13, 2008, http://www.hathitrust.org/press_10-13-2008 (accessed January 2014).
6. Wilkin, J. HathiTrust's past, present, and future. Perspectives from HathiTrust, posted 10/17/11, http://www.hathitrust.org/blogs/perspectives-from-hathitrust/hathitrust039s-past-present-and-future (accessed January 2014).
7. Malpas, Constance. OCLC Research, Cloud-sourcing research collections: managing print in the mass-digitized library environment. Last modified January 01, 2011 (accessed January 14, 2014).
8. HathiTrust, Ingest tools. http://www.hathitrust.org/ingest_tools (accessed January 14, 2014).
9. HathiTrust. Access out-of-print and brittle or missing items, http://www.hathitrust.org/out-of-print-brittle (accessed January 14, 2014).
10. Center for Research Libraries, Trustworthy repositories audit & certification: criteria and checklist, 2007, http://www.crl.edu/sites/default/files/attachments/pages/trac_0.pdf (accessed January 14, 2014).

11. HathiTrust, HathiTrust trustworthy repository audit and certification. http://www.hathitrust.org/trac/ (accessed January 14 2014).

12. HathiTrust, Constitutional convention ballot proposals, http://www.hathitrust.org/constitutional_convention2011_ballot_proposals (accessed January 14, 2014).

13. HathiTrust, Our research center. http://www.hathitrust.org/htrc (accessed January 14, 2014).

14. HathiTrust, mPach, http://www.hathitrust.org/mpach (accessed January 14, 2014).

15. HathiTrust, Zephir, http://www.hathitrust.org/zephir (accessed January 14, 2014).

16. HathiTrust, Creating a registry of US federal government documents, http://www.hathitrust.org/usgovdocs_registry (accessed January 14, 2014).

17. The Digital Preservation Network, The DPN vision. http://www.dpn.org/about/ (accessed January 14, 2014).

18. HathiTrust. HathiTrust announces intention to become a DPN replicating node, http://www.hathitrust.org/hathitrust_dpn_announcement (accessed January 14, 2014).

19. Wikipedia, Authors Guild v. Google, http://en.wikipedia.org/wiki/Authors_Guild_v._Google (accessed January 14, 2014).

20. Authors Guild, Inc.v. HathiTrust, No. 11 CV 6351 (S.D.N.Y. Sept. 12, 2011). http://docs.justia.com/cases/federal/district-courts/new-york/nysdce/1:2011cv06351/384619/173 (accessed January 14, 2014).

21. University of Michigan Libraries, Orphan access and use policies, http://www.lib.umich.edu/orphan-works/access-and-use-policies (accessed January 14, 2104).

22. University of Michigan Libraries. Copyright holders—we want to hear from you! http://www.lib.umich.edu/orphan-works/copyright-holders (accessed January 14, 2014).

23. University of Michigan Libraries. U-M Library statement on the Orphan Works Project, http://www.lib.umich.edu/news/u-m-library-statement-orphan-works-project (accessed January 14, 2014).

24. Authors Guild, Inc. v. HathiTrust, No. 11 CV 6351 (S.D.N.Y. Oct. 10, 2012). http://docs.justia.com/cases/federal/district-courts/new-york/nysdce/1:2011cv06351/384619/156 (accessed January 14, 2014).

Health Science Professional Literatures and Their Users

Cheryl Dee
School of Library and Information Science, University of South Florida, Tampa, Florida, U.S.A.

Jocelyn Rankin
Centers for Disease Control and Prevention Library, Atlanta, Georgia, U.S.A.

Abstract

Information behaviors of the major health sciences professionals are described, in particular those of physicians, nurses, and public health workers. Biomedical researchers are mentioned to illustrate new approaches to information. Continuing barriers to information use include information overload and lack of time, but there is also increasing use of Web resources and growing self-sufficiency. Strong preferences are apparent for information resources that are convenient, accessible, customized, and "just in time." Challenges remain in motivating busy health care professionals to adopt routine information-seeking strategies. Future work should focus on embedding information in workflows by using new technologies and new workers such as informationists.

The dynamics between health care professionals and their information use forms the basis for bridging the gap between the biomedical knowledge base and the use of it in daily medical practice and clinical decision-making. Health care professionals' information needs typically require responses within a short time frame. They need information that is credible, current, and relevant to the specific case at hand. While the knowledge base of the health sciences is the biomedical literature, primarily the journals, additional sources such as collegial expertise, continuing education programs, drug information resources, and various online knowledge services augment the published literature. Library services and technologies that connect the health care professional with this knowledge base in a meaningful and efficient way must be grounded in information-seeking and information-use studies.

Today's health professionals span many areas of practice. This entry focuses primarily on information behaviors of three major professional groups: physicians, nurses, and public health workers. Biomedical researchers who support clinical practice are mentioned briefly because their transforming approach to information may well foreshadow the future information behaviors of all health scientists. Allied health professionals are not addressed in this entry as there is still a need for a solid base of information studies in most of these disciplines.

PHYSICIANS

The 760,000 physicians in the United States are found largely in medical practice; they also work in medical education, health care administration, and research. Physician education programs add to this workforce through 8500 residency programs that train 11,000 residents. The 126 schools of medicine maintain enrollments of more than 70,000 students, and the 20 schools of osteopathic medicine educate another 13,500 students. [1–3]

During the last 25 years, research has contributed to a better understanding of information needs and information-seeking practices of physicians. The published literature in the 1980s and early 1990s set the stage for subsequent studies on physicians' information-related behaviors. Much of this research focused on physicians' preferred information sources, whether patient care questions were being answered, and whether physicians' information needs were being met. These studies showed that physicians frequently asked colleagues for information, used their personal libraries, and consulted textbook sources.[4–6] Covell found that many information needs were not recognized by practicing physicians, and that others went unanswered.[7] Osheroff analyzed information requests during clinical teaching and found that there were frequent requests but that often these requests required synthesis of patients' information and medical knowledge and therefore were difficult to fulfill.[8] Gorman showed how the biomedical literature could answer primary-care information needs, while Dee's study of rural physicians proposed a new information-retrieval system that would build on the positive factors related to collegial consults and would provide concise, relevant, and synthesized answers to specific questions in a format conducive to rapid comprehension and immediate use.[4,9]

Numerous factors influence physicians when they consider using an information resource. These factors include convenience of access, habit, reliability, quality, speed of use, and applicability.[10] Also availability, credibility, currency, rapid delivery, compatibility with their own and their colleagues' experience, and cost in time, effort, and

Encyclopedia of Library and Information Sciences, Fourth Edition DOI: 10.1081/E-ELIS4-120044279

money have been found to affect physicians' preferences for information resources.[6,11–14] The organizational culture and an emphasis on use of the biomedical knowledge base, along with searching skills, may be leading factors stimulating use of online systems by health care professionals.[15]

Common barriers to health professionals' information seeking include lack of time to search, information overload, the belief that there is likely to be no answer, and lack of urgency.[10] When searching for answers to physicians' questions, Ely developed a taxonomy of obstacles encountered. Of the 59 obstacles identified, six were considered particularly prominent, including not having adequate time to find information, difficulty framing a complex issue into an answerable question, difficulty selecting the best search strategy, failure of a seemingly appropriate resource to answer the question, uncertainty in knowing when all the relevant evidence had been gathered, and lack of prepackaged syntheses of multiple bits of evidence.[16]

After a slow uptake of the use of technology, physicians are now employing and benefiting from the Internet and online information resources. An important early study of use of the National Library of Medicine's MEDLINE database by physicians for clinical problem-solving found that MEDLINE searches were performed by and for physicians to meet a diversity of clinical-information needs. Physicians reported that in situations involving individual patients, rapid access to the biomedical literature via MEDLINE was at times critical to a patient's care, and that such rapid access favorably influenced patients' outcomes.[17] More recent studies are showing that Web-based information resources are playing an increasingly central role in the delivery of care. The use of multiple online information resources has been shown to enhance the accuracy of answers provided by experienced clinicians to typical clinical problems.[18] And Bennett found that the average time spent by physicians on the Internet had doubled between 2001 and 2003, with the primary reasons being to access the latest research, locate information in a specific disease area, and find information for patients' problems.[19] While information overload on the Internet remains a barrier, physicians are now more skilled in using preferred Web sites, and they are encountering fewer technical challenges and becoming increasingly confident that they will find needed information.[20] Patterns of use of Web-based resources may vary somewhat by physician specialty, as was shown in a study comparing family physicians with specialists' use of the Internet. Family physicians were more likely to seek patient-oriented information while specialists searched the literature and exchanged information with colleagues. Almost half of the family physicians involved in this study utilized handheld computers, primarily for drug reference. [11]

The emphasis on the practice of evidence-based medicine (EBM), a formal process that enables patient-care decisions to be based on "the conscientious, explicit and judicious use of current best evidence" that has been complied through systematic research,[21] has led to new efforts to convey the biomedical knowledge base to the point of care. The need to overcome barriers to accessing the evidence base was underscored by the Institute of Medicine's report on improving the quality of our nation's health care system.[22] There are formidable challenges in locating the best evidence and applying it at the point of care given the ever-growing amount of biomedical literature and its sometimes conflicting viewpoints, the distance between the evidence and patient care, and the variables inherent in individual patient cases. The market place has stepped up with several electronic evidence-summary services. In a small study of EBM summary databases, Schwartz found that slightly more than half of clinical questions could be fully or partially answered, and that these answers often did modify physicians' opinions and influence patient care. However, the time spent in searching for answers was greater than most clinical settings would allow.[23] When an online evidence system was readily available to health professionals in Australia, it was used by almost half of the clinicians. Use was shown to be associated with patient care, particularly hospital admissions, often influencing clinical decision-making.[18]

Slawson proposes that while patient care based on evidence is important, EBM at the bedside is not yet always feasible. Therefore medical school and residency curricula also need to emphasize effective information management. The three skills needed are the abilities to select the correct tools for staying up-to-date; to find the right "just-in-time" information that is appropriate, easily accessed, and speedily available as well as usable at the point of care; and to combine the best evidence with patient-centered care, considering both the needs and perspective of the patient.[24]

Another strong influence on physicians' information needs and behaviors is the growing use of the Internet by their patients. Fox estimates in the 2008 Pew Internet & American Life Project that between 75% and 80% of Internet users have looked online for health information. Fox's comparison of the Pew estimate with Harris Interactive's latest data on health-information seekers shows that 81% of Internet users and 66% of all adults have sought health information online. Pew's data show that 67% of Americans expect to find reliable information about health or medical conditions online. When asked where they would go the next time they need health or medical information, 46% of Internet users said they would use the Internet and 47% said they would contact a medical professional. Overall (i.e., Internet users and nonusers), 31% of all Americans say they would try to find health information online, while 59% say they would contact a medical professional.[25]

As a result, more patients are better informed about their health conditions, and they ask their physicians more questions. When searching the Internet, they may be supplementing information received from their physicians, looking for a second opinion, discussing sensitive issues with patient groups, or looking for information for another person or for a child.[26] Web-based resources for consumer health information require careful evaluation. Credible Web sites are maintained by medical professional groups such as the American Academy of Family Physicians; by health associations such as the American Cancer Society; and by patient advocacy groups. The award-winning National Library of Medicine's MedlinePlus Web site provides a well-organized portal to health care information on a wide range of topics.[27] Physicians' information needs that relate to communications with their Internet-literate patients will only increase in the coming years as the United States meets the challenge of improving the overall health literacy of the general population.[28]

NURSES

Nurses make up the largest professional group in the health care community, numbering more than 2,200,000 in the United States. About 80% of these registered nurses work part-time or full-time. With 1500 schools offering registered nursing degrees, close to 100,000 new graduates are added each year to the workforce.[1] However, the nursing shortage continues to be severe and, with the aging of those in nursing profession, the shortage is only expected to increase in the coming decade. The shortage is also a reflection of the limited capacity of the nation's training programs as compared with the demand.

These nursing professionals' health information needs are broad and varied addressing both their clinical and educational needs. A small pilot study demonstrated that nurses' information needs are indeed quite different from those of physicians.[29] Research has shown that nurses often need information for their practice and those with advanced degrees may recognize these information needs more frequently than their colleagues. Their information requirements are typically patient-centered, frequently relating to nursing procedures and protocols.[29–32] Cogdill found that nurse practitioners' information needs most often related to drug therapy and diagnosis.[33]

As is the case with other health care professionals, nurses appear to prefer obtaining information from resources that are convenient and accessible.[34] Colleagues are favorite resources for nursing information. Print materials are another group of preferred resources of information, including nursing textbooks and journals. [33–36]

The literature however, indicates an underutilization of the available nursing literature. As with other health care professionals, nurses find that time is a leading obstacle to using the literature. Additional barriers include lack of value for research in practice, lack of organizational

support, lack of understanding of electronic resources and their structures, difficulty in accessing research materials including electronic resources in clinical areas, and lack of critical appraisal and searching skills.[31,37] The need to achieve a supportive culture in the profession for use of the literature is reinforced in McKnight's study, which found that many nurses believed that taking time to read published information on duty was not only difficult, but perhaps also ethically wrong.[30] For these and other reasons, nurses do not pursue all of their information needs. Nurse practitioners self-reported that they followed up on slightly more than half of their information needs; however, a second measure in the same study indicated that significantly fewer information needs were actually pursued.[33]

Mid-1990s research found that electronic sources of information such as CINAHL and MEDLINE were increasing in popularity with nurses, but usage reports differed from study to study. Estabrooks suggested that database searching as a source of nursing information appeared to be much less appealing to some nurses than did personal experience and colleagues. While nurses' Internet and e-mail use at home has increased, Internet use at work is low despite adequate workplace access.[38] In a national survey, Pravikoff found that nurses acknowledged their need for information, but they had greater confidence in consulting the Internet or colleagues than they did in using bibliographic databases such as PubMed or CINAHL.[31]

Ready availability of information resources and training do appear to facilitate greater use by nurses of the knowledge base. A recent report of an evaluation of the information-seeking practices of nurses before and after access to a library's electronic collection of information resources showed that at the inception of the project, nurses used colleagues and print textbooks or journals to satisfy their information needs. However after 1 year with access to the electronic library, 20% of the nurses had begun to use the electronic resources.[36] A smaller but similar project initiated by the same library suggested practicing clinical nurses will use online information resources with appropriate training and accessibility.[39] In a clinical setting with unlimited access to the Internet, nurses used and accessed the Internet for a combination of work and nonwork-related activities. Information enthusiasts emerged who facilitated use for other nurses. Again, training was a recommendation from this study.[40] Recent research showed that more nursing students than clinical nurses used online databases, including CINAHL and PubMed, to locate health information, and that nursing students were more likely than clinical nurses to report performing a database search at least one to five times a week.[35] Confirming this consensus in the value of computer instruction, Secco found that good computer and literature searching skills were positively associated with greater use of electronic information and also with expectations that desktop information would improve practice.[32]

Low use of information resources has led nursing leaders to question the readiness of the nursing profession to transition to a more evidence-based practice. The need for evidence-based practice and access to the latest information is particularly critical in the nursing profession where, as Pavikoff noted, more than two-thirds of those practicing graduated prior to 1990.[31] A systematic review of the literature found that predictors of research use by nurses could be categorized according beliefs and attitudes, involvement in research activities, information seeking, professional characteristics, education, and other socioeconomic factors. Only the beliefs and attitudes category was actually substantiated in the reviewed research.[41] Milner found that clinical nurse educators, clinical nurse specialists, advanced nurse practitioners, and nurses working in research leadership positions are important in facilitating evidence-based practice. However, Milner found also that not all nurses in those categories have the necessary critical appraisal skills and research knowledge to use research effectively in practice.[42] Pravikoff concluded that significant changes are needed through a multifaceted approach involving students, educators, clinicians, and administrators before nurses in the United States fully implement evidence-based practice.[31]

In the era of evidence-based practice and increased accountability for all heath care professionals, facility with searching and using electronic information resources is an important skill for nurses. However, many nurses still do not have the necessary skills to pursue their information needs. Health sciences librarians can play an important role in providing instruction to nurses in accessing and evaluating the literature.

PUBLIC HEALTH

Public health is distinct from other medical fields in that its focus is on the population as a whole, rather than on the individual patient. Information requirements are therefore quite different but nonetheless critical. Ready access to the public health knowledge base is fundamental to achieving the nation's goals established decennially[43] to improve health, including finding the best solutions to community health needs, promoting healthful lifestyles and disease prevention, and providing informed responses to public health issues. And in public health emergencies, public trust requires rapid, well-informed responses to health threats, often of unknown origin and continually unfolding over hours and days.

The public health sector itself is a complex amalgam of federal, state, and local units, health care institutions and providers, as well as many health-related organizations and advocacy groups. The workforce is drawn from at least 35 professions as well as 20+ other job categories. Examples of public health workers included public health medical officers, nurses, environmentalists, nutritionists, sanitarians, inspectors, and laboratorians. Workers' educational backgrounds range from advanced degrees and specialty training to technical backgrounds to those with high school diplomas and on-the-job training. The United States, which is currently experiencing a severe shortage in the public health workforce, has an estimated 450,000 public health workers. Less than 1% are epidemiologists, biostatisticians, or infection-control specialists who have critical responsibilities in the post-9/11 world.[44] Efforts are underway to better define the workforce, accelerate recruitment into the field, and to implement more systematic enumeration strategies.

While there is general consensus on the critical need to make information accessible to the public health community, there have been few formal studies of information needs. These studies can be confounded by the public health workforce's diversity, worker-role variation and overlap, and the fuzzy boundaries of the field. As noted by Revere and colleagues in their literature review, it is not possible to design a comprehensive needs assessment that would neither yield informative data nor design a one-size-fits-all information system solution.[45]

Because information services are often unavailable, information needs, when they occur, may not be recognized by public health workers.[46] When recognized, there may be lack of awareness of what information is available and how to search for answers. A Norwegian study showed that while public health workers value research-based information, they do not appear to identify scientific information as a resource for questions encountered in daily practice.[47] Along with lack of awareness there are other barriers including difficulty in finding the needed information given the breadth of the field, general information overload, limited access to computers and licensed online resources, lack of search skills, limited ability to appraise information quality, and lack of time.[48,49]

A few studies have examined the types of information used by public health workforce segments. LaPelle found that six categories of information were needed: early reports on new risks and preventive behaviors; early reports on public health practices and programs; information on evaluated interventions; synthesized information about public health threats and practices; published research including systematic reviews and meta-analyses; and evidence-based guidelines.[49] In looking at five types of public health workers, Rambo found needs for tools to connect with experts; to get updates on legislative issues; and to find structured information about datasets, best practice resources, templates for frequently used applications, and synthesized knowledge-based information.[50] Other studies have examined specific groups of workers, such as Dobbins' study of public health decision-makers, in whom there was a strong preference for executive summaries and systematic reviews.[51]

Like the workforce, the public health literature is diffuse and appears in many disciplines. There is no single index or database that serves the field. While the National Library of Medicine's PubMed database continues to strengthen its public health content, often other databases are required to locate needed information. As noted by Howes,[52] 44% of the Medical Library Association's list of Core Public Health Journals[53] and 38% of the University of Massachusetts Lamar Souter Library's list[54] are not indexed in MEDLINE. Alpi, in her overview of the major resources for searching in the public health field, notes that the challenges include the range of resources along with the lack of public health indexing terminology in many databases.[55] A useful compilation of free public health databases is provided at the University of Massachusetts' Evidence-Based Practice for Public Health Web site.[54] Examples of specialized resources include the National Library of Medicine's Health Services/Technology Assessment Text (HSTAT) database[56] and the Centers for Disease Control and Prevention's human genome epidemiology (HuGE) knowledge finder.[57]

In addition to the journal literature, influential white papers, government reports, policy, and opinion papers are important information sources in public health. This gray literature can be discovered at the Web sites of federal and state government health agencies and public health organizations. The New York Academy of Medicine Grey Literature Report captures many public health documents.[58] A search for statistics, which are frequently sought in public health, should begin at the Centers for Disease Control and Prevention's National Center for Health Statistics Web site.[59]

As in medicine, there is growing emphasis in public health to use scientific evidence to guide policy making and program planning. Evidence-based public health faces challenges that are different from those of evidence-based medicine: there is considerably less evidence available; the study designs typically cannot match the rigor of controlled clinical trials; population studies generally require a longer time; the workforce has less professional training; and decisions to act on evidence are made by teams as opposed to individual practitioners.[60] Because public health is interdisciplinary and because a significant portion of its knowledge base lies outside the scope of traditional databases, gathering the evidence for systematic reviews and meta-analyses is difficult.[61,62] However, a body of public health evidence is beginning to emerge. The *Guide to Community Preventive Services* is the leading source for evidence-based public health best practices.[63] The well-regarded Cochrane Collaboration includes a Cochrane Health Promotion and Public Health Field group that promotes systematic reviews, identifies new studies, and explores methodology issues in the public health literature.[64] The Canadian Institutes of Health is sponsoring a broad-based initiative to assist with the production, dissemination, and application of public health research evidence in Canada.[65] One outcome is a centralized online registry of systematic reviews, meta-analyses, and evidence-based summaries that are relevant to public health interventions.[66] The European SPHERE (Strengthening Public Health Research in Europe) project is an example of a recent project to examine public health research publications in order to identify new research priorities and to develop ways to facilitate the integration of research findings into public health policy.[67]

Providing information services to the public health workforce has fallen outside the mainstream of library services. Where once there were many state public health libraries, only a handful remain. Very few states have formal arrangements for library and information services for their public health workers. A landmark national conference in 1998 assembled stakeholders, highlighted the need for better information services for the public health community, and initiated discussions about solutions.[48] Progress is now being made in better supporting the information needs of the public health community. One notable result of the 1998 conference was the formation of the Partners in Information Access for the Public Health Workforce, which has developed a public–private collaboration to augment access to and use of information by public health workers at the state and local levels.[68]

BIOMEDICAL RESEARCHERS

Underpinning the practice of medicine is a large community of clinical and biomedical researchers and scientists. While not practitioners of health care, these researchers contribute to the field by discovering the new knowledge that advances the practice of medicine. Their recent approaches to research are transformational, heralding enormous developments in information systems and the information sciences that will eventually permeate other health care professional groups. Advances in technology and large-scale national and international collaborative research efforts are driving these changes, affecting both the way scientific information is generated and the way it is communicated, particularly in the burgeoning fields of molecular biology and genomics.

While colleagues remain an important information resource for these researchers, scientific discovery is now often derived from databases rather than laboratory bench experimentation as was the case for much of the last century. Primary information needs are increasingly being met by complex nonbibliographic databases that constitute the new knowledge base.[69] The success of the Human Genome sequencing project and the recent Framingham Heart Study data release illustrate the power of large collaborations to generate new findings.[70] A leading provider of new research tools is the National

Library of Medicine's National Center for Biotechnology Information (NCBI) that provides a growing list of new resources such as their Entrez databases and the NCBI Map Viewer.[71] Other examples of new approaches to information include ExPlain, a gene expression analysis platform, and Collexis, a knowledge management and text-mining tool.[72,73]

Biomedical researchers are often self-sufficient information users and do use traditional information resources, valuing both online journals and a well-organized library Web site that makes locating information more efficient than an Internet search engine such as Google or Yahoo.[74] However, additionally these researchers work collaboratively, using Web 2.0 methods for rapid dissemination of scientific information. They also work together to build new databases. They require new tools for mining the biomedical literature and the large shared datasets, and tools for synthesizing their retrievals in order to discover relationships and generate new hypotheses.[75] The current emphasis on translational research, that is moving from science to practical application in health care, highlights the need for new workflows, interoperable data repositories, infrastructure and statistical tools for meta-analyses, integrated ontologies, and other approaches that enable collaborative work and data analysis.[76] The challenge for health sciences librarians is to become proficient in the new tools and new ways of managing, accessing, and integrating biomedical research information, particularly as many of these strategies may become standards for all health care information.

CONCLUSION

While researchers and academicians are traditionally more facile in using the biomedical research knowledge base than health care practitioners are, a growing trend toward self-sufficiency in information seeking is apparent in the larger health sciences community. Additionally, the need for "just-in-time" clinical evidence at the point of care was emphasized in the findings of a large medical center's information-needs study.[77] The literature is showing that many health care professionals now expect information services customized to their professional information needs, preferences, and patterns of use.[74]

The emerging solution to customized services at the point of need appears to employ both technological and human interventions. As Bakken pointed out, an informatics infrastructure is essential for evidence-based practice. This infrastructure must include standard terminologies and structures, electronic information resources, data exchange standards to enable transfer of information across heterogeneous systems, processes that enable evidence appropriate to specific patient cases, and informatics competencies. Among the challenges to achieving this goal are building a persuasive business case; achieving

consensus in describing, organizing, accessing, and archiving information resources; designing clinically relevant information-retrieval strategies; and integrating evidence-based processes into the clinical setting and organizational structure.[78] Davidoff and Florance have argued that in addition to informatics tools, a new informationist specialist is needed as a full member of the clinical team: a professional who specializes in information, who possesses information science, informatics and domain knowledge, and who works outside the library in the health care setting.[79] Model informationist programs are now emerging in clinical programs as well as in health policy, public health, biomedical research, and other related domains.[80]

An understanding of each client group's unique information needs and behaviors will result in the development of clearly targeted products and services. Customized services include both technology tools and embedded librarians that together enable successful and seamless integration of information resources and services into the workflow of health care professionals.

REFERENCES

1. National Center for Health Statistics. *Health, United States, 2007 with Chartbook on Trends in the Health of Americans*, NCHS: Hyattsville, MD, 2007.
2. Association of American Medical Colleges, The Association. Washington, DC. http://www.aamc.org (accessed December 29, 2007).
3. American Association of Colleges of Osteopathic Medicine, The Association: Chevy Chase, MD http://www.aacom.org (accessed December 29, 2007).
4. Dee, C.; Blazek, R. Information needs of the rural physician: A descriptive study. Bull. Med. Libr. Assoc. **1993**, *81*(3), 259–264.
5. Timpka, T.; Ekstrom, M.; Bjurulf, P. Information needs and information seeking behaviour in primary health care. Scand. J. Prim. Health Care **1989**, *7*(2), 105–109.
6. Haug, J.D. Physicians' preferences for information sources: A meta-analytic study. Bull. Med. Libr. Assoc. **1997**, *85*(3), 223–232.
7. Covell, D.G.; Uman, G.C.; Manning, P.R. Information needs in office practice: Are they being met?. Ann. Intern. Med. **1985**, *103*(4), 596–599.
8. Osheroff, J.A.; Forsythe, D.E.; Buchanan, B.G.; Bankowitz, R.A.; Blumenfeld, B.H.; Miller, R.A. Physicians' information needs: Analysis of questions posed during clinical teaching. Ann. Intern. Med. **1991**, *114*(7), 576–581.
9. Gorman, P.N.; Ash, J.; Wykoff, L. Can primary care physician's questions be answered using the medical journal literature?. Bull. Med. Libr. Assoc. **1994**, *82*(2), 140–146.
10. Dawes, M.; Sampson, U. Knowledge management in clinical practice: A systematic review of information seeking behavior in physicians. Int. J. Med. Inform. **2003**, *71*(1), 9–15.

11. Bennet, N.L.; Casebeer, L.L.; Kristofco, R.; Collins, B.C. Family physicians' information-seeking behaviors: A survey comparison with other specialties. BMC Med. Inform. Decis. Mak. **2005**, *5*(1), 9.

12. Williamson, J.W.; German, P.S.; Weiss, R.; Skinner, E.A.; Bowes, F. III. Health science information management and continuing education of physicians: A survey of U.S. primary care practitioners and their opinion leaders. Ann. Intern. Med. **1989**, *110*(2), 151–160.

13. Nicholas, D.; Williams, P.; Smith, A.; Longbottom, P. The information needs of perioperative staff: A preparatory study for a proposed specialist library for theatres (NeLH). Health Info. Libr. J. **2005**, *22*(1), 35–43.

14. Connelly, D.P.; Rich, E.C.; Curley, S.P.; Kelly, J.T. Knowledge resource preferences of family physicians. J. Fam. Pract. **1990**, *30*(3), 353–359.

15. Gosling, A.S.; Westbrook, J.I.; Coiera, E.W. Variation in the use of online clinical evidence: a qualitative analysis. Int. J. Med. Inform. **2003**, *69*(1), 1–16.

16. Ely, J.W.; Osheroff, J.A.; Ebell, M.H.; Chambliss, M.L.; Vinson, D.C.; Stevermer, J.J.; Pifer, E.A. Obstacles to answering doctors' questions about patient care with evidence: qualitative study. BMJ **2002**, *324*(7339), 710.

17. Lindberg, D.A.; Siegel, E.R. On assessing the impact of medical information: Does MEDLINE make a difference?. Methods Inf. Med. **1991**, *30*(4), 239–240.

18. Westbrook, J.I.; Coiera, E.W.; Gosling, A.S. Do online information retrieval systems help experienced clinicians answer clinical questions?. J. Am. Med. Inform. Assoc. **2005**, *12*(3), 315–321.

19. Bennett, N.L.; Casebeer, L.L.; Kristofco, R.E.; Strasser, S.M. Physicians' Internet information-seeking behaviors. J. Contin. Educ. Health Prof. **2004**, *24*(1), 31–38.

20. Bennett, N.L.; Casebeer, L.L.; Zheng, S.; Kristofco, R. Information-seeking behaviors and reflective practice. J. Contin. Educ. Health Prof. **2006**, *26*(2), 120–127.

21. Centre for Evidence-Based Medicine, The Centre: Oxford, U.K. http://www.cebm.net (accessed December 29, 2007).

22. Institute of Medicine. *Crossing the Quality Chasm: A New Health System for the 21st Century*, National Academy Press: Washington, DC, 2001.

23. Schwartz, K.; Northrup, J.; Israel, N.; Crowell, K.; Lauder, N.; Neale, A.V. Use of on-line evidence-based resources at the point of care. Fam. Med. **2003**, *35*(4), 251–256.

24. Slawson, D.C.; Shaughnessy, A.F. Teaching evidence-based medicine: Should we be teaching information management instead?. Acad. Med. **2005**, *80*(7), 685–689.

25. Fox, S. *The Engaged e-Patient Population*, Pew Internet & American Life Project: Washington, DC, 2005. http://www.pewinternet.org/pdfs/PIP_Health_Aug08.pdf (accessed September 8, 2008).

26. van Woerkum, C.M. The Internet and primary care physicians: Coping with different expectations. Am. J. Clin. Nutr. **2003**, *77*(4), 1016S–1018S.

27. National Library of Medicine. *MedlinePlus;* The Library: Bethesda, MD. http://medlineplus.gov (accessed December 29, 2007).

28. Nielsen-Bohlman, L. *Health Literacy: A Prescription to End Confusion*, National Academies Press: Washington DC, 2004.

29. Xu, X.; Rocha, R.A.; Bigelow, S.M.; Wallace, C.J.; Hanna, T.; Roemer, L.K. Understanding nurses' information needs and searching behaviour in acute care settings. AMIA Annu. Symp. Proc. **2005**, 839–843.

30. McKnight, M. The information seeking of on-duty critical care nurses: Evidence from participant observation and in-context interviews. J. Med. Libr. Assoc. **2006**, *94*(2), 145–151.

31. Pravikoff, D.S.; Tanner, A.B.; Pierce, S.T. Readiness of U.S. nurses for evidence-based practice. Am. J. Nurs. **2005**, *105*(9), 40–51.

32. Secco, M.L.; Woodgate, R.L.; Hodgson, A.; Kowalski, S.; Plouffe, J.; Rothney, P.R.; Sawatzky-Dickson, D.; Suderman, E. A survey study of pediatric nurses' use of information sources. Comput. Inform. Nurs. **2006**, *24*(2), 105–112.

33. Cogdill, K.W. Information needs and information seeking in primary care: A study of nurse practitioners. J. Med. Libr. Assoc. **2003**, *91*(2), 203–215.

34. Lathey, J.W.; Hodge, B. Information seeking behavior of occupational health nurses: How nurses keep current with health information. AAOHN J. **2001**, *49*(2), 87–95.

35. Dee, C.; Stanley, E.E. Information-seeking behavior of nursing students and clinical nurses: Implications for health sciences librarians. J. Med. Libr. Assoc. **2005**, *93*(2), 213–222.

36. Tannery, N.H.; Wessel, C.B.; Epstein, B.A.; Gadd, C.S. Hospital nurses' use of knowledge-based information resources. Nurs. Outlook **2007**, *55*(1), 15–19.

37. McCaughan, D.; Thompson, C.; Cullum, N.; Sheldon, T.A.; Thompson, D.R. Acute care nurses' perceptions of barriers to using research information in clinical decision-making. J. Adv. Nurs. **2002**, *39*(1), 46–60.

38. Estabrooks, C.A.; O'Leary, K.A.; Ricker, K.L.; Humphrey, C.K. The Internet and access to evidence: How are nurses positioned?. J. Adv. Nurs. **2003**, *42*(1), 73–81.

39. Wozar, J.A.; Worona, P.C. The use of online information resources by nurses. J. Med. Libr. Assoc. **2003**, *91*(2), 216–221.

40. Morris-Docker, S.B.; Tod, A.; Harrison, J.M.; Wolstenholme, D.; Black, R. Nurses' use of the Internet in clinical ward settings. J. Adv. Nurs. **2004**, *48*(2), 157–166.

41. Estabrooks, C.A.; Floyd, J.A.; Scott-Findlay, S.; O'Leary, K.A.; Gushta, M. Individual determinants of research utilization: A systematic review. J. Adv. Nurs. **2003**, *43*(5), 506–520.

42. Milner, M.; Estabrooks, C.A.; Myrick, F. Research utilization and clinical nurse educators: A systematic review. J. Eval. Clin. Pract. **2006**, *12*(6), 639–655.

43. Healthy people 2010; Department of Health and Human Services: Washington, DC, 2000.

44. Gebbie, K.M. *The Public Health Workforce: Enumeration 2000*, Health Resources and Services Administration, Bureau of Health Professions, National Center for Health Workforce Information and Analysis: Washington, DC, 2000.

45. Revere, D.; Turner, A.M.; Madhavan, A.; Rambo, N.; Bugni, P.F.; Kimball, A.; Fuller, S.S. Understanding the information needs of public health practitioners: A literature review to inform design of an interactive digital knowledge management system. J. Biomed. Inform. **2007**, *40*(4), 410–421.

46. Rambo, N.; Zenan, J.S.; Alpi, K.M.; Burroughs, C.M.; Cahn, M.A.; Rankin, J. Public Health Outreach Forum: Lessons learned. Bull. Med. Libr. Assoc. 2001, 89(4), 403–406.

47. Forsetlund, L.; Bjorndal, A. The potential for research-based information in public health: Identifying unrecognised information needs. BMC Public Health 2001, 1, 1.

48. Lasker, R.D. Challenges to accessing useful information in health policy and public health: An introduction to a national forum held at the New York Academy of Medicine, March 23, 1998. J. Urban Health 1998, 75(4), 779–784.

49. LaPelle, N.R.; Luckmann, R.; Simpson, E.H.; Martin, E.R. Identifying strategies to improve access to credible and relevant information for public health professionals: A qualitative study. BMC Public Health 2006, 6, 89.

50. Rambo, N.; Dunham, P. Information needs and uses of the public health workforce—Washington, 1997–1998. MMWR Morb. Mortal. Wkly. Rep. 2000, 49(6), 118–120.

51. Dobbins, M.; Jack, S.; Thomas, H.; Kothari, A. Public health decision-makers' informational needs and preferences for receiving research evidence. Worldviews Evid. Based Nurs. 2007, 4(3), 156–163.

52. Howes, F.; Doyle, J.; Jackson, N.; Waters, E. Evidence-based public health: The importance of finding 'difficult to locate' public health and health promotion intervention studies for systematic reviews. J. Public Health (Oxf.) 2004, 26(1), 101–104.

53. Medical Library Association. Public Health/Health Administration Section. Core Public Health Journals, Vers. 2.0, The Association: Chicago, IL, 2007. http://publichealth.yale.edu/phlibrary/phjournals/v2 (accessed December 29, 2007).

54. University of Massachusetts, The Lamar Soutter Library, Evidence-Based Practice for Public Health, The Library: Worcester, MA. http://library.umassmed.edu/ebpph/freephdbs.cfm (accessed December 29, 2007).

55. Alpi, K.M. Expert searching in public health. J. Med. Libr. Assoc. January 2005, 93(1), 97–103.

56. National Library of Medicine. HSTAT, The Library: Bethesda, MD. http://www.ncbi.nlm.nih.gov/books/bv.fcgi?rid=hstat (accessed December 29, 2007).

57. Centers for Disease Control and Prevention, Human Genome Epidemiology Network (HuGENet), CDC: Atlanta, GA. http://www.cdc.gov/genomics/hugenet/default.htm (accessed December 29, 2007).

58. New York Academy of Medicine. Grey Literature Report, The Library: New York. http://www.nyam.org/library/pages/grey_literature_report (accessed December 29, 2007).

59. National Center for Health Statistics. NCHS: Hyattsville, MD. http://www.cdc.gov/nchs (accessed December 29, 2007).

60. Brownson, R.C. Evidence-Based Public Health, Oxford University Press: Oxford, U.K., 2003.

61. Beahler, C.C.; Sundheim, J.J.; Trapp, N.I. Information retrieval in systematic reviews: Challenges in the public health arena. Am. J. Prev. Med. 2000, 18(4), 6–10.

62. Armstrong, R.; Jackson, N.; Doyle, J.; Waters, E.; Howes, F. It's in your hands: The value of handsearching in conducting systematic reviews of public health interventions. J. Public Health (Oxf.) 2005, 27(4), 388–391.

63. Centers for Disease Control and Prevention. Guide to Community Preventive Services; CDC: Atlanta, GA. http://www.thecommunityguide.org (accessed December 29, 2007).

64. The Cochrane Collaboration, Cochrane health promotion and public health field; John Wiley & Sons: Hoboken, NJ. http://www.mrw.interscience.wiley.com/cochrane/clabout/articles/HEALTHP/frame.html (accessed December 29, 2007).

65. Kiefer, L.; Frank, J.; Di Ruggiero, E.; Dobbins, M.; Manuel, D.; Gully, P.R.; Mowat, D. Fostering evidence-based decision-making in Canada: Examining the need for a Canadian population and public health evidence centre and research network. Can. J. Public Health 2005, 96(3), I1–40 following 200.

66. Health-evidence.ca. McMaster University: Toronto, ON http://health-evidence.ca (accessed December 29, 2007).

67. McCarthy, M.; Clarke, A. European public health research literatures: Measuring progress. Eur. J. Public Health 2007, 17(Suppl 1), 2–5.

68. Cahn, M.A.; Auston, I.; Selden, C.R.; Cogdill, K.; Baker, S.; Cavanaugh, D.; Elliott, S.; Foster, A.J.; Leep, C.J.; Perez, D.J.; Pomietto, B.R. The Partners in Information Access for the Public Health Workforce: Collaboration to improve and protect the public's health, 1995–2006. J. Med. Libr. Assoc. 2007, 95(3), 301–309.

69. Grefsheim, S.; Franklin, J.; Cunningham, D. Biotechnology awareness study, Part 1: Where scientists get their information. Bull. Med. Libr. Assoc. 1991, 79(1), 36–44.

70. Lindberg, D.A.; Humphreys, B.L. Rising expectations: Access to biomedical information. Yearb. Med. Inform. 2008, 3(1), 165–172.

71. National Center for Biotechnology Information, NLM: Bethesda, MD. http://www.ncbi.nlm.nih.gov (accessed September 8, 2008).

72. ExPlain Analysis Platform. BIOBASE Corp: Beverly, MA. http://www.biobase-international.com/index.php?id=286 (accessed September 8, 2008).

73. Collexis, Collexis: Columbia, SC. http://www.collexis.com (accessed September 8, 2008).

74. Grefsheim, S.F.; Rankin, J.A. Information needs and information seeking in a biomedical research setting: A study of scientists and science administrators. J. Med. Libr. Assoc. 2007, 95(4), 426–434.

75. Jensen, L.J.; Saric, J.; Bork, P. Literature mining for the biologist: From information retrieval to biological discovery. Nat. Rev. Genet. 2006, 7(2), 119–129.

76. Burgun, A.; Bodenreider, O. Accessing and integrating data and knowledge for biomedical research. Yearb. Med. Inform 2008, 47(Suppl 1), 91–101.

77. Perley, C.M.; Gentry, C.A.; Fleming, A.S.; Sen, K.M. Conducting a user-centered information needs assessment: The Via Christi Libraries' experience. J. Med. Libr. Assoc. 2007, April 95(2), 173–181 e54–e55.

78. Bakken, S. An informatics infrastructure is essential for evidence-based practice. J. Am. Med. Inform. Assoc. 2001, 8(3), 199–201.

79. Davidoff, F.; Florance, V. The informationist: A new health profession?. Ann. Intern. Med. 2000, 132(12), 996–998.

80. Rankin, J.A.; Grefsheim, S.F.; Canto, C.C. The emerging informationist specialty: A systematic review of the literature. J. Med. Libr. Assoc. 2008, 96(3), 194–206.

Historical and Archaeological Sites: Development and Preservation

Robert B. Pickering
Gilcrease Museum, and Museum Science and Management Program, University of Tulsa, Tulsa, Oklahoma, U.S.A.

Abstract

Historic and archaeological sites provide windows to life in the past. The sites are the in situ repositories of the human activities. Studying these sites helps this and future generations understand the past and our links to it. Preserving these sites honors those who came before and strengthens our connections to our roots. Sites may be as grand as an historic district or an architectural treasure, or as simple as a small campsite used by ancient hunters. Yet, each has an important story to tell about people in the past.

INTRODUCTION

Historic and archaeological sites are important places. Something happened there. Perhaps it was an event that changed history and is the subject of legend and lore. Other times, such sites are small and the people who created the site are nearly forgotten. However, large or small, famous or obscure, historic and archaeological sites are incredibly important windows on the past. They are our history, our heritage, and our link to the people who came before us.

An object, whether from the past or present, can tell a story. The recent obsession with forensic sciences demonstrates how trained researchers use their knowledge and skills to turn something as seemingly insignificant as a hair into a powerful clue to a past event. Archaeologists sometimes call this process "reading" an object. Any object made by humans can be analyzed as to its means of manufacture and its use. Indeed, objects have a "life cycle" from manufacture through use to abandonment. Determining what has happened to the object after abandonment also can be determined from telltale changes to the object. Many times, these processes are natural processes of decay and destruction that leave their own signatures.

If history can be deduced from a single object, then an historical or an archaeological site has even greater potential for revealing past human behavior. The site provides the context for interpreting objects; the locus of activity at which the objects were used. Perhaps there is a progression of understanding here. An object has a specific and limited function. A group of objects found together may reveal the activity in which the objects were used. The site reveals the holistic picture of the human behavior that used the objects and provides information on the who, what, when, and where that helps researchers look back in time to reconstruct entire events and ways of life.

REVEALING THE SITE

Historic and archaeological site museums have multiple functions. At a minimum, they preserve the record of the past in its original location and they present a story for today's students of the past. Revealing the story told by these sites often requires the skills of many kinds of scientific and historical researchers. The tasks often begin with precise and careful examination of the site to determine the details of the human-made structures, whether forts, cliff dwellings, a 200-years-old barn, or the remains of a small campsite used by nomadic hunters thousands of years ago (Fig. 1).

Once the site has been mapped to include the natural features and human-made structures, then decisions will be made about how to take care of those structures. Do structures or buildings need stabilization, renovation, reconstruction, or to be left alone? The term "stabilization" means to make the structure as safe as possible with the least change necessary. Today's conservation ethic, whether in an historical or archaeological context, is that modern changes should be visible and reversible so that future generations of researchers and the public will be able to differentiate between the original structure and any modifications made to it. The reason for making sure that modern changes are visible recognizes that some interpretation is involved in any reconstruction. Over time, the reconstruction may be thought to be original and thereby confuse scholars and the public. As new data is collected, details of the original structure may impact future reconstruction efforts. Each new generation of scholars needs to be able to distinguish between the "original" and the "reconstructed." Making the distinctions obvious allows each new generation of scholars and researchers to use new methods, tools, and materials to start from the original more easily and efficiently.

Encyclopedia of Library and Information Sciences, Fourth Edition DOI: 10.1081/E-ELIS4-120044043

Fig. 1 Prehistoric sites such as Legend Rock have been used by a succession of pre-European cultures. Such sites provide powerful experiences for today's visitors but also must be protected from vandalism.

Renovation and reconstruction implies that efforts will be made to enhance the original structure, perhaps bringing it back to the way it looked when it was being used. Historic houses often have been renovated through time so that the visitor has the experience of being in a "living house" not an old musty and abandoned one. Historic site specialists do not always agree on the extent to which renovations or reconstructions are acceptable. Some historic site specialists prefer to make as few alterations or additions as necessary to provide safety for the structure and the people who work in or visit it. In other cases, the goal is to let the visitor see and experience the site as it would have been at the time it was in use. Both of these perspectives can be seen around the world at various houses, forts, and historical places (Fig. 2).

Historic Oak Park, Illinois, was the home of Frank Lloyd Wright and the location of many of the houses he designed. Many towns, such as Santa Fe, New Mexico, or

Fig. 2 Galena, Illinois, has protected sections of the town to create an historic district that keeps its nineteenth century look.

Charlotte, North Carolina, have entire historic districts of period buildings that are being preserved but also used for contemporary purposes. On the world stage, the great cities of Rome, Beijing, Bangkok, Jerusalem, and Mexico City just to name a few, have extensive districts of historic importance that are still part of the urban milieu. Cities often have strict rules that dictate what kinds of materials or physical changes are allowed in order to maintain individual buildings and the look of the entire district. However, the importance of historic sites is not universally appreciated. As cities strive to modernize, particularly national capitols and centers of industry, whole blocks and quarters are sometimes razed to accommodate the needs of current city dwellers. Beijing's preparation for the 2008 Olympics was an excellent example. While the needs are real, the loss of precious historic resources should not be taken lightly.

Archaeologists have a slightly different challenge when it comes to inventorying archaeological sites. By definition, most archaeological sites are buried by centuries or millennia of debris and natural forces. There are many sites that are known by their aboveground presence, but in fact are simply part of much larger sites that are under foot. Throughout the world spectacular aboveground archaeological sites such as Stonehenge in England, the Pyramids of the Giza Plateau and Saqqara in Egypt, Greece's Parthenon, Peru's Macchu Picchu, Mexico's Teotihuacan, and Nan Madol on the Pacific Island of Pohnpei have attracted countless generations of the curious. Today, these sites often are sources of national pride and sometimes considerable generators of revenue.

Yet, these same sites sometimes become targets of intentional destruction. The massive Buddhas of Bamyan in Afghanistan were destroyed because they represent an earlier religion that is not accepted by some of the current residents of that country. Sometimes, archaeological sites become pawns in contemporary geopolitical affairs.

The great city of Cahokia, on the Illinois side of the Mississippi River across from St. Louis, is no less monumental but differs from many of the world sites in that it was constructed entirely of earth, not stone. Between about 1050–1200 c.e., Cahokia included well over 100 mounds, a great plaza, and extensive housing areas. Cahokia's largest human-made structure, Monk's Mound, can be seen towering above the trees. Its base covers an area larger than the base of the Pyramid of the Sun at Teotihuacan in Mexico. In past decades, excavation was the main method archaeologists used to find buried sites (Fig. 3).

Archaeology is a destructive science. Revealing a buried site requires excavation to see it in detail. Excavating destroys the context. Excavation exposes the buried structures and objects to environmental factors that destroy them much more quickly than if they had been left in the ground. Today, most archaeologists are keenly aware that archaeological sites are like endangered species: If we do

Fig. 3 Monk's Mound at the site Cahokia (the St. Louis Arch in the background), has been encroached up by modern urban development.

not preserve them, they will disappear. Therefore, archaeologists are very careful about what they choose to excavate. Large-scale excavations today must consider not only excavation, but a broad spectrum of data collection and recording, object care, and stabilization of the site. When excavation is initiated, a multidisciplinary team of scientists and technicians are often required so that the record of the site will be as complete as possible and will be preserved through time.

Today, noninvasive tools such as ground penetrating radar, aerial photography with special films and cameras, and magnetometry let archeologists "see" underground structures without having to resort to excavation. Thanks to the technological advances, the need to conduct expansive and expensive excavations to identify architectural features is no longer necessary. In recent years, robotic technology has played a role., Within the Great Pyramid at Giza, there are small shafts that extend out from the tomb chamber. Many theories have been presented as to their function. Using small robots with lights and cameras to explore these shafts might provide new insights into the shafts form and function. Egyptian authorities review

proposals such as these and always have the best interest of the monuments and sites in mind.

Whether in the historical or archaeological context, mapping is only the initial step in creating a great site that can be accessed by the public. Historians and scientists representing many different specialties will analyze the site to determine what actually occurred there. Geologists and soil scientists will help the archaeologist understand what kinds of natural geological formations and processes are important to the site's history. Specialists in conservation, photography, and statistics help preserve and document each piece of the past. Educators and interpreters work with the researchers to help them develop the stories, activities, and information banks which are available to the public. Today, it is common for many of those interpretations to be available on the Web or through other electronic media. This incredible technology makes it possible for people to experience the site, virtually, even if they cannot visit it in person. The experience is not the same, but it is still valuable.

Human beings lived in North America for at least 12,000 years before Christopher Columbus arrived. Some archaeological evidence suggests that North American human history may span 20,000 or more years and that there were numerous waves of migration that brought people to this continent.

In Africa, Asia, Europe, and some other parts of the world, people and even prehuman hominids have lived on the land for longer periods of time. Unfortunately, contemporary human populations often like to live in the same areas as did earlier cultures.

Here then is a conundrum. If people have been here for all those thousands of years and have lived all across the landscape, should we preserve every site that is found? On a shorter timescale, is every old building, farm site, or construction created by humans important enough to save for the future? While it is true that in many ways, each site is unique and definitely each site tells a story, it isn't necessary—it isn't possible—to save all of them. If we did, there would be no land available for this generation and future ones to build their lives. At the same time, is it good enough just to record these sites through images, documents, and to salvage artifacts from those sites, knowing that the bulldozers will destroy the sites? No, every culture needs and wants to preserve the best of its past and its heritage. Disregard for the past would make us a people without a past: a culture with no roots connecting us to previous generations of people and entire cultures that came before us.

SAVING IMPORTANT SITES

Who determines what is worth saving? Does anyone actually decide that some historic or archaeological sites can continue to deteriorate under natural conditions or the quick destruction of bulldozers? These issues are common in local communities and also on the national level. In recent decades, many important Civil War battle sites in the United States have become threatened by real estate and mining development. These pieces of ground saw some of the most terrifying battles in a war that defined this country. To see them become shopping malls was more than many people could bear. The Civil War Preservation Trust was founded to stop the destruction of these historic sites. Their annual report, *History Under Siege*, provides insight into the strong emotional connections that many people feel toward our heritage and shows how individuals can become actively engaged in the preservation effort.

The Civil War Preservation Trust is one of many such preservation organizations that work to save important historic and archaeological sites. From passionate individuals to local historical societies to national organizations, many Americans have joined the preservation efforts. Moreover, many of these sites are not just protected, they are interpreted through many kinds of on-site programs and museums that help visitors understand what they are seeing. Many also go beyond providing just the visual experience; they actually create activities to engage the visitor at the site.

In some countries, the preservation of past sites became an issue long ago. For example, in 1666, Sweden passed a law to protect prehistoric sites and antiquarian monuments. The American Antiquities Act of 1906 was the first significant American law to keep archaeological sites from being desecrated and destroyed. The law was a result of a grassroots effort to preserve important sites from America's pre-European past. Devil's Tower in Wyoming was the first monument designated under the Act by President Theodore Roosevelt. This site is sacred to many Plains tribes including the Crow, Kiowa, Lakota, Cheyenne, and Arapahos. Each tribe had their own name for and legend regarding Devil's Tower. Many of them focused on an association with the bear. Bear Lodge, Bear Lair, and Grizzly Bear Lodge are examples.

In the late 1800s as Euro-American populations increased in the American Southwest, an interest in the region's living and ancient Indian cultures increased. Sadly, some of the interest focused on looting at grand sites in Chaco Canyon, Mesa Verde, and smaller sites across the arid landscape. Without protection, these monuments of the past would become pockmarked fields of destruction. Acts such as the early Swedish law and the American Antiquities Act are courageous efforts to stop the destruction (Fig. 4).

In 1966, the National Historic Preservation Act became law and with it, the National Register of Historic Places (NRHP). This law protects not just single buildings, but also entire sites and even districts that have historical importance. This act also pertains to archaeological, as well as historical sites across the country. Each state has a

Fig. 4 The fine architecture of Mesa Verde is the most visible remnant of ancient life ways that have evolved into the Southwestern Pueblo cultures of today.

State Historic Preservation Officer (SHPO) who is responsible for site protection and overseeing the process by which additional sites are proposed for protection. The SHPO's office normally maintains data on all of the archaeological sites that have been found in the state.

According the NRHP Web site, the criteria for protection are:

> The quality of significance in American history, architecture, archaeology, engineering, and culture is present in districts, sites, buildings, structures, and objects that possess integrity of location, design, setting, materials, workmanship, feeling, and association and:
>
> A. That are associated with events that have made a significant contribution to the broad patterns of our history; or
>
> B. That are associated with the lives of persons significant in our past; or
>
> C. That embody the distinctive characteristics of a type, period, or method of construction, or that represent the work of a master, or that possess high artistic values, or that represent a significant and distinguishable entity whose components may lack individual distinction; or
>
> D. That have yielded or may be likely to yield, information important in prehistory or history." http://www.nps.gov/history/nr/listing.htm(accessed August 2008)

The Archaeological Resources Protection Act (ARPA) of 1979 expands the protection of archaeological sites beyond the American Antiquities Act (1906) and more clearly defines what kinds of activities are prohibited. ARPA also provides for incarceration and larger financial penalties for convicted violators. The law was enacted:

> to secure, for the present and future benefit of the American people, the protection of archaeological resources and sites which are on public lands and Indian lands, and to

foster increased cooperation and exchange of information between governmental authorities, the professional community, and private individuals.

http://www.nps.gov/archeology/tools/Laws/arpa.htm (accessed August 2008)

Many archaeological sites are living sites upon which individuals, families, or entire communities conducted the myriad activities that constituted their lives. Such landed sites can be very large, with boundaries changing through time as the use of the site changed. Moreover, the living sites may represent large numbers of people doing very different things within the boundary of the historic site.

UNDERWATER SITES

Shipwrecks are underwater archaeological sites that tell important stories, too. Recovery of the 17th Swedish *Vasa*, England's *Mary Rose* sinking in 1545, and the *Atocha* which sank in 1622 off the Florida Keys have yielded not only spectacular artifacts, but also insights into their special history and times. Closer to our times, the sinking of the *Titanic* was a traumatic event that continues to generate interest and intrigue. The *Titanic* has not been salvaged, although it has been explored through remote devices. Indeed, the rush to salvage the ship has brought new attention to the need to preserve the ships and keep their human passengers from being disturbed.

Early ships, especially those involved in the early exploration or exploitation of the Americas, were small by today's standards. The number of people on board was limited. The contents of the ship tend to directly reflect the ship as a sailing vessel and a conveyance of people and material. These wrecks represent a very thin slice of time and a limited range of activities—a much more compressed picture than that given by a land site. For those reasons, the proper discovery, recording, and recovery of these sites is both delicate and critical to our understanding of the past.

In the 1960s and 1970s, a movement developed to protect these sites in addition to dryland sites. Various maritime laws already pertained to shipwrecks, e.g., the Law of Salvage and the Law of Finds. However, these laws were more focused on who had rights to the material found on a wreck. The purpose of these laws was not conservation or care of the wreck. Moreover, establishing the exact location of a wreck is important in determining if the wreck comes under specific national or state laws, international laws of the high seas, or international conventions. The U.S. Park Service has created a number of National Marine Sanctuaries to protect underwater cultural sites, such as shipwrecks. The Abandoned Shipwreck Act of 1987 vested the states with the authority to manage abandoned historic shipwrecks. In 2001, the Convention on the Protection of the Underwater Cultural Heritage was adopted by UNESCO to provide uniform definitions and protections for underwater sites. http://www.indiana.edu/~arch/saa/matrix/ael/ael_mod12.htm (accessed August 2008).

In 1985, Mel Fisher and his team found a ship from the Spanish treasure fleet of 1622, *La Nuestra Señora de Atocha*, or, just the *Atocha*, and the *Santa Margarita* (Fig. 5). Both ships sank in a violent storm with all hands on board and a fortune in gold, silver, and emeralds. Fisher's finding of the ships sparked a controversy about who owned the riches, and who had the rights to salvage the riches. In archaeological circles, the controversy also centered on the role of private excavations, or excavations for profit, versus scientific investigation. It is certainly true that much important historic research was conducted on these two important ships. Not only was there gold and silver, but also there were navigation instruments, military arms and swords, personal items, and many, many bones. Some of the objects had been made by new world craftsmen but under Spanish direction—some of these items are unique. The analysis of the animal bones told a fascinating picture of life on board an overcrowded ship of the time. However, regardless of the historic and scientific potential and actual work done, it is the wealth of the *Atocha* that continues to capture the imagination of the public.

Finding the *Atocha* sparked the search for many other sunken treasure ships. The legal arguments resulting from the private recovery of the *Atocha* still have impact today and continue to be tested.

The sinking of the *Sultana* offers another fascinating example of an underwater wreck. However, unlike an oceangoing treasure ship, the *Sultana* was a steamship full of people and commercial goods steaming up the Mississippi River toward St. Louis. On April 27, 1865, the ship exploded and burned. More than 1,500 people were killed, many of them Union POWs recently released from a Confederate prison. The ship sank and eventually its original

Fig. 5 Beautiful artifacts recovered from the *Atocha* spark the imagination but tell only a small portion of the story represented by the shipwreck.

location was lost because the channel of the Mississippi River itself moved. The sunken ship became entombed in earth. Both the *Atocha* and *Sultana* are important shipwrecks that reveal important historical incidents. Both were recovered using many appropriate archaeological techniques and both drew upon the services of professionals and nonprofessional alike. However, the presence of great wealth on the *Atocha* will forever overshadow its historical importance while the *Sultana* will be remembered for the tragic event that caused its sinking.

The Sunken Military Craft Act H.R. 4200 was passed as part of the Ronald W. Reagan National Defense Authorization Act for Fiscal Year 2005.

The House bill contained several provisions (sec. 1021–1028) that would protect sunken U.S. military vessels, aircraft, and spacecraft, as well as the remains and personal effects of their crews from salvage, recovery, or other disturbance without authorization from the secretary of the military department concerned. These provisions would clarify the circumstances under which such sunken craft, entitled to sovereign immunity when they sank, remain the property of the flag state until officially abandoned. They would also encourage the negotiation of international agreements to protect sunken military craft. Finally, the provisions would authorize the secretary of the military department concerned to issue and enforce permits for activities directed at sunken U.S. military craft, including contract salvage. This system would not invalidate any permitting system currently in place nor affect any prior lawful transfer or express abandonment of title to any sunken military craft. The Senate amendment contained no similar provision. The Senate recedes with an amendment that would authorize the Secretary of the Navy, in consultation with the Secretary of State, to apply the permitting system established by these provisions to any foreign sunken military craft located in United States waters, if requested by the flag state of that craft. It would also authorize in rem liability against a vessel involved in a violation of these provisions, and would authorize the Secretary concerned to request the Attorney General to seek other relief in certain cases. It would establish an eight-year statute of limitations for actions to enforce violations of these provisions or any permit issued thereunder. It would also extend the prohibition on applying the law of finds to sunken military craft to foreign craft located in U.S. waters. Finally, it makes technical changes to the definitional section. http://www.history.navy.mil/branches/org12-12b.htm (accessed August 2008)

SITE PRESERVATION IN AN INCREASINGLY CROWDED WORLD

All of these laws recognize that the "site" has the most historic value and integrity when the human-made structure is left on its original location. The laws also recognize the problem of looting of sites for monetary and personal gain. Looting of artifacts for profit is a very old activity

but one that is still vigorous today. Yet, the world does not stand still; the locations of many historical and archaeological sites, per se, make them vulnerable. Archaeological and historic house sites increasingly draw the attention of real estate developers as they try to satisfy the needs of our expanding human population. Perhaps an archaeological site along a river was isolated or an historic farm might have been miles from the nearest town when it was built a 100 or 200 years ago. Today, those same sites may well be in the city or targeted for housing development.

When such sites are endangered, the options are few and rarely ideal from the standpoint of historic preservation. Of course, the best option for the historic structure is to preserve it on its original site and require that any development bypass the site. If the site is of sufficient historical importance and if there is an active preservation community to advocate for preservation, then the site can be saved. Other outcomes are more likely, however.

Sometimes, historic structures are moved from their original sites. While not the best solution from an historical perspective, this solution may put an historic building on a site that can be preserved through time. The Conner Prairie historical site near Indianapolis, Indiana, is an excellent example (Fig. 6). In decades past, architectural and historically significant buildings were moved from their original sites to one expansive private property owned by the philanthropist, Eli Lilly. The buildings were variously conserved and renovated depending on their conditions. Today, Conner Prairie offers a wide variety of excellent living history programs that utilize the period buildings on the site. It is a popular destination for families to not only see a glimpse of the past through the buildings, their contents and interpreters, but also to participate in a wide range of programs for all ages of visitors.

An example of how an historical house can be saved and moved is the Isaac Cody house, built in 1841 in LeClaire, Iowa. Isaac was the father of William F. Cody, later to become known as Buffalo Bill (Fig. 7). In 1933,

Fig. 6 Conner Prairie, near Indianapolis, uses buildings, objects, activities, and in-character presenters to bring the past alive.

Fig. 7 Buffalo Bill's Boyhood Home is an example of an historic structure that has been saved although it has been moved; in this case from Iowa to Wyoming.

Cody's boyhood home was obtained by the Chicago, Burlington & Quincy Railroad Company and moved to its station in Cody, Wyoming. The boyhood home served as a tourist attraction in the town founded by Buffalo Bill in 1896. By 1948, railroad business was rapidly diminishing as a result of the rise of the private automobile. The railroad company donated the 106-years-old house to the Buffalo Bill Memorial Association which placed it on the site of the original museum near downtown Cody, Wyoming. In 1969, the Buffalo Bill Museum moved across Sheridan Avenue to a new museum facility and more expansive space. The boyhood home moved, too. In 2004, the house was moved a fourth time to its present location within the Greever Garden of the Buffalo Bill Historical Center. With each move, the house was thought to be important enough to protect, but as circumstances and ownership changed, so too did the location of the house itself. Hopefully, the house's roaming days are over.

Archaeological sites face other pressures. In North America and much of the world, archaeological sites are not remnants of stone, adobe, or wooden structures that stand above the ground. Rather they are beneath the ground's surface. For that reason, they are difficult to see and sometimes hard to find. Determining the actual physical land area and significance of such sites is often difficult. Archaeological sites, small and large, have been destroyed by the thousands over the last century through expanding mechanized agriculture. Destruction was not the intent of the farmer who tries to make a living and feed the world, but the impact of using larger equipment, deep plowing equipment, and terracing practices to reduce erosion have had negative effects on sites. Making the situation worse, many archeological sites were created by their original inhabitants along the nation's rivers and major streams. These areas provided the richest resources for ancient people who depended on hunting, gathering, and early agriculture to support ancient cultures. Unfortunately, those same rich river valleys are the places that

Euro-American farmers chose for their farms, too. Modern farming and river towns often were built on ancient sites.

Today, states have continuing archaeological survey programs that document sites as they are found. Many historic preservation officers actively work with local farmers, ranchers, and avocational archaeological groups to identify sites and preserve them. The Archaeological Conservancy, founded in 1980, is a national nonprofit organization that seeks to identify threatened sites and provide economic incentives to the owners to preserve such sites. *American Archaeology* is a magazine published by the Conservancy to highlight important sites, research, and issues related to America's prehistoric past. Destruction of archaeological sites is still a problem, but today, there are many more active individuals and organizations who work to save this dwindling resource for future generations.

THE IMPACT OF TOURISM

Historical tourism has been a major factor in preserving many sites and important structures, but it is also a double-edged sword. Increased tourism generates considerable money that can be used for preservation and interpretation of important places. Tourism brings much needed public attention to important sites and provides an economic incentive to local businesses to preserve the resource. At the same time, the increase in foot traffic degrades the site. Increasing tourism has spawned a variety of approaches to presenting the past. In decades past, there were numerous archaeological sites, often burial sites, which exposed ancient human remains and their accoutrement of grave goods, for the benefit of fee-paying visitors. In the late 1960s, some American Indian groups began to object to what they saw as sacrilegious exploitation and cultural commodification of their ancestors for profit.

Initially, mutual distrust was common among the various constituencies. At Dickson Mounds, near Lewistown, Illinois, many local residents believed that Indian people from other parts of the country were unfairly maligning Dickson Mounds and the local people themselves. With picketing, intervention of the Governor, and hard feelings on all sides, Dickson became a flashpoint of controversy. However, out of this conflict have come new sensitivities and new approaches to presenting the past. Dickson Mounds, a branch of the Illinois State Museum, has been a leader in this effort. Today, the skeletons of the ancient dead are no longer on view, but there are excellent life-sized dioramas that depict aspects of past cultures that lived along the Illinois River. In addition to the fine museum exhibits, there are a wide range of living history activities for visitors related to practices of agriculture, tool making, and house construction developed by Indian peoples over thousands of years. Temporary exhibits show that Euro-American inhabitants of the valley farmed, fished, hunted, and collected in the valley and on the river for the same purposes as did generations of Indian peoples millennia earlier.

Other kinds of archaeological sites also have become historical attractions. One of the most common methods for hunting buffalo on the vast American and Canadian Plains was the buffalo jump. In its simplest terms, Indian cultures of the last 10,000 years periodically drove herds of buffalo, sometimes small numbers of animals and sometimes large, over a cliff. Those animals that were not killed by the fall or crushed by the bodies of other buffalo falling on top of them, were killed with lance, club, or arrow. The Head-Smashed-In site, near Fort Macleod, Alberta, Canada and the Vore site, just off Interstate Highway 90 on the southern edge of the Black Hills in Wyoming are examples. Head-Smashed-In offers many programs for the casual visitor to learn more about buffalo jumps and the Indian people who used them. Equally important, the site continues to be an important cultural site to the Blackfeet people.

Mammoth Cave in Kentucky offers yet another unusual type of site. As the name implies, it is a massive natural complex that offers an extraordinary view of underground geology, flora, and fauna. The cave also was used by Indian people to mine minerals. In the eighteenth century, Euro-Americans mined other kinds of minerals in the cave. Truly, Mammoth Cave provides an immersion experience.

MUSEUM EXHIBITS AND LIVING HISTORY SITES

The philosophy of presenting the past to today's visitors may be described as two dichotomies; the museum exhibit versus living history, and description versus interpretation. The "museum exhibit" perspective often provides displays, dioramas, or other constructed means of showing a past event or activity. For the visitor, the experience is usually passive and the methods of communicating the museum's messages are primarily visual and auditory. In contrast, a "living history" approach uses real people wearing period clothing and using period objects to engage the visitor in the experience of an earlier time. Here, the visitor may be immersed in the past and the interpretive messages may impact all the senses. In simplest terms, there is learning by seeing and learning by

doing. Most really good site museums will use many different ways to engage the visitor. Museum interpreters recognize that people learn in a variety of ways and therefore the messages should also be delivered through a variety of methods in order to be effective.

The second dichotomy, description versus interpretation, also underlies presentations at historical and archaeological site museums. Description and interpretation are not independent or mutually exclusive. Perhaps they should be thought of as different points on the same scale. Description tells the visitor what he or she is seeing. The farther one goes back in time or the more distant from today's urban, virtual life, the less likely it is that visitors are able to intuitively determine what they are seeing. Description may tell a person that the object in front of them is a stone-tipped spear point, fastened to a wooden shaft. Naming the type of stone or wood involved may give the viewer additional appreciation of the objects. Interpretation provides a context for the objects on view and helps answer the questions, "Who made this?" and "How was it used?" Interpretation has the power to use a single object to reconstruct an entire culture. Using the stone-tipped spear point as an example, interpretation leads to reconstruction of how the raw material was found, shaped into a tool, and then used. Behind the object, the person who made or used it is revealed. Was the tool made by a man or woman, an aged craftsman, a young hunter, or a child learning the process? From the reconstruction of the event in time, interpretation leads the audience to questions about the society in which the people lived.

CONCLUSION

Historic and archaeological sites are connections to our past. They offer incredible opportunities to not only see, but to vicariously experience what it must have been like to live in another time. Such sites also are like endangered species. They are few in number and under considerable pressure because of the land upon which they occupy. Many individuals and organizations have worked to create laws to protect the most important of these sites. When such sites are managed and interpreted by professional staffs, the site is more likely to be saved. A well interpreted site also is likely to be of greater appeal to audiences who help support the site, and thereby, help preserve it.

Historical Societies

Mark Sgambettera
Bronx County Historical Society, Bronx, New York, U.S.A.

Abstract

The central mission of historical societies, to collect and preserve the records of the past, has remained consistent over the course of the last two centuries, but the scope and the functions associated with these original objectives have changed markedly. This entry will look at some of the major historical developments that shaped the goals of historical societies, while highlighting some of the institutional transformations among historical societies that resulted from new ways of thinking about the collection, preservation, and dissemination of historical records.

INTRODUCTION

Modern historical societies are a product of the developing nation-state. Their development follows the course of public interest in collecting, preserving, and publishing documents of the founding and pioneering generations, indigenous cultures, and natural history. By the turn of the twentieth century, historical societies were adopting professional standards of scholarship and librarianship then being articulated through advanced degree programs and the publication of referenced and peer-reviewed articles and books. At mid-century, many historical societies began to adapt their missions and provide funding in support of public programs. Over the last half-century, historical societies have recognized the need to actively engage a public audience and present historical content through history education and museum programming. Computer technology has enhanced the ability of historical societies to deliver digital content including images, text, and music, anywhere in the world. Currently, historical societies are collaborating with partners from other academic and cultural heritage institutions, as well as professionals in the fields of education and information technology to create digital content that is accessible on the Internet and the World Wide Web. In fulfilling the mission of historical societies to collect, preserve, and provide access to historical records, librarians and archivists will increasingly rely on computer technology such as digital scanners, Web design tools, e-mail, and chat programs to develop and manage their unique collections and provide reference services.

HISTORICAL SOCIETIES TODAY: ORGANIZATION AND MISSION

Historical societies collect, preserve, and provide access to printed records and material culture of enduring value

related to a particular place, people, way of life, or event. Historical societies are typically structured as state-chartered, nonprofit corporations that operate as private and independent institutions or as quasi public–private institutions that receive financial aid from state and local governments. Historical societies define their mission statement, their area of interest, and their goals in a founding charter document; periodically, a society reviews and updates specific policies such as its collections policy. For example, the Georgia Historical Society (GHS), a private, nonprofit corporation chartered by the Georgia General Assembly in 1839, upholds the institutional mission "to collect, preserve, and share Georgia history through a variety of exciting educational outreach programs and research services." More specifically, the GHS collection policy describes its primary areas of interest in terms of geographical boundaries, chronology, and historical themes, including Georgia and Georgians, the original 13 colonies, and immigration to the state. The GHS manages its collections through the processes of acquiring, accessioning, and deaccessioning historical records. Within the bounds of its legal authority, and its technological and financial resources, the GHS builds its collections by acquiring materials through purchase, donation, and deposit. Once records are acquired, librarians or archivists accession the materials into a library catalog or an archival listing, and devote all necessary and available resources to preserve the entire collection. However the GHS also reserves the right to deaccession, or dispose of, previously acquired materials that are no longer considered suitable for its collections.[1]

While the central mission of historical societies to collect and preserve the records of the past has remained consistent over the course of last two centuries, the scope and the functions associated with these original objectives have changed markedly. This entry will look at some of the major historical developments that shaped the goals of historical societies, while highlighting some of the

Encyclopedia of Library and Information Sciences, Fourth Edition DOI: 10.1081/E-ELIS4-120044097

institutional transformations in historical societies that resulted from new ways of thinking about the collection, preservation, and dissemination of historical records.

NATIONALISM AND THE RISE OF THE MODERN HISTORICAL SOCIETY

Modern historical societies are a product of the developing nation-state. Their development follows the course of public interest in collecting, preserving, and publishing documents of the founding and pioneering generations, indigenous cultures, and natural history. The first modern, independent historical societies were established in the United States during the late eighteenth and early nineteenth centuries. In the wake of the American Revolution, bibliophiles and amateur historians such as Reverend Jeremy Belknap (1744–1798) and John Pintard (1759–1844) solicited and combined print resources in private library associations for the purpose of collecting and communicating to the members of the society unpublished manuscripts, printed books and pamphlets, artifacts, and reports on "the natural and political history of America from the earliest times to the present day."[2] Under the stewardship of Reverend Belknap, the Massachusetts Historical Society (MHS) (1791), became the first historical association funded and operated by its members. Other independent historical societies including the New York Historical Society (NYHS) (1804) and the American Antiquarian Society (1812) took the lead in acquiring books, pamphlets, newspaper, and other records that documented the regional cultures of New England, the Mid-Atlantic, Virginia, and the Carolinas and helped to distinguish and connect the history of these societies with the larger Atlantic world. Historical societies made their records accessible to their members through the library and through the sale of published collections. Among the early publications were catalogs of materials held by the larger societies like the MHS and the NYHS.[2]

As an expanding nation, the United States began in the 1790s to organize large western land territories into self-governing states. Emigrants, predominantly from the eastern seaboard states, settled newly constituted territories like Wisconsin (1787). One such immigrant, Lyman Copeland Draper (1815–1891), a seminarian and an avid collector of history and biography, settled in Wisconsin after living many decades in upstate New York. Lyman Draper helped promote the first state-funded historical society in Wisconsin. Draper successfully lobbied the newly constituted Wisconsin State Legislature (1848) to establish a charter for a historical society. The succeeding charter of 1853 stipulated that the state legislature would provide the State Historical Society of Wisconsin (SHSW) with annual subsidies, and that membership to the SHWS would be open to any who paid an annual fee of $1. This aspect of the charter gave the SHSW the character of a public subscription library, which distinguished it from the independent historical societies of the East like the MHS that provided services to a limited membership. The society's institutional mission also spoke of the unique conditions upon which Wisconsin was founded. The charter of 1853 called upon the society "to secure from oblivion the memory of its early pioneers, and to obtain and preserve narratives of their exploits, perils and hardy adventures."[3] Over the course of the nineteenth century, the SHSW collections came to embody Wisconsin state and American historical consciousness, as its members sought to shape the state's historical identity vis-à-vis the nation and the West.[4]

The development of modern historical societies is unique to each nation, state, and locality. During the mid-nineteenth century Russia and Britain, like the United States, were rapidly expanding their continental and oceanic empires. At the same time, explorers and amateur ethnographers were documenting the lands and peoples of Asia, Africa, and the Americas. Institutions of learning such as the Geographical Society of London (1830) and the Russian Geographical Society (RGS) (1845) were established to collect, preserve, and publish ethnographic and historical records about the people who inhabited the imperial domains. The ethnography department of the RGS actually served as the first historical society of St. Petersburg. By 1866, a separate historical society was founded in the same city. The RGS charter called upon its members to "study national culture, arrange archaeological expeditions, and preserve monuments of the past."[5,6]

At the turn of the twentieth century, the breakup of empires around the world led to the rise of independent republican forms of government. The birth of independent republics quickly led to the development of cultural institutions that were capable of expressing national and regional identity through history. Six years after gaining independence, the Republic of Turkey established the Turkish Historical Society (1931) through the patronage of leading nationalist figure and first president of the Republic, Mustafa Kemal, Ataturk.[7] Similarly, the creation of the Commonwealth of Australia in 1901 spurred organizing efforts among local and regional societies including the Royal Australian Historical Society (1901), the Royal Historical Society of Victoria (1909), and the Royal Historical Society of Queensland (1913).[8]

Over the course of the nineteenth and early twentieth centuries historical societies were formed into state and local associations. These societies protected and preserved the past at a time when few other institutions were in place to assume guardianship over the founding documents of the community, state, and nation. The generations of historians, ethnographers, and genealogists who established independent and state historical societies were amateurs and enthusiasts, not trained professionals. Figures like Lyman Draper were not professionally trained historians; they pragmatically developed their skills as librarians and archivists, genealogists and ethnologist, historians and editors. Though as the nineteenth century neared its end, a new generation of professionally trained librarians and historians assumed responsibility for collecting and preserving the past.

PROFESSIONALISM AND LIBRARIANSHIP

By the turn of the twentieth century, the practice of history and librarianship were becoming increasingly professionalized through higher education and the issuance of advanced academic degrees, and the publication of referenced and peer-reviewed articles and books. Beginning with the *Historische Zeitschrift* in Germany in 1859, historical associations published journals featuring original research, analysis, and annotated bibliographies. Journals like *Revue historique* (1876) and the *American Historical Review* (1895) provided a national forum and standards for historical scholarship while also offering university education programs scholarly publications for use in training future historians. In this professional environment, the historical society library came to be seen as a source of authentic historical records to be used by scholars and students. And the increasing scholarship would be published in an expanding array of historical society journals such as *The Pennsylvania Magazine of History and Biography* (1877) and the *Virginia Magazine of History and Biography* (1893).

Historical societies reinforced their role as centers for scholarly research by forming partnerships with state universities and archives. The SHSW was one of several publicly funded historical societies that established an institutional connection with a major research university; in 1900, the SHSW celebrated the opening of its new library on the campus of the University of Wisconsin at Madison. The Georgia Historical Society, on the other hand, established an editorial partnership with the University of Georgia in 1917 through which they published the scholarly journal *Georgia Historical Quarterly*. For some historical societies, legitimacy and institutional standing would become intimately tied to professional standards issued by and judged according to the historical academy. National associations such as the American Library Association (ALA) (1876) and the American Historical Association (AHA) (1884) reinforced professional standards through published resource guides and codes of ethics, annual conferences, and the issuance of accreditation standards.

Reuben Gold Thwaites (1853–1913) was among the generation of professionally trained historians who took an active interest in developing national standards of librarianship and historical research among societies in the United States. Thwaites served as the director of the SHSW from 1887 until his death. During his tenure at the SHSW, Thwaites edited several major historical documents series including 73 volumes of *The Jesuit Relations and Allied Documents* and 10 volumes of the *Collections*

of the State Historical Society. He was also instrumental in relocating the SHSW library collections to the University of Wisconsin at Madison.

As a member of the AHA and as president of the ALA (1900), Thwaites was an outspoken promoter of professional standards for state and local historical societies. In 1906, he wrote a report on behalf of the AHA entitled, "State and Local Historical Societies," in which he laid out general professional guidelines for historical societies to follow. Thwaites urged historical societies to avoid the tendency to passively accept whatever was deposited on their doorstep and to actively collect public and private records and oral history accounts of the pioneering generations. These records, he noted, were to be cataloged and indexed so they may be located upon request.

Thwaites also presciently understood the power of public exhibitions for generating interest in history. Citing evolving standards of museum display, he suggested that historical societies cultivate public interest in history by introducing a rotating schedule of museum exhibits featuring carefully labeled books and objects, and lectures presented to teachers and students. Societies, he argued, could also reach a larger public audience by publishing original essays and primary source documents, monographs, and bibliographic guides to publications held in other state and local history centers. Not satisfied to allow historical societies to continue publishing inaccurate or poorly edited sources, Thwaites sounded a call for a more scholarly approach to historical research.[9]

Historical societies incorporated the theories and practices of librarianship to organize and manage their growing collections. The experience of the Historical Society of Pennsylvania (HSP) demonstrates the fitful approach many historical societies adopted with regard to establishing professional standards of librarianship during the period 1890–1945. On the one hand, the HSP committed to a sustained collections preservation program. Between 1889 and 1910, the society set about renovating or constructing fireproof structures to house its collections. Over the ensuing decades, the HSP added steel bookcases and fireproof enclosures. However, during the renovation process HSP staff uncovered "thousands of documents...that had been allowed to languish unprocessed and uncataloged in boxes in out-of-the-way corners."[10] A lack of financial and human resources was surely a principal reason for the constant backlog of uncataloged materials at the HSP. However, as Sally Griffith noted in her study of the HSP, even by the 1920s, "none of the staff had received formal training."[10] Those employed at the HPS "took pride in holding complete knowledge of their collections in their head" and felt uncomfortable with "the new public libraries and had little interest in standardization or efficiency."[10]

Like many historical societies operating in the first half of the century, the HSP employed a variety of native catalog and classification schemes to organize their collections. Historical society indexes and card catalogs often did not conform to nationally recognized standards such as Melville Dewey's decimal system, the Library of Congress's subject headings classification, or to archival arrangement and description inventories developed by the National Archives. It was enough for historical society librarians to know how to locate items requested by its patrons.

In the 1930s, under the guidance of head librarian Julian Boyd, the HSP revised its collections management program. Boyd sought to improve and monitor access to the society's collections through the use of circulation records and the publication of research guides, indexes, and bibliographies. Boyd recognized that he did not have enough staff to implement the ambitious program; it was difficult simply to reduce the backlog of uncataloged materials—including tens of thousands of pamphlets— let alone catalog current acquisitions. As Boyd himself learned, the mountain of uncataloged materials hid unknown treasures. While preparing a catalog of HSP materials for an exhibit to commemorate the 150th anniversary of the Constitution, Boyd uncovered the only known original copy of the document. Over the ensuing decades, HSP librarians and catalogers tried to keep pace with acquisitions, and in 1944 the manuscript department could claim some measure of satisfaction in having cataloged about 95% of its collections.[10]

The HSP was initially slow in recognizing the advantages to be gained by using technology to improve library services. For example, during the period 1912–1930, when research institutions throughout the United States had begun to use new Photostat copying equipment to reproduce and circulate precious historical documents for use outside their own libraries, the HSP leadership steadfastly refused to give reproductions of its collections to other libraries. However, in the 1930s, as the society became increasingly aware of the extent to which other institutions were accumulating Photostat collections for use as reference and research materials, they adopted new policies that allowed for the photocopying and circulating of materials held in the HSP collections. Whereas the HSP was initially hesitant to adopt Photostat technology, under Boyd's tenure, the HSP adopted the use of microphotography as a method to copy and preserve its own collections and gain permanent access to original materials held by institutions.[10]

Though historical societies were adopting professional standards of scholarship and librarianship during the first half of the twentieth century, most societies were providing library services for a limited clientele. Primarily, historical societies opened their doors to the ranks of historians and librarians; some of these professionals went on to staff historical society libraries, while others made use of historical society collections to write articles for historical society journals. The HSP, for its part, opened its doors to the general public in the twentieth century; it just did not advertise this fact. The HSP leadership and staff "did not consider it part of their purpose to try to attract a broader audience."[10] However, at mid-century, many historical societies began to adapt their missions in order to provide funding and staff support for programs aimed at pubic audiences interested in national and local history. In the process, some historical societies learned how to connect history with popular museum exhibitions and ultimately donor solicitations.

PUBLIC HISTORY AND INSTITUTIONAL GROWTH

Over the last half-century, the number of historical societies has increased markedly in absolute terms. The mission of historical societies has also expanded with the drive to actively inform citizens through history education and public programming.

Jan Partridge, in her article about cultural heritage institutions in Australia, noted that the number of local studies centers has increased significantly since the 1950s. She cites figures based on a 1999 study conducted by Alan Bundy which indicate that 76% of public libraries in Australia possess a local studies collection.[11] Likewise, the number of historical societies operating in the United States has increased dramatically. The Conference of Historical Societies' *Handbook of American Historical Societies* published in 1926 listed 338 national, state, and local historical societies. By the mid-1980s the number of historical societies had surpassed 9000.[12,13]

At the local level, it has often been the case that public support for historical societies follows the commemoration of significant historical events. Jan Partridge noted that the overwhelming majority of public libraries in Australia began collecting local studies materials in the 1980s, a decade that coincided with the bicentennial celebration of white settlement in Australia.[11] Similarly, in 1987, around the time of the centennial anniversary of the founding of Boksburg, South Africa, a local resident, Connie Nelson-Esch,published an article in the *Boksburg Advertiser* about the history of the community.The article spurred other residents to organize the Boksburg Historical Association (1993) to collect and preserve the "history of the city and its people."[14]

Local historical societies around the world have been aided by national organizations such as the American Association for State and Local History (AASLH) (1940), the British Association for Local History (1982), and the Federation of Australian Historical Societies (1977). Since the 1940s, the AASLH has served as a clearinghouse of information for societies in the United States and Canada. The AASLH regularly publishes a *Directory* of members, as well as how-to guides on topics like *Organizing a Local Historical Society, The Management of Small History Museums*, and *A Guide to the Care and Administration of Manuscripts*, as well as bulletins about topics ranging from historic house renovation to public relations.[15]

Today most historical societies offer a good deal more than a research library collection and a catalog of publications. The experience of the Virginia Historical Society (VHS) in the postwar years highlights two significant trends in the development of historical society missions. Over the last 30 years, historical societies have assumed a larger role in educating the public about their collective past. At the same time, historical societies have found it necessary to adopt corporate models of business management particularly in regard to advertising and fund raising.

In 1978, the VHS changed its executive committee structure replacing the formerly self-appointed executive committee with an elected board of trustees. With this institutional change came an incremental shift in the VHS's focus away from its traditional emphasis on developing its research collection and offering library services to a selective academic clientele. In the wake of the United States Bicentennial, the trustees of the VHS became aware of the growing commitment of universities, museums, libraries, and other historical societies to engage students, teachers, and the general public in historical conversations about the nation, freedom, diversity, and unity.[16] In particular, scholarly debate and public discussion embraced a new social history of underrepresented historical figures. Indigenous populations, minorities, and women, and broad social movements for labor and civil rights found expression in public exhibitions, lectures, and education programs.

The VHS began offering its first public museum exhibits in 1987. It would later add theme exhibits such as the Jewish experience in Virginia, racism, and labor. Along with museum exhibits, the VHS took active steps to help shape history education curriculum for teachers and deliver new historical materials to students. The VHS initiated an education program under a separate department in the mid-1990s. Among the many programs initially sponsored by the education department of the VHS were school tours of the museum and library, docent training for volunteer staff, the writing of educational primers for teachers, and guest lectures at affiliated educational institutions. By the mid 1990s, the VHS's mission statement included a research library, a museum and historic houses, traveling exhibits, lectures, and programs, training and services for students, educators, and other local history societies, book and periodical publications, fellowship programs, and collaborative archival projects. With the wealth of public programming being made available, the question became how to pay for it all.[17]

For the VHS, the postwar years were years of growth: by the mid-1970s, the VHS added over 6.5 million processed manuscript items, while the photographic and print collections doubled in size. For most historical societies, meeting the demands of an expanding collection, an aging building, and technology upgrades required the infusion of millions of dollars. In an era of shrinking federal and state budgets, this could only come from private and corporate donors. The VHS undertook its first large-scale donor solicitation program in the late 1980s with the Center for Virginia History and the Fifth Century Campaign to raise $12 million for capital construction. In order to reach its goal, the VHS had to sell itself to the public, and this required publicity. The VHS established a publicity office in 1988 and a development office soon thereafter. The society opened its first corporate-sponsored public event in 1989, an exhibit of the society's premier object collection. Over the next two decades, the VHS solicited close to $100 million with much of the proceeds earmarked for the support of public programming such as a new 10,000 sq. exhibit hall. By the late 1990s, the VHS maintained a permanent museum exhibition, and offered 8–10 temporary installations per year, while drawing an average of over 20,000 visitors annually.[17]

HISTORICAL SOCIETY AS DIGITAL LIBRARY

Historical societies are currently collaborating with partners from other academic and cultural heritage institutions, as well as professionals in the fields of education and information technology to create digital content that is accessible on the Internet and the World Wide Web. Historical societies are making use of digital scanners and camera equipment to capture images of text documents, photographs, and objects that can be easily stored in multiple file formats and integrated into an online public access catalog. The introduction of lower-cost, user-friendly digital capturing, storage, retrieval, and networking technologies, along with the development of nationally recognized standards for digital cataloging and description metadata has greatly enhanced the means through which small and medium-sized historical societies can preserve and provide access to their unique collections such as phone directories, loose sheet maps, or post cards.

Over the course of the last decade, historical societies have developed digital libraries as a means to reach out to larger communities of users and provide a nexus for collaboration between scholars, students, teachers, and amateur historians. State and local repositories including historical societies are establishing digital consortia to facilitate cooperative collecting of historical records that document a particular social theme, historical era, or ethnic group. These cooperative collections emphasize the institutional strengths of individual historical societies and support the needs of educators, researchers, and students. The Oregon Historical Society (OHS), for example, has joined with Washington State University and the state historical societies of Idaho and Washington to create a tristate Columbia River Basin Ethnic History Archive (CRBEHA). The goal of the project "was to identify, digitize, and describe library and museum collections concerning non-Native American ethnic groups of the Columbia River Basin, and to stimulate public use of and discussion of those sources." Principally, the CREBHA project allowed the OHS to pursue its mission to raise public awareness about its collections and develop educational resources.[19] In this regard, the OHS was able to provide public access to some of its vast collection of photographs and family papers.

The Web portal developed by the CREBHA consortium offers direct access to selected historical records and novel ways of collocating records based on key word searches. The Columbia River Basin Ethnic History Archive also offers interpretive tools for users and teaching aids, and allows for the migration of content pointers and metadata from one database or catalog to another through the Open Archives Initiative-Protocol for Metadata Harvesting.[18]

The introduction of new technologies has not significantly altered the mission of historical societies to collect, preserve, and disseminate the records and material culture of a specified place, people, way of life, or event. However, the digital library environment and electronic publishing do offer efficient and inexpensive means for historical societies to provide access to their unique collections, present rich, interactive educational content, and, perhaps most importantly, collaborate with other historical societies and cultural heritage institutions to build fully searchable, subject specific digital catalogs.

CONCLUSIONS

Historical societies will continue to provide a number of services to the public in the digital age. Historical society librarians will produce a variety of research and reference materials including bibliographies, indexes, guides to the collection, and educational materials. As with librarians more generally, society librarians will answer reference questions about local and national history, geography, current events, institutions, and personalities. However, in fulfilling the mission of historical societies to collect, preserve, and provide access to historical records, librarians and archivists will increasingly rely on computer technology such as digital scanners, Web design tools, e-mail, and chat programs to develop and manage their unique collections and provide reference services. The process of digitizing historical collections will raise many significant challenges for historical society staff, not the least of which will be acquiring skills in database design, navigating copyright law and fair use provisions in a digital environment, and securing continued funding for the preservation of digital and non-digital content. Historical societies will, however, find technological, financial, and legal support through consortia partnerships with research universities. Ultimately, the unique collections of historical societies will be widely shared for the purposes of research, pubic exhibitions, and educational programming.

REFERENCES

1. Georgia Historical Society. The Georgia Historical Society Library and Archives Division Collection Development Policy, para. 1. Available at http://www.georgiahistory. com/files/0000/0041/Collection_Development_Policy.pdf. Georgia Historical Society Mission Statement (accessed September 12, 2007). http://www.georgiahistory.com/ containers/32 (accessed June 8, 2008).
2. Whitehall, W.M. *Independent Historical Societies: An Enquiry into Their Research and Publication Function and Their Financial Future;* Harvard University Press: Boston, MA, 1962; 6, 7, 53–55.
3. Laugesen, A. *The Making of Public Historical Culture in the American West, 1880–1910, The Role of Historical Societies;* The Edwin Mellen Press: Lewiston, NY, 2006.
4. Laugesen, A. Keeper of histories: the state historical society of Wisconsin library and its cultural work, 1860–1910. Libr. Cult. **2001**, *39*(1), 13–35.
5. Saint Petersburg Encyclopedia. Historical Societies, para. 1. Available at http://www.encspb.ru/en/article.php? kod=2804011617 (accessed August 5, 2007).
6. Yarukova, L. The contributions of the Russian Geographical Society into the history of the ocean studies. Museum of the World Ocean, theses. Available at http://vitiaz.ru/ congress/en/thesis/70.html (accessed August 15, 2007).
7. Turkish Historical Society. Short history of the Turkish Historical Society. Available at http://www.ttk.org.tr/index. php?Page= Sayfa&No=1 (accessed August 17, 2007).
8. Federation of Australian Historical Societies Inc. Member organizations. Available at http://www.history.org.au/ id9.htm (accessed August 2, 2007).
9. Thwaites, R.G. The State Historical Society of Iowa: Iowa City, IA, 1906; 11–18 State and local historical societies. Reprinted from the April 1906 number of the Iowa Journal of History and Politics.
10. Griffith, S.F. *Serving history in a changing world: The Historical Society of Pennsylvania in the twentieth century;.* The Historical Society of Pennsylvania: Philadelphia, PA, 2001; 37, 67, 79, 89–91, 98, 107, 125.
11. Partridge, J. Local history in Australia: Supporting cultural heritage. INSPEL. **2000**, *34*(1), 31–39.
12. *Handbook of American Historical Societies;* Contwell Printing Company: Madison, WI, 1926; Committee on the Handbook of the Conference of Historical Societies.
13. Smith, B.P. *Directory: Historical Agencies in North America*, 13th Ed. American Association of State and Local History: Nashville, TN, 1986.
14. Boksburg Historical Association. The Boksburg Historical Association—who, what & why?. Available at http://www. geocities. com/boksburghistorical/index_files/Page437.htm (accessed August 22, 2007).
15. Alderson, W.T., Jr. The American Association for State and Local History. West. Hist. Quart. **1970**, *1*, 175–182 JSTOR (accessed August 5, 2007).
16. Virginia Historical Society, Interregnum, 1978–1988. Virg. Mag. Hist. Biogr. **2006**, *114*(1), 144–163 Academic Search Premier (accessed August 21, 2007).
17. Virginia Historical Society, The Center for Virginia History, 1988–2005. Virg. Mag. Hist. Biogr. **2006**, *114*(1),

164–199 Academic Search Premier (accessed August 21, 2007).

18. Wyckoff, L.; Mercier, L.; Bond, T.; Cornish, A. The Columbia River basin ethnic history archive: A tri-state online history database and learning center. Libr. Hi Tech. **2005**, *23*, 252–264 Emerald Publications database (accessed July 23, 2007).

BIBLIOGRAPHY

1. Borgman, C.L. *Scholarship in the Digital Age: Information, Infrastructure, and the Internet;* MIT Press: Cambridge, MA, 2007.
2. Dewe, M. *A Manual of Local Studies Librarianship;* Gower Publications Company: Brookfield, VT, 1987.
3. *Directory of Genealogical and Historical Libraries, Archives, and Collections in the US and Canada,* Iron Gate Publishing: Niwot, CO, 2001.
4. Nichols, H. *Local Studies Librarianship*, K.G. Saur: New York, 1979.
5. Silvestro, C.M. *Organizing a Local Historical Society*, American Association for State and Local History: Nashvile, TN, 1968.

WEB SITES

1. American Association of State and Local History, Available at http://www.aaslh.org.
2. British Association for Local History, Available at http://www.balh.co.uk/index.php.
3. Federation of Australian Historical Societies, Available at http://www.history.org/au.
4. Library of Congress. American Memory, Available at http://memory.loc.gov/ammem/index.html.

Historical Sources and Their Users

Margaret Stieg Dalton
School of Library and Information Studies, University of Alabama, Tuscaloosa, Alabama, U.S.A.

Abstract
This entry discusses the evolution of historical study from its beginnings in the realm of mythology to the present complex world of multiple audiences, multiple approaches, and a scope that touches virtually every area of human endeavor. Paralleling this evolution of scholarship has been a constantly expanding universe of sources deemed appropriate to provide the evidence upon which historians base their assertions. The related topic of scholarly communication among historians also receives attention.

INTRODUCTION

This entry will attempt to show how the world looks from the historian's point of view. It will discuss the values and priorities of historians. It will endeavor to illuminate the relationship between the questions they pose and the sources they use, and to shed light on how both internal and external forces are changing the enterprise.

History—writing about the past, not the past itself, which is also "history"—is an endeavor, activity, and discipline of great complexity, with little unity and an internal logic that is often contradictory. It is like an old mansion with many rooms that has been periodically added to and remodeled to suit succeeding generations. Despite extensive modification, however, a basic structure remains. The business of history was and is to provide answers to two fundamental questions: what happened and why did it happen? New additions have not changed this fundamental purpose.

Answers to those questions require evidence. The evidence may be obtained from written documents, from objects, from pictures, from oral accounts, or from any other source that contains relevant information. Records created at the time the event under investigation took place are called primary sources and offer an inside view of the event; they are the heart of any research project. Sources that interpret and analyze the event are created later and are called secondary sources. The distinction between primary and secondary sources is always relative. If, for example, someone is doing a study of Irish immigration to the United States, records like ships' registers, records of the ports of departure and arrival, and letters written by the immigrants are all primary sources. Newspaper stories and other commentaries about that immigration would be secondary sources, but could themselves be primary sources for a study of popular reaction to Irish immigration. The scholarly writings of historians themselves can become primary sources, as when the views of the nationalist German historian Heinrich von Treitschke

(1834–1896) are examined in a study of the tradition of Prussian militarism.

History depends upon a sense of linear time: there is the present; there was the past; and there will be the future. Each is different from the other and the past does not repeat itself. History also depends on the presence of a belief that an understanding of the past can illuminate present realities and that the present will influence the future.

Historical scholarship and writing serve multiple purposes. The results of such scholarship increase our understanding of human nature. They can be used to glorify the achievements of a group and to strengthen a sense of group identity. They can create myths and they can debunk myths. They provide explanations for present conditions.

It is no accident that the nineteenth century, during which nationalism spread and flourished in Europe, was a period of major development of the discipline. During the nineteenth century, many of its practitioners wrote to reinforce emerging states or to advance the claims of ethnic groups to their own state; Frantisek Palacký's (1798–1876) *Dějiny národu českého w Čechách a v Moravě (History of the Czech Nation and Moravia)* is credited with a major role in the development of Czech national consciousness. Not only did Palacký celebrate the Bohemian past, his use of the Czech language—in the nineteenth century Austro-Hungarian Empire Czech was the language of the peasants of Bohemia—in the volumes published in 1848 and after was highly symbolic. Twentieth century historians interested themselves in additional types of groups, such as those defined by age, by sex, by ethnicity, and by social and economic characteristics.

Those who have helped make history—the events, not the writing about the past—have often written their version of what happened in pride or self-exculpation. Among the best have been the *History of the Rebellion*, a history of the English Civil War by Edward Hyde (1609–1674), advisor to Charles I and Charles II, kings of

Encyclopedia of Library and Information Sciences, Fourth Edition DOI: 10.1081/E-ELIS4-120043658

England, the *Personal Memoirs* of U.S. Grant (1822–1885), General in Chief of the Union forces in the American Civil War, and *The Second World War*, by Winston Churchill (1874–1965), Prime Minister of Great Britain during World War II. Now, a memoir by presidents and commanding generals is almost *de rigueur*.

How history is written can be as important as what is written. Originally, historical writing was one form of literature. Not until the development of professional history in the nineteenth century did the distinction develop between history written for historians and history written for Everyman. Today, both categories of publication flourish, although they are usually quite separate. In addition to the many books published every year by scholars and intended primarily for other scholars, there are many books on historical topics published in the hope that they will sell to and be read by a general, popular audience. In the United States, historical topics of perennial popularity are the American Civil War and World War II.

THE EVOLUTION OF HISTORICAL SCHOLARSHIP: THE BEGINNING

The writing of history has its own long history. Although they are not based on historical evidence, the creation myths that are among the earliest literature to survive are attempts to explain the past. The growth of kingdoms and empires produced annals and chronicles of events; royal chronicles date from the Middle Kingdom period of Egypt (21st–18th century B.C.). Such chronicles tend to be brief recitations of facts, but they are nonetheless a form of historical writing and have their modern counterparts, such as Elizabeth Stone's *American Library Development, 1600–1899* (1977) which gives a chronology of important occasions in American library history, but no narrative establishing connections or interpretations.

The first true historians in the West are considered to be Herodotus (c. 484–after 424 B.C.), who wrote about the Greek wars with Persia, and Thucydides (c. 460/455–399 B.C.), who wrote about the wars between Athens and Sparta. In China Ssu-ma Chien (145–90 B.C.) is usually given that honor. Thucydides wrote about war and politics as did Herodotus, but Herodotus was also interested in different peoples and their cultures. Ssu-ma Chien wrote treatises on the economy of China and on the control of its rivers and canals. What distinguished the work of these historians from that of the chroniclers was that they made an effort not only to state what happened but also to explain why it did. In addition, they paid attention to the accuracy of their sources. This combination of emphasis on sources and interpretation of the information they provide has remained a constant of historical writing through the centuries. As Sir Charles Oman wrote in 1939, "History, then, is the investigation of evidence, written or

sometimes unwritten, about series of events concerning which we are able to make some conclusion."[1]

Historians of the late classical period and the Middle Ages carried on and expanded the genre. Sallust (86–34 B.C.) attempted to make connections between events; he portrayed the rivalry between the Roman generals Marius and Sulla to dramatic effect. Both the Venerable Bede (c. 672/673–785), an English monk, and Einhard (c. 775–840), a German monk, wrote biographies, Bede of the abbots of Wearmouth and Jarrow, Einhard of Charlemagne. In the Islamic world, Ibn al-Athir (1160–1233) produced annals of world history; Ibn Khaldun (1332–1406) constructed a model of dynastic rise and decline in his history of the Arab and Berber dynasties of North Africa. In the writings of these periods one can find examples of persisting features of historical scholarship, such as attention to sources. The Roman historian Tacitus, for example, is known to have used the official records of the Roman state, both the minutes of the Senate and the collection of the acts of the government. Bede used both documentary and oral sources. Writing about events that the historian has participated in, such as the *Anabasis* of Xenophon (431–355 B.C.), is another continuing feature of historical writing, as is the effort to obtain rewards, exemplified by Froissart (c. 1337–1405), the chronicler of the Hundred Years' War, who modified the editions of his Chronicles to appeal to his successive patrons.

THE EVOLUTION OF HISTORICAL SCHOLARSHIP: THE RENAISSANCE AND ENLIGHTENMENT

A shift to greater emphasis on interpretation and historical causation can be observed in the histories written during the Renaissance period. Niccolò Machiavelli (1469–1527), best known as the author of *The Prince*, was the historian of the City of Florence and wrote a history of that city–state. He took the Roman historians Sallust and Livy (59 B.C.–c. 17 A.D.) as his models and sought to illuminate universal principles and general laws. The *History of Florence* can be read as a commentary on historical method.

The Enlightenment of the eighteenth century increased the emphasis on analysis and the description of change over time in historical writing. The eighteenth century also produced the man many consider the greatest historian of all time, Edward Gibbon (1737–1794), author of *The Decline and Fall of the Roman Empire*. Gibbon's approach was to combine the new "philosophic" fashion in historical writing exemplified by such men as David Hume (1711–1776), with the antiquarian tradition and its emphasis on accuracy. Gibbon is also noted for broadening the range of source materials used; his use of the critical geography of Jean Baptiste Bourguignon d'Anville (1697–1782) and the publications of the Académie des Inscriptions are only examples.

THE EVOLUTION OF HISTORICAL SCHOLARSHIP: THE NINETEENTH CENTURY

The nineteenth century brought a constellation of changes. In 1800, most historians in Europe and the United States were amateurs and probably independently wealthy. By the end of the century they were far more likely to be professionally trained university professors. During the century universities expanded both in number and in the range of subjects in which advanced study was possible. New areas of study, of which history was one, were added to curricula that had their roots in ancient Greece. Study beyond the undergraduate level offered a means of professional preparation. The growth in higher education made it possible for those with historical interests but modest means to earn a living as historians. Simultaneously, scholarly periodicals devoted to history were established, such as the *Historische Zeitschrift* in 1859, and organizations dedicated to historical scholarship were founded, such as the American Historical Association in 1884.

In much of this extension and amplification of the historical enterprise, Germany—and one man in particular—led the way. Leopold von Ranke (1795–1886) is often described as the "father" of modern historical scholarship. Responsible for the exhortation to write history "wie es eigentlich gewesen ist" (as it really was), Ranke wrote voluminously. His first major work was the *Geschichten der lateinischen und germanischen Völker* (History of the Latin and German Peoples) which appeared in 1824 and included an appendix in which he set forth a distinctive historical methodology. His last was an ambitious world history that he was working on at the time of his death. In between, came—among others–books on the Ottoman and Spanish empires in the sixteenth and seventeenth centuries, a history of the Roman papacy in the four preceding centuries, books on Germany in the time of the Reformation, and on Prussia, not to mention books on Britain and on France. His work demonstrated what would become the creed of the professional historian: intensive research, usually in records created as close to the events as possible; and interpretation of the findings, which usually meant an attempt to distinguish between significant and details.

His own scholarship, however, was only a part of Ranke's contribution to history. Beginning in the early 1830s, Ranke trained in his seminar at the University of Berlin the first generation of professional historians, men like Georg Waitz, Theodor Mommsen, and Jakob Burckhardt. One student, Maximilian II, king of Bavaria, established an historical commission within the Bavarian Academy of Sciences. For the remainder of the century, German universities were the places to go for the best historical training. American historians who studied in Germany included George Burton Adams (1851–1925) of Yale, William Dunning (1857–1922) of Columbia, Albert Bushnell Hart (1854–1943) of Harvard, and Clarence

Alvord (1868–1928) of the University of Illinois. J. Franklin Jameson (1859–1937), longtime first editor of the *American Historical Review*, was notable as the first American historian of distinction who had not studied in Germany.

Ranke also contributed to the development of the discipline with his attempt to found a scholarly historical periodical. The *Historisch-Politische Zeitschrift* (1832–1834) was in fact more political than historical, but it attempted to provide an historical background for current political problems. A second abortive effort was the *Zeitschrift für Geschictswissenschaft*, founded by Adolf Schmidt (1812–1887) in 1844. The void was eventually filled by the *Historische Zeitschrift*, begun in 1859 by Heinrich von Sybel (1817–1895), which continues today. Both Schmidt and von Sybel were among Ranke's students.

THE EVOLUTION OF HISTORICAL SCHOLARSHIP: THE SPREAD OF HISTORICAL SCHOLARSHIP

By 1900, German innovations were spreading and other features were being added. In the United States, for example, the first doctoral degree in history was awarded in the 1870s. Universities and colleges had begun to establish departments of history. The American Historical Association was founded in 1884 and the *American Historical Review* in 1895. Some universities had set up presses to publish the results of scholarship; historical scholarship was prominent on their lists from the beginning. There were, of course, national variations. In England and France, the pattern was less one of addition than of modification of older forms to new purposes. In non-European countries these developments came later, but today almost every developed country or one with aspirations for development displays similar patterns.

These nineteenth century innovations, the introduction of new canons of scholarship, the development of opportunities for advanced study in history, the foundation of organizations devoted to history, and the creation of media for the dissemination of scholarship did not, however, mean the disappearance of older patterns. Individuals who were not academically trained continued to write history, books on historical topics intended for general readers continued to be published, and articles on historical topics continued to appear in general intellectual periodicals like the *North American Review* and *Atlantic Monthly*. Among examples of American historians without formal historical training who did distinguished work at this time were Francis Parkman (1823–1893), author of the classic *The Oregon Trail*, and Henry Charles Lea (1825–1909), best known for his work on European religious history. Barbara Tuchman (1912–1989), author of *The Guns of August* (1962), is a more recent example.

THE EVOLUTION OF HISTORICAL SCHOLARSHIP: DIVERSIFICATION

The development of this integrated structure of education and publication of research brought expanded opportunities. Historical scholarship increased in quantity and diversified. While the characteristic publication format of the nineteenth century was the multivolume history, the formats of the twentieth century were the scholarly monograph and, increasingly, the scholarly article. These newer formats both contributed to and were the result of the increasing specialization of the field.

Initially, specialization tended to be by geographic area. American historians began to identify themselves as historians of a region, such as the South, the Mississippi Valley, and the West. In departments of history in the United States, the number of historians specializing in various European countries, beginning with Great Britain, increased and other areas like Asia began to be represented as those areas became of interest to Americans. Topical specialization followed; economic history and social history were added to traditional political history. In 2007, the history department of the University of California, Berkeley, a major research university and leader in doctoral study in history, had faculty who identified their specialties as Reformation Germany, comparative civil rights, women in Mexico, the history of biology, the history of crime in the United States, Chinese popular culture, and African health and gender.

Periodicals reflect this trend toward specialization. There are journals to match each of the specializations named in the Berkeley history department, journals of women's history, journals of religious history, journals of German history, journals of African-American and African history, even a journal of criminal justice history, and a journal of the history of biology. Specialization in periodicals has progressed to the point where some journals are doubly specialized, such as the *Journal of African Economic History*. There are also journals that are specialized by what one might call outlook, such as the *History Workshop Journal*, which was founded on the premise that history was a collaborative enterprise involving all interested parties. And there are interdisciplinary journals in which history is an element. When writing an article, the historian must decide which journal is the journal in which he or she would like to have the article published. That choice will affect emphases of presentation and can influence the research process to a certain extent.

University presses, the primary publishers of book length historical scholarship, also show some specialization, but theirs is more limited, since their mission is the much broader one of the advancement of scholarship rather than the advancement of one particular piece of it. A press may have a series in an area as the University of California Press does in the History of the American Cinema. Alternatively, it may lack a named series but still have a recognized interest in an area as the University of Alabama Press does in Alabama history and the University of Notre Dame Press does in Roman Catholic history. In recent years, pressures on university presses to emphasize sales potential have forced many to publish more books on American history, for example, than on European history, as well as more non-scholarly books.

THE EMERGENCE OF THEORY

Another differentiating feature of historical scholarship that has developed in the last century and a half is that of theory. Theory in history is not the same as theory in the natural sciences, although it shares some of the same properties. In the natural sciences, theories are usually the result of experimental research. They are an explanation for a set of data or a model that can be tested by experiment. In history, theories are not subject to testing. They offer explanations, but have more in common with the older and more amorphous concept of world view or *Weltanschauung* than they do with scientific theories. They function as an approach or an intellectual framework rather than a true theory. According to John Tosh, theories in history arise because of the difficulty of understanding the interrelatedness of all aspects of human experience at a given time and because of the nature of historical change and lack of change. A theory may also attempt to provide an explanation of the overall direction of historical events.[2]

Although historical theories have been particularly prominent in the late twentieth century, theory has been part of historical scholarship since Ranke. Until the end of the nineteenth century, the dominant principles of historical scholarship were those of historicism, a creed shaped by Ranke and his students. Historicism (Ger. *Historismus*) was, in fact, so closely identified with historical scholarship that for a longtime historical scholarship was defined by it. It emphasized the importance of close research in historical sources and the centrality of the state and political events and, by extension, defined what constituted proper subjects for historical inquiry. In contrast to Hegel's dialectic theory of history, Ranke's view was that each event is unique and an outgrowth of particular local conditions.

Not until late in the nineteenth century was there a serious challenge to historicism, a challenge usually associated with the name of Karl Lamprecht (1856–1915). Lamprecht criticized both historicism's emphasis on the state and its emphasis on political events. He urged more attention to economic and social issues, and—influenced by the newly emerging area of psychology—can be considered an early proponent of the study of *mentalités*, a concept used to describe the collective attitudes of a group. Stifled by the German historical establishment, Lamprecht's influence in Germany was largely outside the universities and limited to regional and local history. Outside of Germany, however, his ideas were much more favorably received, as in France and the United States.

However novel his ideas about what should be studied, Lamprecht did not challenge the fundamental principle of close attention to sources. Like Ranke, he used archival collections, but where Ranke sought information relative to political developments, Lamprecht sought information relevant to social and economic developments. Ranke used repositories like the Archives nationales in Paris, the Public Record Office in London, the Central State Archives of Moscow, the Vatican, and the Venetian State Archives, Lamprecht used ecclesiastical and city archives in the Rhineland, as well as manuscript collections in libraries and private hands. Ranke's evidence might come from the reports of the Venetian ambassadors, Lamprecht's from manorial records, but the appropriateness of a particular document depended upon the questions asked rather than the form.

In contrast to the relative stability of outlook of nineteenth century historical scholarship, the twentieth century saw a succession of "theories," each one attracting a share of attention and adherents, only to be joined by yet another that attracted its own attention and adherents. The most influential of these multitudinous approaches have been those of the Annales School, the Marxist historians, the historians who have devoted themselves to the study of a particular, hitherto ignored group such as women, and the postmodernists. No single outlook succeeded in vanquishing all others or achieving dominance and the pattern has been one of addition rather than replacement. For the individual historian, these theories have not necessarily been mutually exclusive. It has been entirely possible for a historian to be simultaneously a feminist historian and a Marxist historian; the founders of the Annales group were Marxists. In the twenty-first century, enthusiasm for such intellectual structures seems to be decreasing, as Lynn Hunt, a former president of the American Historical Association, suggested in one of her columns, "Where Have All the Theories Gone?"[3] Historians of different persuasions, however, continue to write history that is influenced by one or another outlook, even if the theoretical controversies are less strident.

The most robust of the various theoretical offerings has probably been that of the Annales group. Named for the journal founded in 1929 by Marc Bloch (1886–1944) and Lucien Febvre (1878–1956), the Annales School was characterized by openness, openness to new methods, and openness to new objects of study. Their guiding principle was that of total history (*histoire totale*); another concept identified with them is that of *mentalités*. One important member of the group, Fernand Braudel (1902–1985), contributed a unique approach to time, conceiving historical phenomena as having three periods: the *longue durée*, a period of long, centuries-long, stability in human experience, determined by such factors as climate and modes of production, the *moyenne durée*, a period of a major trend, particularly economic cycles, and the *courte durée*, a period of a brief phenomenon like a political movement, not lingering enough to be a trend. The breadth of what was considered appropriate for study is reflected in the various names of the *Annales*, one of the more recent of which was *Annales: Économies, Sociétés, Civilisations*. Braudel's book, *The Mediterranean and the Mediterranean World in the Time of Philip II*, (orig. Fr. ed., 1966) epitomizes this breadth, both temporally and in terms of subjects, as well as by the author's attention to the writing of historians from the entire region, not only those of Western Europe. The Annales group also looked to the developing social sciences for methods and insights, early leaders in what would become a common practice.

Marxist history asserts the primacy of economic, rather than political or cultural factors, as "the engine of history." Marx's concepts of class, capitalism, and production are used to interpret events. How these ideas should be applied in historical scholarship has been the subject of debate, and individual Marxist historians have increasingly added additional components to their thinking. They have tended to interest themselves in economic history or in social and cultural matters relating to the lower classes. Frequently cited examples of works by English-speaking Marxist historians are E.P. Thompson's, *The Making of the English Working Class* (1963) and E.J. Hobsbawm's *The Age of Revolution: Europe, 1789–1848* (1962) and *The Age of Capital, 1848–1875* (1975).

Other important approaches have come from historians of gender and historians of other disadvantaged groups. These groups have found new questions to ask, new sources from which to obtain evidence, and new ways to examine previously examined events. Often inspired by personal activism, they have revealed their subjects as actors, not passive objects, and full participants in the creation of the present world. Joan Scott is a prominent gender historian.

One of the most recent schools of thought is that of postmodernism, a complicated constellation of ideas drawn from philosophy, linguistic theories, and textual criticism. In the nineteenth century, historians tended to be positivists, to believe that the past was knowable. Historical knowledge was achieved using the historian's version of the scientific method, immersion in the sources, and generalization from the evidence obtained. Historians assumed that others who used the same sources and the same techniques would come to similar conclusions. In contrast, postmodernism casts doubt on the possibility of a shared understanding of the past, a view reinforced by radical relativism's position that absolute truth does not exist. Instead, understanding depends on the reader's cultural and ideological context and, by virtue of living in another time, the historian can never share the cultural and ideological context of the document. At most, the scholar can situate a text within different discourses. Pushed to its extreme, this position questions the possibility of historical knowledge. On the positive side, it has strengthened interest in cultural history.

These approaches hardly exhaust the varieties of approaches to historical scholarship. Some types, such as quantitative history, are more methodological practices than anything else, offering useful approaches for historians of vastly different interests. Historians, especially economic historians, have long concerned themselves with numbers, but perhaps influenced by the use of statistics in the social sciences, the use of numbers in history has considerably increased in recent years, an expansion facilitated by the development of computers. Quantitative techniques can be applied to a variety of situations; R.W. Fogel (1926–) worked on subjects as diverse as railroads, slavery, and hunger and premature death in modern populations. Other approaches draw on insights from fields outside history, like anthropology and sociology.

THE SOURCES

The character of the primary sources used by scholars in the twentieth century shows somewhat more variety than those of the nineteenth century, but overall there is a remarkable stability. The references in the articles of the first volume of the *American Historical Review* (1895–1896), a journal that has great prestige and includes history of all times, places and subjects, were compared with those in its 111th volume (2006). In both volumes, the primary materials used by the authors were almost exclusively manuscript records or printed primary material. Exceptions in the 2006 volume were a Web site that provided documentary evidence (a speech by the Tony Blair, British Prime Minister from 1997 to 2007) in one article and photographs that were a significant source of information in another article. An exception in the 1895/1896 volume was an interview in which the author of the article on the Underground Railroad had spoken with "an intelligent colored man—a barber, J.J. Minor by name," who had been an agent on the Railroad.[4] The citations to secondary sources in the two volumes, on the other hand, are quite different. In the 2006 volume there are abundant references to the monographs and articles of other scholars. There are virtually no citations to any kind of secondary material in the 1895/1896 volume. That difference reflects the paucity of historical scholarship in the late nineteenth century and its abundance in the early twenty-first.

History has been and continues to be largely identified with written records, but in the twentieth century the definition of appropriate source has expanded to include many kinds of non-written records. The desire to explore the history of peoples who have not left written records behind or who appear only in the written records of others inspired creativity. A particularly good example of this new inclusiveness is recent scholarship on African history. Jan Vansina (1929–), a Belgian who after training in medieval history was appointed a researcher in anthropology in the Belgian Congo, pioneered the use of oral sources. Growth in types of sources used to write African history has progressed to the point where evidence not only from oral sources is used but also evidence from linguistic, botanical, biological, archaeological, and artistic sources.[5] Nor is it only in less well documented fields that such alternative sources are used. Historians in general, impressed by what anthropology and sociology have achieved, show growing interest in their methods and sources of information.

A new project in history can begin in different ways: either a historian finds a question intriguing and decides to investigate it or a historian finds a collection of materials that promises to answer questions about an interesting topic. That collection may be newly discovered, as were the records of Cahokia, the first French settlement in Illinois to survive for any length of time, that were found by Clarence Alvord (1868–1928), or it may be a collection that has used by previous historians, but not used in the way the newcomer envisions. For the historian who begins with a question, the next step is the location of appropriate sources; for the historian who begins with the collection, the next step is immersion in the source.

How does a historian who begins with a question locate appropriate sources? The answer depends on what kind of sources are sought. Primary sources can be identified by the use of guides to archives and special collections, many of which are now available online, bibliographies of manuscripts, and in the bibliographies of scholars who have written on closely related topics. Conversations with knowledgeable archivists can be invaluable. Some primary sources are printed, either transcriptions of manuscript records, like the Monumenta Germaniae Historica, the great series of sources for German history begun by the Prussian statesman Freiherr vom und zu Stein (1757–1831) in 1819 or because the evidence the historian seeks originally appeared in a book, pamphlet, or government document.

For a book on public libraries in Nazi Germany material was located through guides to German archives, through inquiries directed to every provincial and city archives, through inquiries to existing provincial library administrations, and through inquiries to larger libraries about their own records. Printed reports of contemporary library agencies were identified through the German national bibliography. Librarians contacted frequently identified surviving librarians of the period who might be willing to be interviewed; one librarian had an important document in his possession. Secondary material was found through bibliographies and indexes and in books and articles on related topics by other scholars. Imagination, an eye for clues, and persistence are all essential. For that book on public libraries in Nazi Germany, the mention of a 1931 attack on the collection of the public library in Rostock in a document in one repository led the historian to write to the Rostock Public Library, which forwarded the query to the university librarian in Rostock, who had done research on the episode and graciously shared his results.

The importance of archives and manuscript collections to the historian cannot be overstated, although for some topics, particularly those where quantitative methods are used, the same statement could be made about published sources like censuses, statistical reports, etc. Fortunately for the historian, governments, religious bodies, organizations, and other enterprises need to know what their actions and decisions were. Archives, defined as either a collection of records and historical documents or the place in which they are collected, date back to the ancient classical world.[6] For the most part, however, institutions that store and service records are a modern creation. With the exception of the Papacy, heir to the Roman Empire, political entities in Europe did not begin to make formal, centralized arrangements to regulate the preservation of their records until the late eighteenth century. The Archives Nationales of France was created in 1790, the Public Record Office of Great Britain followed in 1838. The National Archives of the United States was finally established in 1934.

Public access to archives followed. After an 1851 petition signed by 83 individuals, including Charles Dickens, Thomas Babington Macaulay, and Thomas Carlyle, the right of access to the Public Record Office for scholarly purposes was granted. By early in the twentieth century, however, the interests of scholars in archives were generally acknowledged, and American historians were among the interest groups that pushed for the National Archives.

Not all records, of course, are open for to the public for use. Some government records may be closed for security reasons or what one might call pseudo-security reasons, such as the attempts of the second Bush presidency to reclassify unclassified documents to protect its actions and policies from scrutiny. Privacy concerns affect access; stringent laws have been passed in some countries to protect the privacy of individuals. Nongovernmental records, such as the records of organizations and businesses and the papers of individuals, are private property and may remain in the custody of the organizations and individuals that created them or of their heirs and successors; they may not have been opened to scholars.

Limitations imposed by inefficiency, bureaucratic indifference, and design also impede historical research. Records may have been destroyed by those who hope to protect reputations; the famous erasures on the Nixon tapes by his loyal secretary, Rose Mary Woods, are a prime example. Less purposeful but no less final is the destruction of records by administrators who considered them no longer worth bothering about. Many records never reach appropriate repositories and will not, therefore, be used; how many records lie buried in dusty file cabinets in the office where they originated or forgotten in some storage area can only be imagined.

Underfunding of archives and records management programs can create major problems. As of the summer of 2006, the National Archives of the United States had over 1,000,000 feet of undescribed records. Those million feet of almost certainly unclassified documents contain useful information on some historians' topics, but they have no way of verifying that fact. A historian should be smart enough to figure out that the records of the Agency for International Development will contain information on United States foreign aid even if there is no guide to them, but in which boxes, folders, and documents the desired facts reside will remain a mystery until they are described at the folder level—unless, of course, the historian is willing to go through, box by box, folder by folder, sheet by sheet, however many hundreds of feet of records there are.

Although many of these limitations are present in the United States today, a rich array of archives is in place, beginning with the National Archives, and includes state and municipal archives, archives of organizations like the Rockefeller Foundation, as well as archives of numerous churches, businesses, and groups. In addition, there are many special collections of the papers of prominent individuals that are either housed in independent institutions like the presidential libraries or have been deposited at some library or archival establishment. Other countries have their own counterparts; the richness depends on the financial resources available and the priorities of those responsible for collecting and preserving the records. These collections make possible historical scholarship, and research in an archives is typically the defining experience of a historian in the same way that field research is usually the defining professional experience for the anthropologist.

Once a relevant source is identified and located, the next question is, is it trustworthy? With modern records, that is rarely a problem. In all probability, the records moved directly from the organization where they were created to the archives. The records themselves may contain information that is untrue or misleading, but the misinformation was either recorded in good faith by a creator who believed it to be true or was recorded by someone who wished to influence an intended reader in a particular direction. It is the historian's job to separate truth from falsehood, to weigh what is in the records, and to compare it with information from other sources. Modern history offers a few examples of deliberate fakes like the Hitler Diaries of 1983, but such frauds are usually detected early.

Earlier sources, however, are more likely to be either fraudulent or altered. In the early modern period, interest in history largely focused on religion and the Church. Concerted efforts to copy and publish manuscripts relating to the lives of saints and the history of the Church began in the late sixteenth century. These great collective enterprises were carried out primarily by the Bollandists, an association of Jesuit scholars, and the Maurists, a congregation of Benedictines.[7] Because the souls of men and women were at stake and because the preceding centuries had seen a flourishing market in religious fakes, standards needed to be developed to identify fraud. In defense of his work on the Benedictine charters of St. Denis, Jean Mabillon (1632–1707) published *De re diplomatica* (about Diplomatics) in 1681. This work defined principles for determining the authenticity of medieval manuscripts and charters and in many respects has not been superseded.

TECHNOLOGY

As far as historians are concerned, technology has had both positive and negative consequences. The introduction of printing, by making possible multiple copies of the same document, increased the chance of its survival. The introduction of the typewriter in the late nineteenth century vastly improved legibility. The telephone, on the other hand, has been detrimental. By its nature a telephone conversation is evanescent. Only in the rare cases in which a recording was made or a conversation summarized in a memorandum or other communication is there a record of what was said.

The development of digital records has affected the historical enterprise in the identification of source materials, in access to source materials, and in the creation of source materials. Historians, like those in other fields, have benefited from the creation of machine-readable bibliographic databases brought by the advance of library technology. There are now numerous databases that include indexes to periodical literature, like *Historical Abstracts*, and some that offer the full texts of articles, like *JSTOR*, as well as online bibliographies and catalogs that list books, pamphlets, and manuscript collections, like *WorldCat*. Because they are so convenient and accessible, historians use them far more readily than they ever used their print counterparts.[8,9] Many guides to individual collections have been made publicly accessible by repositories, like the finding aids for the archives of the American Library Association at the University of Illinois Archives. Some repositories are also making the materials themselves digitally accessible, like the C.S.S. Alabama Digital Collection at the University of Alabama Library (http://www.lib.ua.edu/libraries/hoole/digital/cssala/main.htm). And there are programs underway to digitize books, like the Google Book Project and Project Gutenberg, which will increase access to both primary and secondary source books.

As far as historians are concerned, the leading challenge of digital records lies in the third area, digital records as primary sources. Since about 1960 an increasing proportion of all records has been created digitally, whether the creating body is a government agency, a business firm, or an individual. For many of these records there is no paper equivalent; the electronic voting machine, for example, generates no hard copy register of the votes. As more recent times become the object of historical study, digitally produced sources will increasingly be the sources of the evidence on which historians base their accounts.

Why are they such a challenge? One reason is their sheer volume. The ease of creation of an electronic record, paired with a general trend to ever more documentation by increasingly legalistic and regulated societies, has brought superabundance. Nor is this abundance always well controlled. The physical presence of paper forced individuals and offices to create and use filing systems. Such systems are possible in a digital environment, but individuals appear to use them less consistently.

The inexorable progress of technology, both of hardware and software, brings other problems. Files created before an office's last upgrade often cannot be read. Records were created during the Vietnam War using systems that have long since been superseded and replaced. Their conversion is sometimes possible, but if it is, it is costly. There are also preservation issues. We know the problems the preservation of paper poses; we are only beginning to discover those posed by electronic records. Every other format of information storage degrades; there is no reason to think that digital information will be immune.

HISTORY AND THE PUBLIC

As with many areas of activity, history has popular appeal. Because knowledge of the history of one's own country is regarded as a vital element in the socialization of citizens, some history is included in most high school-level curricula. This practice provides most students with at least a minimum level of knowledge and sometimes stimulates interest in history in later life.

Many publications are available to those who are interested in history. Commercial presses publish numerous biographies and other works of history. Such works involve research, but they are usually written in a more accessible style than works of historical scholarship intended for historians, usually emphasizing the story rather than analysis. Historical fiction is another way in which history reaches a wider audience. It can be very good, like the Captain Horatio Hornblower series of C.S. Forester (1899–1966), or it can be very bad, like the typical "bodice ripper." There are also historical journals intended for the interested public, such as *American Heritage* and *History Today*.

Local history attracts many amateur historians. Many cities and counties have societies dating back to the nineteenth century that hold meetings and offer history-related activities. Frequently, they publish a periodical or some other type of publication. The county of Somerset in England, for example, has both the Somerset Archaeological and Natural History Society, founded in 1849, that publishes proceedings and various other papers and pamphlets, and the Somerset Record Society, founded in 1886, that publishes transcriptions of original documents relating to Somerset, like the 1342 Feodary of Glastonbury Abbey.

Modern means of communication have also been used to create and to disseminate historical products. Many films and television programs have historical themes; those of Ken Burns are both popular and well-regarded. More and more people are contributing to various oral history programs. Story Corps, a national project of the American Folklife Center at the Library of Congress, is a large scale project intended to encourage people from all walks of life to tell their particular stories.

Popular history also has a recreational aspect. Recreations of battles attract numerous participants. Preservation efforts like Williamsburg and Sturbridge Village, two of the most ambitious examples, attempt to portray life in the past with fidelity and are visited by thousands of sightseers annually.

CONCLUSIONS

What is the future of historical scholarship? In the absence of a crystal ball, it seems safe to predict that its future will be one of both stability and change. The foundational questions, what happened and why did it happen, will continue to be asked as long as humans remain curious about their past. The foundational skills of the historian, the ability to identify questions of significance, the ability to find, select, understand, and evaluate evidence, the ability to argue logically and persuasively and to write clearly are not likely to change.

Change will occur in the questions that are posed. Historical scholarship has always had a presentist bias, a truth expressed most eloquently by Benedetto Croce's famous dictum, "All true history is contemporary history." Experience influences what people deem important; depressions are good for economic history and going to war with a country stimulates curiosity about its past. Different generations will have different priorities and concerns and ask different questions.

Already in progress is change in the sources that historians use. Influenced by the success of historians at using nontraditional sources to study the history of peoples without written records, it is probable that historians will expand the range of types of sources even further to supplement traditional sources. The increased use of primary sources in digital form is inevitable as the events of recent years become the object of historians' interests.

Another realm in which change can be expected is that of theory. Both small-scale theories like the Whig theory of history that viewed history as progressing toward parliamentary government on the British model and world view-type theories like the Marxist theory of history will be replaced by new explanations and newer world views.

Less clear is what can be anticipated in the relationship between the historical writing and the public. The distance between scholarly history and popular history appears to be growing. Although many scholars would very much like to reach a wider audience, it is an uncomfortable fact that what entices readers who are not scholars conflicts with the present canons of historical scholarship.

Historical scholarship has its traditions. Standards of scholarship are well-defined. It is not, however, a discipline with paradigms in the sense in which Thomas Kuhn defined paradigm in his book, *The Structure of Scientific Revolutions* (1962). Ultimately, the individual historian decides which questions are worth asking and how they should be examined. Each has his or her own viewpoint and it is entirely possible for two historians to come to quite different conclusions from the same evidence. As the narrator in Dorothy Salisbury Davis's story, "By the Scruff of the Soul," commented, "history's like a story in a way: it depends on who's telling it."[10]

REFERENCES

1. Oman, C. *On the Writing of History*; Barnes & Noble: New York, 1969; Methuen: London, U.K.
2. Tosh, J., Ed. *The Pursuit of History: Aims, Methods and New Directions in the Study of Modern History*, 2nd Ed.; Longman: London, U.K., 1991; 154–155 New York.
3. Hunt, L. Where have all the theories gone?. Perspectives **2002**, *40*(3), 5.
4. Siebert, W.H. Light on the underground railroad. Am. Hist. Rev. **1896**, *1*(3), 456.
5. Philips, J.E., Ed. *Writing African History*; University of Rochester Press: Rochester, NY, 2005.
6. Posner, E. *Archives in the Ancient World*; Harvard University Press: Cambridge, MA, 1972.
7. Knowles, D. *Great Historical Enterprises: Problems in Monastic History*; Nelson: London, U.K., 1963; New York.
8. Stieg, M.F. The information needs of historians: or, how historians don't use libraries. Coll. Res. Libr. **1981**, *42*(6), 549–560.
9. Dalton, M.; Charnigo, L. Historians and their information sources. Coll. Res. Libr. **2004**, *65*(5), 400–425.
10. Davis, D.S. By the scruff of the soul. Ellery Queen's Mystery Mag. **1963**, *41*(1), 6–19.

BIBLIOGRAPHY

1. Ambacher, B.I., Ed. *Thirty Years of Electronic Records*; Scarecrow Press: Lanham, MD, 2003; Oxford, U.K.

2. Boyd, K., Ed. *Encyclopedia of Historians and Historical Writing*; Fitzroy Dearborn: London, U.K., 1999; Chicago, IL.

3. Burke, P. *The French Historical Revolution: The Annales School, 1929–1989*; Polity Press: Cambridge, U.K. Stanford University Press: Stanford, CA, 1990.

4. Cohen, G.A. *Karl Marx's Theory of History: A Defence*; Oxford University Press/New York Princeton University Press: Oxford/Princeton, NJ, 1978.

5. Hine, D.C., Ed. *The State of Afro-American History: Past, Present and Future*; Louisiana State University Press: Baton Rouge, LA, 1986.

6. Iggers, G.G. *Historiography in the Twentieth Century: From Scientific Objectivity to the Postmodern Challenge*; Wesleyan University Press: Middletown, CT, 1997.

7. Jenkins, K., Ed. *The Postmodern History Reader*; Routledge: London, U.K., 1997; New York.

8. Jordanova, L. *History in Practice*, Arnold: London, U.K., 2000.

9. Lukács, G. *History and Class Consciousness: Studies in Marxist Dialectics*, Merlin: London, U.K., 1971; MIT Press: Cambridge, MA.

10. Rigby, S.H. *Marxism and History: A Critical Introduction*; Manchester University Press: Manchester, U.K., 1987; St. Martin's Press: New York.

11. Scott, J.W. *Feminism and History*; Oxford University Press: Oxford, New York, 1996.

12. Scott, J.W. *Gender and the Politics of History*; Columbia University Press: New York, 1988.

13. Stieg, M.F. *The Origin and Development of Scholarly Historical Periodicals*, University of Alabama Press: Tuscaloosa, AL, 1986.

14. Tosh, J. *The Pursuit of History: Aims, Methods and New Directions in the Study of Modern History*, 2nd Ed. Longman: London, U.K., 1991; New York.

15. Tosh, J., Ed. *Historians on History*; Pearson Education: Harlow, Essex, U.K., 2000.

16. Williams, R.C. *The Historian's Toolbox: A Student's Guide to the Theory and Craft of History*, M.E. Sharpe: Armonk, NY, 2003.

17. Wilson, N.J. *History in Crisis? Recent Directions in Historiography*, Pearson, Prentice Hall: Upper Saddle River, NJ, 2005.

History of Libraries

John Mark Tucker
Abilene Christian University, Abilene, Texas, U.S.A.

Edward A. Goedeken
Iowa State University, Ames, Iowa, U.S.A.

Abstract

Society created the library in response to individual, community, and national needs for memory and self-understanding. The development of the library as an institution follows the story of literate humankind and facilitates the telling of the human story in multiple languages and cultures. The library documents growth in intellection and other changes in the human condition. It preserves resources for those of minority as well as majority opinion, ensuring preservation and access for the unorthodox in human affairs. The library respects the full range of human interests and creates networks of resource sharing and international cooperation on behalf of reader interests.

THE ORIGINS OF LIBRARIES

The precise origins of libraries are impossible to trace, although scholars have accumulated knowledge of particular libraries in certain locations. Historians have concluded in general that the invention of writing combined with the impulse to preserve inscriptions have marked the beginnings of the historic era, a period of consciousness about the importance of human memory. The earliest ideas about libraries emerged as a natural outgrowth of interest in preserving such memory, and the library has acted on behalf of society to collect and organize things that are written. The library thus meets a vital social obligation by gathering accounts of the human experience.

DEVELOPING THE INTELLECT: THE ANCIENT WORLD

The creation of libraries likely began with the Sumerians who flourished during the fourth millennia B.C.E. in the region of Mesopotamia between the Tigris and Euphrates rivers. The Sumerians and succeeding civilizations—Akkadians, Babylonians, and Assyrians—inscribed clay tablets using a stylus and imprinting combinations of "wedges" (or Latin *cunei*) into soft clay. With the Sumerian economy based on grain, most of the extant cuneiform tablets describe agricultural transactions. The temples, which were seats of government, stored cuneiform inscriptions in wooden boxes with a tablet labeling the box's contents. Temple storehouses preserved commercial and governmental documents, hymns, prayers, and incantations, and major literary works such as the *Epic of Gilgamesh*.

In the ancient Syrian city of Ebla, a comprehensive, well-organized royal library housed more than 15,000 tablets. The cities of Nippur, Nuzi, and Mari established similar collections. During the seventh century B.C.E., King Assurbanipal (669–633 B.C.E) who ruled Egypt and Babylonia and Assyria, established a great library in the capital at Nineveh. Assurbanipal sought to collect every available work relating to cultural, social, and religious matters within his kingdom. His agents scoured the empire to acquire or to copy such works; his scriptorium in Nineveh produced new editions and his library emerged as an encyclopedic collection of human knowledge.

The growth of ancient libraries continued with the Greeks who developed a taste for book collecting and erected a number of Greek temples that featured libraries. In the sixth century B.C.E., Polycrates of Samos and Pisistratus of Athens established public libraries. During the Age of Pericles (ca. 495–429 B.C.E.), an emerging book trade supported the growth of private collections by philosophers, writers, and other scholars. Aristotle built an extensive manuscript collection to support his catholic intellectual pursuits. Plato's Academy and Aristotle's Peripatetic academy nourished the idea that books were essential to the growth of an educated populace.[1]

The military conquests of Alexander the Great expanded Greek interest in books and learning to a wider audience, and Aristotle's organizational scheme provided the basis for the library in Alexandria, Egypt, which would become the most significant library in the ancient world. Founded by Ptolemy I in the third century and brought to fruition by his son Ptolemy II, the museum and its accompanying library swiftly became the premier site for learning and scholarship. Led by some of the major intellects of its time, including the grammarian Callimachus (ca. 305–240 B.C.E.), the astronomer and writer Eratosthenes (276–

Encyclopedia of Library and Information Sciences, Fourth Edition DOI: 10.1081/E-ELIS4-120043544

194 B.C.E.), and the philosopher Aristophanes of Byzantium (267–180 B.C.E.), the Alexandrian library gathered enormous collections of papyrus and vellum scrolls, which were painstakingly cataloged by Callimachus in his famous *Pinakes*. Eventually, war took its toll on the Alexandrian Library and, by the end of the fifth century C.E., its collections were scattered and lost to the ages.

In Asia Minor, Attalus I (269–197 B.C.E.) and his son Eumenes II (197–159 B.C.E.) established another important library at Pergamum. When Ptolemy II banned the export of papyrus, book makers at Pergamum adopted parchment, which was much more durable since it was made from animal hides, thus marking major progress in preserving library materials. In his history, Plutarch claimed that, with the coming of the Romans in the first century B.C.E., Mark Antony bequeathed to Cleopatra about 200,000 volumes of the Pergamum Library, later absorbed into the Alexandrian Library.

The Romans mirrored Greek interest in books and learning to the extent that Roman emperors—like their counterparts in Alexandria—confiscated and copied books for central libraries. Eminent scholars like Cicero and Seneca created large private collections. Excavations have revealed library rooms in private dwellings in Rome and other major cities throughout the empire. Plutarch and Pliny mentioned that prominent citizens had built extensive private libraries some of which featured separate rooms for Greek and Latin books.

Successful military leaders often acquired books as part of plunder, Mark Antony being the most prominent example. Julius Caesar envisioned the construction of several libraries, some of which were completed after his assassination. The emperors Augustus, Tiberius, Vespasian, Trajan, and Hadrian all established libraries in Rome during the first two centuries C.E. Trajan's Bibliotheca Ulpia, completed about 100 C.E., served as the Public Records Office of Rome until the fifth century. In Byzantium, the emperors Constantine the Great (280–337 C.E.), Julian (331–363 C.E.), and Justinian (482–565 C.E.) sought to expand the holdings of the imperial, patriarchal, and scholarly libraries at Constantinople and elsewhere. Through the efforts of countless scribes and copyists over the centuries, the Byzantine libraries preserved the intellectual heritage of Athens, Rome, and Alexandria, thus preserving ideas from the ancient world and making possible the cultural richness of the Renaissance.[1]

In South Asia, the Aryans, who had established themselves in the Indus Valley in the middle of the second millennia B.C.E., promoted the growth of Jainism and Buddhism, both religious movements with sacred canons. Libraries and archives soon appeared to help organize and preserve this extensive literature. In China, the Han dynasty (206–220 B.C.E.) endeavored to preserve ancient texts that had often been scattered by warfare in earlier centuries. Han emperors encouraged the writing of literature and developed a culture of meticulous record keeping.

The Chinese created a seven-part classification scheme that organized knowledge into Confucian classics, philosophy, prose and poetry, military accounts, medicine, scientific and occult writings, and summaries. The Chinese later revised this system into four parts: the classics, history, philosophy, and miscellaneous works.[2]

DEVOTED TO PRESERVATION: THE MEDIEVAL ERA

With the decline of the ancient libraries in the last years of the Roman Empire, the era of great classical libraries came to an end. For the next thousand years the typical European library—which could more accurately be called a "special" library—consisted of several dozen, or perhaps a few hundred, laboriously copied manuscripts housed in monasteries overseen by learned monks. Religious motivations influenced library development in Western Europe during this period. Copies of the Bible along with letters and commentaries made up the contents of these rudimentary collections.

During the first centuries of the Common Era, the classical format of the book changed both in structure—from scroll to codex—and in type of surface upon which words were written—from papyrus to parchment and vellum. The advent of the emerging Christian culture influenced the eventual adoption of this new format, which led to the construction of a portable and easily readable collection of individual books that became the Bible. Thus the texts contained within the codex became more durable and easier to use and to store. They also had the decided advantage of accommodating the contents on both sides of the codex sheet. Books were shelved on their sides, in chests (*archiva*), or on shelves or desks and, as collections grew, the shelving would sometimes occupy the walls of an entire room, often referred to as a *bibliotheca*. At the outset of the Medieval Era, the *libraria* was a licensed distributor or dealer in books, and the *bibliothecarius* was curator or custodian of the collection. Monasteries often provided space for the library and for the *scriptorium* where copyists plied their craft; eventually, the term "librarian" came to denote one who worked with books in an organized collection.[3]

In the early Middle Ages, two monastic leaders, St. Benedict of Nursia (ca. 480–547) and Flavius Aurelius Cassiodorus (502–597), building on the early precepts of St. Jerome, established rules for transcribing and maintaining manuscripts and general guides for library maintenance. Benedict's rules for copying manuscripts governed that process for the next several centuries. St. Isidore of Seville (ca. 560–636) also wrote standards for operating these fledgling libraries. Such practices continued under the Carolingians, and imperial patronage in Visigothic Spain and Ostrogothic Italy maintained libraries devoted to the preservation of Latin and Greek texts.

More than 220 monasteries existed in Merovingian Gaul although fewer than 300 manuscripts from their collections have survived. By laboriously copying—and thus preserving—numerous classical writings, hardworking monks transmitted an intellectual heritage for future generations. Although the classical texts were not Christian, and therefore considered pagan, early church fathers valued them as precursors of the Christian revelation. By transferring these decaying texts from papyrus to parchment, the church preserved the wisdom of the ancient world.

In contrast to the lands of the Roman West, the Eastern Empire maintained its independence for several centuries, not passing to the control of Islamic forces until 1453. Both Diocletian (245–312) and Constantine (280–337) had promoted the creation and maintenance of imperial libraries at Nicomedia and Constantinople. The great Justinian (527–565) relied on the large palace library to compile his famous code. Photius of Constantinople (820–893) created an influential reference work, the *Myrobiblion*, a classified digest of 280 works. Over the centuries, libraries thrived in great cities and small villages. Given the blending of church and state in the Byzantine Era, it became common practice for imperial and cathedral libraries to organize collections that included secular and religious works. By 1204, the libraries in Constantinople had suffered grievously at the hands of the Crusaders, many never recovering from such devastation.

Meanwhile to the south, a vibrant new civilization was growing from the sands of Arabia based, like Christianity, on the importance of the book. The *Qur'an* encouraged the acquisition of learning and knowledge and, for the Muslim scholar, the private library became essential. Many small libraries were eventually absorbed into larger mosque libraries, the most famous being that of al-Azhar in Cairo, founded in the ninth century. Under the Abbasid Caliphate (750–1258) the *Dar Al-Hikmah* (House of Wisdom) was established in Baghdad in the early 800s. The third most important Islamic collection in the Middle Ages was the court library of the Ummayad rulers of Cordoba, Spain (750–1031), which ultimately boasted a collection of over 400,000 volumes. The steady growth of libraries continued under the Seljuks (1037–1300) and the Ottoman Turks (1299–1923). By the end of the first millennium, Islamic culture supported the construction of numerous libraries, many of which were open to the public. Islamic scholars, moreover, performed an invaluable service for the West by translating Greek and Latin manuscripts into Arabic, thus making them available for future scholars during the Renaissance. The Muslims also acquired knowledge of Chinese papermaking, transmitting this important technology to the West.

While much of Europe sank into cultural depression, King Charlemagne of Frankish Gaul was leading a revival of learning. Under the tutelage of Alcuin of York, who had been influenced by monastery libraries in his native England, Charlemagne founded a school at Aachen, which established the importance of libraries for learning and scholarship. Thus a new educational system emerged, stimulating library growth in the last years of the millennium. This flurry of intellectual activity led to the founding of libraries at monasteries in Mainz, Salzburg, Fulda, Würzburg, and the famous Abbey of St. Gall in Switzerland, which had been erected in honor of the great Irish monk.

During the eleventh and twelfth centuries, production efficiencies vastly reduced costs, thus making it possible for libraries to acquire more volumes. Cathedrals established schools that took the lead in promoting education among the elite, and their libraries provided resources for learning and the professions. The Carthusians (founded in 1084) and Cistercians (founded in 1098) both instituted special rules for the operation of libraries. Meanwhile, during the late thirteenth and fourteenth centuries, fledgling universities—prompted by the earlier appearance of cathedral schools—began to appear at Oxford, Cambridge, and Paris. The universities sought to supply moderately priced books to students, with libraries playing a large role in obtaining duplicates and cheaper editions to distribute freely to young scholars, and keeping extra copies for themselves.[2]

The Vatican had maintained a library at the Lateran Palace since the fourth century, but it had been repeatedly sacked by Rome's invaders. During the exile of the papacy to Avignon in the fourteenth century, the limited collections were further dispersed. Vatican librarian Bartolomeo Platina (1421–1481), who served during the papacy of Sixtus IV, reorganized the collection, carefully describing it, making it available to Catholic scholars and convincing Sixtus to establish consistent funding for new acquisitions.

Princely collections emerged in distributed fashion in the years from 1350 to 1500. In the later Middle Ages, kings began to establish libraries in royal residences. Ruling elites expended great financial resources to obtain and house books, prices for which exceeded what most common people could afford. The nobility viewed a fine library as not merely a scholarly apparatus but also a shrine to the word of God or a monument to individual achievement. Resources such as these could enrich research libraries in a later era. Thus, the French king Charles V installed a library on three floors of the Louvre, which would eventually become the Bibliothèque Nationale, and in England, Henry VI donated some of his private collection to King's College in Cambridge.

REDISCOVERING THE PAST: THE RENAISSANCE

Humanists came to dominate the intellectual climate of the fourteenth and fifteenth centuries, regarding the book—its collection, preservation, reproduction, and distribution—as instrumental in fostering the new learning that would characterize the Renaissance. Humanists devoted themselves to writing and speaking eloquently, to living an upright and moral life, and to serving God as unique individuals, rather than merely as insignificant beings in a massive unfathomable universe.

Seeking fresh perspectives, the fifteenth century reader turned to the classics of ancient Rome and Athens. Scholars rediscovered Cicero, Virgil, Horace, Caesar, and Plato. The advent of the printed book as a result of Johannes Gutenberg's (1400–1468) invention of moveable type in the 1450s—and the subsequent dramatic growth of the craft of printing led by luminaries such as the Venetian Aldus Manutius (1449–1515)—spurred unprecedented expansion in the volume of printed works. This powerful new movement of literary and political expression yielded a vast outpouring of publications in many new subjects which, along with steadily rising literacy rates, promoted libraries as an essential feature of early modern intellectual life.[4]

In Italy, the Venetian book collector Francesco Petrarch (1304–1374) inspired dozens of other scholars to scour European and Middle Eastern countrysides for Greek and Latin manuscripts. Petrarch's personal library numbered only about 200 volumes but contained significant classical works previously unavailable to scholars. In Florence, Coluccio Salutati (1331–1406) and Niccolò de'Niccoli (1346–1437) built libraries exceeding 800 volumes. In Rome, Cardinal Basilius Bessarion (1403–1472), who was of Greek descent, sponsored the collecting and copying of ancient Greek manuscripts and maintained a personal library of more than 1000 volumes. After the fall of Constantinople in 1453, Bessarion's library was donated to the city of Venice. Subsequently, book collectors helped to unearth and make available hundreds of long neglected classical manuscripts. Many private collectors relied on agents who visited bookshops for rare manuscripts, and the literate classes circulated lists of recently published works.

Niccoli's library became the basis of the magnificent Biblioteca Marciana established by Cosimo de' Medici in the mid-sixteenth century and served as one of the first public libraries in Italy. In 1571 Cosimo's grandson, Lorenzo the Magnificent, founded his own public library in a building designed by Michelangelo. While Renaissance humanists might use the term "public library," their notion of it was a collection intended for use by the wealthy, the politically connected, cultural elites rather than by the masses of humankind.

In palatial settings, books were often laid open on pulpit-style lecterns and consulted while standing. By the latter part of the sixteenth century, books were placed on shelves, spines facing inward, with notations on the book's title inscribed on the exposed fore-edge. Collections were managed by library workers who created subject catalogs of their contents and who made initial attempts at classifying books based on prominent subjects such as religious works, canon and civil law, and medicine, followed by philosophy, history, poetry, rhetoric, and grammar.

By the early fifteenth century, the French king Charles V and the British king Henry VI had established royal libraries. In Germany and Central Europe, impressive court collections grew at Augsburg under the influence of the wealthy banker, Jakob Fugger, and at Wolfenbüttel in Lower Saxony, which could boast as its most famous librarian, the philosopher Gottfried Leibniz (1646–1716). Similar libraries appeared in other countries, including the Escorial library in Spain, and in the cities of Vienna, Prague, Munich, and Buda (Hungary). The European intelligentsia developed collections in support of their respective professions. Thus at Ferrara, Italy the physician Nicolò Leoniceno sought ancient Greek manuscripts relating to medicine, and in Seville, Spain, Hernando Colón, son of Christopher Colombus, created an extensive library devoted to ancient and modern geographical sources. Many Renaissance court libraries also housed informal academies filled with collections of scientific instruments.

The growth of libraries during the Renaissance was driven by the dual impact of the printing press and the thirst for both new and rediscovered learning that characterized intellectual life during the fifteenth and early sixteenth centuries. Literate elites sponsored large secular collections which were accompanied by the rise of organized efforts to create bibliographic tools to improve the accessibility of these materials.

NEW HEAVEN AND NEW EARTH: THE REFORMATION

The sixteenth century was a period of intense conflict on the European Continent as the Reformation, beginning with Martin Luther in 1517, shook the very foundations of the established religious order. As a result of the burgeoning Protestant crusade, monastic libraries were damaged, gutted, or razed. The destruction went beyond obvious Catholic Church facilities with even the university libraries in England at Oxford and Cambridge bearing the brunt of anti-Catholic sentiment. The library at Oxford was reduced to such an extent that the furniture was sold, a practical response owing to the loss of so many books. Despite the devastation that resulted from his complaint with Roman Catholicism, Luther fervently supported libraries, and in 1524 he urged in a public letter to all German towns that no expense be spared in establishing good libraries in each community. In response, many new municipal libraries appeared during this time including those at Hamburg (1529) and Augsburg (1537). This period also featured the rise of new universities at Königsberg, Jena, and Marburg, all requiring the acquisition of new book collections.

The rapid expansion of printing promoted the Reformation and the Counter-Reformation as both sides produced thousands of publications to support their positions. Even before 1520, the Catholic Church had sponsored the printing of specialized texts for scholars as well as practical manuals for parish clergy. One significant outcome of the Reformation was the production of numerous translations of the Bible into the vernacular for use among the literate classes. Thus Luther's German Bible appeared in 1534. Meanwhile translations into other languages were published across the Continent: in Dutch (1526), French (1530), Italian (1530), English (1535), and Spanish (1543).[5]

Although literacy was still limited to upper classes or to those educated in Catholic traditions, the Reformation fostered the production of large quantities of popular literature, intended for the common people, resulting in larger numbers of readers and even greater demand for publications. Religious conflict in the sixteenth century stimulated a remarkably powerful output of printed works which emanated from dozens of skilled printers throughout Europe. This vast literature, combined with steadily rising levels of literacy on the Continent, stimulated library growth at impressive rates. The major libraries grew and consolidated their holdings from smaller, private collections. Examples include the Hofbibliothek in Munich (1558), the Escorial Library near Madrid (1575), the Imperial Library in Vienna (1576), and the Ambrosiana Library in Milan (1609). Still the great libraries were not available to most citizens, only the wealthy or those sponsored by well-connected patrons.

ENLIGHTENING THE EYES: THE SEVENTEENTH AND EIGHTEENTH CENTURIES

The rapidly expanding output of published books during the period of the Reformation merged with renewed interest in study and learning that had grown out of the Scientific Revolution to accelerate intellectual life in the early seventeenth century and contributing to growth in all types of libraries. By mid-century, scientists in England, France, Germany, and Italy were expressing the need to move beyond book fairs and the printed lists of booksellers in order to stay abreast of the latest developments. They established the scholarly journal at about the same time that science was becoming more specialized and diverging from *belles lettres* and philosophy. The scholarly journal would come to disseminate research among intellectual communities, fueling the steady growth of private collections.

Libraries were of two kinds: collections built by the wealthy in their homes and those established to support educational, religious, or governmental institutions. Library workers ceased the chaining of books, preferring to place them in cases lining the walls with spines facing outward. Library collections served elite patrons who

were permitted access during limited hours. Private libraries, such as the one developed by French Cardinal Jules Mazarin (1602–1661), grew large enough to require unprecedented organization. Mazarin's library was directed by Gabriel Naudé (1600–1653) who, in his 1627 treatise on library practice *Avis pour dresser une Bibliothèque*, laid the foundation for arranging and managing private libraries. Naudé recommended that books be valued for their content—rather than for their beauty or rarity—and that they be organized by subject and readily available to those with scholarly interests who themselves may have limited resources for building their own libraries. The collection should be described in separate author and subject catalogs. Presciently, Naudé also proposed that libraries be housed in stable and safe environments, free of dirt, moisture, and noise. Following Naudé's instructions, Mazarin's library eventually opened to the public in 1691 and became the basis for the Bibliothèque Nationale following the French Revolution.

The seventeenth century yielded another library-related classic, one that was destined to take its place among the great documents of humankind. In *Areopagitica* [1644], John Milton (1608–1674) addressed an agency of the British Parliament with a sweeping argument that continues to reverberate. Milton argued for a free press, freedom of mind, freedom of conscience, and that ideas freely expressed and heard and deeply considered constituted the highest order of civil liberty. Milton claimed that even bad books deserve a place, but that one who destroys a good book destroys reason itself, something made, as it were, in the image of God. Although the ideas that he integrated into a whole were not original with Milton, he was the one to present them most cogently and eloquently.

Milton thus developed a theoretical framework for the freedom of the reader and for the protectors of books and ideas as rightly oppositional to forces of suppression. Despite an intrusive (though predictable for his time and place) anti-Catholic rhetoric, Milton provided future librarians, professors, readers, and authors with the conceptual tools necessary to argue for the free distribution of printed materials. An important complementary essay written by John Stuart Mill (1806–1873) appeared in 1859. In *On Liberty*, Mill elaborated on Milton, broadening notions of toleration using as foundational ideas an additional two centuries of liberal thought, yet still advocating restricted rather than unfettered access on the part of young people. In the twentieth century, echoes of Milton and Mill have been heard in official documents of library practice in democratic societies. Concepts of intellectual freedom as articulated by librarians, journalists, and professors have tended to proliferate in those societies grounded in well-defined relationships between society and the individual.[6]

Among major libraries appearing in the early seventeenth century was the Bodleian Library at Oxford University (1602), steady growth for which was spurred by its energetic chief benefactor, Sir Thomas Bodley (1545–1613). August, Duke of Braunschweig (1579–1666), founded his library in 1604; it was destined to become one of the finest on the Continent, eventually being renamed the Herzog August Bibliothek at Wolfenbüttel. These were followed soon thereafter by the Ambrosiana Library and the Angelic Library in Rome (1620). Centuries removed, interpretations as to dates of founding may vary as do library names as a result of restructuring and mergers.

In addition to the Bibliothèque Nationale, other nascent national libraries emerged during this period. The library assembled by Friedrich Wilhelm of Brandenburg (1620–1688), starting in 1659, became the Prussian State Library. Catherine II of Russia, an admirer of Voltaire and Diderot, greatly expanded Peter the Great's original collection by capturing as spoils of war the extensive library maintained in Warsaw by Andrej and Jozek Zaluski in the 1790s. The British Museum, which opened in 1753, came about as a merger of the private collections of Sir Hans Sloane (1660–1753), Sir Robert Cotton (1571–1631), and Robert (1661–1724) and Edward (1689–1741) Harley. In 1757 the British Royal Library, which contained works collected by English kings beginning with Edward IV, further enhanced the British Museum's holdings.

The better libraries in early America were assembled by business elites, individual collectors whose books and journals would eventually enrich the great research libraries such as Harvard and Princeton and Yale universities, the New York Public Library, the Library of Congress, and the American Antiquarian Society. Many of the private collectors were motivated by religious interests; the bequest of Puritan minister John Harvard established the Harvard College Library in 1638. Thomas Bray (1656–1730), Anglican minister and bibliographer, devoted to educating clergy and expanding mission work, established some fifty parish libraries throughout the colonies from New York to the Carolinas to Bermuda with about half of them in Maryland. Later he founded some 80 such libraries in England and Wales.

Another movement was underway in North America, that of the social or circulating library. Owned by a private association, books would supply reading matter for members and their families. Benjamin Franklin (1706–1790), scientist and scholar, pioneered in establishing the Library Company of Philadelphia in 1731. Also known as subscription libraries since association members paid fees to become joint owners, the social libraries mirrored similar arrangements in Europe, especially in England where by the mid-eighteenth century more than 250 such libraries were thriving in London and in the countryside. Social libraries established variously by business or working class interests demonstrated the value of reading to an increasingly sophisticated citizenry and became conceptual predecessors to the tax-supported free public library. Robert Keayne's (1595–1656) bequest of 1656 marked an early attempt to create a library in Boston for use by the public; the collection eventually built was destroyed by fire in 1747.

In the Far East, during the Qing Dynasty reigns of K'ang hsi (1662–1722) and Ch'ien-lung (1736–1795), the Imperial Library, palace collections, and governmental agency collections continued to grow. In 1686 K'ang hsi issued instructions about proper maintenance of the Imperial Library. Western works on science and astronomy were translated and added. Ch'ien-lung's (1711–1799) great contribution was to create the Four Treasures Library, an effort resulting in a definitive collection of 36,000 volumes in Chinese philosophy, history, literature, and other subjects.

REVOLUTION IN POLITICS AND SOCIETY: 1776–1875

The fresh winds of democracy blew across the Atlantic from the new United States of America and into France, and the French revolution resulted in expanded access to reading materials. From the fall of the Bastille in 1789 to 1795, the French wrote 20 decrees pertaining to libraries. Rising middle classes confiscated ecclesiastical property and private collections of the nobility, establishing *dépôts littéraires* throughout the nation. This program was visionary, as it included plans for a union catalog and conceived of the scattered collections in urban and district repositories as a commonly held national resource. Two major developments emerged; one involved vastly expanded middle class access to books with middle class defined as white males. The concept of free public libraries also arose, with more robust expressions in Paris than in the countryside. But many provinces had municipal and parish libraries, some of which escaped confiscation due, only in part, to having been considered of minimal value.[7]

A second major trend in the politics of nation building was the movement to establish central libraries with national level responsibilities. In the years from 1793 to 1795, the Bibliothèque Nationale won authorization to obtain first manuscripts and then books from throughout France. Central libraries with nationalizing impulses also arose in Lisbon (1796), The Hague (1798), Washington, DC (1800), Budapest (1802), Buenos Aires and Rio de Janiero (1810), Oslo (1811), Santiago de Chile (1813), and Reykjavik (1818). In the leading cities of Russia, private collections formed the basis of the Imperial Public Library, opened in 1814 in St. Petersburg, along with the N.P. Rumiantsev Library founded posthumously in 1831 and transferred to Moscow 30 years later as the core of the Lenin Library. With the British Museum (more recently the British Library) as forerunner, these national institutions gradually assumed the role of keepers of the cultural record and as leaders in organizing collections and services and in training staff.

The Industrial Revolution in the early nineteenth century brought an influx of rural populations into the great cities of Europe and North America. Millions left the farm, seeking employment in the factory and economic and educational opportunity in the city. Crowded conditions among the new urban masses exacerbated crime and illiteracy. Multiple social responses, both secular and religious, incorporated the tools of self-enlightenment: reading and the distribution of literature, a robust popular press, lyceums, books clubs, and libraries. Literacy emerged to stimulate social critique, but also to quell urban unrest and acculturate youth into the national ethos. Reformers distributed small portable libraries which featured moral instruction but other topics as well.

Reformers also established mechanics institutes representing the reading interests of working class males but most such organizations were eventually absorbed by middle class business interests. The Society for the Distribution of Useful Knowledge (SDUK), established in England in 1826, promoted the expansion of reading and libraries for the working class. In 1839 the SDUK issued *A Manual for Mechanics Institutes*, an early analysis of the value of resource sharing. The *Manual* recommended interlibrary lending that incorporated cathedral libraries, county seat collections, municipal archives, the holdings of book clubs, and the reading rooms of religious denominations.

The Sunday school movement promoted literacy for both genders, something that mechanics', businessmen's, and early subscription libraries had failed to do. The interdenominational Society for Promoting Christian Knowledge (SPCK) had been active in England and Wales for more than a century. The Wesleyans, Presbyterians, and Episcopalians established circulating libraries in North America. Sunday school libraries, partially dependent on the societies, featured not only biblical studies and moral rhetoric but also light fiction, drama, and contemporary nonfiction. In early nineteenth century England, the Religious Tract Society rivaled the SPCK as a distributor of evangelical publications. Sunday schools reached socioeconomic strata below the middle classes and, in fact, provided models for literacy instruction among ethnic minorities. Sunday schools were also among the earliest organizations to take seriously the reading interests of children and young adults in part because of their intense focus on moralistic and middle class behavioral norms. By 1850 Protestant denominations had established more than 2000 Sunday school libraries in the United States and adjoining territories.

Public education at the elementary and secondary levels obtained governmental support, laying the foundation for apprenticeships, vocational training, and civic participation, and providing school libraries. By the 1850s the English common school movement had spurred the establishment of libraries especially in secondary schools. Local control played a larger role in school library support in North America than it did in Europe and the Far East where national leadership became a more powerful determinant.

In the nineteenth century German universities thoughtfully took library functions beyond custodial and scholarly interests. The University of Göttingen established policies to expand professorial and student access. American student, and later founder of the Boston Public Library, George Ticknor (1791–1871) was made to feel welcome enough that he came to regard Göttingen's rich collections as a common treasure not merely for Germany but for the entire world of scholarship. German intellectuals, moreover, sought a wide audience by publishing encyclopedias intended for home use, thus making feasible a collection of searchable knowledge and practical information for the nuclear family.[7]

PROFESSIONALIZATION AND GROWTH: 1876–1988

Landmark events in 1876 marked the dawn of a new era in the professionalization of librarianship. Melvil Dewey (1851–1931) developed a system of classification on the concept of relative location, thus rendering obsolete earlier fixed-location arrangements. Published in 1876, the Dewey Decimal Classification (DDC) found ready acceptance throughout North America. The year 1876 also marked the first issue of *American Library Journal*, retitled *Library Journal*, the first journal in the United States devoted solely to library topics. At the same time, the United States Office of Education issued its massive report, *Public Libraries in the United States of America, Their History Condition and Management: A Special Report of the U.S. Commissioner of Education* [1876], thus launching a large body of professional literature rooted in historical precedent, in contemporary best practices, and in commonly held yet often conflicting assumptions about the social and political purposes of libraries. Librarians established the American Library Association (ALA) in 1876, the first national conference of library practitioners since 1853, which began annually thereafter to address current issues, and to promote the growth of libraries and, to a lesser extent, the professional and economic development of library workers. The Library Association was established in Great Britain in 1877. With the emergence of a professional literature and professional societies, the foundation was laid for the unprecedented expansion of libraries and for the education and training of library workers throughout the English-speaking world.

The editors of *Public Libraries in the United States* considered a public library as any library to which an individual could gain access, a view inclusive enough to incorporate mercantile and subscription libraries, academic libraries, and specialized libraries such as those devoted to law, medicine, and theology. In the year 1876 the origins of such libraries could be traced back more than 200 years. But the tax-supported free public library was altogether different according to William Frederick Poole (1821–1894) who claimed that the free libraries of Europe had served the intelligentsia, rather than the masses, and had not been supported by taxation. Perched atop the public libraries of first Cincinnati and then Chicago, Poole defined the public library much as we know it today—established by state legislation, supported by local taxes and by gifts, and maintained for citizens invited to share equally in its intellectual bounty.

Kathleen Molz describes the tax-supported free public library as essentially an Anglo-American phenomenon, an ameliorating influence responding to the Industrial Revolution in Britain and the United States, an influence associated with reformers who also opposed slavery and promoted education for youth and better treatment for the mentally ill. She observes that the public library movement gained momentum at about the same time in both England and in New England with enabling legislation from the British Parliament in 1850 and 1855 and with locally supported municipal libraries in the United States. Among the American pioneers were Salisbury, Connecticut and Peterborough, New Hampshire, although the first major metropolitan public library opened its doors in Boston, Massachusetts in 1854 and soon emerged as worthy of emulation.[8]

The Boston Public Library has attracted the attention of historians for another reason—research into the motivations of founding elites. In the 1970s Michael Harris studied the Boston Public Library, challenging the previously accepted view of the Library as essentially altruistic, committed to providing reading materials that responded to democratic impulses for political participation and economic opportunity. In "The Role of the Public Library in American Life: A Speculative Essay" Harris pointed to more sinister purposes, that elites created libraries to inculcate compliance from the citizenry, a willingness to accept the *status quo*, not challenging dominant political and cultural norms.[9] A revisionist perspective on social and political purposes thus entered public library historiography and *The Journal of Library History, Philosophy, and Comparative Librarianship* [commonly referred to as *JLH*] recorded much of the vibrant conversation advanced by Elaine Fain,[10] Michael Harris,[11] and Dee Garrison[12] in 1975, Edward G. Holley[13] in 1977, and Michael Harris[14] and Phyllis Dain[15] in 1978.

In collegiate education, Germany had provided a model for her European neighbors and for North American institutions of higher learning in the late nineteenth and early twentieth centuries. Research as a university ideal came first alongside undergraduate liberal arts education then, in many places, eclipsed it. The Universities of Göttingen and Tübingen, for example, led evolving conceptions of critical historical and literary analyses. Germans refined the seminar method of teaching, which featured graduate students making presentations based on examination and comparison of original sources. The intellectual structure for seminar methods was rooted in disciplinary expansion; the social sciences spawned the new disciplines of sociology, economics, political science, and psychology, all of which were growing increasingly sophisticated and examining new paradigms.

German universities attracted scholars from across the globe to pursue studies in the humanities and the emerging social sciences from new, more scientific perspectives. Herbert Baxter Adams (1850–1901), a Johns Hopkins University professor and founder of the American Historical Association, joined the trek of Americans who returned from Germany to the States with the gospel of scholarship for expanding academic libraries into strong retrospective collections organized around disciplinary strength. Rationales for seminar libraries followed inevitably especially from 1880 to 1920 when the broad outlines for the modern university began coming into view, and when new university library buildings featured interior reading rooms organized by discipline and later referred to as subject departmental libraries. Seminar libraries had become powerful symbols of institutional commitments to doctoral research and teaching.

Historians of higher education acknowledge the Social Gospel and Progressive periods as encompassing the formative phases for higher education and its libraries and the twentieth century as the time when university research libraries—based on internal organization and collection size—came to full maturity. Kenneth J. Brough chronicled the transition of the American university library from storehouse to workshop in *Scholar's Workshop: Evolving Conceptions of Library Service* [1953]. He explored the history of the ideas, notions, terms, and phrases for the university library, providing metaphors for its purpose in academe.[16] The leading American university research libraries, based on the depth and range of printed collections, include private universities Harvard, Yale, and Stanford, and public universities Illinois, Michigan, and California at Berkeley. And in the United Kingdom, Oxford and Cambridge had long since set the standard for collections, having been established in the Middle Ages. In 1918, the British Parliament established the University Grants Committee for institutions of higher education throughout England, expanding the national role in financial support. In Italy an 1889 statute had created a council at each university governing library book expenditures. These models differed substantially from the more diverse methods in the United States, which relied on combinations of local, state, and private support.[7]

The Industrial Revolution dominated life in Europe and North America in the late nineteenth century. In those nations most advanced economically, industrialists combined technological innovation with mass production as they constructed factories in big cities. Population centers swelled to unprecedented proportions, creating new wealth amidst unrestrained business expansion. On occasion, a wealthy industrialist would demonstrate civic virtue and cultural influence by supporting colleges, museums, and libraries. One such leader was steel magnate Andrew Carnegie (1835–1919) who contributed funds to construct 3000 library buildings in Canada, England, Ireland, and the United States.

Carnegie used his library contributions to refine the relationship of the municipal library to its constituents and to expand the public library movement throughout the English-speaking world. Precursors of the tax-supported free public library had featured 1) subscription libraries serving upper and middle class, and sometimes working class, interests for members only and 2) municipal reference libraries dependent on wealthy philanthropists. By implementing the requirement that grant recipients collaborate with local governments to elicit tax revenues for library maintenance, Carnegie underscored the value of public–private partnerships but also the importance of continuous public support for cultural institutions. With a new Carnegie library building, even the smallest village was afforded the opportunity to promote literacy, leisure reading, adult education, and political engagement with an institution that stirred a sense of civic pride and accomplishment.

As the great cities had attracted burgeoning populations seeking opportunity, so also they attracted the social problems that followed in the wake of humans as economic commodities in the great industrial engine. The unrestrained rise of industrialization, immigration, and urbanization had created dislocations that permeated Western nations. Individuals felt keenly the loss of belonging and social control formerly inhering in towns and neighborhoods, schools, and churches. Citizens sought order amidst unprecedented change; they felt deeply a loss of community; and they came to see the professions as vital ameliorating influences.[17] A better life, it was hoped, would require more nurses, social workers, teachers, and librarians, thus giving rise to formal education for the helping professions and exemplifying the best Victorian impulses to exercise social control through service for the commonweal.[18]

Educating Library Workers

Since earliest times, aspiring librarians had been apprenticed to the directors of large libraries on the premise that those who oversaw the largest collections dealt with matters of greatest complexity in processing and housing collections, and in making them available to readers. Simultaneously, bibliographers and other library workers continued to develop the core information that would come to be used in formalized training. The writings of Gesner and Naudé advanced this thinking, accompanied by the writings of book collectors, scholars, and philosophers who offered larger intellectual perspectives

and thus helped to establish foundational requirements for practitioners.

As the search for new ideas about the meaning of librarianship intensified, the resulting information provided frameworks for formal instruction. As early as 1821, the Ecole des Chartes in Paris offered conceptual development in the form of archival training. During the early and middle years of the nineteenth century, increasingly nuanced ideas were advanced by the Germans Martin Schrettinger (1772–1851) and Friederich Adolph Ebert (1791–1834), the Danish scholar Christian Molbech (1783–1857), by the Italian Antonio Panizzi (1797–1879) who directed the British Museum, and by Charles Coffin Jewett (1816–1868) in the United States.

As important as these contributions were, they could not match Melvil Dewey's power to educate and to otherwise influence rising generations of library workers. His conceptual grasp of classification and early adoption of standardization laid a solid foundation for library training, a program he launched at Columbia College in 1887 and later moved to the New York State Library in Albany. Dewey had observed vast public and school library movements spreading across a growing nation; he saw the educational potential of libraries and the employment potential of educated librarians. He would prepare individuals for frontline services: his graduates would create catalogs—the essential finding aids for local collections—and they would teach and assist readers and oversee reading rooms. The librarians would become resourceful guides for inquisitive citizens in the big cities and small towns of the rapidly expanding Industrial Age. Though Dewey may have been North America's most visible library educator, he did not labor alone. Indeed, a number of library schools appeared around the turn of the century and soon thereafter, some of them in the public libraries of major cities including Atlanta, Los Angeles, New York, and St. Louis.

Schools flourishing during the first generation of American education for librarianship rode the wave of emphasis on efficiency in business and civil service reform when government workers advanced beyond political patronage into more professionalized settings. The intellectual foundations for library training were quite rigorous and, in fact, schools often required tough entrance exams that assumed knowledge of history, literature, geography, the arts, and foreign languages. Thus early graduates promoted dominant cultural values and mastered the multiple routine tasks that marked librarianship as an entry-level middle class profession. Library education worldwide sprang from independent schools—some of which emulated Dewey and his counterparts—in Munich (1905), Leipzig (1914), Copenhagen (1918), London (1919), Padua (1922), and in Wuhan, China (1920). By the mid-twentieth century many schools had moved into university masters' degree programs. While the master's became the basic requirement for practice in public, academic, and special libraries, undergraduate programs also trained librarians, especially for school libraries, and a small number of nations and states admitted practitioners through examination.[19]

Meanwhile, an alternative model for educating library workers was offered by the redoubtable Karl Dzaiatzko (1843–1903), a German scholar and early adopter who organized cataloging records by interfiling slips alphabetically. In the 1870s Dziatzko restructured library collections at the University of Breslau. By 1886 he was at the University of Göttingen presenting scholarly lectures for librarians-in-training, moving beyond the older systems of patronage and apprenticeships. Holding professorial rank, Dziatzko rooted his lectures in classical scholarship and descriptive bibliography, offering for the Continent a more intellectual approach than either Melvil Dewey or the training programs provided under the aegis of urban public libraries. Unfortunately, the German bibliographer never created a full curriculum and never attracted wide interest on the part of prospective librarians. More scholarly iterations of library education lay dormant until 1926 when the Carnegie Corporation funded the first doctoral program in librarianship at the University of Chicago.

Women Working

Library training programs succeeded in attracting large numbers of females into the profession. As with other helping professions, librarianship was thought by contemporary opinion leaders to be especially suited to women who sought employment beyond home and whose gender traits it was argued were appropriate for successful practice. A male-dominated profession in the nineteenth century and earlier, librarianship transitioned quickly to become female-intensive.

Female participation in the profession has reflected dispositions in the society at large, that women have suffered from discriminatory attitudes and practices. From the earliest years of the twentieth century, according to Mary Niles Maack in "Gender Issues in Librarianship," the library press reported on the absence of women in the top administrative posts of the largest libraries. Maack underscored instances of "hierarchical discrimination," recalling that in 1952 the Public Library Inquiry had documented a dual career structure for males and females and that, in 1987, males constituted 73% of the directorships of member university libraries of the ARL (Association of Research Libraries).[20] The term "glass ceiling" came to describe the barrier faced by women librarians possessed of administrative talent but, due to systemic ideologies arrayed against them, were denied the opportunity to exercise that talent at the highest possible levels.

Maack also identified "territorial discrimination" as the sequestering of women into technical processing and children's and youth services, regarded by many as roles well-suited to female attributes. Another type of territorial

discrimination has been the dispersal of professionals by type of library with men predominant in settings with higher social status, university research libraries, and with women often clustered in less prestigious workplaces such as small public libraries.

Recent scholarship devoted to the history and biography of women librarians has confirmed their skill as resourceful promoters of library services that extend beyond well-connected elites. The impulse of women to transcend the boundaries of gender, class, and race has influenced cultural life as varied as that in China, India, France, Germany, Nigeria, the United States, and the states of the former Soviet Union. Historical precedent has combined with civil rights movements, feminist theories, and case law to provide new tools for the profession to create more equitable settings for women library workers.[20]

Twentieth Century Expansion

Much of the world was engaged in all-consuming war during the early years of the twentieth century. Governments also waged ideological battles, with democracies competing with socialism, fascism, and with repressive governments on virtually every continent. During World War I, libraries supported the war effort with their own special expertise. The American Library Association collaborated with the American Red Cross, the Y.M.C.A., and other social service agencies to support troops through book distribution programs. Librarians shipped 1.5 million books overseas and processed additional millions for libraries for more than 600 military encampments and seagoing vessels, a process that transformed ALA into a much more robust organization.

Military services and related support functions stimulated the expansion of governmental libraries of all types, especially among dominant nation states. These subject collections ranged from patents, to social science data, to foreign affairs, to classified documents. Some of the great libraries in the U.S.S.R., for example, were in Moscow, collections devoted to the social sciences, the sciences, agriculture, and military affairs. Among the finest special libraries in the world were those held by the British Museum. Others of special significance in the United Kingdom include libraries of the Royal Society of Medicine, the Royal Geographical Society, and the School of Economics at the University of London.

Libraries experienced dramatic growth after World War II in the years of economic expansion and the Cold War. Massive federal subventions were designed to prepare nations in the fight against opposing ideologies. Much more was at stake than merely differing points-of-view. The United States and the U.S.S.R. had developed weapons of mass destruction, challenged each other for technological superiority in space, and fought wars of proxy while literate societies began to process the meaning of the Holocaust, and the Israelis carved out of Palestine an economically viable but constantly threatened militarized state. Nations committed support for all levels of education as part of larger movements to establish economic and military superiority. Librarians frequently argued for greater library support as vital to national security, military power, and economic expansion. Libraries devoted to technology and science enjoyed unprecedented growth; a number of academic libraries doubled in collection size every 20 years. During 1968 on college campuses in the United States, 68 major building projects were underway; during 1993, 25 years later, that number had risen to 100.[21]

Sharing Resources

The modern idea of bibliographic control of a library's holdings has developed slowly over the centuries culminating in today's policies and tools for classification, cataloging, and complementary means of bibliographic description. Librarians have come to value such tools, understanding that the local collection rarely meets every request of the local reader, and have thus sought to meet the needs of multiple readers by sharing resources. Since the days of the Sumerians, library keepers were assisting readers in finding materials of interest. This task became especially complex during the Renaissance as the great increase in secular knowledge, produced by a small army of publishers springing up throughout the Western world, resulted in vast new amounts of reading materials and expanding library collections.

The idea that a single volume could guide the inquiring reader and encompass all human knowledge was an idea that had attracted a number of scholars including Konrad von Gesner (1516–1565). In 1545, he published *Bibliotheca Universalis*, a catalog in Greek, Hebrew, and Latin intended to identify all writers (with titles of their works) who ever lived. What may have been the first printed catalog of an academic library appeared in 1595 at the University of Leiden. Most catalogs of this period were arranged into general classes such as theology, medicine, philosophy, and history and then subdivided by the size of the volume. Thomas James (1573–1629), the energetic first librarian of the Bodleian Library, was encouraged by his benefactor, Sir Thomas Bodley, to devise more detailed listings of that library's holdings so that, as a result of book-buying tours of the Continent, the Bodleian would not duplicate what it already owned. The 1620 catalog was likely the first catalog arranged alphabetically by title, an approach vastly improved by 1674 when Thomas Hyde (1636–1703) and later Thomas Hearn (1678–1735) added cross-references to the alphabetical title lists.

A landmark event in resource sharing was the adoption of individual cards to replace entries in static printed volumes, thus providing flexibility and currency in catalog information. Led by such early leaders as Charles Coffin Jewett and Charles Ammi Cutter (1837–1903), American libraries had, by the end of the nineteenth century, begun replacing their printed catalogs with cards. This change yielded fresh interest in improving the description of cataloged works. Sir Antonio Panizzi's groundbreaking 1841 *Catalog of Printed Books in the British Museum* laid the foundation for later efforts by Jewett in 1853 and Cutter in 1876. Influenced by Panizzi and by the 1871 *Prussian Instructions*, catalogers continued to revise rules in subsequent years and throughout the twentieth century. Revisions included those of the American Library Association's *Catalog Rules: Author and Title Entries* (often called the 1908 code), a 1941 revision (sometimes called the 1941 draft code), the 1949 *Rules for Descriptive Cataloging in the Library of Congress*, the 1961 International Conference on Cataloguing Principles (known as the *Paris Principles*), and the well-known 1967 *Anglo American Cataloging Rules*. In 1978 *AACR* was revised to become the *AACR2* which itself was revised in 1988, 1998, and in 2002. Complementary developments included standards for monographic description as reflected in the 1974 International Standard Bibliographic Description which was later applied to nonbook sources.[22]

Description represents only half of the challenge of establishing bibliographic control. The other half is the use of classification to facilitate location in a specific library. A number of classification schemes have been invented with that of Melvil Dewey becoming most widely accepted. While at Amherst College, Dewey created his Dewey Decimal Classification (DDC) which has undergone numerous revisions in order to update nomenclature and concepts, and has become popular in American public, school, and academic libraries. The Library of Congress (LC) developed its own system, drawn initially from an arrangement by Thomas Jefferson (1743–1826) whose approach to classifying knowledge had, in turn, been rooted in concepts of knowledge articulated by Sir Francis Bacon (1561–1626). The LC system was greatly elaborated in the early twentieth century by J. C. M. Hanson (1864–1943) and Charles Martel (1860–1945). In 1901 the Library of Congress began distributing copies of cards to libraries throughout the nation, one important result being the widespread adoption of the LC system especially in academic and research libraries. Other classification systems were the Colon Classification developed by S.R. Ranganathan (1892–1972) in 1933 and the Bibliographic Classification of Henry Evelyn Bliss (1870–1955), which appeared in segments between 1940 and 1953.[23]

By the late nineteenth century, librarians as a learned community had begun to seek professional growth through the formal exchange of ideas both practical and philosophical. Enthusiasm at the inception of the American Library Association spread across the Atlantic Ocean to the first International Conference of Librarians in

London in 1877. Attendees represented the United Kingdom. and the United States as well as Australia, Belgium, Denmark, France, Greece, and Italy. The opening session credited the Germans for contributing the term *bibliothekswissenschaft*, translated "library science." Participants established The Library Association of the U.K., taking note of the differing perspectives of their American counterparts. A second international conference hosted in London in 1897 drew 641 (more than twice the attendance 20 years earlier), representing the Far East as well as Europe and North America. Conferees presented papers on administration, architecture, bibliography, cataloging and classification, children's services, education for librarianship, employment opportunities, and public services.[7]

Cooperative enterprises advanced considerably as a result of the International Conference on Bibliography (Brussels, 1895) which, in turn, established the International Institute of Bibliography (IIB) to develop a universal bibliography on the structure of Dewey's classified subjects. Paul Otlet (1868–1944) and Henri La Fontaine (1854–1943) negotiated with Dewey to adapt the fifth edition of the DDC in order to develop the Universal Decimal Classification (UDC) which they completed in 1907. The UDC, a faceted scheme, was especially well-suited to scientific and technical subjects, and has been widely adopted throughout the world, particularly in Europe, French-speaking North Africa, Spain, and Latin America.

Otlet and La Fontaine pursued a number of educational and organizational ideas, establishing, in 1910, the Union of International Associations. The IIB itself continued UDC development in French, German and English and later became the International Federation for Information and Documentation (FID). The FID subsequently affiliated with other international organizations such as UNESCO (United Nations Educational, Scientific, and Cultural Organization) and IFLA (International Federation of Library Associations and Institutions). In the 1960s and 1970s, FID, IFLA, UNESCO, and others collaborated on library education for developing regions, establishing and strengthening programs in China, Ethiopia, Indonesia, Jamaica, Morocco, Nigeria, the Philippines, Senegal, Uganda, and Venezuela.[24]

In the 1960s in the United States, the Library of Congress led a collaborative effort to create the MARC (Machine-Readable Cataloging) format. With MARC records as a standard, two American networks began distributing online bibliographic records contributed by member libraries: OCLC (Online Computer Library Center, originally Ohio College Library Center) and RLIN (Research Libraries Information Network), affiliated with the Research Libraries Group. OCLC emerged as the core database provider for regional networks, most of which provided a broad range of services including preservation, document delivery, and continuing education. Varieties of MARC were adapted for the United Kingdom, Korea, and other nations, further enriching what functionally became an international database, a vitally essential tool for resource sharing.

Serving Diverse Populations

Ethnic minorities routinely confront multifaceted challenges to economic and educational opportunity, a truism in both free and totalitarian nations. Such circumstances of daily existence describe, for example, Iranians in the United Kingdom, Palestinians in Israel, and African Americans in the United States. Libraries hold the capacity to preserve racial memory, enhance ethnic pride, and acculturate immigrants into the national ethos. The histories of urban public libraries, such as Phyllis Dain's *The New York Public Library: A History of Its Founding and Early Years* [1972], feature discussions of ethnic collections and services to immigrant populations. The role of the librarian, extrapolating from Dain's account, embraces an appreciation for every minority perspective however misunderstood or unusual. Thus, without ignoring the interests of the majority, the librarian incorporates peace literature into a military library, or resources on Islam in a predominantly Christian community, or Hispanic materials in a largely Caucasian city. The library, as it provides resources for minorities, becomes a harbinger of economic and intellectual mobility. A reference source such as the one by Stephan Thernstrom, Ann Orlov, and Oscar Handlin, eds., *Harvard Encyclopedia of American Ethnic Groups* (1980) provides entry into the multiple layers of minority status; and E.J. Josey and Marva L. DeLoach, who edited *Handbook of Black Librarianship* (2nd. ed., 2000), provide a well-informed guide to collections and services for one particular minority culture.

The task of the librarian who would serve the citizens of a pluralistic, multicultural readership constitutes a balance of the tension between advocacy and neutrality. The librarian advocates for access on behalf of the reader who explores the unorthodox in politics, theology, art, sex, and other areas of human interest. At the same time, the librarian—understanding issues of authority and credibility—does not discriminate as to content, preferring as highest priority the task of bringing readers together with the subjects they pursue, regardless of where reader interests might lead. This work is highly political, requiring that people of courage promote professional ideals. Sam Walter Foss (1858–1911) illustrated this professional tension at its best. He wrote that the librarian

is both Greek and Barbarian, Jew and Gentile, realist and romanticist, aristocrat and democrat, theosophist, secularist, orthodox, liberal, populist, and patrician.... the janitor of an amphitheater where warring creeds, beliefs, and tastes contend like gladiators. [The librarian] champions none and antagonizes none, but simply keeps his amphitheater in good repair and takes a sportsman's like delight in seeing the fight go on.[25]

GLOBALIZATION: 1989–PRESENT

Two cataclysmic events in 1989 signaled the arrival of a new age: 1) political revolt in China, fueled by students, professors, and labor activists who had been communicating, in part, through e-mail, culminating in the Tiananmen Square Massacre, and 2) the destruction of the Berlin Wall, the reunification of Germany, and the dispersal of the nations of the U.S.S.R. into independent states. These events symbolized unprecedented intellectual and economic exchange transcending geopolitical borders and barriers of ethnicity, language, and culture. The internet expanded from scientific and military uses into general business and educational purposes, transforming the way the world conducts its affairs. Commercial entities that never before existed came to redefine for-profit and not-for-profit institutions. Thomas L. Friedman heralded the new age in his synthesis, *The World Is Flat [Updated and Expanded]: A Brief History of the Twenty-first Century* (2006). Reading material provided by librarians became available in digital form, accessible anywhere one could find a computer with an Internet connection, no longer bound by a printed or film-based format.

The new age also marks new expressions of religious, economic, and political fundamentalism and militarism. The world of the twenty-first century is as dangerous as in any previous time. Libraries that would pursue successfully their highest ideals require open societies characterized by relative political and economic stability. War, terrorism, and natural disasters destroy libraries, books, the freedom to read, and the unfettered pursuit of ideas. These valued object lessons appeared in sharp relief at Library History Seminar XI, an international symposium hosted October 27–30, 2005 by the University of Illinois Graduate School of Library and Information Science. Hearing tales of fire and flood, bomb and bayonet, conferees recalled once again that the challenges to progress are relentless, but also that the purposes of libraries and the lessons of history have become a narrative intertwined.[26]

WHY SOCIETY NEEDS LIBRARIES

The meaning of the thousands and thousands of stories that make up the library narrative lies embedded in the human impulse to record transactions, experiences, and ideas. Persisting issues in the imperatives to collect and preserve involve the processes and criteria for deciding what content merits preservation, at what levels of expertise and support, and within which formats. The first edition of a literary classic, for example, receives a form of storage, organization, and access that differs from that afforded a current municipal telephone directory. Choices about things to keep, things to treat in a special way, and things to discard must never be made in a vacuum. Such decisions rely inevitably on a mixture of professional perspectives and individual and collective judgments in the context of institutional, cultural, economic, and political priorities and realities. The complex of factors influencing the nature of library collections is thus rooted in historically understood concepts of the library's function in society.

The Library as Repository

Michael Harris defines the library as a collection of graphic materials, intended for specific readers, and that is cared for by individuals familiar with those materials and engaged in making them accessible.[21] The Harris definition may be usefully enriched with the notion of the library story as a foundational chapter in books devoted to the growth of civilization. Pierce Butler (1886–1953) wrote that the library came into existence to meet society's need to preserve accumulated human experience and to transfer it to succeeding generations who would adapt it for contemporary use. The library was a legacy for the living. The story of the library became a narrative with historic roots in people, ideas, and broad environmental trends, yet also with an eye to future generations as a matter of moral obligation.[27]

David Reith has argued that, since the library emerged from a complex of values and social organization, the elements of its structure connect by their nature to cultural phenomena or to components of the social structure.[28] Reith posited the fundamental purpose of the library as a repository, that the library collects and preserves the full range of expressions of human curiosity and intellect, yielding a plethora of resources essential for individual, community, national, and global progress. While some results of human creativity (i.e., art, music, patents, or pharmaceutical formulas) may reside in museums, digital repositories, or research centers, they have, at the root of their creation and distribution, a content-based structure that a specialist can adapt for storage and retrieval. While library classification and arrangement share some concepts with those of museums and archives, the latter institutions are bounded by concerns for format that the library—with its ultimate focus on content—does not share. To place a high value on the organization of materials goes to the very heart of a library's purpose since it considers the interests of future readers in ways that transcend the boundaries of language, culture, ethnicity, gender, ideology, and time.

The Library as Change Agent

The library has also possessed capacities as an agent of change, assuming a dynamic rather than a static universe, and thus a vital work of the library becomes documentation of that change. Although appearing on the surface as a passive and dependent institution, the library has also challenged the status quo, having promoted revision of economic, political, educational, or social norms. The library as change agent represents an important interpretive departure from an earlier view of the library, the public library in particular, as a follower of change rather than a creator of it.[29] While consensus about the library as an agent of change or a follower of change might be elusive, consensus about the library as serving the common good might be more tangible. Historically that good has been regarded as inherent, something understood intuitively by the library and its constituents though too seldom stated in the public square.

The story of the library as an advocate for change is rich with political ideas including that, for example, during the late nineteenth and early twentieth centuries in the United Kingdom and the United States, the library should support the national interest by helping to assimilate immigrant cultures and ethnic minorities, teaching new arrivals the language of democratic participation and economic stability. More recently, library collections have nurtured the goals of civil rights for women and ethnic minorities, for people with physical disabilities, and for those with gay, lesbian, bisexual, and transgendered preferences. This makes the library a potentially safe haven and valued resource for those threatened or intimated by dominant social behaviors, but these value commitments may also make the library an unwelcome target of suppression by fundamentalist impulses. Since libraries depend on the societies into which they are integrated by politics, economics, and ideology, they are rarely positioned for unfettered allegiance to professional ideals but rather offer mixed policies, sometimes promoting change by advocating for minority interests and sometimes limiting change by appealing to the powerful and well-connected.

The Library as Educator

Another role for the library involves that of education, a role that is at once both noble and suspect. Stakeholders in democratized settings tend to disagree about the values the library as educator should promote. Consequently the library, depending on its environment and those interpreting its purpose, has either educated readers to higher levels of perception and understanding or it has suppressed information that readers would find helpful in pursuit of opportunities for intellectual, economic, or political growth.

The librarian as a promoter of certain values, as someone who chooses an educational objective and then pursues that objective by building and promoting collections of a particular character or who simply discerns within an existing collection certain educative potential, is a concept that intellectual and social historians have come to explore with increasing nuance. Seminal monographs by Dee

Garrison,[30] Evelyn Geller,[31] Wayne A. Wiegand,[32] and Louise S. Robbins[33] analyze ambivalent perspectives that have marked the library as promoter of an educational ethos with programming and collections that target identifiable constituents.

In the face of misuse of the library as an educator, it must be recognized that the great religious movements possessed a powerful instructional obligation, honoring the written word, the creeds and liturgies and other sacred writings of prophets and priests. In fact, most religious traditions deserve a debt of gratitude for preserving classical secular texts in literature, history, economics, and government in addition to theological treatises. Scholars and scribes transmitted literature from the past, often migrating content to more durable media, performing such tasks as matters of educational purpose as well as religious observance. Claims to cultural reproduction in this particular way mark the stories of Eastern religions such as Hinduism and the Middle Eastern religions of Judaism, Christianity, and Islam.

Modern iterations of the library as educator may be observed in the adult education movement of the early twentieth century, which valued self-education as a tool of economic opportunity, as well as in twenty-first century literacy programs. The educative power of the library has tended to find its richest expressions in the great universities established in Europe in the Middle Ages and which—along with newer universities in the United States—have been transformed into the multicampus universities of today. These institutions, in concert with great national and private research libraries, have become part and parcel of intellectual and scientific progress—in the most literate nations—in the discovery and production of new knowledge, that most precious of commodities that marks human striving for a better world. The universities are also part of larger public and private educational systems, having been constructed on the foundation of K–12 (kindergarten through 12th grade) schooling wherein the school librarian through the reading and telling of stories, or equally often the public librarian, provides children with their earliest strategic impressions of the learning potential of books and libraries. The special role of the public library remains that of accommodating a wide range of reading tastes, serving citizens with a variety of community programs, welcoming readers in ways for which schools and universities are less well structured, and protecting the freedom to read.

The Ideology of Reading

The desire to use the collections and services of a library or to pursue the practice of library work or research and teaching in library and information science is a desire that, hypothetically at least, is rooted in the desire to read. Biographies and autobiographies in all fields of endeavor, including librarianship, provide abundant testimony to early transformational moments when individuals were mentored by a library worker, or when they spent countless hours browsing library collections and reading books.

Michael Harris defines the ideology of reading as a consensus about the value of reading and the widespread dissemination of books and writing to the growth and progress of a nation or a community. This ideology becomes clear in three particular constructs. The first of these is control, the idea that books and libraries symbolize power exercised by elites in order to support their values and interests. Social control may function to cultivate compliance among lower classes in order to maintain the political *status quo* and avoid civil unrest. Not uniformly shared among library historians, this view likely represents the minority perspective contrasted with the more widely appreciated opinion of the public library as an expression of democratic impulses. A second category is the library as commodity, that it is integral to an elaborate enterprise that incorporates the related work of authors, publishers, marketing specialists, booksellers, and libraries. Partners in the enterprise thrive in those societies with economies diverse enough to support them.

A final category of the library is that of memory. A nation or a municipality develops the capacity to reflect on its progress and to examine and revise its history but also to perform these tasks in settings that are monumental, places that are iconic enough to remind citizens of their cultural and intellectual maturity.[21] Thus millions of words organized into the reading matter of civilizations, confirming and promoting human progress, make up the multitude of stories that constitute the large narrative of the library, and they become essential to the high aspirations of individuals and groups, of families and communities, of movements and nations, of actions and ideas.

ACKNOWLEDGMENT

The authors acknowledge with admiration and gratitude the wise counsel and moral support of Donald G. Davis, Jr.

REFERENCES

1. Casson, L. *Libraries in the Ancient World*; Yale University Press: New Haven, CT, 2001.
2. Staikos, K. *The Great Libraries: From Antiquity to the Renaissance (3000 B.C. to A.D 1600)*; Oak Knoll Press: New Castle, DE, 2000.
3. Christ, K. *The Handbook of Medieval Library History*; Otto, T.M., Trans. Ed.; Scarecrow Press: Metuchen, NJ, 1984.
4. Thompson, L.S. Renaissance libraries. In *Encyclopedia of Library and Information Science*, Suppl. 1, 2nd Ed.; Drake, M.A., Ed.; Marcel Dekker: New York, 2003; 2494–2503.
5. Eisenstein, E. *The Printing Press as an Agent of Change: Communications and Cultural Transformations in Early Modern Europe*, Vols. 1–2, Cambridge University Press: New York, 1979.
6. Swan, J. Intellectual freedom. In *Encyclopedia of Library History*; Wiegand, W.A., Davis, D.G., Jr., Eds.; Garland Publishing: New York, 1994; 280–285.
7. Jackson, S.L. *Libraries and Librarianship in the West: A Brief History*; McGraw-Hill: New York, 1974.
8. Molz, K. Public libraries. In *International Dictionary of Library Histories*, Stam, D.H., Ed.; Fitzroy Dearborn: Chicago, IL, 2001; Vol. 1, 144–150.
9. Harris, M.H. The role of the public library in American life: A speculative essay. University of Illinois Graduate School of Library Science Occasional Papers **1975**, (117), 1–42.
10. Fain, E. Manners and morals in the public library: A glance at some new history. J. Libr. Hist. **1975**, *10* (2), 99–105.
11. Harris, M.H. Externalist or internalist frameworks for the interpretation of American library history—The continuing debate. J. Libr. Hist. **1975**, *10* (2), 106–110.
12. Garrison, D. Rejoinder. J. Libr. Hist. **1975**, *10* (2), 111–116.
13. Holley, E.G. The past as prologue: The work of the library historian. J. Libr. Hist. **1977**, *12* (2), 110–127.
14. Harris, M.H. Antiquarianism, professional piety, and critical scholarship in recent American library historiography. J. Libr. Hist. **1978**, *13* (1), 37–43.
15. Dain, P. A response to issues raised by the ALHRT program "The Nature and Uses of Library History." J. Libr. Hist. **1978**, *13* (1), 44–47.
16. Brough, K.J. *Scholar's Workshop: Evolving Conceptions of Library Service*; University of Illinois Press: Urbana, IL, 1953.
17. Wiebe, R.H. *The Search for Order, 1877–1920*; Hill and Wang: New York, 1967.
18. Bledstein, B.J. *The Culture of Professionalism: The Middle Class and the Development of Higher Education in America*; W.W. Norton: New York, 1976.
19. Davis, D.G., Jr. Education for librarianship. In *Encyclopedia of Library History*; Wiegand, W.A., Davis, D.G., Jr., Eds.; Garland Publishing: New York, 1994; 184–186.
20. Maack, M.N. Gender issues in librarianship. In *Encyclopedia of Library History*; Wiegand, W.A., Davis, D.G., Jr., Eds.; Garland Publishing: New York, 1994; 227–232.
21. Harris, M.H. *History of Libraries in the Western World*, 4th Ed.; Scarecrow Press: Metuchen, NJ, 1995.
22. Carpenter, K. Catalogs and cataloging. In *Encyclopedia of Library History*; Wiegand, W.A., Davis, D.G., Jr., Eds.; Garland Publishing: New York, 1994; 107–117.
23. Miksa, F.L. Classification. In *Encyclopedia of Library History*; Wiegand, W.A., Davis, D.G., Jr., Eds.; Garland Publishing: New York, 1994; 144–153.
24. Rayward, W.B. *The Universe of Information: The Work of Paul Otlet for International Organisation and Documentation*; International Federation for Documentation, All-Union Institute for Scientific and Technical Information: Moscow, 1975.
25. Foss, S.W. Some cardinal principles of a librarian's work. In *American Library Philosophy: An Anthology*;

McCrimmon, B., Ed.; Shoe String Press: Hamden, CT, 1975; 31–32.

26. Rayward, W.B., Jenkins, C., Eds. Libraries in times of war, revolution, and social change. Libr. Trends **2007**, *55* (3), 361–755.
27. Butler, P. *Introduction to Library Science*; University of Chicago Press: Chicago, IL, 1933.
28. Reith, D. The library as a social agency. In *The Library in Society*; Rogers, A.R., McChesney, K., Eds.; Libr. Unlimited: Littleton, CO, 1984; 5–16.
29. Shera, J.H. *Foundations of the Public Library: The Origins of the Public Library Movement in New England, 1692–1855*; University of Chicago Press: Chicago, IL, 1949.
30. Garrison, D. *Apostles of Culture: The Public Librarian and American Society, 1876–1920*, 2nd Ed.; Pawley, C., Ed.; University of Wisconsin Press: Madison, WI, 2003.
31. Geller, E. *Forbidden Books in American Public Libraries, 1876–1939: A Study in Cultural Change*; Greenwood Press: Westport, CT, 1984.
32. Wiegand, W.A. *An Active Instrument for Propaganda: The American Public Library during World War I*; Greenwood Press: Westport, CT, 1989.
33. Robbins, L.S. *The Dismissal of Miss Ruth Brown: Civil Rights, Censorship, and the American Public Library*; University of Oklahoma Press: Norman, Oklahoma, 2000.

BIBLIOGRAPHY

1. Anghelescu, H.G.B.; Poulin, M., Eds. *Books, Libraries, Reading, and Publishing in the Cold War*; Library of Congress Center for the Book: Washington, DC, 2001.
2. Battles, M. *Library: An Unquiet History*; W.W. Norton: New York, 2003.
3. Black, A.; Hoare, P.; Leedham-Green, E.; Mandelbrote, G.; Manley, K.; Webber, T., Eds. *The Cambridge History of Libraries in Britain and Ireland*, Cambridge University Press: Cambridge, U.K., New York, 2006; Vols. 1–3.
4. Buzas, L. *German Library History, 800–1945*; Boyd, W.D., Trans. Ed.; McFarland Publishing: Jefferson, NC, 1986.
5. Feather, J.; Sturges, P., Eds. *International Encyclopedia of Information and Library Science, 2nd Ed.; Routledge: London, U.K., 2003.*
6. Francis, S., Eds. *Libraries in the USSR*; Linnet Books: Hamden, CT, 1971.
7. Grotzinger, L.A.; Carmichael, J.V., Jr.; Maack, M.N. Women's Work: Vision and Change in Librarianship: Papers in Honor of the Centennial of the University of Illinois Graduate School of Library and Information Science. University of Illinois Graduate School of Library and Information Science Occasional Papers **1994** (196/197), 3–130.
8. Jolly, C.; Poulain, M.; Varry, D.; Vernet, A., Eds. *Histoire des Bibliothèques Francaises*, Promodis-Ed. du Cercle de la librairie: Paris, France, 1988–1992; Vols. 1–4.
9. Lerner, F.A. *The Story of Libraries: From the Invention of Writing to the Computer Age*; Continuum International: New York, 1998.
10. Lin, S.C. *Libraries and Librarianship in China*; Greenwood Press: Westport, CT, 1998.
11. Patel, J.; Kumar, K., Eds. *Libraries and Librarianship in India*; Greenwood Press: Westport, CT, 2001.
12. Shera, J.H. *Sociological Foundations of Librarianship*; Asia Publishing House: New York, 1970.
13. Sibai, M.M. *Mosque Libraries: An Historical Study*; Mansell: London, U.K., 1987.
14. Thompson, J. *A History of the Principles of Librarianship*; Clive Bingley: London, U.K., 1977.
15. Weibel, K.; Heim, K.M.; Ellsworth, D.J., Eds. *The Role of Women in Librarianship 1876–1976: The Entry, Advancement, and Struggle for Equalization in One Profession*; Oryx Press: Phoenix, AZ, 1979.
16. Welch, T. *Libraries and Librarianship in Japan*; Greenwood Press: Westport, CT, 1997.
17. Wertheimer, A.B.; Davis Jr, D.G., Eds. *Library History Research in America: Essays Commemorating the Fiftieth Anniversary of the Library History Round Table*; Library of Congress Center for the Book: Washington, DC, 2000.

History of Museums

John Edward Simmons
Museologica, Bellefonte, Pennsylvania, U.S.A.

Abstract
Making collections of objects is a universal human practice. Collections were made long before there were museums. The concept of the museum was developed from the association of objects and learning at the Temple of The Muses of ancient Alexandria. Museums have evolved from the private Renaissance cabinets of curiosities, which were open only to a few, into modern institutions with primarily educational functions that both reflect and shape human society.

INTRODUCTION

When James Smithson (ca. 1765–1829) left his fortune to the U.S. government, he stipulated that it be used for "the increase and diffusion of knowledge."[1] After debating using the gift to establish a library or a university, Congress instead decided that knowledge could best be increased and diffused in the new republic by creating a public museum. The Smithsonian Institution, established in 1846, now includes 19 museums, 9 research centers, and a zoological park.[2]

Museums developed in response to the human need to understand the world by using collections of objects—abstractions of the real world[3]—to make sense of the chaos around them. The collecting and ordering of things is a universal human trait that takes different forms in a diverse array of human cultures.[4] The earliest evidence of collecting is utilitarian objects and grave goods that were part of the material culture of the earliest humans.[2] One writer has suggested that the making and keeping of collections stems from "the human propensity to inquire and acquire" and the "twin concepts of preservation and interpretation."[5]

Collections are distinguished from random assemblages of objects by the presence of order (the recognition of relationships among the objects). All collections have order even if it is an order that is comprehensible only to the collector. Collections are made for a purpose, while assemblages occur by accident.[6] What distinguishes the objects in a collection from other objects is that objects in a collection are musealized—that is, they have been removed from their original natural or cultural environment to become part of the collection.[7,8] In the process of being musealized, objects acquire new meanings and they continue to acquire new meanings as long as they are part of a collection. The history of museums is, in effect, the history of the collection and classification of objects.

COLLECTING IN HISTORY

Collections have a longer history than do museums. Collecting began with the earliest human societies,[2] and there were established collecting traditions in Africa, Arabia, and Asia long before collecting developed in Europe.[9] Ancient collections were assembled for a variety of purposes, including for prestige, as economic hoards, and to promote group loyalty. One of the oldest documented collections dates from ca. 530 BCE in the ancient Sumarian city of Uruk, located in present-day Iraq, about 120 miles north of Basra.[5,10] Excavations of a temple site there by C.L. Woolley and his colleagues in the early 1900s unearthed a collection of antiquities dating back to 2000–2500 BCE that included a boundary stone, a mace head, fragments of a statue, a clay foundation cone, and clay tablets. The objects were documented by inscriptions on a clay drum cylinder on which a scribe had recorded that they were "found in the ruins of Ur, the work of Bur-Sin, King of Ur, which while searching for the ground plan [of the temple] the governor of Ur found, and I saw and wrote out, for the marvel of beholders."[11]

By the third millennium BCE, there were extensive collections in the Sumarian state archives at Ebla, and by the second millennium in Mesopotamia, collections of old inscriptions were being used to teach scribes how to make records. During the Shang dynasty in China (ca. 1600–1025 BCE), gold and bronze artifacts were collected; by the time of the Tang dynasty (CE 618–907), collecting had become very popular among the ruling elite.[10] In what is now Iraq, Nebuchadnezzar (605–562 BCE) acquired a large private collection that included antiquities and natural history specimens, and Nabonidus (555–539 BCE) of Babylonia kept collections of antiquities and natural history objects.[5] Tuthmosis III (1504–1450 BCE) of Egypt had an extensive collection of art, antiquities, flora, and fauna from Asia.[5] In an Egyptian tomb, a fossil sea urchin from the Eocene was found that was inscribed in

Encyclopedia of Library and Information Sciences, Fourth Edition DOI: 10.1081/E-EISA-120053547

hieroglyphs with the date, name of the collector, and locality where it was collected.[12,13] Art collecting was an ancient Greek custom, associated with the exhibition of paintings and sculptures in the entrance peristyles and porches of temples[14-16] in an area known as the pinakotheke or picture gallery. Wealthy Roman citizens collected paintings and objects that were considered to be "unusual and curious."[5] Several private collections of exotic sea shells have been found during the excavation of the ruins of Pompey, and collections of fossils have been found in ancient Greek and Roman cities, as well as collections of precious stones, decorative objects, and antiquities.[9,12] The oldest continuously functioning museum in the world is probably the Shōsōin at the Tōdai Temple in Nara, Japan, founded in the eighth century, which still exhibits secular and sacred artworks.[14]

THE MUSEUM CONCEPT

Both the modern concept of a museum as a place where learning and objects are associated and the source of the word museum (from the Greek *mouseion*, or "seat of the muses") originated in antiquity at a philosophical institution called the Temple of the Muses (a reference to the Greek sister-goddesses).[17] The temple was considered to be "a place of contemplation" in which learning and objects were combined.[9,18,19] The Temple of the Muses was founded in the third-century BCE in the city of Alexandria by Ptolemy Sotor (305–283 BCE). Objects of art and natural history were collected at the institution, and many learned scholars worked there, including Euclid and Heraclitus.[20] The Temple of the Muses had the largest library in the ancient world, lecture halls, gardens, and dormitories for scholars. It continued to flourish under Ptolemy Philadelphius (285–246 BCE). The temple and its collections were ultimately destroyed, probably in a fire that swept Alexandria.[5]

The concept of preservation is closely related to the concept of collecting because for collections to be useful the objects in them have to endure. Some objects are much more durable than others, thus the material the objects were composed of determined, in large part, what went into early collections. For example, preserving organic matter is particularly difficult—animal skins, plant-based materials, leather, and textiles require much more care to preserve so that they can be passed on from one generation to the next than do ceramics or stone.[21] Dehydration (mummification) is the oldest known method of intentional preservation of organic materials. Mummies were made of both humans and other animals on purpose (by removing the soft tissues most prone to deterioration, dehydrating the flesh with salts, wrapping the body in textiles or skins, and treating the bundle with oils and resins to keep pests away) at least 8000 years ago in Peru and at least 5000 years ago in Egypt.[22,23] In classical Greece, the tradition of donating

objects to treasuries at public sanctuaries led to attempts to prevent deterioration by such means as coating metal objects in pitch and preventing dehydration of ivory and wood by the use of oils.[14,24,25]

For collections to be useful in helping understand the world, the objects in them have to be organized or classified. Much like collecting, the organization of objects also stems from an innate human impulse.[26] The organization of objects is based on real or perceived similarities and patterns. In order to sort out objects, people must be able to distinguish them, hence the collection and the organization of collections is closely linked to the establishment of naming systems (taxonomies). In many cultural traditions, establishing a taxonomic system is part of the creation story, as in the Judeo-Christian-Islamic creation myth in which one of the first tasks of the first human is to name the animals.[2]

The first useful and enduring taxonomy of animals was proposed by Aristotle (384–322 BCE), and for plants, by a student of Aristotle named Theophrastus (ca. 372–287 BCE).[27] Aristotle had been a student of Plato in Athens and later moved to Macedonia to become the tutor for the young prince Alexander, the future conqueror of the world.[19] Aristotle arranged all the known animals—about 540 species—in a gradual progression or *scala natura* based on what he perceived to be their degree of perfection, with invertebrates at the lowest part of the scale and humans at the highest.[28] Aristotle's knowledge of animals was based mostly on his own observations and dissections, but he made a few curious mistakes that reflected dominant cultural traditions (e.g., while noting that the internal organs of a dog and a lion were very similar, he also repeated the ancient folklore that a lion has only one bone in its neck; and although familiar with human anatomy, he thought that the heart was the seat of the soul and that the only functions of the brain were to cool the blood and produce mucous).[29] Much of Aristotle's knowledge of non-Mediterranean species was based on specimens or descriptions sent back to Macedonia by Alexander the Great. For example, Aristotle's account of elephants and their natural history in *Historia Animalium* was derived from eyewitness descriptions[27] and possibly from direct examination of bones or pieces of skin (the first elephants that Alexander saw were those used by Darius at the Battle of Gauqamela in 331 BCE).[30] Aristotle's *scala natura* concept had a profound influence on Western perceptions of nature and cultures for the next two thousand years, which was expressed in the way specimens, artifacts, and other objects were arranged in collections.[31]

EVOLUTION OF THE MUSEUM CONCEPT

Between approximately 900 and 1200 CE, a great intellectual awakening took place in the Middle East, including the translation of many Greek texts into Arabic and the development of extensive archives and collections of artistic works/>.[32] At this time, an Arabic collecting tradition was formalized by the Islamic concept of property given for the public good and the donation of objects, similar to the deposition of objects in the treasuries of Greek temples.[5] The work of the Islamic scholars did not reach Europe until the twelfth or thirteenth centuries when the Arabic texts and the Arabic translations of Greek texts were translated into Latin. These translations initiated an admiration for the works of classical antiquity in Europe, which in turn spurred the growth of private collections and encouraged several popes, princes, and other wealthy citizens to fund the excavations of classical sites, particularly between about 1450 and 1550.[2] This is the period when the first *cabinets of curiosities* (also called *Kunst-* or *Wunderkammern*) appeared in Europe.[33]

Pre-Renaissance collecting in Europe was largely confined to collections acquired by churches, which were the centers of intellectual life.[14,33] Church collections included not just sacred art and religious objects, but also rare and unusual things such as the bones of giants, griffin's eggs, classical statuary, and artifacts of historical note.[9,14] Some of the objects in these collections were quite fantastic—the Cathedral in Milan (Italy) claimed a hair from the beard of Noah; the Cathedral of Halberstadt (Germany) exhibited a bone from the whale that swallowed Jonah; the Cathedral in Brunswick boasted a griffin's claw, personally brought back from Palestine by Duke Henry the Lion.[9] From surviving collections, it is now known that goat and antelope horns were often thought to be griffin's claws, fossil sharks teeth were thought to be snake tongues, and elephant bones were assumed to be the bones of giants. Such objects were accepted in the church collections not just because they were unusual, but also because they were thought to be useful in understanding the world. For example, at a time when very few Europeans had seen an ostrich or even an illustration of an ostrich, it was easy to believe that ostrich eggs were the eggs of griffins. However, ostriches were also mentioned in the Biblical book of Job, where it was recorded that the ostrich sometimes forgets its eggs, but when it finds them again, the bird cherishes them all the more, thus ostrich eggs were symbolic of God's love for repentant humans.[9]

MUSEUMS, CLASSIFICATION SYSTEMS, AND SOCIETY

As collections began to be assembled in private cabinets of curiosities in the 1400s, classification schemes were needed to give order to the objects.[34] Initially, objects were simply separated into *mirabilia* (finite marvels) and *miracula* (infinite or divine marvels), or into *artificalia* and *naturalia* (Table 1). As the collections grew larger and more complex, new categories were added, such as *antiquitas* for objects of historical import.[33] The first cabinets of curiosities were small cabinets filled with

Table 1 Some museum collection classification schemes.

Date	Categories	Source of classification
Early 1400s	Mirabilia (finite marvels) Miracula (infinite or divine marvels)	Wunderkammers, Kunstkammers, Cabinets of Curiosities
Mid 1400s	Artificialia Naturalia	
Late 1400s	Artificialia Naturalia Antiquitas	
1565	Material glorifying the founder Handcrafts from antiquity Natural specimens Technical and cultural objects Paintings and sacred objects	Samuel von Quicchebert
1679	Objects from mines Growing things Animals Works of art	Jan Swammerdam
1727	Naturalia Artificialia Curiosa	Caspar Neikelius
1714	Natural history Things sacred and superstitious Artificial rarities Apparatus (philosophical, mathematical, anatomical, surgical, and chemical) Coins and medals	Michael Bernhard Valentini
1759	Manuscripts, medals, and coins Natural and artificial productions Printed books	British Museum
1814	Manuscripts, medals, and coins Natural and artificial productions Printed books Antiquities and art	British Museum
1823	Ancient relics Arms Dresses and implements of half-civilized nations Rarities (gifts, memorials, amulets, curious works of art) Pictures Books and manuscripts Zoological specimens	Ashmolean Museum at Oxford

treasurers of nature and interesting works of art, but the term rapidly evolved to refer to whole rooms filled with treasures. Francis Bacon (1561–1626) described a typical cabinet of curiosities as containing "...whatsoever the hand of man by exquisite art or engine has made rare in stuff, form, or motion; whatsoever singularity, chance and the shuffle of things hath produced; whatsoever Nature has wrought in things that want life and may be kept."[35] The cabinets contained such things as unicorn horns (narwhale tusks), giant's bones (usually the bones of elephants or mastodons), Egyptian mummies, and snake's tongues (fossil shark teeth), as well as relics of saints, religious and secular classical art, statuary, and the occasional object from Asia or Africa.[9] Along with the cabinets of curiosities came a new "...veneration of the rare, the unusual, the wonderful and the miraculous....."[36] The collections in theses cabinets confirmed the existence of a divine being and demonstrated to their collectors that there was a divine order in nature, thus "One of the true raisons d'être behind the growth of cabinets of curiosities was a restless desire to establish a continuity between art and nature. Thus they demonstrate the existence of a supreme unifying principle."[33]

In addition to their value as collectables, many of the objects in the cabinets of curiosities were highly prized for their use in the practice of medicine and alchemy, such as healing stones and mummy dust, or because of the power the objects were believed to possess.[9] Lorenzo the Magnificent (1449–1492), a member of the Medici family of Florence, had a unicorn horn (a narwhale tusk) in his collection, which was particularly valuable as unicorn horns were believed to sweat in the presence of poison.[9] Lorenzo's collections included books, intaglios, precious stones, medals, tapestries, Byzantine icons, sculptures, natural history specimens, and paintings (many of which had miraculous properties).[37] The word *museum* was first used in Europe in the fifteenth century to describe the collection of Lorenzo[38] in reference to the encyclopedic nature of the collections (the word *museum* made its first appearance in an English work in 1615); the word *gallery* is derived from the name of the long, narrow corridors in the Medici palaces where their treasurers were exhibited.[2] Curiously, the word *collector* was not used until 1582, and then only to refer to a literary compiler.[39]

The development of the collections in the Medici palace was based on "Wealth, patronage, and the use of the past..." to glorify the family members based on the role of magic and occult cosmology in giving power to objects.[37] By possessing objects of great power, the Medici family showed that it, too, had great power. The Medici collections were opened to the public at the Uffizi Palace (which had originally housed Florentine administrative offices) in 1582, and ultimately were bequeathed to the state of Tuscany in 1743.[5]

THE POWER OF OBJECTS AND THE TRANSMISSION OF KNOWLEDGE

A common object in the cabinets of curiosities, including that of Lorenzo the Magnificent, was a snake-stone (Fig. 1),

Fig. 1 A snake-stone or ammonite (a fossil cephalopod from the early Cretaceous, *Pulchella veleziensis*).
Source: Photo by J.E. Simmons.

named for its resemblance to a coiled snake.[37] Snake-stones were believed to prevent snake bite and to cure both snake bite and rabies. Another name for a snake-stone was an ammonite, derived from its resemblance to the *Cornu Ammonis*, or Ammon's Horn, a reference to the Egyptian deity who was depicted with the body of a human and the head of a ram with a coiled horn (Alexander the Great had coins struck featuring his profile wearing the Horn of Ammon to affirm his deity).[2] In Medieval times, fossils were thought to be formed by exhalations, as described by Aristotle (fuliginous exhalations formed fossils, orchre, sulfur, and vermillion, while vaporous exhalations formed metals), or believed to grow in the earth.[9] Snake-stones were valued in alchemy because they were thought to be formed by the conjunction of two pure salts. Snake-stones are still common in museums and still popular with collectors even though they are now known to be fossil cephalopods about 400–1400 million years old. The snake-stone shown in Fig. 1 was purchased as an example of the oxidation of pyrite in a geological collection stored at too high a relative humidity. These various conceptions of snake-stones—as medical devices, alchemical substances, scientific specimens, collectables, and teaching aids—are all dependent on the concept that underlies why museums grew and flourished from the cabinets of curiosities onward: *objects are perceived to have power*.[3] The belief in the power of objects greatly influenced what was collected and preserved. For example, "No museum of any repute was considered complete without one or more specimens of unicorn's horn, an article which was believed to possess wonderful virtues, and was much employed in medicine.... The Grand Inquisitor Torquemada always carried about with him the horn of a unicorn to protect him against poison and assassins," and mummies were believed to be "endowed with extraordinary virtues."[9] Mummy dust was used to stop bleeding, to heal bruises and fractures, and to relieve convulsions. Murray notes that "although all museums could not attain an entire mummy, nearly every one had one or more fragments," such as a finger, a foot, or a head.[9]

Since the sixteenth century, collectors have organized their collections in ways that promote the transmission of knowledge.[26] Museum classification systems grew more sophisticated when it became possible to print and circulate collection catalogs.[2] The first museum catalogs were little more than descriptive inventories of collections, but these rapidly evolved into detailed listings of museum contents with illustrations, histories of significant objects, and critiques of the collection.[40] Ulisse Aldrovandi (1522–1605) went so far with his museum catalog as to also produce a "...*Catalogus virorum qui vistarunt Musaeum nostrum*, in which he categorized his visitors according to their geographical origins and social standing."[33]

One of the first printed museum catalogs was prepared by Samuel von Quicchebert (1529–1567), a physician in Antwerp, and published in Munich in 1565.[41] Quicchebert wrote that a collection should be a systematic classification of the materials of the universe, and he provided guidelines for assembling what he considered to be an ideal cabinet of curiosities. Quicchebert proposed an organization scheme (Table 1) that classified objects into five groups that Pearce has pointed out correlate well with modern museum divisions: material glorifying the founder and handcrafts from antiquity (historic objects); natural specimens (natural history materials); technical and cultural objects (applied art and crafts); and paintings and sacred objects (fine art).[3] Quicchebert recommended that a museum include a library, workshop, and apothecary shop, and he described his ideal institution as "A theater of the broadest scope, containing authentic materials and precise reproductions of the whole of the universe."[33] In the same year that Quicchebert's catalog was published (1565), Johannes Kentmann (1518–1574) of Torgau published a catalog of his 1600 rock and mineral specimens, organizing the catalog according to the newly published classification of rocks and minerals in *De re metallica* (1556) developed by Georgius Agricola (1494–1555).[9]

One of the best-known European collections of this time was compiled by Olaus Worm (1588–1654) in Copenhagen beginning in 1620 and described in an extensive catalog, *Museum Wormianum*, published in 1655.[42] Worm's catalog included a woodcut depicting the main room of the museum that has been widely reproduced in many publications about museums. The *Wunderkammer* of Jacobz Swammerdam, a Dutch pharmacist, was cataloged by his son, Jan Swammerdam, after the elder Swammerdam died in 1679.[2] Swammerdam the Younger divided the large and by then famous collection into four categories (Table 1) consisting of objects from mines, growing things, animals, and works of art (which included ethnographic objects). One of the first museum catalogs to be printed in English appeared in 1691, entitled the

"Catalogue of all the chiefest Rarities in the Publick Theater and Anatomie-Hall of the University of Leyden,"[9] prepared primarily for the use of visitors to the museum. The catalog listings included shoes and sandals from Russia, Siam, and Egypt; the skin of a man dressed as parchment; "A drinking cup [made] of the skull of a Moor killed in the beleaguering of Haerlem"; Chinese paper; Egyptian mummies; a Roman lamp believed to be capable of burning eternally; "an Hand of a Meermaide presented by Prince Mauritz"; and a 100-year-old mushroom.[9]

The oldest surviving purpose-built museum building was designed by Wilhelm Egkl and constructed in Munich between 1563 and 1567 to exhibit the paintings of Wilhelm IV and Albrecht V.[38] The building is now known as the Mint (Münzhof) as it housed the Bavarian mint from 1809 to 1983.

Two of the great collectors of the Renaissance were Konrad Gessner (1516–1565) and Ulisse Aldrovandi (1522–1605), both of whom compiled and published detailed, illustrated catalogs of their collections.[31] Gessner, born in Zurich, wrote *Historia animalium*, a work of 3500 pages in four immense folio volumes in which he arranged all the known animal species according to the *scala natura* scheme proposed by Aristotle. After Gessner died of the plague at the age of 49, his collection was acquired by Felix Potter (1536–1614) and then passed on to the Natural History Museum at Basle where some of the specimens are still extant.[38] Aldrovandi, who was from Bologna, taught medicine in Padua and Rome while spending his family's fortune collecting specimens of animals and plants and hiring artists to illustrate them. The Aldrovandi collections are now in the University of Bologna.[38] About this same time, the first herbarium was made by Luca Ghini (1490–1556) in Padua, Italy, when he invented the practice of pressing and drying plants and then attaching them to paper sheets, called a *hortus siccus* or "dry garden."[38,43]

THE MODERN MUSEUM

The modern museum dates to the time when collections began to be made for the specific purpose of exhibiting the objects to the public, but this is not an easy-to-define moment. One of the first public European museums was formed when the Grimani family bequeathed their private collections to the government of Venice between 1523 and 1583.[38] The Grimani collections are now part of the present-day archeological museum of Venice. Many other such donations of collections and the subsequent creation of public museums followed. During this time, systems and scientific methods were being applied to understand both human culture and nature.[38] For example, Francis Bacon (1561–1626) argued for the application of inductive empiricism to the cataloging of knowledge, and

Table 2 Nature of museum collections.

Museum type	Collections description
Art	Aesthetic
History	Documentary
Science	Systematic

René Descartes (1596–1650) sought to rationalize science and religion, developments that were reflected in the nature of museum collections (Table 2).[44]

In England, the Tradescants sought the services of Elias Ashmole (1617–1692) to catalog their own extensive collections, which ultimately became the first public museum in England.[39] John Tradescant the Elder (ca. 1570–1638) and his son John Tradescant the Younger (1608–1662) collected natural history specimens, precious stones, weapons, coins, carvings, paintings, and medallions from all over the world.[34] Tradescant the Elder wrote to the Secretary of the Admiralty in 1625 and asked for help in obtaining things "...that be Rare or Not knowne to us" as well as "Any thing that Is strang."[39] This request came at the same time as the Tradescant collections began to be exhibited to the public at Lambeth.[38] Ashmole's catalog of the Tradescant collection was published in 1656 under the title *Musaeum Tradescantianum.* After the elder Tradescant died, the ownership of the collection passed to the younger Trandescant, and after his death Ashmole moved to take over the collection even though the widow, Hester Tradescant, resisted.[39] Ultimately, after a protracted legal battle, Ashmole gained control over the collection and donated it to Oxford University, where a part of it is still on exhibition as the Ashmolean collection.[45] The Ashmolean Museum established the pattern for what eventually became the modern university museum. Opened in 1683, the Ashmolean included not only space for exhibition and storage of collections, but also offices for the teaching staff associated with the university.[46]

Sir Hans Sloane (1660–1753) made the collections that became the core of the British Museum.[9] Sloane's collections were encyclopedic in scope.[39] The catalog of the collections of the Royal Society of London included listings for "A piece of BONE voided by Sir W. Throgmorton with his urine," "A Weesle Headed Armadillo," and a piece of "skin from the Buttock of a Rhinoceros."[47] Museums had objects like these in their collections largely because "The object of showing such things was that they were expected and that the museum should not seem to be incomplete by their not being there."[9] John Henry Parker, the curator of the Ashmolean Museum, wrote in 1871 that "I do not wish to exclude curiosities from [the museum]; they attract people, and when they are brought hither by curiosity, they may stop to learn something better; they may want to know something of the history of the curiosities they have come to see."[9]

Museums were numerous enough in Europe after 1700 that a museum object dealer from Hamburg named Caspar Neikelius (a pseudonym for Kaspar Freidrich Jenequel)

published a book called *Museographica* in 1727, considered to be the first museological work.[48,49] Neikelius provided guidance for acquisitions; addressed problems of classification of the objects in the collection as naturalia, artificialia, and curiosa (Table 1); presented techniques for caring for collections; and suggested putting a table in the middle of each room "... where things brought from the repository could be studied." Neikelius recommended that museum objects be stored in dry conditions and kept out of direct sunlight, and that museums should have an accession book and a general catalog.[15] Neikelius was the first to articulate the difference between viewing objects clustered in a small room (e.g., as in a cabinet of curiosities) and displayed in a long room (an exhibition hall derived from the *grande sale* of the French medieval chateaux).[48] As late as 1759, the original organization of the British Museum reflected Neikelius' divisions of knowledge with its collections divided into three departments: manuscripts, medals, and coins; natural and artificial productions; and printed books (Table 1).

In 1753, David Hultman published his recommendations for museums, writing that a museum building should be made of brick, be longer than it is wide, and have windows facing north.[9] Despite the appearance of the books by Neikelius and Hultman, collection care in museums at this time was, in general, not terribly good. "...William Swainson compared the storerooms [of the British Museum] with the catacombs at Palermo, each of which was apparently opened once a year to determine how much decay had occurred and to deposit fresh material."[36]

As museums grew larger and more complex early in the eighteenth century, they began to diverge into specialized institutions such as art, ethnographic, history, military, natural history, and technology museums, based on the characteristics of their collections and the systems of order used to categorize the objects in their collection (Table 3).[2] For example, natural history collections benefited greatly from the advent of new taxonomic classification systems for plants (in 1735) and animals (in 1758) developed by the Swedish naturalist, Carl Linnaeus (1707–1778).[50] These efficient, modern classification systems quickly became the principle around which natural history collections were organized and collection growth was directed. An equivalent common universal

Table 3 Generalized systems of order used in museum collections.

Type of museum	Ordering system
Art	Artists' name, period, medium, genre, school
Natural history	Linnaean taxonomy
Geoscience	Epochs, strata, chemical composition
History	Material, topical class (use), style, Chenhall classification
Anthropology	Material, provenance, cultural association

cataloging taxonomy for human-made objects did not become available until 1978.[51] By contrast, the Dewey Decimal system for cataloging library materials in 10 major classes appeared in 1876, the Library of Congress system (using 21 classes) was first published in 1897, and the Universal Decimal Classification was published in Europe in 1895.[2]

Many of the new museums were less encyclopedic and more focused in their collections, such as the first of what are now the Vatican Museums, the Museo Sacro, which opened in Rome in 1756.[52] A number of museums specializing in art, history, and natural history were founded at this time. The first museum devoted exclusively to art, the Pio Clemente Museum, was opened in 1773 in Rome by Pope Clement XIV (the museum's holdings are now part of the Vatican collections).[52] Most early European museums started with collections assembled by happenstance, but some were planned more thoroughly. The first modern art museum was the Hermitage in St. Petersburg, Russia, which was established in 1764.[9] The Czartoryski Museum (Krakow) was founded in 1796 to bring collections from the aristocracy to the general public. In 1779, Christian Von Mechel suggested that the Belvedere Museum in Vienna should be arranged to present "a visible history of art," in a chronological framework.[48] This was followed by the Altes Museum in Berlin (1830), also designed to provide "a visual history of art from its beginnings."[5] The Alte Pinakothek in Munich (1836) opened with a chronological exhibit of art by organized by schools, with gallery spaces designed to protect the artwork from fire, dust, and vibration, with north-facing windows, and moderate heat in the winter.[38]

The first museum in the United States was established in 1773 by the Charleston Library Society, in Charleston, South Carolina.[53] In 1785, the first public museum in the United States was operated by Charles Willson Peale (1741–1827), initially in his home in Philadelphia.[54,55] Based on the European concept of a museum, Peale's innovation was his democratic intention to provide instruction and entertainment to all classes of people. Peale's museum included paintings by himself and his sons, taxidermy mounts, fossils, a mastodon skeleton, ethnographic objects, and live animals.[54] Peale's museum eventually failed when it was confronted with many of the same problems that many museums face today—funding, maintaining audience, and presentations. The Peale collections were dispersed at auction in 1858—of the 1600 bird taxidermy mounts prepared by the Peale family, only 14 are known to exist today.[55]

A number of significant museums were founded around this time (Table 4). The British Museum was opened to the public in 1759 (with free admission), with its collections of art, anthropology, history, science, and a library, making it a universal institution.[38] Charles III of Spain brought together works of art and natural history in 1785 as a museum of natural science, which eventually became

Table 4 Founding dates of some significant museums.

Date of founding	Museum
1523	Grimani collections given to Venice and opened to public
1567	Wilhelm IV and Albrecht V collections established in a purpose-build structure (Munich, Germany)
1582	Medici collections opened to the public at Uffizi Palace (bequeathed to Tuscany in 1743)
1620	Museum of Olaus Worm (Copenhagen)
1625	Tradescant collections on public exhibit in England, to become the Ashmolean Museum at Oxford in 1683
1752	Museo Nacional de Ciencias Naturales (Madrid)
1756	Museo Sacro, Rome (now part of the Vatican Museums)
1759	British Museum (London)
1764	Hermitage (St. Petersburg)
1773	Charleston Library Society (Charleston, South Carolina)
	Pio-Clemente Museum (Rome)
1778	The Batavia Society for Art and Science (now the Central Museum of Indonesian Culture, Jakarta)
1784	The Indian Museum (Calcutta)
1785	The Peale Museum (Philadelphia)
1787	The Prado (Madrid)
1791	The Massachusetts Historical Society (library and public exhibition gallery)
1793	Muséum Central des Artes, now the Louvre (Paris)
1796	Czartoryski Museum (Krakow)
1802	National Museum (Pest)
1814	Asiatic Society of Bengal (Calcutta)
1815	Rijksmuseum (Amsterdam)
	National Museum (Rio de Janeiro)
1818	Moravian Museum (Brno)
1822	Picton Academy, the first Canadian museum (Nova Scotia)
1823	Museo del Pais, now Argentine Museum of Natural History (Buenos Aires)
	Raffles Museum and Library, now Singapore National Museum (Singapore)
1824	National Museum of Colombia (Bogotá)
1825	South African Museum (Capetown)
1830	Altes Museum (Berlin)
1836	Alte Pinakothek Museum (Munich)
1837	Ethnology Museum (Leiden)
1838	National Gallery (London)
1841	Nelson Provincial Museum (New Zealand)
1842	Ancanthe Museum (Hobart)
	Wadsworth Atheneum at Harvard University (Cambridge)
1843	National Museum of Canada, now Canadian Museum of Nature (Ottawa)
	Egyptian Museum (Cairo)
1850	Hasbrouck House (Newburgh)
1853	The Australian Museum (Sydney)

(Continued)

Table 4 Founding dates of some significant museums. *(Continued)*

Date of founding	Museum
1858	Smithsonian Institution (Washington, DC)
1861	Museum of Art, now National Gallery of Victoria (Melbourne)
1862	Municipal Museum and Library (Guayquil)
1864	Lahore Museum (Lahore)
1865	National Museum (Wellington)
1869	American Museum of Natural History (New York)
1870	Metropolitan Museum of Art (New York) Museum of Fine Arts (Boston)
1872	Forerunner of the Tokyo National Museum (Tokyo)
1873	Nordiska Museet, the first folklore museum (Stockholm)
1874	Grand Palace Collections, now the National Museum of Thailand (Bangkok)
1875	Indian Museum (Calcutta)
1877	National Museum (Colombo)
1881	Skansen Museum, (Stockholm)
1887	National Museum (San Jose)
1888	Musée Alaoui, now the National Museum (Tunis)
1889	Brooklyn Children's Museum, the first children's museum (Brooklyn, New York)
1891	Skansen Museum (Stockholm) Geological Museum (Lima)
1901	National Museum (Bulawayo)
1903	Museum of Islamic Art (Cairo)
1905	Nan t'ung Museum (Kiangsu)
1906	Peshawar Museum (Peshawar)
1908	Uganda Museum (Kampala)
1909	National Museum of Kenya (Nairobi)
1912	Openluchtmuseum (Arnhem)
1915	Dar Batha Museum (Fez)
1924	Central Order of Lenin Museum of the Revolution (Moscow)
1926	Colonial Williamsburg (Virginia)
1928	Henry Ford Greenfield Village (Dearborn)
1930	Pergamon Museum (Pergamonmuseum) (Berlin)
1937	Museé national des Arts et Traditions Populaires (Paris)
1949	National Museum of India (New Delhi)
1953	Yad Vashem holocaust memorial museum (Jerusalem)
1964	Museo Nacional de Antropología (Mexico City)
1968	Ontario Science Center (Ottawa) The Exploratorium (San Francisco)
1979	Écomusée du Val de Bièvre (Fresnes)
1986	Musée d'Orsay (Paris)
1990	Vasa Museum (Vasamuseet) (Stockholm)
1997	Nelson Mandella National Museum (Mthatha, South Africa)
2000	Tate Modern (London)
2009	Acropolis Museum (Athens)

the Prado in 1819.[38] The Louvre opened to the public as the Muséum Central des Artes in Paris in 1793, shortly after the French Revolution, exhibiting royal collections that had previously been unavailable to the public, outside of an occasional special exhibition.[38] The new French museum grew rapidly as Napoleon appropriated objects for the collections during his European campaigns, but most of this material was later repatriated, after the Congress of Vienna in 1815.[5,38]

The development of mercantilism, the rise of an affluent merchant class, and the decline of royal patronage systems together led to a greater public interest in the arts beginning early in the eighteenth century.[5] By the middle of the eighteenth century, the dawning Industrial Revolution sparked public interest in technology and science. At the beginning of the nineteenth century, "the first realization of the role of the museum in contributing to national consciousness arose in Europe. With it came the recognition that the museum was the appropriate institution for the preservation of a nation's historic heritage."[38] Thus came the first big museum "boom" in the second half of the nineteenth century in Europe. So much museum growth occurred during this time that the nineteenth century has been called the Golden Age of Museums in Europe; nearly every country in Western Europe opened a comprehensive museum during this time.[14]

One influential museum pioneer in the United States was Phineas T. Barnum (1810–1891), who opened a huge public museum called The American Museum in New York after his purchase of the collection of John Scudder (1775–1821).[56] In his museum, Barnum exhibited more than 600,000 objects,[1] but finally gave up on museums and went into the circus business after a series of disastrous museum fires. In 1842, Barnum acquired a specimen of "a feejee mermade," which he put on exhibit with much fanfare in his New York museum, where it tripled revenues.[57] Once the novelty of the mermaid wore off in New York, he sent it out on tour. Scientists throughout the United States protested the local showings, claiming that the mermaid was an obvious fake, but their protests only served to push ticket sales higher. The mermaid was described in the press as an "ugly dried-up, block-looking, and diminutive specimen about 3 ft long. Its mouth was open, its tail turned over, and its arms thrown up, giving it the appearance of having died in great agony." The mermaid was made from the torso and head of a monkey sewn onto the body of a fish.[58]

THE CHANGING ROLE OF MUSEUMS

In the latter part of the nineteenth century, museums were recast as primarily educational institutions as the "new museum idea" took hold—this was the separation of study collections from exhibition collections.[2] The new museum idea was formally articulated by Sir William Henry Flower

(1831–1899), director of the British Museum, who proposed organizing museums around the dual purposes of research and public education.[59,60] Until this time, museums had been expected to put all of their collections on display, with the result that exhibit halls were often vast arrays of carefully labeled and arranged objects in ordered cases. Although it has become fashionable to criticize this style of exhibit, it was very popular with visitors who sought out museums to see things that they had never seen before, arranged in a ways that brought made sense the chaos around them. The second half of the nineteenth century was also the time of the first period of major growth in museums, with more than 100 new museums opening in the United Kingdom and at least 50 new museums in Germany,[5] and many significant museums opening in the Americas (Table 4).

The first ethnology museum opened in Leiden in 1837.[16] Historic house museums first appeared in the mid-nineteenth century in Europe and the United States, dedicated to preserving buildings because of their significant architecture or association with a significant person or historical event (Fig. 2). The first historic house museum in the United States was Hasbrouck House, founded in 1850 in Newburgh, New York, once the headquarters of General George Washington.[1]

Open air museums or living museums (Fig. 3), which usually include period architecture (often recreated) and historical re-enactors, were developed in the late nineteenth century in Scandinavia.[2] The first open air museum was opened in 1881 near Oslo, Norway, to exhibit the collections of King Oscar II. In 1891, Arthur Hazelius founded the Skansen museum in Stockholm, which became the model for subsequent open air museums around the world.[2] The first outdoor museums in the United States were the historic environment known as Colonial Williamsburg, established in 1926,[23,33] and the Henry Ford Greenfield Village museum, which opened in Dearborn, Michigan, in 1928.[54] The first mobile museum was developed in Liverpool in 1884 to serve school children.[16]

Natural history museums underwent a major change following the publication of *On the Origin of Species* by Charles Darwin (1809–1882) in 1859.[2] The fundamental revolution in biology that was triggered by Darwin's theory of evolution by natural selection had far-reaching effects on how specimens were collected, preserved, and exhibited. Prior to Darwin, species were thought to be immutable, so natural history museum collections contained only one or two specimens of each species, and museums exhibited all of their collections in large synoptic displays, grouped according to the prevailing systems of classification.[2] Darwin's theory demonstrated the importance of studying variation within species, which meant the essentialist or typological natural history collections were no longer very useful for research. In fact, Darwin could not have developed his theory of evolution using just the museum collections of his day because museums did not have sufficient specimens of each species to show the wide degree of variation in nature.[2]

Fig. 2 A historic house museum, the *Casa Museo Antonio Nariño*, Villa de Leyva, Colombia.
Source: Photo by J.E. Simmons.

Fig. 3 An open air museum, the *Prasat Hin Pimai Historic Park*, Nakhon Ratchasima (Khorat), Thailand.
Source: Photo by J.E. Simmons.

At the time that the Smithsonian was founded (in 1846), universities were essentially finishing schools; the creation of knowledge was centered in museums, with the result that "...museums made the fruits of their research available to a general public through exhibits, unlike colleges and universities, which were open only to a few."[61]

There are some significant differences in how museums were established in different regions of the world.[2] In Europe and Canada, museums were usually established through local or national government agencies, but in the United States most new museum growth was initiated by individual or small group patronage at the local level. In other countries, centralized state museum systems were developed, as in France and the former Soviet Union.[62]

Although the idea of the modern public museum is essentially European in origin, it was successfully exported to other parts of the world through trade and colonialism.[38] There were periods of growth in Latin American and Asian museums in the 1800s, and in African museums in the early 1900s.[62] Many of these colonial-era museums evolved into important national museums (Table 4) such that "the emergence of the nation-state, the public, and the public museum in the late eighteenth century, were intimately bound together,"[63] particularly in South America and Asia. As independent nations arose from their colonial roots, some museums became important agencies for developing national identification by offering interpretations of their collections that reflected feelings of national ownership (e.g., defined national culture) as well as defined

nationality compared to other nations and cultures.[63,64] Some of these museums played a significant role in the rejection of colonialism. For example, during the 1970s many Caribbean museums shifted their emphasis from a strong focus on their society's colonial past to present more inclusive cultural and natural histories.[65]

Although two significant American museums were founded in 1870—the Metropolitan Museum in New York and the Museum of Fine Arts in Boston[52]—only 4% of museums in the United States were in existence before 1900.[62] At least 75% of U.S. museums were founded after 1950, and 40% were founded after 1970.[1]

Further changes in museum development have occurred in the twentieth century. Technological developments during the First World War, such as efficient indoor lighting and the production of large sheets of polished plate glass, have allowed museums to make much larger display cases.[3] The population shift in many industrialized countries away from urban centers has spawned the development of community museums.[38] The growth of museums worldwide resulted in the founding of the International Council of Museums (ICOM) in 1946.[62] Not all institutions recognized as museums today even own collections. The definition used by the Accreditation Committee of the American Alliance of Museums states that a museum is "An organized and permanent nonprofit institution, essentially educational or esthetic in purpose, with professional staff, that owns or uses tangible objects, cares for them and exhibits them to the public on some regular schedule," in contrast to the most widely used definition, that of the International Council of Museums, which states that "A museum is a non-profit, permanent institution in the service of society and its development, open to the public, which acquires, conserves, researches, communicates and exhibits the tangible and intangible heritage of humanity and its environment for the purposes of education, study and enjoyment."[2]

Two of the newest concepts in museums are ecomuseums and virtual museums.[66,67] Ecomuseums interpret not just an event, a place, or a culture, but an entire community. Developed by Hugues de Varine in France in 1971, ecomuseums have proven to be popular in parts of Europe, Canada, and much of the developing world. The hundreds of ecomuseums around the world today define themselves by managing heritage in a sustainable environment. In contrast to ecomuseums, virtual museums exist only in cyberspace, although many are usually based on real, physical collections, and show great promise for repatriation of cultural knowledge and a wider sharing of information around the world.[68]

CONCLUSION

The significance of the role of museums in presenting history and defining culture has been demonstrated by such events as Chinese museums being forced to interpret a particular political agenda or be closed during the Cultural Revolution of the 1960s, and the attempt by some members of the United States Congress to interfere with the curator's presentation of the bombing of Hiroshima in the Smithsonian's Enola Gay exhibit.[2] Museums in Eastern Europe both expanded under the post-Communist governments and later struggled to survive in a free market economy. More recently, museums in Iraq and the former Yugoslavia have suffered greatly the ravages of warfare.[2]

History shows that museums have evolved to serve different needs at different times, but have always played a significant role in interpreting nature and culture. Museums have been "...the institutions charged with furthering knowledge and creating order..."[61] due to the fact that they "...assumed intellectual leadership because they fostered original research through the careful and systematic way they dealt with objects."[61] Museums will continue to serve a significant role in society as long as humans remain curious about the world around them.

REFERENCES

1. Pitman, B. Muses, museums, and memories. Daedalus **1999**, *128* (3), 1–31.
2. Simmons, J.E. *Museums: A History*; Rowman and Littlefield: Lanham, MD, 2016.
3. Pearce, S.M. *Museums, Objects, and Collections: A Cultural Study*; Smithsonian Press: Washington, DC, 1992.
4. Muensterberger, W. *Collecting: An Unruly Passion: Psychological Perspectives*; Harcourt Brace and Company: San Diego, CA, 1994.
5. Lewis, G.D. Museums. In *Encyclopedia Britannica*; Encyclopaedia Britannica, Inc.: London, U.K., 1985; 480–492.
6. Pearce, S.M. The urge to collect. In *Interpreting Objects and Collections*; Pearce, S.M., Ed.; Routledge: London, U.K., 1994; 157–159.
7. Desvallées, A.; Mairesse, F. *Key Concepts of Museology*; Armand Colin and ICOM: Paris, France, 2010.
8. Maroević, I. *Introduction to Museology: The European Approach*; C. Müller-Straten: Munich, Germany, 1998.
9. Murray, D. *Museums, Their History, and Their Use: With a Bibliography and List of Museums in the United Kingdom*; James MacLehose and Sons: Glasgow, U.K., 1904.
10. Rigby, D.; Rigby, E. *Lock, Stock and Barrel: The Story of Collecting*; J.B. Lippincott Company: Philadelphia, PA, 1944.
11. Woolley, L. *Excavations at Ur: A Record of Twelve Years' Work*; Ernest Been Limited: New York, 1955.
12. Mayor, A. *The First Fossil Hunters: Paleontology in Greek and Roman Times*; Princeton University Press: Princeton, NJ, 2000.
13. McNamara, K.J. *The Star-Crossed Stone, The Secret Life, Myths, and History of a Fascinating Fossil*; University of Chicago Press: Chicago, IL, 2010.
14. Bazin, G. *The Museum Age*; Universe Books: New York, 1967.
15. Pearce, S.M. *On Collecting: An Investigation into Collecting in the European Tradition*; Routledge: London, U.K., 1995.
16. Zubiaur Carreño, F.J. *Curso de Museología*; Ediciones Trea, S.L.: Gijón, España, 2004.
17. Findlen, P. The museum: its classical etymology and renaissance genealogy. J. Hist. Collect. **1989**, *1* (1), 59–78.
18. Empereur, J.-Y. *Alexandria: Jewel of Egypt*; Harry N. Abrams, Inc.: New York, 2002.
19. Sarton, G. *Ancient Science through the Golden Age of Greece*; W.W. Norton and Company: New York, 1970.
20. Watson, B. Rising sun. Smithsonian **2002**, *33* (1), 78–88.
21. Simmons, J.E.; Muñoz-Saba, Y. The theoretical bases of collections management. Collect. Forum **2003**, *18* (1–2), 38–49.
22. Andrews, C. *Egyptian Mummies*; The British Museum Press: London, U.K., 1998.
23. Arriaza, B.T. *Beyond Death: The Chinchorro Mummies of Ancient Chile*; Smithsonian Institution Press: Washington, DC, 1995.
24. Bounia, A. *The Nature of Classical Collecting: Collectors and Collections, 100 BCE–100 CE*; Ashgate Publishing Limited: Aldershot, U.K., 2004.
25. Ullberg, A.; Ullberg, P.; Grogg, A.H.; Lind, R. A short history of the museum. In *Art and Museum Law: Cases and Materials*; Lind, R.C., Jarvis, R.M., Phelan, M.E., Eds.; Carolina Academic Press: Durham, U.K., 2002; 425–431.
26. Schulz, E. Notes on the history of collecting and of museums. In *Interpreting Objects and Collections*; Pearce, S.M., Ed.; Routledge: London, U.K., 1994; 175–187.
27. French, R. *Ancient Natural History*; Routledge: London, U.K., 1994.

28. Yoon, C.K. *Naming Nature: The Clash between Instinct and Science*; W.W. Norton and Company: New York, 2009.

29. Cole, F.J. *A History of Comparative Anatomy from Aristotle to the Eighteenth Century*; MacMillan and Company, Ltd.: London, U.K., 1944.

30. de Asúa, M.; French, R. *A New World of Animals: Early Modern Europeans on the Creatures of Iberian America*; Ashgate: Burlington, VT, 2005.

31. Simmons, J.E.; Snider, J. Observation and distillation-preservation, depiction, and the perception of nature. Bibliotheca Herpetol. **2012**, *9* (1–2), 115–134.

32. Roberts, J.M.; Westad, O.A. *The Penguin History of the World*, 6th Ed.; Penguin Books: London, U.K., 2013.

33. Mauriès, P. *Cabinets of Curiosities*; Thames and Hudson Ltd.: London, U.K., 2002.

34. Davenne, C.; Fleurent, C. *Cabinets of Wonder*; Abrams: New York, 2012.

35. Bacon, F. *Gesta Grayorum, the History of the High and Mighty Prince Henry*; W. Canning: London, U.K., 1688.

36. Whitehead, P.J.P. Museums in the history of zoology. Museums J. **1970**, *70* (2), 50–57.

37. Hooper-Greenhill, E. *Museums and the Shaping of Knowledge*; Routledge: London, U.K., 1992.

38. Lewis, G. Museums and their precursors: a brief world survey. In *Manual of Curatorship: A Guide to Museum Practice*; Thompson, J.M.A., Ed.; Butterworth-Heinemann: Oxford, U.K., 1992; 5–21.

39. Swann, M. *Curiosities and Texts: The Culture of Collecting in Early Modern England*; University of Pennsylvania Press: Philadelphia, PA, 2001.

40. Findlen, P. Mr. Murray's Cabinet of Wonder. In *Museums, Their History, and Their Use*; Murray, D., Ed.; Pober Publishing: Staten Island, NY, 2000; i–xvii.

41. Meadow, M.A.; Robertson, B. *The First Treatise on Museums. Samuel Quiccheberg's Inscriptiones 1565*; The Getty Research Institute: Los Angeles, CA, 2013.

42. Schepelern, H.D. Natural philosophers and princely collectors: Worm, Paludanus and the Gottorp and Copenhagen collections. In *The Origins of Museums. The Cabinet of Curiosities in Sixteenth- and Seventeenth-Century Europe*; Impey, O., MacGregor, A., Eds.; Clarendon Press: Oxford, U.K., 1985; 121–127.

43. Pavord, A. *The Naming of Names: The Search for Order in the World of Plants*; Bloomsbury Publishing: New York, 2005.

44. Jones, R.F. *Ancients and Moderns, a Study of the Rise of the Scientific Movement in Seventeenth-Century England*, Rev. Ed.; The Washington University Press: St. Louis, MO, 1961.

45. MacGregor, A. *Tradescant's Rarities: Essays on the Foundation of the Asmolean Museum 1683 with a Catalogue of the Surviving Early Collections*; Clarendon Press: Oxford, U.K., 1983.

46. Boylan, P.J. Universities and museums: past, present and future. Museum Manag. Curatorsh. **1999**, *18* (1), 43–56.

47. Grew, N. *Musaeum Regalis Societatis: Or a Catalog and Description of the Natural and Artificial Rarities belonging to the Royal Society and Preserved at Gresham College, Whereunto is Subjoyned the Comparative Anatomy of Stomachs and Guts*; W. Rawlins: London, U.K., 1681.

48. Holdengräber, P. "A visible history of art": the forms and preoccupations of the early museum. In *Studies in Eighteenth-Century Culture*; Yolton, J., Brown, L.E., Eds.; American Society for Eighteenth-Century Studies: East Lansing, MI, 1987; 107–117.

49. Lorente, J.P. *Manual de la Historia de la Museología*; Ediciones Trea: Gijón, España, 2012.

50. Blunt, W. *Linnaeus, The Compleat Naturalist*; Princeton University Press: Princeton, NJ, 2001.

51. Chenall, R.G. *Nomenclature for Museum Cataloguing: A System for Classifying Man-made Objects*; American Association for State and Local History: Nashville, TN, 1978.

52. Alexander, E.P. *Museums in Motion: An Introduction to the History and Functions of Museums*; American Association for State and Local History: Nashville, TN, 1979.

53. Alexander, E.P. Early American museums. From collection of curiosities to popular education. Int. J. Museum Manag. Curatorsh. **1987**, *6* (4), 337–351.

54. Alexander, E.P.; Alexander, M. *Museums in Motion: An Introduction to the History and Functions of Museums*; Altamira Press: Lanham, MD, 2008.

55. Miller, L.B. The Peale family: a lively mixture of art and science. Smithsonian, **1979**, *10* (1), 66–77.

56. Haberly, L. The American museum from Baker to Barnum. N. Y. Hist. Soc. Q. **1959**, *43* (3), 273–287.

57. Kohlstedt, S.G. Entrepreneurs and intellectuals: natural history in early American museums. In *Mermaids, Mummies, and Mastodons: The Emergence of the American Museum*; Alderson, W.T., Ed,; American Association of Museums: Washington, DC, 1992; 23–39.

58. Betts, J.R. P.T. Barnum and the popularization of natural history. J. Hist. Ideas. **1959**, *29* (3), 353–368.

59. Flower, W.H. *Essays on Museums and Other Subjects Connected with Natural History*; MacMillan and Company, Ltd.: London, U.K., 1898.

60. Pyenson, L.; Sheets-Pyenson, S. *Servants of Nature: A History of Scientific Institutions, Enterprises, and Sensibilities*; W.W. Norton and Company: New York, 1999.

61. Conn, S. *Museums and American Intellectual Life, 1876–1926*; University of Chicago Press: Chicago, IL, 1998.

62. Wittlin, A.S. *Museums: In Search of a Usable Future*; The MIT Press: Cambridge, MA, 1970.

63. Macdonald, S.J. Museums, national, postnational and transcultural identities. Museum Soc. **2003**, *1* (1), 1–16.

64. Morales-Moreno, L.G. History and patriotism in the National Museum of Mexico. In *Museums and the Making of "Ourselves." The Role of Objects in National Identity*; Kaplan, F.E.S., Ed.; Leicester University Press: London, U.K., 1994; 171–191.

65. Cummins, A. The "Caribbeanization" of the West Indies: the museum's role in the development of national identity. In *Museums and the Making of "Ourselves." The Role of Objects in National Identity*; Kaplan, F.E.S., Ed.; Leicester University Press: London, U.K., 1994; 192–220.

66. Davis, P. *Ecomuseums: A Sense of Place*; Continuum International Publishing Group: London, U.K., 2011.

67. Latham, K.; Simmons, J.E. *Foundations of Museum Studies: Evolving Systems of Knowledge*; Libraries Unlimited: Santa Barbara, CA, 2014.

68. Schweibenz, W. The development of virtual museums. ICOM News, **2004**, *57* (3), 3.

History of Paper

Sidney E. Berger
Phillips Library, Peabody Essex Museum, Salem, Massachusetts, U.S.A.

Abstract

Centuries before paper was invented, ideas were communicated in various ways other than orally. We know of the paintings on cave walls, and the use of wood, clay, stone, bamboo, wax, silk, palm leaves, and other surfaces. In the West, the immediate predecessors to paper are papyrus and vellum or parchment, the dried skins of animals, which was in use in the West at about the same time as was the earliest papers in the Orient: the second century B.C. But paper has had by far a greater impact on civilization than has any other material ever invented.

INTRODUCTION

Paper is matted fibers.

If that were all there were to it, this entry would not be 9000 words. Paper is an almost magically simple product to make, and it is perhaps—along with printing—one of the most important inventions in history. (Someone suggested that Printing, Paper, and the Alphabet are the "top three" inventions of all times.[1])

ANTECEDENTS TO PAPER

Centuries before paper was invented, ideas were communicated in various ways other than orally. We know of the paintings on cave walls, and of the use of wood, clay, stone, bamboo, wax, silk, and other surfaces, none of which needs to be rehearsed here. In the West, the immediate predecessors to paper are papyrus and vellum or parchment, the dried skins of animals, which was in use in the West at about the same time as was the earliest papers in the Orient: the second century B.C.[2]

Papyrus

Papyrus, used as early as 3500 B.C. in Egypt, is a plant of the sedge family, growing in warm moist climates. It can reach heights of 18 feet or more. Much ignorance about papyrus was passed along to us in the West by scholars knowing little or nothing about it, who made pronouncements based on logic rather than on fact. [Witness this rather ludicrous statement: "Papyrus. . .is only one of the predecessors of paper that together are known by the generic term 'tapa' and are mostly made from the inner bark of paper mulberry, fig and daphne"; quoted from http://www.paperonline.org/history/3000/3000_frame.html (accessed July 29, 2008). This could hardly be more wrong.] Hence, misstatements abound about papyrus'

manufacture. Only through the efforts of Hassan Ragab were we able to rediscover the secrets of the plant and the writing surface made from it. (His dissertation, *Contribution à l'étude du papyrus (Cyperus papyrus.L) et à sa transformation en support de l'écriture (papyrus des anciens)* (L'Institut National Polytechnique de Grenoble, 1979), was self-published into a book, *Le papyrus* in Cairo in 1980.)

As Alia Hanafi writes:

> In 1962, [Hassan Ragab] started the process of re-discovery. But he faced two major obstacles. First, that papyrus was vanished in Egypt, and he had to go to Sudan to re-import the plant. Second, the entire process of papyrus making was maintained as a secret. Therefore, Dr. Ragab read books by Herodotus, Strabo and Theophrastus, but none could describe the process. The only but very vague indication he found in the studies of Pliny the Elder. Nevertheless, this description was so inaccurate that it did not help him in any way. So, he spent the next 4 years researching the method. In July 1966, he produced his first papyrus paper. In 1967, Dr. Ragab founded on a houseboat on the Nile an Institute for the remanufacturing of Papyrus. He started to collect some information from experts, and began his own experiments. Therefore, gradually he found the way to produce sheets in the same quality, the same structure as it was done some thousands years ago [sic].[3]

One thing to remember is that papyrus is *not* paper. Paper is made from matted fibers—fibers that have been macerated and ground down into pieces of tiny lengths. Papyrus fibers have not been macerated. So to call the material "papyrus paper" as Hanafi does is to misrepresent the sheets.

Another common misperception is that sheets of papyrus are "prepared from the pith of the papyrus plant by cutting it in longitudinal strips, arranging them crosswise in two or three layers, soaking them in water, and pressing them into a homogenous surface."[4] This statement has at

Encyclopedia of Library and Information Sciences, Fourth Edition DOI: 10.1081/E-ELIS4-120044852

least two errors. First, the order of events (laying the strips out and then soaking them) is wrong: the soaking of the strips takes place before the arrangement of the strips. Second, "two or three layers" is incorrect. All one needs is two layers and no literature mentions (and no papyrus sheets evidence) a third layer.

A third error, propagated in the nineteenth century by scholars guessing how the sheets were made, is that one must pound the strips of the stalk. Pounding them would disperse the long fibers and mess up the final leaves. We see such statements as, "The strips may have been soaked in water long enough for decomposition to begin, perhaps increasing adhesion, but this is not certain. While still moist, the two layers are hammered together, mashing the layers into a single sheet." (This error comes from the error-prone *Wikipedia*.[5]) The author is following a long tradition of error calling for hammering, smashing, or pounding the layers.

The simple method of making papyrus is as follows:

The stems of the papyrus plant, which are covered with a green "skin" or "bark" and are almost triangular, are filled with a pulpy pith somewhat thicker than but similar in consistency to the pulp of watermelon and with long stringy fibers like those in celery. The stalks are cut down, and then cut into whatever lengths the papyrus maker desires. The green skin is pared off two of the three sides of the stalks, the stalks are sliced into thin strips, and then the last of the green outer "bark" is sliced away.

The strips are then soaked in water to hydrate the fibers. The pith has to be as wet and mushy as possible since it is the blending of this pith within strips lying in different directions that will determine the solidity of the final product.

Various sources talk of how long these strips should be soaked. Soaking for several days, with the water being changed often, will allow for the maximum hydration of the fibers and will allow the pith to break down and become quite soft. The strips are then laid out on a flat surface, first in one direction (slightly overlapping) and then a second layer placed at right angles over the first layer (also overlapping). The strips are then put under great pressure to squeeze out the water and to press the pulp for all of the strips into one solid mass of pulp. Several pressings, each time replacing wet blotting material with dry, pulls the water out of the strips, which are eventually merged into one single leaf of papyrus.

Several leaves can be glued together to make longer and still longer pieces, so that a long text can be written onto a single piece of papyrus. Since the sheet is relatively brittle and will not withstand folding, the standard format of a text on papyrus is either a broadside or a roll (or scroll). The final product is flexible, light and portable, and stable; that is, it has no inherent vice, so it will not deteriorate if it is properly stored and handled. It is generally written on one side only. And while it *is* portable, a long scroll is somewhat unwieldy. Its practicability,

however, and the abundance of such plants made papyrus the most used surface for communication for perhaps 2000 years.

Parchment/Vellum

The word "parchment" has descended from the city Pergamum, an ancient city in Asia Minor, now Bergama, in western Turkey. "Vellum" comes from the French word "velin," a calf (related to "veal").

A good deal of confusion about the terms "parchment" and "vellum" has led to their being used practically interchangeably today. Brown and Lovett say, "It is now usually accepted that parchment is sheep or goat skin and vellum calf skin."[6] Some writers use the term "vellum" only for calf and "parchment" for any other dried animal skin, including horse, pig, goat, and other mammals. There is even a company making what it calls "parchment" out of snakeskin, the skins of various fish and lizards, and other such creatures. It is dried skin, and it is used in bookbinding and for other artistic products. For all practical purposes, and partly because most people cannot distinguish the skin of one mammal from another (especially that of sheep from that of cows), the two terms have become perfectly interchangeable.

Beverly Boyd claims, "Nowadays...manufacturers of stationary have settled these words for the public by using the term 'vellum' to denote a suede-like finish and 'parchment' to denote a crisp finish."[7] Since that was written (in 1973), the distinction has essentially disappeared.

The following description of the preparation of the skin is necessarily brief, leaving out many details. (For a more thorough treatment see books by Reed.[8,9]) The butchered animal is flayed, its skin is soaked in lime then stretched on a frame, and the parchment maker, using a lunellum (a moon-shaped knife), pares down the flesh from one side and shaves off the hair from the other. A fine talcum called "pounce" is sometimes burnished onto the skin to smooth it off and act as a mordant, allowing pigments to adhere to the skin. This yields a fine surface, with a hair side and a flesh side. When the signatures of a book made of sheets of parchment were designed, written or drawn on, folded, and gathered, the artists and scribes knew to have hair sides face hair sides and flesh sides to face flesh sides, since the hair sides tended to be somewhat darker than the flesh sides.

The skins were pared down to be quite thin and were thus easy to fold. The modern codex—the book as we know it with leaves written on both sides, folded, and then sewn together through the folds at the inner margins—is the product of book makers of about the second century A.D.

The skins of young animals were generally preferred to those of older ones, but many a large folio attests to the fact that full-grown cows and sheep, goats and pigs were used as well.

A particularly fine kind of vellum, quite thin, strong, white (or just off-white), and lovely, is called "uterine vellum," presumably because the fetuses were aborted, so that the parchment makers could have such fine skins to work with. Recently, the notion of aborting the fetus has been questioned, especially since an extremely fine skin can be made from a young animal by a skilled craftsman. Using a microscope, an expert may be able to distinguish skin types and follicle patterns to show what animal was used for a particular sheet. But to the naked eye, it is often difficult or impossible to say what animal was used. On the other hand, certain goat skins have a distinct and distinguishable skin.

Naturally, the maker would get out of the skin the largest rectangle he could. But none of the skin would be wasted, for the remainder could be cut into thongs or rendered down to make glue.

Since books were produced one at a time, by hand, the amount of parchment available kept up with the demand for it of the scribes and authors. But certain social forces in the West in the Middle Ages—perhaps the most important of which was the growth of the guild system with a concomitant growth of a middle class—brought about a need for an increasing amount of writing surfaces. Paper in the West was just ripe to be invented.

PAPER

Paper: History

The history of paper is shrouded in mist. We have a few clear facts, like that it was invented in the second century B.C. by the Chinese. We don't know where in China nor do we know the inventor. We can speculate—as many have done—that some genius observed the work of wasps, who made their nests by macerating the pulp of various trees or shrubs, and whose nests were the inspiration for the making of paper. Whether this is true or not is debatable.

One "fact" that has been foisted on the world for many decades is that paper was invented by a court eunuch, Ts'ai Lun (or Cai Lun, or Lung—his name has several other spellings) under the emperor Ho Ti in 105 A.D. This error has been perpetuated so often and for so long that it has taken on a life of its own, and it is difficult to supplant it with the truth. It is wrong, and for the sake of accuracy and historical correctness, I have made this point emphatically in this long paragraph.

We know that paper existed in China in the second century B.C. One source enigmatically says, "True paper is believed to have originated in China in approximately the 2nd Century A.D., although there is some evidence for it being used before this date"; the source follows this with, "Papermaking is considered to be one of the Four Great Inventions of Ancient China, since the first papermaking process was developed in China during the early 2nd century." Then this source says: "the discovery of specimens bearing written Chinese characters in 2006 at north-east China's Gansu province suggest [sic] that paper was in use by the ancient Chinese military more than 100 years before Cai [Lung], in 8 B.C." And finally, from the same source: "Archeologically, however, true paper without writing has been excavated in China dating to the reign of Emperor Wu of Han from the 2nd century B.C., used for purposes of wrapping or padding protection for delicate bronze mirrors."[10]

The Chinese guarded the secret of papermaking for centuries, knowing of the power paper has for transmitting texts. It made its way to Korea and Japan (c. 604 A.D. and 610 A.D., respectively), and then, through Samarkand, to the West in the middle of the twelfth century. By about 1150 the first European papers appear, but how they were made—in a mill or by more primitive methods—no one can determine. We know where the paper came from by what was written on it, so we know that in the last half of the twelfth century paper was being made in Xativa, Spain. And by 1276, the mill in Fabriano, Italy, was at work.

To write a full account of paper's manufacture in the East and the West would take several volumes. In the short space of an encyclopedia entry, only the most superficial information can be imparted. Even when the information may seem minutely detailed, it is really only scratching the surface since the variety of methods, materials, machinery, and practices is measureless.

Manufacture—Asian Methods

Over the centuries, from its earliest practice in China to today, methods of making paper by hand in Asia have evolved tremendously in some respects and have remained the same in others. This brief discussion will look at only one form of Asian papermaking, the so-called Nagashizuki method, since the other (the Tamezuki method) is similar to that of making paper by hand in the West.

To make paper using the Nagashizuki method, the craftsperson must harvest the fibers. Traditionally, the three basic fibers for making paper are kozo, mitsumata, and gampi, the first being the most common. Kozo is *Broussonetia papyrifera*, the Paper Mulberry, common to many cultures throughout the world.

Because the Japanese have become the most prolific and imaginative, creative and artistic papermakers in history, and because they have been practicing the craft for more than 1400 years, this entry uses the Japanese terminology. Papermaking in China over the centuries and even today is light years behind that in Japan.

Though the process of harvesting and preparing the bark is more complicated than this brief discussion reveals, the basic process is described here.

The plant is harvested in the winter once the leaves have fallen off. The stems are cut into pieces about 4 in. long and are cooked until the outer bark is soft and can be scraped off. This outer bark is tied into bundles and dried. They are stored until they are ready to be made into paper in the spring. When it is time to make the paper, the strips are rehydrated until they are soft. They are crushed in running water with the papermakers' feet. The crushing removes the dark outer layer. This is followed by the careful paring and scraping off of the green middle layer, which adheres to the white inner bark. The long white strips of bark are then dried again until the actual paper-making begins.

The bark is then rinsed, removing the last remaining dark or green bark, and is then cooked in an alkaline solution (usually wood ash or caustic soda). After the cooking, the strips are cooled and the scum on the top of the pot is skimmed off. The strips of fibers are now soft; they are lain onto a board and hit with a stick, with automatic stampers, or in a beater—a machine that slices or grinds up the fibers.

When the fibers are all macerated or cut to the right length (the proper length differs with the different kinds of paper to be made), they are floated in water that has a formation aid in it. The formation aid, called tororo aoi, is a slimy gelatinous substance made from the roots of the hibiscus plant. It is called a "formation aid" because it helps the fibers form into a sheet by allowing them to be distributed evenly on the surface of the paper mold.

The mold is dipped into the vat containing the fibers, and a small amount of water and fibers are slid over the mold's surface. This action is done several times until the papermaker has the sheet to the desired thickness.

The mold is in two parts, a su and a geta (or keta). The geta is the frame on which the su (the screen) sits. Once most of the water has dripped through the su, the fibers now distributed on the su are matted into a sheet of paper. The flexible su, made of thin strips of bamboo, detaches from the geta and is taken to a stack of recently made sheets, onto which the fresh sheet is lain. When the su peels away, the newly made sheet transfers onto the stack of other sheets. The laying down of the su must be done from one long edge, while all the strips of bamboo are "rolled" over the stack of sheets beneath it, so that no air bubbles form under the new sheet.

When the stack of sheets is "complete," the papermaker presses it to squeeze out the water and then dries the sheets in various ways. One common way was to peel a sheet off the pile, brush it onto a tall wooden board along with several other sheets (on both sides of the board) and set the board out into the sun to dry. This also whitens the sheets. A more modern method has the papermaker brushing the wet sheet onto the surface of a metal drum that has been heated. This dries the sheet rather quickly. Both methods leave fine brush strokes on the sheet, and the final product has a board (or drum) side and a brush side. This accounts for the different feel of the two sides of many pieces of Washi (handmade Japanese paper).

Manufacture—Western Methods

The method of making paper in the West has many features of that in the Orient, but with a good number of differences. In fact, the Tamezuki style of papermaking in Japan may well come from the Western version of the craft.

To begin with, the fibers in the West were different: there was no kozo, mitsumata, or gampi. In the West, linen and cotton were used. Further, since there was no bamboo, and since metallurgy was well advanced in the West, the paper molds used wires stretched along the long measure of the mold. And finally, since there was no tororo aoi in the West, papermakers developed a method of sheet formation that allowed for only a single dipping of the mold into the vat and that did not allow the sheets to be couched (transferred from the mold) onto previously couched sheets. The sheets had to be couched onto woven woolen felts, which pulled the sheets from the mold.

Before the fibers were macerated, they were usually retted—that is, soaked in a tub until the natural action of bacteria caused the fibers to begin to break down. This is sometimes called "bacterial pulping," though the actual pulping, the final maceration, was a mechanical process.

Macerating the fibers was originally done with stamping mills, essentially large mortars and pestles, the latter driven by water or, in the Netherlands, by wind. Wet pulp was placed into the cups of the mortars, and the pestles, driven up and down, pounded the fibers, beating them into little pieces. In the last quarter of the seventeenth century, the Dutch invented the Hollander beater, a machine consisting of a large oval tub divided partly down the middle, forming a sluice around which the water containing the pulp was forced by a large rotating cylinder on the surface of which were blades running parallel to the width of the cylinder. The rotating cylinder forced the pulp under it, and the blades ground and cut the fibers against a bedplate, breaking them down to the desired length.

The wooden mold—four pieces of wood made sturdy and rigid by having supports affixed across the short measure—had metal wires stretched lengthwise across it. The wires were sewn down with chain stitches along the length of each support. The vatman, scooping up the fibers from the tub onto the mold's surface, shook the mold to distribute the fibers evenly over the wires. The fibers settled evenly over the surface except where the chain stitches ran along the supports, at which points the fibers fell more thinly since the chain stitches were above the rest of the surface of the wires. Since the fibers were more thinly distributed where the chain stitches were, when the sheet was held up to the light, more light would shine through the sheet where it was thinner. These so-called "chain lines" distinguished the handmade papers of the day. Holding a sheet of such paper up to the light, the viewer could see the wire lines going horizontally along the long measure of the sheet and chain lines, separated by a half inch or an inch, going in the other direction.

Also, when the sheet was pressed onto the felt, the supports beneath the wires pressed the fibers above them densely, so when a piece of laid paper was held up to the light, the densely packed fibers would create a dark area around the chain lines, like shadows. What one would see in this so-called "antique laid paper" were the wire lines and chain lines, with shadows around the chain lines.

To avoid the appearance of these shadows, mold makers stretched a second layer of wires across the long measure of the mold, a fraction of an inch above the first layer of wires. Now when the sheet was pressed onto the felt, the supports did not exert any pressure where the chain lines were, so no shadow was formed along them. This new mold created "modern laid paper," sheets showing the wire lines and chain lines, but no shadows around the chain lines.

After dipping the mold into the vat and distributing the fibers over its surface, the vatman would give the mold to a coucher or layman, who couched the sheet (pressed the mold containing the wet sheet to the felt, transferring the sheet to the felt). (The words are pronounced /koocher/ and /koocht/.) The newly formed sheet would be covered by another felt, and another sheet would be couched upon that, and so forth, until there was a large stack consisting of sheets interleaved with felts. This was called a "post."

The post was pressed in a large machine and much of the water would be squeezed out. In the vat, the percentage of water to fiber was about 96% to 4%. After the first pressing, the percentage was more like 90% fiber and 10% water. The felts were then removed and the remaining "white post" was pressed a second time. After this second pressing, the sheets could then be removed from the post and hung (or laid out in spurs of five or six sheets) to dry.

The mold was flat, of course, and if it were used by itself, the fibers and water from the vat would run off the edges when it was dipped into the vat. To keep the fibers and water on the surface of the mold while the water dripped away through the wires, a deckle, a rectangular frame, was placed over the mold. Fibers would adhere to the inner edges of this deckle or they would slide under the deckle, forming slightly uneven edges on the sheet—called "deckle edges" or "deckled edges."

As Allan Stevenson has shown, a typical commercial hand mold was composed of two molds and one deckle. While the vatman was dipping out a sheet from the vat, the coucher (also called the "layman") was couching another sheet onto a felt from the second mold. When he was done and the sheet had been removed from his mold and deposited onto the post, he would exchange his now-empty mold for the one the vatman had just lifted out of the vat.

The vatman would hand off the mold with the newly formed sheet on it and take the empty mold to begin the process again. If the molds had watermarks, the maker of the molds would try to get the watermarks to look identical and be placed in exactly the same position on the two molds, but that was not always the case, and sometimes we can see variations in watermarks or in their placement on sheets made at the same time by the same makers.[11]

Sheets made with only water and fiber are called "waterleaf." The tiny fibers have infinitesimal air pockets around the matted fibers. These pockets, through capillary action, would draw in ink, which could feather out on a sheet as does fountain pen ink on a modern newspaper. The sheets, therefore, needed to be sized, infusing a glue (usually an animal-based glue) into the sheet. The dried sheets would be soaked in the sizing bath, taking the glue in, filling all the tiny air pockets, and preventing inks from feathering out.

It was possible to size the paper by putting the sizing into the vat during the initial sheet formation, but the result would have been pressing the sized sheets onto the felts, imparting the glue to the felts. This would have necessitated a thorough washing of the felts. More common was sizing the papers in a special bath, after the initial drying of the sheets. Hence, there are two kinds of processes: vat sizing and tub sizing, the latter much more common than the former.

The sizing essentially glues all the fibers together, bonding them to one another. Hence the term "bond paper," which merely designates sized paper, as opposed to waterleaf.

Sheets thus made would be pressed again, and then often calendered—that is, run through a calendering press consisting of two smooth cylinders that put the sheets under great pressure, smoothing off the surfaces. The cylinders could be heated up, so there were hot-pressed and cold-pressed sheets.

In the middle of the eighteenth century, John Baskerville designed a new typeface with fine serifs. If during printing the serif landed exactly on a chain line, where the paper was thin, it may not print perfectly. Baskerville wished to have a smoother, evener distribution of fibers in his printing papers. He, or perhaps the famous paper-maker James Whatman, devised a mold consisting of wires pulled left to right and also top to bottom, woven together. The result was a sheet formed on a smooth screen, showing no wire lines or chain lines. This paper is called "wove," not that the fibers are woven, but that the screen from which the paper was made was woven. On the manufacture of wove paper see Hunter.[12]

Hence, paper can be categorized in several ways: by fiber distribution (modern laid, antique laid, or wove); by content (sized or unsized; and vat sized or tub sized); by surface (calendered or uncalendered; and hot-pressed or cold-pressed papers); and then by other features (colored or not; trimmed or not; watermarked or not; and so forth).

With the invention of wove paper made from a screen, papermakers were no longer forced to use hand molds. The laid wires on the hand mold needed to be held in place by the frame of the mold itself. But a woven screen could be "freestanding." It was only a matter of time before a clever inventor could take a screen, make a huge loop out of it, and attach one end to the other in a loop. This led to the mechanization of papermaking.

Frenchman Nicholas-Louis Robert is generally given credit for the invention of a papermaking machine—in 1798. The formal patent is recorded on January 18, 1799.[13] As Hunter explains, Robert quarreled with his backers, sold and then reacquired the patent, and unsuccessfully tried to get a commercial-level machine built in France. He eventually turned to his contact in England, papermaker John Gamble, who interested Henry and Sealy Fourdrinier, stationers, in the machine. They hired Bryan Donkin, a brilliant engineer, who created his own version of the papermaking machine, based on Robert's patented plans, and on June 23, 1801, the English patent was issued.[14] To this day, all papermaking machines are called Fourdriniers.

A cylinder machine was invented by English papermaker John Dickinson in 1809, and a similar machine was created by Thomas Gilpin in the United States, in 1817, the first papermaking machine in this country.[15]

Eventually, the Fourdriniers got to be quite long, containing rollers for drying, embossing, calendering, and otherwise treating papers, along with parts of the machine that added sizing, color, and other modifications to the basic sheet. One such modification was a watermark, created near the very beginning of the papermaking process, before the fibers had fully settled onto the screen. A large roll, called a "dandy roll," containing the pattern for the watermark disrupted the fibers as they were settling, thinning out the sheet at the point where the dandy roll "landed in" the settling fibers. So lovely watermarks are not necessarily a sign of a handmade sheet.

Similarly, a handmade piece of paper has four deckles around it; such a treatment can be put into a machine-made sheet. And a pattern of chain lines and wire lines can be imparted to the sheet by a dandy roll, so laid paper—which was once purely a handmade product—can also be machine made. Sometimes distinguishing between a handmade and a machine-made sheet can be difficult (but see below under "Grain.")

PAPER FIBERS

For several centuries in the West (say, from the middle of the twelfth century until the middle of the nineteenth century), the supply of rags was sufficient to satisfy the world's paper needs. By the second half of the nineteenth century, however, it was clear that another source of fiber was needed. As early as the late eighteenth century, experiments were being done with straw and certain kinds of wood.

Matthias Koops in England was making paper from straw as early as 1800; and straw was experimented with for decades in the trade. Many other fibers were tried. In fact, since paper is matted fibers, just about any fiber will do. Even synthetic fibers have been used in papermaking. Witness Tyvek®, a synthetic olefin plastic, that makes sturdy, almost untearable paper.

In the last 30 years or so, many hand papermakers have experimented with papermaking by using seriously non-traditional fibers, like vegetables, plants of all kinds, many species of cactus and succulents, and many more unusual materials. They all produce paper of various qualities, and most of them are mere curiosities, not useful for printing or bookbinding.

By the third-quarter of the nineteenth century, wood pulp was adopted as the preferred fiber. It had been experimented with as early as 1765 by Dr. Jacob Christian Schäffer in Germany.[16] (See the book by Hunter for a more detailed treatment of the use of wood fibers in papermaking.) As Hunter points out, "the first ground-wood pulp produced commercially on this continent was the output of a machine based on the patents of Heinrich Voelter." "In 1867, Albrecht Pagenstecher founded at Curtisville (now Interlaken) near Stockbridge, Massachusetts, the first ground-wood pulp mill in the United States."[17]

Because wood pulp is much more difficult to macerate than hemp or cotton, methods were created to break down the pulp chemically, using sulfuric and other acids. The old method, using sticks, stamping mills, or Hollander beaters, was a mechanical way to prepare the fibers. The new method was chemical; and today we make a distinction between mechanical pulp and chemical pulp.

If the pulp is allowed to soak (or to be cooked) in acids, and then the acids are not sufficiently washed out of the fibers before the paper is made, the acid remains in the sheets. The aim of using chemicals to break down the fibers is to "break down, the chemical structure of the lignin and render it soluble in the chemical liquor so that it may be washed from the cellulose fibers. Because lignin holds the plant cells together, chemical pulping frees the fibers and makes pulp."[18] Conservators call the residual acids in the fibers "inherent vice": a deteriorating material inherent in the papers themselves; they will cause the pulp to break down, the acids attacking the fibers, from within. Paper from the third quarter of the nineteenth century on (and especially commercially made paper) was likely to be made from chemical pulp, and thus millions upon millions of books and documents using this paper will have browned and become brittle if not deacidified. But by the time the deterioration is noticed, the paper has already gotten brown, and the damage is done.

If the lignin remains in the paper, the paper will be acidic. Papermakers can remove the lignin and can also add buffers like calcium carbonate or magnesium carbonate, so the paper has an alkaline reserve to make it lignin free and acid free. It took a law (Public Law 101-423), signed by President George Bush in October 1990, to require all government printing to be done on acid-free archival paper. Called The Permanent Paper Law, it encouraged the use of acid-free permanent papers for all government documents.

WATERMARKS

One feature of paper that has been a great help to historians and other scholars is whether the paper is watermarked or not. When one holds sheet up to the light, any area that is thinner–that is, an area that has fewer fibers than the areas around it–will show light through the paper. To make the paper thinner at any give point or points, the papermarker affixes something to the surface of the mold that forces the fibers to fall more thinly there than elsewhere on the mold. If a wire in the shape of the letter "R" were sewn or soldered to the surface of the mold, the fibers would fall thinly over it, and the result would be a watermark in the shape of that letter.

Papermakers often identified themselves in simple or elaborate watermarks, sometimes putting the date into the watermark along with their logo. Often a second mark, called a "countermark," would be put into a sheet, so the final sheet would show a watermark of, say, an animal, a building, a flower, or some other decorative element, along with a countermark of the name of the firm or of the party commissioning the paper.

The word "watermark" is a misnomer since water has little to do with the creation of watermarks.

Watermarks can be produced in several ways, but the key is that the fibers are more thinly (or thickly) distributed where the watermark is than they are in the rest of the sheet. For instance, on a hand-mold, the papermaker can fashion a letter, word, or number out of thin wire and sew or solder it to the surface of the mold. When the fibers fall onto the surface of the mold during the papermaking process, they will fall more thinly where the wire watermark sticks up above the surface. Note that this can be done on any kind of paper mold, antique laid, modern laid, or wove. Also note that the wires themselves are called a "watermark," and so is the resultant pattern seen in the back-lighted sheet.

A second kind of watermark is done in wove paper only. A male and female die with a pattern in it is used. The wove screen is heated to make the metal malleable, and it is then pressed between the two faces of the die, which contains the pattern for the watermark. The result can be a standard watermark, where a part of the woven screen is embossed (raised in relief), making the fibers fall more thinly where the screen is raised, and thus creating a watermark in the paper. But the screen can also be de-bossed, that is, pressed inward so that more fibers fall into the groove. The resultant sheet is thicker where more fibers have fallen, and therefore less light shines through the sheet where the watermark is. The notion that a watermark is always revealed in light is thus not strictly correct, for in this case, the mark consists of darker areas of the paper.

Many such male-and-female-die watermarks have both embossed and de-bossed levels in them, so the watermark they produce can have the light that comes through the rest of the sheet, a lighter area for part of the watermark, and a darker area for the other part. This is called a three-plane watermark.

Another kind of mark is also made from a male and female die, but rather than having only embossed and de-bossed surfaces in it, it has graduated levels, creating a watermark with many shades of light penetration. This is called a shadowmark, a light-and-shade watermark, or a chiaroscuro watermark.

Watermarks were used in paper by the end of the thirteenth century. They can appear anywhere in a sheet that the papermaker desires, but the standard placements are either in the center of the sheet or, more common, in the center of one-half of the sheet. As I have noted, many sheets have two such marks, the main one called the watermark, the other called the countermark. Since they yield a thinness to the paper and might affect the printing of the sheet, printers folded the sheets in such a way that the watermarks usually fell into margins. As noted, they can reveal the name or logo of the paper manufacturer, images of animals, buildings, hands or other body parts, geometrical designs, dates, or anything else desired. Paper made specifically for an artist can be fashioned with the artist's name in the watermark.

There is a vast literature on watermarks, for a study of them can help with the dating and localization of otherwise anonymous documents and books. One should probably start with the monumental volumes compiled by Charles M. Briquet, *Les Filigranes: Dictionnaire Historique des Marques du Papier des Leur Apparition Vers 1282 Jisqu'en 1600* (Geneva: 1907, or one of the later reprints). The Paper Publications Society of Hilversum, Holland, has published many grand volumes that are compendia of watermarks.

PAPER SIZES

Paper made by hand was produced in many sizes, there not being any standard sizes that printers demanded. The size of any handmade sheet is determined by the inner dimensions of the deckle. Throughout Europe, sheets were made from fairly large to quite small, and each size was given a name—though, of course, the dimensions represented by any given name are approximate. The following chart reveals approximate sizes since the dimensions varied from paper mill to paper mill and from country to country. The table uses English terms; the nomenclature in other countries obviously differs. (This listing of Paper Sizes was adapted from Labarre.)[19]

E.J. Labarre, in his extraordinary *Dictionary and Encyclopaedia of Paper and Paper-Making*, lists over 200 paper sizes, each with its own name and particular dimensions. The most common of them are listed here, the dimensions given being approximate since papermakers throughout history used whatever size molds they had available for them, and there was no standard for any given book format, broadside, or other use. Other sources will give the same or similar names, but sometimes with varying dimensions (Table 1).

PAPER WEIGHT

Paper is often spoken of in terms of its weight. We use "20 lb. bond" for professional correspondence, "16 lb. paper" for taking notes, "24 lb. paper" for charts, and so forth. The terminology emanates from the weight of a ream of the full-size sheet. So a ream (in the United States this is 500 sheets; in England it was 480, but now the British use 500 as well) of full sheets of paper that weighs 20 pounds yields "20 lb. paper."

The Wikipedia says it this way:

> The basis weight of paper is the density of paper expressed in terms of the mass of a ream of given dimensions and a sheet count. In the U.S. system, the weight is specified in avoirdupois pounds, and the sheet count of a paper ream is usually 500 sheets.[20]

Papers created for different purposes have different base (or basis) weights since the "standard size" of a sheet differs depending on its use (see Table 2).

The base weight of a sheet of Index bristol is higher than is the weight of Tissue, though two sheets are exactly the same size.

GRAIN OF PAPER

When a sheet of paper is hand made, the vatman shakes the fibers over the surface of the mold, forwards, back, and side to side, in such a way that the fibers get distributed in no particular order of alignment. On a Fourdrinier, however, since the screen on which the paper is formed moves constantly in one direction, the fibers tend to line up in that direction, creating a grain in the sheet. The grain can be seen under a microscope, or one can tear the sheet. If a newspaper is torn in one direction, the tear goes straight—with the grain. If it is torn in the other direction, the tear will be jagged and crooked—against the grain.

Table 1 Names of paper sizes.

Names of paper sizes	Sizes	Paper weight
Emperor	72 × 48	W, D
Quad	56 × 38	P
Double Atlas	55 × 31½	P
Antiquarian	53 × 31	D,B
Quad Royal	50 × 40	P
Quad Demy	45 × 35	P
Double Demy Oblong	42 × 16	W
Double Elephant	40 × 27	W, P, D, B
Double Royal	40 × 25	P, W, D, B
Double Demy	35 × 22½	W, P, D
Colombier	34½ × 23½	W, D, B
Atlas'	34 × 26	W, D, B
Double Folio	34 × 22	W
Double Large Post	33 × 21	W, P, D
Double Post	30½ × 19	W, P, D
Imperial	29 × 22½	Wp
Elephant	28 × 23	W, P, D, Wp
Double Foolscap (also called Chancery)	26½ × 16½	W, P, D, B, Wp
Super Royal	27 × 19	W
Cartridge	26 × 21	Wp
Royal	24 × 19	W, P, D, B, Wp
Sheet and a Half Post	23½ × 19½	P
Demy	22½ × 17½	P
Medium	22 × 17½	W, D
Large Post (also called Draft, Medium, or Double Small Loaf)	21 × 16½	W, P, D, B, Wp
Small Demy (also called Demy)	20 × 15½	W, D
Copy (also called Tea Copy)	20 × 16	W, P, D, Wp
Post	19 × 15½	W, P
Crown (also called Single Small Hand)	20 × 15	W, P, D, B, Wp
Small (also called Pinched Post)	Post 18½ × 14½	W, P, D
Foolscap	17 × 13¼	P
Foolscap (also called Brief, Small Foolscap)	16½ × 13¼	W, D
Pott	15 × 12½	W, P, D
Half Crown	15 × 9½	D
Half Foolscap	14 × 9	D

Dimensions are given in inches, and a letter following each size indicates the use for which the paper was originally intended: W, Writing; P, Printing; D, Drawing; C, Cards; B, Boards; Wp, Wrapping. Smaller sizes of sheets for cards, notes, and envelopes are not listed here.

Printers and bookbinders must be particularly careful in their work, getting the grain to align throughout the work (usually vertically). It should be added, however, that handmade and machine-made sheets, composed of the same fibers and no other additive, will be of just about equal quality. Because a piece of paper is machine made does not mean that it is of inferior quality to a handmade one. The only difference between them may be the grain.

Table 2 Paper sizes.

Paper type	Paper size	Number of sheets
Bond, writing, ledger	17 × 22	500 sheets
Manuscript cover	18 × 31	500 sheets
Blotting	19 × 24	500 sheets
Box cover	20 × 24	500 sheets
Cover	20 × 26	500 or 1000 sheets
Bristol and tag	22½ × 28½	500 sheets
Tissue	24 × 36	480 sheets
Newsprint	24 × 36	500 sheets
Hanging, waxing, bag, etc.	24 × 36	500 sheets
Book, text, offset	25 × 38	500 sheets
Index bristol	25½ × 30½	500 sheets
Paperboard (all types)	12 × 12	1000 sheets (1000 square feet per ream)

PAPER PRESERVATION

Simple waterleaf (that is, unsized paper), if it is made from clean water and basic alkaline fibers, is alkaline (with a pH over 7), and will not deteriorate unless it is exposed to acids, high humidity and water (which will produce mildew), fire, or other deleterious agents. Hence, paper produced in the fourteenth century should be good as new if it has been stored properly.

As noted above (under "Paper fibers"), chemical pulp, and even good papers made from nonacidic materials, exposed to bad conditions (especially high humidity), will tend to show signs of deterioration. Papers that have been in a moist atmosphere may show "foxing," the little orange or black spots that form from spores that are activated by water.

The best environment in which to store paper for its longest preservation is in a deep freeze. But that renders the materials inaccessible and creates other problems when the materials need to be used. For most libraries and other repositories, a steady environment of 68 degrees (±2°) and 50% humidity (±2% points) is ideal.

Further, steady readings of temperature and humidity are better for paper than are fluctuations since paper will expand and contract with such changes. It is better to have paper-based materials in a temperature, say, 75 degrees at all times than it is to have the temperature fluctuating frequently between 65 and 75.

Papers should be kept away from lights, especially fluorescent lights with their ultraviolet rays, which are damaging. Sunlight also has UV rays, so paper should be kept in acid-free folders or in books away from direct light. Even incandescent bulbs can be damaging over time.

Air filtration is a must, since outside air, especially in cities, can have acids that will harm paper. Witness the tombstones in New England graveyards, with their carving completely worn away.

Papers with acid in them can be deacidified, but the process, which leaves an alkaline base (like calcium carbonate) in the sheets, will not strengthen the papers nor whiten them.

Good storage conditions and careful handling will lengthen the life of all paper items.

Finally, paper is a fine material for preservation. In the Florence flood of November 1966, millions of books were damaged. The bindings of most of those bound in leather and vellum were beyond repair. Those in paper survived to a much greater extent. The paper could be washed the way the leathers could not.

PAPER DECORATION

Over the centuries, paper has been decorated in a variety of ways, for many reasons. There are many enhancing techniques, but the most common are marbling and paste paper decoration.

While marbling is probably a sixteenth-century Persian invention, the true history is shrouded in mist. The Japanese had their own version of "marbling," called "Suminagashi," in which the artist, holding one or more brushes containing the pigments, would put droplets of colored pigments onto the surface of a water trough by touching the tips of the ink-laden brushes to the water. The drops would spread out, often with a series of drops placed inside previously laid-on drops. With a fan, a hand, or breath, the artist would make the rings move into various loosely controlled "patterns." When the desired distribution of lines was achieved, the artist would place a sheet of Washi (handmade Japanese paper) onto the surface and the pattern would transfer to the surface of the sheet. If the paper was waterleaf, as were many of the soft Japanese papers, the design would impregnate itself into the sheet and be visible from both sides.

There is no way to know if this decorative paper was known to the West, or if it had any direct or indirect effect on the development of marbling in the Middle East or the West.

Marbling is quite a simple process to do, but preparing all the equipment and supplies for it is not. One needs a tray to marble in, water, a thickener for the water, brushes and combs and other tools to create the patterns, pigments, paper, ox gall, and alum.

Sheets of paper are prepared by having a wash of alum brushed over them as a mordant—that is, the binder that will allow the pigments to stick to the sheet. The sheets are then allowed to dry.

The size is prepared: water slightly thickened with Irish moss, carrageen, or gum tragacanth. When it is poured into the trough, it looks like water, but it is thick enough that drops of pigment will "sit still" on its surface.

The pigments can be any kind: watercolor, gouache, acrylics, or other kinds. A color is put into a container (like a cup) and is mixed with ox gall, the thick, brown, odorous liquid from the gall bladder of an ox. The ox gall allows the pigments to float on the top of the size, to spread out into circles (the more ox gall in the pigment, the more the drops spread), and to touch other drops without blending.

Pigments are placed carefully or dropped stochastically onto the surface of the size. They are then manipulated with combs or needles or other tools into a pattern, still sitting on the size in the trough. A piece of alum-coated paper is placed carefully over the surface and the pattern transfers to the sheet. This lifts most of the pigment off the size, so the process must be done from scratch for each sheet. Hence, no two sheets of marbled paper are alike.

The method produces patterned sheets, many of the patterns with names, many with representational art on them, like flowers, animals, calligraphic words, and so forth. Some of the decorative patterns have become familiar over the centuries: bouquet, French snail, Dutch curl, zigzag, chevron, non pareil, Spanish wave, and so on. The process can also be done with no combs, but with the pigment droplets falling at random onto the size. This produces sheets with no particular pattern, but recognizable nevertheless, and often named (like "vein," "stone," "Stormont," and the like).

While the method of marbling was kept a secret during the earlier centuries of its practice, in the nineteenth century the "secrets" were exposed, and today there is a worldwide interest in the art, with practitioners all over the world.

About contemporaneously to marbling, Paste Paper emerged as a way of enhancing books and other surfaces. Both methods (paste and marbling) were early on used by (and even practiced by) bookbinders, who saw them as a way to enhance the beauty of a book at a fraction of the cost of using leather.

Paste paper decoration is much simpler than marbling and is easier to master. One mixes up a batch of paste (wheat starch or rice starch works fine), mixes in a pigment, and spreads the colored paste with a brush or sponge over a sheet of dampened paper. While the pigment is still wet, any way it is touched will disrupt the smooth lines of the brushed-on paste. Touch the paste with a fingertip and the result is a little circle in the paste.

At this point, the artist's imagination comes into play. Using any of a myriad of tools, the artist manipulates the paste into an endless selection of patterns. When the pattern is as the artist wants it, she or he stops moving the paste around and sets the sheet out to dry. The results can be astonishingly beautiful sheets.

There are many other ways to decorate paper: block printing, batiking, tie-dying, folding and dying, impregnating or covering the sheets with materials like sparkles, pigments, or threads, weaving strips of paper together, stenciling, pricking, and so on.

The use of decorated papers in books has been around for two millennia. The attractive materials enhance the volumes and protect them. The papers are less expensive than leathers or parchments, and they do not deteriorate the way poorly processed leathers will.

Modern Papermaking

Today, the basic methods of papermaking that were invented in China more than 2000 years ago still hold: identification and gathering of fibers, preparation of fibers (breaking the raw materials down into tiny fibers); distributing the fibers over a screen to form the paper; removing the paper from the screen and drying it.

Even before the coming of the Industrial Revolution, papermaking was mechanized with the inventions of wove screens, the steam engine, and the Fourdrinier. The need for increasing amounts of paper in the nineteenth century led to experimentation with nontraditional fibers (hemp and cotton—essentially old rags–and various grasses). Wood pulp was the "final" choice since it is abundant, relatively renewable, manipulable, and inexpensive.

Just about all commercially made paper today comes from Fourdriniers, giant machines that perform many functions beyond the initial formation of the paper. Modern papermaking begins in the forest, with the harvesting of the trees, which are taken to the mill and debarked and chipped (the bark is removed and the wood is broken down into chips). It is then macerated, usually after being subjected to an acid bath which begins the breaking-down process. The pulp is then washed, refined, cleaned, and usually bleached. At this stage, if the washing does not remove all of the acids used to break down the pulp, or if the bleaching leaves an acid deposit in the pulp, inherent vice may wind up in the final paper.

At this point, the paper is transferred to the part of the Fourdrinier that actually forms the paper. Many kinds of additives can be put into the giant vats, like colors, inclusions to add tiny flecks to the papers, deacidifying agents like calcium carbonate, coating materials, sizing, and so on.

The pulp is then pumped over the moving screen, and the actual paper formation takes place. Just as the fibers are beginning to settle onto the screen, a dandy roll, a large cylinder containing a raised pattern, rolls over the screen, displacing the fibers to thin out the papers to create watermarks. Water drips through the screen and the paper is now formed into sheets that are as long as the manufacturer wants them to be. That is, if the machine keeps running and the screen keeps moving, and if the pulp continues to be distributed over the screen, an "endless web" of fibers will continue to form paper.

The paper now leaves the "wet end" of the Fourdrinier and enters the "press section," then it goes on to the "dryer section," and finally it goes to the "calender section."

The machine performs many functions, so on the Fourdrinier are other rolls and other features: vacuum pumps to remove water, warm cylinders to dry the paper, calendering cylinders to burnish (smooth out) the paper, and so forth.

Paper is also produced from recycled materials, but each time old papers are prepared for new manufacture, the fibers are macerated further than they were the first time, they get smaller, and the resulting paper is generally not as strong as was the paper created from "new" materials. Often recycled pulp is added to new pulp to reduce costs and to keep the papers fairly strong. Though part of the manufacture of recycled paper is de-inking, the process still yields paper that costs less than does paper manufactured from new materials. More than half of the paper produced in the United States today contains recycled fibers.

If one considers the vast number of uses of paper today and the thousands of manufacturers of so many kinds of paper worldwide, it is easy to see why statistics on the quantities of paper manufacture are difficult to compile.

University of Illinois Library School Professor F.W. Lancaster, in the 1970s, predicted a "paperless society." He did not mean this literally, but he did predict that, early in the computer age, society would be in a position to reduce its reliance on paper if it wanted to, thanks to the memories of computers. Taken out of context innumerable times, this phrase has proven correct and incorrect. It is true that a vastly increasing amount of information is being stored in digital form, thus reducing the need for paper. But the computer has given the world the capacity to print out (download) draft after draft of documents, millions of bits of information from the World Wide Web, photographs and other illustrative matter, and an endless stream of other materials, thus immeasurably increasing the amount of paper used today.

Hence, the amount of paper produced today continues to accelerate, and there is no end in sight.

Modern Hand Papermaking

While the great preponderance of paper today is machine made, there has been, for more than 60 years, a desire to return to the hand crafts.

Douglas Morse Howell was one of the earliest proponents of "modern hand papermaking," having set up his own paper mill in 1946, making paper for artists such as Jackson Pollock and Lee Krasner. Many others followed his lead, and today there is a small but thriving hand papermaking community in the United States. There is even a fine magazine/journal, *Hand Papermaking*, that in 2008 hit its 25th year of publication and is still going strong.

There is still a call for handmade papers throughout the art and book world, for printers, artists, and those who love the feel and rattle of a handmade product.

Several operations have been around for decades, like Henry Morris' private press, The Bird & Bull Press, which has specialized in publishing books about books, with a sub-specialty on handmade paper. Morris' own work *Omnibus* (Bird & Bull Press: North Hills, Pennsylvania, 1967) is a classic in the field, along with Walter Hamady's *Hand Papermaking* (Perishable Press: Mt. Horeb, Wisconsin, 1982).

Many artists, Like Robbin Ami Silverberg in Brooklyn, produce their own handmade papers for the books they print. And in fact, an extensive network of fine presses in the United States (and throughout the world) use only handmade papers in their work.

While Wookey Hole Mill in Somerset, England, and its compatriot mill in Maidstone run by Barcham Green and then by Simon Green, have closed, other mills are still holding on. For nearly 40 years, Kathryn and Howard Clark have run Twinrocker Paper Mill in Indiana. Tim Barrett, with extensive training in Japanese papermaking, teaches the subject at the University of Iowa. And papermaking classes are offered throughout the country, as a glance at any of the *Hand Papermaking* newsletters attests.

Running alongside the papermakers are those decorating the papers: marblers, paste paper makers, book artists needing specific decorative sheets for their publications, and many others. In the United States alone there are hundreds of marblers and scores of people working in paste papers.

In Europe the situation is comparable, with active mills in Germany, France, Czechoslovakia, Italy, and Spain, to name just a few countries. While some mills are there for demonstration only, others, with many private practitioners, are at work producing papers for printers and artists. And in the Far East, the Chinese, Japanese, Thais, Nepalese, Indians, Koreans, and many others are making splendid papers. Even in Africa there is a rudimentary handmade-paper industry. The continued demand for the product from artists, kite makers, scrapbook enthusiasts, origami experts, bookbinders, printers, and even people looking for lovely wrapping papers or greeting cards has spurred interest in the craft, and the production of handmade paper in the world today seems endless.

OTHER MATTERS

Today there are several associations of papermakers, including the International Association of Paper Historians (see http://www.paperhistory.org/); the International Association of Hand Papermakers and Paper Artists (http://www.iapma.info/); many professional and commercial paper associations; and smaller groups throughout the world whose interest is commercial, noncommercial, handmade, decorative, or other kinds of paper. (For instance, there are the American Forest and Paper Association, the National Paper Trade Association, Pulp & Paper

Product Council, Canada, and dozens of others in North America alone.) Worth repeating is the fact that in the United States an important magazine has been published for over 25 years, *Hand Papermaking*, keeping its readers up to date on all kinds of hand papermaking throughout the world.

The medium is important enough to have several museums devoted to it. For instance, The Robert C. Williams Paper Museum at the Institute of Paper Science and Technology in Atlanta, Georgia, contains, among many other things, the original Dard Hunter Collection of Paper. In Europe there are more than three dozen paper museums,[21] and in Asia there are several, including the Pan Asian Paper Museum in Korea, The Paper Museum in Tokyo, and the Ino-Cho Paper Museum in Kochi Prefecture.

The importance of paper in our lives cannot be understated. It is perhaps the most vital material in the world for the advancement of learning, the recording of history, and for thousands of other common uses. It is also one of the most versatile materials, manifesting itself in endless appearances, decorations, shapes, thicknesses, and colors. In the library world, there would be no library world without it.

REFERENCES

1. Levenson, R. *Lecture at the Graduate School of Librarianship*; Berkeley, CA, 1971.
2. Brown, M.P.; Lovett, P. *The Historical Source Book for Scribes*; University of Toronto Press: Toronto, ON, Canada, 1999; 13.
3. Hanafi, A. Available at http://www.ulb.ac.be/assoc/aip/ragab.htm (accessed July 29, 2008).
4. Philip, B.G., Ed. *Webster's Third New International Dictionary of the English Language Unabridged*; Merriam-Webster Inc.: Springfield, MA, 2002; 16–34.
5. Wikipedia. Available at http://en.wikipedia.org/wiki/Papyrus.
6. Brown, M.P.; Lovett, P. *The Historical Source Book for Scribes*; University of Toronto Press: Toronto, ON, Canada, 1999; 14.
7. Boyd, B. *Chaucer and the Medieval Book*; The Huntington Library, 1973; 6–7 N.p. [San Marino, CA].
8. Reed, R. *Ancient Skins, Parchments and Leathers*; Seminar Press: New York, 1972.
9. Reed, R. *The Nature and Making of Parchment*; Elmete Press: Leeds, U.K., 1975.
10. Wikipedia, "Paper". *The Wikipedia cites the following source: Joseph Needham, Science and Civilization in China: Volume 5, Chemicals and Chemical Technology, Part 1, Paper and Printing*; Cambridge University Press: New York, 1985 (accessed July 29, 2008).
11. Stevenson, A. Watermarks are twins. Stud. Bibliogr. **1951–1952**, *4*, 57–91.
12. Hunter, D. *Papermaking: The History and Technique of an Ancient Craft*; 2nd Ed. Knopf: New York, 1947; rpt. Dover: New York, 1978; 125–128.
13. Hunter, D. *Papermaking: The History and Technique of an Ancient Craft*; 2nd Ed. Knopf: New York, 1947; rpt. Dover: New York, 1978, 348.
14. Hunter, D. *Papermaking: The History and Technique of an Ancient Craft*; 2nd Ed. Knopf: New York, 1947; rpt. Dover: New York, 1978, 349.
15. Hunter, D. *Papermaking: The History and Technique of an Ancient Craft*; 2nd Ed. Knopf: New York, 1947; rpt. Dover: New York, 1978; 350–351.
16. Hunter, D. *Papermaking: The History and Technique of an Ancient Craft*; 2nd Ed. Knopf: New York, 1947; rpt. Dover: New York, 1978, 375.
17. Hunter, D. *Papermaking: The History and Technique of an Ancient Craft*; 2nd Ed. Knopf: New York, 1947; rpt. Dover: New York, 1978; 377–378.
18. Wikipedia. Available at http://en.wikipedia.org/wiki/Paper.
19. Labarre, E.J. *Dictionary and Encyclopaedia of Paper and Paper-Making*; 2nd Ed. Swets & Zeitlinger: Amsterdam, the Netherlands, 1952.
20. Wikipedia. Available at http://en.wikipedia.org/wiki/Paper_density.
21. http://www.paperonline.org/links/museu/museu_frame.html.

BIBLIOGRAPHY

1. Boyd, B. *Chaucer and the Medieval Book*; The Huntington Library: San Marino, CA, 1973; N.p.
2. Brown, M.P.; Lovett, P. *The Historical Source Book for Scribes*; University of Toronto Press: Toronto, ON, Canada, 1999.
3. Hanafi, A. In Memoriam Hassan RAGAB, 1911–2004. Available at http://www.ulb.ac.be/assoc/aip/ragab.htm (accessed July 29, 2008).
4. Hunter, D. *Papermaking: The History and Technique of an Ancient Craft*; Knopf: New York, 1947; rpt. Dover: New York, 1978.
5. Labarre, E.J. *Dictionary and Encyclopaedia of Paper and Paper-Making*; 2nd Ed. Swets & Zeitlinger: Amsterdam, the Netherlands, 1952.
6. Paper online, Available at http://www.paperonline.org/history/3000/3000_frame.html (accessed July 29, 2008).
7. Ragab, H. *Contribution à l'étude du papyrus (Cyperus papyrus.L [sic] et à sa transformation en support de l'écriture (papyrus des anciens)*; Dissertation, L'Institut National Polytechnique de Grenoble: Grenoble, France 1979. Published into a book as *Le papyrus*. Dr. Ragab Papyrus Institute: Cairo, Egypt, 1980.
8. Reed, R. *Ancient Skins, Parchments and Leathers*; Seminar Press: New York, 1972.
9. Reed, R. *The Nature and Making of Parchment*; Elmete Press: Leeds, U.K., 1975.
10. Wikipedia. Papyrus, Available at http://en.wikipedia.org/wiki/Papyrus (accessed July 29, 2008).
11. Wikipedia. Paper. Available at http://en.wikipedia.org/wiki/Paper (accessed July 29, 2008). The Wikipedia cites as its source Needham, J. *Science and Civilization in China*: Vol. 5, *Chemicals and Chemical Technology, Part 1, Paper and Printing*; Cambridge University Press: New York, 1985.

History of Public Libraries [ELIS Classic]

Frank B. Sessa
University of Pittsburgh, Pittsburgh, Pennsylvania, U.S.A.

Abstract

The history of public libraries is surveyed, with particular emphasis on public libraries in the United States.

—*ELIS Classic, from 1978*

INTRODUCTION

It was suggested that the contemporary public library in the United States can be "understood to some degree through the historical perspectives of its origins in the 19th century...." The library described in that context is a public institution supported by taxation, one that opens its collections, facilities, and services, without distinction, to all citizens. With minor variations because of differences in political philosophy, national experience, and state of educational development, this statement may be applied equally to the public libraries of Asian countries, of Eastern and Western Europe, of Australia and New Zealand, and of other parts of the world today in which public libraries have been established. The fact remains, however, that the "public library as we understand it is an Anglo-Saxon idea." It developed in England and America at about the same time, "and was original in both countries."[1]

HISTORY OF THE PUBLIC LIBRARY

A century ago, William Frederick Poole, then librarian of the Chicago Public Library, wrote:

> The public library is established by state laws, is supported by local taxation and voluntary gifts, is managed as a public trust, and every citizen of the city and town which maintains it has an equal share in its privileges of reference and circulation.[2]

At that point, three-quarters of the way through the nineteenth century, Poole was writing of a well-established social and educational agency. Its roots, however, lay at least two millenia in the past. The term "public library" may be applied to some libraries in the pre-Christian era, but its meaning differed considerably from that of today; the libraries were public in a far different sense than present public libraries. It might be said that they were public as opposed to the libraries that were the private possessions of individuals who restricted use to their own purposes. Ancient "public" libraries were, of course, for the use of the founder but also for scholars, students, priests, and officials who were permitted to use their collections for approved study.

It was suggested by the writer Aulus Gellius that near the middle of the sixth century B.C. the tyrant Pisistratus "collected a large library of books and later gave it to the city of Athens, where it was opened to the public." There is no corroboration of the account, however.[3]

Julius Caesar had the idea of founding a national or public library in Rome "to open to the public the greatest possible libraries of Greek and Latin books." He planned to place Marcus Terentius Varro in charge, an erudite and prolific writer.[3,4] Caesar was assassinated before he could carry out such a project. It fell then to C. Asinius Pollio to provide the first public library in Rome in the Atrium Libertatis, 39 B.C.[3]

Rome, by the end of the fourth century, was reputed to have 28–30 public libraries. Again, these were not the public libraries of today but were available to those who could and would use them. Rome had, after all, in the imperial period, an increasing number of persons who were literate. There were booksellers in Rome and in many of the larger cities of the provinces. It was fashionable, too, to have books in one's home. As the Roman Empire declined in the West, the libraries also declined, as did book publishing and acquisition.[5]

A step closer to the modern public library was the "town library" that came into existence in the fifteenth to nineteenth centuries in England, Scotland, France, and Germany.

The early libraries in England were founded as gifts of individuals or by a "public and joint-stock contribution, and then entrusted to the guardianship of the respective municipalities." Norwich, Leicester, and Bristol in England had examples of such town libraries founded in the first third of the seventeenth century, but their books and quarters after some vicissitudes ended up in a state of neglect or in the possession of a private society. In Bristol, as an example, the library, the structure provided to house it (Library House), and the books came into the possession of a private subscription library that relieved the Town Council of the need of its support. At Leicester, the town

Encyclopedia of Library and Information Sciences, Fourth Edition DOI: 10.1081/E-ELIS4-120009005

library, founded in 1632, was in the latter part of the seventeenth century permitted to sink "into careless guardianship and ultimate neglect."[6] Scotland had to wait until late in the eighteenth century (1791) for a library, which soon was forced to become a subscription library to continue in existence.[7]

There was at least one other English public library that deserves mention, the Chetham Library in Manchester, founded in 1653, and the gift of Humphrey Chetham, wool-factor and money-lender, who left £1000 to be used for books "for or towards a Library within the town of Manchester and an additional £1000 for the purchase of 'some fit place for the said library.'" There were £200 additional for the purchase of "godly English books, such as Calvin's, Preston's, and Perkin's works." After other bequests—including a Hospital for Maintenance and Education of poor boys—had been met, the residue of the estate was to go for the further purchase of books. The income ran between £750 and £500 annually. By 1826, the library was reputed to have 14,276 items, the larger portion of which were folios and quartos. The next several decades did not do much for the library.[6,8]

Many of the town libraries in France suffered the same fate—"a gross breach of trust"—as those in England, and disappeared. In many other cases, however, the library was quite successful and continued in existence.[7] The library at Caen, for example, was established in 1431, and after suffering from the effects of religious wars and suppression, it was restored in 1736. Subsequently, it received books at the time of the suppression of the Jesuits and further contributions of books were made after the Revolution. In 1809, "when it was organized for public use," it had some 25,000 volumes and continued to grow.[7] Edwards also mentioned a library at Lyons, established in 1530, that early in the nineteenth century had 120,000 volumes and 1500 manuscripts.[7] Edwards was particularly impressed with the state of libraries in the provinces of France at the time he was writing (1850s), the result of the fact "that in some eminent instances French Municipal Councils have consistently displayed, during a series of years, an enlightened appreciation of the value of store-houses of learning."[7]

In Germany, town libraries were established in Ratisbon (1430), Ulm (ca. 1440), Erfurt (1440), Nuremburg (1445), Hamburg (1529), and Lübeck (1530), to cite a few. In general, they grew out of bequests. In the early days, their contents were largely juridical, but when the religious houses were dissolved, many came into a number of rare manuscripts. As in France, a number continued in existence and had important collections by the mid-nineteenth century.[7]

THE UNITED KINGDOM

In the United Kingdom, there were a number of other forerunners of the public library. There were the parish

libraries of the Reverend Thomas Bray that provided collections for laymen as well as for clerics. In Scotland, the Reverend James Kirkwood developed an elaborate scheme for "founding and maintaining bibliothecks in every paroch throughout this kingdom." The scheme entailed providing a place for books in each parish, handing over to the library the personal books of the minister, cataloging of books, and making of four copies of each catalog, one of which would go to the principal library in Edinburgh that would make a general catalog of all books in kingdom. The scheme called for compensation to the minister for his books, cooperation between parishes, the lending of books, book binding, and ultimately, a "Printing-House and Paper Manufactory."[9] The Reverend Samuel Brown of East Lothian developed a plan involving "itinerating libraries," through which there would be provided "a library or division of 50 books in each town or village of a county." The library would remain in the town 2 years, move to another town, then move again in another 2 years, and so on. In each case, the collection would be replaced by another. The plan went into operation in 1817 in Haddington, where Reverend Brown was then provost, and in four other villages. In general, the circulation was good in the first year and fell off fairly sharply in the second year. The books had a strongly religious cast, but there were books of a "plain and popular nature" in the arts and sciences as well as in history, biography, and travel. The plan developed to the point that by 1836 there were some 47 libraries with 2380 volumes. After the death of Reverend Brown in 1839, the project slowly declined, partly because there was no one to offer the management and financial support he had supplied.[9]

Also a forerunner of the public library was the social library: both proprietary and subscription. In larger cities, circulating libraries (strictly profit-making ventures) appeared, particularly in Scotland in the early eighteenth century.[9] For the workers, there were apprentices' libraries and mechanics' institutes. These will be discussed in some detail later.

Toward the middle of the nineteenth century, the modern public library moved closer to reality by the passage of the Museums Act of 1845, primarily the work of William Ewart, who had been a member of Parliament for Liverpool (1830–1837) and was then member for Dumfries. Impetus for passage of the act had come from a meeting held in Manchester in November 1844, a meeting presided over by Richard Cobden. Joseph Brotherton, member for Salford (also in attendance), was influenced to appeal to William Ewart to work on the proposal. The result was passage of an act "Encouraging the Establishment of Museums in Large Towns." It authorized the levying of a ½ d. rate in towns of not less than 10,000 population for the erection of museums of science and art; the act provided only for the building. An admission charge of 1 d. was authorized for support. Within a short time, three towns—Canterbury, Warrington, and Salford—had taken advantage of the act to set up combined museums and libraries. The library at Canterbury, established in 1847, grew out of the purchase of the museum and library of the Philosophical and Library Institution. Warrington followed in the next year with the location together in rented quarters of the museum of the Warrington Natural History Society and the collections of the Warrington Subscription Library. There was a full-time curator who also served as librarian. Salford established a museum and library in 1849, although it was not opened until the following year.[10]

William Ewart was further stimulated to work toward a public library act by an article written by Edward Edwards, "Statistical View of the Principal Libraries in Europe and the United States." Edwards, a prolific writer on the subject of libraries, was then a supernumerary assistant at the British Museum and had testified before an earlier Select Committee inquiry into British Museum activities. Ewart drew upon Edward's knowledge of libraries and by 1849 had convinced Parliament to establish a Select Committee to inquire into the establishment of "libraries freely open to the Public, especially in large towns." The committee and its successor recommended, after inquiring into libraries on the Continent and in the United States, that Parliament authorize town councils to levy a small rate to establish and support public libraries.[6,9,10] In February 1850, Ewart moved for permission to introduce "a Bill for enabling Town Councils to establish Public Libraries and Museums." After considerable debate, the motion passed. After further debate and some amendments, the bill went to the House of Lords and then "received Royal assent" on August 14.[6] The main provisions of the act were that corporate towns of 10,000 persons might levy a ½ d. rate to buy land and build buildings for libraries. The act of 1850 applied to England and Wales. It was extended in 1853 to the "Municipal Boroughs in Ireland and the Royal and Parliamentary Burghs in Scotland."[9]

The Museums Act passed with rather general support, but the Public Library Act ran into considerable opposition. Whatever popular support for it there might have been, it was not marshaled, partly because the franchise was not then as widely extended as later. It can be said that it was sponsored by a strong, determined minority drawn from members of the library profession and from the upper strata of society. In general, the arguments ran to extending the benefits of reading to the lower classes. The benefits were seen as social, moral, and educational. Brotherton argued that reading would reduce crime and "provide the cheapest police that could be gathered." Others argued that it would keep workers from the evils of the gin shops. Opposition came from those who objected to an increase in rates and those who feared that agitation and social unrest would result.[10,11]

Libraries were rather slow to appear. Edward Edwards suggested that Manchester was the first to establish a library

under the act, for the "preliminary subscription towards the expenses of its foundation had been set on foot, whilst the Bill was still pending in the House of Commons, by Sir John Potter...." The poll at Manchester was not taken until August 1852, "when a library of 21,000 volumes was in complete working order." The subscription raised amounted to £12,823.[6] The first city in which a poll was taken was Norwich, however. Although the poll was taken on September 17, 1850, no service was begun until 1857.[8,10] Twenty-three libraries were opened between the years 1851 and 1862, and 98 more between 1868 and 1886, for a total of (with the four previously established) 125.[8,10]

Ewart attempted to have the act of 1850 amended in 1854, but it was not until the next year that the amended act became law: *An Act for further promoting the establishment of Free Public Libraries and Museums in Municipal Towns, and for extending it to Towns governed under Local Improvement Acts, and to Parishes*. It reduced the number of inhabitants necessary to qualify under the act from 10,000 to over 5000. Two neighboring parishes with populations that together aggregated more than 5000 persons and with vestries that chose to unite to establish a public library might do so. The rate was set at "one Penny in the Pound on the rateable value of the property assessed," and "Books, Newspapers, Maps, and Specimens of Art and Science, Fuel, Lighting and other similar matters" might be purchased.[6]

Over the years, there were a number of Public Libraries Acts, but the changes were minor, "no more than further provisions for adoption, area definitions and powers for Authorities to take joint action."[8] In 1892 (June 27), a new Public Libraries Bill received royal assent. The act repealed former legislation and, in effect, consolidated previous advances and changes. The act of 1919 not only permitted the development of urban library service by removing the rate limitation, but it also gave library powers to counties. A major drawback of the national library legislation of the latter half of the nineteenth century had been the continuation of the penny rate limitation. A number of library authorities, about 30 by 1900, had freed themselves of the limitation "by means of clauses in Local Acts."[8] It was not until the close of the year 1919 (December 23), however, that the rate limitation was removed. Other provisions of the act were important too. County Councils might now adopt the Public Libraries Acts for all or part of their areas. They might accept library powers from existing library authorities or give up, with approval of the Education Committee, their powers "in respect of any part of its library area to permit the establishment of an independent library service."[8,10] As Lionel McColvin pointed out, the county system was in position to serve "people living under a variety of circumstances—in isolated farms, in little villages, in mining and industrial townships or market towns, in new towns and in the suburbs."[12] This act was a dominant factor in library development from 1919 to 1965.

Andrew Carnegie contributed significantly to the public library movement in the United Kingdom, as he did in the United States. His first gift was that of £8000 to his native Dunfermline in 1879. By 1883, the library had opened.[8]

Carnegie made subsequent grants in Scotland and in England. As in America, grants were usually for buildings and equipment, not for books or operation. By the time of his death, about half the library authorities in England and Wales and more than half in Scotland had profited from his generosity. In 1913, he created the Carnegie United Kingdom Trust (CUKT) with a capital of £2,000,000, and he indicated libraries were a high priority. Most of the public library development had come in the larger cities and towns. It was logical, therefore, that the Carnegie Trust would turn its attention toward helping the rural areas of the counties. Various local "schemes" for assisting public libraries were used as experiments, such as the Workshop Authority project to supply book service for the nearby rural parishes of Nottinghamshire.[8] At Staffordshire, the Trustees of CUKT funded a "central Repository of books...from which should be dispatched to the Schools of the County consignments of books which would reach their readers through the agency of the schoolmasters and the schoolchildren." The plan had first been suggested to Oxford, which turned down the offer of funding in the amount of £5000. When the new Public Library Act of 1919 provided for the establishment of County Library Authorities, the trustees of the foundation began to make grants to the authorities in terms of books, book boxes, shelving, and other equipment.[8] One measure taken by the trustees to further the cause of county libraries was a grant of £4000 for the provision of a County Library sign that became a familiar reminder of library service across the countryside and of Carnegie "benefaction to a grand total of £500,000." For the early years following the passage of the 1919 act, service consisted of boxes of books that eventually gave way to the "library van" or bookmobile. Gradually, in the smaller urban areas subject to the County Library Authority, a room or library building was provided. Utilizing a provision of the 1919 act that permitted the levy of a rate above the normal county rate to provide branch library service, counties began to provide service on the urban pattern.[8]

Library service remained uneven, however, for the populations served by local authorities varied from 30,000 to 1,000,000 or more persons. The smaller authorities had neither the manpower nor the financial resources to provide a satisfactory level of library service.

The number of public library authorities in England and Wales was sharply reduced (345 to 83) by comprehensive local government legislation, the Local Government Act of 1972. The amalgamation was to be accomplished by April 1, 1974. Most of the new authorities had populations of 200,000 or more persons, which made it possible to have greater financial resources than before. The London area, reorganized in 1965, was not changed.

THE UNITED STATES

In America, the first library to meet the test of a modern public library was that established in Peterborough, New Hampshire, in 1833. Money originally appropriated by the state for other purposes (a state university) was put into a Literary Fund and made available to towns to devote to the support and maintenance of "common free schools, or to other purposes of education."[13] The purpose to which Peterborough put the money was to provide books for a town library to which there would be access without charge. The collection, reports Jesse Shera, was rather like those of the social libraries of the day.[13] The library's true significance, however, was that

for the first time an institution was founded by a town with the deliberate purpose of creating a free library that would be open without restriction to all classes of the community—a library supported from the beginning by public funds.[13]

Before the establishment of the Peterborough library, there had been books and libraries in America for some two centuries, for a number of private libraries had come with the early settlers. Several—like those of Elder William Brewster of Plymouth Colony and John Winthrop, Jr., governor of Connecticut—were, in the early part of the seventeenth century, quite impressive. In New England at the close of the century, the largest private libraries were those of Increase and Cotton Mather; in Westover, Virginia, Colonel William Byrd is reputed to have had a library of 4000 volumes, and in Philadelphia, James Logan, a library of 3000 volumes.[3,14] The number of those who read was, as in the mother country, rather limited, although there were presses in the colonies and booksellers as well.

Robert Keayne—a merchant described variously as "a consciencious & upright man in the generall," an "extortioner," "contentious and stubborn," and fined for "profiteering"—bequeathed a public library to Boston in the 1650s. In his will, written between August and December 1653, he provided that £300 were to be set aside for public use, in particular, a Town House in which a room was to be provided for a public library. Included in the bequest were his "three great writing bookes which are intended as an Exposition or Interpretation of the whole Bible." His son and his wife were to choose from his personal books those they wished, the balance to go to the library. In the event the town of Boston failed to act upon his gift by providing the Town House, the money and books would go to Harvard College. The building was erected and put into use, but it suffered two fires. One in 1711 destroyed the building, but the library was largely saved. The restored structure and the library were totally consumed by fire in 1747. No more was heard of the library. Keayne had hoped his example would lead others to donate books, but few books came by way of contribution. The library served for almost a century as a repository of town records and was generally known as a public library owned by the town and supported by it.[13,15] Another early library for the public resulted from the will of Theophilus Eaton, governor of New Haven, which provided that the books formerly belonging to his late brother Samuel be held in trust for a college that was to be established in New Haven by John Davenport. Davenport left the colony, and the college failed to materialize. The books then belonged to the town and are believed to have eventually found their way into the schoolhouse, where they were kept but seldom used until sold in 1689 for "forty pounds of rye and thirty-two bushels of Indian corn, appraised at 12 pounds, 18 shillings."[13,15] Concord, Massachusetts also had a library owned and supported by the town before 1672. There were other towns in New England that owned and supported libraries in the early years of the eighteenth century. Shera mentions three in Massachusetts: Oxford (1719), Lancaster (1731), and East Sudbury (1726). The first collection was a gift, but the latter two were purchased at town expense, kept in the meeting house, and made available to the townspeople.[13]

At the beginning of the eighteenth century, there appeared for the colonists another source of books, the parish and provincial libraries instigated by the Reverend Thomas Bray. Dr. Bray was appointed commissary of the Anglican Church in the Colony of Maryland in 1695. He early realized that to supply ministers and missionaries for the relatively unappealing parishes in the colony, he was going to have to draw upon the "poorer and less influential men," men who would have difficulty supporting themselves and could not be expected to provide themselves with a library, which Bray considered essential. A minister could do "his best only if he had ready access to a library...."[16] Bray was assisted in his work of getting libraries to America by two groups he was instrumental in forming: the Society for the Promotion of Christian Knowledge and the Society for the Propagation of the Gospel in Foreign Parts (SPG). Later in his life when he fell ill, he was assisted by a group known as Dr. Bray's Associates.[16]

Although his primary interest lay in Maryland, Bray made the effort to extend such libraries to all of the colonies. He thought of one large library in each colony, a provincial or general library, and of a parochial library for each parish. He also provided libraries for laymen. Bray served as commissary for Maryland from 1695 to 1704. In that period of less than a decade, he and those who worked with him established:

> provincial libraries at Boston, New York, Philadelphia, Annapolis, Charleston and Bath, North Carolina. He provided thirty-nine parochial libraries, of which twenty-five were located in Maryland, although each of the other colonies had at least one such library. Finally he provided

over thirty-five layman's libraries and sent over 35,000 religious books and tracts to the colonies for three distribution.[16]

The libraries were not large; the largest, 1095 volumes, was in Annapolis and was considered the "Publick Library" of the colony. Governor Francis Nicholson, with a view to enlarging the collection, suggested that the king be asked for permission to divert some military defense funds for library. The Assembly, however, did not acquiesce.[15] The library in Charleston had support from Bray, the Assembly, and the proprietors of the colony. In 1700, the Assembly of South Carolina passed a law, one of the earliest in America, that put the books in the "care" of the minister of Charleston, with a board of nine commissioners appointed by the Assembly to manage it. Use was without restriction. Books might be borrowed, the length of time depending upon the size of the books: "if a *Folio*, in four months time; if a *Quarto*, in two months time; if an *Octavo*, or under, in one month, upon Penalty of paying three times the full Value of the said Book or Books so borrowed, or damnifying the same." The collections of the libraries were heavily theological but they were not entirely so. More than one-third of the initial purchase of books for the Charleston library were nonreligious. It was not Bray's intention to supply a complete library for the parish. He hoped, although the hope was seldom realized, that there would be additions made locally to the collections.[13,15,16]

In the main, the Bray libraries were not public libraries, even though a few were so designated. Quite a number of laymen had access to all of the libraries, for ministers permitted members of the parish to use some of their books. Their significance was that they "did much to enrich the book resources of the clergy in the American Colonies at the beginning of the eighteenth century." Shera suggested further that their relationship to the public library movement was "more symptomatic than influential." Laugher counters with the observation that "if the libraries had no effect, the SPG would not have continued sending such reading matter to the colonies, in an amount estimated to exceed 100,000 volumes."[13,16]

Of more significance in the chronicle of the predecessors of the public library in America was the social library, a library resulting from the association of a group of persons who contributed or subscribed money for the purchase of books. Title to the books remained with the association, although all contributors could use or borrow them. The library might be proprietary, that is, the members of the group subscribed to stock and owned shares; or it might be a subscription library for which the members of the group subscribed an initial fee, with which the first books were bought, and followed the initial subscription with the payment of an annual fee. Both the proprietary and the subscription libraries soon permitted nonsubscribers to use the collections upon payment of a set fee. In general, these libraries were legal entities operating on a charter issued by the individual colonies and later by the states.[13]

The movement toward the social library was started in America by Benjamin Franklin, who in late 1720s, was the organizer of a group interested in "socializing and debating," the Junto. An experiment of pooling personal books to provide a resource for their debating material and for other use was not a success. Franklin then proposed a library provided by the subscription of 40 shillings by each member of the Junto and an annual fee of 10 shillings. Out of this proposal came the Library Company of Philadelphia, founded in 1731, often referred to as the mother of the social library in America. Before long, subscription libraries began to appear in all of the colonies.[13]

Three other early major social libraries—like the Library Company of Philadelphia, still in existence—are the Redwood Library of Newport, Rhode Island, the New York Society Library of New York City, and the Charleston Library Society of Charleston, South Carolina.

The Redwood Library was founded in 1747 and was the first of these libraries in America to receive a charter. It too grew out of a discussion group, the Literary and Philosophical Society dating back to 1730, or at least the society seems to have been influential in Abraham Redwood's offer to donate £500 if a company for the establishment of a library were formed. The offer was accepted, and money was pledged for a building on property donated by one of the society's members. The Provincial Assembly issued a charter in 1747. By 1750, the library was in its own building, and 5 years later, Dr. Ezra Stiles (pastor at Newport, who later became president of Yale University) became its librarian. He seems to have devoted some of his time each week to the library, but the founder decried the Anglican influence of Stiles and those who controlled the library.[15] According to Horace Scudder, the character of the original collection attracted Stiles to Newport. "The books bought with Mr. Redwood's money were considered at the time the finest collection of works on theology, history, the arts and sciences in the American Colonies."[17] The library suffered during the Revolution, and in 1790, it was described as "in a sad plight and in the period of stagnation many books disappeared and about three quarters of the collection was lost." The library achieved a "renewed prosperity" in the nineteenth century. In 1952, the library began a buying campaign to restore the original collection.[18]

The New York Society Library, organized in 1754 as the City Library, held its first board meeting at the City Arms on Broadway. The meeting was concerned with the raising of money to erect and maintain a "publick Library." It was reported that "not less than 70 gentlemen have already subscribed Five Pounds Principal and Ten Shillings per Annum, for that Purpose." Soon, the 118 subscribers were asked to submit a list of books each considered to be desirable. To books purchased was added a collection of about 2000 volumes, known as the corporation library. This was a gift to the city from two Anglican clergymen who were distressed with the paucity of reading material in New York: the Reverend John Sharpe, chaplain of Queen Anne's forces in New York, who observed "there being no place I know of in America where it [learning] is less encouraged or regarded"; and the Reverend John Millington of Kensington, England, who found New York an "uncultured little city of seven thousand souls in the 'Plantations in America.'" The latter left his books to the SPG to be shipped to New York. The library was open not only to city residents as subscribers but also to those who lived in the colony. Nonsubscribers might borrow books by leaving a deposit of more than one-third the value of the book or books taken. The library was first located in a room in City Hall with Benjamin Hildreth as library keeper, "who received £6 annually for 'his Trouble and Care while in that Office.'"

By 1795, the library had erected its own building. It had fallen upon evil days during the Revolution but began to move toward recovery in 1788, when operations were resumed. A catalog of 1793 listed 5000 titles. In 1840, the library was located at Broadway and Leonard and remained there for 13 years. A large lecture room in these quarters permitted varied entertainment, discussions, and assemblies. Among those who appeared were Fanny Kemble, the Swiss Bell Ringers, Campbell's Minstrels, and Edgar Allan Poe, who lectured on American poetry.[17,19]

The Charleston Library Society was founded in 1748, the earliest proprietary library in America according to Edgar Reinke. Established by 17 young men, the number of members increased to 160 before mid-century. The library was granted a charter by the colony, confirmed by the crown in 1755. It began with the intent of acquiring magazine and pamphlet material but soon acquired books as well. The library prospered because the early members "were all of the aristocratic, paternalistic class prevalent in much of the South at that period." Many of them had received their formal education abroad and sent their sons and daughters abroad for education. There were weekly meetings to which members came, usually 20 to 30. A part of the income of the society was invested in bonds, with the result that by 1775, the funds amounted to £18,000. With sophisticated, well-educated members, the library emphasized the classics and had a fine collection of classical literature. It suffered some from the occupation of Charleston by British troops during the Revolution but was largely destroyed by a major fire. It continued for some years as a social club, and then in 1790, it was reorganized with the remaining books as part of its collections.[17,20]

Shortly after the successful beginning of Franklin's Library Company of Philadelphia, subscription libraries of varying sizes began to proliferate in the middle colonies and particularly in New England. Prior to the Revolutionary War, however, there were only two or three in the South.[20] The social libraries, like the parochial libraries that preceded them, filled a need in the colonies, which were beginning to expand in population. Their collections were quite different, with less emphasis upon religion and more upon secular matters of concern: history, biography, travel, poetry, grammar and rhetoric, agriculture, arithmetic, and natural science are examples of the areas of more prevalent works. Shera suggested that the year 1790 was the midpoint in the effective life of the social library, with its period of most vigorous activity from 1790 to 1815 and a gradual decline from 1815 to 1850.[13] Like most social agencies, the social library suffered in periods of economic decline. The social library declined largely as a result of a number of factors of which the rise of the public library was but one. For one thing, it could not "meet the expanding demand for library resources"; it was restrictive, that is, its clientele was limited at a time when the movement toward popular education was becoming strong. It made a major contribution to the library movement:

> Almost from the very beginning the social library movement assumed the central attributes of a public library system. . . . By virtue of the implications for the future, as well as of the character of its past, the social library is an important factor in the evolution of the modern public library.[13]

A strictly commercial library was the circulating library, perhaps more accurately, a collection of books gathered together for those who wanted them for home use. And the intent of the proprietor was profit. He was more likely than not to cater to popular taste and to avoid concentrating on "good literature." Quite often, circulating libraries were operated in conjunction with bookstores. Although they had been in existence on the Continent and in England much earlier, these libraries became active in the latter half of the eighteenth century in America. One of the earliest, that of William Rind of Annapolis, opened in the fall of 1762. This library and many of those that followed it had a relatively short life. One of the major problems was that of relending on the part of patrons, a practice that deprived the proprietor of needed revenue. It was necessary, too, for the circulating library to anticipate and keep up with the more ephemeral materials. A major criticism of this form of library was that it relied heavily on fiction, "a discredited literary form."[13]

Other types of libraries rose to fill a need for books prior to the appearance of the public library. While rather similar in character, they were known variously as mercantile libraries, mechanics' libraries, young men's libraries, and apprentices' libraries. These libraries were closely related to the growth of the education movement in the first half of the nineteenth century. Mechanics and apprentices turned to libraries for satisfaction of their need for education, and the form of library they used was a

modification of the social library.[13] In England at the turn of the century, workers' institutes devoted to the "intellectual development" of the workers appeared with emphasis upon science in the beginning but expanding later to include literature, history, and the arts. There were libraries, lectures, and discussions as part of their programs. The movement was extensive in England and spread to America.[13] Most of such libraries in America, according to F.B. Perkins, had an education department or school as a principal activity. Classes were offered in bookkeeping, arithmetic, writing, and language. Some also had, in addition to a reading room, a game or chess room, and in some instances, a gymnasium. Perkins further suggested that they were "planned rather like a sort of business college, as if to furnish a general higher education to those who were not able to go as far as desirable at school."[21] Their collections, he reported, varied, were "founded on old and solid libraries," and were "of much positive value." Most were, however, "to a predominating extent. . . as they must necessarily be, collections of popular literature." Like most other libraries of their era, there was a major lack of money. They overcame a part of their difficulty by bringing in a group of older men whose concern was control of the property interests of the group.[21]

Mercantile libraries, "as distinct from other social libraries. . .may be described as primarily for the use of merchants' clerks; secondarily, also, for all general readers."[21] More specifically, they were intended to satisfy the reading requirements of the merchants' clerks and were supported in part by merchants and a periodic fee. They differed from mechanics' and apprentices' libraries in that they began as libraries; their educational aspects came later. There was also a greater emphasis not only on business-related areas but upon history and literature.[13]

Still another type of library providing books primarily to young men and artisans, but to others as well, was the YMCA Library. The first Young Men's Christian Association in America was founded in Boston in 1851, "for the improvement of the spiritual and mental condition of young men." The YMCA Libraries, therefore, developed in the period when the "public" library, as exemplified by the Boston Public Library, was emerging. By 1859, there were 145 associations with libraries, 12 of which had 1000 or more volumes. In 1875, it was calculated that there were 478 associations with an aggregate membership of 43,612; of these associations, 180 reported having libraries, with a total of 164,188 volumes. The largest of these libraries was said to be that in Washington, with a collection of about 15,000 books. Like the mercantile, mechanics', and apprentices' libraries, they also had lectures. In the larger towns, the YMCA was apt to have classes in "those branches of practical knowledge which are especially available in business pursuits." In many towns, the only library "open to the public" was that of the Young Men's Christian Association. The reading rooms "are always free to the general public." An effort was made to have the libraries open "at hours when they will be conveniently accessible to the young men of the community." Occasionally, they were open on Sunday. The library in New York was reputed to have the best collection. The information in Table 1 indicates its breadth.

The libraries described in the preceding paragraphs served as forerunners of the tax-supported library that provided free access to all comers. They provided access to books for several levels of society, when in most cases, there would otherwise have been little access to them. While the social library was still in the ascendant, the first moves toward the public library were made.[22,23]

Caleb Bingham, a Boston bookseller and publisher, in 1803 made a donation of 150 titles to his native town of Salisbury, Connecticut, to serve as a library that would provide reading he did not have as a boy. A self-perpetuating Board of Trustees was to have control of the Bingham Library for Youth, open "freely" to those between 9 and 16 years of age. The library was accepted gratefully by the town, which appropriated $100 for the purchase of "suitable books." Such support continued fitfully for years, and then the library was entirely neglected until it was absorbed toward the end of the century by the Salisbury Library Association, which became the Scoville Memorial Library Association.[13]

The town of Lexington, Massachusetts, also had a library, funds for which were appropriated in 1827. By 1839, however, the town discontinued its periodic payments for support. Shera suggested that a pattern had begun to emerge, that municipal support had been given to these two libraries, and that the next step was "institutional permanence and stability" for the public library derived from municipal support. This came with the establishment of the Peterborough Library in 1833.[13]

In 1835, New York State passed legislation that permitted the levying of a tax to support school district libraries. Other states followed, but by 1876, the impetus was lost. Oliver Garceau credited their decline to the fact that they were artificially created by state planners, following no local pattern of cultural loyalties; they served too small an area—in New York, only 267 persons to the district; they were inadequately housed, poorly supervised by school trustees, and badly managed by elected librarians.[24]

Table 1 Holdings of New York YMCA library.

Category	Percent of holdings
History	11½
Biography	4
Travel and geography	3½
Bibles and biblical works	6
Theology	3½
General literature	18
Poetry and drama	7
Fiction and tales	29½
Arts and sciences	17

In Indiana, an attempt was made to set up county libraries under the constitution of 1816. Because of the frontier conditions, it failed.

The first large municipality to establish a library that met the requirements of a modern public library was Boston, which opened the doors of its library to the public on March 20, 1854. The concept of a public library for Boston had been suggested in a letter written by George Ticknor, Smith Professor of the French and Spanish Languages at Harvard, to Daniel Webster in 1826, 7 years before the Peterborough Library was established. Ticknor, a trustee of the Boston Athenaeum—once called a public library by Charles Coffin Jewett ("practically it is such")—wrote that he had a project to join all of the libraries of Boston, including the Athenaeum, into "one establishment." He would let "the whole circulate." He envisioned elimination of duplication of books, of quarters, and of librarians and their salaries. With the money saved, he would buy more books. Nothing came of the proposal.[25] Suggestions as to combining the libraries of Boston into one large unit also came from a Frenchman, Alexandre Vattemare, a ventriloquist whose stage name was M. Alexandre. Vattemare had visions of bringing peoples closer together by an international exchange of books—as had the Reverend Brown's associates before him.[9] He appeared in New York in 1839 and over the next 2 years he advocated his plan during his various appearances in the United States and Canada. In Boston in 1841, he interested a group of young men who used the Boston Mercantile Library and several prominent citizens, notably, Charles Francis Adams. No project materialized, but there was an exchange of gift books between Vattemare in Paris and the City of Boston. One of the gifts, a rather handsome one of nearly 100 volumes, led to the appointment by the City Council of a Select Committee to recommend a suitable return gift and a place where the gift books should be kept. The committee recommended a room in City Hall. It also included the recommendation that there be established a public library and advised that an anonymous donor (Mayor Quincy) was offering $5000 toward the project with the proviso that $10,000 for the purpose be raised "at large." The library was to be "fully used by all, as may be consistent with the safe-keeping of the property." As a result of this proposal, the council in November 1847 appointed the Joint Special Committee on the Public Library, which among other charges, was to consider the feasibility of applying to the legislature for the authority to establish and operate a public library. In early 1848, a new City Council directed the mayor to apply to the legislature for such authorization, which resulted in an act authorizing the City of Boston to establish and maintain a public library. The governor of Massachusetts signed the act on March 18, 1848.[25] A prime force in the progress toward the establishment of the library was the zeal of Mayor Josiah Quincy. Also important in the movement were

George Ticknor, Edward Everett, and Mayor Joseph Bigelow, who followed Josiah Quincy as mayor in 1849. Quincy, treasurer of the Boston Athenaeum, naturally favored joining the two libraries. The Athenaeum had been established in 1805, an outgrowth of the Anthology Society organized to continue publication of the *Monthly Anthology and Boston Review*, about to go out of existence. The next step was an Anthology Reading Room and Library, a subscription to which would cost $10 per annum. Soon there were 160 subscribers. When the library opened on January 1, 1807, there were more than 1000 volumes and English, French, and American periodicals.[15] The Athenaeum grew and prospered, although it was in some difficulty in mid-century because of unanticipated costs in the construction of its new building. The proposal to join the two libraries fared well until it was put to the proprietors for approval. The proprietors postponed the matter indefinitely, and the Public Library proceeded on its own.[25]

The library began operation by opening to the public the first of its two rooms in the Mason Street Schoolhouse on March 20, 1854. It was open daily (except Sunday) from 9:00 A.M. to 9:30 P.M. and all "inhabitants" of Boston over 16 years of age might use it. A single volume might be withdrawn for home use for 14 days on signature and agreement to observe library rules by a select list of people including, among others, city officials and employees, ordained ministers, teachers in private schools, and benefactors (contributors of $100 or more). Other inhabitants of Boston who wished to borrow a book had to deposit the full value of the book with the librarian.[25] The first librarian appointed by the council, Edward Capen, was a Harvard M.A. who later became a graduate of Harvard Divinity School, and who had served as a clergyman for several years. He was appointed in May 1852. While he was still serving as librarian, the council at the behest of the trustees appointed a superintendent who would have the general responsibilities of administration. The appointment was an annual one, and the position might remain vacant by decision of the council or by the trustees' decision not to make a nomination. The first appointee was Charles Coffin Jewett, who served from 1858 until his death a decade later. Jewett had been librarian of the Smithsonian Institution in Washington and had come to Boston to work with the books received through the munificence of Joshua Bates. For that purpose, the trustees rented a house on Boylston Place in 1855, wherein Jewett was installed.[25] Joshua Bates, a poor boy of Boston who grew up with nothing to spend on books, had the good fortune to be able to satisfy his great desire to read in the bookstore of Hastings, Ethridge, and Bliss, after his long work hours in a counting house. Remembering his own lack, Bates, who was senior partner of the London Banking House of Baring Brothers and Company, offered the sum of $50,000 for books. When the council put a new building under construction, Joshua Bates offered a second gift, the purchase of a "considerable" number of books to be held in trust for the new quarters so that when they opened there would be an adequate number on hand. He estimated the cost would run $20,000 to $30,000. It was this latter gift that Jewett was hired to prepare (in the temporary quarters on Boylston Place) for use in the new building.[25]

Under Jewett's administration, the library made substantial progress. The library had moved into its new building on Boyleston Street on New Year's Day, 1858, and Jewett became its new superintendent almost immediately. On Jewett's death, January 8, 1868, he was succeeded by a trustee, Justin Winsor, under whom the library continued to progress. When he resigned and became librarian of Harvard in July 1877, it was an outstanding library.[25] By 1868, it had a collection of 144,000 volumes and 50,000 pamphlets, second then only to the Library of Congress, which had 175,000 volumes and 70,000 pamphlets. At that time, Winsor noted that only two other public libraries had fairly sizable collections: New Bedford, 21,000 volumes; Cincinnati, 20,000. He noted that Liverpool, the largest of the English public libraries supported by the penny rate, had 84,000 volumes. By 1877, too, there were six branches, several stations, and regular deliveries of books to 13 firehouses and a fireboat.

The motives of those who were largely instrumental in the founding of the Boston Public Library and libraries in larger cities have come under question. Michael Harris, in an article entitled the "Purpose of the American Public Library," attacked what he called the comfortable concept, widely held, that the public library movement was "launched in the 1850's by an intelligent middle class led by a group of enlightened civic leaders." George Ticknor is seen as insisting that the public library should be "dedicated to the continuing education of the 'common man.'" Actually, public libraries, Harris argued, were always "generally cold, rigidly inflexible and elitist institutions." He makes a strong case to support his contention that the founders were men of substance, conservative, and dedicated to the preservation of the form of the society they ruled over. The library, as they saw it, would help educate the new residents of the city, for they were not capable of understanding the country's free institutions. They would be brought "in willing subjection to our own institutions." Harris continued with the concept that those who were hired to run the libraries were "technicians" who were "dedicated" to the founders' concept of the library. Carnegie, when he appeared, was equally authoritarian in his approach to the founding of libraries, and he saw them as a means of helping persons to help themselves, to "make men not violent revolutionists, but cautious evolutionists; not destroyers, but careful improvers."[26] Harris further saw librarians as moving the public library in the first half of the twentieth century toward assuming the role of a bastion of democracy "by assisting the successful working of self government."[26] The library would do so by providing information on both sides of a subject. The user would decide for himself, and the librarians' traditional "passivity" would not be brought into question. Harris's "revisionist interpretation" has not gone unchallenged. Phyllis Dain in her article "Ambivalence and Paradox" pointed out that Ticknor was "aristocratic and conservative" and that his choice of the public library as a means to open opportunities to people, rather than to close them, was "an expression of the 18th century rationalists' faith that the lower classes could be integrated into society through education."[27] She also pointed out that in view of the urban masses' lack of leisure time, lack of access to those who controlled the money, and low level of education, none but an "elite group" was left to foster the public library. As noted earlier, there were many other forms of libraries—mercantile, apprentices', mechanics'—supported in part and used by groups who were not elitist. Phyllis Dain also challenged Harris's criticism that librarians had become technicians and bureaucrats. The increase in numbers of libraries, size of collections, and in staff naturally led librarians to "rationalize procedures and bureaucratize personnel."[27] The Harris thesis, too, does not account for the large numbers of public libraries established in modest-sized towns that lacked urban poor. It might be noted in passing that in England, there were in Parliament members of the "elitist" group who "almost feared that these libraries might be converted into normal schools of agitation."

The public library movement in the latter part of the nineteenth century was stimulated by the philanthropy of many who had made their fortunes in America's burgeoning industries. One very early benefactor was John Jacob Astor, who in a codicil to his will, in August 1839, set aside $400,000 for the establishment of a public library. He was directed toward this philanthropic move by Joseph Green Cogswell, who subsequently (at Astor's request) moved in with him and spent some years prior to Astor's death in 1848 in buying books, preparing catalogs, and seeing to it that the benefactor did not change his mind about his bequest. He helped plan the building and served as superintendent of the library from its establishment until 1861 and as a trustee until 1864. Cogswell thought of the Astor Library as a reference library and primarily for those engaged in research. No circulation was permitted. Its hours were short and access difficult. As a result, it enjoyed a poor press, and complaints were widespread. Members of the Astor family continued to contribute to the library for some years, so that it was able to grow and to achieve preeminence. From 1876 to 1894, however, "it had lost its pre-eminent position and slipped into somnolence."[28,29] James Lenox, a wealthy and prominent New Yorker, founded a second reference library in New York City. The founder, a merchant and large property owner, was a bibliophile who gathered a fine library of 20,000 volumes, which in 1870, he had incorporated into a public library. If anything, it enjoyed an even poorer reputation as a public institution than the Astor Library. It was some years after its establishment before it was finally opened to the public. Because of its great treasures and the fear of its founder that they would be lost or vandalized, access was limited. Further, "stress was placed not on use of materials but on viewing them."[29] A third major bequest for the establishment of a library was that contained in the will of Samuel J. Tilden, which placed the largest part of his estate, $5,000,000, in the Tilden Trust. Tilden, a successful lawyer, had established his reputation by prosecuting successfully the Tweed Ring. He had run on the Democratic ticket for the presidency of the United States in 1876 but lost the election in the recount of votes made in three southern states. The trust was attacked by members of the family, nieces and nephews. Although the court suit went against the trust, there was eventually an agreement to partition the estate, which provided the trust with something between $2 and $2½ million. In 1895, the two libraries, Astor and Lenox, were merged with the Tilden Trust to create the New York Public Library. The first director was John Shaw Billings under "whose forceful leadership they [the trustees] saw the New York Public Library built almost overnight into the illustrious institution of their ambitions."[29] The library created in 1895 was a reference library. The circulation function was achieved when an agreement of consolidation was completed with the New York Free Circulating Library, January 8, 1901. The Free Circulating Library, incorporated in 1880, was the outgrowth of the efforts of the teachers of a sewing class in Grace Church who wished to raise the reading level of the children. As interest grew in the project and more women became involved, a reading room was provided for the 500 books collected. The project expanded, was incorporated, and at the time of the consolidation, the library possessed some $300,000 in cash and securities and five buildings (valued at $300,000) and operated 11 branches with 160,000 books that accounted for an annual circulation of 1,600,000.[28]

In Baltimore, Enoch Pratt, a successful merchant and investor and a native of New England, presented the city in 1882 with a sum of $1,058,333.33 for a library, provided the city would agree to create an annuity that would provide $50,000 per annum. The gift consisted of a building already under construction that would cost $225,000 and "upon its completion, the additional sum of eight hundred and thirty-three thousand three hundred and thirty-three and one-third dollars." The library grew rapidly, and in a decade, had a collection of 150,000 volumes and five branches. Andrew Carnegie in 1905 offered $500,000 with which to build 20 branch libraries. The branches were built over a period of years. The City of Baltimore, too, began adding money each year to supplement the annuity's yield as operations expanded and expenses rose. Much of the later success of this library may be attributed to Joseph L. Wheeler, who became its director in 1926; he was an outstanding administrator who later became a sought-after library building and management consultant.[30]

Many libraries, some quite large and others designed to serve relatively small towns, were established by gifts of wealthy men and women in the next few decades. The major benefactor of libraries, of course, was Andrew Carnegie. Born in Dunfermline, Scotland, in 1835, he came when a boy (1846) to the United States with his parents, who settled in Allegheny, Pennsylvania, a city across the Allegheny River from Pittsburgh. Successively a bobbin boy in a cotton mill, a telegraph messenger, a telegrapher, and a section superintendent for the Pennsylvania Railroad, he began to invest his money in profitable projects and then entered the iron and steel business. From his various sources of income, Carnegie amassed a huge fortune for the day. About 90% of that fortune went into various charitable and philanthropic projects—more than $333,000,000.[31] He donated $56,162,622 to construct 2509 library buildings in the English-speaking world. Except for a few instances, Carnegie donated money only for buildings and did not support or endow libraries. The support of the building by the municipality was a stipulation required before the grant was made. In America, he provided $41,033,850 to construct 1412 buildings.[31] With the library acting as his agent, he entered into an agreement with New York City on July 17, 1901, to provide the city with funds to acquire in the boroughs of Manhattan, Bronx, and Richmond "not more than 42 [later raised to 50] library sites" and erect buildings on them. Earlier, Carnegie had made a contribution to the Free Circulating Library.

The Carnegie library grants were given between the years 1886 and 1919. The bulk of the gifts were made in what he called the "wholesale" period, 1898–1919, to libraries in 1406 communities in the amount of $39,172,981.[31]

At the time of publication of the Bureau of Education's Special Report, *Public Libraries in the United States of America* (1876), the editors were able to include a "Table of public libraries numbering 300 volumes and upwards" which included 3649 libraries. The majority of those listed were university, college, academy, public school, mercantile, and social, and were not municipally supported. There was a fair sprinkling of libraries bearing the title "public library." In 1890, however, of America's 16 largest cities, only seven had municipally supported central libraries.[27] The period of the Carnegie gifts changed this situation markedly. Not only did his gifts account for more than 1400 library buildings, but they stimulated communities that had avoided applying to Carnegie initially to provide libraries on their own at a later date. Libraries had spread over the United States in increasing numbers as the last decades of the nineteenth century were reached, but the major growth came after the Carnegie period.

The growth of the public library movement was slowed somewhat by the great depression of the 1930s. As with many other public agencies, the libraries found themselves with shrinking appropriations and revenues but with increasing use. Library adult book circulation, particularly nonfiction, was up. Total expenditures were down, but expenditures for books dropped relatively more than did salary expenditures. Two of the economic factors that explain increased use of the public library are unemployment and the reduced earnings of those employed.[32]

During World War II, a definite move toward improved public library service in the years to follow the close of hostilities was the *Postwar Standards for Public Libraries* (1943), followed in 1948 by the publication of *A National Plan for Public Library Service* prepared for the Committee on Postwar Planning of the American Library Association by Carleton B. Joeckel and Amy Winslow. In 1950 came the Public Library Inquiry, which was designed to be "a thorough and comprehensive study of the American free public library."

By 1956, the Coordinating Committee on the Revision of Public Library Standards, Public Libraries Division of the American Library Association, had produced *Public Library Service: A Guide to Evaluation with Minimum Standards*. The document was made up of principles and standards and covered subjects, books and nonbook materials, personnel, the organization and control of materials, and physical facilities. The *Standards*, as they came to be called, were criticized by some librarians as being goals rather than standards, for they were impossible to attain by most libraries. Other librarians complained that there were not enough "measurements" given. A supplementary publication subsequently provided such statistical measures for libraries in several categories by size. In 1967, the American Library Association published an updating of the *Standards* entitled *Minimum Standards for Public Library Systems, 1966*. This publication contained a number of finite standards as well as the principles and broad standards.

The 1956 *Standards* contained a statement that was to affect public library development for some years to come:

> Libraries working together, sharing their services and materials, can meet the full needs of their users. *This cooperative approach on the part of libraries is the most important single recommendation of this document.* Without joint action, most American libraries will probably never be able to come up to the standard necessary to meet the needs of their constituencies.[33]

Library systems were not new. They had developed out of county libraries at the turn of the century. In particular, they developed into county systems in California. By 1916 "thirty-seven of California's fifty-eight counties were persuaded to establish libraries."[24] From the county system, it was but a small step to the multi-county library system or regional library system. In 1969, the American Library Association (ALA) published a survey of systems. The system concept has become an integral part of most state public library plans, to which are being added networking and resource sharing. These techniques are being made more effective through the use of computer bibliographic data banks like the Ohio College Library Information Center (OCLC), which extends its service over a large part of the United States. Another benefit of OCLC is its classification and cataloging service.

Despite the efforts of the ALA to improve library service after the end of World War I and the efforts of its committees as noted above, there were still over 85 million Americans without adequate library service in mid-century, particularly in rural areas. In 1956, a U.S. Office of Education report revealed that 26 million rural residents were without any public library service. An additional 50 million rural residents had inadequate service. A strong effort with farm block support succeeded in passing the Library Service Act in that year (1956). It authorized the appropriation of $7.5 million annually for 5 years. The funds were for "services" and were limited to rural areas (10,000 or less). No money was appropriated until 1957, when the Congress appropriated $2,050,000. The next year it appropriated $5 million, and $6 million for each of the next 2 years.[34] In 1961, the act was renewed for another 5 years, but in 1964, it was amended to become the Library Services and Construction Act. It contained two titles: I. Services; II. Construction. Funding was in the amounts of $25 million and $20 million, respectively, and the restriction of funds to rural areas was removed. The act again was amended to provide two additional titles in 1966: III. Interlibrary cooperation; IV-A. State Institutional Library Service, and IV-B. State Library Services to the Physically Handicapped. The act was renewed in 1970 and continued through fiscal year 1976. Title IV was joined with Title I, which resulted in some fear that both Title I activities and services to the handicapped might suffer if funds ran out.

The Library Services and Construction Act has generally been considered to have had a beneficial effect upon public library programs. It resulted in the institution of service to many unserved rural people, in service to the disadvantaged, in the upgrading of services at the state agency level, and in a great number of new library buildings. Federal funds were provided for demonstration projects that resulted in the provision of local funding for their continuation. One criticism levied at the program was that too much of the federal allotment in many states went into agency operational costs, to the detriment of libraries in need of support. Of particular importance was the money (relatively less than for other titles) awarded under Title III for cooperation between types of libraries.[35] Out of early experiments have come "networking" and "resource sharing" that may well cut into duplication of materials, services, and costs.

Until the mid-1960s, funding for public libraries under the Library Services and Construction Act seemed to be growing at a rate quite satisfactory to librarians and their supporters. The amended act of 1966 projected a total authorization over the next 5 years of $700 million for the four titles of the act. As the extent of the United States' involvement in Southeast Asia became a major factor in the nation's economic life and inflation increased accordingly, there was less funding available for social and educational programs at the national level. Table 2, covering fiscal years 1969, 1972, and 1973, indicates the changes that occurred.

The figures in Table 2, taken from *The Bowker Annual* for the years cited, do not tell the complete story, for funds could be and were impounded by executive order. To replace categorical funding such as LSCA, the president proposed in 1972 a new type of funding, revenue sharing, which provided funds for state and local governments over a 5-year period. These funds were to be spent for "priority expenditures," which included libraries but placed them somewhat down the list of priorities. In many instances, local governments had other programs they preferred to fund, and some municipalities merely substituted revenue sharing funds for local funds they had been appropriating for libraries.

The public library in America in the 1960s and early 1970s moved actively to take materials and programs to the people who were not accustomed to coming to the library for them. More specifically, librarians were seeking ways to stimulate minority groups and others who did not have library use in their backgrounds to take advantage of and use library services. One major approach was "outreach," taking programs and services to the inner city or wherever these persons might live. Reference and information services were greatly improved, and the library became responsive to the multimedia orientation of the country's youth. The public library too, became actively involved in continuing education. It was suggested by one of the library's strong supporters that it had "become the most economically effective educational institution evolved by mankind." It served as the resource center for those enrolled in "external university" or "university without walls" courses, and for high school students preparing for the College Level Examination Program (CLEP).

Table 2 LSCA appropriations, 1969–1973.

Fiscal year	Title	Authorization ($)	Appropriation ($)
1969	I	55,000,000	35,000,000
	II	60,000,000	9,185,000
	III	10,000,000	2,281,000
1972	I	112,000,000	46,568,500
	II	80,000,000	9,500,000
	III	15,000,000	2,640,500
1973	I	117,600,000	30,000,000
	II	84,000,000	0
	III	15,750,000	2,640,500

Some of the larger city libraries, too, entered cooperatively into continuing education programs sponsored by nearby colleges and universities. For the individual proceeding on his own, it provided the source of information and materials for his self-education. Librarians enrolled in courses designed to train them to work with patrons who wished to retrain themselves or raise the level of their knowledge. The public library thus provided information, books, and nonbook materials supportive of individual and group educational efforts.

CONCLUSION

As the public library approached the last quarter of the twentieth century, it was beset with a number of difficult problems. The principal one continued to be that of adequate financial support. Urban libraries, particularly those in the older cities of the Northeast and Midwest, were suffering from the effects of urban blight, the flight to the suburbs, and sharply increasing expenses of operations. The library, a part of municipal government that unfortunately did not command as high a priority as some other functions, was forced in many instances to close some branch operations and curtail the hours of opening at the main building. To cope with these problems and to pressure for federal support, the Urban Library Council, made up of the librarians of nearly 50 major urban libraries, was formed. Despite what seemed to be a rather dark picture, a number of cities have managed to keep the library operation on a fairly even level and, in some instances, to float bond issues to construct new main libraries and branches. During the year 1976, there were 277 public library construction projects completed, of which 90 were building alterations. The total expenditure for the projects was $66,374,466, with the majority of this construction for medium-sized and small buildings. Most librarians who considered the problems of administration and who wrote of their reactions were not pessimistic about the future.

REFERENCES

1. Jast, L.S. *Libraries and Living: Essays and Addresses of a Public Librarian*, Books for Libraries Press: Freeport, NY, 1969; 45.
2. Poole, W.F. The origin and management of public libraries. *Public Libraries in the United States of America: Their History, Condition, and Management*, Government Printing Office: Washington, DC, 1876; 477.
3. Johnson, E.D. *A History of Libraries in the Western World*, Scarecrow Press: New York, 1965; 48, 64, 66, 282.
4. Gaverse, J., Ed. Suetonius, In *The Lives of the Twelve Caesars;* Modern Library: New York, 1931; 27.
5. Irwin, R. Ancient and medieval libraries. In *Encyclopedia of Library and Information Science*; Kent, A., Lancour, H., Eds.; Dekker: New York, 1968; Vol. 1., 405 Irwin sets the date of Pollio's library as ca. 33 B.C.
6. Edwards, E. *Memoirs of Libraries: Including a Handbook of Library Economy*, Burt Franklin: New York Vol. 1 635, 749, 782, 785–786, 788–791, 793, 801.
7. Edwards, E. *Memoirs of Libraries: Including a Handbook of Library Economy*, Burt Franklin: New York Vol. 2 28, 29, 315, 316, 322, 333, 434.
8. Munford, W.A. *Penny Rate: Aspects of British Public Library History, 1850–1950*, The Library Association: London, U.K., 1951; 9, 29, 33, 34, 37, 42, 115, 116, 117, 119, 120.
9. Aitken, W.R. *A History of the Public Library Movement in Scotland*, Scottish Library Association: Glasgow, Scotland, 1971; 6–8, 16, 30–33, 38, 44–53.
10. Kelly, T. *A History of Public Libraries in Great Britain, 1845–1965*, The Library Association: London, U.K., 1973; 9–11, 13–15, 23, 209–217.
11. Murison, W.J. *The Public Library: Its Origin, Purpose, and Significance*, G.G. Harrap & Co.: London, U.K., 1971; 23–25, 34–37.
12. McColvin, L.R. *The Chance to Read: Public Libraries in the World Today*, Phoenix House: London,U.K., 1956; 42.
13. Shera, J.H. *Foundations of the Public Library: The Origins of the Public Library Movement in New England, 1629–1855*, Shoe String Press: Metuchen, NJ, 1965; 20–22, 24, 25, 28–32, 57–60, 68, 85, 126, 131, 158–161, 162–164, 169, 229, 230, 232, 233.
14. Morrison, S.E. *The Intellectual Life of Colonial New England*, New York Univ. Press: New York, 1956; 133–143.
15. Thompson, C.S. *Evolution of the American Public Library, 1653–1876*, Scarecrow Press: Washington, DC, 1952; 4–7, 15–17, 25, 27, 52, 53, 66–70.
16. Laugher, C.T. *Thomas Bray's Grand Design: Libraries of the Church of England in America*, American Library Association: Chicago, IL, 1973; 11, 14, 19, 20, 24, 38, 54, 76.
17. Scudder, H. Public libraries a hundred years Ago. *Public Libraries in the United States of America...*; Government Printing Office: Washington, DC, 1876; 12–14, 16.
18. Libr. J. December 15, **1952**, 77, 2084.
19. Libr. J. June 1, **1954**, 79, 1010–1011.
20. Reinke, E.C. A classical debate of the charleston, South Carolina, Library Society, Bibliographical Society of America. Papers **1967**, 61, 13, 84–86.
21. Perkins, F.B. Young Men's Mercantile Libraries. *Public Libraries in the United States of America...*; Government Printing Office: Washington, DC, 1876; 379; 380, 382.
22. Brainerd, C. The libraries of the Young Men's Christian Associations. *Public Libraries in the United States of America...*; Government Printing Office: Washington, DC, 1876; 386–387.
23. Kraus, J.W. Libraries of the Young Men's Christian Associations in the nineteenth century. J. Libr. Hist. **1975**, 10, 3–21.
24. Garceau, O. *The Public Library and the Political Process*, Columbia Univ. Press: New York, 1949; 24, 41.
25. Whitehill, W.M. *Boston Public Library: A Centennial History*, Harvard Univ. Press: Cambridge, MA, 1956; 2, 3, 13–15, 34–36, 43, 44, 48, 53, 54, 77, 88, 89, 108.
26. Harris, M. The purpose of the American public library: a revisionist interpretation of history. Libr. J. September 15, **1973**, 98, 2510–2514.

27. Dain, P. Ambivalence and paradox. Libr. J. February 1, 1975, *100*, 110, 262.

28. Lydenberg, H.M. *History of the New York Public Library: Astor, Lenox and Tilden Foundations*, New York Public Library: New York, 1923; 6–8, 199–202, 213, 405, 410, 411.

29. Dain, P. *The New York Public Library: A History of Its Founding and Early Years*. Dissertation; Columbia University, 1966; 23, 24, 36, 90–99, 185.

30. Castagna, E. Enoch Pratt free library. In *Encyclopedia of Library and Information Science*; Kent, A., Lancour, H., Eds.; Dekker: New York, 1972; Vol. 8, 117–120.

31. Bobinski, G.S. *Carnegie Libraries: Their History and Impact on American Public Library Development*, American Library Association: Chicago, IL, 1969; 3, 13, 14, 17, 19.

32. Herdman, M.M. The public library in the depression. Libr. Q. **1943**, *13*, 310.

33. *Public Library Service: A Guide to Evaluation with Minimum Standards*; American Library Association: Chicago, 1956; 7.

34. Fry, J.W. LSA and LSCA, 1956–1973: a legislative history. Libr. Trends **1975**, *24*, 7–15.

35. Schubert, J.F. The impact of the federal library services and construction act. Libr. Trends **1975**, *24*, 27–44.

History of Records and Information Management

William Benedon
Benedon & Associates, Encino, California, U.S.A.

Abstract

Records management is the information management discipline that addresses the "life cycle" or "birth-to-death" concept of records and the information they contain. It includes the principles and practices that cover the creation, processing, storage, retrieval, protection, and final disposition of records. Records management also evaluates the administrative, financial, legal, operational, and historical need for records. These principles and practices apply to all records, regardless of media, and have been of significant value as business and government transactions have moved from paper, to micrographic, to electronic format. This entry presents an historical overview of the discipline, the factors that brought it into being, the events and individuals that contributed to its development, acceptance, and use as a valuable management tool.

INTRODUCTION

One of the major problems facing business, industry, and government today is how to most effectively and economically manage and utilize a continually expanding accumulation of information. Technological and social changes have resulted in the creation and dissemination of an endless volume of data in a wide variety of records formats. While much of the information demanded and produced is needed, there is also a proliferation of useless and duplicated materials. The object of an organized approach to the management of information must have two principal goals—first, to obtain the maximum value from all information disciplines and second, to obtain that value in an orderly, productive, and cost-effective manner.

Information management is the process of identifying and utilizing all of the information disciplines and information resources enterprise-wide to achieve efficient, effective, and competitive management decisions. Records Management is an information management discipline that involves the principles and practices used by an organization to properly manage its records from their creation to final disposition. A record is recorded information, regardless of medium or characteristic, made or received by an organization that is evidence of its operations and has value requiring its retention for a specified period of time. Since it deals with the information content of records as well, the discipline is popularly referred to as records and information management (RIM). Records management has also been identified as the "life cycle" or the "birth-to-death" concept of records and includes such elements as

- Forms/reports management—The establishment of procedures for the control and design of forms and reports needed in the processing of transactions and summarization of data. This program may also include directive and manual preparation.

- Correspondence management—Assuring the proper preparation, routing, and control of internal and external communication.
- Filing systems—Evaluating and selecting the best type of filing and indexing system to be used as well as the equipment being considered for housing records.
- Retention scheduling—The physical flow requirements of records and their value at each action location (office, storage, and final disposition). The term "records retention or control schedule" is preferred to "disposition schedule." This avoids concern that the program is being used primarily for throwing out records.
- Records centers—The establishment and use of central repositories, as may be required, for the low-cost housing of inactive, vital, and archival records, and to maintain such repositories in an orderly, efficient, and economical manner. Such facilities may be operated in-house or outsourced to commercial companies specializing in the records storage business.
- Records protection—Providing records classifications, procedures, and facilities necessary for the protection of records needed to continue or resume business following a disaster.
- Image management—Making effective use of image processing technologies (micrographics, optical disk, and the like) for the handling, processing, protection, and retention of records.
- Archives management—Providing for the continuing evaluation and preservation of records having historical value and to assure their proper housing and indexing.
- Information technology—Carefully reviewing new technologies that impact on the manner in which businesses use such technologies to manage their records and assuring the proper administrative and legal uses of such technologies.

Encyclopedia of Library and Information Sciences, Fourth Edition DOI: 10.1081/E-ELIS4-120043074

The past 50 years have produced significant technological developments in the information and records management field. The above principles are applicable regardless of media being used. The first major transition came from the application of microfilm for replacing paper copies. It had two primary values as a replacement for storing paper records and for duplicating vital records. It was hailed as the panacea for reducing the volume of stored records. This quality disappeared as the use of low-cost records centers proved to be a more cost-effective approach. This competitive element shifted the focus of microfilm to systems applications and brought about its major value in the form of computer output microfilm (COM)—a system of converting computer output to microfilm, computer-assisted retrieval (CAR)—rapid retrieval of information on microfilm, and computer output to laser disk (COLD). Further advances included optical disks, bar coding systems [upgraded to radio-frequency identification (RFID)]. All became part of the computerization age and the birth of the electronic record.

Records management has proven to be of particular value when applied to electronic records. An *electronic record* is a record created, generated, sent, communicated, received, or stored by electronic means. Usually the term applies to all electronic records systems, whether in microcomputers, minicomputers, or mainframe computers, regardless of storage media, in networked or stand-alone systems, including small computers, such as memory typewriters, calculators, and embedded systems. Examples include records stored on a server, or on magnetic media, such as tapes, disk packs, compact disks, or optical disks.

Electronic records keeping or e*lectronic records management* is the use of records management principles for records maintained electronically. An e*lectronic record keeping system* (ERS) is primarily a software-based methodology used by an organization to manage all its records, regardless of format, over the entire record's life cycle. Primary records keeping functions of these systems must include categorizing, locating, identifying, and controlling record disposition requirements, including management of the storage, retrieval, protection, and disposition of the records regardless of repository.

BEGINNING OF MODERN RECORDS MANAGEMENT

Records management is an outgrowth of archives management and is concerned with the need to preserve records that have long term or permanent value. The rapid growth of business, government, and industry resulted in a significant growth in the amount of documentation needed to manage and operate such activities. This growth resulted in an uncontrollable amount of records, with related administrative costs. Records management has provided the principles and practices needed to properly balance the cost of providing needed records and their retrieval and maintenance costs.

Following World War II, President Harry Truman established the *Commission on the Reorganization of the Federal Government* to address the many operating issues of the U.S. Government resulting from its growth and expansion from the war years. Former president Herbert Hoover was named head of the commission (thus the popular name Hoover Commission). One of the Task Forces under the commission was given the responsibility for examining the government paperwork growth and to recommend methods for its management. Emmett Leahy (a former member of the National Archives and responsible for organizing the records of the Navy Department and a private consultant following his government career) was named chairman of the Paperwork Task Force. The study results were significant. They applied the previously mentioned elements of records management to government paperwork activities with a significant reference to cost savings. Although the term "paperwork management" was used in the report, the term was soon broadened to "records management" to address all records media. These actions were the beginning of records management as it is practiced today.

Two major legislative acts resulted from the Hoover Commission efforts. The Federal Property and Administrative Services Act of 1949 transferred the National Archives to the newly created General Services Agency. The name, National Archives, was changed to the National Archives and Records Services (NARS) to reflect its responsibility for current records as well as archival records. The Federal Records Act of 1950 defined "records management," further clarified and expanded the records management role of NARS (requiring each agency to establish an active and ongoing records management program), and NARS began establishing a series of records centers to store semi-active federal records. NARS remained part of the General Services Agency until 1985, when, through the efforts of the then archivist Robert M. Warner, the National Archives again attained independent status as an agency and became known as the National Archives and Records Administration (NARA).

Emmett Leahy

Emmett Leahy was the leading figure in the introduction of the concept of "modern records management." He joined the staff of the National Archives in 1935 as a Special Examiner to inspect records classified as "useless records" in agency lists. Such records could be destroyed or otherwise disposed of because they had no "permanent value or historical interest." He soon determined that the federal agencies had no systematic means of identifying records of permanent value and the only way to address this issue was involvement in the creation and filing of records. This would provide a process for segregating records of temporary value from those of permanent value. Emmett Leahy became a principal leader in the emerging government records administration program.

In 1941 Leahy left the National Archives to become the Director of Records Coordination for the Navy in the Office of the Secretary of the Navy. In that position he established a model records management program that introduced new records management concepts and techniques similar to those defining records management at the beginning of this entry. In this position he installed the first centralized records centers in the world for the storage of inactive Navy records. In 1945, with World War II coming to an end, he decided to join the civilian market and accepted the position of National Sales Manager in the Microfilm Division of Remington Rand. He left Remington Rand in 1947 to form the National Records Management Council (NAREMCO), a nonprofit records management consulting company, and the Leahy Business Archives, the first commercial records center in the United States. Based upon his experiences with the navy records centers, the records center's principal equipment was standard sized cardboard containers housed on steel shelving. The container was $10'' \times 12'' \times 15''$. Referred to as the "cubic foot" box it could accommodate legal as well as letter-sized documents. It is to this day the main storage container used in records center operations, both in-house and in commercial repositories. It was in this capacity, as a private consultant, that he was named chairman of the task force on records management for the Hoover Commission. In 1953, he left NAREMCO and formed Leahy & Co., a consulting firm, which also included the Leahy Business Archives, Inc.

Emmett Leahy died on June 23, 1964. An award in his name was established and sponsored in 1968 by Rodd Exelbert, then Editor and Publisher of the *Information and Records Management Journal*, and Leahy & Co. It is currently underwritten by the Huron Consulting Company and is presented annually by the Institute of Certified Record Managers. It is considered to be the most prestigious award given in the RIM field today. The Web site devoted to the Leahy Award (http://www.leahyaward. com) includes comments made by peers of Emmett Leahy that provide a personal insight into his influence in the development of the records management profession. The 1968 recipient of the award and author of this entry provided the following comments.

> I was teaching junior–senior high school in the 1947–1950 period and taking my master's degree at NYU in accounting and foreign trade. I selected as my thesis "The Preservation of Accounting Records" (I don't really know why). I felt I didn't really want to be an accountant but I wondered what such practitioners did with all their records. Bob Schiff, a senior officer in the National Records Management Council (NAREMCO) was teaching at NYU at the time, had read my thesis, *Preservation of Accounting*

Records and suggested I make an appointment to meet Ed Leahy, president of NAREMCO and discuss a fellowship with the organization. Thus started a long and happy career in records management, but the real inspiration was my first meeting with Ed Leahy.

I was impressed the moment I met him. He had an exciting gleam in his eyes, an award winning smile, and an air of dignity and knowledge. He immediately put me at ease with his relaxing approach to talking about me and my interests with his personal anecdotes injected as we went along. From that day forward I felt the confidence to make a mark in the records management profession. At the time Ed Leahy also operated the Leahy Business Archives (the first commercial records center system) and I spent the first six months as a records center clerk in that operation. Then I quickly graduated to consulting analyst and worked on projects at Union Carbide, Monsanto Chemical, the City of New York, Oneida Knitting Mills, and Mine Safety Appliances (my first solo operation). While I had the opportunity to work with such notables as Bob Schiff, Bob Weil, and Art Barken, Ed was always available for comments and concerns. He had a practice of taking his analysts out to lunch when they were in town at his favorite Irish restaurant on 23rd Street in New York. The purpose of such get-togethers was to make us feel a part of a great adventure into this exciting world of records management.

I had the opportunity to attend many of Ed Leahy's speeches and accompany him on visits to company president's offices to talk about impending projects. Each trip was a learning experience and critiques that followed these meetings left long-range values for individual growth. I was continually impressed with his ease of presentation and ability to sell his ideas to all levels of management. I remember his telling me that 80% of records management was salesmanship, making certain your clients felt at ease by listening to them and taking their ideas into account. Salesman extraordinaire, you bet, and only in the most positive manner.

With Ed Leahy as a mentor, success was guaranteed. He had the dedication, the personality, and the knowledge to inspire confidence and commitment. What better advocate could there have been to address the records management needs of business, government and industry.

Professional organizations today grant a series of awards for records management based upon government and business program accomplishments, individual accomplishments, and literary awards. The Records Management Association of Australasia sponsors the J. Eddis Linton Award for the individual they consider to be the "father of records management" in Australia. Early in his career Eddis Linton formulated ideas about the need to manage business records in an organized and systematic way. He developed and implemented these ideas incorporating keyword filing systems, inactive records storage, and micrographic systems long before they became mainstream practices. "Fellow" designations are also granted by records and archival management organizations to individuals making major contribution to the profession.

ACHIEVING RECOGNITION

The Hoover Commission Paperwork Task Force study resulted in the disposition of a significant amount of government records and clearly demonstrated the operating efficiencies possible through proper records administration. The results of studies subsequently conducted by Emmett Leahy through his consulting efforts showed similar results could be achieved in business. Through the development of retention schedules based upon careful value analysis, 30% of the records maintained by an organization could be destroyed, 30% could be transferred to low-cost records center facilities due to their reduced activity, and the balance would represent the currently needed and referenced records. Although these figures only represented one facet of records management (proper appraisal of records) they became the driving force for total records programs.

Many of the staff people from the NAREMCO took lead records management positions in government and business (Bethlehem Steel, State of New Jersey, Lockheed Corporation, IBM). The NARA, by virtue of the Hoover Study and the legislation that followed, began extending its program to government agencies and publishing training aids for records programs. Its publications, although directed to governmental operations, have been applicable to the private sector and it is one of the prime resources for all aspects of the subject. Under the able leadership of Everett O. Alldredge (Assistant Archivist for Records Management) and Herbert Angel (Assistant Archivist for Federal Records Centers), NARA took a major role in the development of the profession. One of its major contributions of this government agency in the early years of the professions was the preparation of an annual "Compendium of Federal Recordkeeping Requirements." This booklet covered all the records retention requirements by government agencies. It was organized by government department, described each record, and indicated the period of time the records had to be retained. Unfortunately, this valuable publication became the victim of one of the government's austerity programs. Private firms offering this information on a subscription update basis soon addressed the void. Another former government employee, Frank Knox, joined the commercial consulting world and introduced *Functional Forms Filing*, a system for analyzing business forms to assure better design for processing, to consolidate forms serving the same purpose, and to eliminate unnecessary forms.

Companies started to implement promotional programs to increase exposure to records management and to demonstrate the savings and efficiencies possible through a constant application of records management techniques.

They carried such names as "Operation Round File" (Northrup Aircraft), "Mile High File Pile" (Cleveland Electric Illuminating Company), and "Operation Trim" (Lockheed Corporation) and were further supported by a designated "National Records Management Weeks" [American Records Management Association (ARMA)]. Natural and man-made disasters, in the form of floods, earthquakes, and civil unrest, also put a major focus on records management as organizations became concerned about the need to assure business continuity in the event of a disaster.

Low-cost storage facilities, or records centers, modeled after those used in the U.S. government and the Leahy Business Archives, became a standard part of organizations' records programs. They were the first major part of records management outsourcing as commercial records centers started offering services for the storage, referencing, protection, and disposition of records. The increasing number of organizations providing such services resulted in the formation of the *Professional Records and Information Management, International Association* (PRISM) (http://www.prismintl.org). PRISM publishes an annual directory of its members' locations and services. There are independent non-PRISM member companies as well.

The NAREMCO had issued several reports on the impact the bombings in England during World War II had on the preservation of government and business records. This concern was further emphasized subsequently in the United States by the "Cold War," the "Cuban Crisis" situations, civil riots in Detroit, Michigan and Newark, New Jersey, the New York twin towers destruction, floods in North Dakota and Louisiana. Records protection programs identifying vital records needed to resume or continue business after a given disaster became a priority. Such programs have become an critical part of an overall records management programs.

Over the years, company and commercial facilities have been established to assure dispersal of backup records, including the use of abandoned railroad tunnels, underground limestone and mushroom caves, abandoned mines, and company facilities at company-owned locations remote from central business districts. The National Fire Protection Association (NFPA) in Quincy, Massachusetts (http://www.nfpa.org) issues a standard, NFPA 232, *Standard for the Protection of Records*. It primarily addresses the types of facilities that best serve to protect records. ARMA, International has also issued a standard covering vital records identification and management.

PROFESSIONAL ORGANIZATION GROWTH

For many years prior to the popular introduction of modern records management there had been several associations concerned primarily with the filing and maintenance of records. In 1955 several of these filing associations

(Chicago, Detroit, Minneapolis, Cleveland, Milwaukee, and New York), recognizing the broader professional impact of records management, formed the ARMA. Jack Britt, records manager for Ford Motor Company, was its principal organizer. The Britt Literary Award is presented annually by ARMA for the author of the article the association's magazine judged to be the best in terms of contribution to the field during a given publication year. The association was officially chartered in 1956 with headquarters in Detroit. A separate organization was also established at this time in New York. It was called the Association of Records Executives and Administrators (AREA). The main distinction was in the level of management authority held by the members. ARMA was open to all levels while AREA restricted its membership to the supervisory and managerial level. In 1975 the two organizations merged and became the Association of Records Managers and Administrators but retained the ARMA designation. Membership was open to all levels of practitioners in the field. In 1987, ARMA changed its logo to incorporate "International" in its name, becoming "ARMA, International." The association currently has a chapter in Japan and individual members in 30 countries around the world.

ARMA has had a rapid growth. From its original membership of approximately 375 it today numbers over 10,000. From the founding six filing associations (Filing Association of Chicago, Filing Association of Detroit, Filing Association of New York, etc.) there are currently in excess of 120 ARMA chapters in the United States and Canada in addition to individual members-at-large throughout the world. From an all volunteer operated organization, it progressed to a part-time executive secretary and then to a full time Executive Director with a paid staff headquartered in Lenexa, Kansas. ARMA has become the leading advocate of RIM, sponsoring national conferences and seminars, developing standards, monitoring legislation impacting records management, and providing technical reports on all aspects of the profession. It provides a continuing promotional program involving annual "Records and Information Management Week" utilizing posters and brochures for use by its chapters and by individual companies. It has undertaken special activities to highlight issues at hand. One notable example was the 1980 introduction of "Project ELF" (Eliminate Legal Files), aimed at reducing the paper and filing costs of legal-sized documents vs. letter-sized documents. This project had a positive impact on the filing procedures in many courts and businesses.

The National Association of Government Archivists and Records Administrators (NAGARA) was established as an independent group shortly after the formation of ARMA. Its membership is based solely on federal, state, and local practitioners in the field of archives and records management. It provides a member only quarterly publication covering issues restricted to governmental concerns.

The Association of Information and Image Management (AIIM), formerly the National Microfilm Association (NMA), also supports the records management concepts and provides materials on its website (http://www.aiim.org) and its infonomics Magazine (http://www.infonomicsmag.com). This organization retains the AIIM logo but is now referred to as the *enterprise content management (ECM) organization* ECM, like "re-engineering" and "knowledge management (KM), have been computer age terminology additions to processes for the effective use of information within an organization. AIIM works closely with ARMA on special studies, standards, and research efforts.

Other groups have been formed to address specialty areas concerns for RIM such as the Nuclear Information and Records Management Association (NIMRA) (http://www.nirma.org) and the American Medical Records Association. The latter changed its name in 1991 to American Health Information and Management Association (AHIMA) (http://www.ahima.org). The ARMA organization as part of its educational program also sponsors select groups addressing the interests of specialty fields in business and industry.

RECORDS MANAGEMENT TRAINING

This growing interest in the needs and benefits to be gained by the implementation of records programs by the private and government sectors led to the development of training programs and the establishment of forums to discuss and exchange ideas about the subject. From the mid-1950s to the mid-1980s, many leading universities started offering evening courses in records management. Introduced initially as special evening courses instructed by practitioners in the field, these courses became part of daytime curriculum. In 1964, the ARMA introduced the "Records Management Correspondence Course," authored and instructed by Mr. Benedon and administered by the association. This course was offered until 1985 when the ARMA national headquarters published its own version. This course was supplemented by one offered by North Dakota University in 1969. Many schools of higher learning offer records management courses today in their general business management, library sciences, and computer technology programs.

The first conference completely devoted to records management was held in New York in 1950 and sponsored by the NAREMCO. It introduced records management to a national audience and set the stage for annual conferences on information management. The American Management Association began a series of seminars in New York featuring speakers from companies that were embarking upon programs devoted to records management conferences. In 1956, the Visual Communications Congress, sponsored by the Society of Reproduction Engineers, and the American Institute for Design and Drafting, added ARMA to its program roster. This group is no longer in operation. The ARMA, International organization has sponsored annual conferences since 1956.

PROFESSIONAL STATUS

A profession is recognized when it has developed a body of knowledge, a code of ethics, and a standard for measuring efficiency. ARMA and the other referenced associations have each contributed to the achievement of this recognition. As a professional measurement of these accomplishments and to officially measure the efficiency of practitioners in the RIM field, the Institute of Certified Records Managers (ICRM) was established in 1975 (http://www.icrm.org). Its initial Board consisted of the following representatives from ARMA and the former AREA organizations. Board member backgrounds covered business, government (local, state, and Federal), and education.

President: William Rofes, IBM Corporation.
Vice President: Col. Seymour J. Pomerenz, Department of the Army
Secretary: Dr. L. Ruth Thomas, National Archives & Records Service
Treasurer: Dr. Thornton W. Mitchell, State of North Carolina
Directors: William Benedon, Lockheed Corporation
Maj. Stanley Gordon, City of Los Angeles
Mr. Dudley F. Judd, Exxon Corporation
Mr. H. J. (Mark Koenig), Consultant
Mrs. Katherine A. Mutchler, Lever Brothers Company
Dr. Mary F. Robek, Eastern Michigan University

Following compliance with educational and experience requirements, and the successful completion of a six part examination administered by the Institute, one is granted the Certified Records Manager (CRM) status. The six part examination covers

Part I   Management Principles and the RIM Program
Part II   Records Creation and Use
Part III Records Systems, Storage, and Retrieval.
Part IV   Records Appraisal, Retention, Protection, and Disposition
Part V   Technology, Equipment, and Supplies
Part VI   Case Studies

To assure continued professional competency, a maintenance program based on 5-year cycles is administered. Points are granted for continuing education, writings, presentations, or other professional activities. Training for the certification is provided through a study manual published by the Institute. This study manual also contains an excellent bibliography of reference materials for RIM. Special

examination study sessions are also presented during ARMA's annual conference and through ARMA chapter review programs. The examination can be taken at designated sites or online. The CRM examination is continually updated to reflect the latest applications of technology to the management of records.

The Institute has provided the professional basis for the recognition of records management, as an essential part of managing the information needs of business, government, and industry. Its examination is continually updated to reflect changes in technology and it addresses, as well, all information systems needs, regardless of media involved. Since the early 1990s ARMA attempted to add to this professional status by developing and defining the core competencies of RIM (knowledge, skills, characteristics, or traits that contribute to outstanding performance in a particular profession). This goal was achieved in 2007 with the publication "Records and Information Management Core Competencies." It is expected that this study will also impact on the content of courses being offered in RIM.

The NIRMA, with an additional section on nuclear operations, also uses the CRM certification exam.

LITERATURE

Professional recognition also comes from literary exposure. This availability of this needed resource is reflected in the rapid growth of publications that currently address the records management principles and practices. Prior to the 1950s there were several filing books published. These dealt mainly with filing principles and equipment since that was considered to be the main records maintenance requirement. The first book that covered records scheduling, records centers, and filing was published in 1963 and titled *Modern Records Management* and was authored by Emmett Leahy and Christopher Cameron. The first definitive text on records management addressing all the elements listed in the introduction to this entry was *Records Management* by William Benedon, published in 1969 by Prentice-Hall. From the mid-1970s on there have been several such texts.

The first technical study on records management, "Rules for Alphabetical Filing" was published by ARMA in 1960. This was followed in 1962 by the publication of the "Records Management Workshop" authored by William Benedon and adopted by ARMA as one of its publications. In the late 1970s ARMA expanded its own publication efforts through special studies and standards development and by marketing publications by individual authors. ARMA has a bookstore that provides an abundance of publications on the subject of records management. The bookstore can be accessed at http://www.arma.org.

ARMA's first official general publication for the profession was the *"Records Review"* introduced in 1960. This was an eight-page booklet covering articles on the subject and association news. In an effort to promote records management, the *"Review"* featured a mascot cartoon in the form of a clipboard with arms and legs and called *Scrappy*. This was the brainchild of Bernie Trumbull, a general records manager at Northwestern Bell Telephone Company of Omaha. *Scrappy* became a popular lapel pin for a period of time and was also used on promotional office supply items. In 1974, ARMA and its South Carolina chapter created "Scrappy and Records Management," an instructional video in five parts as an "in-house educational television training environment." ARMA upgraded the *Records Review* to a magazine *Records Management Quarterly* (RMQ) in 1967. This publication was renamed in 1999 (*The Information Management Journal*). Association news was dropped by the magazine and replaced by an insert, "News and Notes" and later "InfoPro" to highlight specific association issues and news. Inserts are now used solely for special studies or white papers. Prior to the merger of ARMA and AREA, the latter published the *Records Management Journal*. This publication was discontinued with the merger. In January 2009, ARMA dropped the word Journal from its magazines title. The only other magazine devoted strictly to records management was the trade journal, *Information and Records Management Journal* (IMJ), edited by Rodd Exelbert. This magazine is no longer published.

AN INTERNATIONAL CONCEPT

The initial interest in records on an international basis came from the archival community's interest in documents such as letters, official papers, photographs, or recorded materials kept for their historical interest. Individual country archival societies existed worldwide to address these interests. In 1948, through the efforts of then U.S. archivist, Solon J. Buck, the International Council on Archives (ICA) was formed. Current records were of secondary concern and referred to as just that—"current records." In 1976, the ICA formed a *Section on Records Management and Archival Professional Organizations* and has had cooperative efforts with records management organizations since that time. ICA has a global network of more than 1400 institutional members in 190 countries. It also has over 200 archivists and records managers as individual members. The records management and archival functions are closely linked today in both the public and private sector.

The traditional international archive community, mainly in Europe, did not initially recognize records management as a distinct discipline and referred to it as "current records." The rapid growth of records management principles in the 1950–1980 period brought about a change in attitude as is evident in 1984 revision of the ICA's "Dictionary of Archival Terminology." It stated:

> This Lexicon was the first attempt on an international scale to draw up a glossary of the main terms then current in archival usage principally in European countries. It was produced in a period of change in the archival world when microforms were in their infancy, when records management was not yet an inseparable component of the archivist's task, and when the application of the computer to the archivist's stock in trade and to his techniques and practices rarely thought of. Now, twenty years on, the archivist's task, his holdings, techniques and practices – and his terminology – have all passed beyond the classical frontiers of his immediate predecessors.

This recognition of the unique principles and practices of records management by archivists has brought about a closer working relationship between the archivists and records managers. Many organization archivists, primarily in the government sector, have expanded their operations to include records management personnel while others coordinate the overall records needs of the organization with separate records management departments. Records management departments, in the private sector, have generally included the identification and collection of historical (archival) records. It has also brought about a cooperative effort in conferences and technical studies between the associations representing the two professions.

In 1969 individual records management group activities were conducted primarily in Melbourne (Victoria) and Sydney (New South Wales) in Australia. This, in turn, led to State Associations being formed in those two states. The pilot committee formed to consider formation of a Federal association, were assisted by a group from the ARMA organization (Eunice Thompson, O. Crawford Jenkins, William P. Southard, John D. Culton, and William Benedon). The ARMA "Records Management Workshop" and the records management objectives it addressed were used in forming the objectives for an association. The Records Management Association of Australia (RMAA) was formed later that year. With the addition of a chapter in New Zealand, the name Australia was changed to Australasia. It currently has nine branches throughout Australasia.

In 1970, Tom Lovett, an RMAA past president, recommended the formation of the International Records Management Council (IRMC) for the worldwide exchange of information and publication on records management. It included, in addition to ARMA and RMAA, the Records Management Society of Great Britain, the Records Management Association of the Philippines, the Records Management Association of South Africa, as well as individual memberships worldwide. It was funded by the individual organizations and published a multilingual International *Records Management Journal* as well as special records management studies and multilingual glossaries (French, German, Japanese, and Portuguese). As the individual country records management associations started to acquire international memberships, support for the IRMC was not provided and it is currently dormant. It currently has a chapter in Japan and individual memberships in 30 countries around the world and maintains an ongoing working relationship with ICA through joint committees, seminars, and publications.

INTERNATIONAL STANDARD

Standards are a part of a profession's efforts to define and promote the "best practices" to be followed in organizing and using any given technology or process. Standards are developed through a sequence of submittals, reviews, and approvals. Organizations have been established in every country to develop standards and in this process to set development procedures, coordinate participation with professional organizations, and to publish approved standards. In the United States it is the American National Standards Institute (ANSI). The major international organization is the International Organization for Standards (ISO), founded in 1947 and located in Geneva, Switzerland.

Most of the international standards relative to records management have been in the area of technologies, such as micrographics and computerized applications. American professional groups have participated in these efforts, mainly AIIM. Individual records management associations have issued individual country approved standards. The first international standard to focus on records management principles was ISO 9000. The global recognition of this standard for measuring product quality in international trade resulted in a coordinated effort for compliance. It brought with it the need for high-level and organization-wide attention to managing quality records. Although the term "records management" is not used directly in the standard, the control element it addresses are clearly founded on records management principles.

The most significant standard, to date, in the history of the development of records management was the issuance of an international standard (ISO15489) in 2001. It addressed all of the principles outlined in the introduction to this entry and set forth guidelines needed for their proper implementation. It provided the needed policy and management involvement and direction for its success. The development of the standard came about through the efforts of the Records Management Association of Australasia. In 1996, as a result of a cooperative effort in Australia between government and public interests, the Australian Records and Information Standard (AS4390) was issued. The positive response from records organizations worldwide led to a concerted effort for an international standard and ISO15489 was the result. The

Association of Records Managers and Administrator (ARMA) held a special program at its Montreal conference in 2001 to launch the standard. It included a Web broadcast to records managers gathered in England for a conference of the Public Records Office.

The NARA, like other government archival organizations worldwide has developed and issued standards that are primarily applicable to government agencies. (http://www.archives.gov) They cover all the standard elements of a records management program. These have been adaptable to business as well. In keeping with the concept of addressing all media, the agency in 1997 adopted the Department of Defense (DOD5025.2) design criteria standards for electronic records management applications. Vendors providing such software to Federal government agencies must abide by this standard.

ARMA, International, through its Standards Development Committee has also issued standards on various aspects of records management that have become approved U.S. standards.

CONCLUSION

The history of RIM has been an uphill struggle to convince management that it was not a file and find occupation but a discipline that, properly applied, could assure the effective and economical use of an important business asset. It elevated an "out of sight, out of mind" approach to inactive records, evidenced by records stored in capitol building domes, basements, attics, moth-balled navy ships, to modern low-cost records center. It assured the orderly and timely disposition of unneeded records. It provided timely access to both active and inactive records needed to conduct daily business and support litigation. Business continuity and the information needed to resume or continue business following a disaster has became a clearly defined program and "vital records" are clearly identified and protected. Records and information management has become an essential ally in the development of systems, the selection of equipment, and the utilization of technologies.

Legislation has also had a major impact on the acceptance and growth of records management. Laws are being continually enacted that address the requirements for proper documentation for business actions and transactions. The Federal Register, issued daily by the NARA, is an ongoing record of rules and procedures that are published for public comment or have been adopted. Records accessibility and access were prominent issues with the passages of the Freedom of Information Act in 1966 and the Privacy Act of 1974. The Paperwork Reduction Act of 1980 addressed efforts to reduce the amount and cost of submitting government reports by requiring agency justification of need and reporting effort. The Occupational Safety and Health Act

(OSHA) and the Employee Retirement Income Security Act (ERISA) impacted the demands for retaining employee records. Health Insurance Portability and Accountability Act (HIPAA) in 2001 established national standards for protecting individual medical records and personal health information. The most significant legislation to date, impacting on the need for and importance of a sound records management program, has been the Sarbanes–Oxley Act of 2002.

The Sarbanes–Oxley Act was a legislative reaction to a series of major corporate accounting scandals involving such companies as WorldCom, Tyco International, and Enron. These scandals, involving corporate executive and leading accounting firms, resulted in investor losses of billions of dollars from share losses. The act mandated new and enhanced standards for all United States public company boards, management, and public accounting firms, including the retention and filing requirements of filing and auditing records.

All regulations regarding the availability and retention of records are applicable regardless of the format in which they are produced. In many cases it is specified that the evidence copy must be produced in paper regardless of the media employed in its generation. The extensive use of electronically stored information today has resulted in changes to the Federal Rules of Civil Procedure (FRCP). Electronic discovery has become a critical factor in litigation and these rules address the requirements for the maintenance and production of records on such media. In 2004, The Sedona Conference addressed the critical issue antitrust law, complex litigation, and intellectual property in the *Sedona Guidelines*: *Best Practices and Commentary for Managing Information and Records in the Electronic Age* (http://www.thesedonaconference.org/contact_html).

Information management is the process of identifying and utilizing all the information disciplines and information resources organization-wide to achieve efficient, effective, and competitive management decisions. An organization can best achieve this goal by implementing a workable system that manages the creation, processing, use, maintenance, protection, and disposition of records, regardless of media. It is, therefore, essential that such a system involves all the disciplines that contribute to the maximum utilization and management of information. This interdisciplinary approach includes records management, computer systems, telecommunications, library sciences, archives management, and general management. This entry has addressed the history and maturing value of records management as part of this "interdisciplinary approach."

BIBLIOGRAPHY

Books

1. Benedon, W. *Records Management*, Prentice-Hall: Englewood Cliffs, NJ, 1969.
2. Cox, R.J. *Closing an Era: Historical Perspective on Modern Archives and Records Management (New Directions on Information Management)*, Greenwood Press: Westport, CT, 2000.
3. Leahy, E.; Cameron, C. *Modern Records Management*, McGraw-Hill: New York, 1963.
4. Read, J.; Ginn, M.L. *Records Management*, 8th Ed. Thompson/South-Western: Mason, OH, 2007.
5. Robek, M.F.; Brown, G.F. Stephens, D.O. *Information and Records Management*, 4th Ed. Glencoe/McGraw-Hill: Hightstown, NJ, 1995.

ORGANIZATIONS

1. Association for Information and Image Management (AIIM International). Available at http://www.aiim.org.
2. Association of Records Managers and Administrators (ARMA International). Available at http://www.arma.org.
3. Institute of Certified Records Managers (ICRM). Available at http://www.icrm.org. Website contains a biography of Emmett Leahy written by Charles Dollar, Cohasset Consultants.
4. International Congress of Archivists (ICA). Available at http://www.ica.org.
5. National Archives and Records Administration (U.S. Federal Government). Available at http://www.archives.gov.
6. The Society of American Archivists. Available at http://www.archivists.org.

PERIODICALS

1. *Infonomics Magazine*. Available at http://www.Infonomicsmag.com.
2. *Records Management Quarterly*, 1967–1984 (Association News Section), Association of Records Managers and Administrators, International, 13725 W. 109th Street, Suite 101, Lexica, KS. This publication's current title is *The Information Management Journal*.
3. *Records Review*, 1961–1966 (Articles and Association News), American Records Management Association (Currently, Association of Records Managers and Administrators, International [ARMA]) 13725 W. 109th Street, Suite 101, Lexeca, KS.

History of the Book

Jonathan Rose

Department of History, Drew University, Madison, New Jersey, U.S.A.

Abstract

The history of the book is a new academic field that explores how books shape society and how society shapes books. It covers not only books per se but all kinds of documents, including manuscripts, periodicals, newspapers, and ephemera. It addresses the social, economic, and cultural history of authorship, editing, scribal and print production, publishing, bookselling, literary property, libraries, censorship, literary criticism, literacy, and reading.

Editor's note: Other scholars sometimes use the term "the new book history" to distinguish this emerging multidisciplinary field from those earlier studies that focused mainly on the physical book and the changes it underwent over time. For coverage of earlier bibliographic and historical studies that focus on books and printers see the following entries in this encyclopedia: "Bibliographical Society of America (BSA)," p. 517; "Bibliographical Society [London]," p. 510; "Bibliography," p. 522; "History of Paper," p. 2107; "History of Three Basic Printing Processes," p. 2148; "Illumination [ELIS Classic]," p. 2233; "Incunabula [ELIS Classic]," p. 2254; "Papyrology," p. 4106; "Private Presses and Fine Printing [ELIS Classic]," p. 4297; and "Provenance of Rare Books," p. 4333.

***

One of the newest fields of academic research—and one of obvious interest to librarians—is the history of the book. Its basic premise is simple: that books shape society, and society shapes books. In the original Anglo-Saxon, *bok* could mean any kind of document, and book historians likewise define the term expansively, to include not only books per se but also manuscripts, periodicals, newspapers, and ephemera. Some scholars prefer the term "print culture history," though that has the disadvantage of excluding written documents. But all book historians agree that, in all literate cultures, script and print are the prime means of communicating information, disseminating ideas, preserving memory, distributing wealth, and exercising power. (This is not to deny the importance of oral and electronic media, but they pose different historiographical questions and involve different methodologies and sources.) Book historians are concerned with the creation, dissemination, uses, storage, and destruction of documents: thus they focus on the social, economic, and cultural history of authorship, editing, scribal and print production, publishing, bookselling, literary property, libraries, censorship, literary criticism, literacy, and reading.

Histories of books and printing go back almost as far as the printing press itself, but only more recently have historians systematically studied books to illuminate larger movements in society. Daniel Mornet's 1910 essay "Les Enseignements des bibliothèques privées" searched 500 prerevolutionary French private libraries and found only one copy of the book that was supposed to have sparked the revolution, Jean-Jacques Rousseau's *The Social Contract*. In *The Puritan Pronaos* (1936), Samuel Eliot Morison recognized that the intellectual climate of seventeenth-century New England could not be understood apart from its printers, booksellers, and libraries. Richard D. Altick's *The English Common Reader 1800–1900* (1957) explored several dimensions of book history avant la lettre: literacy education, public libraries, readers, the book trade, periodicals, and newspapers. In *L'Apparition du livre* (1958) (translated as *The Coming of the Book: The Impact of Printing 1450–1800*), Lucien Febvre and Henri-Jean Martin deployed the methods of the *Annales* school of history to explain the role of print technology in the development of capitalism and Protestantism. In 1979 two major books introduced American historians to the history of the book and popularized the term (from the French *l'histoire du livre*): Elizabeth Eisenstein's *The Printing Press as an Agent of Change* and Robert Darnton's *The Business of Enlightenment: A Publishing History of the Encyclopédie, 1775–1800*. The book was coming to be seen more and more as a driving force in history, a factor that could help explain the dissemination of the Renaissance, the Protestant Reformation, the rise of modern science, and the French Revolution.

In the final years of the twentieth century, book history began to create the structures of an organized academic discipline. The first specialists in the field had to train themselves, until formal graduate programs were set up at the University of Toronto, the University of Wisconsin, the University of Iowa, Florida State University, Drew University, the University of London, the University of Edinburgh, Leiden University, and the Johannes

Encyclopedia of Library and Information Sciences, Fourth Edition DOI: 10.1081/E-ELIS4-120043535

Gutenberg University in Mainz. The first volume of the *Annual Bibliography of the History of the Printed Book and Libraries* was published in 1970: the information therein is now being transferred to *Book History Online*, based at the Koninklijke Bibliotheek (the National Library of the Netherlands). The Society for the History of Authorship, Reading and Publishing (SHARP) was founded in 1991 and held its first annual conference at the CUNY Graduate Center in 1993. It became the leading international organization of book historians, at least in the Anglophone world. Its Web site, at http://www.sharpweb.org, is the most current and extensive listing of resources in the field, with links to publishers' archives, book catalogs, scholarly journals, databases, ephemera collections, research projects, museums, libraries, online exhibits, course syllabi, academic programs, and conferences. In addition to SHARP there arose more specialized scholarly societies defined by nationality or subfields, such as the Book Trade History Group (Britain), the Canadian Association for the Study of Book Culture, the Nederlandse Boekhistorische Vereniging (Netherlands), the Gesellschaft für Buchforschung in Österreich (Austria), the Early Book Society, and the Textbook Colloquium. New journals appeared, such as *Publishing History* (Britain), *Book History* (United States), and the *Jaarboek Nederlandse Boekgeschiedenis* (Netherlands). Textbooks were produced, and monograph series were launched by a growing number of university presses (e.g., Penn State, University of Massachusetts, University of Toronto). Ultimately, all this research was distilled into encyclopedic multivolume histories of the book in the United States, Britain, Scotland, France, Australia, and Canada.

Book history became a highly interdisciplinary discipline, bringing together scholars from a wide range of fields. Sociologists, anthropologists, and reading instructors found it a useful method for studying the uses of literacy. Art historians came to appreciate that the physical book was itself an important art form. Students of theology increasingly understood that books are a prime means of spreading gospels, and that every religious denomination is also a publishing house. (The techniques of mass-market publishing were pioneered by evangelical Christians in early nineteenth-century Britain and America.) And publishing professionals began to take an interest in the history of their business. But most book historians are historians, literary scholars, or librarians—and all three had compelling reasons to be attracted to this new academic enterprise.

By the 1970s intellectual historians found themselves challenged by social historians, who often dismissed the history of ideas as "elitist," oblivious to economic realities and material culture. In fact the project of intellectual history could no longer limit itself to describing conversations among great thinkers: it had to explore how ideas were incarnated in published texts and disseminated to mass audiences. Thus intellectual historians like Robert Darnton met the criticisms of social and economic historians by adopting their methods, studying the *Encyclopédie* as a business venture and tracing the spread of the "low Enlightenment" among common readers. Indeed, book historians reminded social historians of a fact they usually overlooked: that books and the ideas they contain have long been an important part of the everyday lives of ordinary people.

Meanwhile, departments of English and foreign languages were confronted by the rise of postmodern literary theory, which was raising provocative questions about canon formation, reader response, the politics of literary criticism, and the sociology of authorship. These questions needed to be asked, but some Modern Language Association members felt that the answers offered by postmodernists were glib, tendentious, and founded on precious little research. Was the canon simply something constructed by white male critics? Did metropolitan publishers dump European literature on colonized peoples? Do women really read differently from men, and if so, in what ways? (The school of "reader-response critics" was notorious for failing to study actual readers.) "Empirical" was the foulest epithet in the postmodern vocabulary, but some literary scholars began to do the kind of archival research that historians had always done, and their work helped to usher in a "posttheory" revisionist approach to literary history.

Librarians had always felt undervalued in the academic hierarchy, and they were eager to prove that they were more than just warehousers of books. Some of them saw an opportunity in the theories of Michel Foucault, who argued that cultures are defined by how they archive and classify knowledge. In that case, the acquisition, cataloging, borrowing, and culling of books all became vitally important intellectual questions—and librarians, who knew how to find the relevant facts and figures, could make a valuable contribution to writing cultural history.

Regardless of which department they teach in, book historians address the following common questions:

Authorship. Each and every book must be created by someone—or something—but the precise role of the person named on the title page is open to debate. Some literary scholars have gone so far as to proclaim "the death of the author," arguing that books are called into existence by impersonal social, economic, political, and cultural forces, but this is an extreme position. Most of us would agree that, whoever else was involved in creating *The Pickwick Papers*, Charles Dickens had something to do with it. But book historians rightly insist that no book is created *solely* by its author: publishers, printers, illustrators, designers, binders, salesmen, and lawyers all shape the final product in important ways. And all texts are revised, often dramatically, by editors, as A. Scott Berg illustrated in *Max Perkins: Editor of Genius* (1978). Mary Ann Gillies, in *The Professional Literary Agent in Britain,*

1870–1920 (2007), has focused attention on the most under-researched figure in the book trade, who has played a critical editorial role in advising authors to tailor their manuscripts to the demands of publishers and reading publics. Book history is deeply concerned with the sociology of authorship and has generated quite a large body of literature exploring the gender factor: for example, Susan Coultrap-McQuin's *Doing Literary Business: American Women Writers in the Nineteenth Century* (1990), Bette London's *Writing Double: Women's Literary Partnerships* (1999), and Carla Hesse's *The Other Enlightenment: How French Women Became Modern* (2001). Less attention has been paid to class issues, but see Nigel Cross's *The Common Writer: Life in Nineteenth-Century Grub Street* (1985) and Christopher Hilliard's *To Exercise Our Talents: The Democratization of Writing in Britain* (2006).

Printing. The recent volume *Agent of Change: Print Culture Studies after Elizabeth L. Eisenstein*, edited by Sabrina Alcorn Baron, Eric N. Lindquist, and Eleanor F. Shevlin (2007), is only one manifestation of the wide-ranging scholarly debates that her work incited. Did Gutenberg foment a "print revolution," or was his impact on European society less dramatic? Did printing make possible certain kinds of books (such as scientific texts) which were not really possible before? Did it promote "fixity of text" or simply perpetuate textual errors (a question explored in Adrian Johns's *The Nature of the Book* [1998]) Why were certain parts of the world (notably India and the Islamic regions) slow to adopt print technology, and what were the social consequences of that delay? How did the adoption of Western print technology in the nineteenth century transform East and South Asia? As the first mass-production industry, was printing the driving force behind the development of modern capitalism? How did printers change literary texts, with or without the permission of the authors (an issue addressed in Allan C. Dooley's *Author and Printer in Victorian England* [1992]) Print technology changed little between 1450 and 1800, but in the nineteenth century there was arguably a second printing revolution, with the introduction of steam power, rotary presses, stereotype plates, and papermaking machines, all of which made possible mass-market publishing. Book historians also explore reproduction technologies other than movable type, both pre-Gutenberg (xylography) and post-Gutenberg (lithography, mimeographing, microfilm, photocopying, desktop publishing, and the e-book).

Publishing. Publishers have long written or commissioned celebratory "house histories," but book historians have developed this genre to show how particular firms promoted particular kinds of literature—either Tory (David Finkelstein, *The House of Blackwood: Author–Publisher Relations in the Victorian Era* [2002]) or leftist (Sheila Hodges, *Gollancz: The Story of a Publishing House, 1928–1978* [1978]), classics (Jay Satterfield, *The World's Best Books: Taste, Culture, and the Modern*

Library [2002]) or smut (Iain McCalman, *Radical Underworld: Prophets, Revolutionaries and Pornographers in London 1790–1840* [1988]), fine printing (William S. Peterson, *The Kelmscott Press* [1989]) or paperbacks (Thomas L. Bonn, *Heavy Traffic and High Culture: New American Library as Literary Gatekeeper in the Paperback Revolution* [1989]), highbrow (J. H. Willis, Jr., *Leonard and Virginia Woolf as Publishers: The Hogarth Press 1917–41* [1992]), lowbrow (Larry E. Sullivan and Lydia Cushman Schurman, eds., *Pioneers, Passionate Ladies, and Private Eyes: Dime Novels, Series Books, and Paperbacks* [1996]), or somewhere in between (Joan Shelley Rubin, *The Making of Middlebrow Culture* [1992]).

Publishing histories have cast a new light on the work of much-studied authors: see Morton Cohen and Anita Gandalfo, *Lewis Carroll and the House of Macmillan* (1987); Robert L. Patten, *Charles Dickens and His Publishers* (1978); and Peter Shillingsburg, *Pegagsus in Harness: Victorian Publishing and W. M. Thackeray* (1992). The very structure of many Victorian novels was determined by their initial publication in serial form, as illuminated by Linda K. Hughes and Michael Lund, *The Victorian Serial* (1991), and Carol A. Martin, *George Eliot's Serial Fiction* (1994).

In one area in particular, book historians have dramatically revised the conventional narrative of literary history. Modernist authors were once accepted at face value as pure artists resisting the commercial pressures imposed by mercenary publishers. But the close study of publishers' ledgers and correspondence reveals a more mixed reality: it turns out that Joseph Conrad, James Joyce, and D. H. Lawrence were interested in profit maximization as well. Some of the key works on "marketing modernism" include James Nelson, *Elkin Mathews: Publisher to Yeats, Joyce, Pound* (1989); Joyce Piell Wexler, *Who Paid for Modernism? Art, Money, and the Fiction of Conrad, Joyce, and Lawrence* (1997); Peter D. McDonald, *British Literary Culture and Publishing Practice 1880–1914* (1997); Lawrence Rainey, *Institutions of Modernism: Literary Elites and Public Culture* (1998); Josephine M. Guy and Ian Small, *Oscar Wilde's Profession: Writing and the Culture Industry in the Late Nineteenth Century* (2000); Paul Delany, *Literature, Money and the Market: From Trollope to Amis* (2002); Catherine Turner, *Marketing Modernism between the Two World Wars* (2003); and Robert W. Trogdon, *The Lousy Racket: Hemingway, Scribners, and the Business of Literature* (2007).

Bookselling. Bookseller's records can tell us a great deal about the availability and demand for books in a particular time and place. William J. Gilmore used such sources to illuminate literary life in a backwater of the early American republic, in *Reading Becomes a Necessity of Life: Material and Cultural Life in Rural New England, 1780–1835* (1989). Colporteurs (traveling book peddlers) can sometimes convey a very clear picture of what their customers wanted. And so do histories of big modern booselling chains, such as Charles Wilson's *First with the News: The History of W. H. Smith* (1986).

Literary property. The first modern copyright legislation was enacted in Great Britain in 1710, and its impact is described in Mark Rose's *Authors and Owners: The Invention of Copyright* (1993). However, the concept of literary property is almost as old as printing itself, as explained in Cynthia J. Brown's *Poets, Patrons, and Printers: Crisis of Authority in Late Medieval France* (1995) and Joseph Loewenstein's *The Author's Due: Printing and the Prehistory of Copyright* (2002). Until Congress ratified an international copyright treaty in 1891, American readers enjoyed a windfall of cheap pirated foreign literature, as analyzed most recently in Meredith L. McGill's *American Literature and the Culture of Reprinting, 1834–1853* (2003). And Chinese literature has been profoundly shaped by a traditional lack of respect for literary property: see William P. Alford's *To Steal a Book is an Elegant Offense: Intellectual Property Law in Chinese Civilization* (1995) and Andrew C. Mertha's *The Politics of Piracy: Intellectual Property in Contemporary China* (2005).

Libraries. Library history was once a relentlessly uplifting tale about public enlightenment, philanthropic gentlemen, and dedicated collection-builders. Under the influence of book history, however, this field has become more deeply rooted in social history, as exemplified in Alistair Black's *A New History of the English Public Library: Social and Intellectual Contexts, 1850–1914* (1996). In *Reading on the Middle Border: The Culture of Print in Late Nineteenth-Century Osage, Iowa* (2001), Christine Pawley analyzed library records to reconstruct the intellectual milieu of an entire midwestern community. And in *Free to All: Carnegie Libraries and American Culture, 1890–1920* (1995), Abigail Van Slyck used the public library movement as a window into the history of American philanthropy and civic architecture. Wayne Wiegand's *Irrepressible Reformer* (1996) was more than just a biography of Melvil Dewey: it cast light on the invention of information science and the ideological biases built into that profession. One of the distinguishing features of this new approach to library history is a willingness to explore some of its grimmer aspects: for example the McCarthy era, in Louise S. Robbins, *The Dismissal of Miss Ruth Brown: Civil Rights, Censorship, and the American Library* (2000); or convict libraries, in Janet Fyfe, *Books Behind Bars: The Role of Books, Reading, and Libraries in British Prison Reform, 1701–1911* (1992); or James Raven, ed., *Lost Libraries: The Destruction of Great Book Collections since Antiquity* (2004); or, darker still, Ambrus Miskolczy's *Hitler's Library: A Socio-Historical Overview* (2003) and Timothy Ryback's *Hitler's Private Library: The Books That Shaped His Life* (2008). In 12 years the Nazis destroyed an estimated 100 million volumes throughout Europe, as documented in David Shavit, *Hunger for the Printed Word: Books and Libraries in the Jewish Ghettos of Nazi-Occupied Europe* (1997); and Jonathan Rose, ed., *The Holocaust and the Book: Destruction and Preservation* (2001). See also Rebecca Knuth's *Libricide: The Regime-Sponsored Destruction of Books and Libraries in the Twentieth Century* (2003).

Censorship. It is bleakly ironic that the twentieth century, when most Western societies achieved near-universal literacy, also witnessed the most ruthless and extreme suppression of literature. But censorship and expurgation—for moral, political, or religious reasons—have always been with us. Book historians have set themselves the task of explaining why, how, and upon whom censorship was imposed. For example, in *Word Crimes: Blasphemy, Culture, and Literature in Nineteenth-Century England* (1998), Joss Marsh found that blasphemy laws were enforced only against working-class atheists, not gentleman agnostics like T. H. Huxley. Scholars have found that censorship in ancien regime France and Czarist Russia was notoriously leaky and inefficient, allowing in much subversive literature. And we have already begun to study the newest front in the censorship wars: see *The Rushdie File*, ed. Lisa Appignanesi and Sara Maitland (1990). Book historians have also pioneered the serious scholarly study of pornography and its role in culture and politics: see Lynn Hunt, ed., *The Invention of Pornography: Obscenity and the Origins of Modernity, 1500–1800* (1993), and Robert Darnton, *The Forbidden Best-Sellers of Pre-Revolutionary France* (1995).

Literacy and Reading. Where earlier historians focused on estimating rates of literacy, book historians such as David Vincent (*Literacy and Popular Culture: England 1750–1914* [1989]) have delineated the everyday uses of literacy—in the workplace, in political and labor organizations, in everyday letter-writing. A fairly high degree of literacy was necessary to negotiate modern urban environments, as illustrated by Peter Fritzsche in *Reading Berlin 1900* (1996) and David M. Henkin in *City Reading: Written Words and Public Spaces in Antebellum New York* (1998).

Until fairly recently it was widely assumed that recovering the intellectual experiences of ordinary readers in history was impossible, but a growing number of book historians have managed to penetrate that mystery. They have used such sources as probate and booksellers' records, which reveal the ownership and distribution of books. Remarkably detailed sociological surveys of reading were conducted as far back as the 1790s (in the case of *The Statistical Account of Scotland*) and in the old USSR (used by Stephen Lovell to write *The Russian Reading Revolution: Print Culture in the Soviet and Post-Soviet Eras* [2000]). The minutes of reading groups and literary societies can be mined for what they reveal about popular reading habits, as Elizabeth McHenry did in *Forgotten Readers: Recovering the Lost History of African–American Literary Societies* (2002). Equally illuminating are library borrowing records and the memoirs of plebeian readers, as employed in Jonathan Rose's *The Intellectual Life of the British Working Classes* (2001). Much information about learning literacy can be found in the records of educational institutions: Heather Andrea Williams made use of the Freedmen's Bureau archives in *Self-Taught: African American Education in Slavery and Freedom* (2005). No less valuable are letters to magazine and newspaper editors, particularly those that were never published, as studied by David Nord in *Communities of Journalism: A History of American Newspapers and Their Readers* (2001). In his *Faith in Reading: Religious Publishing and the Birth of Mass Media in America* (2004), Nord also made effective use of reports that canvassers sent back to evangelical publishers, essentially an early form of market research. For their book *Everyday Ideas: Socioliterary Experience among Antebellum New Englanders* (2006), Ronald J. Zboray and Mary Saracino Zboray gleaned observations about reading from the letters and diaries of more than 900 individuals. Other revealing sources include interviews (Martyn Lyons and Lucy Taska, *Australian Readers Remember: An Oral History of Reading 1890–1930* [1992]), fan mail (Clarence Karr, *Authors and Audiences: Popular Canadian Fiction in the Early Twentieth Century* [2000]), iconography in illuminated manuscripts (Laurel Amtower, *Engaging Words: The Culture of Reading in the Later Middle Ages* [2000]), and comments scribbled in margins (Heather Jackson, *Marginalia: Readers Writing in Books* [2001]). As Carlo Ginzburg demonstrated in *The Cheese and the Worms* (1980), the Inquisition was keenly interested in what people were reading, and their proceedings are an invaluable historical resource.

Finally, the Reading Experience Database, begun in 1996, is assembling a searchable pool of thousands of individual reading experiences in Britain between 1450 and 1945 (http://www.open.ac.uk/Arts/RED/). And in the United States, the "What Middletown Read" project has constructed a searchable database of the usage of the Muncie Public Library between 1891 and 1902, covering more than 6,000 borrowers, 13,000 volumes, and 400,000 loans (http://www.bsu.edu/middletown/wmr/).

Literary politics. Canon formation has been a hotly contested and highly politicized issue among the last generation of literary scholars. A number of book historians have addressed it in a systematic way, notably Jan Gorak in *The Making of the Modern Canon* (1991), John Guillory in *Cultural Capital: The Problem of Literary Canon Formation* (1993), and Timothy Morris in *Becoming Canonical in American Poetry* (1995). Sex bias in literary criticism, no less controversial a topic, is treated in Nicola Thompson's *Reviewing Sex: Gender and the Reception of Victorian Novels* (1996). For studies of single authors, a model is John Rodden's *The Politics of Literary Reputation* (2nd ed., 2002), which retells the intellectual history of the Cold War though a survey of critical responses to

George Orwell. The question of what gets translated—and how—can also be political, as André Lefevere has explained in *Translation, Rewriting, and the Manipulation of Literary Fame* (1992). Specialized studies in this field have often focused on Germany: Walter Grünzweig, *Constructing the German Walt Whitman* (1995); Bernhard Fabian, *The English Book in Eighteenth-Century Germany* (1992); and Fania Oz-Salzberger, *Translating the Enlightenment: Scottish Civic Discourse in Eighteenth-Century Germany* (1995).

Studies of the development of English as a scholarly discipline, in both the United States and Britain, inevitably focus on academic politics: Chris Baldick's *The Social Mission of English Criticism 1848–1932* (1983) (a Marxist perspective), Franklin Court's *Institutionalizing English Literature* (1992), John Dixon's *A Schooling in "English"* (1991) (more sympathetic than either Baldick or Court), David R. Shumway's *Creating American Civilization: A Genealogy of American Literature as an Academic Discipline* (1994), Kermit Vanderbilt's *American Literature and the Academy* (1986), and Gerald Graff's *Professing Literature: A Institutional History* (2nd ed., 2007). For a devastating treatment of postmodern criticism, see David Lehman, *Signs of the Times: Deconstruction and the Fall of Paul de Man* (1991).

There have also been numerous studies of the political impact of books, including two on *Silent Spring*: Priscilla Coit Murphy's *What a Book Can Do: The Publication and Reception of Silent Spring* (2005) and Mark Hamilton Lytle's *The Gentle Subversive: Rachel Carson, Silent Spring, and the Rise of the Environmental Movement* (2007). Following the lead of Robert Darnton, several historians have looked for the seeds of the French Revolution in print culture: Jack R. Censer in *The French Press in the Age of Enlightenment* (1994), Roger Chartier in *The Cultural Origins of the French Revolution* (1991), Elizabeth Eisenstein in *Grub Street Abroad: Aspects of the French Cosmopolitan Press from the Age of Louis XIV to the French Revolution* (1992), Arlette Farge in *Subversive Words: Public Opinion in Eighteenth-Century France* (1994), Dena Goodman in *The Republic of Letters: A Cultural History of the French Enlightenment* (1994), and Jeremy Popkin in *News and Politics in the Age of Revolution: Jean Luzac's Gazette de Leyde* (1989). An entire volume of critical essays has been devoted to *The Darnton Debate: Books and Revolution in the Eighteenth Century* (ed. Haydn T. Mason, 1998).

Science. Elizabeth Eisenstein argued that print made the scientific revolution possible, and in her wake historians have investigated the publication and reception of scientific ideas. Here the outstanding work is James Secord, *Victorian Sensation: The Extraordinary Publication, Reception, and Secret Authorship of Vestiges of the Natural History of Creation* (2000). But see as well Aileen Fyfe, *Science and Salvation: Evangelical Popular Science Publishing in Victorian Britain* (2004); Lydia Marinelli and Andreas Mayer, *Dreaming by the Book: Freud's Interpretation of Dreams and the History of the Psychoanalytic Movement* (2003); and Marina Frasca-Spada and Nick Jardine, eds., *Books and the Sciences in History* (2000).

Lexicography. Print technology made the national standardization of spelling and vocabulary necessary, and that gave rise to the modern dictionary, which in turn has been an almost irresistible force for defining language. Critics from various points on the ideological compass have charged lexicographers with the crimes of slanginess, "prescriptivism," or linguistic imperialism. Book historians, however, recognize that dictionary makers are publishing professionals who have to balance a host of completing pressures: they must work within deadlines and budgets and space limits, they must coordinate the work of an army of contributors and subeditors, they must track down and historicize and define literally hundreds of thousands of words, and they must produce a book that is both marketable and absolutely accurate. Studies that are particularly sensitive to these problems include Herbert C. Morton's *The Story of Webster's Third: Philip Gove's Controversial Dictionary and Its Critics* (1994), Allen Reddick's *The Making of Johnson's Dictionary, 1746–1773* (2nd ed., 1996), and Lynda Mugglestone's *Lost for Words: The Hidden History of the Oxford English Dictionary* (2005).

Future directions. Until very recently book history was a First World enterprise, concentrating almost exclusively on Europe, North America, and Australasia, but now it is beginning to engage other parts of the globe as well. India in particular has attracted a critical mass of scholars, among them Priya Joshi (*In Another Country: Colonialism, Culture and the English Novel in India* [2002]), Anindita Ghosh (*Power in Print: Popular Publishing and the Politics of Language and Culture in a Colonial Society, 1778–1905* [2006]), and Rimi Chatterjee (*Empires of the Mind: A History of Oxford University Press in India under the Raj* [2006]). Recovering the African common reader might seem to be an impossible task, but it has been accomplished by Wendy Griswold (*Bearing Witness: Readers, Writers and the Novel in Nigeria* [2000]) and Stephanie Newell (*Literary Culture in Colonial Ghana: How to Play the Game of Life* [2002]). For other groundbreaking works, see Christopher A. Reed's *Gutenberg in Shanghai: Chinese Print Capitalism, 1876–1937* (2004)

and Eugenia Roldán Vera's *The British Book Trade and Spanish American Independence: Education and Knowledge Transmission in Transcontinental Perspective* (2003).

As noted at the outset, book history is concerned with all types of documents, so the next logical frontier for the field should be the history of archives. Our culture is defined by the records that we choose to preserve or destroy, their organization and accessibility, and the information they contain, all of which determines the kinds of history we can reconstruct. The importance of this type of scholarship for all historians should be obvious, but archival history is still a very new field, so new that it is scarcely organized. It has no dedicated academic journals or societies, though the International Conference on the History of Records and Archives (I-CHORA) has been meeting since 2003. For examples of some recent work, see *Ancient Archives and Archival Traditions: Concepts of Record-Keeping in the Ancient World*, ed. Maria Brosius (2003). A promising approach to this subject is via the historiography of paperwork, for example Miles Ogborn's *Indian Ink: Script and Print in the Making of the English East India Company* (2007), Cornelia Vismann's *Files: Law and Media Technology* (abridged and translated by Geoffrey Winthrop-Young, 2008), and Jacob Soll's forthcoming *The Information Master: Jean-Baptiste Colbert's Secret State Intelligence System*.

BIBLIOGRAPHY

1. Casper, S.E.; Chaison, J.D.; Groves, J.D., Eds. *Perspectives on American Book History: Artifacts and Commentary*; University of Massachusetts Press: Amherst, MA, 2002.
2. Cavallo, G.; Chartier, R., Eds. *A History of Reading in the West*; trans. Cochrane, L.G; University of Massachusetts Press: Amherst, MA, 1999.
3. Darnton, R. *The Kiss of Lamourette: Reflections in Cultural History*; W. W. Norton: New York, 1990.
4. Eliot, S.; Rose, J., Eds. *A Companion to the History of the Book*; Blackwell: Oxford, U.K., 2007.
5. Febvre, L.; Martin, H.-J. *The Coming of the Book: The Impact of Printing 1450–1800*; trans. Gerard, D, Verso: London, U.K., 1997.
6. Finkelstein, D.; McCleery, A. *An Introduction to Book History*; Routledge: New York and London, U.K., 2005.

History: Three Basic Printing Processes

Sidney E. Berger
Phillips Library, Peabody Essex Museum, Salem, Massachusetts, U.S.A.

Abstract

The present entry will discuss three types of printing processes as they have been practiced in the West for centuries. Moveable type printing that originated with Johannes Gutenberg in Europe is called relief printing because the ink adheres to a raised surface from which is it imparted to the printed surface. The second basic kind of printing in the hand press period is intaglio, that is, printing from inks delivered to a surface from beneath the surface of the printing block. The third type of printing is called planographic and the process is referred to as lithography, which involves printing from the flat surface of a stone.

INTRODUCTION

Printing was developed in China long before Johannes Gutenberg came on the scene. The Chinese were printing from clay maybe by the eighth century and certainly by the ninth century. Also by the ninth century they were printing from wood blocks, carved (in reverse, i.e., in mirror writing) from a flat surface. Hence, the first printing that we know of is one of three types of printing: relief, intaglio, and planographic. The present entry will discuss these three types of printing as they have been practiced in the West for centuries.

RELIEF PRINTING

When something is in relief, it is raised up from a surface below. A relief map shows mountains that actually protrude upward from the surface of the map.

With the growth of the guild system in the Middle Ages, there was a concomitant growth of the middle class, with a simultaneous enlargement of the educational system. With the flow of money to the middle class, there was an increase in leisure time and a parallel demand for education. The number of books produced in the monasteries and by the Stationers—by secular scribes—could not keep up with the demand caused by the expansion of the education system. Manuscript books could be produced only one at a time. But the numbers of students were increasing rapidly.

In this climate, the need arose for a process of book production that would allow multiple copies of books, rather than one at a time. Johannes Gutenberg (1398–February 3, 1468) satisfied this need by adapting several techniques of metallurgy and design to a new craft: printing.

Gutenberg neither invented printing nor did he invent the press, which had existed for centuries before him, for pressing olives or grapes. He did not invent ink, which, of course, had existed for centuries and was used in the production of manuscripts. His genius lay in the use he made of his metal-casting skills, combined with a couple of innovations that made relief printing as we know it possible.

The Chinese could cast words in matrixes (also called matrices), but because they had a pictographic language, every word had to be cast separately. A text with, say, 5000 different words would have required that many individual matrixes. Gutenberg had the good fortune to live in an area of the world that used not pictograms but the individual letters of an alphabet to build up words. The number of matrixes he needed to create was only a tiny fraction of the number needed for a pictographic language.

Gutenberg's first challenge was to design a full font—an alphabet and all the other characters he would need: letters of various sizes, numbers, punctuation signs, and other special figures. With manuscript hands as his model, he designed a font of printing type that perfectly suited his needs, looking sufficiently like the perfectly legible handwriting of scribes.

In fact, though he was creating printed books, to an observer not familiar with printing (and practically no one was since these were the first printed items in the West), what he made looked like multiple, identical copies of manuscripts. Items that were absolutely identical might have received the censure of the Church as being produced with the help of the Devil. Gutenberg got around that potential peril by producing as his first book a Bible.

With a full font designed, Gutenberg set about the kind of work he was familiar with: creating matrixes to cast the type. As a goldsmith, he knew how to create matrixes. He began with a short iron bar, squared off horizontally and vertically. On one end it had a perfectly flat surface onto which he transferred, backward (that is, in mirror writing) the character he wanted to cast. As he carved and filed away, he removed metal from the end of the bar—called a *punch*—leaving behind in relief the character he would eventually cast. As he got closer and closer to the final

Encyclopedia of Library and Information Sciences, Fourth Edition DOI: 10.1081/E-ELIS4-120043541

form, he would take smoke proofs. That is, he would hold the carved end of the punch in a flame, allowing lamp-black to settle on the punch's surface. Then he would press the punch onto a piece of paper to make a print of the character.

If it was not filed or "carved" sufficiently, he would continue, taking further smoke proofs, until it was just as he wanted it. If he went too far, removing too much metal, he would have to begin again. When the punch was exactly as he wanted it, he would hold it in a flame until it glowed to just the right color, and then he would plunge it into cold water to harden it. The steel punch was now ready for the next step: creating the matrix.

A small squared-off bar of copper was the raw matrix. Gutenberg carefully hammered the punch into the copper, creating in it the impression of the character from the tip of the punch. It displaced some copper, so the matrix had to be filed down and squared off—called "justifying the matrix." The punch had to make an impression in the copper to exactly the right depth (the same depth into every matrix for all of the characters). This would assure that every piece of type—every "sort"—would be exactly the same height from its feet to its face. This of course was necessary since all the sorts, when composed into a text, needed to be exactly the same height from foot to face, creating a smooth surface of faces to receive the ink uniformly and to offer up a perfectly uniform impression to the paper or vellum laid upon it.

Once the matrix was justified, it was ready for casting. Here is where Gutenberg's great genius lay: he created an adjustable mold, adjustable "left to right" to accommodate matrices of different horizontal measures. Thus, a matrix of an "I" would fit into the mold with only a narrow "funnel"—formed by the two halves of the mold—above it; while an "M" would be in a matrix that was considerably wider left to right. The mold could slide open to accommodate the wider letter.

With the matrix at the bottom of the mold, which formed a little funnel above it, the type caster would pour molten type metal down the funnel. The metal, which would solidify in a split second, would fill the impression of the character in the matrix and create the sort, with a "jet" of metal above the just-cast sort. This jet, made up of the extra metal poured in that was not needed to create the sort, would be broken off, the sort would be put with other like sorts, the type would be "brushed off" to remove any extra slag or other minute particles of metal that attached to the sort, and the feet of the sort would be created when the point at which the jet was attached would be filed down—thus creating a tiny groove on the bottom of every piece of type, and two "feet" around the groove that the sort would sit on. (All the broken-off jets would be dropped back into the melting pot to be used for further casting.)

When the requisite number of characters was cast from that matrix, it would be removed from the hand mold and another matrix, created in the same way the previous one was, would be put in and used for casting.

Once the typecaster had created all the sorts needed and distributed them into a typecase into little compartments, the compositor would take these sorts and place them one at a time into a handheld device called a composing stick, lining up the sorts to form words, sentences, and paragraphs, or whatever the copy required. When the composing stick was full, the lines of type, all justified to exactly the same length in the stick, would be transferred to a galley, a three-sided tray (usually made of metal). More lines of type from the composing stick would join the earlier ones until the text was completed, or until the galley was full. Additional galleys were needed for longer texts, and, in fact, a whole galley rack holding perhaps dozens of galleys could contain the text of an entire book.

The text would be proofed in the galleys (hence our modern term "galley proofs" or "galleys"), corrected, and proofed again. Eventually the printer would transfer from the galley to the bed of the press, the pages she or he needed to print one side of a sheet. Later the sheet would be "perfected"—that is, the second side of the sheet would be printed. Little by little stacks of printed and perfected sheets would form, and when all the sheets were finished being printed, they would be folded and gathered into groups (called "quires," "gatherings," or "signatures") in the proper sequence to form the continuous text from beginning to end. At this point, the printing was done and the sheets went off to the binder.

* * *

In the hand press period (before, say, 1800), printers faced a dilemma: once they set a book into type, how many copies should they print? If they did a run of 1000 copies and sold only half, they would lose money. If they printed 1000 copies and distributed the type back into the typecases, and then needed more copies, they would have to reset the type. Further, if they printed the 1000 but thought they might need to print more, they could store the type in galleys. But this would take up a good deal of space, and it would render the type unusable for other projects.

The solution was stereotyping, which entailed taking a mold of the pages of type—in plaster, clay, or papier-maché—and using that mold to cast a plate that contained a perfect image of the standing type. (Note that the printing from stereotype plates is indistinguishable from the printing of the text from the type itself. They are both relief printing and will leave the same kind of indentation in the paper. Also, since an edition of a text is constituted by all of the copies printed from a single setting of type, pages printed from type and those printed from stereotype plates cast from that same type are both part of the same edition.)

Many experiments in stereotyping as early as the close of the seventeenth century took place, but it was William Ged in Edinburgh who seems to have made the first practicable stereotype plates about 1725.[1] (This statement is on p. 526. Though this is an old reference book, it is authoritative and reliable.) The process became commercially accepted with its "reinvention" by Andrew Tilloch,[2] the editor of the *Philosophical Magazine*. (The Dictionary says, "Tilloch declared...that he had known nothing of Ged's process, but this is not believed by [Luke] Hansard," the author of a well read printer's manual (p. 527). Tilloch partnered with Andrew Foulis, printer at the University of Glasgow, in 1782. In 1784 they took out four patents for printing with metal plates rather than from standing type.[3]

Stereotyping was almost completely superseded by electrotyping, another way to make a matrix for casting printing plates. The set type is placed in a galvanic bath and a perfect mold of another metal, usually copper, is formed over the type. It is considerably more complicated than this brief statement indicates, but the point is that a printing plate that looks like a stereotype plate, but that is covered with a layer of copper, is formed, and books can be printed from the plates. Copper is much more durable than is the type metal used in stereos, which is a composition of about 80% lead, 10% tin, and 10% antimony. Hence, electros will hold up longer than will stereos.

Electrotype plates, like stereotypes, are of the same edition as was the type they were made from, and they print in relief as do the type and the stereos.[4] (Note that nickel, brass, or steel could be deposited onto the original form of type, but copper was the most common. See the *American Dictionary*, p. 164.) Further, since the printer using these plates is not constrained by thousands of pieces of type, the plates can be bent in such a way as to fit over a cylinder and can be placed into high-speed cylinder presses. Electros can also be made from woodcuts, allowing for the high-speed printing of text and illustration in one operation.

INTAGLIO PRINTING

The second basic kind of printing in the hand press period is intaglio, that is, printing from inks delivered to a surface from beneath the surface of the printing block. (Note that the G in the word "intaglio" is not pronounced.) The text—verbal or pictorial—is incised or carved into the surface of the plate, which traditionally was wood or copper, but later on could be zinc, magnesium, linoleum, or any of several other materials.

Relief printing preceded intaglio by several centuries, probably invented by the Chinese in the second century. "Intaglio engraving, as a method of making prints, was invented in Germany by the 1430s"[5] and the method was soon employed by the Italians and Dutch, though the incising of surfaces of metals clearly predates this by centuries in the decoration of metal objects like armor or trays.

In the most basic method, the artist, using burins and gravers, would incise the image or text into the plate,

leaving grooves of varying widths and depths, then cover the surface of the plate with ink, which was pressed into the grooves. The surface of the plate would then be wiped clean with a tarlatan, a plain-weaved cotton fabric (sometimes the artist would swipe a bare hand over the plate's surface for the final wiping), leaving the ink in the grooves.

A sheet of dampened paper is then placed over the plate, backed with a soft blanket, and run through the press under great pressure. The dampened paper is pressed into the grooves and picks up the ink, transferring the image or text to the sheet.

Additionally, before the printing but after the wiping of the plate, the plate could be colored in various ways on its surface, allowing the artist to add a second, third, or many colors to the final print, creating a monoprint—a print unique in that, while the intaglio-printed text can be reproduced, the coloring on the surface of the plate cannot.

What has just been described is one kind of intaglio printing, engraving, since the artist has engraved the surface of the plate with tools. There is another way to get the grooves into the plate: etching. This is done using acids that burn into the surface of the plate. In etching, the plate is covered in wax, which is impervious to acid. The artist, using a fine metal tool like a needle, scratches off the wax where the image is to go, exposing the metal. When acid is put onto the plate (either being washed over the surface or having the plate dipped into the acid bath), the acid etches the plate. The longer the metal is exposed to the acid, the deeper and wider will be the grooves and dots.[6]

A related method which is not strictly intaglio is drypoint printing. The artist uses the gravers and burins as with engraving, but instead of removing the incised-out metal, the artist leaves a burr of metal at the edges of the incised grooves. These get inked (rather than having the ink go into the grooves) and the print is made from the inked burrs. Since the paper is pressed against the burrs, these burrs do not last long, so only short runs of drypoint prints are made—sometimes fewer than a dozen before the image breaks down.

If the incising is done in wood, the result is a wood engraving, as opposed to a woodcut or woodblock print, which is a relief method. Extremely hard woods can yield exceptionally fine lines, and—as with all of the intaglio methods—prints of exquisite fineness can be produced, with great subtlety in line and shade. Artists like Barry Moser have used a product called Resingrave, which is a synthetic material, mounted on a type-high block, that can be engraved in the same way one cuts into copper.

There is some confusion about the terminology here. Some people see metal engraving as an intaglio process and wood engraving as a relief process. But if the wood is engraved the same way the metal (e.g., copper plate) is, then the ink is delivered to the paper from beneath the surface of the woodblock; hence, this is an intaglio method of printing.

Intaglio-printed texts have a three dimensionality caused by the pressing of the paper into the grooves of the plate. Since this is a labor-intensive, and hence expensive, method of printing, it is highly prized. In the twentieth century a cheaper method of raised printing was invented: thermography. In this process, a newly printed sheet, with the ink still wet, is passed under a part of the press that drops a powder onto the ink. The powder sticks to the ink and the rest of the powder is vacuumed off. The sheet then is exposed to heat, which sets the powder, now raised above the sheet, creating a three-dimensional printed image. It looks from the printed surface like engraving, but from the back of the sheet one can see that the paper has not been pressed into the grooves of a printing plate.[7] Since engraved printing is expensive and looks elegant, it was a sign of wealth and affluence to have engraved such things as business cards, wedding invitations, and stationery. Thermography imparted such a look and cost a fraction of the cost of engraving.

Advances in etching have to do with the use of lutemakers' varnish or acid-resistant resin rather than wax, the use of steel plates rather than copper, the incorporation of photography, and so forth. But the basic method of printing is nonetheless intaglio.

PLANOGRAPHIC PRINTING

In 1796 a Bavarian actor, Alois Senefelder (1771–1834), looking for an inexpensive way of printing music, invented lithography, printing from the flat surface of a stone. The invention was more of a discovery, for he was apparently not actively looking for the method that he came up with.[8]

The basic principle is simple: oil and water do not mix. Senefelder was fortunate to be living where a particular kind of limestone was quarried. It had the properties of being able to hold on its surface an oil-based ink—called tusche—and being covered completely with water where the tusche was not, and holding both water and tusche with equal full coverage. The artist would draw the words and/or images onto the perfectly flat surface of the stone. Since the tusche was oil based, when the stone was covered with water, the tusche would repel the water and remain exposed to the air. But the rest of the stone would be covered with the water. Then an oil-based ink would be rolled on, adhering to the tusche, but being repelled by the water, hence not adhering to any other part of the stone. The paper or other material to be printed would be laid over the stone and rolled in a press similar to an etching or engraving press, and the ink would be transferred to the printing surface of the stone to the printed surface. The printing surface was absolutely flat, not in relief or in intaglio, as in the other two methods of printing described here. Hence it is called "planographic printing," having been done from a flat plane.

The tusche is drawn onto the stone with crayons or fine pens, and under the hands of a master artist, pictures of great beauty and fineness can be created. Also, written text could be created, simply by having the lithographer write or "print out" the text in writing. Since the tusche "lies chiefly on the surface of the stone it is liable to be rubbed off, and therefore a coating which will resist any application of water is applied to it."[9]

The stone can be reused once the printer is finished with its image: it is reground, removing the fine layer of tusche and rendering the stone clear. The thick stones, hence, can be used over and over. By the middle of the nineteenth century the stones were printed on steam presses, speeding up the process considerably from the old method of handprinting. The thick stones are quite heavy, so a method of planographic printing was developed using zinc plates. This method was called zincography. "In 1834, the Frenchman Breugnot patented a zincographic printing process, producing large maps called géoramas."[10] (For this information, Wikipedia cites the dissertation of Pearson.[11])

In 1818 Senefelder himself wrote about printing in color using lithography,[12] and by the 1830s, chromolithography was being used in much of Europe. Chromolithographs (or "chromos") sometimes had a dozen or more colors built up to produce the final pictures. The products from the presses often combine printing processes: usually chromos are printed first, followed by letterpress (i.e., relief) printing and/or intaglio (i.e., engraved) printing.

[More modern printing techniques are not covered in this entry. They include offset printing, rotary-press printing, flexography, screen printing, dye-sublamation printing, photocopying (Xerography), laser printing, dot matrix printing, thermal printing, inkjet printing, digital printing, and three-dimensional printing.]

REFERENCES

1. *American Dictionary of Printing and Bookmaking*; Lenox Hill: New York, 1894; 526–529 (Reprinted 1970).
2. *American Dictionary of Printing and Bookmaking*; Lenox Hill: New York, 1894; 527 (Reprinted 1970).
3. http://www.oldandsold.com/articles09/stereotype-8.shtml See.
4. *American Dictionary of Printing and Bookmaking*; Lenox Hill: New York, 1894; 157–166 (Reprinted 1970).
5. http://en.wikipedia.org/wiki/Intaglio_(printmaking) Wikipedia.
6. http://en.wikipedia.org/wiki/Etching Wikipedia.
7. Old and Sold. *Antiques Digest*, http://www.thermographers.org/thermupd.asp (accessed February 17, 2008).
8. *American Dictionary of Printing and Bookmaking*; Lenox Hill: New York, 1894; 341–346 (Reprinted 1970).
9. *American Dictionary of Printing and Bookmaking*; Lenox Hill: New York, 1894; 343 (Reprinted 1970).

10. http://en.wikipedia.org/wiki/Zincography Wikipedia.

11. Pearson, K. *Lithographic maps in nineteenth-century geographical journals*, The University of Wisconsin-Madison: Madison, WI, 1978; 69 Ph. dissertation.

12. Meggs, P.B. *A History of Graphic Design*; John Wiley & Sons, Inc.: New York, 1998; 146.

BIBLIOGRAPHY

1. Goudy, F. *Typologia: Studies in Type Design & Type Making, with Comments on the Invention of Typography, the First Types, Legibility, and Fine Printing*; University of California Press: Berkeley and Los Angeles, CA, 1940.

2. Hind, A.M. *Guide to the Processes and Schools of Engraving: With Notes on Some of the Most Important Masters*, British Museum Department of Prints and Drawings: London, U.K., 1952.

3. Lawson, A. *Printing Types: An Introduction*. Beacon Press: Boston, MA, 1971.

4. Legros, L.A.; Grant, J.C. *Typographical Printing-Surfaces: The Technology and Mechanism of Their Production*; Longmans, Green and Co.: London, U.K. and New York, 1916.

5. Senefelder, A. *A Complete Course of Lithography: Containing Clear and Explicit Instructions in All the Different Branches and Manners of That Art: Accompanied by Illustrative Specimens of Drawings. To Which Is Prefixed a History of Lithography, from Its Origin to the Present Time*, R. Ackermann: London, U.K., 1818. Several reprints available.

6. Wakeman, G. *The Literature of Letterpress Printing, 1849–1900*; Plough Press: Oxford, U.K., 1985.

Hospital Libraries

Rosalind K. Lett
Information-2-Knowledge, Atlanta, Georgia, U.S.A.

Abstract

Hospital libraries, defined as specialized professional health sciences libraries, located in hospitals, medical centers, acute care facilities, and even long term care facilities, provide biomedical information and clinical evidence-based resources to healthcare professionals, and affiliated hospital staff. In addition, many hospital libraries provide consumer health information services to patients, their families and the community. Clinical resources, particularly those focused on patient care and patient safety, differentiate hospital libraries and distinguish them from academic medical center libraries.

INTRODUCTION

Hospital libraries, defined as specialized professional health sciences libraries, located in hospitals, medical centers, acute care facilities, and even some long term care facilities, provide biomedical information and clinical evidence-based resources to healthcare professionals, and affiliated hospital staff. In addition, some hospital libraries provide consumer health information services to patients, their families and the community. Clinical resources, particularly those focused on patient care and patient safety, differentiate hospital libraries and distinguish them from academic medical center libraries. Academic medical libraries generally provide research, medical education, and clinical information to faculty, students and staff of the academic medical institution. The hospital library staff conscientiously responds to day-to-day information needs yet is always ready to handle clinical information emergencies. Hospital libraries satisfy the individual and collective needs for knowledge-based and evidence-based health information of physicians, nurses, lab technicians, students, hospital administrators, and many others. The physical library space meets multiple needs serving as a place for study, scholarly enrichment, collaborative meetings, consultations, discussions, debates, and solitude. The hospital library offers a peaceful refuge for physicians and medical school students, as well as an activity center for scholarly research and hospital-wide operational and strategic collaborations.[1] Many other factors such as the clinical demands of the clientele, specialized print-based medical resources, electronic clinical resources, and emphasis on point-of-care patient centered information services set the hospital library apart from other medical libraries. Hospitals, especially community hospitals usually employ minimal staff for the library, often only staffing, a one-person library. Minimal square footage, limited budgets, and small resource collections are often characteristics associated with community hospital libraries. Yet even in these less than optimum conditions a special commitment to the environment of care is demonstrated through the vision, expertise, and dedication to service of hospital librarians.

This encyclopedia entry on hospital libraries is designed to promote a deeper understanding of the:

- Value and role,
- Programs, services and information products
- Clientele and community access, and
- Changes and adaptation being made by hospital libraries

The impact of new healthcare policies, changes in the healthcare environment, new development in educational standards and evidence-based medicine, new and innovative technologies, and developing trends and patterns in hospital librarianship will serve as the basis for discussion of the above stated criteria.

HISTORICAL OVERVIEW

The hospital library of today has roots extending back to Colonial America. Dr. John Fothergill presented the Pennsylvania Hospital with its first book *An Experimental History of Materia Medica* by William Lewis, which served as the catalyst for the allocation of fund and the establishment of a Medical Library. Many hospital libraries originated from medical staff libraries, whereas others evolved from nursing libraries that supported hospital-based nurse diploma programs.[2] The earliest medical libraries were often the results of pooled physician resources. The oldest medical library in America, established in Pennsylvania Hospital in Philadelphia, was founded in 1762. In 1847 the American Medical Association designated it as the first, largest and most important medical library in the United States. Many early hospital library collections were supported by student admission fees to

Encyclopedia of Library and Information Sciences, Fourth Edition DOI: 10.1081/E-ELIS4-120043928

clinical lectures, bequest, gift and purchases. Through the help of Benjamin Franklin,[3–5] John Winthrop founded a collection for the New York Hospital that was transferred in later years to form the New York Academy of Medicine. The 1800s ushered in the establishment of several notable medical libraries: the Treadwell Library of Massachusetts General Hospital in 1847, Mt. Sinai Hospital Library in 1883,[6] and the largest hospital library at Johns Hopkins Hospital.

MISSION OF THE HOSPITAL LIBRARY

Hospital libraries, also known in some hospitals as medical libraries or health sciences libraries, are an integral part of the health care environment, which provides essential evidence-based information services.[7] Hospital libraries, much like the hospitals and medical centers that they occupy, vary in size, scope of service, subject focus, access to resources, character and clientele.[8] Some hospital libraries operate as independent departments, whereas others are subunits of departments, such as hospital education medical records, the medical staff office, or even quality improvement. Others are blended departments such as the Medical Library and Continuing Medical Education. The hospital's mission, vision, areas of specialty, educational offerings, participation in research and the needs of its clientele dictate the services and functions of the hospital library. Timely needs assessments and frequent usage evaluations conducted by hospital librarians provide the evidence librarians need to support the sustainability of current programs and the development of new programs and services. As hospitals add new services and expand to form multicampus systems, hospital libraries continue to develop library services to complement, strengthen and support the information needs of distance learners and the evolving needs of on-site and off-site health care providers.

In the American Hospital Association's publication, *Hospital Statistics*, hospital libraries were found to comprise the largest group of Health Sciences Libraries.[9,10] According to statistics compiled from the National Library of Medicine's Docline records, hospital libraries in the United States currently total 3355. Today's hospital library is a uniquely specialized, patient-focused, service-oriented hub of continuous activity.[11] Much like other departments and units of the hospital, the library contributes to the primary mission of providing service excellence and quality health care to the hospital's patients. The hospital library supports the delivery of patient care by providing library services to various types of students and health care professionals, including physicians, nurses, allied health professionals, and hospital administrators. Depending on the setting, some hospital libraries also serve nonaffiliated health professionals, such as pharmaceutical representative, and the community at large, represented by patients and their families. The hospital library provides health care professionals with access to information used in their day-to-day clinical practice and answers to difficult health information questions.[12] Hospital libraries also provide consumer health information and layman-oriented resources for patients, families, and the community.

Hospital libraries are the source of vital patient care information, resources to enhance education, and knowledge-based information resources needed for research endeavors. Knowledge-based information is vital to the hospital, in that it supports patient care; strategic decision making; performance improvement, patient safety, lifelong learning and reflective practice, research initiatives, patient and family education, and professional competency of hospital and medical staff. Lessons traditionally taught by hospital librarians, such as how to cite references, how to use indices, and how to develop search strategies are now being accompanied by lessons on how to search electronic resources, and how to seamlessly access health information on the web. Study shows hospital libraries save lives; ammunition in the fight to reinstate required medical libraries, the survey shows library information was often the key to proper diagnosis and treatment.[13] Hospital librarians guided by changing roles and technology, train hospital staff to develop search strategies, search electronic books, journals and databases, seamlessly access health information from their desktop and provide training in how to analyze and filter health information.[14] Hospital libraries also play a key role in supplying the hospital's administrative staff with information critical to making ongoing data-driven decisions.

ROLE OF HOSPITAL LIBRARIES

Historically, the hospital library has been viewed as a non-revenue generating department of the hospital, which existed predominantly to provide information and library resources to the medical staff for patient care, education, or research. The increased emphasis on the value of the hospital library in clinical care, patient safety and health literacy are presenting new roles and responsibilities for hospital librarians. These new roles have contributed to the expansion of the target audience for library services to include "all" hospital staff, patients, families, and the community served by the hospital.[15] There are numerous types of hospitals: large and small, general and specialty, teaching and nonteaching, and acute and long-term facilities. Larger hospital libraries and multisystem hospital libraries often have more staff, larger budgets, and more resources available than smaller hospital libraries. Teaching hospitals benefit from the abundant access to monetary and physical resources particularly electronic resources of the affiliated Academic Medical Center. The library serves as a vital component in the clinical training of future physicians, and it also serves the work-oriented need of all hospital personnel.[16] In community hospitals, physicians and other health care professionals are made aware of the unlimited resources that the library can provide through networking with other libraries, usage of health resources on the World Wide Web and participating in consortia resource purchases and collaborative ventures.

The role of hospital libraries continues to change and evolve as information is recognized as a corporate asset.[17] Evidence-based medicine, medical information filtering, patient safety and JCAHO requirements all focus on the quality of information and its value to the field of medicine. Providing accessibility of up-to-date, accurate, and authoritative information while the primary role of hospital libraries in not the only role. The role of the hospital library is to be agile and flexible enough to rapidly respond within the changing environment of the hospital and to provide accessibility to information for crucial data-driven decision making. However, with more emphasis on return on investment hospital libraries struggle to define themselves in such a way that the true value of intangible library services can be recognized and valuated.

TYPES OF HOSPITAL LIBRARIES

Community Hospital Library

Many small community hospital libraries are designed as core medical libraries that make optimal use of limited resources. They offer a basic core collection of medical journals and texts that cover the major areas of medical practice, such as Family Medicine, Internal Medicine, Surgery, Obstetrics and Gynecology, Radiology, Public Health and Emergency Medicine. Hospital libraries provide free access to Web-based resources such as the National Library of Medicine's (NLM) Databases; Pub-Med, MedlinePlus, and several other Web-based NLM resources. Due to dramatic changes in access facilitated by journal publisher with input from hospital librarians, even small libraries have access to some electronic journals with the purchase of print journals. Local, regional, and national consortia affiliations help facilitate access for small libraries to electronic books, journals, and databases from recognized medical resource vendors.

Doody's Core Titles for the selection of books for the core print collection has replaced the Brandon Hill List of Books and Journals for the Small Medical Library as the resource tool of choice used to develop medical library collections.[18] These resource collections tools are logically arranged using the National Libraries of Medicine's, NLM Classification Scheme.[19] The smaller hospital libraries, like their larger counterparts, provide invaluable library services that include document delivery, online searching, and access to Web-based resources. The librarians in these libraries serve as facilitators, guides, information providers, expert searchers, and negotiators.[20] Most smaller community hospital libraries have access to the Internet, either dial-up through an Internet provider or more commonly now, through the institution-wide direct Internet connection.[21]

Teaching Hospital Library

According to the Association of American Medical Colleges (AAMC) teaching hospitals are providers of primary care and routine patient services, as well as centers for experimental, innovative, and technically sophisticated services.[22] Hospital libraries in teaching hospitals are vital information centers associated with teaching programs serving the hospital's objectives of patient care, education, innovation, and research. Hospital Libraries strive to develop library services that support the AAMC curricula objectives. Studies show that work-related activities are the starting point for learning for medical residents. Subsequently their information literacy skills and knowledge base are the result of the interpretation and the level of understanding that they draw from instruction and experiences such as library skills training.[23] Teaching hospital libraries incorporate interaction into the learning process through hands-on database training, problem-based learning, the incorporation of new technologies and medical informatics applications. These libraries not only provide the core resources of the community hospital including access to point of care resources in the electronic medical record, e-textbooks, print medical text and other clinical educational resources needed in a teaching environment, but go a step further to evaluate services, analyze collections and develop more value added services for their clientele. The services of a teaching hospital's library are expanded to include bibliographic instruction (basic searching techniques), virtual reference, clinical medical librarianship, morning report, information retrieval and the incorporation of new technologies such as PDA's, iPods, smartphones and learning e-portfolios for student centered learning and the integration of resources into the electronic medical record. Many teaching hospital libraries have even begun to use some of the new social technologies, i.e., blogs, wikis. MySpace, Facebook and others social networking tools "leveraging the connectivity of the sites and using them to form communities around library products, media or information services to really be in contact with users."[24]

Specialty Hospital Library

Specialty hospitals include acute care hospitals with one or more area of special concentration. Specialty hospitals include specialties such as pediatrics, obstetrics and gynecology, ophthalmology, otorhinolaryngology, orthopedic, sports medicine, diabetes treatment, spinal cord injury treatment, general and plastic surgery, and diagnostic breast care. Other types of specialty hospitals are long-term care facilities such as psychiatric, rehabilitation and Veteran's Administration hospitals. Specialty Hospital Libraries foster innovation and improvement in the specialty learning environment with increased attention on residency programs and improving faculty research and patient care outcomes. Specialty hospital libraries offer residents and attending physicians a "space" in which to make connections between clinical experience, bench research projects, and program learning objectives as set forth by their program directors and department chairs. These specialty hospital libraries have in-depth collections aligned with the mission and specialization of the hospital. The collections in these facilities are comprised of core clinical journals and text, however, the primary focus of these collections is on the area of specialization of the organization.

Nursing Library

Nursing libraries provide access and preservation of scholarly records and nursing text to nursing student and nurse educators. In the 1980s, the proportion of registered staff nurses, the patient–nurse ratio increase, and a growing demand for nurses with bachelor's and master's degrees fueled the evolution of nursing. These trends toward the requirement of a bachelor's degree for nurses and the growth of nursing literature brought about by the upgrading of academic programs of nursing schools prompted the development of nursing libraries.[25] Nursing libraries use Doody's core titles to select nursing text as well as other selection tools to build strong nursing collections. CINAHL the Cumulated Index to Nursing and Allied Health Literature is one of the Web-based resources used to locate nursing and allied health journal articles. "In many hospitals the nursing library was formalized before the medical library."[26] Nursing libraries today are more often found in nursing schools than hospitals; however, hospital libraries provide well-developed nursing collections within their library resources, as nurses are quite often the largest user group of hospital libraries. Nursing excellence requires access to evidence-based information resources appropriate to guide health care decisions. Many hospitals today are seeking the powerful Magnet Status, recognition by the American Nurses Credentialing Centers (ANCC) Magnet Recognition Program that support nursing excellence and enhanced nursing practice, yet is very difficult to achieve. Hospital librarians are instrumental in hospitals achieving this recognition. They contribute support to the application process in many ways yet specifically by providing evidence for care delivery models, access to high quality resources and encouraging nursing research and publication.[27–29]

IMPACT ON CLINICAL DECISIONS

Federal legislation enacted in 1986 by the Health Care Financing Administration (HCFA) eliminated the requirement that hospitals maintain a library to be eligible for Medicare and Medicaid funding. Decisions for maintaining hospital libraries were left up to the individual hospitals. The JCAHO in the 1994 standards integrated hospital libraries into the Management of Information giving hospital libraries the opportunity to explore new roles as part of the team charged with managing the organizations information.[26] HCFA and the JCAHO have noticeably impacted decisions about the necessity of hospital libraries. As a result of the HCFA decision, the need for developing new approaches to evaluating and determining the value of hospital library services has become more apparent. Although value studies conducted by the Special Libraries Association measured monetary and time saving, additional studies of the impact of hospital library services on patient care were needed. The Rochester study was devised with objectives "to encourage hospital libraries to develop methods of analyzing current user services in order to improve the visibility and status of the library." Health care professionals make many decisions while treating patients, which are crucial to patient care outcomes and quality of care. Using the Chicago study of the contribution of the hospital library to clinical care as a model, the Rochester group developed a questionnaire to measure the impact of information on clinical decision making. This study confirmed the Chicago study findings that information provided for physicians by hospital libraries is perceived to have significant impact on clinical decision making and helps to establish the relative value of information provided by the hospital library. The Rochester study reported the information provided by librarians saved time, contributed new knowledge, improved patient care, and saved cost for 85% of participating physicians.[27] Hospital libraries are in need of more current validation of their value. A new version of the Rochester study is being planned to help provide hospital libraries with the evidence that they need to visibly illustrate the positive impact hospital libraries have on patient care, education, research, patient safety, and health literacy. In an American Medical Association (AMA) study of New York physicians, "information provided by the library was rated more highly by the physicians than other information sources such as diagnostic imaging, laboratory tests, and discussions with colleagues."[28,29]

LIBRARY STANDARDS

Two important sets of standards affecting hospital libraries have been significantly revised. These are the Medical Libraries Association Hospital Libraries Standards and the Joint Commission on Accreditation of HealthCare Organizations (JCAHO) Standards.

The Medical Library Association Standards

The Medical Libraries Association (MLA) is the organization representing health sciences librarians and other health information professionals dedicated to improving their leadership and quality to foster the art and science of health information services. The Hospital Libraries section of MLA composed standards for hospital libraries that were approved in 1952. A major revision to the Hospital Library Standards was performed in 2002 with updates made in 2004. The Medical Library Association's *Standards for Hospital Libraries 2002* were developed as a guide for hospital administrators, librarians, and accrediting bodies to ensure that hospitals have the resources and services to effectively meet their needs for knowledge-based information (KBI).[30]

JCAHO STANDARDS

The Joint Commission on Accreditation of Healthcare Organizations (JCAHO) is the major accrediting agency for hospitals. In the JCAHO standards for information management, the importance of the need for access to knowledge-based information provided by hospital libraries is outlined in the Agenda for Change. JCAHO has identified expert knowledge-based information as vital to an organization's ability to provide patient care. Knowledge-based information refers to current expert information, produced externally to the organization, including:

- Journals, texts, documents, and databases in print or electronic format;
- Benchmarks, best practices, guidelines, consensus development statements;
- Research studies;
- Quality-filtered Internet resources

According to JCAHO, knowledge-based information is a collection of stored facts, models, and information that can be used for designing and redesigning processes and for problem resolution.[31] Knowledge-based information is found in the clinical and management literature, derived from in-house library collections and external databases. The JCAHO standards for information management focus on the accessibility, availability, and the authoritative nature of knowledge-based information included in the institution-wide planning.[26] "Knowledge-based information supports clinical decision making, continuing education of staff, administrative planning and management, performance assessment and improvement, patient and family education, and research."[32] JCAHO regards information management as a function composed of seven strategic processes that look at needs identification, systems design, information definition and capture, data analysis, data transformation, data transmission, data reporting, and

information assimilation and usage. The newly revised integrated JCAHO standards incorporate information management as a component of quality improvement. As part of the continuous efforts to monitor the library services within the health care environment, the JCAHO developed a new vision of information that is critical to quality care and thus integral to all JCAHO standards.

The JCAHO has changed standards affecting hospital libraries. While the standards state that access to knowledge-based information is needed for the hospital environment, they no longer definitively state that the hospital library is the place for this access. The JCAHO is currently proposing revisions to the management of information standards that could classify hospital libraries standards as nonessential standards. MLA and the hospital library community are providing valuable feedback to the JCAHO to maintain the recognition of the value and need for the hospital library.[33–37]

LIBRARY CLIENTELE

Hospital libraries serve the entire hospital community. Research, training, and information resources are provided to physicians, nurses, allied health professionals and other hospital staff. Drug information and pharmaceutical reference materials are available for pharmacists and other clientele needed drug information. Patient education materials are provided to case managers and staff who plan patient discharge strategies. Dietary information is provided to dieticians and nutritionist. Information on the environment-of-care is provided to administration, hospital safety personnel and public safety officers. Comparative data is provided to quality improvement teams and senior administration to make critical data-driven decisions. New technological developments and innovations are provided to information systems personnel and informatics researchers. Knowledge-based, data-driven decisions are made by hospital administrators based on information obtained by the hospital library from business, statistical, technological, and hospital administrative literature resources. Hospital libraries also serve students, interns, and residents by offering bibliographic instruction, reference assistance, seamless access to print and nonprint resources, paper-based and online catalogs, dictionary, thesauri, controlled vocabularies, and standard nomenclatures.

The information explosion has made us acutely aware that medical literature is growing at an astronomical rate.[38] The number of medical articles available on the Internet increased from zero in 1992 to 107 in 1995 to 3.8 million in 1997 and continues to grow exponentially.[39] A quick Google search reveals 217,000,000 medical articles. Physicians find they can't keep up with the enormous volumes of biomedical information published, even when regularly reviewing current literature. The information explosion has brought about a new age of technology for hospital libraries and a new value to hospital librarians as information experts.[40] The hospital library also plays a major role in the service to patients and their families. Information can increase consumers' receptivity to treatment by improving their knowledge about disorders and treatment alternatives. Information also enhances the patient–clinician relationship by facilitating informed consent and fostering patients' active participation in their treatment. Some hospital librarians have gone as far as to participate in training consumers of health information to make sense of medical data by supporting literacy initiatives.[41]

The current emphasis of the JCAHO on patient education and the rights of consumers to be informed before consenting to test, treatment, and drug therapy have led to a renewed interest in patient libraries.[42] A resurgence of patient libraries is being seen in all types of hospital libraries. Patient and consumer library services in today's hospital provide layman's level, easy to understand information about illness and wellness for the general public. The educated e-health consumer of today seeks direction in searching the literature and locating alternative avenues of health care.

LIBRARY STAFF

Role of the Hospital Librarian

Hospital librarians function as problem solvers, change agents, and invaluable resources of timely information delivery, yet they also serve as generalist. Although generalism contributes greatly to library work, specialized skills are especially critical to developing quality collections and first rate services.[43] As medical librarianship became more widely accepted as a profession, standards for certification were established, which have evolved into the present day Academy of Health Information Professionals (AHIP).[44,45] The staffing of hospital libraries is uniquely different, depending on the size of the hospital, the availability of funding for library resources, and the organizational commitment to lifelong learning.

The medical librarian, a specialized information professional, is uniquely prepared to provide oversight and management of knowledge-based information (KBI) resources and services to hospital or healthcare system. The hospital librarian plays a significant role in bringing specialized competencies to the institution, for the selection, organization, dissemination, evaluation, and expert retrieval of information in support of knowledge-based and evidence-based clinical, administrative, and scientific decisions. Hospital libraries have a vested interest in training health sciences practitioners and other library clientele in the best methods of information retrieval for knowledge-based and evidence-based practice, research, and lifelong learning.

Today's hospital librarians function in the roles of library manager, information specialist, webmaster, database manager, clinical medical librarian, information analyst, chief information officer, informationist, and internal consultant. The hospital library manager works closely with hospital managers and professionals in other disciplines on a daily basis. The job of hospital library manager is accompanied to a great degree by autonomy that allows flexibility and rapid response to the ever-changing needs of the hospital staff. As information specialist, hospital librarians focus on providing expertise in the location and delivery of information resources. The role of web master taps the creative and organizational skills of hospital librarians. Designing, organizing, and maintaining a web site for the library and sometimes multiple sites for the organization, provide a different dimension to the hospital librarian's job. As database manager, hospital librarians develop, classify, and maintain databases of pertinent information, making it available for rapid retrieval. Clinical medical librarians connect with the clinical staff as a part of the clinical team to provide information at the point-of-care. In the role of chief information officer, the librarian is the architect of the organizations' strategic information plan.[46] As internal consultants, hospital librarians cultivating entrepreneurial spirit, evaluate current processes and contribute to the development of new services such as competitive intelligence. These services are the basis of ideas that produce new income streams and incorporate significant cost savings for the organization.

Educational Requirements for Hospital Librarians

The staff of hospital libraries ranges from the one-person librarian experiencing a wide variety of work interactions, to a library staffed with three or more full-time staff members, each devoted to one or more specific aspect of library operations (i.e., document delivery and circulation). Most hospital librarians hired today to manage hospital libraries have earned a master's degree in library science from an American Libraries Association accredited library school. The master's degree provides general, multidisciplined preparation for library work. Specialized course work in medical librarianship provides the subject concentration in medical and health sciences resources. The educational background of library staff varies from certified medical librarians with master's degrees in library science, to library specialist with undergraduate degrees in related disciplines, to library assistants with 2 or more years of college and library experience.[47] Although having a science background is not a requirement to become a hospital or health sciences librarian, the knowledge-base of the life sciences curriculum prepares librarians for in-depth analysis, research, and filtering of biomedical information which proves invaluable in biomedical informatics. The staff of hospital libraries provide valuable database search training, while offering service assistance in retrieval of information from Web-based resources, locating and delivering needed documents, developing resource collections, providing access to electronic resources and supplying other vital information services.[48]

Most hospital libraries not employing a full-time certified medical librarian seek support from the services of a degreed medical librarian, either as a consultant or circuit rider librarian. Library consultants assist libraries in the day-to-day maintenance of the library and keep the library's operational policies in compliance with JCAHO standards. Library consultants provide a variety of services onsite or virtually. Circuit rider librarians usually serve a number of hospitals. They travel from library to library providing basic information services and collection maintenance for several hospital libraries, usually in rural areas.[49] Library and information services provided by professional librarians are critical to the organization's ability to not only respond to information requests but also proactively meet the ever changing needs and systematically link current, standard evidence from the literature with health care processes.

SERVICES

The Medical Library Association sites 19 services as being essential to hospital libraries. These essential services are categorized as distinct functional areas that include Technical Services, Reference and Information Service, Educational and Outreach Services, and Administrative and Management Services.[50,51]

TECHNICAL SERVICE

One of two major functions of libraries, technical services includes processes for acquiring, arranging, indexing, and storing the collection. The constant replenishing of selected materials and the routine update of standard library references fulfill the mission of acquisitions. The acquisitions process includes tasks that involve ordering, receiving, and paying for information resources.[52] For most library clientele, the processing of books, journals, A-Vs, CD-ROMs, electronic resources and software is invisible. The process-oriented functions that convert collection development decisions into acquisition are the backbone of the development of a strong authoritative library collection. Many methods, such as analysis of citations and resources, library usage studies, and subject expert collection evaluation, are used to judge the value of library resources.[53] The acquisitions staff of hospital libraries, one-person or larger, perform a variety of tasks that address many complex issues concerning licensure, contracts, discounts, and electronic format of resources.

Collection Development

The library's mission, objectives, and goals reflect those of the parent organization, as do the library's collection development policies. The information needs of the organization served by the hospital library are figured prominently into the collection development plan.[54] Selecting materials for inclusion in the collection of a hospital library can be a complex process. The needs of library clientele, the current collection strengths and weaknesses, the demands of cooperative collection agreements, the need to preserve historically important documents, the available space, in-house and online journal use counts, and impact factors enable a balanced, objective approach when making difficult choices of how to spend limited collection development budgets.[55,56] The scope of the collection development plan parallels the organizations commitment to various activities and disciplines. The proliferation of published materials, in all forms, is so vast that no single hospital library, not even the largest, can hope to acquire everything. Selection is necessary to ensure the viability of the collection and the incorporation of various materials in subject specialties. The underlying principle of the selection policy defines what the library should get rather than what it does get.[57] The basic principle of selection is derived from assessing and understanding the needs and interests of the clientele and applying basic selection principles. Assessment of information use, demand, and needs of library user groups, both potential and immediate, provides a context for the library staff to make selection decisions for the library.

Medical books correlate information from many primary sources such as journal articles and present the subject in context, often revealing both past and present advances, and future trends. Medical books provide tremendous timesaving when clientele need comprehensive literature analysis, review and comparisons to finds different perspective, interpretations, and outlooks.[58] The transformation of traditional print medical books to online digital electronic books is occurring very rapidly. Online medical books are an important resource for digital library collection building, especially in the context of clinical medicine. Hospital libraries have a unique obligation to advocate for the shift from print book collections to electronic book collections. Hospital Libraries have been successful in increasing their electronic book collections by focusing on the elimination of space requirements for electronic books, the convenience of access, and the cost benefits of acquiring e-books within database packages, such as in the case of MD Consult. Consortial collaborative purchases of product such as STAT!Ref or Books@Ovid are other ways Hospital Libraries facilitate the shift to electronic books.

The hospital librarian has a responsibility to establish and maintain library liaison groups, to evaluate information trends, and to be proactive in response to changes in health care.[53] An important aspect of selection is learning about new publications that can enhance and strengthen the library's collection and purchasing the most appropriate format of that resource. Information is being packaged in a variety of innovative formats, yet budgetary constraints drive hospital libraries to develop more rigorous selection methodologies and to redefine the criteria and processes by which decisions are made to insure accessibility to resources and efficient allocation and use of funds.

Circulation

A major function of the hospital library is to provide conditions for optimal, seamless use of library resources by clientele both inside and outside of the library. Development of circulation policies and procedures for hospital libraries begins with the identification of the population to be served. The policies governing the use of the library by the clientele reflect and enhance the vision and mission of the hospital. Establishing use policies in hospitals often involves collaboration between the librarian(s), the library committee, and hospital administration. The library circulation policies reflect a wide range of library clientele with varying and unique needs.[59] Circulation of print resources has been significantly impacted by the introduction and proliferation of electronic resources, yet many high use titles are maintained in both electronic and print format.

Access to the Library Collection

Information is viewed as a basic commodity in the health care field. Access to up-to-date, authoritative information is critical to the success of a hospital library in serving the needs of its clientele. The library collection is comprised of its information sources (i.e., journals, e-journals, books, e-books, audiovisuals, databases, practice guidelines, patient education materials and Web-based resources. Many hospital libraries, historically, have limited access to physicians, because of the limitations of spaces and staff, and the technical level of the library resources.[60] Today's access to the hospital library collection is provided to all hospital staff and the community during normal business hours. After hours access is provided for clinical staff and hospital administrators, which give them 24-hr access to the resources of the library. The availability of books and journals in electronic Web-based formats provide opportunities for desktop access to library resources virtually 24 hrs a day. Desktop access to online catalogs, bibliographic databases, full-text journals, electronic reserves, and virtual reference services has visibly changed library use patterns. These new formats provide searching, filtering, analytical and access capabilities that aid in rapid location and critical appraisal of information. Libraries are experiencing decreases of in-house use of

library resources, with patrons opting to use the convenience of online full-text resources made freely available from the hospital library. The provision of resources in the myriad of formats currently available support the "equal access to health information resources" called for in MLA's WHCLIS platform.[61]

Access to Bibliographic Information

Two types of documents (indexes and abstracts) contain catalogs and bibliographies of original materials, primarily articles in periodicals. The National Library of Medicine created Index Medicus, a finding aid for biomedical journal articles. Index Medicus was produced as a monthly listing of current articles and cumulated yearly into the Cumulated Index Medicus. Index Medicus is the paper index whose entries dating back to 1966 comprised the MEDLINE database.[62] Most indexes and abstracts used by hospital libraries are currently available electronically. The "List of Serials Indexed for Online Users" (LSIOU), listing 5164 journal titles, provides bibliographic information for all journals ever indexed over time for MEDLINE®. It includes titles that ceased publication, changed titles, or those that were deselected.[63,64] CINAHL, the Cumulative Index to Nursing and Allied Health Literature was originally a print index to the literature of nursing and eventually allied health information. The CINAHL® database has emerged as a comprehensive, authoritative and versatile guide to current periodical literature for nurses, allied health professionals and to an exploding body of health related knowledge, which now extends beyond the limits of a bibliographic print index. Approximately 2900 nursing, allied health, and health related journals are regularly reviewed and indexed for inclusion. Full text articles are available for selected nursing standards, practice acts, pamphlets, state nursing journals, research instruments, and critical paths.[65]

For subject areas not highly demanded, hospital libraries obtain journal article information by searching other indices and databases. For subject areas in high demand, libraries purchase a site license to the Web-based content, access databases through resources purchased in consortia packages, call upon colleagues at academic medical center for help, or use resources of statewide library resource sharing project such as Georgia's GALILEO. GALILEO, or GeorgiA LIbrary LEarning Online, is a world wide Web-based virtual library, providing access to multiple information resources, including secured access to licensed products. GALILEO provides access to over 100 databases indexing thousands of periodicals and scholarly journals, 2000 full-text journal titles and other resources including encyclopedias, business directories, and government publications available primarily to citizens of Georgia.[66] Many states have similar resources that hospital libraries tap to locate needed resources. One major advantage of electronic indexes and abstracts is the feature that enables clientele to search for information using words from titles and abstracts in addition to the author and subject access provided in print versions. This significantly expands the number of information paths available to locate bibliographic information.

Library catalogs are used in the circulation and location of library resources. The early systems still used by only a few hospital libraries are catalog card dependent. This type of card catalog facilitates location of library materials though access to cards organized by subject, title, and author. Hospital libraries now use computerized integrated library systems (OPAC) Online Public Access Catalogs, which record information about both the user and the circulating materials. The OPAC records are created from the library's electronic bibliographic records. The records are accessible through searching software. OPACs can be a part of an integrated system or self-contained packages, as they are in many hospital libraries.[63] The online catalog provides menu-driven searching of book, journals, and audiovisual databases by author, subject, title, format, and keyword. These catalogs provide features such as browsing by title, limiting searches by date, access from remote terminals and other specialized features.

EDUCATIONAL SERVICES

End-User Training in Database Searching

Bibliographic instruction (BI) of medical literature searching in the hospital setting focuses on teaching effective use of appropriate health information resources. Many hospital librarians provide BI to new and seasoned employees, residents, nursing students, house staff, and liaison groups of the hospital. Topics traditionally taught include accessing and organizing information, using library locator tools, citation verification, computerized bibliographic database use, searching electronic journals, utilizing interlibrary loan services, and using Medical Subject Headings (MeSH).[67] Internet searches for information constitute one of the most popular applications taught in BI. Training of end user (library clientele) to search in-house databases, Web-based resources and electronic full text journals are high-profile services common in hospital libraries. Alper and Visnon conclude in a study at the University of Missouri, that introducing students to useful Web sites, practicing answering clinical questions, and integrating this process with clinical rotation experiences can reduce the effort that students need to find answers and improve the quality of answers they find.[68]

The introduction of end user searching systems beginning in the late 1980s initiated a wave of change at the traditional reference desk as users began to discover new ways to utilize library services. With the introduction of end user MEDLINE in the 1980s, many hospital libraries found an increase in requests for individualized instruction, technical assistance, and in-depth reference assistance. With the availability of new information resources, library users find reference services helpful in helping them adapt to newly emerging information landscapes. Enabling end-user access has contributed to a decline in traditional reference services such as mediated searching yet has stimulated the development of new roles of hospital librarians performing more comprehensive subject focused expert searching, filtering, and critically appraising literature.[69] Critical appraisal is the study of two main elements of research; how the research was performed and how the research and findings are presented. When hospital librarians critically appraising a study they are attempting to reduce the uncertainty, focus on important issues, dissect complex problems and corral group participation. Critical appraisal is an essential step in evidence-based decision making. The decision to implement change can be made more accurately after conducting a critical appraisal.[70]

The need to assess the quality of end-user training has drawn attention to the need to evaluate both search ability and the ability to use the resulting information to accomplish a clinical task. End-user searching is usually conducted using electronic bibliographic databases such as PubMed and CINAHL. These databases allow searching by keyword and retrieval of references list. The end user must then sort, read, and critically evaluate the results to uncover answers and results for patients. New third generation evidence-based medicine search engines allow access to hundreds of the best known therapy options through clinical knowledge management systems. These systems use simple "ask a question" interfaces to retrieve the latest peer reviewed research. Results are synthesized into article summaries, tables and graphs with links to original articles. Hospital librarians teach end users to search these databases focusing on their ability to synthesize large bodies of information, and the expanded modules available. Up-to-Date, Dynamed, Cochrane, Google Scholar, Pubmed, and Medical Evidence Matters are valuable resources for obtaining new evidence-based medicine information.[71]

REFERENCE AND INFORMATION SERVICES

Reference and Information Services are the services that range from provision of quick answers to simple questions, to providing in-depth research to answer complex questions. The challenge of reference services is providing precisely what the client needs, in the allotted time, and format.[72] Day-to-day reference work in a hospital library follows a pattern influenced by the nature of the requests for services. Hospital librarians conduct reference interviews, the process of asking open-ended questions, to clarify the client's request, in-person, via telephone, and even virtually. Request for information takes several forms: factual or "direct" inquiries, bibliographic or "indirect" inquiries, and verification request. Factual inquiries include statistics, biographies, locations, a historical data, a formula, a definition, or some similar fact. Five filters are used by librarians to translate request into searchable questions. They include defining or qualifying the subject, establishing the need for the information, pinpointing personal traits of the requester, exploring the relationship of the inquiry to the organization, and determining acceptable answers.[73] The rise in electronic document access has revolutionized rapid delivery of health sciences information, making desktop access to and electronic delivery of health sciences information the preferred method.

Reference

The reference process consists of three primary elements: information, the user, and the librarian.[74] Hospital libraries house a myriad of sources, which prove to be useful for answering factual questions. Virtually every book and journal in the collection is a potential information source. However, dictionaries, directories, catalogs, handbooks, encyclopedia, or similar publications are typically referred to as reference resources because of their format. The user or client is the person posing the question, who generally is unsure of what information they need or the best method of locating needed information.

The role of librarians in the current problem-based hospital environment is to provide the knowledge that facilitates expert performance. The hospital librarian interprets the reference question, evaluates available resources, and identifies the exact resource to supply the answer.[9] Reference services can be broadly divided into three functional areas: 1) information retrieval; 2) information access; and 3) information management. Performing reference services, librarians have traditionally given personal assistance to clientele making the best use of collections to satisfy their information needs. Librarians use their skills and acquired techniques to access, sort, transfer, evaluate, filter, and disseminate information.[75] The publication of printed catalogs and bibliographies, the accessibility of online catalogs and multimedia databases, along with the organizing of the national interlibrary loan system (DOCLINE) have widened the range of resources available to the individual library client.[76] As a result, librarians are increasingly called on to help clientele determine the most efficient tools to use in their research. In hospital libraries, assistance includes explaining the layout of the library, the process of locating material, and the availability of services. Also, providing guidance about information on subject-specific medical resources is a popular service. This process is greatly expanded by the enormous increases in research worldwide, the virtual explosion of Web-based electronic resources, and the quantity of language formats available for media and publications.

Virtual reference, the delivery of personalized information resources to users physically outside of the library, is a sophisticated use of Web-based technology, yet only being explored and contemplated in the majority of hospital libraries.[77] The potential benefits of using a virtual reference chat service to answer remote patron questions has not been convincing conveyed to hospital librarians. Providing key services through the Internet has challenged hospital libraries to embrace the library without walls philosophy. It has become increasingly important to reach those people who don't come to the library to request library services. Chat services offering personal and immediate connections provide a place to connect with users and non-library users offering them both convenience and information service. Questions directed to virtual reference services ideally are ready reference questions that can be answered quickly. Complex labor intensive reference questions are often answered via e-mail following the chat session, if additional resources are need. Many question can be answered satisfactorily using, features such as co-browsing or page pushing that facilitate librarians demonstrating use of electronic resources. Firewall issues and Hospital Information Technology department restrictions block many hospital libraries from using popular free chat based utilities like AOL instant messenger, MSN messenger, Yahoo! Messenger, Google Talk, or trillion basic. Commercial services such as Docutek, Tutor.com, Live Chat and QuestionPoint are expensive and often out of reach for hospital libraries. Hospital libraries are finding ways to work cooperatively with Information Technology to uncover the benefit of the free virtual reference environment.[77]

Information Services

The subject search is one of the areas on which advancing technology has had the greatest impact. The transformation from timed fee-based database searching, to CD-ROM access, to free Web-based access to MEDLINE has provided hospital librarians the opportunity to search more thoroughly and use specialized features to create a variety of enhanced services. In many hospital libraries, a variety of computer-based information retrieval systems provide access to materials on- and off-site. For example, one development in subject access increases the amount of information that is available within library catalogs by including details from the table of contents, a book's index or keywords us. Other systems provide enhanced features that include full-text articles, and links to related articles. "These full-text references eliminate intermediate steps characteristic of older systems requiring users to first perform an electronic search and then obtain the articles themselves in print."[78]

MEDLINE

The availability of electronic resources has made a dramatic impact on today's health care professionals' access to information. The need for information services in a hospital setting has rapidly changed as the virtual library emerges. A trend equally important is the ongoing role hospital librarians play in creating, strengthening, reshaping, and transforming hospital libraries into integrated knowledge management centers.[63]

The literature search is one of the primary services of hospital libraries. MEDLINE, the National Library of Medicine's database of references provide access to more than 16 million articles published in 5000 biomedical journals. The subject scope of MEDLINE is biomedicine and health, broadly defined to encompass those areas of the life sciences, behavioral sciences, chemical sciences, and bioengineering needed by health professionals and others engaged in basic research and clinical care, public health, health policy development, or related educational activities. MEDLINE also covers life sciences vital to biomedical practitioners, researchers, and educators, including aspects of biology, environmental science, marine biology, plant and animal science as well as biophysics and chemistry."[79] Many of the listings also have short summaries of the article (abstracts) and quite often a link to the complete article (full-text) through BioMed Central or a link to the journal. Most of the articles found in MEDLINE are written for health professionals and thus are complex and not easily understood by layman.[80]

In 1997, the National Library of Medicine opened up MEDLINE (the world's largest database of medical literature) to the public on the Internet free of charge. PubMed is the National Library of Medicine's search service that provides access to MEDLINE, PreMEDLINE, and other related databases, with links to participating on-line journals. Access to medical information is provided by a number of aggregators supporting access to several biomedical databases and electronic journals using one common search protocol. Aggregators such as OVID, EBSCO, Thomson, Elsevier, and McGraw Hill producing such products as MD Consult, Up-to-Date, DynaMed, STAT! Ref, and many other products are commonly used in larger hospital libraries and those affiliated with teaching hospitals, whereas smaller hospital libraries depend primarily on free access to PubMed and its related biomedical resources.[9]

Current Awareness Services

Hospital libraries provide current awareness services sometimes called SDI's (Selective Dissemination of Information or Alert Services). These services set up literature searches on specific topics that are run automatically to provide current updated information. Patrons are alerted periodically via e-mail, receiving URLs to web pages of automatically generated updates to their selected topic and of new journal issues, and new publications pertinent to their field. This type of service can increase a user's ability to keep current and may have a positive impact on efficiency and productivity.[81] Some hospital libraries use (TOC) or Table of Content Services as a means of promoting review of current article titles. The TOC allows library clientele to view online contents pages of journals selected from the hospital's list of serials. These services are ideal for keeping patrons up-to-date on their areas of interest.[82] For those hospital libraries unable to subscribe to fee-based TOC services, free alerting service such as Pubcrawler, BioMail and Jade whose scans are updated daily to PubMed databases and provides individuals with listings of new database entries that match their research interests.[83] Other less expensive alternative methods such as scanning of tables of content pages and locally distributing them to enables libraries to increase access to journals and, more importantly, provides a viable alternative to routing and potentially losing journals. Some small hospital libraries still use routing of new journals from office to office as their method of increasing clientele awareness of recent journal literature.

Interlibrary Loan and Document Delivery

Interlibrary loan (ILL) is the process of borrowing and lending books, audiovisuals, and journal issues to other libraries for use by library clientele. Interlibrary loan is a long-time cooperative effort among all types of libraries, as are serials union list and cooperative cataloging projects on the Internet, such as EPIC/OCLC (Online Computer Library Center) and RLIN (Research Libraries Information Network).[84] Document delivery is the process of delivering journal articles or photocopies of needed documents. Hospital libraries use DOCLINE, a comprehensive routing system of the National Library of Medicine to facilitate reciprocal borrowing and lending of library materials from hospitals and major medical libraries around the world. Hospital libraries routinely use DOCLINE as their primary electronic network for requesting loans and lending resources.[85] More than 57,000 libraries in 112 countries and territories around the world use the Online Computer Library Center (OCLC) services to locate, acquire, catalog, lend and preserve library materials. Hospital libraries use OCLC to locate nonmedical documents, reports, proceedings, and other nontraditional resources.[86] Larger hospital libraries sometimes purchase software that allows them to manage their resource sharing activities. OCLC's ILLiad Resource Sharing Management Software helps libraries automate routine interlibrary loan functions, which increases productivity and dramatically reduces paperwork.[87] All of the library's borrowing, lending and document delivery activities are managed through a single Windows-based interface, which allows library patrons to submit and track their own requests via the Web. Prospero, an open access Document Delivery System is available free of charge to libraries seeking low cost resources management software.[88]

Outsourcing

An alternative to in-house initiation of document delivery, cataloging and other library services used by some hospital libraries is the contracting of library services to independent information professionals, information brokers and consultants. Hospital libraries use independent information professionals or consultants when patron expectation of rapid delivery increases and more comprehensive document delivery services are needed. When budgetary constraints prevent hospital libraries from supplying needed materials, library clientele are sometimes referred directly to independent information professionals or consultants often affiliated with the Association of Independent Information Professionals (AIIP).[89] The Association of Independent Information Professional members are owners of firms providing such information-related services as online and manual research, document delivery, database design, library support, consulting, writing, publishing, library space planning, website design strategic planning and overall information architecture.[90]

Online Access to Other Library Collections

For years, libraries shared information about the resources held in library collection through union catalogs available on microfiche or in print using the consortium approach. Access to Web-based union catalogs has enhanced the hospital libraries access to library resources owned by other libraries. These catalogs have been redesigned and have evolved to Web-based products, such as WorldCat, OCLC's union catalog. WorldCat is the world's largest collaboratively-produced network of library services built upon a massive database of bibliographic, ownership and other forms of metadata. The core WorldCat database contains the merged catalogs of thousands of OCLC member libraries and is collectively maintained by those members' information professionals. WorldCat includes over 88 million bibliographic records and serves more than 57,000 participating libraries worldwide.[91] Hospital librarians search the computerized catalog holding of libraries around the world to locate needed resources. The National Libraries of Medicine offers hospital libraries an invaluable resource for locating hard to find materials, foreign journal titles, and obscure publications.[92,93] Hospital libraries use NLM's online catalog, LocatorPlus (http://locatorplus.gov) to find biomedical articles held by academic medical centers, hospitals, and other health care agencies. LocatorPlus is continuously updated and includes: over 1.2 million catalog records for books, audiovisuals, journals, computer files, and other materials in the Library's collections. Holdings information for journals and other materials, links from catalog records to Internet resources, including online journals and circulation status information for materials, even those on-order or in-process at NLM can be found in LocatorPlus.[94]

ADMINISTRATIVE AND MANAGEMENT

The hospital library manager will spend much time in the future developing analytical skills to look more at what can be rather than at what presently is the state of hospital libraries. Steven O'Connor notes that a change in thinking must occur, suggesting that library managers must understand not only what business the hospital library is in but what business it should or could be in.[95] The use of new cutting edge technologies, more stringent legal requirements, heightened standards of accountability and outcomes driven services have dramatically impacted the management of services, staffing, and physical facilities of hospital libraries. Hospital library managers are responsible for budgeting and personnel management, as well as developing policies for acquisitions, planning, marketing, fundraising and service evaluation. Hospital library managers analyze customer satisfaction data to restructure priorities, functions, and supporting services of the library. Keeping up with the enormous amount of information available, forging new methods for 24/7 access to up-to-date biomedical resources, and mapping out unique approaches to outreach are only a fraction of the managerial decisions that hospital librarians face each day. Like managers of other hospital departments, hospital library managers use tried and true participatory and shared models of management to engage employees in the day-to-day operations of the library. In addition to making organizational information decisions, hospital library managers review policies and procedures, comply with internal organizational mandates and create, implement and sustain a vision of service for the hospital library. Hospital library manager must face the hard cold fact that perception of service bears far greater importance than reality. These managers exhibiting intelligence, creativity, and leadership must be willing to leave their comfort zone and begin to mold and shape the perception of reality of their clientele.

Fiscal Management

A mission statement quickly and concisely identifies the role of the one-person or multiperson library, connects it to the parent organizations' mission, and describes briefly what the library does. As part of their administrative duties, hospital managers develop skills in preparing, presenting, and negotiating appropriate budgets. Collective concortial purchasing, creative fund-raising, and project-specific grant writing are alternative means of acquiring needed funds for operational, personnel, and capital expenditures. The hospital funding environment, particularly for technology purchases has become very competitive. Many hospital libraries must prepare business cases and cost savings analysis that illustrate the return-on-investment expected to justifying expenditure of large technology purchases. The National Networks of

Libraries of Medicine and the Institute for Museums and Libraries Services are but a few of the national organizations that offer to large and small hospital libraries, funding options through grants proposal solicitation.

Human Resources

Hospital library managers are responsible for the recruitment, hiring, evaluation, professional development, and ultimately the retention of staff in the hospital library. It is not uncommon to have a library staff range from .5fte to 5fte. Regardless of staff size, staff development is important to personnel enrichment. In today's hospital setting, library team dynamics are extremely important. Librarians serve on teams with their library colleagues, as well as with colleagues from other hospital departments and other hospital affiliates. Working in a library presents unique service-oriented situations, as a vast percentage of your requests come from unscheduled encounters, walk in, phone in or e-mail request. This creates special time management challenges, whereas in most other professional environments clients are meticulously scheduled.[96] Balancing the management of time, setting goals and priorities and appropriately delegating responsibilities are proven strategic skill sets that hospital librarians and hospital library managers must fully embrace. In the fast paced clinical environment where scheduled agendas can quickly be erased by the need for clinical information to deal with a medical emergency, it is imperative that hospital librarians master the art of providing just in time, right on time health information.

Marketing

Marketing perpetuates the hospital library focus on customer-centered approaches to promoting health and wellness. Hospital librarians continuously reevaluate services and target markets to assess the true value of library services. Establishing library advocates among library users and supporters to champion library causes is a strategically insightful way of avoiding budget cuts and staff downsizing. The Internet and newly created social technologies have presented fresh approaches to reaching target markets. Using resources like Blogs, Wikis, Podcast and unlikely sources for advertising like Facebook or Utube hospital libraries can provide the visibility that the library needs to attract new patrons and meet the new generation of users where they connect. For many hospital libraries word-of-mouth marketing has worked for years, however, as hospital systems grow and expand, more and more hospital libraries develop more formalized marketing efforts. National Medical Librarians month in October and National Library Week in April are great times to devote to marketing of current and new services for the library. New marketing techniques such as merchandising can be useful to hospital libraries in drawing attention to

their consumer health information collection.[97] The fundamental function of merchandising is to encourage the customer to discover and select more than they anticipated. Strategically placed, book features prominently displayed and other powerful illustration play a crucial role in steering customer traffic. Merchandising does the job of maximizing turnover of popular categories or drawing attention to under-utilized parts of the collection. The overall objective is to create interest and prompt impulse loans.[98]

Planning

The rapid pace of change and the transformation from traditional library roles to new roles supporting advanced technology and electronic environments requires library staff to routinely conduct service audits and environmental scans. Strategic planning and scenario planning are critical component of an efficient, cost effective hospital library operation plan. To stay agile and responsive to client needs hospital libraries need to examine their services, processes, and structure.[99] Using the mission and vision of the hospital the hospital librarian examines the environment to develop an environmental scan, conducts a SWOT analysis, and map out goals supported by measurable SMART objectives. Developing a staff strategic plan for 3–5 years is recommend, although the library staff should review the strategic plan often to make sure that their services, collection development, educational programs, and capital expenditure are aligned with the stated goals.

Space planning supports the library's strategic direction, creating a reality of collaborations and virtual service. The hospital library manager charged with the task of planning renovations and new construction of hospital libraries space seeks to blend high tech and high touch services. Using vision, knowledge of operations, functional process analysis, and flexibility, library managers can assist architects in designing space that is both aesthetically pleasing and functionally sound. The current trend in libraries is to devote a significant portion of the space to computers and collaborative meeting space.[100] Electronic resources have reduced some of the needs for collection space but surplus workspace in hospitals is always at a premium and rarely available.

As demands for hospital resources increase, hospital library managers face competition for limited resources, and therefore, must continuously cultivate their management skills and fiscal resources to be competitive and effective. The future hospital library manager will need to have a more global outlook, applying more flexible and creating more options for developing plans for the hospital library.

Assessment

The Medical Library Association Standards 6 for medical librarians recommends that librarians provide evidence of an ongoing assessment of the knowledge-based information needs of the organization and best practice.[101,102] The hospital librarian is charged with developing and implementing a plan to provide appropriate resources, services, and technology to meet those identified needs. Library decision makers can more accurately evaluate the quality of current library services, and appropriately allocate scarce resources when assessments of library performance are properly designed.[103]

Using many adapted variations of formal and informal tools, techniques and methodologies hospital librarians assess the knowledge-based information needs of the hospital or health care organization. Assessments that incorporate, opinions and feedback from library users and nonusers can play a significant role in directing the library's strategic path.[104] Some of the more popular techniques used include focus groups, surveys, usage patterns analysis, environmental scans, strategic planning, inventory, budgetary planning, and one-on-one interactions with health care leaders focusing on clinical and organizational information needs.

ORGANIZATIONAL CONTRIBUTIONS

Access to the Internet

Staff access to Internet services is available in most hospital libraries; however, public access to the Internet may not be as accessible, depending on the size of the library, the availability of computer workstations, and type of Internet connections available. When the computer to user ratio changes from "one to one" to "many to one" a significant change in how people relate to health information can be expected. Libraries use the Internet to access resources in response to reference questions, for searches on specific data, providing public access to customers, participating in listserv or discussion groups, and relaying resources electronically to their customer.[74] Constructing home pages for World Wide Web access has become a vital activity in hospital libraries. Library staff participates in defining policies and setting guidelines, designing user-friendly interfaces, and producing easy access to all inclusive electronic information resources. Community hospitals in rural and isolated areas have traditionally lacked the infrastructure for institution-wide access to the Internet, so dial-up access is used as a low-cost, low-risk means of access to the Internet for the hospital library. Using the Internet to connect community hospitals with major research centers is particularly important especially in areas sparsely populated and where large distances separate facilities.[74] Advances in telecommunication and information technologies have been the foundation of connectivity for small and community hospitals.[105] Hospital libraries that directly access the Internet are connected through the organizations' computer network. As with so many other

initiative in community hospitals cost remains a major barrier to establishing direct connections to the Internet. The National Libraries of Medicine recognizes the role of information in the provision of care and have developed, through the Regional Medical Libraries, Library Improvement Project Grants and Express Welcome Grants to assist community hospitals in getting equipment and Internet Service Providers to connected to the Internet.[106]

Hospital librarians play a central role in introducing the Internet to clinical settings. Trends show a rapid increase in the Internet's importance as a source of medical information. The Internet has the potential to empower patients and to bring evidence into medical practice, but also to facilitate reference questions, instruction and seamless access to endless health sciences resources. External information resources continue to be more affordable and more readily available to hospital libraries of all sizes. These external resources help create a network of virtual resources that expands the collection of even the smallest hospital library. To meet the information needs of health professionals, many librarians are using the Internet to access NLM databases and other specialized databases for document transmission, search training tutorials, extend library hours with after hours access, connect directly to NLM publications and other resources, and participate in professional discussion groups and electronic mail.[107] The vast amount of current information on the Internet and the relative ease with which it can be searched make it today's best medium for health research.

Customized Services

Hospital librarians are information experts who can decipher the vast body of information available in print and nonprint resources. Along with providing information on what is available additionally they customize search strategies that help locate the exact information needed. As an accepted organizational information experts hospital librarians participate on internal committees, special task force, new project initiative and as vital members of the information management team.

As educational programs and the need for continuing education expand, hospital libraries provide medical students, residents, health care providers and hospital staff with resources for participation in distance learning, technology application, social networking connections and system-wide collaborations. Likewise they provide opportunities to access continuing education programs using cutting-edge technologies, such as podcasting, webinars, video streaming, web casting, and using other digitally formatted media.

Services for Decision Makers

Hospital administrators play a vital role, managing hospitals, outpatient clinics, hospices, long-term care facilities and drug-abuse treatment centers. The hospital administrator's primary job is to make sure the hospital operates efficiently and provide optimal medical care to patients. Their abundant responsibilities sometimes require the assistance of support staff such as hospital librarians. Administrators focus on expanding existing programs and services and developing new ones for preventive medicine and systematic research, in research oriented hospital. Administrators in teaching hospitals focus on pursuits necessary to educate future doctors. They plan and monitor departmental activities, evaluate health care professionals, create and update policies, develop medical treatment standards, continuously improve quality patient care services, and proactively participate in fund-raising and community health planning.[108] Hospital administrators must keep up with innovations and advances in the medical and health care environment, computer and information technology, diagnostic and therapeutic equipment, government regulations, health insurance industry trends, and financial options. Hospital libraries provide the comprehensive, reliable information.[108] Hospital administrators need to make critical decisions about the myriad relevant health issues and the exponential changes and challenges in health care. The hospital library serves the administrative and health care needs of the administrators, supplying them with the tool needed to compare cost, review trends, assess feasibility and analyze return-on-investment. The foundation for administrators' priority setting criteria are interwoven in the mission of hospital libraries. Hospital library services support the organizations' strategic direction, supplies research for government regulation compliance, reinforces education and research through scholarly resource access, provides clinical evidence to insure clinical competence, and partners with patients and communities encouraging coordination, collaboration and seamless access to health information resources.[109] Business resources such as *Business Week*, and the *Harvard Business Review*, in addition to newspapers, news wires and other business related databases are frequently searched and filtered by hospital librarians, to retrieve data, statistics, trends, regulations, standards, and data-driven information that impacts hospital policies and procedures. While doctors strive to keep the pulse regulated and the heart beating, the hospital administrators keep the hospital alive and vibrant with the expert assistance of hospital librarians who keep them well-informed and data-driven.

Clinical Medical Librarianship

Clinical medical librarians (CML) provide special services to teaching hospitals by participating in medical staff rounds with assigned clinical teams noting clinical questions as they arise. Clinical medical librarian services allow hospital librarians to be highly visible and integrated into research, teaching, and clinical services.[110] The presence of the clinical medical librarian in the hospital corridors often inspires clinicians to remember questions they had forgotten to pursue with the library. The clinical medical librarian is seen as a valuable team member in health care education and delivery. When clinical cases are presented, and discussed the clinical medical librarian is able to recognize and respond to information needs that are never formally voiced or directly requested. The clinical medical librarian sees medical problem solving and decision making take place in the actions and the informal, abbreviated language of the health care practitioner. This gives the clinical medical librarian an opportunity to learn how knowledge-based information is used and to understand clinicians' requests more clearly.[111] The future of clinical librarianship is deeply rooted in health sciences informatics and the Informationist. Health Sciences informatics has been defined as science that deals with the structure, acquisition, and use of health related information. Florance defines an informationist as one who is "cross-trained in medicine, computer science and information science."[112] The role of the Informationist is to clearly understand the principles of clinical work and information science. The ultimate responsibility is to enable clinicians to apply better judgment based on improved use of medical literature.[109] Davidoff estimates that of the 6500 U.S. acute care hospitals, only about 200 have implemented clinical librarianship programs due to the lack of financial incentives, Several funding ideas have surfaced such as, inclusion of cost in telemedicine grants and demonstrating information value to improved outcomes and cost reduction to the Health Care Finance Administration to justify reimbursement.[112]

Health Literacy

Physician–patient communication is vital to patients complying with physician instruction; however, research shows that patients have problems understanding medical instructions from physicians. The use of medical jargon, the lack of confirmation that patients understand instructions, and the delivery of too much information at one time contribute to low health literacy. At the end of the medical encounter, patients remember less than half of what the physician tried to explain, and they may be uncertain about what steps to take next.[113]

Thirty million Americans are below basic literacy levels and are unable to perform literacy task above simple, basic interactions, according to the 2003 National Assessment of Adult Literacy. Another 63 million are only able to read and understand short, everyday text, placing them at the Basic literacy level.[114] Health Literacy is defined simply as the ability to read, write, and understand health information. Increasing attention has been given to the provision of health information to patients, families, caregivers, and the public. The American Hospital Association (AHA) has stated that health education is an integral part of high-quality patient care and has issued a Patient's Bill of

Rights, expressing patient's rights to obtain understandable information concerning diagnosis, treatment, prognosis, and support documentation for informed consent.[115] Hospital libraries have been increasingly engaged in exhibiting their capabilities to provide easy to read, understandable information to patients. At the same time, new consumer health information services have been incorporated in hospital libraries, aiming to combine the subject expertise of the hospital library with the accessibility of the public library. The amount of published literature on health topics for lay people has expanded exponentially. The shift to consumer health information has been encouraged by government health policies that emphasize consumer's right to choose. In 1991, the Patient's Charter, which emphasizes patient's rights to receive health care on the basis of clinical need, regardless of their ability to pay, was launched by the government. More importantly for libraries, the charter guarantees patients the right to be given clear explanations of any treatment proposed, including risks or alternatives, before they decide on treatment.[116] The Center for Clear Health Communication provides many tools to help libraries and health educators select easy to read materials and create health care documents using minimal jargon and simple easy to follow instructions.

Many contemporary patients expect to be educated about their medical conditions and treatment options. In response to these expectations, hospital libraries provide consumer health information written in layman terms to patients and their families. Books, magazines, videos, and computer-based resources are available to answer questions dealing with patient health concerns. The Medical Library Association has defined the role of the medical librarian in the provision of consumer health information. Their responsibilities are to determine the most prevalent diseases and to identify the most authoritative resources pertaining to these diseases.[117]

Hospital librarians often use the National Library of Medicine's (NLM) MedlinePlus database, http://www.medlineplus.gov to locate easy to read patient education materials, drug information, and interactive tutorials. MedlinePlus provides access to MEDLINE and numerous other helpful tools, including a medical encyclopedia, several medical dictionaries, a drug reference guide, and general health information. MedlinePlus also includes detailed reports on the diagnosis, prognosis, and treatment of numerous medical conditions, along with links to hundreds of reputable health organizations.[118] Hundreds of consumer health and layman-oriented web sites are currently available on the World Wide Web; however, the absence of authority of much of the information is a formidable problem. Different methods of quality control are being proposed for information on the Internet. One promising approach is automatic downstream filtering, the process of software (browser) checking of metadata-labeled information to determine if the information meets the personal quality requirement of the searcher. Metadata

describes the content and context of the information, thus allowing the user to determine suitability of the information for individual use.[119] Hospital librarian also provide guidance on evaluating health information Web-site for accuracy and quality.

In recent years, there has been a growing body of research producing evidence on the positive effects of the provision of information to patients. These positive effects are noted as improved patient satisfaction, reductions in pain, fewer postoperative complications, shorter hospital stays, reduction in blood pressure, and improved self-management of conditions such as diabetes and kidney disease.[120] In 1991, a consensus statement was issued "underlining the effect of information giving." Two key areas were identified as benefits of giving health information: reduction of anxiety in patients and families and increased compliance with medical instruction given by care providers.[121] The power of information to produce a more informed, thus more compliant patient population is becoming evident. The provision of information to patients is equated to raising expectations, challenging professional mystiques and outdated ideas, sharing decision making, and most importantly, sharing power. All health care consumers need access to a wide variety of unbiased health information resources, regardless of their age, sex, educational level, socioeconomic status, or ethnicity.[122]

CONTRIBUTIONS TO OTHER HEALTH CARE ORGANIZATIONS

Participation in Cooperative Networks

"The focus of library cooperation is the network. The network is defined as, a group of individuals or organizations that are interconnected to form a system to accomplish some specific goal." Hospital librarians serve as knowledgeable guides through the maze of resources and as liaisons to networks with other libraries for resource sharing.[123] Hospital libraries participate in cooperative networks with the National Library of Medicine, other hospitals, and academic health science libraries to expand their base of available resources. Hospital libraries band together to form consortia that provide enrichment opportunities for hospital librarians, maximize purchasing power, and address community health needs. Hospital library consortia support law librarians and their thirst for medical information, public librarians, in their quest for medical information retrieval skills, and other special libraries seeking comparative medical information for benchmarking, innovative research and scholarly enrichment.

Loansome Doc

Library staff are extremely service-oriented, providing access not only to all categories of staff at the parent institution but frequently also to community health professionals not affiliated with the institution and to patients and their families. Many hospital libraries participate in the National Library of Medicine's program of supplying medical documents to health professionals not affiliated with their parent institution. Recent surveys show that usage of Loansome Doc is low. Additionally, the major barriers to use are cost and timeliness of the service.[124] Greater promotion of what Loansome Doc is and how it can benefit libraries can increase the number of participating libraries. While satisfaction of Loansome Doc end users is high, satisfaction could be increased with more help on the PubMed screen, more library training, and faster delivery methods.[125]

Loansome Doc is a service that allows nonaffiliated groups or individuals to set up an agreement to have a specified hospital library serve as their "home" library for retrieval of articles and library resources that they need. Independent unaffiliated physicians, attorneys, pharmaceutical companies, and other health care organization representatives search MEDLINE and then request photocopies of articles of interest via Loansome Doc. Copies are provided from the home library collection or requested by using the DOCLINE network.[126] These services are generally provided on a cost-recovery basis.

Hospital libraries advocate for access to authoritative up-to-date health information for all affiliated users. Hospital librarians provide an environment that discourages the digital divide by providing libraries with computers for access to technology and fostering an open attitude of cooperation.

FUTURE CHALLENGES

In the information age, sensitivity to the stresses of change affect information utilities like libraries as much as they do other organizations. In a time characterized by layoff, downsizing, rightsizing, restructuring and reengineering, the ability to look forward reflectively, and plan for significant transformation in health care is a huge challenge to all types of libraries, but especially hospital libraries. Future challenges for hospital libraries and the librarians that staff them will center on finding solutions to budgetary constraints, significant changes in user demands, and effects of massive technological changes. The continued need to reach out globally beyond physical walls, firewalls and country boundaries drives the vision of the global virtual library. Heighten pressure will engulf hospital libraries forcing them to continuously demonstrate their contribution to better health care outcomes through the provision of point-of-care access to information resources and services. The visual illustration of the hospital libraries' positive impact on the bottom line of the organization will also be a point of concern. Hospital libraries continue to be challenged to demonstrate their value through

research, outreach, making multiple resources available to patrons onsite and offsite, and revising data gathering. Concentrated effort will also be centered on improvement of dissemination operations, analyzing and evaluating self-help information access, mapping information activities to outcome measures analysis, and visibly supporting innovative problem-based learning, and evidence-based medicine practice.

Electronic Resources

Desktop access to online catalogs, bibliographic databases, and full-text journals is changing library use patterns.[127] Hospital libraries' shift from ownership of physical collections to licensing content for electronic resources has occurred quickly in support of medicine and science, despite budgetary limitations.[128] Changes in the practice of medicine and technological developments offer hospital librarians unprecedented opportunities to select and organize electronic resources, use the web to deliver content throughout the organization, and improve knowledge at the point-of-need. Due to the vast array of available electronic products, access protocol, and pricing structures hospital librarians are faced with anticipating the electronic resource needs of users, identifying leading resources, making sound budgetary decisions, efficiently managing the collection, and seamlessly organizing health information resources. The electronic resource marketplace requires much vigilance, considerable patience, and continuous evaluation. Hospital librarians employ several strategies to proactively stay ahead of the electronic resource curve, including accepting and marketing free trials from publishers; conducting user-based new product evaluation; monitoring and testing products directly marketed to clientele; beta testing new products and services; working with aggregators or re-publishers; joining vendor advisory boards; benchmarking institutional resources against competitors; and forming or joining a consortium for group negotiating and purchasing.[129] Access to electronic books and journals in large and small hospital libraries is due in part to publishers providing limited free access to electronic journals when print copies are purchased, and greatly attributed to shifts in physician's demands for easy to access information resources onsite and offsite. Hospital libraries continue to struggle with journal issues such as access vs. ownership. Constantly faced with electronic access issues ranging from content, licenses, cost, interfaces, technical presentation, and management of electronic journals, hospital librarians are called upon to develop new strategies for building the library's collection and integrate digital resources. Recent trends in hospital libraries shows evidence of a growing shift toward totally digital libraries in hospital settings.[130]

Electronic document delivery systems are setting the stage for exploitation of image technology and providing more global access to full-text digital images. The development of document delivery enhancement products, such as ILLiad and Prospero, to assist in the efficient management of document delivery processes have helped hospital librarians reduce turnaround time on delivered health care documents, improve customer service and better manage their electronic resource.[131] The quality standards of electronically delivered documents continues to improve as PDF (Portable Document Format) formatting of electronic documents is adopted nearly universally as the format of choice.[132] Hospital librarians join their academic counterparts to advocate for the adoption of HTML (Hypertext Markup Language), SGML (Standard Generalized Markup Language) and Open eBook, XML-based formats as the new standards for electronic content.[133]

Training in the use of electronic resources is extremely important in the hospital library. Not only are hospital librarians responsible for acquiring and organizing electronic content but they must assess the best ways to train hospital personnel in the effective location, access method and utilization of electronic resources.

Social Networking Technologies

Witnessing a rapid increase in the use of Web-based "collaborationware" in recent years has made hospital librarians begin to seek ways to implement this technology in the hospital library. Web 2.0 applications, particularly wikis, blogs, and podcasts, have been increasingly adopted by many health sciences libraries. This "collaborationware" offers the opportunity for powerful information sharing and ease of collaboration. Their ease of use and ability for rapid deployment make them desirable particularly for hospital libraries however, often hospital system firewalls prevent their implementation.[134]

Wikis are Web sites that can be edited by anyone who has access to them. The word "blog" is a contraction of "Web Log"—an online Web journal that can offer a resource rich multimedia environment. Podcasts are repositories of audio and video materials that can be "pushed" to subscribers, even without user intervention. These audio and video files can be downloaded to portable media players that can be taken anywhere, providing the potential for "anytime, anywhere" learning experiences (mobile learning). Wikis, blogs, and podcasts are all relatively easy to use, which partly accounts for their proliferation. The fact that there are many free and Open Source versions of these tools may also be responsible for their explosive growth. Web 2.0 sociable technologies and social software are presented as enablers in health care environments.[135] The most prevalent social networking technology includes: social networking services, collaborative filtering, social bookmarking, folksonomies, social search engines, file sharing and tagging, mashups, instant messaging, and online multiplayer games. The more popular Web 2.0 applications in education, namely wikis, blogs, and podcasts, are but the tip of the social software iceberg. Web 2.0 technologies represent a quite revolutionary way of managing and repurposing/remixing online information and knowledge repositories, including clinical and research information.[136]

As internal organization Information Technology departments loosen their restrictions on the use of social technologies in the hospital environment, hospital libraries will be challenged to incorporate these "collaborationware" technologies to more seamlessly connect, and collaborate with library patrons. The new social technologies combined with innovations with instructional technology create new digital learning environments for educating hospital staff in the use and location of digital resources. Research centered on information-retrieving patterns of clinicians and other focused groups will become more important in the design of libraries and the introduction of new services. As hospital libraries grapple with staffing issues, they will see an increased need for development of instructional interactive video media for provision of more seamless library tours, orientations, and bibliographic instruction.[137]

Evidence-Based Librarianship

The evidence-based movement has changed in response to health care; as a result, evidence-based healthcare has evolved with greater flexibility and adaptability for disciplines outside clinical medicine. Evidence-based librarianship (EBL) incorporates the decision-making framework, the basic process, and many similar research methods apparent in evidence-based medicine yet its' flexibility and adaptability are characteristics of evidence based health care.[138] The conceptual framework of evidence-based librarianship seeks to improve library practice using a combination of librarian experience and best evidence. It encourages the application of best evidence and the pursuit of increasingly rigorous research strategies. Hospital librarians are incorporating evidence based librarianship as they convert clinical information needs into answerable questions, tracking down and critically reviewing the best possible evidence, estimating benefits, judging value and ultimately developing clinical practice guidelines to efficiently guide future similar decisions.[139] The EBL process enables hospital librarians to focus on a specific problem in need of immediate attention thus integrating research findings into their daily practice.

The EBL process consists of formulating a practical question, searching for the evidence needed to answer the question, and systematically evaluating the gathered evidence for its usefulness and validity for answering the initial question.[138]

Health care professionals suffer from information overload and struggle to filter evidence relevant to their field. Hospital librarians provide filtering and delivery of information specifically tailored to the meet the needs of researchers and practitioner. One special need filled by hospital librarians is the production of systemic reviews. The systematic review process is the concept of evidence-based medicine (EBM), which Sackett defines as "the conscientious, explicit and judicious use of current evidence in making decisions about the care of individual patients."[140] One way hospital librarians provide support for EBM is by using the Cochrane method of conducting systematic reviews of the literature. The hospital librarian's training as an expert searcher, organizer, and analyzer uniquely quality them to conduct systematic reviews.[141]

Educational Role in Outreach

Hospital librarians are defining new expanded roles for supporting the educational needs of the hospital. As they do this they present a variety of opportunities to bring professional expertise to ongoing assessment and the development of best practice. New technologies provide new forums including using online instructional technology like Moodle to provide Web-based training.

Disparities in health between minority and majority populations have become a topic of high interest in the health care and information communities. Hospital librarians are aggressively embracing their role in working with physicians to develop solutions to issues addressing health disparities, patient safety, and environmental justice.[142] They design and implement personal digital assistants (PDA) programs to assist physicians in getting information at the point-of-care, and institute clinical librarianship programs allowing them to make clinical rounds with physicians, thus impacting decisions from the question's origin.

Hospital librarians play a significant role in reaching out to teach information access skill but also in teaching courses on information filtering, evidence-based medicine, interactive learning techniques, critical appraisal, editing and refereeing of online journal articles, and the construction of specialized knowledge bases to other health professionals in the community.[143] Teaching hands-on information retrieval instruction enhanced by computer-assisted instruction programs to facilitate problem-based learning skills and simulations for decision processes and strategies will strengthen patient-centered librarianship and solidify the role of hospital librarians as evidence educators. Hospital librarians will be challenged to search more complex information, analyzing and synthesizing results into packaged reviews while interacting with their clientele primarily by using electronic mail, blogs, wikis, electronic teaching platforms, podcasts, and other electronically linked networks.[144,145]

Digital Resources

As more hospitals merge into integrated health care systems, hospital librarians are challenged to function as outreach consultants, serving the needs of staff at off-site facilities. The rapid growth of scanning and digitizing technologies has provided new methods for retrieval and delivery of print documents, pictures, graphs, charts, and full text to off-site hospital staff. Portable Document Format (PDF) is the standard format for delivering full text of electronic journal and book resources.

The shift to wireless computer access, flat-screen technology, iPods and other Mp3 players, eBooks, sharper image handheld devices (as easy to read as paper), are presenting unique planning challenges for all health sciences libraries. Recent developments in computer technology have introduced us to the optical mouse, wireless networking, USB ports, jump drives, fiber optic and video transmission systems, for distance education, webinars for teleconferencing, Desktop computer applications have become more adaptable and interface with more customizable technology. Cellular telephone devices such as the iPhone now integrating telephones, iPod, Internet, cameras, blue tooth, and other technologies provide consumers with endless communication options.[146] Voice over Internet Providers (VoIP) are providing access to telephone service through internet connections. Given these innovative options hospital librarian focus on finding ways to integrate these new technologies to enhance seamless delivery of information solutions. The future for hospital libraries holds possibilities of teledesk located throughout the hospital allowing interactive visual and voice connections. Hospital libraries are faced with designing facilities and reallocating space to support wired and wireless technology while building platforms to integrate innovative connectivity and point-of-care information access.

In addition to the changes in the methods of information delivery, new forms of information that include "hypertext, cd and digital video interactives, expert systems, knowledge bases and virtual reality" show significant promise in providing a new qualitative approach to information delivery.

Value Added Service

"Value-added" is a marketing concept that expands or modified a product or service so that it has added value to the customer. For example, offering a MEDLINE search may be a basic service provided by the library; a value-added MEDLINE search is one where, the librarian has analyzed the search, selected several of the most relevant articles, and included full-text copies of these articles in a complete package.[147,148] Hospital librarians may even filter the articles included to provide a summary of the pertinent points outlined in the articles. Quality filtering is a service usually performed on research studies or clinical trial articles. It involves identifying the hypothesis of the study and extracting vital information from the article to give clinicians a clear picture of the type of research study conducted and the validity of the results.[149]

Hospital libraries continually seek to develop and promote value-added services to ensure customer satisfaction and quality service. One of the significant challenges for hospital librarians continues to be the use of knowledge-based information resources and new technologies to create Web portals for the provision of easy access to resources tailored to suit the institutions' unique needs. License agreements and institutional restrictions often limit patron access depending on their affiliation with the hospital.

Occurrence screening is a service that provides the opportunity for librarians to independently analyze raw quality improvement data to determine the overall need for information. Information provided through information screenings is distinctive in that it isn't a response to a specific case presented in the morning report; rather, occurrence screening educational packages address best practice patterns or state-of-the-art methods of patient care to anticipate and diminish future clinical problems.[150]

Communicating the role of information in the provision of care continues to challenge hospital librarians. However, as Quality Oversight Organizations (QOO) encourage community hospitals to embrace the concept of integrated information management for the improvement of quality, hospital librarians have begun to realize opportunities to incorporate Internet usage as a clinically indispensable tool.[151]

Knowledge Management

Knowledge is defined by Peter Drucker as "Information that changes something or somebody—either by becoming grounds for actions or by making an individual (or an institution) capable of different or more effective action."[152] Knowledge Management (KM) is a platform for implementing organizational change; by getting people to record knowledge (as opposed to data) and then share it. In short, it is a way of channeling raw data, into meaningful information.

The concepts of knowledge management is providing a new dimension in library service, as the collection and preservation of explicit (informal) internal knowledge is further explored and meshed with the application and use of tacit (formal) knowledge. KM is linked to what people know, and how what they know can support the organizational objectives. Based on assumptions of strategic planning, the time value of information, and cross-functional teams, KM deals with the most meaningful, practical, and purposeful ideas. KM is ever changing, value added, and visionary. The constant revision and updates of knowledge illustrate the importance of viewing KM as an ongoing process that draws upon pooled expertise, relationships, and alliances. The role of the hospital library in KM is to introduce the concept, provide knowledge expertise and generate enthusiasm, buy-in, and motivation, encouraging managers to work together toward reaching common knowledge preservation goals.[153]

Hospital Librarians will be challenged to share their expertise in categorization and segregation of knowledge to create and update working databases and digital libraries, allowing more efficient access to specific, recent, relevant information through keyword or subject searching. Hospital librarians can also provide more information support through participation in research teams that use information-based techniques such as meta-analysis to blend integral digital and traditions knowledge.[154]

Electronic Health Record and Electronic LATCH

The merging of information technology and health care has contributed to the shifting of attitudes from health care provider to consumer and facilitated the creation of the Electronic Health Record (EHR). The patient centered electronic health record is designed as a cross-institutional, longitudinal information record aimed at establishing a record that contains all consumer health information from "the cradle to the grave."[155] Hospital libraries have the opportunity to challenge conventional thinking about the (EHR) to offer Literature Attached to Chart (LATCH) programs to expand the library's patient care support and compliment other health information. LATCH programs will enable health care personnel to request and review, up-to-date disease specific articles attached directly to the electronic medical record as URLs, PDF or scanned document. Librarians will be able to document evidence to support clinical decisions, thus potentially contributing to reduction in medical errors and cost. LATCH programs will also provide documentation of physician's verbal request for literature to support a diagnosis or treatment, thus providing supporting documentation to help resolve legal disputes.[156]

Good communication between patients, providers and librarians is an essential component of high-quality patient centered health care. Communication between patients and providers has traditionally occurred through in-person, telephone, or paper-based encounters. Due to the evolution of technology patients and providers are enabled to communicate electronically to obtain follow-up test results, collect information before a visit, schedule appointments, send reminders, ask questions, renew prescriptions and in the near future to request health information for addition to their electronic medical record.[157] The EHR offers great potential for hospital librarians to develop and evaluate access protocol, research information seeking behaviors, manage personalized health information web page development and facilitate usage of digital resources.

Consumer Health Trends

One of the highest priorities in today's hospital is the provision of quality care to patients. Consumer health information services make important contributions to consumer choice, safety, literacy, and quality health care. They indicate the need to set up networks for shared development of quality standards and training. Consumer health databases in all formats and the extension of services into new areas that examine quality of care and effectiveness of treatment are warranted. Attention needs to be focused on developing networks to maintain current awareness and creating more standards for best practice.[158] Hospital librarians will be challenged to assist consumers and hospital staff in checking the authenticity and integrity of Internet sites and providing consumers with a higher level of decision-enabling information. A congressional report published in 1988 points to new emphasis on scientific reviews of the outcome and effectiveness of treatment.

> The report states that providing information to consumers on quality of care enables people to avoid poor quality providers and educates the public on the concept of quality. It also injects competition into the medical marketplace and stimulates clinicians to improve practice.[159]

For this to take place, hospital libraries must begin to support consumers with a more focused level of information. Information should be provided on the mortality rates of hospitals and the adverse effects of treatment, including nosocomal (hospital acquired) infections. Disciplinary actions against doctors and patient satisfaction results should be readily available to help individuals make informed personal choices.[160] Evidence-based Librarianship seeks to provide replicable standards for information retrieval and dissemination. The challenge of information providers is to find a way to translate this technical information into digestible information that patients and their families can understand and use to make more informed health care decisions. The creation of the individual health record is an excellent start. This record will allow patients to track their medical care in all aspects of care. This record is a logical place to have literature searches about conditions and disordered recorded to assist the physician in providing optimal care and monitoring the literature as it related to your health conditions.[161]

CONCLUSION

"Clearly, for hospital libraries to survive, their existence must be validated and their contributions must be shown to be consistent with the overall goals of the hospitals they serve."[162] The future of hospital libraries depend on their ability to promulgate new images of hospital librarian's work that convey professionalism, documented value and quality. Hospital libraries are transforming into hubs of electronically based research, where hospital librarians provide practical, workable solutions to the information

challenges of the constantly changing world of evidence-based health care. Balancing information resource formats, cutting edge technologies, patient safety concerns, innovative social networks of communication, and an environment centered on Evidence Based Health Care will continue to create unique challenges for hospital libraries.[163] As hospital libraries continue to reengineer themselves, define new roles, focus on resource access and service excellence, the intangible and tangible value of health care information at-the-point of care will become more apparent. Hospital libraries and librarians must take the lead in proactively identifying and adopting new and changing responsibilities. Hospital librarians must take the lead in developing essential evaluative measures, ideas, energy, and relationships through out the hospital to promote and market the vision, mission and value of the hospital library. As Garfield states, "unless the hospital library becomes fully recognized as a legitimate part of the medical facility, cost-conscious administrators will use outdated models of library service to cut library budgets."[164]

Hospital libraries will serve as the gateway to the application of new creative ways to use internal wikis, comment-enabled internal blogs and other collaborative tools. Hospital libraries will more thoroughly explore the applications of web 2.0 technology, such as creating internal podcast lab to enable users to generate podcast, and creating user generated content tagging, making content easier to locate.[165] Hospital Libraries will be challenged to help create new knowledge tools, using such as organization-specific mashups, to integrate internal information with open source content, creating new discovery tools.[166]

REFERENCES

1. Myers, G.W. Medical libraries in hospitals. Med. Libr. Hist. J. 1905, 3 (4), 282–287.
2. Wolfgram, P.A. Hospital libraries in the United States: Historical antecedents. Bull. Med. Libr. Assoc. 1985, 73, 32–38.
3. Thompson, K.S. America's oldest medical library: The Pennsylvania Hospital. Bull. Med. Libr. Assoc. 1956, 44 (4), 428–430.
4. http://www.uphs.upenn.edu/paharc/timeline/1751/tline4.html.
5. Holst, R. Hospital libraries in perspective. Bull. Med. Libr. Assoc. 1991, 79 (1), 1–9.
6. Culp, R.W. The Mount Sinai Hospital Library, 1883 to 1970. Bull. Med. Libr. Assoc. 1972, 60 (3), 471–490.
7. Annan, G. The Medical Library Association in retrospect 1937–1967. Bull. Med. Libr. Assoc. 1998, 86 (2), 270–278.
8. Brandon, A.; Hill, D. Selected list of books and journals for the small medical library. Bull. Med. Libr. Assoc. 1985, 73 (2), 176–205.
9. Kellerman, F.R. Introduction to Health Sciences Librarianship: A Management Handbook, Greenwood Press: Westport, CT, 1997; 21–73.

10. *AHA Hospital Statistics 2009*. American Hospital Association: Washington, 2008.

11. *National Library of Medicine Classification*, 4th Revised Ed.; National Library of Medicine: Bethesda, MD, 1981.

12. Glitz, B. The changing status of hospital libraries 1984 to 1989: Characteristics and services in Region 7 of the national network of libraries of medicine. Bull. Med. Libr. Assoc. **1992**, *80*, 179–184.

13. Quinn, J.; Rogers, M. Study shows hospital libraries save lives. Libr. J. October 15, **1991**, *116* (17), 12.

14. Lorri Zipperer, M.A.; Sykes, J. The role of librarians in patient safety: Gaps and strengths in the current culture. J. Med. Libr. Assoc. **2004**, *92* (4), 498–500.

15. Bloomquist, H., Rees, A.M., Stearns, N.S., Yast, H., Eds. *Library Practice in Hospitals: A Basic Guide;* Press of Case Western Reserve University: Cleveland, OH, 1972; 13.

16. Johnson, B.C. Services an integrated hospital library can and cannot provide. ALA Bull. **1969**, *63*, 1554–1559.

17. Schwartz, D.G. Medical education and faculty development: A new role for the health sciences librarian. Bull. Med. Libr. Assoc. **1995**, *83* (4), 483–489.

18. Hill, D.R.; Stickell, H.N. Brandon/Hill selected list of books and journals for the small medical library. Bull. Med. Libr. Assoc. **1999**, *87* (2), 145–148.

19. *National Library of Medicine Classification*, 4th Ed. U.S. Dept. of Health and Human Services, NIH: Bethesda, MD, 1981; vii.

20. McVoy, J.M. Program planning for the community teaching hospital medical library. Bull. Med. Libr. Assoc. **1987**, *75*, 122–124.

21. http://www.aamc.org/teachinghospitals.htm.

22. http://www.aamc.org.

23. Teunissen, P.W.; Scheele, F.; Scherpbier, A.J.; van der Vleuten, C.P.; Boor, K.; van Luijk, S.J.; van Diemen-Steenvoorde, J.A. How residents learn: Qualitative evidence for the pivotal role of clinical activities. Med. Educ. August **2007**, *41* (8), 763–770.

24. MySpace, Facebook and Other Social Networking Sites: Hot Today, Gone Tomorrow? Published May 03, 2006 in Knowledge@Wharton.

25. Bunyan, L.E.; Lutz, E.M. Marketing the hospital library to nurses. Bull. Med. Libr. Assoc. **1991**, *79* (2), 223–225.

26. Doyle, J.D. Knowledge-based information management: Implications for information services. Med. Ref. Serv. Q. Summer **1994**, *13* (2), 85–97.

27. Westendorf, J.J. Magnet recognition program. Plast. Surg. Nurs. April **2007**, *27* (2), 102–104.

28. Weeks, S.K.; Smith, B.C.; Hubbartt, E. Magnet recognition for nursing excellence—Is your organization there yet?. Rehabil. Nurs. **2006**, *31* (2), 48–51.

29. Lundmark, V.A.; Hickey, J.V. The magnet recognition program: Developing a national magnet research agenda. J. Nurs. Care Qual. **2007**, *22* (3), 195–198.

30. Gilbert, C.M. Challenges in health care information transfer: The role of hospital libraries. Bull. Med. Libr. Assoc. **1991**, *79* (4), 405–408.

31. Paradise, A. Why the Joint Commission on Accreditation of Healthcare Organizations should add new regulations regarding libraries. J. Med. Libr. Assoc. **2004**, *92* (2), 166–168.

32. *The Complete Guide to the 1997 Hospital Survey Process*; JCAHO: Oakbrook Terrace, IL, 1997; 168–170.

33. Schyve, P.D. *Access to Information: A Critical Component of Continuous Quality Improvement in Hospitals.* Information STAT: RX for Hospital Quality National Library of Medicine Teleconference, 1992.

34. Oliver, K.B.; Roderer, N.K. Working towards the informationist. Health Inform. J **2006**, *12* (1), 41–48.

35. JCAHO. The Joint Commission releases improving America's hospitals: A report on quality and safety. Joint Comm. Perspect **2007**, *27* (5), 3 1.

36. Gluck, J.C. Supporting JCAHO accreditation activities. Natl. Netw **2004**, *29* (2), 21.

37. Rollins, G. Quality. New Joint Commission measures in the works. Hosp Health Netw **2007**, *81* (7), 32.

38. Silverstein, J.L. Strengthening the links between health sciences information users and providers. Bull. Med. Libr. Assoc. **1995**, *83* (4), 407–417.

39. Committee on Psychopathology of the Group for the Advancement of Psychiatry, Patient Care and the Information Explosion. Psychiatr. Serv. **2002**, *53* (6), 657.

40. Association, American Medical, Policy, Group of Health Service, Policy, Division of Health, Evaluation, Program and Resources, Department of Health Care. *Diagnosis-Related Groups (DRGs) and the Prospective Payment System: A Guide for Physicians*, AMA: Chicago, IL, 1984.

41. Burkell, J. What are the chances? Evaluating risk and benefit information in consumer health materials. Med. Libr. Assoc. **2004**, April *92* (2), 200–208.

42. Moore, D., Ed. *Guide for the Development of Nursing Libraries and Information Resources*; NLN Press: New York, 1997; 112–113.

43. de, H.M.; Mendes, C. End-user searching: Impetus for an expanding information management and technology role for the hospital librarian. J. Libr. Inform. Sci. (Folkestone, England) **1997**, *29*, 189–193.

44. Postell, W.D. The Medical Librarian. *Medical Library Association Handbook of Medical Library Practice, with a Bibliography of the Reference Works and Histories in Medicine and the Allied Sciences*, 2nd Ed.; Doe, J., Marshall, M.L., Eds.; American Library Association: Chicago, IL, 1956; 30–41.

45. Baker, L.M.; Kars, M.; Petty, J. More research needed on the Academy of Health Information Professionals, the profession, and the Medical Library Association. J. Med. Libr. Assoc. **2005**, *93* (1), 5–6.

46. Greer, M.C. The medical librarian as chief information officer. Bull. Med. Libr. Assoc. **1998**, *86* (1), 88–94.

47. DeWitt, J. The challenging world of hospital librarians. J. Med. Libr. Assoc. **2005**, *93* (1), 5.

48. Wender, R. Lambremont, J. *Guidelines for Hospital Library Consulting;* Southeastern/Atlantic Regional Medical Library Services, Baltimore, MD, 1984. National Network of Libraries of Medicine SouthEastern Atlantic Region.

49. Reel, L.B. Expanded role for hospital libraries: A direction for successful change. Bull. Med. Libr. Assoc. **1985**, *73* (1), 55–58.

50. Hassig, R.A.; Balogh, L.; Bandy, M.; Doyle, J.D.; Gluck, J. C.; Lindner, K.L.; Reich, B.; Varner, D. Standards for hospital libraries 2002 with 2004 revisions. National Network January **2005**, *29* (3), 11–17.

51. Glitz, B.; Flack, V.; Lovas, I.M.; Newell, P. Hospital library service and the changes in national standards. Bull. Med. Libr. Assoc. **1988**, *86* (1), 77–87.

52. Richards, D.T. Eakin, D. Collection development and assessment in health sciences libraries. In *Current Practice in Health Sciences Librarianship*; Bunting, A., Ed.; Scarecrow Press, Inc.: Lanham, MD, 1997; Vol. 4, 68–76 Med. Libr. Assoc.

53. Hamasu, C. Collection development policy of the library of the American Hospital Association (book review). HLA J **1984**, *41*, 45–47.

54. Schmidt, C.M.; Eckerman, N.L. Circulation of core collection monographs in an academic medical library. Bull. Med. Libr. Assoc. **2001**, *89* (2), 165–169.

55. MacCall, S.L. Online medical books: Their availability and an assessment of how health sciences libraries provide access on their public Websites. J. Med. Libr. Assoc. **2006**, *94* (1), 75–80.

56. Hull, E. "Mapping the literature" useful for collection development. J. Med. Libr. Assoc. **2003**, *91* (1), 11.

57. Carmel, M., Ed. *Health care librarianship and information work;* Library Association Publishing: London, UK, 1995; 142–143.

58. Saha, S.; Saint, S.; Christakis, D.A. Impact factor: A valid measure of journal quality?. J. Med. Libr. Assoc. **2003**, *91* (1), 42–46.

59. Clair, G. St. Williamson, J. *Managing the New One-Person Library*, Bowker Saur: London, 1992; 108–109.

60. Katz, B., Fraley, R.A., Eds. In *Ethics and Reference Services*; Hawthorne Press: New York, 1982; 76–77.

61. Braude, R.M. Medical librarians and the White House Conference: From complacency, to concern, to commitment. Bull. Med. Libr. Assoc. April **1981**, *69* (2), 231–235.

62. Dudden, R.F. Evaluation of online catalog systems for the hospital library. Bull. Med. Libr. Assoc. **1991**, *79*, 422–423.

63. Bibliographic management of information in health sciences. In *Current Practice in Health Sciences Librarianship*; Thompson, L., Ed.; Medical Library Association and The Scarecrow Press, Inc.: Lanham, MD, 2001; Vol. 6, 2–6.

64. http://www.nlm.nih.gov/tsd/serials/lsiou.html.

65. http://www.cinahl.com/prodsvcs/cinahldb.htm.

66. http://galfe2.gsu.edu/cgi-bin/homepage.cgi?.

67. Educational services in health sciences libraries. In *Current Practice in Health Sciences Librarianship*; Allegri, F., Ed.; Medical Library Association and The Scarecrow Press, Inc.: Lanham, MD, 1995; Vol. 2, 37–38.

68. Alper, B.S.; Vinson, D.C. Experiential curriculum improves medical students' ability to answer clinical questions using the internet. Fam. Med. **2005**, *37* (8), 565–569.

69. Rethlefsen, M.L. MEDLINE: A guide to effective searching in PubMed and other interfaces. Rev. J. Med. Libr. Assoc. **2007**, *95* (2), 212–213.

70. Glynn, L. A critical appraisal tool for library and information research. Libr. Hi Tech. **2006**, *24* (3), 387–399.

71. Timm, D. Evidence matters. J. Med. Libr. Assoc. **2006**, *94* (4), 480–482.

72. Taylor, R.S. Question-negotiation and information seeking in libraries. Coll. Res. Libr. **1968**, *29* (3), 178–194.

73. Moore, D., Ed. *Guide for the Development of Nursing Libraries and Information Resources*; NLN Press: New York, 1997; 112–113.

74. Katz, W.A. *Introduction to Reference Work, Vol I. Basic Information Services*, 7th Ed. McGraw Hill: New York, 1997; 10–11.

75. McClure, L.W. The promise of fruit ... and light. Bull. Med. Libr. Assoc. **1985**, *73* (4), 319–329.

76. Reference and information services in health sciences libraries. In *Current Practice in Health Sciences Librarianship*; Bunting, A., Ed. Medical Library Association and Scarecrow Press: Metuchen, NJ, 1994; Vol. 1, 24–34.

77. Alison, M.; Bobal, M.A.; Schmidt, C.M.; Cox, R. One library's experience with live, virtual reference. J. Med. Libr. Assoc. **2005**, *93* (1), 123–125.

78. Breeding, M. Providing virtual reference service. Inform. Today **2001**, *18* (4), 42.

79. http://www.nlm.nih.gov.

80. Killoran, E. Electronic information retrieval by physicians and medical librarians [letter]. JAMA **1999**, *281* (14), 1272–1273.

81. Shultz, M.M.S.; De Groote, S.L. MEDLINE SDI services: How do they compare?. J. Med. Libr. Assoc. October **2003**, *91* (4), 460–467.

82. Kleinmuntz, D.S. TACOS: TAble of COntents Service in the hospital library. Med. Ref. Serv. Q. Fall **1985**, *4*, 17–26.

83. Hokamp, K.; Wolfe, K.H. PubCrawler: Keeping up comfortably with PubMed and GenBank. Nucleic Acids Res. **2004**, *1* (32), (Web Server issue): W16–19.

84. Matthews, J.R. *Public Access to Online Catalogs: A Planning Guide for Managers Online*, Online, Inc.: Weston, CT, 1982.

85. Ben-Shir, R. Fast inter library loans and statistics, enhanced version 2.8. Med. Ref. Serv. Q. **1986**, Spring *5* (1), 17–39.

86. Klein, P.; Hewison, N.S. QuickDoc: An interlibrary loan department in a microcomputer. Med. Ref. Serv. Q. Summer **1991**, *10* (2), 11–32.

87. http://www.oclc.org/illiad.

88. http://www.prospero.com.

89. Davis, F.L.; Waverchak, G.; Coffey, J.B. The use of independent information brokers for document delivery service in hospital libraries. Bull. Med. Libr. Assoc. **1992**, *80*, 185–187.

90. http://www.aiip.org.

91. Lynch, C.A. Preston, C.M. Internet access to information resources. In *Annual Review of Information Science and Technology*; Williams, M.E., Ed.; Elsevier Science Publishers: Amsterdam, the Netherlands, 1990; Vol. 25, 261–311.

92. http://www.worldcat.org.

93. Ohles, J.A. The Internet: A valuable resource for the hospital librarian. Bull. Med. Libr. Assoc. **1996**, *84*, 110–111.

94. http://www.locatorplus.gov.

95. O'Connor, S. The heretical library manager of the future information. Outlook **2007**, *11* (3), 11.

96. Siess, J.A. *The New OPL Sourcebook: A Guide for Solo and Small Libraries*, Information Today, Inc.: Medford, NJ, 2006; 427.

97. Siess, J.A. *Time Management, Planning and Prioritization for Librarians*, Scarecrow Press: Latham, MD, 2002.

98. Delumeau, A. Time management for library professionals. Available at http://www.liscareer.com/delumeau_time.htm.

99. Kuntz, J.; Tennant, M.; Case, A.; Meakin, F. Staff driven strategic planning learning from the past embracing the future. J. Med. Libr. Assoc. **2003**, *91* (1), 79–82.

100. Weise, F. Being there: the library as place. J. Med. Libr. Assoc. **2004**, *92* (1), 6–13.

101. Hassig, R.A.; Balogh, L.; Bandy, M.; Doyle, J.D.; Gluck, J.C.; Lindner, K.L.; Reich, B.; Varner, D. Standards for hospital libraries 2002 with 2004 revision. J. Med. Libr. Assoc. **2005**, *93* (2), 282–283.

102. Perley, C.M.; Gentry, C.A.; Fleming, A.S.; Sen, K.M. Conducting a user-centered information needs assessment: The Via Christi Libraries' experience. J. Med. Libr. Assoc. *95* (2), 173–181.

103. Lancaster, F.W. *If You Want to Evaluate Your Library*, 2nd Ed. University of Illinois Urbana-Champaign: Champaign, IL, 1993.

104. Crabtree, A.B.; Crawford, J.H. Assessing and addressing the library needs of health care personnel in a large regional hospital. Bull. Med. Libr. Assoc. **1997**, *85* (2), 167–175.

105. Lonsdale, M.; Hutchinson, G.I. Patient's desire for information about anaesthesia. Scottish and Canadian attitudes. Anaesthesia **1991**, *46*, 410–412.

106. Fuller, S.S. Internet connectivity for hospitals and hospital libraries: Strategies. Bull. Med. Libr. Assoc. **1995**, *83* (1), 32–36.

107. Rauch, S.; Holt, M.C.; Horner, M.; Rambo, N. Community hospitals and the Internet: Lessons from pilot connections. Bull. Med. Libr. Assoc. October **1994**, *82* (4), 401–406.

108. http://www.princetonreview.com/cte/profiles/dayInLife. asp?careerID = 203.

109. Wagner, K.C.; Byrd, G.D. Evaluating the effectiveness of clinical medical librarian programs: A systematic review of the literature. J. Med. Libr. Assoc. **2004**, *92* (1), 14–33.

110. Winning, M.A.; Beverley, C.A. Clinical librarianship: A systematic review of the literature. Health Info. Libr. J. **2003**, *20* (1), 10–21.

111. Gilbert, C.M. Adapting clinical librarianship. Med. Ref. Serv. Q. Spring **1999**, *18* (1), 69–72.

112. Davidoff, F.; Valerie, F. The informationist: A new health profession?. Ann. Intern. Med. **2000**, *132*, 996–998.

113. Kripalani, S.; Weiss, B.D. Teaching about health literacy and clear communication. Gen Intern Med. August **2006**, *21* (8), 888–890.

114. Laramee, A.S.; Morris, N.; Littenberg, B. Relationship of literacy and heart failure in adults with diabetes. BMC Health Serv. Res. **2007**, *7* (98), doi:10.1186/1472-6963-7-98.

115. American Hospital Association. *A Patient's Bill of Rights;* American Hospital Association: Chicago, IL, 1992.

116. Gann, R. Needham, G. *Promoting Choice: Consumer Health Information in the 1990s;* Consumer Health Information Consortiumt, Winchester, UK, 1992.

117. Medical Library Association. The librarian's role in the provision of consumer health information and patient education. Bull. Med. Libr. Assoc. **1996**, *84* (2), 238–239.

118. Lambremont, J.A. Consumer health information services in the hospital setting. Med. Ref. Serv. Q. Summer **1997**, *16*, 61–67.

119. Eysenbach, G.; Diepgen, T.L. Towards quality management of medical information of the internet: Evaluation, labeling, and filtering of information. BMJ **1998**, *317* (7171), 1496–1500.

120. Phillips, S.A. Assessing consumer health information needs in a community hospital. Bull. Med. Libr. Assoc. **1994**, *82*, 288–293.

121. Katz, B., Fraley, R.A., Eds. *Ethics and Reference Services;* Hawthorne Press: New York, 1982; 76–77.

122. Tracey, C. Planetree health information services: Public access to the health information people want. Bull. Med. Libr. Assoc. **1994**, *82* (1), 57–63.

123. Martin, S.K. *Library Networks, 1986–1987, Libraries in Partnership*, Knowledge Industry Publications, Inc.: New York, 1986; 2.

124. Light, J.; Chapple-Sokol, A. Loansome doc. J. Med. Libr. Assoc. **2002**, *90* (1), 111.

125. Paden, S.L.; Batson, A.L.; Wallace, R.L. Web-based Loansome Doc, librarians, and end users: results from a survey of the Southeast Region. J. Med. Libr. Assoc. **2002**, *90* (1), 111.

126. Fishel, M.R. Loansome Doc: Push a button, get a document. NLM News. **1991**, *46* (3–4), 1–3.

127. Shedlock, J.; Barkey, D.C.; Ross, F. Building the electronic health sciences library for the twenty-first century: The Galter Library experience. Med. Ref. Serv. Q. **1996**, *15* (4), 1–12.

128. Blansit, B.D.; Connor, E. Making sense of the electronic resource marketplace: Trends in health-related electronic resources. Bull. Med. Libr. Assoc. **1999**, *87* (3), 243–250.

129. Chhanabhai, P.; Holt, A. Consumers are ready to accept the transition to online and electronic records if they can be assured of the security measures. MedGenMed. **2007**, *9* (1), 8 11.

130. Luther, J. Selection of full-text online resources: What you need to know: A joint program co-sponsored by the RUSA Collection Development and Evaluation Section and the ACRL Science and Technology Section. Library Acquis. **1997**, *21* (4), 522–525.

131. Harry, K. *Success of OCLC ILLiad at Virginia Tech.* Available at http://www.oclc.org/us/en/illiad/about/success/default.htm (accessed September 2009), 1–5.

132. Craig, J.P. Electronic collection development: A practical guide. J. Med. Libr. Assoc. **2003**, *91* (1), 91.

133. Boyce, P.B. It is time to become discriminating consumers. Against Grain **1997**, *9* (5), 86–87. Available at http://www.against-the-grain.com.

134. Kroski, E. The social tools of Web 2.0: Opportunities for academic libraries choice. Res. Libr. **2007**, *44* (12), 2011.

135. Boulos, M.N.; Maramba, I.; Wheeler, S. Wikis, blogs and podcasts: A new generation of Web-based tools for virtual collaborative clinical practice and education. BMC Med. Educ. **2006**, *15* (6), 41.

136. Kamel Boulos, M.N.; Wheeler, S. The emerging Web 2.0 social software: An enabling suite of sociable technologies in health and health care education. Health Info. Libr. J. **2007**, *24* (1), 2–23.

137. Kautz, B.A.; Rodkewich, P.M.; Philipson, W.D. The evolution of a new library instruction concept: Interactive video (at the University of Minnesota, Minneapolis—St. Paul). Res. Strateg. Summer **1988**, *6*, 109–117.

138. Eldredge, J.D. Evidence based librarianship: An overview. Bull. Med. Libr. Assoc. **2000**, *88* (4), 289–302.

139. Atreja, A.; Messinger-Rapport, B.; Jain, A.; Mehta, N. Using Web 2.0 technologies to develop a resource

for evidence based medicine. AMIA Ann. Symp. Proc. **2006**, 847.

140. Sackett, D.L.; Rosenberg, W.M.C.; Gray, J.A.M.; Haynes, R.B.; Richardson, W.S. Evidence based medicine: What it is and what it isn't. BMJ, **1996**, *312* (7023), 71–72.

141. Harris, M.R. The librarian's roles in the systematic review process: A case study. Med. Libr. Assoc. **2005**, *93* (1), 81–87.

142. Dutcher, G.A.; Spann, M.; Gaines, C. Addressing health disparities and environmental justice: The National Library of Medicine's Environmental Health Information Outreach Program. J. Med. Libr. Assoc. **2007**, *95* (3), 330–336.

143. Lancaster, W.F. Future librarianship: Preparing for an unconventional career. Wilson Libr. Bull. **1983**, *57*, 747–753.

144. Li, X. Library as incubating space for innovations: practices, trends and skill sets. Libr. Manage. **2006**, *27* (6/7), 370–378.

145. Apple's New Calling: The iPhone. Available at http://www.time.com/time/nation/article/0,8599,1575743-1,00.html .

146. Butler, M.A. Editor libraries as user-centered. *Organizations: Imperatives for Organizational Change*, Hawthorne Press Inc.: New York, 1993; 128–131.

147. Jajko, P. A microcomputer teaching lab for information management education. Med. Ref. Serv. Q. Spring **1992**, *11* (1), 63–66.

148. Jajko, P. Hospital and corporate information services: Introducing a new column. Med. Ref. Serv. Q. Spring **1992**, *11* (10), 63–67.

149. Kuller, A.B.; Wessel, C.B.; Glinn, D.S.; Martin, T.P. Quality filtering of the clinical literature by librarians and physicians. Bull. Med. Libr. Assoc. **1993**, *81* (1), 38–43.

150. Howell, P.B.; Jones, C.J. A focus on quality—The library's role in occurrence screening. Med. Ref. Serv. Q. Summer **1993**,*12* (2), 83–89.

151. Hard, R. New HCFA rule calls for electronic cost reports. Hospitals **1991**, *65* (24), 44–45.

152. Covey, S.R. *The Seven Habits of Highly Effective People: Restoring the Character Ethic*, Simon & Schuster: New York, 1989.

153. Knowledge Management—Can You Identify The Six Main Characteristics? Available at http://www.about-goal-setting.com/KM-Library/ (accessed July 2007).

154. van Rooi, H.; Snyman, R. A content analysis of literature regarding knowledge management opportunities for librarians. Aslib Proc. **2006**, *58* (3), 261–271 (accessed September 2007).

155. Lucier, R.E. Knowledge management: Redefining the roles in scientific communication. Educom. Rev. Fall **1990**, *25* (3), 21–27.

156. Berner, E.S.; Moss, J. Informatics challenges for the impending patient information explosion. Am Med. Inform. Assoc. **2005**, *12* (6), 614–617.

157. Nippert, C.C. Online LATCH. Med. Ref. Serv. Q. **1985**, *4*, 23–29.

158. Amatayakul, M. EHRs and the consumer: A new opportunity. In *Electronic Health Records Changing the Vision*; Murphy, G.F., Hanken, M.A., Waters, K.A., Eds.; WB Saunders Co. Philadelphia, PA 26–68.

159. Gann, R. Consumer health information: The growth of an information specialism. J. Doc. **1991**, *47* (3), 284–308.

160. Calabretta, N. The hospital library as provider of consumer health information. Med. Ref. Serv. Q. Fall **1996**, *15*, 13–22.

161. Cann, R. Assuring the quality of consumer health information. In *Performance Measurement: The Quality Assurance Approach*; Taylor, M.H., Wilson, T., Eds.; Library Association/Canadian Library Association: Ottawa, 1990.

162. Cuddy, T.M. Value of hospital libraries: The Fuld Campus study. Med. Libr. Assoc. October **2005**, *93* (4), 446–449.

163. Zipperer, L.; Sykes, J. The role of librarians in patient safety: Gaps and strengths in the current culture. J. Med. Libr. Assoc. **2004**, *92* (4), 489–500.

164. Garfield, E. The impact of health information delivery on the quality of patient care: Whither medical information science?. Health Libr. Rev. **1985**, (4), 159–169.

165. Bates, M.E. Info pro on the edge. EContent **2006**, *29* (10), 17.

166. Mash Up: Web Application Hybrid. Available at http://en.wikipedia.org/wiki/Mashup_(web_application_hybrid).

Human–Computer Interaction Research in Information Retrieval

Shin-jeng Lin
Department of Business Administration, Le Moyne College, Syracuse, New York, U.S.A.

Abstract

Human–computer interaction is a very important topic in studying computerized information retrieval systems, as it takes into account both the human searchers and the information system features. This entry surveys the major research streams and applications of interactive information seeking and retrieval. It also presents how the expectations and requirements for interactive information seeking and retrieval have been expanded and what the challenges are ahead for evaluating such systems.

INTRODUCTION

Human–computer interaction research has increasingly become an important component of information retrieval studies, as the information infrastructure has become largely dependent on computer technology, at personal, group, or organizational levels.

Human–computer interaction research in information retrieval is about identifying the key characteristics of searchers, tasks, and contexts, that affect the search tactics and behaviors of searchers and proposing system features for proper supports. Various streams of research are under this umbrella, including:

1. Interactive information retrieval, which Ingwersen[1] defines as "the interactive communication processes that occur during the retrieval of information by involving all the major participants in information retrieval (IR), i.e., the user, the intermediary, and the IR system."
2. Information retrieval in context, or situated information retrieval, i.e., to incorporate aspects of the searcher or environment that are typically not reflected in queries or search statements, such as the time, place, and history of interaction, the tasks motivating the interaction and the technical possibilities of the information systems.
3. Human–computer information retrieval, which "aims to empower people to explore large-scale information bases but demands that people also take responsibility for this control by expending cognitive and physical energy".[2]
4. Cognitive information retrieval, which takes into account interface issues, the role of information retrieval system interaction in the total range of people's information behaviors, and the information situation, task situation, and problem situation of users when using an IR system (pp. 3,4).[3]

This entry will first describe the history of how we get to this research paradigm in section "History" and then proceed to cover the major research streams in section "General Research Streams," the applications and tools proposed and developed in section "Applications, Tools, and Techniques for Interactive Information Seeking and Retrieval," the evaluation methods for studying the interactive information retrieval systems in section "Evaluation of Interactive Information Retrieval Systems and Interfaces," the important conferences, workshops, organizations, and institutions in section "Important Conferences, Workshops, Organizations, and Institutions." It will conclude with the expectation of the bright future for this research paradigm.

HISTORY

Information retrieval is defined as the process of searching a collection of documents with the goal of identifying documents pertaining to a particular topic.[4,5] The process of information retrieval is inherently interactive between the information searcher and an information environment/system,[6,7] as such a process depends on initiatives on the part of the information searcher, feedback from the information environment, and decisions on subsequent initiatives based on this feedback (p. 17).[8]

The factors associated with both searchers (e.g., type, context of use, kinds of information needs, and immediacy of information needs, etc.) and systems (e.g., size and subject coverage of document collection or database, information representation, indexing methods, algorithms of matching queries against document collections, etc.) plus those associated with the interaction process between the two (e.g., revision of queries or search statements, search logics, and tactics) all could affect the performance of information retrieval.[7,9–12]

Encyclopedia of Library and Information Sciences, Fourth Edition DOI: 10.1081/E-ELIS4-120044556

Despite the interactive nature of the information retrieval process, the information retrieval field has its tradition in "system-centered" research or the matching paradigm, which focuses "solely" on improving the match between query terms and document representations, without taking into account the complexities of the users.[11,13,14] A closely related research community takes the "user-centered" approach, mainly focusing on information seeking behavior/processes, as well as contextual, cognitive, and even affective factors related to such information seeking processes.[1,15,16] While related, the two research communities hold a critical stance toward each other,[17] and much of the user-centered research does not directly address the design of information systems. From the user-centered perspective, the term "information retrieval" is too confined to cover a wide spectrum of information searching phenomenon, as it implicitly connotes that the information searcher already has clearly-defined "information needs" and only needs to "retrieve" the documents from the system that can fittingly answer those needs. The uncertainty of user "information needs" that users are still struggling to form into shape is overlooked. In other words, if the user is not sure what he/she is or even should be looking for, how could the system possibly provide the best answer to his/her "information needs?" Information seeking, thus, is a preferred term over information retrieval in the user-centered studies.

The gaps between the two schools of thought are self-evident, as both have their significant shortcomings. The system-centered studies could contribute to effective information retrieval, but may not be efficient. The success of an information retrieval system totally relies on 1) whether the user can produce the queries that "perfectly" reflect the user's information needs, which could be still evolving, and 2) on its own capability of matching its document collection against those "perfect" queries. It is a daunting, if not impossible, task, given that many studies have shown the non-specificity of "information needs."[4,18–21]

Moreover, the information retrieval process is more than just simply articulating queries and evaluating search outcomes.[22] Marchionini[23] argued that most of information retrieval systems focus on query formulation and results examination functions but ignore problem identification/clarification and information extraction.

Other common search tactics are found, including but not limited to, chaining, differentiating, and extracting, scanning, listing ideas, and many others to either tolerate uncertainty about "information needs" or develop the "information needs."[15,18,24]

In addition, the fact that the information retrieval process frequently takes place over multiple search sessions is often overlooked in system-centered studies.[25–31] Failure to consider the nature, evolution or stages of the information seeking processes likely results in an IR system that requires more effort and time from the searchers to find satisfactory results.

Studies also have reported that searchers often engage in multiple tasks at the same time.[28,32] By concentrating on the information retrieval task itself without considering its context or broadening its perspective, the questions of "could've" and "should've" linger, as other information tasks that are associated with information retrieval, such as question answering, information assimilation, and personal knowledge management, are isolated and thus the information flow and transition among them not supported.

Traditional IR systems are designed primarily to support individuals. Yet, individuals often need to collaborate on information seeking, searching, and retrieval.[33] Research on information retrieval thus expanded to collaborative information seeking and retrieval, just as research efforts in Human–Computer Interaction expanded beyond the individual levels to support collaborative computer work. Research on collaborative information seeking and retrieval has drawn heavily from studies on computer-supported collaborative work (CSCW), information science, information retrieval, and human–computer interaction studies. Foster[33] provided a literature review of the social and collaborative approaches to information seeking and retrieval in the four specific contexts: academy, industry, medicine, and the military. Understanding how people work together has direct implications on designing effective and efficient collaborative information retrieval applications.

The problems of user-centered studies are just the opposite to those of the system-centered ones. Vakkari and Järvelin[34] noted that the user-oriented Information Science approach suspects the realism of the Computer Science system-oriented experimental approach, while the latter suspects the usefulness of the former. While user-centered studies have provided a great understanding of human information tasks and cognitive processes, they often failed to empirically demonstrate the effects and magnitudes of the factors that could affect the information seeking processes.[35] Moreover, many of the studies under this paradigm do not pragmatically suggest possible system solutions for the problems identified.

The differences in the research foci of the "system-centered" vs. "user-centered" research streams were mainly due to the lack of interdisciplinary studies in the earlier IR research community. The "system-centered" IR studies were likely from the computer science discipline, while the "user-centered" IR studies were likely from the disciplines of library and information science, communication, etc.

The cry for the interaction approach that takes both the system and the user into account was heard first in the early 1970s.[36,37] For example, the workshop on The User Interface for Interactive Search of Bibliographic Databases is considered the first occasion on which the general problem of user interfaces for computer systems was raised.[6] The effort to bridge the two camps went extensively into the 1980s and 1990s, and has continued today.

With more and more information systems going electronic and an increasing amount of information collections being digitized, the fields of human–computer interaction (HCI), library and information science (LIS) and computer science (CS) inevitably converge on interactive information retrieval/seeking. On the one hand, HCI sheds light on how to bridge the user-centered vs. system-centered paradigms with the HCI concepts and research models being applied to the studies of IR systems.[11,38–42] On the other hand, the work of the LIS researchers[26,34,43–55] and CS researchers,[56–64] who respond to this outcry, are HCI per se, as they aim to streamline the collaboration between the human searchers and system enablers to improve the overall performances and outcomes of information retrieval processes by considering both users characteristics and system features in the design of information retrieval systems.

GENERAL RESEARCH STREAMS

Major Theories and Models on HCI Research in IR

Although the major theories and models on HCI research in IR might utilize some HCI concepts, such as two-way communication between message sender and receivers and interaction with texts or content rather than information systems (p. 857),[65] they hardly adopt entirely well-established HCI theories or models. For example, the Goals, Operators, Methods, and Selections model (GOMS), a human information processor model,[66] is considered best suitable for routine, more structured and predictable information tasks and behavioral patterns.[67,68] The information seeking/retrieval process could be too interactive and too highly complex to be explained by GOMS.[65,68,69] Consequently, the major theories and models on HCI research in IR are likely to be developed from within the field of information science and meet the following criteria:

1. They must enumerate the variables that are associated with both users and computerized IR systems.
2. They must describe, explain and/or predict the interactions between the variables associated with the human searcher and the computerized IR system for the information retrieval/seeking tasks.
3. The description, explanation, and/or predictions of interactions between the searchers and the IR systems would serve as a conceptual framework to provide design implications for IR systems.

Ingwersen's cognitive IR theory

Ingwersen's cognitive IR theory[1,17] identified cognitive processes that occur in information processing. The main

model components are 1) IR system objects which consist of text/knowledge representation (e.g., meta data), semantic entities like full text and pictures, 2) IR system setting, including search languages/IR techniques, database structure, indexing rules/computational logics, 3) intermediaries that facilitate the information retrieval process, e.g., computer interfaces, human intermediaries and 4) individual searchers' cognitive space, including work task/interest, current cognitive state (the currently known, drawing upon emotions, tacit knowledge, and external factors influencing the searcher), problem space, uncertainty, information need, and information IR behavior, and 5) social/organizational environment, including such variables as domains, strategies, and tasks and preferences.

Ingwersen described the following interactions among these model components: 1) Users interact not only with IR systems, but with information objects, i.e., "texts," "documents," etc.; more specifically, it is the cognitive space of the user that interacts with the "information space" of IR systems; 2) The social and organizational environment influences and shapes the individual cognitive space; 3) From the system design perspective, for the five model components to interact to produce the more effective IR outcome, each of them can "model" or profile how other components would behave cognitively; and 4) The success of the IR process relies on the polyrepresentation in IR. Searchers' queries requested can be enhanced with problem/goal statement and work task/interest description, because in the searchers' cognitive space, work task and interest domains define what is known (current cognitive state) and prompt for what is unknown (problem space) and the gap in between the two (information need). In the information space of IR, different methods of knowledge representations can facilitate the matching of the representations of searcher's cognitive space against semantic entities.

Saracevic[11] pointed out that the strength of the Ingwersen's model lies in the detailed description of the interactions between the searchers and the systems, while the weaknesses of the model could be its testability and application to the evaluation of interactive IR system. Such an assessment is accurate to some degrees, as the main purpose of the Ingwersen's model was to inform the design of an interactive IR system with a descriptive account of the essential processes from both the user and system perspectives; the model did not intend to enumerate the key performance variables for evaluation.

Belkin's episode model

Belkin's episode model[22,70,71] postulates that because the searchers may not always be capable of best representing their information problems with effective query terms, a variety of information interactions to clarify the information problems would be necessary. Sixteen types of information seeking strategies are identified and characterized with four dimensions or factors, each of which has two possible values: method of interaction (scanning vs. searching), goal of interaction (learning vs. selecting), mode of retrieval (recognition vs. specification), and resources considered (information vs. meta information). Based on an empirical study of knowledge workers, Cool and Belkin[72] extended these facets to create information behavior facets, consisting of access, objects interacted with, common dimensions of interaction, and interaction criteria. The access facet includes two sub-facets from the four original ones: method and mode of interaction. The "objects to interact with" facet includes level (information vs. meta-information), medium (e.g., image, written text, speech, etc.) and quantity (e.g., one object, set of objects, database, etc.). The "common dimensions of interaction" facet entails information objects (part vs. whole), systematicity (random vs. systematic), and degree (selective vs. exhaustive). The "interaction criteria" facet is about evaluation criteria or tactics, including accuracy, alphabet, authority, date, person, etc.

Belkin and his colleague suggested that all the information seeking strategies can be supported with a combination of a variety of IR techniques, including representation, comparison, summarization, navigation, and visualization. The initially proposed idea was to use a script-based dialogue to assist the searchers in utilizing proper information seeking strategies that are optimally supported by specific combinations of IR techniques. Yuan and Belkin[54] prototyped an IR system, that simply provides a small selection of information seeking strategies to the searcher. They found that subjects using the prototyped system were likely to spend a fewer number of iterations in submitting queries and the query was likely to be longer than the baseline system. They also found that in terms of usability, the integrated system was significantly easier to use and significantly more useful than the baseline system.

Saracevic[11] made the following critiques of Belkin's episode model. On the plus side, the model directly addresses a greater range of various interactions in the activity level that are so specific that they can easily be mapped onto the designed system features. On the potentially negative side, Saracevic wondered whether the scripts identified would be insufficient to reflect the full complexity and extension of human–computer interaction in IR. However, the Belkin's episode model has proven a great starting point in designing and evaluating interactive IR system. The fact that Yuan and Belkin[54] only focused on a portion of the model not only shows the complexity of the model that is too much to be covered in one single system, but also demonstrates the practical applicability of the model in designing and evaluating IR system artifacts.

Saracevic's stratified interaction model

Saracevic's stratified interaction model[7,11,73] borrows from the concepts elucidated in HCI and from the notions incorporated in the stratification theory in linguistics and communication. The model postulates that the IR interaction is a dialogue between the participants, searcher and "computer," through an interface with the main purpose being to affect the cognitive state of the searcher for effective use in order to apply a found solution to an information problem or task at hand. The model components are users (with such variables as knowledge, intent, and belief, etc.) related to a situation (task, problem-at-hand) within an environment, while interacting with computers to seek for/retrieve information. "Computer" is depicted as having computational resources and capacities, but also separately informational resources—"texts" as cognitive structures, representations, meta-information about texts, and informational and computational resources, and possibly other information for adaptation to different kinds of interactions and user intents.

The model depicts three levels of interaction between the searcher and the system and in some ways, seems to integrate the Belkin's model with Ingwersen's. First, it is on the surface level, where the user engages in a variety of interactions with the IR system as portrayed in Belkin's model. Second, on the cognitive level, users interact with the "texts" (including images, data, and their representations) in the information resources, considering them as cognitive structures, to learn or to assimilate information in order to update their current cognitive state and revise the problem space, as argued by Ingwersen. Third, on the situation level, like Ingwersen, it is about how the environment interacts with or affects the searcher's cognitive activity. However, Saracevic emphasized the effects of the application of the information found to the information problem at hand. Utility becomes a prominent relevance feedback criterion, which could change the information problem at hand and affect the decisions made.

Saracevic[73] further extended the stratified model to encompass specific processes or phenomena that play a crucial role in various IR interactions, including the notion of relevance, user modeling, and feedback types. For the notion of relevance, the stratified model helps distinguish between the following manifestations of relevance as presented in Table 1.

For user modeling, the stratified model helps identify eight types of communication factors or artifacts that manifest the interactions taking place during IR processes, as summarized in Table 2.

For relevance feedback, the stratified model of IR interaction has served as a framework to observe and categorize the following different relevance feedback types in IR in Table 3.

Spink and Saracevic[7] further elaborated the stratified interaction model with how relevance feedback is

Table 1 Types of relevance identified from the stratified model.

Type of relevance	Definition	Inferred criteria
System or algorithmic relevance	Relation between a query and information objects (texts) in the file of a system as retrieved, or as failed to be retrieved, by a given procedure or algorithm	• Comparative effectiveness
Topical or subject relevance	Relation between the subject or topic expressed in a query, and topic or subject covered by retrieved texts, or more broadly, by texts in the systems file, or even in existence	• Aboutness
Cognitive relevance or pertinence	Relation between the state of knowledge and cognitive information need of a user, and texts retrieved, or in the file of a system, or even in existence	• Informativeness • Novelty • Information quality
Situational relevance or utility	Relation between the situation, task, or problem at hand, and texts retrieved by a systems or in the file of a system, or even in existence	• Usefulness in decision making • Appropriateness of information in resolution of a problem • Reduction of uncertainty
Motivational or affective relevance	Relation between the intents, goals, and motivations of a user, and texts retrieved by a system or in the file of a system, or even in existence	• Satisfaction • Success • Accomplishment

represented by the interplay between levels (i.e., the cognitive, affective and situation levels on the user side and the engineering, processing, and content levels on the system side), giving rise to the following types of feedback in Table 3. But Spink and Saracevic[7] stopped short of illustrating how the engineering, processing, and content dimensions of IR systems can make use of this feedback in supporting the searchers. Kelly[50] examined the decisions during interactive information retrieval as to what to examine, retain (save, print), reference, annotate, and the like. Such decisions are assumed to indicate relevance implicitly, which would be very operationalizable for IR systems to make use of and support the searchers.

Saracevic[11] himself noted that the strength of the stratified model lies in decomposition of different types of interactions as related to different elements involved, while the decomposition is not easy and depiction of interplays between levels is hard to specify and consequently the model is difficult to test. But the works of Saracevic[73] and Spink and Saracevic[7] have provided a positive direction to test the model by focusing on the manifestations of specific interactions or communications in IR processes, such as search terms, relevance feedback, etc.

Bates's cascade of interaction model

Bates's cascade of interaction model[74] proclaims that the design of IR systems needs to take into account many design layers, including user understanding and motivations, user searching activities, interface design, search capabilities, system front end, search engine, information in searchable form, database structure, computer system, network, actual indexing, system of metadata and information content. The term, "cascade," is to describe how design features of earlier layers would affect the success

of those of later layers, while the latter could affect the effectiveness of the former.

Although the cascade model is neither a human–computer interaction model nor an interaction in information retrieval model per se (p. 385),[74] it, as a design model for operational online IR systems, in a way, does summarize Bates's series of work[12,75,76] in depicting how different factors concerning both the information searchers and the IR systems affect the performance of information seeking and retrieval. For example, the details of user search capabilities have been described by Bates.[12] Moreover, the different design layers in the cascade model respectively correspond to the factors about the system infrastructure (i.e., the upper left part of the model), the information infrastructure (i.e., the bottom left part of the model), the interface infrastructure (i.e., the middle part of the model), and the human searchers (i.e., the right part of the model). The interactions between the human searchers and the interface infrastructure as well as between the human searchers and the information infrastructure are what substantiate human–computer interaction in IR.

Thus, even though the cascade model does not directly enumerate the variables that are associated with both users and computerized IR systems and instead focuses solely on the interactions of different layers of IR systems, the cascade model, under the broader context of Bates's works to date, still can be considered as a theoretical model in provision of a rich description of HCI in IR. Wilson et al.[77] pointed out that Bates' cascade model actually can be perceived as extending the Saracevic's stratified model in greater detail with additional levels that interact and affect each other.

The strength of the cascade model is the emphasis on the tight coupling of different layers in IR system design. The weakness might be that additional works to directly identify variables in the layers in the cascade model may

Table 2 Factors or artifacts that manifest IR interactions identified through the stratified model.

1. Context	User's problem or task at hand; information seeking stage; information if any collected so far; expectations and other aspects underlying the question; user domain and problem knowledge; user plans.
2. Terminology and restrictions	Elaboration on and modification of concepts, terms, keywords, descriptors; generation of terms; specification of borderlines; restrictions such as to language, years; spelling of technical terms.
3. Systems explanations	Workings and technical aspects of system used; technical explanation of searching; characteristics of databases and documents in system; other possible information sources; obtaining texts; costs involved.
4. Search tactics and procedures	Selection and variation of terms, fields, morphology, logic in search statements; commands; selection and variation in magnitude and output sizes, formats, order; output specification; correcting mistakes.
5. Review and relevance	Review of tactics as to the output; evaluation of output sources or content; relevance judgments of and feedback from outputs; decisions or questions on what is wanted based on tactics or output.
6. Action	Description of an ongoing or impending activity e.g., thesaurus lookup, output formats, printing; explanation of what is happening.
7. Backchanneling— prompts, echoes	Communication prompts, fillers, acknowledgments, formulaic expressions etc. indicating listeners involvement, e.g., "O.K.," "Wow!" "Unhuh," "Right;" echoes and requests for repetitions e.g., "What?" "Pardon?" "Say that again"; pauses.
8. Extraneous	Utterances extraneous to the search interaction—greetings, formulaic courtesies, social comments, and questions; personal matters.

Table 3 Relevance feedback types identified with the stratified model.

Content relevance feedback	User query followed by an IR system output of retrieved items then judged by the user for relevance followed by a query or reformulation.
Term relevance feedback	User query followed by an IR system output of retrieved items and user selection of a new search term(s) from the retrieved output used in a subsequent query.
Magnitude feedback	User query followed by a judgment based on the size of the output from a query that effects the next query.
Tactical review feedback	User input followed by a strategy related judgment to display the search strategy history influencing the subsequent query.
Term review feedback	User input followed by a strategy related judgment to display terms in the inverted file influencing the subsequent query.

still be needed to create a prescriptive evaluation procedure for interactive IR systems.

Lin's MISE model

The MISE model by Lin and Belkin[25,26] and Lin[51] continues in the footsteps of Ingwersen[1,17] and Belkin et al.[71,22] to incorporate the following components into the model: 1) searcher (including variables pertaining to problematic situation and information problems), 2) IR

system, 3) search activity in which the searcher actually interacts with an IR system, 4) search contextual factors (e.g., time, perception of information availability, etc.), 5) information attainment (i.e., with the emphasis of interaction with text, particularly collected information objects), and 6) information use activity (e.g., like Saracevic's situational interaction level, with the emphasis on the impacts of the information sought on the evolution of the information problem, including such factors as decision making, cooperation, communication, commercial transactions, etc.). The model attempted a comprehensive list of variables that matter in successive multisessions information searches and depicted how the variables in these components interplay with each other.

The point of departure is the phenomenological perspective. MISE highlights how different search episodes of the same or similar information problems could be connected. MISE identifies eight different scenarios that a searcher could engage in successive searches based on the nature of how an information problem evolves. They are 1) transmuting information problems which a searcher learns to define or clarify over sessions, 2) spawned information problems which are derived from the main problem and take over the priority, 3) transiting information problems in which the solution of one information problem leads to the beginning of another, 4) rolled-back information problems resulting from the feedback of information use activity, 5) lost-answer problems in which the efficiency of locating the solution may be more important than effectiveness, 6) unanswered information problems, 7) cultivating information problems due to long-term interests, and 8) anticipating information problems foreseen to materialize in the near future.

The MISE model does not include the interface or computer intermediary directly in the model. Instead, it uses the variables associated with the model components to characterize the problems a searcher could encounter during the different processes of search activity (i.e., articulation of information problems, navigation of the information space, evaluation of search outcomes, monitoring the state of the problem space) and consequently propose system features to mitigate the problems and support those processes.

Lin[52] described an actual prototype, PERsonalized and Successive Information Search Tools (PERSIST), which assists the searches for transmuting information problems; PERIST enables the searcher to visualize his/her information collection by using representative words to label and categorize (i.e., explicit coding) his/her own information collection. Such an information collection and their associated labels/category terms can further be dynamically reorganized, expanded, modified, removed, and potentially filtered as the information problem of the searcher evolves. The design goal is to improve monitoring the state of the problem space and navigating the information space (e.g., revisiting information objects) to interact with information objects. The same goal is shared by Komlodi and her colleagues,[53,78,79] who explored how automatically and manually recorded search histories can support information seekers in finding and using information. Komlodi[80] and Komlodi and Soergel[81] proposed three search-history-based user interface tools, including 1) user-manipulable search history displays, 2) a scratchpad interface to allow users to take notes and to save various granules of information and the search history, and 3) an organized collection tool to allow searchers to bridge the gap between finding and using information. All three of these user interface tools include functions to support planning, monitoring, evaluation, task integration, and context preservation.

The main strengths of the MISE model include broadening the scope of searcher-system interactions from single episode to multiple episodes and the apparent applicability from the conceptual model to the design and evaluation of system features (e.g., PERSIST). The major weakness could be that the system component is not as detailed and as well-layered as the stratified model and the cascade model; the design of system features to mitigate the problems occurred in the search process may not be as intuitive or as straight-forward as it could have been.

User-Centered Studies with Design Implications

More and more of the user-centered information search theories, models and their extensions have begun to explore the design implications for interactive information retrieval. Below are a few selected models.

Vakkari and his colleagues[30,31,34,82–84] elaborated Kuhlthau's ISP model[15,16] by providing more specific variable values in characteristics of information search processes and how those variables interact with each other through time. Particularly, Vakkari and his colleagues have focused on how the number and type of search terms and operators and search tactics evolve over time as the information problem continues to develop, which could potentially have very operationalizable design implications for IR systems.

Cole[85] described the interaction between searcher and system as a message coding and encoding process, proposing the idea of "enabling IR system" that would employ interactive devices (e.g., a visualized representation of comparing and contrasting concepts) to help the searcher clarify the state of his/her information problem. Extending Cole's work, Propper's model of the communication process, and Pask's conversation theory, Ford[86] argued that an enabling IR system would be equipped with pedagogic structuring and intervention (e.g., computer-as-assisted learning technologies, such as conceptual maps, summaries, abstracts, classifications, and ontologies, etc.) to enable the searcher to process and build on his/her descriptive knowledge and procedural knowledge in need and help the searcher develop effective metacognitive information handling skills. Cole et al.[47] made a similar argument as Ford, proposing the selection state-information channel model, urging an interactive IR system to develop mechanisms to interactively stimulate the searcher's cognitive ability in reaching a "selection state," which can be seen as a refined, better-defined "information need" or information problem. In other words, instead of asking the searchers to represent their "information needs" that are still in need of clarification in query terms, the system should understand the task that prompts the searchers to seek for information and interact with them to clarify their "information needs."

A growing number of user-centered studies focus on human information interaction, as opposed to human–computer interaction, in the process of interactive information retrieval and seeking. For example, Spink and her colleagues[3,46,87–89] are developing the theory of human information behavior (HIB), postulating that information seeking should be tightly connected to other information processing behavior such as information organization and use. Under this theory, an interactive IR system could be integrated into a greater information system that would function for more than just information retrieval and should support other forms of information organization and use. Fidel et al.[90] used the cognitive work analysis framework to observe how collaborative information seeking and retrieval takes place in the form of human information interaction, suggesting that interactive IR systems should include "mechanisms that support the interactions between the collaborating actors and enhance their access to one another's knowledge, ideas, and opinions or help them keep on track" (p. 951).

APPLICATIONS, TOOLS, AND TECHNIQUES FOR INTERACTIVE INFORMATION SEEKING AND RETRIEVAL

The theories, models and conceptual framework reviewed in section "General Research Streams" have directly or indirectly helped develop or called for the following interactive IR applications, tools, and techniques: user profiling,[17,73] automatic or user-controlled relevance feedback to adjust or expand the users' queries,[7,73] computer-assisted learning technologies, such as conceptual maps, summaries, abstracts, classifications, and ontologies,[86] pedagogic structuring and intervention mechanisms to help clarify and develop the searchers' explicit representation of their information problems,[44,47,86] supports beyond searchers' representation of their information problems to facilitate overall information retrieval, such as browsing, learning, evaluating search outcomes, monitoring the evolution of information problems, annotating and preserving the context, and organizing information collections.[22,25,26,53,71,78,79,91]

More detailed reviews of the types of the applications, techniques, and tools that have been developed during various periods of research in interactive IR can be found in the works of Shaw,[39] Marchionini and Komlodi,[37] and Savage-Knepshield and Belkin.[6]

EVALUATION OF INTERACTIVE INFORMATION RETRIEVAL SYSTEMS AND INTERFACES

The evaluation of information retrieval systems have traditionally used the two measures, precision and recall, developed by the system-driven approach to IR,[92–94] which typically takes place in controlled laboratory tests. These measures, however, are not the best to evaluate interactive IR systems, due to their restricted assumptions on the cognitive and behavioral aspects of the searcher,[93] as described in the previous sections about the limitations of the system-centered approach on IR system design. In addition, finding information on the Web has its specific characteristics, making the applicability of the findings from traditional IR research questionable. Traditional IR research focuses on the development of retrieval strategies for relatively small, static, and relatively homogeneous text corpora. Web information, on the other hand, is massive in size, diverse and dynamic in content and format, and uncontrollable in quality. This makes it impossible to construct a representative test collection to support the conventional evaluation measures such as precision and recall.[95]

Robertson and Hancock-Beaulieu (pp. 458–459)[96] set forth three revolutions: the cognitive revolution, the relevance revolution and the interactive revolution. The cognitive and relevance revolutions require realism with reference to the formation of information need, and relevance assessment processes. This means that an information need ought to be treated as a potentially dynamic concept, and the multidimensional (rather than just topically relevant) and dynamic nature of relevance should be taken into account. Likewise, relevance should be judged against the problematic situation in which the information need arises, not merely the explicit representation of that information need such as query or request statement, and it should be judged by the user. The "interactive revolution" requires the evaluation of IIR systems to include the user's interactive information searching and retrieval processes, where evaluation of the search outcomes can be fluid itself, depending on the stage of information searches[15] or the nature of the information problem.[26]

While the user-centered information seeking studies potentially could help generate measures to fulfill the three requirements described above,[97] they seldom directly design or implement an interactive IR system, let alone providing evaluation measurements. For the studies that do evaluate interactive IR systems, many of them quantify performance effectiveness as "relative" recall and precision ratios in spite of collecting non-binary-based relevance assessments[97] or use the measures that are ad hoc in nature or not universally agreed upon (e.g., satisfaction, the amount of time required to complete a search task, etc). Also, the operationalization of these measures is often not derived from previously well-established questionnaire inventory items.

Performance Measures

Combining the elements from both system-centered and user-centered approaches, Borlund[97] developed a hybrid evaluation approach to evaluate the systems "in a way which takes into account the dynamic natures of information needs and relevance as well as reflects the interactive information searching and retrieval processes." The highlights of Borlund's approach include 1) the emphasis in use of simulated work task situations to trigger simulated information needs and as the platform for the assessment of situational relevance in the context of IR, and 2) the development of alternative performance measures: relative relevance (RR), ranked half-life (RHL).[98] The RR measure acknowledges the fact that different types of relevance[99,100] are involved in evaluation of IR systems. The RR measure computes the degree of agreement between two results of relevance assessments; for example, one may represent the system's output (algorithmic relevance) and the other the user's subjective assessments (e.g., intellectual topicality, pertinence or situational relevance) of the retrieved output. The RR measure proposes a pragmatic solution of how to bridge the gap between subjective and objective relevance. The RHL indicator, a position-oriented measure, denotes the degree to which relevant documents are located on the top of a ranked retrieval result, using two parameters: 1) the algorithmically ranked order, which represents a list of decreasing degrees of predicted objective relevance to the user's information need and 2) the applied subjective types and values of the relevance assessments representing the assessor's or user's interpretations of the ranked information objects.

There are several position-oriented single performance measures already developed. Based on the binary approach to relevant ranked information objects, Losee[101,102] developed average search length (ASL), to indicate the expected position of a relevant information object in the ranked list of information objects. The expected search length (ESL) measure[103] and Expected Search Duration (ESD),[104] which is a modification of the ESL, both calculate the number of non-relevant information objects that the user has to view in the process of retrieving a chosen relevant information object. Seeking to estimate the cumulative relevance gain the user receives by examining the retrieval result up to a given rank, Järvelin and his colleagues[105,113] developed cumulated gain (CG) and cumulated gain with discount (DCG). Both CG and DCG are positional oriented performance measures, but the CG measure builds upon the fact that highly relevant documents are more valuable than marginally relevant documents, while the DCG measure takes into account the relevance assessment behavior of users. The DCG measure has the following advantages not provided by the ASL or RHL measures: 1) it realistically weights down the gain received through the documents found later in the ranked list of results; and 2) it allows modeling the user persistence in examining long ranked result lists by adjusting the discount factor (p. 43).[105]

Evaluation methods for non-traditional IR system, such as question-answering systems, have also been developed. Wacholder et al.[106] described a procedure for quantitative evaluation of interactive question-answering systems and illustrated it with application to the High-Quality Interactive Question-Answering (HITIQA) system. Kelly et al.[107] identified potential evaluation criteria for interactive, analytical question-answering (QA) systems by analyzing evaluative comments made by users of such a system.

Non-performance Measures

As stated in the major theoretical section of this entry, interactive information seeking is considered as a term that more properly portrays the actual interaction of the searcher with the IR system than interactive information retrieval, in that it covers a wider spectrum of the IR system user's search behavior. In addition, as Belkin et al.[71,22] and Lin and Belkin[26] pointed out, a variety of interactions other than querying and document matching is necessary in the design of interactive IR systems. Performance or retrieval effectiveness, alone, cannot completely

measure the success of an interactive IR system. Other important measures could concern efficiency (e.g., spending less time, cognitive efforts, cost effectiveness, etc., in seeking for the information), satisfaction, and goal-oriented effectiveness (e.g., meeting the goal of learning more about the subject) and will require more development in the near future.

Multi-dimensional relevance remains a key measure in interactive IR system. Saracevic[73,100] provided an excellent review of relevance measures up to date.

Continuing the thread of research that promotes the idea of broadening information retrieval to its contexts,[108] particularly the task that prompts for information retrieval,[30,82–84] for achieving overall effectiveness and efficiency of information searches, Järvelin and Ingwersen[105] proposed the nested contexts and evaluation criteria for task-based information seeking and retrieval in an interactive IR system. From the inner to the outer, the four contexts are the information retrieval context, the information seeking context, the work task context, and the social-organizational and cultural context. The information retrieval context is evaluated based on traditional IR performance measures such as recall and precision plus efficiency and quality of information/process. The information seeking context is evaluated in terms of usability and quality of information/process. The work task context is evaluated with the criteria like quality of information and work process/result. The social-organizational and cultural context is evaluated with social-cognitive relevance and quality of work task result.

Measures other than performance, such as described above, should increasingly affect the design and evaluation of interactive IR systems in the future, as the expectations and requirements of interactive IR systems continue to expand.

Validity and Reliability of Methodologies

In general, there is still a long way to achieve the robustness of evaluation measures in interactive information retrieval. Crudge and Johnson[109] reported that the repertory grid technique is a suitable method of eliciting a definite set of constructs from an ordinary information seeker without instilling unacceptable levels of bias. Käki and Aula[110] present methods for controlling the complexity of user-centered evaluations of search user interfaces through within-subjects designs, balanced task sets, time limitations, preformulated queries, cached result pages, and through limiting the users' access to result documents. Kelly et al.[111] investigate the relationship between questionnaire mode (pen-and-paper, electronic and interview) and subjects' responses to a usability questionnaire comprised of closed and open questions administered during an interactive IR experiment. Their findings suggest that researchers should use the interview mode to elicit responses to closed questions from subjects and either pen-and-paper or electronic modes to elicit responses to open questions.

IMPORTANT CONFERENCES, WORKSHOPS, ORGANIZATIONS, AND INSTITUTIONS

The Text REtrieval Conference (TREC) is co-sponsored by the National Institute of Standards and Technology (NIST) and the U.S. Department of Defense. It started in 1992 as part of the TIPSTER Text program with the purpose of supporting research within the information retrieval community by providing the infrastructure necessary for large-scale evaluation of text retrieval methodologies. There have been four research tracks in TREC particularly pertaining to interactive information retrieval. The first and the one most relevant to interactive information retrieval is the interactive track. The participating groups developed a consensus experimental protocol and carried out studies with real users using a common collection and set of user queries, but used their own interfaces and each group could add additional focus on different research topics. Relevance feedback was a predominant topic in this track. The interactive track last ran as an adjunct to the Web Track in TREC 2003. The second is the Web track, featuring search tasks on a document set that is a snapshot of the World Wide Web. It last ran in TREC 2004. The third is the HARD track. The track aims to achieve High Accuracy Retrieval from Documents by leveraging additional information about the searcher and/ or the search context, through techniques such as passage retrieval and using very targeted interaction with the searchers. It last ran in TREC 2005. The most current one is the question answering track, designed to take a step closer to information retrieval rather than document retrieval. The relevance to interactive IR studies lies in one of its sub-tracks, the complex interactive QA task.

Dumais and Belkin[112] provided a great summary of the history and the evolving experimental framework of these interactive tracks in TREC. The summary reflected the following main points. First, the main contribution lies in the development of standard methodologies for studying interactive IR and comparing performance of interactive IR systems, including experimental designs, techniques for reporting event logs, and detailed narrative description of the search process. Second, many interesting systems have been developed to support interactive query formulation and reformulation as well as results presentations and explorations, which enabled the investigation of individual differences in the search process. Third, the reported results have been often variable or not statistically significant. Fourth, the lack of consistent and significant findings could be due to a small number of analysis units (e.g., tasks, subjects) and/or the complexity

of the interactive search process that is hard or insufficient to control during experiments. Fifth, the interactive tracks have continued to at least bring to the surface various important theoretical and pragmatic issues in conducting experiments with human participants. With the points above, various tracks that looked into interactive IR have ceased or evolved, while the goal remains the same: providing a focal point for work in designing and evaluating interactive IR systems.

The annual conferences of Special Interest Group on Information Retrieval (SIGIR) and Special Interest Group on Computer–Human Interaction (SIGCHI) in the Association for Computing Machinery publish many quality research articles and hold workshops on the topics of human–computer interaction research in information retrieval.

The MIT Computer Science and Artificial Intelligence Laboratory, or CSAIL, was born on July 1, 2003 by the merger of the Artificial Intelligence Lab and the Laboratory for Computer Science. It held the first Workshop on Human–Computer Information Retrieval in 2007.

The Annual Symposium of the Human–Computer Interaction Lab at the University of Maryland often includes research on human–computer interaction vs. information retrieval/information seeking. It marked its 25th anniversary in 2008.

CONCLUSION

Human–computer interaction research in information retrieval is a very rigorous research stream. It brings two distinctly separate research communities, system-centered information retrieval research and user-centered information seeking research, closer, if not together, for the same research goal: a more effective and efficient information search system that would take advantages of the respective strengths of humans and computers for interactions. In practice, the Web has also propelled highly interactive IR interfaces that demand that these two communities work together, as information retrieval on the Web faces the challenges of supporting different information interaction purposes and motivations from very diverse end users who may have unpredictable information seeking behaviors.[2,95]

Many studies in the field of CS have started to treat the user as a dynamic and evolving participant in the IR process, designing IR systems that are adaptable and personalizable, while an increasing number of user-centered studies in the field of LIS have attempted to draw design implications from their findings. This entry has addressed the main efforts made by both research communities so far to bridge the gap, in terms of theoretical models, system designs, and ever evolving evaluation metrics and methodologies. In the future, it can be fully expected that the overall research stream will flourish with the emphasis on human–computer interaction as the means, as well as the goal of effective and efficient information searches as the end.

ACKNOWLEDGMENT

The author would like to express gratitude to Dr. Ping Zhang at Syracuse University, whose valuable suggestions helped shape this entry, and to Dr. Marcia Bates at University of California, Los Angeles, who has generously helped edit this entry.

REFERENCES

1. Ingwersen, P. *Information Retrieval Interaction*, Taylor Graham: London, 1992.
2. Marchionini, G. Toward human-computer information retrieval. ASIST Bull. June/July 2006. Available at http://www.asis.org/Bulletin/June-06/marchionini.html (accessed December 27, 2007).
3. Spink, A.; Cole, C. Introduction: New directions in cognitive information retrieval. In *New Directions in Cognitive Information Retrieval*; Spink, A., Cole, C., Eds.; The Information Retrieval Series, Springer: Berlin, Germany, 2005; Vol. 19, 3–12.
4. Belkin, N.J.; Seeger, T.; Wersig, G. Distributed expert problem treatment as a model for information system analysis and design. J. Inform. Sci. 1983, 5(5), 152–167.
5. Lancaster, F.W. *Information Retrieval Systems: Characteristics, Testing and Evaluation*, 2nd Ed. Wiley: New York, 1979.
6. Savage-Knepshield, P.; Belkin, N.J. Interaction in information retrieval: Trends over time. J. Am. Soc. Inform. Sci. Technol. 1999, 50(12), 1067–1082.
7. Spink, A.; Saracevic, T. Human-computer interaction in information retrieval: Nature and manifestations of feedback. Interact. Comput. Interdiscipl. J. Hum-Comput. Interact. 1998, 10(3), 241–267.
8. Marchionini, G. *Information Seeking in Electronic Environments*, Cambridge University Press: New York, 1995.
9. Tague-Sutcliffe, J. The pragmatics of information retrieval. Inform. Process. Manag. 1992, 34(4), 467–490.
10. Belkin, N.J.; Croft, B. Information filtering and information retrieval: Two sides of the same coin?. Commun. ACM 1992, 35(12), 29–38.
11. Saracevic, T. Modeling interaction in information retrieval (IR): A review and proposal Proceedings of the 59th American Society for Information Science Medford, NJ 1996; 33, 3–9 Information Today.
12. Bates, M.J. Where should the person stop and the information search interface start?. Inform. Process. Manag. 1990, 26, 575–591.
13. Hearst, M. User interfaces and visualization. In *Modern Information Retrieval*; Baeza-Yates, R., Ribeiro-Neto, B., Eds.; Addison-Wesley: Reading, MA, 1999; 257–322.
14. Hert, C. *Understanding Information Retrieval Interactions: Theoretical and Practical Implications*, Ablex Publishing Corporation: Greenwich, CT, 1997.
15. Kuhlthau, C.C. Inside the search process: Information seeking from the user's perspective. J. Am. Soc. Inform. Sci. 1991, 42(5), 361–371.
16. Kuhlthau, C.C. *Seeking Meaning: A Process Approach to Library and Information Services*, Ablex Publishing: Norwood, NJ, 1993.
17. Ingwersen, P. Cognitive perspectives of information retrieval interaction. Elements of a cognitive IR theory. J. Doc. 1996, 52(1), 3–50.
18. Bates, M.J. The design of browsing and berry-picking techniques for the online search interface. Online Rev. 1989, 13, 407–424.
19. Belkin, N.J.; Oddy, R.N.; Brooks, H.M. ASK for information retrieval: Parts 1 & 2. J. Doc. 1982, 38(2/3), 61–71, 145–164.
20. Oddy, R.N. Information retrieval through man-machine dialogue. J. Doc. 1977, 33(1), 1–14.
21. Taylor, R.S. Question negotiation and information seeking in libraries. Coll. Res. Libr. 1968, 29, 178–194.
22. Belkin, N.J.; Marchetti, P.G.; Cool, C. BRAQUE: Design of an interface to support user interaction in information retrieval. Inform. Process. Manag. 1993, 29(3), 325–344.
23. Marchionini, G. Interfaces for end-user information seeking. J. Am. Soc. Inform. Sci. 1992, 43(2), 156–163.
24. Ellis, D. A behavioural approach to information retrieval system design. J. Doc. 1989, 45(3), 171–212.
25. Lin, S.J.; Belkin, N.J. Modeling multiple information seeking episodes. *Proceedings of the 20th Annual Meeting of American Society for Information Science*, Chicago, IL, 2000; 133–147.
26. Lin, S.J.; Belkin, N. Validation of a model of information seeking over multiple search sessions. J. Am. Soc. Inform. Sci. Technol. 2005, 56(4), 393–415.
27. Spink, A. Multiple search sessions model of end-user behavior: An exploratory study. J. Am. Soc. Inform. Sci. 1996, 47(8), 603–609.
28. Spink, A.; Greisdorf, H. Partial relevance judgments during interactive information retrieval: An exploratory study. Proc. 60th Annu. Meet. Am. Soc. Inform. Sci. 1997, 34, 111–122.
29. Spink, A.; Ozmultu, H.C.; Ozmultu, S. Multitasking information seeking and searching processes. J. Am. Soc. Inform. Sci. Technol. 2002, 53(8), 639–652.
30. Vakkari, P. A theory of the task-based information retrieval process. J. Doc. 2001, 57(1), 44–60.
31. Vakkari, P.; Hakala, N. Changes in relevance criteria and problem stages in task performance. J. Doc. 2000, 56(5), 540–562.
32. Spink, A.; Park, M. Information and non-information task interplay. J. Doc. 2005, 61(4), 548–554.
33. Foster, J. Collaborative information seeking and retrieval. Annu. Rev. Inform. Sci. Technol. 2006, 40(1), 329–356.
34. Vakkari, P.; Järvelin, K. Explanation in information seeking and retrieval. In *New Directions in Cognitive Information Retrieval*; Spink, A., Cole, C., Eds.; The Information Retrieval Series, Springer: Berlin, Germany, 2005; Vol. 19, 113–138.

35. Fidel, R.; Soergel, D. Factors affecting online bibliographic retrieval: A conceptual framework for research. J. Am. Soc. Informa. Sci. **1983**, *34*(3), 163–80.

36. Bennett, J.L. The user interface in interactive systems. Annu. Rev. Inform. Sci. **1972**, 7, 159–196.

37. Marchionini, G.; Komlodi, A. Design of interfaces for information seeking. Annu. Rev. Inform. Sci. **1998**, 89–130.

38. Rogers, Y. New theoretical approaches for human-computer interaction. Annu. Rev. Inform. Sci. **2004**, *38*, 87–144.

39. Shaw, D. The human-computer interface for information retrieval. Annu. Rev. Inform. Sci. **1991**, *26*, 155–195.

40. Xu, Y. The dynamics of interactive information retrieval behavior, Part I: An activity theory perspective. J. Am. Soc. Inform. Sci. Technol **2007**, *58*(7), 958.

41. Xu, Y.; Liu, C. The dynamics of interactive information retrieval, part II: An empirical study from the activity theory perspective. J. Am. Soc. Inform. Sci. Technol. **2007**, *58*(7), 987.

42. Storrs, G. A conceptualization of multiparty interaction. Interact. Comput. **1994**, *6*(2), 173–189.

43. Belkin, N.J. Anomalous states of knowledge as a basis for information retrieval. Can. J. Inform. Sci. **1980**, *5*, 133–143.

44. Ford, N. New cognitive directions. In *New Directions in Cognitive Information Retrieval*; Spink, A., Cole, C., Eds.; The Information Retrieval Series, Springer: Berlin, Germany, 2005; Vol. 19, 81–98.

45. Larsen, B.; Ingwersen, P. Cognitive overlaps along the polyrepresentation continuum. In *New Directions in Cognitive Information Retrieval*; Spink, A., Cole, C., Eds.; The Information Retrieval Series, Springer: Berlin, Germany, 2005; Vol. 19, 43–60.

46. Spink, A.; Cole, C. A multitasking framework for cognitive information retrieval. In *New Directions in Cognitive Information Retrieval*; Spink, A., Cole, C., Eds.; The Information Retrieval Series, Springer: Berlin, Germany, 2005; Vol. 19, 99–132.

47. Cole, C.; Beheshti, J.; Leide, J.E.; Large, A. Interactive information retrieval: Bridging the user to a selection state. In *New Directions in Cognitive Information Retrieval*; Spink, A., Cole, C., Eds.; The Information Retrieval Series, Springer: Berlin, Germany, 2005; Vol. 19, 13–42.

48. Ruthven, I. Integrating approaches to relevance. In *New Directions in Cognitive Information Retrieval*; Spink, A., Cole, C., Eds.; The Information Retrieval Series, Springer: Berlin, Germany, 2005; Vol. 19, 61–80.

49. Beheshti, J.; Bowler, L.; Large, A.; Nesset, V. Towards an alternative information retrieval system for children. In *New Directions in Cognitive Information Retrieval*; Spink, A., Cole, C., Eds.; The Information Retrieval Series, Springer: Berlin, Germany, 2005; Vol. 19, 139–168. .

50. Kelly, D. Implicit feedback: Using behavior to infer relevance. In *New Directions in Cognitive Information Retrieval*; Spink, A., Cole, C., Eds.; The Information Retrieval Series, Springer: Berlin, 2005; Vol. 19, 169–186.

51. Lin, S. Internetworking of factors affecting successive searches over multiple episodes. J. Am. Soc. Inform. Sci. Technol. **2005**, *56*(4), 416–436.

52. Lin, S.J. Design space of personalized indexing: Enhancing successive web searches for transmuting information problems Proceedings of 2002 American Conference on Information Systems Dallas, TX August, 9–11, 2002.

53. Komlodi, A.; Marchionini, G.; Soergel, D. Search history support for finding information: User interface design recommendations from a user study. Inform. Process. Manag. **2007**, *43*, 10–29.

54. Yuan, X.; Belkin, N.J. *Interaction: Supporting Multiple Information-Seeking Strategies in a Single System Framework,* Proceedings of the 30th Annual International ACM SIGIR Amsterdam, the Netherlands, 2007; 247–254.

55. Xu, Y.; Yin, H. Novelty and topicality in interactive information retrieval. J. Am. Soc. Inform. Sci. Technol. **2008**, *59*(2), 201–215.

56. Chen, H.; Dhar, V. Cognitive process as a basis for intelligent retrieval systems design. J. Am. Soc. Inform. Sci. **1991**, *27*(5), 405–432.

57. Hendry, D.G.; Harper, D.J. An informal information-seeking environment. J. Am. Soc. Inform. Sci. **1997**, *48*(11), 1036–1048.

58. Kintsch, W. How readers construct situation models for stories: The role of syntactic cues and causal inferences. In *From Learning Processes to Cognitive Processes. Essays in Honor of William K. Estes*; Healy, A.E., Kosslyn, S.M., Shiffrin, R.M., Eds.; Erlbaum: Hillsdale, NJ, 1992; Vol. 2, 261–27.

59. Kitajima, M.; Polson, P.G. *A Comprehension-Based Model of Exploration*, CHI96' Proceedings of the SIGCHI Conference on Human Factors in Computing Systems Vancouver, BC, Canada ACM Press: New York, April 13–18, 1996; 324–331.

60. Kitajima, M.; Polson, P.G. *A Computational Model of Skilled Use of a Graphic User Interface*, CHI92' Proceedings of the SIGCHI Conference on Human Factors in Computing Systems Monterey, CA ACM Press: New York, 1992; May 3–8, 1992; 241–249.

61. Terwilliger, R.B.; Polson, P.G. *Relationships Between Users and Interfaces' Task Representations*, CHI97' Proceedings of the SIGCHI Conference on Human Factors in Computing Systems Atlanta, GA, March, 22–27, 1997 ACM Press: New York; 99–106.

62. Buchanan, G.; Blanford, A.; Jones, M. Integrating information seeking and structuring: Exploring the role of spatial hypertext in a digital library Proceedings of the Fifteenth ACM Conference on Hypertext & Hypermedia ACM Press: New York, 2004; 225–234.

63. Zhou, M.X.; Houck, K.; Pan, S.; Shaw, J.; Aggarwal, V.; Wen, Z. *Enabling Context-Sensitive Information Seeking*, Proceedings of the 11th International Conference on Intelligent User Interfaces Sydney, Australia, 2006; 116–123.

64. Oard, D.W.; He, D.; Wang, J. User-assisted query translation for interactive cross-language information retrieval. Inform. Process. Manag. **2008**, *44*(1), 181–211.

65. Toms, E.G. Information interaction: Providing a framework for information architecture. J. Am. Soc. Inform. Sci. Technol. **2002**, *53*(10), 855–862.

66. Card, S.; Moran, T.P.; Newell, A. *The Psychology of Human Computer Interaction*, Lawrence Erlbaum Associates: Hillsdale, NJ, 1983.

67. Carroll, J.M. Human-computer interaction: Psychology as a science of design. Int. J. Hum-Comput. Stud. **1997**, *46*(4), 501–522.

68. Simon, T.; Young, R.M. GOMS meets STRIPS: The integration of planning with skilled procedure execution in human-computer interaction. *In People and Computers IV*, Proceedings of the Fourth Conference of the British Computer Society Human Computer Interaction Special Group September 5–9, 1988 Cambridge University Press: New York, 1998; 581–594. University of Manchester.

69. Toms, E.G. *Browsing Digital Information: Examining the "Affordances" in the Interaction of User and Text*, Unpublished Ph.D. dissertation; University of West Ontario, 1997.

70. Belkin, N.J. Interaction with texts: Information retrieval as information-seeking behavior. In *Information Retrieval*; Knorz, G., Krause, J., Womser-Hacker, C., Eds.; 1993; 55–66. Von der Mode Zoe Anwendung. Kaustanz, Universitaires de lang Loustanz.

71. Belkin, N.J.; Cool, C.; Stein, A.; Thiel, U. Cases, scripts, and information seeking strategies: On the design of interactive information retrieval systems. Expert Syst. Appl. **1995**, *9*(3), 379–395.

72. Cool, C.; Belkin, N.J. A classification of interactions with information Proceedings of the Fourth International Conference on Conceptions of Library and Information Science, 2002; 1–15.

73. Saracevic, T. The stratified model of information retrieval interaction: Extension and applications. Proceedings of the 60th American Society for Information Science, Information Today: Medford, NJ, 1997; Vol. 34, 313–327.

74. Bates, M.J. The cascade of interactions in the digital library interface. Inform. Process. Manag. **2002**, *38*, 381–400.

75. Bates, M.J. Indexing and access for digital libraries and the internet: Human, database, and domain factors. J. Am. Soc. Inform. Sci. Technol. **1998**, *49*, 1185–1205.

76. Bates, M.J. Subject access in online catalogs: A design model. J. Am. Soc. Inform. Sci. Technol. **1986**, *37*, 357–376.

77. Wilson, M.L.; Schraefel, M.C.; White, R. Evaluating advanced search interfaces using established information-seeking models, 2007, Technical Report UNSPECIFIED, School of Electronics and Computer Science, University of Southampton. Available at http://eprints.ecs.soton.ac.uk/13737/1/sigir.pdf (accessed January 2009).

78. Komlodi, A. Task management support in information seeking: A case for search histories. Comput. Hum. Behav. **2004**, *20*, 163–184.

79. Komlodi, A.; Soergel, D.; Marchionini, G. Search histories for user support in user interfaces. J. Am. Soc. Inform. Sci. Technol. **2006**, *57*(6), 803–807.

80. Komlodi, A. The role of interaction histories in mental model building and knowledge sharing in the legal domain. J. Univ. Comput. Sci. **2002**, *8*(5), 557–566.

81. Komlodi, A.; Soergel, D. Attorneys interacting with legal information systems: Tools for mental model building and task integration Proceedings of Annual Meetings of the American Society for Information Science and Technology Philadelphia, PA, 2002.

82. Vakkari, P.; Kuokkanen, M. Theory growth in information science: Applications of the theory of science to a theory of information seeking. J. Doc. **1997**, *53*(5), 497–519.

83. Vakkari, P. Growth of theories on information seeking. An analysis of growth of a theoretical research program on relation between task complexity and information seeking. Inform. Process. Manag. **1998**, *34*(3/4), 361–382.

84. Vakkari, P. Task complexity, problem structure and information actions. Integrating studies on information seeking and retrieval. Inform. Process. Manag. **1999**, *35*(6), 819–837.

85. Cole, C. Interaction with an enabling information retrieval system: Modeling the user's decoding and encoding operations. J. Am. Soc. Inform. Sci. Technol. **2000**, *51*(5), 417–426.

86. Ford, N. Modeling cognitive processes in information seeking: From Popper to Pask. J. Am. Soc. Inform. Sci. Technol. **2004**, *55*(9), 769–782.

87. Spink, A.; Wilson, T.D.; Ford, N.; Foster, D.; Ellis, D. Information seeking and searching study. Part 3. Successive searching. J. Am. Soc. Inform. Sci. Technol. **2002**, *53*(9), 716–727.

88. Spink, A.; Currier, J. Toward an evolutionary perspective on human information behavior: An exploratory study. J. Doc. **2006**, *62*(2), 171–193.

89. Spink, A.; Cole, C. Human information behavior: Integrating diverse approaches and information use. J. Am. Soc. Inform. Sci. Technol. **2006**, *57*(1), 25–35.

90. Fidel, R.; Pejtersen, A.M.; Cleal, B.; Bruce, H. A multidimensional approach to the study of human-information interaction: A case study of collaborative information retrieval. J. Am. Soc. Inform. Sci. **2004**, *55*(11), 939–953.

91. Bates, M.J. The berry-picking search: User interface design. In *Interfaces for Information Retrieval and Online Systems: The State of the Art*; Dillon, M., Ed.; Greenwood Press: New York, 1991; 55–61.

92. Salton, G.; Buckley, C. Term-weighting approaches in automatic text retrieval. Inform. Process. Manag. **1988**, *24*(5), 513–523.

93. Ellis, D. *Progress and Problems in Information Retrieval*, Library Association Publishing: London, U.K., 1996.

94. Ellis, D. The dilemma of measurement in information retrieval research. J. Doc. **1996**, *45*(3), 23–36.

95. Yang, K. Information retrieval on the web. Annu. Rev. Inform. Sci. **2005**, *39*, 33–80.

96. Robertson, S.E.; Hancock-Beaulieu, M.M. On the evaluation of IR systems. Inform. Process. Manag. **1992**, *28*(4), 457–466.

97. Borlund, P. The IIR evaluation model: A framework for evaluation of interactive information retrieval systems. Inform. Res. **2003**, *8*(3). Available at http://informationr.net/ir/8-3/paper152.html (accessed December 27, 2007).

98. Borlund, P.; Ingwersen, P. Measures of relative relevance and ranked half-life: Performance indicators for interactive IR Proceedings of the 21st Annual International ACM SIGIR; Croft, B.W., Moffat, A., van Rijsbergen, C.J., Wilkinson, R., Zobel, J., Eds.; Melbourne, VIC, Australia, 1999; 324–331.

99. Saracevic, T. Relevance: A review of the literature and a framework for thinking on the notion in information

science. Part II: Nature and manifestations of relevance. J. Am. Soc. Inform. Sci. Technol. **2007**, *58*(13), 1915–1933.

100. Saracevic, T. Relevance: A review of the literature and a framework for thinking on the notion in information science. Part III: Behavior and effects of relevance. J. Am. Soc. Inform. Sci. Technol. **2007**, *58*(13), 2126–2144.

101. Losee, R.M. Evaluating retrieval performance given database and query characteristics: Analytical determination of performance surfaces. J. Am. Soc. Inform. Sci. **1996**, *47*(1), 95–105.

102. Losee, R.M. *Text Retrieval and Filtering: Analytical Methods of Performance*, Kluwer Academic Publishers: Norwell, MA, 1998.

103. Cooper, W.S. Expected search length: A single measure of retrieval effectiveness based on the weak ordering action of retrieval systems. Am. Doc. **1968**, *19*(1), 30–41.

104. Dunlop, M. Time, relevance and interaction modeling for information retrieval Proceedings of the 20th ACM SIGIR Conference on Research and Development of Information Retrieval Philadelphia, PA; Belkin, N.J., Rarasimhalu, A. D., Willett, P., Eds., ACM Press: New York, 1997; 206–213.

105. Järvelin, K.; Ingwersen, P. Information seeking research needs extension toward tasks and technology. Inform. Res. **2004**, *10*(1), paper 212. Available at http://InformationR.net/ir/10-1/paper212.html (accessed December 27, 2007).

106. Wacholder, N.; Kelly, D.; Kantor, P.; Rittman, P. A model for quantitative evaluation of an end-to-end question-answering system. J. Am. Soc. Inform. Sci. Technol. **2007**, *58*(8), 1082.

107. Kelly, D.; Wacholder, N.; Rittman, R.; Sun, Y. Using interview data to identify evaluation criteria for interactive, analytical question-answering systems. J. Am. Soc. Inform. Sci. Technol. **2007**, *58*(7), 1032.

108. Pejtersen, A.M.; Rasmussen, J. Ecological information systems and support of learning: Coupling work domain information to user characteristics. In *Handbook of Human-Computer Interaction*; Helander, M.G., Landauer, T.K., Prabhu, P.V., Eds.; Elsevier: Amsterdam, the Netherlands, 1997; 315–345.

109. Crudge, S.E.; Johnson, F.C. Using the information seeker to elicit construct models for search engine evaluation. J. Am. Soc. Inform. Sci. Technol. **2004**, *55*(9), 794–806.

110. Käki, M.; Aula, A. Controlling the complexity in comparing search user interfaces via user studies. Inform. Process. Manag. **2008**, *44*(1), 82–91.

111. Kelly, D.; Harper, D.J.; Landau, B. Questionnaire mode effects in interactive information retrieval experiments. Inform. Process. Manag. **2008**, *44*(1), 122–141.

112. Dumais, S.T.; Belkin, N.J. The TREC interactive tracks: Putting the user into search. In *TREC: Experiment and Evaluation in Information Retrieval*; Voorhees, E.M., Harman, D.K., Eds.; MIT Press: Cambridge, MA, 2005; 123–153.

113. Järvelin, K.; Kekäläinen, J. IR evaluation methods for retrieving highly relevant documents Proceedings of the 23rd ACM SIGIR Conference on Research and Development of Information Retrieval Athens, Greece; Belkin, N. J., Ingwersen, P., Leong, M-K., Eds.; ACM Press: New York, 2000; 41–48.

Humanities Literatures and Their Users

Stephen E. Wiberley, Jr.
University of Illinois at Chicago, Chicago, Illinois, U.S.A.

Abstract

This entry discusses definition of the humanities, reviews briefly the history of study of uses of information in the humanities, presents the characteristics of different types of literature used in humanistic scholarship in various fields, outlines how scholars identify and access different types of literature, and discusses the use of digital information by humanities scholars.

INTRODUCTION

This entry has five goals. First, the entry aims to show the range of approaches toward definition of the humanities. Most relevant to library and information science (LIS) is a definition that distinguishes the humanities from the sciences and social sciences in terms of the sources of information that provide humanists with their basic evidence. Second, the entry gives a very brief history of the study of use of different types of literature in the humanities. Third, the entry explains what primary literature is, its importance for humanistic scholarship, and how humanists identify and locate the primary literature they use. Fourth, the entry explains what secondary literature is, its importance for humanistic scholarship, the distinguishing characteristics of the secondary literature of the humanities, and how humanists identify and locate the secondary literature they use. The discussions of identification and location of primary and secondary literature review what is known about how humanists use access services (sometimes called tertiary literature) and consult with archivists and librarians as they seek relevant literature. Finally, the entry talks about where information seeking and use fit into the workflow of humanities scholars.

At several places, the entry refers to the use of digital literature and access services in the humanities. Until recently digital information has played a limited role in the humanities. This is likely because only a small portion of primary and secondary literature for humanities scholarship was available in digital form. The entry asserts that, now that a substantial and expanding body of literature is available in digital form, the major challenge for future research about humanities users and their literatures will be charting growth in use of digital sources and the ways in which use of them affects the conduct of humanities scholarship.

DEFINITION OF THE HUMANITIES

Approaches toward definition of the term "the humanities" vary. First, many do not define the term, but list disciplines they think constitute the humanities. The most influential example of this approach is the legislation that established the National Endowment for the Humanities in 1965. This law asserted

> The term 'humanities' includes, but is not limited to, the study of the following: language, both modern and classical; linguistics; literature; history; jurisprudence; philosophy; archaeology; comparative religion; ethics; the history, criticism and theory of the arts; those aspects of social sciences which have humanistic content and employ humanistic methods; and the study and application of the humanities to the human environment with particular attention to reflecting our diverse heritage, traditions, and history and to the relevance of the humanities to the current conditions of national life.[1]

Others assert the humanities cannot be defined, but only characterized. In LIS, an influential example of this approach is Allen who states "the nature of the humanities is better understood through observation of their characteristics than by reading definitions." She finds the humanities have

> concern for the individual and for the thoughts, imagination, achievement, creativity, performance, and impact of individuals. There is a concern for culture and for all kinds of human behaviors that produce cultural artifacts. And perhaps all these concerns are framed by the larger concern for values, for quality, and for expression (p. xi).[2]

Finally, some do define the term. In LIS, an important instance of this approach is Blazek and Aversa's *The Humanities* (2000) that follows the Commission on the Humanities and defines the humanities as "those fields of scholarship and study that are 'dedicated to the disciplined development of verbal, perceptual, and imaginative skills needed to understand experience.'" (p. 1)[3]

Also within LIS, Wiberley and Jones have defined the humanities as those fields of scholarship that strive to reconstruct, describe, and interpret the activities and accomplishments of people by establishing and studying

Encyclopedia of Library and Information Sciences, Fourth Edition DOI: 10.1081/E-ELIS4-120043276

documents and other artifacts created by those people. They recognize that all scholarship is a continuum from the sciences to the social sciences to the humanities. There is overlap between the social sciences and the humanities, but clear difference between the core of each area.[4]

Following Wiberley and Jones, the present entry contrasts the humanities to the physical sciences that strive to describe and explain the world through evidence derived from observation and experimentation and the social sciences that strive to describe and explain the activities and behaviors of people through evidence developed by experiment, field work, and survey. Unlike scientists and social scientists, humanities scholars do not construct data gathering instruments (e.g., digital sensors or survey questionnaires) that shape their basic evidence and initially record it. Instead the basic evidence for humanities scholars are artifacts, including documents, that other people created.

The grounding of a definition of the humanities in sources of information makes it relevant to LIS. Tibbo, for example, followed Wiberley and Jones's definition in her discussion of user instruction for database searching in the humanities.[5] The definition, in effect, includes most of the fields normally associated with the humanities: classics; archaeology; literary studies; and history, criticism and theory of the arts, including both fine arts and music. Nevertheless, the definition is unconventional in that it, in effect, includes most of history, often categorized as a social science, and excludes philosophy in the Anglo-American tradition and most of linguistics that are usually grouped with the humanities in universities and by funding agencies and are included in a number of LIS studies about the humanities. This entry discusses philosophy and linguistics, but its conclusion summarizes the article in relation to the Wiberley/Jones definition.

HISTORY OF STUDY OF USES OF INFORMATION IN THE HUMANITIES

In 1975, Bebout, Davis, and Oehlerts asked why there were so few user studies in the humanities, when user studies in the sciences and engineering had a long history and user studies in the social sciences were a growing interest.[6] Four of the five studies of humanities users they referenced were citation studies. Less than a decade later, Stone, citing over 80 different sources, summarized what had been learned to that point about humanities scholars. Few of the sources Stone cited were user studies, most were informed opinion of an individual about the humanities and the work of humanities' scholars. Among the user studies were a handful of surveys from the United Kingdom and the United States.[7] In 1994, Watson-Boone synthesized the findings from seven interview or questionnaire studies and six studies of sources used, including two studies covered by Bebout, Davis, and Oehlerts and one that Stone had reviewed.[8]

Since 1994, researchers have conducted additional questionnaire and interview studies as well as more citation studies. Some scholars, including Bates,[9] Cole,[10] Cullars,[11] Dalton,[12] Heinzkill,[13] Knieval and Kelsey,[14] Palmer and Neumann,[15] Tibbo,[16] and Wiberley and Jones,[17] have published multiple studies that build on their previous work. Because the most recent, relevant publications by these authors cite their earlier work and many other germane publications, this entry generally cites only their latest work.

Unlike Bebout, Davis, and Oehlert, we today know much about how humanities scholars use the literatures of their fields. At the same time, there is more to learn, both because our knowledge is incomplete and the rapid growth of digital primary and secondary literature is likely to change greatly humanities scholarship. Among other things, we need to learn about the predominant types of humanities scholarship so that information professionals can understand humanists better and serve them more effectively.

TYPES OF LITERATURE USED IN THE HUMANITIES

This entry is about the literatures of the humanities. By literature is meant written sources, usually called documents. The social sciences and the sciences have two kinds of literature. First, there is the literature in which social scientists and scientists write about the results of their scholarship. Second, there is a literature that describes and indexes the publications written by social scientists and scientists. This second kind of literature is often called access services. For scholarship in the humanities there are three kinds of literature: primary literature that contains the evidence on which humanists base their scholarship, secondary literature in which humanists write up their scholarship, and access services that describe and index the publications written by humanists. This entry will focus on the primary and secondary literature because there has been substantial research about use of them. It will discuss access literature in relation to them.

Use of primary sources is essential for any work in the humanities. Use of secondary literature is not essential. For example, some significant twentieth century literary criticism cited no secondary sources. But today, the more one aspires for expertise and recognition in the humanities, the more one must engage and cite the secondary literature.

Primary Literature

The primary literature is that which is written by the persons whose activities and accomplishments the humanist seeks to describe or interpret or by persons who observed first-hand the subject whose activities and accomplishments the humanist studies. For a study of George Washington during his presidential years, the following are examples of primary literature a humanities scholar might use: the correspondence of Washington, his family, friends, political allies, and opponents, and diaries, newspapers, and magazines from his era. For a study of Mark Twain's *Huckleberry Finn*, primary literature could include editions of the novel prepared with the author's participation, Twain's notebooks and correspondence, the papers of the novel's publisher, the records of the persons who manufactured copies of it, and publications and personal papers that contained responses to it.

There are a variety of perspectives for analyzing and classifying sources that can be considered primary literature. Does the source exist only in its original version or are there later versions of the source? Was the source unpublished, that is, created only for personal use or limited, controlled distribution or was the source published, that is, purposely disseminated to the public through established channels of distribution? Does only one copy or do many copies survive? Is the source in the possession of an individual or in an institutional collection? If in an institutional collection, is the collection organized as an archive or as a library? In what medium does the source exist: paper, microform, or digital?

Each of the characteristics of primary literature outlined above affects use. Generally speaking, the more public a source, the easier it is for people to use that source. That is, if a source was initially published in many copies (e.g., a popular novel), it is more likely to be available than if it has only existed in one copy that was made for personal use (e.g., a letter to a friend). Similarly, if a source is in a publicly accessible repository, it is easier to locate and use than if it is in private hands.

While there are numerous cases of scholars using primary sources from private, including personal, collections, for the most part humanists use sources held in institutions—libraries, archives, and museums. This is especially true of older sources in original format. As time passes, few artifacts survive for scholars' use unless they are under institutional care.

Primary literature also includes the digital file of a document. An interesting question is whether a digital file is in itself primary literature or its display on a screen or in print is primary literature. The characteristics that make it primary literature are not apparent until they are displayed, yet without the stored file their appearance is impossible.

Extent of use of primary literature

The landmark work of Cullars on citation patterns in humanities monographs is the best starting point for learning about the extent of use of primary sources in humanities scholarship. Cullars's research and his review of other studies tell us that approximately half of all references in humanities scholarship are to primary sources. In fine arts scholarship, references to primary literature range from 30% to 45% of all references. When references to art objects (also primary sources) are added to references to primary literature, the percentage ranges from slightly less than 50% to more than 60%. In investigations of studies of literature in western European languages, Cullars found that the percentage of primary literature cited ranged from 49% to 61%.[18] Other research has found that citations to primary sources are normally more than half of all citations.[12,13] Interestingly, Cullars's discussion of characteristics of citations in philosophy questions the applicability of the distinction between primary and secondary sources for that discipline because essentially all philosophical writing interprets other philosophical writing. He finds that it is impossible to make a distinction between teachers (in other humanities disciplines the authors of secondary sources, e.g., literary critics) and practitioners (in other disciplines the authors of primary sources, e.g., novelists).[11]

Access to primary literature

How do humanities scholars gain access to the primary literature that they use? Normally to gain access a person first has to identify a given source as relevant and then locate a copy. Sometimes location comes first and then identification follows. For example, location precedes identification in browsing of book stacks.

Presuming the normal sequence of identification preceding location, we can ask how identification occurs. This question has two parts. First, what terminology do humanities scholars use when they seek primary literature? Second, what sources do humanities scholars use when they seek primary literature?

Regarding terminology, the Getty End-User Online Searching Project showed that humanists distinguish themselves from scientists and social scientists by using proper terms in their information seeking.[19] Proper terms include names of people (Charles Dickens), places (London), and time periods (Victorian Era). While the Getty study was about retrieval of secondary literature, its findings about use of proper terms apply to primary sources. Reports about users of archives and manuscript collections also tell us that they use names of people and organizations to find relevant sources. In addition, the evidence indicates that humanities scholars use proper terms to organize their notes and to build their understanding of their topics.[10,20] Humanities scholars do use common terms in their searching, but when they have a topic that lends itself to being described or pursued with proper terms, they use them.

There are several means that humanities scholars use to locate primary literature. For primary literature in archives and manuscript collections, Tibbo's survey of historians in 2001 is the most informative study about historians' self-reported approaches to archival materials at the turn of the century. First, almost all scholars, at some time, identify relevant collections through leads and citations in printed books and articles. Roughly four-fifths use printed bibliographies, finding aids, and repository guides as well as their home institution's online catalog. Approximately three-fifths search other institutions' online catalogs and bibliographic utilities like OCLC (Online Computer Library Center), and visit repository Web sites. About two-fifths use Web search engines. Younger historians tend to use electronic means more than older historians. Because an increasing number of finding aids and archival documents are appearing on the Web, it will be important to chart change in use of electronic means of identifying relevant collections. Scholars also consult curators and colleagues to find needed materials. Approximately four-fifths ask colleagues, and most ask repository personnel for assistance whether by writing, telephoning, or e-mailing.[16]

Once at the archives, scholars make great use of finding aids.[12,16,20] Finding aids describe the individual or corporate body that created or gathered the records, and they enumerate, usually at the folder but sometimes at the document level, the collection's components. While at the archives, scholars also seek help of curators. Because archive and manuscript collections contain unique materials that are not described and cataloged in standardized ways as are books and journals, they are not as easy to find. Interviews with scholars who use archives and manuscripts reveal that most report enlisting the help of collection curators to tell them of recent acquisitions not yet processed, to identify collections the scholar has not found by other means, and to pinpoint relevant materials within collections that the scholar has identified as relevant but not yet examined.[20]

By no means are all primary sources found in archives and manuscript collections. Literary critics or theorists, for instance, may never use an archival source. For many topics, most relevant primary literature was published. Published literature may include books, magazines, newspapers, and government publications. It also includes modern scholarly editions of older sources, for example, the University of California Press edition of the works of Mark Twain and the University Press of Virginia edition of the papers of George Washington. To locate published sources, use of library catalogs—ranging from the global WorldCat to the local catalog—is essential.[12]

It should be noted that scholarly editions are an important exception to the general rule that humanists do not contribute to the development of their basic evidence. In scholarly editing, editors make choices, sometimes numerous and sometimes debatable, that shape the content of the scholarly edition. To be sure, editors must be faithful to the content of the original primary literature that initially recorded the basic evidence and must have evidence to justify changes they make. Nevertheless, scholarly

editions differ, even if slightly, from manuscript correspondence, first editions of novels and the like on which they are based.

Digital primary literature

Since the 1980s, studies of humanities scholars have explored the role of digital primary literature in their work. In general, these studies found that few scholars used digital sources and those who did were usually at the margins of their disciplines. This led to the claim that humanities scholars were intrinsically not just opposed to digital sources, but to information technology. Research, however, has shown that, in general, humanists adopt information technology whenever it benefits their work. Most important, the limited use of digital literature appears to have been a function of the scarcity of sources in that format.

The case of ancient Greek texts is instructive in this regard. Since the mid-1980s, the *Thesaurus Linguae Graecae* (TLG) has made available a vast digitized dataset of those texts. Once available, these were used widely by classicists.[21] The advantage that classics had was that Greek primary literature was limited in scope and much of it could be digitized with the given technology available at the time. For many years, other fields, where the potential primary literature was vast or innumerable, were not in a position to launch such a conversion.

In the present century, the availability of digitized primary literature has grown enormously, largely driven by commercial firms that convert microfilmed sources into digital form or digitize books from partner libraries' collections. Presumably use of these digitized sources is following. A major challenge and obligation for future research about the use of primary literature by humanities scholars is to chart the growth in use of digital literature and how that growth changes use of information and humanities scholarship. To give a simple example of how scholarship might change, we can consider that traditionally historians have identified relevant passages in archival sources by what Cole aptly calls "scan reading."[10] With computers, scholars can have the machine identify relevant passages either by simple keyword matching or more sophisticated software analysis. Traditionally, scholars have debated each other's judgment and thoroughness in examining the primary literature. In the future, debate may center on choice of keywords or on software selected to screen primary literature.

Because primary literature, often in its original state, is important for humanities scholarship, the preservation of born-digital sources is essential. So far there is no demonstrated ability to preserve digital information over the long-term as well as we can preserve print-on-paper information. Even the most basic forms of documents, for example, e-mails and word-processed letters or drafts of literary works, are at risk. Beyond the fundamental need to preserve the character strings, it is highly desirable, in some cases at least, to preserve digital information so that it has the same appearance as in its original state. Preservation of the original look of a text may prove extraordinarily difficult, if not impossible. An important question is whether future humanities scholars will be able to analyze the appearance of decades-old, born-digital literature, the way their predecessors analyzed the layout and typography of literature from the print era.

Secondary Literature

In the humanities, secondary literature is writing that describes or interprets what people, usually scholars, find or conclude when they study primary sources about the activities and accomplishments of other people. A book about Washington's presidency and an article in a literary journal about *Huckleberry Finn* are examples of secondary literature. One distinctive characteristic of secondary literature in the humanities is that it normally is the work of a single author. In much of the social sciences and most of the sciences, coauthorship is the norm. Single authorship does not mean that humanities scholars never interact with other scholars. In fact, they normally consult colleagues as well as information professionals. But they do more of their work in isolation than scientists and social scientists.

Also noteworthy about the secondary literature of the humanities is the possibility that it can become primary literature. For instance, scholars may study the evaluation that other scholars have given to Washington's presidency over the years, or they may study critical reaction to *Huckleberry Finn* during different eras. In these cases, books about Washington's presidency or journal articles that interpret *Huckleberry Finn* become primary literature.

A portion of the secondary literature that humanities scholars use is published during their careers. As a result, given natural patterns of book purchase and journal subscription, scholars often use personal copies of secondary literature. For many humanists, use of personal copies of secondary literature contrasts with use of primary literature that is often available only in repositories. At the same time, topical and temporal scatter of secondary literature is normally so great in the humanities that few humanists will own more than a fraction of the secondary sources they use and will rely on libraries for the rest.

Format

In the humanities, the formats in which scholars publish their research are books and journals. Most books are monographs by a single author about a single topic, but a small percentage is books that contain chapters by different authors. Research about formats cited in humanities publications has almost always reported the percentages of books without differentiating between those single-authored and those with different chapter authors. Also, almost all reports about format are separate from reports about proportions of primary and secondary sources, so there is little to say about the proportions of primary and secondary sources among books and journals. As a result, a synthesis of citation studies cannot present a detailed picture. Despite difficulties in generalization, one trend seems clear. Scholars today cite more literature than their predecessors.[12,22]

While most research has not differentiated between format of primary and secondary literature, two studies of citations to secondary literature have found that about 75% to 80% of those citations were to books and 20% to 25% to journals.[12,14] Interestingly, these percentages for books and journals also hold with small variations when citations to primary and secondary literature are combined.[8,11,13] Linguistics appears not to fit this pattern. In linguistics, studies have found books to be 50% to 60% of citations and journals 40% to 50%.[14,23]

Age

Humanities scholars are noted for the age of the literature that they use. While in many scientific and social scientific fields it is unusual to cite literature that is more than 10 years old; in the humanities, it is normal to cite literature that is more than a decade old or older. How much of this difference in age of sources is attributable to secondary sources is impossible to say because citation studies in the humanities have not differentiated age of primary sources from age of secondary sources. Furthermore, because different studies use different time frames to report their findings, we can only generalize broadly about their results. That said, the available data are worth presenting, if only to reinforce the overall difference in the use of literature by humanities scholars from the use of literature by scientists and social scientists. Watson-Boone's summary of eight studies shows that roughly one-third of sources cited or used are more than 30 years old.[8] Later research supports this generalization, except for linguistics.[11,13,18] In linguistics, almost 90% of the citations are to publications less than 30 years old.[14,23]

Language

Increasingly after World War II, English became the language of science and today most of the important scientific publications are in that language. The social sciences are less tied to English, but many important international journals are in that language. In the humanities, non-English language publications remain important. As with age, some of the difference stems from citations to primary literature. Nevertheless, Knieval and Kellsey's study of citations to secondary sources in English-language journals in eight humanities disciplines found that the percentage of non-English language publications cited ranged from one-sixth to one-third, except for linguistics (10%) and philosophy (1%).[14] Other research supports the finding for linguistics, but not philosophy.[11,23] Topic of study and the language of a study's author affect language of sources cited. Thirty percent of citations in a sample of English-language monographs in fine arts that included titles about artists from non-English speaking countries were to non-English language publications. German and French fine arts monographs cited their native language about 70% of the time.[18] In English-language journals about English and American literature nearly 100% of the sources cited were in English.[13]

Identifying and locating secondary literature

While there are few studies of the use of bibliographic databases like *Historical Abstracts* or the *Modern Language Association International Bibliography* by humanities scholars, evidence indicates that these databases are used more today than their print counterparts were in the past. Dalton and Charnigo found that in 2003 historians preferred bibliographic databases more than other means to identify secondary literature relevant to their research. This contrasts with Dalton's 1981 survey that found abstracts or indexes ranked fifth among means to identify relevant secondary sources.[12] Increased reliance on bibliographic databases makes sense given that they are easier to use than print indexes—searching of the entire database can be done at the scholar's desktop, eliminating a trip to the library and a series of lookups in separate index volumes—and given the growth in the literature with which scholars must cope.

Besides using bibliographic databases, scholars employ traditional methods of following references in publications they read, looking at specialized bibliographies (e.g., one about the American revolutionary war), searching library catalogs, and reading book reviews and listings of new books and journals. To a lesser extent, scholars consult colleagues and other experts, and, to a slightly lesser extent, librarians. Interestingly, online discussion forums of various sorts seem to have almost no value for identifying secondary literature.[12]

The previously mentioned Getty End-User Online Searching Project showed that when searching for secondary literature in bibliographic databases, humanists use proper nouns much more than scientists and social scientists. The Getty researchers compared queries of humanists whom they studied with queries of scientists and social scientists found in a study by Saracevic and Kantor. Only 18% of the science and social science queries used proper terms, while 84% of the humanities queries did. Among proper terms, nearly 50% of the humanities queries used the names of individuals. From the perspective of common terms, 100% of the science and social science queries used common terms, while only 57% of the humanities statements did.[19]

Digital secondary literature

During the past 10 years, more and more of the secondary literature of the humanities has become available in digital format. Major university presses have begun to release digital copies of their books, and humanities journals are increasingly available over the Web. How humanities scholars are using digital secondary literature needs investigation. The book is the most important format for humanists, yet the length of books makes it difficult to read them on screen and impractical to print them out. After scholars discover online relevant books, they may obtain printed copies for reading by purchase or borrowing from a library. Because journal articles are shorter than books, online versions may be what all libraries need to acquire. Scholars who do not read journal articles on-screen can print them out for reading. Even if scholars read only the digital version of a book or journal, they likely will find it easier to cite those articles in traditional form without their URLs. Thus citation data may not necessarily tell what format of a publication the scholar actually used. Survey research will be necessary, while recognizing that what people say they do does not necessarily correspond to their behavior. Important too will be learning if there is a difference between use of digital primary literature and use of digital secondary literature. One hypothesis to test is that humanists use computers to identify relevant passages of primary literature and then read only these passages, but read through secondary sources and use information technology only to deliver the source, not parse it.

How humanities scholars integrate information into their work

Thus far this entry has discussed use of the literatures of the humanities from the perspective of the literatures themselves, both primary and secondary, characteristics of those literatures, mechanisms of access, and digital formats.

Another way to discuss literatures is in terms of how they fit into the scholar's workflow. At what points in a project do humanities scholars normally seek primary and secondary literatures? When do they read those literatures? For literary critics, Chu has proposed a model and noted common variants to it. Not surprisingly, the greatest concentration of searching for primary and secondary literatures occurs after the scholar decides to pursue a topic and before the scholar drafts the write-up. Between those two points, the scholar reads the sources that the search has identified. For some projects of mature scholars, there is no initial search to identify relevant primary and secondary literature, because the scholar already knows what they are. Nevertheless, in all cases, whether the topic is new or familiar, analysis and writing reveal that the scholar needs slight to moderate amounts of additional information and this revelation leads to searching for that information and reading of the sources identified by the search. An important difference between literary critics, on the one hand, and scientists and social scientists on the other, is that literary critics do not spend time constructing data gathering instruments to record initially their basic evidence. Construction of instruments for initial data recording is unnecessary in the humanities because that evidence already exists.[24]

Other research by Case on how historians work concludes that "stages of research are illusory" and that "choosing and refining topics, planning and conducting studies, gathering and interpreting evidence, and writing and revising manuscripts can go on concurrently, both within and across individual projects."[25] It may be that humanists, like Chu's literary critics, who begin with an interest in specific works of art, literature, and music and then study those works differ from humanists, like Case's historians, who begin with topics and then explore bodies of archival materials and other blocks of primary sources like newspapers in order to understand those topics. The projects of the latter group of humanists are usually more open ended than those of the former group necessitating more iterations of seeking additional information, refining the topic, and revising the write-up.

Exposition of the elements of the workflow of humanities scholars is an important advance in our understanding of their use of information. With models in mind, practitioners can be more sensitive to the needs of humanists with whom they work. For example, while identifying a long list of relevant literature can help a humanist at the start of a project, a long list probably will be a hindrance after the analysis and writing stage when the humanist is addressing specific information needs.

There is still much to learn about how humanists use information for different types of scholarship. Tibbo, for example, found that social historians differ from biographers in the ways they seek information about archival collections.[16] We know that critical and documentary editions differ from publications of interpretative types of humanities scholarship like criticism, history, and theory. But we lack analyses of the nature of these and other differences, their relationships to searching for and use of primary and secondary literatures, and their meaning for practice by information professionals. This is a challenge because to understand well humanities scholarship, one must study both scholars in many disciplines and books that are far more difficult to analyze than journal articles. The greater availability of digital versions of books should help in this regard, because it provides machine-readable data for such analyses.

CONCLUSION

The literatures of the humanities and the uses of them have several characteristics that distinguish them from the literatures of the sciences and the social sciences and use of those literatures. While the sciences have as their basic evidence results of observation and experiment and the social sciences the results of experiment, field work, and survey, the humanities study artifacts, especially documents, created by other people. The documents that are the humanist's basic evidence constitute the primary literature of the humanities. Scientists and social scientists do not have a comparable literature. Almost half of the citations in humanities scholars' publications are to primary literature or other primary sources. Because the humanities study what people have done in different places and at different times, proper terms, especially the names of individuals, are very important in retrieval of literature, both primary and secondary. Also, because humanities scholarship builds upon documents and artifacts created by different people in different places and times and not by the humanist who uses them, there is less possibility for conventions of method or uniformity in procedure in humanities scholarship than there is in the sciences and social sciences where scholars themselves initially record their basic data. Without a role in the initial recording of their basic data, humanists are less able to construct paradigms than are scientists and social scientists. One consequence of uniqueness of setting and basic evidence and the lack of paradigms and conventions of method is that publications in the humanities generally have to be longer than those in the sciences and social sciences in order to explain the context of the findings and the way in which the scholar developed them. As a result, the book, rather than the journal article, is the predominant form of publication. Lacking paradigms and conventions of method, humanities publications do not build on a sequence of preceding scholarship as easily as do the sciences and social sciences, and so are less likely to cite new scholarship than scientific or social scientific publications. Given that they discuss past activities and accomplishments in different places around the world, there is greater diversity in language of sources cited in the humanities publications than in scientific and social scientific publications.

Because humanists generally do not have a role in the development of their basic evidence as do scientists and social scientists, they have applied more slowly information technology to their scholarship. Since the turn of the century, the availability of digital primary literature has increased very significantly, as countless documents are born digital and innumerable paper-based sources are converted into digital form. Increased digitization of primary evidence and secondary literature is likely to change greatly humanities scholarship. Today, the primary task for research about use of literatures in the humanities is to study effects of this digitization on humanities scholarship.

ACKNOWLEDGMENTS

The author thanks Marcia Bates, John Cullars, Joan B. Fiscella, and Valerie Harris for commenting on drafts of this entry.

REFERENCES

1. National Endowment for the Humanities, What are the Humanities, http://www.neh.gov/whoweare/overview.html.
2. Allen, N. Introduction. *The Humanities and the Library*, 2nd Ed.; Couch, N., Allen, N., Eds.; American Library Association: Chicago, IL, 1993; xi–xviii.
3. Blazek, R.; Aversa, E. *The Humanities: A Selective Guide to Information Resources*, 5th Ed. Libraries Unlimited: Littleton, CO, 2000.
4. Wiberley, S.E.; Jones, W.G. Humanists revisited: a longitudinal look at the adoption of information technology. Coll. Res. Libr. **1994**, *55*(6), 499–509.
5. Tibbo, H. User instruction issues: database searching in the humanities. *Encyclopedia of Library and Information Science*, 1st Ed.; Kent, A., Hall, C.M., Eds.; Marcel Dekker, Inc.: New York, 1999; Vol. 65, 330–354.
6. Bebout, L.; Davis, D.; Oehlerts, D. User studies in the humanities: a survey and a proposal. RQ **1975**, *15*(1), 40–44.
7. Stone, S. Humanities scholars: information needs and uses. J. Doc. **1982**, *38*(4), 292–313.
8. Watson-Boone, R. The information needs and habits of humanities scholars. RQ **1994**, *34*(2), 203–216.
9. Bates, M.J. The Getty end-user searching project in the humanities: Report no. 6: Overview and conclusions. Coll. Res. Libr. **1996**, *57*(6), 514–523.
10. Cole, C. Name collection by Ph.D. history students: Inducing expertise. J. Am. Soc. Inf. Sci. **2000**, *51*(5), 444–455.
11. Cullars, J. Citation characteristics of English-language monographs in philosophy. Lib. Inf. Sci. Res. **1998**, *20*(1), 41–68.
12. Dalton, M.S.; Charnigo, L. Historians and their information sources. Coll. Res. Libr. **2004**, *65*(5), 400–425.
13. Heinzkill, R. References in scholarly English and American literary journals thirty years later: a citation study. Coll. Res. Libr. **2007**, *68*(2), 141–153.
14. Knieval, J.E.; Kelsey, C. Citation analysis for collection development: a comparative study of eight humanities fields. Libr. Quart. **2005**, *75*(2), 142–168.
15. Palmer, C.L.; Neumann, L.J. The information work of interdisciplinary humanities scholars: exploration and translation. Libr. Quart. **2002**, *72*(1), 85–117.
16. Tibbo, H.R. Primarily history in America: how U.S. historians search for primary materials at the dawn of the digital age. Am. Archivist **2003**, *66*(1), 9–50.
17. Wiberley, S.E.; Jones, W.G. Time and technology: a decade-long look at humanists' use of electronic information technology. Coll. Res. Libr. **2000**, *61*(5), 421–431.
18. Cullars, J. Citation characteristics of French and German fine arts monographs. Libr. Quart. **1996**, *66*(2), 138–160.
19. Bates, M.J.; Wilde, D.N.; Siegfried, S. An analysis of search terminology used by humanities scholars: The Getty online searching project report number 1. Libr. Quart. **1993**, *63*(1), 1–39.
20. Duff, W.M.; Johnson, C.A. Accidentally found on purpose: information seeking behavior of historians in archives. Libr. Quart. **2002**, *72*(4), 472–496.
21. Brunner, T.F. The Thesaurus Linguae Graecae: classics and the computer. Libr. Hi Tech **1991**, *9*(1), 61–67.
22. Kellsey, C.; Knievel, J. Global English in the humanities? A longitudinal citation study of foreign-language use by humanities scholars. Coll. Res. Libr. **2004**, *65*(3), 194–204.
23. Georgas, H.; Cullars, J. A citation study of the characteristics of the linguistics literature. Coll. Res. Libr. **2005**, *66*(6), 496–515.
24. Chu, C.M. Literary critics at work and their information needs: a research-phases model. Libr. Inform. Sci. Res. **1999**, *21*(2), 247–273.
25. Case, D.O. The collection and use of information by some American historians: a study of motives and methods. Libr. Quart. **1991**, *61*(1), 61–82.

BIBLIOGRAPHY

1. Al, U.; Sahiner, S.; Tonta, Y. Arts and humanities literature: bibliometric characteristics of contributions by Turkish authors. J. Am. Soc. Inf. Sci. Tech. **2006**, *57*(8), 1011–1022.
2. Day, B.H., Wortman, W.A., Eds. *Literature in English: A Guide for Librarians in the Digital Age*; Association of College and Research Libraries: Chicago, IL, 2000; ACRL Publications in Librarianship No. 54.
3. Gould, C.C. *Information Needs in the Humanities: An Assessment*, Research Libraries Group, Program for Research Information Management: Stanford, CA, 1988.
4. Romanos de Tiratel, S. Accessing information use by humanists and social scientists: a study at the universidad de Buenos Aires, Argentina. J. Acad. Libr. **2000**, *26*(5), 346–354.
5. Schreibman, S. Siemens, R. Unsworth, J. *A Companion to Digital Humanities*; Blackwell Publishing: Malden, MA, 2004.

Hungary: Libraries, Archives, and Museums

Katalin Radics

Research Library, University of California—Los Angeles, Los Angeles, California, U.S.A.

Abstract

After briefly introducing the history of Hungarian literacy, libraries, publishing, record keeping, and museums, this entry gives an overview of Hungarian libraries, the discipline of information science, and the library and information profession, including education for library professionals, and professional associations in the country. A similar review follows about archives: an overview of the different kinds of archives, archival science, education for archivists, and the issue of electronic records. The last section of this entry describes the various kinds of museums, museology, education for curatorship, and professional associations in Hungary.

INTRODUCTION

Historical Context

Hungary is a country in Central-Eastern Europe. 10.3 million inhabitants live in a territory of 35,907 miles^2 (93,000 km^2) (see Fig. 1). The capital is Budapest. Its official language is Hungarian, a Finno-Ougric language. The Hungarian alphabet consists of Latin with the addition of diacritics and two or three letter combinations in order to cover the characteristics of Hungarian phonemes.

The history of literacy and the currently used Latin alphabet is 1000 years old: it goes back to the years after 1000 A.D. when the Hungarian state was established. István I (Stephan I, 1001–1038) Christianized the formerly tribal and pagan people that had used a special type of cuneiform as their writing system. Literature had been orally transmitted during the nomadic period, with written literature appearing shortly after 1000. István I founded monasteries that fulfilled not only religious but also educational functions. Most of the early monasteries probably had libraries holding handwritten literature for ecclesiastic purposes. The most famous was the monastery and library of Pannonhalma, founded in 1001, that operated the first school of the country. An inventory from 1093 indicates the ownership of 80 books. Very little from the early monastic library holdings remained as they were all destroyed during the Mongol invasion (1241).

Early texts as well as the official documents of the royal court were written in Latin. Charters recorded medieval land transactions from the turn of the eleventh century onward. Béla IV (1235–1270) ordered the compulsory recording of land transactions and other legal acts. Systematic tracking of regal decrees (Regestrum) started from 1308 on. The earliest extant Hungarian text is a funeral sermon, "Halotti Beszéd," which has been found in the Latin *Pray Codex*, a work from 1192.

The first universities were founded in the second half of the fourteenth century in Pécs (1367) and Ó-Buda (1387), but were closed during the Turkish occupation of the country (1541–1699). The earliest predecessor of the current universities was founded by the Catholic Church during the first half of the seventeenth century in Nagyszombat (now Trnava, Slovakia) where the Esztergom Archbishopric moved from the territory occupied by the Turcs.

Book culture was restricted to the church until the end of the fourteenth century, but extended to secular areas during the Humanist Movement of the fourteenth and fifteenth centuries when lay people began to collect books and build small libraries. The first printed book written in Hungarian dates from the first half of the fifteenth century.

The great Humanist ruler Matthias Corvinus (Corvina Mátyás, 1458–1490) represented the high point of early book culture. Matthias' library, the *Corvinae*, included 2000–2500 mainly handwritten illustrated codices in Greek and Latin, their topics ranging from physics and mathematics to philosophy. Most of these books, created by some of the famous Italian workshops, were richly illustrated, decorated with gold, and individualized by Matthias' coat of arms. The library was open to those who needed to use the books, particularly scholars, many of them visiting Hungary because of the library itself. Only 216 pieces of this famous collection remain: 52 in Hungarian libraries, the rest in the libraries of 43 different cities in 16 different countries. Rulers succeeding Matthias were not interested in preserving or developing his library, and the collection was given away; what remained was destroyed during the Turkish occupation of the country.[1]

Andras Hess founded and operated the first printing press in Buda in 1473, during the reign of King Matthias. The workshop's first product was a book entitled *Chronicle of Buda* (*Chronicon Budense*). This press closed after a few years, and Hungarian books were printed abroad for almost a half century.

Encyclopedia of Library and Information Sciences, Fourth Edition DOI: 10.1081/E-ELIS3-120043841

Fig. 1   Map of Hungary.
Source: *CIA World Factbook.*[59]

During the Turkish occupation (1526–1699) of a large part of Hungary's territory, book culture and the Humanist Movement continued in the territory held by Austria and in Transylvania. Printing presses were established in these territories rather than in Hungary because the Sultan officially forbade the printing of books in occupied land.

Government documents of the Hungarian Kingdom were systematically archived from 1613 on, but the documents stayed in private property, and were sometimes destroyed or distributed by the heirs until 1723 when a law ordered their deposition in specific governmental archives.

The foundation of the first university (Nagyszombat) and Catholic and Protestant colleges (Debrecen, Sárospatak, Pápa) from the mid-sixteenth century on paralleled the establishment and development of new libraries. Book printing spread all over the country; important Catholic printing firms operated in Vienna, Pozsony (now Bratislava, Slovakia), and Nagyszombat. The most important figure of early Hungarian book printing, *Misztótfalusi Kis Miklós* (1650–1702), studied in Amsterdam in the workshop of the Bleau family and published more than 100 books, the most famous of which was the *Golden Bible* (*Aranyos Biblia*, 1685). The Reformation gained momentum and had a positive effect on the diffusion of the use of Hungarian language and printing. Protestant printing presses were established in Debrecen, Pápa, and Eperjes (now Prešov, Slovakia). The first Hungarian journal, *Magyar Hirmondó*, was started in 1780 in Pozsony.

Building library collections in richly furnished library rooms became fashionable among high-level aristocrats and clergymen during the seventeenth and eighteenth centuries. The Festetics Library in Keszthely has been preserved in its wonderful original state as has the Teleki Family's library in Marosvásárhely (now Târgu-Mureş, Romania).[2]

The spirit of Romanticism and the emergence of national consciousness generated an increased interest in language standardization and the establishment of a broad range of new institutions, among them the Hungarian Academy of Sciences (*Magyar Tudományos Akadémia*), the Budapest University Library (*Egyetemi Könyvtár*), and other libraries, archives, and museums. The most important among them was the Hungarian National Museum and Library (*Magyar Nemzeti Múzeum és Könyvtár*), created in 1802 by count Ferenc Széchényi who donated to the new institution his library, his collections of coins and sculptures, as well as other valuable objects. A law proclaimed the foundation in 1807. The current building of the museum, planned by architect *Mihály Pollack*, was completed in 1846. Before the close of the century, several new museums emerged from the collections of the National Museum. The current Museum of Science (*Természettudományi Múzeum*) grew out of a large collection of minerals donated by Ferenc Széchényi's wife. The Ethnographic Museum (*Néprajzi Múzeum*) split from the National Museum at a later date. The second part of the nineteenth century saw the foundation of a series of new museums (Museum of Applied Art, *Iparművészeti Múzeum*; Museum of Fine Arts, *Szépművészeti Múzeum*, the *Zoo*, etc.) due mainly to the enhanced economic conditions after 1867 and the activity of a few great scholar-managers, e.g., *Ferenc Pulszky, Flóris Rómer, Károly Pulszky*, and *György Ráth*.[3] Libraries and museums have been overseen together by the Main Supervisory Office of Museums and Libraries since the end of the nineteenth century. The main goal of this cosupervision was to increase cooperation between the two types of institutions. This governmental office started the first periodical of the two fields, the *Múzeumi és könyvtári értesítő* (Museum and Library Bulletin) in 1907.

A nationwide effort to standardize the national language began in the second half of the eighteenth century; in this era, the greatest writers and poets created those linguistic forms that effectively determined classical national literature and language. In 1844, Hungarian became official language of Hungary instead of Latin; official documents had to be composed in the national language from this time on. Compulsory sixth grade education begun in 1868.

Formerly, Hungary's governmental documents had been written in Latin and had been collected and stored together with Austria's governmental documents in the *Haus-, Hof- und Staatsarchiv* of the Austro-Hungarian Monarchy since 1749. In 1756, however, a separate archive was created for holding the governmental documents of Hungary, now part of the Habsburg empire. The Palatine, lieutenant-governor of the emperor, exercised supervision over its operations; he was responsible for collecting, preserving, and passing along the documents to the office of the next Palatine.

Independence from Austria, the main goal of the 1848 revolution, failed but a few decades later, the Compromise (Kiegyezés, 1867) established a dual state structure and numerous measures that assured partial independence, self-government, and economic growth. Among many other changes, the Palatine's Archive (*Archivum Palatinum*) was transformed into *National Archives* (Országos Levéltár), signifying the relative independence of Hungary from Austria. A renowned historian, *Gyula Pauler* was appointed chief archivist; he introduced new regulations that permitted scholarly research in the institution. The new Archive took over the documents of the feudal governmental institutions and juridical courts collected by its predecessors. More appropriate space for this immense set of historical holdings was built and opened in 1923. This building still houses the Archives and is located at the southern entrance of the castle area in Budapest.[4]

Citizens and families were allowed to deposit their own private documents in a different archive that was part of the National Museum and Library; this archive later split off from the parent institution, and became independent under the name Museum-Archives (*Múzeumi Archívum*) in 1926 until its ultimate merger with the National Archives (*Országos Levéltár*) around 1934.

Book printing became an important industry in the nineteenth century when several technologically advanced printing companies were established together with major editorial firms (*Franklin, Athaeneum*). *Izidor Kner* and *Andor Tevan* were the most outstanding representatives of artisan bookmaking. Popular demand for broader ranges of books resulted in the opening of public libraries; the first among them was the *Fővárosi Könyvtár* (Library of the Capital), opened in 1904 by *Ervin Szabó*, a social scientist-librarian, who successfully convinced book producers and traders that public libraries will not ruin the flourishing book industry. He established a large network of public libraries in the capital based on the Anglo-American model; its book circulation in 1914 was 190,000 volumes.

During the interwar period, Hungarian libraries—with a few exceptions—were in decline due to insufficient funding. The only library that made some progress was the National Széchényi Library where special collections were enhanced by the return of 16 Corvina codices, the Picture Chronicle, and the Gesta Hungarorum among other texts from the Habsburg Court Library of Vienna. The National Library developed its classification system as well by abandoning the Munich subject system for the Universal Decimal Classification that is still the organizational principle of the books in the stacks. According to Charlotte Réthi's calculations, about 1000 academic and specialized libraries held about 11 million volumes by 1939, while the holdings of the school, public, union, and other libraries was under 1 million.[5] During World War II, many of the libraries were destroyed, and their holdings decimated, in part by looting and confiscation.

Three general trends characterized the development of libraries, archives, and museums after 1945 when Soviet-type state socialism was introduced: the radical nationalization of private institutions, the ambitious creation of village and union libraries, and the centralization of management. Library and museum collections that had been confiscated from private institutions, except a portion of those belonging to the Church, were either added to the holdings of the National Library of state-owned museums, destroyed, or distributed among other libraries. County and municipal archives were taken over by the state. Central managerial organizations were created: the National Library Center (*Országos Könyvtári Központ*) and the National Center of Archives (*Levéltárak Országos Központja*). The Central Economic Archives (*Központi Gazdasági Archivum*) was created to collect documents of the nationalized firms, factories, and other economic units, and the National Museum Center (*Országos Múzeumi Központ*) was developed to govern every single institution on the basis of 5 year plans. This structure only changed in 1968 when municipal and metropolitan libraries were again subordinated to the municipalities. According to Charlotte Réthi, the number of libraries skyrocketed: almost 10,000 libraries operated around 1953, holding more than 27 million volumes, circulating about 8 million, and serving 1.2 million users.[6] (Works by Madas and Monok,[7] Blazovich and Müller,[8] Dóka,[9] Varjas,[10] and Kent and Lancour[11] are consulted on the history of literacy, book publishing, libraries, archives, and museums.)

State socialism collapsed in 1989–1990 as capitalism and democracy gained momentum. Previously confiscated holdings whose former owners could be identified were returned to church libraries, archives, and museums. Private individuals founded art galleries and other institutions, and hidden private art collections became known. On the other hand, most of the small union libraries and hospital libraries have been shut down.

Some of the archives experienced unprecedented numbers of clients requesting documents in support of restitution requests for the Shoah, prisoners of war, victims of expulsion, those turned in to the secret police, and so on. Within 4 years, almost 2 million people turned to the Hungarian archives. A number of new laws were passed about the freedom of information and the operation of archives, libraries, museums, and historical monuments. An unparalleled effort to overcome technological backwardness began: computerization and automation accelerated due to the disappearance of internal (ideological, financial) and external (trade embargo) obstacles. By 2005, 25% of Hungarian households had an Internet connection, about half of the average found in the 15 most developed European Union countries. This technological level has facilitated Hungarians' access to the growing number of digital library, archive, and museum collections and services.

From 2001–2005, the number of registered library users in Hungary grew by 19%, a feat hailed by the library profession and government authorities as an achievement in an era when libraries now compete with the Internet. The number of computer terminals in libraries grew by 47% during that same period, raising the proportion of libraries equipped with computers to 52.9%. The biggest change has been a 145% rise in interlibrary loan/document delivery transactions, contributing to more equal access to library holdings across the Hungarian population. The number of items checked out and the number of items read in the libraries themselves has remained the same—a tendency that experts interpret as a shift in the user behavior, i.e., users are turning more and more to electronic resources instead of the print.[12]

LIBRARY AND INFORMATION PROFESSIONS, SYSTEMS, AND SERVICES[13]

Overview of Legislation

The rights to intellectual freedom and free access to information are declared in the Constitution: "In the Republic of Hungary everyone has the right to the free declaration of his views and opinions, and has the right of access to information of public interest, and also the freedom to disseminate such information."[14]

The law that specifically regulates Hungarian libraries is part of a larger legal document: the 1997 CXL Law on the Protection of Cultural Heritage, Museums, Public Libraries, and Continuing Education.[15] The section about libraries guarantees Hungarian citizens' rights as library users, and regulates the operation and development of "libraries open to all users" (a concept broader than "public libraries"). As defined in the law, the following are "libraries open to all users": the National Library (Országos Széchényi Könyvtár), local municipal libraries, county libraries, the libraries of state universities, and 11 national specialized research libraries and documentary centers listed in the appendix as the National Technical Information Center and Library (Országos Műszaki Információs Központ és Könyvtár), the National Health Policy Library (Országos Egészségpolitikai Könyvtár), the Library of the Hungarian Academy of Sciences (Magyar Tudományos Akadémia Könyvtára), the National Library and Information Center for Agriculture (Országos Mezőgazdasági Könyvtár és Dokumentációs Központ), the Library of the Parliament (Országgyűlési Könyvtár), the National Library of Foreign Literatures (Országos Idegennyelvű Könyvtár), National Educational Library and Museum (Országos Pedagógiai Könyvtár és Múzeum), the Metropolitan Ervin Szabó Library (Fővárosi Szabó Ervin Könyvtár), the Library and Documentation Service of the Central Statistical Office (Központi Statisztikai Hivatal Könyvtár és Dokumentációs Szolgálat), the Library of the Hungarian Film Institute (Magyar Filmintézet Könyvtára), and the Library of the Institute of Military History (Hadtörténeti Intézet Könyvtára).

Those institutions that have their own libraries, like churches, may request and receive the "library open to all users" status and, as a result, receive state support for their institutions if they fulfill all those requirements that the law stipulates. Libraries open to all users are cosupported by their parent institutions or local municipalities (if they have one) and the state.

The law guarantees free in-house access to library materials in these institutions. Users' names, addresses, ID numbers, and date and place of birth may be recorded. Additional services (borrowing, etc.) are available for a membership fee that is waived for persons under 16 or over 70 and for the disabled.

Libraries open to all users are required to employ professional librarians, develop their collections, and provide access to their own and other library collections. They participate in interlibrary loan activities, and supply statistical data about their operations.

An official current list of libraries open to all users is maintained by the Ministry for Education and Culture, the government agency that is responsible for the strategic development and supervision of the Hungarian library systems. Libraries listed by the Ministry receive financial support from the state. The Minister for Culture and Education is required to assure a national network and database of library materials including a catalog of library holdings, a system of interlibrary loans, and a method of forwarding weeded/withdrawn materials to those libraries that want to add them to their collections. The law regulates the responsibilities of the national library, the academic and research libraries, and public municipal libraries and directs publishers to provide depository copies of books and periodicals. Specific sections deal with the management and financial regulation of public libraries.

Fair use is regulated in the 1999 LXXVI Copyright Law.[16]

The 2003 XXIV "Transparent Pocket" ("Üvegzseb") Law requires public institutions to publicize the amounts and use of their public funding. Most public institutions—among them, libraries, archives, and museums—publicize the details of their budgets and spending on their Web sites.

The Ministry for Education and Culture appoints two supervisory bodies: the National Library Board (Országos Könyvtári Kuratórium), which oversees the operations of the national library and the Library Institute, and the Accreditation Committee of Libraries (Könyvtári Akkreditációs Szakbizottság) which makes accreditation decisions regarding programs for the education of librarians and library assistants.

National Library

The Hungarian Széchényi National Library (Országos Széchényi Könyvtár) collects, processes, and preserves the written heritage of Hungary and all documents pertaining to it. The Library's complete collection of Hungarica (books and other documents published in Hungary, as well as publications related to Hungary or Hungarians published abroad) is available for users in all formats: parchment, paper, and electronic. The National Széchényi Library is the largest depository library for copyrighted materials published in the country. Its special collections include manuscripts, ephemera, photographs, old imprints, theatrical publications, maps, and musical scores. Hundreds of medieval codices, incunabula, and the most precious first-known Hungarian texts are held in these special collection sections. Surviving pieces of the library of King Matthias, the Corvinae, also belong to the Library's exceptional collections.[17]

The collections of the National Library are part of Hungary's national cultural heritage; hence their use is regulated by the Ministry differently from the use of the materials held in other libraries. The main difference is that its holdings can be consulted only in-house; its collections are noncirculating. Unlike in other public libraries or libraries open to the general public, users have to buy a day ticket or membership card for in-house consultation of the collections.

The Hungarian National Bibliography (specific lists of published books, periodicals, maps, music scores, and recordings) is produced in the National Széchényi Library, and its most recent 5 years are available freely through the Internet. The library became the host and central agent of the Hungarian National Union Library Catalog (MOKKA), which currently unites the holdings of 17 large Hungarian libraries. MOKKA was founded during the 1980s and has thrived since 2002. Another database housed in the National Library, the National Document Delivery System, provides the software which is the basis for nationwide interlibrary loans.

Several special databases are being developed by the Széchényi Library: they provide access to the Bibliographia Hungarica, a searchable catalog of 73,000 foreign language translations of Hungarian literary authors since 1800. Currently in development is Bibliotheca Eruditionis, a database of 1500–1700 imprints published in the Carpathian basin. A virtual reconstruction of King Matthias' Library, the Bibliotheca Corviniana Digitalis, is also in the making.

The Library Institute (Könyvtári Intézet), housed and operated in the National Széchényi Library, is a library and information science research center responsible for creating the national strategic plan, providing certain central services for librarians and libraries, offering courses for education, and conducting research in library and information science. One of the central concerns of the Institute's 2003–2007 strategic plan is the coordination with and adjustment of Hungarian librarianship to the standards and requirements of the European Union.

The National Library was founded by Count Ferenc Széchényi on November 25th, 1802 with these words: "[This institution] I bestow upon for the good and benefit of my beloved country and the community for ever and irrevocably." The foundational holdings included 13,000 printed books, more than 1200 manuscripts, hundreds of maps, coats of arms, etchings, coins, and more. The opening ceremony was held in 1803. A nationwide campaign was launched to raise the necessary funds from private citizens and other sources for its operations and maintenance. These financial resources made possible the foundation of the Hungarian National Museum, of which the National Széchényi Library was a part. Both institutions moved into the classical-style building of the National Museum in 1846–1847. The library later became independent from the museum in 1949. In 1985, the institution moved into the F building of the Royal Castle in Buda. Most of the collections—now about 7.5 million—are held in storage, but the most important works of reference, essential works in the different disciplines, and a certain part of the university textbook collections are available on the shelves of the reading rooms. General reading rooms are two floors above the entrance (on the seventh floor of the building). Special collections are located on the fifth, sixth, and seventh floors. Guided tours of the library, both for individuals and groups, are available by appointment. The most valuable pieces from the collections are displayed in temporary exhibitions.

Academic and Research Libraries

The National Library, the *Central Library of the Lajos Kossuth University*, the libraries of the state universities, and the 11 research libraries listed in the 1997 CXL Law are the main institutions providing library materials for research in Hungary.

The most famous among them is the Library of the Hungarian Academy of Sciences (*Magyar Tudományos Akadémia Könyvtára*). The library is adjacent to the nineteenth-century neo-Renaissance central building of the Academy on the Pest (east) side of the river Danube. This institution was founded in 1836 by the donation of *József Teleki*'s collection of 30,000 volumes, shortly after the foundation of the Academy itself in 1825 by count *István Széchenyi*. The library's main function has been to support research within the most important scholarly institution of the country. Its special collections currently include a world famous collection of Tibetan, Turkish, Persian, and Central Asian materials, as well as Hebraica. The central library of the Academy, holding more than 2 million volumes, collects materials on languages and literatures, classics, Oriental research, science-related policy, research management, and the history and methodology of science. Members of the broad network of research institutes of the Academy all include discipline-specific libraries collecting scholarly materials in a broad range of the sciences, social sciences, and humanities.

The National Technical Information Center and Library (*Országos Műszaki Könyvtár és Dokumentációs Központ*) collects materials and provides services in the sciences, economics, and engineering. More than 2 million items are held in the institution. The Center builds and provides access to a number of important databases, including the Hungarian Repertory of Technical and Economic Information (*Magyar Műszaki és Gazdasági Repertórium*), and the Hungarian Research and Development Abstracts (in English).

The National Library of Health (*Országos Egészségpolitikai Szakkönyvtár*) compiles the Hungarian Medical Bibliography and extensively collects materials related to public policy, international health organizations, and management of medical institutions.[18–20]

The National Library and Information Center for Agriculture (*Országos Mezőgazdasági Könyvtár és Információs Központ*) compiles the Hungarian Agricultural Bibliography. Its comprehensive agricultural collections serve a broad range of academic and practical needs for professional institutions as well as the general public.

The holdings of the National Educational Library and Museum (*Országos Pedagógiai Könyvtár és Múzeum*) include a comprehensive Hungarian and selective foreign collection of publications—monographs and periodicals—on pedagogy and its interdisciplinary fields (psychology, sociology, etc.). Its special collections include publications (yearbooks) of Hungarian schools as well as children's and youth periodicals. This institution houses the Hungarian branch of the Center to Promote Language Education in Europe, an institution of the Council of Europe helping European Union (EU) member countries to encourage excellence and innovation in foreign language teaching. This library produces the Hungarian Educational Technology Database.

The Library of the Parliament (*Országgyűlési Könyvtár*), founded around 1866, is located in the renowned nineteenth-century neo-Gothic building of the Hungarian Parliament, on the east bank of the river Danube. Its main collections focus on law, government information (as a depository library of the EU), and the social sciences (particularly political science and sociology).

The Library of the Central Statistical Office (*Központi Statisztikai Hivatal Könyvtára*), one of Europe's largest statistical collections, was founded together with the Hungarian governmental statistical service in 1867, and became a research library open to the public as of 1897. The library collects comprehensively in Hungarian and selectively in foreign materials on statistics, demography, and other social sciences, especially the economic–statistical aspects of the other social sciences.

The National Library of Foreign Literatures (*Országos Idegennyelvű Könyvtár*) is the newest from among the large Hungarian research libraries. Belles lettres—especially contemporary literature—linguistics, and music constitute the core of its collections which are primarily in English, French, German, Italian, Russian, and Spanish. This library is a research center and coordinator of public libraries serving minorities (Slovak, German, Serbian, etc.) living in Hungary. The library has borne its current name since 1989; its predecessor, the Gorky Library, founded in 1956, was a center for Russian culture.

More than 200 private- and state-funded university and college libraries served higher education and the general public in 2002.

University and college libraries demonstrate considerable strength in their print collections: the collections of the libraries of *Eötvös Loránd University* (Budapest), *Attila József University* (Szeged), and *Janus Pannonius University* (Pécs) number in the range of 3.5, 1.2, and 1.6 million volumes, respectively.

A sharp increase in the number of college students, the economic conditions of the transformation period from state socialism to capitalism and democracy, and the required merger of small specialized institutions into larger organizations brought many challenges to these libraries during the 1990s and early 2000s. These changes generated more active cooperation and resource sharing especially in the fields of digitization, delivery of online services, license negotiation, and electronic resource management.

Public Libraries

Budapest, the capital city, has its own central public library, the Metropolitan Szabó Ervin Library (*Fővárosi Szabó Ervin Könyvtár*), named after an early twentieth-century social scientist and librarian. The city also hosts a broad network of metropolitan district libraries (57 in 2007). The central library is located in the beautifully renovated building of the Wenckheim palace and extends to the neighboring Pálffy palace, home of the music collections. All 19 counties and all of the nearly 300 municipalities are required by law to operate a public library. Small settlements have to run their own public libraries if their population exceeds 2500–3000. These towns may choose to run their own libraries, or, order library services through the Service System for Rural Areas. Mobile libraries are routed to villages with fewer than 1000 inhabitants. In 2007, more than 2500 villages had their own public libraries that, in addition to supporting primary, secondary, and continuous education, information, and leisure-reading, have a special role in collecting and preserving locally published documents and documents of local interest.[21,22]

The National Document Delivery System (*Országos Dokumentum-ellátási Rendszer*) ensures enhanced access for users to library holdings not held in their local public library or at libraries open to the general public. Established in 1998 and operated by the Hungarian National Library, it provides a searchable database for locating library materials for interlibrary loan. The Hungarian government supports this program by not only financing the central database, but also by funding the acquisition of materials and their postal or electronic delivery to the patrons located anywhere, including small villages. This program is one of the central elements of the government's strategic initiative that considers public libraries and libraries open to all users as pivotal institutions of the information society. The program helps library services in rural areas reach the same level of access as any larger library. Services include physical and electronic document delivery, online information services, organization of exhibitions, and events.

School Libraries

Teaching library skills has been part of the National Curriculum since 1995. The 2003 Law of Public Education stipulates the existence of libraries and the hiring of librarian-teachers in most public schools. However, the quality of these school libraries, their holdings, and their equipment is not always up to the required level; their conditions depend mostly on the economic circumstances and leadership of the given educational institutions. The number of school libraries in Hungary exceeds 4000. The National Pedagogical Library and Museum (NPLM) develops their standards and coordinates their professional work. The NPLM provides a wide array of resources for librarian-teachers. Libraries of private educational institutions have to satisfy the same standards and requirements as public schools.[23,24]

Special Libraries

In spite of the early appearance of the first book collections in hospitals (like Rókus Hospital at the end of eighteenth century, and a number of libraries from the early twentieth century on) most medical libraries were founded after the 1956 Library Law. The medical library network counted more than 300 specialized libraries during the early 1960s and more than 400 during the mid-1970s. This abundance was followed by a period of mergers and shutdowns during the 1980s and 1990s that paralleled a controversial integration and reform process for medical institutions. The Hungarian Medical Library Association counted 171 medical libraries in 2000, excluding the libraries of medical schools.[25,26]

The Library of the Parliament (*Országgyűlési Könyvtár*) and the libraries of the law schools are the special legal libraries in Hungary. Though law firms have book collections, law libraries have not been institutionalized. The first searchable online law collections appeared during the late 2000s.

Religiously affiliated libraries are maintained by the Catholic, Calvinist, Lutheran, Eastern Orthodox, and Unitarian churches, and Jewish religious communities, and offer access to their collections for users within and outside of their religious institutions and communities. *Theca*, the shared bibliographic database of religiously affiliated libraries, provides access to a growing proportion of their post-1850 holdings.

Digital Library Collections and Services

The Hungarian Electronic Library (*Magyar Elektronikus Könyvtár*[27]) collects and preserves freely available documents on Hungary and Central Europe in the areas of culture, education, and scholarly research. The depository is open to the public not only for access, but also for uploading materials. A description helps prospective contributors with content and format criteria. Added works must be out of copyright or accompanied by the permission of the copyright holder. Contributed documents are uploaded via file transfer protocol to the depository. People are invited to send their own works and suggest documents stored on other servers for transfer. This archive of books—and, in small proportion, maps and music scores—was a private initiative of enthusiastic librarians in 1994. It became a project of the National Information Infrastructure Development Program as well as a later popular movement. In 2007, the number of works archived in the depository exceeded 5000. Part of the archives is the result of a major digitization project:

the Digital Library of Hungarian Studies (*Hungarológiai Alapkönyvtár*), making almost 4000 classical texts and reference materials available in the area of Hungarian studies. Both the latter project and the Hungarian Electronic Library are coordinated by the National Széchényi Library.

The National Electronic Periodicals Archive and Database (*Elektronikus Periodika Archívum és Adatbázis*[28]) is a catalog and archive of Hungarian and Hungary-related periodicals. The archives also include digitized or born-digital resources which are either stored here or are linked from other sites. Users can search by title, year, subject, and full text (if the resource is locally archived). In conjunction with the periodical titles, the depository presents the text of the copyright agreement with the publishers of the resources about the use of the full text. Opened in 2004, the EPA is rapidly growing; its aim is to become a comprehensive gateway to Hungarian and Hungarian-related periodical literature. In 2007, it included about 1200 periodical titles of which 153 were locally archived and more than 1500 were linked from another site.

The John von Neumann Digital Library (*Neumann János Digitális Könyvtár*[29]), named after the Hungarian-born American mathematician, is a state-funded institution performing digitization projects of Hungarian cultural heritage. Its collections are selected from among the most valuable and respected literary works and secondary literature. The Neumann Library supports e-learning from early childhood to continuing education. The deposited works are freely available for reading and full-text searching. Parts of the Neumann Library include: the Bibliotheca Hungarica Internetiana, a virtual collection of critical and popular editions of the works of Hungarian—literary and nonfiction—classical authors; the Digital Literary Academy (*Digitális Irodalmi Akadémia*), a gateway to the works of the best living Hungarian literary authors; a collection of children's readings, audio and visual materials, animated stories, videos and games, and the Reading is Fun program (*Olvasni jó*); The latter part includes carefully selected educational materials for the youngest generation.

The Hungarian National Library is digitizing the available pieces of King Matthias' fifteenth-century library. In 2007, the *Bibliotheca Corviniana Digitalis*[30] included 36 codices—all held in the National Library—and provided information about the other "Corvinae" held in libraries in 16 countries. Full codicological description, an analysis of their art historical context, and a full bibliography completes the collection.

The National Digital Data Archive (*Nemzeti Digitális Adattár*[31]) is a searchable catalog of metadata representing Hungarian and Hungary-related content: virtual libraries, museums, archives, and other digital documents (including the items held in the above-mentioned databases). The cooperation, including more than 50 partner institutions, is based on the use of a standard metadata

system and shared data operation. The NDA provides a catalog of metadata, a search engine, and their technological background; it does not run digitization projects itself.

A large number of other archives, catalogs, and databases are available at their own Web sites or through the National Digital Data Archive: e.g., Fine Arts in Hungary (*Képzőművészet Magyarországon*[32]), Budapest Photo Archive (*Budapest Képarchívum*[33]), Hungarian Film History Online (*Magyar Filmtörténet online*[34]), the Data Archive of the Social Research Center *TÁRKI* (*Társadalomtudományi Digitális Adattár*[35]), and the *BMC* Hungarian Music Information Center (*BMC Magyar Zenei Információs Központ*[36]), among many others.

LIBINFO[37] is a Hungarian national online reference service. A few dozen listed librarians provide answers to e-mailed reference questions within 48 hr. The service operates on a consortial basis; questions are triaged to the most appropriate librarian expert on the list. The service is hosted and coordinated by the Hungarian National Library.

Library and Information Science as Discipline and Profession

Scholar bibliographers were the first representatives of library science in Hungary in the eighteenth and nineteenth centuries (*Péter Bod*, 1712–1769 *Károly Szabó*, 1824–1890, *Géza Petrik*, 1845–1925), and bibliographies and collections of authors' biographies were the first works of the discipline. *József Szinnyei* (1830–1913), founder-director of the Periodicals Collections of the National Library wrote the most comprehensive 14-volume Hungarian biobibliography on pre-1900 authors published between 1890 and 1913.[38] He also published the first comprehensive repertory of Hungarian and foreign serials in three volumes.[39] Library science became an academic discipline in 1901 at the University of Kolozsvár (now Cluj) and in Budapest in 1914. *Pál Gulyás* continued Szinnyei's work, publishing a main bio-bibliographical work on post-1900 authors. Early twentieth-century librarians wrote the first works on specific issues (cataloging etc.) of librarianship, and the first research center dealing with the discipline (*Országos Könyvforgalmi és Bibliográfiai Központ*, National Center for the Book Trade and Bibliography) was established in 1923; it was transformed into a National Center for Libraries in 1945. The successor of this center is the *Institute of Librarianship* (Könyvtártudományi Intézet), operating within the framework and in the building of the National Library (Országos Széchényi Könyvtár).

Several prizes honor libraries and librarians: the *Library of the Year Award*, the *Széchényi Ferenc*, and the *Szinnyei József prize* are the most important ones.

Journals of librarianship include the *Könyvtári Figyelő* (Library Review) and the *Könyv, Könyvtár, Könyvtáros* (Book, Library, Librarian)—the latter more interested in international issues and technology, the former aimed for a broader audience more focused on current issues in Hungarian librarianship. These journals are published by the National Library and the Library Institute, respectively. The journal *Tudományos és Műszaki Tájékoztatás* (Scientific and Technical Information) deals with information science and promotes the latest developments in information technology. *Hungarian Library and Information Science Abstracts* reviews Hungarian publications of the discipline for an international audience.

Education for LIS

Prior to World War II, experts with degrees in some of the humanities disciplines were recruited to librarianship. University-level librarian programs started in 1948. Currently, two levels of librarian programs are offered at colleges and universities: BA and MA, some of them with an information studies specialization. Four of the universities (Budapest, Pécs, Szeged, and Debrecen) have Ph.D. programs.

Institutions such as the National Library offer midlevel education for future library assistants. A high school diploma is the prerequisite for these programs.

Professional librarians are required to participate in 120 hr of organized continuing education every 7 years; certificates are provided by institutions accredited specifically to offer these courses.

Professional Associations

Founded in 1935, the Association of Hungarian Librarians (*Magyar Könyvtárosok Egyesülete*) is a civil nonprofit organization with more than 2000 individual and 60 institutional members. Its ten professional sections reflect the main interests and specializations of Hungarian librarians. The Association abides by the Code of Ethics of Hungarian Librarians that sets behavioral standards for professionals.

The Alliance of Libraries and Information Institutes (*Informatikai és Könyvtári Szövetség*) is a national organization of about 230 member institutions. Its mission is to enhance library services and cooperation as well as increase the profile of member libraries. A series of further associations bring together special types of libraries (*Magyar Orvosi Könyvtárak Szövetsége*, Association of Medical Libraries; *Publika Magyar Könyvtári Kör*, Public Library Group; *Egyházi Könyvtárak Egyesülése*, Association of Ecclesiastic Libraries, etc.)

ARCHIVES AND ARCHIVAL SCIENCE

(The main sources of this section are works by Blazovich and Müller[8] and Dóka.[40])

Overview of Legislation

The 1995 LXVI Law regulates the charge and operation of Hungarian archives. The conditions for research in archival resources are specified partly by this law and partly by the 1992 LXIII Law dealing with the protection of private personnel data and the availability of public data. These laws apply equally to repositories holding documents of archival value whether they are financed and/or operated by the state, municipalities, organizations, churches, trade unions, or private citizens.

National Archives and Services

The holdings of the Hungarian National Archives (*Magyar Országos Levéltár*) include an immense historical collection of governmental and private documents. They also provide access to the complete archives of the ruling party of the 1945–1989 period, large historical collections of maps, coins, photos, stamps, and microfilm. The National Archives include materials formerly held in the New Hungarian Central Archives (*Új Magyar Központi Levéltár*), an institution that operated and collected current governmental documents between 1970 and 1992. The National Archives manages the e-Archives (*e-Archívum*), an online union catalog of nationwide archival holdings. Since e-Archives is a relatively new tool, retrospective conversion is still going on. A number of the finding aids are digitized, and full-text digitization of a few important holdings has also begun. The database of digitized materials (*Digitarchív*) is searchable.

A special state archive, the Historical Archives of the Hungarian State Security (*Állambiztonsági Szolgálatok Történeti Levéltára*), was established in 2003 holding documents produced between December 21, 1944 and February, 1990. Its collections include documents of state security organizations, state security documents of the Ministry of Defense and the Hungarian People's Army— all operating during the period of state socialism.

A few additional archives are operated and funded by the state: the Archives of Military History (*Hadtörténeti Levéltár*) holding historical and current governmental documents of the military and its predecessors, the Archives of Environmental and Water Issues (*Környezetvédelmi és Vízügyi Levéltár*), and the Archives of the Central Statistical Office (*Központi Statisztikai Hivatal Levéltára*).

Hungary's 19 counties, the capital city, Budapest, as well as some towns have their own archives collecting local official and private documents.

College and University Archives

Documents on Hungarian higher education held in different collections go back to the seventeenth century. However, the first university archive was not established until 1958 at the Loránd Eötvös University, Budapest. In the second half of the 1970s and early 1980s, six universities deposited their documents into specialized archives, soon followed by the rest of the universities.[41] From 1992 on, college and university archives united into an association to assist member institutions to organize their documents more quickly and to publish the most important sources.

Film Archives and Other Audiovisual Archives

The Hungarian National Film Archives (*Magyar Nemzeti Filmarchívum*) collects, processes, preserves, and stores films and other documents related to Hungarian motion picture production and reception. The Film Archives serves as a depository for films created in Hungary.

The National Audiovisual Archive (*Nemzeti Audiovizuális Archívum*) is a depository of the locally produced programs of the most important Hungarian television channels and radio stations. The cataloging records of the programs are freely accessible for searching through the Internet. An amended Hungarian copyright law made access to the full content of the records and recordings possible for education and research purposes via a network of public terminals ("NAVA points") located in libraries open to the public, in schools, in museums, and in print, visual and audio archives.

Other Kinds of Archives: Corporate and Religious Archives, Manuscript Repositories, Historical Societies

The Archives of the Hungarian Academy of Sciences (*MTA Levéltára*) holds the historical and current documents of the central governing bodies and offices of the organization. Since the Academy plays a pivotal role in granting postgraduate degrees in all disciplines, the archives hold these documents as well.

Private archives open to the public include the archives of the trade unions (*Szakszervezetek Archívuma*), the Institute of Political History (*Politikatörténeti Intézet*), some parties (e.g., *Független Kisgazda és Polgári Párt*), and a variety of religious archives.

The Catholic Primatial Archives of Esztergom (*Esztergomi Prímási Levéltár*) is the largest ecclesiastic archive. Its importance follows from the size of its territory as well as the importance of the Bishop residing here. Highlights of the huge collection include 1200 pre-1526 charters and all minutes from the Canonica Visitation (1557–1940). Other religiously affiliated archives include a number of Protestant, Serbian Orthodox, Jewish, and Unitarian institutions.

The Open Society Archives, a product of the philanthropic activity of the Soros Foundations network, obtains, preserves, and makes available research resources for the study of Communism and the Cold War, particularly in Central and Eastern Europe. The archives of the research institute of Radio Free Europe constitute the core of the OSA's collections. They also hold the complete documentation of the *Index of Censorship*, a journal published in London.

Archival Science as a Discipline and Profession

Traditionally, the profession of archivist has been closely connected to the profession of historian in Hungary. Degrees in economics, German, Latin, library science, and others may also be an educational basis for archivists. Only somewhat more than half of the professionals working in Hungarian archives have a degree in Archival Science. Scholar archivists mainly publish works on historical sources rather than the methodological, theoretical, and technological issues of the profession.

The Educational and Methodological Center in the National Archives (*Oktatási és Módszertani Központ*) offers courses on all levels and provides certificates for archivists and archivist assistants. The College of Archives (*Levéltári Kollégium*), an expert body appointed by the Ministry, participates in the governing, quality control, and strategic planning of the field. Current strategic plans (e.g., *A levéltárak középtávú informatikai stratégiája és feladatterve, 2006–2010*,[42] Medium Term Information Technology Strategy and Goals in Archives, 2006–2010) target the need for archivists who are skilled in information technology, the need for archives better equipped with current technology, and the need to archive electronic documents.

Two main journals are published in the field: the *Levéltári Közlemények* (*Archival Digest*, published since 1923) is the publication of the National Archives, and deals with the analysis and publication of primary historical sources, as well as main issues of archival science nationally and internationally. The *Levéltári Szemle* (*Archival Review*, published since 1951) is the publication of the Association of Hungarian Archivists; it targets the practical work of archivists, facilitates cooperation, and publicizes main Hungarian events of the profession. The *ArchivNet* (subtitled "Historical Sources") is a new online periodical edited by the National Archives since 2001. Its main goal is full-text electronic publishing of twentieth-century historical sources.

Prizes that recognize archivists' outstanding achievements include: the *Ervin Szabó Medal* and the *Gyula Pauler prize*.

Education for Archivists and Records Managers: Examinations, Certification, University-Level Programs, and Continuing Education

Higher education for archivists is provided by some universities (currently the Eötvös Loránd in Budapest, the Debrecen, Miskolc, and Szombathely) offering BA and MA programs in history. History majors may specialize in Archivist Studies and get a BA or MA degree. History and other MAs and PhDs may take specialized postgraduate courses offered by the National Archives and other major archives in order to earn a certificate. Accredited archival institutions (e.g., the National Archives) offer courses and certificates for future archivist assistants. The prerequisite for these courses is a high school diploma. This system of education is in flux and modifications are expected. Accreditation of educational institutions is provided by the Committee of Archivist Accreditation (*Levéltári Akkreditációs Szakbizottság*) appointed by the Ministry for Education and Culture.

Professional Associations

Several associations unite archivists in Hungary. The largest is the Association of Hungarian Archivists (*Magyar Levéltárosok Egyesülete*), which, until 1986, was a section of the Association of Librarians. Three other associations bring together archivists specializing in particular areas: The Council of Municipal Archives (*Önkormányzati Levéltárak Tanácsa*), The Alliance of Religious Archives (*Magyarországi Egyházi Levéltárosok Egyesülete*), and the Coalition of Hungarian University and College Archivists (*Magyar Felsőoktatási Levéltári Szövetség*) focus on professional issues relating to a specific type of archives and to archivists working in these institutions.

Electronic Records as Archival Documents

The issue of electronic documents and their preservation has been a key concern in the twenty-first century. Standards, equipment, skilled archivists, and funding for the handling, storing, and processing of the electronic documents have been lacking. Archivists are aware of the need, and their strategic plan[42] contains action items related to the institutional, technological, and personnel aspects of archiving electronic documents. The realization of this strategic plan is expected in the near future.

Preservation of Documents in All Forms and Formats

The Ministry for Education and Culture exercises quality control over state-financed and municipal archives, as well as private archives open to the public, via a body of experts—the College of Archives (*Levéltári Kollégium*)—that conducts annual surveys and analyses of the individual archives. These analyses include a review of preservation activities among other issues. Lack of space is a major problem as well as lack of funding for improved air-conditioning and climate control. The annual reviews oversee preservation efforts that produce surrogate copies: archives make microform and, increasingly, digitized copies of endangered paper-based materials. Recently, the College raised the issue of the preservation of nonpaper-based documents (photos, sound and video recordings, films, CDs,

DVDs, and electronic documents) and suggested solutions. Preservation standards for these nontraditional materials are under consideration.

MUSEUMS

(Most of the information on individual museums is based on data published in *Magyarország múzeumai. Múzeumlátogatók kézikönyve*.[43])

Overview of Laws

The 1997 CXL Law pertains to museums as well as to libraries. The law lays down the rules for the protection of cultural heritage monuments and objects as well as the ways in which they may be declared protected (e.g., change of ownership has to be traced under specific circumstances; the Ministry has to give permission if they are taken abroad, etc.). It specifies conditions for archeological digs and the protection of these sites. With regard to museums, it defines the prerequisites and methods for the founding and closure of museum institutions. Additionally, it defines the specifications for types of museums in relation to the ways they operate and get funding.

Seven hundred and seventy-two museums and galleries operate all over the country. The Ministry for Education and Culture oversees the activity of museums partly directly and partly via a number of expert bodies: the National Museum Council (*Országos Múzeumi Tanács*), the Accreditation Committees for Museology and Protection of Objects of Museological Value (*Műtárgyvédelmi és Muzeológiai Akkreditációs Bizottságok*), and the Museum College (*Múzeumi Kollégium*), a body that evaluates grant applications.

Museums of National Jurisdiction

The National Museum (*Nemzeti Múzeum*) is located in its nineteenth-century neoclassical building and holds more than 1 million archaeological, numismatic, historical, and artistic artifacts.[44] Highlights of the collections include the coronation cloak of the Hungarian kings and the sword of Saint Stephan (*Szent István*), the first king of the country. The most valuable crown jewels (the crown, the orb, and the scepter) are permanently exhibited under the main dome of the Parliament building and can be seen during guided tours. The following sections present the vast collections of the National Museum and are divided into sections encompassing archeological and historical materials, photographs, coins, and historical paintings. Staff dedicated to data processing, information technology, preservation, restoration, and library services ensure the professional operation of the museum.

The Ethnographic Museum (*Néprajzi Múzeum*) is one of Europe's largest ethnographic collections with 140,000

Hungarian artifacts and more than 50,000 international artifacts. Its permanent exhibit presents traditional Hungarian culture.

The most complete historical collection of Hungarian fine arts (more than 100,000 pieces) is held and part of it permanently exhibited at the Hungarian National Gallery (*Magyar Nemzeti Galéria*), located in one of the most spectacular buildings of the Buda castle. The Gallery provides a variety of services such as research service on Hungarian works of fine arts; this service is available to the public. The Gallery also supplies permissions for transporting Hungarian works of art abroad. Housed in a neoclassical building located with the *Műcsarnok* (a gallery of contemporary art) on the large and impressive Heroes' Square, the Museum of Fine Arts (*Szépművészeti Múzeum*) holds an internationally renowned collection of fine arts, which includes an exceptional series of Spanish paintings by El Greco, Velàzquez, Murillo, and Goya. For a fee, the museum's museologists and art historians will provide expert opinions about the authorship, quality, authenticity, etc. of the art pieces submitted for appraisal by patrons.

Documents and objects related to Hungarian literature are collected and exhibited in the Petőfi Museum of Literature (*Petőfi Irodalmi Múzeum*). The Manuscript Archive of the Museum is the largest collection of its kind in Hungary. The Audiovisual Collections hold recordings of interviews and conversations with the most eminent representatives of Hungarian literature. The Reception Databank monitors, collects and processes the German, French, English, and Italian reception and criticism of Hungarian literature, and makes these results accessible for the public.

The stunning majolica-roofed and eclectic Secession-style building of the Museum of Applied Art (*Iparművészeti Múzeum*) is Ödön Lechner's work; the museum was the third of its kind in the world in 1857 after the opening of similar museums of design in London and Vienna. Its four major collection areas are ceramics, glass, and china; textiles; furniture; and gold and silversmithing.

Additional government-sponsored museums are the Museum of Medical History (*Orvostörténeti Múzeum*), the National Technical Museum (*Országos Műszaki Múzeum*), the Agricultural Museum (*Mezőgazdasági Múzeum*), the Museum of Transportation (*Közlekedési Múzeum*), the Museum of Military History (*Hadtörténeti Múzeum*), and the Budapest Historical Museum (*Budapesti Történeti Múzeum*)—all located in the capital, Budapest; and the Outdoor Ethnographic Museum (*Szabadtéri Néprajzi Múzeum*) located in Szentendre, a small township north of Budapest.

Since the early 1970s, a number of national parks have been opened. The Hortobágy National Park (*Hortobágyi Nemzeti Park*) was the first, presenting the natural history and current wildlife of the Hungarian plain, followed by national parks representing different regions, landscapes, fauna, and flora, such as the *Kiskunság, Bükk, Aggtelek*, and *Őrség*.

Major Art Museums and Galleries

In Budapest, in addition to the Museum of Fine Arts and National Gallery, a series of museums maintain permanent exhibits of art (e.g., the Ludwig Museum, *Ludwig Múzeum*, in the royal castle area, the Picture Gallery of the Capital Museum of Kiscell, *Fővárosi Képtár Kiscelli Múzeum*, etc.). A number of smaller museums present the works of individual artists, (e.g., *Victor Vasarely*, a Hungarian-born French painter; *Imre Varga*, a twentieth-century sculptor, etc.). Galleries such as the *Műcsarnok* (Palace of the Arts), *Vigadó Galéria* (Vigadó Gallery), and the *Ernst Múzeum* (Ernst Museum) offer exhibition spaces for contemporary art. The *Sculpture Garden* (Szoborpark) is an unusual collection of public sculptures which have been removed from their original location and gathered together in one place. These sculptures, produced 1945–1989, express the spirit of state socialism.

A few other cities have a high concentration of museums and galleries. Szentendre has been a favorite town of artists, and subsequently is home to the many memorial museums which have been created to display their artistic achievements. For example, there are museums for the works of *Margit Anna, Imre Ámos, Jenő Barcsay, Béla Czóbel, János Kmetty, and Lajos Vajda* (twentieth-century painters) the *Ferenczy family* (nineteenth- and twentieth-century painters and sculptors), *Margit Kovács* (twentieth-century ceramic artist). The latter, located in a late eighteenth-century building, and presenting ceramic sculptures of unique character, consistently attracts record numbers of visitors.[45]

On the museum walk of the southern Hungarian city of Pécs, the Janus Pannonius Muzeum (*Janus Pannonius Múzeum*) is an umbrella organization for a number of local museums which include, among others, the collections of the Modern Hungarian Picture Gallery (*Modern Magyar Képtár*); the Exhibit of Zsolnai Ceramics (*Zsolnai Kerámia Kiállítás*); a museum for the works of *Victor Vasarely* and another for the works of *Amerigo Tot*, both born in Hungary; the most complete collection of works by early twentieth-century expressionist Hungarian painter, *Tivadar Csontváry Kosztka*; and a large collection of works by *Erzsébet Schaár* (a twentieth-century sculptor).

Kecskemét, a township southeast of the capital, became a center of folk art. The Museum of Hungarian Folk Design (*Magyar Népi Iparművészeti Múzeum*) holds a rich collection of folk arts and crafts. *Szórakaténusz*—the name is part of a counting rhyme—is a museum of folk childrens' games and toys. The Museum of Hungarian Naïve Art (*Magyar Naív Művészek Múzeuma*) also presents paintings and sculptures originating of folk art.

Science and Natural History Museums

The Science Museum (*Természettudományi Múzeum*) split from the National Museum in 1934. Its animals, plants, humans, minerals, and geology sections hold millions of species and other scientific objects. About the history of the main Hungarian museums see work by Holló.[46] The National Technical Museum (*Országos Műszaki Múzeum*) holds historical artifacts of Hungarian science, technology, and industry.

An interesting series of museums hold historical artifacts related to industry and transport. The Museum of Transportation (*Közlekedési Múzeum*) opened in 1899 in Budapest, preserving the objects exhibited at the large 1896 show that commemorated the 1000th anniversary of the conquest of Hungary. The museum collects boats, trains, cars, and other transportation vehicles. The exhibition in the Expo of Flying and Space (*Repüléstörténeti és Űrhajózási Kiállítás*) completes this collection—all of the above are located in Budapest. The Kner Printing Museum (*Kner Nyomdaipari Múzeum*) in Gyomaendrőd displays books and other imprints as well as the workshop of a famous nineteenth-century bookmaker. The Tokaj Museum (*Tokaji Múzeum*) in Tokaj collects tools, objects, and documents related to winemaking. Two museums in the west Hungarian town of Sopron (*Bányászati Múzeum, Bányászati Emlékmúzeum*) and museums in Oroszlány and Tatabánya—all mining areas—present objects and historical documents related to mining. In the city of Herend, in the original late classicist style building of the Herend china factory, the Museum of the Art of China (*Porcelánművészeti Múzeum*) presents the history of this world famous company established in 1839.

Religiously Affiliated Museums

The Christian Museum in Esztergom (*Keresztény Múzeum*) is the richest among the private collections in Hungary.[47] Highlights of the holdings include a late medieval collection (Passion paintings of Master MS, the Calvary altar of Tamás Kolozsvári, etc.) and a collection of postmedieval paintings, design, and graphics. The museum is located in a seventeenth-century Jesuit monastery.

Established in 1909, the Jewish Museum (*Zsidó Múzeum*) collects and preserves cultural, historical, and religious objects of Hungarian Jewry.[48] In spite of a successful 1938 exhibit presenting the long history of Hungarian–Jewish life beginning with King Béla IV's charter (1256) and a large exhibit of Jewish artists in 1939, the museum had to close due to the anti-Semitic laws and government. Thanks to two museologists of the National Museum, the most important pieces of the collections were hidden in the cellars of the National Museum, survived the war, and were given back to the institution afterward. The museum is now located in a building right next to the main synagogue of the capital,

on the place of the house where Tivadar Herzl, founder of the Zionist movement, was born. More than 800,000 items are held in the collections, the largest such collection in Central Europe.

Szentendre, the small artist city north of Budapest, is the home of the Serbian Orthodox Museum (*Szerb Ortodox Múzeum*) located in a building of the Orthodox Church. Icons, goldsmith works, and other objects reflect the culture of seventeenth- and eighteenth-century Serbs in Hungary.

Historical, Anthropological, and Archaeological Museums

A number of larger cities have their own general historical museums. The Ferenc Móra Museum (*Móra Ferenc Múzeum*) in Szeged owns 273,000 objects, and offers permanent exhibitions, among them an exhibition of Avar finds and another on pharmacies. The István Dobó Castle Museum (*Dobó István Vármúzeum*) in Eger presents spectacularly the castle's Turkish siege of 1552 through the objects that have remained from the sixteenth century. The collections of the King Stephan Museum (*Szent István Király Múzeum*) in the city of Székesfehérvár present the ruins of the medieval cathedral, along with archaeological finds and a large collection of paintings.

A number of historical sites became museums. *Aquincum*'s Roman ruins present the remains–mosaic floor, organ, water pipes, etc.–of a prospering city on the border of the Roman Empire (currently in north Budapest). *Visegrád*, the ruins of King Matthias' castle have been transformed into a museum. The National Historical Park (*Nemzeti Történeti Emlékpark*) in Ópusztaszer is the site where, according to the legend, Hungarian tribes, went into a blood union with Árpád's leadership after the conquest of the Carpathian basin in 896. A painting of exceptional size (about 18,000 sq.ft) depicts the historical event. One site in Budapest and another one in Sopron, west Hungary, keep alive the memory of Hungarian Jewish communities: the Medieval Jewish Prayer House (*Középkori Zsidó Imaház*) exhibits the remains of Jewish tombstones and gothic carved stones of the synagogue. The Medieval Old Synagogue (*Középkori Ó-Zsinagóga*) in Sopron goes back to the early gothic era around 1300.

Many historic homes have been preserved and turned into museums all over the country; each municipality pays special attention to those houses and sites that recall memories of a great artist, writer, or politician. Homes of great statesmen (e.g., *Széchenyi István* in Nagycenk, *Lajos Kossuth* in Monok), aristocrats (the *Duke Esterházy* family in Fertőd), poets, and writers (e.g., *Ferenc Kazinczy* in Sátoraljaújhely, *János Arany* in Nagykőrös), artists (e.g., *József Rippl-Rónai* in Kaposvár, *Lajos Kassák* in Budapest), and musicians (e.g., *Ludwig van Beethoven* in Martonvásár, *Franz Liszt, Béla Bartók, Zoltán Kodály* in

Budapest) are preserved, maintained, and presented to the general public.

Zoos and Botanical Gardens

The Budapest Zoo, officially called *Fővárosi Állat- és Növénykert* (Animal and Plant Garden of the Capital), opened in 1866 with 500 diverse animals. *János Xántus*, an ethnographer–traveler, was its first director. The zoo became a research institution during the 1950s. The institution is widely known for its nature conservation activities.

The Botanical Garden of Vácrátót (*Vácrátóti Botanikus Kert*) is the largest of its kind in Hungary with the largest collection of living plants. Its creation dates back to the first half of the nineteenth century. The garden became the site of the Botanical Research Institute of the Hungarian Academy later on. Twelve other botanical gardens present the fauna of the other Hungarian regions; the most important of them is the Arboretum of Szarvas (*Szarvasi Arborétum*), the site of the University of Horticulture and Food.

Digital Museum Exhibits and Services

Every museum and gallery has a Web site offering basic information about services and collections as well as digital samples of the holdings.

Access to the most important digital museums and exhibits is provided by the National Digital Data Archive (*Nemzeti Digitális Adattár*[31]). The digital collection Fine Arts in Hungary (*Képzőművészet Magyarországon*[32]) provides a comprehensive history of the fine arts (painting and sculpture) in Hungary from the eleventh century to the twentieth century. It does not include contemporary fine arts. In 2007, the collection held 5200 digital reproductions. The permanent digital exhibition of the National Gallery (*Nemzeti Galéria*[31]) presents 1000 digital reproductions of its most important holdings; viewers may choose to visit the exhibit with the help of a virtual guide. A smaller collection of the holdings of the Christian Museum of Esztergom (*Keresztény Múzeum*[49]), 164 digital reproductions, is also available through the NDA. Archaeological sites, historical buildings, and objects protected by the state are cataloged (11,000 records) by the Office of Cultural Heritage (*Kulturális Örökségvédelmi Hivatal*[50]). Digital photos and descriptions of 3200 historical buildings (fortresses, castles, churches, etc.) are also available through the NDA database among a number of further collections.

Museology as a Discipline and Profession[51]

Museum professionals are experts in art history, archaeology, ethnography, and history, as well as the sciences and engineering, specializing in museological aspects of their respective fields. Leading figures of the field have conducted research and contributed to the emergence of a museology discourse from the early nineteenth century on. Thanks to their scholarly activity, the legal and institutional framework of this field has developed steadily since the 1880s. The first organization dealing with the inventory and protection of historical monuments (*Műemlékek Országos Bizottsága*) was created in 1881. This institutional background helped professionals produce a series of comprehensive works on Hungary's historical monuments[52–54] that served as a basis for the creation of a thorough register, topography, and standardized approach to sites and buildings of historical importance. Though collecting of ethnographic, historical, scientific, and other types of artifacts as well as art started in the eighteenth century among the aristocracy, and extended to the affluent middle class in the third part of the nineteenth century, no laws and institutions protected collections held by collectors and museums until 1949. The decree on museums (1949) at last made it compulsory to keep standardized records and statistics of museum holdings as well as private property of museum value. These legal and institutional changes have provided a data-oriented background and overview to the type of museological research that deals with the collection, preservation, exhibition, etc. of museum holdings nationwide. The outstanding scholarly production of nineteenth and early twentieth century paved the way for museologists on individual collections, objects, and institutions, and for approaches that map and evaluate the whole cultural heritage. Efforts have been made (especially by the publications of *László Mravik*[55]) to identify and reclaim art works illegally moved out of the country before and during the Second World War.

Magyar múzeumi arcképcsarnok, a recently published biographical lexicon lists all those experts who worked and published during the last two centuries. About 2000 expert professionals have been working in Hungary's 772 museums in 2005;[56] their research contributions are published in books and scholarly periodicals.

Several periodicals focus on museums. *Múzeumi Közlemények* (Museum Proceedings) concentrates on theoretical and methodological issues of museology. The content of *Múzeumi Hírlevél*'s (Museum Newsletter) is more practical; its articles describe current issues and events pertinent to Hungarian museums. *Magyar Múzeumok* (Hungarian Museums), published by the Pulszky Society, is an illustrated magazine targeting a broader audience; it publishes special issues dealing with specific types of museums and subjects related to them.

The best museologists, curators, and managers are annually recognized by the *Ferenc Pulszky* and *Károly Pulszky Prizes*, museums by the *Museum of the Year Award*.

The main academic frameworks for museum research are departments of history and ethnography of the major universities (in Budapest, Debrecen, Miskolc). Expert museum curators and managers conduct research at their institutions; publications are requirements for promotion.

In 2004, the International Council of Museums (ICOM) accepted the Code of Ethics of Museums that has been subsequently accepted by the Hungarian National Committee of ICOM. The document has been translated and published in Hungarian. This code sets standards for professional activity and performance.

Education for Curatorship and Museum Administration

Archeologists, historian-museologists, art historians, and other experts may become museologists. The history and ethnography departments of a few universities offer BA and MA degrees in "museologist specialization" within their disciplines. Postgraduate courses and certificates are offered for future curators at the Hungarian University of Fine Arts (*Magyar Képzőművészeti Egyetem*) and the Management Section of the Pulszky Society (*Pulszky Társaság*). Courses for cultural managers are also offered by the Pulszky Society as well as within the framework of continuing education at some universities (e.g., *Janus Pannonius University*, Pécs).

Professional Associations for Curators and Museum Administrators

The Pulszky Society, Hungarian Association of Museology (*Pulszky Társaság, Magyar Múzeumi Egyesület*) is the largest Hungarian association of museum professionals; its sections deal with such concerns as preservation, management, art history, and continuing education. The association promotes museums and museology, facilitates cooperation among institutions and professionals, publishes a journal, and votes annually on two awards—one for a museum, and one for a professional. Other associations unite special interest museums and museologists including the Association of Public Collections (*Közgyűjtemények Szövetsége*) and the Association of County Museums (*Megyei Múzeumok Igazgatóságainak Szövetsége*).

Key Contemporary Issues

Current priorities are listed in the *Alpha Program*,[57] the mid-range plan for Hungarian museums—most of these priorities relate to the strategic plan of the cultural government of Hungary as a new member country of the European Union. Broadening access to the collections, and strengthening their educational role is the top priority. The second major priority is to develop requirements for open and visitor-friendly museums in each museum service. This goal has consequences for infrastructure as well as for the level and quality of cooperation between schools and museums. The government supports this goal by not only providing free access to museums for schoolchildren, but also providing free public transportation (including long distance train) to groups of schoolchildren to 14 major museums of national jurisdiction. Annual special events like the Museum May Day (*Múzeumi Majális*) and Museum Night (*Múzeumok Éjszakája*) attract more and more people to these institutions, and transform museums into popular meeting places. The third major priority is qualitative development and preventive preservation of the collections, as well as digital access to collections information. This complex professional goal also harmonizes with the EU strategy of preservation declared by the International Centre for the Study of the Preservation and Restauration of Cultural Property (ICCROM) in Vantaa, Finland, in 2000.

CONCLUSION

Current tendencies and future plans of Hungarian libraries, archives, and museums harmonize with trends that characterize these areas worldwide and interests (and financial resources) that the European Union has elaborated for its member countries. The Strategy of Libraries for 2008–2013 (*A könyvtárügy stratégiája 2008–2013*) is currently (in 2007) being widely discussed.[12] Its main goals are the continuation of the development of libraries and library access in rural areas; delivery of around-the-clock access to library materials from any location; and improved ability for the disabled to access libraries. The digitization of extant primary and secondary Hungarian literature as well as current publications will also continue.

The mid-range strategic plan of Hungarian archives identifies the major deficiencies in the current situation as follows: lack of financial resources, lack of appropriate technological knowledge and skills among archivists; lack of theoretical–methodological background. In order to resolve these problems, the mid-range plan (*A levéltárak középtávú informatikai stratégiája és feladatterve, 2006–2010*[42]) projects the transformation of archives from institutions providing merely storage and preservation for the materials, and access to the materials for researchers into institutions that provide access to their materials 24/7 from any location. The document defines future archives as basic institutions of a democratic society, and proposes that the government finance a breakthrough project of e-government and e-public-administration. The plan envisages the creation of an e-archive within the framework of the Hungarian National Archives, and the establishment of a degree in information and archive management as well as records management—both related to public administration rather than to traditional history.

The most important efforts in the museum field will continue to be related to the Alpha Modernization Program which has as goals making museums more accessible and user-friendly, further developing their relationships to education, and increasing the mobility of collections and professionals nationwide and internationally.

Every major trend of Hungarian libraries, archives, and museums over the next 7 years (2007–2013) will certainly be harmonized with or based on the "culture program" of the European Union, accepted for the aforementioned period of time by the European Parliament.[58] The general objective of this program is to "enhance the cultural area common to Europeans with a view to encouraging the emergence of European citizenship." Its central objectives are "supporting the transnational mobility of professionals in the cultural sector; encouraging the circulation of works of art and artistic and cultural products beyond national borders; and promoting intercultural dialog."

ACKNOWLEDGMENTS

I wish to thank Dr. Antal Stark, Assistant State Secretary; Dr. Annamária Vígh, Head of the Department of Public Collections; Prof. György Sebestyén, Director, Institute of Library and Information Science; Dr. Péter Fodor, Director, Ervin Szabó Könyvtár; as well as the expert librarians of the Könyvtári Intézet and Országos Levéltár for giving me opportunities for consultation, supplying materials not readily available in the United States and answering my numerous queries regarding many issues of this entry. I am grateful to Dr. Annamária Vígh and Dr. Antal Stark, Hungarian Ministry for Education and Culture for the statistical data.

APPENDIX: KEY DATES

896	Hungarian tribes settle in the Carpathian Basin.
997–1038	Stephen of the Árpád dynasty rules the country.
1000	Stephen is converted to Christianity. Christianization of the population follows.
1001	Foundation of the first monastery and monastic library (Pannonhalma).
1055	The earliest written record extant in the Hungarian language: the foundation charter of the Tihany abbey.
1192	The earliest Hungarian text, a funeral sermon, inserted in the Latin Pray Codex.
1241	Mongolian Tatars invade and devastate the country.
1367	Foundation of the first university (Pécs).
1458–1490	King Matthias, a true Renaissance ruler, elevates the country to a high European standard.
1460	Foundation of the Bibliotheca Corviniana, King Matthias' library.
1473	Publication of the first printed book (in Latin), *Chronicle of Buda*.

1526	Turks defeat the Hungarian army at Mohács, and the King dies in the battle.
1533	The first book in Hungarian language is published in Krakow.
1541	Turks occupy Buda. Hungary is split into three parts.
1613	Official documents of the Habsburg Monarchy start to be deposited in archives.
1686	Buda is recaptured from the Turks.
1703–1711	Ferenc Rákóczi II, Prince of Transylvania, leads an unsuccessful uprising against the Habsburgs.
1749	Foundation of the Habsburg monarchic archives in Vienna, the *Haus-, Hof-, und Staatsarchiv*.
1756	Foundation of the Hungarian Royal Archives, predecessor of the Hungarian National Archives.
1780	Publication of the first Hungarian journal, *Magyar Hírmondó*.

First half of the nineteenth century

	A national reform movement is launched for the political and economic modernization of the country and the development of its Hungarian national identity.
1802	Foundation of the Hungarian National Museum and Library by count Ferenc Széchenyi.
1825	István Széchenyi founds the Hungarian Academy of Sciences.
1844	Hungarian becomes Hungary's official language.
1848–1849	Revolution and war for independence.
1866	Opening of the Budapest Zoo. Foundation of the Library of the Parliament.
1870–1900	A series of new museums are opened: Ethnographic, Fine Arts, Applied Arts, etc.)
1867	Compromise with the Habsburgs; beginning of a double-centered monarchy of Austria-Hungary. Foundation of the Hungarian Statistical Office and its Library.
1907	Publication of the first periodical on libraries and museums, *Múzeumi és Könyvtári Értesítő*.
1904	Opening of the first public library, *Fővárosi Könyvtár*.
1914–1918	World War I; the Austro-Hungarian monarchy is Germany's ally. After the defeat, the Monarchy disintegrates.
1920	The Trianon Treaty reduces Hungary's territory.
1923	Publication of the first periodical on archives, *Levéltári Közlemények*.

1935	Foundation of the Association of Hungarian Librarians, includes archivists until 1986.
1944	Hungary is occupied by Nazi Germany.
1945	The Soviet Army liberates Hungary.
	Central institutions are founded to administer libraries, archives, and museums.
1946–	Nationalization of most private libraries, archives, museums.
1947	Beginning of Communist control; establishment of Stalinist dictatorship.
1948	University level program for librarian education is established.
1956	Uprising against Stalinism.
	Foundation of the Gorky Library, a center for Russian culture.
	The first Library Law is accepted.
1965	Cautious economic market reforms, the New Economic Mechanism, are launched.
1985	The Hungarian National Library moves to a building of the Royal Castle.
1986	Foundation of the Association of Hungarian Archivists.
1988	Beginning of transition from state socialism to capitalism and democracy.
1990	Multiparty parliamentary democracy is established. The Soviet army leaves Hungary.
1995	LXVI Law regulates Hungarian archives.
1997	CXL Law regulates Hungarian libraries and museums.
1999	Hungary becomes a full member of NATO.
2002	The first online union catalog, *MOKKA*, goes live.
2004	Hungary joins the European Union.

REFERENCES

1. Csapodi, Cs. Csapodi-Gárdonyi, K. *Bibliotheca Corviniana. The Library of King Matthias Corvinus of Hungary*, Corvina: Budapest, Hungary, 1981; 334.
2. Keresztury, D. *Híres Magyar Könyvtárak*, RTV-Minerva: Budapest, Hungary, 1982; 144.
3. Bodó, S., Viga, Gy., Eds. *Magyar Múzeumi Arcképcsarnok*; Pulszky Társaság: Budapest, Hungary, 2002; 984.
4. Érszegi, G., Ed. *Archivum Regni, Regnum Archivi*; Hungarian National Archives: Budapest, Hungary, 2006; 79.
5. Réthi, Ch. Das ungarische Bibliothekswesen. Geschichte und Gegenwart. Bibliothek und Wissenschaft **1967**, *4*, 159–173.
6. Réthi, Ch. Das ungarische Bibliothekswesen. Geschichte und Gegenwart. Bibliothek und Wissenschaft **1967**, *4*, 178–179.
7. Madas, E. Monok, I. *Könyvkultúra Magyarországon a kezdetektől 1800-ig*, Balassi: Budapest, Hungary, 2003; 238.
8. Blazovich, L. Müller, V. *Magyarország levéltárai*, Magyar Levéltárosok Egyesülete: Budapest, Hungary, 1996; 179.
9. Dóka, K., Ed. *Levéltári ismeretek;* Magyar Országos Levéltár: Budapest, Hungary, 1998; 266, Part 1.
10. Varjas, B. *The Development of Librarianship in Hungary*, National Szechényi Library: Budapest, Hungary, 1956; 58.
11. Libraries in Hungary. In *Encyclopedia of Library and Information Science*; Kent, A., Lancour, H., Eds.; Dekker: New York. 1980; Vol. 11, 84–123.
12. *A könyvtárügy stratégiája 2008–2013. Portál program (munkaanyag)*, 195. Available at http://www.ki.oszk.hu/107/download.php?view.
13. *The Hungarian Library System Today*. Könyvtári Intézet: Budapest. Available at http://www.ki.oszk.hu/old/dok/kiadv_2006/system.html (accessed September 11, 2007).
14. Republic of Hungary, Constitution. Available at http://www.lectlaw.com/files/int05.htm.
15. évi CXL. Törvény, 1997. Available at http://www.1000ev.hu/index.php?a=3&param=9559.
16. évi LXXVI. Törvény, 1999. Available at http://www.1000ev.hu/index.php?a=3&param=9747.
17. *The National Széchényi Library*; National Széchenyi Library: Budapest, Hungary, 1985; 143.
18. Csapodi, Cs. *A Magyar Tudományos Akadémia Könyvtárának ősnyomtatvány-gyűjteménye*, MTA: Budapest, Hungary, 1967; 34.
19. Csanak, F.D. *Az Akadémiai Könyvtár története a szabadságharcig*, MTA: Budapest, Hungary, 1959; 29.
20. Simon, M.A. *A Magyar Tudományos Akadémia kutatóintézeti könyvtári hálózata*, MTA: Budapest, Hungary, 1966; 53.
21. Katsányi, S. *A főváros könyvtárának története 1945-ig*, Fővárosi Szabó Ervin Könyvtár: Budapest, Hungary, 2004; 417.
22. Fővárosi Szabó Ervin Könyvtár. *Jelentés, 2006*, FSzEK: Budapest, Hungary, 2006; 134.
23. Dán, K. *Az iskolai könyvtárak fejlesztési stratégiája*, August 22, 2007. Available at http://www.oki.hu/oldal.php?tipus=cikk&kod=konyvtar-Dan-Iskolai (accessed August 22, 2007).
24. Dán, K. *Az iskolai könyvtár mint információs forrásközpont*, August 22, 2007. Available at http://www.oki.hu/oldal.php?tipus=cikk&kod=iii-Dan (accessed August 22, 2007).
25. Erdeiné, T.K.; Kührner, É. A kórházi könyvtárak múltja, jelene, ... jövője?. Tudományos és Műszaki Tájékoztatás, August 1, **2007,** *50*(3). Available at http://tmt.omikk.bme.hu/show_news.html?id=1801&issue_id=49 (accessed August 1, 2007).
26. Magyar Orvosi Könyvtárak Szövetsége. *Alapszabály*, Budapest, 2003. Available at http://moksz.lib.unideb.hu/ (accessed August 20, 2007).
27. Magyar Elektronikus Könyvtár. Available at http://www.mek.iif.hu/.
28. Elektronikus Periodika Archívum és Adatbázis. Available at http://epa.oszk.hu/.
29. Neumann János Digitális Könyvtár. Available at http://www.neumann-haz.hu/index.html.
30. Bibliotheca Corviniana Digitalis. Available at http://www.corvina.oszk.hu/.
31. Nemzeti Digitális Adattár. Available at http://www.nda.hu/Engine.aspx.

32. Képzőművészet Magyarországon. Available at http://www. hung-art.hu/.

33. Budapest Képarchívum. Available at http://www.fszek.hu/ ?tPath=/adatbazisok/sajat_adatbazisok/budapest-keparchivum.

34. Hungarian Film History Online. Available at http://www. filmtortenet.hu/.

35. Társadalomtudományi Digitális Adattár. Available at http://www.tarki.hu/adatbank-h/katalog/index.html.

36. BMC Magyar Zenei Információs Központ. Available at http://www.bmc.hu/.

37. LIBINFO. Available at http://libinfo.oszk.hu/.

38. A könyvtártudomány legkiemelkedőbb képviselői. A könyvtárosképzés. A könyvtárügyi szakirodalom. Available at http://mek.oszk.hu/02100/02185/html/1352.html.

39. *Hazai és külföldi folyóiratok magyar tudományos repertóriuma*; Athenaeum: Budapest, Hungary 1874–1885; 3 Vols.

40. Dóka, K., Ed. *Levéltári ismeretek*; Magyar Országos Levéltár: Budapest, Hungary, 1998; 266, Part 1.

41. Szögi, L. *Az egyetemi levéltárügy és a Magyar Felsőoktatási Levéltári Szövetség története*. Available at http://www.mflsz.hu/fooldal/index.php?page=tortenet/tort_ magyar.html (accessed August 1, 2007).

42. *A levéltárak középtávú informatikai stratégiája és feladatterve, 2006–2010*. Available at http://infoszek.free base.hu/images/leveltari.doc.

43. Balassa, M.I., Ed. *Magyarország múzeumai. Múzeumlátogatók kézikönyve*; Vince: Budapest, Hungary, 2001; 290.

44. Fülep, F., Ed. *The Hungarian National Museum: published for the 175th anniversary of the Museum*; Corvina: Budapest, Hungary, 1978; 351.

45. Brestyánszky, I.P. *Margit Kovács*, 2nd Ed. Corvina: Budapest, Hungary, 1976; 192.

46. Holló Sz, A. *Múzsák kertje. A magyar múzeumok születése*, Pulszky: Budapest, Hungary, 2002; 228.

47. Cséfalvi, P. Buzási, E. *Christian Museum Esztergom*, Corvina: Budapest, Hungary, 1993; 260.

48. Beneschofsky, I. Scheiber, S. *The Jewish Museum of Buda-pest*, Corvina: Budapest, Hungary, 1987; 241.

49. http://www.keresztenymuzeum.hu/ (accessed September 1, 2007).

50. http://www.koh.hu (accessed September 1, 2007).

51. Museology in Hungary (11 articles). Museum. (Paris, France) 35, 4, 202–257.

52. Henszlmann, I. *Magyarország műemlékei a Vallás- és Közoktatásügyi M. Kir. Miniszter úr meghagyásából Magyar Kir.* Egyet. Könyvny: Budapest, Hungary, 1876.

53. Forster, Gy. *Magyarország műemlékei*, Hornyánszky: Budapest, Hungary, 1905; 2 Vols.

54. The monographic series: *Magyarország műemleki topografiája* published from 1948 to present.

55. Mravik, L. Berecky, L. *The "Sacco di Budapest" and Depredation of Hungary, 1938–1949: Works of Art missing from Hungary as a Result of the Second World War: Looted, Smuggled, Captured, Lost and Destroyed Art Works, Books and Archival Documents: Preliminary and Provisional Catalog*, Hungarian National Gallery: Budapest, Hungary, 1998; 468.

56. *Magyar múzeumi arcképcsarnok*; Pulszky Társaság: Budapest, Hungary, 2002; 984.

57. Oktatási és Kulturális Minisztérium. *Alfa program*. Available at http://www.okm.gov.hu/main.php?folderID= 1473.

58. Decision No 1855/2006/EC of the European Parliament and of the Council of 12 December 2006 establishing the Culture Programme (2007 to 2013). Official Journal of the European Union, December 27, 2006. Available at http:// eur-lex.europa.eu/LexUriServ/site/en/oj/2006/l_372/ l_3722006122 7en00010011.pdf.

59. *CIA World Factbook*, article on Hungary. Available at https://www.ciu.gov/library/publications/the-world-factbook/ geos/Hu.html/ (accessed September 17, 2007).

Hypertext and Hypercard: Early Development *[ELIS Classic]*

Susan K. Kinnell
Consultant, Santa Barbara, California, U.S.A.

Carl Franklin
Consultant, Columbus, Ohio, U.S.A.

Abstract

The ease of linking and hopping from one text to another that we associate today with the World Wide Web was implemented in a different context prior to the Web. The creation of "hypertext" has a long and interesting history prior to the Web, as this entry demonstrates. At the time it was issued, the HyperCard software application was expected to be the foundation of a widely-used new means of information organization. We can see now that the key ideas of hypertext were present in HyperCard, without the ease of use of subsequent World Wide Web features.

—ELIS Classic, from 1992

INTRODUCTION AND DEFINITION

Hypertext has been defined by many people in different ways. It has been called nonsequential writing,[1–3] the creation and representation of links between discrete pieces of data,[4] an associative information management system,[5,6] and a database with "active" cross references.[7] However defined, the point is this: electronic links are created between pieces of information in a machine-readable document and a computer is used to make the quick leaps between those pieces of linked information. A computer is required to define those links in the course of creating a hypertext document, and a computer is required to execute those links during the course of reading or using that document. It can be described, written, and talked about, but the essence of hypertext comes from using the speed of a computer to make those links.

Imagine the scope and contents of an extensive reference work. Generally, it will have title and cataloging information; a contents page; various entries that each contain headings, subheadings, footnotes, see and see also references, and notes; there might also be charts, maps, illustrations, or photographs; and in the back, a bibliography, index, glossary, and one or more appendices. When using such a volume, the researcher scans the title first, then probably the contents and index pages, looking for the desired material. Once an appropriate entry is found, its contents are scanned, key word definitions are checked, the notes and references are scanned, and then the bibliography is reviewed. All of this requires considerable page turning and page flipping, as the researcher verifies that the book contains essential information, before he or she even starts to read it and take notes from it. Consider the options available to any researcher if all of this material was linked electronically and could be called up at the stroke of one key. To access a glossary with specific definitions, double check the source of a quote, to consider further study along somewhat different lines, verify the extent of a particular source, or even jot down the salient facts and figures culled from that source—all of these things can now be done electronically (even taking notes on the sources being utilized) without great amounts of effort and time being expended.

As mentioned earlier, reference books often contain illustrations such as maps, charts, or photographs. Given the speed and memory capabilities of modern computers, this has become one of the most appealing features available when creating a hypertext document. Modern computers can access plain photographs such as exist now in reference books, and they can also provide moving video pictures from a variety of sources and audio capability by accessing tape recorders, CD-ROM players, or prerecorded sounds on a floppy disk. The hypertext reference work can provide, for example, a life of Beethoven, a picture of him, a related discussion of his country and fellow composers, and a sample of sounds from his compositions. It might even include access to some video footage from a film or documentary of his life.

As the user moves through such a collection of reference material (called hypermedia if more than one medium is being used), he or she has the ability to select and choose the most pertinent material. The user can move through the material and select paths or links to other pieces of information that are the most relevant. Presumably no two people use a reference work with exactly the same motives or needs, and their paths through the material are now no longer restricted to structured, linear information. Each may select the same material, but in a different order, or each may spend varying amounts of time in different areas. This flexibility and user-defined

Encyclopedia of Library and Information Sciences, Fourth Edition DOI: 10.1081/E-ELIS4-120044769

approach is probably the most significant area of hypertext research currently being undertaken at major universities.

The relationship between the way people think, and the way they learn is of considerable consequence to researchers in education and psychology, as well as in the newer fields of computer and cognitive science. Hypertext presents a new way of looking at material, free from the constraints of linear access. People do not think in a linear fashion and their minds are structured into associative patterns. Access to material or information that allows and even encourages associative browsing is highly desirable, and test results just beginning to be reported in academia are highly supportive of this theory. "Learning by discovery" is becoming a popular basis for hypotheses in educational research.

Finally, in understanding the concept of hypertext, it is necessary to learn a few new words in context. There are four elements to a hypertext program that must be understood, and although software packages may name them differently, their meaning does not change. These four words are: node, button, link, and jump. Node refers to a discrete collection of information. This may range from a single word to a picture, a video clip, or supplementary text. A button represents the beginning point of a connection from one node to another. The link is that connection between nodes and a jump represents taking the link to a new node. In its simplest fashion, therefore, a hypertext document may have two nodes: for example, a paragraph describing a picture and the picture itself. Within the paragraph is a button that links the paragraph to the picture. When the button is pressed, the user jumps to the picture via a link that was pre-established during the creation of the hypertext document.

Another way of looking at this kind of system is to imagine a telephone network. In the simple system described above, there are two nodes (two telephones), one button to press (the dial), and a jump (or call) to make across one link (telephone line). In a more complex telephone system, many calls can be made from one telephone, but it is entirely dependent on how many lines have been strung across the land by telephone workers first.

Electronic technology allows us to access a number of places or things (telephones, video broadcasts, nodes, etc.) from a single unit on our desk or in our home. Keeping this electronic network idea in mind will help in understanding the concepts of a hypertext document and the links it contains.

HISTORY

Popular knowledge of the technology known as hypertext began with the introduction of HyperCard by Apple Computer, Inc. at MacWorld Expo in August 1987. But before that time, a surprising number of people were working on

hypertext projects, or had contributed substantially to the growing field of knowledge in this area. Chief among these people are H.G. Wells,[8] Vannevar Bush,[9,10] Ted Nelson,[1–3] Doug Engelbart,[11] and Alan Kay.[12]

H. G. Wells

In 1936, H.G. Wells delivered a lecture at the Royal Institution of Great Britain, entitled "World Encyclopaedia." In it, Wells posited the theory that man would be faced with too much information to be able to deal with it logically, and that he would not be able to find the material he needed. To rectify this situation, Wells came up with the idea of a world encyclopedia which would be continuously updated and easily accessible to anyone anywhere. He did not trouble himself with the technical details of how this would be achieved, only that it would definitely be necessary.

Vannevar Bush

The article by Vannevar Bush entitled "As We May Think," was published in the August 1945 issue of *Atlantic Monthly* magazine. In it, Bush, science advisor to President Roosevelt, describes a machine he calls the memex (p. 77),

> a device in which an individual stores all of his books, records, and communications, and which is mechanized so that it may be consulted with exceeding speed and flexibility. It is an enlarged supplement to his memory. . . . . It affords an immediate step, however, to associative indexing, the basic idea of which is a provision whereby any item can be caused at will to select immediately and automatically another. This is the essential feature of the memex. The process of tying two things together is the important thing.

Even today, there is no better way to describe or define hypertext. When you consider that Bush described an earlier version of his memex in 1939 (more than 50 years ago!), you realize that Bush is indeed one of the most visionary of the hypertext pioneers.

When his entry was published in *Atlantic Monthly* (and another version in *Life* shortly thereafter), Bush found that his ideas created a great deal of controversy and inspired a number of other researchers. He continued to write about his ideas and belief that mechanization was one way to sort through the ever-increasing piles of information that confront researchers. This process of sorting and selection by means of association was central to the memex and recurs throughout all of Bush's writing.

In 1967, Bush wrote "Memex Revisited" in which he discussed his earlier entry and the technical developments that had taken place since 1945. He concluded that the transistor, video tape, high-speed circuitry, and the ability to compress information storage had all contributed to the theoretical practicality of his memex. Bush reiterated his belief that the mechanization of "selection by association" would bring about a successful personal machine that would allow a human being to "think creatively and wisely, unencumbered by unworthy tasks ..." and that he will be able to "face an increasingly complex existence with hope" (p. 100). In words very reminiscent of Wells, Bush said: "Each generation will receive from its predecessor, not a conglomerate mass of discrete facts and theories, but an interconnected web which covers all that the race has thus far attained" (p. 99).

An interesting sidelight to the work going on during this period was a project at MIT known as Intrex (Information Transfer Experiments). Described in Stephen Salmon's book, *Library Automation Systems*,[13] Intrex began in 1965 and was terminated in 1973. Its principal aim was to provide an "augmented catalog" (p. 121) for libraries that would provide more information online beyond the usual bibliographic references and subject headings. It also attempted to provide the storage and retrieval of full-text documents to library patrons using terminals. When the project was introduced in 1965 to a large conference of librarians, engineers, publishers, government officials, and others, one of those present was Vannevar Bush. He praised the efforts of the Intrex group as reaching far beyond his original ideas of "analytical machinery" (p. 5).

Theodor Holm Nelson

Ted Nelson[1–3] is considered by many to be the father of hypertext. Certainly he was the one who gave it the name, as well as the term hypermedia. He would be the first to laugh at the "overnight" success of hypertext since he began working on his theories and articulating them back in the 1960s. His first published work on the subject was "The Hypertext" in the *Proceedings of the World Documentation Federation* in 1965. A more well-known work, *Computer Lib/Dream Machines*, was published in 1974 and then reissued in 1987 by Microsoft Press. This marvelous collage of ideas, facts, fantasies, drawings, trivia, and profound thinking is must reading for anyone interested in computers or hypertext.

One of Nelson's biggest projects is called Xanadu (after Samuel Taylor Coleridge's "magic place" in the poem *Kubla Khan*), which he started as a graduate student in 1960. Nelson wanted the Xanadu project to store all of the world's literary resources in an electronic format and to link parts of those documents and pieces of text to create new composite documents. In 1988 the Xanadu project was taken over by Autodesk, creators of large information management systems.

Nelson also has a special interest in education and was one of the first to recognize the value of hypertext in both teaching and learning. In an entry entitled. "No more teachers dirty looks. . . ", he said:

Let the student pick what he wishes to study next, decide when he wishes to be tested, and give him a variety of interesting materials, events, and opportunities.... Under such circumstances, students will actually be interested, motivated to achieve far more than they have ever achieved within the normal instructional framework.

Nelson continues his work today, lecturing at conferences and workshops, and further developing the concepts of the Xanadu project.

Douglas Engelbart

Douglas Engelbart[11] began his work at the Stanford Research Institute in the 1960s and was heavily influenced by Vannevar Bush's theories. He worked on a system called NLS (ON Line System) that was designed to link text segments of 3000 words or less. In addition, there was a filter capability that selected information from the database of segments, and a visual capability that allowed the user to view the results of his linked (filtered) selection. NLS subsequently evolved into a hypertext system called Augment, used internally and marketed by McDonnell Douglas. Augment is used primarily for text editing, and features windows and electronic conferencing for multiple users. Engelbart used the term "augment" to describe his system because it augments or extends the human intellect, and his major goal is to aid "knowledge workers." Engelbart is also the developer of the mouse, windows, and numerous other technological advances, and works today at Stanford University on Operation Bootstrap.

Alan Kay

Alan Kay[12] was present at a demonstration done by Engelbart in 1968 on the system he had developed, and it had a profound effect on him. Kay had been formulating his ideas on education and computers during the time he had spent learning to program computers in the Air Force and doing his doctoral work at the University of Utah. There he became involved with the domain of artificial intelligence research as well as the work of Seymour Papert[14] at MIT, who designed the programming language for children called LOGO.

Kay was convinced that the ultimate goal of all software was the enhancement of the ability to learn. He subsequently wrote a language called Smalltalk and began work on the ultimate, small personal computer—something he called the "Dynabook."

Kay was working in those days at Xerox PARC, and he was very concerned with the effect of different kinds of media on children. He wrote an entry in 1977 in which he described the Dynabook as a "dynamic medium for creative thought" and from there he went on to explore the idea's enormous potential for education as well as creative processes in computer simulation. Defining simulation as the power to see what you can imagine. Kay has gone on to develop what he calls the "fantasy amplifier," to preserve and extend that sense of wonder that children have. Kay also pioneered the use of symbols (icons) instead of words for telling a computer what to do next.

After PARC, Alan Kay went to work for Atari as chief scientist. He now works for Apple Computer as an Apple Fellow and indulges his lifelong interests in education and music.

ACADEMIC AND CORPORATE PROJECTS

At the academic and corporate level, a number of prominent scientists and researchers have been working on research projects over the past several years. These hardworking and dedicated people are contributing vital elements to the growing body of knowledge on hypertext and hypermedia.

The Jefferson notebook

Mark Chignell and Tyde Richards are two members of the Jefferson Notebook team at the University of Southern California in Los Angeles. Formerly called Project Jefferson, the project was conceived and designed as a tool for writing research papers in the Freshman Writing Program at USC. Organized as an electronic notebook with access to the instructors assignments, background information, citations of relevant documents, and commercial databases loaded on the mainframe computer at the USC library. Project Jefferson has become the basis for a number of similar applications in varying disciplines such as psychology, anthropology, and library science.

Project Emperor-I

Professor Ching-chih Chen[15] is the Associate Dean of the Graduate School of Library Science at Simmons College in Boston. Dr. Chen has authored many entries and books on the subject of information technology and management for libraries and scholars. She is also editor of the journal *Microcomputers for Information Management* and is the principal director of Project Emperor-1, a project supported by a number of government and business organizations as well as Simmons. The project combines videodisc and microcomputer technology, providing over 100,000 graphic images of the first emperor of China and his terracotta army of warriors and horses excavated in 1973 in Xian, China. Using a HyperCard interface, the project provides not only these images, but film footage, audio tracks of interviews, and related study materials and it also provides the audio and textual materials (including screen design) in Chinese as well as English. It is a major humanities project that has been utilized by Apple's new Visual Almanac, and the videodiscs will soon be available to schools in this country.

Notecards

Randall Trigg. Frank Halasz, and Tom Moran have contributed substantially to the NoteCards project at the Intelligent Systems Lab at Xerox PARC in Palo Alto, California. Trigg is the author of the first doctoral dissertation on the subject of hypertext. NoteCards is a network-based system designed for processing ideas, and has formed the basis for a number of important discoveries on the storage, linking, and retrieval of information, and the concept of the card as a structure for pieces of information has been widely used by HyperCard as well.

Intermedia

The Institute for Research in Information and Scholarship (IRIS) at Brown University in Providence. Rhode Island, has been doing hypertext research for over 20 years. Andries van Dam, Paul Kahn, and Nicole Yankelovich, along with Karen Smith, Norman Meyrowitz and many others have made substantial contributions to our knowledge of hypertext in education. The current project at Brown is Intermedia, a complex and interactive system for creating hypermedia courseware that allows the student to make links to related materials in other areas.

Hyperties

Another university that has devoted time and energy to hypertext research is the University of Maryland. Here Ben Schneiderman, long interested in the human–computer interface, helped develop Hyperties (ties = The Interactive Encyclopedia System) project. Other hypertext research has been done at the University of Maryland by Gary Marchionini. Ronald Weissman, and others.

Bioquest

At the University of Oregon in Portland under the direction of Nils Peterson, a major effort has been made to create a computer-based introductory biology course. Complete with elaborate laboratory simulations. BioQUEST intends to enhance the students' ability to recognize and solve problems. BioQUEST includes text materials, applications software, and an online reference source in HyperCard.

Project Perseus

Elli Mylonas, Kenneth Morrell, and Gregory Crane are three researchers on Project Perseus at Harvard University in Boston. This project is a collection of materials on the classical Greek world, and includes 100 megabytes of text and several thousand images.

Superbook

The Bell Communications Research (Bellcore) lab in Morristown, New Jersey, has done some superlative work in hypertext and hypermedia, including SuperBook. Developed by Tom Landauer among others, SuperBook is a system that reads in an existing (and usually very large) document already in electronic format, and then allows the reader—via the dynamic table of contents, search capabilities, and windows—to access specific parts of the document. It has proven particularly effective in the use of very large technical documents.

HYPERMEDIA AND HYPERTEXT SOFTWARE

Implementations of hypermedia and hypertext for personal computers vary greatly in price, ease of use, and capability. In general, some packages have special facilities for working with electronic text or graphics while others excel at integrating computers with other devices such as videodisc or CD-ROM players. Some are useful for developing applications while others are standalone products. Ideally, the choice of software should be based on a combination of price, ease of use, number of features, and use, but a previous hardware commitment can significantly affect this decision. Therefore, the next entry will provide an overview of hypermedia and hypertext on three personal computer/software systems: the Apple II, MS-DOS, and Macintosh computers.

Apple II Software

HyperScreen

Published in early 1990 by Scholastic Software and developed by George Brackett, HyperScreen works with all members of the Apple II family. HyperScreen supports graphics, sound, animation, and video.

HyperStudio

Unlike HyperScreen and Tutor-Tech, Roger Wagner's HyperStudio will run only on the Apple IIGS. Like HyperCard, each screen is a card and a collection of cards is a stack. HyperStudio is unique among the packages discussed here because it comes with software and hardware to allow the digitization and playback of audio from a variety of sources. In addition, it works with Apple's Video Overlay Card, allowing a developer to integrate video with other forms of hypermedia.

Tutor-Tech

Techware began selling its Tutor-Tech software in 1985. Like many other hypermedia programs, the basic building block is the page. A page is one screen of information and may contain buttons for linking to other pages or to control external devices such as videodisc players and speech synthesizers. Although Tutor-Tech is neither as powerful nor as flexible as HyperCard, it offers the basics of hypermedia to a wide audience.

MS-DOS Software

Guide

Introduced in mid-1987 for computers running Microsoft Windows, Guide 2.0 for the PC performs almost identically to its counterpart on the Macintosh. This can be an important selling point for schools that have both Macintosh and MS-DOS equipment. As noted above, Guide works particularly well with large amounts of text although it also can incorporate graphics. Version 2.0 does not come with a programming language. Guide 3.0 for Windows, just announced, adds a programming language and support for dynamic data exchange with other programs.

HyperPAD

Billed as a HyperCard clone for the PC, HyperPAD runs on machines with a minimum of 384K of RAM and MS-DOS 2.0. The program has basic hypertext features and an excellent built-in programming language called PADtalk. In Hyper-PAD, a file is a pad and a screen of information, a page. Pages can use only character-based graphics since the program runs on monochrome monitors. A good touch is the ability to use either the keyboard or a mouse to control all the functions of the program. Like HyperCard, the package comes with several built-in programs: a calculator, a telephone dialer, a puzzle, and so on. In short, Jim Lawyer and his team at Brightbill-Roberts have done a reasonable job of transferring the non-graphics-related functionality of HyperCard to MS-DOS computers.

Hyperties

Hyperties was originally developed by Dr. Ben Shneiderman and others at the University of Maryland in the early 1980s. Cognetics Corporation now distributes the program. Hyperties provides basic hypertext capabilities to machines with as little as 256K of RAM. Applications can be developed as text-only or a combination of text and graphics. Each application is built around one or more entries and a collection of entries is called a database. In line with its straightforward approach, users can choose between running the program using the keyboard or a mouse.

KnowledgePro

Created by Bev and Bill Thompson. KnowledgePro for DOS combines hypertext and expert systems technology and requires 512K RAM to run. In KnowledgePro, a file is called a knowledge base and consists of a number of topics. Users can add sophisticated features to topics using the built-in programming language. Although KnowledgePro for DOS uses character graphics, bit-mapped images can be added via the Graphics Toolkit. For those interested in more advanced forms of hyperme-dia, the Videodisc Toolkit enables KnowledgePro to con-trol the Sony LDP 2000 videodisc player.

LinkWay

Developed in response to Apple's HyperCard, LinkWay is IBM's flagship hypermedia product. Created by Larry Kheriaty, it requires a minimum of 384K, a CGA display, a Microsoft-compatible mouse, and one floppy drive. A LinkWay file is called a folder and a screen of informa-tion, a page. A page may contain data, buttons, and graphics. LinkWay comes with a paint program, a text editor, a font editor, and sample applications. Although not as powerful as HyperCard, LinkWay does bring some excellent hypermedia tools to the PC.

Macintosh Software

More hypertext/hypermedia software is available for Apple Computer's Macintosh line than any other type of computer. Sporting a mouse and windowing interface, the Macintosh is a natural for hypertext and hypermedia. Development environments include ArchiText, Business Filevision, Guide, Intermedia, Plus, and SuperCard. Inasmuch as HyperCard is the most well-known hypertext software, it will be treated in a separate entry following that describing other Macintosh software.

Business Filevision

An early form of Business Filevision was introduced in August 1984, making it the first hypermedia software for the Macintosh. The product, created by Howard Metcalfe, combines hypermedia with a flat-file database. The result is a synergistic product with more power than HyperCard for certain applications such as geographic information systems. Like ArchiText, Business Filevision lacks a pro-gramming language and this makes it less versatile than other products.

Guide

Guide 2.0 draws on several years of research on reading electronic documents conducted by Dr. Peter Brown at the University of Kent in Canterbury, England. In 1985, Guide was ported to the Macintosh and then, 2 years later, to the IBM PC. Basically, Guide acts like a word proces-sor with extra features for linking text and graphics. Its trademark is its ease of use.

Intermedia

Developed by Norman Meyrowitz and others at Brown University, Intermedia runs under the A/UX operating system (Apple's version of UNIX). A copy may be obtained through the Apple Programmers and Developers' Association. Intermedia comes with elegant drawing, mapping, and writing tools. Although few schools have the necessary computer resources to run Intermedia, its sophistication points the way for the future of hypermedia software on the Macintosh.

Plus

Plus is available in the United States from Spinnaker Soft-ware under a special agreement with its West German developers. While Plus can run most HyperCard stacks, it is much more than a clone. Its programming language, PPL, is a superset of HyperTalk. Overall, it is an excellent development environment for those who find the limita-tions of HyperCard too restricting. More importantly, Spinnaker expects to release versions of Plus for Microsoft Windows and OS/2 in 1990, which should make it possible to run HyperCard stacks on IBM and compati-ble computers.

SuperCard

Like Plus, SuperCard from Silicon Beach Software is not a clone of HyperCard, but an extension. Its extra capabilities come at a price, however. For example, running the pro-gram in color requires 2 MB of RAM. HyperCard stacks may be imported into this environment, but they run more slowly than applications developed using SuperCard. SuperCard also uses some unexpected terminology: a group of cards is called a window and a group of windows, a project. The program's strengths are its animation/draw-ing tools and its SuperTalk programming language.

HYPERCARD

Bill Atkinson and the beginning of HyperCard

Bill Atkinson, developer of HyperCard, graduated from the University of California at San Diego with a Bachelor's degree in chemistry, and went on to get a Master's in electrical engineering at the University of Washington in Seattle. After graduation, he worked for

Rah Systems, and was president of Synaptic Systems Corporation, a company he founded in Seattle.

Atkinson went to work for Apple Computer, Inc. in 1978, adapting a Pascal program to the Apple II. He wrote the first graphics program for the Macintosh, MacPaint, but he is most well known for the development of HyperCard. He calls HyperCard a "software erector set" for building other kinds of applications and programs. His insistence that this new program be given away by Apple with every new Macintosh computer is certainly one of the major reasons for the success not only of this particular program but of the whole concept of hypertext itself. He believes strongly in the concept of sharing knowledge, both in the immediate sense (he visualized hundreds and thousands of people sharing "stacks" of information through HyperCard), and in the overall sense, in which information and results are linked and shared so that duplication of effort is avoided.

Atkinson is currently an Apple Fellow and is investigating the factors that go into the makeup of a good teacher, with the hope of incorporating those factors into future software developments.

Hypercard basics

HyperCard uses an index card metaphor. That is, a screen of information is a card and a collection of cards is a stack. (See Figs. 1 and 2.) The mouse is used to select choices from pull-down menus as well as to navigate among cards in a stack. One innovation to the basic card file concept is the use of backgrounds. The same background may be shared by all of the cards in a stack or each card can have its own distinctive look.

Ready-to-run stacks included in the standard HyperCard package are a rolodex card file, a calendar, an appointment book, and a notebook with activities. There are also demonstration stacks with pictures, quotations,

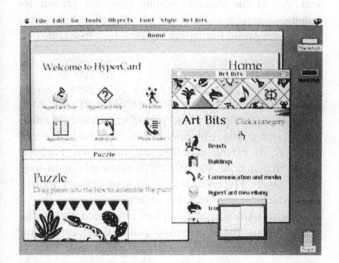

Fig. 1 HyperCard.

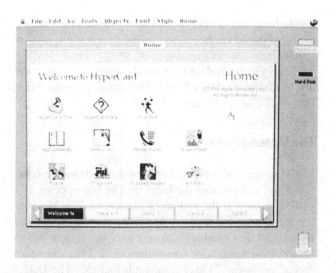

Fig. 2 The Home Card in HyperCard.

and ideas for buttons, cards, and stacks. Going through any of these sample stacks of working through the Intro Stack is a good way to get to know HyperCard.

HOW HYPERCARD WORKS

There are nine major elements in the HyperCard browsing environment: buttons, fields, cards, backgrounds, stacks, the Home Stack. Recent, the Help Stack, and the Message Box. The first five are the basic elements of a HyperCard application: the next three are navigational aids (ways to help move around and through stacks); and the Message Box is a communications device between the user and the HyperCard.

Building a Stack

Every HyperCard application (or stack) consists of a number of cards. A card is equivalent to a screen of information and may contain fields, buttons, and backgrounds. Fields contain text and buttons signal the existence of a link between two cards or fields. Fields and buttons can be layered on top of each other in the card foreground. The background of each card in a stack may be the same or each card may have a different look.

Navigational AIDS

The Home Stack is the index to the entire program. The first card in the Home Stack is the Home Card and is displayed when HyperCard is launched. There are icons on the Home Card that connect to the applications or stacks currently available.

Clicking on Recent shows up to 42 of the most recently viewed cards in the program. This function helps the user keeps track of his or her location in the program by highlighting the current card. It also permits direct access to any of the 42 cards.

The Help icon (a question mark on the Home Card) or the keyboard equivalent Command-? takes the user to the first Card in the Help Stack. This stack contains basic information about HyperCard.

The Message box

The Message box is brought up by holding down the command key and pressing the letter m. The box appears as a small text field at the bottom of the screen. The Message box may be used to send any one-line command directly to HyperCard. For example, the user may tell HyperCard to "Find" something, "Go" somewhere, or "Play" a noise like "beep" or "boing." Other commands include "The Date," "The Time," and "Show" (which displays a particular card or series of cards). (See Figs. 3 and 4.)

USING HYPERCARD

HyperCard has five levels of accessibility that accommodate the novice as well as the experienced user. In order of increasing complexity these are browsing, typing, painting, authoring, and scripting. Each level builds on the capabilities of the previous level.

Browsing: The Browsing level provides access to short file and edit menus, permits movement form card to card, and allows the use of the Browse tool.

Typing: The typing level allows the user to explore HyperCard's stacks search for text, and edit text.

Painting: By moving to this level, the user gains full File and Edit menus. Paint tools (but not Button and Field tools), and the Power Keys option.

Authoring: At this point, the user has access to the Object menu and the Button and Field tools.

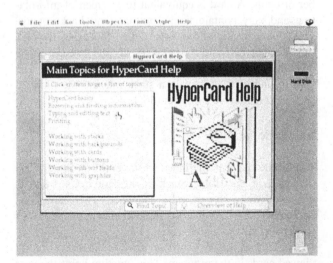

Fig. 3   HyperCard Help.

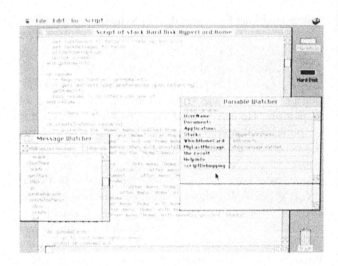

Fig. 4   HyperTalk Script.

Scripting: Finally, the scripting level places all the capabilities of HyperCard at the user's fingertips. Features available only at this level include script editing and access to the Message box even when it is hidden.

GETTING STARTED

The first time HyperCard is launched, the Home Card will appear. Pointing and clicking with the mouse on one of the icons takes the user to the linked stack. One of the easiest ways to get started is to change existing stacks by altering the text or the pictures on the various cards. More adventuresome users may decide to create a new stack via the pull-down menu.

Text Editing

HyperCard has basic facilities for entering and editing text. All of the standard editing tools are present for adding, changing, and deleting text as well as for moving blocks of text and formatting margins, font styles, etc.

Graphics

HyperCard comes with a complete set of painting tools very similar to those in MacPaint. These tools help create bit-mapped graphics by turning pixels (picture elements) on or off. An extension of this capability is the "Fat Bits" option that enlarges the painting to allow editing of individual pixels. HyperCard does not have drawing tools— tools which create graphics as objects.

When a particular painting tool is selected, three additional menus (paint, options, patterns) appear in the menubar. These new menus provide additional tools to enhance or modify a painting. These menus can also be "torn off" and placed in convenient spots on the screen so

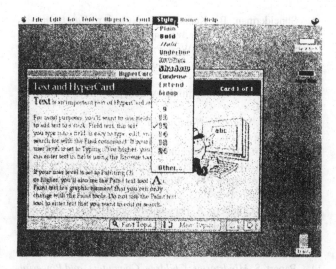

Fig. 5 Text and HyperCard.

they are visible while working on a painting but do not interfere with the image.

HyperCard's graphics tools are moderately sophisticated and powerful. They are also easy to use and follow the patterns of other similar graphics programs. Combined with the Cut-Copy-Paste tools that are also available in the text-editing mode, the graphics tools are more than adequate for most tasks. (See Figs. 5 and 6.)

Scripting with Hypertalk

The most sophisticated and powerful part of HyperCard is its built-in programming language called HyperTalk. Just as text or graphics may be edited, it is also possible to alter the way things work by using the authoring tools. The first step is to switch to the Scripting level. This level is adjusted by going to the Home Card and clicking on the arrow for the previous card (the User Preferences Card). This card allows the user to select any one of the five levels desired.

Fig. 6 A customized Home Card.

One advantage of HyperTalk is that it looks and sounds like ordinary English. Jargon is not needed in order to write simple scripts. Other advantages are that it closely resembles object-oriented programming, which has a simplicity of approach and design. Message passing between objects is the basis of object-oriented programming, and also of HyperTalk. All activity in HyperCard involves messages, whether from the system itself, between stacks, or among cards. HyperCard's major strength is its programmability. Virtually any application can be created using HyperTalk. This is the main reason for the proliferation of stacks all over the country—and even throughout the world. Teachers, librarians, students, and business people alike can use HyperCard to create a unique application.

Advanced features

The power of HyperCard does not end with scripting. The programmers at Apple Computer have made it possible to actually add features to HyperTalk through XCMDs and XFCNs. XCMDS are external commands (written in another programming language such as Pascal). XFCNs are external functions that are similar to XCMDs except that when they finish executing, they return a value. In effect, XCMDs and XFCNs make HyperTalk one of the most flexible programming environments in existence.

Hypermedia Interface

A number of options are available to produce sophisticated educational stacks involving hypermedia. For example, Apple Computer sells the CD-ROM and Videodisc. Toolkits to enable HyperCard to communicate with optical disc systems. Additionally, hypermedia developers can add synthesized speech to their projects through the public-domain HyperMacinTalk stack. For those interested in sound effects or digitized speech, there's the MacRecorder from Farallon. Animation buffs, on the other hand, will want to look into Video Works II from MacroMind and HyperAnimator from Bright Star. VideoWorks II allows the creation of digital movies that can be accessed from HyperCard. Hyper Animator adds talking actors with realistic expressions to stacks. In short, almost any conceivable enhancement can be made to HyperCard for a price.

SUMMARY

HyperCard is only one of the software packages available that enables the user to experiment with the world of hypertext and hypermedia. It is the most widespread, however, and probably the cheapest and easiest to obtain. As more sophisticated applications are developed that use video, laserdisc, sound, and graphics, more and more people will find a way to integrate them into their work and personal information management. The changes that have taken place within the computing world in the last two decades alone are astounding, and the promise is for many more. Voice-operated computers, virtual realities, and fully integrated applications will become the norm. The idea of *linking* that is so central to hypertext is a powerful feature of all of the current and promised technologies. The associations that we have in our minds for the management of the information we need and use are the associations we will actually be able to employ through our computers, thanks to hypertext and hypermedia technology. The world of tomorrow is on our doorstep.

REFERENCES

Note

Portions of this entry are reprinted from Carl Franklin and Susan K. Kinnell. Hypertext Hypermedia in Schools: A Resource Book. ABCCLIO, Inc., Santa Barbara, 1990.

1. Nelson, T.H. No more teachers' dirty looks. Computer December, **1970**, September 16–23.
2. Nelson, T.H. *Computer Lib/Dream Machines*; Microsoft: Redmond, WA, 1987.
3. Nelson, T.H. *Literary Machines*; Nelson: San Antonio,TX, 1987.
4. Parsaye, K.; Chignell, M.; Khoshafian, S.; Wong, H. *Intelligent Databases: Object-Oriented, Deductive Hypermedia Technologies;* John Wiley & Sons, Inc.: New York, 1989.
5. Franklin, C. Hypertext defined and applied. Online, **1989**, *13*, 37–49.
6. Franklin, C.; Kinnell, S. *Hypertext/hypermedia in Schools: A Resource Book*; ABC-CLIO: Santa Barbara, CA, 1990.
7. Shneiderman, B.; Kearsley, G. *Hypertext Hands-on! An Introduction to a New Way of Organizing and Accessing Information*; Addison-Wesley: Menlo Park, CA, 1989.
8. Wells, H.G. *World Brain*; Books for Libraries Press: Freeport, NY, 1971.
9. Bush, V. As we may think. Atlantic Monthly. **1945**, *176*, 101–108.
10. Bush, V. *Science Is Not Enough*; William Morrow & Company: New York, 1967.
11. Engelbart, D.C. A Conceptual Framework for the Augmentation of Man's Intellect.. In *Vistas in Information Handling*; Howerton, P.W., Weeks, D.C., Eds.; Spartan Books: Washington, DC, 1963, Vol. 1, 1–29.
12. Kay, A.; Goldberg, A. Personal dynamic media. Computer, **1977**, *10*(3), 31–41.
13. Salmon, S.R. *Library Automation Systems*; Marcel Dekker: New York, 1975.
14. Papert, S. *Mindstorms: Children, Computers, and Powerful Ideas*; Basic Books: New York, 1980.
15. Chen, C. As We Think: Thriving in the hyperweb environment. Microcomp. Inform. Mgmt. **1989**, *6*, 77–97.

BIBLIOGRAPHY

1. Brand, S. *The Media Lab: Inventing the Future at MIT*; Viking: New York, 1987.
2. Conklin, J. Hypertext, An Introduction and Survey. Computer. **1987**, *20*, 17–41.
3. Overhage, C.F.J.; Harman, R.J. *Intrex: Report of a Planning Conference on Information Transfer Experiments*; MIT Press: Cambridge,U.K., 1965; (September 3, 1965).
4. Rheingold, H. *Tools for Thought: The People and Ideas Behind the Next Computer Revolution*; Simon and Shuster: New York, 1985.
5. U.S. Congress, Office of Technology Assessment. *Power On! New Tools for Teaching and Learning*; U.S. Government Printing Office: Washington, DC, 1988.

Illumination [ELIS Classic]

Abdul Moid
University of Karachi, Karachi, Pakistan

Abstract

"Illumination is the art of embellishing manuscripts with gold or silver and bright colors," according to the author. "The art of illumination or manuscript painting is ancient and widespread. It flourished in Japan, China, India, Central Asia, the Near East, and Europe, as well as in pre-Columbian America. Basically, however, illumination is a medieval art *par excellence* that flourished mostly in Europe and the Orient until the introduction of engraved illustrations in printed books." The history of ancient and medieval illumination is traced, with emphasis on Europe, the near East, and Central Asia.

—ELIS Classic, from 1974

INTRODUCTION

Illumination is the art of embellishing manuscripts with gold or silver and bright colors. In contemporary usage illumination incorporates illustration, historiation, miniatures, paintings, and designs not only in polychrome but also in monochrome. Illumination is derived from the French *enluminure* and Latin *illuminare* meaning "to light." The art of illumination, though ancient, is generally restricted to medieval manuscripts on parchment characterized by the use of gold or, rarely, silver to light the ornamented letters, chapterheads, marginal borders, painted scenes, and sometimes the whole page.

COLOR ILLUSTRATION

Illustration in color is an ancient technique basically employed to clarify the contents of a manuscript. The ancient Egyptians used the technique on papyrus rolls. Historiation or the illustration of texts by relevant paintings or continuous scenes in historical sequence is also an ancient practice.

Miniature, derived from *miniare* in Latin, means to paint in red or with *minium*, a brilliant red pigment. The word "miniature" is commonly used for painted individual illustrations in ancient manuscripts and medieval codices. It is also applied to portraits, landscapes, and figural scenes of minuscule dimension in a manuscript. Paintings in Islamic manuscripts are usually referred to as miniatures. Miniatures may be executed without the use of gold or silver, while in illumination the use of gold is a must.

The main colors used in the embellishment of manuscripts were red, blue, and gold, and less frequently purple, yellow green, plain black, and white. These colors were made from earth minerals or plants, for example red from minium, and later from cinnabar, purple from turnsole or shellfish (Murex), yellow from turmeric roots, white from burnt bones, black from sloe berries, green from copper, etc.

The art of illumination or manuscript painting is ancient and widespread. It flourished in Japan, China, India, Central Asia, the Near East, and Europe, as well as in pre-Columbian America. Basically, however, illumination is a medieval art *par excellence* that flourished mostly in Europe and the Orient until the introduction of engraved illustrations in printed books.

ANCIENT AND CLASSICAL ILLUMINATION

Ancient Egypt

Illumination owes much for its origin to the techniques of illustration used on papyrus rolls by ancient Egyptians. These illustrations were pictorial rather than ornamental, an artistic development due to the fact that one of the earliest forms of Egyptian writing was pictographic. The illustrations in continuous scenes are used to explain the text.

Several of these earliest texts of the second millennium B.C. are now preserved in the British Museum, and are commonly called the *Book of the Dead* as they used to be kept along with a dead body in the tomb.

The earliest known copies containing the *Heliopolitan Recension* are assigned to the eighteenth dynasty (1570-ca. 1350 B.C.). The texts are written in black ink, but the titles and the first words of the chapters are written in red ink, and the designs or vignettes are in black outline.

Another text, known as *Papyrus of Ani*, has a border of two colored lines, the inner one brick red and the other dull yellow. The vertical columns of text are broken at intervals by pictures and vignettes in brilliant color, illustrating the passage of Ani and his wife to the other world. Numerous gods are also represented.

Encyclopedia of Library and Information Sciences, Fourth Edition DOI: 10.1081/E-ELIS4-120008989

Hunefer Papyrus shows the use of systematic pictorial designs in continuous scenes in monochrome and water colors of great delicacy and brilliance. The illustration depicts scenes of a funeral procession with the mourners, wailing women, and a reader who recites the funeral services, and another Anubis holds the outer coffin before the family of Hunefer.

Another copy of the *Book of the Dead* shows Orisis, outlined in black, wearing a garment decorated with bright red dots and a crown and neck ornament of inlaid gold. Border and outlines are drawn in black ink. This color scheme marks the beginning of illumination, which was continued in Christian and Islamic examples.

Greco-Roman Period

Greek art, which mainly flourished in Hellenistic Alexandria, shows a strong ancient Egyptian influence of papyrus style. A fragment of a papyrus roll (Bibliotheque Nationale, Paris) assigned to the second century, has three columns of writing, each bearing illustration in Egyptian style. The figures, however, are drawn in black and have heavy brush strokes. The garments are pink and blue-gray and the faces are brown.

The surviving materials of the classical Greek period are very few and most of them were found in Egypt, apparently dating from about the fourth century B.C. to the seventh century A.D. In the early fourth century, vellum and parchment superseded papyrus and became the chief material for ornamental writing.

The *Ambrosian Ilaid* (Biblioteca Ambrosiana, Milan) is the earliest extant fragmentary example of an ancient Greek manuscript on vellum in roll form. Only 58 illustrations on the verso of the 52 leaves of the vellum have survived, probably out of 386 leaves with 240 pictures. The colors used are red, blue, purple, and green with outlines in ink, and a bright yellow in place of gold. Landscape appears in the backgrounds. Frames of red and blue bands of varying heights surround all miniatures. The scenes, however, are not well proportioned. The date of origin of the *Iliad* is uncertain, but the text on the recto of the leaves is in Greek uncial script characteristic of the fourth to fifth century.

Vienna Dioscorides or *Canstantinopolitanus* (National Library, Vienna) is another ancient Greek illustrated text on science by the great Greek botanist Dioscrides of Anozarbos. It consists of 431 leaves each about 15 1/4 × 13 1/4 in. It is the earliest known codex with gold background. No illustrated Latin manuscript has survived from the early Roman period.

Vatican Virgil (Vatican Library) has 76 leaves, about 12 in. wide and over 12 in. in length. Its 50 pictures are uneven in quality but some of them are very well executed. The codex constitute one-sixth to one-fourth of the original manuscript. The main colors used are dark and light blue, light yellow, brown, green, red, pink, light

purple, orange, gray, white, black, and gold. Flesh has the color of brick red. Miniatures are of Roman origin. The text is in rustic capital of fourth or fifth century.

Roman Virgil (Vatican Library) has 309 square leaves of about 13 1/2 × 13 1/2 in., with 19 miniatures painted in gold, black, white, yellow, brown, purple, blue, green, yellow green, and red. The painting reflects a decadent classical style.

Alexandria, Antioch, and Rome were the important centers where Greco-Roman art flourished.

BYZANTINE ILLUMINATION

In A.D. 330 Constantine shifted his capital from Rome to Byzantium and renamed it Constantinople (presently Istanbul in Turkey). He also declared Christianity the state religion. Constantinople became not only the seat of the Roman empire or the new Byzantine Empire, but also flourished for over 1000 years as one of the great intellectual and artistic centers of the whole ancient world. In true sense, illumination developed in Constantinople around A.D. 500. The main components of the Alexandrian school and the Eastern heritage of the Syrian school centered in Antioch.

The first period of the fourth and fifth centuries is formative and marks the beginning of early Christian elements of rather pagan symbolism. At this time, books were in roll form and illustration was more common. The *Joshua Roll* (ca. A.D. 472, Vatican Library) is a good example of this period. Its origin, however, is debatable. It is written in the script of tenth century minuscule. Until 1902 it remained in roll form, measuring 35 ft. × 1 ft., but since then it has been divided into separate sheets and gathered into an album.

In the sixth century A.D., during the reign of Justinian (527–657), Byzantine illumination reached its first golden age, and became a Christian rather than East Christian art. Main features were the use of vellum in the form of codex comparable to the book of today, decoration of manuscripts of gospels with brilliantly painted ornamental designs, use of gold or silver lettering, superbly executed miniatures embellished with highly gilded backgrounds, angularity of outline, meagerness and elongation of form, and richness of costume, which indicated oriental influences. But very few manuscripts of this period could be preserved. The style and color combination of the period, however, are noticeable in mosaics and frescoes of Roman Churches of medieval times.

The period of iconoclasm (a movement against image worship due probably to Judaeo-Islamic influence) from 726–843 wrought havoc to the art of illumination. Precious illuminated manuscripts were destroyed and mutilated. The artists of this period substituted ornamentation for miniature, and flora, fauna, and geometric forms for figure paintints. In the second half of the ninth century there were two divergent styles: those of the court, "aristocratic" or aulic, based on the sixth century Alexandrian Hellenistic pattern for dogmatic and liturgical canons; and the monastic, based on the Eastern manner of Syria-Palestine called "Cappadocia," in which the illustration of contemporary life became more common. Revival of image worship in 843 brought about the return of figures to paintings, which gradually helped in producing the best miniatures of the Byzantine period.

The most glorious period of Byzantine art is from the tenth to the twelfth centuries, which can be called the age of brilliant miniaturists. *Paris Psalter* (Bibliotheque Nationale, Paris) of the tenth century is a good example in presenting freshness and brilliancy in life. *Vatican Psalter* (Vatican Library) of 1059 has rich miniatures of brilliant coloring. *Vienna Genesis* (National Library, Vienna), an illuminated manuscript, claimed to be of much earlier date, was actually produced later. Its decorative pattern, such as arcades surmounted by monsters, beasts, birds, vases, trees, plants, flowers, interlaced borders and crosses, became very popular in medieval Europe.

The most marked influences of the period could be seen in tessellated and mosaic pattern, interlaced fret work, or twining branches of gold or white over a background of variegated colors, which became a general style in Western Europe.

Byzantine art received a heavy setback by the Latin occupation of Constantinople in 1204, and it ended in 1453 when Constantinople fell to the Ottoman Turks. This was also the time when national styles of illumination were highly developed in Western Europe and also in the Orient. The influence of Byzantine artists was manifested in later works. The areas that were predominantly in the Byzantine sphere of influence were Syria, Palestine, Coptic areas, Armenia, Georgia, the Balkans, and Russia.

EUROPEAN WEST, SIXTH TO ELEVENTH CENTURIES

Western illumination, while it reflects a strong Eastern influence, developed its own original pattern, tendencies, and styles, which in a true sense were more decorative than illustrative. Three outstanding traditions of illumination, the Hiberno-Saxon, Carolingian, and Ottonian are noteworthy.

Hiberno-Saxon Illumination

The seventh and eighth centuries gave rise to the most outstanding schools of Hiberno-Saxon illumination, also called Celtic art. Main features of Celtic illumination are introduction of initials and margins, and full page designs with intricacy of interlacing spirals, zigzags, and ribbons that entangle animal and human shaped fancies, knots and other designs, all executed with a marvelous precision of

mathematical accuracy, delicate touch, and brilliant coloring. Irish illumination is decidedly oriental in execution and conception. The decorative schemes are more similar to the Arabic than to any other.

The best example of Celtic illumination is the *Lindisfarne Bible* (British Museum) written in the early eighth century in honor of Saint Cuthbert. Insular majuscule for initial letters and half uncial script for text are used. Figures show the influence of Byzantine models.

Another most outstanding work is "Q" *Codex* or the *Book of Kells* (Trinity College, Dublin). The 339 surviving leaves contain an incomplete Latin text of the gospels written in combination of uncial and round half uncial script. The ornamentation includes leaf and plant forms, zoomorphic forms, interlaced geometrical patterns, and curious figures. The use of lapis-lazulic blue, the unusual square punctuation marks, and introduction of vine foliage as a new decorative element suggest a later date than seventh to eighth century as usually assigned. No gold was used in *Book of Kells*.

Another example is the *Book of Durrow* of late seventh or early eighth century origin. It is in four colors, dark brown, brick-red, bright yellow, and green.

In Southern England, the Canterbury Scriptorium became an important center of illumination. Here the art was based on early Christian figural tradition in stiffly outlined forms and partly on the Hiberno-Saxon style ornamentation.

In the last decade of the tenth and early eleventh centuries an independent style of illumination flourished in England at Winchester. Borders with foliage in soft shades or in gold, and large initials were the chief characteristics of Winchester style. Later, Hiberno-Saxon art strongly influenced Western European illumination.

Carolingian Illumination

The flowering of Carolingian illumination began with the crowning of Charlemagne (Charles the Great, 742–814) as Emperor of the West in A.D. 800. Charlemagne's court was the scene of great splendor where many cultures met and fused.

A large number of superbly illuminated purple codices of gospels and sacred texts were produced at the monastic and imperial scriptoriums. Carolingian illumination reflects the influence of Byzantine art in the arcaded canon tables, brilliant miniatures, and lavish use of gold or silver in letters as well as illustrations on purple ground, Celtic style can be seen in large initial page designs, and the inclusion of exotic birds seems of Syrian origin. Miniatures represent historical themes. Carolingian illumination, however, shows a tendency to coarseness of workmanship and clumsiness of figure painting on purple vellum.

The Carolingian art flourished in Germany, France, and Italy. The main centers included Tours, Rheims, Aachen

(Aix-la-Chapelle), Metz, Fulda, Lorsch, and Hautvillers. *Otto Gospels* (John Ryland Library, Manchester) of the second half of the tenth century is a good example. It has a full page of decorative patterns in purple and gold and was executed at Cologne or Saint Gallen.

In the second half of the tenth century there was a great influx of Byzantine artists due to the marriage of Otto II to the Byzantine Princess Theophano in 972. The combined technique was an improvement in that facial expressions were more human and had better sense of proportion.

Important centers were the Benedictine Abbey of Reichenan; Regensburg, the seat of the Bavarian School of Illumination; Salzburg; Bamberg; Magdeburg; Trier; Mainz; the Monastery of Fulda; and the Scriptorium of Hildesheim.

ROMANESQUE PERIOD

The eleventh century marked the beginning of Romanesque style. The principal features were monumentality, growth of distinct national styles in art and architecture, religious fervor due to the crusades, large scale building of monasteries and scriptoria, and production of large bibles, psalters, gospel books, missals, biblical commentaries, particularly on the Apocalypse, and other liturgical and religious works, lectionaries, homilies, lives of saints, sacramentaries, and secular codices.

The Romanesque style had as its model the later Hiberno-Saxon and Ottonian as well as Byzantine works. Its main characteristics were elaborate decoration of initial letters ornamented with interlaced ribbons. Gold ground became more popular, and borders and backgrounds composed of a system of frames were used. Illustration directly related to the texts became very common.

During the Romanesque period the development of national styles of illumination in England, France and Low Countries, Spain, Germany, and Italy was notable.

England

The Romanesque or Norman period of the eleventh and twelfth centuries is the greatest in the history of English illumination, with Winchester, Canterbury, Durham, Westminster, St. Albans, Bury St. Edmunds, Hereford, Peterborough, and Croyland as the main centers. Fine bibles, psalters, missals, and liturgical books were the principal products.

The main features of Norman illumination were reflection of Romanesque style of architectures, Byzantine and Syrian influence in striking use of gold and heavy color, mushroom trees in the background, interlacing foliations and fantastic animals, and scenes illustrating the text of Hiberno-Saxon origin, elegant figures with elongated forms, and often full page illumination revealing Carolingian influence. The full page miniature and the stately and monumental size are important features of the twelfth century books. The *Winchester Bible* (Winchester Cathedral Library) is a good example of this period. Originally it was in two, but is now in three stately volumes, and is generally considered the finest of the monumental bibles. It has beautiful miniatures, full page outlines of drawings, good proportion of figures, with rich and beautiful coloring in dark deep tones, deep blue-green historiated initials, human figures, plants, and luxuriant foliage.

France and the Low Countries

Two schools of illumination, Southern and Northern, developed in the eleventh century. The Northern School had the influence of the Anglo-Saxon while the Southern developed on Italian and Spanish models of illumination. The color scheme shows Mozarabic influence as practiced in Moorish Spain.

At the scriptoria of various abbeys in Paris, Rheims, and in Alsace and Lorraine, magnificiently illuminated bibles, psalters, gospels, sacramentaries, lectionaries, homilies, lives of saints, and commentaries on holy books, as well as secular works, were produced. Illumination rather than calligraphic work excelled in ornamental draftsmanship. The color scheme included red ink with blue, green, or yellow backgrounds. The decoration had interlacings and coils, foliage, and panels of ornamental lettering. The human figure, however, is not well portrayed. Initials were done in gold and silver on a purple background. The decline of scriptoria of the great monasteries dates from the middle of the twelfth century.

An important example of the period is the copy of the *Commentary on the Apocalypse* (Bibliotheque Nationale, Paris). Its color schemes and decoration reflect the Mozarabic character of Spanish models. In the regions now known as Belgium a great number of huge bibles were produced. The best known is *Stavelot Bible* (now in the British Museum).

Spain

A new style developed by the Christians under the influence of Muslims in Spain is called Mozarabic art. Early Mozarabic manuscripts had primitive illumination consisting of ornamented colored initials, with green, yellow, and violet colors. Mozarabic illumination greatly influenced medieval art particularly in Spain, Italy, and Southern France. About 25 manuscripts of this period are extant and are known as *Beatus Manuscripts*.

Germany

In Germany and German speaking areas, the Ottonian tradition of illumination remained strong. Typical variations are productions of great bibles with illustrations of tiny framed scenes, huge initials of gold, silver, and other colors, and arcaded canon tables.

The main features of German illumination of this period are artistic design of linear outline, fine drawings with rich and massive grouping of foliage presented in the ornamental initials of white foliated branch outlines in red on soft blue and green fields, and dignified border designs. Emphasis was also placed on artistic calligraphy. Initials became smaller but were exquisitely drawn; dragons and birds were often added to the intertwining stems and leaves to form effective head and tail pieces to the letters, and occasionally human figures were added as part of the decorative scheme.

Italy

Italian illumination had the influences of Byzantine, Carolingian, Ottonian, and Hiberno-Saxon elements. Illuminated manuscripts, produced at Benevento in southern Italy from the eleventh to the thirteenth centuries, consisted of long rolls of parchment or vellum. The color scheme contrasted light blue, pale-green fields with ultramarine or crimson background, on which orange-yellow or gold letters paneled with geometric patterns in red, white and blue, filled with intertwining white vine tendrils, stood in sharp relief. Decorative work was of high quality, although the historiated initials with portrait miniatures were flat, wooden, and generally monotonous.

GOTHIC PERIOD

The rise of Gothic art in the thirteenth century was supremely demonstrated in its architecture with pointed arch and stained glass, which eventually had its great impact upon the book decoration. The main feature of this period was the production of smaller books intended for individual or family use in large numbers. Large and bold characters were replaced by neat minuscules. Historiated initials became more popular. Full page pictures, common in the Romanesque period, became rare and were much reduced in size. Besides liturgical works, private devotional works such as the *Book of Hours* became very popular. In addition, many secular works such as histories, chronicles, and romances began to appear. Gradually, the interest of the monasteries showed a marked decline because of Cistercian disapproval of extravagant forms of illumination. The influence of glass painting became manifest in manuscripts. Interest in landscape and contemporary life became more apparent in painting, and the use of burnished gold leaf became more common.

Gothic initials had elongated terminals, from which sprang rich borders gradually surrounding the text on all four sides. The main part was first straight and rigid, called bar border, but gradually developed a trend toward transforming the bar into a thin cylindrical rod adorned with rings and other ornaments.

Gothic illumination first flourished in France, and then in England, Italy, and elsewhere in Europe.

France

The rise of universities and the growing interest of abbots, kings, dukes, feudal lords, and rich merchants in books made Paris the main center of art, culture, and learning in Europe. Urban bookshops, traveling artists, and guilds of scribes, binders, and illuminators were organized and developed.

The main products consisted of psalters, breviaries, and especially Books of Hours, which were superbly illuminated. Contemporary scenes of knights, ladies, troubadours, and minstrels were depicted in the art, including a background of landscape with richness of color, abundant in gold. In the Grisaille technique developed in Paris, the picture is not fully painted. The color, in part pale semilucent monochrome, creates a harmony between picture and script and transforms illumination into something foreshadowing painting and other graphic arts. The figures are on a colored ground and are faintly shaded and modeled in a cold gray so that they appear as if carved in relief against brocaded and tessellated gold grounds and bright colors.

The examples of this period are numerous, but some of the important illuminated manuscripts are *St. Louis Psalter* (Bibliotheque Nationale, Paris), which has a linear and supremely elegant style, and *Roger of Parmas Treatise on Surgery* (British Museum), which has fully illuminated pages in gold and colors.

In the late thirteenth and early fourteenth centuries richly illuminated books were in great demand by laymen. Illustrated books such as *Biblia Pauperum*, the *Legenda Aurea*, and *Speculum Humanae Salvationis* became very popular.

Paris also was the center of famous artists such as Honore and his son-in-law, Richard de Verdun, and Jean Pucelle, a pioneer in the study of nature, the invention of marginal drolleries, the exposition of traditional iconography, and in rendering buildings in perspective. Pucelle's works, *Belleville Breviary* (Bibliotheque Nationale, Paris) and the *Hours of Jeanne de Evreux* (Cloister, New York City) are good examples. His workshop dominated the first half of the fourteenth century.

Low Countries

Illumination in the Low Countries was of Northern French and Northern German origin. The principal characteristics were plain burnished-gold background, deep blue coloring paling toward the horizon, and natural landscape in the background.

The abbey scriptorium of Stavelot was very famous for its excellent illuminated works. Its chef d'oeuvre, a great two-volume bible, is a good example of the work produced there.

Zwolle Scriptorium in Northern Holland was famous for calligraphic ornament, the painting of the initial letters, and the decoration of the borders with flourished scrolls of penwork, neatly drawn and finely painted.

Flemish psalters of outstanding beauty and elegance were produced by the middle of the thirteenth century. The most famous, the *Maastricht Hours* (British Museum), measuring only 3 3/4 × 3 3/4 in., represents scenes such as a fox shamming death, and three living and three dead kings.

England

England of the thirteenth and fourteenth centuries had two predominant traditions, Gothic and East Anglican.

The Gothic style had delicacy of drawing and refinement of taste with luxuriant decoration of bar borders and margins full of whimsical animals, birds, and creatures of fantasy. Human figures had a softer, more rounded and gracious contour.

The color scheme frequently used included deep rich blue, balanced by red and light green and lightly shaded with buff, gray, and pink. All psalters contained superbly illuminated initials, "B" for Beatus, and historiated initials. Spaces at the end of verses were usually filled in with pen designs in blue and red with flourishes, geometric patterns, or witty drawings of animals.

The main features of the illuminated manuscripts are their small size (sometimes like pocket books), firm, delicate draftmanship, and neat calligraphic script with ornamentation restricted to foliated initials in burnished gold and warm coloring at the beginning of each book.

The Abbey of St. Albans was a great center for the production of illuminated manuscripts. *Windmill Psalter* (Pierpont Morgan Library, New York) and *Tickhill Psalter* (New York Public Library) are some of its outstanding surviving examples.

Norwich was the center of East Anglican style. Its manuscripts have large borders, decorated with ornamental foliage interspersed with human figures, birds, animals, little grotesque armorial bearings, and the like. The principal characteristics are a rich and harmonious color scheme, with ornament in the design of frame borders, and initial decoration. A good example of this style is *Robert de Lisle* (British Museum).

Germany and German-Speaking Countries

In Germany, Byzantine and Romanesque traditions continued. But the Thuringian-Saxon School and the Benedictine monastery of Weingarten produced exquisite psalters; *Berthold Missal* is the chief product of the latter school.

The late thirteenth century Gothic style of Southern France influenced Germany. Austria also became important for its delicate pen drawings. In Bohemia, the Austrian and Italian influences could be seen in the Prague School, their main characteristics being soft, curling foliage, and fresh colored flowers. A detached initial "U," representing the Holy Trinity (National Gallery, Washington) is a good example of Bohemian style. This school influenced English illumination in the late fourteenth century due to the marriage of Charle's daughter, Princess Ann, to Richard II of England. Another work is *Passional* (University Library, Prague) with fine allegorical miniatures in water color. It shows architectural details in Gothic style. A copy of the *Golden Bull* (National Library, Vienna), the constitution of the Holy Roman Empire, is at its best in its style.

Italy

The Gothic style in Italy developed in the thirteenth century. In addition to liturgical works, the main products were law books and legal commentaries, mainly produced at the University of Bologna. Although the period had strong French Gothic influence, Byzantine influence also continued. The main features of illumination were conventional border ornament, long pointed leaves with lobes generally on one side only, cup shaped beads threaded on the wands and stems, and comical use of human, animal, and grotesque figures, such as a hare hunting a man, as can be seen in a small bible now in the British Museum. Fourteenth century illumination is like fresco or panel painting on a small scale, found in municipal accounts books.

In the middle of the fourteenth century English illumination came to a sudden end due to the plague. In the late fourteenth century, however, a new style of illumination on the model of the German School, particularly Rhenish or Bohemian, is noticeable. Its chief characteristics were independent borders with stem and leaves throwing off thin twisted tendrils with gold balls at the end, greater softness in the treatment of the face, depending more on use of brush than pen and pencil, a more harmonious color scheme, a more skillful use of architectural ornament, and the introduction of new forms of foliage and of a white scroll with sinuated edges, wrapped round the upright shafts of pillars or initials. Landscapes were presented in gilded ground, tapestried, or checkered backgrounds.

John Siferwas, a Dominican friar, is famous for his work, particularly his masterpiece the *Sherborne Missal* (Alawick Castle Collection, Northumberland).

FIFTEENTH CENTURY TO THE DECLINE OF ILLUMINATION

In the fifteenth century or during the Renaissance, illumination became a pursuit of professional artists patronized by ruling kings, dukes, and the Papal Court, and developed as a true art. The painting was more real, depicting men and women of flesh and blood. The modeling of flesh became three dimensional, portraying a true feeling of life.

Luxuriously illuminated manuscripts were produced during this period. The main features were decorative frameworks and a transition from the miniature, with its three dimensional space construction, to the flatness of the empty ground of the page.

In this period illumination flourished most in Italy, France, and the Low Countries. Each region had its own distinct characteristics.

Italy

In Italy, calligraphy and illumination both flourished as independent arts. The use of humanistic script in manuscripts became more popular. The manuscript was regarded not only as a show piece but also as something that could be used by scholars; illumination began to be confined only to the frontispiece. Its main feature was border illumination, consisting of narrow gold bands in a rectangular frame interlaced with scrolls of vine tendrils in white, on grounds of alternating blue, green, and crimson. The border enclosed putti, animal forms, and medallions in wreaths of foliage. Sometimes human figures, heraldic or symbolic designs, or busts, were copied from antique models. Miniature painting was linked with monumental painting. In Florence, the cradle of the Renaissance, famous artists such as Fra Angelico, Botticelli, Lorenzo Monace, and Attavante degle Attavanti developed their own styles. The masterpiece of illumination of this period is *Lorenzo Hours* (Biblioteca Laurenziana, Florence) a small book of 4 in. × 6 in., with lovely borders with scrolls of foliage and flowers and rayed gilt disks painted on plain white vellum.

Another great work is the illuminated bible made for Borso d'Este, the *Borso Bible* (Modena Estense Library), a product of the Ferrara School of illumination, which is famous for its distinct character and elaborate margins. Sixteenth century Italy marked the decline of illumination, but the products of such famous miniaturists as Giulio Clovio are notable. Clovio attempted to translate the most monumental qualities of Renaissance frescoes into miniature. The *Book of Hours*, which he illuminated for Cardinal Alessandro Farnese in 1546 (Pierpont Morgan Library, New York), is a good example of his work.

France

In the fifteenth century, France saw the greatest flowering of illumination. Books of Hours were the finest and most numerous. Three great masters were Rohan Master, Jean Fouquet, and the painter of *Livre du Coeur d'Amour e pris* (National Library, Vienna). Rohan Master's art can be

seen in the *Grandes Heures de Rohan* (Bibliotheque Nationale, Paris).

The Limbourg brothers's (Pol de Limbourg and his brothers) *Très-Riches Heures* of the Duc de Berry (Musée Conde, Chantilly), which they left unfinished at their death, is a sumptuous codex. Every page has a luxuriant full border with brilliant title medallion miniatures and superb portrait pages.

Jean Fouqet of Tours spent his early days in Italy, and shows that influence in both panel and miniature painting. He was an artist of international fame in his own time. His illumination in the 47 preserved pages of *Hours of Etienne Chevalier* (Bibliotheque Nationale, Louvre; British Museum, Musée Conde) created miniatures which are elegant and show the influence of the Limbourg brothers.

The third important work, the *Livre du Coeur d'Amour e pris* was written and illustrated by King Rane of Anjou. The miniatures depict the spirit of late medieval chivalry.

In the Low Countries, Trounai, Ypres, Bruges, Ghent, and Brussels were important centers of illumination. Paintings in grisaille were also popular.

Germany

German illumination in the fifteenth and sixteenth centuries can be characterized by putty-colored border frames in which green and scarlet often appear. Franco-Flemish influence is very strong, as can be seen in a seven volume bible with richly illuminated border now preserved in Rome.

Masterpiece of the Glockendons, a prayer book executed by Albrecht Glockendon for the Duke of Bavaria (Biblioteca Estense, Modena) contains 41 full page miniatures and numerous colored initials on gold. Other rich illuminated manuscripts are those that were commissioned by the Emperor Maximilian.

The sixteenth century finally marked the end of illumination in Germany and elsewhere in Europe except for casual execution of religious books and invitation cards.

ISLAMIC ILLUMINATION

Islamic illumination developed from a modest beginning. The early art was purely calligraphic and centered around the development of script, style of writing, and beautification of letters. Then came decoration, first with the use of gold and then with colors. Early illuminated manuscripts basically consisted of Quranic texts and had no illustration or painting depicting any life, as they are not allowed in Islam. Illustrations and paintings were included later in secular works only. The art of miniature painting, which attained an independent pictorial composition, developed in Persia and strongly influenced Turkey and Mughal India.

Arabic script written from right to left became the main script of the Islamic world, and it played the same role as Latin in medieval Europe. It has five variants: Kufic, Naskh, Maghribi, Taliq, and Nastaliq.

Kufic (angular vertical) was named after Kufa in Mesopotamia. It remained the chief script of the Quran for over four centuries, and for about a century for general use. It was a most popular early script and is used even now for epigraphy. After the ninth century, letters evolved into distinctive ornamental style, were elaborately intertwined with shafts, and linked closely with the leaf scrollery of the ground, and are usually called Kufic fleuri.

Naskh (round and cursive and later developed into calligraphic form) originally was the cursive form of Kufic, but it is generally said to have been developed by Ibn-i-Muqla in the early ninth century. Naskh became most popular for religious as well as secular writing. By the twelfth century it finally replaced Kufic. Now the Quran is universally written in the Naskh script.

Maghribi (round and heavy) is a variant of Naskh script, which became popular in Islamic West or Northern Africa. In Moorish Spain it was called institutional script, as it was used for both religious and secular works at Cordova.

Taliq (cursive) was developed in Iran by Hasan Farsi in the early tenth century and was used for popular writing. It became popular in Turkey by the name of "Diwani" or court style. Later on it became popular in India also.

Nastaliq (elegant and round with thick and thin strokes) is an Iranian variant of Naskh but quite independent and distinctive in style, developed by Mir Ali Tabrizi in the late fourteenth century. Nastaliq gradually became the main writing style in Iran and India for secular subjects. The best illuminated manuscripts in Iran and India are in Nastaliq script, except for Quranic text, for which Naskh script is universally used.

Style

Twelve different styles were developed from Kufic script by Ishaq bin Hammad in the early ninth century. They are: Tumar, bold letters for Quran and inscriptions; Sajalat, or Court style; Ohud, for deeds; Amanat, for agreement; Madih, for eulogy; Ghubar, the use of dots to give an impression of cloud, for beauty; Moammerat, for official deliberations; Dibaj, writing on silk; Murassa, ornamental; Hasan, elegant and thin; Riyash, or pictorial; and Bayaz, for documents.

In the late ninth century the famous calligrapher Ibni-Muqla (886–940) developed six styles: Thulth, or one-third, just like uncial script, was bold and was used for Quran and religious texts; Naskh, round and cursive, for religious text; Toqi, bold letters used for official statement; Riqa, for correspondence and accounts; Muhaqiq, book style used by scholars; and Rehan, thin letters used by ladies.

In the beginning, the calligrapher had to illuminate and rubricate, but gradually each of these functions was performed independently by the calligrapher, the illuminator, and the painter. Ink was made from soot and arabic gum, with vitriol or alum; pigments were prepared from gold leaf, powdered lapis lazuli, orpiment, yellow ocher and the like, again with the use of arabic gum.

Decoration included a title page, which always had double headings of the chapter and border medallions. Later, it became a fashion to include in the text the name of the calligrapher, and the date and place of production in a modestly worded tail colophon following the text at the end of the page.

Illumination, though still in fashion for Quranic texts, basically flourished in the Islamic world from the eight to eighteenth centuries. The following periods and areas are important for developing their own distinctive styles of illumination.

EARLY ISLAMIC PERIOD

The Muslim era begins from September 13, A.D. 622. Most of the manuscripts, including the complete text of Quran and the letters of Prophet Mohammed (560–632), were written after this date. The earliest preserved Quranic manuscript is the one used by Hazrat Uthman, the third Caliph (644–656) at the time of his martyrdom in A.D. 656. It is now in the State Library, Tashkent, and a photocopy is in the National Museum of Pakistan, Karachi. It is on a broad parchment sheet written in large early Kufic letters. The earliest dated copy of Quran is of A.D. 784 (National Library, Cairo).

The earliest style of decoration developed in Mesopotamia, Syria, Northern Africa, and Moorish Spain.

In Mesopotamia, the earliest center was Kufa, where Kufic script originated. The Kufic writings of this period were thick and rounded, with short verticals and large horizontals. For decoration, gold was used, and later a few colors, more frequently natural or colored blue, violet or red, and black were also added. Illuminated pages at first had interlacing, foliate forms, and palmette scrolls outlined in brown ink. This style was common in Syria and Egypt.

MAGHRIBI SCHOOL

The term Maghribi or Western Islamic is used for Northern Africa and Moorish Spain. Syrian style of illumination had strong influence in these regions. Damascus in Syria, the capital of Umayyad Caliphs (661–749), had developed a distinctive style of writing which, unlike Kufic, was very close to Naskh. The same variant spread in Northern Africa, particularly in Spain where a fugitive, Umayyad

Prince Abdur Rahman I (756–788), laid the foundation of Moorish rule in Spain with his capital at Cordova.

MOORISH SCHOOL (756–1492)

In the whole of Maghrib (Islamic West) the calligraphic form has not been so well developed and refined as in the east, but the illumination on parchment in polychrome is exquisitely rich. The Moorish codices with arabesque work, executed primarily in gold and blue, surrounding the pages in variants, twining round the headings, and the marginal decoration are superb.

In the fourteenth and fifteenth centuries, Granada became very famous for its vivid color composition, and Alhambra style became an established model for embellishment of a codex. Some texts have free drawing of tree forms with their branches spreading across the text, and can be associated with Sicily in decorative pattern.

Examples of early illuminated Maghribi manuscripts are rare. There are some from the later period in Morocco and Tunis but they are not brilliant examples.

MOZARABIC ILLUMINATION

Under Muslim influence, a new style of book decoration was developed by Jews and Christians in Spain, generally called Mozarabic art. For example, Jewish illumination of *Exodus* (British Museum) shows a marked influence of Islamic style. The majority of the Hebrew codices from the tenth to fifteenth centuries were produced in Spain. The illuminations are executed in bright colors on a gold background. Besides religious manuscripts, there are also illustrated secular works, for example a finely illuminated fourteenth century copy of Avicenna's *Canon of Medicine* (Biblioteca University, Bologna, Manuscript 2197).

Christians in Spain were influenced by Moorish style, particularly in ornamentation of initials, as can be seen in *Beatus Manuscripts* produced in Spain, Italy, and Southern France.

FATIMIDE SCHOOL (909–1171)

The Fatimides, after defeating Aghlabides in Tunis in A.D. 908, became master of almost the whole of North Africa and first made their capital at Mahdiya near Tunis. A half century later they added Egypt and Syria, and founded the city of Cairo, which became one of the greatest intellectual centers of Islamic learning, particularly at the famous Al-Azhar University, which they founded. The Fatimides patronized the Nestorians and Jacobite Christians from Syria who were famous illustrators and illuminators. Many richly illuminated manuscripts of this period are found in the Cairo National Library and the Vienna National Library. The style of writing is very close to Naskh, with rather heavy strokes. Illuminations are rich.

MAMELUKE SCHOOL (1250–1516)

After Fatimides, Ayubides (1169–1250) came into power, followed by Mamelukes or white slaves (1250–1516). Both of the later dynasties were of Central Asian rather than Turkish origin.

Mamelukes are noted for building great mosques and having inscriptions on walls and arches in majestic Tumar (bold) like Thulth, a variant of Naskh form. The large luxury Qurans in Tumar or Thulth, in gold on blue and brown ground, usually have title pages without text and are divided up geometrically into lattice or star shaped compartments with arabesques and palmettes. The chapter headings are generally in Kufic-like letters on a ground of leaf scrolls and surrounded by a border of interlacery. The illuminated texts of the Quran executed in this period and now preserved in great quantities (National Library, Cairo, and National Library, Vienna) are the best examples of Egyptian illumination.

ABBASIDE PERIOD (750–1258)

The Abbaside period was an age of great splendor in Islamic history. Harun-al-Rashid (786–809), of Arabian nights fame, and his successors, Mamun, Moatasim, and Matawakkil, were great patrons of art, learning, and scholarship. Charlemagne (742–814) had close cultural contacts with Harun. The court of Abbasi Caliphs at Baghdad witnessed the scenes of great cultural fusion. Baghdad, Samarrah, Mousal, Basra, Nishapur, Dayar-i-Bakr, and Bukhara, were the chief centers of book art, particularly noted for the development of calligraphic styles. Two schools, those of Baghdad and Seljuk, were famous.

Baghdad School

The Baghdad School is noted for book art. It had the master minds of Ibn Muqla (886–940), Ibn Bawwab (991–1032), and Yaqut-al-Mustasemi (1221–1268), who developed various exquisite styles from Kufic and Naskh forms. The early form of writing was Kufic, and then ordinary cursive Naskhi, the most important features being the curving and elegant Thulth (bold) generally used for the Quran.

The Caliph Mamun-al-Rahid (813–833), son of Harun, patronized Manichian style from its founder, Mani, one of the greatest Iranian painters. The style had central Asian elements and was executed in Baghdad earlier than in Iran. Other famous painters were Abdullah Ibn al Fadhl and Yahya al Wasiti. Ornamentation included designs of rosettes or palmettes, and the colors used were yellow, red, blue, green purple, and gold.

Not many illuminated copies of the Quran of this period have survived, but some are in the National Library, Cairo; Quran manuscripts of A.D. 883 and 890 are in the Bibliotheque Nationale, Paris. Another manuscript of A.D. 870 is in the Cambridge University Library.

Some of the old secular illustrated manuscripts such as *Kalila wa dimna* (fables of Bidpai), dated A.D. 1222, and *Maqamat Hariri*, dated A.D. 1237, are now in the Bibliotheque Nationale, Paris.

Seljuk School (1055–1256)

Seljuks were Turks. At the time of their appearance the empire of the Caliphate was vanishing. Art and learning flourished during the reigns of the great Seljuks Tughral Beg (1037–1063), Alp Arsalan (1062–1072), and Malik Shah (1072–1092). They made Nishapur their capital. Besides Baghdad, other important centers were Raqqa, Ardh-Rome (Konya), Ray, and Kashan. The manuscripts available are of late Seljuk period of the twelfth and thirteenth centuries. Naskh style predominates in manuscripts, on metal works, and pottery. Decorations are executed in miniature style representing single figures, episodes from legends, and court scenes. The colors used are pink, olive green, cobalt blue, violet, brown, black, and gold on white or turquoise blue ground.

MONGOL PERIOD (1258–1500)

The Mongol period, though noted for ruthless wars, is equally famous for the development of sumptuous book art. Two important styles of writing, those of Taliq (cursive) and Nastaliq (round), were developed. Calligraphy and illumination attained highly rich and ornamental styles, with predominant influences of Chinese, Central Asian, and Iranian color composition. Two schools of illumination, those of Ilkhani (1258–1336) and Timuride (1387–1500), are important.

The glorious period of Abbasides ended with the sack of Baghdad by the Mongol invader Hilaku Khan (1256–1265) in 1258, Hilaku, or Hulagu, and his successors ruled Persia and part of Iraq, and were known as Il-Khanis. Tabriz, in Persia, and Maragha, just across the Eurphrates in Iraq, were their capitals. Ghazan (1295–1304), the grandson of Hilaku, accepted Islam, and while he continued the Abbaside tradition of illumination, he also encouraged the development of a new Mongol art.

Early Il-khani styles had Arabic influences, but gradually they developed their own pattern. The Naskh script, for example, became more angular and cursive and came to be known as Taliq. Illumination brought more Chinese and Persian elements in color scheme, and it became more figurative.

The earliest manuscript is that of *Manafeul-haiwan* (Morgan Library, New York), a bestiary executed by the order of Ghazan (1295–1304) at Maragha, with 94 illustrations. Miniatures show landscapes, clouds, plants, and peony flowers of Chinese origin.

Another manuscript is *Jameut-Tawarikh*, a world chronicle written in 1306 by Rashidal-Din, the Wazir of Ghazan and Uljaitun, at Tabriz. It has exceptionally rich illuminations with strong Chinese influence, particularly in costume, landscape, and the pale colors applied in washes. The manuscript has 55 miniatures superbly executed, of which a few have survived and are preserved in the Edinburgh University Library and in several private collections. Smaller copies of *Shah Nameh* (Book of King) of Firdausi (935–1010) are illustrated at Tabriz in 1320, and a few manuscripts are preserved in the Kofler-Truniger Collection, Lucerne, and in the Vever Collection, Paris. The pictures are placed in strips between the text with figures, costumes, and bright colors. Shiraz, next to Tabriz, was famous for illumination, but its work is less elaborate. Painting is generally in black outline on red or ocher background, with additional colors in blue, red olive, green lilac, and gold.

Ahmad Musa is regarded as one of the greatest artists of the Ilkhani School.

Timuride School (1386–1500)

The Timuride School is noted for an extraordinary artistic productivity and quality of illumination. Timur Lang (1335–1405), the founder of the Timuride dynasty, was a great conqueror and lover of art. He invaded India, Iraq, and Turkey and made himself the unchallenged ruler of Central and Western Asia. He brought artists from Baghdad and Tabriz to his capital at Samarkand. Some of the famous artists were Abdul Hayee and Junaid from Baghdad and Mir Babar Ali (1330–1404), the originator of the famous *Nastaliq* style, from Tabriz. Unfortunately, no manuscript of this period survives, except inscriptions on walls and frescoes.

Herat

Shah Rukh (1404–1447), one of the younger sons of Timur, and his own sons Baisunkur Mirza (1399–1433) and Ulugh Beg (1447–1449), beautified their capital, Herat, which became one of the greatest centers of illumination. Baisunkur was a great bibliophile. He founded a library and the Academy of Book Arts, which included 40 calligraphers, painters, illuminators, and miniaturists. Famous artists like Khalil; Jafar Baisunkuri; Abdullah, son of Mir Ali, and his pupil, Mawlana jafar Tabrizi, chief of 40 copyists; and a host of others were at his academy. Most of the masterpieces of the Timuride period were produced at Herat during the time of Shah Rikh, Baisunkur, and later, during the time of Sultan Husain Mirza.

A beautiful copy of *Gulistan* (Rose Garden) of Saadi (1184–1292) is preserved in Chester Beaty Library, Dublin. *Shah-Nameth* (Book of Kings) of Firdausi, elaborately illuminated in polychrome, is dated Herat, 1430, and is in Gulistan Museum, Tehran. *Fables Kalila and Dimna*, ca. 1420, Herat, is in the Gulistan Museum, Tehran.

Notable features of the Herat School are delicate rendering of figures, Iranian landscape with high horizon, and spongy mountains. Naturalistic plants and ornaments are derived from China, and are combined with birds and animals. Color combination shows Chinese influence, but is vivid and harmonious.

Shiraz

Another famous center of illumination that had a longer tradition than Herat was Shiraz, the capital of Ibrahim Sultan, son of Shah Rukh. Two styles of writing, Diwani (official) and Dashti (Tughra script) were developed. Some of the very superbly executed works extant are three copies of *Khamsa Nizami*, magnificently illustrated in 1444, now in John Ryland Library, Manchester; Royal Asiatic Society Library, London; and in Victoria and Albert Museum, London. The usual feature is that texts are on main and on border while pictures are between the texts. *Shah Nameth*, a finely executed copy in the Gulbenkian Collection, Lisbon, is a good example. A very fine copy of *Khamsa of Nizami* is in the Museum Dahlam, Berlin.

The main features of Shiraz style are cooler, lighter, but pale gold color scheme with dark blue ground. *Transoxiana*, the capital of Ulug Beg, son of Shah Rukh, was also an important center, but had the strong influence of Herat style.

The most prominent period of illumination flourished under Sultan Husain Mirza Bayaqara (1458–1505) at Herat, the last of the Timuride Sultans, Bihzad, Sultan Ali Meshadi, and his teacher Mawlana Azhar, the three versatile artists of their time, were at the court of Sultan Husain Mirza and were equally patronized by Mir Ali Sher Nawaii, a great poet, musician, and painter. The Wazir of Sultan Husain was also a great patron of these artists.

The chief characteristics of this period were grace and elegance and a larger freedom of movement, gold, and brilliance in range of colors.

PERSIAN ILLUMINATION (1502–1736)

Shah Ismail, the founder of Safvide Dynasty, and his successors were great patrons of art, architecture, and learning. The period of Safvide rule over Iran for over 200 years, from 1502–1736, is the most glorious in the history of Persian illumination. Tabriz and then Isfahan became the centers of art. This was an age when the quality of the work depended very much upon the fame of the artists, and the fame of the artists of the Safvide School was such that their works became models for Turkish and Mogul miniatures.

Safvide School

Tabriz, the new capital of Shah Ismail (1510–1524), once again became the leading center of book art. Shah Ismail appointed Kamaluddin Bihzad (ca. 1440–1536), a great calligrapher and artist, director of the Royal Library.

Bihzad had previously worked at Herat under the patronage of Sultan Husain Mirza, the last of Timurides, from 1470–1506. After the defeat of Timurides by Shaibanides in 1507, Bihzad remained in Herat and worked for Uzbek Sultan Shaibani Khan (1500–1510). But when Shah Ismail Safvi conquered Herat in 1510, Bihzad moved to Tabriz.

Bizhad built up a famous school of court painters at Tabriz and organized works separately for copyists, painters, gilders, margin drawers, gold mixers, gold beaters, and washers of lapis lazuli. Bihzad trained a good number of gifted pupils who continued his tradition at Herat, Bukhara, Tabriz, and Shiraz. Among his famous disciples were Qasim Ali Mirak, Shaikh Zadeh Mahmud, Abdullah, and Sultan Muhammad Nur.

Illuminated manuscripts of Bihzad are very few. The most artistic works were executed for Shah Tahmasp (1524–1576), one of the famous among them being *Shah Nameh* (British Museum). It contains 285 miniatures, some of them by Bihzad. *Khamsa Nizami* (British Museum) is also a richly illuminated copy. *Bustan of Saadi* (National Library, Cairo) has six miniatures by Bihzad, four of them signed. A copy of *Khamsa Nizami* (British Museum) illustrated by one of Bihzad's pupils, Qasim Ali, generally called Mirak, contains 16 beautiful miniatures. There are a large number of miniatures, now preserved in single leaves in various important libraries, art galleries, museums, and private collections in Europe and America, but the majority of them are in the Gulistan Museum, Tehran.

The characteristics of the Bihzad School are painting of borders in water colors in several tones of gold with a cool color scheme of blue, gray, and green, around a text of fine calligraphy. Later, Sultan Muhammad and Ustad Muhammadi employed pure wash technique in painting without any reference to a text. The other technique was the use of brush or red pencil, which became very popular during the time of Shah Abbas when he was at Qazvin.

Shah Abbas (1587–1629) made Isfahan, his capital, the center of decorated palaces and mosques. He established an academy of arts and employed leading artists of the time. The most famous were Mir Imad of Qazvin (d-1615), a master calligrapher, and Riza Abbasi (1587–1629), a great artist. Shafi Abbasi (son of Riza Abbasi), Muin, Yousuf, and Mohammad were other gifted artists.

The main work of Riza Abbasi is Nizami's *Khusrau and Shirin* (Victoria and Albert Museum, London). A large number of his signed paintings are preserved in the Tehran Museum. His style can be characterized with his keen observation of life, and use of green, light blue, black, and gold colors on pale ground, with curves and short strokes in calligraphic form.

By the end of the seventeenth century a decline in Persian painting began. Shah Abbas II (1642–1667) tried to check it by sending some artists to Rome, but this admixture of foreign style finally finished the originality of the great art of manuscript painting in Iran.

TURKISH ILLUMINATION (1451–1900)

Ottoman Turks, as long as they had their capital at Konya, had Mongol-Persian models before them for book decoration. But after the conquest of Constantinople by Sultan Muhammad in 1453, a preference for Byzantine style developed. Therefore, European artists, along with Persian, were employed.

Characteristics of Turkish calligraphy and illumination are use of Naskh as standard script for religious works, development of Diwani, a variant of Naskh as official script, and use of Tughra, or decorative signature of the reigning Sultan with three long uprights and a large sweeping loop to the left. Production of finely executed texts of the Quran in pocket size became very popular. The color scheme included blue, black, and gold.

Turkish book art, however, remained essentially Persian in style and execution. The decline began toward the end of the seventeenth century.

Among famous calligraphers and artists who were either Turks or came to Turkey from other places were the following: Sanaullah of Brussa, a poet and a painter who worked under Murad II (1422–1451); Bellini, an Italian painter, who also trained Prince Ahmad and worked under Sultan Mohammad (1430–1481); Osman; Hyder; and Shah Kuli and Wali Jan of Tabriz, who were at the court of Sulaiman the Magnificent (1520–1566).

There is a large stock of illuminated manuscripts in the rich libraries of Turkey, but unfortunately all of them have not yet been explored.

MOGUL MINIATURES (1525–1707)

Mogul emperors were great lovers of art and architecture. The Mogul period is noted for the production of richly illuminated works usually called Mogul miniatures. There was no tradition of manuscript painting in India before the Moguls.

Babar, the first Mogul emperor of India (1525–1530), had remarkable talents. He wrote a vivid account of his life in Tartar language, Tuzak-i-Baburi, which is now among the classics of the world. He collected finely illuminated books, several of them now preserved in the princely collection of Alwar State. One painting depicting a sea fight, said to have been in the album of Emperor Jehangir, is now in the State Library, Berlin. Babar attracted artists from Bukhara who introduced Bihzad style and cooler gouache tone.

Humayun (1530–1556), while in exile in Iran for 10 years, met the two leading artists, Khwaja Abdus Samad Shirazi and Mir Sayyed Ali at the court of Shah Tahmasp in Tabriz. Both were invited to Kabul and then to India to supervise the illustration of Amir Hamza, which is said to be the work of 50 painters and was completed during the reign of Akbar. It contains 1400 paintings on linen pages 22 in. × 28 in. Its leaves are now scattered in the libraries of the British Museum, National Library, Vienna, and Metropolitan Museum, New York. The completion of Amir Hamza marks the beginning of the Mogul School of miniature painting in India.

Akbar the Great (1556–1605) made Fatehpur Sikri his capital and built palaces decorated with mural paintings, executed by Iranian and Indian artists. While the Persian influence of Bihzad, Mirak, and Sultan Nur was strong, a new influence of Indian national style also took a firm root during his reign. Akbar established an Academy of Arts and employed 100 painters, the majority of them being Hindus. The work of all the painters is said to have been submitted to him every week. Akbar imposed his own ideas and themes upon the artists, but he also accepted the ideas of Hindu painters who introduced Hindu legends and religious epics. One of the best illuminated manuscripts of this time is the Mahabharata (Razm Namah), containing 169 miniatures, and now preserved in Jaipur. The execution of this sumptuous volume cost £40,000.

Some of Akbar's famous artists from Kashmir, Gujrat, and Punjab were Dharam Das, Sanwlah, Shankar lal, Sur Das, Nar Singh, Mukand and Govardhan, Daswanth, Manohar, and Khem Karan. A good number of them were pupils of Khwaja Abdus Samad. The principal characteristics of their works were gradations of tone and effects of light and shade with atmospheric landscape and perspective and modeling in faces and costumes.

Jehangir (1605–1628) intensified painting, although his interest in illustration lessened. Artists were required to be more realistic and to describe court life, receptions, and audiences, festivities, hunts, and polo tournaments, and to chronicle noteworthy episodes from the life of the ruler. He liked western paintings and introduced them to his artists. Mansur, Murad, Manohar, and Abul Hasan (son of Riza Abbasi) were some of Jehangir's famous painters.

Shah Jehan (1628–1658) was a great calligrapher. Portrait art and ceremonial group painting received greatest attention during his reign. Famous artists of his time were Mohammad Fakirullah Khan, Mir Hashim, Bichitr, Anup Chhatar, and Sayed Amir Khan. Abdur Rashid Dailami, nephew of Mir Imad, also came from Isfanan. He was tutor of Dara Shikoh and also the founder of the Indian School of Calligraphy.

Aurangzeb (1659–1707), the last of the great Mogul emperors, was himself a calligrapher and wrote the Quran for himself and for the princes. Being an orthodox Muslim, he discouraged painting and turned out the court painters, who then took refuge at the court of nobles and rajahs. This princely patronization to artists gave birth to a native style of painting, usually called the Rajput School of Painting.

Rajput School of Painting

Under the influence of the Mogul School of painting the Rajput School was developed. The same Hindu artists who had worked at the Mogul courts, along with their pupils, developed the Rajput style.

Characteristic features of the style were depiction of themes and ideas from Hindu religion, and epic, folklore, and cultural mode of life, which were more romantic and musical. The colors most frequently used were bright red, blue, and gold.

There are two predominant styles of the Rajput School, those of Rajasthani, covering Rajputana and Bundel Khand, and Pahari, covering Kangra, Basohli, Guler, and Jammu. The best examples are the scenes portrayed from *Krishna Lila* and *Nala Damyanti*, both of eighteenth century Kangra School.

The nineteenth century marks the total decline of illumination due to lack of princely patronage and also the vanishing skill of the artists.

BIBLIOGRAPHY

1. Alexander, J.J. *Norman Illumination at Mont St. Michel, 966–1100*, Oxford Univ. Press: London, U.K., 1970.
2. Arnold, T. *Painting in Islam*, Oxford Univ. Press: London, U.K., 1928.
3. Binyon, L. et al. *Persian Miniature Painting*, Oxford Univ. Press: London, U.K., 1933.
4. Blochet, M.E. *Les Paintures Manuscripts Orientaux*, Bibliotheque Nationale: Paris, France, 1922.
5. Bradley, J.W. *Dictionary of Miniaturists, Illuminatores, Calligraphers, and Copyists*, Franklin: New York, 1968; (Reprint of 1898 edition).
6. Crane, W. *Of the Decorative Illustration of Book, Old and New*, Gale: Detroit, MI, 1968; (Reprint of 1905 edition).
7. Daghir, Y.A. *Dalilul-aarib ila ilm il-Kutub wa fannil Makatib*, Darul Kutub al-Labnania: Beirut, Lebanon, 1947 (in Arabic).
8. Delaisse, L.M. *Century of Dutch Manuscript Illumination*, Univ. California Press: Berkeley, CA, 1968.
9. Dimand, M.S. *A Handbook of Muhammadan Art*, Metropolitan Museum of Art: New York, 1958.
10. Dominquez-Bordona, J. *Spanish Illumination*, Hacker: New York, 1969; 2 Vol. in 1 (Reprint of 1929 edition).
11. Dringer, D. *Illuminated Book*, Faber and Faber: London, U.K., 1967.
12. Gluck, V.H. *Die Indischen Miniaturen*, Des Hammzae Ramanes: Zurich, Switzerland.
13. Goldschmidt, A. *German Illumination*, Hacker: New York, 1969; 2 Vol. in 1 (Reprint of 1928 edition).
14. Hasan, Z.M. *Al-funun-al-Iraniyia fi al-asr-al-Isr-al-Islami*, Darul-Kutub-al-Misriya: Cairo, Egypt, 1946 (in Arabic).
15. *Iran, Persian Miniatures—Imperial Library*, New York Graphic Society: New York, 1957.
16. Kuhnel, E. *Islamic Arts*, G. Bell: London, U.K., 1970.
17. Marzooq, A.A. *Al-fannul Islam*, Matba: Asad, Baghdad, 1965; (in Arabic).
18. Meiss, M. *French Painting in the Time of Jean De Barry*, Praeger: New York, 1967; 2 Vol.
19. Morand, K.T. *Jean Puccelle*, Oxford Univ. Press: New York, 1962.
20. Moritz, B. *Arabic Paleography*, Fertig: New York, 1905.
21. Pacht, O. Alexander, J.J. *Illuminated Manuscripts in the Bodlein Library*, Oxford Univ. Press: London, U.K., 2 vols. (Vol. 1: German, Dutch, Flemish, French, and Spanish Schools, 1966, Vol. 2: Italian School, 1970).
22. Pinder-Wilson, R., Ed. *Paintings from Islamic Lands*; Univ. Southern California Press: Los Angeles, CA, 1970.
23. Pope, A.U. *Survey of Persian Art*, Oxford Univ. Press: London, U.K., 1939; 9 Vol.
24. Randall, L.M. *Images in the Margins of Gothic Manuscripts*, Univ. California Press: Berkeley, CA, 1966.
25. Rice, D.T. *Islamic Art*, Thames and Hudson: London, U.K., 1965.
26. Ruthe, E., Ed. *Medieval Book Illumination in Europe*; Norton: New York, 1968.
27. Saunders, O.E. *English Illumination*, Hacker: New York, 1969; 2 Vol. in 1 (Reprint of 1928 edition).
28. Sweeney, J.J. Introduction. *Irish Illuminated Manuscripts of the Early Christian Period*; New American Library: New York, 1965.
29. Turkey: *Ancient Miniatures*, New York Graphic Society: New York, 1961.
30. *Urdu Encyclopedia of Islam Univ. Punjab*: Lahore, 1958; 4 Vol.
31. Weitzmann, K.; Kessler, H. *Studies in Classical and Byzantine Manuscripts Illumination*, Univ. Chicago, Press: Chicago, IL, 1971.

Impact Assessment of Cultural Institutions

Sara Selwood
Department of Cultural Policy and Management, City University, London, U.K.

Abstract

In the United Kingdom, and in England in particular, concern with the "impact" of cultural institutions, cultural activities, and cultural policies has grown exponentially. Prompted by the government's requirement for greater accountability within the public sector and its desire to implement evidence-based policy, this has particularly affected organizations in receipt of public funding. In the United Kingdom, these include the majority of cultural institutions.

This entry considers the context within which a preoccupation with the "impact" of cultural sector institutions came about. It examines the background to the introduction of the impact assessment of cultural institutions, the requirements made of them, and the impacts considered desirable for them to exert. It explores some of the difficulties of assessing those impacts, including definitions, approaches, and the problematic relationship between assessment and advocacy. The entry closes with a discussion of developments of impact assessment within the cultural sector. The principal focus of this entry is museums in England.

INTRODUCTION AND BACKGROUND

Since the 1997 general election, when New Labour came to power, the ways in which cultural policy in the United Kingdom have been articulated, disseminated, and assessed have been transformed. Prior to this, cultural policy was, to all intents and purposes, implied by the actions of such agencies as the former Museums & Galleries Commission and Arts Council of Great Britain. Despite being directly funded by government, these organizations tangibly operated at "arms' length" from it. Indeed, it has been suggested that they functioned in what was, effectively, a "policy vacuum." At best, the successive government departments responsible for funding the cultural sector reviewed current provision, sought to improve the management of advisory and funding bodies, and promoted examples of best practice. Performance measurement was generally considered inappropriate for cultural provision and was effectively steered clear of.

The requirement to evaluate policies and performance in the public sector was initially recognized by the Conservative government's Financial Management Initiative of 1982. This called for greater efficiency, effectiveness, and "value for money" at central and local government levels—demands which were largely implemented through the National Audit Office and the Audit Commission both of which were established in 1983. The former was responsible for reporting on public spending programs in England, Scotland, and Wales; the latter for auditing and examining the management of local authority auditing in England and Wales. While neither body was, or is, specifically responsible for cultural services—museums, galleries, and the arts, nevertheless, fall within

their remits and are subject to the philosophy which they represent.

At this time, the museums sector had almost no measures to assess its success or progress except for the most basic indicators of attendances, budget size, staff size, etc. From the late 1980s various initiatives were introduced in an attempt to introduce a more sophisticated degree of performance management for national and regional museums and galleries including a registration scheme based on minimum standards and intended to provide an assurance of quality and professionalism.[1]

Once in government, Labour insisted on greater accountability than previous Conservative administrations and emphasized the delivery of evidence-based policy making by central, regional, and local government. In that context, the question, "what works?" became a reference point for designing new policies and measuring performance. Analysis and the use of evidence were prescribed as core skills within the civil service.[2–4]

The establishment of the Department for Culture, Media and Sport (DCMS) in July 1997 was marked by responsibility for cultural policy strategically being "reclaimed" by central government. By 1998, it had made it clear that cultural institutions' increases in funding, and specially earmarked initiatives for the sector, were designed to meet the Department's expectations and would directly influence the sector's development.[5] Predicated on the assumption that cultural provision is instrumental and can deliver on government objectives, DCMS's "sponsored" (or subsidized) bodies have been required to commit to agreed targets, specified through a series of linked agreements which cascade down from the Treasury. Not only did the arts and culture become subject

Encyclopedia of Library and Information Sciences, Fourth Edition DOI: 10.1081/E-ELIS4-120043734

to the same policies and regime of impact assessment, but they were all committed to achieving cross-government objectives which were intended to achieve broader economic and social policy aspirations. It was assumed that the impact of their particular contributions could be assessed (this is explored in Selwood[6]).

Museums, which are the focus of attention in this entry, have been particularly close to DCMS's heart. They account for about a quarter of its total grant in aid and, therefore, carry considerable responsibility for delivering on the government's objectives. Indeed, from 2000 onward the Department has specifically credited museums with stimulating economic impact; creating employment; stimulating the development of ancillary services;[7] tackling social exclusion;[8] contributing to social and environmental impacts through transformational projects;[9] and playing a part in the well-being of local authority areas.[10] It has also referred to them as "centres of social change" and "learning."[11]

Against a background of DCMS's interest in monitoring "outputs" and "outcomes" against its "investment" and its increased scrutiny of the performance of subsidized organizations, this entry considers the impact assessment of cultural institutions, museums in England in particular. It comprises four sections:

- The first section describes the requirements made of cultural institutions, and the kind of impacts that they are expected to exert;
- The second considers some of the difficulties of assessing the impact of cultural institutions;
- The third section comments on developments in thinking about impact assessment within the cultural sector; and
- The fourth, and final, section concludes with some observations.

Given that they share the same policy regime, both the arts and culture are occasionally referred to in this entry.

THE REQUIREMENTS OF CULTURAL INSTITUTIONS

The Department for Culture, Media and Sport's pledge that its sectors would deliver on a multitude of central government agendas was set out in its strategy document, A New Cultural Framework (1988) and its first annual report. This described its aims as being

> ... guided by four central themes: the promotion of access, for the many not just the few; the pursuit of excellence and innovation; the nurturing of educational opportunity and the fostering of the creative industries, which provide a growing proportion of Britain's employment

and wealth... aims which resonate across every other department of Government.[12]

This section considers the application of those themes to the cultural sector and the instrumentalist values with which it became associated.

Although it has been argued that many museums were already committed to a community-based agenda, the Department incentivized the wider cultural sector's engagement through a combination of increases in funding and formal requirements. As Labour's first Secretary of State for Culture, Media and Sport, Chris Smith, put it, public funding would no longer to be regarded as

> .... 'something for nothing'. We want to see measurable outcomes for the investment which is being made. From now on, there will be real partnership with obligations and responsibilities.[13]

As the Treasury's guidelines for departmental bids to the 2004 Spending Review made clear:

> In principle, all spending decisions should be supported by evidence, demonstrating that the money being spent will achieve the desired effects as efficiently as possible.[14]

Smith later admitted that this kind of climate demanded a particular kind of response from government departments:

> Spare a thought... for the poor old Minister, faced with the daunting task of getting the increased funding out of the Treasury to start with. The Treasury won't be interested in the intrinsic merits of nurturing beauty or fostering poetry or even 'enhancing the quality of life'. So I acknowledge unashamedly that when I was Secretary of State, going into what always seemed like a battle with the Treasury, I would try and touch the buttons that would work. I would talk about the educational value of what was being done. I would be passionate about artists working in schools. I would refer to the economic value that can be generated from creative and cultural activity. I would count the added numbers who would flock into a free museum. If it helped to get more funds flowing into the arts, the argument was worth deploying.[15]

These comments demonstrate the values that DCMS was encouraged to assume and the way in which it promoted the cultural sector within the wider political economy. Such political expediency set the tone for assessing the impact—or rather, the impacts of cultural institutions. Public subsidies were ostensibly invested in culture for any number of reasons—to reduce the incidence of social exclusion; contribute to education to encourage social regeneration; create destination locations; boost employment in service industries and inward investment in cities. But, in return, cultural institutions were obliged to provide evidence of how effective their contributions were.

Assuming that cultural institutions were making a difference was one thing, but quantifying, if not qualifying, the precise impact of such cultural institutions' effectiveness was another. As one arts minister explained: "I know that Arts and Culture make a contribution ... but I don't always know how to evaluate or describe it. We have to find a language and a way of describing its worth. It's the only way we'll secure the greater support we need."[16]

DIFFICULTIES IN ASSESSING THE IMPACT OF CULTURAL INSTITUTIONS

The model of accountability established by DCMS suggests that the relationship between policy, implementation, the delivery, and effectiveness of outcomes was highly determined as well as relatively simple. It assumes that the impact of various forms of cultural provision can be identified and quantified through the collection of "evidence," defined—"the end result of a complex analytical process beginning with the collection of raw data" (Table. 1). Indeed, for DCMS, an enhanced understanding of impacts was part of a virtuous circle in which the gathering and use of evidence would ensure that policies had maximum effect on key priorities and delivery targets.

However, DCMS's model conceals a number of difficulties which were not easily resolved and which, 5 years on, remain problematic. These include defining "impact"; the creation of objective and robust approaches to its measurement; and, the relationship between evidence and advocacy (for a more detailed discussion of these issues, see Selwood[17]). These are addressed in the following paragraphs.

Definitions

The term "impact" is often used synonymously with "output" and "outcome." But in differentiating between these terms, "impact" has been defined as

...the effect of the outcomes on the environment... using that term very broadly to include people and society at large - and is usually in the long term. An example here

Table. 1 DCMS's understanding of the relationship between raw data and evidence.

Raw data	whether counted or measured once codified, checked and systematically set out/tabulated >
Information	which in turn when focussed on a particular set of hypotheses/policies yields >
Analysis	which when weighed, reviewed assessed and subject to professional judgement and scrutiny becomes >
Evidence	on the impact of a particular hypothesis, policy/programme/or projects

Source: DCMS.[18]

might be the growth in literacy (or even improvements in mental well-being) as a result of reading library books.[19]

By comparison, outputs are

...the things that the organisation produced. They might be book or videotape issues, reference questions answered or seats occupied by readers. Very often, measurement consists of counting the number of outputs produced.

And outcomes are "...the short to medium-term results of applying outputs. The number of books read might be an outcome of book issuing."

Approaches

There have been a number of criticisms of impact assessments of cultural institutions, not least by DCMS itself. These stem from the early 2000s when the Department's systems of performance management were new. They pertain to the relative absence of hard evidence on cultural institutions' impact on tackling social exclusion: "Demonstrating the impact of activities to combat social exclusion is not easy, and it may be some time before the benefits are fully evident."[20] The lack of robustness of the evidence on cultural activities generally in relation to wider social and economic polices was also criticized. Beyond DCMS's immediate funding stream, gaps in local authorities' cultural services' evidence-base were identified—stories about the performance of cultural services tended to be based on anecdote "rather than hard evidence through monitoring and evaluation."[21]

The quantitative data collected was described as "patchy, inconsistent, and incomplete." According to conventional wisdom, this was not only regarded as inadequate but as inappropriate for evidencing the sector's contribution toward the achievement of the government's learning, access, inclusion, and economic development agendas. Acknowledging this, DCMS regarded quantitative evidence as proxies for qualitative outcomes. Thus, opening hours were interpreted as "a good measure of the availability of the collections for access"[22] and numbers of repeat visits to museums as indicative of the likelihood that visitors' quality of life was being enhanced. But emerging research[23] suggests that habitual visiting may be more indicative of visitors' dogged pursuit of personal interests than their satisfaction with particular venues.

Although data collection is becoming more sophisticated (for the most recent advice to DCMS on its museum performance indicators see Morris Hargreaves McIntyre[24]), this has not detracted from the need for the cultural sector having to construct an increasingly more robust "evidence" base. Yet, the collection of data still emphasizes "the quantitative in a field where qualitative assessments have been regarded as central"[25] and although impact is logically only discernable over the long-term, the government's system of performance measurement, driven by biennial funding reviews, militates against this.

> There are no cheap thrills in art, but there are real thrills. They come slowly, gradually, over years and as a result of effort. How do you market such an unappealing message, which happens to be the real message of the arts, the core—to use the market-speak—of their 'Unique Selling Proposition'?[26]

Thus, DCMS's agencies' habit of collecting short-term "evidence" on "new audiences" (as determined by the funding cycle) is likely to be relatively meaningless.

Reviews of the available evidence on the social impact of cultural projects have covered meta-analyses and critiques of single studies (see, for instance, Wavell et al.[27]). The consensus is that much of the evidence presented is insufficiently robust for a variety of reasons including the non-substantiation of claims; the antagonism of cultural institutions towards the collection and use of data; the fact that projects have limited jurisdiction and limited potential to influence outcomes; the lack of robustness of the methodologies used; the quality of evidence gathered and a failure of reporting of methods; the difficulties of attributing causality; and the preponderance of short-term, as opposed to long-term, evaluations.[28] More recently, issues of sustainability have come to the fore.

A prevailing theme has been economic impact. The assumption that various forms of culture are economically significant informs any number of policy papers published by DCMS, its agencies, regional bodies, and local authorities.

> Culture, whether as a central part of a regeneration initiative, or as a substantial component of a broader programme, can play a distinctive role in bringing economic benefits to an area. It does not just bring direct economic improvement by providing employment and generating revenue, but can have a wider economic impact on the general prospects of an area by making it a more desirable place to live and work, and, subsequently, for businesses to invest.[29]

Although DCMS initially regarded museums as being of marginal economic importance in terms of wealth and job creation,[30] by January 2005, the Secretary of State for Culture, Media and Sport insisted that "Museums and galleries are . . . major employers and an important part of the economy."[31] And although the case for investment in museums on the basis of their impact on tourism, education, or the economy had apparently already been won,[32] the commissioning of economic impact studies remains standard practice.

While it might be supposed that economic impact studies provide neutral assessments of the economic consequences of specific strategic interventions and that they provide evidence for future planning, they are primarily

recognized as a lobbying and advocacy tool. It was not by chance that Tate Modern celebrated its first and fifth birthdays by publishing an economic impact studies[33–35] or that the National Museums Directors' Conference (which represents the leaders of the U.K.'s national museums and galleries) thought it appropriate to commission major reports on their collective economic impact in anticipation of government's spending reviews.[36,37]

However, economic impact studies of the cultural sector are considered contentions and a considerable, specialist critical literature exists on the subject. (There is insufficient room here to review the literature. Readers are, therefore, referred to Reeves.[38]) Direct impacts are considered at personal, community, local, regional, and national levels; indirect impacts, at ancillary levels (e.g. suppliers, restaurants, and accommodation) and in relation to the "wider community." Sometimes economic impact is calculated through analyses of inputs and outputs, although more sophisticated theoretical applications include cost-benefit analysis; hedonic pricing; travel cost; contingent valuation; multipliers; displacement; and isolating the many variables that contribute to the impact of any activity or group of activities.

Highlighting the shortcomings of impact studies, of course, runs counter to the desire of DCMS and its agencies to report positive and demonstrable benefits, and to defend the sector against criticisms that it is not fulfilling the task it set itself.

Advocacy

From the outset of New Labour's project to assess the impact of cultural institutions, critics have suggested that

> The evidence, such as it is and it is limited, seems to indicate that museums have had really very little impact on their communities. No research results are available that prove that museums have an impact upon the problems of social exclusion.[39]

Moreover, the political neutrality of "evidence" and, by extension, assertions of impacts, have often been contested. A fundamental reason for this is that evidence of impacts tends to be conceived positively, not least in terms of advocacy.

> Evidence provides the proof of our 'case'—whatever that case may be. It should, for example, prove beyond contradiction that investment in museums, libraries and archives will deliver social, educational, economic or political benefits on a scale that clearly makes investment highly attractive to government, a lottery distributor or some other funding body.[40]

Over the past decade, the default among DCMS's agencies has been to commission impact studies—especially in anticipation of biennial Spending Reviews. Guided by the government's continuing commitment to social and economic aspects of the nation's well-being, these exercises are invariably intended to present the best possible evidence on effective activity.

But since DCMS's evidence-base primarily depends on data provided by institutions with obligations determined by their funding, distinguishing between advocacy-inspired research and objective social science enquiry is of fundamental importance. It is hardly surprising that those agencies, whose raison d'être is to promote the subsidized cultural sector and whose objective is to increase their funding, should be most interested in findings likely to serve their institutional goals. Indeed, in Britain, cultural institutions such as Museums, Libraries and Archives (MLA) Council and Arts Council England make no apology for their interest in research that fuels advocacy.[41] In a bureaucratic culture encouraged to pursue evidence-based policy, it has been suggested that what agencies actually produce is "policy-based evidence."

The pursuit of advocacy obviously imposes severe restrictions on the kind of research conducted, if not what is published and disseminated. Cultures of advocacy tend to lead to biased reporting.[42] For example, DCMS has consistently celebrated the national museums' success in attracting increased audiences since the introduction of free admission for all in December 2001. It has claimed that "the national museums are giving millions of people the opportunity to be stimulated, educated and inspired"[43] and that "Free admission has democratised the nation's treasures making them accessible to all."[44] But early objective and careful scrutiny of the data suggested that that while attendance was increasing, the most significant rises in visit numbers were among those who had always been well represented in museums and gallery.[45] Moreover, subsequent analyses of attendance data reveals that it is not possible to tell how many more people from lower social groups, for whom this policy was designed, have attended museums and galleries as a result of free admission.[46]

DEVELOPING THE IMPACT ASSESSMENT OF CULTURAL INSTITUTIONS

Assessing the impact of cultural institutions has been subject to issues of definition, methodology, and advocacy. But, underlying this has been a more fundamental uncertainty about the appropriateness of even attaching instrumental value to cultural institutions and products.

It appears that even as the former Secretary of State for Culture, Media, and Sport was putting a system of performance indicators in place to measure the impact of cultural institutions, he was aware of several drawbacks:

> The first is that it ignores the fundamental life-force of the cultural activity that gives rise to the educational or

economic value in the first place. (Not, I hasten to add, that there is anything wrong in hailing the value of the educational or economic impact of culture; culture can be profoundly important for a fulfilling education and for a flourishing economy; it is simply that these should not be elevated above the innate value of the art of itself.) The second drawback is that any measurement of numbers, quantity, or added value by figures is necessarily going to be inadequate.[47]

As this section reveals, such reservations are affecting changes in attitudes toward the impact assessment of cultural institutions.

Over the years, cultural institutions have accounted for themselves in relation to expectations of policy. Broadly speaking, they have described their putative contributions to employment and improvements in health and education, crime reduction, the strong communities, the economy and the nation's well-being;[48] neighborhood renewal and regeneration.[49] It has been assumed that they possess a sufficiently detailed "knowledge of, or interest in, the cultural needs of communities,"[50] that this is central to their missions, and that they are "key to achieving the Government's overall goals of a safe, just and tolerant society and providing the opportunity for everyone to realize their true potential."[51]

But, the rejection of instrumentalist arguments to justify support for cultural provision is becoming more vociferous. Twenty years ago, the publication of Myerscough's *The Economic Importance of the Arts in Britain* (1988) prompted economists to observe that the primary function of the arts was not to create economic impact.[52] More recently a number of commentators have similarly disputed the political expectations of culture to solve social problems:

> We assume, ludicrously, that the effect is embedded in the cultural form itself, released when it is 'consumed'. If this were true, then it would be relatively easy to give each of us doses of good culture, making us into model citizens. Few carry faith in cultural effect that far. Yet the popular accounts of the Mozart effect implied just that—a dose of a sonata would improve brain wiring and math ability.[53]

The notion that culture can make the world a better place is arguably no more than a form of political displacement activity:

> If we want to improve our children, our schools, our inner cities, and the lives of the marginal, the elderly, the impoverished, then we should do so directly, rather than argue for a an injection of 'more arts.'

In some cases, improvements to such social and economic agendas could be addressed that more efficiently elsewhere. Measuring culture in relation to these and other political ambitions has come to be regarded by many practitioners as "naïve"[54] "extraneous" and potentially "antithetical to their basic functions and purposes,"[55] and DCMS's ambitions fundamentally appear to deny the "inherent value" of culture.

For its part, DCMS is discernibly moving away from its earlier commitment to the instrumentality of cultural provision. Conceivably prompted by the work of the think tank, Demos, which has sought to revitalize the importance of cultural value,[56,57] Labour's successive Secretaries of State for Culture, Media and Sport have not only indicated that their thinking has moved on, but have expressed doubts about the adequacy of attempts to measure their impact. Smith's successor, Tessa Jowell, published a personal essay on *Culture and the Value of Culture* in which she proposed that culture should be "faced on its own terms and with recognition of what it does"[58] and that the debate should be shifted back to "cultural value."

Her successor and Labour's third Secretary of State for Culture, James Purnell, pursued a similar train of thought. While maintaining that targets were probably necessary in 1997, he considered that public subsidy of culture needed less defense now than it once did. "We no longer need to quote export figures to get a hearing." But despite still believing that culture and the arts remain "the most effective ways of reaching disaffected teenagers, of helping people to think about mental health, of regenerating inner cities or coastal towns," he insisted that they would still matter

> ...even if they did none of those things. They are intrinsically valuable before they are instrumentally so. The arts hold the ring for our national conversation. They are where we find our meanings, individually and collectively.[59]

He maintained that although encouraging attendance by priority groups was still vital, DCMS's focus should shift to "... what people have access to. If any part of our cultural sector is substandard, doesn't take risks, doesn't push barriers, ducks difficult questions, it's not worth subsidising. Garbage in, garbage out."[60] Indeed, he commissioned a review of the role that government and public funding can play in enabling excellence, "how we can move from top-down targets, to empowering and risk-taking."

But even as the substance of the impact assessment of cultural institutions is changing, it is still assumed that the "inherent value of culture" is synonymous with its "transformative power" and that can raise levels of aspiration. For the Arts Council's outgoing Chief Executive, this realization potentially shifted the focus of impact studies. He called "investigation into the value of culture itself in terms of its inherent power to move people, change people, and give people new meaning in their lives."

> ...the issue is for researchers to try and understand better how that transformative value might be captured. This

raises some challenging questions: First, how can we begin to describe transformative experience? ... Second, can we find out what conditions need to be in place for transformative experience to happen?'...'What research techniques would be most applicable to an investigation of this nature?[61]

CONCLUSION

This entry has explored the introduction of the impact assessment of cultural institutions by the New Labour government which came to power in the 1997 general election. It has considered the rationale of the Department for Culture in doing so, as well as setting out the pragmatic and philosophical difficulties encountered. In tracking the development of impact assessment, particularly as it pertains to the English museums sector, this entry has demonstrated how the government's attitude to the impact assessment of cultural institutions has shifted away from instrumentalism to cultural value. However, assessing impact still remains central.

ACKNOWLEDGMENTS

This entry draws on previous publications by the same author including "Great Expectations: Museums and Regional Economic Development in England" (2006) *Curator*, 49.1, 65-80 and "Taking Stock: Cultural Capital, Social Exclusion and Cultural Policy in England" (2004) Unpublished paper prepared for symposium, *Cultural Capital and Social Exclusion: A Critical Investigation*, by the Pavis Centre for Social and Cultural Research, Open University and held at St Hugh's College, University of Oxford.

REFERENCES

1. Selwood, S. Access, efficiency and excellence: Measuring non-economic performance in the English subsidised cultural sector. Cult. Trends. **1999**, *35*, 87–141.
2. Office of Science and Innovation. *Science review of the Department for Culture, Media and Sport*, 2004. Available at http://www.dti.gov.uk/science/science-in-govt/science-reviews/review/dcms/page24896.html (accessed December 2007).
3. Cabinet Office. *Memorandum to the committee*, 2007; Vol. II In Public Administration Select Committee: *Skills for Government*, Ninth Report of Session 2006–07; HC 93-II, Evidence 57 2007.
4. Civil Service. *Capability Review of the Department for Culture, Media and Sport*, 2007. Available at http://www.culture.gov.uk/reference_library/publications/archive_2007/capability_review.htm (accessed December 2007).
5. DCMS. *A New Cultural Framework*, Department for Culture, Media and Sport: London, U.K., 1998.

6. Selwood, S. The politics of data collection: Gathering, analysing and using data in the subsidised cultural sector in England. Cult. Trends. **2004**, *47*, 13–84.

7. DCMS. *Culture at the Heart of Regeneration*, Department for Culture, Media and Sport: London, U.K., 2004.

8. DCMS. *Libraries, Museums Galleries and Archives for All. Co-Operating across the Sectors to Tackle Social Exclusion*, Department for Culture, Media and Sport: London, U.K., 2001.

9. DCMS. *Culture at the Heart of Regeneration: Summary of Responses*, Department for Culture, Media and Sport: London, U.K., 2005.

10. DCMS. *Creating Opportunities: Guidance for Local Authorities in England on Local Cultural Strategies*, Department for Culture, Media and Sport: London, U.K., 2000.

11. DCMS. *Libraries, Museums Galleries and Archives for All. Co-operating across the Sectors to Tackle Social Exclusion*, Department for Culture, Media and Sport: London, U.K., 2001.

12. DCMS. *DCMS Annual Report 1998. The Government's Expenditure Plans 1998–1999*. The Stationery Office: London, U.K., 1998.

13. DCMS. *A New Cultural Framework*, Department for Culture, Media and Sport: London, U.K., 1998.

14. Selwood, S. Intentions and effects: The rhetorics of current cultural policy in England, University of Westminster, 2005; Unpublished Ph.D. thesis.

15. Smith, C. Valuing culture, Demos, 2003. Available at http://www.demos.co.uk/publications//valuingculture-speeches (accessed December 2007).

16. Morris, E. Speech to Cheltenham Festival of Literature October, 16, 2003. Available at http://www.culture.gov.uk/Reference_library/Press_notices/archive_2003/Estelle_Morris_speech_16Oct_2003.htm (accessed December 2007).

17. Selwood, S. Access, efficiency and excellence: Measuring non-economic performance in the English subsidised cultural sector. Cult. Trends. **1999**, *35*, 87–141.

18. DCMS A Research Strategy for DCMS, 2003–2005/06. Technical Paper No 3. Department for Culture, Media and Sport: London, 2003.

19. Cultural Heritage Consortium. Impact evaluation of museums, archives and libraries: quantitative time series data identification exercise; Archives and Libraries, 2002. An unpublished report for Resource: The Council for Museums.

20. DCMS, Centres for Social Change: Museums, Galleries and Archives for All. Policy guidance on social inclusion for DCMS funded and local authority museums, galleries and archives in England; Department for Culture, Media and Sport: London, 2000.

21. Coalter, F. *Realising the Potential of Cultural Services: Making a Difference to the Quality of Life*, Local Government Association: London, U.K., 2001.

22. DCMS *Review of the Efficiency and Effectiveness of the National Museums and Galleries*, Department for Culture, Media and Sport: London, U.K., 1999.

23. Newman, A. Whitehead, C. On behalf of International Centre for Cultural and Heritage Studies, University of Newcastle University. Fivearts Cities: An evaluative report on the impact on over 50s people of participation in activities related to British Art Show 6. Unpublished paper for Five and Arts Council England, 2006.

24. Morris Hargreaves McIntyre. Balancing the Scorecard: Review of DCMS Performance Indicator Framework, 2007. Available at http://www.culture.gov.uk/Reference_library/Publications/archive_2007/dcms_piframework.htm?contextId=%7B6E27314D-E0EC-4C5B-A175-F667D1F9C1FD%7D (accessed December 2007).

25. Ellis, A. Valuing culture; A background note. 2003; Unpublished paper for *Valuing Culture*, Demos Available at http://www.demos.co.uk/publications//valuingculture-speeches (retrieved December 2007).

26. Tusa, J. *Art Matters. Reflecting on Culture*, Methuen: London, U.K., 1999.

27. Wavell, C. Baxter, G. Johnson, I. Williams, D. *Impact Evaluation of Museums, Archives and Libraries: Available Evidence Project*, Aberdeen Business School, The Robert Gordon University: Aberdeen, U.K., 2002.

28. Selwood, S. The politics of data collection: Gathering, analysing and using data in the subsidised cultural sector in England. Cult. Trends. **2004**, *47*, 13–84.

29. DCMS. *Culture at the Heart of Regeneration*, Department for Culture, Media and Sport: London, U.K., 2004.

30. DCMS. *Creative Industries Mapping Document 1998*, Department for Culture, Media and Sport: London, U.K., 1998.

31. DCMS. *Understanding the Future: Museums and 21st Century Life. The Value of Museums*, Department for Culture Media ad Sport: London, U.K., 2005.

32. DCMS. Estelle Morris Sets Out Government Vision for Museums in the 21st Century, 2005; Press notice 008\05 (January 21, 2005). Available at http://www.culture.gov.uk/Reference_library/Press_notices/archive_2005/dcms008_05.htm (accessed December 2007).

33. Tate. Economic Impact of Tate Modern, 2001; Press information (11.05.01). Available at http://www.tate.org.uk/home/news/110501_3.htm (accessed December 2007).

34. Tate. *Tate Modern: The First Five Years*, Tate: London, U.K., 2005.

35. Travers, T. Renewing London. In *Tate Modern: The First Five Years*; Tate, Ed.; Tate: London, U.K., 2005; 23–28.

36. Travers, T. Glaister, S. *Valuing Museums. Impact and Innovation Among National Museums*, National Museum Directors' Conference: London, U.K., 2004.

37. Travers, T. *Museums and Galleries in Britain: Economic, Social and Creative Impacts*, National Museum Directors' Conference: London, U.K., 2006.

38. Reeves, M. *Measuring the Economic and Social Impact of the Arts*, Arts Council of England: London, U.K., 2002. Research report 24.

39. Newman, A.; McLean, F. Museums as agents of social inclusion. Trans. Museums Professionals Group **2000**. *3*, 3–8.

40. Davies, S. Research and evidence: Thinking about the potency of evidence for the museums and galleries domain Unpublished paper for the Counting Culture conference at the University of Greenwich September, 12, 2003.

41. Schuster, J.M. *Informing Cultural Policy: The Research and Information Infrastructure*, Centre for Urban Policy Research, Rutgers, NJ, 2002.

42. Best, J. *Damned Lies and Statistics. Untangling Numbers from the Media, Politicians, and Activists*, University of California Press: London, U.K., 2002.

43. DCMS, Visitor numbers for national museums and galleries up twenty percent. *Chris Smith hails new figures as a 'success for art, heritage and education'*; Department for Culture, Media and Sport: London, U.K., 2001. Press Release 104/01.

44. DCMS. *Free Admission to Museums 'a spectacular success' says Tessa Jowell*, Department for Culture, Media and Sport: London, U.K., 2002. Press Release 2/02.

45. Martin, A. The impact of free entry to museums. Cult. Trends. **2002**, *47*, 1–12.

46. Selwood, S. Free admission: Has it worked?. University of Newcastle on Tyne: London, Demos, January 2007. Unpublished paper given at *Questions of Access: Research and Practice* seminar.

47. Smith, C. Valuing culture. In *Valuing Culture—Event Speeches*; Holden, J., Ed.; http://www.demos.co.uk/catalogue/valuingculturespeeches/ (accessed December 2007).

48. Morris, E. Speech to Cheltenham Festival of Literature, October 16, 2003. Available at http://www.culture.gov.uk/Reference_library/Press_notices/archive_2003/Estelle_Morris_speech_16 Oct_2003.htm (accessed December 2007).

49. Evans, G. Shaw, P. Allen, K. *The Contribution of Culture to Regeneration in the UK*, Department for Culture, Media and Sport: London, U.K., 2003 for London Metropolitan University.

50. Worts, D. On the brink of irrelevance? Art museums in contemporary society. In *Researching Visual Arts Education in Museums and Galleries: An International Reader*; Tickle, L., Secules, V., Xanthoudaki, M., Eds.; Kluwer Academic Publishers: Dordrecht, the Netherlands, 2003; 215–232.

51. In *For Art's Sake: Society and the Arts in the 21st Century*; Cowling, J., Ed.; Institute for Public Policy Research: London, U.K., 2004.

52. van Puffelen, F. Abuses of conventional impact studies in the arts. Cult. Policy. **1996**, *2* (2), 241–254.

53. Jensen, J. *Is Art Good for Us? Beliefs about High Culture in American Life*, Rowman & Littlefield Publishers: Oxford, U.K., 2002.

54. Hytner, N. To hell with targets. The Observer, **2003**. Available at http://www.observer.co.uk/review/story/0,6903,872985,00.html (accessed December 2007).

55. Tusa, J. Thou shalt worship the arts for what they are. Spiked. August 29, **2002**. Available at http://www.spiked-online.com/Articles/00000006DA07.htm (accessed December 2007).

56. Holden, J. *Creating Cultural Value. How Culture Has Become a Tool of Government Policy*, Demos: London, U.K., 2004.

57. Holden, J. *Cultural Value and the Crisis of Legitimacy. Why Culture Needs a Democratic Mandate*, Demos: London, U.K., 2006.

58. Jowell, T. *Government and the Value of Culture*, Department for Culture, Media and Sport: London, U.K., 2004.

59. Purnell, J. World-class from the grassroots up: Culture in the next ten years; Speech given at the National Portrait Gallery, July 6, 2007. Available at http://www.culture.gov.uk/Reference_library/Minister_Speeches/James_Purnell/jamespurnellsos_speechcultureinthenexttenyrs.htm (accessed December 2007).

60. Purnell J. World-class from the grassroots up: Culture in the next ten years. Speech by Secretary of State, Rt Hon James Purnell MP, at the National Portrait Gallery, July 6, 2007.

61. Hewitt, P. The value of evidence and the evidence of value. In *For Art's Sake: Society and the Arts in the 21st Century*; Cowling, J., Ed.; Institute for Public Policy Research: London, U.K., 2004; 14–24.

Incunabula [ELIS Classic]

John P. Immroth
University of Pittsburgh, Pittsburgh, Pennsylvania, U.S.A.

Romano Stephen Almagno
International College of St. Bonaventure, Rome, Italy

Abstract

The word "incunabula" derives from the Latin word meaning "cradle." Incunabula are books from the "cradle" of modern printing, that is, those printed with movable metal type in the fifty years from the invention of movable type to January 1, 1501. These books are the focus of special interest in the study of the history of books, and are designated with this special term. The development of printing during those years, and the search for, discovery, and analysis of books printed during that period are discussed in this entry.

—ELIS Classic, from 1974

INTRODUCTION

Incunabula are any books printed with movable metal type prior to January 1, 1501. This definition includes only the first 50 years of typographic printing. Block books or xylographic books of the same time period are normally not considered to be incunabula because they would not have been printed typographically (i.e., with movable metal type). It may also be noted that the exactness of the date of January 1, 1501, precludes many similar but later works. Most scholars today, however, accept this date as appropriate. Edwin Emerson states,

> In correct English usage, the word "incunabula," in my opinion, should be strictly limited to printed texts or titles or printers' marks from the middle of the fifteenth century to its end. While previous blockbooks, printed from fullpage woodcuts with text, or the later products of some of the first printing presses of the early sixteenth century in England, Spain, Portugal, Mexico and Scandinavia are undoubtedly as rare and primitive as those of preceding printers in Germany, Bohemia, Switzerland, Italy, France and the Netherlands, so that the former books fitly could be said to be in their infancy or cradle, nevertheless neither they nor still earlier Chinese, Korean and Japanese prints from movable types or full page blocks are rated by competent scholars as incunabula. After all, even the most comprehensive students and insatiable collectors of early prints must draw the line somewhere in their ever extending researches. So they might as well draw the incunabula line between the Spring of 1450 and the last day of the year 1500.[1]

Alfred Pollard defines this term in the eleventh edition of the *Encyclopedia Britannica*,

> ... a Latin neuter-plural meaning "swaddling-clothes," a "cradle," "Birthplace," and so the beginning of anything, now curiously specialized to denote books printed in the 15th century. Its use in this sense may have originated with the title of the first separately published list of 15th-century books. Cornelius Beughem's *Incunabula typographiae* (Amsterdam, 1688). The word is generally recognized all over Europe and has produced vernacular forms such as the French *incunables*, German *Inkunabeln* (*Wiegendrucke*), Italian *incunaboli* though the anglicized *incunables* is not yet fully accepted. If its original meaning had been regarded the application of the word would have been confined to books printed before a much earlier date, such as 1475, or to the first few printed in any country or town. By the end of the 15th century book-production in the great centres of the trade such as Venice, Lyons, Paris and Cologne, had already lost much of its primitive character, and in many countries there is no natural halting-place between 1490 and 1520 or later. The attractions of a round date have prevailed, however, over these considerations, and the year 1500 is taken as a halting-place, or more often a terminus, in all the chief works devoted to the registration and description of early printed books.[2]

The extension of this date beyond the end of 1500 is found in Svend Dahl's *History of the Book*. He states about his native area, "In the Scandinavian countries, when printing did not begin until the 1480's the incunabulum period is extended to 1550."[3] Occasionally and inaccurately, the term incunabula may be applied to the first 50 or so years of printing in a country (i.e., American incunabula for early printed books in the United States). Konrad Haebler, a famous German scholar of incunabula, presents the following argument for justifying the January 1, 1501, date.

> To-day, the end of the year 1500 is quite generally accepted as the close of the incunabula period. It agrees with the usage prevailing from early times to the present,

Encyclopedia of Library and Information Sciences, Fourth Edition DOI: 10.1081/E-ELIS4-120008990

and is easily justifiable as an average date. The year 1500 is a very fitting limit for the early printing of Germany in particular, and as the home of the invention of the "black art" this country may well lay claim to special consideration. The mechanical side of the printing process had begun to gain footing in some places in Germany even before the year 1500. The prominent workshops in which that was the case, those of Anton Koberger in Nuremberg, Johann Grüninger in Strassburg, Peter Drach in Speyer, nevertheless had so undeniably gotten their start in the incunabula period, and so, not with standing their attention to the commercial aspect, still retained so much feeling for the scholarly and artistic conception of printing that it would be wrong to deny their books the characteristics of true incunabula. In any case, most of the smaller printing-shops which appeared in Germany up to the year 1500 bore quite unmistakable marks of the incunabula period. As far as Germany is concerned, we might feel in favor of extending the limit of this period still further, to the Reformation, for that was the first event to mark a general and obvious change in the field of printing. To do this, however, would be unfortunate, for the years 1501–17 in Germany were a time in which printing played a considerably diminished role as much in comparison with the preceding as with the following period.

In Italy we find a somewhat different situation. Here one must make a distinction between the printing of Venice, which began as early as the seventies to assume the leading role in the printing art in general, and the workshops of the rest of Italy, for their existence developed under essentially different circumstances. The incunabula period, as we have herein characterized its essentials, ended in Venice about 1480, for not in vain was Venice in the second half of the fifteenth century the indisputable centre of European commerce…. In the other Italian states conditions were almost the same as in Germany…. In fact, the introduction of italic by Aldus Manutius in the year 1501 plainly strengthens our conception of the end of the incunabula period as the year 1500.

In France, too, a distinction should be made between the printing of Paris and that of other cities. The limit for Paris was a considerably later one, however, than for Venice; yet about the middle of the nineties bookmaking even in Paris saw the introduction of methods of management which were contrary to the fundamental principles of their incunabula period….

The situation was similar in other countries into which printing found its way before the end of the fifteenth century. Up to that time, however, Spain and England entirely lacked a centre in which, as had happened for example in Venice or Paris, the art should have had a chance to develop earlier than was possible in the provinces. Not with standing all their presses, in comparison to Italy and France, they remained provincial, their entire output persistently retaining the characteristics of incunabula even down to the sixteenth century. In the north and east we find printing only sporadic, often as offshoots of the workshops which we have already met with in the

older centres of culture. For all these countries, then, the limit of the year 1500 is altogether too early; yet this is not very significant, relatively speaking, since the entire book production in these regions in comparison with that of Germany, Italy or France is of no great importance. For all the reasons here set forth, then, the year 1500 is almost universally recognized as the limit of the incunabula period.[4]

Attempting to make no such defense as Haebler does, the Encyclopedia Britannica simply states, "The limit is convenient but arbitrary, since no special development in the printing art can be connected with it."[5]

The first established use of this Latin word in relation to printing occurs in a tract, De ortu et progressu artis typographicae written by Bernard von Mallinckrodt, dean of Münster Cathedral, and published in 1639 in Cologne. This work was issued as part of the second centenary celebration of Gutenberg's invention of typography. Mallinckrodt described the period from mid-fifteenth century to 1500 as "prima typographiae incunabula."[6] The first bibliographic use of this newly indicated time period was 4 years later in 1643 by J. Saubertus in Historia bibliothecae reipublicae Noribergensis…Accessit…appendix de inventore typographiae itemque catalogus librorum proximis ab inventione annis usque ad a. Chr. 1500 editorium.[4] In 1653, Philippe Labbé equated the word with the time period in his Nova bibliotheca mss. librorum s. specimen antiquarum lectionum latinarum et graecarum.[4] According to Haebler

> The first independent catalogue of incunabula was that by Cornelis à Beughem, Incunabula typographiae s. catalogus librorum scriptorumque proximis ab inventione typographiae annis ad annum Christi MD inclusive in quavis lingua editorum, Amstelodami 1688, 8°. This was no longer the inventory of a single collection but a first attempt to comprehend the collected literature of the period of early printing, the author having brought together approximately three thousand titles.[4]

Additional major incunabula catalogs and bibliographies will be covered in the following sections of this entry.

As the term incunabula became more commonly used to designate a particular period of typographic production, various vernacular forms developed. In English, the following three terms have all been used as a vernacular equivalent: incunables, fifteeners, and cradle-books; of these, incunables is the most common English term today. Three terms have also developed in French: incunable, impression ancienne, and impression primitive. Incunable is the most commonly used term of these three. In German, four terms have evolved: Inkunabel, Wiegendruck, Frühdruck, and Erstlingsdruck. Of these four terms, Weigendruck is the most common. In Dutch, there are two terms: incunabel and weigedruk. The Spanish term is incunable. Incunabulo is the Italian term. The Russian is

ИНРУНаВУЛ (*inkunabul*). There are two terms used by the Scandinavian languages (Swedish, Danish, and Norwegian): *inkunabel* and *paletoyp*. In Finnish, there are three terms: *inkunaabeli, paleotyyppi,* and *kehtopaino.* The Polish term is *inkunabul.* The Greek is τυπωμααρχατοογ (typoma archaion). The Bulgarian term is ИНКПУНаВУЛ (inkunabul). The student of incunable bibliographic literature should be aware of all these different terms that may be used to refer to *incunabula.* The catalogs of foreign collections will often have titles in the vernacular, although the entities will usually be listed in the original languages.

CHIEF REFERENCE WORKS

Possibly no other period in the history of printing has been so well covered (i.e., studied and described) by that which so nearly approaches a complete bibliography, as the period of the incunabula. As early as the end of the eighteenth century ("early" understood with reference to Sir Walter Greg's dating for the beginning of true bibliographical scholarship), George W.F. Panzer published at Nuremberg, during the period 1793–1803, an 11-volume study titled *Annales typographici ab artis inventae origine ad annum MD.* The first five volumes covered the history of typography from the invention of printing to 1500; in 1803, the study was carried on to 1536 and six more volumes were added. This work is considered by some scholars the first important modern bibliography.

Inspired by Maittaire's work, *Annales typographici ab artis inventae origine ad annum MDCLXIV* (Hagae-Comitum, 1719–1725), Panzer borrowed both Maittaire's title and basic method and set out to trace the course of early printing. In the *Annales typographici,* Panzer's principle of division is alphabetical. Listing the main printing centers alphabetically by their Latin names, he then arranged in seniority all the printers who worked in these centers and followed this by a chronological listing of their publications.

The *Annales typographici* is divided into two parts: the first lists books printed up to and including 1500, whereas the second part covers the years 1501–1535. Panzer's annalistic approach gives the *Annales* a rather pronounced scientific tone. And the entries (although brief) include a detailed reference to sources and are more complete and technical than those of his predecessor, Maittaire. Furthermore, by a careful examination of types, Panzer was successful, especially when studying the Strassburg printers, in assigning certain books, published without a printer's name, to a definite printer of that city.

Panzer's work was criticized by Proctor, who in his preface to the *Index to the Early Printed Books in the British Museum,* wrote that:

Panzer's method of grouping of books by years rather than printers has many merits, but obscures the work of the individual printers, and is unsuitable to a work in which the chief stress is laid in this point, and on the types which the printers used.[7]

Despite its limitations, Panzer's work is an early example of how the scientific method can add much to the knowledge of a printed book.

Twenty-three years after Panzer's *Annales,* Ludwig Hain published the *Repterorium bibliographicum in quo libri omnes ab arte typographica inventa usque ad annum MD. typis expressi ordine alphabetico vel simpliciter enumerantur vel adcuratius, recensentur* (Stuttgart, 1826 – 1838, 2 vols. in 4 parts). This is still considered the standard reference work for incunabula studies; but as Roy Stokes has rightly noted, in view of Greg's accomplishments, standard does not necessarily imply the note of immutability. It may nevertheless be considered and used as the first bibliographical tool and as a springboard to other studies in this period of printing history.

The *Repertorium* lists alphabetically and numbers consecutively (by author order) 16,000 books printed before the end of the fifteenth century. Because of Hain's death, the later part of the alphabet is incomplete.

Although the entries preceded by an asterisk were compiled by Hain himself from copies under his care at the Hof und Staatsbibliothek (Munich) and are, therefore, more detailed and descriptive, the others, relying on earlier (XVI, XVII) and contemporary bibliographers, are less descriptive and informative. Each entry is composed of an assigned heading and transcripts. The assigned heading includes the author's name and a brief title. The transcripts are of the incipit, major section titles, and colophon. A folio number is given with reference to the place of the incipit, explicit, and colophon in the incunabula. Thus, for example, in entry 13387, *F 1 a* plus the title caption means that this is to be found on recto of the first folio. When, however, the title caption is printed on a subsequent leaf, the form *F 1 a vacat* is used and the transcript made with the appropriate folio reference. (Cf., e.g., Hain 13463.) The explicit transcript (or colophon) is always preceded by the words *In fine* and is made in full in the style of the type used in the original text. (Cf., e.g., Hain 13408.) The collation of the incunabula is given in code (i.e., in a series of initials and abbreviations that need some practice to decipher). Thus, the collation for Hain 5530 reads: s. 1. a. et typ. n. f. g. ch. s.s. c. et pp. n. 2. col. 421. 304ff. This reads (when deciphered): *sine loco, anno et typo*graphici *nomine, folio, goticis ch*aracteribus, *sine, signatoribus, c*ustrodibus *et p*aginarum *n*umeris, *2 col*umnae, *42l*ineae, *304 folia.* And when translated means: without place, year and printer's name, in folio, in gothic characters, without signatures, catchwords and page numbers, 2 columns, 42 lines to the page, 304 folios. It should be noted, as a point of useful information to students, that a list of the abbreviations used by Hain can be found in Stillwell's *Incunabula and Americana 1450–1800*, pp. 223–225.

Hain's *Repertorium* is, as has been stated, important on account of the wealth of description that it affords the consultor. Although earlier bibliographers furnished the reader with a title for the incunabula based on the incunabula's contents, Hain faithfully recorded the incipit and explicit of each book. This exactness made it possible, for the first time, to identify books with a good amount of certitude and to check them for their completeness.

The *Repertorium* does fall short of the mark, however, on two counts: first, Hain's failure to furnish information that would help to link the books described with their printer; second, his failure to collate the signatures (when present).

To the *Repertorium*, there have been added a series of supplements, which have both augmented and corrected with the original material furnished by Hain. One of the most important of these supplements is the work prepared by W.A. Copinger and titled *Supplement to Hain's Repertorium Bibliographicum*. This work, published between 1895 and 1902, is—as scholars know, and students soon discover—far less accurate than Hain's and should be used with the greatest caution.

Copinger's *Supplement* comprises two volumes, divided into three parts. Volume I, Part I, lists 7000 corrections of collations and additions to collations of works already described or mentioned in Hain. This volume and part was severely criticized because of its many errors and because of the absence of certain authorities (whose presence, as quoted, cited, and referred to, scholars felt to be indispensable). The entries in Volume I, Part I, retain Hain's original numbering and are referred to as H–C (= Hain as corrected or added to by Copinger). Thus, for example, H–C 12259 is the same number in Hain as augmented/corrected by Copinger.

Volume I, Part II, furnishes the user with a list of numerous collations and bibliographical particulars concerning nearly 6000 volumes printed in the fifteenth century and not referred to by Hain. Here Copinger seems to have profited from previous criticism, for the level of his work is considerably better and he is careful to refer to authorities. The entries for this section are in Hain's style, but their numbering is Copinger's own, and an entry in this section is referred to as *Copinger*, *Cop*, or just *C* (always, of course, followed by the corresponding number). Copinger gives the collation before the transcript of the incipit and explicit (colophon). Although in Hain, undated editions are merely listed prior to the dated editions, Copinger instead based his order for undated editions by studying the number of lines per page. It was his contention that a smaller number of lines and a larger number of leaves probably indicated an earlier edition, and so he used this as his criterion for dating undated editions. He also retained (in Volume I, Part II) some of Hain's abbreviations and introduced the *sine notâ*

(without place, name of printer, or date) to be used if these were lacking.

Volume I, Part II, covers the alphabet from letter A to O, and Volume II completes the list of works not mentioned in Hain, covering letters from P to Z. It then furnishes an Addenda to Parts I and II.

Immediately after the Addenda to Part II, there was published as an index to Copinger's *Supplement*, Konrad Burger's *The Printers and Publishers of the XVth Century With a List of Their Works*. Some scholars think that the inclusion of Burger's study (which they consider to be the best brief chronological record of the output of each fifteenth century press) helped somewhat to redeem Copinger's work and give it a certain, acceptable status.

Burger's masterful work was, as he himself notes in the preface, a labor of love to which he could attend only after the day's work was over. What Burger did was to extract all the printers mentioned in Hain and list them (by their self-adopted names) in alphabetical order. Under each printer he then placed the dated books (in chronological order) and then (in alphabetical order) those issued *s. a.* and *s. n.* In his entries, usually kept to a single line to afford easy reference, Burger includes not only the books listed by Hain and Copinger but also adds material from Proctor, Pellechet, and Haebler. Burger also appended to his list a second listing of books which, although dated, bear no indication of printer or place of printing. Relying on Proctor's dating, he assigned to these impressions an approximate date.

Finally Burger, writing in the *Preface* to his *Printers and Publishers of the XVth Century*, apologized for not enumerating about 2000 books, which had appeared without indication of printer's name, place, and date. He also regretted not furnishing his readers with a listing of printing centers and indications concerning their printers and publishers. But he suggested that:

> Whoever desires to gather information on this point may use Proctor's *Index*, which I recommend as a standard work for those engaged in the study of incunabula, and as a book from which further researches must start.[8,9]

In 1905 D. Reichling published the first of six fascicles titled *Appendices ad Hain-Copingeri Repertorium Bibliographicum* (Munich 1905–1911, with a Supplement added in 1914). This work, which is much more authoritative than Copinger's *Supplement to Hain's Repertorium Bibliographicum*, is considered as a further step toward the goal of a complete bibliography of all fifteenth century books. Reichling furnished notices for more than 2000 incunabula not listed in Hain or Copinger and augmented/corrected about 3400 of their descriptions.

The Appendices is, as stated, published in six fascicles (fascicles I–VI, followed by an *Indices fasciculorum* numbered as I.VI, and then closing with a *Supplementum*) with two sequences running through them, all of which does not make this work very easy to use.

The first sequence, numbered consecutively, consists of books unknown to Hain and Copinger. This section is titled: *I. Additiones. Incunabula typographica Hainio–Copingero ignota.* The second sequence, consisting of additions, corrections, and emendations to entries in Hain, Hain–Copinger, and Copinger is titled: *II. Emendationes. Incunabula Typographica ab Hainio–Copingero minus accurate recensita.* Each entry in this second sequence or section is preceded by the appropriate number reference to (sic.) H. = *Hain, Repertorium bibliographicum.* H.C. = *Hain, Repertorium, et Copinger, Supplement P.I.: Corrections.* And Cop. = *Copinger, Supplement P.II., et vol. I. et II.: Additions.* Thus, for example, in Fascicle I: pp. 1–81 are the *Additiones* and pp. 83–206, the *Emendationes.*

The index for this work is to be found in Fascicle I.VI (*Indices* Fasciculorm I.VI) and is quite comprehensive. But in the *Supplementum* there is (besides additional entries) a General Index, which brings together in one alphabetical listing all the items listed in the preceding fascicle.

Again, it is suggested that before a student begins consulting Reichling, he page through the fascicles and become thoroughly familiar with the general layout and arrangement of the material. The *Appendices* may not be a very easy bibliographical tool with which to work, but it is nevertheless a very important one.

Influenced by the insights and contributions of previous and contemporary scholars, but most especially Henry Bradshaw, Robert Proctor (as V. Scholderer has remarked) found the history of early printing guesswork and left it a science.[10]

Proctor's aim was to illustrate the history of early printing by listing (as far as possible) in chronological order all the fifteenth century presses and types. When he came to publish *An Index to the Early Printed Books in the British Museum: from the invention of printing to the year MD with notes on those in the Bodleian Library* (2 vols. K. Paul, 1898–1899; 4 Supplements 1899–1902), he had sorted out (on the basis of typographical evidence) and brought order to some 10,000 volumes, a third of which were, perhaps, without printer's names.

Basically, Proctor applied on a large scale Bradshaw's principle of natural history order. Going from the known to the unknown (as all science must), Proctor compared the types used in signed and dated books against those in books without date, name of printer, or even place of publication. He was so proficient at this identification that A.W. Pollard, writing in the *Introduction* to Volume I of the *British Museum Catalogue of Books Printed in the Fifteenth Century* (1908, p. xi) stated that Proctor could identify types almost always on sight. Pollard's remark is no exaggeration, for not only was Proctor able to identify the vast majority of the unsigned books that he studied, but subsequent studies have by and large attested to his accuracy. His work has, in fact, become the basis for the still incomplete *British Museum Catalogue of Books Printed in the Fifteenth Century.*

Proctor's *Index* is arranged in what is now commonly known as Proctor Order. That is, the books are sorted out, on the basis of typographical evidence, under their countries, towns, presses, and dates.

Proctor intended that his *Index* should include all books printed up to 1520. He selected 1520 rather than the more commonly accepted date of 1500 because he felt that the initial period of printing really ended at this date.

The *Index* is divided into two parts. The first lists all fifteenth century books and concludes with an index listing places, printers, and publishers (all in alphabetical order). There are also—at the end of this first part—other indexes of authors arranged by their Hain or Campbell number and in alphabetical order. Part II lists books printed in Germany during the period 1501–1520. Proctor's death in 1903 left the *Index* unfinished. At his death he had completed only the first section of Part II (i.e., that covering Germany). It was left to Frank Isaac to complete sections 2 and 3 (covering Italy, Switzerland, and Eastern Europe). These were published in 1938.

Proctor's entries are brief: each book is given a short title and the general format is noted, but there are no further collational details. It must be remembered that Proctor's work was meant to be in fact, what it was in name, that is, *An Index.*

Some critics have objected that, properly speaking, Proctor's *Index* is more a catalog than a bibliography. The novelty and complexity of his approach was defended by Proctor himself in the Preface to his *Index*, when he stated:

> They (the books) are arranged, mainly in chronological order, under the printers of them; the printers are arranged in their order under the towns, and the towns under the countries; the precedence assigned to countries, towns, and printers is the same in principle, and is determined by the *terminus a quo* in point of date, in each case.[7]

When the first volume of the *British Museum Catalogue of Books Printed in the Fifteenth Century* appeared in 1908, Pollard set the question to rest when he noted in his Introduction that Proctor's experience with his *Index* had made this the obvious arrangement for a much more expanded catalog.[11] Much of the importance of this superb bibliographical tool depends on its arrangement, which is in the Proctor Order.

It is good to remark here, as Roy Stokes has stressed all these years (in the classroom and in print), that although the student may make his first acquaintance with these bibliographical tools by general descriptions and introductions, he must do everything possible to enable himself to handle the books themselves. The student must become familiar with the scope and the arrangement of these bibliographical tools, for on his knowledge and skillful use of them rests much of the efficiency that he is expected to exercise in the whole area of bibliographical scholarship.[12]

EXTANT INCUNABULA

The normal reaction to the tremendous amount of work and superb scholarship that have been expended in the study and description of the incunabula is to wonder whether, indeed, there is anything left to uncover or discover, much less to describe. Pollard himself wondered if at times the game (in incunabula scholarship) was not played for its own sake without any great consideration of practical utility.[2]

A solution to this questioning can be had by both remembering the past and keeping a keen eye on present developments in this area of historical bibliography.

Pollard believed that the total output of the fifteenth century presses is not likely to have exceeded 40,000 editions and that given the number of copies produced by an individual printer (250 copies by Roman printers, 300 by Venetian printers or even 500 copies toward the end of the century), a possible total of 20 million books were placed on the European market.[13] Today, scholars believe they know about the existence of at least 48,000 incunabula (about three times the amount originally recorded by Hain). But these are neither all registered in a single listing, nor is their description always adequate or complete. Furthermore, it is not infrequent to come across the word/note "unrecorded" in sale catalogs.

Extreme caution must be exercised with regard to new discoveries and the word "unrecorded" in sale catalogs. In this matter, one need only recall the latest hoax uncovered by the Italian bibliographer Roberto Ridolfi, which was fully described and explained in his article, "'Un incunabulo sconosciuto' (e inesistente)" in *La Bibliofilia*, Firenze, 1971, pp. 191–195.

All this does not mean that there is absolutely nothing else to be discovered/uncovered. Rather it means that new discoveries will be difficult if not improbable. History, of course, will be the final judge, and the margin of possibility together with scholarly scepticism will always serve to make the future interesting.

An area of work does exist, however, in searching out libraries and private collections, and in aiming toward both a more accurate/exact description and a cumulative bibliography of all incunabula.

TYPOGRAPHICAL DETECTIVES

The study of typography, with the intention of using the types as bibliographical evidence for dating books is, certainly, one of the more scientific branches of bibliography.

Typography is not unlike paleography because the early types were imitations of the book hand.

Most of the fifteenth century printers both designed and cast their own types. Therefore, books not bearing a printer's name can be assigned to a printer through the comparison and identification of the fonts. This theory is called the "one type, one printer" theory. Because a printer could (and, in fact, did) sell his fonts to others or even pass down his type to successors; many thought that the one type, one printer theory was no longer valid.

But the work of Bradshaw, Proctor, and Haebler (which to a large extent supported this theory) has in no way suffered from these doubts. In fact, their method has been vindicated by subsequent studies and scholars. Today all agree and know that types can be the most reliable guide to both determining a printer and dating a volume.

Henry Bradshaw, whom Greg has called "the founder, or one of the founders, of the modern study of typography, . . ."[14] developed for the study of incunabula a theory based on Darwinism, which he called the natural history method. By grouping books together by origin, he was able to compare them and draw conclusions concerning their genus (i.e., press on which they were printed). His natural history method was worked out in *A Classified Index of the Fifteenth Century Books in the De Meyer Collection* and can be found in *The Collected Papers of Henry Bradshaw*, University Press, Cambridge, 1889, pp. 208–236.

Robert Proctor, who based his work on that of Henry Bradshaw, Holtrop and Campbell, was the first to study the identification of early types in great detail. The result of his labor, *An Index to the Early Printed Books in the British Museum: from the invention of printing to the year 1500 with notes on those in the Bodleian Library*, gave the world of incunabula scholarship the first clear picture of the development of fifteenth century printing and presses.

Useful and important as is Proctor's *Index*, however, the best and to date most important handbook for typographical detection is Konrad Haebler's *Typenrepertorium der Wiegendrucke*. The user will soon come to know—and so should be previously warned—that Haebler's book is a difficult, but important, bibliographical tool. The *Typenrepertorium* is, in fact, a highly detailed classification of types based on the characteristics of design and (in part) of sizes. Haebler selected 102 forms of the upper case M (for Gothic types) and Qu (distinguishing between those printed as two letters or as a logo type) for Roman types. These two letters were selected because it was these that underwent the greatest amount of changes and variations.

The *Typenrepertorium* is divided into two parts: the first on the types of Germany and those countries, which were directly influenced by German printers, and the second covering the types of Italy, France, Portugal, England, and the Netherlands. Under each country, Haebler listed the towns alphabetically and then their printers in chronological order.

The types used by each printer are provided by a series of symbols and numbers. But most important for a fruitful use of Haebler's work is a frequent consultation and familiarity with the two indexes he provides—one for Gothic and a second for Roman type.

Haebler's work, of course, is not the final word, nor does it provide easy solutions to typographical detection. When the user can come to the conclusion that a type compares as closely as possible with what he finds in Haebler, then the next step is to check further in facsimiles, etc. But, as Roy Stokes has rightly remarked, great discretion is needed, and hasty identification is a snare, particularly after 1480.

EXAMPLES OF FAMOUS INCUNABLES

Of the approximately 40,000 editions printed during the incunable period, there are a few that are truly outstanding. These include examples of very fine printing as well as various notable first occurrences. The following discussion includes only a small number of these famous incunables.

Perhaps the most famous incunable is the so-called "Gutenberg Bible." Although there is no absolute proof that Johann Gutenberg of Mainz printed or rather supervised the printing of this Bible, he is generally given credit for planning and at least supervising the early stages of its printing. The completion of the work is assumed to have been done by Gutenberg's successors, Johann Fust and Peter Schoeffer in approximately 1455. A copy that was housed in the Mazarine Library in Paris is signed and dated August 15, 1456, by its rubricator and binder, Heinrich Cremer. The final version of the Bible was in two columns of 42 lines each; hence, this Bible is often called the 42-line Bible. It is the first printed book extant. Margaret B. Stillwell states, "There is a grandeur about this Bible, a superb air of finality, that stands in curious contrast to the fact that it is the first book to have been printed with movable metal types, and thus the starting point in the history of modern book-making."[15] Of the estimated 150 copies on paper and 30 on vellum, there are 21 surviving, 3 of which are on vellum. A large paper copy was placed on sale for $2,500,000 by Kraus.[16] One of the vellum copies is on permanent exhibition at the U.S. Library of Congress. The type design in the 42-line Bible is textura or Lettre de Forme. Textura is the most formal of the types of the Gothic family and is sometimes called "Wedding text" or "Old English" by printers today.

The *Mainz Psalter* is the first printed book to have a complete colophon. It was issued by Gutenberg's successors, Fust and Schoeffer. It is a Latin Psalter dated 1457. The catalog of the famous Printing and the Mind of Man exhibition of 1963 describes it.

This famous masterpiece of printing surpasses even the 42-line Bible in the beauty of its type and the richness of

its ornament. It is the first printed book to give the name of its printer and the date of printing. One of the printers, Johann Fust, had been in partnership with Gutenberg and had advanced money for the first essays in printing. It is supposed that a lawsuit between the partners in 1455 led to the dissolution of the partnership and that thereafter Fust exploited Gutenberg's invention with the help of his son-in-law, Peter Schoeffer, the other printer named in this book.

The colophon at the end may be translated from the Latin as follows:

"The present volume of the psalms, adorned with beautiful initial letters and with the proper rubrics in red, has been given this form artificially by means of a contrivance for printing and inscribing without any use of a pen, and laboriously brought to completion for the service of God by Johann Fust, citizen of Mainz, and Peter Schoeffer of Gernsheim in the year of our Lord 1457 on the Eve of the Assumption" (i.e., on 14 August).

It is an extremely elaborate book, set in two founts of type, excellently cut and cast, with 292 impressions of initial letters cut in metal and printed in colours. The text was printed in black and red and the big initials in red and blue or grey and printed for the most part at one pull, but here and there by two impressions and some stamping by hand. The inking was remarkably laborious: the red and blue letters were picked out of the forme before each impression and separately inked; in the case of the two-colour initials, the block for background ornament, given its colouring, and put back (probably fastened in also) before each copy was printed. Many changes were made in the formes during the run, so that no two of the surviving ten copies, all on vellum, are alike.

Some authorities contend that Gutenberg had a hand in the early stages of the printing; but this can be no more than conjecture.[17]

The type design is textura. Another edition was printed in 1459 by Fust and Schoeffer.

A third important book printed in Mainz is the 1460 *Catholicon*. It is a thirteenth century Latin dictionary compiled by Johannes Balbus and printed in Mainz in 1460. It is thought that Gutenberg may have been the printer. Binns says, "There is no definite evidence that he was, in fact, its printer, but most experts are agreed in crediting the work to him in default of any other person to whom it can be assigned."[18] It is "the first printed publication of any work in the field of secular knowledge."[16] A less formal Gothic type called Fere-Humanistica or Lettre de Somme is first used in this book.

Another important Latin Bible is the 48-line Bible printed by Fust and Schoeffer in Mainz in 1462. This is the first printed Bible to contain a colophon and the first printed appearance of the twin shields printer's device of Fust and Schoeffer. The Gothic type used is called

Fust–Schoeffer Bible type and has the overall appearance of Fere–Humanistica.

The *Subiaco Lactantius* is the first dated book to be printed in Italy. Two German printers from Mainz, Conrad Sweynheym and Arnold Pannartz, settled for a short time in Subiaco, Italy, and printed this book in 1465. The text is *De Divinis Institutionibus* or simply Opera of Lucius Coelius Firmianus Lactantius. The type is a semi-Roman or transitional face. It is also the first printed book to contain short passages of Greek type.

The Recuyell of the Histories of Troy, written by Raoul Le Fevre and translated by William Caxton, is the first book printed in English. Although the book is not dated, Binns says "...it is generally agreed that it was printed at Bruges between 1472 and 1475."[18] In his epilogue Caxton states,

> I have practysed & lerned at my grete charge and dispense to ordeyne this said book in prynte after the maner & forme as ye may here see, and is not wreton with penne and ynke as other bokes ben, to thende that every man may have them attones, ffor all the bookes of this storye named the recule of the historyes of Troyes thus enpryntid as ye here see were begonne in oon day, and also fynysshid in oon day.[16]

This type face is of the Gothic family of a French Bastarda or Lettre Bâtarde. An edition of the French original, *Le Recueil des Histoires de Troyes*, appeared in 1476 and may have been printed also by Caxton. It is probably the earliest French literary work in print (see also *Caxton, William*).

Nicholas Jenson's first important book is probably Eusebius' *De evangelica praeparatione* printed in Venice in 1470. The type designed for this work is of the Roman family and called Venetian. It is considered to be one of the most beautiful Roman text types. B.A. Uhlendorf states, "...Jenson created the most beautiful Roman type we have: a perfect symmetry in size and form, an unparalleled imitation of the lapidary forms of Roman inscriptions, meeting at the same time all the requirements of a printing type."[19]

A very famous book from Nuremberg was printed by Anton Koberger in 1493. Although commonly called the Nuremberg Chronicle, its correct title is *Das Buch der Chroniken* or *Liber Chronicarum* by Hartman Schedel and Georg Alt. It is a massive folio volume of 596 pages containing some 1809 illustrations from woodcuts by Michael Wohlgemuth and Wilhelm Pleydenwurff. Only 645 different wood blocks were used to make the many illustrations so that many illustrations are used more than once.

The *Hypnerotomachia Poliphili*, printed by Aldus Manutius in Venice in 1499, is often considered one of the true masterpieces of the incunable period. The Roman type face is Old Face designed by Francesco da Bologna.

The book is illustrated by delicate woodcuts and intribate initials. William M. Ivins analyzes this book in the following quotation.

> It would be possible to name but few objects that have had the influence on subsequent design that this book had. In Venice and Italy it had little popular acclaim, its text too erudite and its illustrations too familiar in type and style, to arouse much interest. It took forty-odd years to sell off its first edition of six hundred copies, and with the possible exception of the *Nuremberg Chronicle*, which was too big to be read or used, it is today the commonest of fifteenth-century books. In the year of its second edition, 1546, a translation of it into French, accompanied by French copies of the woodcuts of the original, was published at Paris. This translation went through four or five editions, the last of which found a market after the beginning of the seventeenth century. It is doubtful whether any one set of designs has ever played so extraordinary a role as did this in the conversion of France from its Gothic to its Renaissance. It was the first and the greatest of the printed carriers of the revived classical feeling to the peoples of the north.
>
> The *Hypnerotomachia* thus immediately raises several questions that are of extreme importance in any critical discussion of book design and illustration. As far as its text went it was an impossible, erudite, silly romance, fittingly written in a jargon that is almost macaronic, devoted in largest measure to abstruse symbolism and the maundering of a mad collector of classical remains. It describes, as only an Italian platonic humanist could, temples, groves, palaces, ruins, gods and godesses, and fragments of ancient art.... And it was illustrated with pictures of many of these things. Thus it happened that within the covers of this crazy book were to be found more representations, clear, lucid, and simple, of the architectural and monumental forms that intelligent Italy had evolved from the classical, than had ever before been printed.... A richly illustrated book, filled with outline drawings of architectural motifs and details, vases, capitals, arches, pilasters, and other such things, it could not well escape being itself a rather effective object.... Its draftsman was anything but a great artist, but its subject matter and the traditional technique in which he worked lent themselves most admirably to the creation of a homogeneous object of art. Between its letter press and its illustration there was no conflict or color or linear form—a result purely accidental, possible only because the draftsman lacked personality and his subject forbade it. Its success from the typographic point of view is grounded in the fact that its figures display almost as little personality or color or draftsmanship as those in a Euclid. The result is that by many in these modern times it has been declared to be the most beautiful of all illustrated books.[20]

CONCLUSION

Many outstanding collections of incunabula exist in European libraries. The four most important collections, perhaps, are in the British Museum, the Bibliotheque Nationale in

Paris, the Staatsbibliothek in Munich (formerly the Royal Library), and the Vatican Library. In addition, there are major collections in the libraries of Berlin, Milan, Vienna, Manchester (including the John Rylands Library), Brussels, and The Hague. There are also many smaller European collections.

Although none of the American collections can truly match these European ones, the following libraries are noteworthy in this country: the Library of Congress, the Lenox collections of the New York Public Library, Harvard University Library, the Pierpont Morgan Library in New York, the Henry E. Huntington Library in San Marino, California, the Hispanic Society of America in New York, Columbia University Library, Yale University Library, Cornell University Library, the University of Michigan Library, the Chapin Library at Williams College, both the Newberry Library and the John Crerar Library in Chicago, the University of Chicago Library, the Free Library of Philadelphia, the National Library of Medicine, the Boston Athenaeum, the Grolier Club Library of New York, the General Theological Seminary Library, the Annmary Brown Memorial at Brown University, and the Lilly Library at the University of Indiana.[15]

REFERENCES

1. Emerson, E. *Incunabulum Incunabulorum: The Gutenberg Bible on Vellum in the Vollbehr Collection*, Tudor Press: New York, 1928; 54.
2. Pollard, A. W. Incunabula. *The Encyclopedia Britannica*, 11th Ed., 1910; Vol. 14, 369, 370.
3. Dahl, S. *History of the Book*, Scarecrow Press: Metuchen, NJ, 1968; 113.
4. Haebler, K. *The Study of Incunabula*, Grolier Club: New York, 1933; 2–8 (translated from the German by L.E. Osborne with a Foreword by A.W. Pollard).
5. Scholderer, J. V. Incunabula. *The Encyclopedia Britannica*, 1965; Vol. 12, 27.
6. Steinberg, S. H. *Five Hundred Years of Printing*, Penguin Books: Baltimore, MA, 1961; 15, with a Foreword by B. Warde.
7. Proctor, R. *An Index to the Early Printed Books in the British Museum: From the Invention of Printing to the Year 1500*, Holland Press: London, U.K., 1960; 8. with Notes of Those in the Bodleian Library.
8. Burger, K. *The Printers and Publishers of the XV Century, with Lists of Their Works: Index to the Supplement of Hain's Retertorium Bibliographicum, etc.*, Sotheran: London, U.K., 1902; xiii.
9. Copinger, W. A. *Supplement to Hain's Repertorium Bibliographicum, Part 2*, Sotheran: London, U.K., 1902; Vol. 2.
10. Scholderer, V. Early printed books. *The Bibliographical Society, 1892–1942: Studies in Retrospect*; Bibliographical Society: London, U.K., 1945.
11. Pollard, A. W. Introduction. *Catalogue of Books Printed in the XVth Century Now in the British Museum*; British Museum: London, 1908; ix.
12. Strokes, R. *Esdaile's Manual of Bibliography*, Rev. Ed. Allen & Unwin: London, U.K., 1967; 293.
13. Lenhart, J. M. *Pre-reformation Printed Books: A Study in Statistical and Applied Bibliography*, Wagner: New York, 1935; 10.
14. Greg, W. W. The present position of bibliography. In *Collected Papers*; Maxwell, J. C., Ed.; Clarendon Press: Oxford, U.K., 1966; 213.
15. Stillwell, M. B. *Incunabula and America: 1450–1800; A Key to Bibliographical Study*, Columbia Univ. Press: New York, 1931; 5, 15–18.
16. *Monumenta Xylographica et Typographica; The Cradle of Printing, Part II*, Catalogue Kraus: New York, 1972; Vol. 1311;9–75.
17. *Printing and the Mind of Man;* Catalogue of the Exhibitions at the British Museum and at Earls Court London July, 16–27, 1963; Bridges and the Association of British Manufacturers of Printers' Machinery: London, U.K., 1963; 31–32.
18. Binns, N. *An Introduction to Historical Bibliography*, 2nd Ed., Rev. and Enl. Association of Assistant Librarians: London, U.K., 1962; 48, 49, 106.
19. Uhlendorf, B. A. The invention of printing and its spread till 1470 with special reference to social and economic factors. Libr. Q. July **1932**, *2*, 222.
20. Ivins, W. M. Artistic aspects of fifteenth-century printing. Pap. Bibliogr. Soc. Am. **1932**, *26*, 40–41.

BIBLIOGRAPHY

Basic Checklist

1. Burger, K. Supplement zu Hain und Panzer. Beiträge zur Inkunabelbibliographie. *Nummerconcordanz von Panzers Lateinischen und Deutschen Annalen und Ludwig Hains Repertorium Bibliographieum*; Hiersemann: Leipzig, Germany, 1908 (Reprint, Olms, Hildesheim, 1966).
2. Copinger, W.A. *Supplement to Hain's Reportorium Bibliographicum; or Collections Towards a New Edition of that Work*, Sotheran: London, U.K., 1895–1902. In two parts, the first containing nearly 7000 corrections of and additions to the collations of works described or mentioned by Hain; the second, a list with numerous collations and bibliographical particulars of nearly 6000 volumes printed in the fifteenth century, not referred to by Hain. With addenda to Parts I and II and Index by Konrad Burger, 2 Vols. in 3 (Reprint, Görlich Editore, Milan, 1950).
3. Hain, L. *Repertorium Bibliographicum, in quo Libri Omnes ab Arte Typographica Inventa usque ad Annum M. D. Typis Expressi Ordine Alphabetico vel Simpliciter Enumeratur vel Adcuratius Recensentur*, Cotta: Stuttgart, Germany, 1826–1838; 2 Vols. in 4. (Reprint, Görlich Editore, Milan, 1948).
4. Panzer, G. Wolfgang, F. *Annales Typographici, ab Artis Inventae Origine ad Annum 1500*, Zeh: Norimbergae, Germany, 1793–1797; 5 Vols.

5. Panzer, G. Wolfgang, F. *Annales Typographici, ab Anno 1501 ad Annum 1586*, Zeh: Norimbergae, Germany, 1798–1803; 6 Vols. (Reprint, Olms, Hildesheim, 1963–1964, 11 Vols.).

6. Reichling, D. *Appendices ad Hainnii–Copingeri Repertorium Bibliographicum additiones et emendationes edidit*, Görlich: Milan, Italy, 1953; 7 Vols. (Vols. 1–4 in 1, Vols. 5–7 in 2).

7. Reichling, D. *Svpplementvm (maximam partem e bibliotheeis Helvetiae collectvm) cvm indice vrbivm et typographorvm. Accedit index avctorvm generalis totivs operis* (bound with Book 2 of above).

Catalogs and Bibliographies

1. Berkowitz, D. S. *Bibliotheca Bibliographica Incunabula; A Manual of Bibliographical Guides to Inventories of Printing, of Holdings, and of Reference Aids with an Appendix of Useful Information on Place–Names and Dating; Collected and Classified for the Use of Researchers in Incunabulistics*, The Author: Waltham, MA, 1967; (Multigraph copy, 337).

2. Besterman, T. *Early Printed Books to the End of the Sixteenth Century: A Bibliography of Bibliographies*, 2nd Ed. Rowman and Littlefield: New York, 1969.

3. British Museum, Department of Printed Books. *Catalogue of Books Printed in the XVth Century now in the British Museum*, British Museum: London, U.K., 1908–1971; Parts 1–10.

4. Brunet, G. *Imprimeurs Imaginaires et Libraires Supposes; Etude Bibliographique Suivie de Recherches sur Quelques Oevrages Imprimes avec des Indications Fictives de Lieux ou avec des Dates Singulieres*, Tross: Paris, France, 1866 (Reprint, Franklin, New York, 1962).

5. Brunet, J.-C. *Manual du Libraire et de l'Amateur de Livres*, 5th Ed. Firmin Didot: Paris, France, 1860–1880, originale entierement refondue et augmentee d'un tiers, 8 Vols. in 7.

6. Butler, P. *A Check List of Fifteenth Century Books in the Newberry Library and in Other Libraries of Chicago*, Newberry Library: Chicago, IL, 1993.

7. Cambridge University Library. *Early English Printed Books in the University Library Cambridge (1475 to 1640)*, University Press: Cambridge, MA, 1900–1907; 4 Vols.

8. Duff, E.G. *Fifteenth Century English Books: A Biography of Books and Documents Printed in England and of Books for the English Market Printed Abroad*, Illustrated Monography Oxford University Press: London, U.K., 1917; Vol. 18, Printed for the Bibliographical Society (Reprint, Hain, Meisenheim, 1964).

9. Eaton, T. Bibliographical research. Libr. Trends **1964**, July 13, 42–53.

10. *Gesamtkatalog der Wiegendrucke*, Herausgegeben von der Kommission fur der Gesamtkatalog der Wiegendrucke; Hiersemann: Leipzig, Germany, 1925–1940; Vols. 1–81, A-Federicis.

11. Goff, F. *Incunabula in American Libraries; a Third Census of Fifteenth-Century Books Recorded in North American Collections*, Bibliographical Society of America: New York, 1964.

12. 2141. Graesse, J.G.T. *Tresor de Livres Rares et Precieux; ou, Noveau Dictionnaire Bibliographique*, Kuntze: Dresden, 1859–1869; 7 Vols. (Reprint, Görlich Editore, Milan, 1950, 8 Vols.).

13. Greg, W. W. *A Bibliography of the English Printed Drama to the Restoration*, Bibliographical Society: London, U.K., 1939–1957; 4 Vols.

14. Klebs, A. C. *Incunabula Scientifica et Medica*, Olms: Hildesheim, Germany, 1963.

15. McMurtie, D. C.In *The Invention of Printing: A Bibliography*; McMurtie, D. C., Adamson, J., Eds.; Chicago Club of Printing House Craftsmen: Chicago, IL, 1942, prepared as an activity of the Work Projects Administration (Illinois), Chicago Public Library Omnibus Project…section on printing bibliography, co-sponsored by the Chicago Club of Printing House Craftsmen.

16. Pellechet, M. *Catalogue général des incunables des bibliothèques publiques de France*, Krauss-Thomson: Nendeln, Liechtenstein, 1970. Avec une introduction ecrite pour la reimpression par Frederick P. Goff, 26 Vols.

17. Pollard, A. W. Redgrave, G. R. *A Short-Title Catalogue of Books Printed in England, Scotland and Ireland, and of English Books Printed Abroad, 1475–1640*, Bibliographical Society: London, U.K., 1926.

18. *Printing and the Mind of Man;* Catalogue of the Exhibitions at the British Museum and at Earls Court London July, 16–27, 1963; Bridges and the Association of British Manufacturers of Printers' Machinery: London, U.K., 1963.

19. Roberts, J. Printed books to 1640. Libr. Trends **1959**, 7, 517–536.

Handbooks and Reference Sources

1. Bowers, F. *Principles of Bibliographical Description*, Russell and Russell: New York, 1962.

2. Briquet, C. M. *Les filigranes; dictionnaire historique des marques du papier dès leur apparition vers 1282 jusqu'en 1600*, 2nd Ed. Hacker Art Books: New York, 1966; 4 Vols.

3. Cowley, J. D. *Bibliographical Description and Cataloguing*, Grafton: London, U.K., 1939.

4. Davies, H. W. *Devices of the Early Printers, 1457–1560, Their History and Development, with a Chapter on Portrait Figures of Printers*, Grafton: London, U.K., 1935.

5. Dunkin, P. S. *How to Catalogue a Rare Book*, 2nd Ed. Rev. American Library Association: Chicago, IL, 1973.

6. Glaister, G. A. *An Encyclopedia of the Book: Terms Used in Paper-Making, Printing, Bookbinding and Publishing with Notes on Illuminated Manuscripts, Bibiliophiles, Private Presses and Printing Societies*, World: Cleveland, OH, 1960, including illustrations and translated extracts from Grafisk Uppslagsbok (Esselte, Stockholm), The British edition has the title: *A Glossary of the Book.*

7. Haebler, K. *Handbuch der Inkunabelkunde*, Hiersemann: Leipzig, Germany, 1925.

8. Horne, T. H. *An Introduction to the Study of Bibliography*, G. Woodfall: London, U.K., 1814, to which is prefixed a Memoir on the Public Libraries of the Ancients. Printed for T. Cadell and W. Davies, 2 Vols. (Reprint, Gale Research, Detroit, 1967).

9. McKerrow, R. B. *Printers' and Publishers' Devices in England and Scotland, 1485–1640*, Bibliographical Society: London, U.K., 1913.

10. McKerrow, R. B. *An Introduction to Bibliography for Literary Students*, Clarendon Press: Oxford, U.K., 1928.

11. Stokes, R. *Esdaile's Manual of Bibliography*, Rev. Ed. Allen & Unwin: London, U.K., 1967.

12. Willoughby, E. E. *The Uses of Bibliography to the Students of Literature and History*, Shoe String Press: Hamden, CT, 1957.

Monographs and Collections

1. *Bibliographical Essays*; Harvard Univ. Press: Cambridge, MA, 1924. A Tribute to W. Eames.

2. Blades, W. *The Bibliography and Typography of William Caxton, England's First Printer*, Rowman and Littlefield: Totowa, 1971, with an introduction by J. Moran.

3. Bradshaw, H. *Collected Papers of Henry Bradshaw ... Comprising 1. 'Memoranda', 2. 'Communications' Read Before the Cambridge Antiquarian Society Together with an Article Contributed to the 'Bibliographer' and Two Papers not Previously Published*, University Press: Cambridge, 1889. Edited for the Syndics of the University Press.

4. Bradshaw, H. In *Henry Bradshaw's Correspondence on Incunabula with J.W. Holtrop and M.F.A.G. Campbell*; Wytze, Hellinga, L., Eds.; Menno Hertzberger: Amsterdam, the Netherlands, 1966; (i.e., 1968).

5. Bühler, C. F. *The Fifteenth Century Book; The Scribes, the Printers, the Decorators*, Univ. of Pennsylvania Press: Philadelphia, PA, 1960.

6. Consentius, E. *Die Typen der Inkunabelzeit; Eine Betrachtung*, de Gruyter: Berlin, Germany, 1929.

7. Didot, A. *Alde Manuce et l'Hellenisme a Venise*, Firmin-Didot: Paris, France, 1875.

8. Emerson, E. *Incunabulum Incunabulorium; The Gutenberg Bible on Vellum in the Vollbehr Collection; An Authentic Story of the Choicest Book of Christendom*, Tudor Press: New York, 1928.

9. Goldschmidt, E. P. *Medieval Texts and Their First Appearance in Print*, Supplement to the Bibliographical Society's Transactions University Press: Oxford, London, U.K., 1943; Vol. 16, printed for the Bibliographical Society.

10. Greg, W. W.In *Collected Papers*; Maxwell, J. C., Ed.; Clarendon Press: Oxford, U.K., 1966.

11. Hirsch, R. *Printing, Selling and Reading, 1450–1550*, Harrassowitz: Wiesbaden, Germany, 1967.

12. Hobson, G. D. *English Binding Before 1500*, University Press: Cambridge, U.K., 1929 (Sandars Lectures, 1927).

13. Jackson, W. A. *Records of a Bibliographer; Selected Papers*, Belknap Press of Harvard University: Cambridge, MA, 1967. Edited with an Introduction and Bibliography by W.H. Bond.

14. Johnson, A. F. *Type Designs; Their History and Development*, 3rd Ed. Deutsch: London, U.K., 1966.

15. Lenhart, J.M. *Pre-reformation Printed Books; A Study in Statistical and Applied Bibliography*, (Franciscan Studies, no. 14) Wagner: New York, 1935.

16. Lone, E. M. *Some Noteworthy First in Europe During the Fifteenth Century*, Lathrop C. Harper: New York, 1930.

17. Manuzio, A. P. *Aldus Manutius and His Thesaurus Cornucopiae of 1496*, Syracuse Univ. Press: Syracuse, NY, 1958. Containing the first appearance in English of the prologue in which Aldus announces his plans to publish the first printed editions of Aristotle's works and describes his *Thesaurus* as containing "practically everything that anyone could desire in order to achieve perfect knowledge of Greek literature," translated by A. Lemke.

18. Ongania, F. *Early Venetian Printing, Illustrated*, Ongania: Venice, Italy, 1958.

19. Pollard, A. W. *Early Illustrated Books; A History of the Decoration and Illustration of Books in the 15th and 16th Centuries*, Kegan Paul, Trench Trübner: London, U.K., 1903.

20. Proctor, R. *Bibliographical Essays*, Franklin: New York, 1969.

21. Schneider, G. *Theory and History of Bibliography*, Columbia Univ. Press: New York, 1934, translated by R.R. Shaw.

22. Scholderer, V. In *Fifty Essays in Fifteenth- and Sixteenth-Century Bibliography*; Rhodes, D.E., Ed.; Menno Hertzberger: Amsterdam, the Netherlands, 1966.

23. Scholderer, V. *Johann Gutenberg; The Inventor of Printing*, 2nd Ed., Rev. Trustees of the British Museum: London, U.K., 1970.

24. Schulz, E. *Collections of Incunabula and Their Value for Scholars with Special Reference to the Vollbehr Collection*, William Edwin Rudge: Mount Vernon, NY, translated by P. Spring.

25. Updike, D. B. *Printing Types, Their History, Forms and Use; A Study in Survivals*, 3rd Ed. Belknap Press: Cambridge, MA, 1962, with illustrations, 2 Vols.

26. Winship, G. P. *Gutenberg to Plantin; An Outline of the Early History of Printing*, Harvard Univ. Press: Cambridge, MA, 1926.

27. Winship, G. P. *Printing in the Fifteenth Century*, Univ. of Pennsylvania Press: Philadelphia, PA, 1940.

Serials

1. *Beitrage zur Inkunabelkunde*, Dritte Folge, Heft 1, Akademic Verlag: Berlin, 1965.

2. Bibliographical Society. *Transactions* 1893–1919; Vols. 1–15. All published of the first series. (In its second series, merged with "The Library," fourth series); Second Series, Vols. 1–26, 1920–1946, and Third Series, Vol. 1, 1947–date. Cole, G.W. An Index to Bibliographical Papers; Published by the Bibliographical Society and the Library Association, London, 1877–1932. Published for the Bibliographical Society of America at the Univ. Chicago Press, Chicago, 1933.

3. Cambridge Bibliographical Society. *Transactions*; Cambridge, 1949.

4. *Gutenberg Jahrbuch*, Gutenberg Gesellschaft: Mainz, Germany, 1926.

5. *Harvard Library Bulletin*, Cambridge, MA, 1947–1960; 1967.

6. *Huntington Library Quarterly*; Huntington Library and Art Gallery: San Marino, CA, 1937.

7. John Rylands Library. *Bulletin*, Manchester, 1903.

8. *La Bibliofilia*, Rivista di Storia del Libro e di Bibliografia: Olschki, Florence, 1899.

9. *Library Quarterly*; Univ. Chicago Press, 1931–date.

10. New York Public Library. *Bulletin*; New York, 1897.

11. Oxford Bibliographical Society. *Proceedings and Papers*; Oxford, 1923.

12. *Papers*; Bibliographical Society of America: New York, 1904.

13. *Princeton University Library Chronicle*, Princeton, 1939.

14. Simon, O., Morison, S., Eds. *The Fleuron*; University Press: Cambridge, England, 1923–1930. A journal of typography, 7 Vols.

15. *The Colophon*, 1930–1935; Vols. 1–5; New Series, Vols. 1–3, 1935–1938; New Graphic Series. Vol. 1, 1–4, 1939–1940; (See also The New Colophon); The Colophon. Index, 1930–1935. Vols. I–V, 20 parts, with a History of the Quarterly by John T. Winterich and a Listing of Types and Papers by Peter Beilenson, New York, 1935; The Colophon. The Annual of Book-Making (1927–1937), The Colophon, New York, 1938.

16. *The Dolphin*; Limited Editions Club: New York, 1933–1940; Nos. 1–4.

17. *The Library*; Oxford Univ. Press: London, 1888; Series I, Vols. 1–10; Series II, Vols. 1–10; Series III, Vols. 1–10, 1889–1919; Fourth Series, Vols. 1–26, 1920–1946; Fifth Series, Vols. 1, 1947. (From the Fourth Series on contains the Transactions of the Bibliographical Society); Cole, G. W. An Index to Bibliographical Papers, Published by the Bibliographical Society and the Library Association, London, 1877–1932. Published for the Bibliographical Society of America at the University of Chicago Press, Chicago, 1933.

18. *The New Colophon*; Duschnes Crawford: New York, 1948–1950; 3 Vols.

19. University of Virginia. In *Studies in Bibliography*; Bowers, F., Ed.; 1948–1949. Papers of the Bibliographical Society of the University of Virginia, Charlottesville, VA.

20. U.S. Library of Congress. *The Quarterly Journal*, 1943, Washington, DC.

21. Yale University Library. *Gazette*; New Haven, CT, 1926.

Indexing: History and Theory

Bella Hass Weinberg
*Division of Library and Information Science, St. John's University, Queens, New York,
New York, U.S.A.*

Abstract

The history and theory of human textual indexing are surveyed. Basic terms are defined, the extent of the
literature is discussed, and key concepts are explained, with an emphasis on thesaurus-based indexing. A
section on the consistency of human indexing leads to a discussion of automatic indexing algorithms. An
assessment of the future of human indexing concludes the entry. Pages from an early printed index and a
manuscript index illustrate the structural elements of index entries as well as features of the format of early
indexes that are still found in contemporary publications.

SCOPE AND ORGANIZATION OF THE ENTRY

The focus of this entry is on the history of indexing practices and the theory of indexing. The emphasis is on serial/database indexing, but implications are drawn for related techniques in back-of-the-book indexing, concordances, and various indexing-related activities. Other articles in this encyclopedia address a variety of related topics, such as subject headings, descriptive cataloging, metadata, thesauri, and citation indexing. Although Anderson believes that indexing and classification are the same thing,[1] this entry treats index headings that are arranged alphabetically, while hierarchical display of content indicators is discussed in other articles.

This entry begins with definitions of basic terms, proceeds to vogue words, and then surveys the literature of indexing. A history of indexing is followed by sections on the theory of indexing and on the use of thesauri in the indexing process. A discussion of the consistency of indexing serves as a segue to the section on automatic indexing, a method of content analysis that is always consistent. The entry closes with a summary and a discussion of the future prospects of indexing.

THE TERMINOLOGY OF INDEXING

Definitions of Basic Terms

An *index* leads from a known order of symbols to an unknown order of information. An index is in a different order from the document or collection to which it provides access. The card catalog of a library is a type of index. The book collection of a library is generally classified by subject. If one knows the author or title of a book of interest, one may use one's knowledge of the alphabet to locate entries for the author or title of the book in the card catalog. The bibliographic record will provide the call number of the book, which indicates its location within the classified collection.

The type of index most familiar to us is one in which the entries are arranged in alphabetical order, with *locators*, such as page references, pointing to a text that is arranged in a logical, hierarchical sequence. The most common example of this is a book index: The text is in an order established by the author, usually treating general topics before specific ones. The index arranges the terms representing specific topics alphabetically.

In discussing the history of the word *index*, Wellisch[2] noted that the term was once used to refer to many types of information structures: abstracts, titles, etc. The word *index* is still encountered today as a heading for tables of contents, although these are far less sophisticated information structures than indexes. A table of contents lists the chapter titles and headings of a systematically organized work; such a list can be generated automatically. An index, in contrast, provides efficient access to the specific topics covered in a document. Compilation of an index requires far more cerebration than does preparing a table of contents.

Although the word *index* has acquired a specific meaning, a recent article on the history of indexes[3] calls an ancient pictorial catalog—not arranged in a known order—the first index. Many finding aids on the web that are called *site indexes* are in fact *site maps*; the latter are the equivalents of tables of contents.

An index *entry* consists of three elements: a heading, a subheading, and a locator. Of these, the first and last are required, and a subheading is optional. An example of an index entry with all three elements is

Libraries
  Georgia, 365

These structural elements are found in the earliest indexes. Index entries with Roman numerals as locators can be

Encyclopedia of Library and Information Sciences, Fourth Edition DOI: 10.1081/E-ELIS4-140000154

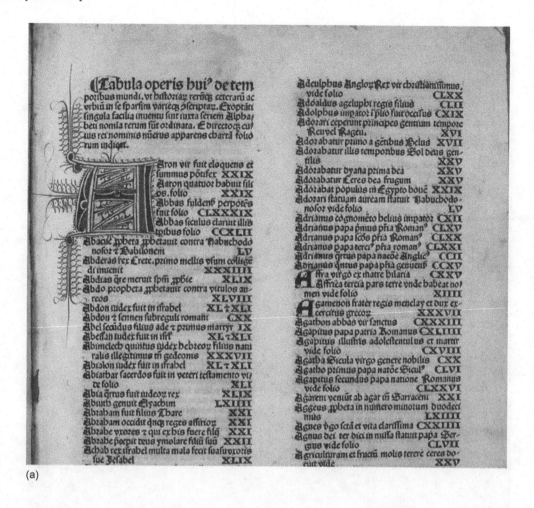

(a)

Fig. 1 (a) Part of the first page of the index to *Liber Cronicarum*, an incunable. Copyright Plantin-Moretus Museum, Antwerp (R 38.4). The introductory note begins with the word *tabula* [= index]. The locators are folio numbers in Roman numerals. The initial A was decorated by hand (cf. Fig. 1c).

seen in Figure 1a–c. Indented subheadings are in Fig. 1b. These illustrations come from an *incunable*, a book issued during the infancy of printing from movable type—before the year 1500.[4]

The sample entry above could occur in the index to a book or to a single volume of a journal. In an index to multiple volumes of a journal, a volume number would precede the page reference. In an index to *multiple journals*, the full bibliographic reference would serve as the locator:

Smith, John. Libraries in Georgia. *American Libraries* 14 (1): 25–26, January 1999.

A wide variety of locator formats has been described by Weinberg.[5] Fig. 2 illustrates the use of a homily number, rather than a page number, in a manuscript index.[6] Section number is often the locator in legal texts, while chapter and verse numbers generally constitute the locator in indexes to the Bible. Browne advocates the use of section

and paragraph numbers as locators to increase the granularity of indexing.[7]

Klement[8] has introduced the term "open- vs. closed-system indexing" to explain the difference between the indexing of journals and books, respectively. A key difference lies in the nature of subheadings for the two formats. Subheadings in books are *coined modifications*,[9] i.e., phrases formulated by the indexer, while those in journals or databases are standardized; the former are more specific. In a book index, for example, one might encounter the heading–subheading combination "caffeine: effect on sleep"; in a database index, the combination may read "caffeine—adverse effects." The introductory sections of controlled vocabularies (such as *Medical Subject Headings*) usually list their standard subdivisions along with rules for assigning them.

Both book indexes and journal indexes include (or should include) cross-references, although the number of such references should be minimized to save the time

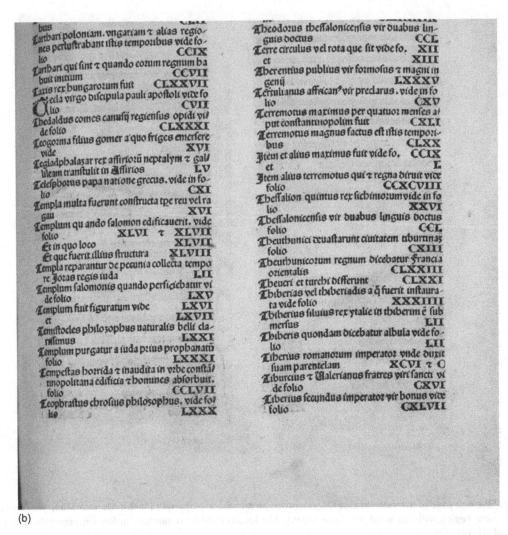

(b)

Fig. 1 (b) Part of a page with entries beginning with T from the index to *Liber Cronicarum*. Copyright Plantin-Moretus Museum, Antwerp (R 38.4). Indented subheadings are in the left-hand column.

of the user. The network of cross-references is called a *syndetic structure*, a term coined by Cutter in his guidelines for a dictionary catalog.[10] A book index has an ad hoc syndetic structure—one created by the indexer to link the synonyms and related terms relevant to that book. The cross-references in journal/database indexes are generally drawn from a thesaurus with preestablished term relationships.

Wellisch[11] has published a glossary of indexing terminology. Dictionaries of library and information science also include definitions of indexing terms.

Vogue Words

Perhaps because the compilation of an index seems as simple as the ABC, the field of indexing is subject to the general linguistic phenomenon of *vogue words*, fashionable words that may not last long in the active vocabulary of speakers. Examples of vogue words germane to the field of indexing follow.

The term *metadata*, once reserved for data about websites, has been applied retroactively to all cataloging and indexing data. A recent article on early encyclopedias and indexes calls them *knowledge management tools*.[12] This is ironic because the focus of the field of knowledge management is on the *unrecorded* information stored in experts' brains, while indexing deals with recorded documents.

Indexing is a type of *content analysis*, now often termed *knowledge representation*. (Abstracting is another type of content analysis, often done by indexers.) Amateurs call the process of assigning index terms *keywording*, although the term *keyword* usually means *free-text term*, not subject to vocabulary control. The controlled vocabularies used in indexing are now frequently called *taxonomies* or *ontologies*. Not long ago, they were called *knowledge bases*.[13]

It takes some effort to analyze the vogue words of indexing in order to determine whether they are renaming a familiar phenomenon or naming a new one.

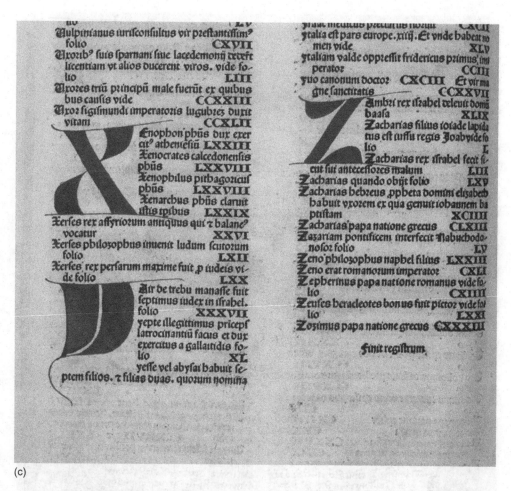

(c)

Fig. 1 (c) Part of the last page of the index to *Liber Cronicarum*, from a second copy of the incunable held by the Plantin-Moretus Museum. Copyright Plantin-Moretus Museum, Antwerp (R 9.7). The different style of the rubrics, as compared with the decorated A in (a), proves that the large initials were drawn by hand. Note the final line, "Finit registrum"; the latter word is a synonym for *tabula*, used at the head of the index.

THE LITERATURE OF INDEXING

The vastness of the literature about indexing is evident from the two book-length bibliographies on this subject compiled by Wellisch.[14] Supplements to these appeared in *The Indexer*, the primary journal of the field.[15] Recent publications on indexing have occasionally been cited in the state-of-the-art reviews entitled "The year's work in subject analysis" in *Library Resources & Technical Services*,[16] the journal of the division of the American Library Association that is most concerned with cataloging. The journal *Knowledge Organization* (formerly *International Classification*) until 2008 had a current-awareness bibliography[17] that included many items germane to the field of indexing. Current issues (2017) have a column entitled "Books Recently Published." State-of-the-art reviews on subject analysis in general, or on special aspects of indexing, were published periodically in the *Annual Review of Information Science and Technology*, which ceased publication in 2011.[18] Coe reviewed the literature on the usability of book indexes.[19] Bell published a bibliography on the indexing of biographies and fiction.[20]

The subject of indexing is also covered by the major print indexes and databases in the field of library and information science. Reviews of books on indexing have been collected in an anthology by Weinberg.[21]

Several editions of a standard for indexes were approved by the American National Standards Institute (ANSI).[22] The most recent revision failed to achieve consensus among the Voting Representatives of the National Information Standards Organization (formerly ANSI Committee Z39); the draft standard was published as a technical report.[23] There are British and international standards for indexing as well; the British adopted the 1996 international standard[24] as their own. Related standards were surveyed by Shuter.[25] A standard for indexes to e-books is under development.[26] These standards cover the principles and the format of indexes; the *process* of indexing is detailed in book-length manuals.

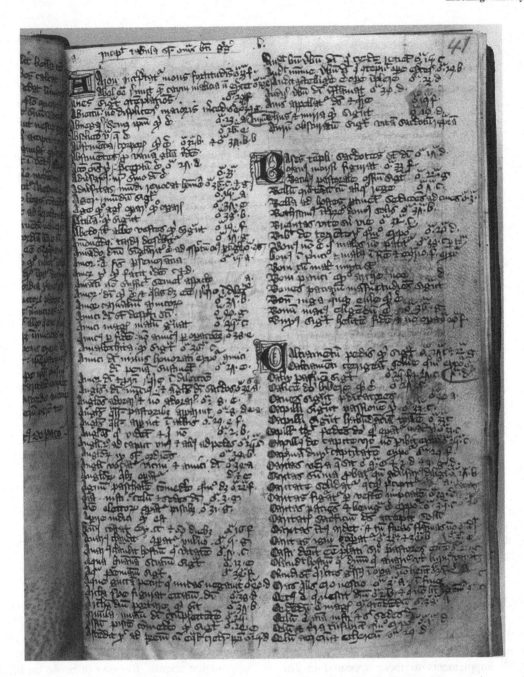

Fig. 2 Initial page of the manuscript index to the homilies of St. Gregory. Copyright Plantin-Moretus Museum, Antwerp (M 216).

DISCIPLINES RELATED TO INDEXING

The preceding section on the literature of indexing provides some clues as to the disciplines related to indexing. The primary one is information science, formerly called *documentation*, with an emphasis on the detailed analysis of information contained in documents. Indexing is often taught in schools of library and information science, but about 50% of book indexers lack a degree in library and information science, and many journal/database indexers are trained in-house.

Indexing is germane to every discipline. The National Library of Medicine has rigorous rules for indexing the literature that it acquires.[27] The policies of databases in other disciplines are often unpublished.

A discipline particularly concerned with indexing is genealogy, as the indexing of names is the primary focus of genealogists. Indexing manuals used to have their own rules for the formulation of name headings, but in recent years these manuals deferred to the rules of the library cataloging community published in *Anglo-American Cataloguing Rules*, 2nd ed. (AACR2), which as of June 5, 2007, is no longer updated.[28] AACR2 has been replaced by RDA (*Resource Description and Access*). Appendix F of the 2014[29] edition of RDA contains guidelines for names in some languages other than English. Spidal discussed these cataloging codes as well as other sources of name headings.[30]

The international journal *The Indexer* has since 2006 been publishing a series of "Centrepieces" focusing on rules for formulating headings for names in a variety of languages;[31] these articles provide more detailed guidance than AACR2 or RDA on the entry element of names in languages other than English, such as La Fontaine, Da Vinci, and Van der Camp.

The expansion of the Internet has stimulated interest in the history of the book and the organization of information. Evidence for this statement is the large number of books and articles published since the year 2000 that deal with the history of books and the impact of printing. Scholars of intellectual history and the Renaissance often write about early indexes and the encyclopedists. The literature of indexing is thus widely scattered. In documenting the history of citation indexes, Weinberg[32] observed that early Hebrew citation indexes were described in journals in the field of religion, not in the literature of information science.

Indexing is of interest not only to academic communities but also to individuals, both scholars and laypersons. Within the context of information science, Jones[33] has written about personal information management, which includes indexing the documents that one decides to keep. "Professional organizers" provide advice on the organization of personal files, focusing on the creation of category structures in which to file personal papers. Weinberg[34] has reviewed a great many manuals authored by professional organizers and found most of the indexing advice incorrect. Many of these manuals advise their readers to file personal papers under the *broadest* heading they can think of, while *specificity* is considered praiseworthy in the field of indexing. Golub[35] cites studies of how people organize their machine-readable files, notably e-mail.

HISTORY OF INDEXING

An index is a form of auxiliary memory. Historian Daniel Boorstin[36] observed that indexing begins when memory declines. If one has not memorized a text that one has read, an index helps one locate the passage(s) of interest quickly, obviating the need for a sequential search of the text. An index also serves those who have *not* read the text. The title pages of early printed books (in Hebrew as well as Latin) that contain indexes often mention their time-saving nature.

Our knowledge of the history of indexing is limited because so much of the evidence has been destroyed by the ravages of time, the burning of books, and the fragility of materials on which information has been recorded. This is especially true for Hebrew books, which were often subjected to censorship and burnings. Furthermore, as Beit-Arié pointed out,[37] Hebrew books tended to be copied for personal use, while Latin books were copied in institutional settings, notably monasteries. In comparing the state of early Hebrew citation indexes with manuscripts of the first Latin citation index, Weinberg[38] commented on the beautiful calligraphy and ornamentation in the latter.

Kilgour[39] described the underlining of keywords in red in hieroglyphics documents. This is analogous to the marking of *indexable matter* (terms to be indexed) on the page proofs of books. Berger[40] detailed the history of alphabetical order, which is essential to many indexes. Witty[41] published one of the first papers on the history of indexing, beginning from antiquity and proceeding to the Middle Ages. Witty emphasized the concept of the *known order* of index entries as a means of facilitating access to written records.

Wellisch[42] dated the origins of indexing to a fourth-century Greek work entitled *Apothegmata*, a collection of sayings of the Church Fathers. Weinberg[43] has demonstrated that most early indexes were in the domain of religion, which was considered the "queen of sciences" in the Middle Ages. Fig. 2, a page from a manuscript index to the homilies of Pope Gregory, illustrates this point. Painting-Stubbs wrote about the early English indexes (1576–1587) of Abraham Fleming, many of which provided access to religious books.[44]

Richard and Mary Rouse[45] have described the earliest Latin Biblical concordances (word indexes), which date back to the early thirteenth century. Sophisticated concordances contained the three elements of index entries: a word from the Bible (the heading), the phrase in which the word occurs (subheading), and the chapter number (locator). Weinberg[46] has demonstrated that selected lists of words from the Hebrew Bible were compiled by the Masoretes at least three centuries earlier, while Busa[47] theorized that concordances to the Bible probably existed in the seventh century.

Rouse[48] stated that subject indexes were invented in France; some of those compiled in the thirteenth century have sophisticated features, such as networks of cross-references. Weinberg[49] described medieval indexes and concordances compiled in France, analyzing their structure and format. Failing to cite Wellisch, Cevolini[50] cites Rouse and other authors who believe that indexing began in the thirteenth century. Humphreys posited that the oldest index is the 3000-yr-old *I Ching*, as she translated its hexagram structure into that of an alphabetical index.[51]

Among the features of medieval indexes that are emulated today is the *introductory note*, which explains the structure of locators or some other aspect of an index. Introductory notes are evident in Figs. 1a and 2. Early printed indexes emulated the format of manuscript indexes, as was noted by Wellisch.[52] This can be seen in Fig. 1a and c, which contain images from two copies of an incunable (a book from the infancy of printing, i.e., fifteenth century) with initial letters calligraphed in different styles.

Thesauri are considered to be an invention of the middle of the twentieth century, but work on synonym control and lexicography dates back to the ancient period. Krovetz[53] has demonstrated that hierarchical relationships are embedded in definitions, e.g., "a *horse* is a *mammal*." Thus, the roots of broader-term relationships in thesauri are in early dictionaries. Hlava[54] reviews the history of such relationships, i.e., taxonomy.

Multilingual thesauri are considered a modern phenomenon, but Wellisch[55] has described medieval multilingual herbals, in which plant names were provided in several languages and scripts. Wellisch[42] also described a graphic display of relationships among index entries in an incunable.

Vocabulary switching is viewed as a contemporary problem, but sophisticated work was done in the 1930s on the translation of the American Library Association's subject headings into Library of Congress subject headings.[56]

Wellisch[57] described and translated a sixteenth-century manual of indexing written by Conrad Gessner, the "Father of bibliography." Gessner provided detailed instructions for the technique of indexing: one should write index entries on sheets of paper and then cut the entries apart in order to arrange them in the desired order. In the twenty-first century, this method may seem laughable, but it is not as obsolete as one may think. As president of the American Society of Indexers, I chaired the jury of the H. W. Wilson Award for Excellence in Indexing; the award-winning indexer used a technique similar to that of Gessner: typing entries on adding-machine tape and later cutting them apart and alphabetizing them!

The Society of Indexers (in England) recently reprinted an early twentieth-century manual of indexing, considered a classic.[58] Wheatley's book devoted a lot of attention to the format of indexes, but he also articulated important principles of indexing that are still cited. His dictum "one index, indivisible" is often violated in contemporary works, resulting in confusion on the part of the user of books with multiple indexes, online catalogs with unclear search options (e.g., subject/keyword), or websites that lack a single search box and require the user to select a category.

In sum, content analysis is an ancient activity; sophisticated indexes were created in the medieval period; and work on vocabulary switching antedates online searching and the Internet era.

THEORY OF INDEXING

Indexing is not really a theory-based profession. John O'Connor's dictum, "Good indexing permits good retrieval" (stated at a conference of the American Society for Information Science), crystallizes the essence of the field, emphasizing its practical purpose. Principles of indexing have been inferred from practice. Wellisch[59] criticized the high percentage of articles about indexing that describe individual projects without reference to principles or the prior literature.

Jonker[60] wrote a book of indexing theory that was cited in Borko's paper "Toward a theory of indexing."[61] Svenonius[62] questioned the theoretical basis of indexing and suggested directions for research, while noting the methodological difficulties of comparing indexing systems with different structures. Quinn[63] reviewed more recent theoretical approaches, focusing on the subjectivity of indexing and on attempts to delineate the steps in the indexing process. Quinn also noted the lack of American theoretical contributions to the literature of indexing and classification.

The textbook of indexing authored by Lancaster[64] records important principles, such as specificity, and demonstrates that all so-called theories of indexing in fact are not. He devoted particular attention to the "axioms" of Robert Fugmann. And yet, Hjorland has classified theories of indexing, including his own.[65]

A key concept in the indexing literature is *aboutness*. Weinberg[66] has suggested that the linguistic concepts of *topic* and *comment* should be applied to enhance the quality of indexes. This would, for example, facilitate the retrieval of documents containing negative views of a topic while excluding those with positive views. Andersen and Christensen[67] also took a linguistic approach to indexing theory, suggesting that it be based on a philosophy of language, with particular attention to the theory of meaning. The authors applied the ideas of Ludwig Wittgenstein to indexing by stating that this process must take into account the social, historical, and linguistic contexts of documents.

While there is no generally accepted theory of indexing, there are standard measures of the characteristics of indexes. *Exhaustivity* of indexing is measured by the number of terms assigned to a document, such as a journal article, or by the number of index entries assigned to a page in a book. Weinberg[68] discussed the exhaustivity of indexes in books, journals, and full text. She has attempted to get the indexing community to use the terms *entry* and *heading* consistently because the definition of entry has implications for the fee structure of indexers.[69,70] Weinberg's letters to *Key Words* contain numerous references to publications on the density of indexing and related terminology. For example, the following line of an index with a heading and multiple locators represents four entries, although some indexers charge by the number of *lines* in an index:

Libraries, 40, 86, 112, 256

Density and *depth* of indexing are often-used synonyms for exhaustivity, although Wellisch[71] defined depth of indexing as a combination of exhaustivity and specificity. Anderson[72] has explained *specificity* as "goodness of fit"; in other words, a term in isolation cannot be called specific; its specificity can be evaluated only with reference to the text being indexed. For example, the term Birds is a specific descriptor for an article about birds in general, but it is not specific for an article about robins.

Ranganathan[73] developed the concept of *coextensiveness* of classification numbers and index terms, i.e., that the full scope of a document should be expressed in a single classification number or index term. For example, if a document deals with the topic "The manufacture of silk shirts in 20th-century Italy," Ranganathan believed that all facets of the topic should be represented in one classification number, synthesized from the elements that designate the key concepts. Alternatively, a single indexing string should contain all the concepts in a specified order.

The use of machines in the indexing process led to the concepts of *precoordination* (combination of terms at the indexing stage) and *postcoordination* (combination of terms at the searching stage). An example of a precoordinated index entry is the heading–subheading combination "Boston—Museums." In a postcoordinate system, the two terms would be indexed separately and combined only at the searching stage. Kilgour[74] wrote that the latter system began to replace precoordinated subject indexing in the mid-1930s. Taube[75] worked extensively in the 1950s and 1960s on the development of [post]coordinate indexing.

Although postcoordination has been presented as superior to precoordinate indexing, the disadvantages of the former method of indexing have been pointed out by several experts in the organization of information and summarized by Weinberg.[76] Milstead[77] noted that it is not a question of better or worse: precoordination is the *only* appropriate method in the print environment. Human beings were not designed to compare lists of document numbers posted to keywords in order to locate a combination of concepts. In using printed indexes or card catalogs, humans require subheadings in order to quickly locate documents that deal with the aspect of interest.

Soon after the implementation of postcoordinate indexing, it was recognized that the loss of word order led to many *false drops*, i.e., the retrieval of documents that were not relevant to the query. If one were seeking information on the Philosophy of History, for example, one would retrieve documents on the History of Philosophy. To deal with this problem, information scientists developed the devices of *roles* and *links* to connect related descriptors. It was quickly recognized that these artificial devices were not assigned consistently, and they were abandoned. Weinberg[78] has reviewed many complex indexing systems that were dropped, including those based

on contemporary linguistic theories. Craven[79] described numerous *string indexing* systems—systems in which a set of terms is selected by a human indexer but manipulated by computer.

In library and information science, there has long been a distinction between technical services and public services. But just as reference librarians must understand the structure of a catalog, so must online search intermediaries understand how databases are indexed. Kesselman and Perry[80] have discussed this, with particular reference to the way precoordinated or multiword terms are processed by online vendors. Searching is the obverse of indexing. As searching of the World Wide Web by end users has increased, consultation of fee-based databases has declined.

Frohmann[81] criticized those who wrote about the mental process of indexing. Anderson responded to the criticisms in his textbook.[82] Bates[83] reviewed research findings on indexing that are germane in the Internet era. She focused on the mismatch between the terms used by the indexer and the searcher, the inconsistency of naming concepts and objects, and on folk classification. The last-mentioned topic is currently receiving a lot of attention in the context of social networks and tagging by laypersons.

Indexing is an art, not a science. Many intelligent people lack the ability to distill the essence of a document and to represent its main topics in a few words. Some people who have gone through formal training will never make good indexers, while others who are self-taught are excellent indexers and have even won awards in the field.

An indexer must be something of a prophet—envisioning the concepts likely to be sought by users of a document, expressing those concepts in terms likely to be sought by users, and providing cross-references from synonyms and alternative spellings as well as links to related terms to assist users in finding all the information that is relevant to their topics of interest.

THE USE OF THESAURI IN INDEXING

This section explains how the features of thesauri are used in the indexing process. The most common term for a preferred heading in a thesaurus, i.e., a term that may be assigned in indexing, is *descriptor*. Numerous synonyms exist for descriptor, including *postable term*, i.e., a term on which index entries may be "posted."

An indexer scans a document and thinks of terms that represent its "aboutness." If the term selected by the indexer is a synonym of the preferred term in the thesaurus, there will (or should) be a USE reference from the nonpreferred term to the descriptor, e.g., "attorneys USE lawyers." If the term selected by the indexer is more specific than any of the descriptors, the thesaurus may provide a USE reference from a *quasi-synonym* (not a true synonym), e.g., "chairs USE furniture." The reciprocal of USE is UF (Used For). By examining the terms coded UF, the indexer sees which terms are considered equivalent:

> lawyers
>> UF attorneys
>>> barristers

The rationale for the USE/UF relationship is that the time of the user will be saved if information is not scattered among synonymous or nearly synonymous headings. The equivalent of USE in book indexes is the command *see*.

A descriptor may be followed by a scope note (SN) that tells the indexer when to assign the term; SNs often refer to related headings. An example of an SN that does this is taken from the Educational Resources Information Center (ERIC) Thesaurus.[84]

Occupational Home Economics

> SN formal preparation for occupations using home economics knowledge and skills—below the baccalaureate level. (Note: For the baccalaureate level and above, use "Home Economics Education.")

A study conducted in Israel found that for nearly a third of the index terms assigned to books by librarians using a Hebrew thesaurus, there was no information relating to those terms in the books.[85] This was explained by the lack, or inadequacy, of SNs in the thesaurus used for indexing.

A thesaurus record for a descriptor often displays narrower terms, coded NT. If an indexer has selected too general a term, the NTs lead the indexer to the most specific term available:

> plants
>> NT flowers

> flowers
>> NT roses

Reference librarians are well aware that users express their information needs in more general terms than they actually require; such librarians are trained to draw out the true information need via a reference interview. When users consult indexes on their own, the downward cross-references serve this function. In a book index, *see also* is the (rough) equivalent of NT.

The reciprocal of NT is BT, for *broader term*. BTs set the hierarchical context of a descriptor:

> flowers
>> BT plants

Some indexing systems have the practice of *upposting*, i.e., assigning a more general term in addition to the descriptor that matches the scope of the document. In older subject heading lists and in book indexes, *see also* references to BTs are usually not provided, although some argue that such cross-references would be especially useful to children, who may have a hard time thinking of BTs if they find little information on a specific topic of interest. For example, if the subject of interest is Turtles, and all the books on that subject have been borrowed from the library, a child may not think to look under the broader term Reptiles.

The final code for semantic relationships in standard thesaurus format is RT, for *related term*. RTs are descriptors that are neither broader nor narrower than the selected term, but semantically related to it. Usually, RT relationships in thesauri are symmetrical: Gold RT Money; Money RT Gold. In older subject heading lists and in book indexes, RT is represented as *see also* in both directions. In light of recent studies of user persistence, showing that laypersons input one or two words to a search box and do not try synonyms or related terms if the search fails, RT references are essential to help users modify or expand their searches.

USE references are called *prescriptive*; they give an instruction to the indexer: You may not use this term; you must use the preferred term. BTs, NTs, and RTs are *suggestive* references; they ask the indexer to consider other terms that may be more appropriate for the document in hand.

James Anderson believes that indexers should not be constrained by controlled vocabularies. (He has expressed this opinion at conferences of the American Society for Information Science.) Anderson recommends that indexers assign the terms they feel are appropriate, and that *post-control* be done by a thesaurus editor: identifying synonyms and related terms, and coding them appropriately.

In indexing operations that use thesauri, indexers are (or should be) encouraged to propose new terms and semantic relationships through paper or electronic forms. The speed with which new terms are added to an indexing thesaurus affects users' perceptions of the quality of an index. Obsolete descriptors make a poor impression.

Some indexing operations use a combination of descriptors and *identifiers*. ERIC has descriptors for topical terms, and *identifiers* for proper names and newly minted terms. ERIC has been controlling (i.e., standardizing) its proper name identifiers, just as libraries establish name headings in authority files. Topical identifiers in ERIC, such as *burnout*, may later be upgraded to descriptors.

Some indexing systems have a combination of descriptors and *free terms*; the latter are uncontrolled terms made up by the indexer, usually for highly specific topics not represented in the thesaurus. Keywords made up by authors may also complement the descriptors assigned by indexers, as is mentioned in Wikipedia's article on "Subject indexing."[86]

A wide variety of thesaurus display formats and codes exist. These are explained in the NISO thesaurus standard.[87] Translating one structure into another requires considerable training. Indexers as well as searchers—not to mention end users—may not comprehend the structure of complex thesauri, and this may affect the quality of indexing and retrieval.

Most members of indexing societies work on books, creating ad hoc syndetic structures, as was noted earlier. Workshops and tutorials about thesauri are increasingly being offered to such indexers.[88] Thesauri may be constructed to enhance searching, i.e., they operate behind the scenes to add synonyms and, perhaps, related terms, to the search terms input by an end user. Studies of this practice have been reviewed by Shiri.[89] Errors in, and omissions from, Shiri's references to thesaurus standards are in a review of his book.[90] Hlava[91] describes more recent standards for thesauri.

One of the rationales for indexing with a thesaurus is that this enhances consistency. Indexing consistency is considered a measure of indexing quality; this is discussed in the following section.

CONSISTENCY OF INDEXING

The fact that there are no rigorous theories or rules for indexing is reflected in the repeated finding that human indexing is highly inconsistent. A thorough review of the literature on indexing consistency published through 1975 was done by Leonard.[92] Saracevic,[93] who conducted an important study of the consistency of *searching*, cited more recent studies of indexing consistency and observed that in all phenomena related to words, consistency rarely exceeds 25%. This has become evident in the Internet environment, with social tagging, i.e., the assignment of "keywords" by laypersons, as is noted by Golub.[94]

It is to be expected that terms assigned to electronic documents and images by those not trained in indexing will be highly inconsistent, but a low percentage of inter-indexer consistency is obtained even among professionals using a controlled vocabulary.

As Lancaster pointed out, there is no single correct set of index terms for a document.[95] Indexing may be slanted to the purpose of an organization, in which case it is called *mission-oriented* indexing. Stibic's book on personal documentation for professionals[96] takes this idea to the level of an individual. Index terms assigned by individuals may have nothing to do with "aboutness."

INDEXING THEORY AND AUTOMATIC INDEXING

One of the arguments for automatic indexing is that it is always perfectly consistent. In order to develop an algorithm for automatic indexing, one must have a theory of human indexing. Most of the early algorithms for automatic indexing were statistically based: they theorized either that the most frequent words—excluding function words (e.g., *the*, *for*)—in a text are the content indicators, that the rarest words in a collection are significant, or that terms that are relatively more frequent in a single document than in a collection are significant. In research done for her dissertation, Weinberg[97] tested all these theories and found that none of them yields results that match those of human indexing.

Another approach to automatic indexing is *positional*. It is based on the assumption that words in certain fields, such as titles and figure legends, are significant. Human indexers also look closely at such components of a document to select index terms. In fact, an international standard[98] suggests doing precisely this.

Most automatic indexing is *extractive* (or *derivative*) indexing—pulling out terms from a recorded text, while human indexing entails *assignment* indexing—assigning terms from a controlled vocabulary, or composing index headings and subheadings without reference to a standardized list. Terms assigned by humans may not occur in the text at all, or they may appear as morphological variants of the standardized term, e.g., *registration* (a noun) for *register* (a verb in the text).

The main reason that automatic indexing algorithms fail to do a thorough job of content analysis is that a substantial percentage of humanly assigned index terms are not expressed in the text. Human beings are good at identifying concepts that are not explicitly named in a text; computers perform poorly in this regard.

Machine-aided indexing projects include those that have a computer select terms from a text and then consult a machine-readable thesaurus. If a synonym of the selected text term is the preferred term in the thesaurus, the computer assigns the latter to the document. An early system of this kind was implemented at the American Petroleum Institute;[99] that system still serves as the basis of Machine Aided Indexer, a software package of Data Harmony. Hlava's *Taxobook* includes a screenshot of this software in which a pop-up window displays suggested terms for assignment to a text.[100]

At information science conferences, the concern has been expressed that when computers suggest terms to indexers, these people will view the machines as oracles and will accept the suggestions without evaluation of their validity and without thinking of errors of omission.

Most of the early experiments on automatic indexing were done on journal articles. For a short while, a product was available whose developers claimed could index books automatically. Two prominent indexers tested the product and wrote such a critical review of it in 1994[101] that the software was withdrawn from the market. Fifteen years later, a software package called TExtract received mixed reviews.[102]

Book indexers use specialized software to assist them with the clerical aspects of indexing, but term selection and entry formulation are done by human beings. As Hirschmann observed in 2011, "Although we currently have several tools that assist in the preparation of back-of-the-book indexes, their preparation by computers without human intervention seems to be beyond their reach, at least for now."[103]

SUMMARY

Indexing is an intellectual activity with a practical purpose—fast retrieval of information. This activity began in ancient times and was highly developed in the Middle Ages.

The selection of content indicators is not subject to rigorous rules, but a scholarly terminology has been developed to characterize various aspects of indexing, such as its depth, and whether the index terms are pre- or postcoordinate. Theories of the mental process of indexing have been subjected to sharp criticism. Indexing remains an art.

FUTURE PROSPECTS

In the late 1990s, I was asked by an editor of *The Indexer* to predict the future of indexing after the millennium. Many of the observations made in that article[104] remain true 25 years later.

The paperless society has arrived far less quickly than predicted. Despite improvements in the format of e-books, traditional books continue to be printed, and the nonfiction ones (at least) require indexes.

Automatic indexing experiments on journal articles have not eliminated human indexers and thesaurus designers. In fact, indexers have found new markets in developing indexes for websites, as many users recognize the limitations of keyword retrieval. Browne and Jermey[105] produced a manual of website indexing that covers both concepts and software.

Anderson[72] expressed the view that only important documents merit human indexing; the rest should be indexed by machine. In the Middle Ages, texts in the domain of religion were considered important and thus received detailed indexes. Today, medical texts are more likely to get thorough indexes, compiled by a professional. When the managers of an organization realize the advantages of fast and thorough access to information, they will pay for the compilation of indexes to printed corporate documents as well as websites.

The Semantic Web is a nice vision, but far from being implemented. As Moore wrote, "The semantic web has so far failed to live up to the initial hype surrounding it at the turn of the millennium."[106] Many of the writers on the Semantic Web seem to have no background in library–information science. Northedge demonstrated that the origins of *topic maps*, which are considered a Semantic Web technology, lie in indexing.[107]

There must be substantial advances in computational linguistics and natural language processing before the need for human indexing is eliminated. Artandi[108] made a similar observation more than four decades ago: ". . . additional research is needed, both in linguistics and in the theory of indexing, to develop methods which will compare favorably with good human indexing."

The recent founding of indexing societies in countries including China, South Africa, Germany, and the Netherlands—as documented in *The Indexer*[109]— provides evidence for the viability of the profession of indexing and for international interest in the principles and best practices of providing efficient access to information.

ACKNOWLEDGMENTS

Much of the historical research reported in this entry was done with travel grants from the Eugene Garfield Foundation. I am grateful to all the libraries that graciously afforded me access to their rare indexes.

REFERENCES

1. Anderson, J.D. Indexing and classification: File organization and display for information retrieval. In *Indexing: The State of Our Knowledge and the State of Our Ignorance*. Proceedings of the 20th Annual Meeting of the American Society of Indexers, New York, May 13, 1998; Weinberg, B.H., Ed.; Learned Information: Medford, NJ, 1989; 69–77.
2. Wellisch, H.H. Index: The word, its history and meanings. In *Indexing from A to Z*, 2nd Ed.; H.W. Wilson: New York, 1996; 199–213.
3. Beare, G. Past, present and future. Indexer **2007**, *25* (4), 257–264.
4. Schedel, H. Liber Cronicarum cum Figures et Ymaginibus ab Inicio Mundi; Koberger: Nurimberge, 1493, (The unpaginated index precedes the foliated text.) Museum Plantin-Moretus R 9.7; R 38.4.
5. Weinberg, B.H. Known orders: Unusual locators in indexes. Indexer **2007**, *25* (4), 243–252.
6. Tabula super omelias beati Gregorii pape super Evangelia. In Sermons de St. Augustin (folios 41–45); 14th c. (The text of the homilies is on folios 261–328. A list of the 40 homilies is on folio 336.) Museum Plantin-Moretus M 216.
7. Browne, G. Section and paragraph number indexing. Indexer **2012**, *30* (4), 177–179.
8. Klement, S. Open-system versus closed-system indexing: A vital distinction. Indexer **2002**, *23* (1), 23–31.
9. Borko, H.; Bernier, C.L. *Indexing Concepts and Methods*; Academic Press: New York, 1978; 17.

10. Cutter, C.A. *Rules for a Printed Dictionary Catalogue*; Government Printing Office: Washington, DC, 1876; 15. (Public Libraries in the United States of America: Their History, Condition, and Management: Special Report, Part II.).

11. Wellisch, H. *Glossary of Terminology in Abstracting, Classification, Indexing and Thesaurus Construction*, 2nd Ed.; Information Today: Medford, NJ, 2000.

12. Zedelmaier, H. *Facilitas inveniendi*: The alphabetical index as a knowledge management tool. Indexer **2007**, *25* (4), 235–241.

13. Weinberg, B.H. Vogue words in information science. Bull. Am. Soc. Inform. Sci. **1990**, *16* (4), 15.

14. Wellisch, H. *Indexing and Abstracting: An International Bibliography*; Clio Press: Santa Barbara, CA, 1980, Supplement 1984.

15. Wheeler, J. Indexing: A current awareness bibliography. Indexer **1993–1998**, *15* (1)–*16* (4).

16. Stone, A.T. That elusive concept of "Aboutness": The year's work in subject analysis, 1992. Libr. Resour. Tech. Serv. **1993**, *37* (3), 277–298. [Web of Science ®], [CSA].

17. Knowledge organization literature. Knowl. Organ. 1993, *20* (last column: 2008, *35* (4)); formerly Classification literature. Int. Classif. 1974, *1* (1). Replaced by a column entitled Books recently published; latest issue examined **2017**, *44* (1).

18. Annual Review of Information Science and Technology. American Society for Information Science: Washington, DC, 1966; Vol. 1, Examples (in chronological order) include: Lancaster, F.M.; Elliker, C.; Connell, T.H. Subject analysis. **1989**, *24*, 35–84; Hjorland, B.; Nielsen, L.K.; Subject access points in electronic retrieval. **2001**, *35*, 249–298; Rasmussen, E.M. Indexing and retrieval for the Web. **2003**, *37*, 91–124; Smeaton, A.F. Indexing, browsing and searching of digital video. **2004**, *38*, 371–407; Khoo, C.S.G.; Na, J.C. Semantic relations in information science. **2006**, *40*, 157–228; Legg, C. Ontologies on the Semantic Web. **2007**, *41*, 407–451; Hunter, J. Collaborative semantic tagging and annotation systems. **2009**, *43*, 187–239; La Barre, K. Facet analysis. **2010**, *44*, 243–284; Blake, C. Text mining. **2011**, *45*, 123–155.

19. Coe, M. Where is the evidence?: A review of the literature on the usability of book indexes. Indexer **2014**, *32* (4), 161–168.

20. Bell, H.K. A bibliography for indexing lives. Indexer **2012**, *30* (3), 147.

21. Weinberg, B.H. *Can You Recommend a Good Book on Indexing?: Collected Reviews on the Organization of Information*; Information Today: Medford, NJ, 1998.

22. American National Standards Institute *USA Standard Basic Criteria for Indexes*, ANSI: New York, 1968, USAS Z39.4-1968 (R1974); reaffirmed 1974. Revision: American National Standard for Library and Information Sciences and Related Publishing Practices: *Basic Criteria for Indexes*, ANSI Z39.4-1984.

23. Anderson, J.D., Ed. *Guidelines for Indexes and Related Information Retrieval Devices*, NISO Technical Report 2. NISO Press: Bethesda, MD, 1997.

24. International Organization for Standardization. Information and Documentation: *Guidelines for the Content, Organization and Presentation of Indexes*; ISO: Geneva, Switzerland, 1996, ISO 999: 1996 (E).

25. Shuter, J. New and revised indexing standards. Indexer **2008**, *26* (2), 96.

26. Combs, M.; Ream, D.K. Understanding the IDF EPUB3 indexes specification. Indexer **2014**, *32* (3), 121–129.

27. Charen, T. MEDLARS Indexing Manual, Pt. 2; National Library of Medicine: Bethesda, MD, 1983, PB 84-104280; Current indexing policies are published on the Library's website: http://www.nlm.nih.gov.

28. Anglo-American Cataloguing Rules, 2nd Ed.; American Library Association: Chicago, IL, 1978. Revised 1988, 1998; issued in looseleaf format (2002–2007).

29. RDA: Resource Description and Access. American Library Association: Chicago, Il, 2014.

30. Cataloging rules and tools: An aid for the indexing of names. Indexer **2012**, *30* (4), 186–190.

31. Centrepiece: Indexing personal names. Indexer **2006**, *25* (2). Other Centrepieces you might find useful [bibliography]. Indexer **2011**, *29* (2), C20. Bridge, N. Personal names as phrases. Indexer **2011**, *29* (4), C1–C4.

32. Weinberg, B.H. The earliest Hebrew citation indexes. J. Am. Soc. Inform. Sci. **1997**, *48* (4), 318–330. Reprinted with a postscript in Historical Studies in Information Science; Hahn, T.B., Buckland, M., Eds.; Information Today: Medford, NJ, 1998; 51–63. [CrossRef], [Web of Science ®], [CSA].

33. Jones, W. Personal information management. Ann. Rev. Inform. Sci. Technol. **2007**, *41*, 453–504. [CrossRef], [Web of Science ®].

34. Weinberg, B.H. Indexing advice in publications on paper management. Indexer **2003**, *23* (4), 218–223.

35. Golub, K. *Subject Access to Information: An Interdisciplinary Approach*; Libraries Unlimited: Santa Barbara, CA, 2015; 30.

36. Boorstin, D. *The Discoverers*; Random House: New York, 1983; 485.

37. Beit-Arié, M. *Hebrew Manuscripts of East and West: Towards a Comparative Codicology*; British Library: London, U.K., 1983; 81.

38. Weinberg, B.H. Predecessors of scientific indexing structures in the domain of religion. In *The History and Heritage of Scientific and Technological Information Systems*, Proceedings of the 2002 Conference; Rayward, W.B., Bowden, M.E., Eds.; Information Today: Medford, NJ, 2004; 126–134.

39. Kilgour, F. Brief communication: Locating information in an Egyptian text of the 17th century B.C . J. Am. Soc. Inform. Sci. **1993**, *44* (5), 292–297. [Web of Science ®], [CSA].

40. Berger, J. Indexation, memory, power, and representations at the beginning of the 12th century: The rediscovery of pages from the tables to the *Liber de Honoribus*, the first cartulary of the Collegiate Church of St. Julian of Auvergne (Brioude). Indexer **2006**, *25* (2), 95–99.

41. Witty, F.J. The beginnings of indexing and abstracting: Some notes towards a history of indexing and abstracting in antiquity and the Middle Ages. Indexer **1973**, *8* (4), 193–198.

42. Wellisch, H.H. Indexing. In *Encyclopedia of Library History*; Wiegand, W., Davis, D., Eds.; Garland: New York, 1994; 268–270.

43. Weinberg, B.H. Indexes and religion: Reflections on research in the history of indexes. Indexer **1999**, *21* (3), 111–118. [CSA].

44. Painting-Stubbs, C. Abraham Fleming: Elizabethan maker of indexes and 'tables'. Indexer **2011**, *29* (3), 109–113.

45. Rouse, R.H.; Rouse, M.A. Concordances et index. In *Mise en Page et Mise en Texte du Livre Manuscrit*; Martin, H., Vezin, J., Eds.; Editions du Cercle: Paris, France, 1990; 218–228.

46. Weinberg, B.H. Index structures in early Hebrew Biblical word lists: Preludes to the first Latin concordances. Indexer **2001**, *22* (4), 178–186. [CSA].

47. Busa, R. Concordances. In *Encyclopedia of Library and Information Science*; Kent, A., Lancour, H., Eds.; Marcel Dekker: New York, 1971; 592–604.

48. Rouse, R.H.; Rouse, M.A. *Preachers, Florilegia and Sermons: Studies on the 'Manipulus florum' of Thomas of Ireland*; Pontifical Institute of Mediaeval Studies: Ontario, Canada, 1979; 11.

49. Weinberg, B.H. Book indexes in France: Medieval specimens and modern practices. Indexer **2000**, *22* (1), 2–13. [CSA].

50. Cevolini, A. Indexing as preadaptive advance: A socio-evolutionary perspective. Indexer **2014**, *32* (4), 50–57.

51. Humphreys, N. The world's oldest profession: Indexing? Indexer **2011**, *29* (4), 161–165.

52. Wellisch, H.H. Incunabula indexes. Indexer **1994**, *19* (1), 3–12. [CSA].

53. Krovetz, R. Viewing the dictionary as a classification system. In *Advances in Classification Research*. Proceedings of the 1st ASIS SIG/CR Classification Research Workshop; Learned Information: Medford, NJ, 1991; 85–91.

54. Hlava, M.M.K. *The Taxobook, Part !: History, Theories and Concepts of Knowledge Organization*; Morgan & Claypool: San Rafael, CA, 2014.

55. Wellisch, H.H. Early multilingual and multiscript indexes in herbals. Indexer **1978**, *11* (2), 81–102.

56. MacPherson, H.D. *Some Practical Problems in Cataloging*; American Library Association: Chicago, IL, 1936; 82–83.

57. Wellisch, H.H.; Gessner, C. How to make an index—16th century style: Conrad Gessner on indexes and catalogs. Int. Classif. **1981**, *8* (1), 10–15.

58. Wheatley, H.B. *How to Make an Index*; Elliot Stock: London, U.K., 1902, Facsimile edition: Society of Indexers: Sheffield, England, 2002.

59. Wellisch, H. The literature of indexing. In *Indexing: The State of Our Knowledge and the State of Our Ignorance*. Proceedings of the 20th Annual Meeting of the American Society of Indexers, New York, May, 13, 1998; Weinberg, B.H., Ed.; Learned Information: Medford, NJ, 1989; 1–15.

60. Jonker, F. *Indexing Theory, Indexing Methods and Search Devices*; Scarecrow Press: New York, 1964.

61. Borko, H. Toward a theory of indexing. Inform. Process. Manage. **1977**, *13* (6), 355–365. [CrossRef], [Web of Science ®], [CSA].

62. Svenonius, E. Directions for research in indexing, classification, and cataloging. Libr. Resour. Tech. Serv. **1981**, *25* (1), 88–103. [Web of Science ®], [CSA].

63. Quinn, B. Recent theoretical approaches in classification and indexing. Knowl. Organ. **1994**, *21* (3), 140–147. [Web of Science ®], [CSA].

64. Lancaster, F.W. *Indexing and Abstracting in Theory and Practice*, 3rd Ed.; Facet: London, U.K., 2003.

65. Hjorland, B. The importance of theories of knowledge: Indexing and information retrieval as an example. J. Am. Soc. Inf. Sci. Technol. **2011**, *62* (1), 72–77.

66. Weinberg, B.H. Why indexing fails the researcher. Indexer **1988**, *16* (1), 3–6. [CSA].

67. Andersen, J.; Christensen, F.S., Wittgenstein and indexing theory. In *Advances in Classification Research*. Proceedings of the 10th ASIS SIG/CR Classification Research Workshop, Washington, DC, November, 1–5, 1999; Albrechtsen, H., Mai, J. Eds.; Information Today: Medford, NJ, 1999; Vol. 10, 1–25.

68. Weinberg, B.H. Exhaustivity of indexes: Books, journals, and electronic full text: Summary of a Workshop presented at the 1999 ASI Annual Conference. Key Words **1999**, *7* (5), 1, 6–19.

69. Weinberg, B.H. Letter to the Editor: Index density. Key Words **2002**, *10* (1), 6.

70. Weinberg, B.H. Letter to the Editor: On index matrices and arrays. Key Words **2004**, *12* (2), 42.

71. Wellisch, H.H. Depth of Indexing. In *Indexing from A to Z*, 2nd Ed.; H.W. Wilson: New York, 1995; 137–138.

72. Anderson, J.D.; Perez-Carballo, J. *Information Retrieval Design: Principles and Options for Information Description, Organization, Display, and Access in Information Retrieval Databases, Digital Libraries, Catalogs, and Indexes*; Ometeca Institute: St. Petersburg, FL, 2005, 171, 185.

73. Ranganathan, S.R. *Prolegomena to Library Classification*, 3rd Ed.; Asia Publishing House: London, U.K., 1967; 287.

74. Kilgour, F.G. Origins of coordinate searching . J. Am. Soc. Inform. Sci. **1997**, *48* (4), 340–348. Reprinted in *Historical Studies in Information Science*; Hahn, T.B., Buckland, M., Eds.; Information Today: Medford, NJ, 1998; 107–115. [Web of Science ®], [CSA].

75. Taube, M. *Studies in Coordinate Indexing*; Documentation Incorporated: Washington, DC, 1953–1965; 6 vols.

76. Weinberg, B.H. Why postcoordination fails the searcher. Indexer **1995**, *19* (3), 155–159. [CSA].

77. Milstead, J. *Subject Access Systems: Alternatives in Design*; Academic Press: Orlando, FL, 1984; 187.

78. Weinberg, B.H. Complexity in indexing systems—Abandonment and failure: Implications for organizing the Internet. In *Global Complexity: Information, Chaos and Control*. Proceedings of the 59th ASIS Annual Meeting, Baltimore, MD, 1996; Hardin, S., Ed.; Information Today: Medford, NJ, 1996; 84–90.

79. Craven, T.C. *String Indexing*; Academic Press: Orlando, FL, 1986.

80. Kesselman, M.; Perry, I. What online searchers should know about indexing, and what indexers should know about online searching. In Proceedings of the Fifth National Online Meeting, New York, April 10–12, 1984; 141–148.

81. Frohmann, B. Rules of indexing: A critique of mentalism in information retrieval theory. J. Doc. **1990**, *46* (2), 81–101. [Web of Science ®], [CSA].

82. Anderson, J.D.; Perez-Carballo, J. *Information Retrieval Design: Principles and Options for Information Description, Organization, Display, and Access in Information Retrieval Databases, Digital Libraries, Catalogs, and*

Indexes; Ometeca Institute: St. Petersburg, FL, 2005; 130–135.

83. Bates, M.J. Indexing and access for digital libraries and the Internet: Human, database, and domain factors. J. Am. Soc. Inform. Sci. **1998**, *49* (13), 1185–1205. [CrossRef], [Web of Science ®], [CSA].

84. Educational Resources Information Center (U.S.). *Thesaurus of ERIC Descriptors*, 14th Ed.; Houston, J.E., Ed.; Oryx Press: Phoenix, AZ, 2001; 222, http://www.eric.ed.gov (accessed May 24, 2017).

85. Keidar, R.; Shoham, S. Miftuah monografyot be-emtsa'ut "Otsar Munhe Miftuah" = Indexing monographs using the Hebrew Thesaurus of Indexing Terms. Yad La-Kore: Israel J. Lib. Informa. Arch. Sci. **2003**, *35*, 24–36. (In Hebrew; English abstract, 104).

86. Subject indexing. Wikipedia, http://en.wikipedia.org/wiki/Subject_indexing. Last modified 31 January 2017. (accessed May 24, 2017).

87. National Information Standards Organization (U.S.). *Guidelines for the Construction, Format, and Management of Monolingual Thesauri: An American National Standard*, ANSI/NISO Z39.19-1993; NISO Press: Bethesda, MD, 1994, Latest edition: Guidelines for the Construction, Format, and Management of Monolingual Controlled Vocabularies, ANSI/NISO Z39.19-2005; Reaffirmed 2010.

88. Leise, F. Controlled vocabularies: An introduction. Indexer **2008**, *26* (3), 121–126; Hedden, H. Opportunities in free-lance taxonomy work. Key Words: Bull. Am. Soc. Index. **2014**, *22* (12), 165–167.

89. Shiri, A. *Powering Search: The Role of Thesauri in New Information Environments*; Published on behalf of the American Society for Information Science and Technology by Information Today: Medford, NJ, 2012.

90. Weinberg, B.H. Book review: Powering Search. J. Assoc. Inform. Sci. Technol. **2014**, *65* (5), 1085–1088.

91. Hlava, M.M.K. *The Taxobook, Part 2: Principles and Practices of Taxonomy Construction*; Morgan & Claypool: San Rafael, CA, 2015; 105–116.

92. Leonard, L.E. Inter-indexer consistency studies, 1954–1975: A review of the literature and summary of study results. University of Illinois Graduate School of Library Science, Chicago, IL, 1977; Occasional Papers, Vol. 131.

93. Saracevic, T. Indexing, searching, and relevance. In *Indexing: The State of Our Knowledge and the State of Our Ignorance*. Proceedings of the 20th Annual Meeting of the American Society of Indexers, New York, 1988;

94. Weinberg, B.H., Ed.; Learned Information: Medford, NJ, 1989; 101–109.

94. Golub, K. *Subject Access to Information: An Interdisciplinary Approach*; Libraries Unlimited: Santa Barbara, CA, 2015; 53.

95. Lancaster, F.W. *Indexing and Abstracting in Theory and Practice*, 3rd Ed.; Facet: London, U.K., 2003; 9.

96. Stibic, V. *Personal Documentation for Professionals: Means and Methods*; North-Holland Publishing Company: New York, 1980.

97. Weinberg, B.H. *Word Frequency and Automatic Indexing*; Columbia University, School of Library Service: New York, 1981, Dissertation.

98. International Organization for Standardization. *Documentation—Methods for Examining Documents, Determining their Subjects, and Selecting Index Terms*; ISO: Geneva, Switzerland, 1985, ISO 5963-1985 (E).

99. Brenner, E.H.; Lucey, J.H.; Martinez, C.L.; Meleka, A. American Petroleum Institute's machine-aided indexing and searching project. Sci. Technol. Libr. **1984**, *5* (1), 49–62. [Taylor & Francis Online].

100. Hlava, M.M.K. *The Taxobook, Part 3: Applications, Implementation and Integration in Search*; Morgan & Claypool: San Rafael, CA, 2015; 79.

101. Mulvany, N.; Milstead, J. Indexicon, the only fully automatic indexer: A review. Key Words **1994**, *2* (5), 1–23.

102. Bennett, R. TExtract: A regular user's view. Indexer **2009**, *27* (2), 84–87.

103. Hirschmann, R. Patterns and hidden meanings: The dawn of automated indexing. Indexer **2011**, *29* (1), 19.

104. Weinberg, B.H. Indexing after the millennium 5: Future conditional. Indexer **1998**, *21* (2), 62–63. [CSA].

105. Browne, G.; Jermey, J. *Website Indexing: Enhancing Access to Information within Websites*, 2nd Ed.; Auslib Press: Adelaide, SA, 2004.

106. Moore, M. The semantic web: An introduction for information professionals. Indexer **2012**, *30* (1), 42.

107. Northedge, R. The medium is not the message: Topic maps and the separation of presentation and content in indexes. Indexer **2008**, *26* (2), 60–64.

108. Artandi, S. *An Introduction to Computers in Information Science*, 2nd Ed.; Scarecrow Press: Metuchen, NJ, 1972; 180.

109. Indexing Societies around the world: A brief survey. Indexer **2011**, *29* (4), C5–C8; International agreement of indexing societies. Indexer **2012**, *30* (3), 151–152.

India: Libraries, Archives and Museums

Krishan Kumar
Former Head, Department of Library and Information Science, University of Delhi, New Delhi, India

V. Jeyaraj
Hepzibah Institute of Conversion, Chennai, India

Ramesh C. Gaur
Kalanidhi Division, Indira Gandhi National Centre for the Arts (IGNCA), New Delhi, India

Abstract

The National Library, Kolkata, is the largest single library that serves as the depository as well as the repository of all the published material of India. It also has built up a large collection of foreign publications. Besides, there are two other national libraries, namely, National Science Library, New Delhi and National Medical Library, New Delhi. There are a large number of academic, research, public and special libraries. Steps are being undertaken to modernize the libraries to meet the increasing demands of users. The National Archives of India (NAI), New Delhi, is the premier records repository of India. It has set up four regional archival repositories in Bhopal, Bhubaneswar, Jaipur, and Pondicherry. Each State has its own archives. There are a large number of college and university archives, corporate archives, religious archives, manuscript repositories, etc. India is a country that is rich in culture, heritage, science, and artifacts. Its museums and art galleries house a great cultural heritage. The National Museum, New Delhi, is the apex museum in the country. In addition to State museums and art galleries, there are a large number of art museums and galleries (noncommercial) that display India's rich heritage. India is also rich in biodiversity. The National Zoological Park, Delhi, is one of the finest zoological parks in India. Some of the best jewels of Indian wilderness include the Great Himalayan National Park, Dachigam National Park, Corbett National Park, Ranthambore National Park, Sundarbans National Park, and Kaziranga National Park.

INTRODUCTION

With a rich cultural heritage, India has one of the oldest civilizations in the world. With a population of 1.14 billion, India is the world's largest democracy. It has made tremendous socioeconomic progress during the last 62 years since its independence (1947). Today, India has become the tenth most industrialized country in the world.

Geography and Population

India covers an area of 32,87,263 sq km. It is bounded by the Great Himalayas in the north, the Indian Ocean on the east, and the Arabian Sea on the west. The population of India was 1,028,737,436 based on the 2001 census, but the projected population as of March, 1, 2008 is 1,147,677,000 (592,245,000 males and 555,432,000 females).[1]

Government

India, also known as Bharat, is a Union of States. It is a Sovereign Socialist Democratic Republic with a parliamentary system of government. The constitutional head of the Executive branch of the Union is the President. But the real executive power lies with the Council of Ministers that has the Prime Minister as its head. There are 28 states and 7 Union territories in the country. In the states, the Governor, as the representative of the President, is the head of the Executive body. However, Union Territories are administered by the President through an Administrator appointed by him.

History

The History of India begins with the birth of the Indus Valley Civilization, more precisely referred to as the Harappan Civilization. It flourished around 2500 B.C. in the western part of South Asia (present Pakistan and Western India). By 1500 B.C., the Harappan Civilization came to an end.

In the third century B.C., King Ashoka united large parts of India. During the reign of the Mauryas (322–185 B.C.E.), Hinduism (the major religion of India today) as a religion took a form that basically exists even now. It was during the eighth century that Islam first came to India. However, by the eleventh century, it had established itself as a strong

Encyclopedia of Library and Information Sciences, Fourth Edition DOI: 10.1081/E-ELIS4-120044942

political force. The North Indian dynasties of the Lodhis, Tughlaqs, and others ruled India and were succeeded by the Mughal Kings.

From the mid-eighteenth century to the mid nineteenth century, India was gradually annexed by the British East India Company. The dissatisfaction with the rule of the East India Company resulted in a revolt that assumed the form of the 1857 Mutiny. This led to the First War of Indian Independence (1857–1858). After this war, India was incorporated into the British Empire completely and began to be directly administered by the British. During the first half of the twentieth century, a nationwide struggle for independence from British rule was initiated by the Indian National Congress. It was a long struggle. In 1947, the subcontinent of India gained freedom from British rule and the subcontinent was partitioned into the countries of India and Pakistan.

Education

The national level pattern exists with 12 years of schooling (8 + 2 + 2), consisting of 8 years of elementary education (that is, 5 years of primary and 3 years of middle school education for the age groups of 6 –11 and 11–14 years, respectively), followed by secondary and higher secondary education, of 2 years of each, besides 2 years of preprimary education. The entry age in class 1 is 5+. Preprimary classes form age group 3 to 4. The higher secondary school certificate enables students to pursue studies either in universities or in colleges for higher education in general academic streams and in technical and professional courses.

According to the recent report of the National Sample Survey Organisation (NSSO), in 2005–2006 the literacy rate was 68.3%.[2] Thus, goal of universal elementary education and total eradication of illiteracy has not been achieved so far. To achieve the goal would require higher level of investment in school education, especially at the elementary level.

The higher secondary school certificate enables students to pursue studies either in universities or in colleges of higher education, in general academic streams and in technical and professional courses. Today, India has a well-developed system of higher education, especially in engineering, technology, and management science.

The Emerging New India

India's greatest asset is a large pool of talent with more than 620 million people of working age. A large majority of its population is young, ambitious and dynamic, and has great aspirations. Its economy is growing rapidly. John. F. Welch, Chief Operating Officer of General Electric, said "India is a developing country, but it is a developed country as far as its intellectual infrastructure is concerned. We get the highest intellectual capital per dollar here."[3]

Toward the end of twentieth century, R. Mashelkar in his presidential address to the Indian Science Congress, made a prediction that "The next century will belong to India, which will become a unique intellectual and economic power to reckon with, recapturing all its glory, which it had in the millennia gone by...."[4]

LIBRARY AND INFORMATION PROFESSIONS, SYSTEMS AND SERVICES

Library Legislation

Pre-independence period

The first landmark in the pre-independence history of the public library movement in India was the enactment of the Delivery and Registration of Publications Act of Bombay Government in May 1808. Almost a century later, on January 31 1902, the Imperial Library Act was passed, creating the Imperial Library at Calcutta (now called Kolkata). In the history of library legislation, passage of the Kolhapur Public Libraries Act, 1945, remains a landmark event. It was the first public libraries act to be enacted in pre-independent India. This Act is now defunct.

Post-independence period (1947–2000)

The Imperial Library (Change of Name) Act, 1948 (Act no. 51 of 1948) was enacted on September 8, 1948. Thereafter, the Imperial Library came to be known as "The National Library". The Delivery of Books "and Newspapers" (Public Libraries) Act, 1954 [The delivery of Books (Public Libraries) Act, 1954: No. 27 of 1954, as amended by the Delivery of Books (Public Libraries) Amendment Act, 1956: No. 99 of 1956.] is another important Act. This is an Act that provides for Delivery of Books to the National Library, Calcutta, and to three other public libraries (Delhi Public Library, Delhi; Connemara Public Library, Chennai; and State Central Library, Mumbai).

Indian Copyright Act, 1957 and as amended in 1994/1995 governs matters related to copyright, including computer software. The act, as amended in 1994/1995, has incorporated many provisions keeping in view the changes in information technology. The Information Technology Act, 2000 (No. 21 Of 2000) [June 9, 2000] deals with issues concerning transactions carried out by means of electronic data interchange and other means of electronic communication, that fall under "electronic commerce."

"Through the good offices of the then Minister for Education, Avinaslingam Chettiar, a modified Bill was introduced in the state legislature which was passed as the Madras Public Libraries Act in 1948."[5] Thus, due to the efforts of Dr S. R. Ranganathan, Father of Library Science in India, the Madras (Tamil Nadu) Public

Libraries Act was enacted in 1948. This was the first public libraries act to be passed in independent India.

The following public libraries acts were passed:

1. Madras (Tamil Nadu) Public Libraries Act (1948)
2. Andhra Pradesh Public Libraries Act (1960)
3. Mysore (Karnataka) Public Libraries Act (1965)
4. Maharashtra Public Libraries (1967)
5. West Bengal Public Libraries Act (1979)
6. Manipur Public Libraries Act (1988)
7. Kerala Public Libraries Act (1989)
8. Haryana Public Libraries Act (1989)
9. Goa Public Libraries Act (1993)
10. Mizoram Public Libraries Act (1993)

Twenty-first century

The following public libraries acts were passed:

1. Gujarat Public Libraries Act (2002)
2. Orissa Public Libraries Act (2002)
3. Uttaranchal Public Libraries Act (2005)
4. Rajasthan Public Libraries Act (2006)
5. Uttar Pradesh Public Libraries Act (2006)

Thus, through 2008, out of 28 states and 7 Union territories in the country, only 15 states have enacted library laws.

National Library and Information Services

Introduction

There are three national libraries of India, namely, the National Library, Kolkata; the National Medical Library, New Delhi; and the National Science Library, New Delhi. Other important libraries include the Central Reference Library, Kolkata that compiles *Indian National Bibliography* and *Index Indiana*. As mentioned above, Delhi Public Library (DPL), Connemara Public Library, Chennai and the State Central Library, Mumbai, are the depositories for the printed cultural heritage of India under the Delivery of Books "and Newspapers" (Public Libraries) Act. These depository libraries are not the national libraries in the strict sense of the term but form a very important part of the National Library sector because India is a vast, multi-lingual country with a rich written heritage in different Indian languages, including English. Thus, the need to cover the large country is realized through a network of national libraries and depository libraries.

There are a number of national documentation centers in different fields. These include the National Institute of Science Communication and Information Resources (NISCAIR) (formerly called Indian National Scientific Documentation Centre), the National Social Science Documentation Centre (NASSDOC) and the Small Enterprises National Documentation Centre (SENDOC). In this list,

we may also include the Defence Science Information and Documentation Centre (DESIDOC). These documentation centers were set up mainly to serve the fields of science, social sciences, small-scale industries and defense science respectively.

National Information System for Science and Technology (NISSAT), New Delhi, was launched in September 1977 as a national level coordinating and funding agency for creating information infrastructure in the area of Science and Technology. This agency was set up and supported by the Department of Scientific and Industrial Research, Government of India. NISSAT created and supported over 13 sectoral information centers, in specific subjects, such as leather, drugs, machine tools, food, etc. By 2004, the NISSAT program ended but the host institutions are continuing the centers with their own resources.

The University Grants Commission (UGC) is the apex body that monitors and funds higher education in the country. It established three information centers covering different disciplines as given below:

- National Centre for Science Information (NCSI) at Indian Institute of Science, Bangalore,
- National Social Science Information Centre (NASSIC) at M.S. University, Baroda (now called Vadodara), and
- National Information Centre (NIC) at SNDT Women's University, Mumbai.

NCSI covers science and engineering, while NASSIC and NIC deal with the social sciences (such as economics, political science, education, and psychology) and other disciplines (such as sociology, women's studies, home science, special education and library science) respectively.

Role of Government of India in relation to libraries

Under the Government of India (Allocation of Business) Rules,

> the work pertaining to the Central Libraries of national importance, the Delivery of Books Act and publication of rare manuscripts is assigned to the Department of Culture. The Central Government, is not a lawmaker for a library system of the country as a whole as the subject 'Libraries' is included in the State list. However, the Central Government takes initiative to secure the voluntary cooperation of the State Governments and to promote coordinated development of national, and State Library system... Apart from maintaining and developing the libraries of national importance, the Central Government is giving financial assistance to libraries sponsored by voluntary organizations throughout the country.[6]

The National Library, Kolkata

The National Library, India is the largest library in the country (see Table 1), located at Kolkata (formerly

Table 1 National Library Statistics as of 31 March 2006.

Books	2,402,579
Books in Indian languages	6,006,508
Maps	88,047
Manuscripts	3227
Books received under the D.B. Act	1,009,182
Current periodical titles	17,530
Bound volumes of periodicals	139,961
Newspapers (titles)	905
Bound volumes of newspapers	11,745
Indian Official Documents	499,509
Microfilms	5553
Microfiche	96,997
Shelf space	More than 45 km
Area of Belvedre Campus	30 acres

Source: http://nlindia.org/useful_info.html[7].

Calcutta City). It is an institution of national importance under the "Department of Culture, Ministry of Tourism and Culture, Government of India." The major aim of the library is to collect, disseminate and preserve the printed material produced in the country. Another important aim of the National Library is to collect all the books published on India, in any part of the world, in any language. At the same time, it is also collecting foreign materials in different languages for the use of the country.

The National Library receives books and periodicals in almost all the Indian languages under the Delivery of Books and Newspapers (Public Libraries) Act 1954 (D.B. Act). It also has

> an invaluable collection in English language, because of the systematic collection development by Calcutta Public Library as well as by the Imperial Library. Way back in 1848 itself, an attempt was being made to acquire journals issued by the foreign learned institutions. Serious works were purchased in large numbers than the light literature. Now a days also the same policy is being continued.

It has a strong collection in the humanities, British and Indian history and literature.[8] Digitization of books is a useful project, undertaken by the Library. To date, 6600 selected books in Indian and English languages have been scanned and stored on 548 CDs, covering a total of over 2,500,000 pages.

The library has separate reading rooms in all of its four buildings, and for each language division, the Foreign Language Division, Foreign Official Documents, Rare Books, Maps and Prints, Science and Technology Division, and Asutosh Collection. Any person above 18 years can use the reading room facilities.

Limited number of books are lent out to the readers (local members) under certain terms and conditions. To use this facility, one has to become a member of the Lending Division of the library. Outstation persons (members living outside Kolkata) are allowed to borrow books through post.

Selected lists of reading materials or bibliographies are prepared by the library on request. Special bibliographies are also compiled when exhibitions are held. Compilation of exhaustive bibliographies is underway on special topics, such as Indology. The library is responsible for providing bibliographies and/or bibliographic statistics to national and international organizations.

Central Reference Library (CRL), Kolkata

The Central Reference Library is a subordinate office of the Ministry of Culture, Government of India. It was carved out of the National Library, for the compilation of the *Indian National Bibliography* and *Index Indiana* (an index to selected articles appearing in current language periodicals).

National Medical Library, New Delhi

The National Medical Library (NML) aims to provide wide and efficient library and information services to the health science (HS) professionals in India. The Library is mainly a reference library in the field of Medical and Allied Sciences. It is open for consultation by Medical, Paramedical and Allied Professionals. The National Medical Library is considered one of the largest medical libraries in South Asia. It has 360,000 volumes of books, reports, bound volumes of journals and other literature and adds about 3000 books and serials every year. It subscribes to 2000 current periodicals. NML is also the National Focal Point of HELLIS (Health Literature Library and Information Service) Network set up by WHO in Southeast Asia in 1982.[9]

NML has established a network of health science libraries in India. For this purpose, it has identified six Regional Medical Libraries (RML) and eight Resource Medical Libraries (RL) in the country. All RMLs and RLs have been provided with equipment such as microcomputers, CD-ROM Drives, the MEDLINE database and a photocopier. A grant-in-aid has been provided to each RML and RL to strengthen their document collection.

National Science Library, New Delhi

The National Science Library (NSL) was set up in 1964 as a part of Insdoc (now named National Institute of Science Communication and Information Resources (NISCAIR)). NSL aims at acquiring all-important Science and Technology publications published in the country and strengthening its resource base for foreign periodicals by acquiring the journals on CD-ROM or other electronic form as far as possible. The library is open to the public. Individuals and institutions can become members to use its collection.

NSL has a collection of over 200,000 volumes including monographs and bound volumes of journals in the fields of science and technology. E-Resources include

CD-ROM databases of primary and secondary sources and E-Journals. NSL has an Electronic Library Division with a collection of more than 5000 foreign journals, conference proceedings, etc. and a large number of databases on CD-ROMs. Services include Readers' Service, Technical Query Service, Copying Service, Inter-Library Loan Service, e-Journals Access (The library provides free access to electronic journals from 13 leading international publishers).

The Indian Agricultural Research Institute Library, New Delhi

The Indian Agricultural Research Institute Library (IARI Library) is a focal point for collecting, organizing and disseminating agrobiological information generated within the country as well as abroad. Due to its rich collection and services, it may be regarded as a national library in the field of agriculture. However, it has not been formally designated as such.

IARI Library has the largest collection in the field of agriculture and is considered a primary library in this field in India. The Library has over 600,000 highly specialized research publications on agriculture and related sciences. The collection is growing annually at the rate of 8000 to 9000 documents. The Library has 10,500 serial files, and 4000 current serials are being procured from 80 countries through subscription, gifts and exchanges.[10]

National Institute of Science Communication and Information Resources, New Delhi

The National Institute of Science Communication and Information Resources (NISCAIR) came into existence on September 30, 2002 through the merger of the National Institute of Science Communication (NISCOM) and the Indian National Scientific Documentation Centre (INSDOC) (Set up in 1952). Its mission is to become the

> prime custodian of all information resources on current and traditional knowledge systems in science and technology in the country, and to promote communication in science to diverse constituents at all levels, using the most appropriate technologies.[11]

NISCAIR is basically concerned with collection, storage, publication and dissemination of science and technology information. It is a premier institution of information science engaged in dissemination of information in the field of S&T.

National Social Science Documentation Centre, New Delhi

The Indian Council of Social Science Research (ICSSR) was set up in 1969 as an autonomous organization to promote research in social sciences in the country. In 1970, ICSSR established the Social Science Documentation Centre that was renamed the National Social Science Documentation Centre (NASSDOC) in 1986. It has a rich collection of reference sources, bibliographies, 5000 doctoral theses, 3500 research project reports (funded by the ICSSR) and 12,500 books and documents. NASSDOC has created a number of databases and information locating tools.

Defence Scientific Information and Documentation Centre (DESIDOC), Delhi

DESIDOC functions as a central information resource for DRDO (Defense Research and Development Organization). It provides science and technology information, based on its library and other information resources, to the DRDO headquarters as well as its various laboratories located at various locations in India. DESIDOC maintains an excellent library in the defense sector. It has more than 262,000 documents and provides document supply to its users quite fast. The library management activities have been computerized. More than 1000 DRDO scientists (and a few others) are provided monthly SDI (Selective Dissemination of Information) services, based on about 10 CD-ROM databases. It also brings out a number of publications to serve its users.

Small Enterprises National Documentation Centre, Hyderabad

The Small Enterprises National Documentation Centre (SENDOC), Hyderabad, was set up in 1971 as an organ of the SIET Institute. This Institute is now called National Institute for Micro, Small and Medium Enterprises. The Centre serves as a national bibliographic center to meet the information needs of micro, small and medium enterprises.

Inter-library cooperation

Today, there are several library networks that have come into existence to advance inter-library cooperation. A number of library networks were originally sponsored by NISSAT (National Information System for Science and Technology), such as ADINET (Ahmedabad Libraries Network), BALINET (Bangalore Library Network), BONET (Bombay Libraries Network), CALIBNET (Calcutta Libraries Network), DELNET (Delhi Libraries Network, now Developing Library Network), MYLIBNET (Mysore Libraries Network) and PUNENET (Pune Libraries Network). MANLIBNET (Management Library Network) was formed by libraries in the field of management.

A number of consortia have been formed. These include Indian National Digital Library in Engineering Sciences and Technology (INDEST), Council of Scientific and Industrial Research Consortium, UGC-INFONET (established by INFLIBNET Centre links more than 172 universities across the country) and ICICI Virtual Information Centre. One of the major activities of these consortia is resource sharing.

National planning

Planning at the national level is done through five-year plans. At present, XI Plan (2007–2012) is in operation. The following thrust has been identified by the Ministry of Culture as a major Thrust Area for the XI Plan (2007–2012):

> Overhauling the library sector to meet the needs of a knowledge society has been found to be the need of the hour by the Ministry... The recommendations of the National Knowledge Commission will be taken into account while formulating the XI Plan proposals in the Library sector.[12]

With the efforts that are going on, it is hoped that it will bring major changes in the library sector, including the national libraries.

Academic and Research Libraries

Size of the sector

As of March 31, 2006, 355 universities and 18,064 colleges existed in the Higher Education sector. During the academic year 2005–2006, the total enrolment in all courses and levels in regular stream had been 11,028,000 including 4,466,000 female students (40.5%). The strength of the teaching faculty in universities and colleges was 488,000. The number of research degrees (Ph.D.) awarded during 2004–2005 was 17,898.[13] The above data shows that the higher education sector is a massive one.

Main players in the higher education sector

The University Grants Commission (UGC) is "responsible for coordination, determination and maintenance of standards, release of grants." Professional Councils are "responsible for recognition of courses, promotion of professional institutions and providing grants to undergraduate programs and various awards." Central Government is "responsible for major policy relating to higher education in the country. It provides grants to the UGC and establishes central universities in the country." State Governments are "responsible for establishment of State Universities and colleges, and provide plan grants for their development and non-plan grants for their maintenance."[14]

Higher education—history

Problems of educational reforms were reviewed by several commissions and committees, notably the University Education Commission (1948–1949) and the Secondary Education Commission (1952–1953). Some steps to implement the recommendations of the Commissions were taken and a Resolution on Scientific Policy was passed under the leadership of Jawaharlal Nehru, the then Prime Minister of India. As a consequence of the resolution, development of science, technology and scientific research received special emphasis. The Education Commission (1964–1966) was appointed to advise the Government on the national pattern of education and other matters. Its recommendations on education are a landmark in the history of education in India. A new education policy (NPE) was adopted by the Parliament in 1986. A revised Programme of Action (POA) was placed in the Parliament on August 9, 1992, and approved by it. The eighth five-year plan (1992–1997) was prepared keeping in mind 1986 NPE and 1992 POA.

The National Knowledge Commission (NKC) is a high-level advisory body to the Prime Minister of India, formed with the objective of transforming India into a knowledge society. In 2007, it gave its recommendations for higher education.[15] The recommendations of the NKC are far reaching in nature. For example, it recommended creation of 50 National Universities that can provide education of the highest standard. These can result in revolutionary changes leading to excellence in higher education.

College libraries

A college, in general, is an institution of higher learning that offers a three-year degree after higher secondary school. However, most professional degrees are of four-year duration. Some colleges offer postgraduate courses of two-year duration. Usually, research is the prerogative of universities rather than colleges.

Colleges in India are regarded as the forerunners of universities. The same is true for college and university libraries as well. Collections of college libraries usually consist of books and periodicals. They may have some nonbook materials. However, the situation is changing. College libraries are increasingly acquiring nonbook materials. Most of them do not provide open access. The majority of the libraries use the *Dewey Decimal Classification* system and *Anglo-American Cataloging Rules*. As regards services, they render lending service, help to users in the location of materials and the use of the library catalog, and provide library orientation to new members. Some college libraries also provide bibliographical services. Teachers are usually provided with intensive reference service and inter-library loan. As regards the photocopying service, it is usually provided by a private vendor appointed by the authorities under the conditions laid out by the authorities. The vendor may set up his machine within the library or anywhere on the college campus.

In recent years, many college libraries have automated their operations. The University Grants Commission (UGC) provides one-time grants for computerization of college libraries. In Delhi, a large number of college libraries have been computerized. Recently, the University of Delhi provided 40 computers to each college library affiliated with it, along with network facility and access to databases available at Delhi University Library System. Thus, faculty and students of colleges have free access to the total resources of the Delhi University Library System. Some of the colleges are using IT to provide highly specialized services. For instance, Farook College, Kozhikode, has set up the Digital Talking Book Library for the benefit of visually challenged students and named it "Insight."[16] College libraries in metropolitan towns are well developed. However, libraries in small towns in economically underdeveloped states are in a poor state of development. UGC has recognized some leading colleges as autonomous colleges that get special assistance from UGC. Libraries attached to autonomous colleges are especially well equipped and maintained.

University libraries

The University Grants Commission. The University Grants Commission (UGC) was set up by the Central Government in 1953. However, in November 1956 the UGC was formally established through an Act of Parliament as a statutory body of the Government of India for the coordination, determination and maintenance of standards of university education in India. The UGC is the only grant-making agency in the country that has been given two responsibilities, namely: 1) providing funds and 2) coordination, determination and maintenance of standards in institutions of higher education. It also advises the union and state governments on measures to be taken in higher education.

UGC formulates rules and regulations for overall teaching and research at higher education. It also looks after the academic libraries (sets various standards for library education, library staff, library services, etc.). Committees are set up by the UGC from time to time for the support of higher education in general and the library services in academic (university and college) libraries in particular.

The UGC Panel on Library and Information Science is a standing body that examines and makes recommendations about issues and library problems. In 1957 UGC appointed the Committee on University and College Libraries to advise it regarding functioning and management of libraries. UGC adopted many of the recommendations from the report of that Committee as norms for college and university libraries.

Present Scenario. University libraries in India have developed steadily but have not succeeded fully in their objective to build up sound library collections as a base for providing satisfactory services. However, the scene is changing due to the application of information and communication technology (ICT).

The UGC meets most of the total expenses of central universities. However, in the cases of state universities and institutions deemed universities, UGC adds to their funds for various development activities under the five-year plans. Libraries attached to central universities receive large financial support compared with libraries of state universities. Very often, state university libraries all over the country are starved of funds.

Information and Library Network (INFLIBNET Centre), has been a boon to university libraries. It is an autonomous Inter-University Centre of the UGC. It has supported many university libraries for creating computer facilities, databases and automation of libraries. It has also given training on a large scale to library staff in computer application, thus preparing them for modernization of libraries and their operations. The UGC-Infonet Digital Library Consortium launched by INFLIBNET Centre provides current as well as archival access to

> more than 4500 core and peer-reviewed journals and nine bibliographic databases from 23 publishers and aggregators in different disciplines. So far 120 Universities out of 171 that come under the purview of UGC, have been provided differential access to subscribed e-resources.[17]

University libraries have participated very actively in information and library networks that have been set up in recent years and benefitted considerably from these networks.

The above mentioned consortium is a program wholly funded by the UGC and executed by the INFLIBNET (Information and Library Network) Centre, Ahmedabad. The benefit of subscription to e-resources will soon also be extended to colleges, to begin with the College for Potential with Excellence (CPE). The Consortium also "plans to launch its "Associate Membership Programme" wherein private universities and other research organizations, would be allowed to join the Consortium for selected e-resources."[18]

Public Libraries

The nineteenth century

The enactment of Delivery and Registration of Publications Act of Bombay Government in May 1808 is considered as the first landmark in the pre-independence history of public libraries in India. Calcutta Public Library was established in 1836. It was not a Government institution. It was being run on a proprietary basis. The Calcutta Public Library is regarded as the first public library in this region of the country. Khuda Bux Oriental Public Library, Patna, was established in 1875. In 1969, it was declared, an institution of national importance under an Act (the Khuda Bakhsh Oriental Public Library Act, 1969) of the Parliament. On March 22, 1890 the foundation stone of Connemara Pubic Library was laid at Madras (now Chennai) and on December 5th 1896, it was formally opened. It is today, an excellent library with a rich collection and is heavily used by the public.

The Imperial Library was formed in 1891 by combining a number of Secretariat libraries. The most important one was the Library of the Home Department. However, the use of the library was restricted to the senior officers of the Government.

By the middle of nineteenth century, the towns of Bombay, Calcutta and Madras had subscription libraries, established with the active support of Europeans. By the end of nineteenth century,

> all the provincial capitals and many district towns had so-called public libraries. In addition many princely states had public libraries in their capitals (e.g., Indore, Travancore-Cochin, Patiala). However, in general the masses did not take full advantage of those institutions.[19]

The beginnings of the "public library movement in India can be traced to 1885, when the Indian National Congress was founded. This was the time when national awakening was taking place, leading to cultural renaissance. The Swadeshi movement was taking root."[19] Towards the end of the century, political, economic, and social pre-conditions necessary for the origin of public libraries were coming into being due to the awakening of national pride in national culture and heritage. National leaders, such as Bipinchandra Pal and Lala Lajpat Rai were responsible for this awakening.

The twentieth century (up to 1947)

On January 31, 1902, the Imperial Library Act was passed. This is considered as another landmark in the pre-independence history of public libraries in India. The Imperial Library, then located at Metcalf Hall, Calcutta (now called Kolkata) was formally opened to the public on January 30, 1903. The aims and objectives of the Imperial Library, were defined in a Notification in the "Gazette of India."

> It is intended that it should be a library of reference, a working place for students and a repository of material for the future historians of India, in which, so far as possible, every work written about India, at any time, can be seen and read.[20]

Maharaja Sayajirao III, Gaekwar of Baroda, an enlightened ruler, thought of establishing public libraries along modern lines throughout the State of Baroda. Therefore, he invited W.A. Borden, the Librarian of the Young Men's Institute, New Haven, Connecticut, to fulfill his dream. During the period of Borden's stay, 1910–1913, he established the Central Library and initiated a public library system. The modern public library movement in India began in Baroda during the first decade of the century, due to the efforts of Borden, who was fully supported by the enlightened Maharaja.

In the year 1914, a public Library was established in the Seshadri Iyer Memorial Hall at Cubbon Park, Bangalore. In 1966, this library was taken over by the Government of Karnataka and was given the status of the Central Library. However, in 1986, this library was redesignated as State Central Reference Library.

Post-independence period (twentieth century, from August 15, 1947 onward)

After independence, the Government of India changed the name of the Imperial Library to the National Library, through an enactment of the Imperial Library (change of name) Act, 1948. Delhi Public Library was started initially by Government of India in 1951, as a UNESCO project. The purpose of the Library was to serve as a model public library for Asia. It is claimed that today, Delhi Public Library is the biggest Public Library System in India and also one of the busiest Public Libraries in South East Asia.

Public library scene in the states

The public library scene is briefly described for five states that have developed, comparatively speaking, better public library systems. These are Andhra Pradesh, Karnataka, Kerala, Tamil Nadu, and West Bengal. In the state of Andhra Pradesh, there are nearly 5000 public libraries including 2348 village libraries.[21] The Department of Public Libraries of Karnataka State has established a large network of public libraries consisting of 3778 libraries including 3251 Gram Panchayat (rural) Libraries. There are, in addition, 42 aided libraries.[22] In Kerala State, the State Central Library is a separate independent Department, functioning in isolation. Kerala State Library Council looks after public libraries in the state. The Government releases grant-in-aid to 3458 public libraries of different categories through Kerala State Library Council. Library Service is provided to the public cent per cent in cities and towns and 90% in villages.[21] The public libraries in Kerala are well developed. The coverage of rural population is of a very high order, compared with other states. The State of Tamil Nadu has set up a network of public libraries. The total number of public libraries is 3751 including 1492 village libraries. Besides this, there are three Government aided libraries.[23] West Bengal is the only state in India having a separate Minister in-charge of library services. It has 2465 public libraries including 2209 rural libraries.[24] The state has a fairly well-developed public library system.

Raja Rammohun Roy Library Foundation, Kolkata

The Raja Rammohun Roy Library Foundation (RRRLF), established in 1972, is a central autonomous organization. It is the nodal agency of the Government of India for supporting public library services and systems as well as promoting the public library movement in the country. It also functions as an advisory and consultancy organization and a funding body for public library development in India. Since its inception, the Foundation has "assisted 31,274 libraries in the country under various schemes," such as construction of library buildings, increasing book stock, centenary celebrations, preservation, TV-VCP, computer application in libraries, children section, mobile library services, public library research, etc.[25]

The twenty-first century

Computer Applications. The public libraries are being modernized. Toward this aim, they are undergoing the process of computerization. Computerization of public libraries started in early 1990s. Initially, it was slow and now it has picked up. RRRLF has played a significant role in computerization of public libraries. It has provided computers to all state central libraries and district central libraries. For instance, Delhi Public Library started automation of library activities in the year 1995 by installing Computers.[26] During the last decade of the twentieth century, computerization was started at Connemara Public Library. However, it was in 1998 that 2 servers and 12 nodes were added. The staff input 350,000 records.[27] In June 2003, OPAC (Online Public Access Catalog) was introduced. A touch screen system for library information was also added. An Internet Browsing center, a separate CD Room Section and book bar code were introduced in 2005. Now renewal of books due can be done online. Computerization facility has been "extended to 17 District Central libraries in Tamil Nadu... The remaining 12 District Central Libraries will be provided with computers in 2004–2005."[28] The Directorate of Library Services, West Bengal, has created a database of the Public Libraries of West Bengal. All data regarding the Government Sponsored Public Libraries is available in the database.

Public Libraries Acts. In twenty-first century, five states have enacted public libraries acts. These are Gujarat Public Libraries Act (2002), Orissa Public Libraries Act (2002), Uttaranchal Public Libraries Act (2005), Rajasthan Public Libraries Act (2006), and Uttar Pradesh Public Libraries Act (2006). Thus, today out of 28 states and 7 Union territories in the country, only 15 states have enacted library law.

Table 2 Penetration of public libraries.

Category (number)	Library type (number)	Coverage
States and Union Territories (35)	State Central Libraries (28)	80.0%
Districts (592)	District Libraries (451)	76.0%
Talukas[a](3987)	Taluka Libraries (501)	2.5%
Villages (587,226)	Rural Libraries (28,820)	4.9%

[a]A taluka is an administrative division forming part of a district within a state or union territory.
Source: Cited in Das and Banwari.[29]

Penetration of Public Libraries in India. From Table 2, we may conclude that urban areas are comparatively well covered by libraries but talukas (sub-areas below district level) and rural areas are almost totally neglected. This data is quite old. Today, there may be around 100,000 public libraries (an estimate). Now, there is a greater stress on development of public libraries in rural areas. In recent years, a number of schemes for public library development in talukas and villages have been introduced.

Rural Libraries. "Lack of resource is another serious bottleneck in developing library services. The condition of the majority of rural libraries, particularly, in the heartland of India, is extremely miserable." The situation of majority of rural public libraries is indeed truly miserable. This is in spite of the efforts of a national agency like RRRLF and state governments. "On analysing the trend of assistance rendered by Raja Rammohun Roy Library Foundation in the course of 28 years, it is found that the lion's share of assistance ... in the current year goes for the rural people of our country."[21]

Till recently, public libraries in rural areas were neglected as an area for library growth and development. But now, these areas are getting special attention from the center and state governments. For instance, in Tamil Nadu, a District Rural Development Agency (DRDA) has been set up in each district. One of the DRDA's aims is to establish rural libraries.

The School Education Minister of Tamil Nadu announced the State Government's proposal "to set up about 12,400 rural libraries within the next five years under the scheme 'Anaithu Grama Anna Marumalarchi Thittam' to benefit the rural population."[30] Similar schemes are being implemented in rural areas of different states. Nongovernmental organizations, such as Rajiv Gandhi Foundation have been quite active in this regard.

Role of nongovernmental organizations

Maharashtra and West Bengal have a long tradition of voluntary organizations providing public library services. "From 1830s, 100s of voluntary organizations came up in the States, more so during the freedom struggle this led to establishment of 1000 of subscription libraries which charged annual subscription and a deposit to finance the library." The Manipur Government passed the library legislation in 1967 and declared subscription libraries as public libraries. The Government of West Bengal passed its library law in 1979 and covered most of the subscription libraries as sponsored libraries.[21]

Nongovernmental organizations are becoming more active in recent years, aiming to empower women, rural areas and backward areas through public libraries. One such example is that of the Rajiv Gandhi Foundation (established in 1991). The Foundation has nurtured a countrywide village library program since 1993. "In all, since 1993, RGF has established a total of 1444 libraries in 22 states, which includes 1344 village and 100 slum libraries."[31]

National policy

In October 1985, the Government of India constituted a committee under the chairmanship of D.P. Chattopadhyaya to formulate the National Policy on Library and Information System (NAPLIS). The final report was submitted, via a letter of May 30, 1986. It is an excellent report. However, the national policy was never approved by the Parliament. Another report that deserves special mention was submitted by the National Knowledge Commission, appointed by the Government of India. In its report on libraries dated December 7, 2006, it recommended setting of a National Commission on Libraries, modernizing of library management, encouragement of greater community participation in library management, promotion of information and computer technology (ICT) applications, etc. Some of the steps have already been taken to implement the recommendations. However, there is a lack of public library policy at the national level that could give direction to library movement in the country.

Current priorities

The following area has been identified by the Ministry of Culture, Government of India, as a major Thrust Area for the XI Plan (2007–2012): "In the Public Library sector, the main thrust will be on Rural Public Libraries. Existing plan schemes of RRRLF will be enlarged and intensified during the XI Plan."[12] With the efforts that are ongoing, it is hoped that this Plan will bring major changes in the public library sector.

School Libraries

Educational system

Introduction. The Indian educational system is regarded as the second-largest system in the world in terms of the number of students, teachers, and institutions. The system is also highly diversified.

Size. The *All India School Education Survey*, seventh in the series of All India Educational Surveys (AIESs), was conducted with reference date as 30 September 2002. The survey covered 1,031,000 schools functioning in 587,000 villages and around 5300 towns/urban areas. It also provided information about 5.53 million teachers imparting education to more than 200 million pupils in the country. The survey is comprehensive in its scope. There are 883,667 elementary (primary and upper primary), 90,741 secondary schools and 43,869 higher secondary schools in the country.[32] Thus, the Indian school education system is quite large.

National education policy

Today, the Central Government continues to play a

> leading role in the evolution and monitoring of educational policies and programs, the most notable of which are the National Policy on Education (NPE), as updated in 1992 envisages a National System of education to bring about uniformity in education...

The National System of Education as envisaged in the NPE is based on "a national curricular framework, which envisages a common core along with other flexible and region-specific components."[33] The country is certainly moving towards the goals. The scheme of Navodaya Vidyalayas, aims to promote excellence along with equity and social justice. It has been a trend setter and a great success.

Library facilities

Salient findings of the *Seventh All India School Education Survey* (7th AISES)[32] regarding library facility in Secondary and Higher Secondary Schools are as follows: 70,090 (77.24%) secondary schools and 39,301 (89.59%) higher secondary schools have library facilities. 73.99% of rural secondary schools have library facility, whereas 84.85% of urban secondary schools have library facility. Similarly, 87.21% of rural higher secondary schools have library facility as against 92.17% of urban higher secondary schools. In secondary and higher secondary schools with a library facility a proportion of 14.98% secondary schools and 41.03% higher secondary schools have full-time librarians. Only 10.07% secondary schools and 12.49% higher secondary schools have part-time librarians. In secondary schools with a library facility, the largest proportion of schools, i.e., 32,615 (46.53%) schools have book strength of up to 500 books. Only 2700 (3.85%) schools have book strength of more than 5000 books. Among higher secondary schools with library facility, the largest proportion of schools, i.e., 10,126 (25.77%) schools have a book strength of 2001 to 5000 books. Only 7190 (18.29%) schools have a book strength of more than 5000 books."[32] As per 7th AISES, "70,090 (77.24%) secondary schools and 39,301 (89.59%) higher secondary schools have a library facility."

These figures are quite impressive. However, the majority of these libraries do not meet the minimum standards for a school library. Only 46.53% of secondary schools have a library facility housing up to 500 books. This indicates the existing situation.

As per 7th AISES, "70,090 (77.24%) secondary schools and 39,301 (89.59%) higher secondary schools are having library facility." The figures are quite impressive. The data must be taken with a pinch of salt as the library facilities in a large majority of libraries are inadequate.

The data indicates that a large majority of so-called school libraries do not have a full time librarian. The size of collections in the majority of the libraries is meager. The usual library services provided by school libraries include circulation and some reference service. Library use instruction provided to students is rare.

The best schools in India are mainly those that come under the category of public schools, members of Indian Public School's Conference. These schools have excellent library facilities, usually with individual libraries for the junior and senior classes. Their libraries are computerized with access to the Internet for students and faculty. The collection usually ranges from 30 to 40 thousand volumes, including multimedia collections. They provide a variety of services to students and teachers, such as reference service, circulation of materials and often, some sort of library use instruction is also provided.

Disparities in Facilities and Standards. There are wide disparities in facilities and standards among different types of schools, varying from rural to urban areas and from state to state. Schools in rural areas are a neglected lot. Some states have done better than others. The "public schools" designed after the British models, along with schools called Navodaya Vidyalayas (established by the central government) and Kendriya Vidyalayas (also called central schools) are well-equipped, well-staffed and adequately supervised. However, government rural or municipal schools are ill-equipped, understaffed and poorly supervised. There are a variety of private schools; some are quite good, and others are poor. On the whole, primary education has been in a very bad shape. The above situation is equally applicable to school libraries.

Special Libraries

History

The history of special libraries in India is interrelated with the growth of research institutions and learned societies. It was only after World War I that learned societies and research institutions began to be established. As a consequence, research activities began to receive a boost at that time. Thus arose the need for improved library facilities. In order to meet the demand for improved library services and facilities, special libraries were established.

Several learned societies or research institutions and their libraries were established as early as the eighteenth century. The Survey of India, The National Survey and Mapping Organisation of the country under the Department of Science and Technology, Government of India, was set up in 1767. It is the oldest scientific department of the Government of India and is India's principal mapping agency. The Asiatic Society, Calcutta, formed in 1784, is an institution of national importance. It is the oldest institution of learning. It has made a tremendous contribution to the growth and development of antiquarian, scientific and literary institutions in India.

Several others were established in the latter part of the nineteenth or early twentieth centuries, before World War I. The Geological Survey of India (GSI), established in 1851, is considered one of the oldest surveys in the World. It is a premier organization of Earth Science Studies with a strength of 2100 geoscientists and technical professionals. The Khuda Bakhsh Oriental Library, Patna, was established in 1875 by Md. Khuda Bakhsh in 1891. Now, this library is an institution of National Importance. The Botanical Survey of India was formally constituted on February 13, 1890. The Survey, with its headquarter at Kolkata, co-ordinates the botanical works of regional centers and botanical explorations. In 1911, the Government of India established the Indian Research Fund Association (IRFA) for the "purpose of sponsoring and coordinating medical research in the country."

In 1949, It was renamed as the Indian Council of Medical Research (ICMR) with expanded functions. Today, the ICMR is funded by the Government of India through the Ministry of Health and Family Welfare.[34] It is the apex body in the field of biomedical research.

After World War I special libraries grew more rapidly. The Indian Council of Agricultural Research (ICAR) was established in 1929 along with associated committees for research. ICAR network is a vast one that includes Institutes, Bureaux, National Research Centres and Project Directorates.

It employs, a manpower of about 30,000 personnel. Out of which nearly 7000 consist of research and management personnel. There are thirty-eight Agricultural Universities (SAUs) that employ about 26,000 scientists for teaching, research and extension education.[35]

Second World War II provided an impetus to the development of scientific and industrial research activities. Thus, the Council of Scientific and Industrial Research

(CSIR) was formed in 1942. This is considered a turning point in the history of scientific and industrial research in India. Today, "it has a network of 38 laboratories/institutes, 39 outreach centers, employing 4555 scientists and 8001 technical persons." CSIR is "amongst the largest R&D organizations in the world for scientific and industrial research"[36] The Indian Atomic Energy Commission was set up in Aug 1948 in the Department of Scientific Research, Government of India. The Department of Atomic Energy (DAE) was established on August 3, 1954 under the direct charge of the Prime Minister. The Defence Science Organization was set up in 1949. Defence Research and Development Organization (DRDO) was formed in 1958 from the amalgamation of various defense organizations. Today, DRDO has 50 laboratories and is engaged in developing Defense technologies. At present, the Organization employs over 5000 scientists and about 25,000 other scientific, technical and supporting personnel.

The Sahitya Akademi, New Delhi, was formally inaugurated in 1954. Indian Council of Social Science Research (ICSSR) was established in the year of 1969 by the Government of India to promote research in social sciences in the country. Central Institute of Indian Languages was established in 1969, to coordinate the development of Indian Languages. Under it, there are 12 centers and 7 regional centers.

The National Information System in Science and Technology (NISSAT) was launched with the assistance of UNESCO in September 1977. It gave a push to special libraries through the establishment of sectoral information centers in various fields of research. Today, there are 13 sectoral information centers in different areas of science and technology, such as leather technology, food technology, marine science etc., although NISSAT itself ceased operations in 2004.

The Indira Gandhi National Centre for Arts (IGNCA), New Delhi, is a multilingual, multimedia, and multidisciplinary organization. It was set up in 1985, as a Centre in the field of the arts. The Centre is a premier research and academic institute engaged in preservation and documentation of Indian Cultural Heritage. The Kala Nidhi Division of the Centre is "responsible for preservation and dissemination of Indian Cultural Heritage Knowledge Resources."[37]

The above description shows that it was only after independence (1947) that a large number of scientific laboratories, research organizations and learned societies were set up. In the same time period India has experienced rapid industrialization. This resulted in growing demand for library facilities and services. Thus, special libraries were established to meet growing demand. The majority of them came into being during the last six decades or so.

The institutions and learned bodies that excel in their field of specialization usually have excellent libraries attached to them.

Health sciences libraries

There are three leading libraries specializing in health sciences. These are the National Library of Medicine, the All India Institute of Medical Sciences Library, and the National Documentation Center of National Institute of Health and Family Welfare. All of them are located in New Delhi.

Another institution also has an excellent health sciences related library. The CDRI (Central Drug Research Institute) Library, Lucknow, established in 1951, is a modern and well-managed Library, with a rich collection. It has systematically built up a specialized collection of reading materials consisting of books, periodicals, reference works, serials and various macro and micro-documents in the areas of Biomedical Research and Drugs and Pharmaceuticals. NICDAP (National Information Center for Drugs and Pharmaceuticals), a Sectoral Information Centre on Drugs and Pharmaceuticals came into being in 1977 at CDRI Library.

Food Science and Technology Information Services (FOSTIS) is the central library of Food Technological Research Institute (CFTRI), Mysore and India's National Information Centre for Food Science and Technology (NICFOS). The library is one of the major information resource centers serving the food processing profession with an extensive collection of print and non-print materials.

The National Medical Library (NML) has set up a network of health science libraries in India. It has with the support from WHO, identified six Regional Medical Libraries (RML) and eight Resource Medical Libraries (RL) in the country. A grant-in-aid was given to each RML and RL to strengthen their document collection.[38]

Law libraries

There are three types of law libraries: academic, judicial and research law libraries.

The leading academic law libraries include Bangalore University College of Law Library, Government Law College (Mumbai) Library, Bombay University Library, Calcutta University Law Library, Delhi University Law Library, Kashmir University Law Library, Madras Law College Library, NALSAR University of Law (Hyderabad), and the National Law School of India University (Bangalore). Delhi University Law Library is regarded as one of the best law libraries in the country.

Recently established National law school libraries are modern, well equipped and provide wide-ranging services. Libraries attached to NALSAR University of Law (Hyderabad), National University of Judicial Sciences (Kolkata), National Law University (Jodhpur), Hidayatullah National University of Law (Raipur) and Gujarat National Law University (Gandhinagar) have good legal collections.

National Law School of India (NLSIU), Bangalore, has one of the best academic law libraries in the country. It has set up a state-of-the art digital library. The library has computerized its library facilities for house keeping and information retrieval. It possesses modern gadgets with wi-fi Internet connectivity and modern audio–visual equipment with teleconferencing capability. In addition, the library provides the facility access to a library portal through which the users can access contents of the current journals, the holdings of current print journals, e-journals, special collections of the library, and information about the library, its staff and services.

Judicial libraries include the Supreme Court Library (New Delhi), High Court Libraries in the states (many of these have good legal collections), bar association libraries attached to the Supreme Court and the high Courts. The Supreme Court Library is the largest law library in the country. Other leading judicial libraries include Calcutta High Court Library, Karnataka High Court Library (Bangalore) and Madras High Court Library. Bar Association libraries serve their lawyer-members and are financed by membership subscription.

Organizations involved in legal research maintain their own libraries. Indian Law Institute Library (New Delhi) is a major library having a rich collection. The Legal Information Resource Centre has been established for

> "retrieving legal information from Indian and foreign Web sites of the Apex Courts, International Courts, Legal Information Institutions, Law Commissions, Human Right Commission. The library subscribes to about 150 legal journals, national and international, and receives nearly 200 periodicals as gifts or in exchange... The library currently houses a collection of 70,000 books and periodicals. In addition, has 25 CD-ROM titles."

It provides Indexing of Indian Legal Periodicals, Indexing of Indian Legislation, Newspapers Clippings Service, Internet Service, Documentation and Bibliographical Services. It has an online library catalog.[39] Besides the above libraries, National Law Institute (Bhopal) Library is another good library.

An example of a modern special library

The Institute for Plasma Research (IPR) Library, Gandhinagar, is a good example of a modern special library. It is a state-of-the-art library. It has a rich collection, helpful staff, wide-ranging services, a soothing ambience, and an atmosphere conducive to scientific research. It gives access to more than 2200 e-journals. The Library has designed a Web site that serves as a gateway to plasma information and provides links to the OPAC, electronic journals, local resources, web resources, etc.[40]

Conclusion

Special libraries are

> primarily, a twentieth-century phenomenon in India. Although a handful existed in the nineteenth century, the majority of these libraries came into being only during the last five decades or so. They are largely concentrated in major towns like Bangalore, Calcutta, Delhi, Hyderabad, Mumbai, and Madras. On the whole, special libraries have succeeded in building a better image than academic and public libraries. They have shown initiative and done better than other types of libraries. They have been forerunners in computer application in Indian libraries.[41]

Thus, special libraries in India have been trendsetters in many ways.

Digital Library Collections and Services

Introduction

In India, a number of libraries, information centers and other institutions have initiated digital library projects by creating databases and e-journals, or by digitizing their own valuable collections. Some of these are described in the next few paragraphs.

General

The Digital Library of India (DLI) is a major project that aims to "digitize all the significant works of mankind." The DLI has three sites which are mirrors of each other, IIIT-H being one of them, as given below:

http://www.new.dli.ernet.in/index.html.en
http://dli.iiit.ac.in/
http://www.dli.cdacnoida.in/

DLI covers primarily books.[42] Though some newspapers and manuscripts are mentioned in one of the sites, they actually point to the external site of the respective newspapers. That is why, what is shown as "manuscripts" or "journals" is really not correct. It is a project hosted by Indian Institute of Science, Bangalore, in cooperation with CMU, IIIT, NSF, ERNET, and MCIT, for the Government of India and 21 participating centers. The mission is to "create a portal for the Digital Library of India which will foster creativity and free access to all human knowledge." Indian Institute of Science, Bangalore, is coordinating the Digital Library of India project along with Carnegie Mellon University.[43]

The UGC-Infonet Digital Library Consortium was formally launched in December, 2003. The Consortium provides current as well as archival "access to more than 4500 core and peer-reviewed journals and nine bibliographic databases from 23 publishers and aggregators in different disciplines." The program is funded by the UGC and administered by the INFLIBNET (Information and Library Network) Centre, Ahmedabad.[44]

Vidyanidhi is India's premier "Digital library initiative to facilitate the creation, archiving and accessing of doctoral theses." Vidyanidhi Database offers "access to more than 1,00,000 Indian theses metadata records...Vidyanidhi provides access to 6500 Full Text Theses Database." It is supported by NISSAT, DSIR, Government of India, the Ford Foundation and Microsoft India.[45]

INLIBNET Centre under "Electronic Theses and Dissertations Project," hosts a bibliographic database of 200,000 dissertations from about 200 Indian universities going back to 1905. Panjab University Digital Library provides access to Library OPAC, online journals, online books, e-reference sources, theses and dissertations, conference proceedings, UN and other information agencies publications, subject gateways, INFLIBNET databases, DELNET databases, LIS portal and miscellaneous.

Indira Gandhi Memorial Library, University of Hyderabad, is one of the first libraries in India to start digitization of books. Since 2002, the library has digitized around 250,000 pages, primarily theses and dissertations, as well as 300 books in English and Indian languages.[46]

University of Delhi has initiated a repository called University of Delhi Eprint Archive. This repository uses GNU Eprints open repository software. Many other universities have also created institutional repositories.

Science

e-Prints is a repository at Indian Institute of Science (IISc), Bangalore, that collects, preserves and disseminates in digital format the research output created by the IISc research community (depository of their preprints, post prints and other scholarly publications). It uses a web interface, and organizes these publications for easy retrieval.[47]

The National Centre for Scientific Information (NCSI), Bangalore provides a

> variety of electronic information services to the Institute's scholars. These include: intranet and Internet access to world's leading bibliographic databases; gateway services for electronic journals and open access resources on the Internet; customized web access ('MySciGate'); IISc e-print archive; and document delivery services.[48]

NISCAIR (New Delhi) has already started the work on the project known as National Science Digital Library (NSDL). It is first of its kind in the country that aims at providing access to digital resources for students.

There are a number of digital repositories of scientific materials at leading scientific institutions using DSpace. These include the Indian Institute of Astrophysics, Bangalore; Raman Research Institute, Bangalore; National Chemical Laboratory, Pune; and the National Institute of Oceanography, Goa.

Medicine

Bioinformatics digital library at Jaypee University of Information Technology, Solan (HP), provides a centralized access for existing resources in bioinformatics.

Traditional Knowledge Digital Library (TKDL) for Indian Systems of Medicine is a collaborative project of the National Institute of Science Communication and Information Resources (NISCAIR), the Council of Scientific and Industrial Research, the Ministry of Science & Technology and Department of AYUSH, and the Ministry of Health and Family Welfare. The project is being implemented at NISCAIR.[49]

Engineering and technology

The Ministry of Human Resource Development (MHRD) set up the Indian National Digital Library in Engineering Sciences and Technology (INDEST) Consortium.

> The Ministry provides funds required for subscription to electronic resources for[33] institutions including IISc, IITs, NITs, IIMs and a few other centrally-funded Government institutions through the consortium headquarters set-up at the IIT Delhi. Besides, 60 Government or Government-aided engineering colleges and technical departments in universities have joined the Consortium with financial support from the AICTE.

Later on, it was renamed INDEST-AICTE Consortium.[50]

The Indian Institute of Technology, New Delhi (EPrints @IIT Delhi) provides access to Online courseware, older volumes of journals, more than 500 theses and dissertations are available in the repository. There are facilities for submitting material to the repository.

The Indian Institute of Technology, Bombay repository provides bibliographic information and abstracts for dissertations from 1965 onward. The masters thesis database has bibliographic information and abstracts from 1999 onward. There are more than 3000 full text theses and Dissertations available in the ETD database.

Nalanda, the Digital Library initiated in 1999 at the National Institute of Technology, Calicut, is one of the largest digital libraries in the country. The repository contains theses and dissertations, course materials, articles, and annual reports. It serves members of the campus with value added services in all the areas of Science/Engineering/Technology.

Social sciences

The Archives of Indian Labour is a unique digital project initiated at the V.V. Giri National Labour Institute (NOIDA, UP), in collaboration with the Association of Indian Labour Historians (AILH). The archive, is a prime repository of labor related records in the country, that aims at preservation of rapidly decaying documents and material on labor.

A Digital Library of electronic publications was set up in 1997, at the Parliament Library (New Delhi), to serve the information needs of members of the Parliament and officers of Lok Sabha Secretariat. The digital collections consist of reference books (atlases, directories etc), reports, e-journals, etc.

Humanities

India has one of the oldest and largest collections of manuscripts in the world. A significant proportion of them have not been preserved scientifically. National Mission for Manuscripts was established specially to tackle the problems related to manuscripts. The mission has already started a pilot project for digitizing the manuscripts in five states.[51] The National Library has undertaken a project for Digitization (Down the memory lane). The scanning and archiving of rare and brittle books and other documents on compact disc has been under taken. English books and documents published before 1900 and Indian publications of pre 1920 are being digitized. Up to now, 6600 selected books in Indian and English languages have already been scanned and stored on 548 CDs.

The Centre for Development of Advanced Computing (C-DAC) Digital Library of Art Masterpieces is "the first initiative of its kind in Asia. It will digitize 200 rare paintings of Rabindranath Tagore and Amrita Shergill from the National Gallery of Modern Arts (NGMA)."[46] The Indira Gandhi National Centre for the Arts (IGNCA), New Delhi, in collaboration with the Ministry of Communication and Information Technology, initiated a project, KALASAMPADA (Digital Library: Resources of Indian Cultural Heritage), for the development of databank of cultural heritage. Kalasampada facilitates the scholars (users) to access and view the materials including over 200,000 of manuscripts, over 100,000 slides, "thousands of rare books, rare photographs, audio and video along with highly researched publications of the IGNCA, from a single window."[52] It is a rich resource of information on Indian art and culture.

Other subjects

Indian Institute of Management, Kozikode (IIM-K), has established a repository for documents limited to the IIMK research community. They can submit preprints, postprints, and other scholarly publications for archiving. The Librarian's Digital Library is a repository set up at the Documentation Research Training Centre, Indian Statistical Institute, Bangalore. It aims to cover material of interest to librarians world-wide. The repository contains articles, theses and dissertations, presentations, multi-lingual documents, photographs, etc.

Information Science as a Discipline and Profession

Discipline

Today, Information Science is considered as a discipline in its own right, an interdisciplinary area of study. Its growth in India has been rather slow. There are very few information schools. They are coming into being slowly. There are only a few institutions conducting courses in information science as given below:

Birla Institute Of Technology, Ranchi (Jharkhand)

The Department of Information Science, Mersa, Ranchi, offers courses leading to an M.Sc. (Information Science) (two-year integrated program) (1993–) and a Ph.D.

Documentation Research and Training Centre, Bangalore (Karnataka), Indian Statistical Institute

From 2008, DRTC has introduced MS (LIS), that is Master of Science in Library and Information Science, that offers comprehensive instruction in the theory and practice of documentation and information science. DRTC also conducts a Research fellowship program, where the emphasis is on special libraries.

National Institute of Science Communication and Information Resources (NISCAIR) (formerly INSDOC), New Delhi

The Education and Training Division of NISCAIR, offers a two-year course leading to Associateship in Information Science (AIS) since 1976. AIS is a two-year program equivalent to Master's degree in Library and Information Science, recognized by Government of India and many Indian Universities.

University of Madras

In 1995, the Department of Library and Information Science, University of Madras, replaced its Master of library and Information Science, with a Master of Science (M.Sc.) in Library and Information Science. In 2004, the Department of Library and Information Science, University of Madras, was renamed Department of Information Science, as the first of its kind. Master of Library and Information Science course was replaced by "Master of Science" in Information Science (that is M.Sc. [Information Science]) beginning in academic session 2004–2005. It has also a provision for Ph.D. in Information Science.

The University of Mysore

Mysore, has established a new generation centre called the International School of Information Management

(I-SiM). ISiM, is a new age school for the knowledge Society. ISiM offers the following programs:

M.Tech. in Information Systems & Management (started in 2008), Doctoral Degree Program (Ph.D.) in Information Systems & Management, Executive Education Programs, Corporate Training.

Impact of information science on library science

In the 1970s, library schools introduced topics from information science. The UGC Panel on Library and Information Science (1982), recommended that library schools might consider changing the nomenclature of library science courses named B.Lib.Sc. and M.Lib.Sc. to BLISc. (Bachelor of Library and Information Science) and MLISc. (Master of Library and Information Science) respectively, so as to reflect the changes introduced in their curriculum. As a result, Library Schools have changed the names of their degrees.

At one time, a library school in India was generally called a "Department of Library Science." Beginning in the late 1970s, most were renamed as a "Department of Library and Information Science," as most of the library schools are called today. Thus, traditional library schools are teaching both library science and information science and their names and their degrees include the term "library and information science."

Profession

Information science as a profession is emerging slowly. The Society for Information Science (SIS) was formed during 1975, to look after the interests of people in the profession.[53] SIS is an all India professional body devoted to encouraging interaction among information professionals, scientists, managers, and users of information. Many of the members are also members of library associations. Another association that looks after the interests of information professionals is IASLIC (Indian Association of Special Libraries and Information Centres). It has created Special Interest Groups (SIGs) to bring together persons of common interests.

Librarianship as a Discipline and Profession

Discipline

Today, librarianship is a full-fledged discipline in its own right. It is recognized as a subject of study and research, worthy of study at the university level at par with other disciplines. There are separate library schools at university, college and institute level, often called Department of Library and Information Science. Librarianship as a discipline is taught at universities, colleges and institutes with curricula leading to the following degrees:

- Bachelor of library and Information Science
- Master of Library and Information Science
- M.Phil.
- Ph.D.
- Post-doctoral degree

The trend is toward establishing two-year integrated Master of Library and Information Science, and abolishing the Bachelor's degree. In recent years, there is also a trend toward offering specialized postgraduate courses. For professional jobs, a degree in library and information science, from a library school affiliated to a university, is a basic requirement. Thus, librarianship as a discipline is well established.

Profession

A profession is an occupation, vocation or career where specialized knowledge of a subject, field, or science is applied.[54]

To become a library professional in India, one is required to possess a degree in library and information science, obtained from a library school attached to a university or college/institute (affiliated to a university). Standards for library education have been formulated by the University Grants Commission (UGC), a coordinating and grant-giving body at the national level. There is an increasing emphasis on continuing education. There is a trend toward providing internship in libraries. For the job of an assistant librarian in a university library or a college librarian, one is required to pass a UGC Net or state level test. In India, the provision of "Licensed practitioners" has not been applied. Joint Council of Library Associations of India (JOCLAI) has formulated a Code of Ethics for the library profession in India. From the above, it follows that librarianship in India fulfills most of the major characteristics of a profession.

Education for LIS

History

William Alanson Borden (1853–1931), an American-trained librarian, was invited by His Highness the Maharaja Sayajirao III, Gaekwar of Baroda (1862–1939), to establish libraries in the princely State of Baroda. Borden started a training program in the State in 1911. It was the first library school to be established in India. Thus, the history of library education in India began in the year 1911. In 1937, the University of Madras introduced, effective from July 1937, a one-year postgraduate diploma course. This was the first full-time course conducted in India, another land mark in the history of library education. This was also the first diploma course conducted by a university.

The Department of Library Science at the University of Delhi initiated a postgraduate course in 1947. In 1948, the University of Delhi became the first university in India to institute a degree course in Library Science (a post-graduate course of study). In 1949, the first batch of students completed the two-year study program. They received their B.Lib.Sc. (Bachelor of Library Science) degrees in 1949. In 1949, a two-year course leading to the award of M.Lib.Sc. (Master of Library Science) degree was introduced to replace the previous program of B.Lib.Sc. The first cohort of students received their M.Lib.Sc. degree in 1951.

The University of Delhi was the first university in the British Commonwealth to introduce this course at the master's level. In 1951, it also became the first university in the country, as well as in the British Commonwealth to introduce doctoral studies in library science by framing regulations for such a doctoral program. A Ph.D. candidate was registered at the University of Delhi in the 1952–1953 academic session. The first Ph.D. in library science was awarded in 1957 to D.B. Krishna Rao by University of Delhi under the guidance of Dr S.R. Ranganathan.

The period of growth of LIS (Library and Information Science) education started in the early 1960s, when there was sudden growth of library education. Many new library schools were started in the 1960s. Realizing the need for standardization of syllabi, examination, qualifications of teachers, etc in the field of library science, UGC in 1961, appointed a Review Committee, under the Chairmanship of S.R. Ranganathan. The Committee submitted its report in 1965.[55] The report made many useful and far reaching recommendations regarding syllabi, standards, etc. This report is a landmark in the history of library education in India.

The Indian Association of Teachers of Library and Information Science (IATLIS) was founded in 1969. It has played a significant role in LIS education.

UGC set up in July 1977, a Specialist Panel, called UGC Panel on Library Science. Its aim was to advise the Commission regarding measures for improvement of standards and facilities for teaching and research, and for the development of interdisciplinary and multidisciplinary programs, etc.

The period of modernization started in the early 1990s. Library schools started revising their curriculum, introducing courses on computer application in libraries, and also included substantial amount of information science. It is also during this period that the library schools began to establish computer laboratories for giving hands-on experience to their students.

Growth of library schools

In 1947, at the time of independence, there were just five library schools at the university level. By the end of 1950s, there were 13 such schools. According to the *Directory of* *library and information schools in India* published in 1988, that covers information about 93 schools and other institutions in India offering training in library and information science at different levels, there are 66 university departments that offer a bachelor's degree in library and information science, 38 of which also offer a master's degree in library and information science, and four of which offer a master of philosophy degree in library and information science. There are 19 schools that offer a doctoral program in library and information science.[56] Today, there are 167 library schools (including information schools) conducting postgraduate courses (121 university level library schools and 46 colleges and institutes conducting library and information science programs including one organization, namely, NISCAIR (formerly INSDOC) that offers two-year Associateship in Information Science). There are 41 universities offering library and information science courses through correspondence or distance education. 129 universities are offering bachelor's degree including four offering a Post-graduate Diploma in Library Automation and Networking and one a Diploma in Health Science Librarianship; 118 offer master's degrees including 37 library schools that conduct two-year integrated master's program; 22 offer M.Phil. degree; 72 offer Ph.D. degree (based on data gathered by the present authors from various sources).

Levels of courses

Basically, Indian library Schools are providing library education at four levels:

1. B.LISc. (Bachelor of Library and Information Science)
2. M.LISc. (Master of Library and Information Science)
3. M.Phil (Master of Philosophy)
4. Ph.D.

Now, most of the universities award Bachelor of Library and Information Science (B.LISc.) degree. There are 118 library schools that are offering master's degrees. Out of these, 37 offer two-year integrated programs.

It was a guideline from UGC to universities that recommended introduction of M.Phil. program as a research degree between Master's and Ph.D. degrees. As a result, some library schools introduced M.Phil.

There are more than 50 Ph.D.s being produced annually. Ph.D. programs are now well established.

Admission requirements

For admission to bachelor's degree in LIS or two-year integrated master's course, the usual minimum qualification is a B.A./B.Sc. Some library schools, they conduct an admission test and/or interviews for admission, in addition to minimum academic qualifications prescribed for the purpose. For admission to one-year master's degree course, bachelor's degree in library and information science is prescribed. Many library schools conduct an admission test. Some schools have also prescribed professional experience as an essential requirement as well.

Qualifications for admission to M.Phil. and Ph.D. vary from school to school. To obtain a Ph.D., 2–3 years of residence is essential in many universities. In some universities, only a short period of residence is required.

Course content (outline)

Typical course content (outline) for Master of Library and Information Science (two-year integrated course) at University of Mysore is given below:

Foundations of Information Science and Society; Fundamentals of Information Technology; Information organization; Personality Development and Communication Sills; Content Organization (DDC)—Practicum; Information Resources; Organizing Information Resources-I; Information Retrieval Systems; Information Technology Skills—Practicum; Content Organization (UDC)—Practicum; Managing information Resources-II; Managing information and information centre; Data communication and networking; organizing information resources—Practicum I; Technology for information management—Practicum; Digital libraries; Information resources, systems and services; Research methods and project management; Organizing information resources—Practicum II; Project.[57]

The above two-year integrated program is spread over four semesters. The stress is on information science and technology. There is less stress on traditional library science.

The Indira Gandhi National Open University (IGNOU) is one of the premier institutions in the country providing Library and Information Science (LIS) courses through distance education. An outline of the syllabi is given below:

Syllabus for B.LISc.

Library and Society; Library Management; Library Classification Theory; Library Classification Practice; Library Cataloging Theory; Library Cataloging Practice; Reference and Information Sources; Information Services; Information Technology: Basics.

Syllabus for M.LISc.

The Program has been designed and developed keeping in view the handling of information rather than library materials as a whole. The program consists of six core courses, one project and six electives (out of which two have to be selected). Information, Communication and Society; Information Sources, Systems and Services; Information Processing and Retrieval; Management of Library and Information Centres; Fundamentals of Information Communication Technologies; Information Communication Technologies: Application; Project.

Electives (any two are to be chosen by the learner)

Preservation and Conservation of Library Materials (Elective); Research Methodology (Elective); Academic Library System (Elective); Technical Writing (Elective); Scientometrics and Informetrics (Elective); Public Library System and Services (Elective).

The school follows a multi-media approach for instruction. The students are offered self-instructional learning course material packages along with:

- Assignments for assessment and feedback
- Supporting audio–video programs
- Face-to-face interaction with academic counselors at Study Centers
- Practical work at designated institutions
- Telecast of Video Programmes on National Network DD1 and EDUSTAT
- Broadcast of Audio Programmes by All India Radio (Selected Stations)
- Teleconference sessions through Gyan Darshan.
- Interactive Radio Counselling Programmes.[58]

IGNOU conducts BLISc. (one-academic year) and MLISc. (one-academic year) courses, as well as PGDLAN (Post Graduate Diploma in Library Automation and Networking) (one-academic year) through distance mode. BLISc. and MLISc. courses at IGNOU provide a combination of library science and information science. It has introduced many innovative approaches for providing distance learning to the learners. The courses offered by IGNOU are very popular. They have set new trends in multi-media based LIS education in the country. In 2008, IGNOU has introduced MLISc. online. The course was inaugurated in June. This the first online course in LIS to be introduced in India.

Methods of teaching and evaluation

There are a variety of methods of teaching being used in Indian library schools. However, the lecture method predominates.

Usually, evaluation is based on performance on a written examination. The students are tested through written examination at the end of the year or at the end of each semester. The written examination is based on essay type questions. There may be some questions requiring writing of short notes or questions involving objective questions or multiple-choice questions. The examination may last for 2–3 hours.

Oral examinations are used to assess dissertation/ project report, sessional work, etc. Increasingly library schools are introducing internal assessment. Internal assessment is done by the teacher teaching the course, based on written assignments, seminar, practical work, etc.

As regards internship, the system varies from library school to library school. In some library schools, it is a compulsory part of the course.

Accreditation

There is no system of accreditation of library schools by a national organization in India. UGC, Association of Indian Universities, and the Ministry of Human Resource Development (Government of India) have played a definite role in the matter of equating degrees within India and degrees awarded by foreign universities. Each university has a specified procedure to equate degrees. Usually, they follow the advice of higher bodies as mentioned above. The National Assessment and Accreditation Council (NAAC) is an autonomous body established by the University Grants Commission (UGC) of India to assess and accredit institutions of higher education in the country. It has started the process. In due course of time, library schools will also be covered. However, courses conducted by IGNOU have been accredited by the Council responsible for accreditation of courses run by the open universities.

Continuing education

The University Grants Commission, in pursuance of the National Policy on Education 1986 and its program of action, had set up 57 Academic Staff Colleges (ASCs) in different Universities/Institutions in the country. These Academic Staff Colleges conduct specially designed Academic Staff orientation programs for newly appointed lecturers and refresher courses for in-service teachers. These programs have proved to be quite useful for LIS teachers and librarians working in universities and colleges, coming under the purview of UGC.

In regards to librarians and teachers of LIS, library associations, library schools, institutions like DRTC, NISCAIR, DESIDOC, etc. also conduct continuing education programs for their benefit.

Conclusion

There has been a proliferation of library schools. Emergence of such a large number of library schools (i.e., 167) has led to an oversupply of library professionals. Library schools are beginning to regularly revise their courses, keeping in mind the latest developments in LIS as well as in ICT. Reports of the UGC Curriculum Development Committee[59,60] have proven to be quite useful in this regard.

Professional Associations

Introduction

There are a variety of professional organizations and associations in India that are organized at national, state, and local levels. They number more than 200, if students' associations are included. Some of the major organizations are described here.

Indian Association of Teachers of Library and Information Science

IATLIS is a professional association of about 500 teachers and library professionals. Since its inception in 1969, IATLIS has been involved in issues of LIS Education in India, especially curriculum development, teaching methods, infrastructure, teachers' training, etc. It looks after promotion of the professional interests of LIS teachers. It conducts national seminars, workshops, training programs etc and brings out *IATLIS Communications* (official journal) and publishes pre-conference volumes and other books.

The Indian Library Association

At the second session (September 13, 1933) of the first "All India Library Conference" held at Calcutta during September 12–14, 1933, a resolution was passed, that led to the formation of Indian Library Association. The objectives of the Association:

1. Promotion of library movement and improvement in library services in all its aspects in India
2. Promotion of library science education and improvement in the training of librarians in India
3. Establishment of libraries, documentation and information centers and assistance in their establishment and working
4. Promotion of appropriate library legislation in India
5. Providing a common forum to all persons engaged or interested in library and information work by holding conferences and meetings for discussion of professional, technical and organizational issues
6. Accreditation of institutions imparting library and information science education and training
7. Promotion as well as formulation of standards, norms, guidelines, etc. for management of library and information systems and services[61]

In 1933, ILA had 70 members and in 2006, it had 7218 members. In a large country like India, where around ten thousand professionals (degree holders) are estimated to be produced every year and the total number of professionals may be around 200,000; the membership figure is low. This is a matter of concern.

The ILA has a president, six vice-presidents, a general secretary and an executive committee. It is organized so as to operate through 11 sectional committees. Major activities of ILA include sponsoring conferences, seminars, conventions, training programs, lectures, etc. It organized an International Conference on Ranganathan's Philosophy at New Delhi in 1985. In the same year, in collaboration with Sarada Ranganathan Endowment for Library Science, it organized the Second Regional FID Conference. ILA hosted the 1992 IFLA Conference at New Delhi. It was a great success. It brings out *ILA Bulletin* and *ILA Newsletter* on a regular basis. It publishes professional tools, conference and seminar proceedings, and annual reports.

ILA was founded in 1933. Thus, the year 2008 was the Platinum Jubilee Year of ILA. It was being celebrated by ILA through various programs. The year 2010 is the Centenary Year of Library Movement in the country. Plans for celebration are underway. ILA has been in the forefront, in taking up issues facing Indian librarianship, such as salary scales, library legislation, status of librarians, etc.

IASLIC

A meeting of librarians was held on September 3, 1955 at the Lecture Hall of the Indian Museum, Calcutta. This is the meeting in which the Indian Association of Special Libraries and Information Centres (IASLIC) was formally established.[62] The major objectives are:

> To improve the quality of library and information services and documentation work;
> To coordinate the activities of and to foster mutual co-operation and assistance among the special libraries, scientific, technological and research institutions, learned societies, commercial organisations, industrial research establishments, as well as other information and documentation centres to the fullest extent;
> To serve as a field of active contact for libraries, information bureaus, documentation centres, scientists, research workers, specialists, and others having common interest;
> To improve the technical efficiency of the workers in special libraries, and information and documentation centres; and to look after their professional welfare;...[63]

IASLIC publishes monographs and other types of documents. *IASLIC Bulletin* is the official journal, published quarterly since 1956 and The *IASLIC Newsletter* has been published bimonthly since 1966. The Association conducts short-term courses, workshops, round tables, seminars etc. It provides consultancy services. It has created Special Interest Groups (SIGs) to bring together persons of common interest. In addition, it organizes conferences, seminars, lectures and study circles.

State level associations

There are a large number of associations at the state level. Each state and union territory has a separate association, sometimes even more than one. The leading associations include Andhra Library Association, Bengal Library Association, Delhi Library Association, Madras Library Association, etc.

Conclusion

The National Library, Kolkata, is the largest single library that serves as the depository as well as the repository of all the published material of India. In addition, there are two other national libraries, namely, the National Science Library and the National Medical Library. India is a large country having one of the largest education systems in the world. Academic and research libraries are under tremendous pressure due to lack of resources and increasing number of students, research scholars and faculty to be served by them.

Public libraries in India have made much progress after independence. However, their penetration is inadequate. They have yet to reach the masses spread over remote corners of the country especially in rural areas.

School libraries form the weakest link. Public schools and schools run by central government are doing a better job in providing good school libraries. Schools located in metropolitan towns have better libraries. However, libraries attached to rural schools need a massive reform.

Special libraries exist in great variety and have done fairly well compared with other kinds of libraries. There are many special libraries, especially in the field of science and technology, that are well-equipped to provide highly satisfactory services to meet the needs of their users.

Today, there are 167 library schools (including information schools). There are 41 universities offering LIS courses through correspondence or distance education. 118 schools offer master's degree and 72 of them offer Ph.D. program. Thus, India has a fairly large system of LIS education.

ARCHIVES AND ARCHIVAL SCIENCE

Introduction

The valuable history of India is embedded in millions of records that exist in the form of manuscripts, inscriptions, and other kinds of records. Unfortunately, most such materials have yet to be preserved and restored in a scientific manner. However, efforts are being made in this direction.

Archival studies has been a rather neglected field in India. It has fewer than 100 archives. However, the situation is changing. Industrial houses, universities and research institutions are beginning to set up their archives.

Legislation Concerning Archives and Regulations That Relate to Record Keeping

The Public Records Act was passed by the Indian Parliament in 1993 to regulate the Management, Administration, and Preservation of Public Records of the Union Government, Union Territories, Public Sector Undertakings, Statutory Bodies and Corporations, Commissions and Committees constituted by the Union Government or Union Territory Administrations. The functioning of the Act is given in detail under the Public Records Rules, 1997.[64] Under the Act, the National Archives of India (NAI) has been given the major responsibility regarding management, administration, and preservation of public records.

National Archives and Services

The National Archives of India, New Delhi

The National Archives of India (NAI), New Delhi, is the premier organized record repository in India. It was set up in March 1891 at Calcutta (now called Kolkata) as the Imperial Record Department. It was shifted to New Delhi after the transfer of the Capital from Calcutta to New Delhi in 1911. It has set up four regional repositories in Bhopal, Bhubaneswar, Jaipur, and Pondicherry.

Activities. NAI is the repository of the noncurrent records of the Government of India and holds them in trust for the use of administrators and scholars. It is an Attached Office of the Department of Culture under the Ministry of Tourism and Culture. NAI performs a wide range of activities. Its main activity is concerned with "Preserving the records of Government of India in its custody, and regulating the Access and Record Management policy of the Government" as per the provisions laid down in Public Record Act.[65]

Holdings. The holdings of records in the National Archives

run into 40 Kms. of shelf-space area and are in a regular series from the year 1748 onwards, though there are stray records of the earlier period as well...Apart from records on paper, we also have records on palm leaf, birch bark, parchment etc. The records are broadly of four categories: Public Records, Oriental Records, Manuscripts and Private Papers. These records throw light on the activities of the later Mughals, the East India Company and British

Rule and the emergence and growth of the freedom struggle in India. They also shed valuable light on our social, political, economic and cultural life. In addition, there is a rich collection of Private Papers and more than 7500 microfilm rolls of records acquired from different countries...

The total holdings in the custody of NAI comprises of 3,875,332 files; 64,221 volumes; 110,332 maps and cartographic items; 3601 Bills assented to by the President(s) of India; 1065 Treaties; 2442 rare manuscripts. NAI has a wide ranging and an extremely rich collection, including government records and private papers especially records of national importance that are invaluable to research scholars.[66]

Services. NAI offers xeroxing, microfilming and photocopying facilities and also undertakes search for records on behalf of scholars and institutions on payment. Facilities for online access to records are available from the Research Room of the Department.

Finding Aids. To facilitate retrieval of information, there are various types of finding aids that have been designed. These include Guide to Records, Indices, Press Lists, Calendars, Descriptive Lists, Subject Lists etc.

Eleventh Five-Year Plan. The report of the Working Group on Art and Culture of the Ministry of Culture, Government of India for the 11th five-year plan (2007–2012) recommended "six new schemes to be taken up by National Archives of India during the 11th Five Year Plan. These schemes are aimed at modernizing the National Archives and enhancing the quality of services besides conservation of public records."[67] The work on some of the schemes has already started.

Other national repositories

Other national repositories include:

> Archives of Indian Labour, Noida (UP)
> Indira Gandhi National Centre for the Arts, New Delhi[68]
> National Library, Kolkata[69]
> Nehru Memorial Museum and Library, New Delhi
> Parliamentary Museum and Archives, New Delhi
> Reserve Bank of India Archives, Pune

State archives

Some of the leading state archives are listed below:

Gujarat State Archives, Gandhinagar. Gujarat State Archives have been created from records (files and manuscripts) of several Princely States and Political Agencies of British India. The records holdings of the Gujarat State Archives are broadly divided into two series, namely, the records of the former princely states and the secretariat records. Gujarat is very rich in terms of archival wealth.

The Karnataka State Archives, Bangalore. The Karnataka State Archives is a repository of non-current records of the Government. It also has Ecclesiastical (Religious) Archives, Business Archives, Industrial Archives and other Private Archives. Work has been initiated to computerize all the required information about the documents. The State Archives has undertaken a program called "Oral History."

The Kerala State Archives Department, Thiruvananthapuram. It is the custodian of all public records (non-current) of permanent value of State Government and its various departments. The records received from private individuals and institutions are also being maintained in the department.

Punjab State Archives (Patiala and Chandigarh). Punjab State Archives have nearly 1 million records in its custody. "Punjab archives have illustrated manuscripts, including copies of *Ain-I-Akbari*, *Zaffarnama* of Guru Gobind Singh, *Shahnama* of Firdausi, *Adi Granth* of 1666, tales of *Laila Majnu*, rare Tibetan palm-leaf manuscripts etc."[70] Punjab Archives has inherited a large number of records from the various princely states that got merged into the present Punjab.

The Tamil Nadu Archives, Chennai. Tamil Nadu Archives and Historical Research is regarded as one of the biggest Archives and Research Institutions in South East Asia. It is a rich resource of records going back to the seventeenth century. It houses

> ...the records of various Departments of the Secretariat, erstwhile Board of Revenue, a few Heads of Departments, premutiny records of Collectorate and District Courts and records of defunct Departments. The records dating back to 1657 A.D. (Dutch Records) are preserved in this Archives.[71]

West Bengal State Archives, Kolkata. The

> collections include East India Company's administrative records from 1770 to 1858, some Persian and Bengali records from 1624. Dutch records relating to Chinsurah from 1702 to 1827, some Danish records on Serampore, records of the Secretariat Departments and records of the Crown period 1858 –1947 and indices.[72]

College and university archives

There is an increasing awareness in academic institutions about the value of archives. Therefore, a number of colleges, universities and other academic institutions have set up their archives. Some of these are described below:

Indian Institute of Astrophysics Archives, Bangalore
Indian Institute of Astrophysics archives has important
    collections, "some of which are more than 200 years
    old."[73]
Indian Institute of Science Archives, Bangalore
The Institute has established an Archives and Publications
    Cell to collect, catalog and preserve all documents of
    relevance to the Institute.
Jawaharlal Nehru University, New Delhi
The Archives on Contemporary History set up in 1970 at
    the Jawaharlal Nehru University, New Delhi, is a
    "repository of variety of materials on the leftwing
    movement in India."[74]
Jesuit Madurai Province Archives, Sacred Heart College,
    Kodaikanal
Jesuit Madurai Province Archives has a large collection of
    rare books, manuscripts, personal papers, antique instruments (pocket watches used by missionaries, old French
    medical instruments) etc.[75]
Maulana Azad Library, Aligarh
Maulana Azad Library of Aligarh Muslim University has a
    wide-ranging collection consisting of books, periodicals, pamphlets, manuscripts, paintings and photographs. The Library "performs the functions of a
    National Library so far as its collection of Oriental
    manuscripts are concerned. It is because of these rich
    collections of immense research value that this Library
    is reckoned among major libraries of the world."[76]
The library has a rich collection of manuscripts, rare
books, manuscripts and early paintings.

Film archives

The mission of the National Film Archive of India is

> to safeguard the heritage of Indian Cinema for posterity and act as a centre for dissemination of a healthy film culture in the country. Promotion of film scholarship and research on various aspects of cinema also form part of its Charter. Familiarizing foreign audiences with Indian Cinema and to make it more visible across the globe is another declared objective of the Archive.

The National Film Archive of India acquires

> National and State Award winning films, Indian Panorama films, Box-office hits and films shown in international film festivals. Film adaptations of famous literary works, films

representing different genres of Indian Cinema, news-reels, documentaries representing the categories mentioned above also find their way to the Archive. Selected foreign films representing national cultures, different genres and landmark works of major filmmakers from different countries are also acquired and used for archival and research purposes.

Books and periodicals covering

Indian and World Cinema, Festival Publications, ancillary material like Song booklets, photographs, wall posters, pamphlets, folders, disc records and other memorabilia on Cinema are also collected and preserved by the Research & Documentation Section.

The treasures of the NFAI's film collection include "the surviving fragments of the films of D.G. Phalke and Baburao Painter, the silent films of Himansu Rai and Franz Osten, a representative collection of films of the great film companies and studios of the 1930s and 1940s..."[77] NFAI has a rich and unique collection about Indian Cinema, not to be found anywhere else.

Other kinds of repositories

A few of the other kinds of repositories are described below:

The Archives of Krishnamurti Foundation India (KFI), Chennai
The materials include

documents and records of Krishnamurti's life, books, manuscripts, transcripts, journals, letters, newspaper cuttings, organizational documents, photographs, audio tapes (including digital audio tapes), gramophone records, videotapes, films, and CD-Rom.[78]

J. Krishnamurti was a great scholar and thinker.
Godrej Archives, Mumbai
It is a record of the contribution made by the Godrej Group to the "industrial history of India, as well as the country's future." Being company archives,

it houses an assortment of agreements, letters, technical drawings, press clippings, old catalogs, advertisements, testimonials from clients and customers, audio-visual recordings, photographs, awards, medals and unique memorabilia items.

The collection consists of manuscripts, photographs, audio–visual materials, memorabilia, printed materials and oral history records. The Manuscript Collection (1836–2007) includes old documents (553 accessioned files). Based on information provided by Ms. Vrunda Pathare, Godrej Archives, Godrej & Boyce Mfg. Co. Ltd., Mumbai.
The French Institute of Pondicherry, Pondicherry

The major collection consists of 8187 palm-leaf bundles, 360 paper codices and 1144 recent paper transcripts (i.e., post-1950 paper manuscripts commissioned or copied by employees of the IFP), which are now on-line.[79]
Mukul Dey Archives, Santiniketan
Mukul Dey was a pioneer Indian graphic artist, who has left behind a large body of work. The work throws light on the early twentieth century Indian art scene. This is a private archives. The entire body of the Archives consists of "anywhere between 500 –750 individual files and more."[80]
The Roja Muthiah Research Library, Chennai
The Roja Muthiah Research Library (RMRL), founded in 1994, provides research materials and facilities for students of Tamil studies.[81]
Sarasvati Mahal Library, Thanjavur
The Thanjavur Maharaja Serfoji's Sarasvati Mahal Library is one gem among a few medieval libraries existing in the world. "It is an unparalleled repository of culture and an inexhaustible treasure house of knowledge built up by successive dynasties of Nayaks and the Marathas of Thanjavur."[82] It is considered as a great treasure house of manuscripts, maps, paintings and books on art, literature and culture.
Tata Institute of Fundamental Research Archives, Mumbai
TIFR Archives, Mumbai, stores the collective memory of the institute by preserving records that tell the history of the Institute from 1945 to the present. The holdings include manuscripts, photographs, oral histories; print and audio-visual material; fine arts and scientific instruments as well as digitized recordings of lectures given by distinguished visitors to the Tata Institute Based on notes provided by Dr Indira Chowdhury, Consultant Archivist, TIFR Archives, Mumbai. Under one roof, researchers can find a rich resource for not only history of TIFR, but also for history of science in India.
The Tata Central Archives, Pune
The Tata Central Archives (TCA) is the first ISO 9001:2000 Certified Business Archives in India. They "collect, and retain letters, documents, images, printed books, group publications and ephemera of potential historical and critical significance to the Tata Group, one of the largest and most respected business houses in India."[83]
Realizing the importance of archives, many other corporate groups also have set up their archives. These include Ambanis, Indian Aluminum Company and DCM group.

Digital archival collections and digital finding aids

There are many projects for digitization of archival collections that have been undertaken during the last few years. Some of these are described here.

Computerization and digitalization program at NAI, for an "Automated Retrieval System" has been undertaken and

> computerization of reference media to records of the Home (Pub.) (1748–1859), Home (Pol.) (1907–1968), Foreign & Political Deptt. (1860–1946), Ministry of External Affairs (1947–1970) and Ministry of State (1947–1953) has been completed.

NAI has also computerized the reference media of Library Books. A Project for WAN Connectivity of five Libraries under Ministry of Culture is in progress. NAI has also undertaken a project with the assistance of the National Institute of Advanced Studies, Bangalore, for digitalization of rare and valuable manuscripts.[84]

Under five-year plan (2007–2012), it has been proposed that

> In order to minimize deterioration of rare and old records due to continuous handling, a new scheme of digitization of rare and old records may be implemented by NAI... Under the new proposed scheme for 11th Five Year Plan, NAI is to launch an archives of E-Records in collaboration with those Ministries where e-governance has made considerable head way.[67]

The work is going on under this scheme.

The Indira Gandhi National Centre for the Arts (IGNCA), has created a digital library on Indian art and culture.[85] The digital library of IGNCA is a tremendous effort and a valuable asset, covering a wide range of records.

Archival Science as a Discipline and Profession

Archival science in India has become a discipline in its own right. It has a growing body of knowledge. The theoretical issues are coming to the forefront. Archival science as a subject of study is being taught in India at the university/college/institute level.

Archivists are mostly employed by the National Archives and its branches, in state and local archival departments. However, increasingly, industrial and commercial firms, business houses, universities, religious institutions and libraries also have positions for archivists.

Education for Archivists and Records Managers

The NAI has been conducting training course in Archives Keeping since 1941. Archival education at the formal level can be traced to 1976, when the Institute of Archival Training was established at New Delhi. It was later, in 1980, renamed as the School of Archival Studies. Today, there are a number of universities and institutes that impart education for archivists and record managers.

The information about the courses offered is given in the next few paragraphs.

School of Archival Studies, National Archives of India, New Delhi

The School offers a one-year diploma course in Archives and Records Management. This School also offers certificate courses in Care and Conservation of Books, Manuscripts and Archives (8 weeks) and Reprography (4 weeks). Short-term certificate courses in Archives Management and Record Management and sub-professional courses in Servicing and Repair of Records are also being run by it.

Institutes/Universities offering post-graduate diploma, postgraduate certificate and undergraduate degree in archival studies include:

Post-graduate diploma courses

1. Diploma in Archival Studies (one-year)
   School of Archival Studies, NAI
2. PG Diploma in Archives Keeping (part-time)
   Annamalai University, Annamalai Nagar
3. PG Diploma in Archives and Documentation and Management
4. PG Diploma in Archival Science and Manuscriptology, Osmania University, Administrative Building, Hyderabad
5. PG Diploma in Archival Studies
   Pondicherry University, Pondicherry
   Postgraduate certificate courses
6. PG Certificate in Archives, Gujarat Vidyapith, Ahmedabad
   Undergraduate courses
7. BA in Archival Science, Maharishi Dayanand Saraswati University, Ajmer—Eligibility: 10 + 2

According to Johare,

> There is little evidence of concern for education and training of record keepers in managing electronic records in India. ...the curriculum content remains traditional in approach due to the lack of local expertise and facilities to deliver education and training programs on ERM.[86]

In view of the significance of electronic records management (ERM), this area needs to be covered adequately in courses for education and training of record keepers.

There are no advance courses at the Master's level and there is also a need to start a Ph.D. program. Need exists for starting separate departments of archival science at universities.

Professional Associations

There are two major professional bodies in the country. These are The National Committee of Archivists and the Indian Historical Records Commission as described below:

The National Committee of Archivists

The National Committee of Archivists is a professional body of archivists from all the States and Union Territories. It has a purely advisory role.[87]

The Indian Historical Records Commission

The Indian Historical Records Commission was set up by the Government of India in 1919 as a consulting body[88] The Commission has played a significant role in various matters relating to different aspects of archives. Its opinions carry a great deal of weight with different levels of the government.

Association of Indian Archivists, New Delhi

Association of Indian Archivists is a national association. Archivists and archival institutions are its members. The association is rather inactive and many archivists are not aware of its activities.

Electronic Records as Archival Documents

Under the 11th five-year plan (2007–2012), it has been proposed that "...NAI is to launch an archives of E-Records in collaboration with those Ministries where e-governance has made considerable head way."[67] ERM presents many challenges. One main challenge is to ensure that digital records remain sustainable, authentic and accessible over a period of time.

Preservation of Documents

Preservation of documents is a major issue. In recent years, the state has taken active steps in this direction. For the latest five-year plan (2007–2012), the Working Group of the Ministry of Culture,

> also recommended implementation of a new scheme: 'Assistance to the State Archives to Conserve and Digitize Records of National Importance.' Under the scheme, identification of records of national importance held by the State Governments Archives will be undertaken so that these Archives could be assisted on a project mode to conserve and digitize the same.[89]

A scheme of financial assistance to support Archival Repositories, Government Libraries/Museums of State/Union Territory Administrations for their developmental activities and preservation of records, books and manuscripts, is available. The Department of Culture, Government of India has set up a Grants Committee under the above scheme for allotting grants in aid of preservation of records. The above scheme is being used by state archives, libraries and other institutions for preservation/conservation/repair of the records.

NFAI is taking good care of its film collection.

> In the beginning, the NFAI film collection was stored in improvised film vaults in the premises of the Film and TV Institute of India. Since the inauguration of its new building in 1994, NFAI has its own film vaults designed according to international film preservation standards.[90]

Other Issues

Archival studies in India face a large number of issues.

> Many records collections are still without any guides or hand-book let alone comprehensive descriptive lists, and very few repositories, public or private, have yet developed a well-articulated program of documents-publication. Most of the collections still continue to be housed in primitive conditions...Very little systematic effort has been made to survey, describe, organize or make use of records in private custody, and particularly, those of institutional, religious or commercial provenance. Lack of trained archivists continues seriously to impede the archival work in the country...[88]

Similar issues have been raised by Rakesh Mohan. He has pointed out that "Establishing physical, administrative and intellectual control over our documentary heritage is the most challenging job because of sheer variety of media on which records are stored."[91]

Conclusion

Up to now, the field of archival studies in India has been a rather neglected one. In recent years, business houses such as Ambanis, TATA, DCM, Godrej, Indian Aluminum Company, etc. have set up their archives. In addition, a number of academic and research institutions have taken initiative to establish their archives.

Under the Eleventh Five-Year Plan (2007–12) of the Government of India, a number of schemes and projects are being implemented for collection of private papers, networking of state and national archives, digitization and preservation of records and modernization of archives. In view of these developments, the demand for trained archivists should increase. There is going to be an increasing potential for employment in this area.

MUSEUMS AND MUSEOLOGY

Introduction

History of museums

In India, precursors of the museum included prehistoric cave paintings, *alekhyagrihas* (*Ranga Mahal*—Hall of paintings), *chitrasalas* (Paintings Gallery), *devakulas*, *visvakarma mandirs* and monasteries, that served the purpose of education and healthy entertainment. The great stupa at Bharhut with its inscriptions in the contemporary *Brahmi* for identification of schemes did exist as an open-air museum. Even today, temples, monasteries etc., function as museums in the country. The genesis of the present day museum goes back to the foundation of the Asiatic Society of Bengal in 1784. For the first time, the Asiatic Society of Bengal, by a historical decision in 1796 to open its collection to the public, established the Indian Museum, Calcutta in 1814. Six provincial museums were established in South India around that time. This period was a great incentive for other parts of the country to accelerate the museum movement slowly but steadily.

The outburst of Indian Mutiny in 1857 left its impact on the growth of the cultural institutions. By the year 1857, there were twelve museums in India. The progress of the Indian Museum Movement was slowed down for a short while. During the coronation year of Queen Victoria, 1887, many museums were established.

The dawn of the twentieth century was an era of awakening and great reforms. Because of the efforts of Lord Curzon many on-site museums were opened at important sites through the Archaeological Survey of India. During the visit of the Prince of Wales to India, in order to commemorate this occasion, the Prince of Wales Museum was opened. It was completed in 1914. In 1936, there were 105 museums of all sorts in India. In 1946, all the museums under the Archaeological Survey of India were brought under the control of the Museum Branch of the Archaeological Survey of India. In the middle of the twentieth century State Museum of Assam, Guwahati (1940), Central Museum, Arunachal Pradesh (1956), Punjab Government Museum (1959), Orissa State Museum (1963), and Manipur State Museum (1969) were established. As of 2008, there are about 700 museums in India.

In recent times, there has been a tremendous interest taken by national policy makers, scholars and cultural icons in museums. This has led to an extraordinary growth in museums of different kinds. During the last 10 years are so, major changes in the filed of museology in India have taken place. Museums are using ICT (information and computer technology) in the display of museum objects, digitization of museum objects, dissemination of knowledge through the Web sites, publications, e-governance, ticketing, security, audio-guide, etc.

A National Mission on Monuments and Antiquities has been established. It has launched its activities throughout the country with independent functional strategy in each state and union territory. It is envisaged that the mandate of the Mission should be achieved within a stipulated time frame of 5 years i.e., 2007–2012. These are positive developments.

Legislation

The cultural renaissance of the early nineteenth century included enactment of the first ever-antiquarian legislation in India known as Bengal Regulation XIX of 1810. This was soon followed by another legislation called as Madras Regulation VII of 1817. Both these regulations vested the Government with a power to intervene whenever the public buildings were under threat of misuse. The Act XX of 1863, was therefore enacted to empower the Government to prevent injury to and preserve buildings remarkable for their antiquity or for their historical or architectural value.

The Indian Treasures Trove Act, 1878 (Act No. VI of 1878) was promulgated to protect and preserve treasures found accidentally but had the archeological and historical value. In a landmark development in 1886, James Burgess, the then Director General, succeeded in prevailing upon the Government for issuing these directions: forbidding any person or agency to undertake excavation without prior consent of the Archaeological Survey of India and debarring officers from disposing of antiquities found or acquired without the permission of the Government.

Cultural heritage ushered in a new era when The Ancient Monuments Preservation Act, 1904 (Act No. VII of 1904) was promulgated. This Act provided effective preservation and authority over monuments particularly those, which were under the custody of individual or private ownership. The next important act was The Antiquities Export Control Act, 1947 (Act No. XXXI of 1947).

When the Ancient and Historical Monuments and Archaeological Sites and Remains (Declaration of National Importance) Act, 1951 (No LXXI of 1951) was enacted, all the ancient and historical monuments and archaeological sites and remains protected earlier under "The Ancient Monuments Preservation Act, 1904" were re-declared as monuments and archaeological sites of national importance. Another 450 monuments and sites of Part 'B' States were also added. Some more monuments and archaeological sites were also declared as of national importance under Section 126 of the States Reorganization Act, 1956.

The Ancient Monuments and Archaeological Sites and Remains Act 1958 (No 24 of 1958) was enacted on August 28, 1958. This Act provides for the preservation of ancient and historical monuments and archeological sites and remains of national importance, for the regulation of archeological excavations, and for the protection of sculptures, carvings and other like objects. The Antiquities and Art Treasures Act 1972 (No. 52 of 1972) is the latest Act, enacted on September 9, 1972 for effective control over the moveable cultural property of antiquities and art treasures.[92]

The Archaeological Survey of India (ASI), under the Ministry of Culture, is the premier organization for archaeological research and protection of the cultural heritage of the nation. Maintenance of ancient monuments and archaeological sites and remains of national importance are the prime concerns of the ASI. Besides, it regulates all archaeological activities in the country under the Acts of 1958 and 1972. At present there are 41 site museums under the control of ASI.

National Museums

Indian Museum, Kolkata

This Museum is an autonomous institution of national importance, funded by the Department of Culture, Government of India. It was established on February 2, 1814 at the Asiatic Society, the earliest learned body in the country. It is considered one of the oldest regular museums of the world and repository of the largest number of museum objects in India.

National Museum, New Delhi

On August 15, 1949, C. Rajagopalachari, the then Governor General of India inaugurated an exhibition at the Audience Hall of the Rashtrapati Bhavan that later formed the nucleus of the National Museum. The exhibition at the Audience Hall consisted of items which had been sent to the Royal Academy, London for an exhibition earlier in 1949. The objects received from various museums for the purpose of the exhibition were not returned to the respective museums. Instead it was decided to keep the objects in New Delhi to form the National Museum. The National Museum, New Delhi, started functioning in a true sense only with the inauguration of the first unit of its building on December 18, 1960. Apart from collections of Prehistory, Archaeology, Jewellery, Paintings, Decorative Arts, Manuscripts, Central Asian Antiquities, Anthropology, Pre-Columbian and Western Art, Arms and Armour and Numismatics and Epigraphy, the museum today has separate branches of Publications, Public Relations, Education, Library, Exhibition, Display, Modeling, Photography, Security and Administration. A well-equipped Conservation Laboratory not only provides restoration to all the art objects but also training facilities to the students and deserving professionals. There are galleries for Prehistory, Indus Valley Civilization, Maurya, Satavahana and Sunga Art, Late Medieval Art, Indian Bronzes, Central Asian Art, Chamba Rangmahal, Indian Miniature Paintings, Manuscripts, Pre-Columbian and Western Art, Indian Coins and Copper Plates, Arms and Armour, Wood-carvings and Musical Instruments. New galleries include Buddhist Art, Tantra Art, Evolution of Indian Scripts and Coins, Decorative Arts, Paintings from Tanjore and Mysore, Tribal Life Style of North-East India, Jewellery, Indian Textiles have been set up recently. An exhibition of India's maritime heritage set up by the Indian Navy in the National Museum covers the evolution of maritime activity of India.

National Museum of Natural History, New Delhi

In 1972, it was decided that the country needed a museum of Natural History to depict its flora, fauna and mineral wealth, to provide an out of school facility for education of children and to promote environmental awareness among the masses. The museum opened its doors to the public on June 5, 1978, with a gallery on Natural History. Since then it has added three galleries, a Discovery and Activity Room for pre-school children. It has also conducted a variety of educational programs and brought out popular literature. In addition, the museum started three regional centers at Mysore, Bhopal and Bhubaneshwar. The museum has four exhibit galleries, namely: The Introduction of Natural History, Nature's Network Ecology, Conservation and Cell—The Basic Unit of Life. These not only provide useful information to the visitors but also serve as valuable resources in supplementing classroom teaching.

National Children's Museum, New Delhi

The National Children's Museum displays a rich collection of toys and dolls from different countries, stone and bronze objects, traditional jewelry, arts and crafts, musical instruments, currency of various countries, etc. The Children's Creative Work Gallery, displays the pieces of arts created by children. Summer camps are organized, with workshops on arts, theatre, painting, music, dance, etc. The Museum also provides drama kits, stories, puppets, toys, costumes and puppet shows. The museum complex includes a hostel, sports facilities, science park, aquarium, jet fighter, functional mini train, etc.

National Rail Museum, New Delhi

The National Rail Museum is a museum in Chanakyapuri, New Delhi which focuses on the rail heritage of India. It opened on the February 1, 1977. It is located in over 10 acres of land with both indoor and outdoor exhibits. A toy train offers rides around its site on regular days. The Museum houses the world's oldest operational steam locomotive (certified by the Guinness Book of Records), the Fairy Queen, built in 1855.

National Gandhi Museum, Delhi

The National Gandhi Museum, Rajghat, has an extremely impressive collection of books, journals and documents, audio–visual materials, exhibits, photographs, relics, memorabilia and art pieces that are related to Mahatma Gandhi, Father of the Nation (India). This museum was opened in the year 1961. It is an excellent place for researchers and students interested in Gandhian thoughts and the Indian Freedom Struggle.

The Allahabad Museum, Allahabad

The Allahabad Museum, Allahabad, was declared as an institution of national importance by the Government of India in 1985. This Museum is famous for its collection of Bharhut, Bhumara and Jamsot, Sculptures and for the terracotta from Kausambi, Bhita, Jhusi, Patliputra, Sarnath, Rajghat and Ahichhatra. The Museum also has paraphernalia and heirlooms of the Nehru family, including manuscripts of *An Autobiography* by Jawaharlal Nehru and a large volume of correspondence. Among the Museum collections are paintings by members of the Bengal School of Painters and Vijayavargiya. Among the foreign painters, mention may be made of Nicholas Roerich, his son Svetoslav Roerich and Anagarika Govinda.[93]

The National Gallery of Modern Art, New Delhi

The National Gallery of Modern Art was inaugurated on March 29, 1954. The Gallery is the premier institution of its kind in India. The NGMA has two branches at Mumbai and Bangalore. The gallery is a repository of the cultural ethos of the country and showcases the changing art forms in the field of Visual and Plastic arts, starting from about 1857.

National Gallery of Portraits, Chandigarh

The visuals and documents which are displayed in the gallery tell the story of how the people of India waged a struggle to win back their freedom and to build a new India. These give a glimpse of the reawakening of India from the time of first war of independence of 1857 to the achievement of freedom in 1947. The gallery displays forty- one well researched computer generated photo and document panels. The panels are supported by the oil paintings of portraits, metal and plaster cast sculptures of selected freedom fighters, murals and dioramas.

The Government Museum and Art Gallery, Chandigarh

The Government Museum and Art Gallery, Chandigarh is an art gallery. Established in August 1947, the building is square (165 feet by 165 feet) and was designed by Le Corbusier (Charles-Édouard Jeanneret-Gris).

Other than the gallery itself, it has the following sections:

- The National History Museum
- The National Gallery of Portraits
- The Chandigarh Architecture Museum

The museum/art gallery exhibits 10,000 mostly Indian artwork such as sculptures and paintings. The attached reference library houses approximately 10,000 media.

National Philatelic Museum, New Delhi

The Museum is located in the Dak Bhavan which has a post office with a popular outlet for the philatelists interested in Indian stamps. The National Philatelic Museum has an elaborate collection of stamps both of the pre- and the post-independence periods. The museum depicts the story of Indian Philatelic Heritage and also the stamps issued by the Indian government. The postal history of India is displayed in the museum, which serves to be an education for visitors. The stamps, which were cancelled, are also displayed in the National Philatelic Museum, New Delhi. The sales counter of the museum sells stamps from all over the world.

National Science Centre, New Delhi

This Centre houses a unique collection of science models to arouse interest among children. The children are made aware of the effective use of science in our lives. It is one of the best science centers of the National Council of Science Museum (NCSM) exhibiting scientific models and intriguing artifacts. Several galleries in the centre pertaining to various themes have a plethora of exhibits. These exhibits are based on different laws and theories of science.

Strengthening and Modernization of Museums

Emphasis has been given for Modernization of Museums in four metropolitan areas, namely Delhi, Kolkata, Mumbai and Chennai during the 11th five year plan (2007–2012). Accordingly, a new scheme for "Modernization of Museums in Metro Cities" will be taken up for its implementation during the Eleventh Plan. As such, technological up-grades of various important museums/galleries such as the National Museum, National Gallery of Modern Art, Salar Jung Museum and Indian Museum are being taken up.

The existing Scheme of Promotion and Strengthening of Regional and Local Museums also has been revised to make those museums effective and much more relevant. In order to develop the Gandhi Darshan at Rajghat, Gandhi Smriti and Darshan Samiti (GSDS) will take up the development work of the complex to make it into a tourist destination and a Center of Excellence.[94]

Major Art Museums and Galleries (Noncommercial)

Chhatrapati Shivaji Maharaj Museum (Prince of Wales Museum), Mumbai

The Museum was opened to the public on January 10th, 1922. The collection of the museum includes the collections of Sir Purushottam Mavji (1915), the gift of Sir Ratan Tata (1921), the collection of Sir Dorab Tata (1933) and the collection of sculptures and coins from the Poona Museum and Bombay Branch of Royal Asiatic Society. There are terracotta objects of the Indus Valley civilization, Buddhist sculptures like Bodhisathva, Maithreya, Uma Maheswara panel, a panel of Brahma, Vishnu on the Sesha, clay and stone tablets, personal emblems of traders, jewellery, paintings, thankas, Bidri work, decorative art works, glass, jade, porcelain wares, mammals, birds, and fishes are the important collections of the museum.

Goa State Museum, Goa

The Goa State Museum is known as much for its impressive architecture as for the splendid collection of ancient artifacts and sculptures. It houses an eclectic collection of over 8000 items including stone sculptures, wooden objects, bronzes, paintings, manuscripts, numismatic collection, and anthropological objects.

Government Central Museum, Jaipur

Government Central Museum not only houses many rarities and beautiful objects but its own building is also a sight to behold. The upper floor/level of the Museum mainly has portraits of royalty and Jaipur Maharajas. It has an extensive collection of jewelry, metalwork and sculpture. There are also many objects made of brass, which display the skills of the expert hands that have hammered and chiseled them to perfection. The Museum also has a huge collection of miniature paintings from the Udaipur, Jaipur, Bundi, Kota, and Kishangarh schools of painting. There are also fine specimens of woodwork, metal objects and other arts & crafts.

Government Museum, Chennai

The Madras Museum was organized during the year 1851, with about 1100 geological specimens. Museum doors were thrown open to the public on April 29, 1851. In 1896, the Front Building with the Museum Theatre and The Connemara Library was built. In 1909, Victoria Memorial, the present National Art Gallery Building, was constructed. In 1939, the New Extension Building, i.e., the main entrance building was opened. In 1963, the buildings for the Bronze Gallery, Birds' Gallery and the Chemical Conservation and Research Laboratory were added to the museum. The Contemporary Art Gallery and the Children's Museum were added to the museum in 1984 and 1988 respectively.

This museum is the oldest museum in the country, having its own conservation laboratory. The laboratory of the museum was established in 1930. In the beginning it was catering to the needs of the Madras Museum, especially to preserve the bronzes and metallic objects. Now it

is meeting the conservation needs of the Central museum and the 15 district museums. Training programs are conducted for the museologists, archivists, executive officers of the Hindu Religious and Charitable Endowments Department and others.

International Dolls Museum, Chandigarh

International Dolls Museum in Chandigarh, established in 1985, is one of the best museums of India. It houses splendid dolls and puppets gathered from all over the world. It has about 250 different kinds of dolls collected from countries like Denmark, Germany, the Netherlands, Spain, Russia, Korea, etc. An added attraction for children is the toy train.

Salar Jung Museum, Hyderabad

Salar Jung Museum, Hyderabad, has a great history behind its formation. Its collection grew out of the rich and variegated collection made by the family of Salar Jungs. In 1961, through an Act of the Parliament, the museum, along with its Library, was declared as a Museum of National Importance. Salar Jung Museum has a total collection of 48,361 items. These objects are being classified into Indian, Western, Middle Eastern and Far Eastern collections. It is a very popular museum.

Thanjavur Art Gallery, Thanjavur

The Art Gallery at Thanjavur is housed in the former palace of the Nayaks, who were once the viceroys of the Vijayanagara rulers and later became rulers themselves. The gallery houses a treasured collection of bronze icons, stone sculptures and other artifacts. The examples of art that we see today at this gallery are the finest of their kind. Most of the pieces belong to the Chola period between the ninth and the thirteenth centuries A.D., to the post-Chola period and to the Nayak period, from the seventeenth to the eighteenth Century A.D. The gallery also houses a few sculptures from the Pallava period.

India's First Sex Museum (Antarang), Mumbai

The clinic-cum-museum, Antarang, was the brainchild of Grant Medical College alumnus and artist Dr. Prakash Sarang. City authorities in Mumbai in 2002 opened a sex museum to raise understanding about sex and related issues. This is the city's—and probably India's—first such museum.[95]

Science and Natural History Museums

Science museums

From the early days of its independence (1947), an emphasis was placed on research in science and technology that transformed India into an important industrial and technological power in the twenty-first century. Science museums have played an important role in creating a social awareness about scientific progress made by the country. Some of the leading science museums are described in the next few paragraphs.

Birla Industrial and Technological Museum, Kolkata. Birla Industrial and Technological Museum was established in 1956, by the Council of Scientific and Industrial Research. Since 1978, the museum has come under the National Council of Science Museums (NCSM). The primary objective of the museum is to arouse scientific curiosity and an understanding of science and technology among the common people, especially the student-community.

It has a large number of exhibits. Galleries cover models showing Electricity, Nuclear Physics, Iron and Steel, Optics, Motive Power, Communication and Mining. The Optics Gallery has since been converted into a Popular Science Gallery. Popular activities of the Museum include films shows, demonstration-lectures, hobby activities, and periodical programs of sky-observation through telescopes. The museum also has a small "animalorium" with live snakes, reptiles, rabbits, an aviary and aquariums. An Underground Mock-up Coal Mine, Rabbit House, Snake Pits, Aquarium, Aviary, Bonsai and Cacti Garden are some of the other attractions.

Nehru Science Centre, Mumbai. Nehru Science Centre uses innovative ways to communicate science in ways that enthuse, entertain, initiate, excite and to enhance public understanding of science and spread scientific literacy. The galleries in the main building are full of exciting, interactive and interesting exhibits on topics quite relevant to school curriculum and general interest in science. These exhibits also facilitate people in general to understand and appreciate principles of science through fun and pleasure.

The National Science Centre, Delhi. The National Science Centre, Delhi, was inaugurated on the January 9, 1992, is a pioneering institute engaged in the organization of science among the people of the northern part of India in general and among students in particular. Since opening, the Centre has rendered yeoman service to the cause of science organizations.

Periyar Science and Technology Centre, Chennai. The Periyar Science and Technology Centre was established in 1986. It is a Science and Technology Museum run by the Government of Tamil Nadu. This thrust of the museum is to popularize science and technology among students, the general public and tourists. This museum has seven galleries popularizing scientific and technological aspects through working models. Most of the exhibits are interactive. It also has a Science Park, Eco Park, Energy Park, Traffic Park and a model meteorological observatory.

The Regional Science Centre, Bhopal. The Regional Science Centre, Bhopal was opened on January 12, 1995. Umbrella—The Atmosphere, Fun Science, Life Science, 3D Science Show Theatre, Children's Activity Corner, Science Park are some of the important galleries of the Centre. The Fun Science Gallery of the Centre offers learning through play.

The Regional Science Centre, Lucknow. The Regional Science Centre has been functioning since 1989 as a centre of interactive science learning. The upgrade of the Centre to the Regional Science City was effected on September 21, 2007. The objective of the upgrade is to create scientific awareness and temperaments among students and the public, and to supplement formal science education and create interest in science among students. Some of the attractions include underwater Exploration, Bio-technological Revolution and Being Human, 3-D Science Show and Space Theatre where Large Format Film Projection.[96]

Science City, Kolkata. The Science City, Kolkata, was built recently, in the twenty-first century. The concept of science city is simply mind-blowing. There are cable cars, a toy train and a children's playground with jungle gyms and slides. Dynamotion is a great favorite among children, with its large exhibit on physics and mechanics. Life-size dinosaurs, aquariums, insectariums and the butterfly corner are also great attractions. Science City also has a Time Machine, which simulates a journey into the past and future with sights and sounds. The Space Theatre is by far the most popular attraction.

Visvesvaraya Industrial and Technological Museum, Bangalore. The museum opened to the public in 1965, has seven permanent exhibition halls viz. Engine Hall, Electro-technic, Fun Science, Space-Emerging Technology in the service of mankind, Biotechnological Revolution, BEL-Hall of Electronics, Science for Children and two special exhibits viz. Dinosaur Corner and Wright Brothers' Aero- plane.

Natural history museums

The Natural History Museum, Chandigarh. In 2001, the existing museum of Evolution of Life was upgraded to its present status as the Natural History Museum with five major sections:

- Cyclorama of Evolution of Life
- Nature in Art section
- Manuscript section

- Evolution of Man section
- Dinosaurs of India section

The Nehru Planetarium, New Delhi.   The Nehru Planetarium in New Delhi is situated in the sprawling surroundings of the Teen Murti House. In 1964, the Jawaharlal Nehru Memorial Fund was set up to promote ideas of Jawaharlal Nehru and subsequently it undertook to build the Nehru Planetarium. The primary aim of the Planetarium is the promotion of astronomy and space education.

Historical, Anthropological, and Archaeological Museums

Nehru Memorial Museum and Library, New Delhi

This museum revolves around the life and works of Jawaharlal Nehru (former Prime Minister), especially those objects pertaining to the freedom struggle. A collection of photographs and newspapers enables one to have a feel of the stirring events that led to the birth of the Indian Republic. The Museum has a library also which is a storehouse of books on Indian history and Indian national movement.

Birla House, New Delhi

The Gandhi Smriti or Birla House or Birla Bhavan, in New Delhi, is the location where Mahatma Gandhi (the Father of the Nation) spent the last 144 days of his life and was assassinated on January 30, 1948. It was originally the house of the Indian business tycoons, the Birlas. It was acquired by the Government of India in 1971 and opened for the public on August 15, 1973 and renamed the Gandhi Smriti (or *Gandhi Remembrance*). The museum in the building houses a number of articles associated with Gandhi's life and death. Visitors can view the preserved room where Gandhi lived and also visit the place on the grounds where he was shot while holding his nightly public walk. The Martyr's Column now marks the place where Gandhi, the "Father of the Nation" was assassinated.

Anthropological Museum (Department of Anthropology, University of Delhi), Delhi

The Museum consists of

> a large number of material cultural objects associated with different economic and social types, such as hunting and food-gathering, fishing, horticulture, animal breeding, farming and agriculture. Musical instruments from different societies are also kept in the Museum. So are the models of different types of habitation from Indian tribes. Dresses and ornaments, and weapons, constitute a separate section in the Museum.

The museum has a

> rich collection of stone and bone implements ...The Museum also had a handsome collection of the casts of fossil man. Stuffed great apes are also kept, so are the bones of the nonhuman primates. All these are used for physical anthropological work.[97]

The Museum is considered one of the best anthropological museums in the country.

The Archaeological Museum, Khajuraho (Madhya Pradesh)

It was established in 1904 and has excellent exhibits of sculptures from the temples of Khajuraho.

Sarnath Archaeological Museum

Amongst the exhibits at the museum are the figures and sculptures that date back to the Mauryan, Kushan and Gupta period of Sarnath. While holidaying in Sarnath one should not miss the Asokan Pillar, the prime attraction of the archaeological museum.

The Archaeological Museum, Nalanda

The Archaeological Museum at Nalanda in Bihar is a storehouse of the excavations from Nalanda and Rajgir. The exhibits at the museum include sculptures and various other archaeological remains.

The Archaeological Museum, Delhi

The Archaeological Museum of Delhi is situated in the Mumtaz Mahal (Palace) of the Red Fort. The museum has on display some of the rare relics dating back to the Mughal era, along with specimens of the fine calligraphy of the past. The main reason to establish the museum was to bring together all the items reminiscent of the history of the city of Delhi under one roof. The Museum includes excavated objects belonging to the Maurya, Sunga, Kushana, Rajput, and the Muslim period.[98]

Surveys of India

There are various Surveys in India that take stock of the situations in respective disciplines such as anthropology, archaeology, botany, geology and zoology. These Surveys are under the control of the Government of India. They are closely connected with museums and museology.

The Archaeological Survey of India (ASI), under the Ministry of Culture, is the premier organization for archaeological research and protection of the cultural heritage of the nation.

The Anthropological Survey of India (AnSI) is a unique organization dealing with the anthropological research in public or private sector and regulates the anthropological activities such as studying tribes and other communities.

The Botanical Survey of India (BSI) is an institution under the supervision of the Union Ministry of Environment and Forests that surveys the plant resources of the Indian empire.

The Geological Survey of India (GSI), one of the oldest surveys in the world, is a premier organization of Earth Science Studies in the sub-continent. The Zoological Survey of India (ZSI), as the premier national organization under the Government of India engaged in field survey and laboratory investigation on faunal resources of India.

Zoos

There are 169 recognized zoos in the country. Leading zoos are described below:

The Alipore Zoological Gardens, Kolkata

The Alipore Zoological Gardens (also informally called the Alipore Zoo, Calcutta Zoo or Kolkata Zoo) is India's oldest formally stated zoological park (as opposed to royal and British menageries) and a big tourist attraction in Kolkata. It is home to one of the few captive breeding projects involving the Manipur Brown-antlered Deer.

Arignar Anna Zoological Park, Chennai

Chennai has the distinction of having the first zoo in India, which was started in 1855. It has a Lion safari, Bird aviaries, Reptile House, Nocturnal House, and Mountain Cave Entrance.

Indira Gandhi Zoological Park, Visakhapatnam

Indira Gandhi Zoological Park is located amidst Kambalakonda Reserve Forest in Visakhapatnam. Nearly 80 species numbering about 800 animals are found in the zoo. The Zoo Park has different sections for primates, carnivores, lesser carnivores, small mammals, reptiles, ungulates and birds caged in their natural ambiance.

Madras Crocodile Bank Trust

The Madras Crocodile Bank Trust or CrocBank is a reptile zoo and herpetology research station, located near Mahabalipuram, 40 km south of the city of Chennai. It was established in 1976 with the aim of saving the three Indian species of crocodiles—the marsh or mugger crocodile, the saltwater crocodile, and the gharial—which at the time were all nearing extinction. The captive breeding program of CrocBank has been highly successful, with

thousands of crocodiles reintroduced to the wild and more still sent to zoos and wildlife parks around the world. The CrocBank is currently home to over 2400 crocodiles, and also houses many species of turtles, snakes, and lizards which are viewable by the public.

Mysore Zoo, Mysore

The Mysore Zoo was established under royal patronage in 1892, making it one of the oldest zoos in the world. It is home to a wide range of wild species. The official name for the zoo is Shri Chamarajendra Zoological Gardens, though it is known commonly by its shortened name. Mysore Zoo is one of the city's most popular attractions.

Nandan Kanan Zoological Park, Bhubaneswar

The zoo was established in 1960–1961. A major renovation was done during 2000. Nandan Kanan is famous for its white tiger population, the species it claims to have produced. Endangered species such as the Asiatic lion, three Indian crocodilians, Sangal lion-tailed macaque, Nilgiri langur, Indian pangolin, mouse deer and countless birds, reptiles and fish have been breeding successfully at Nandan Kanan. Some of the other attractions of Nandan Kanan are the 34 aquaria which are home to a large variety of fresh water fishes. Around 67 kinds of mammals, 18 varieties of reptiles, 81 species of birds, and overall more than 1200 (as of 2005–2006) wild animals coexist in the deep forest. The zoo enjoys a good reputation, internationally, for successfully breeding black panthers, gharial crocodiles and white tigers in captivity. This is one of the few zoos in India where one can see animals in their natural environments.

National Zoological Park, New Delhi

The Delhi National Zoological Park is among the finest Zoological Gardens in the country. It has 2,000 varieties of animals and birds. The animals include Gir Lions, Zebras, Spider Monkeys, and Chimpanzees as well as innumerable reptiles and birds. There are also about 200 varieties of trees in the Park.

Nehru Zoological Park, Hyderabad

Nehru Zoological Park is the largest zoo in India. It was established in 1963. It has a wide selection of nearly 1500 species of birds, animals and reptiles housed here. The zoo runs different safari trips, like Lion Safari, Tiger Safari, Bear Safari, and Butterfly Safari. Other attractions include elephant rides, a Natural History Museum, and a children's train.

Padmaja Naidu Himalayan Zoological Park, Darjeeling

This Zoological Park specializes in breeding animals adapted to alpine conditions, and has done successfully captive breeding of the snow leopard, the critically endangered Himalayan wolf and red panda. The zoo now contains endangered animals like snow leopards, red pandas, gorals (mountain goat), Siberian tigers and a variety of endangered birds.

Parassinkkadavu Snake Park, Kannur, Kerala

There are about 150 varieties of snakes including the spectacled cobra, King cobra, Russell's Viper, Krait, and Pit Viper living in the park. The park also has a large collection of nonpoisonous snakes, including pythons.

Sakkarbaug Zoological Garden, Junagadh

Sakkarbaug Zoological Garden is also known as Sakkarbaug Zoo or Junagadh Zoo. It is famous worldwide for providing purebred Asiatic Lions for the Indian and the international endangered species captive breeding program for critically endangered Asiatic Lions. Wild free ranging Asiatic Lions have become extinct all over Asia and are today found only in the nearby Gir Forest.

Trivandrum Zoo, Thiruvananthapuram

This is one of the best designed zoos in Asia. It is also one of the oldest in the country, established as an annexe to the Museum (Napier Museum) in 1857 by the erstwhile Maharaja of Travancore. The Zoo has 75 different species of animals, not only from India but also from abroad.

Taraporewala Aquarium, Mumbai

Here one can view beautiful marine life, such as rare species of fish, and wonderful pearl jewelry.

National Parks

Indian National Parks provide many opportunities to the visitors to have a close encounter with the wild. But what is so fascinating about the Indian National Parks is that they have a great deal of variety. Seeing the flora, avifauna, and aquafauna, or witnessing various wild forms in their natural surroundings on an elephant or inside a jeep, or through wild ventures is a great experience not to be missed.

Some of the best jewels of Indian wilderness include the Great Himalayan National Park, Dachigam National Park near Srinagar, Corbett National Park in Uttar Pradesh (also a famous tiger reserve), Ranthambore National Park

in Rajasthan, and Sundarbans National Park in West Bengal. Worth visiting in the East Indian part of the country, in "The Land of Rhino" Assam, is Kaziranga.[99]

Great Himalayan National Park (GHNP)

This national park, built in the year 1984, is located in Kullu region in the state of Himachal Pradesh. It is home to more than 375 faunal species. So far, 31 mammals, 181 birds, 3 reptiles, 9 amphibians, 11 annelids, 17 mollusks and 127 insects have been identified. A trek of 35–45 km. takes one to the high altitude habitat (3500 m and above) of various animals such as blue sheep, snow leopard, Himalayan brown bear, Himalayan tahr, and musk deer.[100]

Dachigam National Park

Dachigam National Park is located 22 km from Srinagar, Jammu and Kashmir. The park has been a protected area since 1910. It was declared a National Park in the year 1981. The main animal species that Dachigam is most famous for is the Hangul, or the Kashmir stag. Other species that inhabit its interiors include musk deer, leopards, Himalayan gray langurs, leopard cats, Himalayan black bear, Himalayan brown bear, jackals, hill fox, Himalayan weasel, yellow-throated martens, jungle cats, long-tailed marmots and otters.[101]

Corbett National Park, Ramnagar

This is the oldest national park in India. The park was established in 1936 as Hailey National Park. Located in Ramnagar, Nainital district of Uttarakhand State, the park is a protected area for the critically endangered Bengal tiger of India under the Project Tiger, an Indian wildlife protection initiative.

Ranthambore National Park

Ranthambore National Park is one of the largest and most famous national parks in India. It is situated in Sawai Madhopur district of Rajasthan, about 130 km from Jaipur. This Park was established as the Sawai Madhopur Game Sanctuary in 1955 by the Government of India. It was declared one of the Project Tiger reserves in 1973. Ranthambore became a national park in 1980. In 1984, the adjacent forests were declared the Sawai Man Singh Sanctuary and Keladevi Sanctuary. In 1991, the tiger reserve was enlarged to include both Sawai Man Singh and Keladevi sanctuaries as well. The park is famous for its tiger population. The major wild animals include the tiger, leopard, nilgai, dhole, wild pig, sambar and chital. It also has a wide variety of trees, plants, birds and reptiles. Ranthambore has one of the largest Banyan trees in India.

Sundarbans National Park

Sundarbans National Park (since 1984) is a Tiger Reserve, UNESCO World Heritage Site (since 1987) and a Biosphere Reserve (since 1989). It is located in the Sundarbans delta in West Bengal, lying in a region that is densely covered by mangrove forests. It is considered one of the largest reserves of the Bengal tiger. The park has a large variety of bird, reptile and invertebrate species, as well as salt-water crocodiles.

Kaziranga National Park

Kaziranga National Park is in the Golaghat and Nagaon districts of Assam. It was established in 1905 as a reserve forest. It is both a national park and World Heritage Site. Two-thirds of the Great One-horned Rhinoceroses of the world live in the park. Kaziranga has the highest density of tigers among protected areas in the world. It was declared a Tiger Reserve in the year 2006. The park has also a large population of elephants, water buffalo and swamp deer. Kaziranga is recognized as an Important Bird Area for the conservation of avifaunal species.

Digital Museum Exhibits and Services

Indian museums have been lagging behind in creating digital museums. However, there are signs that they are getting involved in this seriously. Some of the examples of museums that have ventured into this field are given below:

The Government Museum and Art Gallery, Chandigarh

A few years back, the Museum established the "Data Collection Management" section. Inputting of inventory data, object description and conservation data of the collection was started with a pilot project of 627 pieces of Gandharan sculptures. Inputting data about Indian miniatures, contemporary paintings, Indian Medieval and contemporary sculptures is also in progress.

Digital Library of India (Program)

The mission is to create a portal for the Digital Library of India (DLI) which will foster creativity and free access to all human knowledge. This portal will also become an aggregator of all the knowledge and digital contents created by other digital library initiatives in India. The Digital Library of India is mirrored at several locations so as to protect the integrity and availability of the data. The DLI is also a partner with other country specific Digital

Libraries initiatives as part of the Universal Library Project (http://www.ulib.org) spearheaded by Prof. Raj Reddy and Carnegie Mellon University.

Indian National Museum, New Delhi

Computerization and digitization for an automated retrieval system for the Museum has been completed. Computerization of reference media for certain records (such as records for the Ministry of External Affairs (1947–1970), Ministry of State (1947–1953), etc.) has also been completed. A project for digitization of rare and valuable manuscripts is ongoing.

The Indira Gandhi National Centre for the Arts (IGNCA), New Delhi

The National Mission for Manuscripts is one of the departments of IGNCA, created in February 2003 with an aim to protect the manuscripts culture of this country and it is also to carry out the digitization of the manuscripts.

Museology as a Discipline and Profession

Museology has come of age. Today, it has become a multi-disciplinary and increasingly interdisciplinary area of studies. At one time it was a minor area of studies, but now it has become a subject forming part of the mainstream.

Museology in India has grown into a profession in its own right. Museum scholars belong to different disciplines and backgrounds, bringing together a broad range of perspectives. Museology fulfills the characteristics of a profession. In recent years, there has been recognition of the need for trained professionals. Today, museum professionals are expected to posses professional qualifications obtained from recognized institutions.

Education for Curatorship and Museum Administration

Due to the recognition of need for professional training, a number of university level courses have been started.

The National Museum Institute of History of Art, Conservation and Museology came into existence in 1983 and now is deemed to be a University. It provides various Courses with its campus at National Museum (New Delhi).

Some of the Universities offering courses are:
Aligarh Muslim University, Aligarh
    M.A. Program besides one-year diploma in museology
       and Ph.D. Programs
Banaras Hindu University, Varanasi

Diploma in Museology, M.A. in Museology after graduation and Ph.D

Jiwaji University, Gwalior

M.A. in Ancient History, Culture and Archaelogy

M.A. (Museology)

PG Diploma in Archaelogy

Maharaja Sayajirao University, Baroda

M.A. (Fine) Museology and Ph.D. Courses as well as 1 year Diploma Course for in-service people.

National Museum Institute of History of Arts and Conservation and Museology, New Delhi

M.A. (Arts History), M.A. (Conservation), M.A. (Museology); Ph. D (Art History), Ph.D (Conservation), Ph.D (Museology). Besides, the Institute also runs short-term courses in the History of Art stream for general public. The courses are:

• Art Appreciation Course (English)
• India Art and Culture Course (English)
• Bhartiya Kala Nidhi (Hindi)

University of Calcutta, Kolkata

Diploma in Museology after graduation, M.A. in Museology, PG diploma in Museology and Ph.D. in museology.

Vikram University, Ujjain

1-year PG Diploma in Museology

Besides these many museums also provide training in museology and related subjects.

Chemical Conservation and Research Laboratory, Government Museum, Chennai, started a refresher course in 1974 on Care of Museum Objects. At present, it offers one-month long training in Care of Museum Objects for those who are working in museums in allied departments; Course on Care of Temple Antiquities for the Executive Officers of the Hindu Religious and Charitable Endowments Department, Government of Tamil Nadu, Chennai, a course on Care of Archival Materials exclusively for the Archivists, a Course on Care of Library Materials for Librarians etc.[102]

The Conservation Laboratory of the National Museum, New Delhi organizes training programs for students, curators and conservators and also provides training facilities to students and professionals, including restoration of oil paintings. It organizes workshops and seminars at various places from time to time on conserving the vast cultural heritage of the country.

INTACH, Indian Conservation Institute offers various courses in Conservation of Paintings, Documents, and Manuscripts to graduates in Science or Chemistry graduates or BFA degrees at New Delhi and Lucknow.

Professional Associations for Curators and Museum Administrators

The following are the major professional associations:

Indian Council of Historical Research, New Delhi

The Indian council of Historical Research, New Delhi is an autonomous body established by the Government of India with a view to providing funds for historical research and to fostering objective and scientific writing of history. The Council has taken a broad view of history so as to include in its fold archaeology, socio-economic formations and allied subjects.

National Council for Science Museums, Kolkata

The National council of Science Museums, an autonomous organization under the Department of Culture, was set up in 1978 and is primarily engaged in the task of popularization of science and technology among the students in particular and the masses in general through a wide range of interactive programs and activities. It administers 21 science museums/centers/parks throughout the country.

Museum Association of India (MAI), New Delhi, c/o National Museum, New Delhi

The Museum Association of India was founded in 1944. The aim of the Association is to further the cause of museums in India by making them popular with the public by providing new ideas through seminars and publications, and by promoting mutual appreciation of mutual problems by holding museum conferences. The Association has also taken up the responsibility for representing the cause of museums and their personnel. The Museum Association of India brings out the *Journal of Indian Museums* and *Museum's Newsletter*.

Indian Association for the Study of Conservation of Cultural Property in India (IASC) c/o National Museum Institute, Janpath, New Delhi—110011

The Indian Association for the Study of Conservation of Cultural Property was started in New Delhi to create a common platform for conservation scientists, conservation chemists, conservators, architectural conservation engineers etc. It provides a professional centre devoted to the cause of conservation and study of cultural property including historic, archaeological, ethnological, artistic, archival and other material in libraries, manuscript repositories and museums. It brings out a journal called Conservation of Cultural Property India annually and Conservation Newsletter in August every year. Besides these, it also publishes books on special topics.

Indian National Trust for Art and Cultural Heritage (INTACH) Indian Conservation Institute

The main aims and objectives are: To take up conservation and restoration of different types of objects, to impart training in different branches of conservation and to create awareness among the public about the need for conservation and the problems involved through periodical exhibitions, seminars and workshops.

The Indian Conservation Institute has branches at Bangalore, Bhubaneswar, New Delhi, Rampur, Jaipur, Trissur, etc.

Key Contemporary Issues

Publicity

An on-going study by the National Museum Institute has revealed that "about 90 percent of the people standing at the bus stop right outside the museum did not know where the museum was or what was in it?"[103] This may be true to a large extent, even today. This shows lack of publicity.

Procurement

A large number of rare items of Indian origin are held by museums and private individuals in Europe and in Southeast Asian countries. From time to time they appear at auctions. Indian museums sometimes have tried to acquire them, but due to lack of sufficient budget, they have not been able to acquire many pieces.

Preservation

The contemporary scene in India is abysmal and needs to be redressed for any meaningful discussion on plunder of the heritage. Although the ASI has declared over 3000 monuments as nationally important, it is the sixteen sites that have been declared as part of World Heritage that receive greater attention. Thus there is clearly an imbalance in regional coverage both of heritage sites and protected monuments. Similarly there are far more museums in cities than in rural areas, though even within the cities the situation is far from satisfactory.[104]

Access

The social service role of Museums and Art Galleries in making their resources accessible to all is an important issue. There is a need for a National Policy on Museum Accessibility that gives due importance to accessibility factors.

Museums are currently creating Web sites. The question arises as to what should be the role of museum Web sites? Should each be a separate entity from the museum itself? Should the Web site be a mere advertising medium for a museum?

Education

In a country as large as India, only 25 university departments across the country conduct archaeological fieldwork and offer post-graduate education on the subject. Even in the national capital, none of the prestigious universities has a full-fledged department of archaeology at the undergraduate or postgraduate level.[104]

There is a need for setting up full-fledged departments of archaeology at universities for teaching and research.

Presentation techniques

Museums in India are not updating their presentation techniques due to lack of funds and training of the curators. New lighting methodologies have been adapted in national museums and other large State museums. But all small museums, such as the district level museums, school and college museums do not have adequate funds for updating the museums.

Conservation

Major museums have their own conservation laboratories. There are also regional conservation laboratories in various regions. But they are inadequate to meet the needs of existing museums. There is a need for more conservation laboratories to serve the increasing number of museums.

Conservation of Extinct Species of Wild Animals. India once had rich biodiversity that has become considerably depleted. The question arises as to how this fall in biodiversity can be checked and also reversed.

Project Tiger was launched in 1973 to provide tigers an opportunity to breathe and grow in their natural habitat. However, as administration focus has dwindled and priorities have changed, implementation of the program has certainly suffered and funds sanctioned for Project Tiger have also not been properly utilized. There is a need for such projects to cover other species as well that are facing extinction.

Present Situation

India is a country that is rich in culture, heritage, science and artifacts. Its museums and art galleries house a great cultural heritage. The National Museum, New Delhi is the top museum in the country. In addition to State museums and art galleries, there are a large number of art museums and galleries (non-commercial) that display India's rich heritage. Strengthening and modernization of museums in four metros, namely, Delhi, Kolkata, Mumbai, and Chennai is taking place under the 11th five year plan (2007–2012). Hopefully, this will lead to resurgence of Museums and Museology.

India–Information Behavior

India also has a rich biodiversity. The country possesses bountiful forest areas that display the richness of species and the range of habitat types. The National Zoological Park, Delhi, is the finest Zoological Gardens in India. Some of the best jewels of Indian wilderness include the Great Himalayan National Park in Himachal Pradesh, Dachigam National Park near Srinagar, Corbett National Park in Uttar Pradesh (which is also a famous tiger reserve), Ranthambore National Park in Rajasthan, and Sundarbans National Park in West Bengal, and Kaziranga in Assam (the land of rhino).

CONCLUSION

With a population of over one billion, India is the world's largest democracy. It has a large pool of talents with over 620 million people of working age. Its economy is growing at an average rate of 8%. With booming IT services, state-of-the-art communication, and fast growing service industries, India is poised to become a global power.

Convergence of Libraries, Archives, and Museums

There are certain areas and issues of common interest among the three fields of specialization. Areas of common interest include acquisition, organization, preservation, and digitization of documents, designing of Web sites, organization of exhibitions, display of items, management problems, status in the society, etc. These areas can serve as a starting point for a fruitful dialog. Today, the situation is such in India is that there is very little interaction between these three areas.

There is little convergence happening in India. The National Mission for Manuscripts is an example of convergence, where libraries, museums and archives are involved in the effort. The post of Librarian at Jawaharlal Nehru University was advertised recently, the desirable qualification was M.Phil./Ph.D. degree in library science/ information science/documentation/archives and manuscript-keeping. This is a step toward convergence. There are very few examples of this kind.

There is a need to create linkages across different kinds of information institutions in India. Librarians, archivists, and museologists need to work out common strategies for making collections accessible and facilitating inter-linkages between different kinds of collections. Plans for common content strategies can be worked out in various programs and projects involving digital work. In fact, there are common problems faced by information professionals, such as that new materials often are in unstable digital formats.

They should work together joining hands to do a better job, in spite of differences in focus, practices, perception, standards for digital format, etc. It may be kept in mind that often users want information, rather than a specific book, an archival folio, or a museum object. Let there be cross-fertilization of ideas, practices and experiences. This will do a lot of good for information professionals and institutions in India.

Cooperation among Information Institutions

There are some ongoing projects involving cooperation among information institutions such as the Digital Library of India, National Mission for Manuscripts, etc. The Digital Library of India is hosted by the Indian Institute of Science, Bangalore in cooperation with CMU, IIIT, NSF, ERNET, and MCIT for the Government of India and 21 participating centers. The National Mission for Manuscripts was launched in February 2003 by the Ministry of Culture, Government of India, to save the manuscripts, one of the most valuable but less visible cultural heritage. The main aim of the mission being to create an electronic database of manuscripts.

Trends

In memory institutions, there is a definite shift in emphasis toward access to information instead of ownership of information. Digitization of documents has helped in this shift. Computerization of libraries, archives and museums is taking place. All major information institutions have their own Web sites. Large number of digital libraries have been designed. Museums are putting out digital exhibitions and digitizing their collections. Archives are also digitizing their collections.

Digital libraries in information institutions are beginning to become the center of information services Information institutions are increasingly participating in creating open sources. The open source movement in India is getting quite strong. These are healthy signs.

Issues

The question arises, are the graduates being produced by the schools of library science, archival science and museology employable? The quality of graduates being turned out in India leaves much to be desired. The quality of education needs to be improved to bring it up to the international level.

There is not enough financial support available for the information sector. However, there are signs that in the 11th five-year plan (2007–2012), the Government of India is committed to providing better support for preserving the national heritage and making it accessible to the people.

Lack of a good image is a matter of concern. Improvement in quality of education can go a long way in this respect. In addition, the theoretical basis of the disciplines of library science, archaeology and museology needs to be strengthened, so that they are considered on a par with other disciplines in higher education.

REFERENCES

1. http://www.censusindia.gov.in/Census_Data_2001/India_at_glance/popu1.aspx.
2. http://news.indiainfo.com/2008/02/01/0802010844_india_rate.html.
3. http://www.sciencemag.org/cgi/content/full/307/5714/1415.
4. http://www.sciencemag.org/cgi/content/full/307/5714/1415.
5. Kumbar, B.D. Growth and development of public library system in India with special reference to Karnataka. International Workshop on Democratization of Information: Focus on Libraries. Available at http://www.nigd.org/libraries/mumbai/reports/article-4.pdf (accessed April 20, 2008).
6. http://www.education.nic.in/cd50years/12/8i/6W/8I6W0J01.htm.
7. http://nlindia.org/useful_info.html(accessed April 10, 2008).
8. http://nlindia.org/collection_english_foreign.html.
9. http://www.nml.nic.in/geninfo.html.
10. http://www.wisard.org/rwc/shared/asp/generalinfoserver/intermediate.asp?InstitutionID = 5038.
11. http://www.niscair.res.in/aboutus/about.asp?a = topframe.htm&b = leftcon.asp&c = mission.htm&d = test.
12. http://www.planningcommission.nic.in/aboutus/committee/wrkgrp11/wg11_culture.pdf.
13. http://www.ugc.ac.in/pub/#annual UGC, Annual Report, 2005–06.
14. http://www.education.nic.in/higedu.asp.
15. http://knowledgecommission.gov.in/downloads/recommendations/HigherEducationLetterPM.pdf.
16. http://publication.samachar.com/pub_article.php?id = 753195.
17. http://202.141.12.215/.
18. http://202.141.12.215/.
19. Patel, J. Kumar, K. *Libraries and Librarianship in India*, Greenwood Press: Westport, CT, 2001; 81.
20. http://www.nlindia.org/history.html.
21. Bhattacharjee, R. *Public Library Services in India: Systems and Deficiencies.* http://www.ifla.org/VII/s8/annual/cr02-in.htm (accessed May 2, 2008).
22. http://www.kar.nic.in/publib/SOMEFACTS.htm.
23. http://www.tn.gov.in/policynotes/archives/policy2004–05/sedu/edu2004–5–13.htm.
24. http://banglargranthagar.nic.in/html/public_library_system1.html.
25. http://www.rrrlf.nic.in/achivfrm.htm.
26. http://www.dpl.gov.in/.
27. http://www.connemarapubliclibrarychennai.com/modernisation.htm.
28. http://www.tn.gov.in/policynotes/archives/policy2004–05/sedu/edu2004–5–13.htm.
29. Das, A.K.; Banwari, L. Cited in Information literacy and public libraries in India. Available at http://eprints.rclis.org/archive/00005697/01/Information_Literacy_Public_Libraries_India.pdf (accessed May 2, 2008) (Data given by the two authors is based on Census of India, 1991; and Ghosh, M. The public library system in India: challenges and opportunities. Lib. Rev. **2005**, *54* (3), 180–191).
30. http://www.hindu.com/2007/10/03/stories/2007100360180200.htm.
31. http://www.rgfindia.com/education.htm#slum.
32. http://www.ncert.nic.in/html/pdf/Publication/Journal2008/Survey_reports2007/Specific_%20Facilities/Specific_Facilities.pdf.
33. http://india.gov.in/sectors/education/education_overview.php.
34. http://www.icmr.nic.in/abouticmr.htm.
35. http://www.icar.org.in/icar1.htm.
36. http://www.csir.res.in/External/Utilities/Frames/aboutcsir/main_page.asp?a = topframe.htm&b = leftcon.htm&c = ../../../Heads/aboutcsir/network_map.htm.
37. http://bl125w.blu125.mail.live.com/mail/mail.aspx?wa = wsignin1.0&n = 26868272.
38. http://www.nml.nic.in/regionallab.html.
39. http://www.ilidelhi.org/library.htm.
40. Das, S. Pathak, P.J. Facilitating scientific research with library services: a case study of the IPR Library. Libr. Philos. and Pract. 2008; April, 1–7. Available at http://libr.unl.edu:2000/LPP/das-pathak.htm (accessed April 20, 2008).
41. Patel, J. Kumar, K. *Libraries and Librarianship in India*, Greenwood Press: Westport, CT, 2001; 131.
42. http://www.new.dli.ernet.in/.
43. http://knowledgecommission.gov.in/downloads/documents/wg_open_course.pdf.
44. http://202.141.130.70/.
45. http://210.212.200.226/.
46. http://www.webpages.uidaho.edu/~mbolin/vara-chandra.htm.
47. E-Prints at IISc. Available at http://www.ncsi.iisc.ernet.in.
48. http://www.ncsi.iisc.ernet.in/about_ncsi.php.
49. http://www.tkdl.res.in/tkdl/langdefault/common/AboutTKDL.asp#present.
50. http://paniit.iitd.ac.in/indest/.
51. http://namami.nic.in/digitizationinside.htm.
52. http://www.ignca.nic.in/kalasampada.pdf.
53. http://sis-india.netfirms.com/about.htm.
54. *Oxford English Dictionary*, 2nd Ed. Oxford University Press: Oxford, U.K., 1989.
55. University Grants Commission (India), Review Committee, UGC: New Delhi, India, 1965; Library science in Indian universities; a report, 1965; University Grants Commission (India), Review Committee, UGC: New Delhi, India.
56. Chopra, H.R. et al. *Directory of Library and Information Schools in India*, Arun Publishing House: Chandigarh, India, 1988, preface.
57. http://www.uni-mysore.ac.in/unity/course/view?id = 29.
58. http://www.ignou.ac.in/.
59. Report of the Curriculum Development Committee in Library and information science (Chairman: PN Kaula), 1993. University Grants Commission (India), UGC: New Delhi, India.
60. UGC model curriculum: Library and information science (Chairman: C R Karisiddappa), 2001. University Grants Commission (India), UGC: New Delhi, India.
61. http://www.ila-india.org/constitution.asp.
62. http://www.iaslic1955.org/history.htm.
63. http://www.iaslic1955.org/aims.htm.
64. http://nationalarchives.nic.in/record_mgmt.html.
65. http://nationalarchives.nic.in/activities.html.
66. http://nationalarchives.nic.in/holdings.html.

67. http://www.planningcommission.nic.in/aboutus/committee/wrkgrp11/wg11_culture.pdf.
68. http://ignca.nic.in/about.htm.
69. http://www.nlindia.org/collection_dev.html.
70. http://eurindia.pc.unicatt.it/english/psa.html.
71. http://www.tn.gov.in/citizen/archives.htm.
72. http://www.wbtourism.com/art_culture/museum3.htm.
73. http://www.iiap.res.in/lib_archives; http://prints.iiap.res.in.
74. http://www.jnu.ac.in/main.asp?sendval = SocialArchives.
75. http://www.iiap.res.in/archives/pdfs/Fr_Joseph_Antoniswamy_compress.pdf.
76. http://www.amu.ac.in/index2.asp?sublinkid = 194&linkid = 52.
77. http://www.nfaipune.gov.in/films.htm.
78. http://www.kfionline.org/foundation/archives.asp.
79. http://www.ifpindia.org/-Map-archives-.html.
80. http://www.chitralekha.org/archives.htm.
81. http://www.lib.uchicago.edu/e/su/southasia/about-rmrl.html #Heading9.
82. http://www.sarasvatimahallibrary.tn.nic.in/library/library.html.
83. http://www.tatacentralarchives.com/collections/documents/documents.htm.
84. http://nationalarchives.nic.in/computer.html.
85. http://ignca.nic.in/.
86. Johare, R. Education and training in electronic records management (ERM): the need for partnership building Proceedings of the Asia-Pacific Conference on Library & Information Education & Practice, 2006; Khoo, C., Singh, D., Chaudhry, A.S., Eds.; School of Communication & Information, Nanyang Technological University: Singapore, 2006; 541–549. Available at http://dlist.sir.arizona.edu/1433/01/77.Rusnah_Johare_pp541–549.long.pdf (accessed April 5, 2008).
87. http://nationalarchives.gov.in/nca.html.
88. http://nationalarchives.nic.in/ihrc.html.
89. http://www.planningcommission.nic.in/aboutus/committee/wrkgrp11/wg11_culture.pdf.
90. http://www.nfaipune.gov.in/preservation.htm.
91. Mohan, R. Reserve Bank of India archives—some reflections and the way forward; Inaugural address by Dr Rakesh Mohan, Deputy Governor of the Reserve Bank of India, at the Silver Jubilee Inaugural Function of the Reserve Bank of India Archives, Pune, September 29, 2006. Available at http://www.bis.org/review/r061110d.pdf (accessed April 5, 2008).
92. http://asi.nic.in/asi_legislations.asp.
93. http://www.indianngos.com/issue/culture&heritage/govt/members/schemes1.htm.
94. http://www.planningcommission.nic.in/aboutus/committee/wrkgrp11/wg11_culture.pdf.
95. http://news.bbc.co.uk/2/hi/south_asia/2514387.stm; http://www.newindpress.com.
96. http://www.rsclucknow.org/.
97. http://www.du.ac.in/show_department.html? Department_id = Anthropology.
98. http://www.bharatonline.com/delhi/museum/archaeological-museum.html.
99. http://www.indianwildlifeportal.com/national-parks/.
100. http://www.greathimalayannationalpark.com/GHNP_biodiv Anim.htm.
101. http://www.indiawildliferesorts.com/national-parks/dachigam-national-park.html.
102. http://www.chennaimuseum.org/draft/gallery/09/chemcons.htm.
103. The Hindu, November 29,2002. http://www.hindu.com/2002/11/29/99hdline.htm (accessed June 8, 2008).
104. http://www.iicdelhi.nic.in/program/program_detail.asp? ProgId = 52&CatgId = 2.

Indigenous Librarianship

Kathleen Burns
Beinecke Rare Book and Manuscript Library, Yale University, New Haven, Connecticut, U.S.A.

Ann Doyle
X̱wi7x̱wa Library, First Nations House of Learning, University of British Columbia, Vancouver, British Columbia, Canada

Gene Joseph
Aboriginal Library Consultant, Langley, British Columbia, Canada

Allison Krebs
University of Arizona, Tucson, Arizona, U.S.A.

Abstract

Indigenous librarianship unites the discipline of librarianship with Indigenous approaches to knowledge, theory, and research methodology. It has a developing bibliography and local, national, and international professional associations devoted to its growth. A focus of Indigenous librarianship is the provision of culturally relevant library and information collections and services by, for, and with Indigenous people. Grounded in the contemporary realities of Indigenous people and Indigenous aspirations for self-governance and sovereignty, it has a critical theoretical base. Its practice may be carried out in spaces from small Indigenous community libraries to specialized collections in large research institutions. As an emergent scholarship the field is in the process of defining itself. This entry serves as an introductory overview to the history, practice, issues, and theoretical approaches associated with Indigenous librarianship.

INTRODUCTION

Indigenous librarianship unites the discipline of librarianship with Indigenous approaches to knowledge, theory, and methodology. It emerged as a distinct field of practice and an arena for international scholarship in the late twentieth century bolstered by a global recognition of the value and vulnerability of Indigenous knowledge systems, and of the right of Indigenous peoples to control them.[1,2] Its growth converges with the development of Indigenous research paradigms that place Indigenous control, benefit, and values at the center of research.[3] The field of Indigenous librarianship is rooted in long-standing and established practices that Indigenous peoples employ to create, transmit, and preserve knowledge. These practices maintain Indigenous cultural and social systems and provide protocols for ownership and the appropriate use of community knowledge.[4,5]

Indigenous librarianship has a developing bibliography and local, national, and international professional associations devoted to its growth.[6] Its foundations rest on strong understandings of the concerns of Indigenous people about the intersections between Indigenous knowledge and culture, and library and information science. Indigenous cultural principles are considered critical to restoring and continuing the principles of Indigenous knowledge management and sharing. Indigenous librarianship encourages the broader profession to move beyond its own disciplinary knowledge base and engage in multidisciplinary approaches with Indigenous cultural experts, information technology (IT) developers, governments, and other institutions.[7]

The purpose of the entry is to survey this protean field through establishing its social and historical contexts, profiling leading practitioners, and highlighting some of the key issues. This entry focuses on Indigenous librarianship within the United States and Canada, and is informed by Indigenous scholarship in Aotearoa/New Zealand and Australia with reference to other international initiatives in order to give a sense of the breadth and the diversity of the provision of library and information services by, for, and with Indigenous peoples. As an emergent scholarship, the parameters and scope of Indigenous librarianship are fluid and although it has a rich discourse there is as yet no codified definition of the field. This entry therefore describes some of the features and begins to map the landscape of Indigenous librarianship.

Methodology

The reality of the practice of Indigenous librarianship is underreported and exists beyond the literature: it exists in the lives of those who work directly with Indigenous peoples.[8] Indigenous library workers who often work outside

Encyclopedia of Library and Information Sciences, Fourth Edition DOI: 10.1081/E-ELIS4-120044735

of the mainstream and librarians in Indigenous cultural and collecting institutions that are outside of state or public systems are the "local heroes" who serve as a link between the past and present generations.[9] This entry incorporates a biographical approach in order to recognize and celebrate the achievements of Indigenous librarians and library workers. This approach is informed by Indigenous research methodologies that strive to surface the contributions and legacies of Indigenous people, and aligns with Linda Tuhiwai Smith's Indigenous projects of testimony, storytelling, sharing, and returning.[10]

Terminology

The original inhabitants of North and South America, Australasia, Africa, and Asia are often identified as a type of collectivity that is seen in contradistinction to the Western or dominant society. Terminology that represents this collectivity includes words such as *Tribal*, *Native*, *Aboriginal*, and *Indigenous*. Original inhabitants within a specific country are culturally and linguistically diverse although they may also be classified as a single group within their countries. The terminology used by the state often reflects a classification established by the force of law within a country and imposes external concepts of identity that may or may not be accepted by an Indigenous individual or collective. This is a complex area with its own literatures and discourses where meanings are constructed in legal, social, cultural, and political contexts.[11] In addition to specific names of nations, communities, cultural, and language groups, there are various generic terms used to denote Indigenous peoples.

In Canada the term Aboriginal is defined under Section 35 of the Constitution Act (1982) to include Indian, Métis, and Inuit peoples. For the purposes of this entry it is used more broadly to include all First Nations, status and non-status Indians, Métis, and Inuit people. First Nations is a term that arose in the 1970s to replace the word "Indian" which is sometimes considered offensive, and refers to a body of Aboriginal people with a shared national identity. First Nations is also used to replace the word "band," a term defined by the Indian Act to mean a body of people defined as Indian by the government. A status Indian is a person who is registered as an Indian under the Indian Act; conversely a non-status Indian is a person not registered as an Indian under the Indian Act. Métis people are of mixed First Nations or Inuit and European ancestry who may also identify as a nation, often the Métis Nation within Western Canada.[12]

Within the United States, the collective term Native American may include American Indian, Alaska Native, and Native Hawaiian. In Canada, the United States, Australia, and New Zealand, Indigenous people claim the right to define their own cultural identity and membership and may not accept the definitions of the state. Within international arenas, the term Indigenous peoples is pluralized to denote the great diversity among Indigenous groups at the same time as it serves as a collective term. Indigenous peoples are seen to be

the inheritors and practitioners of unique living cultures and ways of relating to other people and to the environment who have retained social, cultural, economic, and political characteristics that are distinct from those of the dominant societies in which they live.[13]

INDIGENOUS PEOPLES AND LIBRARIES

The United Nations (UN) estimates that there are 4000 to 5000 Indigenous cultures existing in the world, and over 370 million individuals belonging to these cultures, living in more than 70 countries.[14] This enormous cultural and linguistic diversity among Indigenous peoples belies a shared common experience of historic and ongoing colonialism. Indigenous peoples globally continue to face the ongoing effects of the dispossession of their lands, languages, cultures, and knowledge. Many Indigenous people face economic marginalization, lack of access to social services and educational opportunities, and racial discrimination. Consequently, Indigenous people share concerns relating to the protection of their rights, lands, resources, and their cultural and intellectual property. As Lynette Russell, Director of Monash University's Centre for Australian Indigenous Studies observes, "The First peoples in Aotearoa/New Zealand, Canada, the United States of America along with many other Indigenous peoples face similar issues relating to access to, and control of, information about their cultures and communities."[15]

United States

According to the 2000 census, 4.1 million American Indians and Alaska Natives comprise 1.5% of the total population of the United States.[16] Approximately one-third live on one of 300 reservations with the remainder living in urban and rural areas. The population is young in comparison with the general population. One-third of the population lives below the poverty line, experiencing lower high school graduation rates, and less presence in higher education.[17] There are 175 Indigenous languages spoken in the United States however, 55 are spoken by fewer than 10 people; 70 are spoken only by Elders; and only 50 of them are spoken by two or more generations. As in other countries, Indigenous language loss is considered a key factor in cultural erosion, and Native language maintenance and revitalization are a high priority.[18]

The relationship between Native Americans in the United States and librarianship is fundamentally different from that of other cultural groups because tribal nations have a formal relationship with the federal government. This relationship is set out in treaties and court decisions intended to assure tribal groups of certain benefits, such as, health, education, and general welfare.[19] Although education is a treaty right of American Indians in the United States, and access to libraries and information is integral to the education process, library services to reservations were not available until the 1970s.[20] During the 1970s, fostered by a convergence of changes in federal legislation, court decisions, and an increased receptivity to American Indian self-determination efforts, tribal libraries slowly began to develop. The National Commission on Libraries and Information Science (NCLIS) hearings in 1974 examined library services to urban and on-reserve American Indians and identified the great need in these communities and an "abysmal" lack of formal policy. The *White House Pre-Conference on Indian Library and Information Services On or Near Reservations* (1978) brought together 103 tribes to lay the groundwork to improve library services for American Indians and shape U.S. Federal library and information policy. Native Americans actively promoted and advocated for tribal libraries, the spaces that foster and preserve cultural heritage and protect a tribe's heritage for future generations, which were a keystone in this national library service framework. Tribal libraries support oral traditions through preservation programs and the dissemination offered by print and new media. They also serve the educational, informational, and recreational information needs of Native Americans and provide vital access to government data that supports self-governance activities.

Nonetheless, the comprehensive NCLIS report *Pathways to Excellence: A Report on Improving Library and Information Services to Native American Peoples* (1992) documented inadequate library services for Native Americans characterized by discrimination and lack of culturally appropriate services for off-reserve populations, and geographic barriers to access on-reserve.[21] Ten challenges were identified for the development of tribal libraries: consistent funding at federal, state, local, and tribal government levels; training and technical support for Native American communities; relevant collection development; improved access; state and local partnerships; identification of model programs; the expansion of the tribal library program to include museum and archival services; support for literacy and job skills training; support for IT; and the establishment of federal responsibilities.

Currently, support of tribal libraries crosses multiple jurisdictional boundaries: tribal, local, county, state, regional, and federal. Each represents potential revenue streams to buttress tribal library sustainability and capacity building. At the federal level, the Institute for Museum and Library Services (IMLS) pursues a multidimensional strategy including basic noncompetitive support for local tribal libraries, enhanced support for innovative developments within tribal libraries, national leadership initiatives designed to promote collaborative efforts and develop best

practices, and funding capacity building diversity scholarship program initiatives such as Knowledge River at the University of Arizona and Honoring Generations at the University of Texas, Austin. At the state level, some examples of tribal library initiatives are found in Arizona, New Mexico, Montana, and Oklahoma. The Arizona Gathering of Tribal Librarians is currently planning its seventh Gathering for the Spring of 2008, and a Tribal Library Consultant is employed within the Arizona State Library, Archives and Public Records. The New Mexico State Library's Tribal Libraries Program (TLP) includes the TLP Direct noncompetitive grant for tribal libraries[22] and the Indigenous Nations Library Program (INLP) at the University of New Mexico.[23] In Montana, the Tribal College Librarians Professional Development Institute has been held annually since 1990 at Montana State University in Bozeman.[24]

The Tribal Archives, Libraries and Museums conferences held biannually since 2003 are excellent examples of cross-jurisdictional collaboration in support of the development of tribal libraries. Originating from an IMLS National Leadership Grant awarded in Arizona in 2003 and 2005, the concept was expanded through an IMLS Laura Bush Librarians for the twenty-first Century Grant to the Western Council of State Libraries for 2007–2009. The Oklahoma Department of Libraries hosted the 2007 National Tribal Archives, Libraries and Museums Conference. Four National Immersion Institutes followed in 2008, one each focusing on Archives, Caring for Native American Objects, Photographic Preservation, and Tribal Libraries. The final conference of this grant cycle will be hosted by the Oregon State Library and Tamástslikt Cultural Institute in Oregon in 2009.[25] The ability to create these platforms for collaboration and professional exchange are essential to the development, definition, and vitality of the emergent field of Indigenous librarianship. They provide the opportunity to discuss issues from Indigenous standpoints, meet other practitioners, and allow Indigenous librarians to center their practice within their ways of knowing (Fig. 1).

Canada

Canada's Aboriginal population is young and growing six times faster than the general population. It is now over 1 million. The increase may be attributed to a variety of factors, including tendency to self-identification, birth rate, and legislative changes in definitions. The Aboriginal population consists of approximately 60% First Nations people, 33% Métis people, and 4% Inuit who live primarily in the Arctic regions. Over half of the Aboriginal population lives in urban areas. By 2017 it is projected that the Aboriginal young adult population (aged 20–29) will comprise one-third of the young adults in the province of Saskatchewan; 24% in Manitoba; 40% in the Yukon Territory and 58% in the Northwest Territories.[28] In Canada

Fig. 1   Profile: Lotsee Patterson.

Dr. Lotsee Patterson, an enrolled member of the Comanche Nation raised on her mother's allotment in southwestern Oklahoma, is Professor Emeritus at the University of Oklahoma School of Library and Information Studies. Dr. Patterson is a founder and past president of the AILA. She is a well-known lobbyist for national legislation to fund and improve library services to United States tribes, and for helping to establish tribal libraries in the United States. Beginning in the early 1970s, Dr. Patterson wrote successful grant applications to hold training institutes for American Indian library aides, believing that training staff would pave the way for tribal libraries. Patterson carried out a series of groundbreaking tribal library demonstration projects in the 1970s, eventually publishing the seminal TRAILS (Training and Assistance for Indian Library Services) manual in 1984, a key resource for tribal librarians. Dr. Patterson cochaired both the 1979 and 1991 Native American preconferences to the White House Conference on Library and Information Services, and has mentored hundreds of American Indian librarians and students throughout her career while persistently spotlighting the critical need to fund tribal libraries and commit resources to library services for American Indians. In 2005, Dr. Patterson was recognized as "one of the most outspoken advocates for equitable library services for American Indians" with an honorary ALA membership award for her outstanding and lasting contributions to the field of librarianship.[26,27]

there are 615 First Nations, 10 unique language families and over 60 different Aboriginal languages spoken in the country although, many Aboriginal languages in Canada are endangered or have been lost. The Indian residential school system which operated from the nineteenth century to the 1980s resulted in the dislocation of Aboriginal families, communities and cultures, and in the loss of Aboriginal languages. The ongoing intergenerational impacts of the residential school system continue to be felt today.[29] On June 11, 2008, the Prime Minister of Canada and the Federal party leaders issued an official apology to the Aboriginal people of Canada for the damage and suffering caused by the assimilationist policies of the Canadian government.[30] The courage and resilience of Aboriginal people and the strengths of Aboriginal cultures were acknowledged, and a Truth and Reconciliation commission established to foster reconciliation between Aboriginal people and all Canadians, and to rectify the public historic record of the past.

Public library services for Aboriginal people are uneven across the country. In some provinces, jurisdictional issues are cited as a rationale for the lack of free access to the public library system for Aboriginal people. As First Nations and Métis people are considered federal jurisdiction[31] and public libraries are often funded at the municipal level, the principle of universal access to public institutions does not extend in practice to Indigenous peoples. In British Columbia (B.C), there are no public

libraries on reserve, and the libraries that do exist on reserve are generally small, underfunded band council collections, and band school libraries.[32] In Ontario, the provincial government contributes to the development of public libraries in First Nations communities. However in 2001–2002, only 52 of 141 First Nation libraries in Ontario received operating grants, and because the operating grants are based on population size many small communities are underfunded.[33] Among First Nations communities, libraries are not always a priority when there are pressing needs in the areas of rights and title claims, infrastructure, education, and health. A First Nations library worker explains: "We need all our money to fund our land claims. If we don't have land, we don't have community. If we don't have community, we don't need a library."[34]

The province of Saskatchewan is among the leaders in developing equitable, culturally relevant Aboriginal library and information services in Canada. The Saskatchewan Minister's Advisory Committee on Library Service for Aboriginal people report, *Information is for Everyone* (2001), makes 46 recommendations for improved library and information services for Aboriginal people. It highlights universal access to library services for all Aboriginal people, including on-reserve and off-reserve; partnerships for equitable access; increased awareness, and public education regarding Aboriginal people.[31] A key recommendation, similar to repeated earlier ones in Ontario service reviews, is that First Nations retain control of library services on reserve, and responsibility for determining the kind of library services on reserve. The Library Services for Saskatchewan's Aboriginal Peoples Committee is composed of Aboriginal and public sector representatives who meet six times a year to advise on the implementation of the recommendations.

Public libraries in urban centers tend not to differentiate between Aboriginal people and the general population. As a consequence urban Aboriginal peoples are often not well served. There are exceptions, such as the Albert Library branch of the Regina Public Library[35] and the Spadina branch of the Toronto Public Library that work closely with the local urban Aboriginal communities. The Edmonton Public Library conducted a survey in order to improve library services and programs for the urban Aboriginal community in Edmonton. The final report, *Library Services to Aboriginal Peoples:Task Force Report* (2005), includes an environmental scan with recommendations.[36]

At the national level, a Library and Archives Canada national consultation on Aboriginal library services resulted in a report that included 10 focus areas for improvement in the areas of consultation and partnerships; funding and resources; jurisdiction; planning and administration; universal and equitable access; education and training; advocacy; promotion; authenticity of voice; and outreach and networking (Fig. 2).[37]

Fig. 2 Profile: Charles Angus Cook (Thawennersere) (1870–1958).

The tenacity and vision of Charles Angus Cook (Thawennensere or Da-ha-wen-nen-se-re), a Kanesatake Mohawk, set a standard for the aspirations of Aboriginal library services in Canada. Da-ha-wen-nen-se-re (Charles Cook) worked for the Canadian Indian Affairs Records Branch from 1893 to 1926 as a clerk who classified documents relating to Indians in Canada, and as a translator who translated Iroquois dialects into English. Early in his career he envisioned and advocated for a National Indian Library. He also lobbied tirelessly for the development and proper organization of the Department of Indian Affairs' collection of Indian materials and recommended supplementing the government collection with materials contributed by Aboriginal people in order to reflect Aboriginal perspectives and understandings. He recommended free access to the collections for departmental staff and for all status Indians. In later years, Da-ha-wen-nen-se compiled a Mohawk dictionary and published a Mohawk language newspaper, *Onkweonwe*, the first newspaper in Canada to be produced and published solely by an Aboriginal person.[38]

Australia

Aboriginal Australians and Torres Strait Islander people are two culturally distinct Indigenous peoples of Australia. The Torres Strait Islanders are the traditional inhabitants of the Torres Strait Islands which lie north of Cape York, Queensland; Aboriginal people are located primarily in mainland Australia, including Tasmania. In 2006, 2.5% of Australia's total population of over 21 million are identified as Indigenous.[39] The Indigenous population in Australia is growing rapidly and is also young; 39% are under 15 years of age. While the largest proportion of Indigenous people live in urban areas (30%), a high proportion live in Outer Regional (23%), Remote (9%), and Very Remote (18%) areas when compared against national statistics.[40]

Before European contact, Indigenous peoples in Australia comprised over 500 different language groups. Beginning in the late 1700s, British colonization violently suppressed Aboriginal cultures: colonial legislation regulated segregation, restricted movement, and forcibly removed children from their families.[41] The Australian government's *Bringing Them Home* report (1997) documented the impact of over 150 years of these policies that dislocated families, impacted physical and mental health, resulted in losses of language, culture, and connection to traditional land. On February 13, 2008, a historic parliamentary vote adopted Prime Minister Kevin Rudd's apology on behalf of all Australians for the harm done to the Indigenous people of Australia.[42]

A 1993 report revealed that Australian Indigenous library services relied on erratic grant funding and were usually initiated by community or educational organizations.[43] A year later, an Indigenous Advisory Committee was established to assist with the development of equitable access and inclusive services. The Library and Information Service of Western Australia (LISWA) generated a number of Indigenous-focused service plans aimed at improvement, including *Public Libraries: Good Places for Aboriginal People* (1995) and *Services to Aboriginal and Torres Strait Island Peoples* (1997).

The State Library of Queensland, acknowledging that Indigenous Australians had been "denied, excluded, and/or discouraged access," implemented an Indigenous Library Services Strategy in 2002 focusing on the establishment of Indigenous Knowledge Centres (IKCs) in remote communities, improving public library services, raising the profile of Indigenous people in libraries particularly the State Library, and increasing employment and training opportunities.[44] By 2008, the State Library of Queensland had established 17 IKCs in partnership with Indigenous communities who own and manage the IKCs. An IKC is a community space that offers traditional library services and can be located in community Keeping Places and small museums. In addition to the initial setup costs, the State Library of Queensland provides ongoing support to IKCs in the form of training and development support, and community training programs to help preserve and share local Indigenous Knowledge, orally and digitally, and access cultural material in collecting and cultural institutions throughout the world. The State Library of Queensland has established the first Indigenous Knowledge Centre in a State Library called *kuril dhagun* which welcomes Indigenous and non-Indigenous people to engage with traditional and contemporary expressions of Queensland Indigenous knowledge. The Library has been instrumental in the development of the *National Policy Framework for Aboriginal and Torres Strait Islander Library Services and Collections*,[45,46] as well it has developed its own policies and strategies on reconciliation, cultural protocols, language preservation and maintenance, public library services, and employment and training in the library and information sector.[47]

In 2006, an evaluation of the Northern Territory's Libraries and Knowledge Centre (LKC) model led by Dr. Martin Nakata, a Torres Strait Islander, and Director of Indigenous Academic Programs at Jumbunna Indigenous House of Learning, University of Technology Sydney, concluded that the model had the potential for extension across the Northern Territory.[48] The model incorporates Indigenous knowledge as part of a community-centered information and knowledge base to support the goals of community-building through libraries, and the provision of sustainable public library services that are relevant to multilingual, clan-based, Indigenous communities. Indigenous knowledge centres are also being established in Africa, Latin America, and Asia to revitalize endangered cultures and languages, contribute to economic development, and center Indigenous planning and development (Fig. 3).[49]

Fig. 3 Profile: Joe Gumbala.

Joe Neparrŋa Gumbala, a Gupapuyngu Yolŋu Elder and
musician from North East Arnhem Land is a leading authority on
Yolŋu intellectual and legal traditions. Gumbala is respected for
his Yolŋu knowledge and his ability to interpret other knowledge
systems using traditional frames of reference.[50] As a
Community Liaison Officer at the Galiwin'ku Indigenous
Knowledge Centre in northeast Arnhem Land, Gumbala travels
throughout Australia locating collections of Yolŋu family
histories and other cultural heritage materials, and returning
digital copies to Gupapuyngu communities for local access.
Gumbala applies the Yolŋu traditional knowledge organization
systems to the management of the knowledge centre's digital
collections. Yolŋu knowledge, ceremony, and law have three
strata—restricted, peri-restricted, and public. All Yolŋu
materials are bound by these access and ownership principles.
Kinship relations define related secondary rights to intellectual
and physical property, and determine access to both historic and
contemporary Yolŋu materials at the Galiwin'ku IKC.[51]

Aotearoa/New Zealand

Māori people are the *tangata whenua* ("indigenous people") of New Zealand. The Māori call their traditional
lands Aotearoa, Land of the Long White Cloud. In
Aotearoa/New Zealand, Māori people represent about
15% of the population and are expected to reach 21% by
the year 2051. Like many Indigenous people, Māori are
increasingly urbanized, and they experience social and
economic challenges, including comparatively high unemployment, incarceration, and mortality rates, and lower
outcomes in educational achievement, health, and
income.[52]

The colonization period in Aotearoa/New Zealand
began during the mid-nineteenth century after the signing
of the Treaty of Waitangi in 1840. Signed by over 500
chiefs, the Treaty of Waitangi guaranteed ongoing ownership of lands, fisheries, and other possessions to the Māori,
and granted full British citizenship to the Māori. The
orthography of the early missionaries was readily adopted
by the Māori and resulted in a significant body of manuscript and printed materials written in the Māori language.
In 1975 a permanent commission of enquiry, the Waitangi
Tribunal, was established to address ongoing infringements
on Treaty of Waitangi provisions and enable Māori people
to contest breaches of promises and make claims. Evidence
used in Treaty claims frequently relies on the documentary
materials held in libraries and archives throughout
Aotearora/New Zealand. The Tribunal has been instructed
to make its decisions based on both the English and the
Māori text. Māori access to library and archive holdings is
therefore central to the ongoing settlement of Māori claims
and to the national reconciliation process. In addition,
libraries and archives in New Zealand also play a central
role in supporting Māori language revitalization efforts.

This socio-legal background sets the stage for Indigenous
librarianship in New Zealand and for understanding the
development of the Ngā Ūpoko Tukutuku/Māori subject
headings and their role in the provision of access to Māori
collections for and by Māori people.

In 1993 the Library and Information Association of
New Zealand Aotearoa (LIANZA) initiated a two-phase
national research project on biculturalism issues and services to Māori, *Te Ara Tika* (translated as "the right
path"). The first phase undertook an analysis from the
perspective of the library profession; the next phase surveyed Māori information needs and Māori opinion about
libraries and library services. The findings are documented
in *Te Ara Tika Guiding Voices* report (1997) which identified strong Māori interest in library and information services within six dominant themes that emerged as
intellectual access and information literacy; relationships
between youth literacy, libraries, and schools; Māori
staffing; establishing libraries in Māori communities; and
intellectual property issues. These findings echoed a 1960s
report conducted by the New Zealand Library Association, and the replication of results highlights a persistent
Māori interest in library-centered issues.[53]

The library community's response to *Te Ara Tika Guiding Voices* report has included the National Library of
New Zealand's *Te Kaupapa Mahi Tahi—A Plan for Partnership* (2001), a renewable five-year plan focused on the
National Library's service to Māori. It also includes the
Manukau Libraries' *Te Ao Marama* (2002), a Māori service strategy from one of the country's largest public
libraries. In addition, a new National Library Act (2003)
was passed that acknowledges Māori interests in library
collections and services: it specifically references
Mātauranga Māori (Māori knowledge), and has
established the Library and Information Advisory Commission Ngā Kaiwhakamārama i ngā Kohikohinga Kōrero
(LIAC) as an advisory body on the role of library and
information services in the social, cultural, and economic
life, including Mātauranga Māori. The LIANZA includes
knowledge of Mātauranga Māori and the Treaty of
Waitangi as essential components of professional competence for the library and information sector (Fig. 4).

Indigenous Libraries and Their Intersections

From Māori perspectives the past and the present are seen
as a continuum: the past is a taonga (knowledge/treasure)
to understand the present, to learn and grow from. The
past forms part of the Māori living traditions that connect
Māori to their past, and to their identity.[56] Traditional
taonga knowledge comes in many forms: it may be carried
in carving, woven into wall panels, as well as inscribed in
early Māori writings, archival documents, and other forms
of transmission. For millennia Indigenous peoples have
passed on their unique legacies through the chain of oral
tradition. It is transmitted through habits and customs as

Fig. 4 Profile: Chris Szekely.

Chris Szekely served as a lead on the *Te Ara Tika Guiding Voices* national research project on library and information services for Māori, and has written widely in support of improved library services for Indigenous New Zealanders and on issues related to Indigenous librarianship. On March 19, 2007, Mr. Szekely became the first Māori Chief Librarian of the Alexander Turnbull Library, a division of the National Library of New Zealand and the country's leading heritage research library and storehouse of the nation's documentary collections. One of his first tasks is to provide leadership on a major expansion of the facility to be completed in 2011.[54] Prior to this appointment, Chris Szekely served as City Librarian at Manukau City Council heading one of the largest and fastest growing public library service regions in New Zealand. During his tenure as City Librarian, he opened a number of new branches, including one designed with and for Pacific Islander youth, and established a bilingual catalogue and Web site for the library.[55] He is a founding member of Te Rōpū Whakahau, the National Association of Māori library and information workers, and was instrumental in the formation of the International Indigenous Librarians' Forum (IILF).

well as through those Elders who serve as the living libraries of their communities: the carriers of knowledge of traditional governance, science, technology, philosophy, values, healing, and history. This type of knowledge is often largely undocumented and Indigenous peoples are developing more permanent structures such as libraries, and utilizing new media technologies, to protect and preserve it. At the same time Indigenous nations require access to all of the information resources and technologies required for self-governance and activities related to education, social services, economic development, law, and environmental issues in the twenty-first century.[21]

Indigenous understandings of knowledge continua are sometimes manifest in institutional convergences between libraries, archives, and museums. As a function of both worldview and resource constraints, Indigenous libraries may traverse the conventional institutional boundaries separating library–archive–museum and creatively converge these institutions for Indigenous purposes. The locations of knowledge centers may range from an ecotourism center to a school media center, or postsecondary academic library, to a literacy program, treaty office, health services unit, or urban friendship center. There is extensive variation in locale, clientele, services, and governance and with the local and external institutions with which they intersect (Fig. 5).

KEY ISSUES IN INDIGENOUS LIBRARIANSHIP

While the practice and the location varies, a focus of Indigenous librarianship is the provision of culturally relevant library and information collections and services for Indigenous people. Within Indigenous communities there are standard information requirements in addition to unique information needs that are related to the maintenance and revitalization of Indigenous cultures and languages; Indigenous self-governance; rights and title claims; stewardship of traditional territories and resources; preservation of traditional knowledge systems; and the protection of intellectual and cultural property. The web of service provision ideally begin with Indigenous-controlled libraries in Indigenous communities and extends to the networks of small, rural, urban, academic, legal, special libraries, archives, and other institutions. All of these sites offer rich ground for the development of practice, theory, scholarship, and methodology in Indigenous librarianship. Several overarching themes that recur in practice and in the literature have been selected as key issues for Indigenous librarianship under the umbrella concepts of library development, access, and intellectual property. The development of Indigenous-controlled libraries and other forms of memory institutions is fundamental for Indigenous cultural and intellectual sovereignty. Social justice demands that Indigenous people have equitable access to public institutions and their resources. Equitable access includes a range of considerations including resolution of jurisdictional barriers, the provision of culturally appropriate and meaningful collections and services, and development of accurate knowledge representation tools: these may be bilingual or multilingual depending on the locale and clientele. Public institutions have a responsibility to staff their services with a diverse staff that represents the clientele being served and to explore innovative measures to ensure diversity. Prerequisites to the provision of equitable access include the basic infrastructure and skills to utilize library services and collections, such as Internet access, telecommunications, and multiple literacies. Literacy forms pathways composed of skills and knowledge that facilitate various levels of access to the resources offered by libraries and is therefore a fundamental issue for Indigenous librarianship. The protection of and protocols for use of Indigenous cultural and intellectual property (ICIP) guide the design of appropriate services, and collections and inform standards of professional ethics: virtual repatriation, an emergent area within the field may be included within this purview.

Indigenous Libraries

Against the odds Indigenous libraries endure and continue to grow. Although diverse in form, size, purpose, and location, Indigenous libraries share many similar challenges: they often compete for funds with basic services, such as roads, utilities, and more urgent priorities on reserve and are staffed by nondegreed personnel with little training.[57] Perennial funding challenges contribute to high staff turnover, inadequate facilities, and a lack of

Fig. 5 Profile: Gene Joseph.

Gene Joseph, Wet'suwet'en Dakehl, has been involved in developing First Nations libraries in Canada for many years. She also manages First Nation litigation research for cultural and legal issues, and served as the librarian for the Gitxsan Wet'suwet'en in the precedent setting Delgamuukw case in the Supreme Court of Canada. Gene Joseph reflects on her experiences during this landmark trial.

"On December 11, 1997 the Supreme Court of Canada handed down its decision in the court case Delgamuukw vs. British Columbia, [1997] 3 S.C.R. 1010 which affirmed the inherent meaning of aboriginal title. It was also the first court to rule that oral history or oral evidence be placed on equal footing with that given to historical documents.

In 1984 two First Nations, the Wet'suwet'en and the Gitxsan, filed their statement of claim to 58,000 km² which was divided into 133 territories with traditional ownership accorded to 71 Houses of the Gitxsan and Wet'suwet'en people.

In 1982 I had graduated from the University of British Columbia School of Library and Archival Sciences and it was an honor to me that in 1984 I was recruited by the Gitxsan and Wet'suwet'en to work on a collection of oral history materials from the elders and chiefs. I returned to my home in Hagwilget, a Wet'suwet'en village near Hazelton. There, I worked on the oral evidence with senior Gitxsan and Wet'suwet'en researchers: oral evidence was thoroughly reviewed, transcribed, and translated by the chiefs and elders.

In 1986 Mass Gaak (Don Ryan) again recruited me to return to Hazelton, this time to work on the historical documents that had been collected as evidence. I continued to work through the trial. The trial ran for 374 days starting May 11, 1987 and ending February 7, 1990. The trial had 9200 exhibits with thousands more documents previously listed in numerous document lists, and 26,000 pages of transcripts. The decision was handed down on March 8, 1991. This was followed by the B.C. court of Appeal. This decision came down on June 25, 1993 and was appealed by the Gitxsan and the Wet'suwet'en to the Supreme Court of Canada, which rendered its decision on December 11, 1997.

Delgamuukw drew upon the technical skills I had learned at the Union of B.C. Indian Chief's Library, and the organizational, archival, and computing skills learned at Library school. The oral recordings needed to be preserved and treated as archival as they recorded people who were in ill health or quite elderly. Their knowledge was invaluable. The case started just as personal computers began to be introduced into office environments, which in turn required the development of new software programs, database structures, and the incorporation of continually developing and advancing hardware and software. The Delgamuukw Gisdaywa case was one of the first court rooms in Canada to use personal computers by the court and counsel.

Historical documents had been collected from various archives in Canada, England, and the United States. There were numerous scientists from various fields: archaeologists, anthropologists, linguists, historians, geographers, and genealogists gave evidence and presented documents. Therefore the language, classification, and headings covered many streams of knowledge, both Western and Indigenous. Litigation support as well drew upon court requirements, counsel's needs, and court reporters which were in the throes of moving from the traditional hard copy to an electronic court room.

Most of all, the trial drew upon the knowledge of the traditional systems, history, and culture that I had learned from my family, and then from the elders and chiefs with whom I worked among the Gitxsan and Wet'suwet'en people. While I did not speak the language, I was constantly surrounded and worked with sound and video recordings, translators, and linguists who were for the first time having to spell personal, place, and spiritual names. We worked closely with the cartographer as he recorded these names onto the new maps of the territories, continually cross-checking with the chiefs, elders, and researchers. The map was named "The map that roared" by the court.

collections and technology. Indigenous communities in remote areas face transportation and communications difficulties. These barriers to the development of Indigenous libraries have remained much the same over time, however, the priorities are changing due to the ubiquity of information and communication technologies (ICTs) in a global networked world. ICTs present the added challenges of an ever-changing technical environment that requires the acquisition and maintenance of hardware and software, the skills sets to utilize them, and broadband access. Even if funds are available, Internet connectivity may be inadequate in remote locations, and distance may also discourage the recruitment and retention of qualified IT staff.[18]

Digital Divide

ICTs have been defined as "a diverse set of technological tools and resources used to communicate, and to create, disseminate, store, and manage information."[58] The term digital divide is generally understood as the gap between ICT "haves" and "have-nots." It encompasses issues, such

as infrastructure and access to ICTs, use and barriers to use, and the critical role of ICT skills and literacy in an information society. From Indigenous perspectives ICTs support the revitalization of culture and language, and they serve as knowledge and communication building blocks that enable the development of community infrastructure in a range of areas from education to health, from economic development to environmental protection.[59] They enable access to the global web of information, and perhaps more importantly they provide the means to participate in local and distributed communities of interest. As authorial tools ICTs have the potential to create and distribute Indigenous perspectives in order to correct some of the ubiquitous stereotypes and misrepresentations, to shape attitudes, and to change the ways in which history is understood. National information policy in Canada and the United States aims to provide affordable access to the Internet and to the skills required to use it. However, in the National Telecommunications Information Administration (NTIA) in the United States reported that only 9% of Native Americans in rural areas have home Internet access and that access tends to be through schools or libraries.[60]

In Canada, the BC First Nations Technology Council research shows that in one-third of BC First Nations communities 75% of the homes are without Internet access, and in almost 20% of BC First Nations communities there are homes without basic telephone service.[61] In Canada, the Community Access Program (CAP) is one of the primary federal connectivity programs that benefits Aboriginal communities and the Gates Foundation is making improvements to technology access, equipment, and support in both the United States and Canada. The digital divide, the ICT gap in access, services, and skills, however, continues to exist for Aboriginal people.

Profile: Jean Whitehorse

Jean Whitehorse, a Navajo member of the Towering House clan and Born for Bitter Water clan, is making a difference. As a training and outreach coordinator for the New Mexico State Library, Whitehorse conducts IT training at libraries and Navajo chapter houses in New Mexico. Exclaiming "get ready the world is going to change with or without you!" her advocacy has resulted in the hiring of more Native American trainers and in a new internship program for tribal college student ICT trainers working with the tribes. Whitehorse believes that as comfort with technology increases the tribal community members are empowered with new skills, and this in turn encourages the children, the future leaders, to explore the benefits of the virtual world. She draws an analogy between the artistry and expertise involved in weaving a Navajo rug and that of weaving technology education for the nations (Fig. 6).[62]

This type of multidimensional model of ICT access underlines the many threads that must be woven together for effective use of technology, including political support at multiple levels, funding, perceived relevance to Indigenous interests, culturally based evaluation and training, social relationships and skills sets.

Fig. 6 Profile: Jean Whitehorse. Cyber sovereignty: Digital diné.

* Navajo weavers	NM State legislatures supporting Senator Tsosie
* Raw material in the wool	State funding and grants
* Shearing the sheep	Advocacy at the chapter houses
* Tools: shears/combs/spindle/batten	Infrastructure, planning and program development
* Loom	Networking
* Wash the wool	Outreach to the chapters and tribal leaders
* Card the wool	Collaborating with the Gates Foundation
* Dye the wool	Collaborating with Navajo Community Development
* Spinning, grandma can teach you	TLP Tech support and computer training
* Design and pattern	Trainings evaluations

Universal Access

Librarians have long upheld the principle of universal access to public libraries because as the UNESCO Public Library Manifesto states, "The public library, the local gateway to knowledge, provides a basic condition for lifelong learning, independent decision-making and cultural development of the individual and social groups."[63] However, universal access to the public library is not a reality for Indigenous people in North America although it is a cornerstone of the national educational and information infrastructure in the United States and Canada. For Indigenous people who do "technically" live inside a library service catchment area, there continue to be many visible and invisible barriers presented through library practices, collections, and services. Many public institutions are seeking to improve their services for Indigenous people, after all, Indigenous people are community members in urban centers as well as in rural communities. Indigenous students, teachers, and faculty members populate the schools and academic institutions, and are within the ever-expanding circles of the digital community.[64]

Literacy

From Indigenous perspectives the notion of literacy is conceptualized as being multidimensional one that may extend from an ability to read the land to an ability to read text. It includes the range of skills and knowledge required to read and interpret meaning, to allow deeper understandings, and ultimately to become the authors of new meaning. Indigenous approaches to literacy seek to honor and build bridges from existing knowledge and skills to strengthen Indigenous cultural identity, languages, and values. They are centered on local issues at the same time as they connect with an awareness of the global world. The legacies of cultural and language disruption left by colonial education systems and education designed for assimilation are integral to understandings of Aboriginal literacy and Aboriginal literacy education.[65] Low text literacy levels are frequently a challenge in Indigenous communities. In Canada, the rate of illiteracy on-reserve is almost two times the rate of the off-reserve Aboriginal population and three times that of the general Canadian population.[66] Within Indigenous contexts, it is important to acknowledge familial and social networks of authority and various types of literacy, in addition to English language text literacy. The relationships between ideas and knowledge, social practices, and responsibilities are considered to be important.[67] English may be a second language for some learners, and for some learners Aboriginal English is the dialect used in the home, not mainstream English. Successful literacy strategies therefore

Fig. 7 Profile: Loriene Roy.

Loriene Roy is Anishinabe, an enrolled member of the Minnesota Chippewa Tribe, White Earth Reservation, and a Professor at the University of Texas at Austin School of Information since 1987. Dr. Roy has devoted her career to improving literacy and instruction services for Native youth, advocating for library services for and by Native communities, and supporting the education of American Indian librarians. Guided by Indigenous protocols and Anishinabe teachings in her teaching and writing, Dr. Roy is a respected and visible advocate for Indigenous perspectives on national literacy and library issues in the United States, and has been an active participant in international Indigenous librarianship gatherings, serving on committees that organized the first and second IILF in 1999 and 2001. In 2007, Dr. Roy became the first American Indian president of the American Library Association, a role she filled with the same spirit and vision that she brought to her presidency of the AILA in 1997–1998. In addition to her national and international leadership, she has served as the director of the Native American youth reading club program, "If I Can Read, I Can Do Anything" since its founding in 1999; established the "Honoring Generations" scholarship program for tribal librarians at University of Texas at Austin; assisted tribal schools with developing culturally responsive curriculum; created online resources for tribal college students; and inspired successive generations of American Indian librarians and students.[68,69]

incorporate programming by and for Aboriginal people that are designed for a specific cultural clienteles to develop the range of literacy skills required to succeed in education, and to succeed in integrating Aboriginal approaches to education into twenty-first century Indigenous pedagogies (Fig. 7).

Indigenous Knowledge Organization

The dominant North American classification and subject heading systems, the Dewey Decimal Classification and the Library of Congress systems, are not adept at representing Indigenous peoples and topics. These types of knowledge organization systems are shaped by culture and they reflect world view through the selection of terminology, concepts, and the ways in which they show or do not show relationships.[70] The literature documents that the mainstream systems tend to marginalize, omit, or misrepresent Indigenous topics. These types of inaccuracies can occur through historicization, lack of specificity, lack of relevance, lack of recognition of sovereign nations, and the omission of the historical realities of colonization.[71,72] Cataloging practice for Indigenous topics must recognize the names, relationships, places, histories, and concepts used by Indigenous peoples. If Indigenous perspectives are not incorporated into knowledge organization tools, it creates another barrier to access for Indigenous peoples at the same time as perpetuating inaccurate and culturally inappropriate representation for the

general public. From Indigenous perspectives, intellectual access to public collections in libraries, archives, and museums is important for educational and informational purposes, and also for claims research, genealogy, and the revitalization of traditions, languages, and histories.[73] The dominant classification and subject heading systems are now used on a global scale, and while this enables unprecedented sharing of knowledge, it also has unprecedented power to marginalize Indigenous knowledge domains, and to establish the cultural perspectives of mainstream North America as a global norm.[74] Ambitious national Indigenous thesaurus projects have been undertaken in both Australia and New Zealand to provide more balanced representation and access: the Māori subject headings provide access to the Māori body of knowledge held in public institutions for Māori people.[75] The Australian Aboriginal and Torres Strait Islander Thesaurus aims to improve access to Aboriginal and Torres Strait Islander materials: "It is important that the Indigenous voices of Australia are heard and felt through proper representation in catalogues."[76] International bodies, such as, the UN and the International Federation of Library Associations and Institutions (IFLA), assert the importance of preserving Indigenous knowledge and protecting the individual and collective rights of Indigenous people.

Intellectual and Cultural Property (ICIP)

The concept of ICIP rights refers to past, present, and future tangible and intangible expressions of heritage. These expressions exist within a body of cultural practices, knowledge systems, and resources that serve to define cultural identity.[77] The results of a global study of Indigenous heritage led by Professor Erica-Irene Daes, Chairperson of the UN Working Group on Indigenous Populations, is widely cited as a standard and it shaped The Declaration on the Rights of Indigenous Peoples[78] which was adopted by the UN General Assembly on September 13, 2007. One of the most comprehensive statements on the individual and collective rights of Indigenous people, the Declaration states:

> Indigenous peoples have the right to practice and revitalize their cultural traditions and customs. This includes the right to maintain, protect and develop the past, present and future manifestations of their cultures ...taken without their free and informed consent or in violation of their laws, traditions and customs."[79] When knowledge is removed from communities and the systems are disrupted, there is a community loss of control over ways they are represented and used. Some Indigenous legal concepts, such as, the notion of collective rights, do not easily fit into existing legal frameworks. Public institutions, such as libraries, archives and museums that hold Indigenous collections face a range of ICIP issues, such as, the retrospective identification of heritage materials; identification of the community of origin; the determination of copyright

and ownership; ascertaining restrictions on access.[80] Because existing copyright law and intellectual property law do not wholly protect ICIP, protocols have been developed as guidelines for institutions and organizations to use in their interactions with Indigenous people.

Indigenous Protocols

Protocols are seen as a bridge between Indigenous customary law and existing legal instruments. Protocols guide practice, and are localized in order to reflect the approaches of specific communities and the contexts of each institution's mission and collections.[81]*The Aboriginal and Torres Strait Islander Library and Information Resource Network (ATSILIRN) Protocols* are considered to be a leading guide for libraries. They serve as a compass for discussion, policy, and practice related to the care of Indigenous materials and to the development of relationships between Indigenous communities and individuals, and institutions. First published in 1995, the protocols were revised in 2005, and are considered to be living documents that are continuously updated.[81] Some of the primary concerns regarding information issues from Indigenous perspectives are governance and policy, education and training, and increased Indigenous employment and staffing.[82] In addition Indigenous peoples have concerns regarding community ownership and rights management, guidelines for access to sensitive or sacred knowledge, and ownership of oral traditions and songs.

Virtual Repatriation

Indigenous communities have had their knowledge systems disrupted in many ways. One significant outcome is that collecting institutions, such as museums, libraries, and archives throughout the world hold large collections of materials collected from or of significance to Indigenous people. Virtual repatriation is the process by which digital copies of objects, recordings, images, and documents are returned to the originating Indigenous community. In some cases virtual repatriation partnerships exist between Indigenous groups and collecting institutions, such as, the Smithsonian National Museum of the American Indian (NMAI) Spiral of Knowledge project. In other cases, Indigenous communities repatriate digital copies from collecting institutions or churches, or from individual collectors such as anthropologists, missionaries, and others. The returned digital materials gradually amass to form local Indigenous knowledge bases which in themselves may present significant IT issues, and ethical and knowledge organization challenges for the community.[83] Frequently multidisciplinary in scope with various types of content and different file formats, these knowledge bases use software and hardware that are vulnerable to change. Systematic planning for data migration, attention

to standards compliance, and consideration of sustainability, interoperability, and portability issues are therefore required at the community level. Intellectual property and copyright guidelines, and digital rights management are increasingly important in these types of environment where the boundaries of collecting institutions are coalescing and technologies are converging. Collecting institutions meet their own ownership and access requirements in order to repatriate materials to communities, and Indigenous communities then face ongoing intellectual property issues related to both the returned materials and to contemporary materials. Communities may face a range of ICIP considerations, including different kinds rights for different types of knowledge and material formats; considerations for individual viewing, public viewing, and reproduction of materials by Indigenous people or external groups; and considerations regarding community members adding their own annotations to shared databases. The rights management systems utilized must satisfy Indigenous customary approaches, as well as national laws and institutional regulations. Dr. Martin Nakata suggests that coordinated approaches at the community level, the state level, or possibly national level may be beneficial as the number of knowledge bases and amount of content can only be expected to increase over time both within individual communities and among communities. The complexities of these virtual repatriation processes are beginning to constitute a specialist area of practice.[84]

RESEARCH IN INDIGENOUS LIBRARIANSHIP

Indigenous scholars are asking new questions of research and creating an emergent scholarship that speaks to Indigenous interests in reclaiming languages, histories and knowledge, and creating new solutions to address the negative impacts of colonialism.[85] These processes require (re)conceptualizing research as a transformative practice: capable of transforming the world and capable of transforming itself. Indigenous research methodology offers expanded systems of knowledge and ways of knowing that hold potential for sustainable research practices with global applicability in the twenty-first century.

Practitioners of Indigenous librarianship are positioned to take up the new methodologies of Indigenous theorists to inform research practice: there is a need for empirical, theoretical, evaluation, and policy research in Indigenous librarianship. In 1992 Cheryl Metoyer-Duran observed a lack of baseline data needed to conduct research in order to plan, develop, implement, or evaluate services in tribal communities. "At present, there is no comprehensive study which considers the definition of tribal libraries, their location, description of resources and services, staffing or clientele."[86] This still holds true in 2008 and continues to impede the further development of planning, preservation, and the dissemination and evaluation of services and collections.

The key issues for Indigenous librarianship highlighted in this entry suggest a range of areas for future research. Areas of applied research could include, best practices in Indigenous library development, Indigenous approaches to digitization, local and national information policy, literacy education, cultural and intellectual property rights, knowledge organization and representation, professional ethics and professional competencies. There is a need for further development of social justice, critical and Indigenous theoretical frameworks within library and information science. Linda Tuhiwai Smith's work on decolonizing methodologies could be used to provide a map of the terrain of research relationships: some research will be undertaken only by Indigenous researchers in Indigenous communities, other types of research will be controlled by Indigenous people with outside partners, and some will constitute a whole range of collaborative research partnerships with Indigenous people and others.[87] A fundamental issue for research and for practice is the education of Indigenous librarians and education for Indigenous librarianship.

EDUCATION FOR INDIGENOUS LIBRARIANSHIP

Kelly Webster, past president of the American Indian Library Association (AILA) and a member of the Oneida Tribe of Indians of Wisconsin, recalls her experience in library school.

> I went to library school in the mid-1990's, and like most other students I did not hear a word about library services to American Indians in my classes, meet another Native person in the program, or encounter anything in my assigned readings on the topic[88]

Employment and education of Indigenous people across the library and information sector is repeatedly cited as a high priority in the United States, Canada, Aotearoa/New Zealand, and Australia. However, there has been limited success at recruitment and relevant curriculum development. The Association for Library and Information Science Education (ALISE) statistics on ALA accredited programs in the United States and Canada (2004) show full-time American Indian LIS faculty represented six positions (0.8%) of the faculty in 51 schools.[89] In 2002–2003, only 26 American Indian graduates were awarded LIS degrees out of a total of 7284 graduates: there were no American Indian doctoral graduates.[90] Part of the recruitment challenge hinges on the development of culturally relevant and responsive curriculum. The Knowledge River program at the School of Information Resources and Library Science (SIRLS), University of Arizona; the University of New Mexico, INLP; and Honoring Generations at the University of Texas at Austin Information School are promising initiatives in education and recruitment of Indigenous people.[91–93] The LIANZA statement of core competencies includes awareness of Indigenous knowledge paradigms and describes it in sufficient detail to guide to curriculum development by education providers.[94]

There is a need to educate tribal librarians who can plan and implement infrastructure for twenty-first century community library and information services, and professionals who can design and manage Indigenous memory institutions, facilitate repatriation efforts, and navigate the complex relationships required to build alliances. At the same time, the broader profession and collecting institutions require education to address widespread issues of ignorance and misunderstandings that are a legacy of past educational failures. An example of staff professional development is modeled by the University of Queensland where Indigenous and non-Indigenous library staff have partnered on developing a staff education program about Indigenous issues and histories. This occurred within an organizational climate that has a Senate-approved mandate to improve Indigenous education by challenging preconceived ideas of knowledge creation, dissemination, and recognition.[95]

PROFESSIONAL ASSOCIATIONS

From the seminal work of the National Indian Education Association with the American Library Association that produced the Goals for Indian Library and Information Service (1973) to the formation of the International Indigenous Librarians' Forum (IILF) in 1999, the initiatives of Indigenous peoples' associations guide the field. The following are key groups at national and international levels.

The IILF was formed in 1999 for Indigenous library, archives and information workers to share experiences and to discuss common issues and concerns. The IILF meets every 2 years and publishes conference proceedings on an irregular basis. The first forum was convened by the Māori in Auckland Aotearoa/New Zealand in November 1999. Subsequent forums have been hosted by local Indigenous groups in Jokmokk, Sweden in 2001; Santa Fe, New Mexico in 2003; Regina, Saskatchewan in 2005; Brisbane Australia 2007; Otaki in Aotearoa/New Zealand in 2009.

The AILA, founded in 1979 as a result of the 1978 White House Pre-Conference, has a mandate to improve library services to American Indians and Alaska Natives in school, public, and research libraries, both on- and off-reservation, and to disseminate information about American Indian and Alaska Native library issues. AILA holds meetings twice a year in conjunction with the American Library Association, runs an e-mail list that networks American Indian librarians and librarians serving American Indian communities, publishes a quarterly newsletter, and has formed a classification and subject access committee that plays a leadership role in shaping culturally appropriate subject representation.

The Aboriginal and Torres Strait Islander Library and Information Resource Network (ATSILIRN) was established in 1993 to provide an information network and support for Aboriginal and Torres Strait Islander peoples working in libraries. The organization also includes members and institutions whose work addresses the information needs of Australian Indigenous peoples. ATSILIRN holds annual conferences and has participated in the development of protocols for libraries and archives serving Aboriginal and Torres Strait Islanders and the compilation of the Aboriginal and Torres Strait Islander Thesaurus.

In 1992, Māori library workers established a professional association, Te Rōpū Whakahau (TRW, the Māori Library and Information Workers' Association). Its goals are to provide cultural and professional support to Māori working in libraries, and to create a forum for Māori voices to inform policies and practices relating to the care of Māori material in libraries and archives. The TRW publishes a regular newsletter, makes policy submissions, participates in research projects, organizes *hui* (gatherings/conferences), and produces publications related to Māori library issues.

In addition, there are numerous professional associations at the local, state/provincial, and national levels within the United States, Canada, Australia, and Aotearoa/New Zealand that are involved with the development of Indigenous library and information services, and educating the general population about Indigenous issues, histories, and diverse approaches to knowledge and ways of knowing. At the international level, a proposal to form a Special Interest Group (SIG) on Indigenous knowledge was submitted to the International Federation of Libraries and Institutions Association (IFLA) at its annual conference in Quebec City (2008).

CONCLUSION

In the United States, Canada, Australia, and Aotearoa/New Zealand Indigenous librarianship is located within policy environments of Indigenous self-governance and national reconciliation. Two clear implications for librarianship are: (1) Indigenous information demands will continue to grow exponentially due to expanding Indigenous self-governance activities and the exigencies of demographics and (2) Indigenous library and information services can only succeed under the direction of Indigenous nations, or in ethical partnerships between Indigenous and non-Indigenous partners.[96] The development of Indigenous libraries and information services is key for cultural revitalization and maintenance, and for the economic and educational interests of Indigenous communities and

individuals. At the same time rapidly growing young Indigenous populations can be expected to increase demands for youth programs, education, and bridging programs from public institutions.[97] Equitable access to public institutions and infrastructure are necessary to avoid creating systemic two-tiered systems that will further marginalize an increasingly large proportion of national populations.

The scholarship of Indigenous librarianship has important contributions to make to library and information science as a discipline that speaks to real-world issues in local and global contexts. It has the potential to mobilize Indigenous knowledge to shape the theory and practice of the broader profession, including curriculum development and research in library and information science faculties. As Indigenous librarianship serves Indigenous interests, it is also serves the education of all learners who are citizens of countries where Indigenous peoples are the First Peoples.

ACKNOWLEDGMENTS

Olivia Robinson, Senior Policy and Project Officer, Indigenous Library Services. State Library of Queensland, Australia.

Amanda Simard, Library Specialist, Assembly of Manitoba Chiefs, Manitoba.

Wendy Sinclair Sparvier, Head, Albert Community Branch, Regina Saskatchewan.

Jean Whitehorse, Navajo member of the Towering House clan and Born for Bitter Water clan. Training and Outreach Librarian, New Mexico State Library.

Xwi7xwa Library Staff: Eleanore Wellwood, Library Assistant; Jenna Walsh, Graduate Academic Assistant; Kim Lawson, Reference Librarian; Linda Allen, Library Assistant.

AUTHORS

Kathleen T. Burns, Mixed-blood Nlaka'pamux. Archivist, Beinecke Rare Book and Manuscript Library, Yale University; American Indian Library Association; Society of American Archivists.

Ann Doyle, Librarian, First Nations House of Learning, Xwi7xwa Library, University of British Columbia; Canadian Library Association, Library and Information Needs of Native Peoples Interest Group.

Gene Joseph, Wet'suwet'en Dakehl. Librarian, Environmental Aboriginal Guardianship through Law and Education (EAGLE); British Columbia Library Association, First Nations Interest Group.

Allison Boucher Krebs, Anishinaabe, member Sault Ste. Marie Tribe of the Chippewa Indians. M.L.S. Knowledge River Scholar, University of Arizona (2008); Native

India–Information Behavior

American Roundtable Steering Committee of the Society of American Archivists; Member of the Board of Directors, Michigan Indian Education Council.

REFERENCES

1. Nakata, M.; Byrne, A.; Nakata, V.; Gardiner, G. Indigenous knowledge, the library and information service sector, and protocols. In *Australian Indigenous Knowledge and Libraries*; Nakata, M., Langton, M., Eds.; Australian Academic & Research Libraries: Canberra, Australian Capital Territory, Australia, 2005; 9–24.

2. Patterson, L. International issues. In *Library Services to Indigenous Populations: Viewpoints and Resources*; Webster, K., Ed.; Office for Literacy and Outreach Services, American Library Association: Chicago, IL, 2005; 24–29.

3. Denzin, N.K.; Lincoln, Y.S.; Smith, L.T. *Handbook of Critical and Indigenous Methodologies*, Sage Publications: Thousand Oaks, CA, 2008.

4. Lawson, K.L. *Precious fragments: First Nations materials in archives, libraries and museums*, University of British Columbia: Vancouver, BC, 2004, M.L.I.S. thesis.

5. Adams, N. Professional legacies: The significance of careers in cultural preservation. Winds Change 2005, 20 (4), 44–48.

6. Webster, K., Ed. In *Library Services to Indigenous Populations: Viewpoints and Resources*; Office for Literacy and Outreach Services, American Library Association: Chicago, IL, 2005.

7. In *Australian Indigenous Knowledge and Libraries*; Nakata, M., Langton, M., Eds.; Australian Academic & Research Libraries: Canberra, Australian Capital Territory, Australia, 2005; 216.

8. Roy, L.; Smith, A.A. Preface. In *Library Services to Indigenous Populations: Viewpoints and Resources*; Webster, K., Ed.; Office for Literacy and Outreach Services, American Library Association: Chicago, IL, 2005; v.

9. Roy, L.; Smith, A.A. Preface. In *Library Services to Indigenous Populations: Viewpoints and Resources*; Webster, K., Ed.; Office for Literacy and Outreach Services, American Library Association: Chicago, IL, 2005; vi.

10. Smith, L.T. Twenty-five Indigenous projects. *Decolonizing Methodologies: Research and Indigenous Peoples*; Zed Books: New York, 1999; 142–162.

11. Sawchuck, J., Ed. In *Identities and State Structures of Readings in Aboriginal Studies*; Bearpaw Publishing: Brandon, Manitoba, 1992; Vol. 2.

12. Indians and Northern Affairs. *Words First: An Evolving Terminology Relating to Aboriginal Peoples in Canada*, Communications Branch: Canada, October 2002. Available at http://www.ainc-inac.gc.ca/ap/pubs/wf/wf-eng.pdf (accessed June 2008).

13. Baer, L.A. Protection of rights of holders of traditional knowledge, Indigenous peoples and local communities. World Libr. 2002, 12(1), 15. Available at http://www.worlib.org/vol12no1/baer_v12n1.shtml (accessed June 2008).

14. United Nations. United Nations Permanent Forum on Indigenous Peoples. *Factsheet—Who are Indigenous Peoples?* Available at http://www.un.org/esa/socdev/unpfii/documents/5session_factsheet1.pdf.

15. Russell, L. Indigenous knowledge and archives: Accessing hidden history and understandings. In *Australian Indigenous Knowledge and Libraries*; Nakata, M., Langton, M., Eds.; Australian Academic & Research Libraries: Canberra, Australian Capital Territory, Australia, 2005; 178.

16. United States. Census Bureau. United States Census 2000. Available at http://www.census.gov/main/www/cen2000.html United States. Census Bureau. *United States Census 2000*.

17. Roy, L. Indigenous peoples and library services in the United States. In *Issues and Initiatives in Indigenous Librarianship: Some International Perspectives*; Szekely, C., Ed.; Te Rōpū Whakahau: Auckland, NZ, 1999; 36–47.

18. Patterson, L. History and development of libraries on American Indian reservations. *International Indigenous Librarians' Forum*, Proceedings, International Indigenous Librarians' Forum, Waipapa University of Auckland, NZ November, 1–5, 1999; Sullivan, R., Ed.; Te Rōpū Whakahau: Wellington, NZ, 2001; 38–43.

19. Patterson, L. History and status of Native Americans in librarianship. Libr. Trends 2000, 49(1), 182–193.

20. Metoyer-Duran, C. *Gatekeepers in Ethnolinguistic Communities*, Ablex Pub. Corp.: Norwood, NJ, 1993.

21. United States, National Commission on Libraries and Information Science. *Pathways to Excellence: A Report on Improving Library and Information Services for Native American Peoples*; U.S. National Commission on Libraries and Information Science: Washington, DC, 1992.

22. New Mexico State Library. Tribal Libraries Program Direct Grant. Available at http://www.nmstatelibrary.org/index.php?option=com_content&view=article&id=85&Itemid=628.

23. University of New Mexico. Indigenous Nations Library Program. About INLP. Available at http://elibrary.unm.edu/inlp/about.php.

24. Montana State University. Libraries. The Tribal College Librarians Professional Development Institute. Available at http://www.lib.montana.edu/tcli/ Montana State University. Libraries. *The Tribal College Librarians Professional Development Institute*.

25. Streams of Language, Memory and Lifeways 2009 National Tribal Archives, Libraries, and Museums Conference Portland, OR October, 18–22, 2009. Available at http://www.tribalconference.org/index.html (accessed December 2008).

26. Biggs, B. Bright child of Oklahoma: Lotsee Patterson and the development of America's tribal libraries. Am. Indian Cult. Res. J. 2000, 24(4), 55–67. Available at http://aisc.metapress.com/content/e4q72xwq12668875/fulltext.pdf (accessed October 2008).

27. Oklahoma State University. Library, Oklahoma Library Legends: Lotsee Patterson. Available at http://www.library.okstate.edu/dean/jpaust/legends/people/patterson.htm.

28. Canada, Statistics Canada. *Aboriginal Peoples in Canada in 2006: Inuit, Métis and First Nations*, 2006; Census Findings, Statistics Canada: Ottawa, Ontario, Canada. 2008. Available at http://www12.statcan.ca/english/census06/analysis/Aboriginal/index.cfm (accessed June 2008).

29. Canada, Royal Commission on Aboriginal Peoples. *Report of the Royal Commission on Aboriginal Peoples*, Commission; Ottawa, Ontario, Canada 1996. Available at http://www.ainc-inac.gc.ca/ap/pubs/sg/sg-eng.asp (accessed December 2008).

30. Canada. Apology to former students of Indian residential schools. In House of Commons Debates (Hansard), 39th Parl., 2nd Sess. (June 11, 2008) (Online). Available at http://www2.parl.gc.ca/HousePublications/Publication.aspx?Language=E&Mode=1&Parl=39&Ses=2&DocId=3568890.

31. Saskatchewan. Minister's Advisory Committee on Library Services for Aboriginal People. *Information Is for Everyone: Final Report of the Minister's Advisory Committee on Library Services for Aboriginal People*, Saskatchewan Provincial Library; Regina, Saskatchewan, Canada, 2001. Available at http://www.lib.sk.ca/staff/minAboriginal/ablib/ablibfinal.html (accessed February 2008).

32. Joseph, G.; Lawson, K. First Nations and British Columbia public libraries. Feliciter **2003**, *49*(5), 245–247.

33. Lawlor, P. Ontario's First Nations public libraries: An overview with observations. Feliciter **2003**, *49*(5), 240–244.

34. Lawlor, P. Ontario's First Nations public libraries: An overview with observations. Feliciter **2003**, *49*(5), 243.

35. Sinclair-Sparvier, W. Improving and delivering effective library services for Aboriginal peoples in Saskatchewan: A Canadian province's approach to answering the needs of the Aboriginal community. World Libr. **2002**, *12*(1), 32–45. Available at http://www.worlib.org/vol12no1/sinclair_v12n1.shtml (accessed December 2008).

36. Edmonton Public Library, *Report of the Task Force on Library Services for Aboriginal Peoples (LSAP)*, Edmonton Public Library: Edmonton, Alberta, Canada, November 2005. Available at http://www.epl.ca/ResourcesPDF/ReportOfTaskForceOnLSAPFeb2006.pdf (accessed June 2008).

37. Blake, D.; Martin, L.; Pelletier, D. *Report and Recommendations of the Consultation on Aboriginal Resources and Services*, Library and Archives Canada: Ottawa, Ontario, Canada, 2004. Available at http://epe.lac-bac.gc.ca/100/200/301/lac-bac/rep_consult_aboriginal-e/index.html (accessed June 2008).

38. Edwards, B.F.R. *Paper Talk: A History of Libraries, Print Culture, and Aboriginal Peoples in Canada Before 1960*, Scarecrow Press: Lanham, MD, 2005.

39. Australia, Australian Bureau of Statistics. *Census of Population and Housing*; Australian Bureau of Statistics: Canberra, Australian Capital territory, Australia, 2006. Available at http://www.abs.gov.au/websitedbs/D3310114.nsf/Home/census (accessed October 2008).

40. Australia, Australian Bureau of Statistics. *1301.0—Year Book of Australia, 2004*, Australian Bureau of Statistics: Canberra, 2004. Available at http://www.abs.gov.au/AUSSTATS/abs@.nsf/featurearticlesbytitle/06E6409495FF5247CA256DEA00053A04?OpenDocument (accessed June 2008).

41. Williams, L. Issues and initiatives in Indigenous librarianship: An Australian perspective. In *Issues and Initiatives in Indigenous Librarianship: Some International Perspectives*; Szekely, C., Ed.; Te Rōpū Whakahau: Auckland, NZ, 1999; 13–23.

42. Australia. Parliament of Australia. House of Representatives. Speech by the Honourable Kevin Rudd MP—Apology to Australia's Indigenous peoples. Wednesday February 13, 2008. Available at http://www.aph.gov.au/house/Rudd_Speech.pdf.

43. Garlick, M. Aborigines and public libraries: Nightmare or dream(ing). Aust. Libr. Rev. **1993**, *10*(2), 218–231.

44. Taylor, S. State Library of Queensland Indigenous Library Services: Overcoming barriers and building bridges. Aust. Acad. Res. Libr. **2003**, *34*(4), 278–287. Available at http://alia.org.au/publishing/aarl/34.4/full.text/taylor.html (accessed June 2008).

45. National and State Libraries of Australasia Consortium. *National Policy Framework for Aboriginal and Torres Strait Islander Library Services and Collections*, National and State Libraries Australasia: Melbourne, Australia, 2006. Available at http://www.slq.qld.gov.au/__data/assets/pdf_file/0017/74141/NSLA_National_Policy_Framework_for_Aboriginal_and_Torres_Strait_Islander_Library_Services_and_Collections.pdf (accessed October 2008).

46. National and State Libraries of Australasia Consortium, NSLA Indigenous Library Services and Collections Working Group. *National Policy Framework for Aboriginal and Torres Strait Islander Library Services and Collections: 2008 Initiatives: Responding to the National Policy Framework*. Available at http://www.nsla.org.au/publications/papers/2008/doc/NSLA.Discussion-Paper-20080201-Indigenous.Services.Initiatives.2008.doc (accessed October 2008).

47. Queensland, State Library of Queensland. *Aboriginal People and Torres Strait Islanders: Strategic Documents*, State Library of Queensland: South Brisbane, Queensland, Australia. Available at http://www.slq.qld.gov.au/info/ind#strategic (accessed October 2008).

48. Nakata, M. *Evaluation of the Northern Territory Library's Libraries and Knowledge Centres Model*, Northern Territory Government: Darwin, Northern Territory, Australia, 2006. Available at http://www.ntl.nt.gov.au/__data/assets/pdf_file/0018/4680/nakata_finalreport.pdf (accessed April 2008).

49. Hunter, J. The role of information technologies in Indigenous knowledge management. In *Australian Indigenous Knowledge and Libraries*; Nakata, M., Langton, M., Eds.; Australian Academic & Research Libraries: Canberra, Austalian Capital Territory, Australia, 2005; 113–128.

50. Ji, J. Sydney welcomes its first Indigenous research fellow. Sydney Alumni Magazine **2006**, *Summer*, 8–9. Available at http://www.usyd.edu.au/alumni/images/content/activities/magazine/2006-summer/sam.pdf (accessed June 2008).

51. Gumbula, J.N. Exploring the Gupapuyna legacy: Strategies for developing the Galiwin'ku Indigenous Knowledge Centre. In *Australian Indigenous Knowledge and Libraries*; Nakata, M., Langton, M., Eds.; Australian Academic & Research Libraries: Canberra, Austalian Capital Territory, Australia, 2005; 25–28.

52. In *Issues and Initiatives in Indigenous Librarianship: Some International Perspectives*; Szekely, C., Ed.; Te Rōpū Whakahau: Auckland, NZ, 1999; 48.

53. Szekely, C. Te ara tika: Māori and libraries in New Zealand—staying the distance. World Libr. **2002**, *12*(1), 46–53. Available at http://www.worlib.org/vol12no1/szekely_v12n1.shtml (accessed June 2008).

54. Wilson, C.; Szekely, C. Upbeat: Chris Szekely Episode podcast. Radio New Zealand, Wednesday, May 28, **2008**. Available at http://www.trumix.com/podshows/2879205 (accessed November 2008).

55. New Zealand Library Association, *National Library Announces Appointment of Alexander Turnbull Chief Librarian*, January 10, 2007. Available at http://www.lianza.org.nz/news/newsroom/news1168401381.html (accessed June 2008).

56. Wikaira, J. Kaitiakitanga. The role of the Māori archivist. Archifacts **2004**, *April*, 46–49.

57. Patterson, L. Tribal and reservation libraries. Rural Libr. **2001**, *22*(1), 19–24.

58. Blurton, C.G. New directions in education. In *World Communication and Information Report 1999–2000*; Bartagnon, G., Courrier, Y., Eds.; UNESCO Publishing: Paris, France, 1999; 46–61. Available at http://www.unesco.org/webworld/wcir/en/pdf_report/chap2.pdf (accessed November 2008).

59. Gordon, A.C.; Dorr, J.; Gordon, M. Native American technology access: The Gates Foundation in Four Corners. Electron. Libr. **2003**, *21*(5), 428–434.

60. Patterson, L. History and status of Native Americans in librarianship. Libr. Trends **2000**, *49*(1), 192.

61. First Nations Technology Council. Information and communications technology in B.C. First Nations communities, March 2005. Available at http://www.fntc.info/files/documents/Environmental_Scan_Final_Report.pdf.

62. Whitehorse, J. Cyber sovereignty: Digital Diné International Indigenous Librarians' Forum III: Closer to the Fire: Ensuring Culturally Responsive Library Practices Santa Fe, NM November, 10–13, 2003; Ongley, D.; Ed.; American Indian Library Association: Norman, OK, 2005; 145–146.

63. International Federation of Library Associations and Institutions, *IFLA/UNESCO Public Library Manifesto*, 1994 Available at http://www.ifla.org/VII/s8/unesco/eng.htm (accessed February 2008).

64. Webster, K. Introduction. In *Library Services to Indigenous Populations: Viewpoints and Resources*; Webster, K., Ed.; Office for Literacy and Outreach Services, American Library Association: Chicago, IL, 2005; ix–x.

65. Hare, J. To 'know papers': Aboriginal perspectives on literacy. In *Portraits of Literacy Across Families, Communities and Schools: Tensions and Intersections*; Anderson, J., Kendrick, M., Rogers, T., Smythe, S., Eds.; Lawrence Erlbaum Associates: Mahwah, NJ, 2005; 243–263.

66. Canada, Indian Affairs and Northern Affairs Canada. *Highlights of Aboriginal Conditions 1991, 1986: Demographic, Social and Economic Characteristics*, Indian Affairs and Northern Development: Ottawa, Ontario, Canada, 1995 Available at http://www.ainc-inac.gc.ca/ai/rs/pubs/sts/hilts/hilts-eng.pdf (accessed December 2008).

67. Hermes, M.; Uran, C. Treaties that dominate and literacy that empowers? I wish it was all in Ojibwemowin. Anthropol. Educ. Quart. **2006**, *37*(4), 393–398.

68. Roy, L. To support and model Native American library services. Texas Libr. J. **2000**, *76*(1), 32–35. Available at http://www.txla.org/pubs/tlj76_1/native.html (accessed February 2008).

69. Roy, L. *Dr. Roy's Web site*, Loriene Roy: Professor of Library and Information Science. Available at http://www.ischool.utexas.edu/~loriene/ (accessed June 2008).

70. Foskett, A.C. *The Subject Approach to Information*, 4th Ed. Clive Bingley Ltd.: London, U.K., 1982.

71. Carter, N.C. American Indians and law libraries: Acknowledging the third sovereign. Law Libr. J. **2002**, *94*(1), 7–26. Available at http://www.aallnet.org/products/pub_llj_v94n01/2002-01.pdf (accessed December 2008).

72. Moorcroft, H. The construction of silence. Aust. Libr. J. **1993**, *42*(1), 27–32.

73. Joseph, G. Library services to First Nations in British Columbia. BCLA Report. **1995**, *39*(4), 37.

74. Olson, H.A. *The Power to Name: Locating the Limits of Subject Representation in Libraries*, Kluwer Academic Publishers: Dordrecht, the Netherlands, 2002.

75. Simpson, S. *Te ara tika: Guiding Words: Ngā ingoa kaupapa Māori: Māori Subject Headings: Pūrongo tuatoru: Phase Three Research Report*, Te Rōpū Whakahau, in association with the National Library of New Zealand and LIANZA: Auckland, NZ, 2005. Available at http://www.trw.org.nz/publications/Te_Ara_Tika_Guiding_Words.pdf (accessed June 2008).

76. National Library of Australia. *The Aboriginal Thesaurum First Roundtable on Library and Archives Collections and Services of Relevance to Aboriginal and Torres Strait Islander People*; State Library of South Australia: Adelaide, 1995; May 41. Available at http://www.nla.gov.au/niac/libs/thesaurus.html (accessed June 2008).

77. Janke, T. Managing Indigenous knowledge and Indigenous cultural and intellectual property. In *Australian Indigenous Knowledge and Libraries*; Nakata, M., Langton, M., Eds.; Australian Academic & Research Libraries: Canberra, Australian Capital Territory, Australia, 2005; 99–111.

78. Daes, E. *Discrimination against Indigenous Peoples: Protection of the Heritage of Indigenous People. Final Report of the Special Rapporteur, Mrs. Erica-Irene Daes, in Conformity with Subcommission Resolution 1993/44 and Decision 1994/105 of the Commission on Human Rights, E/CN.4/Sub.2/1995/26*, United Nations, Office of the UN High Commissioner on Human Rights: Geneva, Switzerland, 1995. Available at http://www.unhchr.ch/Huridocda/Huridoca.nsf/0/c6646bc7fe89406f802566c0005cd3f0?Opendocument (accessed June 2008).

79. United Nations. General Assembly, *United Nations Declaration on the Rights of Indigenous Peoples. Article 13.1*, United Nations: New York, 2007, A/Res/61/295; Available at http://www.un.org/esa/socdev/unpfii/en/declaration.html (accessed June 2008).

80. Nakata, N.M. Indigenous digital collections. Aust. Acad. Res. Libr. **2007**, *38*(2), 101.

81. Aboriginal and Torres Straits Islander Library Information and Resource Network Inc. *ATSILIRN Protocols*. Available at http://www1.aiatsis.gov.au/atsilirn/protocols.atsilirn.asn.au/index0c51.html?option=com_frontpage&Itemid=1 (accessed June 2008).

82. Garwood-Houng, A. Protocols: Meeting the challenges of Indigenous information needs. In *Australian Indigenous Knowledge and Libraries*; Nakata, M., Langton, M., Eds.;

Australian Academic & Research Libraries: Canberra, Australian Capital Territory, Australia, 2005; 149–157.

83. Hunter, J. The role of information technologies in Indigenous knowledge management. Austr. Acad. Res. Libr. **2007**, *38*(2), 113–128.

84. Nakata, N.M. Indigenous digital collections. Aust. Acad. Res. Libr. **2007**, *38*(2), 99–110.

85. Smith, L.T. On tricky ground: Researching the native in the age of uncertainty. *The SAGE Handbook of Qualitative Research*, 3rd Ed.; Denzin, N.K., Lincoln, Y.S., Eds.; Sage Publications: Thousand Oaks, CA, 2005; 85–107.

86. Metoyer-Duran, C. Native American library and information services. Govern. Inform. Quart. **1992**, *9*(3), 359.

87. Smith, L.T. *Decolonizing Methodologies: Research and Indigenous Peoples*, Zed Books: New York, 1999.

88. Webster, K. Introduction. In *Library Services to Indigenous Populations: Viewpoints and Resources*; Webster, K., Ed.; Office for Literacy and Outreach Services, American Library Association: Chicago, IL, 2005; vii.

89. Association for Library and Information Science Education (ALISE). *Table I-17: Ethnic Background of Full-Time Faculty*, January 1, 2004. Available at http://ils.unc.edu/ALISE/2004/Faculty/Table%20I-17.htm (accessed June 2008).

90. Association for Library and Information Science Education (ALISE). *Table II-3-a:Degrees and Certificates Awarded by Gender and Ethnic Origin 2002–2003*. Available at http://ils.unc.edu/ALISE/2004/Students/Table%20II-3-a. htm (accessed June 2008).

91. Aguilar, P.L. University of New Mexico libraries' Indigenous nations library program (INLP): Reaching out and serving the UNM American Indian community and New Mexico American Indians. Coll. Res. Libr. News **2006**, *67* (3), 158–160.

92. Berry, J.N. Knowledge river. Libr. J. (1976) **2004**, *129*(7), 55. Available at http://www.libraryjournal.com/article/CA408335.html (accessed December 2008).

93. School of Information. University of Texas at Austin. Developing the next generation of Native librarians, Honoring Generations Home Page Web site. Available at http://www.ischool.utexas.edu/~hg/.

94. New Zealand Library Association Inc. *LIANZA Statement: The Library and Information Sector: Core Knowledge, Skills and Qualities. Appendix.* Available at http://www.lianza.org.nz/registration/files/Body_of_Knowledge_Appendix_Oct08.pdf.

95. Austalian Library and Information Association. InCite **2008**, *29*(7). Special Issue. Indigenous Librarianship.

96. Metoyer-Duran, C. Native American library and information services. Govern. Inform. Quart. **1992**, *9*(3), 359–362.

97. Townley, C.T. American Indian library service. In *Advances in Librarianship*; Michael, H. Harris., Ed.; Academic Press: New York, 1978; 152–159.

Information

Marcia J. Bates
*Department of Information Studies, Graduate School of Education and Information Studies,
University of California, Los Angeles (UCLA), Los Angeles, CA, U.S.A.*

Abstract

A selection of representative definitions of information is drawn from information science and related disciplines and discussed and compared. Defining information remains such a contested project that any claim to present a unified, singular vision of the topic would be disingenuous. Seven categories of definitions are described: communicatory or semiotic, activity-based (i.e., information as event), propositional, structural, social, multi-type, and deconstructionist. The impact of Norbert Wiener and Claude Shannon is discussed, as well as the widespread influence of Karl Popper's ideas. The data–information–knowledge–wisdom continuum is also addressed.

The work of these authors are reviewed: Marcia J. Bates, Gregory Bateson, Paul Beynon-Davies, B.C. Brookes, Michael Buckland, Ian Cornelius, Ronald Day, Richard Derr, Brenda Dervin, Fred Dretske, Jason Farradane, Christopher Fox, Bernd Frohmann, Jonathan Furner, J.A. Goguen, Robert Losee, A.D. Madden, D.M. McKay, Doede Nauta, A.D. Pratt, Frederick Thompson.

INTRODUCTION

The concept "information" is of signal importance to all the information disciplines. Perhaps for that reason, it is a term that has been defined in countless ways over many decades. It would be fair to say that there is no widely agreed-upon definition or theoretical conception of the term. The meaning of this term is still highly contested. In this regard, the status of the term is similar to that of "communication" in the communication sciences.

In light of the lack of agreement about the definition of the term "information," the main objective of this entry will be to lay out some of the major classes of definitions and theoretical constructions of the term that are currently or recently in play. No effort will be made to capture and discuss every definition that has been provided in the literature; rather, major types will be presented, as well as popular ideas that are recurrent in the literature. The discussion draws from writings over the last sixty years; the approach is by category rather than by chronology.

The effort to define information is active in other disciplines besides those explicitly concerned with the topic; philosophy, cognitive science, electrical engineering, computer science, and systems theory, among others, have been active players on this scene as well. The objective of this entry, however, is to concentrate on the ideas about information either that have been developed within the information disciplines or, in a few cases, that have come from other fields but have also been influential in the information disciplines. For coverage of other approaches to the concept, the reader is directed to reviews by Aspray,[1] Belkin,[2] Capurro and Hjørland,[3] Cornelius,[4] Furner,[5] Meadow and Yuan,[6] and Wersig.[7]

A different way of acquainting oneself with the numerous issues and debates across the disciplines about information would be to examine several collections of articles written by authors bringing a variety of perspectives to the question. See Kornwachs and Jacoby,[8] Davies and Gregersen,[9] and Ibekwe-San Juan and Dousa.[10] In the latter volume, Furner takes an amusing, but highly illustrative, approach by citing and discussing 18 papers across the disciplines—almost entirely not in information science—that have the title "What is information?" and that have appeared between 1955 and 2012.[11]

Some authors embed a discussion of information within a much larger philosophical or theoretical program. In other words, exposition of the meaning of the term "information" is not a primary goal, but only incidental to much larger projects. It is beyond the focus of this article to attempt a review of these larger intellectual programs. Prime examples include Søren Brier's "cybersemiotics";[12] Benny Karpatschof's dissertation on "Human Activity";[13] Howard Resnikoff's analysis of information within a mathematical, physical, and signal detection framework;[14] Jan Kåhre's "mathematical theory of information";[15] and separate disquisitions on the relationships among physics, biology, and information by Roederer[16] and by Stonier.[17–19] A recent book by Reading[20] in the biosciences is intended to be broad, readable, and compact on the subject of information in those fields. Another author in this category is Luciano Floridi, a philosopher, who is developing and promoting an area of philosophy to be known as "philosophy of information."[21] He develops his own view of information as a philosopher, with attention to the issues of concern to that discipline in the article "Information,"[22] as well as in a

Encyclopedia of Library and Information Sciences, Fourth Edition DOI: 10.1081/E-ELIS4-120053334

short book.[23] Floridi's recent book, *The 4th Revolution: How the Infosphere is Reshaping Human Reality*,[24] has been reviewed scathingly by the philosopher John Searle, who comes from a distinctly different perspective on information.[25]

Because Norbert Wiener's and Claude Shannon's ideas of information were so influential at the dawn of the "Information Age," their influence is discussed in a preamble in the following text. Shannon's actual "information theory," however, is reviewed elsewhere in an entry by that name in this encyclopedia.

After the preamble, conceptions of information of the following types will be reviewed in succession:

- Communicatory or semiotic
- Activity-based (i.e., information as event)
- Propositional
- Structural
- Social
- Multi-type
- Deconstructionist

Between these categories, we will take two interludes, one to discuss the "Problem of Popper's Worlds," regarding the philosopher Karl Popper, and the other to address "DIKW" or the commonly discussed sequence known as "data–information–knowledge–wisdom." Both of these, Popper's "three worlds" concept and the DIKW sequence, have motivated so much discussion in the information sciences around information that they merit separate discussion.

In the process, the work of the following people will be addressed: Marcia J. Bates, Gregory Bateson, Paul Beynon-Davies, B.C. Brookes, Michael Buckland, Ian Cornelius, Ronald Day, Richard Derr, Brenda Dervin, Fred Dretske, Jason Farradane, Christopher Fox, Bernd Frohmann, Jonathan Furner, J.A. Goguen, Robert Losee, A.D. Madden, D.M. McKay, Doede Nauta, A.D. Pratt, and Frederick Thompson.

In this entry, no summary conclusion is made about "the best" or "the truest" understanding of the concept of information. Rather, the purpose is to present the array of ideas flowing around this core concept in the information disciplines, so that the reader may become acquainted with the issues.

PREAMBLE: THE ROLES OF WIENER AND SHANNON

It is almost impossible to overestimate the impact of Claude Shannon's ideas about information on the (American) intellectual culture of the 1950s and 1960s. In that era, there was a tremendous amount of attention directed to the technical revolution(s) that had become possible with the development of computers, television, new communication technologies, and a new way of thinking about information. This new way of thinking percolated out of the academic world into the society at large and imbued at a subconscious level the thinking of people who had no understanding of Shannon's ideas per se.

Today, many scholars write dismissively about the concept of information (see the last portion of this entry) and reject the earlier excitement around the "Information Age" and the "Information Society" as a love affair with a cold, technical, even militaristic conception of the technology-driven society.[26] Indeed, Frank Webster, writing in this encyclopedia about the "Information Society," analyzes the term's many weaknesses and confusions, without seeming to recognize the positive value originally gained from the ideas carried by the concept. Shannon appears in Webster's discussion only in terms of the "deracinated" definition of information that arises out of Shannon's writing. Ironically, as we shall see, it was, in fact, the very fecund power of that deracinated definition of information—i.e., a concept of information as independent of meaning—that allowed an explosion of scientific and social development around information and its social and technical role.

The new conception of information that came with Shannon was so fundamental, so pervasive in science and engineering, that today's critics do not actually see *it as it was to people then*. The several streams of new thinking on information were startling, different, and stimulating, compared to prior understanding. I believe that the impact was so fundamental that an earlier generation can be forgiven for inventing ideas like the "Information Age," the "Information Society," and "Information Explosion." The consciousness of information was so new and changed so many established ideas that it really felt to the participants like a new age marked by the new awareness of information.

It is fashionable now to deride that earlier absorption with the new concepts, but we are *able* to deride these concepts only because we have so thoroughly absorbed the learning from that time that it feels easy to dismiss it in favor of newer ideas. The ever-present fact is that people both build on and react to what was present earlier in their lives. Today's critics are, of course, doing that too. This author is old enough to remember that earlier time, and I choose to present that era as I understood it, as a bit of a counter to the somewhat dismissive attitude toward it that is popular nowadays.

Boulding wrote about three levels of organization in life: 1) static structures; 2) clockwork, that is, the world of mechanics; and 3) thermostats, that is, control mechanisms that maintain a stable condition by responding to feedback from their environment.[27] These three levels have some parallel in the development of science in the Western world—the medieval belief in a static world created by God, followed by the Newtonian discovery and analysis of dynamic processes, followed by the cybernetic understanding of the role of information in life processes.

The world of Newton and his epigones was one in which the theory of forces and impacts of recognizable regular, measurable change was developed. The quintessential model of the mechanical universe is that of billiard balls being hit and rolling into other balls and making them move in a certain direction with a certain force.

The movement of the planets was closely measured, the mathematics of change in the form of the calculus was developed, and a deep threat to the medieval concept of the static universe arose. The long history of religious controversy, with Galileo as a prime example and proceeding through the inquisition, the Reformation, and the Counter-Reformation, was in no small part due to the fundamental challenge offered by this new dynamic idea of how the universe worked.

In the twentieth century, information began to become important in the thinking of science and society. Problems of observation and the impact of observation emerged in early twentieth-century physics. Finally, during the 1940s and 1950s, the role of information was made theoretically explicit in the theory of cybernetics. The term came from a Greek root word meaning to govern or steer. Norbert Wiener's conception of cybernetics involved the governing of action through the feedback of information.[28]

"Feedback" is a tediously trite term nowadays, usually employed in the context of customer relations or group therapy. But the idea behind it was revolutionary in Wiener's day. Wiener illustrated just how significant the idea was in his description of research that he conducted with a physician on physiological processes.[29] Again, grossly simplifying, the thinking in that day in physiology was that when I reach out to pick up a pencil, this process is achieved by my brain sending a signal to muscles and tendons along the lines of "go get it," and the machinery of my arm goes into action and picks up the pencil. This was a classically mechanical concept of my actions. A pulse goes out to my arm to do a certain thing, I act, and then the pulse diminishes.

Wiener and his colleague demonstrated that the process did not work that way. Instead, when I start to pick up the pencil, I extend my arm in the direction of the pencil, and then, *utilizing constant kinesthetic and visual feedback,* I micro-adjust the position of my arm repeatedly and successively until it successfully lands on the pencil, grasps it, and picks it up. Picking up the pencil is not a single, mechanical, act, but rather an extended behavior utilizing continuous information feedback telling me whether my hand is on or off course and, if off course, enabling me to adjust the tension in muscles and the direction of my reach so that I can successfully touch and pick up the pencil.[30]

Thus, in cybernetic situations, two processes are going on continuously in parallel—the physical forces and the detection and utilization of information about the physical forces, information that is used to affect the physical actions. While the billiard ball model was the one commonly used for the mechanical understanding of the universe, with the impact of cybernetic thinking, the household thermostat became the standard model of cybernetics and feedback. In the summer heat, I set the thermostat for a certain temperature. When the heat in the room affects a sensing mechanism in the thermostat beyond a certain point, the air conditioning starts, and cools the room down to where the sensing mechanism again achieves its desired temperature, and the air conditioning shuts off. The sensing mechanism provides continuous information, and the design of the thermostat is such that when the information indicates that the room temperature is outside a desired range, the air conditioning comes on. Governing, or steering, is about utilizing information feedback to direct the ship of action.

In the larger history of scientific thinking, the development of cybernetics drew attention to the *distinct role of information* in physical and social processes. Previously, the kinesthetic and visual feedback I get while picking up the pencil—as well as in countless other information-based processes—had been almost entirely invisible in the thinking of science. This may be one reason why the 1950s and 1960s were so obsessed with information—the role of information had at last emerged as a focal topic of interest in science; its role in influencing physical and social processes at last came to the fore and, once seen, was studied with fascination in many domains of science.

So what was Claude Shannon's role in all this scientific development? Shannon and Wiener worked on some of the same ideas during this fertile period. Shannon, working at Bell Laboratories, however, developed the mathematical and engineering theory to put an understanding of information on a firm basis.[31] Strictly speaking, Shannon did not define information at all, at least in any conventionally understandable way. Shannon found a way to measure the *amount* of information going over a transmission channel. As Wiener puts it, "...we had to develop a statistical theory of the *amount of information*, in which the unit amount of information was that transmitted as a single decision between equally probably alternatives."[32]

Since the alternative messages, letters, words, or other units of communication are not always sent with equal probability, the formula Shannon developed measured the amount of information as a function of two things—the number of alternatives out of which a message might be selected for sending and the probabilities of the various messages. The more possible messages from which the sent message is selected and the more equiprobable the messages, the greater the amount of information transmitted.

Shannon's analysis was revolutionary in several senses. Before him, engineers really did not have a means of computing the maximum amount of information that could be transmitted through a channel of a given size or configuration. It was assumed that it would be possible to go on improving channels to carry more and more information. Shannon's formulas enable the calculation of the maximum possible information transmission for a given physical configuration.

Once Shannon developed a firm model of the amount of information, actual and possible, in a channel, he could clarify the role of redundancy, of error rates, and noise in a channel. For example, since the letters of the alphabet do not appear in written text with equal probabilities, the amount of information conveyed with English text is well less than 100% of the amount of information that could be conveyed if each letter were equiprobable. Further, Shannon mathematically analyzed the role of noise in a channel and the ways in which redundancy could compensate for the noise. These discoveries were immensely important for all sorts of communication engineering situations. Go to the right section of an engineering library, and you can find textbooks full of hundreds of mathematical formulas developed out of these crucial insights by Shannon. Shannon's work revolutionized communication engineering. His key paper has been cited over 7000 times in the ISI "Web of Science" database.[33]

His impact went well beyond engineering, however. It was as if for the first time people saw the informational regularities beneath the surface variety of the text sent over a wire or the words spoken on the telephone or written in a book. Shannon's model of information is dismissed today because he separated information from meaning. What is currently forgotten, however, is that this separation was in fact an *achievement*. People had not been able to make that differentiation before. Now, with far greater clarity and understanding, the handling of information in quantitative terms at last came into its own. In 1951, the psychologist and linguist George Miller wrote the book *Language and Communication,* which essentially consisted of working out the implications of Shannon's work for those disciplines.[34] In the process, Miller educated a generation of social scientists on this way of thinking.

The fundamental clarification of the relationship between messages and the amount of information they convey (Shannon) and the concomitant recognition of the important role of information throughout life processes (Wiener) led to an enormous surge of research and theorizing throughout science about information. (Other researchers, such as John von Neumann and Oskar Morgenstern, had important roles as well.) Just as those hundreds of mathematical formulas had to be worked out in the engineering world, so also did the social sciences need to work with these same ideas and transform some parts of those disciplines.

The application of Shannon's approach to the social and behavioral sciences was not straightforward, however. There were many insights gained, but many problems encountered as well. After a while, the initial enthusiasm in the social sciences waned—to the point where it is now fashionable to deride these post-War ideas. But we are shaped by those ideas so thoroughly nonetheless that we can only attempt to throw off their influence.

COMMUNICATORY OR SEMIOTIC DEFINITIONS OF INFORMATION

We begin with definitions/conceptions of information that are framed within a communicatory or signaling context. Some authors even take the approach to the point of identifying meaning with information.

A.D. Madden

As a recent example, in 2000 Madden defined information as "a stimulus originating in one system that affects the interpretation by another system of either the second system's relationship to the first or of the relationship the two systems share with a given environment. ..."[35] In 2004, he simplified it to "a stimulus which expands or amends the World View of the informed."[36] The latter definition is reminiscent of Boulding's concept of the "image," which is the grand total of my (or any individual's) subjective knowledge, my mental image of the world, and my place in it.[37] Boulding argued that behavior depends on this image. So in Madden's approach, information is, in effect, something that alters the image.

Gregory Bateson

Gregory Bateson applied concepts of information and feedback to the psychodynamics of human relations, most famously writing of the pathological, feedback-based, "Double Bind" relationship.[38] He also wrote about information science. Expressing the semiotic approach still more generally, Bateson said that information is a difference that makes a difference.[39] This approach has its roots in the idea of the single difference being the elementary unit of amount of information, the single bit, the zero or one. The difference that makes a difference, presumably, makes that difference to a sensing being.

B.C. Brookes

Brookes, one of the grand old men of British information science, took a similar tack. The following is his "fundamental equation" for the relationship between information and knowledge:

$K[S] + \Delta I = K[S + \Delta S]$, which states in its very general way that the knowledge structure $K[S]$ is changed to the new modified structure $K[S + \Delta S]$ by the information ΔI, the ΔS indicating the effect of the modification.[40]

Thus the (human) knowledge structure in the mind is changed in some way with the input of information.

Doede Nauta

Nauta takes information quite explicitly to be meaning but in a particular sense. "Information is that which is common to all representations that are synonymous to the interpreter (synonymity is identity of meaning)."[41] Thus, information is the meaning that is common to all the different ways of expressing that meaning. Here, it would seem that only representations can contain redundancies, because information is the common meaning core to all the different possible representations. In this approach, Nauta drew on both semiotic and (Shannon) information theoretic approaches.

Robert Losee

Losee developed what he calls a "discipline-independent definition" of information. "Information is produced by all processes and it is the values in the characteristics of the processes' output that are information."[42]

> Information is always informative about something, being a component of the output or result of the process. This 'aboutness' or representation is the result of a process or function producing the representation of the input, which might, in turn, be the output of another function and represent its input, and so forth.[43]

Losee takes as his central example the baking of a cake. "Examining the cake provides information about both the process and the original ingredients.... The choice of high quality ingredients...will affect the outcome.... Varying the process, such as the amount of time in the oven...also changes the final product...."[43]

This definition raises a couple of questions. First, what about situations that are not processes? Can there be no information there? Or is process so universal that everything is a result of it?

Second, it is with cake baking, as with many physical processes, that the information produced from the process is often quite incomplete and can be misleading. Losee says that examining the cake provides information both about process and original ingredients. But, in fact, the person who had never seen a cake before almost certainly would not know enough to be able to figure out from the output alone all that went into making it, both in ingredients and processes. This is true with many processes. Often, there is an emergent result—yeast does things in the cake not in evidence when the baking begins. The baking causes chemical processes that lead to the final result being very different in qualities from the starting dough.

Thus, in the experience of human observers, information can be limited and distorted coming out of a process, and it can be also be quite unambiguous and complete, as when we know of the process "add +1 to the output of prior process." In the latter case, the information we derive from the result is presumably complete and correct. Thus, it would appear that Losee's general formulation of information includes many situations where the information is limited or distorted, as well as situations where the information resulting from a process is unambiguously clear.

INFORMATION AS EVENT

Allan Pratt

Pratt provided probably the most developed version of a conception of information in which information is an *event*, that is, he looks at the process of being informed and derives the term "information" from that. Pratt, too, draws on Boulding's concept of "the image." He says: "My Image of the world, and my relationships in it, which includes my perception of cause and effect, of time, of space, of values, of everything which impinges on my consciousness, is different from yours, and from that of every other person in the world."[44]

> After a person has received and understood the content of a message, in ordinary speech we say that he has become informed about the matter at hand. This is a surprisingly precise and accurate statement. He has been 'in-formed.' .... He has been inwardly shaped or formed; his Image has been altered or affected.

> In-formation is the alteration of the Image which occurs when it receives a message. Information is thus an event; an event which occurs at some unique point in time and space, to some particular individual.[45]

He compares the concept "information" to the concept "explosion." "Every explosion is unique; no two are identical." "Further, explosions cannot be stored or retrieved. One may, of course, store and retrieve potentially explosive substances...." Later, he admits: "informative event" may be a more felicitous term than "an 'information'."[45] Here he comes upon the practical problem of the mass-noun usage of the word "information"; "an information" as a count noun just does not fit into English usage.

PROPOSITIONAL DEFINITIONS OF INFORMATION

Propositional definitions are ones in which a piece of information is considered to be a claim about the world, a proposition.

Richard Derr

Perhaps the most accessible such definition is that of Derr: "...information is an abstract, meaningful representation of determinations which have been made of objects." "A determination is a judgment of what is the case."[46] Using the example of an ordinary sentence, he elaborates as follows:

Five necessary conditions of the truth of the first sentence have been identified. In order for Sentence 1 to be true, it is necessary that

1. information be a representation,
2. the representation be abstract,
3. the representation be meaningful,
4. the representation consists of determinations which have been made,
5. the determinations have been made of certain objects.[46]

Derr states that "[n]one of these conditions by itself is sufficient to insure the truth of this sentence; however, jointly, they constitute a set of sufficient conditions."[46] He goes on to argue that, based on these five essential properties, four derivative properties of information can be identified as well: Information is *communicable, informing, empowering,* that is, one can take action based on having the information, and *quantitative,* that is, information varies in amount.[47]

Fred Dretske

Dretske, a philosopher, has been widely influential in his conceptualization of information. He draws heavily on the Shannon conception of information. Much of his book is taken up with working through the logical and philosophical implications of his position, and no attempt will be made to expatiate that here. Instead, let us take his simpler, introductory description of information:

Roughly speaking, information is that commodity capable of yielding knowledge, and what information a signal carries is what we can learn from it. If everything I say to you is false, then I have given you no information. At least I have given you no information of the kind I purported to be giving.[48]

Later, "Information is what is capable of yielding knowledge, and since knowledge requires truth, information requires it also."[49] Thus, to be information, a proposition must be true. Dretske takes his analysis through many complex arguments, but at the heart of every argument is the core statement "s is F." The latter is the generic statement of a proposition, a claim.

He distinguishes information from meaning in the following way. A sentence, such as "Joe is at the office," has a meaning that arises straightforwardly from interpreting the sentence for anyone literate in English. A sentence may, however, carry much more information as well, beyond the meaning of the sentence itself. "The acoustic signal that tells us someone is at our door carries not only the information that someone is at the door, but also the

information that the door button is depressed, that electricity is flowing through the doorbell circuit, that the clapper on the doorbell is vibrating, and much else besides."[50] Thus, Dretske's sense of information includes all the demonstrable implications of a proposition, not only the (more limited) meaning of the proposition itself.

Christopher Fox

Fox takes his propositional view of information through many transformations as well. Again, using the simplest formulation for our discussion here, Fox is essentially claiming that the information (if any) contained in a set of sentences in a particular context is the proposition p such that, first, p is the conglomerate proposition expressed by the set of sentences in that particular context and, second, that the agent of that context is in a position to know that p.[51] Put still more colloquially, information is the collective propositional claim of a set of statements in a given context, provided the agent in that context is in a position to know that p.

Fox titles his book *Information and Misinformation* and spends some time analyzing the latter concept as well. He disagrees with Dretske in that he does not feel that the act of "informing" necessarily means informing someone of a *true* proposition. He concludes, through a series of arguments based on the logical and linguistic character of true and false statements, that *informing* does not require truth, that is, the claim "that p" need not be true for someone to be informed of it. He argues, however, that we use "misinform" in a stronger sense—that to misinform someone necessarily means that the person is being informed of something that is not true. So we *inform* people of things that may or may not be true, but when we *misinform* someone, it necessarily involves telling the person something that is not true.[52]

We are now in a position to return to Losee's conception of information. Losee's position admits of misinformation too. He says, "The value of a variable is information about the input; when the information is only partial and is tainted by error, it is better understood as misinformation. Essentially, this is information that is partly or wholly false."[53] So in Losee's conception, the value produced by a process may indeed be inadequate or inaccurate and should then be known as misinformation.

STRUCTURAL DEFINITIONS

In addition to Frederick Thompson, discussed in the following section, we will review two other authors whose definitions are largely structural, D.M. MacKay and Marcia Bates. Their definitions are "multi-type," however, and will be reviewed in the section on multi-type definitions.

Frederick Thompson

Thompson makes a discursive argument about information as a kind of structure. He recognizes the ways in which the structuring and organizing of information contains its own information, and is therefore likewise informative. He describes information as "a product that results from applying the processes of organization to the raw material of experience, much like steel is obtained from iron ore."[54] He also compares the scientist to the artist in that "[d]ata are to the scientist like the colors on the palette of the painter. It is by the artistry of his theories that we are informed. It is the organization that is the information."[55]

Commonly, in daily life, the forms of organization of information are seen to be neutral, content-free. Indeed, they are often taken for granted and not even noticed. Thompson brings out the ways in which these organizing activities are themselves content, influencing, to a greater or lesser extent, the overall meaning of the text or other body of information. This is an intellectual position—highlighting the impacts of the form and organization of information—that has been taken up by many more recent scholars, for example, Geoffrey Bowker and Leigh Star.[56]

SOCIAL DEFINITIONS

The definitions considered to this point are drawn largely from logical and scientific points of view. This is sometimes known as a *nomothetic* approach; the fundamental effort in the sciences is to discover causes, effects, patterns, and tendencies that underlie the surface variety and particularity of life. The humanities perspective of valuing and studying the unique, specific characteristics of a situation, social group, or event, known as an *idiographic* approach, has not yet been represented here. In fact, probably due to the influence of the post–World War II scientific interest in information, many people coming from a humanities point of view have dismissed "information" as a specifically technological and heartless concept to be perennially contrasted with the rich detail of specific institutions and historical moments, such as a study of the library in nineteenth-century Illinois. However, the authors discussed in this section do embrace the concept of information, but argue that it must be seen as embedded in a social context.

Ian Cornelius

In 1996, Ian Cornelius wrote about an "interpretive viewpoint" to information. Taking the practice of law for his example, he argued that information should be seen as socially constructed within a set of practices. A practice is a "coherent set of actions and beliefs which we conform to along with the other people in our practice (whatever it may be, profession or game), and it has its own internal logic and ethic."[57]

> My claim is that information is properly seen not as an objective independent entity as part of a 'real world,' but that it is a human artefact, constructed and reconstructed within social situations. As in law, every bit of information is only information when understood within its own cultural packaging which allows us to interpret it.[58]

Further,

> ...[T]here is no separate entity of information to discover independent of our practices. Up to the point that it is sought by a practitioner within a practice it is not information and cannot be interpreted.

> When a practice is seeking to impose meaning on something, that thing will already have come within the interpretive range of that practice and will already be at an early stage in a process of interpretation.[59]

Thus, information must be seen within the dense context of social relations, negotiations, and understandings operative in a particular social context. Cornelius compares the embeddedness of information received and interpreted with the embeddedness of most interpretations of the law.

Joseph Goguen

Writing a year later, Joseph Goguen developed a more detailed conception of a socially embedded information.[60] His more idiographic approach may have succeeded in humanizing and detechnologizing the concept for those of a more social science or humanities bent. He defines information as follows: "An item of information is an interpretation of a configuration of signs for which members of some social group are accountable."[61]

He argues that all information is situated within a context and can only be fully understood within that context. He then addresses the question of whether any information is ever context-free; is some information more bound within a specific context than other information is? He describes a continuum of the character of information, from "wet" to "dry." He states that processes of abstraction and formalization are attempts to take information out of contexts and make it as generally applicable as possible. The more decontextualized, the "drier" the information.[62]

Certainly, many scientific results fit this description. We do not need to know the specific circumstances in which Robert Boyle discovered Boyle's law (physics) in order to gain full value from the use of Boyle's law. On the other hand, enormous amounts of contextual knowledge is needed in order properly to interpret the reasoning and strategy involved in directing the prosecution of World War II or, in the information system design context, the hostile attitudes toward use of an information system in a particular government agency.

According to Goguen

> In general, information cannot be fully context sensitive (for then it could only be understood when and where it is produced) nor fully context insensitive (for then it could be understood by anyone in any time and place).

> According to our social theory of information, meaning is an ongoing achievement of some social group; it takes *work* to interpret configurations of signs, and this work necessarily occurs in some particular context, including a particular time, place, and group. The meaning of an item of information consists of the relations of accountability that are attached to it in that context, and... the narratives in which it is embedded.[63]

He draws on ethnomethodology for the *principle of accountability:* "Members are held accountable for certain actions by their social groups; exactly those actions are the ones constructed as socially significant by those groups."[64]

It should be understood that Goguen is developing this concept of information in the context of information system design and usability testing. He refers to the numerous instances where massively expensive information systems were abandoned because they were dysfunctional for the organization for which they were designed. He argues that the close observation of people as called for in ethnomethodology is the gold standard for learning how a group organizes the work of their institution—what systems of categories, what contrasts, what relationships matter to the group, and how the group divides up the processes and objects in their world in order to carry out their ongoing activities. Goguen: "In particular, ethnomethodology looks at the *categories* and *methods* members use to render their actions intelligible to one another; this contrasts with presupposing that the categories and methods of the analyst are necessarily superior to those of members."[64]

This is a powerful conceptualization of information that incorporates its social role. Goguen argues that information, as understood through his construction of the term, is *situated, local, emergent, contingent, embodied, vague,* and *open*.[63] Recall Derr's characterization of information and compare it to Goguen's view: "abstract, meaningful representation of determinations which have been made of objects."[46] The idiographic and nomothetic world views are on display in this contrast. For my part, they both carry a lot of truth. I do not see that one or the other approach has to "win" in the culture wars. By incorporating both approaches in our thinking, we may end up with the richest possible understanding.

FIRST INTERLUDE: THE PROBLEM OF POPPER'S WORLDS

We interrupt this recital of different approaches to the concept of information in order to consider the role of the work of Karl Popper, a well-known twentieth-century philosopher of science, in discussions of the nature of information. Popper was not himself interested in the concept of information and used the word very little. However, he developed another idea, of three worlds in the scientist's life, which has had enormous impact in information science and recurs again and again through the literature on information. Popper wrote over a number of years about what he called three "worlds": "We can call the physical world 'world 1,' the world of our conscious experiences 'world 2,' and the world of the logical *contents* of books, libraries, computer memories, and suchlike 'world 3'" (his italics).[65]

It was important to Popper to distinguish one person's subjective understanding of a scientific topic from a more objective existence of knowledge of science that is independent of individual people. Once Robert Boyle died, the knowledge of "Boyle's law" did not die with him. It was expressed and recorded in the literature of science and was in the minds of many people who studied science. In short, scientific learning has a public, independent, and thus reasonably objective existence apart from any one person's subjective understanding of a scientific finding.

It is the daily bread of the work of people in the information disciplines to address the recorded, "exosomatic" (outside the body) forms of information. When a philosopher writes about objective knowledge, argues for its importance, and is at pains to distinguish it from other "worlds," it may seem that at last someone from outside the information disciplines has paid recorded knowledge the attention that it deserves. At last, the very heart of the work of information managers has been recognized and validated as a key part of science!

Unfortunately, however, a close reading of Popper indicates that he did not view information resources in the way that information professionals do. Though he would sometimes refer to objective knowledge in books and journals, thus making it easy to conflate the "thingness" of books in with the objective nature of scientific findings, in fact, it is evident again and again in Popper's writing that when he is speaking of the objective nature of world 3, he means, as his definition earlier indicates, the *logical contents* of the books and journals, not the objects themselves. When he pays attention to the books themselves, he always calls them a part of world 1. Indeed, the scientific examples he uses are generally of the very "driest" sort, in Goguen's terms—generally mathematical and physical examples. To make his point about objective science, he is determined to select examples that can live independently in the most unambiguous way from individual knowers.

Popper was a philosopher of science and was concerned about various debates he was having with his philosopher colleagues. It was important to him to argue for the idea that the body of scientific learning can be thought of as independent from any one individual's (world 2) experience. He called this "epistemology without a knowing subject."[66] A prime argument of his was that we can learn more about epistemological issues associated with science if we attend to the world 3 form of science, rather than to questions of how an individual person comes to know and believe something, the traditional subject matter of philosophical epistemology.

But it appears that he was not particularly conscious of the contents of libraries as a domain of study or professional practice. Indeed, Popper appears to have been unaware of John Ziman's book: *Public Knowledge: An Essay Concerning The Social Dimension of Science,* published in 1968, which took a more socially sophisticated look at the senses in which science has a public existence.[67] Popper was not a social scientist, and he rather ignored distinctions that would be important in the social sciences. He saw libraries as the abode of the logical content, but it was only the logical content that interested him—not the vast infrastructure of information institutions, professional associations, and laboratories supporting these exosomatic forms of information storage. In fairness to Popper, it was the philosophical, not the social or professional dimensions of the material aspects of science that interested him.

Nonetheless, Popper has held a continuing fascination for information studies, and discussion of his three worlds appears in the work of many, including Brookes,[68] Rudd,[69] Neill,[70,71] Capurro and Hjørland,[3] and other information scientists' work. It is not my objective here to analyze these appearances of Popper in information studies, except to say that Popper is often misunderstood, or the subtle distinctions he made are ignored. To take just one example, Capurro and Hjørland define Popper's world 3 as follows: "intellectual contents such as books, documents, scientific theories, etc."[72] Treating scientific theories as being in the same category as books and documents, thus conflating world 1 with world 3, misunderstands Popper in a fundamental way. Again, scientific knowledge has a public and objective existence (world 3), apart from either an individual's subjective knowledge of science (world 2) or the physical embodiment of that knowledge in texts and documents (world 1). Scientific knowledge is objective not just because it is recorded in objects called books or disks. Popper's third world is different from the librarian's sense of recorded information existing in physical objects or electronic networks.

If the reader finds tackling the large body of writings by Popper to be daunting, J.W. Grove[73] provides a good, knowledgeable discussion of world 3. The best places to find Popper's own discussions of world 3 are in his book *Objective Knowledge*[74] and in Chapter P2 of Popper and Eccles' *The Self and Its Brain.*[75]

MULTI-TYPE INFORMATION DEFINITIONS

Donald MacKay

Donald MacKay, writing at about the same time as Thompson, who was reviewed previously, also saw information structurally, specifically, "Information: that which determines form."[76] MacKay took a more rigorous scientific approach to conceptualizing information than Thompson did. Elsewhere, he defines it as "that which adds to a representation."[77] Within this general formulation, three senses of information are distinguished:

1. Structural information content, measured by "logons"
2. Metrical information content, measured by "metrons"
3. Selective information content, measured by "bits"

MacKay divided the three measures mentioned earlier into two types, constructive and selective. The first two measures are labeled "constructive." The third measure, "bits," corresponds to Shannon-type information and is labeled "selective." Since the Shannon approach measures amount of information, in part, by the number of options from which a message is selected—a message chosen from 100 possible equiprobable messages is more informative that a message selected from 10 possible equiprobable messages—the amount is measured in an indirect way, in terms of the number of messages *not* sent, hence "selective."

It is interesting, therefore, to contemplate MacKay's effort to measure information in a more direct, or positive, way, with his first two "constructive" measures, logons and metrons. The logons he sees as "[t]he number of *distinguishable groups or clusters* in a representation...its *dimensionality* or *number of degrees of freedom*"[78] The metron, on the other hand, is "that which supplies one element for a pattern." Later, "Thus the amount of metrical information in a pattern measures the *weight of evidence* to which it is equivalent."[79] This approach is redolent of inferential statistics, though it appears to have been intended to be still more general than that. Whatever the case, it does not appear to have caught on as a general means of measuring information.

Brenda Dervin

Brenda Dervin developed an Information[1–3] formulation of information, drawing heavily on the work of Richard Carter, though the distinctions she makes bear some resemblance to Popper's. (Carter's works were notoriously fugitive, seldom appearing in conventional publication venues.)

Dervin states: "In the most general sense, Information1 refers to external reality; Information[2] refers to internal reality." This distinction "forces our attention to the notion that information can be whatever an individual finds 'informing.' It moves our attention away from 'objective' information, toward assessing the 'cognitive maps or pictures' of an individual."[80] She then asks how the individual moves between these two realities. "How does he impose sense on reality when he finds none there?"[81]

She argues that "[b]oth an individual's selection and use of Information,[1] and his creation of Information[2] result from some kind of behavior. It is suggested here that these behaviors are in themselves legitimate informational inputs: Information."[3,81] In other words, Dervin sees Information[3] as all the ways in which people make sense of their worlds, the set of techniques they have to make this reconciliation between internal and external worlds. She then provides examples of different ways that people make sense of their experiences: by "decisioning," by using a "liking–disliking procedure," by a "relating to others" strategy, that is, getting advice from others. In sum, we can say that in Dervin's terms, Information[1] is the external world, Information[2] is the internal world, and Information[3] is the procedures used to reconcile these two worlds.

Michael Buckland

Buckland argues for three types of information:

1. Information-as-process: "When someone is informed, what they know is changed." This definition is similar to Pratt's concept of "in-formation" (see "Allan Pratt" under "Information as Event").
2. Information-as-knowledge: "'Information' is also used to denote that which is perceived in 'information-as-process'"
3. Information-as-thing: "The term 'information' is also used attributively for objects, such as data and documents that are referred to as 'information' because they are regarded as being informative. . . ."[82]

Buckland titled his article "Information as thing" and addresses this sense of information the most in the article's discussion. He sees the information disciplines as primarily being concerned with information in this sense. ". . .[T]he means provided, what is handled and operated upon, what is stored and retrieved, is physical information (information-as-thing)."[83] In this regard, his thinking most resembles that of Jason Farradane, who defined information as a "physical surrogate of knowledge."[84] Farradane argued that such a tangible concept was needed in order to develop a proper science out of information science.

Citing examples of documents, statistical data, statutes, photographs, etc., Buckland says, "In each case it is reasonable to view information-as-thing as *evidence,* though without implying that what was read, viewed, listened to, or otherwise perceived or observed was necessarily accurate, useful, or even pertinent to the user's purposes." Later, "If something cannot be viewed as having the characteristics of evidence, then it is difficult to see how it could be regarded as information."[85] This characterization does leave the reader wondering if Buckland always distinguishes information-as-knowledge from information-as-thing. Suppose a legal precedent is considered evidence. Is the physical book where the precedent is published the evidence, or is it the "information-as-knowledge" within the book that is the evidence? It would seem to be important to distinguish the physical form of the record from its logical content.

Buckland goes on to say that most anything can be informative; therefore information is everything. "We conclude that *we are unable to say confidently of anything that it could not be information.*"[86]

Buckland concludes by suggesting areas in information science where distinguishing "information-as-thing" could be helpful. He notes that historical bibliography, the study of books as physical objects, and statistical analysis of information objects (now known as "informetrics") are areas where information-as-thing has primacy. Second, in the professional activity of the information disciplines, an understanding of the physical handling of different kinds of objects and materials is vital to the effective management of those resources.

Marcia J. Bates

Marcia Bates sets out self-consciously to build a conception of information that is suitable and productive for the information disciplines to use in theory and practice.[87,88]

Her basic definition is a structural one—arguably the most suitable approach for disciplines concerned with material storage and access to information: "Information is the pattern of organization of matter and energy."[89]

She aligns with Wiener on the nature of information: Wiener has said, "Information is information, not matter or energy."[90] That is, she argues that information is not identical to the physical material that composes it; rather information is the *pattern of organization* of that material, not the material itself. (This contrasts with Buckland's conclusion that information is everything.)

On the other hand, though the material world is indisputably materially "there" and not a figment of solipsistic imagination, how living beings perceive and conceive of that pattern of organization is immensely variable across species and across individuals and across the same individual at different times. In this sense, information may be both objective (called "information 1") and subjective (called "information 2"—pattern of organization of matter and energy given meaning by a living thing). Thus, nature has a physical reality independent of human beings, in which we can posit the existence of patterns of organization, even if we perceive them poorly or not at all, while living beings experience patterns of organization in their lives that may be uniquely their own, either as a species or an individual.

At the same time, she addresses information in the larger context of the development of life on earth, drawing on a conception developed by Susantha Goonatilake of the evolution of information transfer over the history of life on earth. Goonatilake's view of the broad fundamental channels of information is well suited to the needs of the information disciplines.[91]

He argues that over the history of life on earth, information has been stored and transmitted in three fundamental ways: genetically, neural-culturally, and exosomatically, that is, through the genome, through cultural transmission, and through storage devices external to the body, such as stelae, scrolls, books, photos, and videos. Animals moved beyond just genetic information transfer to neural-cultural information transfer when they began to teach their young to hunt and otherwise survive as adults. Humans took neural-cultural information still further when they developed language and began memorizing and telling stories to pass on culture through the neural-cultural channel. Humans then developed an explosively growing capacity for exosomatic storage and transmission once they began to carve, draw, and write on more or less durable surfaces.

In developing her conception of information, Bates argues that in living organisms, information tends to move back and forth between encoded and embodied forms. Genetic information is encoded in the genome and embodied in the living animal, the phenotype. The phenotype, in turn, encodes the genome in reproductive material to the next generation. Neural-cultural information is encoded in the brain of an animal and embodied in the experiences, actions, and communications of the animal, respectively, called experienced information, enacted information, and expressed information. Exosomatic information is encoded in the external materials in which it is stored, whence it is again embodied in human experience during reading, touching, or observing.

It is the exosomatic information that is of greatest interest in the managerial practice of the information disciplines. Types of exosomatic information include embedded and recorded information. Embedded information comes from the enduring effects of animals on the earth—from a path beaten through the woods to deliberately fashioned tools, homes, and other objects. For example, a ceramic storage vessel dating from Roman times contains embedded information in its design, in any painting on it, in any residue of its contents, etc. These aspects were generally not designed for intentional communication with later generations; but we can discern many informative things from examining them. Recorded information is communicatory or memorial

information preserved in a durable medium. This type of information is the prime domain of most of the information disciplines—librarianship, archival science, knowledge management, etc.

To Goonatilake's three channels of information transmission, she adds a fourth channel, "Residue." Residue is the flow line of extinction, where previously encoded or embodied information degrades, as in the Biblical "dust to dust." This flow line is important in the information disciplines, because relatively durable information storage does not endure forever and can degrade to the point where no socially meaningful evidence remains.

Thus, in parallel to Goonatilake's three flow lines, Bates defined the following forms of information:

- The genetic flow line is associated with genetic information.
- The neural-cultural flow line is associated with experienced information (in the mind), enacted information (actions in the world), and expressed information (nondurable communications).
- The exosomatic flow line is associated with embedded information and recorded information.
- Finally, residue is associated with trace information—the pattern of organization of the residue that is incidental to living processes or which remains after living processes are finished with it. The importance of trace information to the archaeological and museum worlds is self-evident.

Bates argues for the value of such an approach by describing several example applications of these multi-type terms for information in information studies. For example, the study of information seeking behavior needs to incorporate an awareness of *all* the forms of information a person takes in:

> People get information not just from paper sources, not just from other people, but also from the physical layout of their workspaces, from the design, not just the content, of informational genres, and above all, from the interaction of these various factors in a real situation. All the patterns of organization of matter and energy—cognitive, physical, architectural, social, linguistic—are informative.[92]

Thus, all types and forms of information need to be incorporated in our thinking in doing information research, and having these multiple types of information in mind can promote that awareness and use in research and teaching throughout the information professions.

Paul Beynon-Davies

Beynon-Davies comes at information from the perspective of the information systems discipline. "Significance" is his core concept, rather than information.[93,94] What he calls "the enactment of significance" consists in three levels of systems—data, information, and activity. These are called, respectively, forma, informa, and performa. Core to these three concepts are the ideas of representation, communication, and performance. Thus, a system of representation may be the ones and zeroes of a computer operating system or the alphabet. Persistent data is subject to the classic elements of information system design: read, write, update, and delete.

Information is thought about in Beynon-Davies' work as mostly being about signaling (intentionally or otherwise), that is, as the communication of meaning that is sent by a sender and received and interpreted by a receiver. He draws on the work of biologists and ethologists, with particular attention to research on prairie dog signaling, to demonstrate how even nonlinguistic messages may be produced and interpreted.

Performa consists in the activity of performing a plan or organizational system. According to his Figure 1,[95] moving from the data level through the information level to the performance level consists of the following: The *form* of data is *structured* into *meaning,* from which *intentions* arise, leading to *actions.* Thus, we start with the data, give it meaning and use it to inform, and then perform actions, collaboratively or singly, to achieve goals. As he states elsewhere, "Forma can be seen to encapsulate the objective nature of information, informa its subjective nature and performa its inter-subjective nature."[96]

SECOND INTERLUDE: DIKW

DIKW stands for data–information–knowledge–wisdom. Just as Popper's three worlds frequently show up in considering information, so also does this sequence. Discussion of this sequence is based on the assumption that the terms go from the least to most processed or integrated, with data the rawest and wisdom the most rarefied.

Arguably, this view of these terms comes ultimately from their popular usage. Intuitively, we see each term in the sequence as more developed, "cooked,"[97] or worked through than the term to its left. Discussions of this sequence, in more or less formally worked through thinking, show up in many works, including, at least, those of Houston and Harmon,[98] Hammarberg,[97] Meadow and Yuan,[6] and Ferris.[99] Sharma traced the hierarchy through the knowledge management and information science literature in the 1980s back to the poet T.S. Eliot in 1934.[100] Thompson suggests that "signal" should be a fifth term in the sequence, preceding data ("Telecommunications" in *ELIS*).

Though this sequence may feel intuitively right, it is difficult to take it from its popular meaning and develop it into something sufficiently refined to be useful for research. Most discussions of DIKW really, at base,

elaborate the intuitive understanding and do not take theory much further. Frické concurs and argues that "the DIKW pyramid should be abandoned."[101]

DECONSTRUCTING "INFORMATION"

"Information" has had so much importance in the thinking of many disciplines, including library and information science, over the last 60 or more years that it is not surprising that the time has come where authors set out to debunk or "deflate" the importance of the concept of information. They choose various ways of doing this; three are illustrated in the succeeding text.

Ronald Day

In Ronald Day's deconstruction of *The Modern Invention of Information*, he states that "I attempt to show how professional and authoritative texts about the social importance of information tried to use language (particularly through books) to construct a social, utopian value for information and helped to raise information and its connotations of factuality and quantitative measure to a privileged, even totalitarian, form of knowledge and discourse."[102] He says his objective is not to say what information "really is" nor to conclude that information is good or bad, but "rather that certain connotations of information, and the social and cultural privileging of certain technologies and techniques associated with it, are cultural and social productions that elevate certain values over other values...."[103] Thus, he is not defining so much as critiquing the uses of the term "information."

Bernd Frohmann

Bernd Frohmann's objective in his book *Deflating Information* is to replace the centrality of "information" as the focus of much of information studies and science studies with the centrality of practices surrounding documents.[104] His objective is thus not so much defining or theorizing information, but rather, as his title says, "deflating information."

"One of the aims of this book is to show how rich and varied the practices with scientific documents can be, especially compared to the simplistic idea that there is no more to the informativeness of a document than what happens in the mind of someone who understands it."[105]

Some would complain, however, that good research on information seeking has, from the beginning, also examined scientific practices around documents, and linked those practices to the subjective points of view of the people being studied. Most of the articles on information seeking in the "ancient" 1958 International Conference on Scientific Information[106] or the 1960s era American Psychological Association's Project on Scientific Information in Psychology[107] could be shown to have done that. What we can say of recent decades, though, is that consciousness of all the practices, situations, and cultural beliefs surrounding information seeking and use has grown substantially, and Frohmann's book-length treatment demonstrates that.

Jonathan Furner

Furner suggests that rather than relating information to epistemology, we should relate it to the philosophy of language. Further, "we shall find that philosophers of language have modeled the phenomena fundamental to human communication in ways that do not require us to commit to a separate concept of 'information.'" And "[o]nce the concepts of interest have been labeled with conventional names such as 'data,' 'meaning,' 'communication,' 'relevance,' etc., nothing is left (so it may be argued) to which to apply the term 'information.'" In fact, he claims that the entire field may be misnamed and "that its subject matter should more appropriately be treated as a branch of communication studies, semiotics, or library studies."[108] Furner might not call himself a postmodernist, but the effort to design an approach that does without *the* central concept in a discipline has an objective very much in a postmodernist spirit of deconstructing hitherto core values and ideas.

He identifies what he considers to be the several ways in which "information" is used and discussed in information studies and categorizes them in three broad groupings as follows: "information-as-particular," namely, "utterances," "thoughts," and "situations"; "information-as-action," namely, "communication"; and "information-as-universal," namely, "informativeness" and "relevance."[109] He then argues that other fields address most of these topics with deeper understanding and research results than information studies does and that even in those topic areas where information studies has done much work, such as relevance, we can draw from work in pragmatics and the philosophy of language.[110]

One can certainly agree that we have not advanced as far as desirable in understanding information, and, as well, that we often lack an adequate theoretical basis out of which to develop our ideas. However, one can see this situation as a problem of failing to date to develop our unique intellectual substrate, rather than that we are reinventing lumpy versions of other disciplines' well-wrought wheels.

The universe of study of the physicist is the physical processes and dynamics that govern our universe; the universe of study of the biologist is the world of living things. The primary domain of study in the information disciplines is the world of exosomatic information and human beings' relationship to that world as creators, designers, and users. Heretofore, society has seen that world, if it noticed it at all, as merely an epiphenomenon of the real

world of things that matter. Increasingly, as the twenty-first century develops, we are more and more often grasping the reality that the world of information has become its own universe of study, one of immense importance to human beings, full of intriguing phenomena to observe and understand. That study should surely include identification of key terms, along with the provision of our own disciplinary definitions.

CONCLUSIONS

The understanding of the core concept of "information" in information science remains a highly contested area. Information is seen as

- A proposition, a structure, a message, or an event
- Requiring truth or indifferent to truth
- Socially embedded and under perpetual reinterpretation or as measurable in bits
- A worn-out idea deserving of dispatch or as an exciting conception understandable in terms of evolutionary forces

The much-debated concept of information remains at the lively heart of information science.

REFERENCES

1. Aspray, W. The scientific conceptualization of information: A survey. Ann. Hist. Comput. **1985**, *7* (2), 117–140.
2. Belkin, N.J. Information concepts for information science. J. Doc. **1978**, *34* (1), 55–85.
3. Capurro, R.; Hjørland, B. The concept of information. Ann. Rev. Inf. Sci. Technol. **2003**, *37*, 343–411.
4. Cornelius, I. Theorizing information for information science. Ann. Rev. Inf. Sci. Technol. **2002**, *36*, 393–425.
5. Furner, J. Philosophy and information studies. Ann. Rev. Inf. Sci. Technol. **2010**, *44*, 161–200.
6. Meadow, C.T.; Yuan, W. Measuring the impact of information: Defining the concepts. Inf. Process. Manage. **1997**, *33* (6), 697–714.
7. Wersig, G.; Neveling, U. The phenomena of interest to information science. Inform. Scientist **1975**, *9* (4), 127–140.
8. Kornwachs, K.; Jacoby, K., Eds. *Information: New Questions to a Multidisciplinary Concept*. Akademie Verlag: Berlin, Germany, 1996.
9. Davies, P.; Gregersen, N.H., Eds. *Information and the Nature of Reality: From Physics to Metaphysics*; Cambridge University Press: Cambridge, U.K., 2010.
10. Ibekwe-San Juan, F.; Dousa, T.M., Eds. *Theories of Information, Communication and Knowledge: A Multidisciplinary Approach*; Springer: Dordrecht, Germany, 2014.
11. Furner, J. Information without information studies. In *Theories of Information, Communication and Knowledge: A Multidisciplinary Approach*; Ibekwe-San Juan, F.,

Dousa, T.M., Eds.; Springer: Dordrecht, the Netherlands, 2014; 143–179.

12. Brier, S. Cybersemiotics: A transdisciplinary framework for information studies. BioSystems **1998**, *46* (1–2), 185–191.

13. Karpatschof, B. *Human Activity: Contributions to the Anthropological Sciences from a Perspective of Activity Theory*; Dansk Psykologisk Forlag: Copenhagen, Denmark, 2000.

14. Resnikoff, H.L. *The Illusion of Reality*; Springer-Verlag: New York, 1989.

15. Kåhre, J. *The Mathematical Theory of Information*; Kluwer Academic: Boston, MA, 2002.

16. Roederer, J.G. *Information and Its Role in Nature*; Springer: Berlin, Germany, 2005.

17. Stonier, T. *Information and the Internal Structure of the Universe: An Exploration into Information Physics*; Springer-Verlag: London, U.K., 1990.

18. Stonier, T. *Beyond Information: The Natural History of Intelligence*; Springer-Verlag: London, U.K., 1992.

19. Stonier, T. *Information and Meaning: An Evolutionary Perspective*; Springer: Berlin, Germany, 1997.

20. Reading, A. *Meaningful Information: The Bridge Between Biology, Brain, and Behavior*; Springer: New York, 2011.

21. Floridi, L. What is the philosophy of information? Metaphilosophy **2002**, *33* (1–2), 123–145.

22. Floridi, L., Ed. Information. In *Blackwell Guide to the Philosophy of Computing and Information*; Blackwell: Oxford, U.K., 2004; 40–61.

23. Floridi, L. *Information: A Very Short Introduction*; Oxford University Press: Oxford, U.K., 2010.

24. Floridi, L. *The 4th Revolution: How the Infosphere is Reshaping Human Reality*; Oxford University Press: Oxford, U.K., 2014.

25. Searle, J.R. What your computer can't know. New York Rev. Books **2014**, *61* (15), 52–55.

26. Day, R.E. *The Modern Invention of Information*; Southern Illinois University Press: Carbondale, IL, 2001.

27. Boulding, K.E. *The Image: Knowledge of Life and Society*; University of Michigan Press: Ann Arbor, MI, 1961; 20.

28. Wiener, N. *Cybernetics: Or Control and Communication in the Animal and the Machine*, 2nd Ed.; MIT Press: Cambridge, MA, 1961.

29. Wiener, N. *Cybernetics: Or Control and Communication in the Animal and the Machine*, 2nd Ed.; MIT Press: Cambridge, MA, 1961, Introduction, Chapter 4.

30. Wiener, N. *Cybernetics: Or Control and Communication in the Animal and the Machine*, 2nd Ed.; MIT Press: Cambridge, MA, 1961, 8.

31. Shannon, C.E.; Weaver, W. *The Mathematical Theory of Communication*; University of Illinois Press: Urbana, IL, 1975.

32. Wiener, N. *Cybernetics: Or Control and Communication in the Animal and the Machine*, 2nd Ed.; MIT Press: Cambridge, MA, 1961; 10.

33. Shannon, C.E. A mathematical theory of communication. Bell Syst. Tech. J. **1948**, *27* (3), 379–423.

34. Miller, G.A. *Language and Communication*; McGraw-Hill: New York, 1951.

35. Madden, A.D. A definition of information. Aslib Proc. **2000**, *52* (9), 348.

36. Madden, A.D. Evolution and information. J. Doc. **2004**, *60* (1), 9.

37. Boulding, K.E. *The Image: Knowledge of Life and Society*; University of Michigan Press: Ann Arbor, MI, 1961.

38. Bateson, G *Steps to an Ecology of Mind*; Ballantine Books: New York, 1972; 271–278.

39. Bateson, G. *Steps to an Ecology of Mind*; Ballantine Books: New York, 1972; 453.

40. Brookes, B.C. The foundations of information science. Part I. Philosophical aspects. J. Inf. Sci. **1980**, *2* (3–4), 131.

41. Nauta, D. *The Meaning of Information*; Mouton: The Hague, the Netherlands, 1972; 201.

42. Losee, R.M. A discipline independent definition of information. J. Am. Soc. Inf. Sci. **1997**, *48* (3), 256.

43. Losee, R.M. A discipline independent definition of information. J. Am. Soc. Inf. Sci. **1997**, *48* (3), 258.

44. Pratt, A.D. The information of the image: A model of the communications process. Libri **1977**, *27* (3), 208.

45. Pratt, A.D. The information of the image: A model of the communications process. Libri **1977**, *27* (3), 215.

46. Derr, R.L. The concept of information in ordinary discourse. Inf. Process. Manage. **1985**, *21* (6), 491.

47. Derr, R.L. The concept of information in ordinary discourse. Inf. Process. Manage. **1985**, *21* (6), 493–494.

48. Dretske, F.I. *Knowledge and the Flow of Information*; MIT Press: Cambridge, MA, 1981; 44.

49. Dretske, F.I. *Knowledge and the Flow of Information*; MIT Press: Cambridge, MA, 1981; 45.

50. Dretske, F.I. *Knowledge and the Flow of Information*; MIT Press: Cambridge, MA, 72.

51. Fox, C.J. *Information and Misinformation: An Investigation of the Notions of Information, Misinformation, Informing and Misinforming*; Greenwood Press: Westport, CT, 1983; 203

52. Fox, C.J. *Information and Misinformation: An Investigation of the Notions of Information, Misinformation, Informing and Misinforming*; Greenwood Press: Westport, CT, 1983; 154

53. Losee, R.M. A discipline independent definition of information. J. Am. Soc. Inf. Sci. **1997**, *48* (3), 267.

54. Thompson, F.B. The organization is the information. Am. Doc. **1968**, *19* (3), 305.

55. Thompson, F.B. The organization is the information. Am. Doc. **1968**, *19* (3), 306.

56. Bowker, G.C.; Star, S.L. *Sorting Things Out: Classification and Its Consequences*; MIT Press: Cambridge, MA, 1999.

57. Cornelius, I. Information and interpretation. In *Integration in Perspective, Proceedings of CoLIS 2: Second International Conference on Conceptions of Library and Information Science*; Ingwersen, P., Pors, N.O., Eds.; Royal School of Librarianship: Copenhagen, Denmark, October 13–16, 1996; 15.

58. Cornelius, I. Information and interpretation. In *Integration in Perspective, Proceedings of CoLIS 2: Second International Conference on Conceptions of Library and Information Science*; Ingwersen, P., Pors, N.O., Eds.; Royal School of Librarianship: Copenhagen, Denmark, October 13–16, 1996; 19.

59. Cornelius, I. Information and interpretation. In *Integration in Perspective, Proceedings of CoLIS 2: Second International Conference on Conceptions of Library and*

Information Science; Ingwersen, P., Pors, N.O., Eds.; Royal School of Librarianship: Copenhagen, Denmark, October 13–16, 1996; 20.

60. Goguen, J.A. Towards a social, ethical theory of information. In *Social Science Research, Technical Systems, and Cooperative Work: Beyond the Great Divide*; Bowker, G., Gasser, L., Star, L., Turner, W., Eds.; Lawrence Erlbaum Associates: Mahwah, NJ, 1997; 27–56.

61. Goguen, J.A. Towards a social, ethical theory of information. In *Social Science Research, Technical Systems, and Cooperative Work: Beyond the Great Divide*; Bowker, G., Gasser, L., Star, L., Turner, W., Eds.; Lawrence Erlbaum Associates: Mahwah, NJ, 1997; 31.

62. Goguen, J.A. Towards a social, ethical theory of information. In *Social Science Research, Technical Systems, and Cooperative Work: Beyond the Great Divide*; Bowker, G., Gasser, L., Star, L., Turner, W., Eds.; Lawrence Erlbaum Associates: Mahwah, NJ, 1997; 32.

63. Goguen, J.A. Towards a social, ethical theory of information. In *Social Science Research, Technical Systems, and Cooperative Work: Beyond the Great Divide*; Bowker, G., Gasser, L., Star, L., Turner, W., Eds.; Lawrence Erlbaum Associates: Mahwah, NJ, 1997; 34.

64. Goguen, J.A. Towards a social, ethical theory of information. In *Social Science Research, Technical Systems, and Cooperative Work: Beyond the Great Divide*; Bowker, G., Gasser, L., Star, L., Turner, W., Eds.; Lawrence Erlbaum Associates: Mahwah, NJ, 1997; 40.

65. Popper, K.R. *Objective Knowledge: An Evolutionary Approach*; Clarendon Press: Oxford, U.K., 1979; 74.

66. Popper, K.R. *Objective Knowledge: An Evolutionary Approach*; Oxford, U.K.: Clarendon Press, 1979; 106–152.

67. Ziman, J.M. *Public Knowledge: An Essay Concerning the Social Dimension of Science*; Cambridge University Press: London, U.K., 1968.

68. Brookes, B.C. The foundations of information science. Part I. Philosophical aspects. J. Inf. Sci. **1980**, *2* (3–4), 125–133.

69. Rudd, D. Do we really need World 3? Information science with or without Popper. J. Inf. Sci. **1983**, *7*, 99–105.

70. Neill, S.D. The dilemma of the subjective in information organisation and retrieval. J. Doc. **1987**, *43* (3), 193–211.

71. Neill, S.D. Brookes, Popper, and objective knowledge. J. Inf. Sci. **1982**, *4* (1), 33–39.

72. Capurro, R.; Hjørland, B. The concept of information. Ann. Rev. Inf. Sci. Technol. **2003**, *37*, 393.

73. Grove, J.W. Popper 'demystified': The curious ideas of Bloor (and some others) about World 3. Philos. Soc.Sci. **1980**, *10*, 173–180.

74. Popper, K.R. *Objective Knowledge: An Evolutionary Approach*; Clarendon Press: Oxford, U.K., 1979.

75. Popper, K.R.; Eccles, J.C. *The Self and Its Brain*; Springer International: Berlin, Germany, 1985.

76. MacKay, D.M. *Information, Mechanism, and Meaning*; MIT Press: Cambridge, MA, 1969; 160.

77. MacKay, D.M. *Information, Mechanism, and Meaning*; MIT Press: Cambridge, MA, 1969; 163.

78. MacKay, D.M. *Information, Mechanism, and Meaning*; MIT Press: Cambridge, MA, 1969; 165.

79. MacKay, D.M. *Information, Mechanism, and Meaning*; MIT Press: Cambridge, MA, 1969; 166.

80. Dervin, B. Useful theory for librarianship: Communication not information. Drexel Libr. Quart. **1977**, *13* (3), 22.

81. Dervin, B. Useful theory for librarianship: Communication not information. Drexel Libr. Quart. **1977**, *13* (3), 23.

82. Buckland, M.K. Information as thing. J. Am. Soc. Inf. Sci. **1991**, *42* (5), 351.

83. Buckland, M.K. Information as thing. J. Am. Soc. Inf. Sci. **1991**, *42* (5), 352.

84. Farradane, J. The nature of information. J. Inf. Sci. **1983**, *1* (1), 17.

85. Buckland, M.K. Information as thing. J. Am. Soc. Inf. Sci. **1991**, *42* (5), 353.

86. Buckland, M.K. Information as thing. J. Am. Soc. Inf. Sci. **1991**, *42* (5), 356.

87. Bates, M.J Information and knowledge: An evolutionary framework for information science. Inf. Res. **2005**, *10*(4), paper 239, http://informationr.net/ir/10-4/paper239.html.

88. Bates, M.J. Fundamental forms of information. J. Am. Soc. Inf. Sci. **2006**, *57* (8), 1033–1045.

89. Bates, M.J. Fundamental forms of information. J. Am. Soc. Inf. Sci. Technol. **2006**, *57* (8), 1033.

90. Wiener, N. *Cybernetics: Or Control and Communication in the Animal and the Machine*, 2nd Ed.; MIT Press: Cambridge, MA, 1961; 132.

91. Goonatilake, S. *The Evolution of Information: Lineages in Gene, Culture, and Artefact*; Pinter: London, U.K., 1991.

92. Bates, M.J. Fundamental forms of information. J. Am. Soc. Inf. Sci. Technol. **2006**, *57* (8), 1043.

93. Beynon-Davies, P. *Significance: Exploring the Nature of Information, Systems and Technology*; Palgrave-Macmillan: New York, 2011.

94. Beynon-Davies, P. In-formation on the prairie: Signs, patterns, systems and prairie dogs. Int. J. Inf. Manage. **2011**, *31* (4), 307–316.

95. Beynon-Davies, P. In-formation on the prairie: Signs, patterns, systems and prairie dogs. Int. J. Inf. Manage. **2011**, *31* (4), 309.

96. Beynon-Davies, P. *Significance: Exploring the Nature of Information, Systems and Technology*; Palgrave-Macmillan: New York, 2011, 288.

97. Hammarberg, R. The cooked and the raw. J. Inf. Sci. **1981**, *3* (6), 261–267.

98. Houston, R.D.; Harmon, E.G. Re-envisioning the information concept: Systematic definitions. In *Emerging Frameworks and Methods, Proceedings of the Fourth International Conference on Conceptions of Library and Information Science (CoLIS 4)*; Bruce, H., Fidel, R., Ingwersen, P., Vakkari, P., Eds.; Libraries Unlimited: Greenwood Village, CO, July 21–25, 2002; 305–308.

99. Ferris, T.L.J. Characteristics of data, information, knowledge, and wisdom. In *Handbook of Measuring System Design*; Sydenham, P.H.; Thorn, R., Eds.; Wiley: Chichester, England, 2005; Vol. 1, 231–234.

100. Sharma, N. The origin of the "data information knowledge wisdom" hierarchy. [Updated Feb. 4, 2008]. http://www-personal.si.umich.edu/~nsharma/dikw_origin.htm (accessed January 2009).

101. Frické, M. The knowledge pyramid: A critique of the DIKW hierarchy. J. Inf. Sci. **2009**, *35* (2), 132.

102. Day, R.E. *The Modern Invention of Information*; Southern Illinois University Press: Carbondale, IL, 2001; 2.

103. Day, R.E. *The Modern Invention of Information*; Southern Illinois University Press: Carbondale, IL, 2001; 117.

104. Frohmann, B. *Deflating Information: From Science Studies to Documentation*; University of Toronto Press: Toronto, Ontario, Canada, 2004.

105. Frohmann, B. *Deflating Information: From Science Studies to Documentation*; University of Toronto Press: Toronto, Ontario, Canada, 2004; 16.

106. Proceedings of the International Conference on Scientific Information Washington, D.C., Nov. 16–21,

1958. National Academy of Sciences, National Research Council: Washington, DC, 1959; 2 vol.

107. American Psychological Association. *Project on Scientific Information Exchange in Psychology*; American Psychological Association: Washington, DC, 1963–1968; 21 reports.

108. Furner, J. Information studies without information. Libr. Trends **2004**, *52* (3), 428.

109. Furner, J. Information studies without information. Libr. Trends **2004**, *52* (3), 438.

110. Furner, J. Information studies without information. Libr. Trends **2004**, *52* (3), 444.

Information Arts

Christiane Paul
Jack Toolin
Whitney Museum of American Art, New York, U.S.A.

Abstract

This entry provides a survey of the field of information arts, an artistic practice that creatively and critically reflects on the collection, filtering, and dissemination of information. The term information arts is relatively new and used mostly as it relates to the information society of the digital age. This entry outlines the roots of contemporary information art practice in processes of information distribution and mass media and places it within the wider art historical context of works that have explored information flow and mass-mediated images. Among the topics addressed are the ways in which recent information artworks process data from sources such as science, humanities, and network technologies and the methods these artworks employ for giving information form, for example, data visualization and the construction of databases. This entry also briefly discusses the challenges that information art using new technologies poses to the traditional art world, ranging from presentation to collection and preservation.

INTRODUCTION

This entry explores the field of information arts and its relationship to information societies, its practitioners, their conceptual motivations, and the various manifestations their artworks take, from projected visualizations to performative interactions. A brief discussion about the historical development of the information society is included in order to elucidate information arts' relevance to that history, as well as its break from past cultural practice.

A data flow diagram depicts the range of data origins, the strategies employed by artists to process the data sets, as well as the various methods of presentation. Using examples, this entry presents two main artistic approaches to working with information, one more focused on formal and aesthetic concerns, the other addressing cultural and political aspects. Finally, this entry considers information arts in the context of the art institution, summarizing approaches to exhibition, and preservation.

DEFINING INFORMATION ARTS

It would be problematic to claim that information arts are a clearly defined field or a term that describes a specific kind of artistic practice in a specific medium. While one could argue that art throughout the centuries has been concerned with or addressed information in some form or another, the term "information arts" has been used only fairly recently. The term was formalized by Stephen Wilson when he published his book of the same name in 2002. Wilson describes the field as one primarily concerned with data as it relates to science and technology, making a strong case for the ubiquitous impact of these areas in the information society.[1] However, this seems too narrow an approach as it excludes valuable contributions by artists who, while working with information and its mechanisms for evaluation and distribution, do not directly comment on or use data derived from science or technology.

If one understands information science as an interdisciplinary field concerned with the collection, storage, classification, retrieval, and dissemination of information, one could say that information arts make the concerns of information science both their content and medium. Information arts consciously explore or critically address the issues surrounding the processing and distribution of information by making information itself the medium and carrier of this exploration.

The term information arts now seems inextricably interconnected with the information society that has been brought about by digital technologies and is occasionally understood as strictly digital or data driven. However, information arts are a wide-ranging category that can also be applied to analog techniques and technologies and has a history within artistic practice, as we will show in the following. We are addressing the topic with a rather broad scope, thinking of information as a cultural as well as numerical entity. While information arts are not identical with digital art or so-called new media art (art that uses digital technologies as a medium for production, storage, and distribution), these fields of artistic practice certainly overlap. One could argue that digital art is a subcategory of the broader field of information arts in that it explores and processes information by means of digital technologies only (e.g., as a data visualization or website) and predominantly understands data as digital binaries. The larger umbrella of information arts, by contrast, potentially engages with its subject

Encyclopedia of Library and Information Sciences, Fourth Edition DOI: 10.1081/E-ELIS4-120053398

across a range of media—from print and analog radio and TV to digital media. Not all of digital art can automatically be understood as information art; a digital artwork that explores hyperlinked storytelling and narrative does not necessarily self-consciously address information processing and distribution. In terms of defining the field, one could therefore suggest that a portion of digital art—in which information is both medium and subject matter—is a subcategory of information arts at large.

A strong link between digital art and information arts in general is established by the use of algorithms or code—a procedure of formal instructions that accomplish a "result" in a finite number of steps—which forms the basis of digital or new media art. Information arts uses a variety of methods, both analog and digital, to process data but a significant portion of the practice relies on digital technologies and algorithms in this processing. The layer of code and instructions constitutes a conceptual level that connects to the artistic explorations of previous decades. Information arts can be understood as a larger category than digital art, as a field of artistic practice that consciously makes information—be it in digital form, contained in genetic code, or circulated by the mass media—its subject matter.

INFORMATION ARTS IN AN INFORMATION SOCIETY

Today, it is nothing new to think of our society as an "information society," so much so that we might take for granted when and how this development occurred. Information, or the communication of information, was an important element in the development of ancient societies and has remained important ever since. The evolution of languages and the means for circulating those languages was a key for extending cultural influences, and the power of the societies generating them, from Babylon to Qatar. But one would not describe the late Roman Empire as an information society, despite the centralized authority over a large expanse and people of disparate backgrounds.

In fact, we typically do not think of information societies occurring until the twentieth century, and more precisely not until the latter half of the century as the economy moved from material goods to information goods. While it is not our intention to examine the evolution of information from its inception, a brief consideration of its growing role and importance to our civilization will allow us to better understand the development and relevance of what one might call the information arts.

When did the collection, classification, storage, and dissemination of information become important to society? Again, one could go back to early civilization, but a crucial moment would be after the Renaissance and the rise of rational humanism, during the Industrial Revolution, when mechanization and automation provided for greater redundancy, predictability, and measurability—Taylorism was a symptom of this trend in business practice and philosophy, and Fordism was its crowning achievement. In the late nineteenth century, Frederick Winslow Taylor proposed that working environments and procedures be based upon analyses of the work to be done, with increased productivity being the goal, as opposed to methods adopted by convention. Fordism, a term coined by the Italian political theorist Antonio Gramsci, refers to the deskilled, task-oriented work common in twentieth-century manufacturing since Henry Ford implemented the assembly line. The economy became increasingly reliant upon efficiency and productivity, and in the meantime developing transportation and communication technologies allowed for a more dispersed clientele and a public whose solidarity increasingly defied geography and genetics.

Immigration was spurred by new technologies both because travel became easier and because booming industries lured people to travel great lengths for financial gain. The influx of immigrants in America precipitated a shift toward a greater use of images in journalism as it went "yellow" and coincided with the rise of the moving image, which was, in this regard, fortunate to be silent.

These changes did not go unnoticed by artists of the time: One can see examples of the influence of mechanization and technological idealism in cubism and futurism, while the Dadaists adopted rule-based methodologies for some of their art making, emphasizing procedure over product. It is not a surprise that today, in societies consumed by computation, the Dadaism is seen as one of the most influential art movements of the twentieth century. The conceptual artists of the late twentieth century are seen as descendents of these earlier explorations, and their de-emphasis of aesthetics and material as the central signifiers of art opened up the door for a growing number of practitioners from disciplines such as computer science, engineering, biology, and philosophy.

It was in the early twentieth century that Madison Avenue and Hollywood (not to mention the military) realized the power to persuade that the mass media possessed. However, despite the growing importance of mass-circulated information in this nascent stage, the economic engine of the West was still largely the production and distribution of hard goods, with the postwar boom yet to happen—information was mostly at the service of engineering and manufacturing. Radio, movies, and magazines made inroads into leisure time, but they all took a hit as television became the mass medium by the late 1950s. Consumerism reached new proportions as the mass media were there to guide and facilitate achieving a proper standard of living for the growing middle class. Art reflected these developments, with overt manifestations in the pop art movements of England and the United States, Richard Hamilton and Andy Warhol being prime examples, respectively. While Hamilton and his colleagues in the Independent Group critiqued the growing trends of consumerism and the corporatization of contemporary society with wry satire, Warhol employed the visual language and marketing strategies of corporate culture to manufacture and disseminate the Warhol brand.

An appropriate parallel to these artists' approaches is the recent work of artist collectives ®TMark and etoy. The former group undermines corporate authority through various strategies, among them the mirroring of websites, a common tactic of activist art projects. Artists register domain names similar to those of corporate entities or institutions, mirror the look of these entities' websites, but subvert their contents as an act of critique. In collaboration with The Yes Men, ®TMark was involved in a December 2002 press release originating from the fake site Dow-Chemical.com that explained why Dow could not take responsibility for the Bhopal catastrophe, which resulted in an estimated 20,000 deaths over the years. The release created public outrage, as well as expansive press coverage and controversy.[2] etoy frequently carry out acts designed to heighten their public profile, and hence increase their value as a cultural entity. In other words, they engage in branding. The work of these artists reveals identity as a cultural construct that is dependent upon the maintenance of a profile in the public, which is widely accepted as an entity established through communication. The value, or impact, of a given identity is reliant upon its circulation via various media, from print to the Internet. As etoy themselves state

The firm represents the core and code of the corporate sculpture, and controls, protects, promotes, and exploits the cultural substance (intellectual property) and the etoy. ART-COLLECTION. etoy intends to reinvest all financial earnings in art—the final link in the value chain.[3] (Fig. 1)

Meanwhile, as corporations extended their reach, their desire for greater productivity was met by the burgeoning computer industry. The UNIversal Automatic Computer, which was capable of computing textual and numerical data, was the first commercially available computer, announced in 1951. While it took some years for computing to be adopted by industry at large and decades longer for it to become a fixture in the home, the concepts and methods that are the foundation of computing had manifestations in rule-based art from the late 1950s through the 1970s and beyond, such as Sol LeWitt's drawings, paintings, and structures, Fluxus' instructions for "being" art (one cannot overlook the relevance of Dada performance/ poetry here), the psychogeographic explorations of the Situationists, the chance operations of John Cage's sound work, and the reiterative music of Steve Reich. Recognizing that technology had extended from the production floor of the factory to the cutting room of culture, artists like Nam June Paik, Vito Acconci, and Bruce Nauman began experimenting with video, and in the mid-1960s Experiments in Art and Technology, founded by engineers Billy Klüver and Fred Waldhauer and artists Robert Rauschenberg and Bob Whitman, melded the skills of engineer and artist to explore the possibilities of technologically enabled art.

Experiments in Art and Technology was far from the first such commingling of art and technology, after all photography and film have their roots in such experimentation; the linear perspective of Early Renaissance painting was based in mathematics, and architecture going back to antiquity followed mathematical principles for design and proportion. So is the emergence of the information arts of the late twentieth century anything new? Yes. While one can argue that information has been key to the existence and propagation of civilizations from their start, it is since the mid-twentieth century that the collection, classification, and dissemination of information has been such a force within society that economics, politics, and social relations depend upon it. In the United States, a

Fig. 1   etoy.CORPORATION History/Share Certificates. Screenshot.

process of deindustrialization began in the mid-1960s when the percentage of manufacturing employment peaked at 28%, dwindling by more than 10% over the next 10 years.[4] This coincided with growth in the information industries and the growing economic activity related to the processing and distribution of information.

FROM DATA TO INFORMATION FLOW: THE PRACTICE AND PRODUCTION CYCLE OF INFORMATION ARTS

Essential to the concept of information arts is the "production cycle" of information itself, which—in its connection to all the previously mentioned aspects of information collection and dissemination—becomes the subject and means of artistic exploration. The Merriam-Webster Online Dictionary defines information as "the communication or reception of knowledge or intelligence" or "knowledge obtained from investigation, study, or instruction."[5] Derived from the Latin verb "informare," which means "to put into form," information is closely connected to the act of informing as imparting learning or instruction. Webster's, as many other dictionaries and common language usage, to some extent conflates information with data, defining data as "factual information (as measurements or statistics) used as a basis for reasoning, discussion, or calculation."[6] A more precise definition and delineation of the two terms might be the understanding of information as processed data. In this sense, information would consist of the conclusions derived from the analysis of figures, statistics, etc. (data), which form the basis of reasoning. This meaning of information would be closer to *Webster*'s description of information as representation of data: "a signal or character (as in a communication system or computer) representing data." On a sidenote, the equation of information and knowledge seems equally problematic. David Sholle suggests to distinguish the two in terms of multiplicity, as well as temporal and spatial categories, arguing that (1) information is piecemeal and fragmented, while knowledge is structured and coherent; (2) information is timely and transitory, while knowledge is enduring and temporally expansive; and (3) information flows across spaces, while knowledge is a stock and located, yet spatially expansive.[7]

Distinguishing characteristics aside, there is no doubt that information and data are closely related and feed into each other. Data commonly function as input into systems or programs that output information. However, information or segments thereof can either become or produce input data. David Sholle has pointed out that in information economics, information functions both as the resource providing input into the production process of commodities and the control of the market itself and as the output that is materialized and sold as a commodity.[8]

The diagram in Fig. 2, which is meant to be a schematic outline rather than a definitive model, sketches some central aspects of the practice of information arts. The source data for an art project can be derived from areas as varied as the sciences (such as biotechnology and genetics or geographic information systems), the humanities (languages and literature, visual arts, and music), network processes (data flowing through or pertaining to digital networks), haptic or acoustic processes, etc.

Information arts process these data through the use of rules, algorithms and codes (instructions that accomplish a "result" in a finite number of steps), or other forms of encoding and transformation. It is important to note that code cannot be understood as separable from its overall structure. As Adrian Ward, Alex McLean, and Geoff Cox

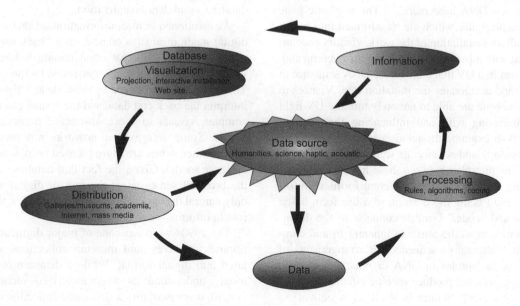

Fig. 2 Paul/Toolin, flow diagram of the practice of information arts.

Fig. 3 Eduardo Kac, Genesis (1999). Transgenic work with artist-created bacteria, ultraviolet light, internet, video (detail), edition of 2, dimensions variable.

pointed out in "The Aesthetics of Generative Code,"[9] the written form of code—as "a notation of an internal structure that the computer is executing, expressing ideas, logic, and decisions"—is "a computer-readable notation of logic" and not what the computer really executes. The execution takes place through various layers of interpreting and compiling. This layered interpretation and processing (by various means and methods) is a basic characteristic of information arts.

Eduardo Kac's *Genesis* (Fig. 3) perfectly illustrates this process of multilayered interpretation. Taking textual and scientific data (from the field of genetics) as its source, Genesis uses encoding and the transformation of different materialities as a means of processing. For the project, Eduardo Kac created a synthetic "artist's gene" by translating a sentence from the biblical book of Genesis ("Let man have dominion over the fish of the sea, and over the fowl of the air, and over every living thing that moves upon the earth") into Morse code and converting the Morse code into DNA base pairs.[10] The synthetic gene is cloned into plasmids, which are transformed into bacteria. In the gallery installation of the work, visitors encounter a pedestal with a petri dish containing the bacteria and, suspended over it, a UV that disrupts the DNA sequence in the plasmid and accelerates the mutation rate. Visitors to the Genesis website are able to remotely turn the UV light on, thus interfering with and influencing the process. Kac's goal is to examine the relationship between information technology and science, as well as belief systems and ethics. The interplay between these fields is achieved by translating and transforming different forms of information, the result being the creation of a life form based on language and "code." Genesis connects to the definition of information as the attribute inherent in and communicated by "alternative sequences or arrangements of something (as nucleotides in DNA or binary digits in a computer program) that produce specific effects."[5]

While Kac's work manifests itself as a networked installation, information art can use numerous methods to give information form, ranging from installation to a virtual reality environment or distribution over mobile devices, such as cell phones or personal digital assistants. The latter play an important role in locative media projects, which use a location in public space as a "canvas" for an art project and have become one of the most active and fast-growing areas in information arts. Locative media employ technologies such as the global positioning system for data gathering or allow their users to contribute to projects and share information via mobile devices. A number of art projects have focused on mapping and enhancing existing physical spaces and architectures, creating a virtual, public repository for information that supplements sites. Others have focused on transforming mobile devices from mere communication tools into personal measurement instruments and enabling people to collect and share data about their surroundings and environment. Other common methods for making information manifest are the construction of databases and data visualization.

As mentioned before, information art that involves the digital medium always consists of a "back end" of algorithms and data sets that often remain hidden behind a visible "front end" that is experienced by the viewer/user. This front end is produced by the code and algorithms that interpret the back end data, and the results can range from complex visuals to more abstract communication processes. Some information artworks are predominantly visual; other works are more focused on raw data and the database model. Given the fact that database structure in the broadest sense lies at the root of digital media, it is only natural that so-called database aesthetics play a major role in information arts.

The 1990s were a decade of major digitization, where libraries, archives, and museum collections were translated into digital format. While a database is now commonly understood as a computerized record keeping system, it is essentially a structured collection of data that stands in the tradition of "data containers" such as a book, a library, an archive, or Wunderkammer. Every "container" of information ultimately constitutes a dataspace and information architecture of its own, even though its characteristics are quite different from the virtual, dynamic dataspace. What distinguishes digital databases from their analog predecessors is their inherent possibility for the retrieval and filtering of data in multiple ways, allowing for new forms of relational connections.

Databases can be distinguished according to different "data models"—that is, data containers and the ways in which data are stored in and retrieved from them. A database essentially is a system that comprises three levels: (1) the hardware that stores the data; (2) the software that allows for housing the data in its respective container and for retrieving, filtering, and processing them; (3) and the users who add a further level in understanding the data as information.

In the field of information arts and digital art, the term "database aesthetics" is frequently used to describe the aesthetic principles that are applied in imposing the logic of the database to any type of information or filtering data collections or visualizing data. In that sense, database aesthetics often becomes a conceptual, potential, and cultural form—a way of constructing information by revealing (visual) patterns of knowledge, beliefs, and social behavior. Generally speaking, the aesthetics of a database are inherently relational, be it on the level of potential (the data stored in the data container) or the actual relationships established by the software component. Database aesthetics suggest the possibilities of tracing process—individual, cultural, communicative—in its various forms on the basis of data. Largely brought about by digital technologies, database aesthetics itself has become

an important cultural narrative in information arts, constituting a shift toward a relational, networked approach to gathering and creating information and knowledge about cultural specifics.

Examples of information arts that apply a database model to reveal information about cultural and individual values are George Legrady's projects *Pockets Full of Memories* (2001) and *Slippery Traces* (1997). Pockets Full of Memories, an installation with an accompanying website,[11] explicitly focuses on the "mechanics" of database construction and the way in which we derive informational value from databases (Fig. 4). It creates an "anatomy" of personal value by inviting visitors to digitally scan an object in their possession at a scanning station and answer a set of questions regarding the object, rating it according to certain attributes (old/new, soft/hard, natural/synthetic, functional/symbolic, personal/nonpersonal, useful/useless, etc.). The algorithm used to process the data is the Kohonen self-organizing algorithm, which classifies the scanned objects in a two-dimensional map based on similarities in their descriptions and attribute ratings. The Kohonen map generates a grid with random values for each point in the grid and all the data categories for each object; the algorithm classifies one object after the other and positions it where it finds the closest values for the respective object, so that over time all the objects are positioned in proximity to the ones with similar values. Users can review each object's data and add their own personal comments and stories. The mapping of these objects illuminates how each object is contextualized by its surrounding data and underscores the absurdities of classifying objects endowed with personal meaning.

Fig. 4 George Legrady, Pockets Full of Memories (2001). Screenshot of the interface.

The information conveyed is obviously very much dependent on the database system as a whole—the interplay between the container, the algorithms, and the interpretation of the user. Database categories and the algorithms filtering them are never value-free but always inscribed with an interpretative angle.

Closely related to the construction of databases, data visualization is another method of making processed data manifest as information. Data visualization can be defined as the creation of dynamic visual models for data sets. For any given set of data, there are multiple possibilities for giving it a visual form, which in turn lend themselves to reconfiguration. The dynamics of the visualization and interface are yet another layer of processing that provides a context for deriving information. Context becomes key when it comes to the success of the visualization process. While there needs to be a certain focus on data changes at any given point, the visualization tends to turn into a form of wallpaper (no matter how beautiful it is) if it loses the larger context of its underlying data set.

The issue of potential relationships between the data structure or data stream and its visualization is perfectly captured by the Radical Software Group's project *Carnivore* (2001–present).[12] The project is inspired by the software DCS1000 (nicknamed "Carnivore"), which is used by the FBI to perform electronic wiretaps and search for certain "suspicious" keywords via packet sniffing—a software-based process of intercepting, logging, and analyzing the data packets sent over a digital network. Using network traffic on a specific local area network as its data source, the project processes the data through software that performs packet sniffing. The resulting data stream is visualized by the numerous "client" applications that

artists have created since the project's inception. At the core of the Carnivore project are the unlimited possibilities of visualizing the server's data stream in a collaborative, open-source way. Jonah Brucker-Cohen's *Police State* (2003) addresses and subverts the process of surveillance itself (Fig. 5). In Police State, the processing of the data stream takes the form of both a visualization and a physical installation. The client sniffs the network looking for keywords relating to domestic U.S. terrorism and assigns the identified text to an active police radio code, which is translated to its binary equivalent and sent to 20 radio-controlled toy police cars as a movement sequence. Controlled by the very data that law enforcement is searching for, the police cars perform a synchronized "dance," driven by their own surveillance.

The previous examples illustrate ways in which data are processed (through algorithms, encoding, and transformation) and methods of engaging with the data to give it form (through installations, construction of databases, or data visualization). As any information, these and other information art projects enter the larger cultural and social sphere through the media—be it the mass media of print publications and television. The technologies and distribution process of the media, as well as the information circulated by them, again produce data that information arts make their subject. An excellent example of this recapitulation of media imagery is a 2006 project by Eva and Franco Mattes (aka 100101110101101) titled *13 Most Beautiful Avatars*. This project consists of "pictures of self-portraits" featuring the avatars made by inhabitants of the virtual world Second Life, which reveal a desire to appear as someone other, someone closer to the ideals of beauty commonly seen in Western mass media. The

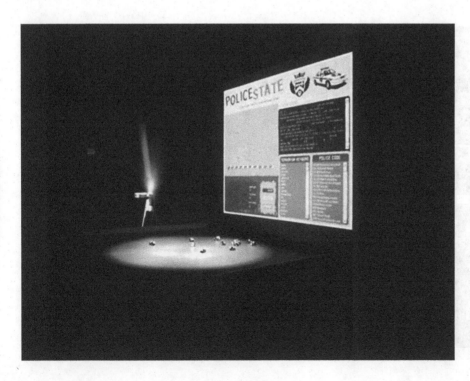

Fig. 5 Jonah Brucker-Cohen, Police State (2003) at the exhibition "Source Code," Eyebeam, New York City (May 31–August 11, 2007).

project directly references two of Andy Warhol's works of the 1960, *Thirteen Most Beautiful Boys* and *Thirteen Most Beautiful Women*. The Mattes' piece is one of the many utilizing the imagery and implications of popular culture in virtual worlds and computer games.

APPROACHES TO INFORMATION ARTS: FORMALISM VERSUS CULTURALISM

The practice and data flow of information arts we have outlined so far makes obvious that the field is not at all unified but spans various artistic media and methods. This raises the question whether it is possible to identify major conceptual categories for understanding information arts rather than relying on the rather formal distinctions between different methods for processing and materializing data. Categories that may be helpful for a conceptual approach are those of formalism versus culturalism, which have been used in software art, a subcategory of digital art that focuses on artist-written code. One can argue that there is a fairly strong connection between software art, which relies on processing through code and algorithms, and information arts, which involve either the same methods or rules and "encoding" in the broadest sense for transforming data.

The jury of the pioneering software art festival Read_Me 1.2 (2002)[13] broadly defined software art as works based on code as formal instructions or offering a cultural reflection of software. The former would apply to forms such as generative art and code poetry that put an emphasis on the aesthetics of formal instructions; the latter would apply to categories such as manipulations of existing software (cracks and patches or plug-ins) or political and activist software (e.g., cease-and-desist-ware and software resistance), which offers a critical reflection of software's cultural status, its encoded political or commercial agenda. Games, artistic tools, and conceptual software could fall into either of these two groups, depending on the execution of the respective project and the weight it places on formal aspects or critical reflection. One can rephrase this classification of software art—as focused either on code as formal instructions or on cultural reflection—as a manifestation of formalism versus culturalism. In his essay "Concepts, Notations, Software, Art," Florian Cramer also suggests this distinction with regard to software art: "a cultural, politically coded construct" versus a focus on "the formal poetics and aesthetics of software code and individual subjectivity expressed in algorithms."[14] Applying the formalism versus culturalism distinction to the information art projects discussed earlier, one could propose that Kac's Genesis offers cultural reflections on biotechnology and belief systems. As opposed to Brucker-Cohen's *Police State*, which explores surveillance and political aspects, Napier's Black and White software is a mostly formally and aesthetically

oriented project (as many other data visualizations). Legrady's projects would also be culturally focused, be it in the interpretation of imagery or the personal value of objects. The projects of etoy, mentioned in the beginning, can be seen as a cultural investigation of the "products" of information society.

It is important to note that, as conceptual art, information arts cannot be evaluated in terms of classical standards of "visual beauty" since they may take the form of a database that concentrates on its own structure and underlying "politics" rather than the visual aspects of its contents. As Cramer puts it, the focus on the purely perceptual aesthetics of art "is a straight continuation of romanticist philosophy and its privileging of aisthesis (perception) over poeisis (construction), cheapened into a restrained concept of art as only that what is tactile, audible, and visible."[15] The range of information art projects combines both aspects and raises issues about the status of representation in an information society, which has been much discussed. If one defines representation as a "likeness" or image of an external referent (an "object" or "scene" in the broadest sense), information arts in general ultimately represent data. One could draw the conclusion that we are facing a major transformation of the status of representation itself, which becomes a process that involves data processing and is concerned at least as much with algorithmic rules and conceptual aspects as visual, textual, and acoustic manifestations.

INFORMATION ARTS IN THE MUSEUM

Over the decades, there have been a number of digital and media art exhibitions that featured information arts and some galleries have consistently presented it, but shows in an institutional context have mostly taken place at media centers and museums such as InterCommunication Center in Tokyo or Zentrum für Kultur und Medien (Center for Culture and Media) in Karlsruhe, Germany, and the art mostly found its exhibition venues under the umbrella of conferences, festivals, and symposia devoted to art and technology, among them the Ars Electronica Festival (Linz, Austria), the art show of the U.S.-based Special Interest Group for Computer Graphics and Interactive Techniques conference and ISEA International (founded in the Netherlands) and festivals such as European Media Art Festival (Osnabrück, Germany), Dutch Electronic Art Festival, Next Five Minutes (Netherlands), and Transmediale (Berlin, Germany). Traditional art institutions so far have not played a major role in the production and development of information art projects, which have been supported mostly by the research labs of educational institutions or media centers, such as V2 in the Netherlands or the Banff New Media Institute in Canada.

Information arts that do not take the form of more traditional media still pose quite a few challenges to the traditional art world, ranging from presentation to collection and preservation. Digital print, photography, and sculpture represent the object-oriented work that museums are equipped for, but time-based, interactive works of information art raise numerous issues. These issues to a large extent are not medium specific but apply to any time-based and interactive work, be it a video, a performance, or a robotic sculpture. Information art often requires audience engagement and does not reveal its content at a glance. The basic rule of museums, "Please do not touch the art," suddenly does not apply anymore and large segments of the audience are still hesitant to physically engage with artwork. Works of information art can be expensive to show and ideally require consistent maintenance. Museum buildings are mostly based on the "white cube" model rather than completely wired and equipped with flexible presentation systems. Information arts make us reconsider our traditional notions of space and architecture and often require the translation of information architecture or characteristics of virtual spaces into physical space. Information arts relying on new technologies ideally require a parallel, distributed, living information space that is open to artistic interference—a space for exchange, collaborative creation, and presentation that is transparent and flexible.

The specific challenges that a digital work of information art poses are dependent on the form it takes, be it a (networked) interactive installation, an online data visualization, a work involving mobile devices, or an immersive virtual reality piece. While some information art projects can be installed according to specified parameters (such as height, width, and defined lighting requirements), the variability and modularity inherent to the digital medium often means that a work can be shown in very different ways and has to be reconfigured for a specific space. Variability entails a fluent transition between the different manifestations that information art can take: The same work might be shown, for example, as an installation, projection, or kiosk setup.

Information art that has been created for the Internet tends to be particularly challenging to show within a gallery. Internet art has been created to be seen by anyone, anywhere, and anytime (provided one has access to the Internet) and doesn't need a museum to be presented or introduced to the public. In the online world, the branding of the physical gallery and museum does not necessarily function as a signifier of status. However, physical art spaces such as galleries, museums, and festivals also play an important role when it comes to net-based art in that they provide context for the work, chronicle its developments, assist in its preservation, and expand its audience. Models for presenting Internet art in an institutional context have been widely discussed.[16] Internet art often requires a relatively private engagement over a longer period of time, and in order to create an environment for this experience, institutions have often presented the art in

a separate area of a public space, which raised the criticism of "ghettoization." The setup in a separate "lounge area" has the advantage of inviting people to spend more time with a piece but prevents that the art can be seen in the context of more traditional media and enter into a dialogue with them.

Ultimately, the physical environment should be defined by what a work of information art requires, and it is important to establish a connection between the physical space and the respective information architecture.

The collection of digitally based information art projects is yet another topic that has been hotly debated. The value of art is—at least when it comes to traditional models of the art world—inextricably connected to its economic value. However, the notion of the original and the scarcity-equals-value model do not necessarily work for information art, which could consist of a set of instructions or a dynamic process. Collecting is less problematic in the case of digital installations, which ultimately are objects, or software art (which sometimes comes with custom hardware), which can be sold as a limited edition as photography or video. Information art can also draw on precedents in the realm of conceptual art; instruction-based works such as Sol LeWitt's wall drawings have been collected by major museums. In the case of Internet art, the hosting of the source code on the respective museum's server constitutes a form of ownership. As opposed to traditional artworks, net projects are on view permanently and not only when the museum decides to mount them in a gallery.

The process of collecting art entails the responsibility of maintaining it, which is one of the biggest challenges posed by information art projects involving new technologies. The process-oriented nature of many of these works makes it evident that preserving the art requires new models and criteria for documentation and preservation. The main strategies for preservation are storage, emulation, and migration. Storage means the archiving of software and hardware as it continues to be developed, an obviously not very elegant solution that quickly requires large storage facilities. Emulation is the use of software for imitating the original version of a project by "re-creating" the software or operating systems that the project requires, and migration means an upgrade to the next version of hardware/software.[17] Worldwide, numerous preservation initiatives are creating standards for preserving media works that involve new technologies. Among them are the Variable Media Network[18]—a consortium project by the University of California Berkeley Art Museum and Pacific Film Archive, the University of Maine, the Solomon R. Guggenheim Museum, Franklin Furnace Archive, and Rhizome.org, among others—and International Network for the Conservation of Contemporary Art.[19] These initiatives are developing vocabulary for catalog records, standards that allow institutions to exchange the metadata gathered for these records, and tools (such as database systems) for the cataloging of process-oriented art. Among these tools is the "Variable Media Questionnaire," which enables artists and museum and media consultants to identify artist-approved strategies for preserving artwork and to define the behaviors of artworks in a media-independent way. Describing artworks according to categories that are not specific to any particular medium but allow to establish a common ground beyond materiality seems to be particularly relevant for approaching the conservation of information arts, which are not bound to any specific medium.

CONCLUSION

Cultural developments in the late twentieth century have produced information societies that make it imperative for artists to be aware of or engage with changing modes of cultural production. The expansion of digital technologies and their impact on our lives and cultures will induce the creation of even more data sets, information, and research and consequentially more information artworks reflecting and critically engaging with this cultural impact. The ways in which artists encode and transform data will presumably evolve along with the latest research and technologies for data processing. The methods and platforms that artworks employ to give information in physical and visual form will also develop along with research and technologies. The pervasiveness of mobile technologies has already led to a proliferation of artwork using networked mobile devices.

The terminology for art forms involving new technologies has always been fluid and gone through numerous changes over the past few decades. Labels aside, the artistic practice that involves information circulating through research, science, technologies, and media distribution systems is certainly here to stay and will grow. Most likely information arts will always be an evolving field and exist in multiple contexts, supported and presented by art and technology centers, research and development labs, and hopefully traditional art institutions.

REFERENCES

1. Wilson, S. *Information Arts*; The MIT Press: Cambridge, MA, 2002.
2. http://yeslab.org/projects; https://www.youtube.com/watch?v=I1vhS26GoEY.
3. https://en.wikipedia.org/wiki/Etoy.
4. Rowthorn, R.; Ramaswamy, R. *Deindustrialization—Its Causes and Implications*; International Monetary Fund: Washington, DC, 1997.
5. https://www.merriam-webster.com/dictionary/information.
6. https://www.merriam-webster.com/dictionary/data.
7. Sholle, D. What Is Information?. In *Democracy and New Media*; Jenkins, H., Thorburn, D., Eds.; The MIT Press: Cambridge, 2004; 347.
8. Sholle, D. What Is Information?. In *Democracy and New Media*; Jenkins, H., Thorburn, D, Eds.; The MIT Press: Cambridge, 2004; 355.
9. Ward, A.; McLean, A.; Cox, G. *The Aesthetics of Generative Code*; http://www.generative.net/papers/aesthetics/ (accessed August 31, 2007).
10. Eduardo, K. *Genesis*; http://www.ekac.org/genesis.html (accessed August 31, 2007).
11. Merriam Webster Online Dictionary. https://www.merriam-webster.com/dictionary/information.
12. http://www.mat.ucsb.edu/g.legrady/glWeb/Projects/pfom2/pfom2.html.
13. http://r-s-g.org/carnivore/.
14. Cramer, F. Concepts, Notations, Software, Art, 2002, http://www.netzliteratur.net/cramer/concepts_notations_software_art.html.
15. http://www.netzliteratur.net/cramer/concepts_notations_software_art.html.
16. Krysa, J. Ed., *Curating Immateriality—The Work of the Curator in the Age of Network Systems*; Autonomedia: New York, 2006.
17. Solomon, R. *Guggenheim Museum*; March 19–May 16 2004, http://www.variablemedia.net/e/seeingdouble/index.html, (accessed August 31, 2007).
18. The Variable Media Network. http://www.variablemedia.net.
19. International Network for the Conservation of Contemporary Art. http://www.incca.org.

Information Behavior

Marcia J. Bates
Department of Information Studies, Graduate School of Education and Information Studies,
University of California, Los Angeles (UCLA), Los Angeles, California, U.S.A.

Abstract

"Information behavior" is the currently preferred term used to describe the many ways in which human beings interact with information, in particular, the ways in which people seek and utilize information. The broad history of research on information-seeking behavior over the last 50–60 years is reviewed, major landmarks are identified, and current directions in research are discussed.

INTRODUCTION

"Information behavior" is the currently preferred term used to describe the many ways in which human beings interact with information, in particular, the ways in which people seek and utilize information. Information behavior is also the term of art used in library and information science to refer to a subdiscipline that engages in a wide range of types of research conducted in order to understand the human relationship to information.

Interest in this area developed out of several streams. Librarians wanted to understand library users better, government agencies wanted to understand how scientists and engineers used technical information in order to promote more rapid uptake of new research results, and social scientists generally were interested in the social uses of information in a variety of senses. In more recent years, social studies of information technology and social informatics have contributed to this area as well. Within library and information science, these various streams of research are drawn on for what they can contribute to a richer understanding of information behavior.

INFORMATION

What, then, is information? Here, rather than review the many senses in which this term has been interpreted in the field (see ELIS entry "Information"), we will rely on a sense of the term that is an extended understanding of the concept as used in general conversation. We all recognize that people search for information on, say, the history of a small town, the population of Turkey, or how to do foreign exchange trading online. All these examples make a reasonable match with the generally understood sense of information as being factual, statistical, and/or procedural.

"Information," however, is used in a broader sense as well in the world of information behavior research. The term is generally assumed to cover all instances where people interact with their environment in any such way that leaves some impression on them—that is, adds or changes their knowledge store. These impressions can include the emotional changes that result from reading a novel or learning that one's friend is ill. These changes can also reflect complex interactions where information combines with preexisting knowledge to make new understandings or enables the individual to deduce or induce new thoughts and ideas. As the Hans Christian Andersen tale suggested, the ugly ducking did not realize that he was a swan until he came in contact with swans, saw his reflection in water, and figured out that he was himself a swan, too.[1]

These information interactions can also leave a negative impact—one may ignore, deny, or reject information.[2] (See also an excellent early analysis of relations to information by Atkin.[3]) One may also simply discover that nothing has changed—the university admissions letter still has not come in the mail. This negative news is, of course, informative in its own way, just as a person who has ignored information has often, in some way or other, nonetheless absorbed it. In fact, probably the largest amount of all information taken in by human beings is that received passively—simply through being aware—that is absorbed in the context of daily living.[4]

Is this not a very broad understanding of information behavior? Indeed, does it not cover all interactions people have with their environment? Bates has argued:

In comparison to other social and behavioral science fields, we are always looking for the red thread of information in the social texture of people's lives. When we study people we do so with the purpose of understanding information creation, seeking, and use. We do not just study people in general. ... In communications research, a cousin to our field, the emphasis is on the communication process and its effects on people; in information science we study that process *in service of information transfer*.[5]

Encyclopedia of Library and Information Sciences, Fourth Edition DOI: 10.1081/E-EISA-120053335

Bates goes on to provide a specific example:

> ... [T]here are social scientists today who are observing people doing collaborative work through new types of networked systems in the field of computer-supported cooperative work (CSCW). The sociologist or social psychologist identifies and describes the network of relationships and the social hierarchy that develops under these circumstances. ...

> The information scientist, on the other hand, follows the information .... That's the red thread in the social tapestry. When we look at that social hierarchy, we are not interested in the hierarchy per se, but, rather, we ask how it impedes or promotes the transfer of information. We ask what kinds of information people prefer to communicate through this or that new channel of information technology. We always follow the information.[5]

Thus, the study of information behavior can cast a very wide net, looking into both individual interactions and large-scale complex group and societal interactions with information. Indeed, as we shall see, the variety of contexts in which information behavior has been studied demonstrates this breadth. But information behavior research is not communication, psychology, education, sociology, or social impacts of technology research, though all those disciplines may find the work interesting to discover. Rather, information behavior research actually studies—and largely limits itself to—information-related behavior.

HISTORY OF INFORMATION BEHAVIOR RESEARCH

From the earliest days, librarianship in the United States had a commitment to care about and serve the users of libraries. In the founding year of American professional librarianship, 1876, Samuel Green wrote to encourage librarians to "mingle freely" with the library's users "and help them in every way."[6] In the mid-twentieth century, the great Indian librarian, S.R. Ranganathan, promulgated his Five Laws of Librarianship, which were very much oriented to the library user:

1. Books are for use.
2. Every reader, his book.
3. Every book its reader.
4. Save the time of the reader.
5. The library is a growing organism.[7]

However, for many decades that commitment remained largely on the plane of values and had little other than anecdotal data upon which to develop library services. In the 1930s, the Graduate Library School at the University of Chicago[8] introduced the first doctoral degree in library science in the United States. Sophisticated social science

researchers, such as Douglas Waples and Bernard Berelson, brought their skills to the field. Waples[9] did research on reader preferences, and Berelson, among other things, produced a compendium of results from dozens of studies on public library use.[10,11]

The experiences associated with the operation of "Big Science" during World War II—major projects such as the development of the atom bomb—led government leaders to see the advantages in improving the distribution and transfer of information on new discoveries to other scientists and engineers. Major conferences on scientific information, in 1948 and 1959, led to a substantial amount of money being invested during the 1950s and 1960s in research on how scientists gathered and used information in their research work. Major example publications were the proceedings of the two science information conferences.[12,13] The 21-report series "Project on Scientific Information Exchange in Psychology" from the American Psychological Association,[14] and the work of Garvey et al. on several disciplines.[15,16] Other influential early works include publications by Derek de Solla Price,[17,18] Diana Crane,[19] and A.J. Meadows.[20] (Note: In order to keep this entry's long bibliography from being even longer, referenced items are often only a sample of a person's work, and when a series of articles comes out from a project, generally only the last article in the series is referenced.)

Early on, studies on information behavior were called "use studies."[21] studies of "information seeking and gathering," or studies of "information needs and uses."[22] Gradually, the term "information-seeking research" was used to include all kinds of research on people's interaction with information.

More recently, however, some researchers came to feel that "information seeking" suggested only explicit efforts to locate information and did not include the many other ways people and information interacted. In the 1990s, the term "information behavior" came into wide use to replace "information seeking." The Old Guard objected that the phrase is a non sequitur—information does not "behave"—but, they lost out, and "information behavior" remains the most commonly used term today.

During the 1960s, in particular, generous funding was available in the United States for social science research, and a great deal of knowledge, based on large, well-designed studies, was developed regarding the social aspects of scientific communication and information use.[23–25] Important studies were also produced on information use and library use by the general public.[26–29] Focus in the larger society during the 1960s and 1970s on identity politics of race, gender, sexual orientation, and the economically underprivileged also led to research attention being directed to information seeking of the corresponding population groups.

In the late 1960s and early 1970s, this research began to be taught in library and information educational programs in North America.[30] As scientists had been studied according to their disciplines—physics, biology, etc.—and many members of the general public had been studied by their social identities—the poor, the elderly, etc.—there was a tendency to study information-related behavior by looking at groups of these sorts. For example, an invited conference on "information service needs of the nation" was funded by the U.S. National Commission on Libraries and Information Science in 1973. Presentations were structured in a parallel format to address the needs of a number of groups, including people working in science, agriculture, business, labor, biomedicine, the arts, social services, as well as children, the geographically remote, the economically and socially deprived, the institutionalized, and the mentally and physically handicapped, among others.[31]

After the earlier attention to the natural sciences, during the 1970s research attention turned to information transfer in the social sciences. Grant funding in the United States receded, and pride of place went to Great Britain, where several researchers engaged in creative and revealing research on information seeking and use in the social sciences.[32–34]

Finally, in the 1980s and 1990s the underfunded humanities at last got their due,[35–38] particularly with the support of large institutions such as the J. Paul Getty Trust.[39] In the 1990s, the needs of interdisciplinary and area studies researchers were addressed.[40] See, especially, Carole Palmer, as Issue Editor, of an issue of *Library Trends* on interdisciplinary information seeking,[41] as well as her subsequent book.[42]

Over the decades, varying amounts of information behavior research has been done in various professional contexts as well, including the health sciences,[43] law,[44] and business.[45] Among the professions, it is almost certainly the health sciences where the largest body of information behavior research has been done—probably due to abundant funding—while the education profession, despite the importance of information seeking for teachers, seems, mysteriously, to have drawn very little attention.[46,47]

In the 2000s, Kari and Hartel made a persuasive case for studying the information behavior of people engaged in activities aimed at fulfillment and self-realization, and their own research provided examples of what could be learned along this line.[48] Caidi, Allard, and Quirke review another recently growing area of research: immigrant information seeking and use.[49]

The sweeping impact of use of the Internet and of mobile devices has increasingly dominated the working and living of all the groups reviewed earlier. Recent extensive studies include Antonijevic and Cahoy's on scholars' information practices,[50] Mizrachi and Bates[51] on the practices of undergraduate college students, and Beheshti and Large's book on current uses by children and teens.[52]

Throughout the years, a number of models have been proposed to characterize various aspects of information behavior. Paisley beautifully characterized the subjective world of the scientist as constituting a series of contexts—local work environment, research specialty, discipline, larger cultural and political world, etc.[24] In 1981, Tom Wilson described information seeking in general in a model[53] that was subsequently very widely used and also reviewed a wide range of information behavior models in 1999.[54] Belkin et al. propounded the concept of "anomalous state of knowledge," or ASK,[55] as characterizing many information needs. That is to say, they argued that the information need is often complex and requires an extensive description to cover all the factors really at play in people's requests. Kuhlthau's Information Search Process model, based on extensive research, demonstrated how intricately the conceptualization of a paper or project was bound up with confusions and problems in searching for information.[56] Bates' "berrypicking," that is, picking up a bit of knowledge here and a bit of knowledge there, was seen to be an appropriate description of much of human searching to meet information needs,[57] in contrast to the previous generally assumed simple query that could be answered by a single retrieval from just one database.

Though extensive research on information seeking inside and outside of library and information science had been going on since the 1950s, it was an article by Dervin and Nilan in 1986,[58] however, that seemed to provide the impetus for a great increase in interest in the subject in library and information science. The authors articulated the value of placing the user/searcher at the center of research, and paying close attention to the internal motivations and needs of the information seeker. From a minority interest of a relatively few people, information behavior research exploded in LIS after that article appeared, and doctoral students flocked to the subject area. For example, the number of articles dubbed "Use studies," the standard term used in Wilson Web's article database *Library Literature and Information Full Text*, doubled per year in the 5 years between 1985 and 1990—from 76 to 155—while in the subsequent 18 years, the annual number has gone up by less than 60% to 245 in 2008 (author's database search). (Of course, these results could be artifacts of the publisher's indexing practices, and a fuller exploration would be needed to verify this conclusion.)

In particular, Dervin's conception of "sensemaking," the effort of people to make sense of many aspects of their lives through information seeking and use, has been a dominating force in recent research on information behavior.[59]

Dervin dismissed prior studies on grounds that "the studies assumed that the information brick was being thrown into the empty bucket"—that is, into the user of information.[60] In one blow, this clever metaphor both characterized and caricatured much of the more classically empirical scientific approaches to research on information behavior and gave qualitative research techniques and philosophies a boost. Dervin's "brick" image was unfair to the many researchers who did not take a simplistic view of information transfer, including many of the people mentioned in this article to this point.[61] However, her emphasis on the importance of sense-making in motivating information seeking legitimated the subsequent emphasis on qualitative techniques in the field and enlarged the perspective of the whole subdiscipline of information behavior.

Indeed, over the years, increasing dissatisfaction was expressed by some researchers toward the prior orientation either to the individual seeking information or to studying the tendencies and preferences of large social groups, such as physicists or older people. These researchers sought to expand information behavior research, drawing on several theoretical paradigms of interest in the social sciences, such as social constructivism, social constructionism, and ethnographic techniques.[62]

The surest sign of this broader interest came in the form of the "Information Seeking in Context (ISIC)" conference that came to be presented every other year, mostly in Europe, beginning in 1996.[63] Conference attendees have sought to study information behavior in a way that goes beyond traditional research designs. They argue that context must be understood in a much fuller sense; they argue for rich, detailed, qualitative study of specific situations and contexts in order to understand the very nuanced ways in which people might receive and shape information.

They draw upon many different information-related theories and models,[64] as well as on the many varieties of metatheoretical and philosophical perspectives that have become popular in the social sciences and humanities.[65] See, as examples of these newer approaches, Ellis' grounded theory approach,[66] Talja's discourse analysis of the culture of music in relation to libraries,[67] Xu's application of activity theory to interactive information retrieval,[68] Reddy and Jansen's ethnographic study of collaborative information behavior in healthcare,[69] Limberg's[70] and Ford's[71,72] use of educational theory, and Srinivasan and Pyati's critical reexamination of information environments for diasporic groups.[73]

At the same time, research drawing on other, more classically scientific and engineering methodologies did not disappear. See Fidel and Pejtersen's use of the Cognitive Work Analysis Framework,[74,75] Sandstrom and Sandstrom's analysis of the methods of scientific anthropology as applied in library and information science,[76] Nicholas et al.'s study of online information seeking through transaction log analysis,[77] and even Bates' use of biological and evolutionary concepts in her recent work on information[78] and browsing.[79]

Perhaps the greatest sign of maturity of the field of information behavior research came with the publication—at last!—of the first book comprehensively addressing information seeking, by Donald Case, in 2002, third edition in 2012.[80]

The popularity of the ISIC conferences demonstrates the recent efflorescence of qualitative information behavior research beyond the borders of the (sometimes self-absorbed) research culture of the United States. Scholars from the United Kingdom (Tom Wilson, David Ellis, Nigel Ford, Elizabeth Davenport), Ireland (Crystal Fulton), Scandinavia (Louise Limberg, Olof Sundin, Annelise Mark Pejtersen), and Finland (Pertti Vakkari, Reijo Savolainen, Sanna Talja, Jannica Heinström) have presented and published at ISIC and elsewhere. Australian (Kirsty Williamson, Theresa Anderson) and Canadian researchers (Heidi Julien, Karen Fisher, Gloria Leckie, Lynne McKechnie, Pam McKenzie, Roma Harris, Chun Wei Choo) have also been very active in recent years.

Recently, Savolainen may have marked the beginning of a new phase in information research when he urged that the qualitative research on information behavior be called instead the study of "information practice."[81] He argued that the concept of "information behavior" is primarily associated with the cognitive viewpoint, while "information practice is mainly inspired by the ideas of social constructivism."[81]

> The concepts of information behavior and information practice both seem to refer to the ways in which people "deal with information." The major difference is that within the discourse on information behavior, the 'dealing with information' is primarily seen to be triggered by needs and motives, while the discourse on information practice accentuates the continuity and habitualization of activities affected and shaped by social and cultural factors ....[82]

More recently, Huizing and Cavanagh have enlarged and systematized the theory and methodology of research on information practice.[83] Their lucid exposition of this methodology is a good fit for the nature of information behavior study. They break down the traditional (and tired) contrast between the subjective and objective, they give physical objects the important role they should have in any theory of people and information, and they identify the dynamic nature of information seeking, without dissolving the study of it into confusing and nongeneralizable sets of very short-term and local acts. Huizing and Cavanagh's approach provides what is perhaps the best guiding philosophy at this time for further information behavior research.

In the last several years, there has also been a very active Special Interest Group on Information Behavior, founded by Barbara Wildemuth and Karen Fisher, among others, in the American Society for Information Science and Technology, which has held a number of preconferences and conference sessions, and offered awards for research in the area.

To follow the development of the research in this area, one can read the several chapters on the subject, starting with Menzel's in 1966[22] and ending with Fisher and Julien's in 2009,[84] which appeared periodically in the *Annual Review of Information Science and Technology.* (That review publication has now been subsumed within the *Journal of the Association for Information Science and Technology.*)

INFORMATION SEARCHING VERSUS INFORMATION SEEKING

This discussion addressed research on how people interact with information, how and when they seek information, and what uses they make of it. But it should be understood that throughout this period of time a parallel body of research and practical application was continuing that addressed the specifics of *the act of searching itself.* That is, in working with paper and online resources, many problems were encountered and skills needed to succeed in the specific acts associated with locating information in a paper or online resource. Bates' articles on information-searching tactics and search techniques[85,86] promoted greater attention to the complexities of identifying sources and working one's way through resources to locate the desired information. A long line of research followed that addressed both search success and desirable design features in information systems to promote ease of use[87–91] (See also ELIS entry "Information searching and search models."). Even browsing, normally seen as the most unstructured method of information searching, came in for considerable attention.[79,92,93]

ROLE OF TECHNOLOGY IN INFORMATION BEHAVIOR RESEARCH

In order to simplify the narrative line, the aforementioned discussion made little mention of the role of technology in information seeking and research on information seeking. But, in fact, the extraordinary changes in information technology (IT) over the last 50–60 years have meant that a great deal of information behavior research has also been concerned with impacts of and reactions to the kinds of interactions people experience when using new technologies for finding and communicating information.

Focus on impacts of, and roles of, IT in information behavior has been intertwined to a greater and lesser extent with the information behavior research over these decades. Early studies took a fairly stable, largely paper-based environment for granted. Indeed, Garvey's research[23] made salient, perhaps for the first time for many readers of his work, the huge, complex scientific publication cycle, from early tentative verbal presentation at talks all the way through conference presentations,

summary reports, journal publication, annual reviews, and, finally, incorporation of the scientific results into the established canon in textbooks.

But consciousness of the complexity of the production and publication of science was soon joined by efforts to improve, especially to speed up, the collection, storage, organization, and dissemination of that information.

Indeed, the entire discipline of information science has, in one sense, been the story of the successive absorption of a long series of IT innovations, followed, in each case, by research on the impacts of those innovations, and efforts to improve access to information through optimal design of those innovations. With the excitement generated by each new technology, the relatively stable underlying human behaviors and reactions were sometimes forgotten, and the new technology instead seen as the source of a totally new information-seeking landscape. One thing we now know, however, after a lot of research on those successive waves of new technology, is that underlying human propensities with regard to information emerge again and again as each new technology becomes familiar and its use second nature. Often, in the end, the new technologies offer speed and ease of use, while otherwise replicating previous social structures and interactions.

We know, for example, that people are willing to commit very little energy and effort to seeking information, in contrast, say, to seeking a fortune, a family, or a reputation. In fact, the truly explosive popularity of the World Wide Web as an information source may be due to the fact that the level of effort the searcher must engage in to find an answer to a question on the Web is at last so very little as to slip in under that minimal level of (least) effort that feels "natural" in information seeking. Most of the information that people eagerly seek online was once available in their local public or academic library, but the effort required to locate that information was seen as excessive in the vast majority of cases.

In the rest of this section, we will follow several IT innovations and consider their impact on information behavior research.

The first major technology in modern times to affect information seeking was the computer. Initially, its use for library information systems was limited—computers were used to capture machine-readable versions of library catalog records ("MARC" records), which, in turn, enabled the publication of computer-produced print-on-paper book catalogs. This was followed, in short succession, by so-called "COM cats," that is, computer output microfiche catalogs, which could update book catalogs between publications of paper editions.[94]

It will be forgotten today that in the age of card catalogs, while in one library, one could not access the catalog of any other branch of the academic or public library, or of any other library, for that matter. In academic libraries, a comprehensive copy of all the materials on campus was generally available only in the main library.

Disseminating multiple copies of the full set of library records through book catalogs and COM cats in branch libraries was a significant, time-saving innovation.

These catalog innovations during the late 1960s and 1970s were followed by a true revolution in catalog accessibility—the online catalog, which was developed in the early 1980s. These constituted the first widely available end user information search systems, and much was learned about how untrained people did and did not succeed in this form of online searching.[95,96]

For a variety of reasons, the card catalog structure could not be simply translated into online form. Questions of redesign of catalog access in the new context, and the development of new and faster system designs to improve access occupied many in LIS research over the next 10–15 years.[97–99] (See also ELIS entry "Online catalog subject searching.")

In the meantime, (at least) four other overlapping information-related revolutions were occupying the field as well. The first revolution occurred in the area of information retrieval, where various forms of automatic indexing and retrieval were experimented with over decades from the 1950s forward, gradually improving the speed and effectiveness of both retrieval and ranking algorithms.[100,101] In the 1990s, search engines, such as Alta Vista and Google, drew upon these retrieval techniques to design their Web systems.

Second, in the early 1970s, online database searching was made practicable through searching against large databases on "dumb" (typewriter-like) terminals receiving and sending data over telephone wires. "Online searching" as then understood, and as then implemented by database vendors, was a complex skill that required considerable training to do well. Teaching these skills became an important part of LIS education and drew a lot of research interest as well. That type of searching required a mix of gifts that not everyone has, and numerous studies of online searching behavior resulted.[88,102,103]

The third revolution was the development of the Internet and World Wide Web, which enabled access to information all over the world from anywhere in the world. We are still working through the many impacts and implications of this capability for all prior information technologies and sources of information.[104–106]

The fourth revolution occurred with the widespread interest in creating digital libraries of all manner of textual and image material—and sometimes online portals to access those resources. The Digital Libraries Initiative in the 1990s marked the moment when, at last, truly substantial amounts of research money entered the information science field. Ann Bishop and colleagues addressed at book length the sociotechnical factors of digital library use.[107] The new capability of storing and easily accessing previously unimaginably large bodies of information in digital libraries led to innovative experiments in the storage and use of primary resources materials.

Example studies are those of children using primary archival materials,[108] uses of texts in the field of classics in a digital library,[109] and use of a medical portal.[110]

During the 1970s to the present, many studies of information behavior involved, to a greater or lesser extent, research on people's use of and success with, these innovations in information access. On the whole, more behavioral research was done in the areas of online catalogs and online database searching than in information retrieval. For a long time, IR researchers were not particularly receptive to, or interested in, the human side of the equation, though in the 1990s they came to realize that people needed attention, too, in the overall effort to improve retrieval. See, for example, the contrasting emphases in the two entries in this encyclopedia by Salton ("SMART System: 1961–1976") and Järvelin and Ingwersen ("User-oriented and cognitive models of information retrieval").

With the development of frequent interaction with microcomputers in the early 1980s, the already-thriving field of human–computer interaction research (HCI) exploded and became a still larger field. HCI paid little attention to LIS research, however, and LIS paid little attention to HCI research, probably to the detriment of both fields. However, there may have been good reasons for this mutual indifference. The specific circumstances of needing and seeking information are not well understood, for the most part, outside of LIS, and required the focused attention of LIS researchers. At the same time, HCI researchers were working to discover general principles applicable to all online and computer access, and therefore tended to ignore the distinctive features of various "application" fields, including information seeking. (See ELIS article "Human–computer interaction for information retrieval.") Perhaps the best blend of information science and HCI approaches to search user interfaces can be found in Hearst.[111]

In this encyclopedia, Diane Nahl's two articles on early and recent "User-centered design," as well as articles by Elaine Toms ("User-centered design of information systems") and Judith Weedman ("Design science in the information sciences") address, in much greater detail, the efforts and results in this area at the intersection of information technology and the study of information behavior.

RANGE OF TOPICS OF INFORMATION BEHAVIOR RESEARCH

What have we learned over the years from the study of information-seeking behavior? This is a hard question to answer briefly, to put it mildly, but a description of the sequence of research topics of interest over the years may give a hint of the growing understanding over time of the human relationship with information. What follows is a mere sampling.

In the 1940s and 1950s, information seeking and gathering tended to be viewed implicitly as the study of the use of various forms of literature—books, journals, handbooks, etc.—and of various types of institutions and their services. How many books were circulated, how many reference questions were asked, how many people of what economic strata used the public library, and so on (see Berelson[10]).

In the 1960s and beyond, studies of information seeking and use by the general public opened out the research to incorporate many sources of information, of which the library was only one.[27,112] The first surprise was to discover how much information—in both personal and professional contexts—people got from friends and colleagues. In a study looking at how scientists' learned of things serendipitously, Menzel found that fellow scientists were immensely important in that process.[113] In fact, in a large number of studies, the human preference to get information from other people was soundly demonstrated.

From early on, the dominance of the "principle of least effort" in human information seeking was demonstrated over and over.[25] It may not seem surprising that people try to minimize effort in finding information, but the research demonstrated that ease of access and ease of use mattered more to people than the quality of the information they found. People have a (sometimes unjustified) belief in their ability to filter the good and valid information from the faulty, hence their tendency to undersearch to find the highest quality information available.

Further, information seeking is often quite unselfconscious. People are trying to solve problems in their lives, not "seek information." Activities that involve information seeking are seldom differentiated from the other actions taken to solve problems. Good research design for the study of information seeking *must* recognize this reality; asking people what they have done lately in the way of information seeking is therefore not the way to get data with high internal validity, as a rule. Dervin has made this point repeatedly and insightfully. For a prime example of her research technique, see Dervin.[114]

Thus, as a rule, people—even including Ph.D. scholars—develop what search skills they have incidentally to their primary efforts at research or problem-solving and often fail to develop a conscious repertoire of search skills and techniques to help them over difficult stages. Particularly among college students, discomfort regarding library research has been found to be severe enough to merit the term "library anxiety," and a number of studies have been done on this topic (see ELIS entry "Library anxiety"). Along with the evidence of student difficulties with libraries, a large literature has developed on the goals and techniques of teaching "information literacy," that is, the capability of finding and effectively evaluating desired information (see ELIS entries "Information literacy" and "Information literacy instruction"). In sum,

people often vastly underutilize available resources and are often quite inefficient in finding what they do find.

In the study of various academic disciplines, the close attention in the 1960s to the rich complexity of the culture of science enabled a subtler analysis of the information seeking in all the academic disciplines studied from the 1970s to the present time. See, for example, Patrick Wilson on the concept of "cognitive authority,"[115] Julie Hurd on implications of information use patterns for library design,[116] Paisley on "information and work,"[117] Robert Taylor on "information use environments,"[118] Cronin on invisible colleges (i.e., informal groups of researchers with shared interests),[119] the model by Leckie et al. of information seeking in the professions,[120] and Budd[121] and Bates[122] comparing the cultures of science and humanities. In the understudied area of archival resources, Barbara Orbach[123] and Wendy Duff and Catherine Johnson[124] have provided insightful descriptions of the use of historical archival materials.

During the 1980s and 1990s, several researchers deepened the understanding of various aspects of information behavior by exploring questions and areas previously not as well understood. Elfreda Chatman looked at the information environments of janitors, women in a retirement home, and prisoners.[125–127] Cheryl Metoyer-Duran applied the concept of gatekeeping to five minority groups in Southern California and developed sophisticated (and sometimes counterintuitive) understandings about information flow within minority communities, and between them and the larger society.[128] The challenge of studying unconventional groups and domains even extended to abused women[129] and abused children.[130]

Carol Kuhlthau is another researcher who has had very wide influence in the information behavior world. She developed a model of student information seeking, which she refined over several studies that are themselves models of the art of research. Her model runs counter to many assumptions in both education and library and information science about how people tackle researching a paper or project, and how that experience can be substantially improved over past approaches.[131] Specifically, she discovered that the combined process of researching and writing a paper is complex and difficult for most people—indeed, the library research is inextricably bound with the understanding and gradual formulation of the thesis of the paper. Consequently, the simple idea of "picking a topic," like picking an apple off a tree, then going to research it in the library, is not how the process reasonably can or should be expected to proceed. Yet generations of teachers and professors have left students floundering and frustrated as they moved, essentially without guidance, through this core process in paper-writing.

David Ellis' empirically based model of common actions associated with scholarly information seeking[132] has also been influential, spurring several follow-on studies to test for similar activities in the work of people in other circumstances. And, of course, Brenda Dervin's concept of "sensemaking" as a motivation for information seeking constituted the underlying model for much information behavior research.[60]

In the 1990s and 2000s, along with the growth of the ISIC community, researchers expanded their look at information behavior by incorporating the whole environment—physical, social, and technological—in the study of people's interactions with information. Social context and social situation were recognized as essential to the understanding of information seeking.[133,134] Karen Fisher (nee Pettigrew) developed the concept of "information grounds"—the joint creation of social environments by people in which to share conversation and information.[135] Disciplinary examples of these rich analyses include science[42] and business.[136] As noted earlier, the study of "information practice," as a shaping paradigm for information behavior research, has emerged strongly in the twenty-first century.[83]

Several recent studies have demonstrated particularly creative approaches to the study of children's information seeking, traditionally an underpopulated area of research. Virginia Walter demonstrated that children's information needs were immense and were in no way limited to requests made of school librarians![137] Joanne Silverstein studied unconventional forms of information use,[138] and Ciaran Trace studied informal information creation and use by children.[139] Research on the "information behavior of a new generation" is discussed in the recent book edited by Beheshti and Large.[52]

During recent decades, a more sophisticated understanding has also developed of information genres and the ways they are shaped by practice. In a particularly elegant study, Kling and McKim showed how preexisting social information practices shaped the design of post-Web online information support in three scientific disciplines.[140] Peiling Wang studied at the micro level how scientists actually make use of and subsequently cite other literature in the course of their research.[141] Ann Bishop[142] and Lisa Covi[143] studied closely the interactions between people and the structure and genres of information.

CONCLUSIONS

Information behavior research has grown immensely from its scattered beginnings earlier in the twentieth century. We now have a much deeper and less simplistic understanding of how people interact with information. We understand information behavior better within social contexts and as integrated with cultural practices and values. The further complexity of information seeking through the use of various technologies and genres is coming to be better understood, though there is much more to be studied. In fact, even as I write, some six billion people are interacting with information

worldwide, drawing on cognitive and evolutionarily shaped behaviors, on social shaping and environmental expectations, and interacting with every information technology from the book to the wireless handheld "smartphone." There is unimaginably much more to learn about information behavior.

The state of our current understandings on these topics is reviewed in over 30 articles in this encyclopedia. See, especially, the section titled "People using cultural resources" in the topical contents list of the encyclopedia.

REFERENCES

1. Andersen, H.C.; Lucas, E. The ugly duckling. In *Fairy Tales from Hans Christian Andersen*, 3rd Ed.; J.M. Dent & Co.: London, U.K., 1907; 379–387.
2. Case, D.O.; Andrews, J.E.; Johnson, J.D.; Allard, S.L. Avoiding versus seeking: the relationship of information seeking to avoidance, blunting, coping, dissonance, and related concepts. J. Med. Libr. Assoc. **2005**, *93* (3), 353–362.
3. Atkin, C. Instrumental utilities and information seeking. In *New Models for Mass Communication Research*; Clarke, P., Ed.; Sage: Beverly Hills, CA, 1973; Vol. 2, 205–239.
4. Bates, M.J. Toward an integrated model of information seeking and searching. New Rev. Inf. Behav. Res. **2002**, *3*, 1–15. Also available at https://pages.gseis.ucla.edu/faculty/bates/ (accessed June 2016).
5. Bates, M.J. The invisible substrate of information science. J. Am. Soc. Inf. Sci. **1999**, *50* (12), 1048.
6. Green, S.S. Personal relations between librarians and readers. Am. Libr. J. **1876**, *1*, 78.
7. Ranganathan, S.R. *The Five laws of Library Science*, 2nd Ed.; Blunt and Sons: London, U.K., 1957. See also http://dlist.sir.arizona.edu/1220/ (accessed December 2008).
8. Richardson, J.V., Jr. *The Spirit of Inquiry; the Graduate Library School at Chicago, 1921–1951*, ACRL Publications in Librarianship; American Library Association: Chicago, IL, 1982; Vol. 42.
9. Waples, D. *People and Print; Social Aspects of Reading in the Depression*; University of Chicago Press: Chicago, IL, 1938.
10. Berelson, B. *Library's Public*; Columbia University Press: New York, 1949.
11. Berelson, B. The public library, book reading, and political behavior. Libr. Q. **1945**, *15* (4), 281–299.
12. Royal Society of London. *Royal Society of London Scientific Information Conference, Report*; Royal Society: London, U.K., 1948.
13. Proceedings of the International Conference on Scientific Information Washington, DC, November 16–21, 1958.; National Academy of Sciences, National Research Council: Washington, DC, 1959; 2 volumes.
14. American Psychological Association. *Project on Scientific Information Exchange in Psychology*; American Psychological Association: Washington, DC, 1963–1968. 21 reports.

15. Garvey, W.D.; Griffith, B.C. Scientific communication as a social system. Science **1967**, *157*, 1011–1016.

16. Garvey, W.D. Communication in the physical and social sciences. Science **1970**, *11*, 1166–1173.

17. Price, D.j.d.S. *Little Science, Big Science*; Columbia University Press: New York, 1963.

18. Price, D.J.d.S. Networks of scientific papers. Science **1965**, *149*, 510–515.

19. Crane, D. *Invisible Colleges: Diffusion of Knowledge in Scientific Communities*; University of Chicago Press: Chicago, IL, 1972.

20. Meadows, A.J. *Communication in Science*; Butterworth: London, U.K., 1974.

21. Davis, R.A.; Bailey, C.A. *Bibliography of Use Studies*; Drexel Institute of Technology, Graduate School of Library Science: Philadelphia, PA, 1964.

22. Menzel, H. Information needs and uses in science and technology. Annu. Rev. Inf. Sci. Technol. **1966**, *1*, 41–69.

23. Garvey, W.D. *Communication: The Essence of Science: Facilitating Information Exchange Among Librarians, Scientists, Engineers, and Students*; Pergamon Press: New York, 1979.

24. Paisley, W.J. Information needs and uses. Ann. Rev. Inf. Sci. Technol. **1968**, *3*, 1–30.

25. Poole, H. *Theories of the Middle Range*; Ablex: Norwood, NJ, 1985.

26. Warner, E.S., et al. *Information Needs of Urban Residents*; Regional Planning Council/Westat Research, Inc.: Baltimore, MD/Rockville, MD, 1973; (ERIC ED 088 464).

27. Dervin, B. *Development of Strategies for Dealing With the Information Needs of Urban Residents: Phase I—Citizen Study. Final Report*; University of Washington, Department of Communication: Seattle, WA, 1976; (ERIC ED 125 640).

28. Bundy, M.L. Metropolitan public library use. Wilson Libr. Bull. **1967**, *41*, 950–961.

29. Bundy, M.L. Factors influencing public library use. Wilson Libr. Bull. **1967**, *42*, 371–382.

30. Bates, M.J. Information science at the University of California at Berkeley in the 1960s: a memoir of student days. Libr. Trends **2004**, *52* (4), 683–701.

31. Cuadra, C.A.; Bates, M.J., Eds. *Library and Information Service Needs of the Nation: Proceedings of a Conference on the Needs of Occupational, Ethnic, and other Groups in the United States*. Sponsored by the National Commission on Libraries and Information Science, University of Denver, 1973; U.S. Government Printing Office: Washington, DC, 1974.

32. Streatfield, D.R.; Wilson, T.D. Information innovations in social services departments: a third report on Project INISS. J. Doc. **1982**, *38*, 273–281.

33. Blake, B.; Morkham, T.; Skinner, A. Inside information: social welfare practitioners and their information needs. Aslib Proc. **1979**, *31*, 275–283.

34. Brittain, J.M. Information services and the structure of knowledge in the social sciences. Int. Soc. Sci. J. **1979**, *31* (4), 711–728.

35. Case, D.O. Conceptual organization and retrieval of text by historians: the role of memory and metaphor. J. Am. Soc. Inf. Sci. **1991**, *42* (9), 657–668.

36. Chu, C.M. Literary critics at work and their information needs: a research-phases model. Libr. Inf. Sci. Res. **1999**, *21* (2), 247–273.

37. Cobbledick, S. Information-seeking behavior of artists: exploratory interviews. Libr. Q. **1996**, *66*, 343–372.

38. Wiberley, S.E., Jr.; Jones, W.G. Patterns of information seeking in the humanities. Coll. Res. Libr. **1989**, *50*, 638–645.

39. Bates, M.J. Getty end-user online searching project in the humanities: report no. 6: overview and conclusions. Coll. Res. Libr. **1996**, *57*, 514–523.

40. Westbrook, L. Information needs and experiences of scholars in women's studies: problems and solutions. Coll. Res. Libr. **2003**, *64* (3), 192–209.

41. Palmer, C.L. Issue Editor. *Libr. Trends* **1996**, *45* (2), 129–366.

42. Palmer, C.L. *Work at the Boundaries of Science: Information and the Interdisciplinary Research Process*; Kluwer Academic Publishers: Boston, MA/Dordrecht, the Netherlands, 2001.

43. Davies, K. The information-seeking behaviour of doctors: a review of the evidence. Health Inf. Libr. J. **2007**, *24* (2), 78–94.

44. Sutton, S.A. Role of attorney mental models of law in case relevance determinations: an exploratory analysis. J. Am. Soc. Inf. Sci. **1994**, *45*, 186–200.

45. Auster, E.; Choo, C.W. Environmental scanning by CEOs in two Canadian industries. J. Am. Soc. Inf. Sci. **1993**, *44* (4), 194–203.

46. Summers, E.G.; Matheson, J.; Conry, R. The effect of personal, professional, and psychological attributes, and information seeking behavior on the use of information sources by educators. J. Am. Soc. Inf. Sci. **1983**, *34* (1), 75–85.

47. Williams, D.; Coles, L. Evidence-based practice in teaching: an information perspective. J. Doc. **2007**, *63* (6), 812–835.

48. Kari, J.; Hartel, J. Information and higher things in life: addressing the pleasurable and the profound in information science. J. Am. Soc. Inf. Sci. Technol. **2007**, *58* (8), 1131–1147.

49. Caidi, N.; Allard, D.; Quirke, L. Information practices of immigrants. Annu. Rev. Inf. Sci. Technol. **2010**, *44*, 493–531.

50. Antonijevic, S.; Cahoy, E.S. Personal library curation: an ethnographic study of scholars' information practices. Portal: Libr. Acad. **2014**, *14* (2), 287–306.

51. Mizrachi, D.; Bates, M.J. Undergraduates' personal academic information management and the consideration of time and task-urgency. J. Am. Soc. Inf. Sci. Technol. **2013**, *64* (8), 1590–1607.

52. Beheshti, J.; Large, A., Eds. *The Information Behavior of a New Generation: Children and Teens on the 21st Century*; Scarecrow Press: Lanham, MD, 2013.

53. Wilson, T.D. On user studies and information needs. J. Doc. **1981**, *37*, 3–15.

54. Wilson, T.D. Models in information behaviour research. J. Doc. **1999**, *55* (3), 249–270.

55. Belkin, N.J.; Oddy, R.N.; Brooks, H.M. ASK for information retrieval: part I. background and theory. J. Doc. **1982**, *38* (2), 61–71.

56. Kuhlthau, C.C. Inside the search process: information seeking from the user's perspective. J. Am. Soc. Inf. Sci. **1991**, *42*, 361–371.

57. Bates, M.J. The design of browsing and berrypicking techniques for the online search interface. Online Rev. **1989**, *13*, 407–424.

58. Dervin, B.; Nilan, M. Information needs and uses. Annu. Rev. Inf. Sci. Technol. **1986**, *21*, 3–33.

59. http://communication.sbs.ohio-state.edu/sense-making/AAauthors/authorlistdervin.html (accessed June 2008).

60. Dervin, B. Information as a user construct: the relevance of perceived information needs to synthesis and interpretation. In *Knowledge Structure and Use: Implications for Synthesis and Interpretation*; Ward, S.A., Reed, L.J., Eds.; Temple University Press: Philadelphia, PA, 1983; 161.

61. Talja, S.; Hartel, J. Revisiting the user-centered turn in information science research: an intellectual history perspective. Inf. Res. **2007**, *12* (4), paper colis04. (available at http://InformationR.net/ir/12-4/colis/colis04.html).

62. Talja, S.; Tuominen, K.; Savolainen, R. 'Isms' in information science: constructivism, collectivism and constructionism. J. Doc. **2005**, *61* (1), 79–101.

63. http://www.kf.vu.lt/~isic2008/?page_id=4 (accessed June 2008).

64. Fisher, K.E.; Erdelez, S.; McKechnie, L.(E.F.), Eds. *Theories of Information Behavior*; American Society for Information Science and Technology by Information Today: Medford, NJ, c2005.

65. Bates, M.J. An introduction to metatheories, theories, and models. In *Theories of Information Behavior*; Fisher, K.E., Erdelez, S., McKechnie, L.(E.F.), Eds.; American Society for Information Science and Technology: Medford, NJ, c2005; 1–24.

66. Ellis, D. Modeling the information-seeking patterns of academic researchers: a grounded theory approach. Libr. Q. **1993**, *63* (4), 469–486.

67. Talja, S. *Music, Culture, and the Library: An Analysis of Discourses*; Scarecrow Press: Lanham, MD, c2001.

68. Xu, Y.; Liu, C. The dynamics of interactive information retrieval, part II: an empirical study from the activity theory perspective. J. Am. Soc. Inf. Sci. Technol. **2007**, *58* (7), 987–998.

69. Reddy, M.C.; Jansen, B.J. A model for understanding collaborative information behavior in context: a study of two healthcare teams. Inf. Process. Manage. **2008**, *44* (1), 256–273.

70. Limberg, L. Experiencing information seeking and learning: a study of the interaction between two phenomena. Inf. Res. **1999**, *5*(1) (available at: http://informationr.net/ir/5-1/paper68.html).

71. Ford, N. Psychological determinants of information needs: a small-scale study of higher education students. J. Librariansh. **1986**, *18* (1), 47–62.

72. Ford, N. Towards a model of learning for educational informatics. J. Doc. **2004**, *60* (2), 183–225.

73. Srinivasan, R.; Pyati, A. Diasporic information environments: reframing immigrant-focused information research. J. Am. Soc. Inf. Sci. Technol. **2007**, *58* (12), 1734–1744.

74. Fidel, R.; Pejtersen, A.M. From information behaviour research to the design of information systems: the Cognitive Work Analysis framework. Inf. Res. **2004**, *10* (1), paper 210. (available at http://InformationR.net/ir/10-1/paper210.html).

75. Fidel, R. *Human Information Interaction: An Ecological Approach to Information Behavior*; MIT Press: Cambridge, MA, 2012.

76. Sandstrom, A.R.; Sandstrom, P.E. The use and misuse of anthropological methods in library and information science research. Libr. Q. **1995**, *65* (2), 161–199.

77. Nicholas, D.; Huntington, P.; Jamali, H.R.; Watkinson, A. The information seeking behaviour of the users of digital scholarly journals. Inf. Process. Manage. **2006**, *42* (5), 1345–1365.

78. Bates, M.J. Information and knowledge: an evolutionary framework for information science. Inf. Res. **2005**, *10*(4), paper 239. (available at http://InformationR.net/ir/10-4/paper239.html).

79. Bates, M.J. What is browsing—really? A model drawing from behavioural science research. Inf. Res. **2007**, *12* (4), paper 330. (available at http://InformationR.net/ir/12-4/paper330.html).

80. Case, D.O. *Looking for Information: A Survey of Research on Information Seeking, Needs, and Behavior*, 3rd Ed.; Emerald Group Publishing: Bingley, U.K., 2012.

81. Savolainen, R. Information behavior and information practice: reviewing the "umbrella concepts" of information-seeking studies. Libr. Q. **2007**, *77* (2), 109–132.

82. Savolainen, R. Information behavior and information practice: reviewing the "umbrella concepts" of information-seeking studies. Libr. Q. **2007**, *77* (2), 126.

83. Huizing, A.; Cavanagh, M. Planting contemporary practice theory in the garden of information science. Inf. Res. **2011**, *16*(4), paper 497. (available at http://InformationR.net/ir/16-4/paper497.html).

84. Fisher, K.E.; Julien, H. Information behavior. Annu. Rev. Inf. Sci. Technol. **2009**, *43*, 1–73.

85. Bates, M.J. Information search tactics. J. Am. Soc. Inf. Sci. **1979**, *30*, 205–214.

86. Bates, M.J. Search techniques. Annu. Rev. Inf. Sci. Technol. **1981**, *16*, 139–169.

87. Cochrane, P.A.; Markey, K. Catalog use studies-before and after the introduction of online interactive catalogs: impact on design for subject access. Libr. Inf. Sci. Res. **1983**, *5* (4), 337–363.

88. Fidel, R. Online searching styles: a case-study-based model of searching behavior. J. Am. Soc. Inf. Sci. **1984**, *35* (4), 211–221.

89. Hsieh-Yee, I. Effects of search experience and subject knowledge on online search behavior: measuring the search tactics of novice and experienced searchers. J. Am. Soc. Inf. Sci. **1993**, *44*, 161–174.

90. Marchionini, G. *Information Seeking in Electronic Environments*; Cambridge University Press: Cambridge, U.K., 1995.

91. Spink, A.; Wolfram, D.; Jansen, B.J.; Saracevic, T. Searching the web: the public and their queries. J. Am. Soc. Inf. Sci. Technol. **2001**, *52* (3), 226–234.

92. O'Connor, B. Browsing: a framework for seeking functional information. Knowl. Creativity Diffus. Util. **1993**, *15* (2), 211–232.

93. Rice, R.E.; McCreadie, M.; Chang, S.L. *Accessing and Browsing Information and Communication*; MIT Press: Cambridge, MA, 2001.

94. Hodges, T.; Bloch, U. Fiche or film for COM catalogs—two use tests. Libr. Q. **1982**, *52* (2), 131–144.

95. Matthews, J.R.; Lawrence, G.S.; Ferguson, D.K., Eds. *Using Online Catalogs: A Nationwide Survey*; Neal-Schuman: New York, 1983.

96. Lynch, C.A. The next generation of public access information retrieval systems for research libraries: lessons from ten years of the MELVYL system. Inf. Technol. Libr. **1992**, *11*, 405–415.

97. Bates, M.J. Subject access in online catalogs: a design model. J. Am. Soc. Inf. Sci. **1986**, *37*, 357–376.

98. Hildreth, C.R. *Intelligent Interfaces and Retrieval Methods for Subject Searching in Bibliographic Retrieval Systems*, Advances in Library Information Technology #2; Library of Congress Cataloging Distribution Service: Washington, DC, 1989.

99. Borgman, C.L. Why are online catalogs still hard to use? J. Am. Soc. Inf. Sci. **1996**, *47*, 493–503.

100. Salton, G.; McGill, J.M. *Introduction to Modern Information Retrieval*; McGraw-Hill: New York, 1983.

101. Voorhees, E.M.; Harman, D.K., Eds. TREC – *Experiment and Evaluation in Information Retrieval*; The MIT Press: Cambridge, MA, 2005.

102. Saracevic, T.; Kantor, P. A study of information seeking and retrieving. III. Searchers, searches, and overlap. J. Am. Soc. Inf. Sci. **1988**, *39*, 197–216.

103. Fidel, R. Searchers' selection of search keys: III. Searching styles. J. Am. Soc. Inf. Sci. **1991**, *42* (7), 515–527.

104. Cronin, B.; Hert, C.A. Scholarly foraging and network discovery tools. J. Doc. **1995**, *51* (4), 388–403.

105. Xie, H.I. Supporting ease-of-use and user control: desired features and structure of web-based online IR systems. Inf. Process. Manage. **2003**, *39* (6), 899–922.

106. Rieh, S.Y. On the web at home: information seeking and web searching in the home environment. J. Am. Soc. Inf. Sci. Technol. **2004**, *55* (8), 743–753.

107. Bishop, A.P.; Van House, N.A.; Buttenfield, B.P. *Digital Library Use: Social Practice in Design and Evaluation*; MIT Press: Cambridge, MA, 2003.

108. Gilliland-Swetland, A.J.; Kafai, Y.; Landis, W.E. Integrating primary sources into the elementary school classroom: a case study of teachers' perspectives. Archivaria **1999**, *48*, 89–116.

109. Marchionini, G.; Crane, G. Evaluating hypermedia and learning: methods and results from the Perseus Project. ACM Trans. Inf. Syst. **1994**, *12* (1), 5–34.

110. Roderer, N.K.; Zambrowicz, C.; Zhang, D.; Zhou, H. User information seeking behavior in a medical web portal environment: a preliminary study. J. Am. Soc. Inf. Sci. Technol. **2004**, *55* (8), 670–684.

111. Hearst, M.A. *Search User Interfaces*; Cambridge University Press: Cambridge, U.K., 2009.

112. Chen, C.; Hernon, P. *Information Seeking: Assessing and Anticipating User Needs*; Neal Schuman Publishers: New York, 1982.

113. Menzel, H. In *Planned and unplanned scientific communication*. Proceedings of the International Conference on Scientific Information, Washington, DC, November 16–21, 1958; National Academy of Sciences, National Research Council: Washington, DC, 1959; 199–243.

114. Dervin, B.; Harpring, J.E.; Foreman-Wernet, L. Moments of concern: a sense-making study of pregnant, drug-addicted women and their information needs. Electron. J. Commun. **1999**, *9*, 2–4. Available at http://www.cios.org/www/ejc/v9n23499.htm.

115. Wilson, P. *Second-Hand Knowledge: An Inquiry into Cognitive Authority*; Greenwood Press: Westport, CT, 1983.

116. Hurd, J.M. Interdisciplinary research in the sciences: implications for library organization. Coll. Res. Libr. **1992**, *53* (4), 283–297.

117. Paisley, W. Information and work. In *Progress in Communication Sciences*; Dervin, B., Voigt, M., Eds.; Ablex: Norwood, NJ, 1980; Vol. 2, 113–165.

118. Taylor, R.S. Information use environments. In *Progress in Communication Sciences*; Dervin, B., Voigt, M., Eds.; Ablex: Norwood, NJ, 1991; Vol. 10, 217–255.

119. Cronin, B. Invisible colleges and information transfer: a review and commentary with particular reference to the social sciences. J. Doc. **1982**, *38* (3), 212–236.

120. Leckie, G.J.; Pettigrew, K.E.; Sylvain, C. Modeling the information seeking of professionals: a general model derived from research on engineers, health care professionals, and lawyers. Libr. Q. **1996**, *66* (2), 161–193.

121. Budd, J.M. Research in the two cultures: the nature of scholarship in science and the humanities. Collect. Manage. **1989**, *11*, 1–21.

122. Bates, M.J. The design of databases and other information resources for humanities scholars: the Getty Online Searching Project Report No. 4. Online CD-ROM Rev. **1994**, *18* (6), 331–340.

123. Orbach, B.C. The view from the researcher's desk: historians' perceptions of research and repositories. Am. Arch. **1991**, *54* (1), 28–43.

124. Duff, W.M.; Johnson, C.A. Where is the list with all the names? Information-seeking behavior of genealogists. Am. Arch. **2003**, *66* (1), 79–95.

125. Chatman, E. The information world of low-skilled workers. Libr. Inf. Sci. Res. **1987**, *9*, 265–283.

126. Chatman, E.A. *The Information World of Retired Women*; Greenwood Press: New York, 1992.

127. Chatman, E.A. A theory of life in the round. J. Am. Soc. Inf. Sci. **1999**, *50* (3), 207–217.

128. Metoyer-Duran, C. *Gatekeepers in Ethnolinguistic Communities*; Ablex: Norwood, NJ, 1993.

129. Harris, R.M.; Dewdney, P. *Barriers to Information: How Formal Help Systems Fail Battered Women*; Greenwood Press: Westport, CT, 1994.

130. Hersberger, J.A.; Murray, A.L.; Sokoloff, S.M. The information use environment of abused and neglected children. Inf. Res. **2006**, *12*(1), paper 277. (Available at http://InformationR.net/ir/12-1/paper277.html).

131. Kuhlthau, C.C. *Seeking Meaning: A Process Approach To Library and Information Services*, 2nd Ed.; Libraries Unlimited: Westport, CT, 2004.

132. Ellis, D. Behavioural approach to information retrieval system design. J. Doc. **1989**, *45* (3), 171–212.

133. Cool, C. The concept of situation in information science. Annu. Rev. Inf. Sci. Technol. **2001**, *35*, 5–42.

134. Courtright, C. Context in information behavior research. Annu. Rev. Inf. Sci. Technol. **2007**, *41*, 273–306.

135. Fisher, K.E.; Durrance, J.C.; Hinton, M.B. Information grounds and the use of need-based services by immigrants in Queens, New York: A context-based, outcome evaluation approach. J. Am. Soc. Inf. Sci. Technol. **2004**, *55* (8), 754–766.

136. Choo, C.W.; Detlor, B.; Turnbull, D. *Web Work: Information Seeking and Knowledge Work on the World Wide Web*; Kluwer Academic: Boston, MA, 2000.

137. Walter, V. Information needs of children. Adv. Librariansh. **1994**, *18*, 111–129.

138. Silverstein, J. Just curious: children's use of digital reference for unimposed queries and its importance in informal education. Libr. Trends **2005**, *54* (2), 228–244.

139. Trace, C.B. Information creation and the notion of membership. J. Doc. **2007**, *63* (1), 142–164.

140. Kling, R.; McKim, G. Not just a matter of time: field differences and the shaping of electronic media in supporting scientific communication. J. Am. Soc. Inf. Sci. **2000**, *51* (14), 1306–1320.

141. Wang, P.; White, M.D. A cognitive model of document use during a research project. Study II. Decisions at the reading and citing stages. J. Am. Soc. Inf. Sci. **1999**, *50* (2), 98–114.

142. Bishop, A.P. Document structure and digital libraries: how researchers mobilize information in journal articles. Inf. Process. Manage. **1999**, *35* (3), 255–279.

143. Covi, L.M. Material mastery: situating digital library use in university research practices. Inf. Process. Manage. **1999**, *35* (3), 293–316.

Information Behavior Models

Thomas D. Wilson
Publisher/Editor in Chief, Information Research, U.K.

Abstract

This entry outlines the development of models of information behavior. The concept of a *model* is defined and the different types of model are identified. Models of information behavior are presented within a typology of descriptive model, decision-based models, and causal models. It is suggested that, in research terms, a movement from descriptive models to causal models is needed if theory development is to take place in the field.

INTRODUCTION

Information behavior has been defined as

> ... the totality of human behavior in relation to sources and channels of information, including both active and passive information seeking, and information use. Thus, it includes face-to-face communication with others, as well as the passive reception of information as in, for example, watching TV advertisements, without any intention to act on the information given.[1]

In addition to the specific aspects mentioned in that definition, we can add that the determination of information needs (or "information requirements" in information systems development) is part of information behavior research, as is the human interaction aspect of information retrieval (excluding, that is, the algorithmic work in the IR field), as exemplified by Ingwersen's work referred to below.

The history of information behavior research has shown a move from the study of the information resources used by people, in an attempt by researchers to identify "information needs", to the investigation of actual behavior in relation to information sources and systems. However, the situation is complicated by disciplinary and methodological divisions within the information disciplines, such that work in the information systems area is rarely put together with work in information science and, within information science, the human interaction aspects of information retrieval are rarely considered together with other aspects of information access and sharing. Much work in information retrieval also has a laboratory experiment basis, while information behavior research (at least over the last several decades) has been mainly qualitative in character, with the result that the two groups of researchers rarely interact.

To a degree, the interest in modeling information behavior arises out of a concern that these differences should at least be identified and recognized, in the hope that, as a result, gaps in research will be revealed and, perhaps through cross-disciplinary collaboration, explored.

MODELS

Definitions of models are numerous and include not only the *conceptual models*[2] with which we are concerned here, but also physical models (such as those employed in architecture) and human models—the "model user" or "the model librarian." All models, of whatever kind, are attempts at the representation, characterization, or exemplification of some aspect of reality or of human behavior. Models may be graphic, mathematical, or simply textual: we can describe a model in words, setting out, for example, a set of theoretical propositions. In this light, stating a set of hypotheses about a subject of investigation is to express a model of anticipated relationships among variables. We can also express those relationships in graphic form and, very often, in quantitative research the results of hypothesis testing are modeled graphically. Finally, we can express the same relationships mathematically, indicating the strength of relationships and again, a graphic model of the results of hypothesis testing may also show the strength of relationships. Mathematical models for weather forecasting, for example, will employ huge amounts of data in complex equations of relationships among many variables, but some mathematical models are quite simple in construction: $E = MC^2$ is a simple equation, modeling the relationship between energy, mass, and the speed of light, with enormous implications.

There are also pseudo-mathematical models (i.e., those for which units of measurement are lacking), which attempt to say something about relationships in information science, the most cited of which is that by Brookes,[3] $K(S) + I = K(S + \Delta I)$. This is simply a more concise way of saying that a new "knowledge state" $K(S + \Delta I)$ is brought about by the addition of information (I) to the existing knowledge state ($K(S)$).

The use of models of these different kinds is as old as scientific endeavor: indeed, geometry itself can be seen as a system for modeling spatial relationships. In astronomy, certainly from the time of Kepler and Copernicus, models

Encyclopedia of Library and Information Sciences, Fourth Edition DOI: 10.1081/E-ELIS4-120043256

of the planetary system, and their representation, subsequently, in the physical model of the orrery, have been commonly used. The same applies in the social sciences, particularly since the introduction of system approaches to social phenomena and, from the social sciences, models, particularly graphical models, have found their way into information science. Case's[4] treatment of models constitutes a valuable supplement to the ideas presented here.

MODELS IN INFORMATION BEHAVIOR RESEARCH

In information behavior research, the word *model* is generally used to describe graphical models: diagrams that express actual or theoretical relationships, or ideal processes of interaction with information. The common elements of such models are the information user and his or her environment or context, the information resources available to the user and the "tools" available (which may include various levels of technology, or, for example, a human intermediary). Inevitably, therefore, because they all attempt to portray the same phenomena, the various models are very similar and, to a large extent, map on to one another.

It is noted above that models probably found their way into information science from the social sciences, and this may well be the case for the behavioral aspects of the subject. However, in other fields, such as bibliometrics and information retrieval, mathematical and pseudo-mathematical models have also been used.

We find three kinds of models in information behavior research: the first is the purely descriptive, which sets out the connections between user, tool, and information resource, showing the general communication flows among these elements. Wilson[5] set out a very generic model of this kind (Fig. 1), which, in spite of changes in the technology between 1981 and the present, can still be used to outline the connections.

This kind of model simply maps out the actions that an information user may engage in to obtain or exchange information, as indicated by the lettered lines: thus, one strategy is indicated by lines f, g, j—an information user seeks the help of an information intermediary, who uses the available technology to access structured information resources. Clearly, in this kind of diagram not all of the lines of communication can be shown without making the diagram virtually unreadable: thus, in this diagram no feedback lines are shown, which would indicate, for example, what happens when information is found or fails to be found.

The model suggests that information seeking can be seen as the interaction of three "systems": the user in his or her life-world and in particular groups in that life-world, with the "reference group" shown to illustrate this notion; the information systems that mediate access to information resources (either used directly by a person or by an intermediary acting on behalf of that person); and the system of information resources, accessed through the information system or directly, for example, in the case of the person browsing library shelves. The whole is shown to exist in a "universe of knowledge," implying that the individual may access other information resources, which are not organized, such as using direct observation of phenomena, or talking to other people. There is no suggestion in Fig. 1 of any limitation of the model to work life or ordinary life, it is sufficiently general to cover both: Savolainen's[6] model of everyday life information

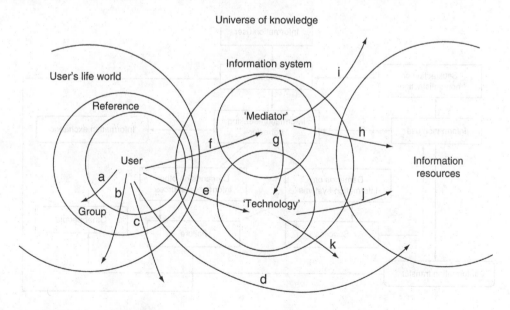

Fig. 1 Information seeking—a generic model.
Source: From Wilson.[5]

seeking elaborates the left-most set of "nested" circles in that particular context, drawing upon sociological theory in a more explicit manner.

We might label models of the kind shown in Fig. 1 as models of "what can be done" in seeking information. Such models are not generally theoretical in character, although theory may inform their construction; thus, reference group theory[7] clearly informs the model and the use of the term "life-world" suggests a phenomenological orientation, since this is a term derived from that field.

The second type can be characterized as models of "what happens." Such models, of which Fig. 2 is an example, have more the character of decision diagrams, showing alternative courses of action and, in some cases "if A then B" situations.

This kind of model makes some things more obvious than models of the kind shown in Fig. 1: it brings in the notion of success or failure to find information, identifies "information sources" as formal or informal ("information systems" and "other information sources"); it brings in "information" use and the idea that use may or may not lead to the satisfaction of the initial "information need." Again, theory is not explicit in the model, but "social exchange theory"[8] has influenced the model in the notion of "information exchange" to show "other people" as sources of information.

Clearly, more lines and more detail could be provided in this model; for example, by showing that a need for information does not always lead to information-seeking behavior, or that a failure to find information does not necessarily lead to a further round of information seeking. However, more boxes and more lines may only serve to confuse and one of the advantages of simple graphical models is that they are easy to understand and the lack of detail allows the reader to think further about what appears to be missing and what further relationships might be embodied in the diagram.

The point that all models of this kind map on to one another can be illustrated by reference to the model by Krikelas,[9] which has similarities to Fig. 2. However, Krikelas introduces the notion of 'deferred need' and specifies 'memory', 'personal files' and 'direct observation' as ways of acquiring information that would be subsumed under 'demands on other information sources' in Fig. 2.

Models with a rather similar intent include those of Leckie et al.[10] and Byström and Järvelin.[11]

Models of the second type are concerned with the individual information-seeking process and probably the best known of these is that proposed by Kuhlthau,[12] which is not usually expressed graphically. However, Kuhlthau does provide a graphic model which associates the stage process of information searching, the feelings experienced by the information seeker, the cognitive dimension and the actions taken (Fig. 3).

An important aspect of Kuhlthau's model is that it is based on theory: thus, the stage process is derived from theories of the construction of learning by Dewey, Bruner and Kelly [12, Ch. 2]. This recognition of the role of theory distinguishes models of this kind from the first type.

Wilson's[13] "problem solving" model is, similarly, a stage process model: however, it is based not on stages of the search process but on the stages in coping with a problem. Thus, it hypothesizes a four-stage model, problem recognition, problem definition, problem resolution and solution statement, and associates the need to seek information with these stages (Fig. 4).

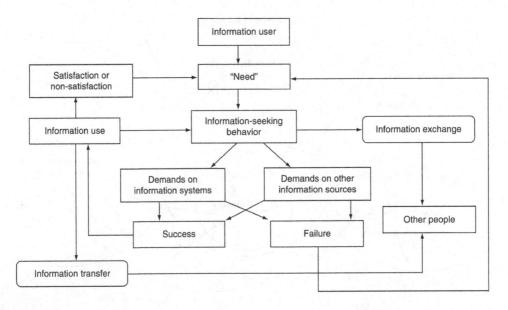

Fig. 2 A model of information behavior.
Source: From Wilson.[5]

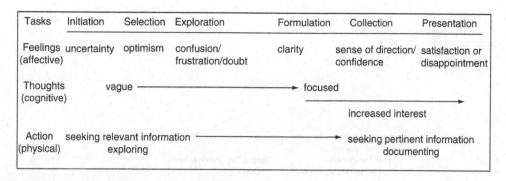

Fig. 3 Kuhlthau's model of the information search process.
Source: From Kuhlthau.[12]

Rather being derived from theory, this model states a theory: that in the course of solving a problem and delivering the solution, the individual's state of uncertainty on how to proceed is resolved by information seeking. It is a modest theoretical statement but, like Kuhlthau's model, serves to associate information-seeking behavior with a more general phenomenon. The information-seeking element is not specifically shown in Fig. 5, but the paper notes that uncertainty is resolved through information seeking and use and the figure could be modified to show this.

A third example of models of this kind is Ingwersen's[14] (Fig. 5) which draws upon cognitive psychology and the idea of mental models as a way of indicating the cognitive processes involved in information searching.

Within this category of models, a slightly different perspective is offered in Wilson's model of 1996 (Fig. 6), which is based on his earlier models: the top level of this model is a simplified version of one of the 1981 models, which is then expanded to indicate the demographic and other variables that influence information seeking, the different modes of information-seeking behavior and theories that may be of explanatory value.

Thus, "stress/coping theory" from the health field[16] is suggested as possibly explaining why some people seek information in response to a problem situation while others do not. For some, the stress created by the "need to know" is not strong enough to overcome the barriers (represented here as "intervening variables") that must be overcome, actually to engage in information seeking.

Choo[17] has produced a model of this kind which seeks to integrate a number of ideas from research on information behavior. Fig. 7 presents three connected triangles:

the top triangle shows the circumstances of information need, while the bottom two triangles show, respectively, purposive information seeking and information use. Choo notes the complexity of the situation regarding information use, commenting:

> How this information is processed and put to use depends on the cognitive style and preferences of the individual, the emotional responses that accompany information processing, and the organizational or social context surrounding information use.

He goes on to use the model to illustrate organizational information use, and its shortcomings, in the *Challenger* and *Columbia* space exploration accidents, showing how gaps in understanding and false shared beliefs contributed to the tragedies.

Finally, there are a limited number of causal models, that is, models that seek to demonstrate not only the processes of information seeking or the relationships of this behavior to other phenomena, but that attempt to show causal relationships. A very generic model of this kind is that of Johnson,[18] which suggests causal relationships in cancer-related information seeking (Fig. 8).

Johnson's model appears to say that demographic characteristics (such as age, sex, and ethnicity) and direct experience of the phenomenon about which information is sought, together with the perceived importance of the search problem and the individual's beliefs about the problem determine the utility of the information "carrier" (source would be a more common term in information science) and these "utilities" together with specific

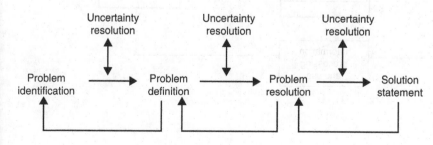

Fig. 4 The problem-solving model.
Source: From Wilson.[13]

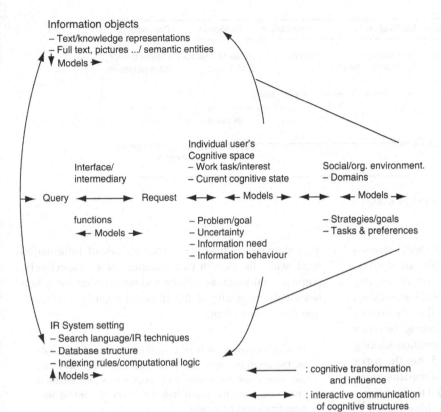

Information objects
– Text/knowledge representations
– Full text, pictures .../ semantic entities
▼ Models ►

Individual user's
Cognitive space
– Work task/interest
– Current cognitive state

Interface/
intermediary

Social/org. environment.
– Domains

Query ◄───► Request ◄─► ◄─ Models ► ◄─► ◄─ Models ►

functions   – Problem/goal   – Strategies/goals
◄─ Models ►   – Uncertainty   – Tasks & preferences
                          – Information need
                          – Information behaviour

IR System setting
– Search language/IR techniques
– Database structure
– Indexing rules/computational logic
▲ Models ►

◄──────► : cognitive transformation
               and influence
◄──────► : interactive communication
               of cognitive structures

Fig. 5 Ingwersen's cognitive model.
Source: From Ingwersen.[14]

characteristics of the source determine the information-seeking actions the individual will carry out.

It can be seen that Johnson's model is much more concerned with the motivations for information seeking (the background factors and the personal relevance factors) than with the specific operations of information

seeking, whereas the models proposed by Krikelas and Wilson are more concerned with the latter.

Finally, in this section, Höglund et al.[19] proposed a theoretical, causal model of the relationship between information and trust in health care. The model was derived from previous research on health information and

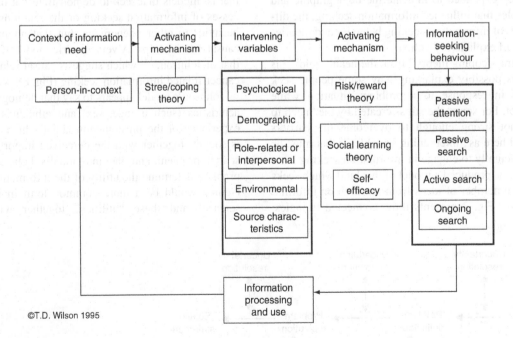

©T.D. Wilson 1995

Fig. 6 Wilson's expanded model.
Source: From Wilson and Walsh.[15]

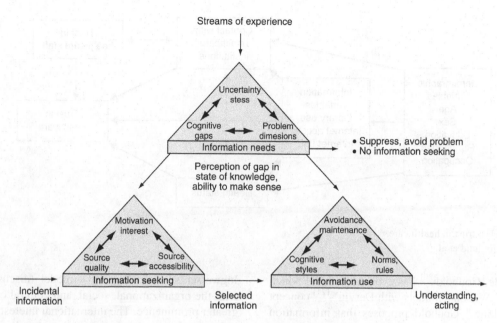

Fig. 7 Choo's model of information needs, seeking and use.
Source: From Choo.[17]

on trust in health care and the test of the model was carried out on a large database of responses to a Swedish national survey (Riks-SOM). The model (Fig. 9) links health status, contact with health institutions, library use, Internet use, and trust in health institutions, variables that were explored in the survey. The study is an example of how large data sets can be used for secondary analysis.

There appears to have been a loss of interest in the idea of modeling information behavior between the early models of the 1980s and those from the mid-1990s onwards. Certainly, since the publication of Wilson's review in 1999, interest has revived and the development, modification, and testing of models has become a significant area of research in the field.

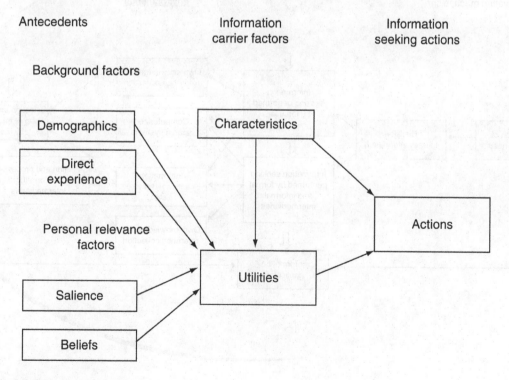

Fig. 8 Johnson's information-seeking model.
Source: Redrawn from Johnson.[18]

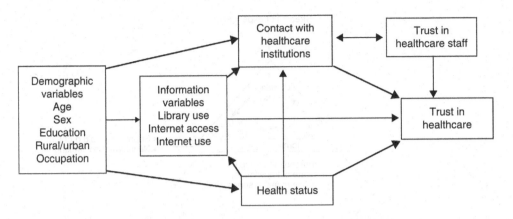

Fig. 9 A model of trust in health care.
Source: From Höglund et al.[19]

For example, Godbold[20] has evolved a model which seeks to marry Wilson's models with Dervin's[21] concept of "sense making." Godbold proposes that information seeking can be seen as a multidirectional activity, rather than a mono-directional activity, and this also appears to be the thrust of Foster's[22] "nonlinear" model. Ingwersen and Järvelin[23] have also developed a general model of the information-seeking process within an overall cognitive framework. This appears to be a generalization of Ingwersen's earlier cognitive model (discussed above), with the organizational, social, and cultural context given greater prominence. The international interest in modeling is shown not only by those mentioned earlier in this paragraph (which come from Australia, the U.K., Finland, and Denmark) but also by Niedźwiedzka's[24] "proposed general model of information behavior" from Poland. Like Godbold, Niedźwiedzka begins with Wilson's 1996 model and expands it in an attempt to incorporate aspects of

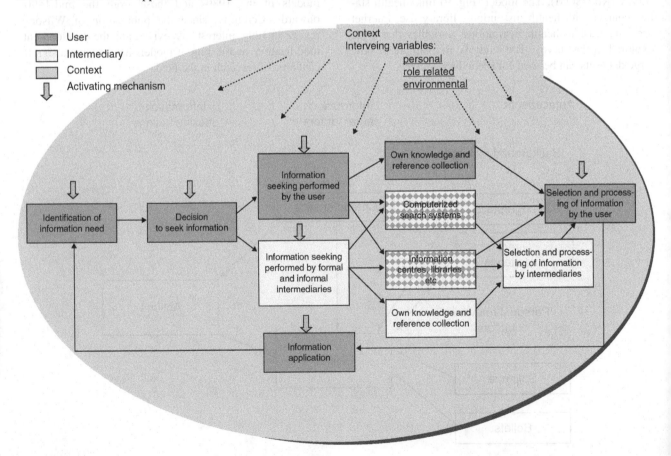

Fig. 10 Niedźwiedzka's general model of information behavior.
Source: From Ingwersen and Järvelin.[23]

information behavior other than information seeking. The result is a kind of combination of Figs. 1 and 2 in this entry (Fig. 10).

CONCLUSION

The three types of models discussed above demonstrate a movement from models of activity, which are generally descriptive, through those that link information seeking to other aspects of behavior or to characteristics of the information user and/or information sources, to those that embody hypotheses about relationships. From the point of view of the genuine development of research in the field, it is desirable, even necessary, that this movement should take place. One can only go so far in refining descriptive models and even those that embody theory can only progress if the underlying theories are tested, and it is the function of the third type of model to graphically illustrate the postulated theoretical relationships. It is to hoped that the sustained level of interest in research into information-seeking behavior will now move away from the refinement of descriptive models and on to the development and testing of theory.

REFERENCES

1. Wilson, T.D. Human information behavior. Inform. Sci. **2000**, *3*(2), 49–55 http://inform.nu/Articles/Vol3/v3n2p49–56.pdf (accessed June 2008).
2. Järvelin, K.; Wilson, T.D. On conceptual models for information seeking and retrieval research. Inform. Res. **2003**, *9* (1), paper 163. http://InformationR.net/ir/9–1/paper163.html (accessed June 2008).
3. Brookes, B.C. The fundamental equation of information science. *Problems of Information Science*; VINITI: Moscow, Russia, 1975; 115–130.
4. Case, D.O. *Looking for Information: A Survey of Research on Information Seeking, Needs, and Behavior*, 2nd Ed. Academic Press: New York, 2007.
5. Wilson, T.D. On user studies and information needs. J. Doc. **1981**, *37*(1), 3–15.
6. Savolainen, R. Everyday life information seeking. In *Theories of Information Behavior*; Fisher, K.E., Erdelez, S., McKechnie, E.F., Eds.; Information Today, Inc.: Medford, NJ, 2005; 143–148.
7. Merton, R.K. Kitt, A. *Contributions to the Theory of Reference Group Behavior*, Free Press: Glencoe, IL, 1950.
8. Thibaut, J.W. Kelley, H.H. *The Social Psychology of Groups*, Wiley: New York, 1959.
9. Krikelas, J. Information-seeking behavior: Patterns and concepts. Drexel Libr. Quart. **1983**, *19*(1), 5–20.
10. Leckie, G.J.; Pettigrew, K.E.; Sylvain, C. Modeling the information seeking of professionals: A general model

derived from research on engineers, health care professionals, and lawyers. Libr. Quart. **1996**, *66*(2), 161–193.
11. Byström, K.; Järvelin, K. Task complexity affects information seeking and use. Inform. Process. Manag. **1995**, *31*(2), 193–213.
12. Kuhlthau, C.C. *Seeking Meaning: A Process Approach to Library and Information Services*, Libraries Unlimited: Westport, CT, 2004.
13. Wilson, T.D. Models in information behavior research. J. Doc. **1999**, *55*(3), 249–270.
14. Ingwersen, P. Cognitive perspectives of information retrieval interaction: Elements of a cognitive IR theory. J. Doc. **1996**, *52*(1), 3–50.
15. Wilson, T.D. Walsh, C. *Information Behavior: An Inter-Disciplinary Perspective*, University of Sheffield, Department of Information Studies: Sheffield, U.K., 1996. British Library Research and Innovation Report, 10. http://informationr.net/tdw/publ/infbehav/index.html (accessed June 2008).
16. Lazarus, R.S. Folkman, S. *Stress, Appraisal and Coping*, Springer Publishing Company Inc.: New York, 1984.
17. Choo, C.W. *The Knowing Organization*, 2nd Ed. Oxford University Press: New York, 2006.
18. Johnson, J.D. *Cancer-Related Information Seeking*, Hampton Press: Cresskill, NJ, 1997.
19. Höglund, L.; Macevičiūtė, E.; Wilson, T.D. Trust in health care: An information perspective. Health Inform. J. **2004**, *10*(1), 37–48.
20. Godbold, N. Beyond information seeking: Towards a general model of information behavior. Inform. Res. **2006**, *11* (4), paper 269. http://InformationR.net/ir/11–4/paper269.html (accessed June 2008).
21. Dervin, B. *Sense-Making Methodology Reader: Selected Writings of Brenda Dervin*, Hampton Press: Cresskill, NJ, 2003.
22. Foster, A.E. A non-linear model of information seeking behavior. J. Am. Soc. Inform. Sci. Technol. **2004**, *55*(3), 228–237.
23. Ingwersen, P. Järvelin, K. *The Turn: Integration of Information Seeking and Retrieval in Context*, Springer/Kluwer: Berlin, Germany, 2005.
24. Niedźwiedzka, B. A proposed general model of information behavior. Inform. Res. **2003**, *9*(1), paper 164. http://InformationR.net/ir/9–1/paper164.html (accessed June 2008).

BIBLIOGRAPHY

1. Dervin, B.; Nilan, M. Information needs and uses. Annu. Rev. Inform. Sci. Technol. **1986**, *21*, 1–25.
2. Ellis, D. A behavioral approach to information retrieval design. J. Doc. **1989**, *45*(3), 171–212.
3. In *Theories of Information Behavior*; Fisher, K.E., Erdelez, S., McKechnie, E.F., Eds.; Information Today, Inc.: Medford, NJ, 2005.
4. Shoemaker, P.J. Tankard, J.W. Lasorsa, D.L. Theoretical models. *How to Build Social Science Theories*; Sage Publications: Thousand Oaks, CA, 2004; Chap. 7.

Information Crises and Crisis Information

Philippe Baumard
School of Engineering, Stanford University, Stanford, California, U.S.A.

Abstract

Information crises are failures of sense-making in organizations, i.e., failures to attribute a meaning and interpretation that can lead to a corrective action. Challenging the hierarchy of data, information, and knowledge, this entry argues that information crises cannot be resolved through normalization and normative prescriptions, but rather by the reinstallment of behavioral-involvement mechanisms, that have been lost in electronic mass-intermediation of postindustrial organizations.

Postmodern societies are highly dependent upon various forms of information, because most of their technical, societal, social, and economic subsystems are consuming as much information that they produce. The rise of machine intermediation has contributed to a lag in the speed and accuracy of human sense-making. By 1999, most experts agreed that machine-to-machine communications could not represent more than half of world traffic before the 2020s. This figure was reached in 2008. Information mostly circulates from machines to machines, from onboard plane maintenance systems to computers on the ground, from an Internet server to a home desktop, from a financial transactions platform to a trader's desk.[1]

One consequence of such an acceleration of information diffusion lies in its autonomous development. Society and local societal organizations rarely possess the mechanisms to influence, forbid, or shape its diffusion. In archaic, and then modern societies, access to information was conditioned, with conditions being the societal strata of groups and communities. But now information is fairly accessible to everyone. The rise of electronic communications, and in particular of the Internet in the late 1990s, has reduced the distance and privileges in accessing, producing, discussing, or emitting information. Machines handle half of the world's communication traffic, and the other half, although not fully automated, has reached an unprecedented level of reliability, not from a sense-making perspective, but from a transmission point of view. The latter half suffers none or few denials of access. While this status has produced tremendous learning opportunities for populations deprived of educational infrastructures, it has also produced on one hand, informational crises, and on the other hand, crisis information management issues.

Informational crises are situations where the opinion-makers, the stakeholders, the potential victims, the organizations, and the policymakers find themselves fully or partially incapable to give sense to critical problems. Plato, in his *Theory of forms*, already addressed what would otherwise seem a contemporary issue. For Plato, universal nature (*phusis*, φύσις) is embodied into recognizable forms or bodies (sōmata, σώματα), which are merely mimetic of their real existence. In other words, information would only be a somatic expression of the likeliness (mimēmata) of a real existence. Modern assumptions on the definition of information follow Plato's intuition: Information is seen as a state of a system that becomes formalized through sense-making, i.e., attributing a message to a given information. Informational crises, in a Plato perspective, would hence be situations where somatic expressions of an event overwhelmed sense-making, either because a recognizable pattern or form cannot be attributed, or because any reliable meaning can be attributed to each individual mirror that compose the information source.

While Plato was trying to understand how mankind accesses nature, modern informational crises have penetrated most societal arenas, from healthcare, politics, and economics to the conduct of business and welfare. Stock markets are dependent upon a mass of information that clearly surpasses the human limitations of sense-making, with or without the support of modern information technologies. Military operations are intertwined with a global information infrastructure that leaves no place hidden from public scrutiny, no rationale unquestioned, and no legitimacy freed of questioning. Dissymmetry of the weak defending against the incumbent makes an intensive use of deliberate information crises, aimed at challenging the rationale, the legitimacy, and the morale of its offensives. One defensive mechanism, not unknown to nature and biological systems, is to develop forms, or information strategies, that defy the larger opponent's sense-making, and hence creates a somatic state within its ranks. Such deliberate informational crises are called "asymmetric campaigning."[2] As organizations are more and more dependent on information for the continuity and stability of their operations, they also become more vulnerable to information crises, either genuine, or deliberate for the purpose of their destabilization.

Encyclopedia of Library and Information Sciences, Fourth Edition DOI: 10.1081/E-ELIS4-120043272

Information crises, and crisis information are, therefore, very close concepts. While crisis information represents the attempt to make sense of a crisis with the purpose of solving it, information crisis represents the state in which organizations are prone to engage in crisis information. One immediate issue relates to sense-making. Attributing sense, i.e., producing a message derived from information, relies on a continuous and ongoing retrospective analysis of plausible forms that attempts to rationalize events and people's actions (p. 409).[3] The first obvious assumption is that to make sense, people or organizations must first notice the concerned events. What people notice or do not notice is not, however, a matter of access, presence, or availability of data and information. Information becomes accessible when one is able or capable of understanding its meaning. When we fail to notice, we might simply fail to understand. Stimuli often do not escape our attention, they escape our sense-making. As R.D. Laing puts it: "The range of what we think and do is limited by what *we fail to notice*. And because we fail to notice that we fail to notice, there is little we can do to change, until we notice, how failing to notice shapes our thoughts and deeds" (quoted by Goleman (p. 24).[4] An informational crisis is often a sense-making crisis, rather than being a problem of availability or quality of the information at hand.

THE MECHANISMS OF INFORMATION CRISES

Information crises grow on the grounds of uncertainty, independently of the nature, the depth, and the reliability of the information at hand. Both the Columbia and the Challenger space shuttle accidents created long and painful information crises, despite dealing with some of the most documented industrial and engineering processes on earth. In contrast, the impossibility to give sense to an event can occur with a very little, ill-mastered information. The development of viruses such as H5N1 or SARS is exemplar: the lack of information about viral behavior creates the information crisis. Hence, many information crises are triggered by a failure to conduct a reductive analysis, either by too numerous interpretations being available and creating causal ambiguity, or by the impossibility of reducing reality and making it stay real (p. 327).[5]

The first conundrum of such a principle lies in knowledge ontology. R.D. Laing's philosophical pun says that knowledge turns in circles, for its substance can only be accessed through teleological means. Data can produce information with a mindful purpose. And knowledge can be derived from information, assuming that the sense that we gave to the data and information has not been filtered by our perceptual biases. But previous knowledge is what biases our perception and the way we select information in the first place. Hence, information crises encompass both the previous learning and knowledge of concerned individuals, as well as disconcerting new information. Crises

arise when individuals are no longer capable of "labeling and categorizing to stabilize the streaming of experience" (p. 411).[3] This situation can either arise from events that an individual has never experienced before, thus depriving them of labels and categories of reference, or from new stimuli coming through familiar channels, but that do not match the existing labels and categories.

The central mechanism of an information crisis is therefore one of imperfect, incomplete, and/or unreliable interpretation. The lack of reliable interpretation has three main sources. First, individuals themselves tend to distort their perception, more or less purposefully. Following Plato, if we accept the idea that information precedes a somatic expression of reality, then traumas, guilt, fears, and pain can lead an individual to see what he or she wants to see, instead of what is presented.[4]

Second, organizations replicate, duplicate, and distort individual distortions, for they reflect collectively the more or less somatic reading of information conducted by individuals. "Those interpretations are generated within the organization in the face of considerable perceptual ambiguity" (p. 19).[6] As Starbuck puts it (p. 91):[7]

Most of the time, organizations generate actions unreflectively and non adaptively. To justify their actions, organizations create problems, successes, threats, and opportunities. These are ideological molecules that mix values, goals, expectations, perceptions, theories, plans, and symbols. The molecules form while people are result watching, guided by the beliefs that they should judge results good or bad, look for the causes of results, and propose needs for action.

Far from being a distinctive reality on which action is acted, information is an integral part of generated action. Information may be generated ahead of time to justify an intended action, and vice versa, information is often generated ex-post to justify a non-intended action. Of course, this production of information does not flow in two separate categories, so people in organizations cannot really tell if information has preceded or followed an ongoing action.[3]

Third, information itself can be destructive. Destructive information can be defined as a set of messages, signals, and stimuli that mislead cognitive and behavioral routines of an organization, and lead an organization or an individual to generate confusion. It also threatens the reliable pursuit of the organization's goals. Goffman, in his study of interaction rituals between individuals, detected such a phenomenon (p. 141),[8] by observing individuals purposefully distorting information to manipulate and mislead others. Others have described destructive information as "guilty knowledge" or "dirty data."[9] Incomplete, truncated, uncertain data can lead individuals to encounter sharp crisis situations, which are either solved by the production of reliable data, or, if not solved, can exhaust reductive analysis, morale, and determination.

Hence, information, or the lack of, can produce decision paralysis, panic, fear and through somatic and secondary effects, and actual pain. While this phenomenon is well-known to the art of medicine, few studies have been conducted in organizational settings other than healthcare and patient safety.

SPIRALING, AUTO-FEEDING, AND SELF-REINFORCEMENT

Sense-making is about presumption. It is social and systemic (p. 412).[3] Presumptions are the products of past experiences, social learning, and education. In nature, presumptions are born through interactions and propagate through interactions. When people face an information crisis, they usually seek help in their immediate surroundings, engage in collective sense-making, seek information in the press, on the internet, try to reinforce their core beliefs to fight disturbing stimuli.[4] They engage in socializations that can reduce their anxiety and the uncertainty surrounding the situation, or reinforce both the uncertainty and the importance given to their interpretation of the new event. This second phenomenon is known as "sense-making spiraling." Seeking help from a knowledgeable source can definitely reduce uncertainty when the lack of knowledge is dissymmetric. When ignorance and incomplete information are mutual, with little expectation to add sense to the ongoing information crisis, individuals provide feedback loops to each other that ignore better-informed sources and may aggravate the situation.[10,11] Over time, these processes trigger more negative outcomes, and turn into vicious cycles, leading to a spiral of counter-productive influences auto-feeding with incomplete information.[12] These deviation-amplifying loops are well-known to the Internet, in a modern version of rumors, grow shorter, more concise, easier to grasp, and to tell as they travel from one individual to another.[13]

As individuals tend to associate the repetition of information as a sign of its reliability, the Internet with its continuous flow of commentaries and self-produced knowledge has become a vector of crisis information vulnerability. Duplication, however, is not to be blamed on individuals, but on society's evolution as a whole. The press, facing an intensive competition from free media, is also forced to outsource most of its information, and therefore often engages in commentaries driven from secondary commercial sources. The cost structures of the press have thus evolved from mostly primary information at its birth, to mostly secondary sources and commentaries in its maturity phase. The process of validating information has become tedious, as competition forces editors and media organizations to deliver news almost instantly. Moreover, the rise of a press deriving benefits from sensational information has progressively blurred the boundaries between institutional and legitimate sources of information and

their look-a-likes. With the rise of electronic intermediation, most people in organizations access information faster through external electronic media than through internal channels. Hence, crisis information spirals are not per se an organizational phenomenon.[14]

Contrary to the phenomenon of rumors, however, people in organizations rarely generate destructive information spirals intentionally. Most informational behavior in organizations is somewhat "positional," in Hirsch's terms.[15] People seek to gain information that allows them to position themselves, reduce ambiguity, and get a perspective that they perceive as slightly better than those their own or than what they witness in their colleagues. Accordingly, people do not see information as having absolute superior value, but rather an immediate, practical leverage for their ongoing actions. Rather than challenging information being used and articulated in ongoing programs, people favor collateral and ad hoc organizations, which would leave their main programs untouched, and their deeds unchallenged.[16] Secrecy that can turn banal information into highly destructive information follows a social psychology that is more embedded in ignorance than maliciousness.[17] Human inferences are imperfect, and turn genuine interpretations into misleading and contaminating shortcuts.[18] Moreover, most information is unconsciously processed by individuals, so that people are generally not able to identify how they gathered, assimilated, and transformed information that leads their actions and deeds.[19] Hence, individuals rarely discriminate between genuine information and its many doubles. Reality is taken for granted, until proven otherwise. Artifacts are as much instrumental as reality, for realities are known as genuine only when they get dismantled.[20] This latter characteristic of informational behavior contributes to sustaining the development of crisis information spirals in most organizations. "Information-generating" behavior is much alike the "action-generating" behavior described by.[7] People generate information while listening upwards; they document expost facto an action-generation whose rationale they might have lost; they fine-tune their past commitments with the new criteria for approval; they reuse uncompleted achievements that have bred frustration and translate them into the new set of core beliefs.

This leads us to the most puzzling characteristic of crisis information: its self-reinforcement and its capacity to feed on itself. Findings in action-generation suggest that the pursuit of programmed behavior is strongly intertwined with the self-reinforcement of an information crisis. Individuals produce learning and information by repeatedly experimenting successfully with behaviors that they turn into programs. When an action fails to produce the expected outcomes, they can either modify the behavior to alter its output, or alter the information so that their unchanged behavior matches the discordant informational output. Large banks and financial institutions have suffered such a phenomenon repeatedly from the early 1980s till today. A trader engages in hazardous investments, realizes that their outcome does not match his or her expectations, and subsequently modifies the informational output with complicities that would prevent a behavioral change, in expectation of a positive reversal of fortune.

Self-reinforcement is often accentuated by group behavior. Janis[21] described how small groups facing crises tend to protect their cohesiveness through collective rationalization, stereotyped views of out-groups, self-censorship, illusion of unanimity, and self-appointed "mindguards." Different from spiraling, "groupthink" aims at protecting the group from a perceived vulnerability, by reaffirming the shared core belief, and developing an illusion of invulnerability. The immediate consequence of groupthink is the cessation of search for alternative interpretations. Group members discount early warnings, and sanction peers who would question the group cohesiveness by doing so. Historical cases discussed by Janis[21] include the attack of Pearl Harbor and the Bay of Pigs crises.

RESOLVING INFORMATION CRISES

Resolving informational crises often involves managing the crisis itself. A crisis is a situation that seriously threatens an individual or an organization. As the etymology of its noun suggests, a crisis is a time for a decision. Crises, however, are usually unnecessary. There is no scientific evidence that crises improve or diminish organizational longevity. There also is no evidence that organizational survival indicates effectiveness (p. 54).[22] In fact, most organizations keep their names to maintain the continuity of their recognition by individuals who deal with them. But most organizations have little to do with their constituents from a decade earlier. Two questions come immediately to mind: if escaping crises does not display any form of correlation with resilience, other than psychological at the individual level, and if organizational survival is not an evidence of their performance, why do organizations continue to manage crises? Why do they not simply leave the environments that created the crisis in the first place?

An answer comes from Staw et al.[23] under the form of threat-rigidity effects. Perceived uncertainty over anticipated events creates slower decision-making, and organizational rigidity, that are often accentuated by groupthink at senior management levels.[21] Accordingly, organizations persist in managing crises because they believe they can repeat their past successes; they want to protect this core belief; they do not want to disavow public commitments, and hence, most often end up escalating their commitments, not to the crisis itself, but to its resolution process. This phenomenon is not completely a stranger to Plato's intuition: information crises are somatic expressions of an inaccessible reality; hence, organizations focus

on the symptoms that are immediately accessible and actionable. But as Nystrom and Starbuck p. 55[22] underscore: "In real crises, weathering-the-storm strategies work only briefly. Then the symptoms of trouble reappear; only this time, the organizations start with fewer resources and less time to act." Not surprisingly, crisis information management techniques are sometimes more somatic and symptomatic that the crises themselves.

Symptoms of crisis information management that ultimately aggravates the crisis include an over-emphasis on prediction (as an attempt to reduce uncertainty), mindguards and preachers of hierarchical control (expected to bring back a sense of control), and increased demands for various rationalizations and justifications (as an attempt to analytically exhaust reality). These three "usual suspects" of inadequate crisis information management are grounded in one solid block, made of five interlocked components: the reproduction of past successes; the defense of legitimacy and legacy of concerned decision makers; preparation for potential scapegoating; the reassurance of the null hypothesis; and the evaluation of senior managers.

Firms try to reproduce their past successes, by approximating their mechanisms and re-enacting environments that approximate the conditions of the past. One obvious rationale lies in mass assets effects, and the attempt to reemploy past expertise into new lines of products and services. That is to say, firms tend to bend environmental conditions so as to fit already deployed assets on a global scale. Over time, this mass asset impact prevents firms from assessing the validity of their learning. They enact environments that tend to self-validate their learning, eventually masking vulnerabilities or misconceptions. A less obvious consideration is that firms try to "do more of the same thing," while adapting to unexpected demands through management by exceptions. Alas, environments of the past are not replicable in the present. While this seems obvious, most organizations develop over time the core belief that efficiency and consistency of successes achieved in the past are replicable in environments that have little to do with the earlier economic, technological, and societal conditions. Hence, usual mismanagement of crisis information is rooted in the belief that trying to replicate conditions of the past will increase the capability of prediction over the present. Unfortunately, learning from repeated success makes future failure very likely.[24]

The second "usual suspect"—i.e., increasing hierarchical control—is mostly grounded in the criteria that are used to assess, reward, or sanction senior managers. People in organizations are judged on one hand on their past legacies, and on the other hand, on the institutional "soundness" of their decision process. Past legacies are made of past successes, but also of past difficulties and the way they were handled. Immediately increasing hierarchical control in a time of crisis presents the advantage of clearly identifying the ownership of the crisis, and eventually, the lack of ownership of the concerned senior manager, if events transform into a real disaster. Hence, an increase of hierarchical control is often a strategy that prepares for potential failure of the crisis management, prompting potential scapegoats, and preparing a defense of probably questioned legitimacy.

The third "usual suspect"—i.e., analytically exhaust reality—has more to do with the search for a reassuring absence of change, and the protection of core beliefs. Not all crises express themselves loudly, and organizations are prone to errors of appreciation. As it might be unclear whether the information crisis at stake may end up in a success or a failure, organization members usually slant interpretations to argue that nothing has really changed in the practices or the behavior of employees. Unfortunately, employees often think along the same lines and are not really willing to share information about mistakes they have made. The consequence is that the sought "null hypothesis" is easily achieved. Senior managers duly question all middle-managers and employees asking them if they had wrongly changed constituents that might have led to a crisis, and the employees and middle managers duly answer that they did not. Paradoxically, this exchange of tense and polite audits is mutually beneficial, by contributing to escapes and scapegoating strategies by both employees and senior management. Accordingly, managers tend to dismiss small failures that challenge the firm's foundation premises, perceive errors as small deviations and experiments, and prepare the ground for justifying that a large failure is fully exogenous to both their management responsibility and their governance techniques.[24]

As discussed earlier, information crises, and information about crises, are primarily failures of interpretation. Not surprisingly, organization members attempt to reinforce their sense-making in the most controlled and predictable manner. But when information has lost its labels, senior managers attempt to invent new ones or force data into old repositories. And while the experience has been destabilized, and the labels left untouched, managers are convinced that relabeling will improve experience. Yet when channels have been unchallenged, and the crisis still occurs, managers ask people to justify once again that they used the same channels as usual. As Nystrom and Starbuck (p. 55)[22] put it: "They know that their current beliefs and procedures have arisen from rational analyses and successful experiences, so they have to see evidence that these beliefs and procedures are seriously deficient before they will even think about major changes."

Crisis information management is about stopping the self-reinforced and auto-feeding phenomenon that surrounds a crisis, and is made of fears, anxiety, rumors, and apprehension about being misjudged. By increasing management control and hierarchical scrutiny, managers often "de-humanize" the crisis and the information surrounding it. Accordingly, people who feel that they need to justify

unintended actions with unintended consequences also perceive a growing distance between them and the people asking the questions. Crises are not systemic. On the contrary, the existence of a crisis explicitly expresses that both the social and the management "systems" have failed to absorb an environmental change. To reapply and reenforce a system that just failed is "doing more of the same thing," i.e., trying to solve an information problem by substituting the same information under another "form," to quote Plato's expression. Increasing control, demanding facts and figures, are somatic responses. They express a mimetic symptom that does not suppress, but rather leverages the original expression of the soma.

In their seminal study of modern crises,[2] Atkinson and Moffat surmise that the rise of information-dependency in modern organizations led to the generalization of "nonlinear dynamics" as a principal, not a peripheral component of organized societal life (Table 1). Atkinson and Moffat (p. 184),[2] reflecting on the organizational roots of the Columbia Shuttle Accident, infer that

> within the rule-based and hierarchical safety control system, information was being lost. The right information existed, but within the almost tangential network of unofficial e-mails, exchanged on a trust basis by engineers and scientists working alongside, but outside, the hierarchical control chain. Truths established by NASAs scientific and engineering networks were not getting through to those who needed them, crucially to those who needed, even if they did not want, to know.

Reflecting on the Challenger Shuttle accident, Weick (p. 397)[25] suggests another characterization of the role of information in crises. Reviewing Diane Vaughan's works on the Challenger accident, Karl Weick notices: "The O-rings were not the only problem with the connecting joints. Rainwater had accumulated in joints on an earlier launch (p. 304), and the putty that was supposed to prevent hot gas from even reaching the O-rings had repeatedly failed (p. 10)." Where Atkinson and Moffat are describing an institutional malformation of modern organizations,

Table 1 Characteristics of complex nonlinear organizations.

Complexity concept	Information age organizations
Nonlinear interaction	The organization is composed of a large number of nonlinearly interacting parts
Self-organization	Local coevolution induces long-range order
Nonequilibrium order	Interactions within the organization proceed far from equilibrium. Correlation of local effects is key
Collective dynamics	Cascades of local effects ripple through the organization

Source: Adapted from Atkinson and Moffat.[2]

i.e., the spreading of uncontrolled electronic communications, Weick sees elements that

> speak to larger issues of the role of chance in organizational outcomes, distraction during moments when embedded signals of danger come across one's desk, credibility as a function of position, and organizational learning in the face of shifting attributions and incomplete data (p. 397).

In other words, the rapid growth of signal-detection opportunities, sensors, and electronic devices in organizations does not seem to improve its sense-making performance, but rather multiplies the number of nonlinear interactions, nonequilibrium orders, and noninteracting or interacting nonlinear parts.[2] Table 1 from Atkinson and Moffat's study of modern crises and insurgencies, illustrates characteristics of postindustrial organizations as envisioned by the authors.

The multiplication of interpretations in organizations is not a new phenomenon, and in a sense, an organization cannot be anything else than the permanent re-combination of random nonlinear interactions. What is new is the loss of correlation between power and social structures and information life in organizations. Whereas information has been subdued and submitted to preexistent and prevalent authority structures for centuries, it is now able to circulate beyond hierarchical boundaries, bypassing legitimate chains of command, for better or for worse. As Karl Weick noted about the Challenger disaster, "in 1985 there was both escalating concern about safety and belief that risk was acceptable, an unusual combination of simultaneous belief and doubt that may be more common than we suspect" (1997: 398). The main difference between Von Braun's NASA in 1951 and the modern NASA in the twenty-first century is that deviance has been heard; not acted upon, but heard beyond the institutional and legitimate boundaries of the organization. The "normalization" of events[26] that used to be a long and maturing process of many social interactions, is now attempted to be achieved by an uncontrollable nonlinear and quasi-instant process of electronic messaging. However, in such a substitution process, involvement is replaced with figuration; facing issues is replaced with declarative safety nets, as noted by Atkinson and Moffat,[2] Weick,[25] and Vaughan.[26] Such attributes are symptomatic of postindustrial organizations. Huber[27] suggested that such organizations "rely upon all available knowledge, always more knowledge," that they must face "complexity, always more complexity" and "turbulence, always more turbulence." They must make very complex decisions, which require "the consideration of an ever-increasing number of variables with ever more complex relationships between them" (1984, p. 933). From this foundation, George Huber then considered the effects of the advent of new information technology, concluding that "postindustrial organizations will be more formal," and that "the acquisition of information will be more directed, more integrated, and specialized" (1984, pp. 933–943). While Huber's premonition proved accurate in most points, a third sequel of postindustrial organizing has been overlooked: postindustrial organizations are not only prone to informational crises, they generate them.

REFERENCES

1. Starbuck, W.H.; Baumard, P. Where are organizational cultures going?. In *The International Handbook of Organizational Culture and Climate*; Cary, C., Christopher, E., Eds.; John Wiley and Sons: New York, 2001; 521–531.
2. Atkinson, S.R.; Moffat, J. *The Agile Organization: From Informal Networks to Complex Effects and Agility*, DoD Command and Control Research Program, Information Age Series: Washington, DC, 2005.
3. Weick, K.E.; Sutcliffe, K.M.; Obstfeld, D. Organizing and the Process of Sensemaking. Org. Sci. **2005**, *16*(4), 409–421.
4. Goleman, D. *Vital Lies, Simple Truths: The Psychology of Self-Deception*, Simon & Schuster: New York, 1985.
5. Macintosh, J.P. Connectivity: the space, tempo and exploitation of risk in information age. In *Cyberwar 2.0: Myths, Mysteries and Reality*; Campen, A.D., Dearth, D.H., Eds.; AFCEA: Fairfax, VA, 1998; 323–345.
6. March, J.G., Olsen, J.P., Eds.; *Ambiguity and Choice in Organizations*; Universitets Forlaget: Bergen, Norway, 1976.
7. Starbuck, W.H. Organizations as action generators. Am. Sociol. Rev. **1983**, *48*, 91–102.
8. Goffman, E. *The Presentation of Self in Everyday Life*, Pelican Books: Harmondsworth, U.K., 1971.
9. Van Maanen, J. On the ethics of fieldwork. In *An Introduction to Social Research: A Handbook of Social Science Methods*; Smith, R., Ed.; Ballinger: Cambridge, MA, 1982; Vol. 1., 227–251.
10. Hambrick, D.C.; Daveni, R.A. Large corporate failures as downward spirals. Admin. Sci. Quart. **1988**, *33*(1), 1–23.
11. Ashforth, B. Petty tyranny in organizations. Hum. Relat **1994**, *47*(7), 755–778.
12. Masuch, M. Vicious circles in organizations. Admin. Sci. Quart **1985**, *30*(1), 14–33.
13. Allport, G.W.; Postman, L. *The Psychology of Rumor*, Russell: New York, 1947.
14. Mitroff, I.I.; Pauchant, T.C.; Shrivastava, P. Conceptual and empirical issues in the development of a general theory of crisis management. Technol. Forecast. Soc. **1988**, *33*, 83–107.
15. Hirsch, F. *Social Limits to Growth*, Routledge & Kegan Paul: London, 1977.
16. Zand, D.E. *Information, Organization and Power: Effective Management in the Knowledge Society*, McGraw-Hill: New York, 1981; 57–88.
17. Simmel, G. The sociology of secrecy and of the secret societies. Am. J. Sociol. **1906**, *11*, 441–498.
18. Nisbett, R.E.; Ross, L. *Human Inferences: Strategies and Shortcomings of Social Judgment*, Prentice Hall: Englewood Cliffs, NJ, 1980.

19. Nisbett, R.E.; Wilson, T.D. Telling more than we know: verbal reports on mental processes. Psychol. Rev. **1977**, *84*, 231–259.
20. Rosset, C. *Le Réel: Traité de l'idiotie*, Editions de Minuit: Paris, France, 1977.
21. Janis, I.L. *Victims of Groupthink*, Houghton Mifflin: Boston, MA, 1972.
22. Nystrom, P.C.; Starbuck, W.H. To avoid organizational crises, unlearn. Organ. Dyn. **1984**, *12*(4), 53–65.
23. Staw, B.M.; Sandelands, L.E.; Dutton, J.E. Threat-rigidity effects in organizational behavior: a multi-level analysis. Admin. Sci. Quart. **1981**, *26*, 501–524.
24. Baumard, P.; Starbuck, W.H. Learning from failures: why it may not happen. Long Range Plann. **2005**, *38*, 281–298.
25. Weick, K.E. The challenger launch decision: risky technology, culture, and deviance at NASA. Admin. Sci. Quart. **1997**, *42*(2), 395–401.

26. Vaughan, D. *The Challenger Launch Decision: Risky Technology, Culture, and Deviance at NASA*; University of Chicago Press: Chicago, IL, 1996.
27. Huber, G.P. The nature and design of post-industrial organizations. Manage. Sci. **1984**, *30*(8), 928–951.

BIBLIOGRAPHY

1. Sheffi, Y. *The Resilient Enterprise: Overcoming Vulnerability for Competitive Advantage*; The MIT Press: Cambridge, MA, 2005.
2. Starbuck, W.H.; Farjoun, M. *Organization at the Limit: Lessons from the Columbia Disaster*; Blackwell Publishing: Oxford, U.K., 2005.

Information Explosion

Ronald E. Day
School of Library and Information Science, Indiana University, Bloomington, Indiana, U.S.A.

Abstract

This entry discusses the concept of the information explosion as an empirical phenomenon and, more so, as a discursive concept. The term is discussed in relation to discourses on the information society and in relation to the concept of information overload.

Within its concept the term "information explosion" most often refers to the extended and largely continual growth and proliferation of "information" (newspapers, books, journal articles, television programs, Internet Web sites, e-mail, radio programs, etc.) during the nineteenth and, particularly, the twentieth and now the twenty-first centuries. It is a term that is central in discourses that demand information management in response to social, institutional, and even personal information growth and proliferation. It is often associated with other terms, such as "the information society" and "information overload," which mark some qualitative social and historical event arising out of these quantitative increases.

The term characterizes the growth and proliferation of data, documents, and communication in both general social and in scientific communication. With such a broad sweep, the term signifies a general cause that demands greater information management across an equally broad sweep of informational forms: bibliographic and other documentary forms; abstracts, catalogs, and other records of initial documents; informal or "grey" literature in the sciences; scientific data; internet and broadcast media. The "information explosion," broadly conceived, brings within its domain much of what we experience in, and as, modernity, and from this viewpoint it may be seen as what has allowed local lives to be understood as global issues, as well as has allowed for the observation and even surveillance of individual lives through national and international agencies. Indeed, any discussion of the "information explosion" would be addressing some of the major social challenges of information management and evaluation in modern societies across a broad range of areas: national intelligence and many other governmental and social policy issues; social and cultural values and welfare; scientific policy; social opinion and thought; and pedagogy, psychology, and human development.

Obviously, such a broad arena exceeds the range of an encyclopedia entry. More importantly, however, we may ask if this very generality of the concept is either informative or useful? With these caveats in mind, this entry takes a more simple, and more materialist, critical, approach.

Instead of focusing on the "information explosion" as a fact, particularly in the general manner in which the term is often couched, we will ask if this term makes any sense and how it does so. Though the concept of the "information explosion" is often taken as representing an empirical fact, in this entry we will suggest that, as a general historical and social concept, at least, it functions as a rhetorical device in "information society" literatures. The term may seem to refer to an empirical fact, but as we will suggest, the term, in its often used generality, is difficult to define and to empirically validate, it is emphatic and emotive ("explosion"), and it is often embedded in arguments that are rhetorically interesting, but empirically specious. The prevalence of the term, particularly in popular accounts of the information age or information society, together with its ambiguity and problematic empirical reference, suggests that the proper approach to this topic is that of critical informatics, as a subset of social informatics, and in particular, as an analysis of the term's rhetorical forms and discursive contexts. From this perspective, the term's meaning may be better understood by its rhetorical deployments in social space and as cultural forms of expression, rather than by countless—and always limited—enumerations of its supposed empirical referents.

The initial task facing a critical understanding of the term "information explosion" is to ask, just what is it that is "information" which is supposed to have "exploded," and if there is a relative overproduction or "overload" of information, then why do we use the rather dramatic term of "explosion" and what are the consequences of the use of such language?

Some of the problems involved with arguing for an information explosion can be gleaned in Peter Lyman and Hal R. Varian's report, "How Much Information? 2003."[1] Lyman and Varian's report covers the growth (and occasional decrease) in information production across the globe across a wide variety of mediums as measured in bytes of information.

Our interest in pointing to Lyman and Varian's report is not that of reproducing their findings, findings that are reported yearly in more scattered form in a variety of

Encyclopedia of Library and Information Sciences, Fourth Edition DOI: 10.1081/E-ELIS4-120044391

governmental and professional yearbooks. Our interest, rather, is to point out a common method of argument in discourses on the "information explosion." The concept of the information explosion is commonly constructed through an argument that begins with asking something of the order of "how much information is produced (consumed, stored, etc.) in a given period of time or in a given geographical or organizational locale?" Such a question is not only difficult to answer because of the problem of finding standardized data pertaining to the different "forms" of information, but moreover, it is possibly unanswerable in its totality because there is not a common understanding of what the word "information" means. (Capurro and Bjørland have discussed the many different senses of the word "information."[2]) For example, by asking "how much information is produced?" are we to include verbal information produced in our ordinary affairs? Are we to include "grey" or informal literature? Are we to include (as Warren Weaver suggested in his commentary on Shannon's *The Mathematical Theory of Communication*) the "affects" of the performing arts (such as dance—and what would this mean)?[3] And, if we limit ourselves to presenting evidence about the information explosion to data on the growth of documents, then we are still faced with the problem of what is considered to be a document.[4,5] And, substituting the term "data" for "documents" and presenting all information measured in terms of bytes blurs the values of different informational forms still further.

Such problems of definition are not marginal to the problem of the information explosion, but rather, their being considered marginal and their being forgotten are at the heart of the term's success in seemingly representing an empirical event. This forgetting is central to its success in discourses arguing for the social need for professional information management techniques and technologies and information management organizations.

For example, if one had consulted in 2007 the homepage of the contemporary "ischools" consortium (http://www.ischools.org), made up of many of the top university schools in information science in the United States, one would have found there an "ExaByte-Counter," which suggested the need for such schools:

> ExaByte-Counter—the number of bytes our world is creating. (One exabyte = 10^{18} bytes)
> **In 2006, the world created 161 exabytes of new information**.
> 161 exabytes would fill 2 billion 80 GB iPods.
> 142,000,000,000,000,000,000 bytes[6]

The reason why the exabyte data is shown on the web page is, as is often the case in this type of discourse, to persuasively suggest the need for new technical, technological, or in this case, organizational and educational tools and bodies in order to "harness" the "power" of information: "The iField addresses this fundamental issue: how do we harness that incredible flow of information for the betterment of society, rather than get swamped by it?"[7]

This statement contains the tropes of "information flow" and, implicitly, "information power" in an unspoken metaphor that equates the ischools with something akin to a hydroelectric plant. Subsequent statements on the ischools' Web site surrounding the above quote stressed that what we refer to as the information explosion is a product of the Information Age and that it creates conditions of information overload. The rhetorical relation of "the information explosion" to "the Information Age" (or, its near synonym, "the Information Society") and to "information overload" will be addressed in the following sections of this entry.

It needs to be mentioned first, however, that there are plentiful historical precedents for this type of discourse. Suzanne Briet, "Madame Documentation," used the same rhetorical strategies as those above to argue for the historical inevitability of the profession of Documentation in the beginning of her 1951 book, *Qu'est-ce que la documentation? (What is Documentation?)*.[8,9] The father of European Documentation, Paul Otlet, in his writings used the trope of the information explosion as a reason to embark upon his own projects, which included not just written works, but the creation of a world documentation organization and dreams of adding to this a world museum and a world bank. One contemporary author, Alex Wright, has even suggested that the information explosion reaches back to prehistoric times—a rather spectacular claim![10] Tefko Saracevic has summarized the view that information science and the development of information technology has been a consequence of the information explosion and the "evolution" of the information society:

> Addressing the problem of information explosion, information science found a niche within the broader context of the evolution of the information society. In its various manifestations and attempted solutions, the niche is getting broader and bigger.[11]

If read deeply, the existence of such discourses suggests that we need to examine not only the rhetorical bases for the deployment of "information explosion" discourses, but we also must examine the larger social forces investing in what are supposedly explained by such discourses and their tropes: namely information infrastructures. This broader task has been undertaken, for example in Geoffrey Bowker's book, *Memory Practices in the Sciences*.[12]

INFORMATION SOCIETY

Frank Webster[13] has well summarized some of the more salient points of a critical analysis of the concept of the "information society." His comments bear repeating and bear further commentary in the context of the concept of the "information explosion," for both terms connote historically unique moments of information mass and overproduction.

One of the most important points that Webster makes in his article is that arguments for asserting the existence of an information society—like arguments asserting the existence of an information explosion—often take the form of asserting a qualitative social change out of the evidence of rhetorically or stylistically impressive data on information production, use, etc. The issue here is that though the data may be rhetorically or stylistically impressive (as in the ischool consortium's "ExaByte counter"), often there is a lack of a standard for discussing why and how such data is to be used as the basis for making assertions about qualitative historical events or social values. Information society literature, for example, often argues for the existence of an information society based on data that show increases in the production and use of information and of information and communication technologies, the use of such technologies in manufacturing and in other traditionally blue-collar jobs, increases in white-collar education requirements, and various other statistical measures. This argument and these types of data are familiar in the writings of the most well-known presenters of "information society" literature: Daniel Bell, Robert Reich, Manuel Castells, etc. These arguments also sometimes appear in Knowledge Management literature as quantitative evidence for arguments asserting the reality of post-Fordism and other "post-industrial" events and values, leading up to the appearance and supposed social importance of Knowledge Management. As Webster argues, however,

...quantitative measures—simply more information—cannot of themselves identify a break with previous systems, while it is at least theoretically possible to regard small but decisive quantitative changes as marking a system break.... What we have here is the assumption that quantitative increases transform—in unspecified ways—into qualitative changes in the social system.[14]

The assumption that quantitative data can give evidence of an historical event or social value without also supplying criteria for the translation of the quantitative data to the qualitative values invites a mischievous use of numbers and statistics for purely persuasive, rather than reasoned, purposes. As we have suggested, this is but one reason for suspecting that information explosion discourse, particularly in the generalist and historicist literature in which it is often found, is more polemical than empirically sound. Another suspicion is aroused by the use of the common standard of bytes for measuring informational units whose meaning and social value cannot be measured by such. (For example, stating that a book is made up of x number of electronic bytes [assuming that it

is in an electronic format] tells us nothing about its informational value in the manner that we usually say that books give their readers information.) No massive number of bytes and no well-known professional authorities can hide the fact that such arguments are specious. Data showing increases in library holdings, publication rates, and data production alone tells us nothing about the qualitative social importance of such numbers unless real historical and social effects are explained and demonstrated. And the ability to demonstrate an "information explosion" across seemingly endless varieties of documentary forms and communication events is very problematic, not only for reasons of reliable statistics, but for the more fundamental reason that the term "information" is a figure of speech that covers many different documentary forms and communication events without a reliable common element which could be pointed to for comparison between, or for combining, these forms and events.

INFORMATION OVERLOAD

If we are to account for the rhetoric of the "information explosion" we may do so in terms of its argumentative forms for evidence (quantitative data, citations to well-known authors, etc.) and in terms of its association to other claimed qualitative events and values (such as "the information society"). If the information society is often discussed as the outward manifestation of an information explosion (or just as often, the information explosion as an outward manifestation of an information society), the "inward" or psychological effect of an information explosion is often argued in terms of "information overload." "Information overload" is often discussed in the literature in terms of a person being "overloaded" either by a single event of too much information or by the effect of an "information explosion" on a social scale.

Mary Jo Rudd and Joel Rudd in an article on the impact of the information explosion on library users distinguish information explosion and information "load" and "overload" in terms of causes and their effects.[15] They suggest that the results of early experiments into information overload should be approached cautiously since such results fail to adequately account for personal selections of information "input" and personal avoidance behaviors for preventing "overload." Further, however, we might add that the information processing metaphors used in Rudd and Rudd's article are especially peculiar, for library patrons are traditionally thought of in terms of seeking information for particular needs, not as information processing systems. Given a needs-based agent it is hard to imagine an overloaded mental apparatus since needs give way to more needs or no needs when the patron is "satisfied" or ready to move on or simply stops or quits his or her search. The point is that the "information overload" trope may not work very well as even traditional explanations explanatory devices in an of information seeking. The "information overload" trope seems to be a personal psychological equivalent to the social "information explosion" trope: both work on an energy flow metaphor for information (as we saw with the ischools consortium Web site). Indeed, these two tropes sometimes cross in the literature so that information overloads are said to occur both in terms of personal psychology and in terms of social systems.

Of course, there are many writers who suggest various psychological conditions resulting from information overload in the sense of what is sometimes called, "media overload." The theme of information or stimulus overload goes back to the beginnings of industrial modernity, while complaints of media overload, specifically, are a bit more recent, tending to become louder in the 1930s, but continuing on through today, now focusing on digital information.

One of the more fascinating commentators on information overload may be the Italian social commentator, Franco Berardi (also known as "Bifo"). What make Berardi's commentary so fascinating are his claims that information overload largely accounts for the rise of certain psychopathologies, such as panic disorder and depression. In many of his writings of the past 15 years, not the least being his book *La fabbrica dell' infelicità* (*The Factory of Unhappiness*),[16] the advent of panic as a psychological disorder (panic disorder became a psychological disorder of its own—derived from the Freudian category of anxiety neurosis—only with the publication of the third edition of the *Diagnostic and Statistical Manual of Mental Disorders* [*DSM* III] in 1980) is linked to information overload, and the subsequent depression which occurs when the person finds him or herself unable to position his or her potential actions in this overload of stimulation. Interestingly, we may recall that Immanuel Kant, too, described a similar psychological phenomenon in his *Critique of Judgment*; the "natural sublime" or the "infinite sublime" are experienced as moments of expansive awe, and even fear and trepidation, leading to a loss of possibilities for personal action, and thus perhaps, we may speculate, eventually resulting in depression. Being in a pre-electric age, of course, Kant did not have access to the electric energy metaphor. Berardi's is a modern account of the origins of psychological diseases (particularly, panic disorder) as caused by information overload, particularly in the form of media overload.

Another account of the effect of information overload is reviewed in Frank Webster's previously mentioned article. This is what is sometimes referred to as a "postmodern" reading of information overload where the referential quality of language is understood as breaking down in the midst of a proliferation of signs. Particularly in the contemporary political sphere, language is sometimes critically viewed as being self-referential, its meaning reinforced by repetition and networks of supporting signification which have no real referent, so that it might be said that "the real" disappears beneath a "simulacrum" of signs. Viewed on the vast plains of culture and society, however, the truth of this claim is difficult to judge. The complaint, really, is much the same as that of Plato and others against the sophists and rhetoriticians in antiquity. What we could add in order to make a theory built around such a claim more useful is the suggestion that what is psychologically lost in the midst of multiple representations of reality are the various manners by which evidence is ascertained and by which claims about reality are justified and proven. The basis for the charge of relativism is often a feeling that criteria for judgment have been left out. The problem may not be with either an accumulation or heterogeneity of stimuli or information resources, but with a demand that all types of information be treated in the same manner. Such a demand can become more pressing or "overloading" when many information types are presented to a viewer or reader simultaneously. Conversely, the problem can also be due to a generalized semiotic grammar that is used to represent all matters in the same general form (such as in the mass media) or it can be caused by the view that many different types of semiotic inscriptions constitute equally necessary and valid "forms" of information that equally need our immediate attention. In some of the literature of this type (e.g., that of Guy Debord, Jean Baudrillard, etc.) it seems that it is not an "overload" of signs, per se, that is the issue, but rather, the problems are those of semiotic similarity and a politically motivated aesthetic leveling or foreclosure of possibilities for analysis and judgment, which these authors then point to as the source for the modern "spectacle" or simulacra. Here, the concept of "overload," in the sense of an "information explosion," can refer to a variety of phenomena rooted in media production, rhetoric, aesthetics, culture, and politics.

CONCLUSION

In this entry we have suggested that the term "information explosion" needs to be treated as a rhetorical device. We are led to this approach by the rhetorical roles that the term serves in arguments suggesting the historical and social necessity of new information technologies and infrastructures and by its association to other tropes such as "the information age," "the information society," and "information overload." What such an analysis does is to force one to explain what are the specific values of information tools, agents, organizations, and other information infrastructures and cyberinfrastructures and what are their specific social and historical origins and possibilities, once we have eliminated explanations based on the reified trope of the "information explosion."

REFERENCES

1. Lyman, P. Varian, H.R. *How Much Information?*, 2003. Available at http://www2.sims.berkeley.edu/research/projects/how-much-info-2003/ (accessed August 20, 2007).
2. Capurro, R.; Hjørland, B. The concept of information. Annu. Rev. Inform. Sci. Technol. **2003**, *37*, 343–411.
3. Weaver, W. Recent contributions to the mathematical theory of communication. In *The Mathematical Theory of Communication*; Shannon, C.E., Weaver, W., Eds.; University of Illinois Press: Urbana, IL, 1949.
4. Buckland, M. What is a document?. J. Am. Soc. Inform. Sci. **1997**, *48* (9), 804–809. Available at http://people.ischool.berkeley.edu/~buckland/whatdoc.html (accessed October 7, 2007).
5. Lund, N.W. Document theory. Annu. Rev. Inform. Sci. Technol. **2008**, *42*.
6. http://www.ischools.org.
7. http://www.ischools.org/oc/study.html.
8. Briet, S.In *What Is Documentation?: English Translation of the Classic French Text*; Translated and edited Day, R.E., Martinet, L., Anghelescu, H., Eds.; Scarecrow Press: Lanham, MD, 2006.http://ella.slis.indiana.edu/roday/briet.html.
9. Day, R.E. Tropes, history, and ethics in professional discourse and information science. J. Am. Soc. Inform. Sci. **2000**, *51* (5), 469–475. Available at http://ella.slis.indiana.edu/~roday/intd.htm.
10. Wright, A. *Glut: Mastering Information through the Ages*, Joseph Henry Press: Washington, DC, 2007.
11. Saracevic, T. Information science. J. Am. Soc. Inform. Sci. **1999**, *50* (12), 1051–1063, 1053.
12. Bowker, G. *Memory Practices in the Sciences*, MIT: Cambridge, MA, 2005.
13. Webster, F. The information society: conceptions and critique. *Encyclopedia of Library and Information Science*, 2nd Ed. Marcel Dekker: New York, 2003; 338–1357.
14. Webster, F. The information society: conceptions and critique. *Encyclopedia of Library and Information Science*, 2nd Ed. Marcel Dekker: New York, 2003; 1350.
15. Rudd, M.J.; Rudd, J. The impact of the information explosion on library users: overload or opportunity?. Acad. Librariansh. **1986**, *12* (5), 304–306.
16. Berardi, F. *La Fabbrica dell'inflicità: New Economy e Movimento del Cognitariato*, DeriveAapprodi: Rome, Italy, 2001.

Information Management

Brian Detlor
Information Systems, McMaster University, Hamilton, Ontario, Canada

Abstract

Information management concerns the control over how information is created, acquired, organized, stored, distributed, and used as a means of promoting efficient and effective information access, processing, and use by people and organizations. Historically, three perspectives of information management have dominated the Library and Information Science literature: the organizational, library, and personal perspectives. Each deals with the management of the processes involved in the information life cycle. Each concerns itself with the management of different types of information resources. Today, a more consolidated view of information management in the LIS literature exists, largely due to driving forces in society such as digital convergence, changing library roles, and the emergence and popularity of Big Data. These forces have elevated the significance of information management and have raised awareness among people and organizations today of the importance and need to manage information both effectively and efficiently.

INTRODUCTION

Information management (IM) is a broad conceptual term that has various meanings and interpretations among different constituencies. Frequently the term is used interchangeably with others. For instance, IM is often equated with the management of information resources, the management of information technology (IT), or the management of information policies or standards.[1] Some suggest that IM draws upon ideas from both librarianship and information science.[2] The purpose of this entry is to clarify the meaning of the term information management, to showcase its major historical perspectives in the Library and Information Science (LIS) literature, and to illustrate how a more consolidated, holistic perspective exists today.

What is IM? IM is the management of the processes and systems that create, acquire, organize, store, distribute, and use information. The goal of IM is to help people and organizations access, process, and use information efficiently and effectively. Doing so helps organizations operate more competitively and strategically, and helps people better accomplish their tasks and become better informed.

This entry adopts a process orientation toward IM where IM is viewed as the control over the information life cycle. Various models of information processes exist; some of the major processes involved in information life cycle concern those that create, acquire, organize, store, distribute, and use information.

Importantly, this entry recognizes three major historical perspectives of IM found in the LIS literature: the organizational, library, and personal perspectives. By far, the organizational perspective has been the most predominant and popular. In a nutshell, this perspective deals with the management of all information processes involved in the information life cycle with the goal of helping an organization reach its competitive and strategic objectives. A variety of information resources are managed by organizations. These include transactional information stored in databases, summarized information found in data warehouses, and unstructured information content found in documents and reports. From the organizational perspective, the management of IT is a major component of any IM plan. It is with this perspective where associated terms like information systems management, IT management, data management, business intelligence, competitive intelligence, content management, and records management have relevance.

The library perspective of IM recognizes the unique role of information provision organizations, such as libraries, whose central mandate is to provide clientele with access to information resources and services. As such, these types of organizations historically have viewed IM primarily as the management of information collections, such as books and journals. With respect to this historical view, libraries are neither the creators nor the users of this information. As such, the historical library perspective deals with the management of a subset of information processes involved in the information life cycle with the goal of helping library patrons access and borrow information items held in collections. It is with the library perspective where associated terms like knowledge organization, classification, cataloguing, digital libraries, indexes, and information retrieval systems have relevance.

The personal perspective of IM, though not strong in the LIS literature, is similar to the organizational perspective in that it involves the management of all information processes in the information life cycle. The major

Encyclopedia of Library and Information Sciences, Fourth Edition DOI: 10.1081/E-EISA-120053391

difference, however, is that the organizational perspective concerns the management of information of interest to the success and well-being of an organization, while the personal perspective deals with the management of information of relevance and concern to the individual.

Importantly, a consolidated view of these three major perspectives has recently emerged over the last few years in the LIS literature. This consolidation is a result of several new shaping forces in society. One is digital convergence—the digitizing of traditional media—where a convergence of ITs and information content is happening. Another is changing library roles where libraries themselves are involved in the creation of information. A third force is Big Data where organizations and people are generating data at unprecedented levels and at an incredible pace, and analyzing this data in the hopes of discovering new patterns, associations, and insights.

In terms of this entry's organization, the remainder is structured to further explain the major points just described. First, description is given on the information life cycle and the process view of IM. This is followed by a detailed discussion on each of the three major historical perspectives of IM from an LIS vantage point: the organizational, library, and personal perspectives. Next, discussion ensues on how societal forces are helping to shape a consolidated view of IM in the LIS literature. Last, concluding remarks are made.

A PROCESS VIEW OF IM

Leading IM scholars and organizations purport a process-driven view of IM. For example, Wilson defines IM as "the application of management principles to the acquisition, organization, control, dissemination and use of information relevant to the effective operation of organizations of all kinds."[3] Similarly, Choo defines IM as the management of processes that acquire, create, organize, distribute, and use information.[1] Likewise, the US Government Accountability Office defines IM as "the planning, budgeting, manipulating, and controlling of information throughout its life cycle."[4]

The conceptualization of IM from a process perspective emerged in the early 1990s.[5,6] Advocates of this approach stress that a process model of IM should encompass all or some parts of the information value chain or life cycle. Choo proposes six discrete information-related processes or activities that need to be managed: 1) identification of information needs, 2) acquisition of information to address those needs, 3) organization and storage of information, 4) design and development of information products, 5) distribution of information, and 6) information use.[1] Wilson positions the creation and use of information outside the IM rubric and purports the following six information-related processes pertain to IM: 1) acquisition, 2) organization, 3) storage, 4) retrieval, 5) access/lending,

and 6) dissemination.[7] Not all IM frameworks include information needs identification and information use as processes to be managed. However, many see the most critical issue facing information managers is eliciting information requirements and matching those information needs in the design and delivery of information systems to promote effective and efficient information use.[1,8,9]

With respect to this entry, the following are considered to be the predominant information processes to be managed in IM: information creation, acquisition, organization, storage, distribution, and use. Information creation is the process where individuals and organizations generate and produce new information artifacts and items. Information acquisition is the process where information items are obtained from external sources. Information organization is the process of indexing or classifying information in ways that support easy retrieval at later points in time. Information storage is the process of physically housing information content in structures such as databases or file systems. Information distribution is the process of disseminating, transporting, or sharing information. Information use is the process where individuals and organizations utilize and apply information made available to them. Effectively managing these information processes helps get the right information to the right people in the right forms at the right times and at reasonable costs.[1,10]

THE ORGANIZATIONAL PERSPECTIVE

The organizational perspective is the most predominant perspective of IM. Under the organizational perspective, IM concerns the management and control over the full life cycle of information processes ranging from creation to use for the betterment of the organization itself. In this sense, the management of information processes is seen as a strategic advantage that affords four kinds of benefits to an organization: 1) a reduction of costs; 2) a reduction of uncertainty or risks; 3) added value to existing products and services; and 4) the creation of new value through the introduction of new information-based products and services.[11]

Information as a Resource

Fundamental to the organizational perspective of IM is the view and treatment of information as a strategic resource—one that needs to be managed like any other critical organizational resource, such as people, equipment, and capital. Many organizations recognize the potential value of information and the need to be aware of what information resources exist in an organization, and the costs associated with acquiring, storing, processing, and using that information. Forward-looking companies consider information as a strategic asset that can be leveraged into a competitive advantage in the markets served by the company.[8]

The concept of managing information as an organizational resource emerged in the late 1970s with the creation of the US Paperwork Reduction Act that was established to resolve the huge costs of managing and handling information by bidders for government contracts.[12] It was at this time that the term information resources management (IRM) became popular and was used to signify the management of both information and ITs.[13,14] In reality though, the IRM concept was more about the management of data than it was about the management of other types of information, such as documents or reports. Case in point, an empirical assessment of the IRM construct defines IRM as "a comprehensive approach to planning, organizing, budgeting, directing, monitoring and controlling the people, funding, technologies and activities associated with acquiring, storing, processing and distributing *data* to meet a business need for the benefit of the enterprise"—not other types of information (italics added for emphasis).[15]

This entry suggests that within the organizational perspective of IM, IM is more than just the management of data (e.g., raw facts stored in transactional databases). Rather, IM in organizations involves the management of a varied set of information resources, ranging from data to information.[16]

Data can be considered as "raw facts" that reflect the characteristics of an event or entity. Examples of data items held in an organization would be a customer name, an order quantity, or a unit price. The management of data in organizations traditionally belonged to the "data management" function or "data resource management" department. Data management deals with the storage and processing of low-level data items found in transaction processing systems. The focus of data management is to maximize the speed, accuracy, and efficiency of processing and maintaining transactions or records.[1] Data management is concerned with the creation and "acquisition of data, its storage in databases, its manipulation or processing to produce new (value-added) data and reports via application programs, and the transmission (communication) of the data or resulting reports."[8]

Information can be viewed as "meaningful data" where data have been converted into a meaningful and useful context, such as in the identification of a best-selling or worst-selling product item from historical sales data for a company. Examples of information items managed in a company would be summarized information pulled from transactional database systems and stored in data warehouses and/or data marts. Such "business intelligent" systems support decision-making and allow for the slicing-and-dicing of summarized transactional information to find patterns and trends in operational data (e.g., sales data, supplier data, customer profile data) of importance and relevance to the organization. For example, the mining of summarized transactional data stored in a data warehouse could be used to justify the promotion of a product or service to an untapped market segment, or to measure the effectiveness of a marketing campaign in a certain geographical area.[16]

Though more emphasis in organizations is placed on the management of data and information that is structured and formalized (i.e., data neatly contained within a transactional database or summarized information stored in a data warehouse), the amount of unstructured information that is created, acquired, organized, stored, distributed, and used within an organization usually far exceeds the amount of structured data and information an organization manages.

Unstructured information is the type of information that can be found in reports, documents, email messages, and PowerPoint presentations, among others. This includes reports and documentation generated internally with a company and outside the enterprise as well. For example, managing information concerning industry trends, legislative regulations, competitor happenings, news bulletins, etc., is key to helping an organization stay abreast and react to competitor threats and environmental concerns. This is where IM intersects with a company's "competitive intelligence" initiatives and "environmental scanning" activities. Competitive intelligence refers to the analysis of information about competitors and competitive conditions in particular industries or regions.[17] Environmental scanning refers to the analysis of information about every sector of the external environment that can help an organization plan for its future.[18,19]

Often, document management systems, also known as content management systems, help manage unstructured information that is created, acquired, organized, stored, distributed, and used within an organization. These systems support the electronic capture, storage, distribution, archiving, and accessing of documents. These systems typically provide a document repository where documents can be housed, indexed, and accessed. In these repositories, metadata information is maintained about each document that tracks each document's editorial history and relationships to other documents. Indexing of documents within these systems, through both manual keyword classifications and automatic indexing techniques, facilitates easy document retrieval by organizational workers at later points in time.[16]

Unstructured information also includes records of transactional information processing such as invoices, contracts, order requisitions, bills of lading, and financial statements. The actual data may be resident in a transaction database and managed elsewhere, but the entire record of the event, often with signatures, are handled as a complete entity that must be generated, stored, processed, retrieved, and archived. The management of such information is referred to as "records management" and involves the application of systematic and scientific control to all recorded information that an organization needs to do business.[20]

Managing Information Processes

A good IM program in an organization will manage the full life cycle of information ranging from creation to use. For example:

- When generating transactional data, steps will be taken to ensure that the data will be stored following database "normalization rules" to promote data integrity, the single sourcing of data, the reduction of wasted database space, and fast transaction processing.
- When acquiring information, such as the purchase of market research data or competitor intelligence information, steps will be taken to reduce duplicate purchases and to increase the accessibility of any purchased data and information across the enterprise.
- Any data or information that is stored will be adequately protected against unauthorized access, as security, privacy, and copyright concerns exist.
- Data and information stewardship programs will be set up to identify those organizational workers or units who are responsible for the quality and management of certain data and information items.
- Data and information will be regularly backed up for recovery purposes.
- Duplicate or mirror copies of data and information items will be created to facilitate access and reduce network congestion and/or an overload of requests on the servers on which the data and information reside.
- Old data and outdated information will be archived and/or deleted.[16]

IT's Role

IT plays a critical role in the management of information in organizations. However, having said that, it should be understood that IT is the technical medium upon which information is housed, accessed, retrieved, distributed, and used, and not the primary entity that is being managed under the IM rubric. Information processes are the entities being managed.

Nevertheless, much confusion exists over the role IT plays in the management of information in organizations, with some equating IM primarily to the management of IT itself. For example, the mission of the Society for Information Management, a professional society for chief information officers and senior IT leaders based in the United States, emphasizes the management and use of IT to achieve business objectives.[21] Likewise, Davis and Hamilton define IM as "the management of information systems and information resources by an individual, a group, or an organization" and describe IM as a "new business function with responsibility to define organizational informational requirements, plan and build an information infrastructure and information systems applications, operate the system, and organize, staff, and manage these activities."[22]

This entry suggests that such descriptions of the IM function in organizations are inappropriate and are better served by alternate terms such as information systems management or IT management. Information systems management refers to the control over the development, design, roll-out, and support of information systems applications that support business processes and workflow. IT management refers to the management and control over IT (e.g., hardware, software).

A variety of factors need to be considered when managing technology in organizations. The appropriate hardware and software needs to be installed and implemented. Repair and maintenance of hardware and software systems must be done. Licensing concerns must be taken into consideration. Information systems professionals (e.g., programmers, network specialists, database administrators, systems analysts) need to be hired and trained.[16]

IT is very important to how information is managed in organizations, and the management of IT should be an integral part of any IM plan.[11] After all, IT facilitates the ability to support information creation, acquisition, organization, storage, distribution, and use in both efficient and effective manners.

Organizational Information Processing

IM is concerned with organizational information processing. Two broad orientations exist in the organizational information processing literature that have implications on IM.[23]

The first, mainly developed at Carnegie Mellon University and represented by Herbert Simon, James March, and Richard Cyert, sees an organization's ability to process information as the core of managerial and organizational competencies and organizations as bounded, rational systems.[24] Here, strategies to improve information processing capabilities concern increasing an organization's information processing capacity and reducing an organization's need for information processing.[25]

The second, represented by Karl Weick and Richard Daft, sees organizations as loosely coupled systems where individual participants collectively develop shared interpretations of the environment and then act on the basis of this interpretation. In this sense, information processing is about reducing the equivocality or ambiguousness of information about the organization's external environment.[26]

Taking these two orientations of organizational information processing together, IM then is about increasing an organization's information processing capacity and reducing both information processing needs and information equivocality.

Of interest, how an organization processes information is influenced by its information culture (i.e., the shared assumptions, values, norms, and behaviors that shape an organization's perception, management, and use of information).[27] Specifically, four types of information cultures exist (results-oriented, rule-following, relationship-based, and risk-taking) and each has influence on how an organization manages information. In a results-oriented culture, the goal of IM is to enable the organization to compete and succeed in the marketplace. In a rule-following culture, information is managed to control internal operations and to reinforce rules and policies. In a relationship culture, information is managed to encourage communication, participation, and a sense of identity. In a risk-taking culture, information is managed to encourage innovation, creativity, and the exploration of new ideas. Most organizations would display varying degrees of each of these four types of IM norms and behaviors.[28]

THE LIBRARY PERSPECTIVE

Outside of the organizational context, IM also has meaning in the library world and to other information provision organizations whose central mandate is to provide clientele with access to information resources and services. IM is of concern to all kinds of libraries, such as public libraries and academic and research libraries. This includes corporate libraries that manage serial subscriptions and electronic access to industry reports and electronic databases for workers and employees in their organizations.

From a library perspective, IM concerns the management of information collections, such as books and journals. The goal of IM from a library perspective is to help library patrons access and borrow information items held in the collection. A variety of activities surround the management of a library collection, including the development of collection policies and materials budgets, the selection of collection items, the analysis of collection usage and end user collection needs, training of collection staff, preservation of collection items, and the development of cooperative collections with other institutions.[29]

Since historically libraries have neither been creators nor users of information, this perspective deals with the management of a subset of information processes involved in the information life cycle. For example, Wilson identifies six information-related processes pertaining to IM that are applicable to the library perspective: 1) acquisition, 2) organization, 3) storage, 4) retrieval, 5) access/lending, and 6) dissemination.[7]

Information acquisition involves the process of buying or securing information from sources external to the library for the collection. Care must be taken to ensure that the correct information items are acquired (those that match the information needs of end users) and at reasonable costs.

Information organization pertains to the process of indexing or classifying information housed in the collection to support easy retrieval at later points in time. Today, this process is sometimes referred to as "knowledge organization" in the library world. For example, the International Society for Knowledge Organization utilizes the term "knowledge organization" to represent the process of how documents, document representations (such as bibliographic records), and concepts (keywords, constructs) are ordered and classified.[30] Likewise, Anderson defines knowledge organization as the "the description of documents, their contents, features and purposes, and the organization of these descriptions so as to make these documents and their parts accessible to persons seeking them or the messages that they contain" and describes how knowledge organization encompasses "every type and method of indexing, abstracting, cataloguing, classification, records management, bibliography and the creation of textual or bibliographic databases for information retrieval."[31] In this sense, knowledge organization deals with both processes and systems.[32] With respect to IM, this entry suggests that the use of the "knowledge organization" label is misleading. In actuality, information items (such as documents and document representations) are being organized or ordered (i.e., indexed, classified, catalogued) rather than knowledge items (concepts, constructs) per se. As such, "information organization" is suggested to be a better label to use when talking about the indexing and classification of items held in a collection, at least from a library perspective of IM.

Information storage refers to physically housing items in the collection. This encompasses the housing of both paper and electronic documents (and their document representations). This could be accomplished by storing books and journals in physical stacks in the library or storing full-text electronic versions of documents in an electronic or digital library.

Information retrieval involves the process of searching and finding information in the collection. Typically, end users will conduct a search query using electronic tools that are Web-based to find items of interest in the collection. In the information retrieval process, end users themselves, or information search intermediaries (librarians) working on the behalf of end users, "pull" the information that is needed from the collection.

Information access/lending involves the process of providing physical or electronic access to the collection and the ability to check out information items of interest. For paper-based documents, this may involve signing out and borrowing a physical information item. For information in electronic form, this may involve viewing the information item online and/or downloading a copy of the information item from the collection.

Information dissemination is the process of circulating physical information items of interest from the collection to end users. Traditionally, methods of dissemination involve the distribution of photocopied journal content pages or the circulation of documents. Today, this has largely been replaced with electronic alert services that "push" information items in the collection of interest to specific users based on stored end user profiles.

The management of library information collections is a complex and ever-evolving process.[33] The extensive digitization of information resources has placed new pressures on libraries to respond to securing the requisite skills, resources, and competencies to successfully manage digital library collections.[34] In order to manage the transition and reliance on digital information collections, it is important more than ever for libraries to consider the expectations and needs of end users, as well as limitations in library staff and budget adaptability.[33] These are critical factors in rolling out any successful IM program from a library perspective.

THE PERSONAL PERSPECTIVE

IM from the personal perspective refers to how individuals create, acquire, organize, store, distribute, and use information for personal purposes.[35,36] This can concern the management of information for everyday use (e.g., personal calendars, schedules, diaries, news items) or work-related reasons (e.g., work schedules, things-to-do, project files). As such, personal IM involves the handling and processing of information over the entire information life cycle, just as in the case of the organizational perspective. However, the personal IM perspective differs from the organizational perspective of IM in that personal IM concerns items of interest to the individual, not the organization.

Central to the personal perspective of IM is the need to manage the information processes of information creation, acquisition, organization, distribution, and use so that the right information is accessible and available in the right place, in the right form, and of sufficient completeness and quality to meet personal information needs. A variety of information items are created, acquired, organized, stored, distributed, and used by people for personal purposes. These include personal notes, personal journals, web pages, email messages, news articles, address books, calendar dates, reminders, fax communications, etc.

Technologies and tools, such as electronic personal information managers like PDAs, help people carry out these processes more efficiently and effectively.[37,38] Cheap and fast search and storage technologies bring stability and order to people's often chaotic and messy personal information environments, and facilitate making the most of people's personal information collections.[39] Despite the benefits of these technological tools, there is some evidence to suggest that technological advances are less important in determining how individuals organize and use information than are the tasks that people perform,[40] and that improvements in personal ITs are required, specifically in terms of minimizing information overload, supporting easier context switching, and providing better integration across a variety of applications.[41]

It is interesting to note that the phrase "personal information management" was first used in the 1980s with the advent of personal computers and their capacity to process and manage information.[42] However, the concept of "personal information management" was most likely first implied back in 1945 by Vannevar Bush when he envisioned using the "Memex" machine for personal IM—a machine that allowed an individual to store all his or her books, records, and communications and consult those personal information sources with great speed and flexibility.[43]

As the proliferation of personal computing devices and the explosion of the amount of information that is created, generated, and used continues to increase, the relevance of IM from the personal perspective will likely gain more attention and importance from both researchers and practitioners alike.

TOWARD A CONSOLIDATED VIEW

Though, historically, the three major perspectives of IM described earlier (i.e., the organizational, library, and personal perspectives) were formed independently from each other, a variety of recent societal forces have led to the formation of a new consolidated view. These forces include digital convergence, changing library roles, and the emergence of Big Data.

Digital convergence involves the coming together of previously distinct products and services that employ digital technologies.[44] According to a report by Deloitte, digital convergence is driven by three underlying trends: 1) the proliferation of digital data, which provides a common base for handling diverse types of information using the same devices, processing techniques, and media; 2) widespread connectivity, which helps bring diverse information together, and extends the value and capabilities of a device beyond its out-of-the-box functionality; and 3) continuous advances in technology, from battery life to processor speed.[45] As digital convergence has occurred, organizations, libraries, and individuals have become accustomed to working with information systems that are not strictly contained to a specific organizational, library, or personal content domain, or restricted to a specific type of IT. Rather, organizations, libraries, and people are now more accustomed to working with digital technologies and devices that allow the gathering, collection, access, and use of information from a wide variety of sources and to using the same type of ITs to do so. As such, organizations, libraries, and people have been accustomed to utilizing the same types of ITs to access, collect, store, and use information.

Libraries have embraced content creation. This is a new and expanded role for libraries. Today, one can easily find libraries involved in the creation of new information through the provision of maker-spaces,[46,47] open-access online journals,[48,49] institutional repositories,[50,51] and the generation of digital storytelling collections.[52,53]

Further, academic libraries now play a lead role in the stewardship of institutional research data.[54,55] This new recent content-creation role has increased the breadth of information processes in the information life cycle for libraries and made libraries more closely aligned with the information processes one would find in the organizational and personal IM perspectives.

Big Data refers to the tools, processes, and procedures that allow an organization to create, manipulate, and manage very large data sets and storage facilities.[56] One of the primary reasons for Big Data is "data explosion," largely due to the widespread accessibility, affordability, and availability of new digital devices, such as smartphones, tablets, and laptops, that make access to the Internet both easy and relatively inexpensive for billions of people worldwide. Another is that the list of data sources keeps growing as organizations and consumers generate different and vast amounts of data every day by emailing, searching, browsing, blogging, tweeting, and texting.[57] Organizations are scrambling to leverage the overwhelming amount of Web-based, mobile, and sensor-generated data arriving at terabyte and even exabyte levels afforded by Big Data by analyzing this highly detailed, contextualized and rich content in the hopes of making insights and new discoveries for competitive and business success.[58] The proliferation of Big Data enables companies to harness the power of predictive analysis.[59] Of importance to this entry, organizations that wish to leverage Big Data recognize the need to follow sound IM principles.[60] In this regard, Big Data has raised awareness of the critical importance of IM and the need to manage information efficiently and effectively more than ever before.

CONCLUSION

This entry provided a review and discussion of the IM concept. Importantly, a process-oriented definition of IM was proposed and three distinct historical perspectives of IM from an LIS vantage point were described: the organizational, library, and personal perspectives. Importantly, a consolidated view of these three historical perspectives was suggested based on recent trends and happenings.

This entry emphasized the importance of IM. IM allows organizations to reach strategic goals and make sound decisions. IM enables libraries and other information provision organizations to manage information collections effectively and efficiently. IM helps people manage their own personal information collections.

This entry also described how IM is not so much about the management of technology, but rather more about the management of the processes of IM, specifically the creation, acquisition, organization, storage, distribution, and usage of information.

According to the current scope of the *International Journal of Information Management*, the challenge for IM now is less about managing activities that collect, store, and disseminate information, and more about placing greater focus on managing activities that make changes in patterns of behavior of customers, people, and organizations, and information that leads to changes in the way people use information.[61] This may not be such an easy task. People and their information behaviors are hard to change. So are organizational cultures.[11] IM is less about solving technical problems and more about addressing the human-side of IM. Humans add the context, meaning, and value to information, and it is humans who benefit and use this information. As such, "mastering information management is an essentially human task."[62]

REFERENCES

1. Choo, C.W. *Information Management for the Intelligent Organization: The Art of Environmental Scanning*, 3rd Ed.; Learned Information: Medford, NJ, 2002.
2. Macevičiūtė, E.; Wilson, T.D. The development of the information management research area. Inf. Res. **2002**, *7* (3), http://InformationR.net/ir/7-3/paper133.html (accessed October 2014).
3. Wilson, T.D. Information management. In *International Encyclopedia of Information and Library Science*; Routledge: London, U.K., 2003; 263–278.
4. U.S. Government Accountability Office. http://www.gao. gov (accessed October 2014).
5. Davenport, T.H. *Process Innovation: Reengineering Work Through Information Technology*; Harvard Business School Press: Boston, MA, 1993.
6. McGee, J.V.; Prusak, L. *Managing Information Strategically*; John Wiley & Sons: Toronto, Ontario, Canada, 1993.
7. Wilson, T.D. 'The nonsense of knowledge management' revisited. In *Introducing Information Management*; Macevičiūtė, E., Wilson, T.D., Eds.; Facet Publishing: London, U.K., 2005, 151–164.
8. Karim, N.S.A.; Hussein, R. Managers' perception of information management and the role of information and knowledge managers: the Malaysian perspectives. Int. J. Inf. Manage. **2008**, *28* (2), 114–127.
9. Detlor, B. *Towards Knowledge Portals: From Human Issues to Intelligent Agents*; Kluwer Academic Publishers: Dordrecht, the Netherlands, 2004.
10. Robertson, J. *Ten principles of effective information management*, November 2005, KM Column, http://www.steptwo. com.au/papers/kmc_effectiveim/index.html (accessed October 2014).
11. Choo, C.W. http://choo.fis.utoronto.ca/Imfaq/ (accessed October 2014).
12. Commission on Federal Paperwork. *Information Resources Management*; U.S. Government Printing Office: Washington, DC, 1977.
13. Horton, F.W. *Information Resources Management: Concept and Cases*; Association for Systems Management: Cleveland, OH, 1979.
14. Horton, F.W. *The Information Management Workbook: IRM Made Simple*; Information Management Press: Washington, DC, 1982.

15. Lewis, B.R.; Snyder, C.A.; Rainer, R.K., Jr. An empirical assessment of the information resource management construct. J. Manag. Inf. Syst. **1995**, *12* (1), 199–223.

16. Baltzan, P.; Detlor, B.; Welsh, C. *Business-Driven Information Systems*, 3rd Canadian Ed.; McGraw-Hill Ryerson: Whitby, Ontario, Canada, 2012.

17. Sutton, H. *Competitive Intelligence*; The Conference Board Inc.: New York, 1988.

18. Aguilar, F.J. *Scanning the Business Environment*; MacMillan Co.: New York, 1967.

19. Choo, C.W.; Auster, E. Scanning the business environment: acquisition and use of information by managers. In *Annual Review of Information Science and Technology*; Williams, M.E., Ed.; Learned Information: Medford, NJ, 1993.

20. Robek, M.F.; Brown, G.F.; Wilmer, O.M. *Information and Records Management*, 3rd Ed.; Glencoe Publishing: Encino, CA, 1987.

21. Society of Information Management (SIM). http://www.simnet.org (accessed October 2014).

22. Davis, G.B.; Hamilton, S. *Managing Information: How Information Systems Impact Organizational Strategy*; Business One Irwin: Homewood, IL, 1993.

23. Choo, C.W. Towards an informational model of organizations. Can. J. Inf. Sci. **1991**, *16* (3), 32–62.

24. Simon, H. *Administrative Behavior: A Study of Decision-Making Processes in Administrative Organization*, 3rd Ed.; The Free Press: New York, 1976.

25. Galbraith, J.R. *Organization Design*; Addison-Wesley: Reading, MA, 1977.

26. Weick, K.E.; Daft, R.L. The effectiveness of interpretation systems. In *Organizational Effectiveness: A Comparison of Multiple Models*; Cameron, K.S.; Whetten, D.A., Eds.; Academic Press: New York, 1983, 71–93.

27. Choo, C.W.; Bergeron, P.; Detlor, B.; Heaton, L. Information culture and information use: An exploratory study of three organizations. J. Am. Soc. Inf. Sci. Technol. **2008**, *59* (5), 792–804.

28. Choo, C.W. Information culture and organizational effectiveness. Int. J. Inf. Manage. **2013**, *33*, 775–779.

29. Branin, J.J., Ed. *Collection Management in the 1990s*; American Library Association: Chicago, IL, 1993.

30. International Society for Knowledge Organization (ISKO). http://www.isko.org/ko.html (accessed October 2014).

31. Anderson, J.D. Organization of knowledge. In *International Encyclopedia of Information and Library science*; Feather, J., Sturges, P., Eds.; Routledge: London, U.K., 1996, 336–353.

32. Hjorland, B. *Lifeboat for Knowledge Organization*, 2008. http://www.iva.dk/bh/lifeboat_ko/home.htm (last accessed October 2014).

33. Branin, J.; Groen, F.; Thorin, S. The changing nature of collection management in research libraries. Libr. Resour. Techn. Serv. **2000**, *44* (1), 23–32.

34. Sreenivasulu, V. The role of a digital librarian in the management of digital information systems (DIS). Electron. Libr. **2000**, *18* (1), 12–20.

35. Jones, W. Personal information management. Annu. Rev. Inf. Sci. Technol. **2007**, *41*, 453–504.

36. Jones, W. *The Future of Personal Information Management, Part I: Our Information, Always and Forever*; Synthesis Lectures on Information Concepts, Retrieval, and Services Morgan & Claypool Publishers: San Rafael, CA, 2012.

37. Jones, W. *Keeping Found Things Found: The Study and Practice of Personal Information Management*; Morgan Kaufmann Publishers: Burlington, MA, 2008.

38. Jones, W. *Transforming Technologies to Manage Our Information: The Future of Personal Information Management, Part 2*; Synthesis Lectures on Information Concepts, Retrieval, and Services, Morgan & Claypool Publishers: San Rafael, CA, 2013; 1–179. ISBN 9781598299373.

39. Teevan, J.; Jones, W.; Bederson, B.B. Personal information management. Commun. ACM **2006**, *49* (1), 40–43.

40. Barreau, D. The persistence of behavior and form in the organization of personal information. J. Am. Soc. Inf. Sci. Technol. **2008**, *59* (2), 307–317.

41. Warren, P. Personal information management: The case for an evolutionary approach. Interact. Comput. **2013**, *26* (3), 208–237.

42. Lansdale, M. The psychology of personal information management. Appl. Ergon. **1988**, *19* (1), 55–66.

43. Bush, V. As we may think. The Atlantic Monthly, **July 1945**, *176* (1), 101–108.

44. Lord, B.; Velez, R.; Ebooks Corporation. *Converge: Transforming Business at the Intersection of Marketing and Technology*; John Wiley & Sons, Inc.: Hoboken, NJ, 2013.

45. Deloitte. Digital convergence: lead, follow or get out of the way. TelecomWeb News Digest. September 11, 2005; p. 6, https://www.highbeam.com/doc/1G1-138498525.html.

46. Britton, L. The makings of maker spaces. Libr. J. **2012**, *137* (16), 20–23.

47. Loertscher, D.V. Maker Spaces and the Learning Commons. Teach. Libr. **2012**, *39* (6), 45–46.

48. Zhao, L. Riding the wave of open access: providing library research support for scholarly publishing literacy. Aust. Acad. Res. Libr. **2014**, *45* (1), 3–18.

49. Chadwell, F.; Sutton, S.C. The future of open access and library publishing. New Libr. World, **2014**, *115* (5/6), 225–236.

50. Armstrong, M. Institutional repository management models that support faculty research dissemination. OCLC Syst. Serv. **2014**, *30* (1), 43–51.

51. Bruns, T.; Knight-Davis, S.; Corrigan, E.K.; Brantley, S. It takes a library: growing a robust institutional repository in two years. Coll. Undergrad. Libr. **2014**, *21* (3/4), 244–262.

52. Conrad, S.K. Documenting local history: a case study in digital storytelling. Libr. Rev. **2013**, *62* (8/9), 459–471.

53. Czarnecki, K. Digital storytelling in different library settings. Libr. Technol. Rep. **2009**, *45* (7), 20–30.

54. Keil, D.E. Research data needs from academic libraries: the perspective of a faculty researcher. J. Libr. Adm. **2014**, *54* (3), 233–240.

55. Kruse, F.; Boserup Thestrup, J. Research libraries' new role in research data management, current trends and visions in Denmark. Libr. Q. J. Eur. Res. Libr. **2014**, *23* (4), 310–335.

56. Knapp, M. Big data. J. Electron. Resour. Med. Libr. **2013**, *10* (4), 215–222.

57. Data, data everywhere, A special report on managing information, The Economist. February 27, 2010; 5–7. Available at http://www.economist.com/node/15557443 (last accessed October 2014).

58. Chen, H.; Chiang, R.H.L.; Storey, V.C. Business intelligence and analytics: From big data to big impact. MIS Q. **2012**, *36* (4), 1165–1188.

59. Seymour, C. The state of Big Data. EContent Mag. **January–February, 2014**; 26–27.

60. Information Management and Big Data: A Reference Architecture, An Oracle White Paper, February 2013. www.oracle. com/technetwork/topics/entarch/articles/info-mgmt-big-data-ref-arch-1902853.pdf (last accessed October 2014).

61. http://www.journals.elsevier.com/international-journal-of-information-management (accessed October 2014).

62. Davenport, T. Putting the I in IT. In *Mastering Information Management*; Pearson Education: London, U.K., 2000.

Information Needs

Charles M. Naumer
Karen E. Fisher
Information School, University of Washington, Seattle, Washington, U.S.A.

Abstract

The following entry describes the concept of "information need." The concept of "information need" has no single definition but is dependent on the perspective from which it is applied. The concept of "information need" is discussed in terms of its definition in other fields, evolvement with the user-centered paradigm, and articulation in key models of information seeking, as well as how it has spurred new avenues of inquiry with in library and information science (LIS).

INTRODUCTION

"Information need" is one of the most central concepts within library and information science (LIS). If people did not have information needs, then libraries and other information systems would cease to exist, even basic interpersonal human communication would be altered. An in-depth understanding of "information needs" is critical to answering some of the larger questions facing LIS from an individual, organizational, and societal perspective. These questions include: (1) how are information needs created? (2) what motivates people to seek information? (3) why do people sometimes avoid information? (4) how do people express information needs? (5) how is relevance considered? (6) how should information be organized and managed to best respond and anticipate people's needs? and (7) how should we organize and plan for the expression of information need? LIS professionals thus require an understanding of what an information need comprises, how it develops, is met, and transforms in order to provide optimal service in collection development, cataloging, and reference—to name a few key library functions. System designers and professionals in other fields require in-depth understanding to meet users' needs through their services as well. However, while libraries have existed for millennia, formal understanding of information needs from a user perspective has only been explored since the 1960s.

SITUATING INFORMATION NEEDS

In order to understand the term "information needs" it is important to understand how it is situated within the general context of "human needs" research as well as within the evolutionary trajectory of LIS. "Needs" or "human needs" is a central concept in many disciplines. In order to fully consider the meaning of the term information needs, it will be examined within the general context of "human needs" research. A multidisciplinary examination of the importance of "needs" research provides an essential context for understanding the concept of "information needs" within LIS and especially from a user-centered perspective. The use of this term will also be explored as part of the historical development of the LIS field and its role in spurring new avenues of inquiry within the field.

The Definition of "Need" in Cognate Fields

The concept of "need" is unsurprisingly central to many different disciplines. Perhaps the best known is psychology and Maslow's hierarchy of needs.[1] Maslow's theory of human motivation contends that human needs can be organized into a hierarchy or a pyramid of five types of needs. At the bottom of the pyramid are basic or physiological needs such as breathing, food, water, sex, and sleep. The next level relates to safety including physical security, employment, property, and resources. Above this level is a sense of love and belonging associated with friendship, family, and intimacy. At the next level is esteem which is reflected in self-esteem, confidence, and respect by others. Lastly, Maslow described the highest level of need being self-actualization, which is characterized as involving personal development associated with morality, creativity, spontaneity, and problem solving. Maslow's hierarchy is often used as the basis for understanding human motivation. Another, simpler, categorization of human need by psychologists is that of: (1) physiological need; (2) affective need; and (3) cognitive need.[2]

Human needs are also of central concern in the field of economics and political science. Human need is considered a driving force in the demand for goods and services. Human needs theory has played a prominent role in political economy research as a means of supporting economic development theory. For example, the political economist

Encyclopedia of Library and Information Sciences, Fourth Edition DOI: 10.1081/E-ELIS4-120043243

and Nobel prize winning scholar Amartya Sen based his arguments on the moral grounds for public spending on a definition of human needs.[3] Political scientists have also used theories of human needs as a way to better understand conditions for peace, conflict resolution, and negotiation.[4]

Perhaps most closely related to many of the inquiries on information need in LIS is the definition of "educational need." The concept of need in the field of education has been used both to assess and express individual needs as well as to measure aggregate needs at the local, state, or federal level.[5–7] Other disciplines, such as health sciences, have conducted their own studies on "information needs" in the context of their fields.[8]

Information Needs and LIS

Despite its centrality to information seeking, use and sharing the concept of "information need" remains ambiguous in the literature. This difficulty may stem from the fact that it is challenging to create a boundary around the concept of "information needs." Wilson suggested that an "information need" is secondary to a primary need such as food, shelter, and clothing.[9] In order to understand an information need, it is often necessary to understand the context of human needs that created a need for information. This approach to understanding information need requires a broad understanding of people's personal situations. Wilson[2] also noted that one of the difficulties faced in defining "information needs" is separating the concept from "wants," "expressed demand," "satisfied demand," and so on. He partially attributed this to the "failure to identify the context within which information needs investigations are carried out" (p. 8).[2] Hjørland[10] later argued that "it is essential not to confuse the concept of need with the concept of demand."[10] To illustrate the difference, Hjørland presented a situation in which the demand for information from a library was low due to factors such as accessibility; yet, the information needs of the people in the community were high.[10] In this situation, need and demand were clearly not equal.

Green[11] also considered the differences between "wants," "demands," and "needs."[11] His identified four aspects as most central to an understanding of the concept of information need: (1) need is necessarily instrumental; (2) needs are usually contestable; (3) need has a strong relationship with necessity; and (4) there is no necessary psychological element in a need. Green also stressed that need does not necessarily mean that information is lacking—a person may need information that they already have.

An explicit information need is often considered to be the motivating force behind a user's action to seek information. Understanding the motivational factors involved in human information behavior is critical to understanding other parts of the information seeking and use processes

and has raised several important questions. For example, motivation is central to research regarding passive and active approaches to information seeking as well as blunting and avoidance behaviors.

The difficulty of ascertaining a person's information need has also been cited as cause for lack of a more thorough consideration of the concept. In the early 1980s, Belkin and Vickery[12] argued that since information needs exist in someone's head they are very difficult to assess.[12] Harter[13] later suggested that information needs are akin to a person's mental state, arguing that they are in a constant state of flux as a person continually acquires new information.[13] Given these considerations and the close relationship between information need and other subdisciplines' consideration of need, it has been suggested that "needs" research may fall outside the scope of LIS and be better suited to other disciplines. Wilson[2] suggests "it may be advisable to remove the term "information needs" from our professional vocabulary and to speak instead of "information seeking towards the satisfaction of needs" (p. 9).[2]

Historical Evolution of Information Need Research within LIS

In a historical context, studies concerning "information need" have evolved greatly. In the famous monograph "The Library's Public," Berelson[14] synthesized the results of library studies from 1930 to 1949, and reported that libraries were used primarily for accessing books and were patronized by the younger, better-schooled, culturally alert members of the community.[14] Despite collecting demographic data, little attention was paid to the types of uses that people made of libraries, especially in connection to particular needs. Most of the studies summarized by Berelson were concerned with "demands" rather than "needs," and were aimed at informing collection development and circulation practices.

The 1940s and mid-1950s were marked by the vast increase in the amount of scientific literature generated and released in the postwar era. Responding to Vannevar Bush's call to "make more accessible a bewildering store of knowledge," researchers began studying how information is used in relation to work focusing particular attention on science and technology.[15] This type of research was primarily focused on determining how information sources could be made more useful to scientists, and in this context the information needs of scientists were studied.

The 1960s and 1970s ushered in an era in which LIS research focused on social and community issues. Several major, large-scale studies were conducted, including the study of the information needs of urban residents of Baltimore and the "The Humphry Report" of Maine.[16,17] These public library-oriented studies sought to identify the information needs of large populations. The federal government through the U.S. Department of Education also demonstrated a strong interest to identify the information needs of citizens. As part of this effort, the U.S. Department of Education funded a study by Ching-chih Chen and Peter Hernon investigating the information seeking patterns of the general public as well as a study by Brenda Dervin examining the information needs of urban residents of Seattle.[18,19]

A similar large publicly funded study was conducted in Britain during this period. The INISS Project directed by Tom Wilson and David Streatfield studied the communication and information flows in local authority social services departments.[2] The project was particularly innovative for its use of action research to foster change in the organizations, and employment of qualitative methods such as structured observation. Wilson credited this 5 year project as being a major influence of the ideas expressed in his seminal 1981 paper on user studies and information needs.

During the 1960s and 1970s a new conceptualization of information need also began to emerge. In 1962, Robert Taylor published an article in which he examined the process of information need development as revealed through question asking and answering dialogue at the reference desk of a library.[20] He followed this article up 4 years later in 1968, with his seminal article "Question-Negotiation and Information Seeking in Libraries."[21] During this period, other researchers, such as Brenda Dervin were beginning to focus their attention on better understanding the process by which information needs are determined and expressed. The work of these researchers launched a new way of viewing information users and information needs.[22] In their landmark 1977 work "Public Library Use, Users, Uses" Zweizig and Dervin challenged researchers with identifying the uses (and *possible* uses) that people make of public libraries by focusing on situational needs.[23] They observed that the time for studying "how much use is made of libraries and by whom" is past, and that focus should be switched from "the user in the life of the library" to "the library in the life of the user."[23]

In their seminal 1986 ARIST chapter, Dervin and Nilan expounded on the paradigm shift that they claimed had occurred within LIS, a switch in focus from the system-oriented paradigm of past decades to a new user-centered or alternative approach that emphasized constructive, active users, subjective information, situationality, holistic views of experience, internal cognition, and systematic individuality.[24] At the heart of this paradigm shift was its view of users and their inherent information needs, which were no longer seen as "empty buckets" that could be filled with "bricks of information" (to use Dervin's terminology). Dervin and Nilan gave three examples of such user-centered scholarship: Taylor's user-values or value-added approach, Dervin's Sense-Making approach, and Belkin and colleagues' anomalous states-of-knowledge approach.[24] Notable definitions of information need cited by Dervin and Nilan include "a conceptual incongruity in which the person's cognitive structure is not adequate to a task,"[24,25] "when a person recognizes something wrong in his or her state of knowledge & wishes to resolve the anomaly,"[26] "when the current state of possessed knowledge is less than needed,"[27] and "when internal sense runs out" (Dervin, 1980). During this period, Dervin and Dewdney proposed neutral questioning, based on Dervin's Sense-Making approach, as a technique for understanding users' information needs at the reference desk.[24] Although the paradigm shift is most often associated with the 1980s, Bates contended that the shift actually began occurring in 1960 at the time Moore's Law was published and as represented by Edwin Parker's 1966 argument that "the system should adapt to the receiver or user, rather than the user to the system" (as cited by Bates).[28] In 1976 Dervin, herself, called for a shift in attention toward designing systems that adapt to users' needs which support their efforts to help themselves to make sense out of information.

Case,[29] views Dervin's work and specifically the Sense-Making approach to be "the most ambitious attempt to explain the origins of information needs" (p. 75).[29] Dervin's Sense-Making approach considers "information need" as being derived from a person's desire to make sense out of a situation.[30] The Sense-Making approach describes a person reaching a point at which they need help to bridge a gap in their understanding. According to the Sense-Making approach, the "gap" represents a crucial point at which a person develops a need for information to allow them to move forward. The "gap" is the point at which a person begins to recognize and articulate their information needs. An important aspect of sense-making as it relates to information need is the recognition that information needs are not isolated but are connected to a larger context. When an information need is considered in a larger context it will be linked to numerous information needs. As one information need is addressed, other needs will likely develop.

The user-centered work of Dervin, Wilson, Kuhlthau, Belkin, and others in the 1970s and 1980s introduced holistic approaches to understanding information behavior and laid the foundation for an exploration of the role of "context" in understanding human information behavior. The 1990s to the present marks a period in which "context" became more deeply considered in all aspects of information behavior. Indeed, in 1996, information seeking in context began developing its own subspecialty within the field of LIS. As research interest coalesced around this topic, a conference was organized in Tampere, Finland and aptly named the Information Seeking in Context (ISIC) conference. According to Pettigrew et al. (2001), "another quantum leap ha[d] occurred within information behavior ... emphasiz[ing] the contextual interplay of cognitive, social, cultural, organizational, affective, and linguistic factors" [Pettigrew, 2001 #463, p. 67]. Kuhlthau described information seeking in context as "focus[ing] on a holistic view of information needs in the course of people's lives" (p. 723).[39]

Social context has been a particularly important aspect of studies of information seeking in context. Chatman's work exemplifies studies that carefully consider the influences of social contexts on all aspects of information behavior. For example, Chatman's study of the information behavior of women prisoners suggests that "life in the round will, for everyday purposes, have a negative effect on information seeking" and that "people will not search for information if there is no need to do so. If members of a social world choose to ignore information, it is because their world is working without it" (p. 214).[32] In this study, Chatman demonstrated a strong connection between information need and the social context or social world of the participants.

Lastly, research on everyday life information seeking (ELIS) has also evolved during this time period [[34] #1276; [35] #1265; [36] #1275; [37] #1203; [38] #433; [39] #282]. This research focused on information seeking behavior as part of people's everyday life experience as compared to job-related information behavior studies.

INFORMATION PARADIGMS AND MODELS

The concept of "information need" can be understood in greater depth according to three theoretical perspectives. As argued by Tuominen, Talja, and Savolainen, information science has evolved in three stages where each stage was dominated by a particular theoretical perspective.[33] These three perspectives were labeled the "information transfer" model, the "constructivist" model, and the "constructionist" model. These three perspectives might also be termed the physical view, cognitive view, and social view, and are discussed in depth below.

Information Transfer Model

The transfer model or physical view of information need is based on the concept of demand for physical objects. This perspective considers an information system as a process for transmitting "information objects" such as books and documents. Based on this conceptualization, information need might be represented as a request for a physical document. The system might then be measured according to its capacity to deliver the physical objects meeting the information need. This view is tied to the conceptualization of information as a thing. This perspective has been influential in the development of methods to evaluate libraries and other information systems according to their ability to deliver books and documents on demand.

Constructivist or Cognitive View

Under the Constructivist or Cognitive View, "information needs" are seen in terms of the knowledge structures of people. This view seeks to understand information needs based on the mental models, processes, and relationships. Therefore, people's information needs are based on knowledge or lack of knowledge about a topic, their level of proficiency regarding a process, and the cognitive processes they engage in to make sense of information.

Taylor's work is exemplary of this constructionist or cognitive view. Considered a pioneer in LIS, before becoming Dean of the School of Information Studies at Syracuse University, Taylor worked as a reference librarian and developed a model of the information seeking process which articulated information need development through question formulation. This concept was described in two articles published in 1962 and 1968, the latter of which is most often cited.[20,21]

Taylor's conception of information need advances the idea that people progress through four levels of question formulation:

Q1—the actual, but unexpressed need for information (the visceral need).
Q2—the conscious, within brain description of the need (the conscious need).
Q3—the formal statement of the need (the formalized need).
Q4—the question as presented to the information system (the compromised need).

Taylor's model is especially important as it was the first time the suggestion was made that a person may experience a sense of need for information before being conscious of it or able to articulate it. The very notion of such a concept creates an awareness of why professionals should support a user in articulating his or her information need and necessitates shifting the focus from information to that of understanding the user. Taylor's model recognizes that the information need presented to a system or person is a compromised need and that a negotiation occurs between the stages of recognizing a need and presenting it to an information system. Therefore, the information need expressed to a system in the form of a query, for example, is only a representation of the information need and is constrained by the ability to fully articulate the need through the use of a language or set of tools. Taylor's work preceded the user-centered shift in information science by close to two decades. Taylor's levels of information need development continues to be often cited and an important underlying work for much research including the development of subsequent information models such as Belkin's ASK model, Kulthau's ISP model, and Dervin's Sense-Making approach.

Informed by Taylor's conception of information need, several theories of information seeking arose that defined "information need" as being motivated by a sense of uncertainty. Theories falling under this category could be considered Belkin's Anomalous State of Knowledge, Kulthau's ISP, and Dervin's Sense-Making methodology.[24,30,34,35] All these theories explain information need and the motivation for searching for information as being derived from a gap in knowledge which manifests itself as a sense of uncertainty. Although in comparison to Wilson's model they do not explicitly represent an external need that preempts an information need, they all recognize information need as a part of a larger situation. Dervin is especially clear in this regard conceptualizing a user as someone situated in context and in the process of defining their situation. Dervin's approach to situating a user in context has strong implications toward understanding the social view of information behavior although sense-making is most often considered as part of the cognitive view.[36]

Social Constructionist or Social View

Those espousing a social constructionist perspective (the third theoretical framework according to Tuominen et al.[33]), criticize the cognitive perspective for failing to fully recognize the impact of the social realm on information behavior. Hjørland, claims that Taylor's information need model is extremely individualistic and argues that "behind the concrete information seeking-process lies an information need that is an integration of the individual and the collective information need" (p. 168).[10] This perspective and other holistic perspectives recognize that information need is not something static located in the user's head but as something dynamic that changes as the user interacts with information and society as a whole.[10] This conception of information need recognizes need development as being socially situated, and that the needs of a group may be different than the needs of an individual, the needs of a group should be considered in addition to or instead of the needs of an individual.

Although Wilson's models are most often associated with the cognitive perspective, Wilson's concept of holistic "information need" might also be classified in the social realm. In his second model of 1981, Wilson made two propositions regarding information need. The first proposition argues that information need is a secondary need emerging from a primary need. A primary need is of a more basic nature encompassing needs such as food, shelter, companionship, and employment. Primary needs can be classified as the following:

1. Physiological needs—need for food, water, shelter, etc.
2. Affective needs—need for attainment, domination, etc.
3. Cognitive needs—need to plan, learn, etc.

The second proposition suggests that in the course of seeking information to satisfy their needs individuals will likely run into barriers of different kinds.[2] In this paper, Wilson also proposed the idea of information behavior in context. The concept of information in context and the development of information needs in context was a precursor to the rise of interest in ISIC.

In his 1996 report Wilson further commented on the lack of progress in assessing information need:

> At the root of the problem of information-seeking behaviour is the concept of *information need*, which has proved intractable for the reason advanced by Wilson in 1981; that is, *need* is a subjective experience which occurs only in the mind of the person in need and, consequently, is not directly accessible to an observer. The experience of need can only be discovered by deduction from behaviour or through the reports of the person in need (p. 6).[37]

Wilson's models of information behavior have evolved throughout the past several decades [[2] #1213; 9 #1118; 37 #1]. The significance of his treatment of information need in relation to information seeking behavior is the holistic or ecological nature of his model, which situates information behavior in a person's contextual setting. In his models of 1996 and 1999, Wilson separated information need from motivation—recognizing that information needs are not always acted upon. Others, such as Bruce have considered information needs in terms of personal information management rather than as the motivating force behind information seeking behavior. The personal anticipated information need (PAIN) hypothesis describes a person's struggle to anticipate their future information needs while making personal information management decisions related to the storage and management of information.[38]

As discussed, there is a growing body of research that addresses information behavior in a social context and within this, research on information need is addressed. Notable research studies include those by Fisher and colleagues regarding information grounds, Harris and Dewdney on battered women, and Chatman's stream on marginalized populations.[32,39–41] As a motivating research question, Chatman discovered that the expression and development of information needs were largely influenced by social factors. In environments such as a prison, she found evidence that information needs were socially constructed[32]—findings that were confirmed by Fisher et al., in their studies of information flow in informal, social settings, or information grounds. Savolainen's[39] model of information seeking in the context of way of life (ELIS) also addresses information behavior in a social context. As described by Savolainen[42] the ELIS model "was developed to elaborate the role of social and cultural factors that affect people's way of preferring and using information sources in everyday settings."[42]

Information need is a central concept to virtually all information models. It represents the starting point and motivation that brings a user to engage in the process of information seeking. The definition of information need is allusive and may best be defined according to the meta-theoretical framework used to guide research.

CONCLUSION

Research on information needs has taken new, exciting directions since the mid-1990s for three primary reasons: (1) important foundational work on "needs" had been carried out thus enabling exploration into new forays; (2) researchers have becoming even more interdisciplinary than in the past, applying rich ideas from other fields to their work; and (3) the advent of the Internet and the World Wide Web along with other new information and communication technologies facilitated more and new information behaviors that are more easily studied than in the past.

Promising research directions include research conducted on community information needs.[39,43,44] Research on nonpurposive information seeking is expressed as serendipity and information encountering.[45,46] Recognizing the role of lay mediaries in the information seeking process in terms of not only searching for information but also helping others realize their information needs through such phenomena as imposed queries and gate-keeping.[47] Lastly, research on the process of knowledge structure transformation on information need development all show promising signs of furthering our understanding of information needs from multiple perspectives.[48]

There is still much to learn about information needs. In his 1981 article "On User Studies and Information Needs" Wilson attempted to "reduce confusion by devoting attention to the definition of some concepts and by proposing the basis for a theory of the motivations for information seeking behavior" (p. 3).[2] Although the LIS field has learned a great deal about information behavior while its theoretical frameworks have matured, questions regarding the nature of information need and how it relates to motivation remain. There is great promise that given the new directions of the past decade and the renewed interest in factors influencing information need, some of these questions will be answered.

REFERENCES

1. Maslow, A.H. A theory of human motivation. Psychol. Rev. **1943**, *50*, 370–396.
2. Wilson, T.D. On user studies and information needs. J. Docum. **1981**, *37*(1), 3–15.
3. Sen, A.K. *Collective Choice and Social Welfare*, Holden-Day: San Francisco, CA, 1970; xii, 225 Mathematical economics texts, 5.
4. Burton, J.W. *Conflict: Human Needs Theory*, St. Martin's Press: New York, 1990; xxv, 358.
5. Dearden, R.F. 'Needs' in education. Br J. Educ. Stud. **1966**, *14*(3), 5–17.
6. White, A.R. Needs and wants. J. Philos. Educ. **1974**, *8*(2), 159–180.
7. Woodhead, M. The needs of children: Is there any value in the concept?. Oxf. Rev. Educ. **1987**, *13*(2).
8. Timmins, F. Exploring the concept of 'information need'. Int. J. Nurs. Pract. **2006**, *12*, 375–381.
9. Wilson, T.D. Models in information behavior research. J. Doc. **1999**, *55*(3), 249–271.
10. Hjørland, B. *Information Seeking and Subject Representation: An Activity-Theoretical Approach to Information Science*, Greenwood Press: Westport, CT, 1997.
11. Green, A. What do we mean by user needs?. Br. J. Acad. Libr. **1990**, *5*(2), 65–78.
12. Belkin, N.J.; Vickery, A. *Interaction in Information Systems: A Review of Research from Document Retrieval to Knowledge-Based Systems*, British Library: London, U.K., 1985; viii, 250 Library and information research report.
13. Harter, S.P. Psychological relevance and information-science. J. Am. Soc. Inform. Sci. **1992**, *43*(9), 602–615.
14. Berelson, B. *The Library's Public: A Report of the Public Library Inquiry*, Columbia University Press: New York, 1947.
15. Bush, V. As we may think. The Atlantic. Monthly **1945**.
16. Humphry, J. *The Humphry Report: Regional Library Service in the State of Main: A Study*, Maine State Library: Portland, MN, 1979.
17. Warner, E.S.; Murray, A.D.; Palmour, V.E. *Information Needs of Urban Residents. Final Report of the Regional Planning Council and Westat Inc. US Dept. of Health, Education and Welfare, Division of Library Programs*, Baltimore, MD, 1973.
18. Chen, C.-C.; Hernon, P. *Information Seeking: Assessing and Anticipating User Needs*, Applications in Information Management and Technology Series Neal-Schuman: New York, 1982.
19. Dervin, B.; Kwan, C. *The Development of Strategies for Dealing with the Information Needs of Urban Residents: Phase I: The Citizen Study*, University of Washington, School of Communications: Seattle, WA, 1976. Final report of Project L0035J to the U.S. Office of Education; Vol. ERIC: ED 125640.
20. Taylor, R.S. The process of asking questions. Am. Doc. **1962**, *13*, 391–396.
21. Taylor, R. Question negotiation and information seeking in libraries. Coll. Res. Libr. **1968**, *29*, 178–194.
22. Dervin, B. et al. *The Development of Strategies for Dealing with the Information Needs of Urban Residents*, US Office of Education, Office of Libraries and Learning Resources: Seattle, WA, 1976.
23. Zweizig, D.; Dervin, B. Public library use, users, uses: Advances in knowledge of the characteristics and needs of the adult clientele of American public libraries. Adv. Libr. **1977**, *7*, 231–255.
24. Dervin, B.; Nilan, M. Information needs and uses. Annu. Rev. Inform. Sci. Technol. **1986**, *21*, 3–33.
25. Ford, N. Relating "information needs" to learner characteristics in higher education. J. Doc. **1980**, *36*(2), 99–114.
26. Belkin, N. Information concepts for information science. J. Doc. **1978**, *34*(1), 55–85.

27. Krikelas, J. Information seeking behavior patterns and concepts. Drexel. Libr. Quart. **1983**, *19*(2), 5–20.

28. Bates, M.J. A tour of information science through the pages of JASIS. J. Am. Soc. Inform. Sci. **1999**, *50*(11), 975–993.

29. Case, D. *Looking for information: A Survey of Research on Information Seeking, Needs, and Behavior*, Academic Press: Amsterdam, the Netherlands, 2007.

30. Dervin, B. From the mind's eye of the user: The sense-making qualitative–quantitative methodology. In *Qualitative Research in Information Management*; Glazier, J., Powell, R., Eds.; Libraries Unlimited: Littleton, CO, 1992; 61–84.

31. Kuhlthau, C.C.; Vakkari, P. Information seeking in context (ISIC). Inform. Process. Manage. **1999**, *35*(6), 723–725.

32. Chatman, E.A. A theory of life in the round. J. Am. Soc. Inform. Sci. **1999**, 207–217.

33. Tuominen, K.; Talja, S.; Savolainen, R. Discourse, cognition and reality: Towards a social constructionist metatheory for library and information science Emerging frameworks and methods: Proceedings of the Fourth International Conference on Conceptions of Library and Information Science (CoLIS4) Seattle, WA July, 21–25; Bruce, H.F.R.I.P.V.P., Ed.; Libraries Unlimited: Greenwood Village, CO, 2002; 271–283.

34. Chatman, E.A. *Life in a small world: Applicability of gratification theory to information seeking behavior*. J. Am. Soc. Inform. Sci. **1991**, *42*, 438–449.

35. Dervin, B. et al. *The Development of Strategies for Dealing with the Information Needs of Urban Residents*, US Office of Education, Office of Libraries and Learning Resources: Seattle, WA, 1976.

36. Durrance, J. *Armed for Action: Library Response to Citizen Information Needs*, Neal-Schuman Publishers: New York, 1984.

37. Harris, R.M.; Dewdney, P. *Barriers to Information: How Formal Help Systems Fail Battered Women*; Greenwood Press: Westport, CT, 1994.

38. Savolainen, R. Everyday life communication and information seeking in networks. Int. Research-Electron. Netw. App. Policy **1997**, *7*(1), 69–70.

39. Savolainen, R. Everyday life information seeking: Approaching information seeking in the context of "way of life.". Lib. Inform. Sci. Res. **1995**, *17*, 259–294.

40. Fisher, K.E.; Landry, C.F.; Naumer, C.M. Social spaces, casual interactions, meaningful exchanges: 'information ground' characteristics based on the college student experience. Inform. Res. **2006**, *12*(2).

41. Harris, R.M.; Dewdney, P. *Barriers to Information: How Formal Help Systems Fail Battered Women*, Greenwood Press: Westport, CN, 1994.

42. Savolainen, R. Everyday life information seeking. In *Theories of Information Behavior*; Fisher, K.E., Erdelez, S., McKechnie, L., Eds.; Information Today, Inc.: Medford, NJ, 2005; 143–148.

43. Durrance, J.C. et al. Community problem-solving framed as a distributed information use environment: Bridging research and practice. Inform. Res. Int. Electron. J. **2006**, *11*(2).

44. Pettigrew, K.E.; Durrance, J.C.; Unruh, K.T. Facilitating community information seeking using the Internet: Findings from three public library–community network systems. J. Am. Soc. Inform. Sci. Technol. **2002**, *53*(11), 894–903.

45. Wilson, T.D. On user studies and information needs. J. Doc. **1981**, *37*(1), 3–15.

46. Wilson, T.D. Models in Information Behavior Research. J. Doc **1999**, *55*(3), 249–271.

47. Wilson, T.D. Information behaviour: An interdisciplinary perspective. Inform. Proces. Manage. **1997**, *35*(4), 551–572.

48. Cole, C. et al. Putting it together online: Information need identification for the domain novice user. J. Am. Soc. Inform. Sci. Technol. **2005**, *56*(7), 684–694.

Information Needs and Behaviors of Diasporic Populations

Ajit K. Pyati
University of Western Ontario, London, Ontario, Canada

Abstract
Diaspora, which refers to the global and transnational spread of certain ethnic and religious groups, has been a reality for a long time. However, the increasing spread and ubiquity of new media technologies has in many instances accelerated the diasporic reality for many immigrant communities, facilitating transnational connections and senses of identity. In particular, the context of diaspora is affecting ways of approaching immigrant information behavior research. Specifically, diasporic information needs and behavior research takes account of the transnational information environments of these populations. Thus, immigrant communities are often part of rich, global information networks. New research is emerging which frames immigrant information research within a diasporic context, bridging local and global information needs and behaviors. Implications exist for rethinking concepts of assimilation, fostering cultural preservation and growth, and the development of enhanced social capital.

INTRODUCTION

In a world characterized by processes of globalization, both capital (often in the form of transnational corporations) and human beings increasingly traverse borders. The immigration of populations, often from the so-called "third-world" to the "first-world," is a major characteristic of the modern age. The movement of human populations around the world is certainly not new, however, as mass displacements of people (both voluntary and forced) have occurred across the centuries. Thus, the African slave trade, which reached its peak in the eighteenth and early to mid-nineteenth centuries, is a prominent example of a forced and brutal migration of a population. On the other hand, however, middle-class immigrants from Asia and Eastern Europe who are working in the information technology industries in the West are examples of voluntary economic immigrants.

While the term "immigration" captures the movement of certain ethnic groups across international borders, the term "diaspora" refers to the global dispersion of various ethnic populations around the world. Diaspora is etymologically derived from the Greek word "diasperien," which means "to sow or scatter seeds," and has historically referred to displaced communities of people who have been dislocated from their native homeland though the movements of migration, immigration, or exile (p. 1).[1] This term was originally applied to Jewish populations living in exile from their homeland, with later references to an African diaspora, accelerated by the slave trade. This term is now extended to refer to the global spread of a host of various ethnic groups, including Chinese, Indian, Haitian, Cuban, and Vietnamese populations, to name just a few. Thus, diaspora refers to a global spread of a population that transcends national boundaries, while

immigration focuses more specifically on communities living in a "host" or "adopted" land. Diaspora studies research is gaining in importance as a field of study, covering a range of disciplines in the humanities and social sciences.

Information needs and behavior research focus on the conscious efforts of individuals or populations to acquire information in response to needs or gaps in knowledge.[2] The information needs and behaviors of immigrant populations have been studied to a modest degree in the literature of library and information science. Given the changing demographics of many Western countries and the increasing importance of immigration to the economic well-being of these countries, however, understanding the information needs and behaviors of immigrant groups is becoming an increasingly important endeavor.[3] Immigrants are a diverse and heterogeneous group, and their information needs and behaviors differ based on a set of various economic, ethnic, and demographic factors.[4] Research on immigrant information needs focuses on a range of issues such as settlement information, economic information, and information for cultural and civic engagement.[4]

The context of diaspora is now being recognized in Library and Information Science (LIS), particularly in relation to the information needs and behaviors of immigrant communities. Diasporic information behavior research is most closely tied to diaspora research within the field of media studies. In the context of globalization, diaspora helps to situate the information environments of immigrant communities on an international scale, as the information realities of many immigrant communities stretch beyond the boundaries of Western nation-states. For instance, immigrant communities are often part of larger diasporic information and media markets, including

Encyclopedia of Library and Information Sciences, Fourth Edition DOI: 10.1081/E-ELIS4-120044049

access to global satellite television and international Web sites.[5] Thus, transnational information networks play an important role in understanding diasporic information needs and behaviors.[6] This entry presents an overview of the current state of diaspora research within the context of LIS, a new area of research within the field, which extends the contours of immigrant information behavior research. The following sections discuss prominent themes in diaspora research, diaspora and media studies, immigrant information-seeking research, and the emerging field of diasporic information research.

DIASPORA RESEARCH: PROMINENT THEMES

The field of diaspora studies is a growing area of study, with coverage in fields as diverse as literature, sociology, anthropology, film studies, queer theory, area studies, and ethnic studies.[1] Some of the leading theorists on diaspora include Arjun Appadurai, Homi Bhabha, Stuart Hall, Paul Gilroy, Lisa Lowe, and Aihwa Ong, to name a few. Diaspora studies is a diverse area, with a wide range of differing perspectives and viewpoints. Diaspora in fact is a contested term, with some scholars focusing on its liberatory potentials, while others are cautious about its limitations and abilities to transcend existing social and power dynamics.[1] Diaspora does not, for instance, transcend differences of race, class, gender, and sexuality, nor can it be disassociated from these categories of analysis [7, as quoted in 1]. In certain cases, diasporic identities might be subject to hegemonic influence by dominant groups and elites, and can reinforce existing ideologies and power structures.[8] Thus, while offering new possibilities for expressing transnational identity, diaspora is also subject to the same power structures and forces that shape other social formations.

Diaspora studies is related to the concept of globalization, but the focus is on the dispersion and movement of populations around the globe, rather than the movement of corporations and global capital. The following subsections will focus on a few prominent themes in diaspora research. The first subsection discusses in detail some of the differences between diaspora, transnationalism, and globalization. The next subsection discusses the related themes of hybridity, imagination, and identity—it is widely argued in the literature that diasporic communities often reside within *in-between spaces* across different cultures, which allows for a fluid and flexible sense of identity. The last subsection focuses on the role of diaspora in critiquing dominant views of the nation-state, as diaspora may allow for a certain *postnational* sensibility for people beyond the traditional rubric of nation-states.[9]

Globalization, Transnationalism, and Diaspora

The importance of diaspora as a framework for understanding the information needs and behaviors of certain ethnic groups cannot be discussed without reference to globalization. Globalization is seemingly the buzzword of the twenty-first century—while a concept that is complex and contested, a certain agreement exists about its occurrence and tangibility. Globalization, whether of the top-down, corporate-dominated variety,[10] or in its more grassroots conception, is fundamentally concerned with the increasing interconnectedness of social, political, economic, and cultural relations in the world. This interconnectedness is manifested in global flows of capital and labor, especially with regard to immigration from the global "South" to the "North." Globalization, however, often is associated with logics of cultural homogenization and the dominance of Western values and interests.[10]

Diaspora, transnationalism, and globalization are related terms, but are not necessarily the same, however. As Braziel and Mannur[1] discuss:

> While diaspora may be accurately described as transnationalist, it is not synonymous with transnationalism. Transnationalism may be defined as the flow of people, ideas, goods, and capital across national territories in a way that undermines nationality and nationalism as discrete categories of identification, economic organization, and political constitution. We differentiate diaspora from transnationalism, however, in that diaspora refers specifically to the movement—forced or voluntary—of people from one or more nation-states to another [p. 8].

A difference between diaspora and transnationalism, therefore, is the distinction between the often impersonal forces of globalization and global capitalism, and the lived experience of migration and dispersion. Transnationalism, in its dominant version of global capitalism and global institutions such as the International Monetary Fund and the World Bank, is often associated with processes of cultural and economic homogenization.[1] In contrast, some argue that a focus on diaspora emphasizes forces of cultural heterogeneity.[9] Diaspora and the networks of people and associations across borders can be viewed as a form of "globalization from below," in contrast to the top-down globalization characterized by large corporations and increasing homogeneity.[5]

Hybridity, Imagination, and Identity

Diaspora is a contested term, with a range of political and cultural meanings. The nostalgic dislocation from a "homeland" has traditionally characterized concepts of diaspora, but increasingly differentiated meanings of the concept now proliferate.[1] For instance, diaspora and the *diasporic identity* of these populations are often marked by hybridity and heterogeneity, in cultural, linguistic, ethnic, and national terms.[1] Hybridity and heterogeneity thus often define diasporic identity, an identity that is not necessarily fixed and is often "deterritorialized" (p. 37).[9]

For instance, Appadurai[9] discusses deterritorialization in the following way:

> As Turkish guest workers in Germany watch Turkish films in their German flats, as Koreans in Philadelphia watch the 1988 Olympics in Seoul through satellite feeds from Korea, and Pakistani cabdrivers in Chicago listen to cassettes of sermons recorded in mosques in Pakistan or Iran, we see moving images meet deterritorialized viewers [p. 4].

Thus, the process of deterritorialization is related to an internationalized sense of identity for many diasporic communities. Diasporic identity formation is a creative process that takes place often at the intersection of various nations and cultures.[9]

Diasporic identity and consciousness is also a "work of the imagination" (p. 5)[9] as diasporic communities endeavor to reimagine homelands and also articulate diverse and hybrid adaptations of cultural reality. Thus, diasporic identity and consciousness can be thought of on the one hand as a process of re-creating cultural spaces, but on the other hand as also part of an imaginary construction of identity. Benedict Anderson's work[11] on the role of print capitalism in the creation of imagined national communities provides a foundation for Appadurai's work, as Appadurai extends this thesis to the role of electronic and new media for the creation of diasporic identity. Thus, according to Appadurai, the role of electronic and new media is important in facilitating these works of the imagination.[9] These media sources and networks help in the process of diasporic identity construction and map out spaces for expressing this identity.[5]

Appadurai's framework for understanding the implications of globalization and new media for diaspora is influential in the field of diaspora studies. He lays out the following dimensions of this framework for understanding the new global economy in terms of "-scapes": 1) ethnoscapes (people who move between nations, such as tourists, immigrants, exiles, guestworkers, and refugees); 2) mediascapes (electronic and new media); 3) technoscapes (technology, often linked to multinational corporations); 4) financescapes (global capital, currency markets, and stock exchanges); and 5) ideoscapes (official state ideologies and counter-ideologies) (p. 25).[12] These -scapes provide a lens to understand the disjunctures in the global cultural economy.[12] All of these dimensions are global in nature, while at the same time diasporic communities develop their own local articulations of these dimensions. The focus on mediascapes has had the most impact on diasporic information behavior research. Appadurai[9] further describes mediascapes as follows:

> Mediascapes refer both to the distribution of the electronic capabilities to produce and disseminate information (newspapers, magazines, television stations, and film-

production studios), which are now available to a growing number of private and public interests throughout the world, and to the images of the world created by these media [p. 35].

In addition to Appadurai, Homi Bhabha[13] discusses the notion of diasporic spaces, which is influential in the field of diaspora studies. He argues, for instance, that the movements of populations around the world have created spaces that are neither part of the "homeland" nor the "adopted country." Bhabha[13] discusses this in-between zone of diasporic communities as a "Third Space," an area of identity articulation outside the homogenizing narratives of Western modernity. Bhabha discusses this Third Space as a way for diasporic communities to engage with and create new articulations of modernity. Beyond the case of diasporic communities, this Third Space of enunciation also problematizes the inherent originality and purity of cultures, as even Western cultures (despite claims to homogeneity) demonstrate hybridity.[13] Thus, diasporic identity (and the concept of identity in general) is viewed as a hybrid and shifting concept, in contrast to notions of a *pure* identity.[14] Diasporic groups are thus able to navigate a range of identity formations, depending on various local and global inflections.

Diaspora and the Narratives of the Nation-State

Another theme that occurs within the literature of diaspora is the disruption of the dominance of nation-states in identity formation and creation. Some scholars argue, for instance, that we are entering a stage of postnationalism,[9] with the nation-state receding into the background, as transnational forces hold greater sway. As Braziel and Mannur[1] state:

> ...diaspora forces us to rethink the rubrics of nation and nationalism, while refiguring the relations of citizens and nation-states. Second, diaspora offers myriad, dislocated sites of contestation to the hegemonic, homogenizing forces of globalization [p. 7].

The transcendence of the nation-state as a main shaper of identity is a theme that is echoed in much of the diaspora literature.[5,9] Appadurai,[9] for instance, argues that the United States needs to examine its understanding of immigration issues and multiculturalism. As he discusses in regard to the United States, "neither popular nor academic thought in this country has come to terms with the difference between being a land of immigrants and being one node in a postnational network of diasporas" (p. 171).[9] The discourse of diaspora appears to challenge dominant narratives of fixed national identity and the primacy of the nation-state as a major cultural shaper. However, other forms of nationalism and ethnic identity may be privileged in lieu of traditional discourses of the nation-state [15, as quoted by 5]. These nationalisms may be chauvinistic in nature or highlight particular politically charged and controversial notions of identity, as in the case of the imagined nation of "Khalistan" for Punjabi Sikhs in the 1980s (p. 36).[12] Thus, diaspora may create different senses of imagined national identity beyond the nation-state.

DIASPORA AND MEDIA

This section provides a brief overview of prominent research in diasporic media studies. Appadurai's work on mediascapes is influential in this line of study, and diasporic media research is closely related to diasporic information needs and behavior research. Electronic media are playing an increasingly important role in the development of diasporic consciousness as "moving images meet deterritorialized audiences" (p. 4).[9] Recent scholarship on diaspora and media spans a wide range of ethnic groups and types of electronic media.[5,14,16,17] For instance, Karim[5] has edited an influential book which highlights some prominent research in the field of diasporic media studies.

In this edited volume, Manas Ray[18] discusses the role that the Mumbai-based film industry of "Bollywood" plays in the identity construction of Fiji Indians. For this ethnic group, which has been displaced from the Indian "homeland" for several generations, Bollywood is playing a role as an information source in the construction of an imagined sense of identity and nationhood.[18] Naficy[19] discusses the role of "narrowcasting" in diaspora, how television programming for diasporic Middle Eastern groups can provide information and entertainment. In the case of Middle Eastern groups and other diasporic groups in general, both ethnic television (usually produced in the host country) and transnational television (media that is imported from overseas) play a role.[19] DeSantis[20] provides examples from the Latin American television environment in North America, as Mexican and Brazilian programming are gaining new audiences in this market. Thus, television can play an important role as a diasporic information source, both for purposes of entertainment and identity formation.

The Internet is also increasingly a space for negotiating diasporic identity and the sharing of diasporic information. Mandaville,[21] for instance, discusses the role of the Internet in the creation of a virtual *ummah* (world community of Muslims) in the Islamic diaspora. In particular, Mandaville[21] discusses how dominant discourses of Islam can be challenged by dissenting voices on the Internet, especially within the context of Western Europe and North America. A sense of virtual community amongst Muslims living abroad can be developed, and this identity often has local inflections and connotations.[21] This ability for the Internet to provide a space for new articulations

of identity is echoed in the experiences of countless other ethnic groups. For instance, in the context of Greek populations, Tsaliki[22] discusses how the Internet can embody Bhabha's[13] notion of the Third Space, as it can provide an "in-between space" between the nation and its diaspora, allowing for rearticulations of national narratives.

In addition, the work of Mitra[23] on immigrant identities in "cybernetic space" discusses how Indian immigrants are interacting in online spaces in a process of identity formation. In the context of local, immigrant country spaces that may be threatening to an expression of immigrant identities (especially in a post-9/11 world in the United States), Mitra[23] argues that online spaces offer an opportunity to re-create some of the physical places that have been lost for Indian immigrant communities. These examples highlight just a small portion of the growing literature on diasporic communities and their often empowering uses of the Internet.

Despite the liberating possibilities of the Internet and new media for diaspora and diasporic identity, research has also shown the potential for fragmentation, homogenization, division, and the replication of inequalities. In the case of the Indian diaspora, for instance, some scholars question the imposition of a monolithic understanding of Indian identity, often defined by Hindi language films and Hinduism.[24] The reality of the Indian diaspora (and all diasporas in general) is that it is a multiplicity of diasporas, influenced by factors such as class, religion, language, and country of residence, to name a few factors.[25] Issues of religious extremism and ethnic chauvinism are also a concern in the discourse of diasporic media research. Economic and technological elites can reproduce understandings of religion and culture that may not reflect the diversity of diaspora.[8] In terms of the Indian diaspora, research has shown that Hindu nationalist discourses are being privileged, along with middle-class Hindu notions of Indian identity.[8,26] However, the Internet can also provide spaces for marginalized voices to contest the hegemony of these dominant narratives.[8,21] Thus, information and communication technology (ICT)-mediated diasporic information sources can both disrupt and reinforce hegemony.

IMMIGRANT INFORMATION-SEEKING BEHAVIOR RESEARCH: KEY THEMES

The reality of globalization and diaspora is affecting information seeking research as well, although it is often not explicitly referenced or referred to as such. This intersection with globalization is manifested in research focusing on the information-seeking behavior of immigrant groups. The cultural diversity of information seeking behaviors and needs is now widely recognized as an important area in the field. In the West, and especially in a post-9/11 world, immigration (both legal and illegal) and discourses about immigration are often center stage in political, economic, and national security debates. Immigrant information-seeking behavior research is related to and has a longer history than diasporic information behavior research, and this section discusses some of the main themes in this research area.

The information needs and behaviors of immigrant groups, as various studies have shown,[4,27–29] often differ from the information needs and behaviors of dominant and mainstream groups in society. Depending on the immigrant community and variations in economic status, information needs vary, covering a wide range such as basic English literacy information, information about basic living skills in the new country to information about maintaining cultural ties to the home country, to name a few. The implications of these types of studies are important in the better design of information services and ICT-enabled information resources that meet these particular behaviors and needs. While immigration occurs at all socioeconomic levels in the United States and other Western countries, particular concerns arise regarding the needs of low-income immigrants and the reality of *information poverty* and the *digital divide*.

A valuable body of work dealing with immigrant information-seeking behavior already exists, and the work of Metoyer-Duran[27] on ethnolinguistic gatekeepers is an important example. Gatekeepers in ethnolinguistic, minority communities in the United States, according to Metoyer-Duran[27] "act as agents of acculturation when they disseminate information within their communities" [p. 320]. Thus, gatekeepers are key information agents and disseminators within these communities. She identifies two major "domains" in which gatekeepers operate—the cognitive and affective. She describes the cognitive domain in relation to established theories of learning that promote the hierarchical acquisition of knowledge, while the affective domain is concerned with the gatekeeper's cultural orientation toward information needs and use. While the details of these domains are not important to this discussion, the subsequent "profiles" that Metoyer-Duran derives in relation to these domains has important consequences for understanding the information seeking behavior of these groups. She defines six different profiles for gatekeepers as: 1) impeder; 2) broker; 3) unaffiliated gatekeeper; 4) affiliated gatekeeper; 5) information professional; and 6) leader/executive.

Another strand of research in immigrant information seeking is the work on "information grounds." According to Fisher, information grounds are "environment(s) temporarily created when people come together for a singular purpose but from whose behavior emerges a social atmosphere that fosters the spontaneous and serendipitous sharing of information" (p. 811).[30] The key qualities of "information grounds" are their temporality and existence in "nontraditional" information environments. Examples

of information grounds include restaurants, hair salons, buses, medical offices, and grocery store queues, to name a few. For example, this particular kind of information grounds research is found in "Information Grounds and the Use of Need-Based Service by Immigrants in Queens, New York: A Context-Based, Outcome Evaluation Approach".[31] The researchers in this article focus on exploring how programs in literacy and coping skills run by the Queens Borough Public Library (QBPL) in New York City might function as information grounds. The researchers conclude that these programs constitute a "grand context," and a rich information grounds for immigrant populations. Some gains achieved in these programs include improved coping skills and technology skills, and better preparation for employment. Other immigrant information grounds research points to the strength of interpersonal networks as sources of information, as the choice of which information ground to visit is related to factors such as ease of communication and perception of increased reliability of sources in these environments.[28] Also, given the language, cultural, and economic barriers and the deep extent of everyday needs that some immigrant communities face, interpersonal sources of information are often preferred sources.[28]

Other prominent studies on immigrant information behavior include Chu's[29] work on immigrant child mediators (ICMs). This study focuses on how immigrant children can serve as cultural, linguistic, and information intermediaries for immigrant parents. Chu provides suggestions for librarians on how to effectively address the needs of this group. While interpersonal networks and the use of intermediaries are important in the discussion of immigrant information behavior, the role of social capital is also important in this area of research. Caidi and Allard[4] discuss how information access for immigrant communities can become part of developing the social capital of these communities. Social capital is a term used in various literatures, and according to Putnam,[32] it is related to "social organization such as networks, norms and social trust that facilitate coordination and cooperation for mutual benefit" (p. 67). Social capital is related to enhanced connections to resources for immigrant communities with the potential for enhanced social inclusion and civic participation.[4] The next section extends these ideas into the context of diasporic communities.

DIASPORIC INFORMATION BEHAVIOR: EXTENDING IMMIGRANT INFORMATION RESEARCH

While many immigrant communities in North America and the Western world are part of rich and layered diasporic communities, much of the research in LIS and information studies does not yet reflect this reality. One of the first major studies exploring the role of diaspora in immigrant information-seeking behavior is Srinivasan and Pyati's[6] article in the *Journal of the American Society for Information Science and Technology*, entitled "Diasporic Information Environments: Reframing Immigrant-Focused Information Research." These authors argue that studies of immigrant information behavior need to be situated within the dynamic contexts of globalization and diaspora. Specifically, they propose a methodology for understanding diasporic information behavior through the lens of what they term a *Diasporic Information Environment Model* (DIEM).[6] This model links the local, place-based information environments of immigrant communities with the global, transnational ICT-mediated information environments of these groups. Methodological frameworks such as reflexive ethnography, social network analyses, and community-based action research are discussed as ways to develop local and global analyses of diasporic information behavior.

Srinivasan and Pyati[6] draw in major part from the work of Arjun Appadurai, one of the leading scholars in theorizing ICT-mediated diasporas. He talks about the increasingly important role of ICTs and ICT-enabled technologies in the process of maintaining and creating diaspora, helping to further create "works of the imagination."[6] As globalization becomes increasingly defined and mediated by ICTs, immigrant groups and their information-seeking behavior are being shaped by diasporic forces enabled by information technology.

The complex association between diasporic groups and ICTs has led to a concept of e-diasporas that actively utilizes ICTs to achieve community-specific goals.[6] A scenario of moving migrants has made e-diasporas critical for the formation and sustenance of community for immigrant groups.[9] Appadurai argues that nation can be formed in cyberspace, and often cyberspace serves as the sole means of providing a sense of aspiration and hope to placeless migrant populations.[33]

The DIEM of Srinivasan and Pyati[6] works to bridge local and global information environments by recognizing the transnational and fluid identities of immigrant and diasporic communities. Thus, these authors acknowledge the importance of local information grounds and local networks, but also recognize the increasing importance of diasporic Web sites and transnational networks for information.[6] The authors illustrate this bridging of local and global information sources through a discussion of the Somali diaspora. Srinivasan[34] has conducted research with Somali refugee communities in Boston, noting that this community is not isolated, as it is in constant communication with refugee pockets in other parts of the United States, Kenya, and Italy. Srinivasan and Pyati[6] discuss how this diasporic community's needs can be effectively studied by the DIEM. For example, they discuss how social network analyses can identify the transnational information networks of this community, which can result in better community service models. The DIEM also

emphasizes community-based research which can help engage local communities to address and articulate their own information needs. The major difference between diasporic and immigrant information behavior research, as identified in the work of Srinivasan and Pyati,[6] is an emphasis and recognition of the globalized nature of information resources for certain immigrant communities. The understanding of connections of immigrant communities to different information networks and resources beyond the local environment is a contribution of a diasporic perspective. Implications exist for the preservation and growth of culture,[6] and this perspective emphasizes the sometimes hidden information assets of immigrant communities.[33]

Related to the diasporic information behavior perspective is the importance of social capital and social inclusion. Caidi and Allard[4] discuss the role that information access can play in furthering these ideals. These authors emphasize an understanding of social inclusion that is not related to social cohesion, but rather makes visible and breaks down barriers that prevent full participation in new host countries.[4] According to these authors, "social inclusion values diverse identities and fundamentally questions both the process and result of social inclusion" (p. 313).[4] Thus, social inclusion can be framed as a way for immigrant communities to embrace diasporic identities, while also taking part in local civic life. This orientation can have implications for information services to these communities as librarians and other information service providers can be more aware of the global and diverse nature of immigrant information environments. Thus, information for social inclusion and cultural preservation may come from diasporic and global sources. As the world becomes more globalized, concepts such as citizenship and assimilation are being problematized.[9] Meeting the information needs of diasporic communities largely overlaps with the domain of traditional immigrant information services but brings the added perspective of providing information for global citizenship and identity. This perspective acknowledges the lived reality of diasporic communities and recognizes the Third Space[13] of diasporic identity, a fluid and hybrid space of agency for these communities. An increasingly globalized and arguably *postnational* world may spur increasing research focused on diaspora within LIS.

CONCLUSION

This survey of the information needs and behaviors of diasporic populations has highlighted the increasing importance of ICTs and new media in the creation of "e-diasporas." Diaspora, which refers to the global and transnational spread of certain ethnic and religious groups, has been a reality for a long time; however, the increasing spread and ubiquity of new media technologies has in many instances accelerated the diasporic consciousness of many immigrant communities. This discussion began with a brief overview of what diaspora means in the context of globalization, and how it is affecting ways of approaching immigrant information behavior research. Specifically, studying the information needs and behaviors of diasporic populations takes into account the often transnational information environments of these populations.

While the information needs and behaviors of diasporic populations mirror key ideas and concepts in standard immigrant and ethnolinguistic minority information behavior research (e.g., gatekeepers, information grounds, importance of personal social networks, etc.), diasporic information needs research is adding a globalized perspective to understanding these information needs and behaviors, providing a space to understand the global–local tension in immigrant information environments. For instance, immigrant groups are increasingly looking toward transnational and ICT-mediated sources of information not necessarily tied to a particular location. Due to the increasing influence of new media technologies, a diasporic consciousness and identity often accompanies information resources for these groups. New research that specifically looks at the relationship between the global and local nature of immigrant information environments is beginning to appear in the LIS literature,[6] and it is likely that more research will continue to emerge that takes into account the larger context of globalization and diaspora.

REFERENCES

1. Braziel, J.E.; Mannur, A. Nation, migration, globalization: points of contention in diaspora studies. In *Theorizing Diaspora*; Braziel, J.E., Mannur, A., Eds.; Blackwell: Malden, MA, 2003.
2. Case, D.O. *Looking for Information: A Survey of Research on Information Seeking, Needs, and Behavior*, Academic Press: New York, 2002.
3. Pyati, A.K. Limited English proficient users and the need for improved reference services. Ref. Serv. Rev. **2003**, *31*(3), 264–271.
4. Caidi, N.; Allard, D. Social inclusion of newcomers to Canada: an information problem?. Lib. Inform. Sci. Res. **2005**, *27*(3), 302–324.
5. Karim, K.H. Mapping diasporic mediascapes. In *The Media of Diaspora*; Karim, K.H., Ed.; Routledge: London, U.K., 2003; 1–17.
6. Srinivasan, R.; Pyati, A.K. Diasporic information environments: re-framing immigrant-focused information research. J. Am. Soc. Inform. Sci. Technol. **2007**, *58*(12), 1734–1744.
7. Urgo, J.R. *Willa Cather and the Myth of American Migration*, University of Illinois Press: Urbana, IL, 1995.
8. Chopra, R. Global primordialities: virtual identity politics in online Hindutva and Dalit discourse. New Med. Soc. **2006**, *8*(2), 187–206.
9. Appadurai, A. *Modernity at Large: Cultural Dimensions of Globalization*, University of Minnesota Press: Minneapolis, MN, 1996.
10. Kellner, D.K. Theorizing globalization. Sociol. Theor. **2002**, *20*(3), 285–305.
11. Anderson, B. *Imagined Communities: Reflections on the Origin and Spread of Nationalism*, Verso: London, 2006.
12. Appadurai, A. Disjuncture and difference in the global cultural economy. In *Theorizing Diaspora*; Braziel, J.E., Mannur, A., Eds.; Blackwell: Malden, MA, 2003; 25–48.
13. Bhabha, H. *The Location of Culture*, Routledge: London, U.K., 1994.
14. Georgiou, M. *Diaspora, Identity, and the Media: Diasporic Transnationalism and Mediated Spatialities*, Hampton Press: Cresskill, NJ, 2006.
15. Hall, S. Cultural identity and diaspora. In *Dangerous Liaisons: Gender, Nation, and Postcolonial Perspectives*; McClintock, A., Mufti, A., Shohat, E., Eds.; University of Minnesota Press: Minneapolis, MN, 1997; 173–187.
16. Sun, W.; Ed. *Media and the Chinese diaspora: Community, Communications, and Commerce;* Routledge: New York, 2006.
17. Bailey, O.G.; Georgiou, M.; Harindranath, R.; Eds. *Transnational Lives and the Media: Re-Imagining Diaspora*; Palgrave Macmillan: New York, 2007.
18. Ray, M. Nation, nostalgia and Bollywood: in the tracks of a twice-displaced community. In *The Media of Diaspora*; Karim, K.H., Ed.; Routledge: London, U.K., 2003; 21–35.
19. Naficy, H. Narrowcasting in diaspora: Middle Eastern television in Los Angeles. In *The Media of Diaspora*; Karim, K.H., Ed.; Routledge: London, U.K., 2003; 51–62.
20. De Santis, H. Mi programa es su programa: tele/visions of a Spanish-language diaspora in North America. In *The Media of Diaspora*; Karim, K.H., Ed.; Routledge: London, U.K., 2003; 63–75.
21. Mandaville, P. Communication and diasporic Islam: a virtual ummah?. In *The Media of Diaspora*; Karim, K.H., Ed.; Routledge: London, U.K., 2003; 135–147.
22. Tsaliki, L. Globalisation and hybridity: the construction of Greekness on the Internet. In *The Media of Diaspora*; Karim, K.H., Ed.; Routledge: London, U.K., 2003; 162–176.
23. Mitra, A. Creating immigrant identities in cybernetic space: examples from a non-resident Indian website. Med. Cult. Soc. **2005**, *27*(3), 371–390.
24. Lal, V. *Reflections on the Indian Diaspora, in the Caribbean and Elsewhere*. Available at http://www.sscnet.ucla.edu/southasia/Diaspora/reflect.html.
25. Lal, B.V. Introduction. In *The Encyclopedia of the Indian Diaspora*; Lal, B.V., Ed.; University of Hawaii Press: Honolulu, HI, 2006.
26. Mallapragada, M. Home, homeland, homepage: belonging and the Indian-American web. New Med. Soc. **2006**, *8*(2), 207–227.
27. Metoyer-Duran, C. Information-seeking behavior of Gatekeepers in Ethnolinguistic communities: overview of a taxonomy. Lib. Inform. Sci. Res. **1991**, *13*, 319–346.
28. Fisher, K.E.; Marcoux, E.; Miller, L.S.; Sanchez, A.; Cunningham, E.R. Information behaviour of migrant Hispanic farm workers and their families in the Pacific

Northwest. Inform. Res. **2004**, *10*. Available at http://informationr.net/ir/10–1/paper199.html (accessed March 4, 2006).

29. Chu, C.M. Immigrant children mediators (ICM): bridging the literacy gap in immigrant communities. New Rev. Child. Literat. Librarian. **1999**, *5*, 85–94.

30. Fisher, K.E. Information grounds. In *Theories of Information Behavior*; Fisher, K.E., Erdelez, S., McKechnie, L., Eds.; Information Today: Medford, NJ, 2005.

31. Fisher, K.E.; Durrance, J.C.; Hinton, M.B. Information grounds and the use of need-based services by immigrants in Queens, New York: a context-based, outcome evaluation approach. J. Am. Soc. Inform. Sci. Technol. **2004**, *55*(8), 754–766.

32. Putnam, R.D. Bowling alone: America's declining social capital. J. Democr. **1995**, *6*(1), 65–78.

33. Appadurai, A. Archive and aspiration. In *Information Is Alive*; Brouwer, J., Mulder, A., Eds.; V2 Publishing/NAI Publishers: Rotterdam, the Netherlands, 2003.

34. Srinivasan, R. Reconstituting the urban through community-articulated digital environments. J. Urban Technol. **2004**, *11*(2), 93–111.

Information Needs and Behaviors of Populations in Less Developed Regions

Innocent I. Ekoja
University Library, University of Abuja, Abuja, Nigeria

Abstract

The information needs of the peoples of the developing regions are for work-related activities, leisure, consumption, and daily survival. Due to low literacy levels and ignorance about other sources, the general information-seeking behaviors include passive quests for information and heavy reliance on opinion leaders, rumors, and oral sources, with the library often the least preferred source for information. Even with an emphasis on the seeking of information for utilitarian purposes, people generally have not adopted the habit of utilizing information resources such as libraries and information centers in their work, life, and study. Due to their urban locations, distance and poor information infrastructures, libraries and information centers are not patronized frequently and regularly by many potential users, who instead resort to the use of their own personal collections and individual contacts. In the face of poor retrieval devices, browsing is the most favored approach to determine the relevance of materials to be consulted. In some instances people use information outside that for which they express interest. The predicament of libraries and information centers in developing regions is made worse by lack of local content, the failure to develop indigenous knowledge systems, and especially the advent of information and communication technologies (ICTs). The latter have brought about further lower patronage because most libraries and information centers cannot afford the ICTs. Finally, the inefficiency of general municipal services makes the information seeker exert more effort and spend more time to access information than might be expected in developed countries.

INTRODUCTION

This entry will provide an understanding of the information needs and behaviors of people in developing regions. "Information needs" refers to the information that people require to conduct their businesses and live their daily lives. "Information behaviors" are the tendencies and approaches exhibited by people while seeking out information.

All human beings need information, regardless of where they live. It is required for individual growth and development, and by extension, societal growth and change, too. Information is needed both for personal, social and/or work-related activities of individuals and for development of societies and states.

As information-dependent organisms, human beings have discernible ways of looking for information to meet their information needs. However, for reasons to be discussed, access to information through libraries and over the Internet, while increasingly common in the developed world, is limited in developing or underdeveloped countries. Rather than drawing on these sources for information, people in developing countries often use a variety of other information-seeking resources that are more readily available.

THE CONCEPT OF DEVELOPING COUNTRIES

Based on their economies, the World Bank has classified the countries of the world into low, middle, and high income economies. According to the Bank, "low income and middle income economies are sometimes referred to as developing economies" or countries.[1]

The developing countries of the world are those with low standard of living, a weak industrial base, and a generally low human development index score. Among the outstanding features of developing countries are widespread poverty and low capital formation. The developing countries are found especially in sub-Saharan Africa, Asia, the Pacific, Latin America, the Caribbean, etc. The factors responsible for the under-development of these countries are many and are subsumed under social, political, and economic considerations. Among the many political and economic considerations is improper access to education and information.[2]

FRAMEWORK OF THE ENTRY

The framework for this entry is based on an adaptation of Ranganathan's categorization of human knowledge.

Encyclopedia of Library and Information Sciences, Fourth Edition DOI: 10.1081/E-ELIS4-120043726

Ranganathan categorized human knowledge using concepts of "personality," "matter," "energy," "space and time" (PMEST) (p. 452).[3] This categorization also can be used to understand human information-seeking behavior by drawing the following analogies:

- "Personality" includes individual information seekers and individual information-seeking behaviors occurring in the information environment, both of users and managers, their social networks, etc.
- "Matter" includes the information and information resources, access systems and technology.
- "Energy" entails the problems/goals, processes and tasks undertaken in the course of information provision.
- "Space" entails the work space, organization, country, or geographic unit.
- "Time" entails episodes, intervals, and total time needed for information to be accessed.

"PERSONALITY": INDIVIDUALS AND INDIVIDUAL INFORMATION SEEKING IN THE DEVELOPING WORLD

At the most basic level, one might simply explore the ways individuals seek information, which could be through any or a combination of the following ways (p. 3):[4]

1. Experiment(s) or adopting a trial and error approach.
2. Asking colleague(s) or discussing with him/her (them).
3. Consulting personal collections for relevant information sources.
4. Observing nature or environment for needed information.
5. Consulting library/information centers for information either through self-help or consulting the librarian/information professional.

Information-seeking behaviors vary considerably from one individual to another according to age, gender, level of education, occupation, location, religion, culture, etc. It is very difficult, if not impossible, to identify common information-seeking behaviors for all the peoples of the developing regions of the world. This entry therefore will not attempt to identify common individual information-seeking behaviors in different countries and cultures of the developing world.

Rather, this entry will explore some general parameters influencing information-seeking behavior of types or groups of individuals in developing countries. Information-seeking behavior is the noticeable, and in some instances, the unnoticeable traits individuals exhibit or ways they adopt in the course of seeking out needed

information. It is the purposive seeking for information as a consequence of a need to satisfy some goals.[5] Information behavioral traits would be exhibited in the course of passive attention, passive search, active search, or ongoing search for information (p. 433).[6] Information-seeking behavior is therefore both a function of recognition of one's needs for information, and knowledge of, availability of, and ability to make use of information services and resources to meet ones perceived information needs. We will consider parameters affecting meeting of the information needs of four types of individuals found in developing countries: students, professionals, farmers, and artisans. For all four groups costs, quality, or availability of information resources such as libraries, information centers, and some information networks more commonly accessible in more developed countries (e.g., professional conferences) limit their information access and contribute to their use of alternative means to obtain information.

There are millions of students engaged in academic pursuits or the pursuit of professional qualifications in the developing countries. Primarily, they require or need information to support or facilitate their academic pursuits. They would also require information for daily survival, such as information on where to get access to health care delivery, foods and drinks, clothing, spiritual needs, etc. Even though there are millions of such students, their social/professional networks are limited because of the constraints of economic resources and technological considerations. They are, therefore, hardly ever able to attend conferences, whether international or local, just as they hardly ever subscribe to journals, newsletters, etc., on their own. Due to high costs, they cannot subscribe to the membership of learned societies on their own either, even in situations where they are offered student rates. Students in developing countries are therefore more dependent for information than those in developed countries on school or university library resources that are often much poorer in quality, breadth, depth and being up to date than those in developed countries—or on other students and professors or teachers with whom they are in direct contact.

Professionals in the developing countries, as in the developed countries, include engineers, health care practitioners, legal practitioners, teachers, administrators, scientists, etc. Professionals require information to support their respective practices, and for their day-to-day living as well. Professionals in developing countries aspire to and do maintain social/professional networks, which afford them the opportunity to attend local and international conferences to discuss and exchange ideas with colleagues; subscribe to journals and newsletters; and subscribe to the membership of learned societies. However, owing to economic and technological constraints, among other reasons, most of them are unable to develop their social/professional networks to be able to acquire the needed material for research and other purposes. This contrasts with the situation of their counterparts in the developed world who can and do develop and sustain such networks. There are, for example, professionals in the developing countries who, because of inadequate remuneration, cannot afford $100 a year to initiate and retain membership of a single learned society. Some other professionals are unwilling to pay that much even if they can afford it because of competing needs for the money. In fact, in Nigerian universities, the highest paid professors are entitled to only $300 a year for learned societies and $600 for journal allowances. These amounts can hardly pay, on the average, for more than two learned societies and two journals from abroad. Due also to poor institutional funding, professionals in developing countries can hardly attend international conferences either, except in the few instances that they are sponsored by international organizations. In general, professionals in developing countries have fewer social/professional networks than their counterparts in developed countries because of these obvious limitations.

The farmer, artisan, and other less skilled workers also require information to further their practices and for their daily survival. It is probably with this category of information seekers that there would be the most major differences in terms of information needs and seeking behaviors when compared to their counterparts in the developed countries. This is so because of the big disparity in the levels of education of farmers, artisans, and less skilled workers in developing countries. In fact, in the developing regions, the majority of farmers, artisans, etc., are generally people with little or no education. Because of their low levels of education and general lack of exposure to a variety of information resources, they may not know how to go about meeting their information needs, or even if they know, they tend to wait passively for their information needs to be met instead of taking proactive measures to meet them.

Another big drawback for farmers, artisans, and less skilled workers is the lack of information in the language or form they would be able to access. Many of the developing countries, especially those in Africa have multi-ethnic groups with their own languages, yet the libraries and information centers provide information mainly in colonial languages such as English, French, Spanish, Portuguese, German, etc. Even then, libraries and information centers are available much more often in urban areas than in rural areas.

"MATTER": INFORMATION AND INFORMATION RESOURCES IN DEVELOPING COUNTRIES

For the developing countries of the world, just as for the developed countries, information ought to be available to support the needs of the people for career-related activities, consumption, leisure, etc. Such information is available from a number of sources. Some developing countries have acknowledged the need for and attempted to provide

information resources to their populations. For example, Cai and O'Keefe (p. 23)[7] report that both scientists and farmers in China have access to information through agricultural journals. It was also reported of China that the Management Data Team and the Library Resource Team disseminated information to village people, including farmers (p. 70).[8] The latter effort was funded by the International Development Research Centre based in Canada. In contrast, in the Philippines urban Filipinos were better served than their rural counterparts (p. 10).[9]

As shown by the above cases, there are a few instances of other developing countries where information is readily available, especially to urban populations. In general terms, however, most of the developing countries are both information-poor and information-starved. They are information-poor because they do not experience the kind of information flood experienced by the developed world. They are information-starved because they do not have the means to acquire the materials and infrastructure that contain needed information, or the economic resources needed to pay personnel to acquire, organize, and maintain access to the information. Developing countries, therefore, in most instances have to wait for donations, and those donations often provide outdated or non-relevant information resources.

In the developing countries, much like the developed world, current information for ready application is required. The information resources available to the populations of the developing world include print but also non-print materials, including databases (both online and offline). Electronic databases are available for use in the few libraries and information centers that have been automated and/or digitized. Where they exist libraries and information centers are located mainly in urban and semi-urban areas, with the implication that rural dwellers often do not have access to the resources to meet their information needs. Book mobiles (whether motor vehicles, boats, donkeys, etc.) are not as popular as they used to be in the past because they are little encouraged.

Information access systems in the developing countries are not well developed and coordinated because of the lack of the wherewithal of individual libraries to develop them, which is made worse by their failure to enter into cooperation and collaboration. The instances of cooperation and collaboration, where they exist, are few. This is even made worse by the fact that in most countries of the developing world, the necessary information and communication technologies (ICTs) and infrastructure required for information handling are not available.

Another issue is that most information professionals lack the necessary and requisite ICT skills. Inadequate training and human resource capacity was identified as a problem threatening the continued existence of the rural knowledge centers (RKC) in East Africa. This lack of capacity is not limited to ICT use, but there is a general lack of human resource capacity to manage even conventional information resources and services in the developing countries such that they can meet the information needs of the communities they are meant for.

Recently and increasingly, however, there has been a considerable measure of investment in ICT acquisition and usage in many parts of the developing world, especially in rural communities, provided through international donors. On this score it has been observed with regard to East Africa that:

> Rural knowledge centers, also known as community telecenters, are becoming a popular model for delivering ICT in rural areas, especially in developing countries where information and communication facilities are limited. The past decade has witnessed an explosion in projects that apply ICTs to support socio-economic development (p. 145).[10]

These RKC include simple telephone shops, market information centers (MIC), market information prints (MIP), multipurpose community telecenters (MCT), etc. The MICs and MIPs are a creation of the Kenya Agricultural Commodity Exchange Limited, aimed at assisting small scale farmers with up-to-date market information services such as good prices for their produce and where to sell and buy at such prices, commodity stocks, etc. The ICT components of the MICs include computers and mobile phones, which farmers use to access current information. From the MICs, information is downloaded and distributed to the MIPs every market day (p. 15).[11]

The multipurpose community centers are the most sophisticated of the RKC. Their services include telephony, Internet searching, satellite broadcasts for radio and video shows, fax, e-mail, etc. Using the examples of MCTs in East Africa, located specifically at Nakaseke, Buwama and Nabweru in Uganda; and Sengerema in Tanzania, it was reported that these centers undertake a number of projects that offer information on agriculture, education, health, and indigenous knowledge (p. 145).[11] The information services deriving from these projects profoundly affect the ways of life of their host communities in several ways. These include opportunities for income-generating activities for farmers and local entrepreneurs who search the Internet for information on markets and agrochemicals, updating professionals with information in the fields of work as well as advertisements for job opportunities, and providing access to learning resources for students.

Despite these recent advances and occasional successes, the general prevailing practice in most developing countries is that ICT use has not impacted on information provision in a widespread way. Apart from the centers often being sparsely used, the general lack of much ICT infrastructure, replacement/update capacity, and trained personnel remain daunting challenges.

Another reason is the failure of most developing countries to develop their indigenous knowledge systems (IKS), which would have complemented the information coming from western knowledge systems (WKS), most of which emanate from the developed countries. It is observed of this situation that information flows in developing countries are segmented, divisive and uncoordinated (p. 2).[12] Although it may arrive late (and already outdated) in printed form, WKS information is much of what can currently be obtained over the Internet and through ICTs. Professionals such as medical doctors in developing countries might be able to obtain WKS information about disease treatment, yet would also require IKS information about the traditions and cultures of the populations they serve in order to serve them well. Otherwise, if WKS information services offend the sensibilities of the populations served, they might not let themselves be served. It was reported of health workers in Upper East Region of Ghana that they required information about the beliefs, taboos, festivals, etc., of the people to be able to deliver acceptable medical practice to them (p. 367).[13] Although developing countries have been slow in making IKS information available through channels such as libraries and information centers, indigenous knowledge items often remain available through rich oral traditions, ceremonial practices, etc. These oral traditions and active practices remain a positively valued alternative source for obtaining a wide variety of information.

"PERSONALITY" AND "MATTER": THE INTERPLAY OF INFORMATION AND INFORMATION RESOURCE AVAILABILITY AND THE USE OF ALTERNATIVE INFORMATION-SEEKING BEHAVIORS

In most developing countries, professionals like engineers, scientists, technologists, medical doctors, pharmacists, etc., are unable to have most of their professional work information needs met because of the many factors reported in the last entry. A study conducted on the information needs of scientists and technologists in Nigeria revealed that libraries and information centers were unable to meet their information needs due to poor stocking and staffing. Current journals and databases lack good retrieval systems and interlibrary loan facilities. The other shortcomings included inadequate information sources and the poor orientation of library and information center staff to responsive reference services (p. 137).[14] This study was conducted in the 1990s but the situations have generally not changed even with ICT availability, which for most libraries and information centers in the developing countries, is still a mirage. It is instructive to mention here that the Academic Staff Union of Nigerian Universities, which in 1991/1992 went on strike for over 6 months due to poor facilities, including libraries, in Nigerian

Universities went on strike again for several months in 2007 because the state of these facilities had deteriorated.

In the course of pursuing his academic or professional education, an average African scholar maximally exploits the limited available learning material to enhance his chances of acquiring the desired certificate(s). For him, therefore, knowledge or information is hardly sought after for purposes other than utilitarian. This is with the consequence that educated Africans, after acquiring certificates from educational institutions and professional bodies, hardly read outside newspapers and magazines. Since few people read for the sake of esthetics, it follows too that information or knowledge for esthetic purposes is hardly sought after. This situation is encouraged by the tantalizing rich oral culture to which many people turn to derive exciting and pleasurable experiences. Instead of turning to novels and other sources of information, whether print, electronic or otherwise to seek information that keeps them entertained; such entertainment can be derived from the happenings in the immediate environment(s).

Even as it was reported that the increased use of the Internet was bringing an end to the two-step flow of information seeking (p. 660)[15] in some parts of the world, the two-step information-seeking approach still thrives very much in developing countries. The two-step information-seeking approach is a situation in which a person obtains information from friends and acquaintances who, in an earlier first step, had obtained such information from some other source. This approach still thrives in developing countries because the Internet is not readily available, especially to rural populations.

Another catalyst for the two-step flow of information seeking is the gregarious nature of the populations in developing countries, especially in Africa and Asia. This also promotes the use of oral sources by information seekers, including reliance on opinion leaders for information. This was acknowledged in a study of Indonesian farmers, who, it was reported, relied on opinion leaders and those with higher socio-economic status to get information about pest management (p. 4).[16] The same is also true of many other settings in developing countries where community members rely for information on chiefs, community leaders, pastors, imams, and others with higher socio-economic status.

Related to the issue of two-step information seeking is that of rumors, which is prevalent and relied upon in Africa because of the propensity of African governments and their agencies to suppress information (p. 5).[17] Rumor is not relied upon as sources of information only in Africa but also in many developing countries where dictatorial governments suppress information. In this situation, information, which one might expect to be readily available, is deliberately withheld, thus giving room to rumor peddling.

Another big barrier to the use of libraries or information centers by many people in developing countries is that

in making information and information resources available, consideration is not given to local languages, visual orientation, and the use of voice interfaces for populations that are to a very big extent illiterate. Because of this (both conventional illiteracy and ICT illiteracy), most of the populations for whom information services are meant are unable to use them, especially in the rural areas. A study on the information needs of community-based organizations indicated that most community development projects and social programs failed because information about them did not reach the people in the form or language that they understood (p. 34).[18] This is also true of library and information services.

These are some of the problems facing information diffusion and use in many developing countries. A typical case is with regard to the developing regions of China of which it was reported that most citizens had not adopted the habit of utilizing information resources in their work, life, and study because of their low literacy levels.[19] The developing regions of China are still better off than most other developing parts of the world because this same report indicated ICT availability to the rural Chinese, who with their ICT literacy, found the use of the Internet popular. The use of the Internet among them for information and services was, however, found to be detrimental to the patronage of reference services in public libraries, which service was obviously on the decline.

The library in most developing countries is the least patronized when users seek to meet their information needs because of irrelevant materials in terms of their language(s), form(s), and up-to-dateness. The language in which information is made available is very important, else people would be unable to use it. For example, for a setting where Kiswahili is the spoken and written language, materials provided in the English language would almost be useless. Similarly, where people are illiterate, print materials like books, journals, etc., would not be required to access information.

There is also the problem of lack of local content that meets the local and immediate information needs of the members of the communities where libraries and information centers are located. The situation is made worse by the failure of information services providers to consult with potential users to determine their information needs, and the failure still to monitor these needs regularly to be able to respond to changes. The result is that libraries and information centers are not providing services that users require.

Another major barrier to information needs and seeking behaviors of populations in the developing regions of the world is that information seekers more often than not use information other than that which they expressed a need for. It was observed in an Indian community that: "The information people usually say they need was not always what they end up using. In the M.S. Swaminathan Pondicherry Project, for example, male farmers originally said they needed information about agriculture. In fact, their largest usage of village info-kiosks was to get information about government programs."[20]

The situation in India could be associated with the finding that:

> Observing human information seeking has demonstrated that people do not always choose actions that would lead them to the optimal result. For example, they may bypass the most knowledgeable information provider to ask questions of someone they know. In fact, the typical findings of information-seeking studies in various settings indicate that accessibility of information is the key factor involved in what sources people select, and that interpersonal sources are preferred over other channels (p. 661).[15]

"ENERGY," "SPACE," AND "TIME": BARRIERS IN OBTAINING INFORMATION TO MEET INFORMATION NEEDS AND IMPACTS ON INFORMATION-SEEKING BEHAVIORS

There are a number of barriers to obtaining information that meets information needs and seeking behaviors in developing countries. These include outright non-availability of information and the information resources that meet the needs of users; availability of inappropriate information, and information resources; non-awareness of the information and information resources that are available; lack of time for searching for information and for learning how to use an information source; lack of the hardware and/or software with which to retrieve information; distance from users' home to points of information, etc.

These problems have been observed to be setbacks to the free flow of information right from the source through the media to users, and have economic, social, environmental, and infrastructural dimensions (p. 5).[15] The economic problems of information seeking relate to cost as it affects information carrying media, time, and labor. The general poverty of the developing regions makes it near impossible to develop the information infrastructure that can make information available to meet the needs of the people. Another major factor accounting for poor information services in developing countries is that they compete with other social services provision like roads, water, energy, etc., for which the people have a preference. Apart from the existence of only a few well-developed libraries and information centers, inadequate ICT development and outright lack of it is also a big factor militating against access to information.

The library and information systems are therefore not well developed to meet the information needs of users. This is especially true of the rural areas because library and information services providers, including telecommunications operators prefer to offer services in urban and semi-urban areas. Due to the poor library and information systems, many professionals rely on their limited personal collections, and the few who can afford it own computers with Internet access. Those who cannot afford it have a Herculean task accessing desired information or are even unable to access it.

Compared to the developed countries, the information seeker in developing countries spends more time and exerts more effort in accessing the required information, which, in some instances, even after rigorous searching, is still not available. This is so because in the first place information facilities, as well as retrieval devices to aid his searching, are often just not available. The scarcity of retrieval devices makes browsing the most favored way to seek for information. It was observed with regard to the knowledge centers in East Africa that one difficulty in ensuring that they become sustainable is the lack of capacity to use ICTs to access and apply relevant information to solve problems (p. 150).[17] This difficulty does not apply to East Africa alone but generally to most of the developing countries because of inadequate training opportunities and poor human capacity to use ICT to access information. The situation is such that it is not just the users alone, but even managers of information systems who often lack the capacity to manage information using ICTs in such a way as to produce the information that users need. Apart from their financial constraints to subscribe to information carrying media on CDs, VCDs, DVDs, and online, many information professionals in developing countries are unable to access open source materials, which can address the information needs of those they serve, due to this lack of human capacity.

Again because of the failure of municipal services provision, the information seeker spends 2–3 times over and above the time and effort he would have required to access information in better-supplied areas. An example is that in trying to access information on the Internet, power outage may be experienced, which will lead to the suspension of the exercise. Power may not be restored until some hours later, only to be interrupted again as the renewed effort to access the information commences. This may go on and on until the seeker succeeds in accessing the required information after several attempts. This makes information seeking more expensive in terms of time and labor, apart from the frustrations encountered. The prevailing poverty also makes access to information very difficult because generally most members of the populations of developing regions are unable to own information resources (books, computers with Internet connectivity, subscribe to journals, etc.) or even pay for Internet access in business centers that can enable them access the information that meets their needs.

Related to the problem of poor utility or municipal services is that of gasoline scarcity and cost that helps limit people's ability to reach libraries or information centers. A lot of time, effort, and cost go into fueling own vehicles or boarding public transport that in the end those who would normally seek after information to meet their needs are unable to do so.

Another major problem is the distance between the residences of information seekers and the points of information services. Such distances affect the frequency and regularity with which information is sought after and used in developing countries because of the time and cost involved. There are other activities such as social, religious, etc., competing for the time that would ordinarily have gone into the use of information. This is especially worse for women and girls because of their disadvantaged position, and the fact that they are saddled with most of the household chores.

CONCLUSION

Information is of strategic importance to the peoples of the developing regions. It is very difficult, if not impossible, to identify common information needs and behaviors for all the peoples of the developing world. However, the problems they face in the course of accessing information to meet their needs have much in common.

The issue of information needs and behaviors of populations in less developed regions was addressed from the perspective of an adaptation of Ranganathan's PMEST categorization, which stands for personality, matter, energy, space, and time. The information seekers in the developing regions include students, professionals, artisans, farmers, etc., whose limited social/professional networks constitute one of the problems for their failure to have their information needs met. Some of the potential information users have very little education, or are even outright illiterate and ignorant, and therefore do not know how to go about meeting their information needs, or at best wait passively for information to be brought to them.

It is only in a few parts of the developing countries that information infrastructures are available to meet the needs of the populace. The majority of the developing countries experience information starvation and information poverty, lack of commitment by concerned authorities to provide effective information systems, and failure to develop IKS to support WKS. The two-step flow of information is the vogue due to vast oral sources, which along with the suppression of information by authorities, is also associated with reliance on rumors, opinion leaders, and community leaders.

The information access systems are generally not well developed, and part of this is explained by the fact that most information professionals lack the requisite skills, both conventional and ICT, for the handling of information. Where ICTs have made in-roads, it is most often with the assistance or intervention of western donor agencies, and in such cases the professionals manning such libraries and information centers have the capacity to offer services using ICTs because the training of personnel is one of the components of such interventions.

The barriers to obtaining information to meet the needs of the populations of the developing regions are many. They include outright non-availability of information and the information resources that meet the needs of users; availability of inappropriate information and information resources, non-awareness of the information and the information resources that are available; lack of time for searching for information and for learning how to use information sources; lack of the hardware and/or software with which to retrieve information; distance from users' homes to points of information; and other factors associated with the problems of daily life in developing countries.

Although the challenges are great, all hope is not lost for the populations of the developing regions to have their information needs met if only their governments and other funding authorities will rise up to make education and information provision priorities. When they do this, it will encourage western donor agencies, which are already doing much to facilitate access to information in the developing regions, to do even more. Another important thing to do is to encourage the development of IKS to complement WKS in the developing countries.

REFERENCES

1. http:web.worldbank.org/WEBSITE/EXTERNAL/DATASTATISTICS/O.
2. http:en.wikipedia. org/wiki/Developing countries.
3. Sonnenwald, D.H.; Iivonen, M. An integrated human information research framework for information studies. Libr. Inform. Sci. Res. 1999, 21(4), 429–453.
4. Afolabi, M. Topical Issues in Information Management, Department of Library and Information Science, Ahmadu Bello University: Zaria, Nigeria, 1998.
5. Wilson, T.D. Human information behavior. Inform. Sci. 2000, 3(2), 49–55.
6. Wilson, T.D. Information behavior: An interdisciplinary perspective. Inform. Process. Manage. 1997, 33, 551–572 Cited by Sonnenwald, D.H.; Iivonen, M. An integrated human information framework for information studies. Libr. Inform. Sci. Res. 1999, 2(4), 429–453.
7. Cai, J.; O'keefe, G. Disseminating agricultural science information by journal publishing in China. IAALD Quart. Bull. 1993, 38(1), 1–7.
8. Shettlesworth, C.; Malakedsuwan, B.; Tungtikul, S.; Blair, J. Thai Agricultural Colleges Transfer of Information Cooperative Service (TACTICS). IAALD Quart. Bull. 1990, 35(2), 69–72.
9. Gregorio, L.B.; Sison, J.C. Agricultural information provision in developing countries. IAALD Quart. Bull. 1989, 34(1), 7–11.
10. Mukhebi, A. Providing marketing and market information services in liberalized agricultural markets: The case of KACE Proceedings of Workshop on Improvement and

Sustainability of Information Supply and Dissemination in the Wider Agricultural Community of Kenya Nairobi, Kenya, February, 18–19, 2003; CAB International and Kenya Agricultural Research Institute: Nairobi, Kenya, 2003.

11. Asaba, J.F.; Musebe, R.; Kimani, M.; Day, R.; Nkonu, M.; Mukhebi, A.; Wesonga, A.; Mbula, R.; Balaba, P.; Nakagwa, A. Bridging the information and knowledge gap between urban and rural communities through rural knowledge centres: Case studies from Kenya and Uganda. IAALD Q. B. **2006**, *51*(3/4), 143–151.

12. Adeyemi, N.M. Issues in the provision of information services to developing countries. Afr. J. Libr. Arch. Inform. Sci. **1991**, *1*(1), 1–8.

13. Apalayine, G.B.; Ehikhamenor, F.A. The information needs and sources of primary health care workers in the Upper East Region of Ghana. J. Inform. Sci. **1996**, *22*(5), 367–373.

14. Adimorah, E.N.O. Information needs of scientists and technologists in Nigeria. Lead. Libr. Inform. Cent. **1993**, *1*(2), 19–26.

15. Case, D.O.; Johson, D.J.; Andrews, J.E.; Allard, S.L.; Kelly, K.M. From two-step flow to internet: The changing array of sources for genetics information-seeking. J. Am. Soc. Inform. Sci. Technol. **2004**, *55*(8), 660–669.

16. Feder, G.; Savastano, S. Diffusing new knowledge among farmers: The role of opinion leaders. World Bank Dig. **2006**, *1*(2), 4.

17. Sturges, P. Veil, R. *The Quiet Struggle: Libraries and Information for Africa*, Mansel: London, U.K., 1990.

18. Kantumuya, A. Public libraries and community information services in Africa. Afr. J. Libr. Arch. Inform. Sci. **1992**, *2*(1), 33–38.

19. Yanru, L. Marketing reference service of public libraries in developing regions World Library and Information Congress, Proceedings of 72nd IFLA General Conference and Council Seoul, Korea, August, 20–24, 2006.

20. Keniston, K. Grassroots ICT projects in India: Some preliminary hypotheses. ASCI J. Manage. **2002**, *31*(1&2), 1–9.

Information Policy: European Union

Debbie Rabina
School of Library and Information Science, Pratt Institute, New York, New York, U.S.A.

Scott Johnston
McPherson Library, University of Victoria, Victoria, British Columbia, Canada

Abstract

This entry provides an overview of European Union (EU) information policy, focusing on its formation, its goals, and its influence. European Union information policy refers to the legislation and strategies pertaining to the European policy for the creation of the information society. It is concerned with economic and industrial competitiveness, with an emphasis on the role that information and communication technologies play in revolutionizing everyday life, a broad goal with far reaching socioeconomic implications. This discussion, however, will be confined to information policy areas of greatest interest to information professionals, namely copyright and intellectual property, data protection and privacy, e-government and digitization.

INTRODUCTION

European Union (EU) information policy refers to the legislation and strategies pertaining to the European policy for the creation of information society. This includes areas such as copyright and intellectual property, data protection and privacy, e-government and digitization. It is also concerned with economic and industrial competitiveness with an emphasis on the role that information and communication technologies play in revolutionizing everyday life. Information policy is viewed as contributing to the larger goals and objectives of the EU itself, particularly in relation to the European economy.

The beginning of a comprehensive information policy for the EU can be traced back to 1994 when the European Council, recognizing the profound effect that global information and communication systems were having on European society, began to establish a foundation for an information and communication infrastructure. At the root of the EU information policy was an effort to build a legal and physical infrastructure designed to promote a global information society.

Following a brief discussion of the key concepts in information policy, we will provide a brief history of the EU, before going on to discuss the formation, legislation, and implementation of information policy in the EU as they pertain to library and information science. Lastly we will discuss some of the major issues facing information policy in the EU and the influence it has had in the United States and on an international stage.

BACKGROUND

Information Policy

Information policy is an umbrella term for official government policies that govern the collection, storage, and dissemination of official information within a specific jurisdiction. Weingarten describes information policy as a set of all public laws, regulations, and policies that encourage, discourage, or regulate the creation, use, storage, and communication of information.[1]

Information policy is a socially constructed concept and should be evaluated in relation to the environment in which it is practiced. The term "information policy" connotes a U.S. perspective and is not the preferred term of the EU. EU policy makers have adopated the term "Information Society" to denote a broader set of issues relating to aspects of information management.

While only one perspective can be presented and developed here, it is important that readers be made aware of alternative views. Keeping in mind the likely readership of the *Encyclopedia of Library and Information Science* and attempting to offer a unified perspective of information policy as expressed in the information policy entry, this entry examines EU information policy in a narrowly defined way that is analogous to the discussion of information policy as generally perceived in the United States.

We limit our discussion to the EU information policy as defined by Hernon and Relyea in the third edition of ELIS and diverge from it when expansion in the framework is necessary for understanding the EU landscape.

Encyclopedia of Library and Information Sciences, Fourth Edition DOI: 10.1081/E-ELIS4-120044551

For purposes of this entry, we have chosen to adopt the definition used by Hernon and Relyea: "Information policy is [...] a set of interrelated principles, laws, guidelines, rules, regulations, and procedures guiding the oversight and management of the information *life cycle*: the production, collection, distribution/dissemination, retrieval and use, and retirement, including preservation, of information."[2]

At the government level, information policy is designed to be operational and is executed by a series of laws, regulations, and court cases that reflect a country's approach to information policy. Cahill and Overman argue that information policy is value-based and that these values are normative in nature and specific to the value system of individual countries.[3] Normative ethics attempt to balance right and wrong behaviors as they are perceived through the underlying morals and arrive at the correct moral principles by which all people should be morally guided.[4]

A research perspective of information policy takes into account various theories that explain and justify information policies. Theoretical frameworks are important to the discussion of information policy in that they provide justification for the policies enacted, serve as the underlying imprint of policies and situate them in a specific time and place. With regard to information policies, legal jurisdictions such as federal governments, as in the United States, or supragovernmental organizations, as in the EU, design and enact policies. Such policies are intended to help resolve inherent problems in information technology and provide pragmatic models for resolving concrete problems. The wide penetration of information technologies highlighted the conflict between policy values, such as information privacy or information ownership, and unconfined use of technology. While there are numerous theoretical approaches to information policy, some of the more widespread approaches include ethical frameworks and economic frameworks.

Many ethical approaches to information policy are based on John Stuart Mill's essay on Utilitarianism, published originally in 1859.[5] Recognizing that absolute ethics are not possible to achieve, Mill promotes pragmatic ethics which results in the greatest good for the greatest number of people affected. A utilitarian approach will result in different policies from an approach based on basic human rights. For example, in the United States many of the areas associated with information policy are based on basic rights of the people as articulated in the U.S. Constitution. In Europe, where a Millsian pragmatic ethics approach is more common, information policy is seen to be serving greater considerations than just those of the citizenry.[6]

Another theoretical framework for understanding information policy in the European context is to understand it as a series of policies that support economic growth. Researchers who advocate this approach contend that

thriving economies depend on uniform laws and regulations of information among and between governments. Such researchers include Samuelson and Varian[7] and Reidenberg.[8] While the scope of this entry does not allow us to delve deep into theoretical frameworks, the utilitarian and economic perspectives contribute to a better understanding of the approach to information policy that directs the EU.

Historical Overview of the European Union

The EU is a supranational body working towards peace and prosperity in Europe. The EU maintains a unique structure. It is not a federation of countries, but rather an organization in which each member state maintains its own independent governments and legislatures, while at the same time agreeing to have common institutions with the power to make decisions on matters of joint interest to other member states.

The origins of the EU can be traced back to 1950 when French Foreign Minister Robert Schuman conceived the idea of European integration. Europe Day is celebrated on May 9 to mark the anniversary (Europa http://europa.eu/abc/symbols/9-may/euday_en.htm).

As of June 2008, there were 27 member states as well as three candidate countries (Turkey, Croatia, and Macedonia) awaiting membership. Many of the most recent countries to join the EU in 2004 were members of the former Soviet bloc and include the Czech Republic, Cyprus, Estonia, Hungary, Latvia, Lithuania, Malta, Poland, Slovakia, and Slovenia. In 2007 Bulgaria and Romania also met the democratic and economic threshold requirements for joining the EU and became member states. They joined the earlier members, comprising Belgium, France, Germany, Italy, Luxembourg, the Netherlands (1957), Denmark, Ireland, United Kingdom (1973), Greece (1981), Portugal, Spain (1986), Austria, Finland, and Sweden (1995). Switzerland and Norway elected not to join the EU in order to preserve their neutrality.

The total population of the EU is nearly half a billion people. It covers an area of 1.67 M sq mi, making it nearly twice as large as the United States in terms of population, and slightly under half its size in area. The EU has no constitution. Attempts to ratify one failed in 2004 when France, followed by the Netherlands, voted against a proposed constitution. The prospect of a unifying constitution has become even more remote with the Irish vote against it in June 2008.

The EU functions on the basis of four founding treaties that, in the absence of a constitution, provide the rationale and justification of all decision-making for the Union. Thus, legislation is always directly linked to specific articles in the founding treaties. The four treaties that form the basis of the EU are *The treaty establishing the European Coal and Steel community, 1951* (commonly referred to as The Treaty of Paris); *The treaty establishing the European economic community, 1957* (The Treaty of Rome); *The treaty establishing the European Atomic Energy Community, 1957* (EURATOM); and the *Treaty on European Union, 1992* (Treaty of Maastricht). Treaties are referred to as Primary Law and are regarded as constitutional in statutes. All other legislation is defined as secondary and based on the treaties. Legislation in the EU is binding to all member nations, citizens living within its borders, and companies that conduct business with the EU.[9]

As the main initiator of legislation within the EU, the European Commission is instrumental in the policy-making process regarding the information society. While the Council and the Parliament pass legislation, they can only act on proposals from the Commission. The Commission, the most powerful of the EU institutions, acts as the executive branch of the EU and is the guardian of EU treaties; as such it is entrusted with the role of initiating legislation stemming from treaties (The European Commission at a glance).[10] The Commission is divided into 26 Directorate-Generals (which are similar to government ministries) overseeing different subject areas. Information policy falls under the domain of the Information Society and Media Directorate-General (DG Infso).

European Union government policy is divided into three "pillars." The first pillar covers policy relating to the three communities of the European Coal and Steel Community, the Economic Community, and EURATOM (European Atomic Energy Community). The second pillar covers common foreign and security policy (CFSP). The third pillar covers justice and home affairs, judicial cooperation in civil and criminal matters, police cooperation, and immigration policy. With few exceptions, policies and legislation relating to information policy fall under the first pillar.

INFORMATION POLICY IN THE EUROPEAN UNION

History

The European Commission's role in the EU is to prepare and implement legislation adopted by the European Council and the European Parliament in connection with EU policies acting as the EU's executive branch. It was not until 1979 that the European Commission became involved in information policy when it issued a report that "addressed the role of networks in economic competition and the necessity of cooperation for developing new networks and services."[11] Not only does information policy in the EU lack the long tradition it has in the United States, the term *information policy* itself is not in frequent use in the European context, the preferred term being *information society* (Europa glossary).[12]

Attempts to address legal and regulatory issues relating to the information society did not begin in earnest until the

1990s, with the publication of the Bangemann report, discussed below.[13]

Objectives

The brief definition provided by the Europa glossary of the term *information society* places emphasis on information and communication technologies and their potential role in revolutionizing everyday life, and in this respect is more similar to the Clinton administration's use of the term *National Information Infrastructure*.[14] The information society is therefore a technologically driven phenomenon and, not surprisingly, many of the efforts of the EU are devoted to developing policies centering on technological issues, specifically policies relating to market regulation, introduction of new technologies, and benefiting from information and communications technologies (Europe's Information Society: Information Society Policies).[15]

Commission report (94) 347 situates the role and vision of the information society as a force for economic growth: *"The information society is on its way. A 'digital revolution' is triggering structural changes comparable to last century's industrial revolution with the corresponding high economic stakes. The process cannot be stopped and will lead eventually to a knowledge-based economy"* (COM (94) 347).[16]

Challenges

The EU, for reasons both historical and pragmatic, focuses more efforts on execution than on vision. While its institutions are democratic, and increased transparency continues to be one of the EU's main goals, it is not in the purest sense a democratic institution since the EU's Parliament, whose members are elected directly by the citizens of the member states, has limited ability to exercise control over the European Commission. Transparency and access to information continue to be a challenge in spite of the adoption of a code of conduct regulating access to EU information.[17]

EUROPEAN INFORMATION SOCIETY

Unlike the United States, where information policy is piecemeal and for the most part reactive, information policy in the EU is preemptive. The EU views information policy as contributing to its larger goals and objectives, and considers it an important part of the European economy.

The 1994 Bangemann report is often identified as the foundation of information policy for the EU. It resulted from the European Council's request for a report outlining measures and steps to be considered when laying a foundation for an information and communication infrastructure. The report recognized the profound effect that global information and communication systems were having on European society, including economic and social life.

The report lays out a vision for a European information society and recommends actions to achieve desired outcomes, but devotes little attention to a thorough analysis of the existing preconditions in Europe. Subsequent reports, particularly by the European Commission Blankert et al.,[18] followed the Bangemann report and advised the Commission on a recommended course of action. The Bangemann report was therefore advisory in nature, while implementation was left to EU executives.

At the root of the EU's information policy is an effort to build a legal and physical infrastructure that will promote a global information society. The European Council's vision is for the goal to be achieved by a combination of free market forces and support from the regulatory system (Bangemann report, 4) that will address the needs of all EU citizens in an equitable way and prevent a digital divide (Bangemann report, 7). The goal is for everyone to benefit from the opportunities offered by technology while controlling its adverse effects. To curb the adverse effects of an information-based society, the Bangemann report recommended emphasis be placed on education and training. Free market forces play a major role in achieving the goals of an information society, and the Bangemann report calls for ending monopolies of telecommunication operators and the system of political burdens that are inherent in them (chap. 2). The action plan of the report perceives the role of government as safeguarding competitive forces (chap. 2).

The report set out 10 areas related to ICT in which Europe needs to strengthen itself in order to compete in the global economy. These areas, included in chapter four of the report, are described as applications, or building blocks, of the information society. They include: teleworking, distance learning, a network for universities and research centers, telematic services for small- and medium-sized enterprises, road traffic management, air traffic control, health care networks, electronic tendering; trans-European public administration networks; city information highways.

To promote the goals of the information society, in 1999 the European Commission launched the eEurope initiative to accelerate Europe's entry into the digital age. The result was eEurope 2002, which sought to create a cheaper, faster, and more secure Internet, to invest in people and skills, and to stimulate the use of the Internet throughout the EU (EU Guide to the Digital Economy, 2003).[19] eEurope 2002 was followed by eEurope 2005, and most recently i2010 (Europe's Information Society).[20] i2010 is "an initiative which will provide an integrated approach to information society and audiovisual policies in the EU, covering regulation, research, and deployment and promoting cultural diversity." i2010 aims to achieve through regulation, funding, and partnerships, a single European information space for competitive society and media services, and is currently the main coordinating body for European information society initiatives and implementation in the EU. i2010 actions are directed toward establishing a single European space for affordable and secure ICT both in terms of diverse content and digital services. Other objectives of i2010 are in developing private-public sector partnerships that promote technological innovation and providing an inclusive framework for ICT public services, particularly in the area of e-governments.

Within the framework of the EU, responsibility for the information society was initially that of the Commissioner for Enterprise and Information Society, but as roles expanded, so did the office, which is now known as the Commissioner for Enterprise and Industry (Enterprise and Industry).[21]

MAJOR ISSUES

Several important directives are included under the umbrella of Information Society legislation. These are conveniently collected and updated on the EU's Web site and updated regularly (Europa. Activities on the EU).[22] The main areas of activity most relevant to information professionals include ICT, Intellectual Property, Electronic Commerce, and Data Protection and Privacy.

Information and Communications Technologies (ICT)

The EU's information policy approach is closely linked with communication policy in general and ICT in particular. Both are perceived as equal contributors to the information society. Information and communication are valued as commodities designed for both high-end markets as well as mass consumption.

The Commission of the European Communities set about implementing the recommendation of the Bangemann report, and the initial recommendations for implementation was articulated in an action plan (COM (94) 347). The action plan reiterates the conclusions of the Bangemann report, emphasizing the role of the private sector in infrastructure development, and of the member states in creating a stable regulatory framework. In addition, the action plan proposes a response in four areas: ICT regulatory framework, intellectual property rights, privacy, and electronic protection.

The current legislative framework relating to information policy has attached information policy areas to a "Telecoms Package" that regulates electronic communications in the public sector. The Telecoms Package includes a directive on data protection,[23] the general framework,[24] access and interconnection,[25] authorization and licensing,[26] and universal access.[27]

The objective of the Telecom Package is to provide a regulatory framework for electronic communication that opens the telecommunication markets to competition. This emerged from the recognition that enabling technologies are converging and that a single horizontal framework is therefore required to support them. The framework addresses regulation harmonization in areas of fixed-line voice telephony, mobile and broadband communications, and cable and satellite television.

The most recent assessment found that significant progress has been made in achieving that goal and that the focus should now be on management of the radio spectrum and the streamlining of market reviews (COM(2006) 334 final).[28] In addition, since revenue growth in the area of electronic communication has outperformed growth in the overall EU economy, the framework is considered a success (COM(2006) 334 final).

The preemptive nature of EU information policy is in evidence in many of the general frameworks such as the regulatory framework for electronic communication outlined above. As in other areas of the information society that draft policy based on predictions of the long-term developments in the area (COM (2005) 229 final), the electronic communication framework also attempts to anticipate future developments in the area. Specifically, the report predicts that four major technological developments will occur by 2016: 1) a migration to "all Internet Protocol (information policy)" networks; 2) increased use of wireless communications and wireless platforms; 3) deployment of fiber-optic connections in the local access networks; and 4) the transition to digital television (COM (2006) 334 final).

Intellectual Property

One of the first official reports to address intellectual property was the 1988 Green Paper (COM (88) 172).[29] It was followed by a Commission Working Programme (COM (90) 584).[30] The most recent version, and currently in effect, is Directive 2001/29/EC[31] on the harmonization of certain aspects of copyright and related rights in the information society, which passed in May 22, 2001. The Directive puts the EU in compliance with the World Intellectual Property Organization (WIPO) Copyright Treaty.

The Directive, which went into effect on December 22, 2002, is a slim document, consisting of 15 articles described in 10 pages, and outlines the EU approach to copyright in the broadest terms, leaving many details to individual member nations.

The purpose of the Directive, as described in the preamble, is primarily to contribute to the economic strength of the EU within the framework of the EU's mandate to establish an information society. While the Directive is most commonly regarded as legislation regulating copyright, some of the related rights mentioned in the law's subtitle are significant to the EU's policy framework and

include freedom and expression (Directive 2001/29/EC preamble sections 1–3).

Although the underlying notion of intellectual property protection as an incentive for creativity lies outside of the scope of the Directive, the document clearly assumes that copyright and other intellectual property are economic engines for growth. Section 4 of the preamble states that the desired outcome of the Directive is increased competitiveness in ICT as well as across industrial sectors. This, it is argued, will in turn encourage new job creation (Directive 2001/29/EC preamble section 4). An additional goal of the Directive is to be in compliance with the WIPO (Directive 2001/29/EC preamble section 15).

The main articles of the Directive address reproduction rights, distribution rights, technological protection, and digital rights management. Fair Use, known in the Directive as "Exceptions to Copyright," is addressed in article 6 ([4]). The Directive takes a strict stand on avoiding technological protections, banning not only circumvention of access control technologies which regulate access to information and protected content, but also copy control technologies which prevent additional reproductions beyond the first sale of a copyrighted work (Directive 2001/29/EC Article 6). This is a departure from the Digital Millennium Copyright Act (DMCA)[32] that only made access circumvention illegal. The Directive is interpreted as more favorable to users than the DMCA in that it tilts the balance in favor of the user.[33]

Moral rights (commonly referred to as "droit d'auteur"), which include the right of authors to have their work properly attributed, to preserve the integrity of their work, and to publish anonymously or under a pseudonym, are outside the scope of the Copyright Directive. Section 19 of the preface leaves the exercise and implementation of moral rights to individual member states to work out the issues in accordance with the Berne Convention and the WIPO Copyright treaty.

Electronic Commerce

Within the framework of the EU, electronic commerce (e-Commerce) is viewed as an integral part of the information society structure in that it is an essential part of the network environment. The Directive on Electronic Commerce[34] addresses electronic commerce, defamation, misleading advertising, and infringement of trademarks. The Directive sets rules and supports regulations for transparency for online service providers, and electronic contracts, and limits the liability of intermediary service providers. In addition to e-Commerce as a means of increasing for profit business transactions, it is also the basis for eGovernment services within the EU. The EU policy in the field of eGovernment is part of the previously mentioned i2010 plan (COM (2005) 229 final)[35] and has five objectives all intended to increase services to citizens. eGovernment encourages the use of ICT in the public sector and public administration to improve service, increase democratic participation, and encourage transparency. Areas directly affected by eGovernment initiatives are research and development and scientific, technical, and medical (STM) publishing. The eGovernment action plan (COM (2006) 173 final).[36] outlines the steps to be taken during 2006–2010 to achieve eGovernment goals.

Data Protection and Privacy

Privacy in the context of the EU is closely linked with data protection. While in the United States the term "privacy" prevails, the legislation that regulates matters relating to privacy in the EU primarily covers the protection of personal data. The EU's concern with data protection is mainly to allow data exchange between member states in a manner that ensures a high level of protection within the EU, as well as guaranteeing citizens the same high level of security when exporting data outside the EU. Thus the main legislation protecting privacy, Directive 95/46/EC,[37] prohibits the transfer of personal data of or about EU citizens held in registered databases, to non-EU countries that do not meet the adequacy standard for data protection. The 1995 Directive went into effect in 1998, and subsequent legislation includes the Directive on privacy and electronic communications (Directive 2002/58/EC), an amendment to the 2002 directive,[38] as well as additional legislation and regulation (for complete list see http://ec.europa.eu/justice_home/fsj/privacy/law/index_en.htm).[39]

In order for U.S. companies to trade database information with the EU, the U.S. Department of Commerce established the Safe Harbor framework, a voluntary system of participation approved in 2000. This framework allows participating American companies to trade information with EU companies (Export gov).[40] The EU has addressed data transfer with the United States in two main areas: air passenger data transfer and safe harbor agreements. Data transfer between the EU and the United States is regulation not by legislation (directive) but by a series of agreements and letters issued by the EU (Commission decisions of Third Countries).[41] These documents allow the transfer of information about EU citizens to the United States for purposes of travel and commerce, with the condition that the United States will afford EU citizens data the same level of protection awarded to them by the EU directives. While some of these decisions are unilateral and take the form of statements issued by the EU, there also include joint agreements between the EU and the United States that enable travel and commerce.

A recent example of the impact of EU legislation can be seen in the opinion of the Article 29 Working Group.[42] It determined that search engine companies, in order to comply with the EU Data Protection Directive, must "delete or irreversibly anonymise personal data" once collection goals have been met. The opinion states that this requirement applies to search engine companies based outside Europe as well as those in Europe, since European privacy laws apply to search engines (Article 29).

In the aftermath of 9/11, privacy protection and violation has changed dramatically in the United States, particularly as a result of the USA PATRIOT Act. The effect in Europe has not been as pronounced. The difference in perspective is the result of Europe's historical experience with terrorism: many European countries were victims of international and internal terrorism prior to the September 11, 2001 attack on the United States such as the Irish Republican Army in England, Bader Meinhof in Germany, and the Red Brigade in Italy. The EU has always viewed terrorism on a domestic level to be handled by each country's own criminal code: criminal law is part of "Justice and Home Affairs" as described in the Third Pillar of the Treaty on the EU. While this approach remained unchanged following the September 11 attacks, the EU did address questions of terrorism in June 2002 with a Decision on Combating Terrorism (2002/475/JHA),[43] which defines terrorist groups and acts with regard to groups, individuals, and supporters and calls on member states to align their legislation so that the uniform definitions apply in all member states.

While human rights were not addressed in the EU's Decision, the Council of Europe did address the matter in its 2002 Guidelines on Human Rights and the Fight against Terrorism (Council of Europe, 2002).[44] The Council of Europe is not part of the EU per se, although they are considered an affiliated organization operating under the flag of the EU and working toward European integration (Council of Europe, 2008).[45] The Guidelines guarantee respect for human rights in the fight against terrorism declaring that states "may not use indiscriminate measures which would only undermine the fundamental values they seek to protect," and prohibiting the use of torture in all circumstances. Sections V and VI of the Guidelines specifically address privacy, including privacy with respect to collection of personal data, searches of body, houses and personal effects, surveillance, and wire tapping. While such actions are permitted as measures to fight terrorism and protect citizens, the Guidelines state that they should be exercised with the utmost caution, only when no other measures exist, and should be employed in accordance with provision of domestic laws. In addition, such actions may be subject for external review and open to challenges before a court of law.

Other Activities of Europe's Information Society

In addition to the areas outlined above, the EU is engaged in other activities to further the development of an information society. These include promoting digital infrastructure, encouraging research and innovation, and promoting a safer Internet. (Europe's Information Society:

information society activities).[46] The safer Internet activities address illegal and harmful content on the Internet and resulted from a green paper issued by the Commission in 1996 (Commission of the European Union COM(96) 487 final)[47] and include a 4-year program that addresses four main issues: fighting against illegal content, tackling unwanted and harmful content, promoting a safer environment, and awareness-raising. More recent activity in the area also includes a recommendation to member states regarding protection of minors and human dignity in online activities.[48] While U.S. case law has supported the view that the Internet is private space and therefore not directed by government action, the EU is more heavily involved in content regulation.

IMPLICATIONS

Information and communication technology, and more specifically the Internet, are making national borders more difficult to manage or control from specific jurisdictions. This trend has been occurring and gradually increasing as Internet activity grows, and is driven by two very different approaches to information on both sides of the Atlantic. The U.S. government does not regulate cyberspace and is concerned only by harmful use of information, while the EU protects its citizens from the wrongful collection of information.

In the United States, this is a *de facto* phenomenon, resulting from market forces that set standards and establish benchmarks for information flow and trade driven by private enterprises for financial benefit. In the EU the de facto eradication of international borders is recognized but not allowed free reign. Rather is it curtailed by de juro legislation and regulation by the EU that in effect imposes European standards of information trade on non-EU countries. This has compelled the U.S. government to diverge from its laissez faire policy and negotiate the Safe Harbor Agreement that enables information exchange between the United States and the EU. Concerns that the Internet will undermine the authority of governments have not materialized. In the case of the EU, the opposite has occurred. The EU's approach to transborder information flow has resulted in imposing these standards and practices on countries wanting to trade with the EU.

CONCLUSION

European Union information policy refers to the legislation and strategies pertaining to the European policy for the creation of information society. The goal of this entry was to provide an overview of the unique and influential nature of the EU's approach to information policy by discussing its formation, goals, and ultimately its influence. In the broadest sense, EU information policy is concerned with economic and industrial competitiveness with an emphasis on the role that information technologies play in revolutionizing everyday life, a broad goal with far reaching socioeconomic implications. Our discussion has focused on several policy areas of greatest interest to information professionals by discussing the approach that the EU has taken addressing areas such as copyright, intellectual property, data protection and privacy, and e-government. In its aim to bring EU information to its citizens, EU information policy has challenged policy notions by establishing new levels of cooperation between major state institutions and all information and communication matters.

GLOSSARY

Directive: Legislation, which is binding to EU member nations.

Green paper: Documents published by the European Commission. Their purpose is to stimulate discussion and may eventually lead to legislation, but their recommendations are not binding. Green papers are often followed by White papers.

Information society: synonymous with "new information and communication technologies" (ICT).

Pillars of the EU: Three pillars form the basic structure of the EU, and are: 1) the Community pillar, corresponding to the three Communities: the European Community, the European Atomic Energy Community, and the former European Coal and Steel Community; 2) the common foreign and security policy, and 3) the policy and judicial cooperation in criminal pillar.

White paper: Documents published by the European Commission that contain proposals for actions in a specific area. When White papers are received favorably they lead to actions in the area they address.

REFERENCES

1. Weingarten, F.W. Federal information policy development: The congressional perspective. In *United States Government Information Policies*; McClure, C., Hernon, P., Relyea, H., Eds.; Ablex Publishing Company: Norwood, NJ, 1989; 77–99.

2. Hernon, P.; Relyea, H.C. Information policy. *Encyclopedia of Library and Information Science*, 2nd Ed.; Drake, M.A., Ed.; Marcel Dekker, Inc.: New York, 2003; Vol. 2, 1300–1315.

3. Cahill, A.G.; Overman, E.S. Information policy: A study of values in the policy process. Policy Stud. Rev. **1990**, 9(4), 803–818.

4. Regan, T. Introduction to moral reasoning. In *Information Ethics: Privacy, Property, and Power*; Moore, A.D., Ed.; University of Washington Press: Seattle, WA, 2005; 30–46.

5. Mill, J.S. Utilitarianism. In *Information Ethics: Privacy, Property, and Power*; Moore, A.D., Ed.; University of Washington Press: Seattle, WA, 2005; 47–65.

6. Sejersted, F. Freedom of information in a modern society World Library and Information Congress: 71th IFLA General Conference and Council, Libraries—A Voyage of Discovery Oslo, Norway August, 14–18, 2005. Available at http://www.ifla.org/IV/ifla71/papers/185-Sejersted.pdf (accessed June 2008).

7. Samuelson, P.; Varian, H.R. Information policy in the Clinton years. *In American Economic Policy in the 1990s, Center for Business and Government*; Kennedy, J.F., Ed.; School of Government, Harvard University: Cambridge, MA, June 27–30, 2001. Available at http://www.hks.harvard.edu/m-rcbg/Conferences/economic_policy/SAMUELSON-VARIAN.pdf (accessed June 2008).

8. Redidenberg, J.R. Lex informatica: The formulation of information policy rules through technology. Texas Law Rev. **1998**, *76*(3), 554–583.

9. Sloan, B. The European Union. *International Information: Documents, Publication, and Electronic Information of International Government Organizations*, 2nd Ed.; Hajnal, P.I., Ed.; Libraries Unlimited: Englewood, CO, 1997; Vol. 1, 51–116.

10. The European Commission at Work: Basic Facts. Available at http://ec.europa.eu/atwork/basicfacts/index_en.htm.

11. Schneider, V. Institutional reform in telecommunications: The European Union in transitional policy diffusion. In *Transforming Europe: Europeanization and Domestic Change*; Cowels, M.G., Caporaso, J., Riesse, T., Eds.; Cornell University Press: Ithaca, NY, 2001; 60–78.

12. Europra: Glossary. Available at http://europa.eu/scadplus/glossary/index_en.htm *Europra: Glossary*.

13. Bangemann, M.; Bonfield, P.L.; Cabral da Fonseca, E.; Davignon, E.; Davis, P.J.; Descarpentries, J.-M.; De Benedetti, C.; Ennis, B.; Gyllenhammer, P.G.; Henkel, H. O.; Knutsen, A.; Lescure, P.; Makropoulos, C.; Maragall, P.; Hunsel, L.; Prodi, R.; Thorn, G.E.; Timmer, J.D. Velazquez Gastelu, C. von Pierer, H. *Report on Europe and the Global Information Society: Recommendations of the High-Level Group on the Information Society to the Corfu European Council (Bangemann Group)*, Office for Official Publications of the European Communities: Luxembourg, 1994; 5–40 Bulletin of the European Union, Supplement No. 2/94. Commonly called the Bangemann Report. Available at http://aei.pitt.edu/1199/01/info_society_bangeman_report. pdf (accessed June 2008). Commonly called the BangemannReport.

14. Goodwin, I.; Spittle, S. The European Union and the information society: Discourse, power and policy. New Med. Soc. **2002**, *4*(2), 225–249.

15. Europe's Information Society: Information society policies at a glance. Available at http://ec.europa.eu/information_society/tl/policy/index_en.htm.

16. Directive 2002/58/EC of the European Parliament and of the Council of 12 July 2002 concerning the processing of personal data and the protection of privacy in the electronic communications sector (directive on privacy and electronic communications). Off. J. Eur. Union July 31, **2002**, *L 201*, 37–47. Available at http://eur-lex.europa.eu/LexUriServ/LexUriServ.do?uri=OJ:L:2002:201:0037:0047:EN:PDF (accessed June 2008).

17. Commission decision 94/90/ECSC, EC, Euratom of 8 February 1994 on public access to Commission documents. Off. J. Eur. UnionFebruary 18, **1994**, *L 46*, 58–61. Available at http://eur-lex.europa.eu/LexUriServ/LexUriServ.do?uri=CELEX:31994D0090:EN:HTML (accessed June 2008).

18. Blankert, H.; Bosch, G.;Castells, M.; Connellan, L.; Carlson, B.; Engelen-Kefer, U.; Freeman, C.; Knudsen, L.; Lasfargue, Y.; Pailliart, I.; Rocha Trindade, A.; Rantanen, J.; Soete, L.; Verderio, P. *Building the European Information Society for Us All: Final Policy Report of the High Level Expert Group*, European Commission Directorate-General for employment, industrial relations and social affairs, April 1997. Available at http://www.epractice.eu/resource/688 or http://ec.europa.eu/employment_social/knowledge_society/buildingen.pdf (accessed June 2008).

19. EU Guide to the Digital Economy. *2003*, The EU Committee of the American Chamber of Commerce in Belgium: Brussels, 2003.

20. Europe's Information Society: i2010—A European information society for growth and employment. Available at http://ec.europa.eu/information_society/eeurope/i2010/index_en.htm.

21. European Commission: Enterprise and Industry. Available at http://ec.europa.eu/enterprise/index_en.htm.

22. Europra, Activities of the European Union: Summaries of Legislation—Information Society. Available at http://europa.eu/scadplus/leg/en/s21012.htm. *Europra, Activities of the European Union: Summaries of Legislation—Information Society*.

23. *Europe's Way to the Information Society, an Action Plan: Communication from the Commission to the Council, the European Parliament, the Economic and Social Committee and the Committee of the Regions*; Commission of the European Communities: Brussels, July 19, 1994; COM (94) 347 final; Available at http://aei.pitt.edu/947/01/info_socieity_action_plan_COM_94_347.pdf (accessed June 2008).

24. Dusollier, S. Fair use by design in the European Copyright Directive of 2001. Commun. ACM **2003**, *46*(4), 51–55.

25. Directive 2002/19/EC of the European Parliament and of the Council of 7 March 2002 on access to, and interconnection of, electronic communications networks and associated facilities (access directive). Off. J. Eur. Union April 24, **2002**, *L 108*, 7–20. Available at http://eur-lex.europa.eu/LexUriServ/LexUriServ.do?uri=OJ:L:2002:108:0007:0020:EN:PDF (accessed June 2008).

26. Directive 2002/20/EC of the European Parliament and of the Council of 7 March 2002 on the authorisation of electronic communications networks and services (authorisation directive). Off. J. Eur. Union April 24, **2002**, *L 108*, 21–32. Available at http://eur-lex.europa.eu/LexUriServ/LexUriServ.do?uri=OJ:L:2002:108:0021:0032:EN:PDF (accessed June 2008).

27. Directive 2002/22/EC of the European Parliament and of the Council of 7 March 2002 on universal service and users' rights relating to electronic communications networks and services (universal service directive). Off. J. Eur. Union

April 24, **2002**, *L 108*, 51–77. Available at http://eur-lex.
europa.eu/LexUriServ/LexUriServ.do?uri=OJ:
L:2002:108:0051:0077:EN:PDF (accessed June 2008).

28. *On the Review of the EU Regulatory Framework for Electronic Communications Networks and Services: Communication from the Commission of 29 June 2006*, COM (2006)
334 final; Commission of the European Communities:
Brussels, June 29, 2006. Available at http://eur-lex.europa.
eu/LexUriServ/LexUriServ.do?uri=COM:2006:0334:FIN:
EN:PDF (accessed June 2008).

29. *Green Paper on Copyright and the Challenge of
Technology—Copyright Issues Requiring Immediate
Action*, COM (88) 172 final; Commission of the European
Communities: Brussels, June 7, 1988. Available at http://
aei.pitt.edu/1209/01/copyright_and_tech_gp_COM_88_
172.pdf (accessed June 2008).

30. *Follow-Up to the Green Paper: Working Programme of the
Commission in the Field of Copyright and Neighbouring
Rights*, COM (90) 584 final; Commission of the European
Communities: Brussels, January 17, 1991. Available at
http://aei.pitt.edu/1210/02/copyright_gp_follow_COM_90_
584.pdf (accessed June 2008).

31. Directive 2001/29/EC of the European Parliament and of the
Council of 22 May 2001 on the harmonisation of certain
aspects of copyright and related rights in the information
society. Off. J. Eur. Union June 22, **2001**, *L 167*, 10–19.
Available at http://eur-lex.europa.eu/pri/en/oj/dat/2001/
l_167/l_16720010622en00100019.pdf (accessed June 2008).

32. Digital Millennium Copyright Act; 17 U.S.C. §1201(a)(1).

33. Directive 2002/21/EC of the European Parliament and of
the Council of 7 March 2002 on a common regulatory
framework for electronic communications networks and
services ("Framework Directive"). Available at http://
europa.eu/scadplus/leg/en/lvb/l24216a.htm.

34. Directive 2000/31/EC of the European Parliament and of the
Council of 8 June 2000 on certain legal aspects of information
society services, in particular electronic commerce, in the
internal market (directive on electronic commerce). Off. J.
Eur. Union July 17, **2000**, *L 178*, 1–16. Available at http://
eur-lex.europa.eu/LexUriServ/LexUriServ.do?uri=OJ:
L:2000:178:0001:0016:EN:PDF (accessed June 2008).

35. *i2010—a European Information Society for Growth and
Employment: Communication from the Commission to the
Council, the European Parliament, the Economic and
Social Committee and the Committee of the Regions*,
COM (2005) 229 final; Commission of the European Com-
munities: Brussels, June 1, 2005. Available at http://eur-
lex.europa.eu/LexUriServ/LexUriServ.do?uri=COM:2005:
0229:FIN:EN:PDF (accessed June 2008).

36. *i2010 eGovernment Action Plan—Accelerating
eGovernment in Europe for the Benefit of all: Communication from the Commission to the Council, the European
Parliament, the Economic and Social Committee and the
Committee of the Regions*, COM (2006) 173 final; Commission of the European Communities: Brussels, April 25,
2006. Available at http://eur-lex.europa.eu/LexUriServ/
LexUriServ.do?uri=COM:2006:0173:FIN:EN:PDF
(accessed June 2008).

37. Directive 95/46/EC of the European Parliament and of the
Council of 24 October 1995 on the protection of individuals with regard to the processing of personal data and on
the free movement of such data. Off. J. Eur. Union November 23, **1995**, *L 281*, 31–50. Available at http://eur-lex.
europa.eu/LexUriServ/LexUriServ.do?uri=CELEX:31995
L0046:EN:HTML (accessed June 2008).

38. Directive 2006/24/EC of the European Parliament and of
the Council of 15 March 2006 on the retention of data
generated or processed in connection with the provision of
publicly available electronic communications services or of
public communications networks and amending Directive
2002/58/EC. Off. J. Eur. Union April 13, **2006**, *L 105*,
54–63. Available at http://eur-lex.europa.eu/LexUriServ/
LexUriServ.do?uri=OJ:L:2006:105:0054:0063:EN:PDF
(accessed June 2008).

39. European Commission: Freedom, Security and Justice—
Data Protection. Available at http://ec.europa.eu/justice_
home/fsj/privacy/index_en.htm.

40. Export.gov: welcome to the safe harbor. Available at http://
www.export.gov/safeharbor/doc_safeharbor_index.asp.

41. Commission decisions on the adequacy of the protection
of personal data in third countries. Available at http://ec.
europa.eu/justice_home/fsj/privacy/thridcountries/index_
en.htm.

42. Article 29 Data Protection Working Party. Opinion on data
protection issues related to search engines. 00989/08/EN
WP 150. May 15, 2008. Available at http://ec.europa.eu/
justice_home/fsj/privacy/docs/wpdocs/2008/wp150_en.pdf.

43. Council framework decision 2002/475/JHA of 13 June
2002 on combating terrorism. Off. J. Eur. Union June 22,
2002, *L 164*, 3–7. Available at http://eur-lex.europa.eu/
LexUriServ/LexUriServ.do?uri=OJ:L:2002:164:0003:0007:
EN:PDF (accessed June 2008).

44. Directorate General of Human Rights. *Guidelines on
Human Rights and the Fight against Terrorism: Adopted
by the Committee of Ministers on 11 July 2002 at the 804th
Meeting of the Ministers*, Deputies, Council of Europe:
Strasbourg, 2002. Available at http://www.coe.int/T/E/
Human_rights/h-inf(2002)8eng.pdf or http://www.coe.int/
t/E/Human_Rights/1Lignes_dir_compendium_en.asp#Top
OfPage (accessed June 2008).

45. About the Council of Europe. Available at http://www.coe.
int/T/e/Com/about_coe/.

46. Europe's Information Society: Information society activities
at a glance. Available at http://ec.europa.eu/information_
society/activities/index_en.htm.

47. *Illegal and Harmful Content on the Internet: Communication from the Commission to the Council, the European
Parliament, the Economic and Social Committee and the
Committee of the Regions*, COM (96) 487 final; Commission of the European Communities: Brussels, October 16,
1996. Available at http://aei.pitt.edu/5895/01/001527_1.
pdf (accessed June 2008).

48. Recommendation 2006/952/EC of the European Parliament
and of the Council of 20 December 2006 on the protection of
minors and human dignity and on the right of reply in relation to the competitiveness of the European audiovisual and
on-line information services industry. Off. J. Eur. Union
December 27, **2006**, *L 378*, 72–77. Available at http://eur-
lex.europa.eu/LexUriServ/LexUriServ.do?uri=OJ:L:2006:
378:0072:0077:EN:PDF (accessed June 2008).

Information Policy: United States

Peter Hernon
Graduate School of Library and Information Science, Simmons College, Boston, Massachusetts, U.S.A.

Harold C. Relyea
Congressional Research Service, Library of Congress, Washington, District of Columbia, U.S.A.

Abstract

Information policy, a field encompassing both public policy and information science, treats information as both a commodity—adheres to the economic theory of property rights—and a resource to be collected, protected, shared, manipulated, and managed. Although the literature often refers to information policy in the singular, there is no single all-encompassing policy. Rather, information *policies* tend to address specific issues and, at times, to be fragmented, overlapping, and contradictory.

INTRODUCTION

Information is "essential to our existence" and assumes a "life of its own."[1] Information policy then is a set of interrelated principles, laws, guidelines, rules, regulations, and procedures guiding the oversight and management of the information *life cycle*: the production, collection, distribution/dissemination, retrieval and use, and retirement, including preservation, of information. Information policy also embraces access to, and use of, information and records; records relate to the conduct of government business and provide an audit trail for holding government accountable. Collectively, policies form a framework that "profoundly affects the manner in which an individual in a society, indeed a society itself, makes political, economic, and social choices."[2]

Much of the discussion of U.S. information policy revolves around actions taken or planned by government, either at the national or subnational levels. Since the mid-1990s, commercial transactions on the Internet—called electronic commerce—have grown substantially. At the same time, governments at various levels within the United States have embraced electronic government (e-government or e-gov). At the federal level, for instance, e-government focuses on the political economy of the nation, and relevant information policies concentrate on issues related to Internet infrastructure, resource management, and the provision of online services and resources. Clearly, the Internet, and its World Wide Web, have become the primary channels for the federal government's dissemination of resources to the public; that public is now global and extends to people of all ages (from youth to the elderly). Still, the private and not-for-profit sectors play a legitimate and important role in the provision of government information to specific constituency groups and to the public at large.

Information policy has global implications, but it also occurs outside of government. It takes place within and among organizations, associations, and other groups. This introductory essay cannot touch on all aspects of information policy and still provide a semblance of unity. For this reason, the essay does not address censorship, telecommunications, the press, broadcasting, First Amendment issues, propaganda, intellectual property rights, patents and trademarks, and archival management. Moreover, the essay focuses on American national government information policy. It discusses some key policy areas and stakeholders, shows how policy is formulated, and identifies issues central to an understanding of information policy in the twenty-first century. There is no single corpus of statutory or administrative law to coordinate information policies of federal agencies and to eliminate ambiguities in federal information policies. Some policies pertain to an agency and specific activities; others apply to a branch of government, have governmentwide application, or have international ramifications. Nonetheless, a group of core policies pertain to the management of government information resources and the information life cycle. For an overview of these policies, see Hernon.[3]

SIGNIFICANCE OF INFORMATION POLICY TO THE LIBRARY COMMUNITY

Government policies provide a framework within which libraries and information centers must function. These policies often determine what types of publications will be issued, the availability of government funds, and how funds will be allocated and spent. They may relate directly

Encyclopedia of Library and Information Sciences, Fourth Edition DOI: 10.1081/E-ELIS4-120009040

to the management of libraries and the types of services provided and address issues such as Internet privacy and security. Obviously, librarians must understand the policy arena and how it affects the services they provide, as well as how to influence the policy-making process, as they try to have their perspective addressed during policy development.

Another reason why librarians should be knowledgeable about information policy is that libraries and information centers are part of a larger organization (e.g., city government, an academic institution, or a corporation). The internal policies set by that organization impact on libraries and information centers and set the constraints under which they function. Moreover, external policies also have an impact on the ability of libraries and information centers to meet stated goals and objectives.

Perhaps two examples of the importance of information policy might be beneficial. First, as part of its Library Awareness Program, during the 1970s and part of the 1980s, the Federal Bureau of Investigation (FBI) visited libraries, tried to solicit information about library users, and compiled investigative records on library personnel. A full understanding of the program and the options open to the library community necessitates knowledge of the Department of Justice's counterintelligence activities and the grounds on which the FBI justified its actions.[4] Any rebuttal of the FBI's justification for its policies that might result in a change of agency policy and practices must address the legal basis on which the FBI justified its actions. To effect change, librarians need extensive knowledge of policy terminology (e.g., the differences among executive orders, circulars, and directives), how policy is formulated, and strategies that might result in policy modification or reversal.

Following the terrorist attacks of September 11, the U.S. Geological Survey requested the Government Printing Office (GPO) to instruct those depository libraries that received a CD-ROM on the characteristics of large surface-water supplies in the United States to destroy their copies. The GPO ordered the libraries to comply and destroy the CD-ROM immediately. "Subsequently, the Federal Bureau of Investigation visited several Federal Depository Libraries to determine whether that order had been carried out. This occurred without consultation with the GPO or the Geological Survey...."[5] In a memorandum, dated March 13, 2002, attorney Thomas Susman of Ropes and Gray observed:

> The delicate balance between responding to concerns relating to homeland security while ensuring public access to government information presents new challenges to many libraries. What limitations, if any, should be on access to selected government information resources? Are there criteria to consider as to whether information resources should be publicly available? Similarly, many libraries that participate in the Federal Depository Library

> Program ... are concerned that changes may be forthcoming in the information access and dissemination policies of federal agencies.[5]

In formulating their response, depository libraries should ask, "What does the law say?" If they are dissatisfied with the answer, they might inquire about "How feasible is it to change the law?" "What support might we gather from other stakeholders?" "Are there any changes in the law under consideration?" "What is the likelihood of those changes being enacted?" and "Can you influence the shaping of those changes?" Clearly, libraries participating in the depository program need to understand their legal responsibilities, as well as those of GPO, as specified in Chapter 19 of Title 44 of the *United States Code*.

HISTORICAL DEVELOPMENT OF INFORMATION POLICY

Information policy existed in America long before the establishment of the federal government in 1789. Indeed, it probably can be said that information policy began with the arrival of the first European colonists who brought with them the information policies of their homeland. The common law rights of Englishmen were particularly important in this regard and were directly influential in the development of the American legal system well into the early nineteenth century.[6]

The experience of the colonists differed regarding patterns of communication and information dissemination.[7] Consequently, their expectations about the availability and accessibility of government information varied from one region to the next. Eventually, however, as England became the predominant power in the Atlantic territories, conflicts over information and "the rights of Englishmen" came to be commonly experienced throughout the American colonies. Disputes arose over the secret activities of royal governors and colonial legislatures, the public accessibility of official records, and proper respect for personal privacy.[8–10] These and other perceived violations of individual rights by George III kindled the fires of revolt and the rebellion that resulted in American independence.

Within the new nation, information policy was given primary expression in the Articles of Confederation and state constitutions, the latter containing expressions of fundamental rights guaranteeing freedom of the press and personal privacy. These documents would later be important sources for James Madison when drafting the Bill of Rights for the U.S. Constitution. Very little historical research, however, has been conducted on the development of information policy during the American colonial and confederation eras. Some general histories of government institutions and practices of the period provide occasional bits of pertinent knowledge, but much work remains to be done before a better understanding of information policy prior to the establishment of the federal government can be realized.[11–13]

The history of federal information policy development begins with the Philadelphia convention of 1787, which, itself, owing to the secrecy in which it occurred, was a special information policy event.[14] The Constitution of the United States created a limited government with some explicit powers and responsibilities. Certain of these concerned information matters. Among the enumerated powers of Congress, for example, are authority to "establish Post Offices and post Roads," to "promote the Progress of Science and useful Arts," by securing for limited Times to Authors and Inventors the exclusive Right to their respective Writings and Discoveries," and "make Rules for the Government and Regulation of the land and naval Forces" (Article I, Section 8, clauses 7, 8, and 14), and to "make all needful Rules and Regulations respecting the Territory or other Property belonging to the United States" (Article IV, Section 3, clause 2).

In the Bill of Rights, which was subsequently appended to the Constitution, guarantees are made concerning speech and press freedoms (Amendment I), the security of personal papers against "unreasonable searches and seizures" (Amendment IV), and not being "compelled in any Criminal Case to be a witness against" oneself (Amendment V). Also included are rights to a public trial in criminal prosecution and "to be informed of the nature and cause of the accusation; to be confronted with the witnesses against [oneself]; [and] to have [a] compulsory process for obtaining witnesses in [one's] favor" (Amendment VI).

The Constitution created a government accountable to the people and itself, as well. There was an expectation that government leaders would keep the citizenry informed of developments, or at least maintain a record of their activities. In this regard, the Constitution specifies that each House of Congress "shall keep a Journal of its Proceedings, and from time to time publish the same, excepting such Parts as may in their Judgement require Secrecy" (Article I, Section 5, clause 3). Concerning the duties of electors, the Twelfth Amendment prescribes that "they shall make distinct lists of all persons voted for as President, and of all persons voted for as Vice-President, and the number of votes for each, which lists they shall sign and certify" (Article II, Section 1, clause 3). With regard to the subnational level of government, the Constitution states: "Full Faith and Credit shall be given in each State to the Public Acts, Records, and judicial Proceedings of every other State" (Article IV, Section 1, clause 1).

Moreover, with its system of checks and balances, the Constitution anticipated that each branch would be knowledgeable of the activities and interests of the other two. In this regard, the Constitution specifically provides that, when the President vetoes a bill, "he shall return it, with his Objections to that House in which it shall have originated, who shall enter the Objections at large

on their Journal; and proceed to reconsider it" (Article I, Section 7, clause 2). Concerning interbranch accountability, provision is made for the President to "require the Opinion, in writing, of the principal Officer in each of the executive Departments, upon any Subject relating to the Duties of their respective Offices" (Article II, Section 2, clause 1). The Constitution also indicates that the President "shall from time to time give to the Congress Information of the State of the Union, and recommend to their Consideration such Measures as he shall judge necessary and expedient" (Article II, Section 3). Finally, as a consequence of the separation of powers doctrine of the Constitution, presidents determined, early in the life of the federal government, that a discretion might be exercised regarding requests for information from the other branches. For example, President Washington contemplated discretion in 1792 and exercised it four years later, the first invocation of what would subsequently be called "executive privilege" or the privilege of the Chief Executive to withhold requested information from Congress or the Judiciary for institutional reasons.[11,15–22] Congress has claimed and exercised similar powers.[23–25]

In many regards, these constitutional references to information matters indicate some fundamental expectations regarding government accountability and communication, the exercise of certain popular rights regarding information, and subsequent legislation on at least a few particular information subjects. Furthermore, historically, as experience and practice suggested that Congress create and refine additional statutory information policies, these, among other constitutional considerations, have guided the legislative and oversight processes.

An information policy area that quickly commanded the attention of the new federal government and continued to be refined throughout the nineteenth century was official publication. The matter had been debated during the Constitutional Convention of 1787. James Wilson of Pennsylvania, addressing a proposal to allow each chamber of the Federal Congress a discretion as to the parts of their journal that would be published, told the delegates: "These people have the right to know what their Agents are doing or have done, and it should not be in the option of the Legislature to conceal their proceedings."[26] The following year, during the Virginia Convention on the new Constitution, James Madison and George Mason raised a similar consideration when speaking about the importance of publishing all receipts and expenditures of public money under the new government.[27]

In deference to views such as these, the federal Congress quickly provided for the printing and distribution of both laws and treaties,[28–35] the preservation of state paper,[36] and the maintenance of official files in the new departments.[28,29,37] In 1813, the printing and distribution of both the Senate and House journals was authorized.[38] Congressional floor debate was variously reported in the *Register of Debates*, *Congressional Globe*, and, beginning in 1873, the *Congressional Record*. See the statutes[39,40] and McPherson[41] and of related interest, see Childs.[42,43]

Provision was initially made in 1846 for the routine printing of all congressional reports, special documents (which included Executive Branch materials), and bills.[44] Although these responsibilities were met for many years through the use of contract printers, such arrangements proved to be subject to considerable political abuse. Consequently, in 1860, Congress established GPO to produce all of its literature and to serve, as well, the printing needs of the Executive Branch.[45] Additional aspects of governmentwide printing and publication policy were set with the Printing Act of 1895, which is the source of much of the basic policy still found in the printing chapters of Title 44 of the *United States Code*.[46,47]

Congress, in addition to providing for publication of the statutes and a variety of legislative literature (and executive materials produced as Senate or House documents), promoting newspaper reprinting of the laws and treaties,[48] and circulating printed documents through official sources, also developed a depository library program to further facilitate public knowledge of government actions. In 1859, the Secretary of the Interior was statutorily tasked with distributing all books printed or purchased for the use of the federal government, except those for the particular use of Congress or Executive Branch entities.[49] A decade later, a subordinate officer in the Department—the Superintendent of Public Documents—was mandated to perform this responsibility.[50] Distributions were made to certain libraries throughout the country that were designated to be depositories for government publications. This arrangement had been begun in 1813 with regard to congressional materials[38] and extended in 1857 to include other federal literature.[51] The Printing Act of 1895 relocated the Superintendent of Public Documents within GPO.[52–54]

In the relocation process, the superintendent was also given responsibility for managing the sale of documents and preparing periodic indices of GPO products. Until 1904, the sales stock available to the superintendent derived entirely from such materials as were provided for this purpose by the departments and agencies or were returned from depository libraries. The situation was altered when the superintendent was granted authority to reprint any departmental publication, with the consent of the pertinent secretary, for public sale.[55] Congress legislated comparable discretion to reproduce its documents in 1922.[56]

Shortly after the dawn of the twentieth century, the federal government entered a new phase—the rise of the administrative state. Among the forces contributing to this development was the Progressive Movement, which sought greater government intervention into, and regulation of, various sectors of American society. With the United States' entry into World War I, regulatory activities further expanded and the number of administrative

agencies so involved increased. In the postwar era, government expansion momentarily slowed but began again with the onset of the Great Depression and the arrival of the New Deal.

As federal regulatory powers and administrative entities dramatically grew during this period, there was a concomitant increase in both the number and variety of controlling directives, regulations, and requirements. Soon, problems of accountability, uniformity in the form and promulgation of agency directives, and public access to agency administrative records arose. To address the first of these issues, an Executive Branch gazette was created—the *Federal Register*—in July 1935.[57] Two years later came the *Code of Federal Regulations*. This cumulation of the authorities appearing in the gazette contained almost all operative agency regulations and was eventually updated annually.[58] Later, the general statutory authority underlying the *Federal Register* was relied on for the creation of other series of publications, namely, the *United States Government Manual* (1939–), the *Public Papers of the President* (1960–), and the *Weekly Compilation of Presidential Documents* (1965–).

The efforts of a study committee established by the Attorney General[59] contributed to the legislating of the Administrative Procedure Act of 1946,[60] which brought uniformity to the form and promulgation of agency regulations. The statute also contained an important public information section that directed the agencies to publish in the *Federal Register* "the established places at which, and methods whereby, the public may secure information or make submittals or requests."[61] However, broad discretionary allowances also were made for protecting information, and a changing climate of opinion within the federal bureaucracy soon transformed this public information mandate into a basis for administrative secrecy. Elements of the press community gave particular attention to the unwillingness of federal agencies, as well as some other government entities, to disclose requested information.[62–66] In 1955, a special subcommittee on government information was established in the House of Representatives; it inaugurated, with assistance from elements of the press, a major probe of agency information access policy and practice.[67]

Subsequently, in 1966, after a long congressional examination and a difficult legislative struggle, the public information section of the Administrative Procedure Act was replaced by a new statute and a new concept in information access. The Freedom of Information (FOI) Act established a presumptive right of public access to department and agency records, specified nine categories of information that could be exempted from the rule of disclosure, and provided for court resolution of disputes over the availability of requested materials.[68] Later amended in 1974, 1976, 1986, and 1996, with portions subject to considerable judicial interpretation, the statute has remained a very effective tool for enabling public access to topical records of the administrative state. It has also served as a model for other information access laws, such as the Privacy Act of 1974,[69] and open government statutes, such as the Federal Advisory Committee Act of 1972[70] and the Government in the Sunshine Act of 1976.[71]

With the end of World War II and the onset of the Cold War, the federal government entered still another new phase—the rise of the national security state. From the outset of the era until the mid-1960s, it was a time of strong, unilateral leadership by the president in the external affairs of the country and was marked by the creation of new agencies and policies to safeguard the nation. Several such innovations were taken regarding information policy.[72,75] These developments, however, built on a few prior policy actions. Since the earliest days of the Republic, for example, government officials had engaged in the practice of assigning a secret status to certain kinds of sensitive information, usually concerning foreign affairs, defense, or intelligence matters. The Executive Branch, including the armed forces, engaged in such information security–secrecy practices for over a half century before they were given direct statutory authorization.[76] Formal military secrecy directives or regulations appeared only after the Civil War. The initial Army General Order of 1869 concerning security-secrecy pertained to the physical protection of forts and coastal defenses. Such facilities were not to be photographed or otherwise depicted without prior permission from appropriate officials. This limited application underwent a series of evolutionary adjustments and, shortly after the United States' entry into World War I, resulted in a fully developed information security classification system.[77] In 1911 and 1917, Congress provided for the criminal punishment of espionage and the acquisition of valuable defense information by spies.[78–80] Neither law, however, specifically sanctioned the information secrecy practices of the military departments or the armed forces. Initially, the military departments made no mention of the espionage laws in their information security orders and directives, but soon such regulations began referring to these laws as a possible basis for their enforcement.

Relying on a 1938 statute concerning the protection of armed forces installations and equipment and "information relative thereto," President Franklin D. Roosevelt assumed responsibility for security classification policy and procedures by issuing an executive order setting such policy. It largely paralleled Army and Navy regulations for marking and handling secret records and gave civilian employees of the military departments authority to classify information. However, the legislative history of the 1938 statute, on which the president relied to issue his directive, provided no indication that Congress anticipated or expected that such a security classification arrangement would be created.[81] Nevertheless, it was the beginning of presidential leadership in setting security classification policy.

Congress seemingly has evidenced a general reluctance to authorize directly or legislate a governmentwide information security classification system. Although it has mandated information security arrangements for special areas such as atomic energy,[82] intelligence,[83] or patent applications having national security implications,[84,85] Congress, through various committees and subcommittees, for 30 years, successfully encouraged and pressured presidents from Eisenhower to Reagan to narrow classification criteria and limit discretionary authority to classify.[77] The Reagan administration's sweeping 1982 executive order reversed the prior historical trend by expanding the categories of classifiable information, by mandating that information falling within these categories be classified, by making reclassification authority available, by admonishing classifiers to favor classification in deciding close cases, and by eliminating automatic declassification arrangements.[86]

Furthermore, with the realization of the national security state at the end of World War II and the onset of the Cold War and the penchant for secrecy, publication of the law of the land became impaired not by circumstances of accident or inadequate means, but, instead, as a consequence of concealment by design. The National Security Act of 1947[87] sought to preserve and perpetuate the nation *by any and all means*. In 1951, President Harry S Truman signed an executive order giving almost every government agency broad discretionary authority to classify information "in order to protect the security of the United States."[88] The following year, a still secret presidential directive created the National Security Agency. Not officially acknowledged to exist until 1957, it remains one of the most reticent components of the national security leviathan.[89]

The heart of the national security state, if for no other reason than its membership, is the National Security Council (NSC). After a modest beginning under President Truman, it gained importance during the Eisenhower administration, waned somewhat during the Kennedy administration, but regained its importance and has remained highly influential ever since. The written policy pronouncements of the president emanating from the NSC increasingly appear to have oftentimes assumed the character of secret law.

Shortly after its creation, the NSC began to produce four types of policy papers: basic comprehensive policy statements on a broad variety of national security problems, together with pertinent political, economic, and military pursuit strategies; situation profiles of large geographic areas or specific countries; assessments of mobilization, arms control, atomic energy, and other functional matters; and organizational statements on the council, foreign intelligence, and internal security structure and activities. The initial products in the series apparently were of the geographic type; the first comprehensive policy statement was completed and given NSC approval in November 1948.[89]

Subsequent presidents have attached different names to the NSC secret papers. For example, Jimmy Carter issued secret Presidential Directives, Ronald Reagan changed the name to National Security Decision Directives, and George H.W. Bush referred to them as National Security Directives. Under William Clinton, they became Presidential Decision Directives, and George W. Bush nominated them as National Security Presidential Directives. (See Hernon, Relyea et al.,[3] Chap. 6 for a discussion of the national security state and the various forms in which a president communicates public policy.)

Now, most of the NSC directives produced up to 1960 have been declassified and are accessible at the relevant presidential libraries, whereas most of those produced in subsequent years remain classified, "and details about them are largely unavailable for congressional or public scrutiny."[89] In summary, as the General Accounting Office has pointed out, unlike executive orders, these directives "embody foreign and military policy-making guidance rather than specific instructions; are classified; are usually directed only to NSC and the most senior executive branch officials; and do not appear to be issued under statutory authority conferred by Congress...."[90] However, these directives embody policy-making guidance, but some of them have provided specific instruction. For example, Presidential Decision Directive 63, issued by President Carter, dealt with the fight against cyberterrorism. Among the tasks it recommended were the development of a plan to improve intelligence gathering and an expansion of international cooperation.

Finally, apart from national security secrecy considerations, information is also lawfully protected to maintain the integrity of persons. In the case of individuals, such protection is understood as privacy. However, in the case of corporate persons, protection extends to proprietary or commercially valuable information.

Individual privacy, the wish not to be intruded on, probably predates recorded history. Certainly it is one of the presocietal or "natural rights" that the founding fathers sought to preserve.[91] When drafting the Bill of Rights, they gave constitutional recognition to privacy expectations in the First, Third, Fourth, Fifth, and Ninth Amendments, which the Supreme Court characterized as comprising a penumbral right of privacy in a landmark 1965 decision.[92,93]

Through the years, for various governmental activities and programs involving the collection and maintenance of personally identifiable information, such as the census and income tax returns, prohibitions have been legislated on the disclosure of such data. These statutory restrictions are recognized in the FOI Act,[94] and the Privacy Act prohibits federal agencies from colleting some kinds of personally identifiable information.[95] The Privacy Act also allows American citizens to gain access to, and make supplementary corrections of, a great many agency records on themselves. Examples of laws that have been enacted to provide citizens with greater control over personal records held by third parties include the Fair Credit Reporting Act,[96] the Privacy Act, the Family Educational Rights and Privacy (or "Buckley") Act,[97] and the Pupils' Rights Act.[98]

Furthermore, more than a century ago, the Supreme Court recognized corporations as being a "person," but it has not vested them with the privacy rights reserved for individuals.[99] Generally, when legal protection has been accorded to the information of corporate entities, it has been done for economic reasons and without explanation in terms of privacy rights. Perhaps the best-known statutory prohibition in this regard is the Trade Secrets Act, which makes the disclosure of trade secrets by a federal officer or employee criminally punishable.[100] A 1977 study prepared by the Department of Justice identified 90 operative statutes "reflecting varied approaches to the regulation of the disclosure by federal agencies of the information they collect from or maintain about business entities.[101] Moreover, open government laws, such as the FOI Act and the Government in the Sunshine Act, contain exemptions for the protection of trade secrets and confidential commercial information.

A number of issues affect the continued growth of the Internet for personal, government, and business purposes. Among these, for instance, are Internet privacy, computer security, access to broadband (high-speed) services, e-commerce, commercial Web site adherence to "fair information practices" proposed by the Federal Trade Commission, the receipt of unsolicited commercial electronic mail (spam or junk e-mail), and government information technology management. The practices include: 1) providing notice to users of their information practices before collecting personal information, 2) allowing the public choice about whether and how personal information is used, 3) allowing users access to data collected and the ability to content its accuracy, and 4) ensuring security of the information from unauthorized use. A critical question relates to whether or not industry can regulate itself, or if legislation is required for the protection of consumer privacy. The Internet makes it easier for the public and private sectors to obtain information about consumers and possibly use that information to the consumers' detriment. That issue focuses on the extent to which webmasters gather personally identifiable information about individuals and share that information with third parties, perhaps without the knowledge or consent of the people concerned.

In the wake of the September 11 terrorist attacks, the issue of law enforcement monitoring of Internet and web activity has become more controversial, with some advocating that law enforcement receive additional tools to combat terrorism, whereas others are concerned about the intrusion on civil liberties. The USA PATRIOT Act (P.L. 107-56) grants law enforcement officials additional authority to monitor Internet activity. Some of the provisions of Title II of that law expand the scope of subpoenas for records of electronic communications to include records commonly associated with Internet usage (e.g., session times and duration); allow Internet Service Providers to divulge records or other information (but not the contents of communications) pertaining to a subscriber if they believe there is immediate danger of death or serious physical injury, or as otherwise authorized, and requires them to divulge such records or information (excluding the contents of communications) to a government entity under certain conditions); and add routing and addressing information (used in Internet communications) that a government agency may capture by using pen registers and trap-and-trace devices as authorized by court order, while excluding the content of any wire or electronic communications.

ELECTRONIC GOVERNMENT

Electronic government is an evolving concept that currently includes four important areas: 1) the delivery of services (government-to-citizen); 2) providing information to the public; 3) facilitating the procurement of goods and services (government-to-business and business-to-government); and 4) facilitating efficient exchanges within and between agencies (government-to-government). FirstGov (http://www.firstgov.gov/) is a portal that facilitates access to digital resources relevant to each of these areas. Regarding the provision of information, it provides access to information at the national and subnational levels and provides a link to FedStats (http://www.fedstats.gov/), which enables users to gain access to statistical information from more than 100 government agencies. For some agencies, a service includes the provision of e-mail reference service; the information seeker will receive a response to his or her query.

Subordinate to the four current areas of electronic government is a fifth area, namely, the government as an on-line retailer. At their Web sites, government bodies (e.g., the Department of Treasury, the U.S. Mint, Amtrak, the General Services Administration, the U.S. Postal Service, the U.S. Geological Survey, the National Park Service, and GPO) conduct on-line sales.[102]

E-government and the various information policy instruments expand the five areas into 11 purposes:[103]

- Communication between an agency and the public, and communication among government bodies.
- Information access and meeting the information needs of the American public, from the nation's youth to senior citizens.

- Service delivery and the provision of online services, including online sales.
- Procurement or the purchase of services and goods from the private sector.
- Security, including the protection of Internet transactions among government entities and between those entities and the public against obstruction, diversion, interception, and falsification. Security also extends to protection against hacking of home pages and safeguarding Web sites and computers against viruses. Furthermore, security pertains to the storage of electronic information to assure its integrity and prevent unauthorized disclosure.
- Privacy of personally identifiable information and unauthorized use of cookies that can be attached to computers so that agencies can monitor the public's use of their Web sites.
- Management of e-government operations and related matters.
- Maintenance of information technology systems that underlie e-government.
- Digital divide and reducing the perceived disparity that results from portions of the population not having the ability to use information technology due to a lack of access, skill, or both. This is why government agencies use standard plug-ins that the public can freely download from the Web, or agencies provide free access to plug-ins that they specially created for some of their products.
- Emergency response, or dealing with a sudden crisis that threatens the nation. For example, following September 11, the public used government Web sites to monitor the situation and report alleged terrorist sightings to the appropriate agency. Special institutions, such as the Federal Emergency Management Agency (FEMA), have been created to respond to, coordinate the efforts of other agencies to respond to, and plan for national emergencies. Such institutions have coordinated and contributed to the preparation and maintenance of emergency plans, such as the Federal Response Plan for the delivery of federal disaster assistance, and standby directives, such as Executive Order 12656 of November 18, 1988, assigning emergency preparedness responsibilities among the federal departments and agencies. In addition, Congress has enacted various laws that provide the president ready authority to address an emergency, as well as some standby statutory powers that may be selectively activated under the terms of the National Emergencies Act of 1976, as amended.
- Oversight of the development of e-government by both the Executive Branch and Congress.

A central issue for policy makers is the development of a comprehensive, but flexible, strategy to coordinate the disparate e-government initiatives across the federal government. In 2001, the Bush administration proposed the concept of plug-and-play e-government, called component-based architecture (CBA), whereby some agencies develop basic components that others can use. In March, the Office of Management and Budget (OMB) released CBA models for 24 cross-agency e-government initiatives, which "will help agencies decide what technology they need to complete their e-government projects and will also help agencies work better together."[104]

As William Clinton prepared to leave the presidency, the National Archives and Records Administration (NARA) revealed that it had treated the White House Web site as a record and had captured images of it every 2 years of his 8-year tenure as president. The various government bodies from the three branches offer millions of pages on their Web sites, and over the years, they have posted an extensive amount of information on these pages. Once the material is removed, most likely, it may not be regarded as a record and reviewed by NARA for possible retention. Nonetheless, federal agencies generate a "torrent of electronic records," and this tendency "has overwhelmed the ability of "NARA to identify, review and determine which ones merit retention, and preserve them."[105]

THE LITERATURE ON INFORMATION POLICY

The Appendix of the *United States Government Information: Policies and Sources*[3] identifies source material (finding aids, monographs, government reports, and Web sites) that covers information policy from the perspective of different disciplines and stakeholders. Some of the better-known sources for keeping abreast of the latest developments include the following:

- *Federal Computer Week.*
- *Government Computer News.*
- *Government Information Quarterly.*
- *Privacy Times.*

The CD-ROM accompanying *United States Government Information* reprints historically significant works on information policy and contains, as well, exercises and self-help guides.

SOME POLICY ISSUES

Overview

Since the publication of the Porat study in 1977,[106] little progress has been made in further developing detailed typologies of policy issues, using sophisticated methods to organize and relate issues or producing better methods of clarifying issues and their interrelationships. Many policy issues are part of both a larger and smaller issue, and resolution of one issue often depends on resolution of another.

The typologies characterize government information policy prior to the emergence of the Internet and electronic government. For example, Hernon and McClure, who analyzed a wide range of policy issues, underscored that:[107]

- The published policy literature is repetitive in the broad themes it addresses.
- Surprisingly, little duplication exists among specific policy issues; each issue tends to emphasize specific and unique aspects of the broader themes.
- The literature devotes little attention to issues related to the role of libraries in the provision of government information and the information needs and gathering behaviors of user segments.
- Policy issues can be isolated in their impact on other policy issues.

Public Access to Government Information

As Hernon and McClure noted, "government information is a broad term that encompasses both published and unpublished information that ... government either does or does not intend to make public."[107] Public information encompasses that which a government department or agency chooses to make available on its own or the courts force it to release. In contrast, private information is intended solely for internal use within government. There is a gray area between public (released) and private (protected) information. The availability of information in the gray area would be determined through the FOI Act, the Privacy Act, judicial review, and such. Clearly, the definition of key terms should be an important component of information policy.

E-government and the various information policies behind it have altered the landscape of public access. The government releases more types of information resources electronically than it did in the past, and FirstGov represents an attempt to create a portal that provides subject access to information resources across the three branches of the federal government. Although far from providing comprehensive access, it does serve as a tool for those unfamiliar with the structure and organizational complexity of the government. Beyond such a portal, the search process becomes more complex, and there are guides to navigating both the electronic and print environments. At the same time, although there is no governmentwide recommendation as to which types of viewers government entities should follow and different entities may use different ones,[108] the government relies on those viewers that the public can download free of charge through the Web. The government has also created specialized software that might have operated in a mainframe environment but has been modified to function in an e-government environment. Thus, the public can download these software packages at an agency's home page and run the application through a personal computer. Examples of such applications include:[108]

- GEODE (GEO-DATA Explorer; U.S. Geological Survey (USGS);http://dss1.er.usgs.gov/), a tool for accessing, viewing, and downloading "information from geospatial databases containing a broad spectrum of data produced by the USGS and other government agencies."
- BASINS (Better Assessment Science Integrating Point and Nonpoint Sources; Environmental Protection Agency's (EPA) Office of Science and Technology; http://www.epa.gov/epahome/gis.htm) "integrates a geographic information system (GIS), national watershed data, and state-of-the-art environmental assessment and modeling tools into one convenient package."
- EXTRACT (U.S. Bureau of the Census,http://www.census.gov/epcd/www/extract.html), "a general purpose data display and extension tool that works with bureau files recorded in dBase format."
- Map-It (U.S. Geological Survey,http://stellwagen.er.usgs.gov/mapit/), a map generator that "takes longitude/latitude pairs as input and plots them on a Mercator projection map along with land/sea and political boundaries."

Another means of informing the public is webcasting, which is an audiovisual presentation, such as a lecture, training session or program, or news conference that can be viewed online in real time or archived for later viewing. The Department of Housing and Urban Development, for instance, provides live webcasts of training and public events (http://www.hud.gov/webcasts/index.cfm), and congressional committees often offer live hearings through webcasting. Most government Web sites recommend RealPlayer from RealNetworks, Inc. (Seattle, WA; http://www.real.com/) to view and hear webcasts.

EPA's Maps on Demand EnviroMapper (http://maps.epa.gov/environmapper/) provides users with interactive GIS functionality using some of the agency's spatial data for the conterminous United States. The USGS's National Atlas Online (http://www-atlas.usgs.gov/atlasvue.html), which uses Macromedia's Shockwave (http://sdc.shockwave.com/shockwave/download/), allows users to customize maps interactively with a user's Web browser. Finally, EPA's "Dumptown Game" (http://www.epa.gov/recyclecity/gameintro.htm) also users Shockwave, but, in this instance, as a browser viewer to watch the images move and change as users interact with the program as the City Manager of Recycle City. The "Dumptown Game" is one of more than 100 government Web sites aimed at the nation's youth.[108]

Federal agencies are cognizant that their web visitors use a variety of workstation platforms (Intel and Apple), browsers (Netscape and Microsoft Internet Explorer), Internet access speeds [telephone, cable, and Digital Subscriber Line (DSL) modems in addition to local area networks], and workstation-installed software productivity applications (e.g., Microsoft and Corel office suites). As a result, government Web sites are making efforts to meet individual user needs by providing the public with alternative choices for viewing information and downloading files based on the speed of their Internet connection and installed viewer. An excellent example is the Video Gallery of the National Aeronautics and Space Administration (NASA) (http://www.nasa.gov/gallery/video/index.html), which provides users with choices of movie format based on file size (large and small versions), desired viewer (the same movie in either Quicktime or RealPlayer format), and movie resolution (which affects file size) based on the speed of the user's connection to the Internet (high resolution for larger files and for cable modems and T1 users, medium resolution and average file sizes for fast dial-up modem users, and low resolutions with smaller file sizes for slower dial-up users).[108]

The on-line "help and customization" services that some government Web sites provide include fully functional advanced search engines with Boolean and document search options, perhaps tailored to the educational level of the information seeker (e.g., Department of Education, http://www.ed.gov/search/advSearchForm.jsp); excellent help pages (e.g., THOMAS of the Library of Congress, http://thomas.loc.gov/tfaqs/tfaq15/pdfhelp.html) and online guides (e.g., for installing GEODE, http://dss1.er.usgs.gov/help/); the establishment of personalized web pages, whereby the public collects their favorite information from the site and receives updates on a regular basis (the user logs onto the site using a password) (e.g., "My TradeNet," http://tradenet.gov/); and the free and convenient access to full-text and bibliographic records of the Department of Energy, such as research and development reports in the sciences and some other disciplines, using a persistent uniform resource locator (PURL) (see "DOE Information Bridge," http://www.osti.gov/bridge/).[108]

An example of private and public sector cooperation involves mapping products that government agencies prepare. These products might be linked to a commercially available GIS that combines mapping and a data set and that permits users to display multiple data items. A GIS is a computerized system that captures, stores, manipulates, analyzes, and presents data coded to a particular location or area on the Earth's surface (latitude and longitude). Federal agencies use GISs for resource management, planning, resource allocation, and the setting of and compliance with regulations. More precisely, they use the computerized systems for land use analysis and planning, natural resource management, land cover interpretation, demographic mapping and analysis, transportation route or traffic corridor selection, natural hazard assessment, global research, military reconnaissance, etc.[109]

Depository Library Programs

The Government Printing Office administers the best-known depository program, in which more than 1300 libraries receive publications that GPO receives and distributes for public use. A key question is: "What is the role of this depository program (as well as other ones) in the environment of e-government that has been briefly sketched in this essay?" Is it more than being a resource for lessening the digital divide (see below) providing access to historical documents, and assisting the public in navigating the government's presence on the Web and furnishing the necessary plug-ins to retrieval needed government information resources? Depository libraries can provide the public with free access to fee-based statistical compilations of the Department of Commerce's STAT-USA.

Complicating matters, the only study to document the number of users of the depository program (actually only academic and public depositories) recorded 167,000 of them for a typical week in the latter 1980s.[110] In contrast, during a typically week, the Bureau of the Census, for instance, has more than 1 million "hits" on its home page. Thus, under e-government, government departments and agencies can directly, efficiently, and effectively provide the public with both information and services, without having to rely on third parties such as depository libraries. Perhaps the major exception to this generalization is the depository program of the Patent and Trademark Office, where anyone seeking patent or trademark information can rely on the special knowledge and search skills of the highly trained staff at these libraries. Seeking information on patent and trademarks can constitute a complex search process, and even the agency's home page acknowledges the program and encourages information seekers to use the resources under the direction of depository library staff.

Policy Framework

At the federal level of government, information policy may be developed in a variety of ways and prescribed in a number of different forms. The prescribed way for Congress to establish information policy is largely through the constitutionally specified legislative process. A member of Congress formally introduces a proposal in the form of a bill or a joint resolution. Usually the measure is one endorsed by the member, but legislation can be offered "by request" on behalf of the president. Ideally, the proposal is referred to the appropriate committee of jurisdiction; given a hearing, where public comment is received; marked up in accordance with committee wishes; reported to the floor; and voted on by the chamber membership. After the other house of Congress completes similar action

on the measure or one nearly like it, a conference committee may be necessary to resolve differences in the two adopted versions. After both houses have agreed to the single compromise bill, the proposal is presented to the president for signature. When signed into law, the measure attains the status of being a statute and, usually, is positioned within the *United States Code*. If the president vetoes it, Congress has an opportunity to override and, if successful, the measure becomes a statute.[3]

There are, however, other techniques and procedures available to Congress for setting policy. Within its own domain, the two houses of Congress adopt rules and standards that constitute policy. In 1980, for example, the Senate adopted a simple resolution that changed the rules of that body to increase public access to its archived records.[111,112] A similar reform was instituted in the House of Representatives in 1989 with the adoption of a simple resolution amending the rules of the House for the 101st Congress.[113,114] Committees of the House and Senate set rules for themselves that constitute information policy. For example, many committees have a rule on how they handle and maintain security classified or other sensitive information.

Congress also appropriates funds for the departments and agencies. This fiscal authority can be directly and indirectly used to set policy. A verbal understanding or committee report language concerning the operation and/or expansion of a program in question may accompany a generous appropriation for an information program. Similarly, funds may be denied or withheld for a program. Moreover, a permanent prohibition may be instituted through the appropriation process.[115]

Finally, policy may be set through informal but, nonetheless, documented agreements. A powerful committee chairman may ask an agency head to conduct some information operation in a particular way; the verbal agreement, extracted at a hearing, is captured in the transcript of the proceeding. In the same regard, an exchange of letters may be used to set policy. For example, shortly after President Kennedy assumed office, the chairman of the House Special Subcommittee on Government Information wrote to him asking for an explanation of how his administration would invoke "executive privilege." By return letter, Kennedy pledged he would exclusively exercise this power and would assume personal responsibility for its use. Sometimes, of course, a record documenting an informal agreement setting policy may be difficult, if not impossible, to locate. Furthermore, sometimes no such record exists.

The federal courts also make information policy. When a judicial decision is rendered on a dispute, it may uphold the status quo or modify an existing policy at issue. Moreover, in writing an opinion on a decision, a judge or judges may offer views or prescribe a procedure that assumes a policy character. For example, law professor Robert Vaughn's FOI Act lawsuit to gain access to Civil Service Commission evaluations of certain agencies' personnel management programs and other similar reports prepared by the Bureau of Personnel Management resulted not only in a ruling in his favor but also inaugurated agency creation of an index that would enable courts to facilitate reference to particular portions of documents and to know the exact exemption being relied on by the government for each controverted section of a document at issue. Such an index allows a requester to prepare better arguments for the disclosure of sought records. An agency must identify specific portions of disputed documents that are being exempted from disclosure and must justify in detail the reasons for protecting particular information under certain exemptions.[116] The FOI Act, in particular, has been subject to a considerable amount of such judicial gloss.

Courts and individual judges also enjoy a considerable amount of authority for setting information policy for their domains. Federal court rules, practices, and procedures, not inconsistent with legislative enactments, have the force and effect of statutes, but any such rule inconsistent with a statute is inoperative. The Supreme Court promulgates rules for itself and the separate lower federal courts.[117] These are for the general guidance of the courts. However, because the individual Courts of Appeals in their circuits and federal District Courts throughout the country encounter special local conditions and circumstances, they are empowered to make their own special rules, not inconsistent with the rules of general applications set down for them by the Supreme Court.[118] Furthermore, within all of these rules, presiding trial judges have some latitude to control information (e.g., issue a protective order, seal documents, or perhaps close a portion of a proceedings). Such actions may be viewed as policy making; their significance will vary depending on their public effect.

Judicial opinions, once filed, are publicly available at least in typescript at the courthouse of the authoring judge (s). Some judges, however, may be slow to file their prepared views. Commercial publishing firms obtain these opinions and produce various compilations, including the well-known *Federal Reporter* and *Federal Supplement* series. Supreme Court opinions, while also available in commercially published form, are produced by GPO in the *United States Reports* series.

Within the Executive Branch, information policy may be prescribed through a wide variety of forms emanating from the Oval Office, an agency fulfilling a governmentwide responsibility, or an agency serving only its own personnel. In the first category, the president may set policy through the issuance of a directive, such as an executive order or a national security decision directive, a letter, a memorandum, or simply an announcement. In almost all cases, such policy making cannot conflict with statutory expressions and is of an administrative nature and internal to the government. Occasionally, however, the president may exercise some constitutional authority (e.g., Commander in Chief powers) resulting in policy expression in conflict with congressionally legislated policy. For example, some speculate that one of the reasons why Congress has not directly legislated information security classification policy, except in very specific program areas, is that the president has the prerogative in this field by virtue of being constitutionally Chief Executive and Commander in Chief. Conflicts between a congressional and a presidential policy expression are sometimes settled by the courts but are oftentimes left to political settlement.

Governmentwide policy on a matter may be set by a particular agency. For many years, OMB, and the Bureau of the Budget before it, has issued circulars, announcements, and guidelines on a variety of fiscal and administrative matters. The Privacy Act of 1974 authorized OMB to issue governmentwide guidance and regulations for implementing the statute.[119]

Finally, each agency produces forms of policy. Again, the expectation is that these agency expressions of policy will not conflict with statutes or other superior policy forms, such as a presidential directive or governmentwide guidance. Agencies issue regulations implementing and interpreting statutes and presidential policy instruments, internal administrative orders and directives governing their organization and operation, and staff manuals, such as security classification guidebooks, all of which contain expressions of policy. Most agency regulations can be found in the *Code of Federal Regulations*. Draft and new regulations, as well as some other agency orders and directives, are published, when first issued, in the *Federal Register*. Nonetheless, some of this material is unpublished and fugitive; however, it might appear on an agency's home page.

Stakeholders Affecting Information Policy

Given the impact of information policies on many facets of one's work and nonwork situations, a listing of stakeholders involved in policy formulation and review would be endless and unproductive. Most professional organizations have a body for presenting their response to draft and newly reported information policies of concern to their membership; those bodies may also try to shape those policies. For example, they might be invited to present their position at a congressional hearing or to interact with committee staff in shaping initial legislation. It is important that different stakeholders be willing to work with each other and, when necessary, to compromise. Clearly, information policy is subject to the political process. As well, policy makers will be sensitive to the costs of any proposed recommendations and will not react well to calls for creating a new government agency or program. There are, as well, competing priorities such as, of late, homeland security matters, including the creation of a new cabinet-level department charged with such responsibilities.

TOWARD NATIONAL INFORMATION POLICY

In July 1976, the Domestic Council within the Executive Office of the President submitted a report, *National Information Policy*, to President Gerald Ford. The principal recommendation was that "the United States set as a goal the development of a coordinated National Information Policy ... that is comprehensive, sufficiently sensitive to new technology, and responsive to the implications of the Information Age."[120] The report advocated a unified approach to information policy coordinated in the Office of the President.

Subsequent discussions of information policy have encouraged the development of a "requisite arterial system" for "the free and equitable flow of all nonproprietary, nonconfidential information to each individual, regardless of location, level of comprehension, economic status, or other circumstances."[121] Such discussions focus on national information policy, but for either government or nongovernment information. Rarely has such policy been viewed as a marriage of all information resources, whether they are government or nongovernment.

Trying to develop national information policy, the National Commission on Libraries and Information Science, the British Library, and the Canadian Institute for Research on Policy formulated the Glenerin Declaration, a trinational statement that could serve as a preamble for national, or international, information policy that recognizes the impact of information on national economies and societies. Although dated, that declaration articulates an agenda of issues, initiatives, and strategies for achieving the marriage of all information resources.[122]

Briefly, national information policy conveys a sense of national purpose and represents guiding principles leading to the integration of all publicly available government information in the United States, regardless of the level of government producing that information. Moreover, that integration combines government and nongovernment information, extends bibliographic control over that information, and produces mechanisms for gaining effective and efficient access to that information. In contrast, federal information policy has the force of law and variously binds the federal government to prescribed courses of action.

One purpose of national information policy is to improve the dissemination of government information and to bring pertinent government information resources produced in the United States to the resolution of various information needs of the citizenry. Of course, national information policy might have another component: the identification of significant foreign source material that, e.g., will lead to a U.S.-based patent or scientific breakthrough. National information policy should encourage differentiation between quantity and quality of information and discourage the generation of information that merely adds to information overload.

The National Commission on Libraries and Information Science (NCLIS), a proponent of national information policy, has reaffirmed its support of national information policy through its declaration of "Principles of Public Information," such as with *Principle 1: The public has the right of access to public information*: Government agencies should guarantee open, timely and uninhibited access to public information except where restricted by law. People should be able to access public information, regardless of its format, without any special training or expertise."[123]

In 2000, NCLIS asked Robert M. Hayes, Professor Emeritus at the University of California, Los Angeles, and chair of the 1982 NCLIS Public Sector/Private Sector Task Force, to reflect on the task force's findings, conclusions, and recommendations 20 years later. In his reflection, he discusses seven principles and 27 recommendations.[124] It is encouraging to note that e-government has met most of the principles and recommendations.

E-government, with its attempt to make government become "citizen-centered,"[125] is achieving national information policy. E-government is forging partnerships and alliances with the private sector and government agencies (even those at subnational levels of government). As a result, more, better organized, and better displayed, government information is readily available. Furthermore, right on their home pages, they tailor access to information for specialized audiences. For example, the Library of Congress's home page (http://www.loc.gov/) enables information seekers to search by whether they are "researchers," "law researchers," "librarians and archivists," "teachers," "publishers," "persons with disabilities," or "blind persons."

Government departments and agencies have too much information—not all of which is conducive to Web delivery—to place the entire set on the Web. They might not have organized some of their information resources sufficiently for electronic delivery, and some information may not be conducive to display on the Web. In other instances, agencies may have overlooked some information resources in their possession, thereby letting information resources evade being captured bibliographically and being presented electronically, if deemed of sufficient public interest and value. Naturally, e-government cannot and does not focus on nongovernment information. It would seem that the declarations of policy principles and the private and public sector roles and responsibilities that these principles lay out merit reconsideration in the age of digital government. The conditions stated in these principles no longer exist.

LOOKING TO THE FUTURE

If there is a single dramatic and profound factor of change in information policy at present and for the future, it is the concept of e-government, which recognizes the civic and business role of government in disseminating both information and services. For a long time, information policy has been viewed and formulated in a context of civil liberties and citizen rights in a democracy. This value will continue to be important but is being joined by the somewhat competing factor of information having economic, global, and national security value, particularly when government information is increasingly available in digital formats that are attractive to information users.

The challenge for the future will be to continue to improve information dissemination through e-government[126] in balance with post-September 11 security concerns. At the same time, government departments and agencies will need to articulate better how they decide what to include and exclude on their home pages and what happens once information is removed from availability there. Is the information removed to a "library," which is a storehouse that may not be easy to search, "archived," or destroyed?

Most definitely, the amount of information produced annually within the federal government and other levels of government is large and ever-increasing. Although the quantity of information increases, so too does its usefulness to diverse segments of the population. Information policy is crucial to national economic well-being and scientific discovery, as well as maintaining an informed and well-educated citizenry that interacts with the government on a regular basis.

CONCLUSION

The availability of information is no longer restricted by national boundaries. Furthermore, the free market is expanding, and geopolitical structures are undergoing radical changes in the name of e-government. As a result, many policies have broad implications. Local libraries and information centers operate within this broad framework. That framework shapes what information is available, in what forms, at what price, etc. Clearly, libraries can play a part in revitalizing U.S. competitiveness in world markets. However, they have other charges as well. The result is that a host of current and potential policy issues have direct and indirect implications for library and information science as e-government continues to unfold and its infrastructure is developed. It is important that these issues be identified and that the library and information science profession develops strategies that define the role of libraries and information centers in the provision of electronic and print information to the public and that complement the goals of e-government.

REFERENCES

1. Chartrand, R.L. Policy imperatives in the information age. Bull. Am. Soc. Inf. Sci. **1986**, February/March, 1986, *12*, 6.

2. Gell Mason, M. *The Federal Role in Library and Information Services*, Knowledge Industry Publications, Inc.: White Pains, NY, 1983; 93.

3. Hernon, P.; Relyea, H.; Dugan, R. Cheverie, J. *United States Government: Policies and Sources*, Libraries Unlimited: Westport, CT, 2002 and the accompanying 1,800 page CD-ROM.

4. Congress House. *Committee on the Judiciary FBI Counterintelligence Visits to Libraries, Hearings* GPO: Washington, DC, 1988.

5. Susman, T. *Memorandum: Removal or Destruction of Federal Depository Library Documents*, Association of Research Libraries: Washington, DC, March 2002; 131. Available at http://www.arl.org/info/frn/gov/Susman.html.

6. Friedman, L.M. *A History of American Law*, Simon and Schuster: New York, 1973; 88–90, 93–100, 148–156, 285–288.

7. Brown, R.D. *Knowledge is Power*, Oxford University Press: New York, 1989.

8. Clarke, M.P. *Parliamentary Privilege in the American Colonies*, Yale University Press: New Haven, CT, 1943.

9. Flaherty, D.H. *Privacy in Colonial New England*, University Press of Virginia: Charlottesville, VA, 1972.

10. Pole, J.R. *The Gift of Government*, The University of Georgia Press: Athens, GA, 1983; especially Chaps. 4–6.

11. Berger, R. *Executive Privilege*, Harvard University Press: Cambridge, MA, 1974; 15–34.

12. Rakove, N. *Beginnings of National Politics*, Alfred A. Knopf: New York, 1979.

13. Sanders, J.B. *Evolution of Executive Departments of the Continental Congress 1997–1789*, The University of North Carolina Press: Durham, NC, 1935; Chap. 3.

14. Hoffman, D.N. *Government Secrecy and the Founding Fathers*, Greenwood Press: Westport, CT, 1981.

15. Berger, R. Executive privilege v. congressional inquiry. UCLA Law Rev. May **1965**, *12*, 1043–1120.

16. Berger, R. Executive privilege v. congressional inquiry. UCLA Law Rev. August **1965**, *12*, 1287–1364.

17. Breckenbridge, A.C. *The Executive Privilege*, University of Nebraska Press: Lincoln, NE, 1974.

18. Kramer, R.; Marcuse, H. Executive privilege—A study of the period 1953–1960. George Washington Law Rev. April **1961**, *29*, 623–718.

19. Kramer, R.; Marcuse, H. Executive privilege—A study of the period 1953–1960. George Washington Law Rev. June **1961**, *29*, 827–916.

20. Wolkinson, H. Demands of Congressional Committees for executive papers. Fed. Bar J. April **1949**, *10*, 103–150.

21. Wolkinson, H. Demands of Congressional Committees for executive papers. Fed. Bar J. July **1949**, *10*, 223–259.

22. Wolkinson, H. Demands of congressional committees for executive papers. Fed. Bar J. October **1949**, *10*, 319–350.

23. Kaye, D. Congressional papers and judicial subpoenas. UCLA Law Rev. October **1975**, *22*, 57–76.

24. Kaye, D. Congressional papers judicial subpoenas, and the constitution. UCLA Law Rev. February **1977**, *24*, 523–580.

25. Reinstein, R.J.; Silvergate, H.A. Legislative privilege and the separation of powers. Harvard Law Rev. May **1973**, *86*, 1113–1182.

26. Farrand, M., Ed. *The Records of the Federal Convention of 1787;* Yale University Press: New Haven, CT, 1937; Vol. 2, 260.

27. Farrand, M., Ed. *The Records of the Federal Convention of 1787;* Yale University Press: New Haven, CT, 1937; Vol. 3 331, 326.

28. 1 Stat 28 (1789).

29. 1 Stat 49 (1789).

30. 1 Stat. 519 (1797).

31. 1 Stat. 724 (1799).

32. 2 Stat. 302 (1804).

33. 3 Stat, 145 (1814).

34. 3 Stat. 439 (1818).

35. 3 Stat. 576 (1820).

36. 1 Stat. 168 (1789).

37. 1 Stat. 65 (1789). These and similar provisions were consolidated in the *Revised Statutes of the United States* (1878) at section 161, which is presently located in the *United States Code* at 5 U.S.C. 301.

38. 3 Stat. 140 (1813).

39. 13 Stat. 460 (1865).

40. 17 Stat. 510 (1873).

41. McPherson, E.G. Reporting the debates of congress. Q.J. Speech April **1942**, *28*, 141–148.

42. Childs, J.B. "Disappeared in the wings of oblivion": the story of the United States house of representatives printed documents at the first session of the first congress, New York, 1798. Pap. Bibliogr. Soc. Am. **1964**, *58*, 91–132 Second Quarter.

43. Childs, J.B. The story of the United States Senate documents, 1st Congress, 1st Session, New York, 1789. Pap. Bibliogr. Soc. Am. **1962**, *56*, 175–194 Second Quarter.

44. 9 Stat. 113 (1846).

45. 12 Stat. 113 (1860).

46. 28 Stat. 601 (1895).

47. Stathis, S.W. The evolution of government printing and publishing in America. Gov. Publ. Rev. **1980**, *7A*, 377–390.

48. Smith, C.H. *The Press, Politics, and Patronage*, University of Georgia Press: Athens, GA, 1977.

49. 11 Stat. 379 (1859).

50. 15 Stat. 292 (1869).

51. 11 Stat. 253 (1857).

52. 28 Stat. 610.

53. Current authority for the depository library program may be found at 44 *U.S.C.* 1901–1915.

54. Hernon, P. McClure, C.R. Purcell, G.R. *GPO's Depository Library Program*, Ablex: Norwood, NJ, 1985.

55. 33 Stat. 584 (1904).

56. 42 Stat. 541 (1922).

57. 49 Stat. 500 (1935).

58. 50 Stat. 304 (1937).

59. U.S. Department of justice, committee on administrative Procedure. *Administrative Procedure in Government Agencies*, GPO: Washington, DC, 1941; S. Doc, 8.

60. 60 Stat. 237 (1946).

61. 60 Stat. 238.

62. Cross, H.L. *The People's Right to Know*, Columbia University Press: Morningside Heights, NY, 1953.

63. Mollenhoff, C.R. *Washington Cover-Up*, Doubleday and Co.: Garden City, NJ, 1962.

64. Wiggins, J.R. *Freedom or Secrecy*, Revised Ed. Oxford University Press: New York, 1964.

65. Rourke, F.E. *Secrecy and Publicity*, The Johns Hopkins Press: Baltimore, MD, 1961.

66. Summers, R.E., Ed. *Federal Information Controls in Peacetime*; The H.W. Wilson Co.: New York, 1949.

67. Congress. House. Committee on government operations. *Availability of Information from Federal Departments and Agencies*, Hearings 84th–86th Congresses GPO: Washington, DC, 1959–1965; 17 parts.

68. 80 Stat. 250 (1966); 5 U.S.C. 552.

69. 88 Stat. 1896 (1974); 5 U.S.C. 552a.

70. 86 Stat. 770 (1972); 5 U.S.C. App.

71. 90 Stat. 1241 (1976); 5 U.S.C. 552b.

72. Cox, A.M. *The Myths of National Security*, Beacon Press: Boston, MA, 1975.

73. Dorsen, N.; Gillers, S.; Eds. *None of Your Business*; Viking Press: New York, 1974.

74. Franck, T.M.; Weisband, E.; Eds. *Secrecy and Foreign Policy*; Oxford University Press: New York, 1974.

75. Halperin, M.H.; Hoffman, D.N. *To Secret*, New Republic Books: Washington, DC, 1977.

76. See 11 Stat. 60 (1857).

77. Ehlke, R.C.; Relyea, H.C. The Reagan administration order on security classification: A critical assessment. Fed. Bar News J. February **1983**, *30*, 91–97.

78. 36 Stat. 1084 (1911).

79. 40 Stat. 217 (1917).

80. Edgar, H.; Schmidt, B.C. The espionage statutes and the publication of defense information. Columbia Law Rev. May **1973**, *73*, 929–1087.

81. See 52 Stat. 3 (1938).

82. See 60 Stat. 755 (1946); 42 U.S.C. 2161–2168.

83. See 61 Stat. 495 (1947); 50 U.S.C. 403(d)(3).

84. See 66 Stat. 1 (1952).

85. 66 Stat. 792–805 (1952); 35 U.S.C. 181–188.

86. Executive Order 12356. Fed. Regist. **1982**, April 6 *47*, 14874–14884 President Clinton later modified this order, as his administration implemented a new declassification policy.

87. 10290, 3 C.F.R. (1949–1953 Comp.), 790–797.

88. Bamford, J. *The Puzzle Palace*, Houghton Mifflin: Boston, MA, 1982.

89. Falk, S.L. The national security council under Truman, Eisenhower, and Kennedy. Polit. Sci. Q. September **1964**, *79*, 410.

90. General Accounting Office, *National Security: The Use of Presidential Directives to Make and Implement U.S. Policy*, GAO: Washington, DC, January 1992; GAO/NSIAD-89-31-2.

91. Hixon, R.F. *Privacy in a Public Society*, Oxford University Press: New York, 1987; especially xiii–xiv.

92. *Griswold* v. *Connecticut*, 383 U.S. 479 (1965).

93. Clark, R.H. Constitutional sources of the penumbral right to privacy. Villanova Law Rev. June **1974**, *19*, 833–884.

94. 5 U.S.C. 552(b) (3) and (6).

95. 5. U.S.C. 552a.

96. 15 U.S.C. 1681–1681t.

97. 20 U.S.C. 1232g.

98. 20 U.S.C. 1232h.

99. *Santa Clara County* v. *Southern Pacific Railroad Company*, 118 U.S. 394 (1885).
100. See 18 U.S.C. 1905.
101. Commission on Federal Paperwork. *Confidentiality and Privacy*, GPO: Washington, DC, 1977; 26.
102. Government e-retail sites. Fed. Computer Week. May 18, 2001. *16*, 28–35.
103. Relyea, H.C. E-Gov comes to the federal government. In *U.S. Government on the Web*; Hernon, P., Dugan, R.E., Shuler, J.A., Eds.; Libraries Unlimited: Littleton, CO, 2001. Chap. 14. This chapter also identifies and discusses the relevant policy instruments. See also Chap. 16, Hernon et al.[3].
104. Frank, D. Plug and play e-government. Fed. Compu. Week. April 1, **2002**, *17*, 16–17.
105. Matthews, W. GAO: E-records overwhelm NARA. Fed. Compu. Week. June 24, **2001**, *16*, 54.
106. Porat, M. *The Information Economy*, GPO: Washington, DC, 1977; Vol. 1, 214–239.
107. Hernon, P.; McClure, C.R. *Federal Information Policies in the 1980s*, Ablex: Norwood, NJ, 1987; 5. Chap. 8.
108. Hernon, P.; Dugan, R.E. Shuler, J.A. *U.S. Government on the Web*, Libraries Unlimited: Littleton, CO, 2001. Chapter 15.
109. Greene, R.W. *GIS in Public Policy, Open Access: GIS in e-Government and Confronting Catastrophe: A GIS Handbook*, ESRI Press: Redlands, CA, 2001.
110. McClure, C.R.; Hernon, P. *Users of Academic and Public GPO Depository Libraries*, GPO: Washington, DC, 1989.
111. Congress, Senate, Committee on Rules and Administration, *Relating to Public Access to Senate Records at the National Archives*, GPO: Washington, DC, 1980. S. Rpt. 96-1042.
112. Congress Rec. December 1,**1980**, *126*, 31188–31189.
113. Congress Rec. January 3, **1989**, *135*, H7–H8.
114. Relyea, H.C. Public access to congressional records: Present policy and reform considerations. Gov. Infom. Q. **1985**, *2*, 235–256.
115. 5 U.S.C. 3107.
116. *Vaughn* v. *Rosen*, 484 F.2d 820 (D.C. Cir., 1973).
117. 18 U.S.C. 3771-3722; 28 U.S.C. 2072.
118. 28 U.S.C/2071.
119. Fed. Regist. July 9, **1975**, *40*, 28948–28978.
120. Domestic council, committee on the right to privacy, *National Information Policy*, National Commission on Libraries and Information Science: Washington, DC, 1976. vi, 183–184.
121. Kaser, D.; Blake, F.; Chelton, M.K.; Josey, E.J.; Malinconcio, S.M.; Sullivan, P.; Scwartz, R. Toward a conceptual foundation for a National Information Policy. Wilson Libr. Bull. March **1978**, *52*, 545.
122. Glenerin declaration: Statement of policy. Fed.Regist. December 10, **1987**, *52*, 46980–46981.
123. National Commission on Libraries and Information Science, *Principles of Public Information*, The Commission: Washington, DC, June 29, 1990. .
124. National Commission on Libraries and Information Science, *Appendix 17: An Invited Retrospective Appraisal of the 1982 NCLIS Public Sector/Private Sector Task Force Report*, The Commission: Washington, DC, August 15, 2000. Available at http://www.nclis.gov/govt/assess/assess.append17.pdf.
125. Daniels, M.E., Jr. *Memorandum for the Heads of Executive Departments and Agencies: Citizen-Centered E-Government: Developing the Action Plan*, Office of Management and Budget: Washington, DC, July 18, 2001. Available at http://www.whitehouse.gov/omb/memoranda/m-01-28.html.
126. Hernon, P.; Relyea, H.C.; Dugan, R.E. Access to government information in a digital environment. Academe. July–August **2002**, *88*, 62–65.

Information Practice

Crystal Fulton
Jean Henefer
School of Information and Communication Studies, University College Dublin, Dublin, Ireland

Abstract

The phrase *information practice* is relatively new to the field of Library and Information Science (LIS). Using the works of individuals, such as Foucault, Vygotsky, and Garfinkel, the concept of information practice questions the historical positioning of the individual as the unit of analysis. Instead, information practice proposes that information behavior is best understood by considering information and knowledge constructed as a sociocultural context. Recent LIS scholarship in regions, such as Australia, North America, and the Nordic countries, has drawn upon explorations of discourse to theorize and apply information practice as an umbrella approach to LIS research. This entry explores the concept of information practice and its place among LIS metatheories and application in LIS research.

INTRODUCTION

To commence this entry, a truism is stated: Library and Information Science is a multidisciplinary field. The discipline embraces a multitude of information-related areas concerned with human information behaviors or practices, including information creation, access, retrieval, organization, etc., necessitating the consideration of a range of social science perspectives in the work of practitioners, researchers, and theorists in this field to legitimize and expand research. Equally, because in the social sciences Library and Information Science is relatively new (particularly in terms of empirical theory building compared to other social science disciplines), it is important to embrace new perspectives that draw upon applicable theories and research. However, it is also vital that the discipline does not ignore or negate the fundamental work that has been done by scholars who have explored and may continue to do so, the ways in which human beings engage with information both to build a theoretical basis for this field as well to guide information professionals, including librarians, in their service delivery.

For some decades, the accepted terminology for this particular area of interest and research in the field has been described as *information behavior* (IB).[1-5] Information behavior researchers and practitioners over the years have dedicated their efforts to exploring and addressing the information needs, information seeking, and information uses of individuals and collectives. All of these endeavors have been undertaken not only to improve information service provision but as well to contribute to theory building in this relatively new field. As embodied by the Association for Information Science and Technology (ASIS&T)'s Special Interest Group: Information Needs, Seeking and Use (SIG USE), the focus of information behavior, encompassing both cognitive and affective behaviors, includes

- Shaping and identifying information needs
- Seeking (and not seeking) information that will address those needs
- Exploring information sources present in one's context/situation
- Retrieving information from available information sources
- Sharing information with others
- Managing personal information collections
- Communicating and collaborating with others concerning an information need or information resources
- Personal and group-based information use[6,7]

In recent years, IB has been challenged both as a term and a research approach by a respected body of researchers who have contributed significant work to empirical and IB theory construction.[8-11] The suggested new nomenclature or "umbrella" term is *information practice*.

This entry includes not only an introduction to information practice, including the philosophical perspectives and the work of the researchers and theorists in this field, but also the recent work being done by individuals who are teasing out this possible "new" term or alternatives to IB for LIS dialog, research, and theory construction from a multidisciplinary perspective.[12] As well, it will consider other works related to the proposed theoretical basis of information practice and review related current work that seems to place information practices within a wider definition of information behavior in a range of different contexts[2,4] and discuss new and potentially exciting interpretations.[2,13,14] Finally, this entry will consider whether there actually is a fundamental difference in perspective between those who describe understanding human activities as information behavior and those who choose information practice, or whether possibly, in reality, this move to an alternative categorization is a semantic

Encyclopedia of Library and Information Sciences, Fourth Edition DOI: 10.1081/E-ELIS4-120053392

issue. The authors' review of the literature from both perspectives finds that there is mutual agreement that an information activity (or indeed inactivity) is determined by context, whether that be personal, organizational, cultural, etc. Therefore, because LIS research is incorporating the importance of context in studies of information behavior and information practice, the authors will reflect upon the possible need in LIS theory building to move away from focusing on what might be a semantic issue to placing context at the forefront of the development of LIS as a rigorous field in the social sciences.

WHAT IS PRACTICE?

The term *practice* may be defined as pertaining to routine or habitual activities, the idea being to convey a custom or tradition in experience. For example, one definition of practice offered by the *Oxford English Dictionary* is "*the habitual doing or carrying on of something*; *usual, customary, or constant action or performance*; *conduct*," a definition debated by Savolainen and Wilson.[15] However, the use of the term *practice* in research has yet to be standardized. Some scholars claim to study *practice* as a theoretical construct, while others refer to *practices* as activity-based experience. Similarly, as they attempt to reconstruct their research identities, some scholars refer to their field of specialization as *information seeking practices* and combine this with *information needs*, referring to the long established field of information behavior.[16] Others have simply appended *information practices* to *information behavior* as an addition to the field of information behavior.[17] The varying adoptions of the term *practice* to relay disciplinary subject are suggestive of the flux around defining practice as a concept and information practice as a field of study.

Library and Information Science scholars who advocate information practice as a theoretical concept for our field have drawn on Schatzki's[18] definition of practice. Schatzki explains practice in terms of *human activities*, explaining "Practices are the bundled activities that one type of component of social orders performs."[18] He summarizes a practice as "a temporally evolving, open-ended set of doings and sayings linked by practical understandings, rules, teleoaffective structure, and general understandings."[18]

EVOLVING CONCEPTUALIZATIONS OF INFORMATION PRACTICE

In their analysis of LIS metatheories, Talja et al.[19] state that "A metatheory enables researchers to determine what kind of entities, for example, information, knowledge, users and information retrieval systems are...bringing into researchers' view a specific object of study and a

way of studying this object." The concept of *information practice* arises from the philosophical perspective that because information and knowledge creation is rooted in a sociocultural context, research approaches that concentrate on the individual as the unit of analysis inadequately address the social nature of information processes.

During the late 1970s, constructivism, or the "cognitive viewpoint,"[20–22] based on educational theories of learning,[23,24] emerged as a dominant research approach in LIS. Rooted in the view that knowledge is created internally through active, individualized engagement and interpretation of information, constructivism focuses specifically on the individual's sense-making[25,26] when faced with a gap or uncertainty.[21] Constructivist researchers[5,21,27,28] explore the cognitive and affective dimensions of human information behavior and the situational contexts that trigger and may determine the nature and outcome of the individual's engagement with information. Wilson[29] states that information needs should be included in any model of human information behavior, as well as the drivers that cause the perception of need, those elements that have an effect on response to need, and the nature of the response.

Criticism of the constructivist approach has been raised on a number of levels. Among these is the view that, because the focus is on the individual and his or her internalized construction of mental models or sense-making, the research is, in essence, a study of subjective meanings. Additionally, the "cognitive viewpoint" implicitly creates a perception that LIS is specifically about the effect of information on the individual,[30] the "information man"[31] replacing "information" as the core theoretical tenet. Despite the increased attention to information seeking in context (ISIC), constructivist research, it has been argued,[19,32] does not adequately explore the effect of sociocultural elements on the creation of knowledge nor attributes to language more than an indistinct role as a tool for acquiring evidence of cognitive processes. Methodologically, constructivism has been challenged as well, in terms of the feasibility, either quantitatively or qualitatively, of acquiring an accurate, objective portrait of the inner workings of the human mind engaged in knowledge formation.[33]

An alternative to constructivism is that of collectivism or social constructivism (reorienting the research approach from the individual to the collective). Based on Vygotsky's[34] view that knowledge is created through both the individual's internal cognitive processes and their engagement with and experience of a particular sociocultural milieu, collectivism explores the ways in which individuals engage with information and form knowledge through their daily experience of, and participation in, the external, social world. At the center of collectivism is the concept that, because people are social and cultural beings, then it is erroneous to explore their information needs and practices purely from a psychological perspective. This approach has been explored particularly in domain analysis studies. Hjorland and Albrechtsen[35] critique the individualistic, cognitive focus of constructivism as being subjective and possibly defective, calling for "investigations of more holistic theories, incorporating knowledge about the cultures in which the information systems are functioning...this implies giving up (or at least supplementing) behavioristic and cognitivistic positions in LIS." Research in this approach has directed its attention away from a unilateral focus on the individual to the information practices inherent in different professions, communities, and environments. Because the empirical work has been conducted predominantly within scholarly discourse communities,[36–38] there is a concern that collectivism may not have applicability to everyday life information seeking. Wenger's[39] theory of communities of practice, with its emphasis on how individuals within a group learn collectively, addresses this issue. Communities of practice exist and can be identified and studied, not only in professional or academic settings, but also in informal, socially based, everyday life settings.

In order to encompass the full dimensions of information seeking and use, social constructionism (or constructionism) is proposed as a potential metatheoretical alternative for LIS. Like collectivism, constructionism is concerned with the social and external use of information, as opposed to the subjective and internal. Knowledge and knowledge structures are not viewed in terms of human beings' individualized mental states, but rather as social and cultural products and processes. Specifically, the constructionist approach emphasizes language, that is linguistic rather than cognitive processes. It differs from collectivism in that it "entails a more direct focus on rhetorics, argumentation and language use...."[19]

Information practice has its roots in the work of several theoreticians. At the center of this discussion is philosopher Michel Foucault, whose writings have informed the development of the concept of information practice, as well as the movement to construct an overarching theory of LIS. As Buschman[40] observes, Foucault "is widely cited, and his insights are adapted in various works that focus on LIS forms of power, discourse, archaeology, silences, exclusion, defining the *other*, domination, and micropractices in the last 15 years of critical-theoretical LIS scholarship." Foucault[41] describes discourses as "practices that systematically form the objects of which they speak." This idea of discourse offers Foucault's most influential idea adopted in LIS theoretical work.[40]

This notion of discourse as the object of analysis has long been explored in the academy, with authors, such as Bernd Frohmann[42,43] and Gary Radford,[44,45] promoting discourse analysis as a means of understanding the "text" of LIS, including collections, documentary practices, etc. For example, Volosinov's[46] work is used to understand discourse by way of classification of discourse through the

selection, organization, and combination of concepts.[44] In addition to Foucault, proponents of the information practice approach cite other influential figures on thinking about this area, such as Mihail Bakhtin,[47] Valentin Volosinov,[46] Harold Garfinkel,[48] and Wayne Wiegand.[49] However, while other philosophers and scholars are linked to Foucault, Foucault remains "far more central to the project at hand."[41]

The underlying assumption of the discursive approach is that language holds the key to understanding or establishing meaning in information-related activities, including information needs, seeking, interaction, and sense-making.[42] Discourse, then, holds a central role in constructing social reality. Information practice research explores "how people give accounts of their information behavior or construct the meanings of technical artifacts in work and everyday life,"[50] the construction of which Talja and McKenzie assert as significant to "understanding information seeking and technology use from a broader sociological perspective."[50] From a theoretical perspective, this reasoning is sound. However, it ignores the fact that discourse, as well as being determined by sociocultural context, is also grounded in cognitive processes. Vygotsky,[34] while emphasizing the importance of the social context for children's development, also concentrated his work in exploring the role of inner speak or self-talk as a key to development and sense-making.

INFORMATION PRACTICE IN INFORMATION SCIENCE

Social constructionists generally explain their approach in juxtaposition with the cognitive perspective attributed to information behavior. Savolainen[11,51] contends that information behavior has been accepted unquestioningly by LIS practitioners, the focus on the individual's internal processes preventing the exploration of alternative ways of understanding information seeking and use. He asserts that information practice and information behavior are actually "umbrella" discourses. He calls for "a self-reflexive and critical attitude among researchers towards their familiar concepts in order to avoid being 'trapped' in their own discursive formations."[11]

In proposing an alternative, social constructionists challenge, in a broad sense, the human information behavior approach adopted by LIS researchers. While interest in human beings' use of information can be traced back to the early decades of the twentieth century, the concept of information behavior is typically perceived to be rooted in the work of researchers, such as William Paisley,[52] in the 1960s, with Tom Wilson's[53] 1981 model of information seeking and use significantly offering an early model that he would later develop to account for human information behavior. By definition, this concept of behavior includes all aspects of the individual's engagement (or, in some cases, nonengagement) with information both internally and externally. This approach, while endeavoring to understand the internal processes of individuals, also explores the external factors including "intervening variables"[54] that help explain the role of information in people's life worlds. While Wilson is typically cited for establishing information behavior as a theoretical concept for LIS, the models and theories of other prominent LIS scholars, including Paisley,[52] Bates,[55] Chatman,[56,57] Sonnenwald,[58] Krikelas[59] (see also Henefer and Fulton[60]), and Kuhlthau,[61] form a canon representing a traditional viewpoint under information behavior.[11] Social constructionists, such as Talja et al.,[33] argue that while researchers in human information behavior have, over time, expanded their frame of reference and elements of research investigation, the term "behavior," with its traditional association with internal, cognitive processes, will never provide real understanding, because it is impossible to observe objectively. Of the familiar pioneer names in LIS, Dervin has moved to adopt the term "practice" over "behavior," placing her in the fold for information practice advocates.[11]

In proposing the need for critical reflection, Savolainen[11] argues that, although information practice and information behavior appear to overlap, the two are distinct, emerging from different theoretical perspectives and, therefore, providing differing positions for considering information seeking. Savolainen explores a selection of texts to investigate the development of information practice. In doing so, his analysis takes on a selective text choice, a problematic difficulty already criticized by Buschman[40] in Foucault's work. This adopted assumption underlying information practice requires further exploration to support the viability of the approach.

Buschman[40] examines the potential for a Foucauldian approach in LIS. Importantly, he quotes Habermas' objections to Foucault's work, which suggest that Foucault's logic is flawed, leaving his theory relativist and unable to escape subjectivity. Selectivity of texts and the "death of the subject" are problematic for many of Foucault's critics, for whom theoretical construct and its language are equally hegemonic. According to Buschman,[40] "without a theoretical subject or the ability to locate a locus of power, transgression is (literally) meaningless and hopeless, and social and economic relations are frozen—in stasis." Issues of power remain problematic, where the danger becomes that "the point of LIS discourse analysis becomes LIS discourse analysis."[40]

While arguing for an alternative "umbrella" concept, Savolainen[11] concedes that information behavior and information practice are overlapping at times, such that "researchers may flexibly draw upon alternative metatheoretical ideas in the empirical study of information seeking." What both perspectives share in common is a belief in context, although implementation may differ. Characterizing context ("the Unruly Beast") as "a label

for a site of struggle," Brenda Dervin, in attempting to define what we mean by context in LIS, states that "the only possible conclusion is that there is no term that is more often used, less often defined, and when defined defined so variously as context."[62] A critical contribution that constructionism offers to the development of LIS research methodologies lies in its approach to context and how, as researchers, we can examine and refine our empirical studies. Again, those who are exploring the validity of identifying information practice as a more encompassing term to define and investigate the role of information in life worlds make a distinction between their approach to context as compared to that of information behavior researchers.

Constructionists' approach to context is described as "interpretative," in that "context is not understood as an independent entity, but as a carrier of meaning."[33] In comparison, context, for those studying information behavior, is defined as "objectified." This implies that information behavior researchers are interested in context in terms of the factors that have an impact on human beings' use of information, identifying the range of variables that will have an effect on individuals' needs, seeking, and use, in order to anticipate information behavior in particular situations and best provide systems to facilitate information resolutions. These studies, it is argued, aim to identify the range of variables (internal and external) that either create or affect the actions (or inactions) related to information behavior that have an effect on the object of the research, that is, the individual. Although there is no argument, superficially, with this research approach, constructionists, interested in the applicability of their theory to empirical endeavors, maintain that the crucial dilemma for information behavior researchers is the assumption that this well-established and inadequately challenged methodology does not sufficiently allow for the subjectivity of language and interpretation.

The interpretative approach, proposed by those advocating information practice as an alternative "umbrella" concept, is helpful in terms of providing LIS researchers with a means to experiment with a methodology that challenges the constant critique of the "softness" of social science research. The interpretative approach to context portends that data cannot be interpreted as clear reflections of reality, but that all data collected during the process of research represent not only participants', but also researchers' and readers' sociocultural background assumptions and experiences. Proponents of information practice assert that only through acknowledging that research participants, researchers, and readers bring their own particular sociocultural meanings and interpretations to information seeking and use, can we hope to arrive at a research methodology that will more adequately serve the development of LIS theory. By focusing on the analyses of sociocultural discourses, and simultaneously recognizing and reiterating the subjectivity of all participants' interpretations (research participant, researcher, and reader), constructionists are advocating a further development in LIS research practices that will contribute to the scientific rigors of our work.

In his consideration of the relevance of a "practice approach" to information science, Cox[13,14] recognizes that "practice theory" is applicable across a range of disciplines to support theory building. "Communities of Practice" have informed IB research for decades, Ellis'[27] model of academics' information seeking being an obvious example. In seeking to ground LIS theory building within a robust social science perspective, IP scholars have adopted practice theory as a solution.

In her work placing information literacy within an information practice framework, Lloyd[63] explores the historical evolution of practice theories, citing the studies of philosophers from Aristotle to Wittgenstein, Bourdieu, and Giddens. She presents the view that practice theories are effective means by which one can study and make sense of "sociality"[63] (p. 248). In other words, they provide a potentially fruitful framework through which we can explore and build theory about the ways in which human beings engage with information (seeking, gathering, processing, etc.) and critically how the individual's subsequent construction and use of knowledge is determined by the particular characteristics of the social site they inhabit,[64] including (but not limited to) cultural norms and expectations, histories, linguistic traditions, economies, and politics. While making an effective argument for conceptualizing information literacy as an information practice, grounded in social sites, Lloyd does concede possible limitations to this approach stating:

> At present, however, there is no unified approach or definition of practice, consequently explications of practice differ depending on the ontological and epistemological orientation and interest of the enquirer[63] (p. 248).

Huizing and Cavanagh[65] similarly note the lack of a unified practice-based approach. They suggest that practice theory has evolved to contemporary practice-based approaches, with five underlying premises: *including objects, stretching interaction, foregrounding dynamics, explicating knowing,* and *articulating practice. Including objects* refers to recognizing the role of material objects in social, organization, and information theories. *Stretching interaction* is about expanding definitions of social interaction to include the influence of human and nonhuman agencies and actions relevant to the interaction. *Foregrounding dynamics* prioritizes actions and practices over actors and organizations in organizing ourselves. *Explicating knowing* offers knowledge as a group, rather than individual, activity. And finally, *articulating practice* refers to the interpretative nature of practice and a contemporary definition of practice.

Bystrom and Lloyd[12] acknowledge that information practice "lacks fixed meaning in the field of studies." They offer information practice as a "social practice" that encompasses all human information activities, including producing, seeking, organizing, distributing, and using information. Lloyd[66] (p. 285), drawing on Schatzki, defines information practice as "an array of information related activities and skills, constituted, justified and organized through the arrangements of a social site, and mediated socially and materially with the aim of producing shared understanding and mutual agreement about ways of knowing and recognizing how performance is enacted, enabled and constrained in collective situated action." However, as Cox[13] points out, practice theory in itself is inconclusive. Corraid et al.[67] highlight that practice-based approaches embrace a range of different perspectives both from an empirical and a theoretical stance. In describing the fluidity, or perhaps fragility of practice theory, these authors describe current work in practice theory as a "bandwagon."

FROM THEORETICAL CONSIDERATIONS TO IMPLEMENTATION

Methodological approaches often follow similar pathways to those adopted to explore other frameworks and theories in LIS. For example, Tuominen et al.[68] cite Garfinkel's[48] ideas on ethnography as an important means of exploring information practice, as well as the case study method used by researchers, such as Veinot.[69] Savolainen[11] cites Volosinov's[46] analysis through classification of concepts as a useful methodological approach. Among the wide array of available research techniques, interviews with individuals and textual analysis remain commonplace in data collection and analysis under the information practice approach.

Recent scholarship has drawn upon these explorations of discourse to theorize and apply an information practice approach to LIS research. As Buschman[40] observes, there exists a core group of LIS scholars who have taken up the challenge of Harris[70] and Wiegand[49] to explore Foucault's work and its implications for LIS theory and research. Leading works have emanated largely from Australia, North America, and the Nordic countries. For example, various publications by Talja, Tuominen, and Savolainen[31,32,68] have explored positioning of information practice theoretically.

Examples of researchers implementing social constructionism as a research approach have expanded in recent years. Michael Olsson, who presented some of his early work on social constructionism at the ISIC conference held in Dublin in 2004,[10] currently incorporates an information practice perspective into his previously information behavior-positioned research on Dervin's sensemaking and Foucault's discourse analysis in his more recent conference and published works.[71–73] Sanna Talja, Annemaree Lloyd, Reijo Savolainen, and others have collaborated variously on works about information practices, for example Lloyd and Talja's edited volume focused on information practice, learning, and information literacy.[74]

Pamela McKenzie, who has been acknowledged by many information practice scholars to be among the most highly active in this area,[9] is known for implementing information practice in empirical fieldwork. For example, McKenzie[75] has applied an information practice framework to clinical midwifery. McKenzie and Stooke[76] also analyzed a public library storytime from a collectivist perspective, concluding that the approach enables the researcher to begin connecting the actions of individuals to those of social actors in other contexts. In her study of the information seeking accounts of pregnant women, McKenzie identifies four modes of information practices that she describes as operating on a continuum: "active seeking," "active scanning," "nondirected monitoring," and "by proxy."[77] The first mode, as its title implies, is purposive, directed and planned information seeking. "Active scanning" would include practices in which the individual browses or scans materials or locations which are likely to offer information. McKenzie states that the third mode of information practice "…involves serendipitously encountering and recognizing a source…in an unlikely place, while not seeking information at all…or while monitoring information sources…with no intent other than to become generally informed." The final information practice mode in McKenzie's model is described as "by proxy" and includes a variety of incidents when an individual would obtain information through the intervention of an external agent or intermediary.

In 2007, McKenzie and Talja edited an issue of *Library Quarterly* (Vol. 77, No. 2), devoted to *Discursive Approaches to Information Seeking in Context*, with articles exploring topics related to communication, information literacy, and work and professional practices. Contributors included Savolainen,[11] with his comparison of cognitive and discursive metatheories, as well as various authors applying information practice to different information contexts. Park[78] analyzed a chat group's textual output to examine communication in an online environment. Veinot[69] focused on a case study of the blue-collar work world of an individual vault inspector at a hydroelectric utility company, using information practice as a framework for exploration of an individual's work role. Lloyd[8] applied information practice to the role of information literacy and workplace learning among firefighters in Australia, in which the process of increasing information literacy required interaction of various textual and personal constructions of collective practice. Having previously explored discourse in various other pieces individually, with others, and together,[79,80] Johannisson and

Sundin[81] examined embedded discourses in the nursing community of practice that produce a professional identity for this issue of *Library Quarterly*. Olsson[82] investigated the relationships among author, text, reader, and researcher for Brenda Dervin as an author in LIS discourse, following on from previous work on this topic mentioned earlier[10] and having presented this entry at the *ASIS&T annual conference* in 2005.[83] Although individuals have previously published about information practice in various venues, this issue of *Library Quarterly* is significant for publishing several pieces on this subject in a single collection.

In more recent times, the authors have found a number of studies that either are grounded in a theoretical IP position[12,63,69,84,85] or mention information practice(s) as an element of information behavior generally. The latter adopt an IB perspective and then describe practices that they categorize as part of the holistic information behaviors of those people they are studying.[1–4,84–87] Of particular interest are Meyer's[2] study of cross sociocultural information exchange with regard to developing communities that explores further Chatman's theory of small worlds, as well as Webber's[4] and Huvila et al.'s[1] investigations of the information behavior of individuals in "Second Lives" (SL), considering the rules and practices within this virtual reality that determine participants' active and passive information behaviors. From his work researching family photography, Cox[14] argues that it is important for theorists and practitioners to engage in discussion about the use of practice theories to understand LIS as a social science. However, he also suggests perhaps a more pragmatic approach (i.e., "information in social practice") stating:

> …information activities are woven through all social practices, and this is even more evident today through ubiquitous access to information resources through the internet. Thus we need to look at the information aspect of all social practices. Escaping a narrow preoccupation with goal-oriented information, we need to first ask within any practice what, for social actors, constitutes information, and then how do they find, use, create and share it[14] (p. 185).

CONCLUSION: OPPORTUNITIES AND THEORETICAL PATHWAYS

It has been clearly established[5] that IB is not fixated unilaterally on the cognitive dimensions of human being interactions with information,[25,28] (etc.). Early models of human information behavior have firmly placed context at the core. The context includes the social dynamic that includes those customs, rules, attitudes, and vernaculars that comprise the multifaceted life worlds of each individual, experienced through their work, their membership in a community and in their personal lives and familial histories. Equally, the unique individuality of the person contributes to the context. These elements not only dictate and determine the individual's information needs but as well direct the manner in which a person goes about finding information and subsequently how they use (or do not use) the information.

Rather than looking for ways to destabilize preliminary theory building semantically in this relatively new field in the social sciences, perhaps the way forward should be exploring the different perspectives of how to study, research, and think about human information behavior with a priority on the context.

The IP argument has and continues to be helpful in that it has provided a basis for scholars to explore further a multidisciplinary perspective in LIS. A pertinent and well-reasoned example would be Lloyd's work[63] in applying Schatzki's site theory to information literacy practices. This type of work is to be welcomed in contributing to theory building. Equally, the IP stance and literature has fuelled others to challenge their discourse, with regard to everyday life information seeking and behavior to consider and reconceptualize the ways in which people engage, or do not engage, with information.[13]

The different approaches described in this entry are "fluid and complementary," contributing to both practical and theoretical applications in LIS. Information practice offers a different approach to understanding information behavior. Although Savolainen[11] argues that, while the cognitive approach has been the dominant discourse in LIS until recently, information practice "must be the primary discourse of LIS" in the future to enable understanding of everyday information worlds, the two perspectives continue to function in parallel in practice. For example, proponents of each approach present varying conceptual approaches in the recent text, *Theories of Information Behavior*,[88] which takes information behavior as its umbrella concept. Similarly, researchers interested in information behavior and information practice participate together in events, such as the SIG USE connected with the ASIS&T, as well as the ISIC conference, supporting the notion and feasibility of co-existence. Advocates of the information practice approach credit some of these venues, such as ISIC, as the beginning of the rise of this rival umbrella concept.[62] For the moment, at least, scholarship seems engaged in an exploration of new possibilities offered by different conceptual approaches.

The range of theoretical approaches offers a variety of choices to researchers exploring behaviors surrounding information. Each contributes to the scientific rigor of our research and the practical value of our efforts in delivering information services. Olsson[82] offers several potentially fruitful areas of development, for example, Foucault's ideas about power offer inspiration in exploring the relationship between power and information behavior. Other potential areas include nonpurposive information behavior, which remains largely unexplored, as well as a refocus on user expertise rather than knowledge gaps.[82]

While some advocate separation and re-boxing of areas, perhaps the perspectives noted herein actually form an evolving continuum, along which a broad field of information behavior has emerged and from which we can draw upon to maximum benefit in our research. Olsson[82] proposes an exciting future for the development of the field of information behavior, in which we can further Dervin and Nilan's[89] call for a more holistic approach, noting "rather than conceiving of information behavior as being driven by the desire to satisfy discrete information needs, any information interaction or encounter should be seen as one chapter in an individual's ongoing engagement with, and construction of, their lifeworld."

REFERENCES

1. Huvila, I.; Ek, S.; Widen, G. Information sharing and the dimensions of social capital in second life. J. Inf. Sci. **2014**, *40* (2), 237–248.
2. Meyer, H.W.J. The influence of information behaviour on information sharing across cultural boundaries in development contexts. Inf. Res. **2009**, *14* (1), paper 393. http://InformationR.net/ir/14-1/paper393.html.
3. von Thaden, T.L. Building a foundation to study distributed information behaviour. Inf. Res. **2007**, *12* (3), paper 312. http://InformationR.net/ir/12-3/paper312.html.
4. Webber, S. Blended information behaviour in second life. J. Inf. Sci. **2013**, *39* (1), 85–100.
5. Wilson, T.D. Models in information behaviour research. J. Doc. **1999**, *55* (3), 249–270.
6. About SIG USE, http://siguse.wordpress.com/about.
7. Fulton, C. Introduction to special section. A decade of SIG/USE: celebrating SIG/USE and information behavior research. Bull. ASIS&T **2010**, *36* (3), 24–26. http://www.asis.org/Bulletin/Feb-10/FebMar10_Fulton.html.
8. Lloyd, A. Learning to put out the red stuff: becoming information literate through discursive practice. Libr. Q. **2007**, *77* (2), 181–198.
9. McKenzie, P.J. A model of information practices in accounts of everyday life information seeking. J. Doc. **2003**, *59* (1), 19–40.
10. Olsson, M. Meaning and authority: the social construction of an 'author' among information behavior researchers. Inf. Res. **2005**, *10* (2), paper 219. http://InformationR.net/ir/10-2/paper219.html.
11. Savolainen, R. Information behavior and information practice: reviewing the "umbrella concepts" of information-seeking studies. Libr. Q. **2007**, *77* (2), 109–132.
12. Bystrom, K.; Lloyd, A. Practice theory and work task performance: how are they related and how can they contribute to a study of information practices. Annual Meeting

of Association for Information Science and Technology (ASIS&T) 2012, Baltimore, MD, October 28–31, 2012.

13. Cox, A.M. An exploration of the practice approach and its place in information science. J. Inf. Sci. **2012**, *38* (2), 176–188.

14. Cox, A.M. Information in social practice: a practice approach to understanding information activities in personal photography. J. Inf. Sci. **2013**, *39* (1), 61–72.

15. The behaviour/practice debate: a discussion prompted by Tom Wilson's review of Reijo Savolainen's everyday information practices: a social phenomenological perspective. Scarecrow Press: Lanham, MD, 2008. Inf. Res. **2009**, *14* (2), paper 403, 25 May, 2009. http://InformationR.net/ir/14-2/paper403.html.

16. Savolainen, R. Homepage. http://people.uta.fi/~liresa.

17. Olsson, M. Homepage. http://www.uts.edu.au/staff/michael.olsson.

18. Schatzki, T.R. *The Site of the Social: A Philosophical Account of the Constitution of Social Life and Change*; Pennsylvania State University Press: University Park, PA, 2002.

19. Talja, S.; Tuominen, K.; Savolainen, R. "Isms" in information studies: constructivism, collectivism and constructionism. J. Doc. **2005**, *61* (1), 93.

20. Belkin, N.J.; Oddy, R.N.; Brooks, H.M. ASK for information retrieval, Part I: background and theory. J. Doc. **1982**, *38*, 61–71.

21. Brookes, B.C. The foundations of information studies, Part I: philosophical aspects. J. Inf. Stud. **1980**, *2* (3–4), 125–133.

22. Ingwersen, P. Search procedures in the library: analysed from the cognitive point of view. J. Doc. **1982**, *38* (3), 165–191.

23. Dewey, J. *How We Think: A Restatement of the Relation of Reflective Thinking to the Education Process*; D.C. Heath and Company: Boston, MA, 1933.

24. Kelly, G. *A Theory of Personality: The Psychology of Personal Constructs*; Norton: New York, 1963.

25. Dervin, B. An overview of sense-making research: concepts, methods, and results to date. Paper presented at the Annual Meeting of the International Communication Association, Dallas, TX, 1983.

26. Dervin, B. On studying information seeking methodology: the implications of connecting metatheory to method. Inf. Process. Manag. **1999**, *35*, 727–750.

27. Ellis, D. A behavioural approach to information retrieval system design. J. Doc. **1989**, *45* (3), 171–212.

28. Kuhlthau, C.C. *Teaching the Library Research Process: A Step by Step Program for Secondary Students*; West Nyack, NY: Center for Applied Research in Education, 1985.

29. Wilson, T.D. Information behavior: an interdisciplinary perspective. Information processing and management **1997**, *33* (4), 39.

30. Capurro, R.; Vakkari, P.; Cronin, B. What is information science for? A philosophical reflection. In *Conceptions of Library and Information Science: Historical, Empirical and Theoretical Perspectives*; Taylor Graham: London, U.K., 1992; 82–96.

31. Talja, S. Constituting "information" and "user" as research objects: a theory of knowledge formations as an alternative to the information man—theory. In *Information Seeking in Context: Proceedings of an International Conference on Research in Information Needs, Seeking and Use in Different Contexts, 14–16 August, 1996, Tampere, Finland*; Vakkari, P., Savolainen, R., Dervin, B., Eds.; Taylor Graham: London, U.K., 1997; 67–80.

32. Tuominen, K.; Savolainen, R. A social constructionist approach to the study of information use as discursive action. In *Information Seeking in Context: Proceedings of an International Conference on Research in Information Needs, Seeking and Use in Different Contexts, 14–16 August, 1996, Tampere, Finland*; Vakkari, P., Savolainen, R., Dervin, B., Eds.; Taylor Graham: London, U.K., 1997. 81–96.

33. Talja, S.; Keso, H.; Pietilainen, T. The production of context in information seeking research: a metatheoretical view. Inf. Process. Manag. **1999**, *35*, 751–756.

34. Vygotsky, L. *Mind in Society*; Harvard University Press: Cambridge, MA, 1978.

35. Hjorland, B.; Albrechtsen, H. Toward a new horizon in information science: domain analysis. J. Am. Assoc. Inf. Sci. **1999**, *46* (6), 412.

36. Fry, J. Scholarly research and information practices: a domain analytic approach. Inf. Process. Manag. **2006**, *42*, 299–313.

37. Orlikowski, W.J. Knowing in practice: enacting a collective capability in distributive organizing. Organ. Sci. **2002**, *13* (3), 249–273.

38. Palmer, C.L. Structures and strategies of interdisciplinary science. J. Am. Soc. Inf. Sci. **1999**, *50* (3), 242–253.

39. Wenger, E. *Communities of Practice: Learning, Meaning, and Identity*; Cambridge University Press: Cambridge, U.K., 1998.

40. Buschman, J. Transgression or stasis? Challenging Foucault in LIS theory. Libr. Q. **2007**, *77* (1), 30–34.

41. Foucault, M. *The Archeology of Knowledge and the Discourse on Language*; Pantheon: New York, 1972.

42. Frohmann, B. Discourse and documentation: some implications for pedagogy and research. J. Libr. Inf. Sci. Educ. **2001**, *42*, 13–28.

43. Frohmann, B. Discourse analysis as a research method. Libr. Inf. Sci. Res. **2004**, *16* (2), 119–138.

44. Radford, G.P. Positivism, Foucault, and the Fantasia of the library: conceptions of knowledge and the modern library experience. Libr. Q. **1992**, *62*, 408–424.

45. Radford, G.P. Trapped in our own discourse formulations: toward an archaeology of library and information science. Libr. Q. **2003**, *73* (1), 1–18.

46. Volosinov, V. *Marxism and Literature*; Harvard University Press: Cambridge, MA, 1986.

47. Bakhtin, M.M. *The Dialogic Imagination: Four Essays*; University of Texas Press: Austin, TX, 1981.

48. Garfinkel, H. *Studies in Ethnomethodology*; Prentice-Hall: Englewood Cliffs, NJ, 1967.

49. Wiegand, W.A. Tunnel vision and blind spots: what the past tells us about the present; Reflections on the twentieth-century history of American librarianship. Libr. Q. **1999**, *69* (1), 1–32.

50. Talja, S.; McKenzie, P.J. Editors' introduction: special issue on discursive approaches to information seeking in context. Libr. Q. **2007**, *77* (2), 97–108.

51. Savolainen, R. *Everyday Information Practices: A Social Phenomenological Perspective*; Scarecrow Press: Lanham, MD, 2008.

52. Paisley, W. Information needs and uses. Annu. Rev. Inf. Sci. Technol. **1968**, *3*, 1–30.

53. Wilson, T.D. On user studies and information needs. J. Doc. **1981**, *37* (1), 3–15.

54. Wilson, T.D. Information needs and uses: fifty years of progress. In *Fifty Years of Information Progress: A Journal of Documentation Review*; Vickery, B.C., Ed.; ASLIB: London, U.K., 1994; 15–51.

55. Bates, M. An introduction to metatheories, theories, and models. In *Theories of Information Behavior*; Fisher, K., Erdelez, S., McKechnie, L., Eds.; Information Today: Medford, NJ, 2005; 1–24.

56. Chatman, E.A. A theory of life in the round. J. Am. Soc. Inf. Sci. **1999**, *50*, 207–217.

57. Chatman, E.A. Framing social life in theory and research. New Rev. Inf. Behav. Res. **2000**, *1*, 3–17.

58. Sonnenwald, D.H. Evolving perspectives of human information behaviour: contexts, situations, social networks and information horizons. In *Exploring the Contexts of Information Behaviour: Proceedings of the Second International Conference in Information Needs, Seeking and Use in Different Contexts, 13–15 August Sheffield, UK*; Wilson, T.D., Allen, D.K., Eds.; Taylor Graham. London, U.K., 1999. 176–190.

59. Krikelas, J. Information-seeking behavior: patterns and concepts. Drexel Libr. Q. **1983**, *19*, 5–20.

60. Henefer, J.; Fulton, C. Krikelas's model of information seeking. In *Theories of Information Behavior*; Fisher, K., Erdelez, S., McKechnie, L., Eds.; Information Today: Medford, NJ, 2005; 225–229.

61. Kuhlthau, C. Students and the information search process: zones of interventions for librarians. Adv. Libr. **1994**, *18*, 57–72.

62. Dervin, B. Given a context by any other name: methodological tools for taming the unruly beast. In *Information Seeking in Context: Proceedings of an International Conference on Research in Information Needs, Seeking and Use in Different Contexts, 14–16 August, 1996, Tampere, Finland*; Vakkari, P., Savolainen, R., Dervin, B., Eds.; Taylor Graham: London, U.K., 1997; 13–38.

63. Lloyd, A. Framing information literacy as information practice: site ontology and practice theory. J. Doc. **2010**, *66* (2), 245–258. http://dx.doi.org/10.1108/00220411011023643.

64. Schatzki, T. Introduction: practice theory. In *The Practice Turn in Contemporary Theory*; Schatzki, T., Knorr Cetina, K., von Savigny, E., Eds.; Routledge: London, U.K., 2001.

65. Huizing, A.; Cavanagh, M. Planting contemporary practice theory in the garden of information science. Inf. Res. **2011**, *16* (4), paper 497. http://InformationR.net/ir/16-4/paper497.html.

66. Lloyd, A. Trapped between a rock and hard place: what counts as information literacy in the workplace and how LIS is conceptualized. Libr. Trends **2011**, *60* (2), 277–296.

67. Corraid, G.; Gherardi, S.; Verzelloni, L. Through the practice lens: where is the Bandwagon of practice-based studies heading? Manag. Learn. **2010**, *41* (3), 265–283.

68. Tuominen, K.; Talja, S.; Savolainen, R. The social constructionist viewpoint on information practices. In *Theories of Information Behavior*; Fisher, K., Erdelez, S., McKechnie, L., Eds.; Information Today: Medford, NJ, 2005; 328–333.

69. Veinot, T.C. "The eyes of the power company": workplace information practices of a vault inspector. Libr. Q. **2007**, *77* (2), 157–180.

70. Harris, M. Review of Michel Foucault, by Didier Eribon. Libr. Q. **1993**, *63* (1), 115–116.

71. Olsson, M.R. All the world's a stage—the information practices and sense-making of theatre professionals. Libri **2010**, *60* (3), 241–251.

72. Olsson, M.R. Gently to hear, kindly to judge: the affective information practices of theatre professionals and journalists untitled publication. In *Information Research, Proceedings of the Eighth International Conference on Conceptions of Library and Information Science, Copenhagen, Denmark, August 2013*; Nicolaisen, J., Eds.; University of Sheffield, Sheffield, U.K., 2013; 1–12.

73. Olsson, M.R.; Heizmann, H.K.; Yerbury, H. Knowledge management: a practice-based perspective. In *Active Citizenship by Knowledge, Management & Innovation. Proceedings of the Management, Knowledge, and Learning International Conference 2013, Zadar, Croatia, June 2013*; Dermol, V., Trunk Sirca, N., Dakovic, G., Eds.; ToKnowPress: Bangkok, Thailand, 2013; 525–532.

74. Lloyd, A.; Talja, S. *Practising Information Literacy: Bringing Theories of Learning, Practice and Information Literacy Together*; Centre for Information Studies, Charles Sturt University: Wagga Wagga, New South Wales, Australia, 2010.

75. McKenzie, P.J. Mapping textually-mediated information practice in clinical midwifery care. In *New Directions in Human Information Behavior*; Spink, A., Cole, C., Eds.; Springer: New York, 2006; 73–92.

76. McKenzie, P.J.; Stooke, R.K. Producing storytime: a collectivist analysis of work in a complex communicative space. Libr. Q. **2007**, *77* (1), 3–20.

77. McKenzie, P.J. Negotiating authoritative knowledge: information practices across a life transition. Doctoral dissertation, University of Western Ontario: London, Ontario, Canada, 2001.

78. Park, J. Interpersonal and affective communication in synchronous online discourse. Libr. Q. **2007**, *77* (2), 133–156.

79. Hedemark, Å.; Hedman, J.; Sundin, O. Speaking of users: on user discourses in the field of public libraries. Inf. Res. **2005**, *10* (2), paper 218. http://InformationR.net/ir/10-2/paper218.html.

80. Sundin, O.; Johannison, J. Pragmatism, neo-pragmatism and sociocultural theory: communicative participation as a perspective in LIS. J. Doc. **2005**, *61* (1), 23–43.

81. Johannisson, J.; Sundin, O. Putting discourse to work: information practices and the professional project of nurses. Libr. Q. **2007**, *77* (2), 199–218.

82. Olsson, M. Power/knowledge: the discursive construction of an author. Libr. Q. **2007**, *77* (2), 219–240.

83. Olsson, M. Beyond "needy" individuals: conceptualizing information behavior as a social construct. Paper presented at the *American Society for Information Science and Technology (ASIS&T) Annual Conference*, Charlotte, North Carolina, October 28–November 2, 2005. Abstract available at: http://www.asis.org/Conferences/AM05/abstracts/61.html.

84. Pilerot, O. A practice theoretical exploration of information sharing and trust in a dispersed community of design scholars. Inf. Res. **2013**, *18* (4), paper 595. http://InformationR.net/ir/18-4/paper595.html.

85. Rivera, G.; Cox, A. An evaluation of the practice based approach to understanding the adoption and use of information systems. J. Doc. **2014**, *70* (5), 878–901.

86. Smiljana, A.; Cahoy, E.S. Personal library curation: an ethnographic study of scholars' information practices. Libr. Acad. **2014**, *14* (2), 287–306.

87. Nathan, L.P. Sustainable information practice: an ethnographic investigation. J. Am. Soc. Inf. Sci. Technol. **2012**, *63* (11), 2254–2268.

88. Fisher, K.; Erdelez, S.; McKechnie, L. *Theories of Information Behavior*; Information Today: Medford, NJ, 2005.

89. Dervin, B.; Nilan, M. Information needs and uses. Ann. Rev. Inf. Sci. Technol. **1986**, *21*, 3–33.

Information Retrieval Experimentation *[ELIS Classic]*

Jean Tague-Sutcliffe
Graduate School of Library and Information Science, University of Western Ontario, London, Ontario, Canada

Abstract

Jean Tague-Sutcliffe was an important figure in information retrieval experimentation. Here, she reviews the history of IR research, and provides a description of the fundamental paradigm of information retrieval experimentation that continues to dominate the field.

—ELIS Classic, from 1996

INTRODUCTION

Information retrieval, the searching through collection of printed or electronic natural language material for items that may satisfy some individual's need or curiosity, has always been a core activity of information professionals. Research into the best way to carry out this activity has been a concern of information science since the field arose in the 1950s.

Information retrieval research belongs to the paradigm of empirical research. Theories are developed about the primary characteristics and relationships of the components of an information retrieval process. Hypotheses are developed about the effect of one or more factors, characteristics, or approaches (the independent variables) on the outcome of the process (the dependent variables). In experimentation, as opposed to other kinds of empirical research such as surveys, there is some control of the independent variable in order to determine the resulting change in the dependent variable.

Some of the components of an information retrieval process, as viewed by information retrieval researchers, are the collection or database that is being searched, the users, the query or verbalization of the user's need or interest, the searchers (end users or intermediaries), the search strategies or ways of searching to satisfy the user, the form of the output from a search, and the way the output is evaluated as to relevance or utility to the user. Each component can usually be further described by a number of characteristics that may vary and that may thus serve as independent variables in an experiment.

In a true laboratory experiment, all of the independent variables and other factors that might affect the outcomes are under the control of the experimenter. In an operational test, at least some will be determined by the operational setting. Some writers would restrict the word *experiment* to the laboratory setting. However, in information retrieval research, there is really a spectrum of researcher control, from situations in which database, searchers, queries, search strategies, and output are all controlled by the experimenter, to situations in which some components are controlled and others are not, to situations in which only one component is controlled. In this entry, we will consider all situations in which there is control of at least one independent variable.

In any information retrieval experiment, the researcher will use databases and develop search strategies and forms of output that embody the variable features, the hypotheses, that he or she is investigating. In a laboratory experiment, all other aspects of the retrieval process will be held constant. At one time, information retrieval researchers ensured an even greater control by creating artificial queries and relevance determinations. A number of test collections of documents and queries with predetermined relevance assessments were developed and used to test a variety of hypotheses. The predominant present-day view of information retrieval, however, is that queries must represent real user needs and that the end user can best determine the relevance or utility of the output with respect to this need.

The advantage of a laboratory experiment is that the control of extraneous sources of variation makes it possible to draw conclusions about the effect of the features under investigation in terms that are not limited to the particular situation in which the retrieval took place. In operational tests, it is not always possible to conclude that the features under investigation really caused the observed results because there are so many uncontrolled sources of variation. However, laboratory tests have their disadvantages: they are expensive to set up, and incorporating real users and queries in a laboratory environment is difficult. If the experimental database is small or if real users and queries are not employed, the results may not apply to operational systems. However, as Hull[1] and Salton[2] have pointed out, there is no reason to disallow experiments with small experimental systems unless specific biases can be demonstrated.

Encyclopedia of Library and Information Sciences, Fourth Edition DOI: 10.1081/E-ELIS4-120044772

The situation is not really one of "either/or" but of "both." Robertson and Hancock-Beaulieu[3] suggest that given the complexity of present-day information retrieval systems and the need to take user characteristics into account, the best solution is a facility intermediate between a laboratory and an operational environment. Called the evaluative facility, this would use real users, queries, and databases, but provide capabilities for easy modification of query and document representations and extensive data gathering and analysis.

Many different features of information retrieval systems have been evaluated in information retrieval research. Most attention has been paid to the way items are represented in the database and the way searches are carried out. In early experiments, the database usually consisted of a set of document surrogates, records that referenced, indexed, and abstracted printed documents outside the system. In more recent times, databases may consist of full-text documents or even hypertext or hypermedia documents, in which the user peruses the document via links, rather than in a predetermined sequence.

The ways in which information is represented in the database and the search strategies are closely related. This relationship can be described by an information system model. A number of these have been developed, the most prominent being the Boolean model and the vector space model. Much information retrieval experimentation has focused on aspects of these two models or on comparisons of the two.

In the Boolean model, the documents in the database are represented as sets of index headings, keywords, or descriptors (called *terms*), possibly with field delimiters such as author, title, abstract, and journal source. Search strategies consist of Boolean expressions involving these terms, possibly delimited, and the Boolean operators "and," "or," and "not." For example, the search expression "interface and (database or information)" would retrieve documents containing the term *interface* and either *database* or *information*. The output from a Boolean model system is a set of retrieved documents.

In the vector space model, both documents and queries are represented as sequences or vectors of weights, one for each term in the database. The weight is a number, usually between zero and one, that indicates the importance of the term in the document or query. Search strategies determine the similarity of document and query using these weights and output documents ranked by this similarity value.

PERFORMANCE MEASURES

A number of performance measures have been used by information retrieval researchers as a basis for comparing different systems features. The best known are recall and precision, originally suggested by Perry et al.[4] in 1956.

They are based on the idea that the purpose of a retrieval system is to present the users with all and only those documents that are relevant to their information needs. Recall is the proportion of the documents relevant to the user that are retrieved by the search. Precision (originally called pertinency) is the proportion of the documents retrieved by the search that are relevant to the user. Both recall and precision represent properties that are important to the user, however, they assume that the user can unambiguously identify relevant documents for an information need, an assumption that has been questioned by a number of investigators, for example Saracevic.[5]

Relevance may not be a binary variable; some investigators have used a ternary scale (relevant, partially relevant, not relevant), others an ordinal scale (i.e., documents are ranked as to relevance), and still others a continuous scale. A distinction is often made between subject relevance (aboutness) and usefulness (pertinence), although Regazzi[6] found experimental evidence of no difference in subjective judgments of subject relevance and utility. Some investigators believe that relevance requires assessment by the end user, the person with the information need, although Burgin[7] found that variations in relevance judgments by four judges did not affect retrieval performance. Finally, Schamber et al.[8] suggest that the relevance of a document is situational and dynamic in that it depends on what the user has already seen.

Despite these difficulties, binary relevance-based values continue to be the basis for evaluation of information retrieval features. Recall and precision are sometimes supplemented with fallout, defined as the proportion of nonrelevant documents that are retrieved. Fallout provides additional evaluative information, as it is sensitive to the size of the collection. For example, a search of a 1,000- and a 1 million-document database could produce the same recall and precision values. However, the search of the 1 million-document database would clearly be superior in terms of discriminating power, and this fact would be evident in the two fallout values.

In some retrieval experiments, performance measures reflect aspects of the retrieval process other than search effectiveness. The efficiency of the data structures and processing algorithms may be measured by such temporal variables as user connect time or number of disk accesses. In experiments concerned with features of the user-system interface, user friendliness may be assessed via user rating scales or more objective criteria such as length of learning time or number of exasperation responses or terminations.

Subjective ratings of overall system success are seen by some investigators (e.g., Su[9]) as being superior to the more objective measures of recall and precision. However, system success is an even more elusive concept to define than relevance, and in most studies in which it is recorded, shows very little variation over users or features. Thus, it can rarely be used in an experimental setting to discriminate good performance from bad.

Hypertext and other interactive full-text systems have complicated the evaluation problem. Users follow search trails, rather than receiving sets of retrieved items. Tague-Sutcliffe[10] suggests that evaluation should compare the actual search trail with an "ideal" one for the user. Ways of describing user actions become important in evaluating information retrieval systems; for example, Qiu[11] suggests that user trails can be described as Markov processes, sequences of search states with certain probabilistic dependencies.

MAJOR INFORMATION RETRIEVAL EXPERIMENTS

Information retrieval experimentation is usually considered to have begun in the late 1950s with the Cranfield tests by Cyril Cleverdon.[12–14] In Cranfield I, a comparative evaluation was made of four systems: the universal decimal classification (UDC), a conventional alphabetical subject index, a facet classification, and Uniterm (keyword) coordinate indexing. During the test, 18,000 papers in the field of aeronautical engineering were indexed by each of the four systems, and 1,200 search questions were obtained from several hundred individuals for questions based on a single document. The search was considered successful if that document was retrieved. The results showed all four systems retrieved the required paper in 74–88% of the cases, with the Uniterm system scoring the highest and faceted classification the lowest. Most failures were due to human error rather than the indexing system. A later comparison with the computer-based metallurgical index at Western Reserve University,[14] which employed sophisticated language analysis features (role indicators and semantic factors), showed that the performance of the new system was not equal to that of the four original systems.

Cranfield II, also carried out by Cleverdon, sought to determine the effect of specific recall-increasing and precision-increasing devices in a laboratory setting. Questions were obtained from 200 authors of recently published papers who were asked to provide questions to which their paper would be an answer. A test collection of 1,400 documents and 279 questions were obtained in this way. The indexing languages evaluated consisted of single terms selected from the natural language of the document, alone or combined with various devices such as synonyms, word form variants, quasi-synonyms, term weighting, links and roles, hierachical linking of terms, phrases, and controlled language terms. Ranked output was obtained by using ten coordination levels.

Indexing devices were evaluated by a single measure, normalized recall, which is essentially recall averaged over the points in the search where relevant documents are retrieved. The results showed that indexing based on single natural language terms, the simplest kind of indexing to implement, performed best by this criterion. The number of index terms assigned to documents, or exhaustivity, was also found to influence performance, with the optimal level being one of thirty-three terms.

Cleverdon,[12] speaking of these tests from a perspective of 30 years, notes that although he found the results of Cranfield II more significant than the earlier tests, "they did not arouse so much general comment, partly, I think, because the results were so unexpected as to appear unbelievable and also because the nature of the test removed it so far from normal experience." He also notes that the tests confirmed the hypothesis that there is an inverse relationship between recall and precision, so that there are no devices that concurrently increase both.

The Cranfield II test collection was subsequently used by two other information retrieval experimenters, Gerard Salton at Cornell University and Karen Sparck Jones at Cambridge University, Salton[2] has developed and used an experimental system, the Smart system, over a period of 30 years, to investigate a number of sophisticated approaches to information retrieval based on the vector space model and a ranked output. The earlier tests are described in Salton[15] and Salton and McGill,[16] and later ones in a series of papers, many of which are listed in the references to Salton's 1992 article.[2] Early results showed that weighted word stem indexing, where the stems are extracted from the document texts, was more effective than such sophisticated methods as phrases and classification hierarchies. A comparison with a subset of the Medlars search system at the National Library of Medicine, which uses a controlled vocabulary, showed that the Smart word stems increased recall by 12% and decreased precision by 9%.[17]

In recent years, the Smart collection has grown to approximately 50,000 documents distributed over six test collections. Each collection covers a different subject area, and queries and relevance assessments have been obtained from a number of different user populations. Improvements, as evaluated by precision averaged over standard recall levels, have been obtained through sophisticated term weighting procedures, relevance feedback techniques, and extended Boolean logic. The optimal term weighting in noninteractive retrieval was found to be a normalized function of the within document frequency divided by the across documents frequency. Relevance feedback is a process in which the results from an initial search, evaluated by the user, are used to supplement and reweight the original query terms to provide a revised query, which can then be used to search the database again. Extended Boolean retrieval includes a set of techniques that permit a ranking of documents retrieved by a Boolean search. Thus, it allows comparison of the output of Boolean and vector space systems.

Another early set of experiments in information retrieval was performed at Cambridge University by Karen Sparck Jones and Roger Needham. Here the interest was in automated classification, and a series of investigations as carried out[18,19] to discover why classification techniques did not prove in experiments to be as effective as simple keyword indexing. Despite a major series of tests concluded in 1976, Sparck Jones was unable to isolate the reasons for failure of classification to improve retrieval. It was at this point that she and Van Rijsbergen proposed the development of the ideal test collection[20] to provide a resource that could be used by the international information retrieval community to test new approaches to retrieval. Although the collection did not materialize at that point, the proposal provided the seed for the TREC tests of the 1990s.

In the 1980s, Tefko Saracevic, Paul Kantor, and others conducted a major series of information retrieval experiments at Case Western Reserve University.[21] These tests used a more operational environment than those just described; the aim of the study was to investigate the elements involved in information seeking and retrieving, particularly related to the cognitive and human decision-making context, in conditions as close to real life as possible.

Forty users were involved, each of whom submitted one question for searching, evaluated items retrieved as to relevance for this question, and provided other information via questionnaire and interview. Each question was searched by nine different searchers from a pool of thirty-nine searchers. Searching was done on DIALOG, with one database searched for each question. The analysis investigated the impact of a number of variables on precision and recall and on the odds that retrieved items were relevant as opposed to not relevant.

An interesting finding of the experiment related to the overlap in search terms used by different searchers. Based on 800 pairs of comparisons, the main overlap was only 27% in search terms and 18% in items retrieved. Items retrieved five or more times were over six times as likely to be relevant or partially relevant as items retrieved once. In general, the more often an item was retrieved by different searchers for the same question, the more likely it was to be relevant.

A number of statistically significant results were found in this study. These were presented in the form of an increase in the odds that (1) items retrieved in association with a given characteristic of a variable would be relevant or partially relevant as opposed to not relevant, and (2) searches associated with a given characteristic of a variable would be of high precision and recall, as opposed to low precision or recall. Recall, in this case, meant relative recall; that is, the proportion of the relevant documents found by any searcher that were found in one particular search for a question.

The following variables increased the indicated odds by a factor of at least two: placing a time limit on years searched increased precision odds; low subject specificity and high complexity in the question increased precision

odds; high searcher scores for abstractness over concreteness increased precision and recall odds; and finally, retrieval by four or more searchers increased relevance odds more than any other variable.

A challenge to the validity of results from a small database was presented by the Blair and Maron full-text evaluation of the 1980s.[22] They investigated the Boolean-based IBM STAIRS full-text document retrieval system by using it to search approximately 350,000 pages of text in a litigation support system. Some 51 queries were generated by two lawyers, who evaluated retrieved documents as relevant (vital, satisfactory, marginally relevant), or irrelevant. Searching was continued until the user stated that he or she was satisfied with the result and believed that at least 75% of the relevant documents had been retrieved. To find the unretrieved relevant documents, in order to estimate recall, the investigators generated samples of subsets of the database they believed to be rich in relevant documents. These samples were also evaluated by the users.

Average precision was 75.5% and average recall 20.3%. The investigators speculate that recall was low because "it is impossibly difficult for users to predict the exact word, word combinations, and phrases that are used by all (or most) relevant documents and *only* (or primarily) by these documents."[22] They suggest that previous results, based on small experimental databases, cannot be transferred to larger operational databases.

Partly in response to this concern that experiments must use realistically sized test collections, the TREC (Text Retrieval Conference) project was launched by Donna Harman in 1992, under the sponsorship of the U.S. National Institute of Standards and Technology and the U.S. Advanced Research Projects Agency. The purpose of the TREC project is to provide a forum in which researchers using a variety of approaches to information representation and retrieval can compare these approaches using a large collection of textual materials, queries and associated relevance judgments, and a uniform scoring procedure. TREC conferences were held in 1992, 1993, and 1994.

TREC is designed to evaluate both adhoc (one-time) querying and routing (filtering) searches. Participants work with approximately 1 million documents, retrieving lists of documents for fifty ad hoc and fifty routing queries. Queries may be automatically or manually constructed and may use relevance feedback. Test data consist of newspaper stories, Associated Press newswire entries, U.S. patent applications, entries from the *Federal Register*, the Ziff Computer Select database, and U.S. Department of the Environment abstracts.

The National Institute of Standards and Technology is responsible for the distribution of the test data, the evaluation of the outputs, and the analysis of the results. Relevance judgments are made by assessors at the institute of the top 100 documents from each participant for each query. Evaluation involves the calculation of precision at standard recall levels (0, .1, .2, .3, .4, .5, .6, .7, .8, .9, 1), precision at fixed numbers of retrieved documents (5, 10, 15, 20, 30, 100, 500, 1000), and two average precision values (over standard recall levels and over the first R retrievals, where R is the number of relevant documents for the query.

There were 25 participating systems in TREC-1 and each participant submitted ranked lists of the top 200 documents retrieved for each topic. Much of the participants' time was spent in organizing the large dataset, so that results were very preliminary in nature. Harman summarizes TREC-1 by saying:[23]

> it was clear that the simple systems did the task well, but it is too early to pass judgment on the more complicated systems. The automatic construction of queries from the topics did as well as, or better than manual construction of the queries, and this is encouraging for groups supporting the use of simple natural language interfaces for retrieval systems.

There were thirty participants in TREC-2 and each group submitted ranked lists of the top 1,000 documents retrieved for each query. In general, TREC-2 results showed an improvement in effectiveness over TREC-1, in part because of the submission of a larger number of retrieved documents (1,000 rather than 200) and in part because of participants' greater experience with the data and their systems.

Approaches in TREC-2 included probabilistic models, vector space models, natural language processing, Bayesian networks, query expansion, Boolean models, combinations of strategies, and document structuring. A preliminary report[24] notes that, as in TREC-2, the simple systems still did the best, but the more complex ones are catching up. Term weighting emerged as being especially important. Harman also notes a problem in looking solely at average measures: "there were 21 groups for which there was at least one topic on which their system had the best average precision."

The TREC tests are likely to continue to set the standard in information retrieval testing for the 1990s, however, it is also likely that more attention will be paid in the future to what is happening at the individual document-query level, using techniques such as failure analysis and analysis of passages (rather than documents) retrieved.

CURRENT RESEARCH CONCERNS

As we have seen, the two major concerns of past retrieval experimentation were first, how documents should be represented in a database, and second, how search strategies should be structured so as to retrieve all and only the relevant documents. These concerns continue to be the focus of much current information retrieval experimentation, as reflected in the *Proceedings of the ACM SIGIR International Conference on Research and Development in Information Retrieval* and other sources listed at the end of this entry.

Recent research has tended to investigate more complicated approaches than simple document-query keyword matching and to look at the interfaces and and special features needed for particular applications. In this entry, we will describe some recent work of particular interest, although it should be understood that this description represents a sampling only and is by no means complete.

A key aspect of the vector space model is the weighting of query terms. Robertson and Sparck Jones[25] introduced an important model, called the probabilistic model, for this weighting; term weights should represent the logarithm of the odds in favor of relevance over nonrelevance for documents indexed by the term. The technique of relevance feedback, in which the user evaluates as relevant or nonrelevant an initial set of documents, makes possible an estimate of these odds for the original and for new query terms. Harman[26] found in experiments on relevance feedback with the Cranfield collection that most improvements in retrieval using relevance feedback come from the addition of a limited number of new query terms. She also found that multiple iterations of feedback are very effective. Aalbersberg[27] notes that despite positive experimental results, relevance feedback has not been implemented in commercial systems because of the user friendliness problem. He suggests a "friendlier" approach (incremental relevance feedback), in which documents are retrieved one at a time and relevance judgments are made directly after documents are retrieved.

Many other experiments in recent years have addressed the problem of optimal methods of term weighting and query expansion. Keen[28] has experimented with document-ranking principles that are based on term position or the proximity of the query terms in the sentences of the document. He found that incorporating term position improved precision by 12–18%, depending on recall. Crouch and Yang[29] and Grefenstette[30] experimented with techniques for extending the querying by automatically generating thesaurus classes, lists of words related to the original query terms.

Despite the poor results that phrase-based indexing, as opposed to simple word retrieval, has produced in the past, a number of investigators have looked at more sophisticated ways of incorporating phrases into retrieval. Fagan[31] showed that incorporation of statistical phrases, defined by co-occurence and proximity of words, sometimes improved retrieval, but that imposing systactic constraints as well did not result in further improvements. Croft et al.[32] extend Fagan's work by incorporating weights that represent the importance of the phrase, as distinct from the individual terms, in the document and query.

Investigators continue to be concerned that retrieval is based on word stems rather than on concepts and have suggested various forms of analysis to overcome the "limitations" of uncontrolled word stem indexing. Linguistic analysis may be used to disambiguating word senses when a word may have more than one meaning. Voorhees[33] experimented with an automatic indexing procedure that uses WordNet, a thesaurus containing hierarchically organized sets of synonyms, to carry out this task. Thus, it permits the construction of vectors of word senses rather than word stems. Deerwester et al.[34] looked at latent semantic analysis, which permits documents to be represented by factors rather than terms. The factors are obtained as weighted combinations of the initial word stems.

Information retrieval systems are increasingly based on collections of full-text documents rather than document surrogates. Thus, the problem of passage retrieval, retrieving the passage or passages within a document that best answers a query, has become an important concern of information retrieval experiments. O'Connor[35] carried out experiments on passage retrieval in the 1970s. More recent work experiments have been done by Salton, Allen, and Buckley.[36] An interesting aspect here relates to the size of the text fragment that should be output and whether or not several text fragments should be combined in an "answer."

Boolean retrieval methods also continue to be investigated. Croft et al.[32] suggest that translating natural language queries into Boolean expressions using "and," "or," and "not" may be more effective than the vector space model of sets of weighted terms, and they have developed some experimental evidence for this statement. The work of Saracevic and Kantor[21] showed that different searchers tended to generate different strategies for the same query. Similarly, Turtle and Croft[37] found that combining natural language and Boolean combinations for the same query increased performance over either one alone. Belkin et al.[38] experimented with five independently generated Boolean query formulations and found that progressive combination of query formulations leads to progressively improving retrieval performance. Pao[39] found that using both term and citation searching on commercial databases improves recall and discrimination of relevant items.

In cluster-based retrieval, documents are grouped together on the basis of similarity in their term vectors. The expectation is that search time will be reduced by confining the search to a subset of clusters. Experiments with clustering have focused on optimal methods for their construction (see, e.g., Willett)[40] and on the question of their meaning; that is, if they represent meaningful groupings or if they are simply random collections of documents. Shaw[41] looked at evidence for clustering structure and the effectiveness of cluster-band retrieval and found an inverse relationship between them.

EXPERIMENTAL DESIGN AND ANALYSIS

In general terms, the problem in information retrieval is to assess the effects of one or more factors or independent variables on a performance measure by means of a sample of experimental units in which each unit is assigned to a combination of factor levels and measured as to performance. Experimental design is concerned with techniques for assigning the experimental units to the factor levels. In order to eliminate bias, it is essential that units be assigned randomly, and in order to assess interactions between variables, it is essential that more than one unit be assigned to combinations of factors.

Information retrieval experiments, the independent variables are the features of the database, the search strategies, the queries, and the users that we are investigating. Other factors relating to the search environment, such as the characteristics of the searcher, the order of searching, equipment problems, time, and temperature, may also affect the outcome and so should be randomized as much as possible over the factors that are of particular concern.

What constitutes an experimental unit in an information retrieval research design will depend on the purpose of the experiment, but in general it will be the smallest unit for which performance is measured. For example, an experimental unit might be a query, a search for documents relevant to the query using one particular strategy, a search using one particular strategy by one particular searcher, a single document retrieved in a search, or a step in a search process. Performance may be measured for each of these, depending on the kind of performance (query-level, strategy-level, searcher/strategy level, document-level, search-step-level).

In a minimal information retrieval experiment, there will be treatments (search strategies or indexing approaches) and queries. A major decision is whether or not to search different queries under the various treatments (independent samples) or repeatedly search each query under all treatments (repeated measures). The advantage of repeated measures is that variation in the difficulty of the query topics will not affect the overall results. The disadvantage is that there may be learning or fatigue effects (sequence effects) as a searcher repeats the same query using a different treatment. Different searchers may be used for each repetition; however, this will not be possible if searching is to be done by the end user.

To eliminate some of the variability among queries in the independent sample design a randomized block design may be used. Here the queries are separated into a number of blocks or groups of queries at approximately the same level of difficulty. Equal numbers of queries from each block are then assigned to the treatments and constitute independent samples. More complicated designs are used when there is more than one kind of treatment. Several of these are described in Tague-Sutcliffe.[42]

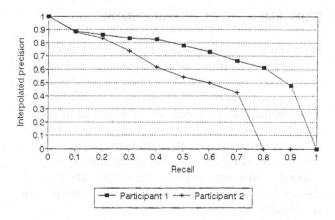

Fig. 1 Interpolated precision at standard recall levels.

Results of information retrieval experiments are usually presented in the form of averages of recall and precision values or, when output is ranked as with the vector-space model, in the form of recall-precision graphs. The most commonly used recall-precision graph shows interpolated precision values at standard recall values from zero to one. Another form shows precision at fixed numbers of retrieved documents. Both forms are shown in Figs. 1 and 2, which present these graphs for two of the participants in TREC-2.

Standard techniques of statistical analysis may be used to test hypotheses regarding differing effects of the treatments or factors in an information retrieval experiment. Analysis of variance may be used to compare mean performance scores for different treatments if the original scores satisfy the assumptions of this technique, namely approximate normality and equality of variance over treatment groups. If these assumptions are not met, then it may be necessary to transform the scores; in particular, it is often helpful to transform recall and precision scores by applying an aresine transformation to their square root in order to stabilize the variance. If performance scores do not satisfy the requirements of ANOVA, as would be the case if they were ordinal rather than quantitative,

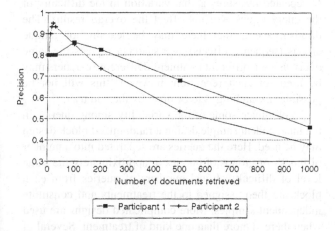

Fig. 2 Precision at retrieved document levels.

nonparametric statistical techniques are used. Hull[1] provides an overview of both classical and nonparametric techniques that may be used in analyzing results of information retrieval experiments.

FUTURE DIRECTIONS

As text and multimedia collections continue to grow worldwide, the core problem of information retrieval—to give the user all and only that information that he or she needs—remains to be solved and, indeed, may be unsolvable. Many subproblems remain, though, that are tractable, and information retrieval research is therefore unlikely to decline.

Some specific problems that have been identified by researchers in the field and that are amendable to the experimental approach are listed below:

- Under what conditions can results from small-scale experiments be applied to large operational systems?
- How can we model user behavior in interactive windowed information retrieval environments in such a way as to be able to use the model to improve retrieval systems?
- Using the Schamber et al.[8] dynamic situational view of relevance, how can we determine the document characteristics that should be in the system in order to satisfy this kind of relevance criteria?
- What kinds of experiments can be designed to improve the user interface to an information retrieval system?
- How can efficiency as well as effectiveness of information retrieval processes be investigated by information retrieval experiments?
- How can information retrieval experimental research have a greater impact on commercial systems development?
- Will Cranfield I ever be disproved?

SOURCES

The best source of information about current information retrieval experimentation is the *Proceedings of the ACM SIGIR International Conference on Research and Development in Information Retrieval*, published by the Association for Computing Machinery (ACM) Special Interest Group in Information Retrieval. Two other ACM publications frequently contain entries about information retrieval experiments: *Transactions on Information Systems* and *Communications of the ACM*. Information science journals such as *Information Processing and Management*, and the *Journal of Documentation* also publish experimental retrieval studies. The July-August 1992 issue of *Information Processing and Management* (vol. 28, no. 4), a special issue on evaluation issues in information retrieval, is particularly useful.

Only one book is exclusively devoted to information retrieval experiment: *Information Retrieval Experiment*; edited by Karen Sparck Jones (Butterworths, London, 1981). Despite the date, it still contains much valuable information. A good general introduction to information retrieval is *Information Retrieval: Data Structures and Algorithms*; edited by W. B. Frakes and R. Baeza-Yates (Prentice-Hall, Englewood Cliffs, N.J., 1992)[43].

REFERENCES

1. Hull, D. Using statistical testing in the evaluation of retrieval experiments. In Proceedings of the ACM SIGIR International Conference on Research and Development in Information Retrieval ACM: New York, 1993; 16, 329–338.
2. Salton, G. The state of retrieval system evaluation. Inform. Proc. Mgmt. **1992**, *28*(4), 441–450.
3. Robertson, S.E.; Hancock-Beaulieu, M.M. On the evaluation of IR systems. Inform. Proc. Mgmt. **1992**, *28*, 457–446.
4. Perry, J.W.; Kent, A.; Berry, M.M. Operational criteria for designing information retrieval systems,. *Machine Literature Searching*, Interscience: New York, 1956; Ch. 8.
5. Saracevic, T. Relevance: A review of and framework for thinking on the notion in information science. J. Am. Soc. Inform. Sci. **1975**, *26*, 321–343.
6. Regazzi, J. Performance measures for information retrieval. J. Am. Soc. Inform. Sci. **1988**, *39*(4), 235–251.
7. Burgin, R. Variations in relevance judgments and the evaluation of retrieval performance. Inform. Proc. Mgmt. **1992**, *28*(5), 619–628.
8. Shamber, L.; Eisenberg, M.; Nilan, M. A re-examination of relevance: Toward a dynamic, situational definition. Inform. Proc. Mgmt. **1990**, *26*(6), 755–776.
9. Su, L.T. The relevance of recall and precision in user evaluation. J. Am. Soc. Inform. Sci. **1994**, *45*(3), 207–217.
10. Tague-Sutcliffe, J. Measuring the informativeness of a retrieval process. In Proceedings of the ACM SIGIR International Conference on Research and Development in Information Retrieval ACM: New York, 1992; 15, 23–36.
11. Li, Q. Markov models of search state patterns in a hypertext information retrieval system. J. Am. Soc. Inform. Sci. **1993**, *44*(7), 413–427.
12. Cleverdon, C.W. *Report on the Testing and Analysis of an Investigation into the Comparative Efficiency of Indexing Systems*, College of Aeronautics: Cranfield, England, 1966, 2 vols.
13. Cleverdon, C.W. The significance of the Cranfield tests on index language. In Proceedings of the ACM SIGIR International Conference on Research and Development in Information Retrieval, 1991; 14, 3–13.
14. Aitchison, J. Cleverdon, C.W. *A Report on a Test of the Index of Metallurgical Literature of Western Reserve University*, College of Aeronautics: Crandfield, England, 1963.
15. In *The SMART Retrieval System: Experiments in Automatic Document Processing*; Salton, G., Ed.; Prentice-Hall: Englewood Cliffs, NJ, 1971.
16. Salton, G. McGill, J. The SMART and SIRE experimental retrieval systems.. In *Introduction to Modern Information Retrieval*, McGraw-Hill: New York, 1983; Chap. 4.
17. Salton, G. A new comparison between conventional indexing (MEDLARS) and automatic text processing (SMART). J. Am. Soc. Inform. Sci. **1972**, *23*, 75–84.
18. Sparck Jones, K. *Automatic Keyword Classification for Information Retrieval*, Butterworths: London, U.K., 1971.
19. Sparck Jones, K. A look back and a look onwards. In Proceedings of the ACM SIGIR International Conference on Research and Development in Information Retrieval ACM: New York, 1988; 11, 13–30.
20. Sarek Jones, K.; Van Rijsbergen, C.J. Information retrieval test collections. J. Doc. **1976**, *32*, 59–75.
21. Saracevic, T.; Kantor, P. et al. A study of information seeking and retrieving, I. Background and methodology, II. Users, questions, and effectiveness: III. Searchers, searchers, and overlap. J. Am. Soc. Inform. Sci. **1988**, *39*(3), 161–216.
22. Blair, D.; Maron, M.E. An evaluation of retrieval effectiveness for a full-text document-retrieval system. Commun. ACM. **1984**, *28*(3), 281–299.
23. Harman, D. An overview of the first text retrieval conference. In Proceedings of the ACM SIGIR International Conference on Research and Development in Information Retrieval, 1993; 16, 36–48.
24. TREC-2 Program Committee. Report on TREC-2 (Text Retrieval Conference) Gaithersburg, MD August, 30, 1993 September 2, SIGIR Forum, **1993**, *27*(3) 14–18.
25. Robertson, S.E.; Sparck Jones, K. Relevance weighting of search terms. J. Am. Soc. Inform. Sci. **1976**, *27*, 129–146.
26. Harman, D. Relevance feedback revisited. In Proceedings of the ACM SIGIR International Conference on Research and Development in Information Retrieval ACM: New York, 1992, 15, 1–10.
27. Aalbersberg, I.J. Incremental relevance feedback. In Proceedings of the ACM SIGIR International Conference on Research and Development in Information Retrieval, 1992, 14, 11–22.
28. Keen, E.M. Presenting results of experimental retrieval comparisons. Inform. Proc. Mgmt. **1992**, *28*, 491–502.
29. Crough, C.; Yang, B. Experiments in automatic statistical thesaurus construction. In Proceedings of the ACM SIGIR International Conference on Research and Development in Information Retrieval, 1992, 14, 77–88.
30. Grefenstette, G. Use of syntactic context to produce term association lists for text retrieval. In Proceedings of the ACM SIGIR International Conference on Research and Development in Information Retrieval, 1992, 14, 89–97.
31. Fagan, J. The effectiveness of a nonsysntactic approach to automatic phrase indexing for document retrieval. J. Am. Soc. Inform. Sci. **1989**, *40*, 115–132.
32. Croft, B.; Turtle, H.; Lewis, D. The use of phrases and structured queries in information retrieval. In Proceedings of the ACM SIGIR International Conference on Research and Development in Information Retrieval ACM: New York, 1991, 14, 32–45.

33. Voorhees, E. Using WordNet to disambiguate word senses for text retrieval. In Proceedings of the ACM SIGIR International Conference on Research and Development in Information Retrieval, 1993, 16, 171–180.

34. Deerwester, S. et al. Indexing by latent semantic analysis. J. Am. Soc. Inform. Sci. **1990**, *41*, 391–407.

35. O'Connor, J. Answer passage retrieval by text searching. J. Am. Soc. Inform. Sci. **1980**, *32*, 227–239.

36. Salton, G.; Allen, J.; Buckley, C. Approaches to passage retrieval in full text information systems. In Proceedings of the ACM SIGIR International Conference on Research and Development in Information Retrieval, 1993, 16, 49–58.

37. Turtle, H.; Croft, B. Evaluation of an inference network-based retrieval model. ACM Trans. Inform. Syst. **1991**, *9*, 187–222.

38. Belkin, N.; Cool, C.; Croft, B.; Callan, J. Effect of multiple query representations on information retrieval system performance. In Proceedings of the ACM SIGIR International Conference on Research and Development in Information Retrieval, 1993, 16, 339–346.

39. Pao, M. Term and citation retrieval: A field study. Inform. Proc. Mgmt. **1993**, *26*, 95–112.

40. Willett, P. Recent trends in hierarchic document clustering: A critical review. Inform. Proc. Mgmt. **1988**, *24*, 577–597.

41. Shaw, W.M., Jr. Subject indexing and citation indexing: Part 1, Clustering structure in the cystic fibrosis document collection; Part II, An evaluation and comparison. Inform. Proc. Mgmt. **1990**, *26*, 693–718.

42. Tague-Sutcliffe, J. The pragmatics of information retrieval experimentation, revisited. Inform. Proc. Mgmt. **1992**, *28*, 467–490.

Index

America Online (AOL), 2521
Amigos, 3922, 3924
Ammonite, *see* Snake stones
Amos Tuck School of Administration and
    Finance, 650
Anacostia Community Museum, 4192
Analytical bibliography, 477–478
Analytico-synthetic classification, 967, 971,
    4786
Anastosi I, 644
Anatolian University Library Consortium
    (ANKOS), 2829
Ancien Régime, 182
Ancient Greece, 999, 1460–1461, 1742, 1744,
    1788, 2677, 3831
Andrew Mellon Foundation, 372, 988
Anglo-American Cataloging Rules (AACR),
    449, 727, 2920–2921, 3062, 4144
Anglo-American Cataloguing Rules, 2nd ed.
    (AACR2), 137, 253, 453, 670,
    1230–1231, 1982–1983, 2921, 2923,
    3131, 3178, 3294, 3396, 4140–4141,
    4144
Anglo-American Cataloguing Rules 3rd ed.
    (AACR3), 670
*An Inquiry into the Wealth of Nations and
    Causes of the Wealth of Nations*, 646
Annales de Mathématiques Pures et Appliquées,
    3024, 3026
*Annales typographici ab artis inventae origine
    ad annum MDCLXIV*, 1968
ANNs, *see* Artificial neural networks
Annual fund, 2836–2837
Annual Meeting of the Document Academy
    (DOCAM), 1379
*Annual Review of Information Science and
    Technology* (ARIST), 312, 489
Anomalous state of knowledge (ASK), 2076,
    2118–2119, 2225, 4526–4527, 4874,
    4879
ANSI, *see* American National Standards
    Institute
ANSI/NISO Z39.50, 2983
Answer Garden (AG), 3865–3866
Anthropogeographie, 1687
Anthropological museum, Hungary, 1929–1930
Antiquarian book, 3820
Antiquarian Booksellers' Association of Amer-
    ica (ABAA), 4344, 4576, 4578, 4585,
    4588
Antiquarian Booksellers database, 4576
Antiquities Act of 1906, 4169
Antiquities Act of 1964, 4511
Antiquities of the Jews, 644
Apache Lucene IR system, 2204
Apache Project, 5025
Apollonios of Citium, 3043
Apologie, 1400
Appeal factors, 3700, 3705, 3850, 3857
Apple's HyperCard, 5023
Application ontologies, 3457
Application programming interfaces (APIs)
    FAST, 1545
    ILSs, 409
    ORCID, 3506–3508
Application Service Definition and Protocol
    Specification, 2983

Application service providers (ASPs), 698
Application software, 1056, 1333, 2272–2273,
    3650, 4805, 5034
Appraisal and selection process, 131
Apprentices' libraries, 1842
The Apprentice's time enterteiner accomptantly:
    *or a methodical means to obtain the
    equisite art of accomptantship*, 645
Approval plan
    history, 96–97
    profiles, 97–98
    transformation, 97
    vendors, 98
Apriori, 2631
Aquaria, 3238
Aquariums and zoological parks, 5077
    archives, 5083
    libraries
        current status and services, 5081–5083
        early libraries, establishment of, 5081
        need for, 5080–5081
    professional development
        animal collections, 5077
        captive wildlife management, 5077
        European collections, 5077–5078
        exotic wild animals, 5078
        modern aquariums, 5078
        modern zoological park management, 5077
        professional associations, 5078
        public aquarium, 5078
    professional literature, growth in, 5078–5080
Aquisitions Section (AS), 328
Arab Federation for Libraries and Information
    (AFLI), 100–101, 3978
    finance, 102
    honors and awards, 103–104
    location, 102
    membership, 101
    objectives, 101
    organizational structures, 101–102
    publications, 103
    relationships and cooperation, 103
    seminars and conferences, 102–103
    training and workshops, 103
Arabian Nights Entertainment, 853
Arabic Union Catalog, 3978
Arab Libraries Association, 100
*Arbetisgemeinschaft der Kunst-und Museumsbi-
    bliotheken* (AKMB), 255
Arboreta, 3238
Archaeological collections, curation of, *see*
    Curation, archaeological artifacts
Archaeological Conservancy, 1777
Archaeological museums
    in Croatia, 1129
    Hungary, 1929–1930
    in Israel, 2551
Archaeological Resources Protection Act
    (ARPA), 1774
Archaeological site museum, 4167–4168
Archie, 2517
Architecture, museum
    eighteenth century
        American Museum in Philadelphia, 3153
        Baroque design, 3152
        Belvedere sculpture court, 3151–3152
        Corinthian loggia, 3151

        courtyard plan, 3151
        curiosity/art cabinets, 3150
        exhibition spaces and galleries, 3151
        Galleria degli Uffizi in Florence, 3152
        Grande Galerie, 3152
        Greek cross, pattern of, 3151
        Inscriptiones vel tituli teatri amplissimi,
            3150–3151
        Louvre in Paris, 3152
        multifunctional institution, 3151
        Musei Capitolini in Rome, 3152
        Museo Nacional del Prado, 3152
        Museo Pio-Clementino, 3151–3152
        Museum Fridericianum, 3152
        neoclassical design, 3152–3153
        Newby Hall's gallery, 3151
        Pennsylvania Academy of the Fine Arts in
            Philadelphia, 3153
    nineteenth century
        Alte Pinakothek, 3153–3154
        Altes Museum, 3153
        Beaux-Arts method, 3153, 3156
        Belvedere statue court, 3154
        courtyard model, 3153–3154
        Dulwich Picture Gallery, 3154
        educational and training, 3155
        Glyptothek, 3153
        growth, specialization, and spatial concen-
            tration, 3154
        instructive decorations, 3155
        iron and glass structure, 3154–3155
        Neo-Gothic brick building, 3155
        Oxford University Museum, 3155
        shallow buildings, 3154
        South Kensington Museum, 3154–3155
        top lighting, 3154
        Victoria and Albert Museum, 3154–3155
    pre-eighteenth century
        arcaded perambulatories, 3149–3150
        Belvedere statue court, 3149
        centrally planned rooms, 3150
        circular and top-lit building, 3150
        curiosity/art cabinets, 3150
        galleries, 3150
        pinacotheca, 3149
        purpose-designed public museum, 3150
    twentieth century and beyond
        Akron Art Museum, 3158
        American metropolitan architecture, 3156
        Beaux-Arts inspired plan, 3156
        central foyer spaces, 3158
        historic museum buildings, 3157
        industrial buildings, 3157–3158
        Milwaukee Art Museum, 3158
        Modernism, 3156
        modernist glass box, 3156–3157
        Museo Civico di Castelvecchio, 3157
        Museo Guggenheim, Bilbao, 3158
        Museumsufer, 3157
        National Gallery of Art, 3156
        New York Museum of Modern Art,
            3157
        open museum concept, 3157
        Quadracci Pavilion, 3158
        Solomon R. Guggenheim Museum, 3156
Architecture of integrated information systems
    (ARIS), 632

Business literature
abstracting services, 652
accounting, 651
banking, finance, and investments, 651
Code of Hammurabi, 643
on computer operations, 652–653
cuneiform clay tablets, 643
in Egypt, 643–644
in England, 645–648
foreign trade, 652
France and Germany, publications in, 648
in Greece, 643–644
in late seventeenth century, 645–646
loose-leaf services, 652
marketing, sales management, and advertising, 651–652
newspaper indexes, 652
periodicals, 653
personnel and industrial relations, 651
professional associations, 651
public relations, 652
real estate and insurance, 651
during Romans, 644
schools of business, 650
scientific management studies
in Europe and United States, 650
list of books, 650–651
in sixteenth and seventeenth centuries, 645
statistics, 648–649
trade associations, publications of, 649–650
in United States, 647–649
in Venice and Florence, 644–645
Business magazines, 641
Business process reengineering (BPR), 2658, 3511
Business productivity software, 3650
Business Reference and Services Section (BRASS), 3909
Business Software Alliance (BSA), 3650–3651
Business Statistics, 649
Business Week, 650
Business writing, 4547–4548
Butterfly effect, 1036
Butter stamp, 540
Byzantine illumination, 1946–1947

C

Cabinets of curiosities, 1814
Cable Communications Policy Act, 1017
Cable Television Consumer Protection and Competition Act, 1017
Calcutta Public Library, 3326
Caldecott Committee, 334
Caldecott Medal, 334
Calendars, 133, 153, 170, 4084
California Digital Library, 1760
California Public Records Act, 1105
California's Meyers-Milias-Brown Act, 4690
California State University (CSU), 6, 9
Caliper Corporation, 1676
The Cambridge Crystallographic Data Centre, 822
Cambridge Structural Database (CSD), 822, 834
Cambridge Tracts in Mathematics and Mathematical Physics, 3028
Camel library, Kenya, 2595

Cameo binding, 543
CaMMS, *see* Cataloging and Metadata Management Section
Campbell Collaboration, 1519
Canada
broadcast archives, 1567
library and archives (*see* Library and Archives Canada)
Canada Institute for Scientific and Technical Information (CISTI), 660–661
Canadiana.org, 667
Canadian Association of Research Libraries (CARL), 659–660, 664–665
Canadian Broadcasting Company (CBC), 1567
Canadian Committee on Archival Description (CCAD), 670
Canadian Council of Archives (CCA), 666
Canadian Federation of Library Associations (CFLA), 665
Canadian Heritage Information Network (CHIN)
Artefacts Canada, 678
BCIN, 676
CIN, 676
international activities, 675–676, 679
knowledge exchange, 678
membership, 679–680
mission, 676–678
NIP, 676
online resources, 675
research, 679
strategies, 675
VMC Investment Program, 676, 678–679
Web sites, 678
Canadian Journal of Mathematics, 3027
Canadian Library Association (CLA), 19
early history, 682
governance, 682
LIS community, 681
roles and activities, 681–682
1970s–2000, 682–683
from 2000 On, 683
Canadian Urban Libraries Council (CULC), 666
Canberra, 186, 389, 1392–1393, 3692
Cancelbot, 785, 786
Canevari bindings, 543
Canned text systems, 431
Canstantinopolitanus, see Vienna Dioscorides
Capen, Edward, 1844
Capital and Finance in the Age of the Renaissance: A Study of the Fuggers and their Connections, 645
Capitalism, 891, 1790, 1859, 1861, 4198–4199
Caracas Declaration, 4887–4890
Card sort, 4797
Careers, 706
ALA's Office on Human Resource Development and Recruitment, 711
categorization analyst, 711
digital services librarian (assistant professor), 711
knowledge systems librarian/taxonomist, law, 711
staff training and development coordinator, 712
Youth Services Department Head, 712
CARIST, 4631

CARL, *see* Canadian Association of Research Libraries
Carlos III University, 4321
Carnegie, Andrew, 1839, 1845–1846
Carnegie Corporation, 3216–3217
Carnegie Library, 2387, 2802–2803, 3325
Carnegie United Kingdom Trust (CUKT), 1839
Carnegie–Whitney endowment, 78
Carnivore project, 2070
Carolingian illumination, 1947–1948
Carolingian leather bindings, 542
Carpenter, Nathaniel, 1685
Carthage National Museum, 4637
Carus Mathematical Monographs, 3028
CAS, *see* Chemical Abstracts Service
Cascading style sheets (CSS) specification, 5021, 5025
Case digests, 2741–2742
Case-study model, 3814–3815
Casinos, 1123
Cason, Hulsey, 500–501
CASREACT database, 818
CAS Registry Numbers®, 824
CASS, *see* Chinese Academy of the Social Sciences
Cassette tapes, 3280
Catalan consortium, 2824
Catalog cards, 3450
Cataloging
bibliographic records, 730–731
components, 726
forms, 724–725
functions, 725–726
Cataloging and Metadata Management Section (CaMMS), 328–329
Cataloging cultural objects (CCO), 3178, 3761, 4935, 4937–4938
assessment of, 740–742
elements
authorities, 739–740
class element, 738
creator information, 736
description element, 738
location and geography, 737–738
object naming, 736
physical characteristics, 737
stylistic, cultural and chronological information, 737
subject element, 738
entity relationship diagram, 735
general guidelines
database design, 735
display and indexing, 735
related works, 735
subjective interpretation, 735
work and image records, 735
historical context of, 733–734
Cataloging in Publication (CIP) program, 450, 3395
Cataloging Rules and Principles, 2921
Catalogs and cataloging
AACR, 2920–2921
archaeological collections, 1149
arrangement, 744
audiovisual archives, 1574–1575
authority control, 2920
BIBFRAME model, 2924

Philosophy
  branches, 3615, 3617–3618
  definitions, 3614–3615
  of information
    epistemology, 3616–3617
    ethics, 3617
    as meta-field, 3610
    metaphysics, 3616
    meta-studies, 3611
  of information sciences
    approaches, 3618
    Becher's model, 3618–3619
    epistemological questions, 3618
    goals, 3618
    hard fields, 3618
    as meta-field, 3611
    nomothetic–idiographic spectrum, 3619
    preparadigmatic communities, 3618
    scientific–humanistic distinction, 3618
    soft fields, 3618–3619
  metaphilosophy, 3615
  meta-questions, 3614, 3619
  personal/professional, 3611–3612
  of philosophy, 3611
Philosophy of science
  library and information sciences, 3631–3632
  organization, 3624–3625
  scope, 3623
Phoenix Central Library, 2791
Phonetics, 2–3
Phonogramm-Archiv, 4299
Phonographs, 4055
Phonological awareness, 3842, 3844
Phonological processing hypothesis, 3842
Photographic images, 1307–1308
Photostat technology, 1782
Phrase headings, 2866
Phrase searching, 4048–4049
Phronesis, 2678
Phronetic leadership, 2446
Physical bibliography
  analytical bibliography, 477–478
  descriptive bibliography, 478
  historical bibliography, 478–468
  textual bibliography, 478
Physical Geography, 1686
Physical Symbol System Hypothesis (PSSH), 283
Physical wayfinding, 4958
Physiological needs, 2115, 2119
PIALA, *see* Pacific Islands Association of Libraries and Archives
Picasso Museum, 1596, 4332
Picture Australia, 1363
Picture books
  alphabet books, 859
  concept books, 859
  counting books, 859
  definitions, 856–857
  engineered books, 860
  graphic novels, 860
  illustration, styles of, 857–859
  text of, 857
  trends in, 860–861
  wordless picture books, 858–859
Pinakes ("tablets"), 468–469
Pio Clemente Museum, 1818

Pipeline architecture, 431–432
Piracy, 4298
Pirate Bay, 3653, 3656
Pittsburgh Project, 1415
Pixelation, 1309
Pixel-level object, 4421
Pixels, 1308–1310
PLA, *see* Public Library Association
Place identity, 3262
Plagiarism of print and electronic resources
  academic dishonesty
    definition, 3665
    faculty attitudes, 3668–3669
    individual differences, 3668–3669
    social factors, 3668
  cheating, 3665
  coping with
    ethical reasoning, 3669–3670
    online instruction, 3670
    prevention techniques, 3670
    software detection programs, 3670
    teacher's role to translate moral ideology, 3669
  definitions, 3664–3665
  effective pedagogical approaches, 3666
  fabrication, 3665
  hidden curriculum, 3669
  inadvertent/unconscious plagiarism, 3665
  paraphrasing plagiarism, 3665
  ProQuest Platinum database, 3665–3666
Planetarium, 3238
Planned-situational interactive IR model, 2247–2248, 4881–4883
Planning and Budget Assembly (PBA), 72
Planning, organizing, staffing, directing, coordinating, reporting, and budgeting (POSDCORB), 3511
Planographic printing, 1868
Plaquette binding, 551
Platform for Internet content selection (PICS), 783, 1393
PLATO, 1029
The Pleasant Art of Money Catching, 1400
PLOS ALM Reports, 47
Plum Analytics, 45
Pluralism, 3811–3812
PMEST
  energy, space, and time, 2135–2136
  matter, 2132–2133
  personality, 2131–2132
PNG format, 1311
POD, *see* Print-on-demand
Poetry, 861–862
Poland
  archives, 3685–3687
  historical background, 3674–3676
  library legislation, 3676–3677
  map of, 3675
  museums, 3685
  national bibliography
    Bibliografia Wydawnictw Ciągłych, 3683
    Bibliografia Zawartości Czasopism, 3683
  digital libraries, 3683–3684
  librarians and libraries, organizations support to, 3684–3685

Polonica Zagraniczne. Bibliografia, 3683
  professional education and training, librarians, 3684
  Przewodnik Bibliograficzny, 3682–3683
  public libraries, 3677–3678
  research libraries
    National Library, 3679–3682
    NUKAT, 3679
  school libraries, 3678
Policy and Standards Division (PSD), 2858–2859
Policy on Loyalty Programs, 2392–2393
Polish ISKO Chapter, 2497
Political Arithmetic, 1402
Political ideologies, 4404–4405
Politics, 644
Politische Discurs, 1401
Politische Geographie, 1687
Polo, Marco, 1684
Polyphonic music, 3267–3268, 3272
Polysemy, 2689
Pompidou Center, 1597
Poor's Manual of Railroads, 1404
Popper, Karl, 2055–2056
Population ecology, 3514
Portable document format (PDF), 1367, 2342
Portico, 1213
Positional formats, 1177
Positive feedback, 1036
Positivism, 3628–3629
Post-cancellation access (PCA), 1335
Postcoordinate indexing, 1985
Poughkeepsie principles, 4565–4566
Power law, 1040–1041
Poznan Foundation of Scientific Libraries, 2828
Practical working ethics, 1473
Practice materials, 2739
Pragmatism, 2613
Prairienet, 1030
Pratt, Allan, 2052
Pratt–Smoot Act, 563, 3576
Precision (P), 3945
Precoordinated index, 1985
Preferential attachment, 1041
Pre-Hellenic mathematics, 3020
Preliterate society, 3831–3832
PrepComs, 5012–5013
Presentational markup, 3073
Preservation, 2468
  of audiovisual material
    analog audio and videotape materials, 1568–1572
    digital formats, 1571
    film, 1567–1568, 2465, 2467
    funding, 1578–1579
    sound and audiovisual collections, 2413, 2416
    UNESCO, 4660–4661
Preservation and Conservation (PAC), 2457
Preservation and Reformatting Section (PARS), 329
Preservation Description Information (PDI), 1366
Preservation Metadata: Implementation Strategies (PREMIS), 1366, 1575
Preserved context indexing system (PRECIS), 3137
Preserving Digital Information (PDI), 3484

Presidential libraries
  history
    Archivist report, 3715
    Claypoole, Richard, 3715
    Clinton Presidential Project, 3715
    Eisenhower Library, 3715
    George H.W. Bush Library, 3715
    Hoover, 3714
    John F. Kennedy Library, 3715
    Johnson, Lyndon B., 3715
    Lyndon Baines Johnson Foundation, 3715
    NARA, 3715
    public–private partnership, 3715
    Roosevelt, Franklin D., 3714
    Truman Grants program, 3714
  list, 3717–3718
  presidential materials
    audiovisual and photographic record, 3716
    Clinton Presidential Materials Project, 3716
    economic indicators and project, 3717
    The Foreign Gifts and Decorations Act, 3716
    library websites, 3717
    National Archives, 3716
    National Study Commission report, 3716
    Nixon Presidential Materials Staff, 3716
    personal papers and historical materials, 3716
    presidential papers, 3715
    PRMPA, 3716
    selective donation and selective destruction, 3716
  public and educational programs, 3717
Presidential Libraries Act of 1955, 3714–3715
Presidential Recordings and Materials Preservation Act (PRMPA), 3716
Presidential Records Act, 3716
Pressure ethics, 1473
Presumed credibility, 1115
Pretty Good Privacy (PGP), 404
Preventive censorship, 3676
Primary mathematics literature
  biological and behavioral sciences, 3025
  book series, 3027–3028
  journals, 3026–3027
  nonserial book, 3025
  publishers, 3026
Primary records
  card catalogs, conversions of, 3722
  definition, 3719–3721
  electronic forms, 3721
  survival and accessibility of
    artifacts, preservation of, 3728–3730
    collection-based institution, 3727
    dematerialization of information, 3726
    ownership and access, 3726
    paper facsimiles, 3727
    physical presentation of verbal texts, 3730
    primary texts, 3726
    print products, 3726
    rare books, 3726
    storage, conservation and preservation, 3727
  uses of, 3722–3725
Primos Library in Secane, Philadelphia, 1638
Principal component analysis (PCA), 3272
Principle of cumulative advantage, 4199

Print DDA programs, 1211–1212
Print disabilities, 3574
Printing
  in China, 1865
  histories, 1861
  intaglio, 1867–1868
  modern techniques, 1868
  planographic, 1868
  relief, 1865–1867
Printing Act of 1895, 2150
Printing press, 999, 3606
Print-on-demand (POD), 3736–3737, 3986, 4055–4056
  authors, opportunities for, 3736
  book publishing, impacts on, 3733–3734
    commercial and vanity publishers, 3735
    long tail, 3734
    nontraditional and traditional publishing, 3734–3735
    ODB, 3735
    suppliers, growth in, 3735
  book retailers, 3736
  digital printing
    art reproductions and artist books, 3736
    digital image, 3733, 3735
    vs. offset printing, 3733
  music publishing, 3736
Prison librarians, 3415
Pritchard, Alan, 497–499, 506
Privacy Act of 1974, 1857, 2151
Privacy Act of 1976, 1555
Privacy vs. information sharing, 2398–2399
Private bureaucracy, 2256
Private libraries, 748
  America, 1839
  Croatia, 1123
  Mexican libraries, 3091
  Peru, 3606
  Poland, 3674
  Saudi Arabia, 3973–3974
  Ukraine, 4642
Private press
  aristocratic plaything, 3739–3740
  author, 3740–3741
  bibliography, 3743
  clandestine, 3741
  educational press, 3739
  fine books, 3741–3742
  little, 3743
  origins, 3738
  quasi-official press, 3738–3739
  scholarly presses, 3739
Private presses, 4337
Probabilistic models, 422–423
Probabilistic Relational Models (PRM), 274
Probability, theory of, 494–496
Probate records, 1658
Problem, intervention, comparison, and outcome (PICO), 1517
Problem-solving model, 2088–2089
Procedural and descriptive markup, 4560
Procedural knowledge, 3535
Procedural markup, 3074
Proceedings of Symposia in Pure Mathematics, 3028
Proceedings of the American Mathematical Society, 3027

Proceedings of the National Academy of Sciences (PNAS), 3469
Proceedings of the Steklov Institute of Mathematics in the Academy of Sciences of the USSR, 3028
Process-based retention schedules, *see* Large aggregation retention schedules
Process knowledge, 3535
Process quality management, 1178
Producer–Archive Interface Methodology Abstract Standard (PAIMAS), 3485
Producer–Archive Interface Specification (PAIS), 3485
Product catalogs, 639
Professional associations, 303, 3377
Professional conference organizer (PCO), 2453
Professional machine bureaucracies, 3512
Professional metadata creators, 3066
Professional recognition, MLA, 3036
Professional Records and Information Management, International Association (PRISM), 1853
Professional registration, 3377
Program for Cooperative Cataloging (PCC), 454, 2871, 3395
Program for Museum Development in Africa (PMDA), *see* Centre for Heritage Development in Africa
Programme on Information and Communication Technologies (PICT), 2255
Progression of actions lifecycle model, 168
Prolegomena to Library Classification, 1534
PROLOG, 272
Promotion and Identification of Emerging Advanced Telecommunications Services (PISTA), 4322
Property rights, 2277
Prophetic Shrine Library, 3976
Propositional knowledge
  belief
    dispositional view, 2610
    state-object view, 2610–2611
  justification
    adequate indication, 2613
    contextualism, 2615–2616
    epistemic coherentism, 2614
    epistemic foundationalism, 2614–2615
    fallibilism, 2613
    inductive justification, 2613–2614
    inferential justification, 2614
    modest foundationalism, 2615
    radical foundationalism, 2615
  vs. non-propositional knowledge, 2610
  truth, 2611–2612
    coherence, 2612–2613
    correspondence, 2612
    pragmatic value, 2613
Propositions, 592–593
ProQuest Coutts Award for Innovation, 332
ProQuest Ebooks, 1211
Prospectus d'un nouveau dictionnaire de commerce, 1403
Protein Data Bank, 836
Prototypical task, 4555
Provenance, 116
Provenance information, 1364

Sound and audio archives (cont'd.)
   funding and support, 4304
   medium-centered archive, 4300
   music archives
      disc program, 4301
      Edison phonograph, 4300
      pulse code modulation (PCM), 4301
      rise of, 4301
   national efforts, 4305
   pay-as-you-go digital distribution, 4304
   Phonogramm-Archiv, 4299
   preservation and access, 4302–4304
   professional associations, 4302–4303
   sound recordings, 4299–4300
   supporting materials, 4302
   technical processing, 4302
   user needs, 4301
Source credibility, 1115
SourceForge, 1063
South Asia Materials Project (SAMP), 791
South Australian Literary Association, 391
South Central Region of National Network of
   Libraries of Medicine, 3034
South Dublin County Library Service, 3786
Southeast Asia Materials Project (SEAM), 791
Southeast Asia-Pacific Audiovisual Archive
   Association (SEAPAVAA), 1579
Southeastern College Art Conference (SECAC),
   4934
Southern Appalachian Information Node
   (SAIN), 3310
Southern California Earthquake Center (SCEC),
   2997
Southern European Libraries Link (SELL),
   2829
South Kensington Museum, 3154–3155
South Korea
   archives and archival science
      as discipline, 4309
      legislative history, 4308–4309
      NARS, 4308
   history, 4307–4308
   libraries
      academic libraries, 4310–4311
      administrative and legal systems,
         4309–4310
      Book Reading Seoul project, 4313
      Bookstart movement, 4312
      Children and Young Adult Services Pro-
         grams, 4312–4313
      education, 4312
      Enhancing Library Service for the Dis-
         abled, 4313
      Miracle Library project, 4312
      National Assembly Library, 4310
      NLK, 4309–4310
      One Book, One City movement, 4313
      professional association, 4312
      public libraries, 4311
      school libraries, 4311
      Small Library movement, 4313
      special libraries, 4311
      Supreme Court Library, 4310
      WLIC, 4313
   map of, 4307–4308
Soviet Mathematics-Doklady, 3027
Space facet, 1536

Spain
   archives and archival science
      administration, 4329–4330
      associations, 4330
      collections, 4330
      education, 4330
      expenditures, 4330
      representative archives profiles, 4330
      user services, 4330
   education, library and information science,
      4327–4328
   government libraries
      museum libraries, 4326
      religious libraries, 4327
      Royal Academies, 4326
   history, 4314–4315
   legislation, 4315–4316
   libraries
      in Peru, 3606
   library cooperation, 4329
   map of, 4315
   museums and museology
      administration, 4331
      associations, 4333
      collections, 4331
      education, 4333
      expenditures, 4331
      representative museum profiles, 4331–4333
      user services, 4331
   National Library
      CATMARC, 4316
      collections, 4317–4318
      cooperation, 4319
      databases and automation, 4318–4319
      digitization, 4319
      expenditures, 4317
      IBERMARC format, 4316
      LibEcon, 4316
      organization and structure, 4316–4317
      publications, 4318
      REBIUN, 4316
      RUECA, 4316
      special collections, 4318
      user services, 4319
   professional library associations, 4328
   public libraries
      administration and staff, 4322–4323
      automation, 4323–4324
      collections, 4323
      expenditures, 4323
      The Inform@tion Society for All, 4322
      Library of Catalonia, 4324
      Pedro Salinas Public Library, 4324
      PISTA Program, 4322
      user services, 4323
   school libraries
      administration, 4324
      automation, 4325
      collections, 4324
      expenditures, 4324
      staff, 4324
      user services, 4324–4325
   special libraries
      administration, 4325
      automation, 4325–4326
      collections, 4325
      expenditures, 4325

      staff, 4325
      user services, 4325
   university and research libraries
      administration and staffing, 4319–4320
      automation, 4320–4321
      collections, 4320
      CSIC libraries, 4321
      expenditures, 4320
      repesentative university library profiles, 4321
      Scientific and Literary Athenaeum of
         Madrid, 4322
      user services, 4320
   virtual and digital libraries, 4327
Spain ISKO Chapter, 2497
Spangler Library, 878
Spanish binding, 545
Spanish illumination, 1948
Spanish Spring Library, 2792
SPARQL, 2939–2941
Special auxiliaries, 4785
Special bulletins, 4937
Special collections, 3820–3821; *see also* Rare
   book collections
   age, 4336, 4344
   area studies collections, 4335
   care and security, 4335
   communication skills, 4348–4349
   condition, 4338, 4346
   core professional requirements, 4348–4349
   definition, 4335–4336
   definitions, 4343–4344
   digitization, 4341
   exhibitions, 4347
   foreign language skill, 4349
   format, 4345
   formats, 4335, 4337
   foundations, 4346
   fundraising, 4348
   future changes, 4349
   grant-writing, 4348
   and manuscripts
      core professional requirements, 4340–4341
      definition, 4336
   market value, 4336–4337, 4344
   modern special collections
      exhibitions and publications, 4339
      fund-raising and grant-writing, 4340
      public programs and performances, 4339
      security, preservation, and posterity, 4340
      teaching and research, 4339–4340
   noncirculating collections, 4335
   preservation, 4349
   provenance, 4337, 4345
   public programs, 4347
   rare book rooms, 4338
   scarcity, 4337–4338, 4345–4346
   securing posterity, 4349
   stand-alone research and independent librar-
      ies, 4336, 4338–4339
   subject matter, 4337, 4345
   teaching and research, 4347–4348
   treasure rooms, 4338
Special Collections in Mass Media & Culture
   (SCMMC), 1561
Special Committee to Review Program Assessment Processes and Procedures
   (SCRPAPP), 71

Index

Index